10 GOOD REASONS FOR CHOOSING

NEW EDITION!

THE UNITED STATES ©1990
A HISTORY OF THE REPUBLIC
by DAVIDSON/LYTLE

GRADES 9-12
PRENTICE HALL

The Western Frontier (1865–1914) 19

CHAPTER OUTLINE

1. Visions of the West
2. Opening of the West
3. Tragedy for the Plains Indians
4. The Cattle Frontier
5. The Sodbusters' Frontier

"I have heard that you intend to settle us on a reservation near the mountains. I don't want to settle. . . . A long time ago this land belonged to our fathers. But when I go up the river I see the camps of soldiers on its banks. These soldiers cut down my timber. They kill my buffalo. . . . I feel as though my heart will burst with sorrow."

The speaker was the Kiowa chief Satanta, or "White Bear." The occasion was a peace council at Medicine Creek Lodge in Kansas. On one side were more than 5,000 Indians—Kiowa, Comanche, Cheyenne, Arapaho. On the other side were commissioners of the United States government.

It was October 1867, and one of the thorniest problems facing Washington policy makers was how to deal with the western Indians. Land-hungry settlers were pouring into Indian territory. They were eager to carve out farms and ranches. But these were Indian lands. At Medicine Creek Lodge, the commissioners presented Congress's plan. If the Indians would sign treaties giving up their hunting grounds,

they would receive tracts of land and be supplied with tools and livestock. They would settle down to become farmers and ranchers.

Such a prospect filled warriors like Satanta with grief. But the treaties promised peace and freedom, and the Indians signed them. In the words of another Kiowa chief, Setangya: "We thank the Great Spirit that . . . the old days of peace and friendship [are] to come again. . . . The green grass will not be stained with the blood of the whites."

But the grass was to be stained—with both white and Indian blood. When promises to supply the Indians with provisions and clothing were not kept, some warriors raided white settlements for food and ammunition. By the time the fighting was over, Satanta was dead, his heart broken by being denied the freedom to ride the plains.

Treaties and peace councils did little to protect the Indians from the steady advance of white settlers. It was only a matter of time before farms and ranches replaced the great open range of the West.

The arrival of white settlers on the Great Plains meant the end of a way of life for the Indians living there. This clash of cultures often led to bloodshed. In this painting by Frederic Remington, Indian scouts help United States Army troops find a trail.

1 Visions of the West

READ TO UNDERSTAND

■ What conditions were like on the Great Plains.

■ How the American Indians lived on the Great Plains.

■ How different groups viewed the land of the West.

In the early 1800s, explorers who visited the region of the Great Plains reported enormous tracts "where the wind has thrown up the sand in all the fanciful forms of the ocean's rolling waves, and on which not a speck of vegetable matter existed." They dubbed the area the "Great American Desert," and for many years settlers were quite content to leave the region to the Indians. After the Civil War, however, settlers began to push into the plains, and their vision of the area quickly came into conflict with that of the Indians who already lived there.

GEOGRAPHY AND HISTORY

Life of the Plains Indians

The Great Plains, stretching from about the 100th meridian to the Rocky Mountains, are a vast semiarid grassland. Far from moist ocean winds, most of the plains get under 20 inches (50 centimeters) of rainfall a year, less than half the amount received by most eastern areas. When the first settlers arrived, the plains were covered with grass and scrub, with occasional trees in a river bottom.

As you have read in Chapter 1, before the arrival of the Europeans, many Plains peoples were nomadic hunters. At that time there were no horses in North America, so the Indians hunted buffalo and other game on foot. Later, Spanish explorers brought European horses to the Americas. Over the years, some horses strayed. Herds of wild horses gradually migrated north from Mexico onto the Great Plains. In the 1700s, Plains Indians began to tame the horses, and by the 1780s, most groups had become accomplished riders.

On horseback, the Kiowa, Sioux, Crow, Comanche, Cheyenne, Arapaho, Blackfeet, and

401

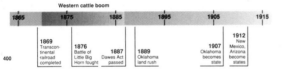

	Western cattle boom					
1865	1875	1885	1895	1905		1915
	1869 Transcontinental railroad completed	1876 Battle of Little Big Horn fought	1887 Dawes Act passed	1889 Oklahoma land rush	1907 Oklahoma becomes state	1912 New Mexico, Arizona become states

400

---

1. STUDENT TEXT (ISBN 139-43697-9) A highly readable text designed for use with students of different ability levels.

Alive with the drama of our history

- A focus on people—on their struggles and achievements
- First-person eyewitness accounts from our past
- The great issues and debates that have enriched our history
- A seamless integration of economic, social, and political history

- Spirit of America features on the special nature of our heritage, such as religion, equality, and ingenuity
- Real-world connections between our past and our present

Geared to the real world of your classroom

- A three-part lesson organization that previews, teache and reviews
- A carefully constructed skills program that instructs, reviews, and enriches in logical steps
- Features and ancillaries specifically geared to studen of different ability levels
- The clearest, most instructive, maps and charts

2. ANNOTATED TEACHER'S EDITION (ISBN 139-43705-3) Helps you adapt instruction to students' different ability levels and learning styles. Look for CLEARLY labeled, idea-filled lesson suggestions keyed to ability level and on-page annotations.

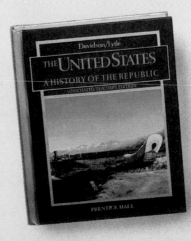

3. TEACHER'S RESOURCE BOOK

(ISBN 139-43739-8) Gives you what you value most—choices! Look for:

For each chapter...
- Advance Planner
- Lesson Suggestions (keyed to ability level)
- Skill Application Worksheet
- Review Worksheet
- Using Historical Sources Worksheet
- Tests, Form A & B

Enrichment Materials To Study Key Topics From Many Different Perspectives...
- Spirit of America Worksheets
- Great Debate Worksheets

- Geography in History Worksheets
- History Through Literature Selections (with annotated correlation to literature)
- History Through Fine Art Transparencies (with lesson ideas and art notes on works in text)

Plus...
- "To the Teacher" Special Essays
  - Teaching Heterogenous Groups
  - Teaching Special Populations
  - Integrating Other Content Areas
  - Teaching Critical and Creative Thinking
- History Writer's Guide
- Citizenship Worksheets

4. COMPUTER TEST BANK

(ISBN 139-68728-9) Create tests, alternate versions of tests, answer keys in minutes! Choose from over 1,200 questions in the test bank booklet by using the software provided, or by requesting your test questions through our unique Dial-A-Test™ toll-free hotline service.

5. CRITICAL THINKING SKILL TRANSPARENCIES

(ISBN 130-27475-5) 48 full-color, easy-to-see projector transparencies of maps, graphs, charts and timelines, plus a detailed Teacher's Guide for developing students' critical thinking skills.

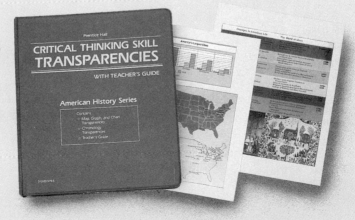

You Can Order These For Your Students

6. STUDENT STUDY GUIDE (ISBN 139-68942-7) Offers self-reviews and self-tests for each chapter, a guide to writing research papers, quick-reference charts, and a special introduction on how to study and take tests. Well worth ordering for students.

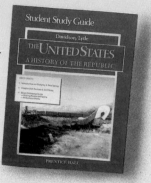

7. HISTORICAL OUTLINE MAP BOOK (ISBN 130-27541-7) By completing the 92 outline maps in this workbook and analyzing the results, your students will gain both valuable geography skills and an understanding of history and its relationship to geography. Teacher's edition contains lesson suggestions.

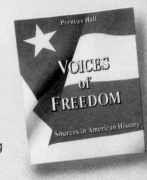

8. CONSTITUTION STUDY GUIDE (ISBN 130-69004-3) Provides in-depth treatment of the Constitution in 15 lively, easy-to-teach, simply written, illustrated lessons. Includes 4 unique YOU ARE THE JUDGE features. A 96-page Teacher's Manual provides lesson plans, activities, transparency masters, Supreme Court cases, a final exam, and more.

9. VOICES OF FREEDOM (ISBN 139-43655-3) Contains 232 letters, poems, diaries, songs, drawings, and other primary sources that give fresh perspectives on topics and events covered in American history. Vocabulary lists precede each reading and critical thinking questions follow each one.

10. SUPERIOR CUSTOMER SERVICE Meeting your needs is our first priority. You can rely on Prentice Hall for total service and support throughout the life of your adoption.

THE UNITED STATES © 1990
A HISTORY OF THE REPUBLIC

The Difference Between "Mentioning" and "Appreciating" History

For more information, or to order, simply contact your Prentice Hall sales representative or call toll free:

1-800-848-9500.

For more information, please write:

PRENTICE HALL
School Division of Simon & Schuster
Englewood Cliffs, NJ 07632

ISBN 139-31502-

ANNOTATED TEACHER'S EDITION

THE UNITED STATES

A HISTORY OF THE REPUBLIC

James West Davidson/Mark H. Lytle

Prentice Hall
Englewood Cliffs, New Jersey
Needham, Massachusetts

CONTENTS

THE UNITED STATES A HISTORY OF THE REPUBLIC

FIFTH EDITION

Annotated Teacher's Edition

ISBN 0-13-943705-3 10 9 8 7 6 5 4 3

Prentice Hall
A Division of Simon & Schuster
Englewood Cliffs, New Jersey

TO THE TEACHER

The United States: A History of the Republic offers the student a chronological narrative treatment of American history. Within this framework, the authors deal with several important themes that reappear throughout American history—such themes as the growth of national unity, the diversity of the population, and the development of democratic institutions.

Several auxiliary components accompany the student edition of *The United States: A History of the Republic:*

- Annotated Teacher's Edition
- Teacher's Resource Book
- Student Study Guide
- Computer Test Bank
- American History Historical Outline Map Book
- Critical Thinking Skill Transparencies, American History Series

The Student Text

The United States: A History of the Republic is divided into ten units. Chronologically organized, each unit covers a period in American history.

Each unit is divided into chapters, which represent about a week of instructional time. The chapters are divided into sections that provide a sharply focused discussion of specific issues.

The Reference Section, pages 838–917, is designed to supplement the body of the text. It is intended for student use throughout the course of study.

READING AIDS

The following features serve as special aids to readability:

Read to Understand statements at the beginning of each section provide a focus for reading.

Vocabulary terms, listed in Read to Understand, are boldfaced and defined when they first appear.

Pronunciations are provided for terms and names that may be unfamiliar to students. The Pronunciation Key can be found on page 854.

The Glossary defines all vocabulary terms and phrases introduced in the text. Each entry is cross-referenced to the text page on which the term first appears.

Footnotes provide further explanation of a term, idea, or event that would be intrusive if placed within the narrative itself.

FEATURES OF THE TEXT

In addition to the reading aids, the student text contains many other helpful features.

Unit Openers contain a colorful, illustrated time line that provides an overview of the political, social, economic, and cultural developments in the unit.

Chapter Openers include a motivational anecdote about a person or event discussed in the chapter and a large related illustration. An outline of section heads and a time line provide an overview of chapter content.

Spirit of America is a four page illustrated feature in each unit that focuses on an important tradition in American history.

Special Features are vignettes, profiles, and primary source documents, including speeches, diary excerpts, and letters that are dispersed throughout the text. Each chapter has at least one special feature.

Skill Lessons integrated in the student text teach important social studies skills. The content of each skill lesson is directly related to the chapter and section in which it appears.

See the table of contents to the student text for a complete list of the skill lessons.

Visual Aids including hundreds of photographs, paintings, cartoons, maps, charts, and graphs reinforce and enrich the narrative.

Metric equivalents appear in parentheses for most measurements presented in traditional form.

Section Reviews include questions that ask students to identify people or events and to define vocabulary terms. Each section concludes with several review questions and a critical thinking question.

Chapter Reviews provide a variety of opportunities for students to test their comprehension, to analyze and synthesize what they have learned, and to practice skills. Each Chapter Review includes the following:

- *Summary* provides a brief summary of each section.
- *Vocabulary* reviews and reinforces boldfaced terms in the text.
- *Chapter Checkup* questions ask students to comprehend, analyze, and synthesize information from the chapter.
- *Critical Thinking* questions ask students to draw inferences from information in the chapter or to defend a point of view.
- *Connecting Past and Present* questions encourage students to recognize parallels between past events and current events and to analyze similarities and differences.
- *Developing Basic Skills* questions ask students to apply such skills as comparing, interpreting visual evidence, reading maps and graphs, and undertaking library research.
- *Writing About History* lessons help students develop the writing and research skills associated with the study of history.

Reference Section, on pages 838–917, contains a number of important elements described below:

- *Atlas* of eight reference maps provide general information about the United States and the world (pages 840–849).
- *Chronology of American History* traces developments in politics and government, exploration and innovation, society and economics, and culture and religion (pages 850–853).
- *Pronunciation Key* explains the phonetic respelling of difficult terms and names used throughout the text (page 854).
- *Glossary* defines key historical terms (pages 854–862).
- *Fifty States Chart* contains basic information about the 50 states.

- *Presidents and Vice Presidents of the United States* list the dates and parties of the forty-one Presidents(pages 863–864).
- *The Declaration of Independence* is reproduced in full (pages 865–866).
- *The Constitution of the United States* is accompanied by annotations explaining the substance of each clause (pages 867–897). The annotations include cross-references to pertinent discussions in the text.
- *Index* (pages 898–917) lists all the important subjects discussed in the text. Charts, maps, and pictures are included, each identified by an italicized letter (*c*, *m*, or *p*) preceding the page reference. Works of art are indicated.

Annotated Teacher's Edition

The Annotated Teacher's Edition is a comprehensive instructional package for use with *The United States: A History of the Republic*. It consists of a complete student text, 160 additional teacher pages, and extensive on-page annotations.

TEACHER PAGES

Overview includes a brief outline of the chapter content.

Sidelights are interesting historical anecdotes and background information. The sidelights are keyed to a page in the student text to indicate the point at which you might wish to introduce them.

Lesson Activities are provided for every section in the student text. Some are class activities, while others are intended to be used in small groups or by individual students. The three lesson activities are designed for students of differing ability levels. The symbols explained below indicate the students for whom each activity is appropriate:

    O average and below-average students
    ☆ all students
    □ average and above-average students

These classifications provide a general guideline. You are the best judge of your students' abilities and should make the final assignment of activities.

Answers to the Section Review questions follow each set of section activities in the teacher pages. Complete answers for all questions in the map and graph captions, Special Features, Skill Lessons, Spirit of America features, and Chapter Reviews are also included in the teacher pages.

On-page Annotations provide additional background information, as well as suggested discussion topics and activities. Annotations are printed in red in the margins of the student pages for easy reference.

Each annotation has a title to identify its content. Annotations also provide cross-references to the answers in the teacher pages for section and chapter reviews, map and graph questions, and special feature questions.

Teacher's Resource Book

The Teacher's Resource Book for *The United States: A History of the Republic* is organized into two basic parts: chapter materials and additional resources.

CHAPTER MATERIALS

The chapter materials are arranged by chapter, behind a unit tab. They include:

Lesson Suggestions are organized into chapters and sections that correspond to the chapters and sections in the text.

- *Chapter Overview* includes Chapter Focus, Planning, and Historical Sidelights. The sidelights contain interesting anecdotes that can be used for motivation.
- *Main Lessons* for each section include specific lesson ideas based on text material. A wide variety of learning strategies is used, and all of them encourage students to become actively involved in the lessons. After completing the steps in each Main Lesson, students will have accomplished several important knowledge and skills objectives.
- *Reinforcement Assignments* involve students in review and mastery of the text material. A wide variety of activities is presented, including completing word puzzles, interpreting visual evidence, and writing historical fiction, to name a few.
- *Enrichment Assignments* encourage students to extend their knowledge beyond the text

by researching in greater depth some of the topics they have learned about or by investigating new ones.

Skill Application Worksheets tie in directly with the lesson suggestions. The worksheets are designed for use either with the Main Lesson for a given section or with a Reinforcement or Enrichment Assignment. The worksheets may be duplicated and distributed.

Review Worksheets are designed to give students of average and below-average ability levels an opportunity to learn and reinforce their knowledge of the key facts and ideas in a chapter. There is one worksheet for every chapter in the text, and each includes five distinct activities: Building Vocabulary, Reviewing Key People, History and Geography, Understanding Chronology, and Writing About the Main Idea.

Using Historical Sources Worksheets are designed as extension activities for students of average and above-average ability. Each contains a lengthy historical source about a topic covered in the chapter. There is one for each chapter.

Tests, which come in two forms, allow you flexibility in assessing your students' understanding. Chapter and unit tests are composed of objective and essay questions. All are designed for completion in one class period. Like the worksheets, the tests are intended for duplication and distribution to your classes.

Answer Keys for the worksheets and tests comes at the end of each set of chapter materials.

OTHER RESOURCES IN THE TEACHER'S RESOURCE BOOK

Spirit of America Worksheets are keyed to each of ten Spirit of America features in the text.

Great Debates in American History focus on an enduring issue in American history, such as states' rights, government regulation, and civil disobedience.

Geography in History focuses on the impact of geography on important historical events.

History Through Literature includes substantial excerpts from important works from a historical period or about a historical period. The worksheet helps students to make connections between the works and the historical event or period it covers.

History Through Fine Art helps students appreciate the place of art in history. Fine art transparencies and lesson ideas help the teacher present fine art to the students.

History Writer's Guide is designed to integrate writing and research skills into the American history course. It consists of two parts. The first part, Writing a Research Paper, which gives step-by-step instructions, is ready for duplication and distribution to students. The second part consists of 14 writing skill worksheets that provide students with the opportunity to develop effective strategies for writing paragraphs, essays, and research papers.

Citizenship Worksheets provide a review of the rights and responsibilities of American citizens. They help students apply major citizenship ideas to their own lives.

Answer Keys can be found at the end of each section of the Teacher's Resource Book that contains questions.

Student Study Guide

The Student Study Guide book contains a useful section on study skills as well as a three-page review worksheet and a one-page self-test for each chapter in *The United States: A History of the Republic*. In addition, a quick reference section includes the organization of the government, a chronology of important events, a biographical dictionary, and a writer's handbook.

Computer Test Bank

The Computer Test Bank that accompanies *The United States: A History of the Republic* enables you to create tests tailored to the needs of your class. You can use the software included with the Test Bank or use DIAL-A-TEST™, a free phone-in test service.

Approximately 50 test items are provided for each of the 37 chapters of the student text. Each item is keyed to the section of the chapter in which the topic is discussed. The Test Bank includes both objective and essay questions divided into four categories: "Skills," such as map and graph reading, "Key People, Places, and Terms," "Chronology," and "Critical Thinking."

Historical Outline Map Book

This book contains 92 outline maps. The first 70 of these are historical outline maps of important developments in American history, including European explorations, the American Revolution, United States expansion, and United States post-World War II policy.

Maps 71 to 81 are outline maps of current world regions. These maps are especially useful when teaching about United States foreign policy. Maps 82 to 92 are outline maps of the United States today, including regional maps that can be used to teach state and local history.

Critical Thinking Skill Transparencies

A package of Critical Thinking Skill Transparencies is available for use with *The United States: A History of the Republic*. Two types of transparencies are included. The 44 map, graph, and chart transparencies provide clear, colorful maps, graphs, diagrams, tables, and charts to reinforce and extend student knowledge of American history. Over half of these contain more than one illustration. The four chronology transparencies provide a chronological overview of American history that traces events and developments in government and citizenship, exploration and innovation, changes in daily life, and the world of ideas.

The Teacher's Guide that accompanies the transparencies contains strategies for using them to develop critical thinking skills. The strategies are developed in three steps, reflecting increasingly sophisticated skills: 1. Reading the illustration, 2. Interpreting, and 3. Analyzing.

Unit One
The Americas

Chapter 1   (pages 2–23)

The American Land and Its People _____

OVERVIEW

Chapter 1 focuses on the geography and peoples of the Americas and on developments in Europe in the 1300s and 1400s. Students learn to apply the five major themes that geographers use to show relationships between geography and history. Then they investigate the physical features and climate regions of the Americas. They also examine the many rich and diverse cultures of the first Americans as well as the developments that led to a spirit of exploration in Europe.

HISTORICAL SIDELIGHTS

The following pieces of historical information can serve as notes of interest during the study of Chapter 1. The page numbers in parentheses indicate the points in the student text at which you may wish to introduce the information.

Indian Ball Games (p. 15)   Many Native Americans played ball games. Such games ranged from the unstructured form of kickball played by the Eskimo to the complex ceremonial ball games performed by the Maya on elaborate stone courts. The Algonquin are generally credited with inventing lacrosse. The lacrosse ball was fashioned from tightly packed deerskin covered with deer hide. In one version, as many as 700 players were on the field at one time.

Mayan Astronomers (p. 16)   The Maya were highly sophisticated mathematicians and astronomers. Their system of arithmetic had a base of 20 — counting fingers and toes instead of only fingers, as in the European system. Mayan astronomers used observations of the moon, sun, and the planet Venus to create a calendar more accurate than European calendars of the time. The Mayan year was divided into 19 months—18 months of 20 days each and one month of 5 days.

SECTION 1	(pages 3–5)
Geography and History	

ACTIVITIES*

○ **Identifying**   Read aloud the following clues or duplicate and distribute copies. Ask students to use the clues to identify the words and then use each word in a sentence of their own. (1) A measure on a map or globe showing distance north or south of the Equator. (2) An account of what has happened in the development of a people, nation, or civilization. (3) The study of people, their environments, and their resources. (4) A measure on a map or globe of the distance east or west of the Prime Meridian. *Answers*: **1.** latitude **2.** history **3.** geography **4.** longitude

☆ **Outlining**   Have students prepare an outline of Section 1. They can begin by listing the subsection titles (Themes of Geography, and so on) and then writing two or three important supporting facts under each.

□ **Applying Themes of Geography**   Have students list the five themes of geography. (Review the meanings of any that they do not understand.) Then have them apply the relevant themes to the Hopi people discussed in the introduction. For example, what is the location of the Hopi community? How did the people interact with their environment?

ANSWERS: SKILL LESSON   (page 4)
1. (a) The American land and its people. **(b)** Prehistory to 1492. **2. (a)** 4 sections. **(b)** Section 2. **(c)** It shows that the early people depended on the land

_____
*See "To the Teacher" for an explanation of the symbols.

to provide food for them to eat. They believed that gods helped the land provide for them. **3. (a)** The connections between history and geography. **(b)** Because understanding the connections will help you understand why things are the way they are today. **4.** Themes of Geography, Location, Place, Interactions Between People and Their Environment, Movement, Regions. **5. (a)** On plains and plateaus. **(b)** Development of nation states and improvements in technology.

ANSWERS: SECTION 1 REVIEW   (page 5)
1. location, place, interaction—p. 4; movement, region—p. 5. **2.** geography, history—p. 3; latitude, longitude—p. 4. **3.** Because there is a connection between where things happen and why they happen; the more you understand about these connections, the more sense you can make out of events and how they affect you. **4.** Technology has greatly speeded up the movement of people, from the use of only human and animal power to today's jet planes and telecommunications. **5.** The themes put information about the world and its peoples into categories that make it easier to see relationships between different regions, for example, or connections between places and why people move there.

SECTION 2   (pages 6–11)
The American Land

ACTIVITIES
○ **Understanding Physical Regions and Climates** Have students study the maps on text pages 7 and 10. Have them identify your state and, based on the maps, write a paragraph describing your state's physical regions and climate. Ask if they can see any connections between the state's physical features and its climate (for example, do mountains cause cooler temperatures?).

☆ **Researching** Have students learn more about one important river or lake in the United States. They should explore such aspects as its location, its usefulness to the people and animals that live near it, its history, ways that it has changed or been changed by people over the years. Ask students to prepare a written report of their findings.

☐ **Understanding Geography** Have students choose one region of the United States other than the one in which you live. Ask them to

study the maps on text pages 7 and 10 to learn more about the region. Then have them plan a trip to that region by deciding what clothes to bring, what kind of recreational activities might be available there, and what local foods might be available to eat. (Reassure students that they might not have all the information they need to plan such a trip, but they should rely on reasonable conclusions they can draw from the available information.)

ANSWERS: MAP STUDY   (page 7)
Appalachian, Rocky, Cascade, Sierra Nevada; the Appalachian range is located in the eastern part of the United States, the other three in the west.

ANSWER: MAP STUDY   (page 10)
Marine, mediterranean, humid continental, humid subtropical; arctic, desert, highland, subarctic; answers will vary.

ANSWERS: SECTION 2 REVIEW   (page 11)
1. plateau—p. 7; marine climate, mediterranean climate, humid continental climate—p. 9; humid subtropical climate—p. 10. **2.** elevation, relief—p. 6; climate—p. 9. **3.** Pacific Coast, Intermountain Region, Rocky Mountains, Interior Plains, Canadian Shield, Appalachian Mountains, Coastal Plains. **4.** Rivers provide transportation, irrigation, drinking water, and hydroelectric power. **5.** Answers will vary.

SECTION 3   (pages 11–17)
The First Americans

ACTIVITIES
○ **Map Reading** Ask students to locate each of the following Native American cultures on the map on text page 12 and decide which cultural region the group is in: Kutchin, Creek, Pawnee, Fox, Maya, Shoshone, Pomo, Bella Coola, Cree, Iroquois, Cheyenne, Navajo, Choctaw, Huron, Hopi. You might make this assignment a game by calling out the names and giving points for correct answers.

☆ **Understanding Geography** List the following Indian nations and culture groups in a column on the chalkboard: Eskimo, Northwest Coast Indians, Great Basin Indians, Anasazi, Pueblo, Navajo, Plains, Algonquin, Iroquois, and Muskogean. Label the next two columns Environment and Adaptations. Then have students fill in the chart by describing the geography of the region where each group lived and telling how each group adapted to their environment.

- ☐ **Comparing** Have students do further research about the scientific accomplishments of the Aztec, Maya, or Inca. They could begin by using an encyclopedia. Then ask them to present an oral report to the class with their findings.

ANSWER: MAP STUDY   (page 12)

Answers will vary.

ANSWERS: ARTS IN AMERICA   (page 16)

1. Students should locate the names in the captions. **2.** You might assume that the things the Maya wrote about were the things that were most important to their culture or most meaningful to them in some way.

ANSWERS: SECTION 3 REVIEW   (page 17)

1. Iroquois League—p. 15; Tenochtitlán—p. 16. **2.** potlatch—p. 13; pictogram, adobe, kiva, matrilineal, nomadic—p. 14; sachem—p. 15. **3.** They probably crossed a land bridge from Asia, which formed when the ocean level dropped as a result of glaciers. **4.** The travois made it easier for the Plains people to carry their possessions. The teepee provided the Plains people with portable shelters. **5.** Possible answers: **(a)** Huge buildings and pyramids, calendar, ability to predict eclipses, ideograms. **(b)** Beautiful buildings and capital city, knowledge of astronomy, calendar. **(c)** Buildings that could withstand earthquakes. **6.** Possible answer: Because they had to spend less time worrying about the basic needs of everyday life, they could concentrate on other developments.

SECTION 4   (pages 18–21)

Europe Awakens

ACTIVITIES

- ○ **Locating Places on a Map** Give students a blank map of Europe, Asia, and the Middle East. On the map, have them locate key places mentioned in the section, such as the Holy Land, China, Venice, and Portugal. (You might ask them to skim the section first to identify the key places.) Then have them notice things on the map such as the distances between Venice and China or between Europe and the

Holy Land or the direction people traveled to get from one place to the other.

- ☆ **Writing a Report** Have students write a report in which they provide background information about one of the following topics: life of serfs, feudal manors, Seljuk Turks, early Crusades, Kublai Khan, one of the African kingdoms. These reports could be shared to enrich the study of the chapter.

- ☐ **Writing a Journal Entry** Have students imagine that they were crew members on a Portuguese caravel in 1432 (that is, before any crew had passed south of Cape Bojador). Ask them to write a journal entry recording their reactions to a trip along the west coast of Africa. Students might want to do research about caravels and early expeditions to make their journal entries more realistic.

ANSWERS: SECTION 4 REVIEW   (page 21)

1. Marco Polo—p. 19; Henry the Navigator—p. 20; Vasco da Gama—p. 21. **2.** serf, vassal, feudalism, manor—p. 18; astrolabe, quadrant—p. 20. **3. (a)** Wars waged by European Christians beginning in 1099 to recapture the city of Jerusalem from Muslims. **(b)** They introduced new ideas and knowledge by bringing back books by Arabic scholars; they brought back items such as spices, perfumes, and fabrics that introduced new ideas of food, fashion, and comfort. **4. (a)** They sparked interest in trade and travel to China. **(b)** It spurred a search for faster and cheaper trade routes to China. **(c)** Through alliance, monarchs and merchants used their wealth to finance expeditions and hence increase their power and influence. **5.** Astrolabe, quadrant, and caravel. **6.** Possible answer: Although the Crusaders lost the territory they had won from the Muslims, they helped introduce Asia, and its ideas and products, to Europeans.

ANSWERS: CHAPTER 1 REVIEW   (pages 22–23)

Vocabulary 1. Geography **2.** History **3.** Elevation **4.** Adobe **5.** kiva **6.** Nomadic

Chapter Checkup 1. (a) Location refers to the exact position of a place, in terms of latitude and longitude, or the relative location of a place. On the other hand, place refers to the physical and human characteristics of a location. **(b)** They may be distinguished according to physical features or according to the characteristics of the people who live there. **2. (a)** The mobility of people, ideas, and goods. **(b)** Movement has been speeded up dramatically by such inventions as railroads and telecommunications. **(c)** The earliest Americans came here from Asia; many people who came to live here later also migrated from other lands.

Many ideas have made their way here from other places. **3**. Landforms and climates affect the kinds of jobs people can do; in addition, crops and vegetation vary according to the type of soil and climate in a place. Also, certain landforms, such as steep mountains, and certain climates, such as an arctic climate, are less attractive for habitation. **4. (a)** The Eskimo hunted seal, walrus, whale, and caribou. Plains Indians hunted buffalo and did some farming. **(b)** Different animals lived in each region because of the climate and vegetation there; the climate was much more severe where the Eskimo lived so they could not farm. **5.** By developing complex irrigation systems for farming and by building dwellings suitable to vast temperature changes. **6. (a)** The Pueblo conducted religious ceremonies for many purposes, such as to ask for rain or heal the sick; that religion was important to them can be seen by the fact that the kiva was in the center of the town. **(b)** Religion affected the daily lives of the Navajo, whose religion taught them to live their lives in harmony with the universe. They also believed that they had to perform certain rituals to please the Holy People. **(c)** The entire social structure of the Muskogean was based on their worship of the sun. **7.** The Renaissance was a time of intellectual revival. People began to investigate their surroundings and question what they found, which encouraged advances in science and technology. This new attitude and the advances it fostered made journeys of exploration possible. **8. (a)** Portugal led the way in overseas exploration. **(b)** Prince Henry made overseas exploration possible by setting up a school, financing expeditions, and encouraging technological advances.

Critical Thinking **1.** Students should refer to the cultures discussed in the text for supporting examples. Differing environments can contribute to a diversity of cultures by requiring people to develop different skills for survival. **2.** Possible answers: They might be living a life similar to the traditional one they had developed before meeting Europeans. They might have developed further technologies to meet their needs (for example, new crops to enhance their diet or new tools or vehicles to lighten their work load); these changes might have led to various changes in their culture or society.

Connecting Past and Present **1. (a)** Sample answer: People have adapted to their environment, for example, by learning to build homes and wear clothing suitable to the climate where they live. They have adapted their environment in such ways as building bridges to cross rivers and dams to harness water power. **(b)** Certain changes in the environment have caused problems, such as pollution or risk of extinction of certain animal species; other changes have had global effects, such as the damage to the ozone layer. **2.** Possible answer: Some advances have brought people physically closer, such as jet planes. Others have brought ideas and information closer; these advances include computers, telecommunications devices, and space satellites. All of these developments have sped up communication or transportation, thus bringing people closer together.

Developing Basic Skills **1.** Answers will vary according to where you live. **2. (a)** "Europe Awakens"; it means that Europe was becoming alert to new ideas. **(b)** Clues include: myths would soon clear away; two worlds that had not known each other would soon be brought together. **(c)** Europe in the Middle Ages, A New Age Dawns, Expanding Horizons Eastward, Exploration and Politics, Changes in Outlook, Geography and History: Portugal Takes the Lead, Early Contacts With the Americas. **(d)** What life was like in Europe during the Middle Ages. **(e)** Expanding Horizons Eastward. **(f)** 1300s and 1400s.

Chapter 2 (pages 24–47)
Europe's Age of Discovery _____

OVERVIEW
Chapter 2 describes the meeting of the Old World and the New World as Europeans arrived in the Western Hemisphere. Students read about early voyages of discovery by Columbus, Magellan, and Balboa, as well as later explorations of the continents. They also examine the Spanish settlement of South and Central America, the activities of the French and the English in North America, and the first English settlements in Virginia and New England.

HISTORICAL SIDELIGHTS
The following pieces of historical information can serve as notes of interest during the study of Chapter 2. The page numbers in parentheses indicate the points in the student text at which you may wish to introduce the information.

Plant and Animal Immigrants to the New World (pp. 31–32) Humans were not the only

Old World "discoverers" of America. Explorers brought plants and animals that often prospered in the New World. Horses and pigs multiplied rapidly and roamed wild. Orange, banana, and olive trees took root. There were even unintended immigrants: the dandelion, the daisy, and "Kentucky" bluegrass all came from Europe. European rats migrated, too. In Bermuda, they honeycombed the earth with their burrows and nested in almost every tree. They became so numerous that they seriously threatened the colonists' food supplies.

Cartier and Donnaconna (p. 35)   European exploration led to significant discoveries, but it also produced some tall tales. When Jacques Cartier sailed up the St. Lawrence River, he met Chief Donnaconna of the Huron Indians. Donnaconna, perhaps hoping to impress the gold-hungry Europeans, told Cartier of the fabulous northern Kingdom of Saguenay, where white people lived and mined gold, silver, and rubies. Some of the inhabitants there, he said, had only one leg, flew like bats, and never ate. Cartier believed the tales and brought Donnaconna to France to tell his story to the king.

SECTION 1   (pages 25–30)
Spanish Conquest in the Americas

ACTIVITIES*

○ **Map Reading**   Ask students to study the map on text page 27 and answer the following questions: (1) Whose expedition was the first to sail around the world? (2) Which Portuguese explorer claimed part of South America for his country? (3) Who was the first European explorer to reach India by sailing around the southern tip of Africa? (4) Which of Columbus's four voyages took him the farthest north?

☆ **Ranking**   Have students list on the chalkboard reasons why Spanish conquistadores were able to destroy the greatest empires of the New World. Discuss the list and then have the class vote to rank the reasons in order of importance.

---

*See "To the Teacher" for an explanation of the symbols.

□ **What If?** Ask students to write an essay describing what might have happened if Columbus had landed in present-day Virginia rather than in the Caribbean on his first voyage. They should speculate about how history might have been different.

ANSWER: MAP STUDY   (page 27)
The Portuguese sailed eastward around Africa, rather than westward across the Atlantic Ocean.

ANSWERS: MAP STUDY   (page 29)
Spain; they visited the southern portion of North America, the West Indies, and the western coast of South America.

ANSWERS: SECTION 1 REVIEW   (page 30)
1. Queen Isabella—p. 25; Montezuma—p. 28; Pizarro—p. 29; Ponce de León—p. 30; Cabeza de Vaca, Estevanico—pp. 24, 30; de Soto, Coronado—p. 30. **2.** circumnavigate, conquistador—p. 27. **3.** Queen Isabella of Spain paid for three ships, provided 90 sailors, and made Columbus an admiral. Without this help, Columbus would not have been able to reach America. **4. (a)** Balboa crossed the Isthmus of Panama and became the first European to see the Pacific Ocean; Magellan's expedition that circled the globe proved that America was a new continent and showed how large the Pacific Ocean was. **(b)** They gave Spain, as well as other countries, more information about the world; they gave Spain an advantage in claiming lands in the Americas and enhanced Spain's position as a world power. **5.** He hoped to find gold and riches to enrich both himself and Spain. **6.** Since Spain is located in the southern part of Europe, Spanish explorers and settlers might have tended to seek out southern locations.

SECTION 2   (pages 30–33)
Settling New Spain

ACTIVITIES

○ **Expressing an Opinion**   Have students write a one- or two-paragraph answer to this question: Why do you think the Spanish were willing to force Native Americans and Africans to do grueling and deadly work on encomiendas and in mines?

☆ **Classifying** Have students make a chart with three columns headed Pueblo, Mission, and Presidio. In each column they should list the major characteristics of life in that type of Spanish settlement. When they have completed the chart, ask them to speculate about which type of settlement they would like to have lived in if they had been Spanish settlers in the 1500s.

☐ **Interviewing** Ask students to imagine that it is 1550 and that the king of Spain has sent them to New Spain to report on conditions there. Part of the report is to consist of an interview with the viceroy and part is an interview with a Native American laborer. Have students make a list of questions they would ask during each interview. Some students may want to do further research about life in New Spain during that period and prepare a written report.

ANSWERS: SECTION 2 REVIEW (page 33)

1. Santo Domingo, New Spain, Philip II—p. 31; Bartolomé de Las Casas—p. 32. **2.** presidio—p. 31; encomienda—p. 32. **3.** Presidios were built for military purposes; missions were centers for bringing Christianity to the Native Americans; pueblos were communities for farming, trade, and town life. **4.** Native Americans were often made to work for the conquistadores as a way of paying required taxes. They had no other way of paying the tax, so the Native Americans soon became bound to the land. **5.** Possible answers include: Planners today still try to keep the beauty of the town in mind when they decide where and what kinds of buildings to put in the community. Communities still have to collect taxes to run the town.

SECTION 3 (pages 33–37)
The French and English Look North

ACTIVITIES

○ **Comparing** Have students review the description of the Spanish conquistadores on text pages 27–28 and of the English sea dogs on pages 35 and 37. Then ask students to write a short essay in which they compare the motivations, goals, activities, and relationship with the crown of the conquistadores and sea dogs.

☆ **Using Visual Evidence** After students have completed the skill lesson on text page 36, ask them to find other early maps of the New World. They might consult *The American Heritage Pictorial Atlas of United States History*. Have them analyze one of the maps as visual evidence by using the steps in the skill lesson. Then ask them to compare the view of the Americas presented in the skill lesson map with that presented in the other map they have analyzed.

☐ **Understanding a Primary Source** Read students the following excerpt from the charter granted Walter Raleigh by Elizabeth I, or duplicate and distribute copies.

Knowe yee that of our especial grace . . . we give and graunt to our trustie and well-beloved servant Walter Ralegh . . . free libertie and licence . . . to discover, search, finde out, and view such remote, heathen and barbarous lands, countries, and territories, not actually possessed of any Christian Prince, nor inhabited by Christian People, . . . the same to have, holde, occupie and enjoy . . . for ever.

Have students rewrite the quotation in their own words. Then ask: (1) What can you conclude about the attitude of Elizabeth toward Native Americans? (2) Why do you think she held this attitude?

ANSWERS: GEOGRAPHIC CONNECTION (page 34)

1. In order to take advantage of the resources within the continent. **2.** Possible answer: Settlements were probably set up along the waterways, because rivers and bays acted as highways into the interior.

ANSWERS: SKILL LESSON (page 36)

1. (a) The people wearing loincloths and carrying bows and arrows probably lived in the territory shown. The people carrying lances and on horseback at the bottom left probably just arrived. They came by ship. **(b)** The territory had trees, rivers, wildlife, and mountains. The waters off the coast were thought to contain sea creatures. **(c)** Florida and Mexico are shown at the top of the map. The map has south at the top. **2. (a)** No. The area was largely unexplored, and many of the things, such as the sea creatures, did not exist. **(b)** One could infer that the artist was French since the detail centers around the area that the French explored. It would be best to use this picture to understand the viewpoint of the French. **(c)** Yes, the source is good for understanding French perceptions of the New World in the 1500s. **3. (a)** People in the mid-1500s viewed the voyage to the Americas as dangerous, as evidenced by the creatures in the sea. **(b)** The perspective is that of the early French explorers, who arrived in the New World from the north, as shown on the map on text page 29. A Spaniard might have drawn this map with north at the top, since Spanish ships arrived in the south and sailed north to explore.

ANSWERS: SECTION 3 REVIEW (page 37)

1. Jacques Cartier, Samuel de Champlain, Sir Francis Drake—p. 35; Armada, Sir Walter Raleigh—p. 37. **2. (a)** To find gold and to discover a faster water route to Asia. **(b)** They began to look for places to set up settlements and ways to exploit the land's natural resources. **3.** They pirated Spanish treasure ships. **4. (a)** Raleigh envisioned a colony that would raise crops and export raw materials to England. **(b)** Roanoke did not survive as a permanent settlement, although the reasons for its disappearance remain a mystery. **5.** Possible answers: It gave them confidence. It eliminated Spain as a serious contender in North America.

SECTION 4 (pages 38–42)
A Gamble in Virginia

ACTIVITIES

○ **Name Game** Read aloud the following clues or duplicate and distribute copies. Ask students to use the clues to identify each person, place, or thing. (1) 1215 document that promised certain rights to English nobles; (2) adapted West Indian tobacco to Virginia; (3) first English colony in Virginia; (4) leader who steered English colony through first years; (5) first representative assembly in the New World; (6) intervened to save leader of English colony.
Answers: **1.** Magna Carta **2.** John Rolfe **3.** Jamestown **4.** John Smith **5.** House of Burgesses **6.** Pocahontas

☆ **Relating Cause and Effect** Have students list the problems faced by settlers in Jamestown before 1620. Then ask students what the colonists did to solve each problem. Ask: What step ensured the survival of Jamestown?

□ **Comparing** Have students make a chart comparing the House of Burgesses in Virginia with Parliament in England. Use the following headings: Origin, Structure, People Who Served, Groups Whose Interests Were Protected.

ANSWER: MAP STUDY (page 39)

Nine Native American groups.

ANSWERS: THE AMERICAN EXPERIENCE (page 40)

1. A letter from John Smith said the best way to the Indies was northwest through North America. **2.** Possible answers: desire to be famous; desire to be the first to accomplish what many had tried.

ANSWERS: SECTION 4 REVIEW (page 42)

1. Plymouth Company, London Company—p. 38; Pocahontas—p. 39; John Rolfe—p. 40; Magna Carta—p. 41. **2.** Joint stock company—p. 38. **3.** The drinking water was brackish, the damp air rotted the wooden buildings, and settlers were infected by malaria-carrying mosquitoes; settlers lacked skills needed to survive in the wilderness, wanted to search for gold rather than work at farming or hunting, and were unable to govern themselves peaceably. **4.** Smith governed sternly. He treated the men like a military battalion and halted the search for gold. **5. (a)** A representative assembly established in Virginia in 1619 consisting of 22 burgesses, or representatives, two from each of the 11 areas of the colony. **(b)** The House of Burgesses was the first representative assembly in the New World; it set the pattern for government in the English colonies. **6.** Possible answer: The London Company told the settlers to search for gold, when there was no gold to find in Virginia.

SECTION 5 (pages 42–45)
The New England Way

ACTIVITIES

○ **Relating Past to Present** Have students re-read the subsection "Search for a More Comfortable Life" on text page 42. Then have them list reasons why families came to the New World in the 1600s. Ask: (1) Why do people from other countries come to the United States today? (2) Which reasons are the same as in the 1600s? Which are different?

☆ **Comparing** Have students write a short essay comparing the government in Virginia with the government in Massachusetts Bay. Ask: Which was the more democratic? Why?

☐ **Writing a Skit** Have students find out more about Roger Williams and his disagreements with Massachusetts leaders. Then have them write a dialogue between Williams and colony leaders. The dialogue should reflect the religious views of each, as well as their attitudes toward each other.

ANSWERS: SECTION 5 REVIEW (page 45)

1. Martin Luther—p. 43; Pilgrims, Mayflower Compact, Puritans—p. 44; Roger Williams, Fundamental Orders of Connecticut—p. 45. **2.** First they had gone to the Netherlands to escape abuse in England. But they missed their English ways, so they decided to move to North America, where they could start a community based on English customs. **3.** Male church members. **4.** Both Rhode Island and Connecticut were founded to guarantee religious toleration, and both had some kind of representative government. **5.** They believed they knew the correct way to worship and to govern accordng to the Bible. Therefore, they did not want to ruin their colony by allowing "incorrect" views to exist.

ANSWERS: CHAPTER 2 REVIEW (pages 46–47)

Vocabulary 1. b **2.** c **3.** a **4.** a **5.** b.

Chapter Checkup 1. (a) It created a bitter dispute. **(b)** He feared this dispute would lead to war and weaken European Christianity. **(c)** He drew a line to divide undiscovered lands between the two. **2.** Conquistadores carried on much of the exploration in the Americas; their discoveries led to land claims for Spain. Each conquistador was permitted by the Spanish government to establish settlements in America. **3.** The laws regulated most aspects of life in the colonies and specified that presidios, missions, and pueblos be set up. They regulated the design of each of these settlements and such details as what crops to plant. **4.** Native Americans were mistreated and enslaved. Bartolomé de Las Casas, a Dominican priest, persuaded the Spanish government to place the Native Americans under the protection of the clergy and import slaves from Africa to take the Indians' place in the mines and ranches. **5.** Internal problems in France distracted French leaders from thinking about setting up colonies; early successes with the fur trade encouraged its continuation. **6.** The London Company did not anticipate the environmental conditions that were the source of many of the colony's problems and wanted settlers to search for gold

and a northwest passage to China. **7.** The Pilgrims wanted to separate from the Church of England, but the Puritans wanted to reform it. **8.** Possible answers: Many ships and settlers arrived in Massachusetts from the very beginning; probably the people had more varied skills than did those who first went to Jamestown. The Massachusetts settlers chose a very able leader. The land they chose was more suited to settlement than was the lowland where Jamestown was located.

Critical Thinking 1. They were adventurous, courageous, and bold; they had to know how to survive in spite of difficult natural obstacles. **2. (a)** The Spanish came first as conquerors and explorers; later they set up settlements that were regulated strictly by the Laws of the Indies. The earliest English colonies struggled until they found a way to grow food and, in the case of Jamestown, to grow a crop they could sell in Europe; there were no central regulations such as the Laws of the Indies. The French relied mostly on fur trapping to gain their foothold in America. **(b)** Possible answers: Spain regulated its colonies very strictly, in order to protect the gold and riches being shipped back to Spain. English colonies, on the other hand, were religious havens or business ventures, set up by joint stock companies; there was less direct involvement by the English government at first. The French were troubled by problems in France and so gave little attention at first to their lands in North America.

Connecting Past and Present 1. Possible answers: In both cases people were going in search of unknown places; they were pitting their courage against nature; people had to plan carefully and carry appropriate supplies for the voyage; both cost a lot of money. **2.** Possible answers: You can still find examples of Spanish architecture in these areas; also the names of many natural and human-made places have Spanish names; popular foods in these areas are similar to Spanish foods.

Developing Basic Skills 1. Check student charts for accuracy. **(a)** Possible answers: All groups were motivated by the desire for wealth. While the Spanish were primarily interested in discovering gold, the English wanted to establish permanent agricultural colonies. **(b)** The desire to spread Christianity and the desire to gain wealth. **2. (a)** Magellan, Drake. **(b)** They were trying to reach Asia around the coast of Africa. **(c)** Da Gama. **3. (a)** West Indies, southern North America. **(b)** Northeastern North America. **(c)** Northeastern North America. **(d)** Hudson Bay, Hudson River area. **(e)** There was not an ice-free passage through or around North America.

SPIRIT OF AMERICA   (pages 48–51)

ANSWERS: RELIGION IN HISTORY (pages 48–49)

1. The Puritans believed that their society in America would serve as a model for the reforming of England, that they were building a "city on a hill" for all to see and imitate. **2.** Possible answers: Religious values of right and wrong have influenced people's actions. Diversity might have made people more tolerant of different beliefs, because they wanted people to be tolerant of their own beliefs. It has made religion an important factor in American life.

ANSWERS: NOTABLE AMERICANS   (page 50)

1. For expressing beliefs that contradicted those of the colony's leaders and for saying that the leaders were doing Satan's work. **2.** Because if her ideas spread, the people might turn against the leaders of the colony; if she were allowed to stay, control of the colony might fall into the hands of people with "wrong ideas," such as Hutchinson's, and the Puritan leaders would see this as harmful to the colony.

ANSWERS: VOICES OF FREEDOM   (page 51)

1. That no one be forced to practice any particular religion and that people be allowed to practice their own religion if they have one. **2.** He states that people should have the freedom to practice their religion if they have one, but that people still must follow the laws of the community in other matters.

Chapter 3   (pages 52–75)

Life in Colonial America

OVERVIEW

Chapter 3 focuses on the political, social, economic, and cultural development of colonial America. Students explore life in the New England, Middle, and Southern colonies and examine how a distinctive American culture began to take shape in spite of regional differences.

HISTORICAL SIDELIGHTS

The following pieces of historical information can serve as notes of interest during the study of Chapter 3. The page numbers in parentheses indicate the points in the student text at which you may wish to introduce the information.

The Heritage of Manhattan (p. 54)   The original Dutch settlement on Manhattan Island left its imprint. By 1650, a blockhouse, several windmills, and houses clustered around the principal street. The street was lined on both sides by a palisade, or wall—hence the name Wall Street. The farms that were scattered beyond the walls were known as "bouweries," a name that survives in the city's Bowery section. Although the settlement of 1650 numbered only about 1,000 people, the inhabitants of Manhattan Island were remarkably diverse. Dutch, French, English, Portuguese, Swedes, Finns, Jews, and Brazilian blacks lived at the trading outpost, where 18 languages were spoken.

Bachelors in New England (p. 60)   In New England, where the virtues of family life were important, colonists frowned on bachelors. Town laws often forbade them to live alone and ordered them to stay with a family of the town's choice until they married.

Voting by Voice (p. 65)   Election days were festive occasions in many colonies, with the candidates giving supporters free food and drink. People cast their votes by voice in the presence of the candidates. The following dialogue from an election in Virginia illustrates the custom:

Sheriff: Mr. Blair, who do you vote for?
Blair: John Marshall.
Marshall: Your vote is appreciated, Mr. Blair.
Sheriff: Who do you vote for, Mr. Buchanan?
Buchanan: For John Clopton.
Clopton: Mr. Buchanan, I shall treasure that vote in my memory. It will be regarded as a feather in my cap forever.

SECTION 1   (pages 53–58)
Developing a Colonial System

ACTIVITIES*

○ **Reading a Chart** Have students study the chart on text page 55. Ask: (1) Which colonies made up the Middle Colonies? (2) Who was

---

*See "To the Teacher" for an explanation of the symbols.

the leader of Georgia? (3) Which colonies were not settled by the English at first? (4) When did New Hampshire become a royal colony? Virginia? (5) Religious freedom was a reason for founding which colonies?

☆ **Biographical Sketch** Ask students to research the background of one of the founders of the American colonies and write a biographical sketch. They should concentrate on the person's reasons for establishing the colony and ideas about how such a colony should be governed.

☐ **Comparing** Have students trace the development of representative government in New York and Pennsylvania. They should consider the original form of government, any changes that were made, and the reasons for the changes. More advanced students may want to do further research and write a report about their findings.

ANSWER: CHART STUDY   (page 55)

New Hampshire, New Jersey, Pennsylvania, Maryland, the Carolinas.

ANSWERS: SECTION 1 REVIEW   (page 58)

1. Maryland Toleration Act, Charles II—p. 54; James Oglethorpe—p. 56; Glorious Revolution—p. 58. **2.** Proprietor—p. 54. **3. (a)** As a refuge for Roman Catholics and as a money-making real estate venture. **(b)** Protestants and Catholics. **4. (a)** As a refuge for fellow Quakers. **(b)** Democratic. **5.** Royal colonies received better protection from the English army and navy, and colonial representatives had more political power. The king gained a share of the profits from the colonies. **6.** Possible answers: Because they had seen how they might be treated if they did not have representative government (for example, when the king created the Dominion of New England). Because they had grown accustomed to being governed by representatives.

SECTION 2   (pages 58–61)

The New England Colonies

ACTIVITIES

○ **Vocabulary Building** Ask students to use a dictionary to define the term "self-sufficient." Have them explain how people on New England farms were self-sufficient. Then have them suggest ways people are self-sufficient today.

☆ **Applying Information** Ask students to reread "Social Classes in New England" on text page 61. Then divide the class into four groups, one representing upper class New Englanders, one a group of wealthy artisans, one a group of farmers, and the last group, members of the Massachusetts General Court. Have the groups debate the law specifying who could wear expensive clothing, described on text page 61.

☐ **Making an Oral Report** Have students work in groups to prepare an oral report on the status of women in the New England colonies. Each group should focus on one of the following topics: property rights, legal rights, educational opportunities, employment opportunities. Possible sources include *We, the American Women* edited by Beth Millstein and Jeanne Bodin and *Daughters of the Promised Land* by Page Smith.

ANSWERS: MAP STUDY   (page 59)

New England—New Hampshire, Massachusetts, Connecticut, Rhode Island; Middle—New York, New Jersey, Pennsylvania, Delaware; Southern—Maryland, Virginia, North Carolina, South Carolina, Georgia; about 800 miles.

ANSWERS: SECTION 2 REVIEW   (page 61)

1. Subsistence farming, self-sufficient—p. 58; town meeting—p. 60. **2.** The New England farm family had the resources to get along without outside help. Men were responsible for the crops and animals; women made clothing, utensils, and other household necessities. **3.** The elders of a congregation requested a tract of land from the colonial legislature. After approval of the request, the tract was surveyed and divided into lots. Each family received land for a house and farm. **4.** It was less rigid. The social system grew more democratic as people became financially able to improve their status. **5.** Possible answer: Because farming conditions were poor, New Englanders developed fishing, shipping, and other industries.

SECTION 3   (pages 61–64)

The Middle Colonies

ACTIVITIES

○ **Map Reading** Have students study the map and graph on text page 62 and answer the following questions: (1) In which colonies did most Scotch-Irish settle? What percentage of the population were they? (2) In which colonies were Africans a major portion of the population? (3) What immigrant groups settled in Pennsylvania? (4) In Massachusetts?

☆ **Understanding a Primary Source** Read aloud the following description of frontier life in 1711 or duplicate and distribute copies.

Women are dear and scarce. I have about a dozen acres of clear ground, and the rest woods; in all, 300 acres. Had I servants and money, I might live very comfortably upon it, raise good corn of all sorts, and cattle, without any great labor. . . . I am forced to work hard with axe, hoe, and spade. I have not a stick to burn for any use but what I cut down with my own hands. I am forced to dig a garden, raise beans, peas, etc. . . . Men are generally of all trades, and women the like within their spheres.

Ask: (1) What problems did the frontier farmer face? (2) Why might life become easier when more settlers moved to the area? (3) How might the role of women on the frontier be different from that of city women?

☐ **Researching** Have students do additional research on slavery in the Middle Colonies between 1650 and 1750. Students should consider the number of slaves in the Middle Colonies, the work slaves did, and how they were treated. A possible source is *From Slavery to Freedom: A History of American Negroes* by John Hope Franklin.

ANSWERS: MAP AND GRAPH STUDY (page 62)
North Carolina; southern coast; 48.7 percent.

ANSWERS : MAP STUDY (page 64)
Along the Atlantic coastline; colonists followed the inland rivers and settled near them to ensure a supply of water.

ANSWERS: SECTION 3 REVIEW (page 64)
1. Scotch-Irish—p. 62; Pennsylvania Dutch—p. 63. **2.** Patroon, fall line—p. 63. **3. (a)** The Scotch-Irish and the Germans, who became known as Pennsylvania Dutch. **(b)** In search of religious toleration and economic prosperity. **4. (a)** Pennsylvania. **(b)** New York. Because of the patroon system of landholding, settlers preferred to settle in other colonies. **(c)** By farming, hunting, and trapping. **5. (a)** The Middle Colonies and New England. **(b)** No, less freedom; most colonies passed laws restricting their activities. **6.** Possible answer: Backcountry settlers lived in virtual isolation.

SECTION 4   (pages 65–69)
The Southern Colonies

ACTIVITIES

○ **Applying Information** Have students review the subsection "Indentured Servants" on text pages 66–67. Then ask them to imagine that they are indentured servants who have just completed their contract. Have them write an essay in which they describe their plans for the future.

☆ **Finding the Main Idea** Write the following excerpt from a poem by Phillis Wheatley on the chalkboard or duplicate and distribute copies. Wheatley was brought to America as a slave. She taught herself to read and write and became a well-known poet. (See text page 72.) Ask students to look up any words in the poem they don't know. Then have them explain in their own words what Wheatley is saying.

I, young in life, by seeming cruel fate
Was snatch'd from Afric's fancy'd happy seat:
What pangs excruciating must molest,
What sorrows labour in my parent's breast?
Steel'd was the soul and by no misery mov'd
That from a father seiz'd his babe belov'd
Such, such my case. And can I then but pray
Others may never feel tyrannic sway?

☐ **Comparing** Have students investigate Bacon's Rebellion in 1676 and the activities of the Regulators in 1771. Then ask them to compare the causes and outcomes of the two rebellions in a short essay or an oral report. They might consult *The American Heritage History of the Thirteen Colonies* edited by L. B. Wright.

ANSWER: CHART STUDY (page 67)
Possible answer: Slavery grew much more rapidly in the South than in the North.

ANSWERS: SECTION 4 REVIEW (page 69)
1. Regulators, Eliza Lucas Pinckney—p. 65; Nathaniel Bacon—p. 67; "middle passage"—p. 68. **2.** Piedmont region, tidewater region, planter, cash crop, indigo—p. 65; indentured servant—p. 66; slave code—p. 69. **3.** They felt unrepresented in the government, thought taxes were unfair, and generally resented the wealth of the planters. **4.** Cash crops such as indigo and rice could be sold for large profits. **5. (a)** An opportunity to acquire

land and become independent. Also, the chance to learn a trade and get an education. **(b)** The inability of indentured servants to meet labor demands, the need to teach skills to a new group every few years, and the presence of embittered former servants in the backcountry. **6.** Possible answer: Because slavery was economically profitable, anti-slavery protests had little effect.

SECTION 5   (pages 69–73)
Colonial Culture

ACTIVITIES

○ **Making an Outline**   Have students review the subsection "The Importance of Education." Then ask them to make an outline of the information presented. Afterward, ask students: What seems to have been the purpose of colonial education? What do they think is the purpose of education today?

☆ **Supporting Generalizations**   Read aloud each of the following generalizations, or duplicate the list and distribute copies. Ask students to write two or three factual statements that support each generalization: (1) No single church was dominant in all the American colonies. (2) American colonists were not tolerant of all religious groups. (3) There was generally more religious tolerance in the American colonies than in Europe. (4) Colonial Americans valued education. (5) Cities had a significant effect on life in colonial America. When students have completed the assignment, review their answers in class.

□ **Finding the Main Idea**   Many of Benjamin Franklin's sayings have remained an important part of American folklore. Read the following maxims to the class and ask students to tell what they think each means in their own words. Ask students whether they think each maxim is still applicable.

If you'd know the value of money, go and borrow some.
Three may keep a secret, if two of them are dead.
When the well's dry, we know the worth of water.
Little strokes fell great oaks.
Beware of little expenses; a small leak will sink a great ship.

No gains without pains.
'Tis easier to prevent bad habits than to break them.
Do not squander time, for that's what life is made of.

ANSWERS: NOTABLE AMERICANS   (page 71)
1. Not drinking beer at breakfast; nude bathing; moderation; exercise; swimming; inoculation against smallpox. **2.** Possible answers: psychologist; newspaper columnist; doctor.

ANSWERS: SKILL LESSON   (page 73)
1. (a) Population. **(b)** Years. **(c)** Population growth of New York, Philadelphia, Boston, and Charleston between 1690 and 1730. **2. (a)** 3,900. **(b)** 1690–1700. **(c)** 3,500. **3. (a)** Boston. **(b)** Boston. **(c)** 2,000. **4. (a)** All four cities experienced population growth. **(b)** Answers should mention trade, transportation, and immigration.

ANSWERS: SECTION 5 REVIEW   (page 73)
1. Established church, primer—p. 70; dame school, literacy rate—p. 72. **2. (a)** Mutual toleration developed as a matter of necessity. **(b)** Roman Catholicism and Judaism. **3. (a)** Massachusetts. **(b)** Puritans believed it provided access to truths in the Bible. **4.** Girls were educated in dame schools, where they learned reading and writing as well as sewing and embroidery. In the South, some were educated by tutors. In New England, boys were educated in public grammar schools, where their instruction prepared them for college. In the other colonies, private schools and tutors existed for those who could afford them. **5.** Possible answer: Many people had come to America seeking religious freedom.

ANSWERS: CHAPTER 3 REVIEW   (pages 74–75)
   Vocabulary   1. Proprietors. **2.** self-sufficient. **3.** patroons. **4.** Cash crops. **5.** Slave codes.
   Chapter Checkup   1. (a) In a royal colony the king appointed the colonial governor and council. **(b)** The governor controlled trade, appointed judges, and served as the colony's chief executive. **(c)** The council advised the governor, approved official appointments, and served as the colony's highest court. **(d)** The assembly had to consent to all proposed laws before they could be passed. **2.** Virginia and Massachusetts had representative government from the earliest days, and the other colonies gradually followed their example. Whether under proprietary colonies or royal colonies, the king provided for the colonists to have some say in their governments. Eventually, the colonists came to prize that self-government and to resent any

attempts to take it away. **3. (a)** Timber, shipbuilding, and fishing; agriculture; agriculture. **(b)** Different climates and geography. **4. (a)** In New England, below the upper class were landowners and merchants. Beneath them were shopkeepers, artisans, and small landowners. Lowest stood city workers, tenant farmers, and agricultural laborers. **(b)** The colonies became more prosperous, enabling people to improve their social status. **5.** Backcountry farming was on a subsistence level; families were much more dependent on each other for survival. Isolation made life in the backcountry different from life along the coast. **6.** Slavery became a more viable way of meeting labor demands. **7.** The economic structures in these regions did not require a large low-cost work force to survive. **8.** Slaves needed permission to leave the plantation; they had only limited rights to testify in court; any slave who killed his or her owner was subject to death. **9. (a)** The Great Awakening was a time of religious revival. **(b)** It led to the splintering of religious groups. **10. (a)** Because education was provided in a variety of schools throughout the colonies. **(b)** It was lower on the frontier; possible answer: On the frontier, life was harder and people had to concentrate on meeting their basic needs.

Critical Thinking 1. Governments in proprietary colonies were less democratic that those in colonies organized under charters. **2.** Slavery deprived the slave of freedom to make choices. Students might point out that the master determined where a slave's spouse and children would live. All slaves knew that they were property. **3.** It served the planters by providing a controlled and steady supply of labor, with no need to retrain every few years. **4.** Possible answer: Girls received some education, because colonists believed in the value of education. But girls received less education because many felt that advanced education was not necessary for a woman to play her most common role of mother and homemaker.

Connecting Past and Present 1. Possible answers: **(a)** Social class is less important today. **(b)** Easier today, where public education gives everyone a more equal start. **2.** Students might say it serves the public by presenting them with points of view to consider. Or they might say it hurts because some people will not be able to distinguish editorial opinions from news, and will thus not get a clear picture of events.

Developing Basic Skills 1. (a) New York, Delaware. **(b)** New Hampshire, New York, Delaware, New Jersey, Pennsylvania, Maryland, the Carolinas, Georgia. **(c)** religious freedom, profit from trade. **2.** From most rigid to least rigid: Southern Colonies coastal area, New England towns, Middle Colonies coastal area, Southern Colonies backcountry, Middle Colonies backcountry. **(a)** The Southern Colonies coastal area had the most rigid social system in that the slaves were absolutely barred from improving their status. Students could place the New England towns in the second rank because people in this area observed sharp distinctions among classes. The Middle Colonies coastal area could be ranked third because it contained manors worked by tenant farmers who could never own their own land. In the backcountry of the Southern and Middle colonies, nearly all farming was on a subsistence level and social distinctions were not important. **(b)** Differences might have resulted from the attitudes of the colonies' founders. Also, unique conditions in the backcountry fostered a kind of equality. **3. (a)** The graph shows the ethnic breakdown of the colonial population in 1775. **(b)** English, African, and Scotch-Irish; Dutch, French, and Swedish. **(c)** Students could suggest that many people in the colonies were of English origin, but other groups were important as well.

Chapter 4 (pages 76–91)
A Struggle for Empire ——

OVERVIEW

Chapter 4 focuses on the competition for empire in North America among the nations of Great Britain, France, and Spain. Students read about the effects of British mercantilism on the American colonies and examine the basis for conflict among the European nations and the result of that conflict—the French and Indian War.

HISTORICAL SIDELIGHTS

The following pieces of historical information can serve as notes of interest during the study of Chapter 4. The page numbers in parentheses indicate the points in the student text at which you may wish to introduce the information.

College Life (p. 81) During the 1600s, Spain established more than 20 universities in the New World, as well as 100 seminaries, colleges, and private schools. College students of the era, both in Spanish America and in the English colonies, were slightly younger than today's students, and they were often boisterous. Practical jokes and brawls with townspeople were common. Spanish officials sometimes set up campus jails to punish offenders. In New England, "rustication"—sending pupils to stay with a country family until their behavior improved—was a favorite discipline.

Quick Thinking at Quebec (pp. 88–89) In the battle for Quebec, the British might never have reached the Plains of Abraham without the quick thinking of a French-speaking Scotsman, General Wolfe. His plan required the British troop boats to drift silently past the French city under cover of darkness. Disaster seemed imminent when a French sentinel spotted them. *"Qui vive?"* (Who goes there?) cried the sentry. *"France!"* replied the Scotsman. *"De quel regiment?"* (What regiment?) responded the sentry. *"De la Reine"* (The queen's regiment), the Scot called back. The sentry was satisfied and let the boats pass.

SECTION 1 (pages 77–80)
Colonies: A Vital Part of the British Empire

ACTIVITIES*

○ **Classifying** Have students make a chart with two columns headed Colonial Imports and Colonial Exports. Remind them that imports are goods brought into a country and exports are goods shipped out of a country. Ask students to refer to the map on text page 79 and in Section 1 to list the items the colonies imported and the items they exported. Then ask: (1) Did the Americas send manufactured goods or raw materials to Europe? (2) What did Europe ship to the New World?

☆ **Relating Past to Present** Have students re-read Sir Walter Raleigh's comment on text page 77 about the value of commerce: "Whoever commands the trade of the world commands the riches of the world and consequently the world itself." Ask whether they think the statement was true at the time and if it still applies to conditions in the world today. For example, they might consider the production and distribution of oil or wheat.

□ **Researching** Have students read about the history of the Netherlands during the mid-1600s. They could consult an encyclopedia or a book of European history. Ask them to write

---

*See "To the Teacher" for an explanation of the symbols.

T 14

a short report about the Dutch role in world trade during that period. Students should explain why the English considered the Dutch their chief commercial competitor.

ANSWER: MAP STUDY (page 79)

Rum for slaves on the west coast of Africa; slaves for molasses in the West Indies.

ANSWERS: SECTION 1 REVIEW (page 80)

1. Molasses Act—p. 80. **2.** mercantilism—p. 77; enumerated commodity—p. 78; triangular trade—p. 80. **3.** Colonies provided essential raw materials and served as a market for finished products. **4.** By prohibiting colonists from using foreign ships, Britain hoped to stop colonial trade with other nations, particularly the Netherlands. **5. (a)** For the most part, yes. **(b)** Colonial benefits included bonuses for producing certain goods and protection from French and Spanish competition. **6.** Possible answer: Because in those days goods could be sent from colonies to Europe only by sea; so a strong navy could help protect the merchant ships.

SECTION 2 (pages 80–85)
Rivalry in North America

ACTIVITIES

○ **Scrambled Names** Write the following scrambled names and clues on the chalkboard or duplicate and distribute copies. Ask students to use the clues to unscramble the names.

1. QSUORIIO	**1.** drove the Algonquins from their hunting grounds
2. NIOK	**2.** set up missions in Arizona in the 1690s
3. ALSAELL	**3.** claimed Louisiana for France
4. NHOUR	**4.** served as middlemen between other Native Americans and French traders
5. METRQUETA	**5.** explored the Mississippi River for France

Answers: **1.** Iroquois **2.** Kino **3.** La Salle **4.** Huron **5.** Marquette

☆ **Classifying** Divide the class into groups of four or five students. Have each group make a chart with the following five headings: European Country, Area Settled, Type of Settler, Factors Aiding Settlement, Factors Hindering

Settlement. Ask them to use text pages 80–85 as well as Chapter 2 to complete the chart for Spain, France, and Great Britain. When the groups have completed their charts, have them compare answers. Then ask: (1) How did the types of settlers differ? (2) What effect did the type of settler have on the density of population in the areas settled by the three countries? (3) What factors encouraged British settlement? (4) What factors hindered French settlement?

☐ **Relating Cause and Effect**   Ask students to write one effect for each of the following developments. (1) In 1783 the Spanish declared that slaves who escaped from the English colonies could live freely in Florida. (2) Louis XIV of France launched a program of empire building. (3) Europeans took an active part in the fur trade. (4) English settlers moved into Indian lands and cleared the forest for planting.

ANSWERS: **SKILL LESSON**   (page 82)
1. **(a)** Land Claims in North America, 1753. **(b)** 1753. **(c)** British, French, Spanish, and Russian claims. **2.** **(a)** Approximately 1950 kilometers; approximately 800 kilometers. **(b)** Britain **(c)** Appalachian Mountains. **(d)** Mississippi and Ohio rivers. **3.** **(a)** To the Appalachian Mountains. The mountains formed a natural barrier to further expansion. **(b)** At the border of present-day Florida. **(c)** West of the Appalachian Mountains.

ANSWER: **MAP STUDY**   (page 83)
With France, because France claimed lands all along the western boundaries of England's colonies.

ANSWERS: **NOTABLE AMERICANS**   (page 84)
1. She was a Creek who married a South Carolina fur trader; she was in a position to help sustain friendly relations between the British and the Creek. **2.** Because in English society women rarely had political power (except when they were born to it, as in the case of a queen).

ANSWERS: **SECTION 2 REVIEW**   (page 85)
1. Louis XIV—p. 82; Joliet, Marquette, La Salle— p. 83; coureur de bois—p. 84; Pequot War—p. 85. **2.** Georgia and Florida. Competition in this area was part of a traditional rivalry between the British and Spanish empires. **3.** **(a)** New France was to be a market for French exports and a food source for the French West Indies. **(b)** The colonists were incapable of producing enough food for themselves, let alone for the West Indies. **(c)** Exploration and fur trading. **4.** Possible answer: Native Americans were forced out of their traditional homes and hunting grounds.

SECTION 3   (pages 86–89)
The French and Indian War

ACTIVITIES

○ **Map Reading**   Have students study the map on text page 88 and answer these questions: (1) In 1763, what nation controlled the lands between the Mississippi River and the Appalachians? Between the Mississippi River and the Rockies? Between the Great Lakes and Hudson Bay? (2) What nation controlled the area of present-day Texas? Colorado? Oregon? Ohio? Alabama?

☆ **Placing Events in Time**   Copy the following time line on the chalkboard. Then read aloud the list of events. Ask students to write the letter of the correct time period for each event on a sheet of paper. Point out that the time line is based on information from the entire chapter.

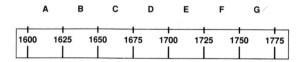

(1) Treaty of Paris signed; (2) Albany Congress held; (3) La Salle reaches Mississippi delta; (4) Father Kino establishes missions in Arizona; (5) Washington defeated at Fort Necessity; (6) French surrender to British at Quebec; (7) Pequot War breaks out; (8) Joliet and Marquette explore the Mississippi; (9) Vizcaino explores northern coast of California; (10) Spanish found Santa Fe.
Answers: **1.** G **2.** G **3.** D **4.** D **5.** G **6.** G **7.** B **8.** C **9.** A **10.** A

☐ **Preparing an Oral Report**   Divide the class into three groups. Have each group research one of the conflicts between France and Britain that preceded the French and Indian War (see pp. 86–87). Have groups prepare oral reports that explain the cause of the war, the major battles, who won, and the results.

ANSWER: **MAP STUDY**   (page 87)
It would have left New France open to British expansion.

ANSWER: **MAP STUDY**   (page 88)
France's claims in North America were almost eliminated; the mainland was divided between Spain

and England; much more territory had been explored by 1763.

ANSWERS: SECTION 3 REVIEW (page 89)

1. Plan of Union, Benjamin Franklin—p. 86; William Pitt—p. 87. **2.** The confrontation of British troops (under George Washington) and French troops in the Ohio Valley. **3.** In response to mounting fears of an attack by the French and their Native American allies, colonists sought to solidify friendship with the Iroquois and to plan for a common defense. **4.** Pitt united the previously divided colonies by guaranteeing them payment for services and supplies. He also replaced older military leaders with more capable younger officers. **5.** Great Britain gained land east of the Mississippi River; Spain gave Florida to Great Britain; Spain received some land west of the Mississippi; France kept a few islands in the Gulf of St. Lawrence and the Caribbean Sea. **6.** Possible answer: Its location on the St. Lawrence River was strategic.

ANSWERS: CHAPTER 4 REVIEW (pages 90–91)

Vocabulary 1. mercantilism. **2.** Enumerated commodities. **3.** triangular trade. **4.** coureurs de bois. **5.** Albany Plan of Union.

Chapter Checkup 1. By controlling trade in the colonies, Britain would be one step closer to "commanding the riches of the world" and then "the world itself." **2.** Colonial merchants were allowed to ship goods on British or colonial vessels only; enumerated commodities could be shipped only to Britain; imported products had to be routed through Britain first. **3.** The acts might have interfered with the rum trade but had little impact because they were not enforced. **4. (a)** Britain and Spain competed for control of Florida. **(b)** Britain competed with France over claims to the Ohio Valley. Control of Canada was also an issue between the two nations. **5. (a)** It stimulated traditional Indian rivalries. **(b)** It pushed Indians out of their traditional lands. **(c)** English settlement, because it would permanently disrupt Indian life. **6.** Pitt, as secretary of state, united the previously divided colonies and brought in new, more capable military officers. A three-pronged attack on the French led to the surrender of Quebec to the British.

Critical Thinking 1. Answers may vary. Students should note that colonialism gave Britain access to raw materials and markets, while the policy of mercantilism guaranteed that Britain would enjoy a favored position in its trade with the colonies. **2.** Answers may vary but should refer to proximate land claims on the North American continent. Students also should refer to the historic antagonism among the British, French, and Spanish.

Connecting Past and Present 1. Yes, importing more than one exports leads to a trade deficit. This causes dollars to leave the United States and leaves the economy vulnerable. **2.** Students might point to examples in current events such as the conflict in the Middle East or troubled United States relations with Latin American countries that are compounded by cultural differences.

Developing Basic Skills 1. (a) East of the Mississippi River and to Canada. **(b)** West of the Mississippi and to Mexico. **(c)** Islands in the Caribbean Sea. **(d)** Spain. **2. (a)** Britain gained the most territory east of the Mississippi River. **(b)** France lost the most.

Unit Two
Creating a Republic

Chapter 5   (pages 94–113)

The Road
to Revolution _____

OVERVIEW

Chapter 5 focuses on the tension that developed
between Britain and the colonies after the French
and Indian War. In this chapter, students examine
British attempts to raise revenue, efforts that
caused growing dissatisfaction in the colonies and
culminated in the First Continental Congress
and the outbreak of fighting at Lexington and
Concord.

HISTORICAL SIDELIGHTS

The following pieces of historical information
can serve as notes of interest during the study
of Chapter 5. The page numbers in parentheses
indicate the points in the student text at which
you may wish to introduce the information.

Tea Party Costumes (pp. 104–105) The "Indians" of the Boston Tea Party were, for the most
part, only thinly disguised. No contemporary account mentions any feathered headbands. The
leaders of the mob wore ragged clothes, perhaps
a hood to cover their heads and shoulders, and
some grease or paint to darken their faces. Most
men carried a hatchet or a pair of pistols. They
charged the wharf, shouting such slogans as
"Boston Harbor a teapot tonight!"

Travel to the Continental Congress (p. 107)
A delegate's journey to the First Continental
Congress was often a broadening experience. For

example, John Adams and the Massachusetts delegation traveled 20 days from Boston to reach Philadelphia. New Haven welcomed the group by ringing
church bells, noted Adams, "and the People Men
Women and Children, were crowding at the Doors
and Windows as it was to see a Coronation." New
York City took the delegation more in stride. New
Yorkers, Adams complained, "talk very loud, very
fast, and all together. If they ask you a Question,
before you can utter 3 words of your Answer, they
will break out upon you again—and talk away."

SECTION 1   (pages 95–100)
Problems of Britain's New Empire

ACTIVITIES*

○ **Map Reading**   Have students study the map
on text page 96. Then ask: (1) About how far
inland was the line drawn by the Proclamation
of 1763? (2) Along which mountain range did
it run? (3) What was done with the land west
of the line? (4) Who controlled the land west
of the Mississippi River? (5) Can you think of
reasons why the Proclamation line was drawn
along the crest of a mountain range?

☆ **Classifying**   Have students make a chart with
these headings: British Problem, British Action,
Colonial Reaction. Ask them to complete the
chart using text pages 95–100. Use the chart
as the basis for a discussion of the mounting
antagonism between British officials and the
colonists.

□ **Analyzing**   Have students reread the statement from the *Gazette* concerning representation for the colonies (text page 98) and then
explain the meaning of the statement in their
own words. Ask students why they think representation was such a concern of the colonists.

---

*See "To the Teacher" for an explanation of
the symbols.

ANSWERS: **MAP STUDY**   (page 96)
Answers will vary.

ANSWER: **GRAPH STUDY**   (page 99)
The graph shows a drop in the value of British imports to the colonies during the periods of the boycotts.

ANSWERS: **SECTION 1 REVIEW**   (page 100)
1. Pontiac, Proclamation of 1763—p. 96; George Grenville—p. 97; Sons of Liberty, Stamp Act Congress, Daughters of Liberty—p. 99. **2.** How to deal with the Native Americans who lived in the new land; whether settlers should be allowed to move west of the Appalachians; how to pay the war debt. **3.** The building of settlements and forts east of the Appalachians in violation of treaties with Native Americans; British General Amherst's refusal to pay Native Americans for land. **4.** Unlike earlier laws, it was an attempt to raise revenues as well as to regulate trade. **5. (a)** Forbade colonial governments from issuing their own paper money, demanded the recall of paper money in circulation, and required British money to be used to pay debts owed to British merchants. **(b)** Passed the responsibility and expense of housing British troops to the colonists. **(c)** Placed a tax on many items, such as legal documents; a tax stamp would be affixed to show the tax had been paid. **6.** Possible answer: The colonists believed that because they did not elect members to Parliament, they were not represented there. Parliament's view was that its members represented all British citizens.

> ## SECTION 2   (pages 100–103)
> # The Quarrel Widens

ACTIVITIES
○ **Placing Events in Time**   Copy the time line below on the chalkboard. Then read aloud the list of events. Ask students to write on a sheet of paper the letter of the correct time period for each event. Then ask: Are there cause-and-effect relationships between any of the events?

A	B	C	D	E	
1766	1767	1768	1769	1770	1771

(1) George III appoints Lord North as prime minister; (2) Boston Massacre; (3) British troops set up camp on the Boston common; (4) colonial merchants sign nonimportation agreement; (5) Townshend Acts passed.
Answers: **1.** E **2.** E **3.** C **4.** C **5.** B

☆ **Applying Information**   Draw a chart on the chalkboard with three columns headed Action, Purpose, Consequences. List the following actions in the first column: (1) Townshend Acts passed; (2) Townshend tries to enforce Townshend Acts; (3) Townshend tries to enforce Quartering Act; (4) British send two regiments of troops to Boston.

Ask students to describe the purpose and consequences of each action. Then add the information to the chart. When the chart is completed, ask: (1) What was Townshend's goal for the American colonies? (2) How did he try to accomplish it? (3) What was the reaction of the colonists? (4) Was Townshend successful? Why or why not?

☐ **Interpreting Visual Evidence**   Ask students to study Paul Revere's engraving of the Boston Massacre on text page 102 and to describe the event as it is shown in the engraving. Then have them compare their description with the description of the incident on text page 102. Ask: (1) Why did Revere portray the incident as he did? (2) What might John Adams have said about Revere's engraving?

ANSWERS: **SECTION 2 REVIEW**   (page 103)
1. Charles Townshend—p. 100; the Boston Massacre, John Adams—p. 102; Lord North—p. 103. **2.** non-importation agreement, writs of assistance —p. 101. **3.** No, because the colonists signed a non-importation agreement and started buying colonial-made goods. **4.** The colonial legislatures showed their support of New York by vowing to resist every tax put on them by Great Britain. **5.** Parliament hoped to quiet colonial outrage and, at the same time, assert their right to tax the colonies. **6.** Possible answer: Strong emotions and anti-British sentiment made it difficult for many eyewitnesses to remain objective.

> ## SECTION 3   (pages 103–107)
> # The Roots of Independence

ACTIVITIES
○ **Comparing and Contrasting**   Have students study the pictures on pages 104 and 105 and

review the information in the text about the burning of the *Gaspée* and the Boston Tea Party. Then ask them to compare the two events in terms of their causes, what happened during the incidents, and the results.

☆ **Making Generalizations** Ask students to write two or three factual statements that support each of the following generalizations: (1) During 1772 tensions between the colonists and Britain increased. (2) Lord North and George III tried to force the colonists to obey British authority. (3) Committees of Correspondence played an important role in unifying the colonies.

☐ **Defending a Position** Ask students to act out the dialogue in the special feature *The Local Tavern: A Communication Center* (text page 106). Then ask each student to imagine that he or she is a British official who entered the tavern and heard the conversation. Have students describe their reaction.

ANSWERS: VOICES OF FREEDOM (page 106)
1. That Parliament might pass a law taxing or taking away their property. **2.** Possible answer: Because he would need the support of the people to take action against Britain.

ANSWERS: SECTION 3 REVIEW (page 107)
1. *Gaspée*—p. 103; British East India Company—p. 104; Intolerable Acts—p. 105; Committees of Correspondence, Samuel Adams—p. 107. **2. (a)** To make tea sold by the British East India Company in the colonies cheaper than Dutch tea, which was smuggled in. **(b)** Complaints by colonial tea merchants about a British monopoly led to a widespread tea boycott. In Massachusetts, colonists dumped the tea on British ships into Boston Harbor. **3.** To punish Boston, the center of colonial resistance, and to spread fear throughout the colonies. **4.** Colonial unity grew as colonists learned more about the issues of the day and their common grievances against Britain. **5.** To discuss a unified response to the Intolerable Acts. **6.** Possible answer: Trial by jury was a fundamental right. If it was in jeopardy, so were other rights.

SECTION 4   (pages 108–111)
From Protest to Revolution

ACTIVITIES
○ **Identifying** Read aloud the following clues and ask students to identify the people:

(1) argued that Parliament could not legislate for the colonies; (2) led British troops at Concord; (3) set up to enforce boycott of British goods; (4) warned colonists that the British were moving through Massachusetts; (5) members of Massachusetts militia; (6) leader of "moderates" at First Continental Congress. *Answers:* **1.** Jefferson **2.** Pitcairn **3.** Association **4.** Revere **5.** Minutemen **6.** Galloway

☆ **Understanding Chronology** Ask students to create a horizontal time line and place the following events on it: (1) The Massachusetts Congress votes to raise 13,600 troops. (2) Coercive Acts passed. (3) Fighting breaks out at Lexington and Concord. (4) First Continental Congress meets. (5) Paul Revere warns colonists about British troops. (6) General Gage orders troops to seize arsenal at Concord. Then ask: What cause-and-effect relationships do you see between any of the events? *Answers:* 2, 4, 6, 5, 3, 1

☐ **Analyzing a Primary Source** Read aloud the following excerpt from Jefferson's "A Summary View of the Rights of British America" or duplicate and distribute copies:

Can any one reason be assigned why 160,000 electors in the island of Great Britain should give law to 4,000,000 in the states of America, every individual of whom is equal to every individual of them in virtue, in understanding, and in bodily strength?

Ask students to restate the quotation in their own words and state its main idea. Ask: Why do you think Jefferson stated that Americans were equal to British electors in virtue, understanding, and strength?

ANSWERS: VOICES OF FREEDOM (page 109)
1. Because the king sent an army to the colonies that could have no other purpose. **2.** Possible answers: repetition of words; calls to God; words such as "We must fight!"; use of questions to involve the listener.

ANSWERS: SKILL LESSON (page 110)
1. (a) Government report. **(b)** Lieutenant-Colonel Smith. Yes. **(c)** April 22, 1775. **2. (a)** He was probably expected to inform his supervisors of the results of the battles. **(b)** He commanded British troops that marched on Concord and Lexington. **(c)** British. From the context it is clear that he is commanding the "king's troops." He might be inclined to exaggerate the bravery of his troops or the numerical strength of the enemy. **(d)** Yes. However, one should take into account the author's need to justify his role to his commanding officer.

3. (a) Smith's troops moved in response to Gage's orders. Smith marched to Concord. When the British arrived, the colonists were lined up on the green. The colonists fired first; the soldiers returned the fire. The British troops were fired upon as they returned to Boston. **(b)** He believed that the colonists' attack on the British was planned. He believed that the British intended no harm. **(c)** They seemed reluctant to engage the colonists in battle.

ANSWERS: **SECTION 4 REVIEW**   (page 111)
1. Joseph Galloway, Thomas Jefferson, *Declaration and Resolves*—p. 108; Continental Association—p. 109. **2.** minutemen—p. 111. **3. (a)** They proposed to unite the colonies under British authority; a colonial representative council would be able to veto laws of Parliament concerning the colonies. **(b)** The radicals believed that Parliament did not have the right to tax or make laws for the colonists. **4.** It issued *Declaration and Resolves;* agreed to cut off trade with Britain and set up the Continental Association; agreed to meet again the next spring. **5.** General Gage received word that the minutemen had an arsenal of weapons at Concord. **6.** Possible answer: As long as they were economically dependent on Britain, they were not really free.

ANSWERS: **CHAPTER 6 REVIEW** (pages 112–113)
   Vocabulary   **1.** b **2.** a **3.** c **4.** c **5.** b
   Chapter Checkup   **1. (a)** Settlers had built forts in western lands in violation of Indian treaties, and the British had not paid Indians for confiscated land. **(b)** The Proclamation of 1763 was a direct result of Pontiac's Rebellion. The British tried to enforce a border between colonial and Indian lands. **2. (a)** The Sugar Act cut taxes on molasses and added a tax on coffee, wine, sugar, and cloth. The Currency Act prohibited colonies from issuing paper money, required the recall of paper money in circulation, and required British debts to be paid with British currency. The Quartering Act required that the colonists provide room and board for British troops. The Stamp Act required that a stamp, representing a paid tax, be affixed to a number of items. **(b)** The colonists objected to these measures and sought their repeal. **3. (a)** Revenue measures passed in 1767 by Parliament. **(b)** By firing customs officials who accepted bribes, by issuing writs of assistance, and by stationing more troops in Boston. **(c)** By manufacturing goods instead of importing them, by signing nonimportation agreements, and by taunting British soldiers in Boston (leading to the Boston Massacre). **4. (a)** The Coercive Acts punished Massachusetts for the Boston Tea Party by closing the port of Boston, revoking the charter of Massachusetts, disbanding the legislature, imposing military rule, forbidding town meetings, and reviving the Quartering Act. **(b)** The colonists considered it a deliberate obstacle to westward expansion because it provided for the expansion of Quebec's boundaries. **5. (a)** The moderates sought a compromise and reconciliation with Great Britain. The radicals wanted to redefine the relationship of the colonies to Britain. For them the British Empire was a loose union of independent states, each with its own legislature and united by loyalty to the king. **(b)** By the end of the Congress, the radical position seemed to dominate. **6.** Compromise would now be more difficult; people had died on both sides so there was now much greater risk of war.
   Critical Thinking   **1. (a)** Both were imposed as revenue-raising measures on the colonies by Parliament, a body 3,000 miles away that had no colonial representatives. **(b)** The Sugar Act and the Stamp Act were passed to raise revenue. The Molasses Act taxed all molasses or rum imported from the West Indies, but its primary purpose was regulating trade. **(c)** The colonists thought that their assemblies had the power to tax them because the members of the assemblies were elected to represent them. **2.** "Massacre" is defined as the "indiscriminate merciless killing of a number of human beings." The incident was a massacre in that British troops fired indiscriminately at the crowd. More important, however, the colonial press may have been trying to arouse the colonists against the British.
   Connecting Past and Present   **1.** Possible answers: rallies, articles, speeches, voter registration. **2.** Possible answers: nuclear war, environmental pollution, abortion, relations with South Africa.
   Developing Basic Skills   **1. (a)** Appalachian Mountains. **(b)** Native Americans. **(c)** Spain. **2.** Check student time lines for accuracy. **(a)** Four months. **(b)** Three years. **(c)** Yes. The time line reflects the increasing refusal of the colonies to submit to Britain's demands.

Chapter 6   (pages 114–135)
A War for Independence

OVERVIEW
Chapter 6 traces the American War for Independence from the first battle at Lexington and Concord in 1775 to the signing of the Treaty of Paris in

1783. Students examine how the colonists organized themselves politically and militarily. They also study the course of the fighting and the terms of the peace.

HISTORICAL SIDELIGHTS

The following pieces of historical information can serve as notes of interest during the study of Chapter 6. The page numbers in parentheses indicate the points in the student text at which you may wish to introduce the information.

Yankees and Buckskin Soldiers (p. 125) Continental soldiers from different colonies were reluctant at first to serve in the same regiment. New Englanders were distrustful of Virginians, whom they called "buckskins" because General Daniel Morgan's recruits wore the fringed hunting shirt of the frontier. Pennsylvanians were often suspicious of residents of New England, or "Yankees." One Philadelphia lady was surprised to discover that New Englanders looked like her own people. "Is he a Yankee?" she asked of one soldier. "I thought he was a Pennsylvanian. I don't see any difference between him and other people."

The Swamp Fox (p. 130) No patriot knew how to use the tactics of guerrilla warfare better than the "Swamp Fox" of South Carolina, Francis Marion. Marion was a prosperous planter, over 40 years old when the fighting broke out. He successfully led his band of patriots on grueling campaigns through the Carolina swamps. The men marched under the cover of darkness, rested during the day, and never camped in the same spot two nights in a row. Young Colonel Banastre Tarleton, the British commander who unsuccessfully pursued Marion, ruefully remarked that "the devil himself" could not catch that "old fox."

SECTION 1	(pages 115–118)

The Revolution Begins

ACTIVITIES*

○ **Studying a Map** Refer students to the map on text page 118. Have them locate the places mentioned in the reading. Then ask: Who were the American officers named on the map? How can you tell? Which British officer is named? What does the map show him doing?

---

*See "To the Teacher" for an explanation of the symbols.

☆ **Recognizing Points of View** Divide the class into small groups. Have half the groups write an account of the Battle of Bunker Hill from the point of view of a colonist strongly critical of British actions over the past two years. Have the other groups write from the point of view of a strong supporter of British policy in the colonies. When students finish, have groups exchange reports. Ask: (1) What facts can you identify? (2) What opinions? (3) How can you recognize the point of view of the writers?

☐ **Making Generalizations** Ask students to make a list of the American military officers mentioned on text pages 115–118. Have them find information about the officers' military experience by consulting an encyclopedia or the *Dictionary of American Biography*. Then ask students to write one generalization about the military experience of army leaders at the beginning of the Revolutionary War. They should provide at least three factual statements to support their generalization.

ANSWERS: MAP STUDY   (page 118)

American victories—Concord, Dorchester Heights, Fort Ticonderoga; American defeats—Lexington, Bunker Hill, Quebec.

ANSWERS: SECTION 1 REVIEW   (page 118)

1. John Dickinson, Committees of Safety, Bunker Hill—p. 116; Israel Putnam, William Howe, Benedict Arnold—p. 117. **2.** Moderates hoped to compromise with Britain, while radicals sought independence. **3.** Soldiers respected George Washington's leadership abilities; the Continental Congress trusted his dedication to the colonial cause; his southern background broadened support for what had been seen as a New England war. **4.** Canadian Governor Carleton planned an invasion of the colonies, so the Congress decided to attack first. **5.** Possible answer: Because the fighting grew out of the reaction to the Coercive Acts, which affected Massachusetts most directly.

SECTION 2	(pages 118–121)

The Road to Independence

ACTIVITIES

○ **Using a Primary Source** Have students re-read the excerpt from Paine's *Common Sense* on text page 119. Ask them to look up any words they do not know and then restate the quotation in their own words. Ask: Why do you think Paine's ideas were popular with Americans?

☆ **Understanding Main Ideas and Supporting Details** Have students turn to the middle section of the Declaration of Independence on text pages 865–866. Ask them to select four of the grievances listed there and explain what each grievance means in their own words. Then have students give at least one specific example to support each grievance. Encourage students to check unfamiliar words in the dictionary.

☐ **Comparing** Ask students to review what they have read about the Mayflower Compact (on text page 44), the Fundamental Orders of Connecticut (on text page 45), and *A Summary View of the Rights of British America* (on text page 108). Have them select one of these documents and compare the political ideas it contains with the ideas found in the Declaration of Independence.

ANSWERS: SECTION 2 REVIEW (page 121)

1. Olive Branch Petition, Prohibitory Act, Thomas Paine, *Common Sense*—p. 119. **2.** The Prohibitory Act and the hiring of Hessian mercenaries. **3.** He argued that all monarchies are evil, that monarchs are "crowned ruffians." **4.** It turned 13 British colonies into the United States of America. It gave the Americans a goal in their struggle against Britain. **5.** The first section is the preamble, which explains why the colonists wanted independence. The second section is a list of complaints against the king and Parliament; its purpose was to justify and bolster the call for independence. The third section declares a new government and severs all ties with Britain. **6.** Possible answer: Paine was strongly opposed to a hereditary monarchy. Locke believed that the right to govern came not from God but from the people.

SECTION 3 (pages 121–125)
The Balance of Forces

ACTIVITIES

○ **Using Visual Evidence** Have students work in small groups to design recruiting posters for the Continental army. Before they begin, ask: What emotions should a recruiting poster arouse?

☆ **Expressing an Opinion** Divide the class into groups of two persons each. Tell each group to imagine they are cousins during the Revolutionary War. Designate one cousin as a Loyalist and the other as a Patriot. Ask students to write letters to their cousin in which they explain why they are Loyalists or Patriots and why they think their side will win the war. When the letters are completed, have students volunteer to read their letters aloud and discuss the arguments.

☐ **Analyzing** Ask students to make a chart with two columns. In the first column, they should list the *powers* the Second Continental Congress assumed during the Revolutionary War. In the second column, they should list the *problems* the Congress faced. When the chart is completed, ask students to write a paragraph describing the additional powers they think the Congress needed to deal with those problems. You might ask students to speculate about why the Congress did not have such powers.

ANSWERS: NOTABLE AMERICANS (page 122)

1. That they were being taxed with no representation in the legislature; that many blacks had fought in the Revolution to end a similar injustice against the colonies by Britain. **2.** He used peaceful means to achieve his goals (petition, refusal to pay taxes).

ANSWERS: SECTION 3 REVIEW (page 125)

1. Loyalists, Patriots—p. 121; redcoats—p. 123; John Paul Jones—p. 125. **2.** pacifism—p. 122; localism—p. 124. **3.** At first, the Congress feared that if large numbers of blacks joined the army to fight for independence, they would encourage slaves to revolt. But once the British started offering to free any slave who joined the British army, the Continental Congress allowed blacks to enlist. **4.** A few women dressed as men and fought in battles; others were successful spies; wives made camp life bearable for their soldier husbands; some women did the work left by men who had gone to war. **5. (a)** Advantages included experienced generals, a well-trained and well-equipped army, and a large navy. Disadvantages included difficulty in obtaining supplies. **(b)** Advantages included a fervent response to the threat against their land, experience with firearms, the leadership of George Washington, and aid from foreign nations. Disadvantages included inexperienced soldiers, a weak navy, shortage of supplies, and localism. **6.** Possible answer: Because they were fighting for the right to rule themselves, the states resented having to surrender any power to a central authority.

SECTION 4   (pages 126–128)
Fighting a Colonial War

SECTION 5   (pages 129–133)
Victory for the Americans

ACTIVITIES
○ **Vocabulary Building** The text refers to the "guerrilla tactics" used by the Americans during the Revolutionary War (p. 128). Ask students to use the dictionary to define "guerrilla." Then have them read about guerrilla warfare in an encyclopedia and answer these questions: (1) What is the origin of the phrase? (2) What type of military action is taken in a guerrilla war?

☆ **Map Reading** Have students study the maps on text page 128 and answer these questions. Ask: (1) Who led British forces south from Quebec? (2) What river did they follow? (3) On what lake is Fort Ticonderoga? (4) Who won the battle fought there? (5) Who led British forces south from New York? (6) Where did these troops suffer a defeat? (7) Who led Patriot troops west from Albany?

□ **What If?** Ask students to write an essay describing what might have happened if General Howe had followed the original British plan in 1777 instead of deciding to take Philadelphia. Students should concentrate on how the course of the war might have changed.

ANSWER: MAP STUDY   (page 127)
In the Middle Colonies.

ANSWERS: MAP STUDY   (page 128)
Gates; Burgoyne; down the St. Lawrence River, then inland.

ANSWERS: SECTION 4 REVIEW   (page 128)
1. Lord Cornwallis, Barry St. Leger—p. 127; John Burgoyne, Horatio Gates—p. 128. 2. Lowered American morale. Soldiers began deserting in large numbers. 3. (a) A plan to split the colonies by capturing New York and isolating New England. (b) General Howe deviated from the plan by moving to capture Philadelphia. He thereby failed to support General Burgoyne in his march south from Canada. Burgoyne surrendered at the Battle of Saratoga. 4. It turned the tide of the war, giving the Americans new hope. 5. Possible answer: When morale was good, more Americans were likely to enlist and to continue fighting in the face of adversity.

ACTIVITIES
○ **Interviewing** Tell students to imagine that they are members of Parliament making an inquiry about the British defeat at Yorktown. Have students prepare a list of questions they would like to ask Lord Cornwallis. Possible topics include (1) the reason for Cornwallis's retreat to Yorktown, (2) the strategy employed by the Americans and French, (3) the reason for Cornwallis's decision to surrender.

☆ **Finding the Main Idea** Divide the class into four groups and assign each group one of the subsections in Section 5. Tell each group first to write a statement that reflects the main idea of the subsection, then two other statements about the subsection. When the groups have finished, have each group write the three statements on the chalkboard in random order. Ask the class to review each subsection and decide which of the three statements is the main idea. Compare the class choices with the group's choice and have students defend their answers if the answers differ.

□ **Biographical Sketch** Have students learn more about Lafayette, Rochambeau, Von Steuben, Kosciusko, or Pulaski. They might consult the *Encyclopedia of the American Revolution* by Mark M. Boatner III or the *Dictionary of American Biography*. Ask students to write a brief report in which they discuss why each person decided to fight for American independence.

ANSWERS: MAP STUDY   (page 129)
The Ohio, Wabash, and Mississippi rivers; it provided the most direct route from the colonies to the West.

ANSWER: MAP STUDY   (page 131)
A combined French and American force cut off his retreat by land; the French navy cut off his retreat by sea.

ANSWER: MAP STUDY   (page 132)
Spain.

ANSWERS: SECTION 5 REVIEW   (page 133)
1. Baron von Steuben—p. 129; Thaddeus Kosciusko, Casimir Pulaski, George Rogers Clark—p. 130; Nathanael Greene—p. 131; Marquis de Lafayette—

T 23

p. 133. **2.** France sent supplies and military experts. The French navy sent ships to patrol American waters. Also, with Britain at war with France, British military pressure on the Americans was reduced. **3.** The British believed that they could easily move troops around by sea and that southern Loyalists would support them. **4.** Britain recognized the U.S. as an independent nation and gave up all land west of the Mississippi between the Great Lakes and Florida. **5.** Possible answer: It paved the way for American victory, which meant the U.S. would become a real nation. Had the U.S. remained under British control, world history would have been very different.

ANSWERS: CHAPTER 6 REVIEW (pages 134–135)

Vocabulary 1. Committees of Safety **2.** Olive Branch Petition **3.** Pacifism **4.** Localism **5.** Patriots **6.** Loyalists

Chapter Checkup 1. Even though the British won, Americans realized they had a chance to defeat the better-trained and better-equipped British troops. **2.** It made the radical position more appealing to more people, because it made Britain seem so unreasonable. **3. (a)** That there are certain rights that belong to all people. **(b)** This principle of human rights became an ideal many hoped to realize. **(c)** The declaration claimed that the British government had violated the natural rights of the colonists. **4. (a)** Many southern leaders owned slaves. They felt that the wide participation of blacks in the army might encourage slaves to revolt to gain their independence. **(b)** Blacks were involved in many battles during the war. Rhode Island had an all-black battalion. **5. (a)** States did not want to give money, supplies, or soldiers to help build a national army. Soldiers felt loyalty to their states, not the nation. **(b)** Not very successfully, because there was no way to force the states to cooperate. **(c)** Few states met their recruitment quotas; Congress could not levy taxes to pay for the war and the states would not cooperate; some states even tried to negotiate separate treaties with foreign nations. **6. (a)** It brought hope after a dismal string of defeats. **(b)** It was the turning point, bringing confidence and a French alliance. **(c)** The last major battle of the war. **7. (a)** The first treaty recognized the U.S. as an independent nation and granted special trading privileges to France. The second treaty specified that if France and Great Britain went to war, France would give up all land east of the Mississippi River and the U.S. would recognize French claims in the West Indies. **(b)** The French wanted to see if Americans could really defeat the British. **8.** Cornwallis refused to give up his European style of fighting; few southerners helped the British; the French naval presence prevented free use of sea transportation by the British; Cornwallis became surrounded at Yorktown.

Critical Thinking 1. (a) God-given rights that no government could take away. **(b)** Since Jefferson believed that the power to rule flowed from the people to the government, the king had no God-given power to rule. Thus, a government that trampled on the natural rights of its citizens could be overthrown. **2.** Answers will vary. Students might mention Israeli problems on the West Bank or South African attempts to maintain Afrikaner rule as examples supporting Burke's opinion.

Connecting Past and Present 1. (a) Possible answers: Israel, South Korea, Japan, India. **(b)** To help our allies or to keep friendly governments in power in areas of strategic or economic importance to the United States. **2.** Possible answers: We would live under a Parliamentary system; we would be loyal to the monarch of Great Britain; our situation might be similar to that of Canada today.

Developing Basic Skills 1. Check student charts for accuracy. **(a), (b), (c)** Accept all justifiable answers. **2.** Between 1763 and 1783, the boundary lines expanded from the Appalachian Mountains westward to the Mississippi River.

SPIRIT OF AMERICA   (pages 136–139)

ANSWERS: AMERICAN INDIVIDUALISM

(pages 136–137)

1. Americans had to be self-reliant, especially on the frontier, and so developed an attitude of individualism. **2.** Possible answer: Because the needs of society represent the needs of a greater number of people, individual rights must have limits.

ANSWERS: NOTABLE AMERICANS

(pages 138–139)

1. Both New Hampshire and New York claimed ownership. **2.** Possible answer: His bravery and daring exploits against the British make the story of Ethan Allen resemble a folk tale.

ANSWERS: VOICES OF FREEDOM   (page 139)

1. In America, with hard work, newcomers could own land, feed their families, and build a better life. **2.** Possible answers: His own experience in America had been so positive. He had seen people improve their lives through hard work and self-reliance.

Chapter 7   (pages 140–157)

An Experimental Era ____

OVERVIEW

Chapter 7 focuses on the period during and after the Revolutionary War. During this time, the newly independent U.S. created a weak central government under the Articles of Confederation. In this chapter, students examine the new nation's accomplishments and the problems it faced.

HISTORICAL SIDELIGHTS

The following pieces of historical information can serve as notes of interest during the study of Chapter 7. The page numbers in parentheses indicate the points in the student text at which you may wish to introduce the information.

Loyalists After the War (p. 142)   Contrary to popular opinion, the newly independent American republic welcomed back Loyalist colonists who had gone to Britain during the war. Approximately 80,000 Tories had left, for the most part voluntarily. And some who left later returned. Loyalist Cadwallader Colden was even elected mayor of New York City upon his return.

Voting by Ballot (p. 146)   States in the young republic increasingly eliminated the old tradition of voting by voice because the practice allowed prominent men to influence other voters. Voting by written ballot or by submitting a preprinted ticket with a candidate's name on it came to be used in elections. This method sometimes led to fraud, however. The printed tickets were "often palmed upon such as cannot write or read," claimed William Paterson of New Jersey, "by which means they sometimes vote in the person they intended to vote out."

SECTION 1   (pages 141–145)
Making a New Start

ACTIVITIES*

○ **Expressing an Opinion**   Have students reread the subsection Moving Toward Greater

----

*See "To the Teacher" for an explanation of the symbols.

Political and Social Equality on text pages 141–142. Then ask students to write a short letter either criticizing or supporting the Cincinnati Society.

☆ **Researching**   Ask students to read about Abigail Adams's ideas on equality for women. They might consult *We the American Women: A Documentary History* edited by Beth Millstein and Jeanne Bodin. Have them write a report in which they list Adams's grievances and her suggestions for reform.

□ **Analyzing a Quotation**   Copy the following quotation from Hector St. John de Crèvecoeur on the chalkboard.

We are the most perfect society now existing in the world. Here man is free, as he ought to be, nor is this pleasing equality . . . temporary as many others are.

Remind students that Crèvecoeur, a native of France, lived in the U.S. for many years and in 1782 published a book of essays entitled *Letters From an American Farmer,* from which this excerpt is taken. Ask students to write an essay in which they either support or dispute Crèvecoeur's view of America as "the most perfect society now existing in the world."

ANSWERS: NOTABLE AMERICANS   (page 145)

1. To rid America of "the king's English." **2.** When people speak the same language, they can more easily share experiences that can be built into shared traditions. They begin to see themselves as a group or a nation with things in common, and they begin to feel loyalty to each other and the nation.

ANSWERS: SECTION 1 REVIEW   (page 145)

1. Society of the Cincinnati, Abigail Adams—p. 142; Noah Webster—p. 144. **2.** segregated—p. 143; manumission—p. 144. **3. (a)** A person had to be male, white, Christian, and a property owner. **(b)** Changes in inheritance laws broke up large land holdings; the government sold land formerly owned by Loyalists and gave soldiers western land as bonuses. **4.** They could not vote (except briefly in New Jersey); few property rights; discriminated against in education. **5. (a)** Free blacks in some states gained more equality in the legal system, constitutional voting rights, and increased opportunities for jobs. **(b)** Segregation in most northern states; few freedoms in the South; possibility of being kidnapped and sold into slavery. **6.** Possible answer: The democratic ideas that spurred the revolution also encouraged social change.

ACTIVITIES

○ **Classifying**   Have students make a chart with these headings: Limitations on the Executive Branch, Limitations on the Legislative Branch. Ask students to list the features of new state governments that belong under each heading. Use the completed chart as the basis for a class discussion about how the state constitutions limited the power of government.

☆ **Making Generalizations** Ask students to write one or two factual statements that support each of the following generalizations: (1) After the Revolutionary War, Americans wanted to guarantee that the newly established state governments would not abuse their power. (2) Representative assemblies have deep roots in American political tradition. (3) Americans opposed aristocratic control of state legislatures. (4) Many state constitutions were formulated with the consent of the people.

□ **Analyzing a Quotation**   Copy the following extract from the Massachusetts Bill of Rights on the chalkboard.

Government is instituted for the common good, for the protection, safety, prosperity, and happiness of the people and not for the profit, honor, or private interest of any one man, family, or class of men; therefore the people alone have an incontestable, unalienable, and indefensible right to institute government; and to reform, alter, or totally change the same, when their protection, safety, prosperity, and happiness require it.

Have students study the quotation and look up any words they don't know. Ask: (1) What type of abuses of power seemed to concern the author of the document? (2) Who had the right to change the state constitution? (3) What developments did the author think might make a change of government necessary?

ANSWERS: SECTION 2 REVIEW (page 147)

1. veto, bicameral legislature—p. 146; unalienable rights—p. 147. **2.** Some colonial assemblies became the new state legislatures; many prewar laws remained; a few royal charters became the new state constitutions. **3. (a)** Executive, legislative, and judicial. **(b)** Colonial governors had represented British rule in America. As a result, Americans were still suspicious of the office of governor.

4. The people of Massachusetts placed the writing of their constitution in the hands of delegates to a special convention. Legislators could not change the constitution without the people's consent. **5.** Possible answer: When rules and rights are written down, it is easier to see what they are; there is less room for interpretation, so it is harder to violate them.

ACTIVITIES

○ **Placing Events in Time**   Ask students to put the following events in correct chronological order: (1) Revolutionary War ends; (2) Land Ordinance of 1785 passed; (3) Continental Congress submits Articles of Confederation to the states; (4) Northwest Ordinance passed; (5) Articles of Confederation ratified by states; (6) A New England group buys over 1 million acres in the Northwest Territory. *Answers:* 3, 5, 1, 2, 6, 4

☆ **Applying Information** Ask students to explain the meaning of the term "confederation." When students have defined the term, describe the following hypothetical governments: Country A is governed by a strong central government. Twenty states exist, but these states may implement only policies established by the national government. Country B is made up of five states, each of which is allowed to make policies in a wide range of areas. The national government may suggest policies to the states but cannot enforce them. Ask: (1) Which country is a confederation? (2) What problems might arise for the government of Country A? Country B?

□ **Expressing an Opinion**   Have students review the discussion of policy for western lands on text pages 149–152. Then have them write letters from Cornplanter or another Native American to George Washington criticizing the land policy. Volunteers can read their letters aloud.

ANSWER: CHART STUDY (page 148)

Congress had the power to raise an army and navy, but could not collect the funds needed to do so itself. Furthermore, the states could freely ignore any attempt Congress made to enforce its powers.

ANSWERS: GEOGRAPHIC CONNECTION
(page 150)

1. Township, section, and quarter. **2.** Possible answer: Because it was created by people who had just moved here from Europe; they used the system that was familiar.

ANSWER: MAP AND GRAPH STUDY (page 151)

The income from the sale of the sixteenth section of each township was reserved for schools.

ANSWERS: SECTION 3 REVIEW (page 153)

1. Articles of Confederation—p. 148; Northwest Territory, Land Ordinance of 1785—p. 150; Northwest Ordinance—p. 151. **2.** confederation—p. 148; ratify—p. 149; squatter—p. 151. **3. (a)** Congress had the power to declare war, commission military officers, enter into treaties and alliances, receive and send ambassadors, establish post offices, borrow money, deal with Native Americans, fix weights and measures. **(b)** Congress could not collect taxes or order men to serve in the army. **4. (a)** Wild terrain could not easily be divided into squares, and squatters had settled illegally. **(b)** When it had a population of 60,000 free inhabitants. **5.** Foreign trade had been disrupted; the war helped industry; southern planters were hurt by loss of markets and slaves; small farmers profited by selling food to armies; inflation lowered the value of continental money. **6.** Possible answer: Until the government they had fought for was firmly established, the revolution was incomplete.

SECTION 4   (pages 153–155)
A Need for Further Experimentation

ACTIVITIES

○ **Classifying** Ask students to review text pages 153–155 and make a list of the problems faced by the new government. Then have students classify the problems under these headings: Economic Problems, Foreign Threats, Political Problems.

☆ **Relating Cause and Effect** Ask students to write one "effect" statement for each of the following "cause" statements: (1) The states usually rejected Congress's requests for money. (2) Under the Articles of Confederation, Congress could only request troops from the states. (3) Many American leaders believed that the U.S. was slipping into economic anarchy.

☐ **Analyzing a Quotation** Copy the following quotation about Shays' Rebellion from Abigail Adams on the chalkboard or duplicate and distribute copies.

With regard to the tumults in my native state which you inquire about, I wish I could say that report had exaggerated them. It is too true, sir, that they have been carried to so alarming a height as to stop the courts of justice in several counties. Ignorant, restless desperados, without conscience or principles, had led a deluded multitude to follow their standard, under pretense of grievances which have no existence but in their imaginations. Some of them were crying out for an equal distribution of property. Some were for annihilating all debts, others complaining that the Senate was a useless branch of government.

Ask: (1) What demands did Shays and his followers make? (2) Why do you think Adams was so hostile to the demands of the rebels?

ANSWERS: SECTION 4 REVIEW (page 155)

1. Shays' Rebellion—p. 155. **2. (a)** The states. **(b)** By asking states for funds, borrowing from foreign governments, printing money, and selling western lands. **3.** States issued their own currencies; they often imposed tariffs on one another. **4. (a)** King George III kept troops in the Northwest Territory, thereby violating the peace treaty. **(b)** Spain pressured western settlers to break away from the U.S. and closed the lower Mississippi to American ships. **5.** Possible answer: Congress's inability to enforce any of its powers made it powerless in any real sense.

ANSWERS: CHAPTER 7 REVIEW (page 156–157)

Vocabulary **1.** c **2.** g **3.** d **4.** f **5.** b **6.** a **7.** h **8.** e

Chapter Checkup **1.** Americans began to question all aspects of their life. Experiments in education: less emphasis on Latin and Greek, coeducation. Experiments in political equality: denunciation of clubs, changes in inheritance laws, easing of restrictions on free blacks, more religious equality. **2. (a)** A typical state government had executive, legislative, and judicial branches of government. **(b)** The legislative branch, because it symbolized the power of the people. **3. (a)** There were strict limits on congressional authority. **(b)** Because abuses of the British Parliament made the states distrust a powerful central authority. **4. (a)** The national government was composed of a congress, which had a variety of powers. Nine of the 13 states had to approve a bill before it became law. There were no provisions for a national court or a chief executive. **(b)** All states were represented equally in Congress. **(c)** States with large populations did not agree, but they recognized the need for a central government. **5.** States that had no western land wanted profits from its sale to benefit the entire country and not just a few states. Ratification was held up until the problem was settled. **6. (a)** Under the Land Ordinance, land was divided into townships, which were subdivided into 36 one-square-mile lots. **(b)** Under the Northwest Ordinance, the western lands were divided into three to five territories. When the adult male population of a territory reached 5,000, it could elect a legislature. Each territory would be governed by a governor, a secretary, and three judges. A territory could apply for statehood once its free population reached 60,000. **7.** Because Congress was weak and the national currency was worthless. State legislatures protected local interests by issuing their own currency and imposing tariffs on interstate commerce. **8.** Spain renewed its interest in claiming western land, and England kept troops stationed in the Northwest Territory, in violation of the peace treaty. Other nations were initially hesitant about entering into trade agreements with the U.S.

Critical Thinking   **1.** A revolution brings a sudden change in government. Because political power and political relationships would be in flux after a revolution, it would be natural to consider change in the social order as well. **2.** Most Americans considered their state government more important than the national government. The organization of government under the Articles of Confederation supports this view.

Connecting Past and Present   **1. (a)** Rights to vote, to an education, to own property, to pursue any occupation. **(b)** Answers will vary. **2. (a)** They still have executive, legislative, and judicial branches; they can still tax. **(b)** They can no longer issue their own currency; raise an army; place tariffs or other restrictions on interstate trade.

Developing Basic Skills   **1. (a)** Congress could declare war and make peace, raise an army and navy, make foreign treaties and alliances, coin and borrow money, regulate weights and measures, establish a post office, and regulate Indian affairs. **(b)** It could not levy taxes, regulate trade, settle disputes among states, collect debts owed Congress by the states, or enforce any of its powers. **(c)** The approval of nine states. **(d)** All other powers not given to Congress. **2. (a)** New York, Connecticut, Virginia, North Carolina, South Carolina, and Georgia. **(b)** Spain. **(c)** Conflicts among the states over land claims could threaten the country's unity.

Chapter 8   (pages 158–175)

A More Perfect Union _____

OVERVIEW

Chapter 8 focuses on the writing and ratification of the Constitution. Students explore the actions of delegates to the Constitutional Convention and examine the document itself, especially federalism and the system of checks and balances. They also read about the ratification struggle and the Bill of Rights.

HISTORICAL SIDELIGHTS

The following pieces of historical information can serve as notes of interest during the study of Chapter 8. The page numbers in parentheses indicate the points in the student text at which you may wish to introduce the information.

Secrecy at the Convention (p. 160)   Anticipating that drafting a new form of government while the old one was still in force would be a delicate matter, convention delegates agreed to keep their proceedings secret. Sentries were placed at the doors of the Pennsylvania statehouse, where the convention met, and delegates could not copy from the official minutes without permission. Benjamin Franklin was reportedly often watched over by a more careful delegate, who did his best to deflect the conversation when one of Franklin's anecdotes threatened to reveal the secrets of the convention.

A National Symbol (p. 163)   Among the many questions debated at the Constitutional Convention was that of a national symbol. Not everyone favored the powerful bald eagle. Benjamin Franklin, for one, argued that the turkey was a more appropriate symbol:

> For my own part, I wish the bald eagle had not been chosen as the representative of our country; he is a bird of bad moral character; he does not get his living honestly; you may have seen him perched on some dead tree, where, too lazy to fish for himself, he watches the labor of the fishing-hawk; and, when that diligent bird has at length taken a fish, and is bearing it to his nest for the support of his mate and young ones, the bald eagle pursues him and takes it from him. . . . in truth, the

turkey is in comparison a much more respectable bird, and withal a true original native of America.

SECTION 1   (pages 159–163)
Producing a New Constitution

ACTIVITIES*

○ **Identification** Ask students to identify the person referred to in each of the following clues: (1) "I smelt a rat"; (2) ambassador to France during the Convention; (3) ambassador to Great Britain during the Convention; (4) one of the oldest and best-known delegates to the Constitutional Convention; (5) wrote the Virginia Plan; (6) proposed the New Jersey Plan; (7) proposed a compromise that satisfied both large and small states.
Answers: **1.** Patrick Henry **2.** Thomas Jefferson **3.** John Adams **4.** Benjamin Franklin **5.** James Madison **6.** William Paterson **7.** Roger Sherman

☆ **Comparing** Ask students to make a chart with three columns headed Virginia Plan, New Jersey Plan, Great Compromise. Have them write the major characteristics of each plan in the appropriate column. Topics considered should include (1) the number of houses in the legislature, (2) how legislators would be selected, (3) how representation would be determined, and (4) extent of powers granted to the central government. When students have completed their charts, lead a class discussion comparing the three plans.

☐ **Analyzing a Quotation** Read students the following extract or duplicate and distribute copies. The quotation is from a letter George Washington wrote to John Jay in 1786 about the reaction to Shays' Rebellion.

What astonishing changes a few years are capable of producing! I am told that even respectable characters speak of a monarchical form of government without horror. . . . What a triumph for the advocates of despotism to find that we are incapable of governing ourselves,

and that systems founded on the basis of equal liberty are merely ideal and fallacious. Would to God that wise measures may be taken in time to avert consequences we have but too much reason to apprehend.

Ask: (1) What change in attitude surprised Washington? (2) What caused such a change? (3) What threat did Washington feel the new attitude posed? (4) What would you assume his attitude toward the opening of the Constitutional Convention would be? (5) Does the quotation help you understand why most delegates were willing to compromise at the Constitutional Convention? Explain.

ANSWERS: VOICES OF FREEDOM   (page 162)
1. Mr. Martin believed the slave trade should be ended or taxed. His argument for ending the slave trade was that it was inconsistent with the principles of the revolution. His argument for a tax was that slavery gave the South benefits and privileges that should be taxed. Mr. Sherman thought it best to leave things as they were, in the interest of avoiding conflict over the new Constitution. Col. Mason felt the trade should be restricted because otherwise Georgia and South Carolina would be able to import many slaves while Virginia had already banned the trade. Gen. Pinckney felt the slave trade must continue because South Carolina and Georgia could not do without it, and besides, according to him, it benefited the whole country. **2.** That he felt slaves were not people, but simply products to be used for economic benefit.

ANSWERS: SECTION 1 REVIEW   (page 163)
1. Virginia Plan, New Jersey Plan—p. 160; the Great Compromise—p. 161. **2.** The new government would have a representative form; have the power to levy taxes, enforce laws, and provide for national defense; and be based on a written constitution. **3. (a)** That the plan gave all the power to large states. **(b)** It maintained most of the features of the Articles of Confederation, which the convention had set out to change. **4.** Three fifths of the slaves in a state were counted for purposes of determining a state's representatives. Congress would not interfere with the slave trade for 20 years from the time the Constitution went into effect. Delegates agreed to prohibit export taxes. They also required a two-thirds-majority vote in the Senate to ratify treaties, including trade agreements. **5.** Possible answer: The name suggests that the country was a union entered into by independent states.

---

*See "To the Teacher" for an explanation of the symbols.

SECTION 2   (pages 163–165)
The Principle of Federalism

ACTIVITIES

○ **Using Diagrams**   Ask students to study the diagram on text page 164 and then answer the following questions: (1) What is the topic of the diagram? (2) Which group of powers were given to the national government? (3) Which group of powers were shared by the national and state governments? (4) Which group of powers were left to the states?

☆ **Relating Past to Present**   Ask students to prepare an oral report about how the system of federalism affects their own lives. They should consider actions of both the national and state governments. You might suggest that they begin by thinking about laws such as traffic regulations and agencies such as the post office.

□ **Analyzing**   Have students write a paragraph in which they explain why they think the delegates to the Constitutional Convention gave the following powers exclusively to the national government: coining money, regulating foreign trade, declaring war. Ask them to consider the possible consequences if each individual state government had those powers.

ANSWER: CHART STUDY   (page 164)
The national government was given greater powers to avoid some of the problems that arose under the Articles.

ANSWERS: SECTION 2 REVIEW   (page 165)
1. popular sovereignty—p. 163; federalism, delegated powers, reserved powers, concurrent powers —p. 164. **2. (a)** Under the Virginia Plan the central government would have been sovereign. **(b)** Under the New Jersey Plan state governments would have been sovereign. **3.** By establishing a system of shared sovereignty between the national and state governments. **4.** Delegated powers include the power to declare war, coin money, regulate foreign and domestic trade, and establish a postal system. Reserved powers include the right to control intrastate trade, create local governments, and establish voting qualifications. Concurrent powers include the right to support education and to enforce laws. **5.** It created a direct link between the people and the national government. They can elect representatives to Congress and they must obey the

laws passed by Congress. **6.** Possible answer: It reserved some powers specifically to the states, thus allowing the states to preserve some of their individuality.

SECTION 3   (pages 166–168)
Limits to Power

ACTIVITIES

○ **Supporting the Main Idea**   Ask students to give at least one specific modern example of the following governmental powers: the power to create armed forces; the power to levy taxes; the power to establish schools; the power to provide for safety; the power to regulate immigration. Write student responses on the chalkboard and then have students decide from their examples which powers are delegated, concurrent, and reserved.

☆ **Expressing an Opinion**   Ask students whether they agree or disagree with the following statement: The framers of the Constitution tried to restrict the direct power of the people too severely. Have students write a paragraph explaining their opinion. Then have volunteers read their paragraphs to the class to start a class discussion.

□ **Biographical Sketch**   Have students read about the life of Montesquieu and write a biographical sketch. They should discuss his background and note how his ideas influenced political thinking in Europe as well as in America. Students could begin by reading about Montesquieu in an encyclopedia. More advanced students might read a biography.

ANSWERS: CHART STUDY   (page 167)
Answers will vary.

ANSWERS: SECTION 3 REVIEW   (page 168)
1. Baron de Montesquieu—p. 166. **2.** separation of powers, checks and balances—p. 166; impeach, unconstitutional—p. 167; electoral college—p. 168. **3.** Legislative branch passes laws; executive branch enforces laws; judicial branch interprets laws. **4. (a)** The President can check the power of Congress by vetoing bills. **(b)** Congress can check the power of the President by refusing to approve presidential appointments. **(c)** The Supreme Court can check the power of Congress by declaring laws unconstitutional. **5.** Possible answers: Suggestions have been made to eliminate the electoral

college and permit the President to be elected by popular vote. Senators were originally elected by state legislatures; now they are elected directly by the people.

SECTION 4   (pages 168–171)
Ratifying the Constitution

ACTIVITIES

○ **Analyzing a Document** Have students re-read the special feature, *A Farmer Argues for the Constitution* (text page 169), and answer these questions: (1) What "black cloud" does the farmer speak of? (2) What effect did it have on the farmer and his neighbors? (3) Why does he say that "anarchy leads to tyranny"? (4) Does the farmer support the Constitution? How can you tell?

☆ **Analyzing** Have students make a list of the arguments the Antifederalists used against ratification of the Constitution. Ask them to explain why they think the Antifederalists made each argument and how the Federalists proba-bly responded.

☐ **Summarizing** Ask students to read one of the *Federalist Papers* and write a short summary of the argument made.

ANSWERS: VOICES OF FREEDOM (page 169)
1. Because Shays' Rebellion left the people with no meaningful government, they would have ac-cepted any leader, even a tyrant, who could re-store order. **2.** Possible answer: The argument that failure to act now might lead the country toward anarchy and then tyranny.

ANSWERS: SECTION 4 REVIEW (page 171)
1. Federalists, *Federalist Papers,* Antifederalists—p. 169. **2.** Federalists argued that a strong national government was needed, that individual states should not have the power to reject national policy, and that states' rights were still protected under the new Constitution. **3.** Antifederalists argued that the new central government would be too strong and the state governments too weak. They said that the electoral college system removed the people from the election process. They also op-posed longer terms of office for Congressional representatives. Most important, they opposed the Constitution because it lacked a bill of rights. **4.** Pennsylvania, Massachusetts, Virginia, and New York. **5.** Possible answer: The experiment with

the Articles of Confederation showed that a system of strong state governments weakened the entire union and put all the states in danger.

SECTION 5   (pages 171–173)
Ensuring Individual Rights

ACTIVITIES

○ **Relating Past to Present** Ask students to find articles or pictures in newspapers and magazines that illustrate one of the rights pro-tected in the Bill of Rights. You might ask them to clip the articles and have the class display them on a bulletin board. Use the in-formation students gather as the basis of a class discussion about the continued impor-tance of the Bill of Rights.

☆ **Relating Information** Have students find out more about several proposed constitutional amendments, for example, the equal rights amendment, balanced budget amendment, or amendment to prohibit abortion. Then divide the class into two groups, one group repre-senting the Senate and the other group the House. Have students debate each amendment and then vote on it.

☐ **Writing an Essay** Have students select one of the first ten amendments to the Constitution and write an essay in which they explain how that amendment reflects the experiences of Americans between 1770 and 1791.

ANSWERS: SECTION 5 REVIEW (page 173)
1. amend—p. 171; writ of habeas corpus, bill of at-tainder, ex post facto law—p. 172; due process—p. 173. **2. (a)** By a two-thirds majority vote of Con-gress or by a special convention ordered by two thirds of the state legislatures. **(b)** Three fourths of the states. **3.** Madison feared that those rights not listed in it might be unprotected. **4.** Check that student responses refer to rights contained in the Bill of Rights. **5.** Answers will vary.

ANSWERS: CHAPTER 8 REVIEW (page 174–175)
Vocabulary 1. Popular sovereignty **2.** concur-rent powers **3.** Separation of powers **4.** checks and balances **5.** amend **6.** bill of attainder.
Chapter Checkup 1. (a) Because the influence of populous and less populous states in Congress was at stake. **(b)** The Virginia Plan proposed a Congress divided into two houses: the House of

Representatives and the Senate. The number of representatives allotted to each state would be based on the size of that state's population. The House would select Senators from candidates proposed by the state legislatures. **(c)** The New Jersey Plan proposed a one-house Congress in which all states, large or small, would have the same number of representatives. **(d)** Two houses were established: a House of Representatives based on proportional representation, and a Senate with two members from each state. **2. (a)** Counting slaves as part of population when figuring representation; continuation of the slave trade; protection against export taxes. **(b)** Three fifths of slaves would be counted; the slave trade would not be interfered with for 20 years; export taxes were outlawed; the Senate had to approve treaties, including trade treaties. **3. (a)** Under the system of federalism, neither the national government nor the states have absolute power. **(b)** Through the separation of powers, no one branch of government could gain too much power. **(c)** Checks and balances allow each of the three branches to prevent any other branch from abusing its power. **4. (a)** Congress must approve presidential appointments and has the power to impeach and remove a President. The Supreme Court can declare presidential action unconstitutional. **(b)** Because they had seen what can happen when the executive becomes tyrannical (as King George did). **5. (a)** Both houses must agree on bills; the President can veto bills; the Supreme Court can declare laws unconstitutional. **(b)** The President appoints federal judges with the consent of the Senate; Congress can impeach and remove judges. **6.** Arguments for ratification: a strong central government was needed; controls on the states were necessary; states' rights would still be protected. Arguments against ratification: the central government would become too strong; the people would be removed from electing the President, Vice President, and senators; congressional terms of office would be too long; no bill of rights. **7. (a)** So the Constitution would be flexible to meet changing times. **(b)** An amendment can be proposed by two thirds of Congress or by a convention called by two thirds of the state legislatures. The amendment must be approved by three fourths of the states. **8. (a)** By guaranteeing the right to a writ of habeas corpus, by prohibiting the passage of bills of attainder, by outlawing ex post facto laws, and by ensuring the right to a jury trial in criminal cases. **(b)** Antifederalists maintained that a specific bill of rights was needed to ensure that the liberties won in the Revolution would be preserved.

Critical Thinking   1. (a) Answers may vary, but they should discuss the fear of another monarch abusing power. **(b)** Students may suggest that a monarch chosen for life would be above politics because he or she would not have to worry about getting reelected. **2.** Both members of Congress and the people might be more sympathetic to the views of a popular President; so more of his proposals might be accepted.

Connecting Past and Present   1. (a) Because they believed that the people might not be sufficiently informed to make wise decisions. **(b)** Answers will vary, but students might mention higher levels of education today and faster communication about current events. **2.** Students might mention such examples as a recent veto or Senate approval of a presidential appointment.

Developing Basic Skills   1. Under Delegated Powers: army, off-shore drilling rights, postal service. Under Reserved Powers: voting age, fishing regulations, police protection, motor-vehicle regulations. Under Concurrent Powers: education, income tax. **2.** Answers will vary.

Unit Three
An Emerging Nation

Chapter 9   (pages 178–195)

A Federalist Beginning —

OVERVIEW
Chapter 9 describes the critical first years of constitutional government, the Federalist era. During this period, the federal government put the nation on a firm financial footing and resolved conflicts with Britain, France, and Spain. After reading about the differences between Alexander Hamilton and Thomas Jefferson, students examine the formation of political parties.

HISTORICAL SIDELIGHTS
The following pieces of historical information can serve as notes of interest during the study of Chapter 9. The page numbers in parentheses indicate the points in the student text at which you may wish to introduce the information.

Cashing in on Washington's Name (p. 179) The fame and reputation of George Washington was so great in his own time that eager manufacturers capitalized on it by using merchandising techniques that have an amazingly modern ring. An observer indignantly complained that Washington's name had been "stamped, in black or blue or red capitals, upon handkerchiefs, ribbons, buttons, and other wares, to render them saleable; and a certain proportion of purchasers considered it a recommendation, until they were gulled out of their money. . . . This trick for the sale of goods," the writer optimistically concluded, "has therefore gone pretty much out of Vogue."

The Growth of the Newspaper Business (p. 188) One consequence of the growth of political parties in the 1790s was the increase of news-

papers designed to air political views. In 1790, the nation had fewer than 100 newspapers; by 1800, that figure had jumped to more than 230. Many of these newspapers were owned by Republicans who opposed Federalist policies. Lower prices, easier-to-read typography, and cartoons increased the papers' popularity. By 1810, Americans were buying over 22 million copies of 376 newspapers every year. No other nation in the world could boast as high a circulation.

SECTION 1   (pages 179–184)
Challenges of the New Government

ACTIVITIES*

○ **Using Visual Evidence**   Ask students to study the painting by James Peale on text page 183 and then answer the following questions: (1) What feelings about President Washington did the artist intend to convey? (2) How did the artist express these feelings in the painting? (3) What would be an appropriate title for this painting?

☆ **Writing a Speech**   Divide the class into two groups. Tell the members of one group to imagine that they are speech writers for Alexander Hamilton. Tell the members of the other group to imagine that they are critics of Hamilton's policies. Have each group write a speech defending or criticizing Hamilton's position on these topics: (1) full funding of the national debt, (2) creation of a national bank, (3) establishment of a protective tariff.

□ **Biographical Sketch**   Have students read about the life of Benjamin Banneker and write a biographical sketch. They should discuss Banneker's almanac (the cover of which is reproduced on text page 182), his work on the capital, and his relationship with Thomas Jefferson. Students could begin reading about

---

*See "To the Teacher" for an explanation of the symbols.

Banneker in an encyclopedia, or they might consult *Eyewitness: The Negro in American History,* edited by William Loren Katz.

ANSWERS: THE AMERICAN EXPERIENCE
(page 181)
1. That it be a capital city worthy of a great republic. **2.** Possible answer: Yes; it is a fine city with many monuments and squares that recognize the contributions of early Americans and the original states.

ANSWERS: SECTION 1 REVIEW   (page 184)
1. John Jay, Thomas Jefferson, Alexander Hamilton—p. 180. **2.** funding—p. 180; assumption—p. 181; strict construction, loose construction—p. 182; protective tariff—p. 183. **3. (a)** Article II of the Constitution authorized the creation of several executive departments. **(b)** They created the first cabinet departments—War, State, and Treasury. **4.** He proposed that the federal government issue new bonds, to be exchanged at face value for war bonds. He also proposed that the national government assume the state debts. He proposed a protective tariff, an excise tax on whiskey and the setting up of a national bank. **5. (a)** The passage of an excise tax on whiskey, which was a major source of income for farmers in western Pennsylvania. **(b)** Brought in the state militia to suppress it. **6.** Possible answer: No one knew exactly what lay ahead.

SECTION 2   (pages 184–187)

A Question of Entangling Alliances

ACTIVITIES

○ **Placing Events in Time** Copy the time line below on the chalkboard. Then read aloud the list of events. Ask students to write on a sheet of paper the letter of the correct time period of each event.

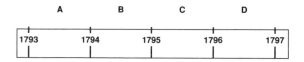

(1) Pinckney Treaty negotiated; (2) Jay Treaty negotiated; (3) President Washington's Farewell Address; (4) Proclamation of Neutrality issued.
Answers: **1.** C **2.** B **3.** D **4.** A

☆ **Making a Chart** Ask students to make a chart with four columns headed Policy, Reasons for Policy, How Implemented, Degree of Success. Have them fill out the chart for each of these policies: (1) to avoid involvement in the war between Britain and France; (2) to remove British forts from American soil; (3) to gain the right to ship cargo down the Mississippi. When the charts are complete, ask: Do you think U.S. foreign policy was generally successful under President Washington? Why or why not?

□ **Relating Past to Present** Read the following excerpt from Washington's Farewell Address: "Europe has a set of primary interests which to us have none or a very remote relation. . . . Hence, therefore, it must be unwise . . . [for] us to implicate ourselves . . . in . . . her politics." Ask students whether they think this advice is still sound today.

ANSWERS: VOICES OF FREEDOM   (page 186)
1. National unity; rights and responsibilities of people in a constitutional government; danger of political parties; need for an active national government. **2.** Answers will vary.

ANSWERS: SECTION 2 REVIEW   (page 187)
1. Edmond Genêt—p. 185; Thomas Pinckney—p. 187. **2.** Hamilton opposed the French Revolution because it attacked the power of the upper class; Jefferson applauded the goals of the rebels. **3.** Genêt outfitted American ships to attack English ships, he organized an attack by Americans on Spanish New Orleans, and he organized pro-French clubs that criticized Washington's policy of neutrality. These actions risked bringing the United States into war against Great Britain and Spain. **4. (a)** Britain would evacuate military posts on U.S. soil and pay damages for ships it had seized. The U.S. would pay debts owed to British merchants. **(b)** Pinckney negotiated a border between Spanish Florida and the U.S. at the 31st parallel. He also won for Americans the right to ship cargo down the Mississippi River and to deposit cargo at New Orleans. **5.** Washington feared alliances would involve the U.S. in European conflicts and threaten the development of the U.S. **6.** Possible answer: Involvement in the war would have caused serious economic problems for the new nation.

SECTION 3   (pages 187–189)
The Birth of Political Parties

ACTIVITIES

○ **Expressing an Opinion** Have students re-read President Washington's comment on political parties on text page 186 and describe what they think he meant. Ask students whether they agree or disagree with Washington's assessment of political parties.

☆ **Applying Information** Have students review the discussion of the political differences between Jefferson and Hamilton on text page 188. Then ask them to consider the following statements: (1) A college degree and ownership of 100 acres of land should be made a requirement for voting. (2) All free adult men should be allowed to hold public office. (3) Congress should pass a law providing aid to manufacturing firms. Have students decide which statements would probably be approved by Hamilton and which statements would probably be approved by Jefferson. Then ask them to write an essay comparing the political ideas of the two men.

☐ **Analyzing a Quotation** Read aloud the following quotation from Thomas Jefferson: "I am not a friend to a very energetic government. It is always oppressive. It places the governors indeed more at their ease; at the expense of the people." Ask students to clip newspaper articles that either support or refute the statement. Have them write a brief report in which they explain how their articles relate to Jefferson's beliefs about government.

ANSWERS: SECTION 3 REVIEW   (page 189)

1. Republican party, Federalist party—p. 188. **2.** Hamilton believed that wealthy, well-educated people should control the government. Jefferson believed that power should be spread among the common people. Hamilton believed that the nation's economy should depend on manufacturing, shipping, and commerce. Jefferson believed that it should be based on farming. Hamilton believed in a strong central government and in a loose interpretation of the Constitution. Jefferson, who believed that states should retain authority, was a strict constructionist. **3.** By traveling to New York to seek out anti-Hamilton people; by arranging for a new pro-Jefferson newspaper to be published. **4.** Candidates with opposing views could be elected President and Vice President. **5.** Possible answer:

The beginnings of the two-party system can be traced to the factions headed by Hamilton and Jefferson.

SECTION 4   (pages 190–193)
John Adams's Sacrifice

ACTIVITIES

○ **Identifying** Ask students to identify each of the following names and terms and use each in a sentence: (1) High Federalists, (2) XYZ Affair, (3) Alien Act, (4) Sedition Act, (5) nullify.

☆ **Making Generalizations** Ask students to write one or two factual statements that support each of the following generalizations: (1) John Adams was able to resist pressure from his party to go to war with France. (2) The Federalists tried to limit Republican criticism of their policies. (3) The Republicans believed that the Alien and Sedition acts were an abuse of governmental power. Then ask students to write a generalization about President Adams's term in office.

☐ **What If?** Have students write an essay describing what might have happened if the XYZ Affair had not taken place. They should concentrate on Federalist relations with the Republican party. Ask them to support their arguments with factual information.

ANSWERS: SECTION 4 REVIEW   (page 193)

1. High Federalists, XYZ Affair—p. 190; Convention of 1800—p. 191; Judiciary Act of 1801—p. 193. **2.** nullify—p. 193. **3. (a)** French seizure of U.S. ships and the XYZ Affair. **(b)** He threatened to resign if the Senate blocked nomination of a new ambassador. The Senate then agreed to a three-person delegation that negotiated successfully and thereby avoided war with France. **4. (a)** The stated purpose of the Alien and Sedition acts was to protect the nation from foreign treachery. In reality, the Alien Act tried to weaken the Republican party by reducing the political influence of immigrants, who usually voted for Republicans. It extended the residency requirement for citizenship and permitted the President to deport or imprison foreigners during time of war. The Sedition Act also weakened the Republican party by providing for the fine or imprisonment of anyone who spoke out against the government (which was led by the Federalist party). **(b)** By turning to the state gov-

T 35

ernments. Kentucky and Virginia both passed resolutions nullifying the Alien and Sedition acts. **5.** Possible answer: In that election, the presidency was passed from one political party to another.

ANSWERS: **CHAPTER 9 REVIEW** (page 194–195)

Vocabulary 1. c **2.** e **3.** a **4.** d **5.** b

Chapter Checkup 1. (a) Washington was a strong, popular leader respected by the American people. **(b)** Established how the Supreme Court should be organized and what its jurisdiction should be. **(c)** Helped the President establish major policies as well as handle administrative details. **2. (a)** Repaying the national debt fully; federal assumption of state debts; creation of a national bank; imposing of a protective tariff and an excise tax on whiskey. **(b)** All but the protective tariff; a tariff was passed but it was much lower than the one proposed by Hamilton. **(c)** Farmers who would have to pay the whiskey tax refused to pay and abused some revenue officers. Washington sent troops to stop the unrest. **3. (a)** He felt it rewarded speculators; he thought only original investors should be fully repaid. **(b)** That full funding would help the reputation of the country; that speculators had helped the country when it needed help and now they should be repaid. **4. (a)** It would issue currency and hold tax revenues. Perhaps more important, it would promote the loyalty of wealthy investors in the national government. **(b)** Because nowhere did the Constitution give Congress the power to set up a bank. **(c)** He thought the elastic clause gave Congress the right because the Constitution did give the right to tax. The bank was a place to deposit tax money. **5. (a)** Jefferson favored France because he approved of the ideals of their revolution. Hamilton supported the British because they were trying to end the French Revolution, which attacked the upper classes; also he felt that the U.S. could not afford another war with Britain, which might result from support of France. **(b)** Washington issued the Proclamation of Neutrality and tried to steer a middle course between France and Britain. **6.(a)** Maintaining forts in the U.S., selling arms to Native Americans, and seizing American ships and sailors suspected of deserting British ships. **(b)** Most were dissatisfied with it. Although it avoided war, it appeared to be a surrender to Great Britain. **7. (a)** They grew out of policy disagreements between Jefferson and his followers and Hamilton and his followers. **(b)** Republican—Jefferson; Federalist—Hamilton. **(c)** Because Jefferson was opposed to political parties, and had not originally intended to start a

party when he opposed Hamilton. **8. (a)** French attacks on American shipping, combined with cries for war within Federalist ranks. **(b)** He negotiated with France. **9. (a)** The Alien Act gave the President power to deport or jail foreigners during wartime and to require a foreigner to live in the U.S. 14 years before becoming a citizen. The Sedition Act outlawed any action that impeded the progress of government or defamed government officials. **(b)** To limit the power of Republicans. **(c)** Because they abused government power and they were aimed at Republicans. **10. (a)** Many voters had been angered by the Alien and Sedition acts and by high taxes; Adams had sent troops to quell a tax revolt in Pennsylvania. **(b)** Jefferson and Burr each received the same number of votes, because the electors each cast two votes without distinguishing between President and Vice President. The election was thrown into the House of Representatives.

Critical Thinking 1. (a) Because of his knowledge of economics and because he had gained Washington's confidence during the Revolutionary War. **(b)** Accept answers that discuss Hamilton's economic programs in relation to his aristocratic leanings and attitude toward the common people. **2. (a)** They declared the Alien and Sedition acts invalid. **(b)** He believed the states had created the federal government, so they could nullify federal laws. **(c)** If they had been supported by other states or if the Alien and Sedition acts had remained in effect longer.

Connecting Past and Present 1. (a) Industries competing with foreign goods of exceptional quality or low cost, such as clothing, cars, electronics. **(b)** For example: Japan, Germany, South Korea, Taiwan. **2. (a)** Democrats tend to favor bigger government to support social programs. Republicans tend to be more conservative in spending money at home and more liberal in supporting military expenditures. **(b)** Maybe a Republican, because he favored the states over the federal government. But he might have been a Democrat, because of their support of the "common citizen" against the upper classes. **(c)** Hamilton would probably be a Republican, because that is generally thought to be the party of the wealthy. But he favored strong central government, as do the Democrats today. **3. (a)** Each party had a newspaper that presented its point of view to the public. **(b)** They inform voters about events and politicians' views. They express editorial opinions about events.

Developing Basic Skills 1. Check charts for accuracy. **2. (a)** It is a speech. **(b)** Accept answers that refer to the themes in the speech. **(c)** Students should refer to the problems cited by Washington.

Chapter 10   (pages 196–215)

The Republicans in Office —————

OVERVIEW

Chapter 10 traces the beginning of a period of national growth and expansion. Students read about Thomas Jefferson's policies of reconciliation and the changes he made as President. They examine the attempts to keep the U.S. out of the conflict between France and Britain and the eventual decision to go to war. Although the war was more or less a draw, many Americans considered it a victory, and the nation emerged with greater self-confidence and pride.

HISTORICAL SIDELIGHTS

The following pieces of historical information can serve as notes of interest during the study of Chapter 10. The page numbers in parentheses indicate the points in the student text at which you may wish to introduce the information.

Tributes to the Barbary Pirates (p. 199)   When Jefferson began his campaign against the Barbary pirates, the U.S. had already paid hundreds of thousands of dollars in "tributes." A treaty with Tripoli in 1797, for example, called for payments of $40,000 in gold and silver coin, thirteen watches, three diamond rings, one sapphire ring, as well as a ring with a small watch on it.

Complications in the Louisiana Purchase (p. 202)   The American purchase of Louisiana required a certain amount of diplomatic scrambling. France had acquired the territory from Spain in October 1800 in the secret Treaty of San Ildefonso. But when Americans arrived in Louisiana in 1803, they discovered that New Orleans had been under French rule for only three weeks and that St. Louis, in "Upper Louisiana," was still run by the Spanish. On March 9, 1804, Captain Amos Stoddard, an American, took command of St. Louis, first acting as an agent for France. Then, on the following day, he went through the formality of transferring the territory to himself, now acting as an agent for the U.S.

SECTION 1   (pages 197–201)
Jefferson and the National Government

ACTIVITIES*

○   **Writing a Diary** Tell students to imagine that they are members of Stephen Decatur's crew during the fighting with the Barbary pirates. Have students write two diary entries in which they describe their experiences in the Mediterranean. You might ask students to seek additional information about the Barbary pirates to supplement the information in the text.

☆   **Researching** Tell students that Thomas Jefferson was a person of many talents. In fact, at a White House dinner honoring Nobel Prize winners in 1962, President John Kennedy remarked that the group was "the most extraordinary collection of talent . . . that has ever been gathered together at the White House—with the possible exception of when Thomas Jefferson dined alone." Ask students to write a short report describing one of Jefferson's talents. Suggest the following vocations: architect, writer, lawyer, inventor, botanist, surveyor, philosopher, archaeologist, educator.

☐   **Applying Information** Point out to students that some Americans at the time referred to Thomas Jefferson's election as the "revolution of 1800." Ask students to review what they learned about Jefferson's presidency and answer the following questions: (1) What does the term "revolution" mean? (2) Why do you think some people thought Jefferson's election was a revolution? (3) In retrospect, would you agree that it was a revolution? Explain.

ANSWERS: MAP STUDY   (page 199)
On the Mediterranean Sea; because many Mediterranean shipping lanes passed Tripoli.

ANSWERS: SECTION 1 REVIEW   (page 201)
1. "Midnight appointments," *Marbury* v. *Madison*—p. 198; Aaron Burr—p. 200. **2.** judicial review—p. 198; laissez-faire—p. 199; secede—p. 200. **3. (a)** By making a conciliatory inaugural address, allowing

———————
*See "To the Teacher" for an explanation of the symbols.

some Federalists to keep their government positions, and retaining some important Federalist policies. **(b)** Allowing the Alien and Sedition acts to expire; refunding all fines that had been paid under those acts; restoring the five-year residence requirement for naturalization; laissez-faire policies; cut in defense spending. **4.** He thought the judiciary, controlled by the Federalists, was assuming too much power and feared that the balance of power among the three branches would be upset. **5. (a)** To avoid the risk of having its merchant ships captured. **(b)** By sending ships to blockade Tripoli harbor and marines to land at Tripoli, which forced the Barbary States to make peace. **6.** Possible answer: Jefferson meant that the two political parties had many common goals.

SECTION 2 (pages 201–204)
Expanding the Nation's Boundaries

ACTIVITIES
○ **Using Visual Evidence** Ask students to study the painting on text page 204 and answer the following questions: (1) What is going on in the painting? (2) Draw one conclusion from the painting.

☆ **Relating Cause and Effect** Have students describe the cause-and-effect relationship between the following pairs of events: (1) Napoleon's decision to sell Louisiana and events in Haiti; (2) Napoleon's decision to sell Louisiana and France's European wars; (3) the Louisiana Purchase and the Lewis and Clark expedition. Ask them to state clearly which event in each pair was the cause and which event was the effect. Have students suggest long-range causes and effects of the decision to buy Louisiana.

□ **Organizing a Debate** Point out to students that some historians believe that except for the Revolutionary War, the Louisiana Purchase is the most important event in American history. Hold a classroom debate on the issue. Students should do research to support their arguments.

ANSWERS: MAP STUDY (page 203)
Lewis and Clark; Pike.

ANSWERS: SECTION 2 REVIEW (page 204)
1. Meriwether Lewis, Napoleon Bonaparte—p. 201; William Clark—p. 202; Sacajawea —p. 203. **2. (a)** He feared that Napoleon would close the port of New Orleans to American shipping. He worried that Napoleon might use the territory as a base to build a colonial empire in America. **(b)** Napoleon needed money for wars in Europe. Also, with the revolt in Haiti, his dreams of an American empire had dissolved. **3. (a)** It does not specify how new territory can be acquired. **(b)** Jefferson based the purchase on his constitutional power to make treaties with foreign nations. **4. (a)** He instructed them to gather information about the flow of rivers and about plants, climate, and geology of the territory. They also were to determine if a Northwest Passage existed. **(b)** That there is no easy way to cross the continent. **5.** Possible answer: The information they gathered made it easier for large numbers of Americans to move westward.

SECTION 3 (pages 204–210)
The Coming of Another War

ACTIVITIES
○ **Identifying** Read aloud the following clues and ask students who or what each describes: (1) led U.S. forces in battle of Fallen Timber; (2) general who was defeated by the Shawnee in 1791; (3) led the Shawnee in 1791 victory over U.S. forces; (4) battle that doomed the confederation of Native Americans organized by Tecumseh; (5) treaty by which Native Americans ceded a large part of present-day Ohio to the U.S.; (6) called on Indians to give up customs adopted from white settlers; (7) governor of Indiana territory in 1811; (8) skilled orator who tried to organize Native Americans to resist white settlement.
Answers: **1.** Wayne **2.** St. Claire **3.** Little Turtle **4.** Tippecanoe **5.** Greenville **6.** Prophet **7.** Harrison **8.** Tecumseh

☆ **Relating Cause and Effect** Remind students that major historical events such as wars usually have multiple causes. Ask students, working in small groups, to list the events and developments that contributed to the outbreak of the War of 1812. Have the groups report to the class, explaining how each was a cause of the war. Then ask: Which of the events or developments do you think had the greatest effect on the outbreak of war? Why?

☐ **Writing a Report** Have students research and write a report about the history of one of the Native American nations shown on the map on text page 208. If possible, students should concentrate on the period from 1789 to 1812. They might begin by consulting *The Indian Heritage of America* by Alvin Josephy or *The Indian in America* by Wilcomb E. Washburn.

ANSWER: GRAPH STUDY   (page 207)

The fluctuations show the effects of unstable U.S. relations with Europe; for example, the Embargo Act of 1807 had a severe effect on American trade.

ANSWER: MAP STUDY   (page 208)

The land ceded by the Greenville Treaty.

ANSWERS: VOICES OF FREEDOM   (page 209)

1. Because the Indians were there first; and no sale of land to the settlers was valid unless all Indians agreed to it. **2.** Probably, because both groups claimed a right to the land, and both could not own the land at the same time.

ANSWERS: SECTION 3 REVIEW   (page 210)

1. Nonintercourse Act—p. 207; Henry Clay, Treaty of Greenville—p. 208; William Henry Harrison—p. 209. **2.** impressment, naturalized citizen—p. 205; embargo—p. 206. **3.(a)** He asked Congress to pass the Embargo Act. **(b)** Many merchants who cooperated with the embargo were ruined; others evaded the law because they depended on trade. **4.** They hoped to win Canada and push the British out of North America. **5.** Possible answer: The alliance could have forced the Americans to divide their military strength. Thus the British might have won the war and the Indians might have won back their land from American settlers.

SECTION 4   (pages 210–213)
A Complex War

ACTIVITIES

○ **Using a Song as a Primary Source** Review with students how the "Star-Spangled Banner" was written (p. 212). Then have them read the lyrics of the song and explain what Francis Scott Key was referring to. Ask them

to speculate about how Key felt when he wrote the song.

☆ **Placing Events in Time** Ask students to construct a horizontal time line for the years 1812–1816. Then have them place each of the following events in the correct place on the time line: (1) Battle of the Thames; (2) British occupy Washington, D.C.; (3) Treaty of Ghent signed; (4) Battle of Lake Erie; (5) General Hull surrenders to British at Detroit; (6) Hartford Convention held; (7) Battle of Horseshoe Bend; (8) Battle of New Orleans; (9) Foreign trade falls to 90 percent of peak in 1807; (10) American victory on Lake Champlain. Then ask students why they think the war was called the War of 1812 even though it lasted until 1814.

☐ **Biographical Sketch** Have students write a biographical sketch of one of the following persons: James Madison, William Henry Harrison, Oliver Hazard Perry, Tecumseh, Dolley Madison, Francis Scott Key, Andrew Jackson. While writing their sketch, students should concentrate on the person's role in the War of 1812.

ANSWER: MAP STUDY   (page 211)

The British blockade of the Atlantic coast and the British presence in the Gulf of Mexico.

ANSWERS: SECTION 4 REVIEW   (page 213)

1. Hartford Convention—p. 211; Andrew Jackson, Creek War, Treaty of Ghent—p. 213. **2.** Small army and small navy, incompetent military leaders, and ineffective strategy. **3.** Because the New England economy depended so much on trade with Britain. **4.** Perry's victory on Lake Erie and Harrison's victory at the Battle of the Thames. **5.** Possible answer: No. The members of the Hartford Convention merely threatened to secede; they did not carry out their threat.

ANSWERS: CHAPTER 10 REVIEW   (pages 214–215)

Vocabulary **1.** f **2.** c **3.** e **4.** d **5.** a **6.** b

Chapter Checkup **1.** He was able to end the Alien and Sedition acts, refund fines collected under it, and restore previous residency requirements for naturalization. **2. (a)** He tried to prevent "midnight judges" from taking office. **(b)** He thought it gave the judiciary too much power and disrupted the balance in the federal government among the three branches. **3. (a)** It was part of his general plan to reduce the role of the federal government. **(b)** The navy was soon needed to fight the Barbary pirates. **4.(a)** To protect the main trade and transportation route for western settlers. **(b)** Because Napoleon had decided to give up his American empire, so he had no use for the Louisiana Territory. **5. (a)** Jefferson believed in a strict interpretation of the Constitution, and the Constitution did not explicitly provide for the purchase of new territory. **(b)** On his power to make treaties with foreign nations. **6.(a)** To explore and gather information about the Louisiana Territory. **(b)** It was used by fur traders, road builders, and settlers as they entered the new territory. **7. (a)** They each issued orders to prevent countries from trading with the other. They seized ships bound for the other country. The British impressed American sailors. **(b)** He proposed the Embargo Act. **(c)** British and French shipping were hurt, but so was American shipping. In 1809, Congress ended the embargo. **8. (a)** Congress passed the Nonintercourse Act. Madison said if France or Britain ended trade restrictions, the U.S. would stop trading with the other. **(b)** No, in the end Madison asked Congress to declare war. **9. (a)** Indians, supported by the British, resisted the westward movement of settlers. **(b)** They tried to unite the Indian nations in resisting American settlement. During the War of 1812, they helped the British. **10. (a)** There were few soldiers, few competent leaders, only a small navy. **(b)** Americans were successful on Lake Erie and at the Battle of the Thames. **11. (a)** None, the war was already over. **(b)** They performed so well that General Jackson singled them out for praise. **12. (a)** Restored prewar conditions. **(b)** Border disputes, which were left to be settled later, and the issue of impressment, which was no longer important since Britain and France were not at war. **(c)** Because the U.S. held its own against a strong European power.

Critical Thinking **1.** Students should refer to impeachment proceedings held by Congress against members of the judicial branch accused of misconduct in office. **2. (a)** War Hawks, because they wanted to control British Canada and believed that the British were supporting Native Americans in the West. **(b)** New Englanders, because it would hurt their trade and industry. **(c)** New Englanders, since the Treaty of Ghent did little to change prewar conditions.

Connecting Past and Present **1.** Possible answers: income taxes, post offices, interstate highways, regulation of the contents of consumer products. Jefferson would probably have thought the government was too involved in people's lives, since he believed in a policy of laissez-faire. **2. (a)** Possible answer: The ban on importing medical drugs that have not been tested by the FDA. **(b)** To prevent the use of drugs whose side effects

are unknown. **(c)** Yes, several drugs that were kept out of the country later proved to be dangerous.

Developing Basic Skills **1. (a)** Oil, natural gas, iron ore, coal, gold, silver, lead, zinc, copper, and uranium. **(b)** Agriculture, livestock, forestry, and mining. **2. (a)** 1807. **(b)** 1807. **(c)** Students should refer to the threat of war and the Embargo Act.

Chapter 11   (pages 216–237)
A Growing Nation ——

OVERVIEW
Chapter 11 focuses on the period of national growth and development following the War of 1812. Students read about industrial growth and westward expansion as well as a vigorous foreign policy. They also examine the growing spirit of nationalism.

HISTORICAL SIDELIGHTS
The following pieces of historical information can serve as notes of interest during the study of Chapter 11. The page numbers in parentheses indicate the points in the student text at which you may wish to introduce the information.

Straw Hats (p. 222)   The widespread effects of the Industrial Revolution extended into the countryside. For example, for years many women and children in the rural town of Franklin, Massachusetts, had woven straw braids for use in women's hats. At first, they only exchanged the braids for merchandise at the local general store. But by 1840, a local firm was making straw bonnets to sell in Boston and Providence. By 1812, workers in Franklin were producing 6,000 straw hats a year. (One of the young boys who braided such hats was Horace Mann, who later became an influential educational reformer.)

A Rocky Ride (p. 228)   Stagecoaches, which provided public transportation over often primitive roads, gave passengers some bone-jolting rides. "The coachman . . . drove most furiously," reported one traveler in 1832. "Ravines and watercourses, which cut up the road in countless numbers, were no impediments; he dashed on at a surprising rate, over rough stones and tottering bridges that would have cracked every spring in an English carriage." The passengers were prevented from being hurled into each other's laps by holding on to a broad leather strap that formed a backrest to the coach seat.

SECTION 1 (pages 217–219)
A Sense of National Unity

ACTIVITIES*

○ **Applying Information** Ask students to define the term Era of Good Feelings. Have them list three ways the period after the War of 1812 was such an era. Ask: Has there been an Era of Good Feelings recently?

☆ **Writing a Report** Divide the class into five groups and assign each group one of the following Supreme Court cases: (1) *Marbury* v. *Madison;* (2) *Fletcher* v. *Peck;* (3) *Dartmouth* v. *Woodward;* (4) *McCulloch* v. *Maryland;* (5) *Gibbons* v. *Ogden.* Tell each group to prepare oral reports describing the case, the decision, and its significance. After the groups have presented their reports, ask: (1) Which case was most significant for the nation in the early 1800s? Why? (2) Which case remains most significant for the present time? Why?

□ **Expressing an Opinion** Read aloud the following quotation by Thomas Jefferson: "To consider the [Supreme Court] judges as the ultimate arbiters of all constitutional questions is a very dangerous doctrine indeed." Then ask students the following questions: (1) Based on what you read in Chapter 10 of your text, why do you think Jefferson held that opinion? (2) Do you think John Marshall would have agreed? Why or why not? (3) Do you agree? Why or why not?

ANSWERS: SECTION 1 REVIEW (page 219)

1. Era of Good Feelings—p. 218. **2.** He was the last President to have been an adult during the Revolution; he dressed in an old-fashioned way; he believed that, except in foreign affairs, the President should not make policy, but should follow the people and Congress; he shared the older mistrust of political parties. **3.** Marshall wrote many decisions during his 35 years on the Supreme Court; he often used his office to strengthen federal power. **4.(a)** *Fletcher* v. *Peck* (1810) and *Dartmouth College* v. *Woodward* (1819). **(b)** *McCulloch* v. *Maryland* (1819) and *Gibbons* v. *Ogden* (1824). **5.** Possible answers: It supported the existence of implied powers; it said that a state could not hinder a national institution within its borders.

---

* See "To the Teacher" for an explanation of the symbols.

SECTION 2 (pages 220–223)
The Industrial Revolution

ACTIVITIES

○ **Writing a Letter** Have students imagine that they worked in one of the Lowell mills during the early years. Ask them to write a letter home to their families telling about life at the mill. They should refer to the material on text pages 222–223 to help them get started.

☆ **Applying Information** Draw a chart on the chalkboard with three columns headed Characteristics, Before the Industrial Revolution, As a Result of the Industrial Revolution. Write these items in the first column: (1) location of manufacturing; (2) sources of money for Investment; (3) technology involved; (4) speed of manufacturing; (5) source of power; (6) type of workers; (7) trade with other nations. Complete the chart as a class activity. Then ask: Was the Industrial Revolution really a revolution? Why or why not?

□ **Writing a Report** Have students research the history of the steamboat and write a report in which they describe the development of a working steamboat from the first steam engine to Robert Fulton's launching of the *Clermont.* Students might consult *Robert Fulton* by John S. Morgan.

ANSWERS: SECTION 2 REVIEW (page 223)

1. James Watt—p. 220; Robert Fulton, Eli Whitney, Samuel Slater—p. 221; Francis Cabot Lowell—p. 222. **2.** factory system, capital, limited liability—p. 220; interchangeable parts—p. 221. **3. (a)** For example, steam engine provided power for factories and in transportation; spinning jenny greatly speeded up the process of spinning cloth; cotton gin greatly speeded the process of cleaning seeds from cotton. **(b)** Through British mechanics who were willing to supply the necessary information. Several state legislatures offered rewards for such information. **4.** Both worked for low wages. Also, children, because they were small, were agile around dangerous machinery. **5. (a)** Industrialization brought Americans closer by helping to create a pride in self-sufficiency. **(b)** Industrialization developed primarily in the North, whereas the South continued to rely on agriculture. This difference contributed to different ways of life and economic interests. **6.** Possible answers: It affected employment opportunities, wages, and working conditions. It led to a gap between workers and factory owners, between rich and poor. **T 41**

SECTION 3   (pages 224–226)
Henry Clay's American System

ACTIVITIES

○ **Finding the Main Idea** Have students write short summaries of each subsection on text pages 224–226, underlining the main idea. Lead a class discussion to arrive at the best statement of the main idea of each subsection.

☆ **Relating Cause and Effect** Ask students to describe one effect of each of the following events or developments: (1) British manufacturers began dumping low-priced goods on the American market after the War of 1812. (2) State banks issued paper currency without backing in gold and silver. (3) In 1819, the second Bank of the U.S. began to call in its loans. (4) European demand for American farm products began to decline.

☐ **Comparing** Ask students to define "protective tariff" and to explain how the Tariff of 1816 was a protective tariff. Then have them write a short essay comparing the positions of Henry Clay, John Calhoun, and Daniel Webster on the tariff.

ANSWERS: SECTION 3 REVIEW   (page 226)
1. Henry Clay, Daniel Webster, John C. Calhoun—p. 224. **2.** bank note—p. 225. **3.** Each supported nationalism at one time or another in his career. **4.** The three main parts were a protective tariff, a new national bank, and a federal program of internal improvements. **5.** Because it raised tariffs and this threatened the shipping industry in New England. **6.** Provide a stable means of issuing money and a safe depository for federal funds. **7.** Possible answer: It might have caused some people to think that the federal government should be more active in economic affairs, that it should take actions such as passing a protective tariff.

SECTION 4   (pages 226–231)
Building Pathways to the West

ACTIVITIES

○ **Using Visual Evidence** Have students find pictures of early steamboats. Ask them to learn what they can about one of them. Have them prepare a short report about the steamboat's

design, where it was meant to be used, and what its advantages were.

☆ **Map Reading** Ask students to study the map on text page 231 and answer these questions: (1) In what direction do most of the major roads go? (2) What bodies of water are connected by each of the major canals? (3) In what region were most major canals located? (4) What states did the National Road pass through? (5) Which cities appear to be developing as transportation centers? (6) How did the system of canals and roads contribute to westward movement? (7) Do you agree with John C. Calhoun that good transportation would bind the nation together? Explain.

☐ **Interpreting a Graph** Have students make a line graph of total population growth between 1790 and 1830 based on the statistics that follow. The horizontal axis should go from 1800 to 1830, the vertical axis from 1 to 13 million.

1790	3,929,000
1800	5,297,000
1810	7,224,000
1820	9,618,000
1830	12,901,000

Source: *Historical Statistics of the United States*

When students have completed their graphs, have them write an essay describing the trend shown and its implications.

ANSWERS: SKILL LESSON   (page 227)
1. (a) 1790–1830. **(b)** 40 years. **(c)** The population of different states at ten-year intervals. **2. (a)** 75,400. **(b)** 145,300. **(c)** 1820. **3. (a)** It grew by over 150,000. **(b)** It grew by 76,900. **(c)** Kentucky; Ohio. **(d)** Ohio grew more quickly. **4. (a)** The region experienced significant population growth. **(b)** Better transportation encouraged population growth in the West. **(c)** Each state benefited from good river transportation. **(d)** Ohio, 1803; Kentucky, 1792; Tennessee, 1796; Mississippi, 1817; Indiana, 1816; Michigan, 1837; Louisiana, 1812; Illinois, 1818; Missouri, 1821; Arkansas, 1836; Alabama, 1819. **(e)** The more heavily populated territories achieved statehood sooner than the less-populated territories.

ANSWER: GRAPH STUDY   (page 229)
In the late 1820s.

ANSWERS: THE GEOGRAPHIC CONNECTION
(page 230)
1. Because each wanted to control the trade with the West, which was a growing area. **2.** First, the Erie Canal was cheaper and easier to build than

other canals because it followed a lowland route; so shipping rates could be kept low. Later, railroads following the same lowland route gave New York a further edge.

ANSWERS: MAP STUDY   (page 231)

Answers will vary.

ANSWERS: SECTION 4 REVIEW   (page 231)

1. National Road, Erie Canal—p. 229. **2.** corduroy roads—p. 229. **3.** Because of high food prices in the East and the availability of rich farmland in the West. **4.** They needed roads to send farm products to the East and to bring manufactured goods back to the West. **5. (a)** It cut the cost of transportation and reduced the travel time between New York City and western markets. **(b)** It made it possible to carry goods even up river; Shreve's steam boat showed that steamboats could be used in shallow waters. **6.** Possible answer: The improvements helped link sections of the country together, encourage national pride, and make future economic growth possible.

SECTION 5   (pages 232–235)

James Monroe and Foreign Affairs

ACTIVITIES

○ **Placing Events in Time** Copy the following time line on the chalkboard. Then read aloud the list of events. Ask students to write on a sheet of paper the letter of the correct time period for each event.

A	B	C	D	E
1814	1816	1818	1820	1822	1824

(1) U.S. grants official recognition to Latin American republics; (2) Rush-Bagot Treaty negotiated; (3) Monroe Doctrine issued; (4) Andrew Jackson leads military party into Florida; (5) Convention that established boundary between Canada and the United States approved.
Answers: **1.** E **2.** B **3.** E **4.** C **5.** C

☆ **Defending a Position** Tell students to imagine that they are presenting a case before an international court of justice in 1818. The issue is Andrew Jackson's excursion into Florida. Ask half the students to imagine that they are representatives of the Spanish government and have them write an essay describing their position on the incident. Ask the other half of the students to imagine that they are representatives of the U.S. government and have them write an essay describing their position on the incident.

☐ **Researching** Ask students to do additional research about the reaction of European nations to the Monroe Doctrine and to write a report about their findings. They might consult *The Era of Good Feeling* by George Dangerfield or *A Diplomatic History of the American People* by Thomas A. Bailey.

ANSWERS: MAP STUDY   (page 233)

Convention of 1818; through the Adams-Onís Treaty; Oregon, because it was jointly occupied by Great Britain and the United States, and its boundaries were not set by any treaties with Britain.

ANSWER: MAP STUDY   (page 234)

Because of the closeness of the new nations to the United States.

ANSWERS: SECTION 5 REVIEW   (page 235)

1. John Quincy Adams, Rush-Bagot Treaty, Convention of 1818—p. 232. **2. (a)** Served as a haven for outlaws and as a refuge for escaped slaves. Also, some Native Americans raided U.S. settlements from there. **(b)** By transferring control over Florida to the U.S. **(c)** It settled the boundary between the Louisiana Purchase and Spanish territory. **3. (a)** The United States feared that recognition might endanger negotiations with Spain over Florida. **(b)** They feared that the alliance in Europe might lead to an attempt to restore Spanish control over its former colonies. **4.** That the United States would not interfere with European countries or existing colonies in the Americas; that the United States would oppose any European intervention in the affairs of independent nations in the Americas. **5.** Possible answer: The refusal to issue a joint declaration with Britain reflected Americans' pride in their nation's independence.

ANSWERS: CHAPTER 11 REVIEW
                                    (pages 236–237)

Vocabulary **1.** c **2.** d **3.** a **4.** e **5.** b

Chapter Checkup **1. (a)** Monroe rejected the idea of political parties and attempted to foster good relations between political opponents. **(b)** In age, dress, and mental outlook. **2. (a)** It became an active, influential branch of the government. **(b)** It confirmed the principle of judicial review. It demonstrated that the Supreme Court could rule state laws unconstitutional, in *Fletcher* v. *Peck.* **(c)** Because it emphasized the importance of national powers. **3. (a)** So much good farmland was available in the vast nation that few people chose to work in factories. Also, skilled artisans, accustomed to working at home, had little interest in factory work. **(b)** Women and children. **(c)** At first, though workers had to work long hours, they were treated fairly well; they were provided with places to live, food, social activities, and educational programs. **4.** It helped unify the country by encouraging the growth of American industries and reducing dependence on foreign goods. But it also divided the country, because the industry was concentrated in the North and, as a result, differences in economic and social patterns grew up in the different regions of the country. **5. (a)** By raising the price of imported goods, the Tariff of 1816 would eliminate lower-priced competition for domestic products. This protection would allow industries to grow and foster self-sufficiency for the U.S. **(b)** The western and Middle Atlantic states believed the revenues would help pay for roads and canals needed for trade. The South supported the tariff because it would protect the cotton industry. **6. (a)** The absence of a uniform currency made commerce difficult, and the federal government needed a secure place to deposits its funds. **(b)** By calling in its loans to state banks, which in turn recalled their loans to land speculators. **(c)** A declining European demand for textile and farm products and a resulting drop in southern cotton prices. **7. (a)** As more people moved west, there was a need for better roads on which to travel and to transport goods. **(b)** These advances made both transportation and communication easier between the parts of the country; this led to a greater feeling of unity. **8. (a)** He wanted to check further European intervention in the Western Hemisphere. **(b)** It demonstrated American independence and pride.

Critical Thinking **1.** President Monroe's desire to avoid struggles between political parties; Supreme Court decisions that strengthened the power of the national government; the tariff; industrialization; transportation improvements that linked East to West; the Monroe Doctrine. **2.** Students should discuss the absence of political parties in the early years of the federal government.

Connecting Past and Present **1.** It supports an interstate highway system; it runs portions of railroad lines; it regulates aspects of air transportation. **2.** Answers will vary. Students might point to certain American industries that have trouble competing with cheap labor in other countries. On the other hand, they might argue that American industries should fend for themselves in world competition. **3.** Certain products are too heavy or bulky to be transported easily by plane or truck. Water transportation is still needed in these cases. **4.** Students might mention the concern over the intervention by communist countries, such as Cuba, in the internal affairs of Latin American nations. American military and economic power is probably more important than the Monroe Doctrine in our relations with Latin America.

Developing Basic Skills **1.** *Marbury* v. *Madison:* Article III, Section 2, Clause 1: "The judicial power shall extend to all cases, in law and equity, arising under this Constitution, the laws of the United States..." *Fletcher* v. *Peck:* Article I, Section 10, Clause 1: "No state shall . . . pass any . . . law impairing the obligation of contracts." *Dartmouth College* v. *Woodward:* See the clause cited for *Fletcher* v. *Peck. McCulloch* v. *Maryland:* Article I, Section 8, Clause 18: "The Congress shall have the power to make all laws which shall be necessary and proper for carrying into execution the foregoing powers." *Gibbons* v. *Ogden:* Article I, Section 8, Clause 3: "The Congress shall have the power . . . to regulate commerce . . . among the several states." **2. (a)** The U.S. in 1824. **(b)** Convention of 1818. **(c)** Adams-Onís Treaty. **(d)** Spain ceded Florida to the U.S. **3.** Clay: U.S. commissioner during peace talks with Great Britain after the War of 1812, member of the House of Representatives, senator. Calhoun: secretary of war, Vice President of the U.S., senator, secretary of state. Webster: member of the House of Representatives, senator. These men held important positions for many years and as such had an opportunity to influence national policy.

ANSWERS: SPIRIT OF AMERICA (pages 238–241)
1. Europeans have thought that Americans put too much emphasis on youth. **2.** Possible answer: There are things people can learn from the experience of others; however, very often people will want to try things for themselves.

Notable Americans **1.** As the oldest child, Catharine had the advantage of much of her parents' time and attention. One disadvantage was that she had much responsibility for the younger children. **2.** Possible answer: The children were provided with a good education and with many advantages, and much was expected of them.

Voices of Freedom **1.** Much of Lincoln's education came from his reading and from what he was able to teach himself. **2.** Possible answer: He reveals his determination, his self-sufficiency, and his lack of pretensions.

Unit Four

An Era of Expansion

Chapter 12   (pages 244–261)

A Democracy for the People _____

OVERVIEW

Chapter 12 focuses on growing democracy in politics and the increasing power of the President. Students examine ways in which people were given more political power. They also explore President Jackson's handling of the nullification and banking crises. The chapter concludes with a discussion of the Panic of 1837 and presidential politics during the early 1840s.

HISTORICAL SIDELIGHTS

The following pieces of historical information can serve as notes of interest during the study of Chapter 12. The page numbers in parentheses indicate the points in the student text at which you may wish to introduce the information.

A Fateful Day (p. 246) In 1826, when the supporters of Andrew Jackson had already begun the campaign that would usher in a new era, two elder statesmen of the old era passed away. At noon on July fourth, Thomas Jefferson died peacefully at his home in Monticello. On the same day, hundreds of miles to the north, John Adams breathed his last not far from the celebrations of independence in his home town of Quincy, Massachusetts. His final words were, "Thomas Jefferson still survives. . . ." The day marked the 50-year anniversary of the signing of the Declaration of Independence.

From Nullification to Secession (p. 255) Andrew Jackson saw with remarkable clarity the implications of the idea of nullification. If a state could nullify a law, Jackson argued, what would prevent a state from seceding from the union— if not because of the tariff, for some other reason? "The next pretext," he predicted, "will be the . . . slavery question." Time was to prove Jackson correct.

> **SECTION 1**   (pages 245–248)
> **Emergence of a**
> **New Party System**

ACTIVITIES*

○ **Identification** Ask students who is referred to by each of the following clues: (1) became secretary of state after the election of 1824; (2) charged that a "corrupt bargain" had deprived him of the presidency; (3) won the presidential election of 1824; (4) charged that Adams was trying to create an aristocracy; (5) won the presidential election of 1828. *Answers:* **1.** Clay **2.** Jackson **3.** Adams **4.** Jackson **5.** Jackson

☆ **Reading a Map, Graph, and Chart** Have students study the map, graph, and chart on text page 247 and answer these questions: (1) What is the topic shown? (2) What areas of the country did Jackson win? (3) What areas did Adams win? (4) How would you explain this territorial breakdown? (5) Was Jackson's victory bigger in the popular vote or the electoral vote? (6) How did the results of the 1828 election compare with the results of the 1824 election? (7) Why do you think the results changed?

_____

* See "To the Teacher" for an explanation of the symbols.

□ **Analyzing a Quotation**   Read aloud the following quotation or duplicate and distribute copies. Explain that the quotation is from a letter written in 1825 by Representative William Plumer, Jr. The letter concerns President Adams's appointment of Henry Clay as secretary of state.

The office of Secretary of State was, at the same time, offered to Mr. Clay. This was anticipated by everybody as a matter of course. The Western states, nine in number, with a population of two or three millions, have never had a President, a Secretary of State, or any other commanding station in the government. Upon every principle, they were entitled to notice. When to this we add that five of these states voted for Mr. Adams, and thereby pledged themselves to his support, and that all this was done by the friends of Mr. Clay, it is hardly necessary to suppose any corrupt bargain, or intrigue between Clay and Adams, to account for the promotion of a man who had already been twice offered a seat in the Cabinet by former Presidents.

Ask: (1) Did Representative Plumer believe there was a "corrupt bargain" between Adams and Clay? (2) According to Plumer, what factors explain Clay's appointment as secretary of state? (3) How do you think Andrew Jackson might have responded had he read this letter?

ANSWER: GRAPH STUDY   (page 246)
Because Jackson had received more of the popular vote and more electoral votes than any other candidate.

ANSWERS: MAP AND GRAPH STUDY   (page 247)
The Northeast; the South and West.

ANSWERS: SECTION 1 REVIEW   (page 248)
1. National Republicans, Democratic Republicans—p. 246; Old Hickory— p. 247. **2.** party platform — p. 247. **3. (a)** Because no candidate won a majority in the electoral college, the President was selected by the House of Representatives. **(b)** Clay persuaded his supporters in the House of Representatives to back Adams; afterward Clay was appointed secretary of state. People suspected a "deal" had been made. **4.** Adams won mainly his region of New England. Jackson took the entire South and West. **5.** Possible answer: The candidates' personalities were given more attention than the issues.

SECTION 2   (pages 248–253)
Rise of the Common People

ACTIVITIES

○ **Using Primary Sources**   Have students re-read the excerpt on page 252 about the Trail of Tears. Then ask: (1) Did the Reverend Jones think the Cherokee were treated fairly? Give two examples to support your answer. (2) How do you think the Reverend felt about the Removal Act? Explain. (3) How might President Jackson have reacted to the Reverend's account of events?

☆ **Making Generalizations**   Ask students to write two factual statements that support each of the following generalizations: (1) There were limits to Jacksonian democracy. (2) Many Native Americans were deprived of their rights during Jackson's presidency. (3) Some Native Americans resisted the government's plan for their removal from the East. Then have students write their own generalization based on this section and list the facts that support it.

□ **Biographical Sketch**   Have students write a biographical sketch of Andrew Jackson in which they discuss Jackson's ideas on democracy. Ask them to investigate aspects of Jackson's life that may have contributed to his support of democracy. They might consult the *Dictionary of American Biography* or a biography of Jackson.

ANSWERS: NOTABLE AMERICANS   (page 251)
1. So they could become informed about events and be independent of white people. **2.** It used symbols to stand for syllables, instead of single letter sounds.

ANSWER: MAP STUDY   (page 252)
Approximately 650 miles.

ANSWERS: SECTION 2 REVIEW   (page 253)
1. Removal Act, Trail of Tears—p. 251; Blackhawk, Osceola—p. 252. **2.** white manhood suffrage—p. 249; caucus—p. 250. **3. (a)** All white males whether or not they owned property. **(b)** By 1832, voters chose electors directly in every state but South Carolina. **4.** Women, black Americans, and Native Americans. **5. (a)** The Court ruled that the laws of Georgia have no force on the Cherokee because they are a separate political entity. **(b)** That he would not enforce the Court's ruling; he challenged the Court to enforce it. **6.** Possible answer:

His statement implied that the Indians had to obey the orders of the government but could not participate in it.

SECTION 3   (pages 253–257)
Strengthening the National Government

ACTIVITIES

○ **Name Game**   Read these clues to the class and ask students to identify the people described: (1) director of the second Bank of the United States; (2) argued that the federal government, not the states, held final authority under the Constitution; (3) proposed a compromise tariff bill in 1833 that ended the nullification crisis; (4) argued that states could nullify a federal law considered unconstitutional; (5) threatened to use force if South Carolina defied federal law.
Answers: **1.** Biddle **2.** Webster **3.** Clay **4.** Calhoun **5.** Jackson

☆ **Relating Cause and Effect**   Write the following statements on the chalkboard or duplicate and distribute copies: (1) President Jackson establishes a spoils system. (2) South Carolina nullifies the Tariff of 1832. (3) President Jackson signs Henry Clay's compromise tariff bill. (4) President Jackson encourages the establishment of the "pet banks." (5) Nicholas Biddle blocks new loans by the second Bank of the United States. Remind students that one historical event is often the result or effect of one event and the cause of another event. Have students write one cause and one effect of each of the events listed. Then ask whether they would classify Jackson as a "strong" or "weak" President based on what they have learned.

☐ **Analyzing a Quotation**   Read aloud the quotation that follows, or duplicate and distribute copies. Explain that the quotation is from the speech given in 1830 by Senator Robert Hayne of South Carolina. (See text page 255.)

Sir, as to the doctrine that the federal government is the exclusive judge of the extent as well as the limitations of its powers, it seems to me to be utterly subversive of the sovereignty and independence of the states. It makes but little difference in my estimation whether Congress or the Supreme Court are invested with this power. If the federal government . . . is to prescribe the limits of its own authority, and the states are bound to submit to the decision and are not allowed to examine and decide for themselves when the barriers of the Constitution shall be overleaped, this is practically "a government without limitation of powers."

Have students look up difficult words in the dictionary. Then ask: (1) Whose power does Senator Hayne want to preserve? (2) Why does Senator Hayne believe that the federal government should not be the "exclusive judge" of its own power? (3) What would Daniel Webster's reaction to the quotation probably have been?

ANSWERS: SECTION 3 REVIEW   (page 257)
1. Kitchen Cabinet, Tariff of Abominations—p. 254; Robert Hayne—p. 255; Nicholas Biddle—p. 256; pet banks—p. 257. **2.** spoils system—p. 254. **3.** He felt it prevented government workers from believing that their job was their personal property. He believed any intelligent person could perform any government job. **4. (a)** The tariff was high and the people of South Carolina felt that it was, in fact, a tax against the South, which imported many goods from Europe. South Carolina moved to nullify the law, claiming that a state had the right to overrule an unreasonable federal law. **(b)** Because Southerners wanted to protect slavery from federal intervention. **5.** Because it represented private stockholders' interests and not those of the United States; the Bank's influence in government was strong, with bribes of officials common. He also believed the bank charter was unconstitutional and viewed it as favoring the rich and powerful owners. **6.** Possible answer: No. Democracy would be furthered by giving offices to the most qualified candidates regardless of party loyalty.

SECTION 4   (pages 257–259)
Hard Times

ACTIVITIES
○ **Using Visual Evidence**   Have students reread the material on the Whigs' strategy during the campaign of 1840. Then have them design a campaign poster that would have furthered

that strategy. Ask each student to present his or her poster to the class and explain why it is designed the way it is.

☆ **Finding the Main Idea** Divide the class into three groups and assign each group one of the subsections in Section 4. Tell each group to write a statement that reflects the main idea of the subsection plus two statements that are true but are not the main idea. Have each group read their statements and ask the class to identify the main idea of each subsection.

☐ **Researching** Ask students to read about the Panic of 1837 in *The Age of Jackson* by Arthur M. Schlesinger, Jr. Have them write a report in which they describe the impact of the panic on either farmers or factory workers.

ANSWERS: SECTION 4 REVIEW (page 259)

1. Whigs—p. 257; Specie Circular—p. 258; John Tyler—p. 259. **2. (a)** To prevent any candidate from winning a majority of electoral votes, thereby throwing the vote into the House of Representatives, as in 1824. **(b)** No, the Democrat Van Buren won a majority of the popular and electoral votes. **3.** Farmers who had borrowed money for land purchases went broke and were unable to repay their loans. Banks failed, land sales stopped, factories closed, and unemployment climbed. Even some states went bankrupt. **4.** Portrayed their candidate as a simple western farmer and attracted voter interest with rallies, parades, bonfires, and barbecues complete with bands and entertainment. **5.** Possible answers: It would be difficult today to present an inaccurate account of a candidate's background without the truth coming to light; some of these techniques are used today, such as rallies, bands, and barbecues.

ANSWERS: CHAPTER 12 REVIEW

(pages 260–261)

Vocabulary **1.** party platform **2.** aristocracy **3.** White manhood suffrage **4.** caucus **5.** spoils system

Chapter Checkup **1.** Factors included: Jackson's claim that a corrupt bargain had been made with Clay; attacks by people who favored a limited role for the federal government; Adams's lack of personal skills. **2. (a)** The National Republicans supported the national programs of John Quincy Adams. The Democratic-Republicans opposed government elitism and stressed ties with common people. **(b)** The National Republicans backed Adams for reelection, while the Democratic-Republicans supported Andrew Jackson. Both parties strongly attacked the other side. **3. (a)** The

right to vote was extended to all white males; by 1832, all states except South Carolina allowed voters to choose presidential electors directly; and within the political parties, national nominating conventions replaced secret caucuses. **(b)** Women, black Americans, and Native Americans. **4. (a)** Congress passed the Removal Act in 1830; then it used troops to forcibly remove the Indians. **(b)** The Sac and the Fox returned to Illinois and launched attacks to regain their homelands. The Seminole refused to leave their homes and fought a war with the American army from 1835 to 1838. **5. (a)** The Kitchen Cabinet was made up of people, some of whom were not regular office holders, whose opinions he trusted. **(b)** He used the spoils system to rotate people in office and prevent anyone from looking at his position as his personal property. **(c)** He opposed the Bank because it was not responsible to the government or to the people, but to a few wealthy stockholders. **6. (a)** He argued that the federal government did not have sovereignty over the individual states. **(b)** He argued that the federal government held the final power under the Constitution and was a direct agent of the people. **7. (a)** Because South Carolina imported large quantities of goods and thought the tariff helped the North at the expense of the South. **(b)** It declared the tariff null and void. **(c)** He threatened to use military force to enforce the new tariff. **(d)** Jackson wanted to avoid an open rebellion by South Carolina. South Carolina benefited from the compromise that would reduce tariffs over the next nine years; and no other state had sided with South Carolina in the dispute. **8. (a)** The federal government deposited all its revenue in the Bank; the Bank could use the federal money without paying interest; the Bank issued all the national currency, thus giving it control over the amount of money in circulation. **(b)** He had all government deposits removed from the Bank and placed in "pet banks." **(c)** Ultimately the Bank went out of business. But in the process, the nation's economy suffered a panic. **9. (a)** During the 1830s, the government put large amounts of land up for sale at low prices. Speculators bought much of the land hoping to sell it later at a profit. Many farmers mortgaged their farms to buy more land and then planted cotton on the land. Later, when cotton prices dropped, they could not repay their loans. **(b)** Much of the money that was available was not backed by gold or silver. When people tried to redeem the money for gold or silver, banks did not always have the necessary specie. **(c)** The Specie Circular required that people buy land with only gold or silver. This caused a slump in the land market. **(d)** Farmers who had mortgaged their farms to buy more land did not earn enough profit from cotton to repay their loans. Without the repayment of the loans, many banks failed. **10. (a)** Because, like Andrew Jackson, he was a popular military hero with western ties. **(b)** To balance the ticket. **(c)** Harrison soon died, and Tyler, who succeeded him, would not support Whig policies.

Critical Thinking **1.** From the Jackson defenders accept answers that refer to his trust in the people and his distrust of elitism. From the Jackson critics accept answers that mention his heavy-handed way of dealing with opposition and his authoritarian manner. **2.** Accept answers that refer to Jackson's origin as a western farmer and his experience fighting Indians in Tennessee.

Connecting Past and Present **1.** Students might mention the fact that so few people actually vote on election day or the fact that economic and educational opportunities do not seem to be equal for all segments of the population. **2.** Possible answers: President Carter left runaway inflation. President Reagan left a huge national deficit and trade imbalance.

Developing Basic Skills **1. (a)** The relocation of Indians, 1830–1842. **(b)** Florida, Georgia, Alabama, Mississippi, Tennessee, and North Carolina. **(c)** The Seminole moved about 1,125 miles (1,800 kilometers) from their homeland; the Choctaw about 500 miles (800 kilometers); the Creek about 600 miles (1,000 kilometers); the Chickasaw 500 miles (800 kilometers); and the Cherokee 750 miles (1,200 kilometers). **2. (a)** Adams and Jackson. **(b)** 1824 electoral: Adams 31 percent, Jackson 43 percent; 1828 electoral: Adams 32 percent, Jackson 68 percent. **(c)** Yes, Jackson won more popular and electoral votes than any one of his opponents and yet he was not elected President.

Chapter 13   (pages 262–283)

From Sea to Sea _____

OVERVIEW

Chapter 13 focuses on the continental expansion of the U.S. during the 1840s. Students examine the settlement and eventual annexation of the western lands. They also read about the cultural diversity that challenged the nation during the era of expansion.

HISTORICAL SIDELIGHTS

The following pieces of historical information can serve as notes of interest during the study of Chapter 13. The page numbers in parentheses indicate the points in the student text at which you may wish to introduce the information.

Some Tall Tales (p. 268)   Along with the factual stories of fertile farmland in Oregon came tall tales that were so much a part of western folklore. Some guidebooks assured eastern emigrants that wheat in Oregon grew as tall as a man, beets grew to three feet in circumference, and turnips to an amazing five feet. A boy whose parents later moved to Oregon recalled the tales of a soapbox orator in Missouri. The orator claimed that out West, the pigs were "running about under the great acorn trees, round and fat, and already cooked, with knives and forks sticking in them so that you can cut off a slice whenever you are hungry!"

Doughboys (p. 277)   Infantrymen in the Mexican War were the first to be popularly called "doughboys," a term used until World War II. "Doughboy" originally referred to a dough cake baked for sailors, but the term was transferred to infantrymen apparently because the large brass buttons of the soldiers' uniforms resembled the dough cake.

SECTION 1	(pages 263–266)
The View From West to East	

ACTIVITIES*

○   **Outlining**   Have students write a sentence outline of Section 1. The titles of the subsections can serve as major topics, but suggest that students rephrase them as questions.

☆   **Writing a Report**   Divide the class into four groups and assign each group one of these areas: California, Arizona and New Mexico, Texas, Oregon. Tell each group to prepare an oral report about the area in the early 1800s, which answers these questions: (1) What are the main geographical features of the area? (See the map on text page 844.) (2) What is the natural vegetation of the area? (See the map on text page 845.) (3) What nation or nations claimed the area in the early 1800s? (4) What was the extent of control and settle-

---

*See "To the Teacher" for an explanation of the symbols.

ment by that nation? (5) What was the relationship between settlers and Native Americans in the area? (6) What attracted the first traders or settlers from the U.S. to the area? Some students might want to do further research or clip pictures from discarded magazines to illustrate their reports. Have each group give their report and ask students to point out similarities and differences among the areas.

☐ **Researching** Ask students to do research on the reasons why Americans founded a colony in Texas during the 1820s. They should note the challenges the settlers faced and how they overcame them. Students could consult *Texas: The Lone Star State* by Rupert Norval Richardson.

ANSWERS: SECTION 1 REVIEW (page 266)

1. Don Gaspar de Portolá, Father Junípero Serra—p. 264; Secularization Act—p. 265; Stephen Austin—p. 266. **2.** ranchero, mortality rate—p. 265. **3.** The missions served as political and economic symbols of Spanish control. **4.** Worked as farmhands or herders. **5.** Mexico hoped Texas would prosper if more settlers moved there. **6.** Possible answer: Perhaps they feared that Americans would take away control of the area from Mexico.

SECTION 2 (pages 267–270)
Oregon and the Fur Trade

ACTIVITIES

○ **Using Visual Evidence** Ask students to study the painting on text page 267 and describe what is shown. Have students suggest a title for the painting. You might ask if any occupation today is similar to that of the trapper shown here.

☆ **Relating Cause and Effect** Ask students to write one "effect" statement for each of the following "cause" statements: (1) Many mountain men trapped animals and traded their pelts. (2) Mountain men reported that rich land was available in the Oregon country. (3) Americans gradually began to outnumber the British in Oregon. Lead a classroom discussion about the long-range effects of these developments.

☐ **Analyzing a Primary Source** Read aloud the following quotation or duplicate and distribute copies. Explain that the extract is from the diary of Eliza Spalding, a missionary who traveled to Oregon in 1836.

June 10. Still traveling along the Platte. . . . I have been quite unwell for several days—and attribute my illness wholly to change of diet, which has been from necessity. Since we reached the Buffalo, our fare has been Buffalo meat.

Fort Wm. June 21. This day we are to leave this post, and have no resting place in view, till we reach Rendevoux, 400 miles distant. . . . Only He who knows all things, knows whether this habitated frame will survive the undertaking. His will, not mine, be done.

August 6th. Yesterday my horse became unmanageable in consequence of stepping into a hornet's nest. I was thrown, and notwithstanding my foot remained a moment in the stirrup, and my body dragged some distance, I received no serious injury. . . . The hand of God has been conspicuous in preserving my life thus far, on this adventurous journey.

August 30, 1836. Passed through the Round today—this is a large and very beautiful plain, derived its name from its appearance, it is circular, surrounded by sloping mountains covered with Pine and Spruce—a beautiful river well timbered passes through it—the soil has the appearance of fertility and to the eye of the traveler who has for many weeks seen nothing but rugged and barren deserts, it presents a very grand appearance.

Ask: (1) What hardships did Eliza Spalding face on her journey to Oregon? (2) What did Spalding believe helped her during the trip? (3) Why was she so impressed by the landscape as she neared the end of her journey in late August?

ANSWERS: GEOGRAPHIC CONNECTION
(page 268)

1. An imaginary line; east of the line rivers flow into the Atlantic Ocean or Gulf of Mexico, west of the line rivers flow into the Pacific Ocean. **2.** Possible answer: It meant that people could not travel west by water until after crossing over the Continental Divide.

ANSWERS: MAP STUDY (page 269)

Oregon Trail and California Trail; Fort Laramie and Sutter's Fort; through the South Pass.

ANSWERS: SECTION 2 REVIEW (page 270)

1. Oregon Trail—p. 269. **2.** They blazed trails west and told stories of the region that made it enticing to settlers. **3.** Most pioneers went to Oregon in search of rich land, some to bring Christianity to the Indians. **4. (a)** Outlined a temporary government for the Oregon country. **(b)** It provided a system of government until a more permanent form could be established. **5.** Possible answer: Even though they opposed the institution of slavery, they still held prejudices about blacks and did not want to share the land with them.

SECTION 3   (pages 270–273)
The Republic of Texas

ACTIVITIES

○ **Using a Letter as a Primary Source** Have students reread the special feature, *The Siege at the Alamo,* on text page 272. Ask: (1) Who wrote the letter? (2) What is he requesting? (3) Why does he say he needs it? (4) Based on your reading, did he receive what he needed? (5) How does this letter help you understand the siege at the Alamo?

☆ **Defending a Position** Ask students to imagine that they are U.S. senators in 1836. Designate one half of the class as southern senators and the other half as northern senators. Ask each student to write a speech stating whether he or she would have supported the annexation of Texas at that time and explain the reasons for his or her position. Have volunteers give their speeches. Then review the reasons the two sides had.

☐ **Finding the Main Idea** Write the following excerpt from the Texas Declaration of Independence on the chalkboard or duplicate and distribute copies. Ask students to read the excerpt and explain in their own words what the declaration states. You might want to ask students to review the U.S. Declaration of Independence (text pages 865–866) and compare its ideas to the ideas expressed in the Texas Declaration.

When a government has ceased to protect the lives, liberty, and property of its people, from whom its legitimate powers are derived . . . [the people] . . . have a sacred obligation to their posterity to abolish such a government and create another in its stead, calculated to rescue them from impending dangers, and to secure their future welfare and happiness.

ANSWERS: MAP STUDY   (page 271)

San Antonio, The Alamo, San Jacinto, Gonzales, and Goliad; San Antonio, Gonzales, and San Jacinto.

ANSWERS: THE AMERICAN EXPERIENCE
                                (page 272)

1. He is asking people to come to the Alamo and help defend it against the Mexicans. **2.** It helped them maintain morale and fight with their full strength.

ANSWERS: SECTION 3 REVIEW   (page 273)

1. Antonio de Santa Anna, Declaration of Causes, Sam Houston—p. 271; "Remember the Alamo"— p. 272. **2. (a)** Americans spoke English; Mexicans spoke Spanish. Americans were mainly Protestant; Mexicans were mainly Catholic. **(b)** Americans had a strong democratic tradition and were accustomed to local rule; Mexicans were accustomed to being ruled by provincial officers and mayors appointed by the crown. The Mexican judicial system was less protective of individual rights than the American; a single judge decided on cases without a jury, and testimony by the parties involved was not customary. Slavery was abolished by Mexico in 1827; most American settlers in Texas were from the South and approved of slavery. **3.** He sent reinforcements into Texas. **4.** One granted independence to Texas; the other established the Rio Grande as its southern border. **5. (a)** He feared war with Mexico. Many northerners were afraid annexation would increase the power of the southern states. **(b)** Jackson formally recognized Texan independence but refused to annex the territory. **6.** Possible answer: The Texans were fighting to defend their land and their homes.

SECTION 4   (pages 273–278)
Surge to the Pacific

ACTIVITIES

○ **Understanding Vocabulary** Ask students to look up in a dictionary the words *manifest* and *destiny*. Then have them write their own definition of Manifest Destiny.

☆ **Making Generalizations** Ask students to write one or two factual statements that support each of the following generalizations: (1) The annexation of Texas aggravated relations with Mexico. (2) President Polk believed in the manifest destiny of the U.S. (3) Americans were divided on the wisdom of war with

Mexico. (4) The U.S. gained territory as a result of the Mexican War. Then ask them to write another generalization based on this section and list facts to support it.

☐ **Biographical Sketch** Have students write a biographical sketch of President James Polk in which they discuss Polk's ideas on American expansion. They might consult *Frontier President: James K. Polk* by Bill Severn.

ANSWERS: MAP STUDY   (page 276)

As far north as San Francisco and as far south as Veracruz; to attack Mexico along the Pacific coast of California and along the Gulf of Mexico coastline.

ANSWERS: MAP STUDY   (page 277)

Washington, Oregon, Idaho, and parts of Montana and Wyoming; Nevada, Utah, and parts of Arizona, New Mexico, Colorado, and Wyoming; parts of Arizona and New Mexico.

ANSWERS: SECTION 4 REVIEW   (page 278)

1. Manifest destiny, James K. Polk—p. 274; "Fifty-four Forty or Fight", John C. Frémont—p. 275; Zachary Taylor—p. 276; Gadsden Purchase—p. 277. **2.** Congress passed a joint resolution calling for the annexation of Texas, and Texas voted to accept annexation. **3.** The U.S. recognized the Rio Grande as the southern border of Texas. Mexico recognized the Nueces River, 200 miles north. Polk ordered the army to cross the Nueces River and move toward the Rio Grande. Mexico saw this action as a provocation. **4.** The U.S. gained control of California and the New Mexico territory, and Mexico recognized the Rio Grande as the southern border of Texas. In return the U.S. paid Mexico $15 million and assumed all debts owed to U.S. citizens by Mexico. **5.** Possible answer: Polk realized that the British were willing to compromise but that tensions between the U.S. and Mexico made compromise impossible.

SECTION 5   (pages 278–281)
The Challenge of Greater Diversity

ACTIVITIES

○ **Writing a Diary** Tell students to imagine that they are Mormons living during the 1830s and 1840s. Have them write diary entries in which they describe the efforts of the Mormons to escape religious persecution.

☆ **Making a Chart** Tell students to draw a chart with four columns headed Groups, Reasons for Immigration to the West, Problems Faced, Accomplishments. Have them write the names of the following—Mormons, Chinese, black Americans—in the first column and complete the chart. Then ask: (1) What experiences did the groups have in common? (2) How did their experiences differ? How might you explain the differences? (3) In what ways was the cultural diversity of the West a challenge?

☐ **Relating Past to Present** Ask students to write an essay in which they respond to the following questions: (1) Is the U.S. still a diverse nation today? Give examples. (2) Does coping with diversity seem as difficult today as it was in the 1840s? Explain.

ANSWERS: SECTION 5 REVIEW   (page 281)

1. Sutter's Mill—p. 279; Joseph Smith—p. 280; Brigham Young—p. 281. **2. (a)** California Indians were driven off their lands and many became ill or starved to death. Some were killed and whole villages were massacred. Their population fell from 250,000 in 1848 to 17,000 20 years later. **(b)** They were treated as foreigners. Land disputes were usually decided against them; vigilantes enforced the decisions. Vigilantes drove Mexicans from the gold fields. **3.** At first they were accepted, but eventually they were met with jealousy, prejudice, discrimination, and denial of political rights. **4.** Prejudice, discrimination, and denial of political rights. **5.** They set up a community based on the teachings of their religion; they used extensive irrigation to make the desert bloom; they avoided conflict with other Americans by choosing an isolated spot for their settlement. **6.** Possible answer: It helped California by encouraging its settlement and eventual statehood.

ANSWERS: CHAPTER 13 REVIEW
                                 (pages 282–283)

Vocabulary 1. rancheros **2.** mortality rate **3.** mountain men **4.** Continental Divide **5.** Manifest destiny **6.** joint resolution

Chapter Checkup 1. (a) The Spanish built missions in California, which claimed most of the land. Large numbers of the local Indians moved onto mission lands and worked as farmers or ranchers. The Indians were provided with food, clothing, and shelter. **(b)** Many Indians converted to Christianity as a result of their exposure to the missions. As time went on, the missionaries saw the Indians as cheap laborers and working conditions became harsher. **2. (a)** Blazed trails and spread word about its abundant resources. **(b)** Relayed stories about natural resources to the East and set up early governments. **(c)** Took friends and families west and encouraged others to join them. **3. (a)** Because of cultural, religious, political, and language differences. **(b)** Some Americans in Texas believed that Santa Anna planned to force the Americans to leave Texas. In fact, he did send troops to the area. Ultimately, the Americans in Texas won a war against Santa Anna's troops and set up an independent nation. **4. (a)** "Manifest destiny" refers to the commonly held belief that all land between the Atlantic and Pacific oceans should belong to the U.S. **(b)** No. Puritans and Quakers believed that God favored their type of settlements because they were superior models for government and living. **5. (a)** Because California represented the completion of U.S. manifest destiny; the United States would span the continent. **(b)** Tried to buy California; supported Californians who favored joining the United States. **(c)** The United States finally acquired California as a result of the treaty ending the Mexican War. **6. (a)** The discovery of gold led to the gold rush as a result of which the population increased tremendously and became extremely diverse. **(b)** There were few rules of behavior; most of the people were men; prices were very high. **7. (a)** Indians' land claims were often ignored, even though they had been guaranteed in the Treaty of Guadalupe-Hidalgo; they were driven from their lands and thousands died. **(b)** Mexicans were treated as foreigners. They were barred from the gold fields and treated unfairly in land disputes. **(c)** At first they were treated with respect. But soon they faced discrimination and scorn. **(d)** Blacks faced discrimination and prejudice. **8. (a)** Some of the religious beliefs of the Mormons angered other Americans. For example, they believed in communal ownership of property and in allowing men to marry more than one wife. **(b)** In the desert around the Great Salt Lake in Utah. **(c)** They established cooperative communities and made the desert bloom with a remarkable system of irrigation.

Critical Thinking   1. (a) Loneliness, danger, the need to survive in the wilderness. **(b)** Resourcefulness, daring, courage, backwoods skills, stamina, wile. **2. (a)** Like the early colonists, Texans were treated as second-class citizens. They had little influence on the government of Mexico. Like the early colonists the Americans in Texas believed in democracy and local control. **(b)** Accept answers that point out there were no language differences or cultural differences behind the American Revolution. The American judicial system was borrowed in part from the English, whereas the Mexican system was completely alien to Americans. Texans were not taxed, as the early colonists were.

Connecting Past and Present   1. The two nations would probably hold meetings to work out the dispute peacefully. **2.** The fastest growing areas today are in the Sun Belt. Increases in population can stimulate the economies and cultures of an area; but they can also overburden the area's resources.

Developing Basic Skills   1. (a) Travelers had to cross the mountains. **(b)** The Oregon Trail was planned to travel through mountain passes. **2. (a)** Treaty. **(b)** France. **(c)** Agree. During the period 1845–1848, Texas, Oregon Country, California, and the Southwest became part of the U.S.

Chapter 14   (pages 284–307)
The Different Worlds of North and South _____

OVERVIEW
Technological advances in the first half of the 1800s transformed both the economy and patterns of living. The North moved rapidly toward an economy based largely on manufacturing, while the South greatly expanded its agricultural production. In this chapter, students read about how economic patterns and immigration widened the differences between North and South.

HISTORICAL SIDELIGHTS
The following pieces of historical information can serve as notes of interest during the study of Chapter 14. The page numbers in parentheses indicate the points in the student text at which you may wish to introduce the information.

An Outrage (p. 287)   Not everyone welcomed the smoke and spark-spitting iron horse of the rails. In 1839, the following poster appeared in Philadelphia: "Philadelphians, your RIGHTS are being invaded! regardless of your interests or the LIVES OF YOUR LITTLE ONES. THE CAMDEN AND AMBOY with the assistance of other companies without a charter, and in VIOLATION OF LAW, as decreed by your Courts, are laying a LOCOMOTIVE RAIL ROAD! RALLY PEOPLE in the Majesty of your Strength and forbid THIS OUTRAGE!"

Out of Work (p. 289)   Many northern laborers suffered from long work hours, but others suffered from short working hours—that is, from underemployment. For example, when a hatter ran out of fur or leather, he or she might be forced to look for a temporary job until a new shipment arrived. Frozen canals and rivers in the winter meant long periods of inactivity for workers who depended on water transportation.

SECTION 1 (pages 285–289)
The Growth of Industry in the North

ACTIVITIES*

○ **Name Game** Read aloud the following clues and ask students who is being described: (1) perfected the telegraph; (2) invented the sewing machine; (3) invented the steel plow; (4) won commercial rights for the U.S. in Japan; (5) invented a steam locomotive; (6) developed a mechanical reaper; (7) developed a method of vulcanizing rubber.
   Answers: **1.** Morse **2.** Howe **3.** Deere **4.** Perry **5.** Stevens **6.** McCormick **7.** Goodyear

☆ **Writing a Dialogue** Ask students to write an imaginary dialogue between a grandparent and grandchild in 1860 in which the grandparent describes some of the many ways life had changed during the preceding 20 years.

□ **Writing a Report** Have students write a report about one of the inventors mentioned in Section 1. They should describe his life, other inventions of his, and the significance of his inventions. Students could do research about other inventors of the period.

ANSWERS: MAP STUDY (page 287)

New Orleans, Memphis, and Cairo.

ANSWERS: SECTION 1 REVIEW (page 289)

1. Charles Goodyear, Samuel F. B. Morse—p. 286; Cyrus McCormick—p. 288; Matthew Perry—p. 289. **2.** feeder line, trunk line—p. 287; clipper ship—p. 289. **3.** Sturdier bridges and roadbeds had to be built and rails had to be improved. **4.** It carried on America's growing trade with Europe and Asia. **5.** Possible answer: The acquisition of a Pacific coast gave the U.S. easier access to Asia.

SECTION 2 (pages 289–294)
Life in the Industrializing North

ACTIVITIES

○ **Applying Information** Tell students to imagine that they work for a steamship company during the late 1840s. Ask them to write an advertisement to attract immigrants to the U.S. Some students may want to illustrate their advertisements.

☆ **Distinguishing Fact and Opinion** Divide the class into six groups and assign each one of the following topics: (1) factory workers between 1820 and 1860; (2) union members between 1820 and 1860; (3) members of workingmen's parties between 1820 and 1860; (4) Irish immigrants between 1820 and 1860; (5) German immigrants between 1820 and 1860; (6) nativists between 1820 and 1860. Tell each group to write four statements about the assigned topic: two facts and two opinions based on information in the text. Have each group read its statements aloud to the class. Then have students decide which of the statements are facts and which are opinions.

□ **Interpreting a Graph** Have students study the graph on text page 292 and answer these questions: (1) What is the topic of the graph? (2) Approximately how many Germans immigrated to the United States between 1841 and 1850? (3) From which area did the largest number of immigrants arrive between 1821 and 1860? (4) How would you describe the change in immigration between 1821 and 1860? (5) What effect did the change have on the American society and economy?

ANSWERS: GRAPH STUDY (page 292)

Ireland; the Irish potato famine of 1845–1850.

ANSWERS: NOTABLE AMERICANS (page 293)

1. He fought with the Union during the Civil War; he spoke out against slavery; he advised the President to give the vote to free blacks as a condition of the southern states rejoining the Union after the Civil War. **2.** Possible answers: women's rights; civil rights.

ANSWERS: SECTION 2 REVIEW (page 294)

1. National Trades Union—p. 290; *Commonwealth* v. *Hunt*—p. 291; Know-Nothing party—p. 294. **2.** strike, union—p. 290; workingmen's party—

*See "To the Teacher" for an explanation of the symbols.

p. 291; nativist, assimilate—p. 294. **3.** Universal white male suffrage, free public education, and an end to imprisonment for failure to pay debts. **4.** The North's economy was expanding and jobs were plentiful; it seemed truly a land of opportunity. **5.** Possible answer: The traditional ways provided something secure and familiar in the midst of a frightening new place.

SECTION 3   (pages 295–298)
Economic Growth in the South

ACTIVITIES

○ **Graph Reading** Ask students to study the graphs on text page 297 and answer these questions: (1) About how many bales of cotton were produced in 1820? In 1860? (2) About how many slaves were there in 1820? In 1860? (3) Were the increases in cotton production and the number of slaves related? Explain.

☆ **Constructing Graphs** Have students use the data below to construct a circle or pie graph. The graph should represent U.S. exports in 1860. When they have completed the graph, ask them to write a paragraph in which they describe the role of cotton in U.S. foreign trade.

Type of U.S. Exports, 1860 (by value)
Cotton 61%
Finished manufactured goods 11%
Others 28%

Source: *Historical Statistics of the United States*

☐ **Researching** Ask students to do further research about William Gregg's textile mill in Graniteville, South Carolina (see text page 298). They should describe the founding of the mill, working conditions there, and the significance of the mill. They might consult *William Gregg: Factory Master of the Old South* by Broadus Mitchell.

ANSWERS: MAP STUDY   (page 296)
In an arc from eastern Texas and Arkansas to South Carolina; westward into Texas and Arkansas, and further southward in Alabama, Georgia, and South Carolina..

ANSWER: GRAPH STUDY   (page 297)
That the growth in cotton production led to a need for more slaves.

ANSWERS: SECTION 3 REVIEW   (page 298)
1. Eli Whitney—p. 295; William Gregg—p. 298. **2.** Invention of the cotton gin. The machine separated cotton seeds from cotton fibers. This greatly speeded up the process and made cotton growing more profitable. **3.** Cotton was still picked by hand. To make a large profit in cotton, a planter needed a large labor supply. Planters met their labor needs with slaves. **4.** A few industries developed, including textiles, iron making, and flour milling. **5.** Possible answer: Since cotton was so successful, the South developed an economy based almost exclusively on that single crop. This discouraged development of other industries.

SECTION 4   (pages 298–301)
Life in the South

ACTIVITIES

○ **Using Visual Evidence** Have students study the painting on text page 300 and describe what they can learn about plantation life from it. Ask them whether the painting reflects what they learned about plantation life in Chapter 14.

☆ **Applying Information** Draw a chart on the chalkboard with four rows and five columns. Label the rows Small Farmers, Poor Whites, Free Blacks, Planters. Label the columns Number, Where They Lived, How They Made a Living, Degree of Wealth, Social Status. Complete the chart as a class. In order to complete each part in detail, you might ask students to do additional research. When the chart is complete, ask: (1) Based on the chart, how did most southerners make a living? (2) Rank the four groups from the group that probably had the highest social status to the group that probably had the lowest social status. Explain your ranking.

☐ **Comparing** Have students read about life in southern cities between 1820 and 1860. They might consult *The Growth of Southern Civilization, 1790–1860* by Clement Eaton. Then ask them to write an essay comparing city life with rural life in the South.

ANSWERS: SECTION 4 REVIEW   (page 301)
1. Owned small farms. **2. (a)** Whites who lived on land that could not be farmed for profit. **(b)** They lived in isolated cabins surrounded by a few rows of vegetables and a few domestic animals. They

might own a small herd of cattle or hogs who foraged in the woods around the cabin. The women did most of the household work as well as the farming. **3.** They could not vote; usually they could not testify in court; they were subject to curfews; their freedom of movement and assembly was restricted. **4. (a)** To be considered a planter, a farmer had to own 20 slaves or more, own a cotton gin, and hire an overseer to supervise the slaves. **(b)** They set the social style and held most of the political power. **5.** Possible answer: They were afraid that if slaves saw that some blacks were free, they would try to become free too.

SECTION 5   (pages 301–305)
The Slaves' World

ACTIVITIES

○ **Comparing Visual Evidence** Ask students to study the pictures on text pages 302 and 304. Then have them answer these questions: (1) What is the subject of each picture? (2) What aspects of slave life are shown in each? (3) Which do you think would probably be the most accurate view of slave life? (4) What can you learn about slavery by using the pictures as visual evidence?

☆ **Analyzing a Quotation** Read the following quotation to students or duplicate and distribute copies. Explain that the quotation is from a speech by Frederick Douglass. (See text page 292.)

I have often been utterly astonished, since I came to the north, to find persons who could speak of the singing among slaves, as evidence of their contentment and happiness. It is impossible to conceive of a greater mistake. Slaves sing most when they are most unhappy. The songs of the slave represent the sorrows of his heart; and he is relieved by them, only as an aching heart is relieved by tears. At least, such is my experience.

Ask: (1) What misunderstanding does Douglass describe? (2) What does he say singing meant to slaves?

☐ **Preparing a Group Report** Divide the class into four groups and assign each group one of the following topics: (1) slavery in ancient Egypt, (2) slavery in ancient Greece, (3) slavery in ancient Rome, (4) slavery in Latin America

under the Spanish. Have the students in each group prepare a report in which they describe the reasons the people became enslaved, the types of work done by the slaves, the living conditions of the slaves, and the possibility of the slaves being freed. They could begin by consulting a world history text. When the groups have completed their reports, have students compare their findings with the description of slavery in the U.S. between 1820 and 1860.

ANSWERS: SKILL LESSON   (page 303)

1. (a) Lyell says the working conditions are not taxing, that slaves have free time. Northup says they work in cotton fields from sunrise past sunset and get little rest. **(b)** According to Lyell the slaves get Indian meal, rice, milk, and occasionally pork and soup. They also raise chickens. According to Northup they get only cold bacon and corn cake, three and a half pounds of bacon per week, and a peck of meal. **(c)** Lyell says the whip is a threat rarely used; Northup says a person would be whipped for staying in the quarters after daybreak. **2. (a)** Lyell may have been sympathetic to the conduct of others in his social class. **(b)** Northup had experienced first hand the bitterness and frustration of slavery so he was more likely to sympathize with the plight of the slaves. **3. (a)** Possible answer: Yes, but neither description should be considered complete; each dealt with only one plantation and each writer had his own personal perspective on what he saw. **(b)** You could conclude that some whippings took place, that slaves received some food from their owners, and that work began early.

ANSWERS: SECTION 5 REVIEW   (page 305)

1. "puttin' on old Massa"—p. 304; Nat Turner—p. 305. **2.** task system, gang system—p. 301. **3. (a)** Hemp, rice, and Sea Island cotton plantations. **(b)** Tobacco, sugar, and inland cotton plantations. **4.** Teachings on family life, marriage, and people's obligations to one another. **5.** Turner's revolt shocked and frightened many southerners. It led to harsher slave laws. **6.** Possible answer: He was free.

ANSWERS: CHAPTER 14 REVIEW
                              (pages 306–307)

   Vocabulary **1.** Trunk lines **2.** strike **3.** unions **4.** Nativists **5.** task system

   Chapter Checkup **1. (a)** Stronger bridges and roadbeds, a uniform track gauge, and better equipment overcame early problems. **(b)** Railroads spurred on the growth of industrialization in the North; they transported goods to markets and natural resources to industry. **2. (a)** America was granted special trading privileges in China and trading rights in Japan. **(b)** For about 20 years, the clipper ships were the fastest merchant ships on the seas. **(c)** Because the steamships could travel faster and carry heavier loads. **3. (a)** It made available labor-saving machines, such as the mechanical reaper and the steel plow. It also brought about the expansion of rail lines that made it easier for farmers to ship their goods to market. **(b)** Farming in the South relied on slaves, which farming in the North did not. Different crops were grown in the two regions. Farming in the North was more diversified than was farming in the South. **4. (a)** During the 1830s, factory owners were not greatly concerned with providing good working conditions; workers were regarded as machinery; increased competition led owners to cut wages in order to lower prices. **(b)** Through strikes, union organizing, political action, legal action. **(c)** Mixed success. Three hundred thousand trained workers belonged to local labor organizations, but conditions remained poor and unskilled workers were unorganized. **5. (a)** Mostly from Germany and Ireland. **(b)** Germans settled largely in the Midwest, some on farms and others in cities such as Chicago, Milwaukee, and St. Louis. The Irish settled in large numbers in Boston and other northern cities. **(c)** Reasons included: fear of competition for jobs; fear of immigrants as strikebreakers; distrust of people with a different religion; slow pace of assimilation by immigrants. **6. (a)** The cotton-growing region expanded inland, more land was put under cultivation, and more cotton was profitably produced. **(b)** The demand for cotton increased. **(c)** The need for an increased labor force contributed to the spread of slavery. **7. (a)** Small farmers grew their own food and produced a small amount of cash crops. "Poor whites" lacked cash crops and raised wild hogs or cattle. **(b)** Most planters owned 20 or more slaves, possessed large land holdings, and raised profitable crops. Their life was modeled after that of wealthy English landed gentry. **8. (a)** By maintaining a semblance of family life; through religion, holidays, and cultural traditions. **(b)** Resistance included: "Puttin' on old Massa," running away, slave revolts. **(c)** Revolts led to more repression and running away usually failed, so day-to-day resistance may have been the best strategy.

Critical Thinking   1. (a) Accept answers that note the isolation of the South from the North, the concentration of railroad lines in the North, and

the tendency for people and industry to move westward to unsettled areas. **(b)** Hastened settlement of the West. **2. (a)** Prejudice and job discrimination. **(b)** Resentment from white workers, laws restricting their movement and assembly, discrimination, and prejudice. **(c)** In neither area did they enjoy full citizenship, respect, or opportunities. **(d)** The degree of political restriction was less in the North and the fear of being sold into slavery was greater in the South. **3.** Possible answer: Their wealth and large land holdings made their actions more significant to the economy of the South as a whole. Because they were better educated than most, they were more likely to be influential in the government. Because others aspired to join their ranks, they were imitated.

Connecting Past and Present   1. (a) Defenders of unions might say that by joining together, workers can protect themselves. Opponents of unions might argue that each person should be responsible for his or her own job security. **(b)** Possible answers: Educational opportunities for all. Job re-training programs. **2.** The whole society loses the contributions that would have been made by the group that is discriminated against.

Developing Basic Skills   1. (a) The distribution of major southern crops. **(b)** South Carolina, Georgia, Alabama, Mississippi, and Louisiana. **(c)** Virginia and North Carolina. **(d)** Because the growing season was too short. **2.** Answers will vary.

SPIRIT OF AMERICA   (pages 308–311)

ANSWERS: AMERICAN INGENUITY   (page 310)

1. After the Civil War, more universities and schools of technology were established. Business and industry began to take research and development very seriously. **2.** Both James and Dewey recognized the importance of learning by doing.

ANSWERS: NOTABLE AMERICANS   (page 311)

1. McCormick extended credit to his customers and provided a written guarantee for his reaper. **2.** Customers came to trust McCormick because of his integrity and became intensely loyal to him and to his products.

ANSWERS: VOICES OF FREEDOM   (page 311)

1. He considers the use of steam to be the greatest achievement of the age, especially its use in improving transportation. **2.** The railroads provided a means of transportation used equally by the rich and the poor.

Chapter 15 (pages 312–329)

A Land of Idealism ———

OVERVIEW
Chapter 15 focuses on the reform movements that developed during the first half of the nineteenth century. Students read about attempts to reform individual lives as well as attempts to improve education, prisons, and care for the mentally ill. They also examine the early campaign for women's rights and the abolitionist movement. The period saw the growth of a characteristic American culture.

HISTORICAL SIDELIGHTS
The following pieces of historical information can serve as notes of interest during the study of Chapter 15. The page numbers in parentheses indicate the points in the student text at which you may wish to introduce the information.

Delicate Sensibilities (p. 319) Some Americans opposed advanced education for women because they believed that women were too delicate to face many of the "harsh realities" of life. For example, male visitors to one female seminary were shocked to see a young woman drawing a heart, arteries, and veins on a blackboard to explain the circulation of blood.

Escape from Slavery (p. 324) Although the underground railroad helped only a small percentage of slaves escape to freedom, the publicity surrounding individual stories raised both the hopes of slaves and the fears of slave owners. One widely publicized episode concerned Henry Brown, a Virginia slave who had himself crated up in a wooden box and shipped to Philadelphia via the Adams Express Company. Brown arrived, cramped but safe. Other slaves used the lyrics of a song, "Follow the Drinking Gourd," to help them escape. The "drinking gourd" stood for the Big Dipper constellation, which pointed to the North Star and gave slaves the direction they needed when traveling at night.

———
*See "To the Teacher" for an explanation of the symbols.

SECTION 1 (pages 313–315)
The Reforming Impulse

ACTIVITIES*
○ **Writing a Diary** Tell students to imagine that they attended a revival during the early 1800s. Ask them to write two or three diary entries in which they describe the revival and what it meant to them.

☆ **Defending an Opinion** Tell students to imagine that the class is a committee of a state legislature in the 1840s, formed to consider a proposed law to ban the sale and use of all alcoholic beverages in the state. Ask committee members to present arguments for and against the bill. Among the topics they could consider are the effects of alcohol on work habits and family life, the popularity of alcohol at social activities, and whether banning the sale and use of alcohol would violate personal liberties. Then have the committee vote on whether to recommend passage of the bill or not.

☐ **Analyzing a Document** Have students turn to the Declaration of Independence and the Constitution in the Reference Section of the text. Ask them to cite parts of the documents that provided a political heritage for reformers in the first half of the 1800s.

ANSWERS: SECTION 1 REVIEW (page 315)
1. revival—p. 314; temperance movement, abstinence—p. 315. **2.** That the promise of these ideals had not been fulfilled. **3.** To make the United States a Christian nation where goodness ruled. **4.** Possible answer: Religious beliefs often dictate people's ideas about what types of behavior are or are not acceptable.

SECTION 2 (pages 315–318)
Social Reform

ACTIVITIES
○ **Applying Information** Ask students to imagine that they are reporters accompanying Dorothea Dix on her crusade to improve care of the mentally ill. Have them write a newspaper article describing her activities. In the article, they should note where she might have spoken and the type of arguments she probably made.

☆ **Writing an Editorial** Divide the class into two sections: one as supporters of educational reformers such as Horace Mann, the other as opponents. Ask each student to write a newspaper editorial on the question of compulsory public education from the point of view assigned to their section. They should describe the issue, state their opinion, explain why they think the opposing point of view is incorrect. Ask volunteers to read their editorials aloud, and lead a class discussion about the strengths of the various editorials.

☐ **Writing a Report** Ask students to research and write a report about one of the utopian communities that existed during the 1800s. They could select one of the communities mentioned in the text (p. 318) or another community such as Brook Farm in Massachusetts, the Amana Colonies in Iowa, or Nashoba in Tennessee. In their reports they should describe life in the community.

ANSWERS: SECTION 2 REVIEW   (page 318)

1. Horace Mann—p. 316; Dorothea Dix—p. 318. **2.** compulsory education—p. 317; utopian—p. 318. **3.** Reforms included: higher state spending for education, higher teachers' salaries, lengthened school year, introduction of compulsory education. **4.** The prison in Auburn, New York, which served as a model for others, introduced a strict schedule for inmates during the day and solitary confinement at night; prisoners were not allowed to communicate with each other. Reforms for the mentally ill included recognizing their condition as a sickness, not a crime, and the introduction of special facilities for the mentally ill. **5.** Under a system of self-government, the people elect their representatives and must make decisions about issues. Education enables people to make informed judgments.

SECTION 3   (pages 319–321)

A Campaign for Women's Rights

ACTIVITIES

○ **Using a Speech as a Primary Source** Ask students to reread the special feature, *Sojourner Truth: Equality for Women* (text page 320), and answer these questions: (1) Who made the speech? (2) On what occasion was it made? (3) What is the main point of Sojourner Truth's

words? (4) How do you think her audience responded? Explain. (5) How do you think an audience today would respond? Explain.

☆ **Making a Chart** Draw a chart on the chalkboard with three columns headed Issue or Problem, Results by 1860, Unmet Goals. Ask students what issues or problems faced women in the first half of the 1800s, and have them write their suggestions in the first column. Complete the rest of the chart as a class. When the chart is complete, ask students to write an essay in which they summarize the results of the campaign for women's rights in the first half of the nineteenth century.

☐ **Writing a Speech** Ask students to imagine that they have been invited to make a speech in favor of women's rights at the Seneca Falls Convention. Have them write a speech around one of the following topics: the right to vote, the right to control one's property, the right to equality before the law. Encourage students to do additional research to make their speeches as accurate as possible.

ANSWERS: VOICES OF FREEDOM   (page 320)

1. She gives examples that show she has done things as well as any man; she also points to the story of Eve in the Bible where a woman turns the whole world on its head. **2.** Possible answers: Because many women worked in the abolitionist movement; because both movements had to do with basic human rights.

ANSWERS: SECTION 3 REVIEW   (page 321)

1. Sarah and Angelina Grimké—p. 319; Elizabeth Cady Stanton, Seneca Falls Convention—p. 320; Elizabeth Blackwell—p. 321. **2.** Because they could see in their work for other reforms that they were not treated equally. Female reformers often faced rejection and ridicule from male reformers. **3.** Advances in education and property rights and recognition as writers. **4.** Possible answers: It gave women some experience with success in their reform efforts; the successes gave people a chance to get used to women having some rights; later they could accept greater rights for women.

SECTION 4   (pages 321–325)

The Battle Against Slavery

ACTIVITIES

○ **Name Game** Read students the following clues and ask who is being described: (1) or-

ganized abolitionists at Lane Seminary in Cin-cinnati; (2) "Black Moses"; (3) leading radical abolitionist; (4) wrote *Appeal to the Colored Citizens of the World;* (5) brothers who founded the Liberty party; (6) leading antislavery po-litical party in 1848; (7) _____ Truth.
Answers: **1.** Weld **2.** Tubman **3.** Garrison **4.** Walker **5.** Tappans **6.** Free Soil **7.** Sojourner

☆ **Defending an Opinion**   Divide the class into groups of four or five students. Tell students to imagine that they are a group of abolitionists meeting during the 1850s. They are to decide on the best way to win freedom for the slaves. Instruct each group to discuss the strengths and weaknesses of the various approaches to abolition. Each group should present their recommendations to the class.

☐ **Analyzing a Quotation**   Read aloud the fol-lowing quotation from philosopher Ralph Waldo Emerson: "If you put a chain around the neck of a slave, the other end fastens itself around your own." Then ask: (1) What do you think the quotation means? (2) Based on the quotation, do you think Emerson op-posed slavery? (3) Do you agree with the state-ment? Explain. Ask students to read works by Emerson to verify their conclusions about his attitude toward slavery.

ANSWERS: VOICES OF FREEDOM   (page 323)
1. Memories of the footsteps and cries of chained slaves being led away to be sold in the deep South. **2.** Because he could speak from personal experi-ence about slavery.

ANSWERS: SECTION 4 REVIEW   (page 325)
1. William Lloyd Garrison—p. 322; Sojourner Truth, Frederick Douglass—p. 323; underground railroad—p. 324. **2.** emancipation, abolitionist—p. 322. **3.** Stop slavery from spreading to new states, end slave trade within the U.S., persuade slave states to free slaves. **4.** The role of women in the antislavery movement and the question of whether political action should be used to achieve its goals. **5. (a)** The Liberty party wanted to abolish slavery. **(b)** The Free Soil party called for a halt to the expansion of slavery into new territories. **6.** Possible answer: It gave slaves some hope to go on with their dreary lives; it might have made them feel a little less powerless. It frightened slave owners into thinking that many of their slaves might escape; it might have made them feel threatened.

| SECTION 5 | (pages 325–327) |

Flowering of an American Culture

ACTIVITIES

○ **Using Visual Evidence**   Have students study the painting by Thomas Cole on text page 326 and answer these questions: (1) What impres-sion of the American landscape do you form from the painting? (2) How do you think the artist viewed nature?

☆ **Analyzing a Document**   Ask students to re-read the lines from Walt Whitman's poem on text page 327. Have them make a list of the types of people Whitman names. Ask them how they think Whitman would describe an American. Have students suggest additional verses to the poem that would reflect Ameri-cans today.

☐ **Analyzing**   Have students read Thoreau's es-say, "On Civil Disobedience." Then ask them to write an essay in which they describe Thoreau's reasons for refusing to pay taxes during the war with Mexico. They should also state whether they think Thoreau's actions were proper.

ANSWERS: SECTION 5 REVIEW   (page 327)
1. Hudson River School—p. 326; Nathaniel Haw-thorne, Walt Whitman—p. 327. **2.** The grandeur and rugged nature of the American landscape. **3.** That people should work to improve themselves and society through closer spiritual ties to nature. **4.** Possible answer: They summarize the ideas and ideals of an age.

ANSWERS: CHAPTER 15 REVIEW (page 328–329)
   Vocabulary   1. Revivals **2.** temperance move-ment **3.** Abstinence **4.** compulsory education **5.** utopian
   Chapter Checkup   1. The reform spirit had its roots in the Revolutionary War, the Declara-tion of Independence, and the Bill of Rights, as well as in the nation's religious heritage. The early colonists hoped the young republic would be an example to the world of a society based on Christian principles and justice. **2. (a)** By encouraging religious renewals and reforming personal habits such as the consumption of alcoholic beverages. **(b)** Thousands of people were touched by the efforts of these reform groups; it could not be

said, however, that all those people changed their ways of life as a result. **3.** In New England, every town was required by law to have a public school; however, laws regarding the support of such schools were unenforced. In the Middle Atlantic states, free education existed for those who claimed poverty. In the South, there was no support for public education. The West had only a few poorly equipped schools. **4. (a)** Some people resented taxation for education, especially people without children and those who sent their children to private schools. **(b)** Poor people and farmers often opposed compulsory education because they needed their children to work. **5. (a)** Towns ignored the educational needs of black Americans or barred them from public schools. New York and Boston segregated black children. It was illegal to teach slaves in the South to read and write. **(b)** Women received little education beyond basic writing and reading. **6.** Beginning with the Seneca Falls Convention, annual meetings were held and state legislatures were petitioned to grant women the vote. The movement remained small until after the Civil War. It did have some success in the areas of education and property rights. **7. (a)** Gradual emancipation through stopping the spread of slavery to new states, the end of the slave trade, and gradual freeing of slaves in the South. **(b)** Immediate emancipation through inclusion of women in the movement, refusal to vote or hold office in protest against the Constitution's recognition of slavery; no use of violence. **(c)** Blacks should rise up and free themselves. **(d)** Favored taking the issue to the voters by setting up a new antislavery political party. **8.** Artists and writers focused on the nation's unique heritage and natural landscape.

Critical Thinking   1. As former slaves they spoke from firsthand experience. They brought conviction and a good deal of passion to their cause. Their intelligence and fervor made them impressive models to follow. They inspired courage in others. **2.** Whitman's boast that his joints are "the limberest joints on earth and the sternest joints on earth" suggests the optimism of the American people. His assertion that "in all people I see myself" represents the American ideal of equality. **3. (a)** Examples include: environmental movement, womens' rights movement, peace movement. **(b)** Both; for example, some social activists use religious justifications for their position; other rights movements, such as women's rights, focus on political rationales.

Connecting Past and Present   1. (a) Women could not vote; in most places they could not own property, make a will, or file a lawsuit. **(b)** Women can vote and have the same legal rights as men. **2.** Accept all reasonable answers.

Developing Basic Skills   1. (a) Primary document. **(b)** Yes. He was an escaped slave. **(c)** To persuade New Yorkers to support the antislavery movement and to fight the slave trade. **(d)** The horror involved in the sale of human beings. **2. (a)** Abolitionism, women's rights, education, temperance, prison reform, improved treatment of the mentally ill. **(b)** There was moderate success in the areas of temperance, women's rights, education, and treatment of the mentally ill. **3.** Answers will vary.

Unit 5
A Nation Torn Apart

Chapter 16 (pages 332–351)
The Cords of Union Broken _____

OVERVIEW

Chapter 16 traces the road to disunion from the Missouri Compromise to the Confederate attack on Fort Sumter. Students read about the aims of the North and the South and efforts to reconcile the differences between them. Students also examine the effect of sectional discord on national political parties.

HISTORICAL SIDELIGHTS

The following pieces of historical information can serve as notes of interest during the study of Chapter 16. The page numbers in parentheses indicate the points in the student text at which you may wish to introduce the information.

Dred Scott's Life (p. 342)   What happened to Dred Scott while the long legal controversy swirled around him? From 1846 to 1852, while his case was before the state courts, he remained under the nominal control of the sheriff in St. Louis, Missouri. The sheriff hired him out at the rate of five dollars a month. Although Scott was ostensibly sold to different owners during the federal trials, he remained in St. Louis with no regular employment. After the Supreme Court decision, Scott was again sold, this time to a person who freed him. Scott then worked as a porter at Barnum's Hotel in St. Louis until his death from tuberculosis in 1858.

John Brown in Boston (p. 345)   John Brown's swashbuckling ways attracted much attention among abolitionists. While visiting Boston to raise money for a raid in Virginia, he acted the part of a "freedom-fighting Kansan" to perfection, sporting frontier clothes and a bowie knife tucked in his boot. Since Brown believed he was never safe from his enemies, he barricaded himself in his room each night. Although some radical abolitionists gave him verbal support, they contributed only about $1,000 to his cause.

SECTION 1 (pages 333–337)
Differences Over Slavery

ACTIVITIES*

○ **Name Game**   Ask students to name the person referred to in each of the following clues: (1) declared that the dispute over Missouri's admission to the Union frightened him "like a firebell in the night. . . ."; (2) proposed that Congress ban slavery in any territory acquired from Mexico; (3) argued that slavery should be permitted in all the territories; (4) championed popular sovereignty; (5) "The Great Compromiser."
Answers: **1.** Thomas Jefferson **2.** David Wilmot **3.** John Calhoun **4.** Stephen Douglas **5.** Henry Clay

☆ **Making an Oral Report**   Divide the class into four groups. Assign two groups to work on the Missouri Compromise, one group to represent the North and the other the South. Inform the other two groups that they will work on the Compromise of 1850, one group to represent the North and the other the South. Each group should prepare an oral report in which it (1) describes the issue or issues over which the compromise was made; (2) explains their section's position on the issue before the compromise was reached; (3) describes the parts of the compromise their section favored; (4) describes the parts of the compromise their section disliked but agreed to accept. After the groups have given their reports, ask: (1) Which section benefited most from the Missouri Compromise? Why? (2) Which section benefited most from the Compromise of 1850? Why?

_____

*See "To the Teacher" for an explanation of the symbols.

☐ **Analyzing a Quotation**   Read aloud the quotation that follows or duplicate and distribute copies. Tell students it is from a newspaper article published in New Haven, Connecticut, after the passage of the Missouri Compromise.

Slavery is extended to Missouri, by a majority of three. The deed is done. The galling chains of slavery are forged for myriads [great numbers] yet unborn. Humble yourselves in the dust, ye high-minded citizens of Connecticut. Let your cheeks be red as crimson. On *your* representatives [in Congress] rests the stigma of this foul disgrace. It is a stain of blood, which oceans of tears and centuries of repentance can never obliterate.

Then ask these questions: (1) On what grounds does the author condemn the Missouri Compromise? (2) Why does the author declare that the citizens of Connecticut ought to feel disgraced? (3) How might a supporter of the Missouri Compromise respond to this article?

ANSWER: MAP STUDY   (page 334)

It set rules governing the status of future territories carved out of the Louisiana Purchase; it did not settle the question of slavery in other areas.

ANSWER: MAP STUDY   (page 336)

By popular sovereignty.

ANSWERS: ARTS IN AMERICA   (page 337)

1. He suggests that even though the nation faces troubled times, the foundation is strong and will hold. **2.** Possible answer: the tensions leading to the Compromise of 1850.

ANSWERS: SECTION 1 REVIEW   (page 337)

1. David Wilmot, Stephen Douglas, Zachary Taylor—p. 335. **2.** free state, slave state—p. 333. **3.** Provided that Congress admit Missouri as a slave state and Maine as a free state; prohibited slavery in the remaining portion of the Louisiana Purchase north of latitude 36°30'. **4. (a)** The extreme northern position held that slavery should be excluded from all territory gained from Mexico. The extreme southern position declared that slavery should be permitted in all the territories. **(b)** One moderate position suggested that the Missouri Compromise line of 36°30' be extended to the Pacific, with slavery prohibited to its north and allowed to its south. Another favored popular sovereignty in the territories. **5.** Northerners would benefit from the admission of California as a free state and from the abolition of the slave trade in the District of Columbia. Southerners would bene-

fit from a strong fugitive slave law, from Congress officially declaring it had no power to abolish the slave trade between states, and by a provision that the rest of the southwestern territory would be open to slavery by popular sovereignty. **6.** Possible answer: He meant the common interest, common heritage, and tradition that united the states.

SECTION 2   (pages 338–341)
A Faltering Compromise

ACTIVITIES

○ **Analyzing Fiction**   Have students do dramatic readings from *Uncle Tom's Cabin*. Ask: Why did the novel become so popular? How do you think an audience would have reacted to these excerpts? Do the students know of any novel today that has had that type of impact on the public?

☆ **Applying Information**   Draw the outline of a chart on the chalkboard with two columns headed Southerners and Northerners. Have students review text pages 338–341 and suggest which of the events described on those pages aggravated southerners and which aggravated northerners. Write their responses on the chart. When the chart is complete, ask: (1) Why were people disturbed by these events? (2) Do you think northerners or southerners had more serious grievances between 1850 and 1856? Explain.

☐ **Researching**   Ask students to read about John Brown's raid on Pottawatomie Creek, Kansas, and write a report in which they discuss the nation's reaction to events in "Bleeding Kansas." They might consult *Ordeal of the Union* by Allan Nevins.

ANSWERS: VOICES OF FREEDOM   (page 339)

1. Because many of the spectators opposed slavery, while the court was trying a runaway slave. **2.** They were openly breaking the law because they thought the law was unjust.

ANSWER: MAP STUDY   (page 341)

It allowed slavery above the Missouri Compromise line if voters in those territories wanted it.

ANSWERS: SECTION 2 REVIEW   (page 341)

1. *Uncle Tom's Cabin*—p. 338; Franklin Pierce—p. 339; Ostend Manifesto, Kansas-Nebraska Act—p. 340; John Brown—p. 341. **2. (a)** Southerners thought the Fugitive Slave Law represented what was due them because the Constitution permitted them to hold slaves as property. **(b)** The law denied a person accused of being a fugitive slave the right to a jury trial and the right to testify and required citizens in the North to assist in capturing fugitive slaves. **3. (a)** A lopsided victory for the proslavery forces. **(b)** Antislavery settlers in Kansas refused to recognize the authority of the territorial government. They established a rival "free state" government at Lawrence. **4.** Possible answer: The Fugitive Slave Law, part of the Compromise of 1850, promoted division between North and South.

SECTION 3 (pages 342–344)
Rise of Sectional Politics

ACTIVITIES

○ **Building Vocabulary** Have students reread the excerpt from Lincoln's campaign speech on text page 344. Ask them to make a list of unfamiliar words and look each up in a dictionary. Then have them explain in their own words what the excerpt says.

☆ **Making Generalizations** Ask students to write at least two factual statements that support each of the following generalizations: (1) The presidential election of 1856 demonstrated that the nation had become divided along sectional lines. (2) The Dred Scott decision strengthened the institution of slavery. (3) Stephen Douglas's Freeport Doctrine helped divide the Democratic party along sectional lines.

☐ **Expressing an Opinion** Ask students to write an essay in which they agree or disagree with the following statement: The Supreme Court, in *Dred Scott* v. *Sandford,* reduced the possibility of a compromise on the issue of slavery.

ANSWERS: SECTION 3 REVIEW (page 344)

1. Dred Scott—p. 342; Freeport Doctrine—p. 344. **2.** Opposition to the extension of slavery into the territories. **3.** Democratic nominee, Buchanan, carried every southern state except Maryland, while Republican Frémont carried most northern states. **4.** The Supreme Court ruled that slaves could not be citizens. Since Scott was bound by Missouri law, he was still a slave. **5.** Possible answer: A debate can make the candidate and his views more widely known.

SECTION 4 (pages 344–349)
The House Divided

ACTIVITIES

○ **Name Game** Read the following clues or duplicate and distribute copies. Have students identify each person: (1) led a raid on the federal arsenal at Harpers Ferry, Virginia; (2) President of the Confederate States of America; (3) presidential candidate of the Constitutional Union party in 1860; (4) presidential candidate of the southern Democrats in 1860; (5) presidential candidate of the northern Democrats in 1860; (6) won the presidential election of 1860.
   Answers: **1.** Brown **2.** Davis **3.** Bell **4.** Breckinridge **5.** Douglas **6.** Lincoln

☆ **Map, Chart, and Graph Reading** Ask students to study the map, chart, and graphs on text page 347 and answer these questions: (1) In which section of the country was Lincoln the strongest? (2) In which section of the country was Breckinridge the strongest? (3) Did any candidate win a majority of the popular vote? (4) Who won the most popular votes? (5) Who won a majority of electoral votes? (6) How does the election map on page 347 of your text reflect sectional divisions?

☐ **Forecasting Alternative Futures** Ask students to speculate how future developments might have been different if Breckinridge, Bell, or Douglas had been elected President in 1860. They should support their forecasts with specific information.

ANSWER: MAP STUDY (page 347)

The votes for each candidate were concentrated in different areas of the nation.

ANSWERS: SKILL LESSON (page 348)

1. (a) The economic conflict between the commercial, industrial North and the agrarian South. **(b)** The moral issue of slavery. **2. (a)** The Great Depression probably caused many people to think in terms of economics. **(b)** The inhumanity of the concentration camps focused thinking on prejudice and human rights. **3. (a)** The North as an industrialized section favored a protective tariff; the South opposed high tariffs because tariffs made manufactured goods more expensive. **(b)** Generated emotions that encouraged extremists on both sides. The highly charged emotional atmosphere made compromise difficult. **(c)** The issue of whether newly created states should be slave or free constantly aggravated tensions between the North and South.

ANSWERS: SECTION 4 REVIEW   (page 349)
1. Harpers Ferry—p. 345; Confederate States of America, Jefferson Davis—p. 347; Fort Sumter—p. 349. **2.** lame duck—p. 348. **3. (a)** It sparked anti-slavery opinion, although many northern leaders dismissed him as a lunatic. **(b)** The North's sympathy for Brown convinced many southerners that their security could be maintained only by seceding from the Union. **4.** They feared that the leading contender, Seward of New York, was too radical to win. Lincoln, a moderate, was acceptable to all factions of the party and came from Illinois, a key state. **5.** Convinced many southerners that the South had lost political power and should secede. **6.** Possible answer: No. Even if Lincoln had allowed the Confederate states to secede, conflicts between North and South could have led eventually to war.

ANSWERS: CHAPTER 16 REVIEW(pages 350–351)
    Vocabulary   1. free **2.** slave **3.** popular sovereignty **4.** lame duck **5.** arsenal
    Chapter Checkup   1. (a) Because most northerners opposed the extension of slavery, while most southerners felt that slave owners should be allowed to take their slaves with them anywhere. **(b)** Each time a slave state entered the Union, a way was found to balance it with a free state; in this way, neither section gained an advantage in the Senate. **2. (a)** Because much of the new territory was southern, northerners feared it would become a vast slave-holding region. **(b)** That slavery be banned forever in the land acquired from Mexico. **(c)** That slavery be permitted in all territories; that the Missouri Compromise line be extended all the way to the Pacific; that the people in each territory decide for themselves whether they wanted to allow slavery. **3. (a)** As an additional free state, it would upset the balance in the Senate. **(b)** California was admitted as a free state, but the rest of the southwestern territory was opened to slavery by popular sovereignty. Slave trading was prohibited in Washington, D.C., but allowed among states. A strong fugitive slave law was enacted. **4. (a)** Because many northerners resented being forced to participate in the capture of runaway slaves. **(b)** It called for the return of all blacks who had ever been slaves, even those who had escaped long before; also, free blacks could be falsely accused of being fugitives. **5. (a)** By popular sovereignty. **(b)** It left the question of whether slavery would be permitted to the people rather than to Congress. **6. (a)** Nullified the Missouri

Compromise by ruling that Congress could not outlaw slavery in any territory. **(b)** It made the goals of their party unconstitutional. **7. (a)** They presented the main arguments dividing the nation. **(b)** A proposal that the people in a territory could prevent slavery by refusing to enact a slave code. **(c)** It split the party, because southern Democrats saw the Freeport Doctrine as a betrayal. **8.** It led southerners to the conclusion that the North supported armed slave uprisings and that the South would be secure only by seceding. **9. (a)** The party split into regional factions: northerners supported Douglas and southerners supported Breckinridge. **(b)** Lincoln won by carrying the more populous North. The South was simply outvoted. **10.** They could see that they had lost all influence in the federal government; the only way they could play a role in national government was to form their own.
    Critical Thinking   1. Because the conflicts between northern and southern supporters led to violence, such as the raid on Pottawatomie Creek and the destruction in Lawrence. **2.** Brown's raid on Harpers Ferry was violent and poorly executed, but his conduct after capture seemed noble and dignified, which made him appear a martyr.
    Connecting Past and Present   1. Possible answers: abortion, nuclear war, the environment. **2.** Probably not; the Republican party in 1856 was filling a political void. The same situation does not exist today.
    Developing Basic Skills   1. (a) The Missouri Compromise outlawed slavery above 36°30'. **(b)** The Compromise of 1850 opened the region to slavery through popular sovereignty. **(c)** The Kansas-Nebraska Act opened territory above 36°30' to slavery through popular sovereignty. **2.** Events of the 1850s point to a likely split. Require students to support conclusions with factual evidence.

Chapter 17   (pages 352–375)
Divided by War _____

OVERVIEW
Chapter 17 focuses on the Civil War, both on the battlefield and behind the lines. Students read about preparation for war, the war itself from Bull Run to Appomattox, and the Emancipation Proclamation. They also examine the effect of the war on life behind the lines.

HISTORICAL SIDELIGHTS

The following pieces of historical information can serve as notes of interest during the study of Chapter 17. The page numbers in parentheses indicate the points in the student text at which you may wish to introduce the information.

Bearded Soldiers (p. 357)   Civil War soldiers often wore beards, partly as protection against the elements and partly because shaving at the front was inconvenient. "Let your beard grow so to protect your throat and lungs," advised one Confederate manual. General Ambrose Burnside started a fashion trend by wearing whiskers that reached from the ear to the moustache—a style first called "burnsides" and later, "sideburns." One Georgia private bucked the trend, however, writing home to his wife, "I shaved off part of my beard the other day for the first time since I left home. I don't want my beard dabbling in my grub, let others do as they may."

Mother Bickerdyke (p. 367)   Of all those who served as nurses during the war, none received more affection and respect from the troops than "Mother" Mary Ann Bickerdyke. Mother Bickerdyke often irritated doctors and officers by her lack of concern for protocol, but she won grudging respect when they saw how effectively she cleaned up field hospitals, ferreted out mismanagement and corruption, and tended the sick. Once, when an army surgeon complained of her conduct to General Grant, Grant replied, "My God, man. Mother Bickerdyke outranks everybody, even Lincoln. If you have run amuck of her, I advise you to get out quickly before she has you under arrest."

SECTION 1   (pages 353–357)
Preparing for War

ACTIVITIES*
○ **Map Reading**   Have students study the map on text page 354 and answer these questions: (1) Which slave states remained loyal to the Union? (2) How many states seceded before the fall of Fort Sumter? (3) How many states were in the Union? (4) How many states were in the Confederate States of America?

☆ **Expressing an Opinion**   Ask students to write an essay in response to the following statement: The Civil War was "a rich man's war

and poor man's fight." They should state whether they agree or disagree with the statement and support their opinion. Tell students to consider the statement from the perspective of both southerners and northerners.

☐ **Applying Information**   Divide the class into two groups. Tell one group of students to imagine that they are representatives of the Union sent to Europe to win support for the war effort. Tell the other group of students to imagine that they are representatives of the Confederacy sent to Europe to win support for the war effort. Ask students to write a speech that they would make when they arrived. They should include any political or economic advantages the European nation might gain as well as any moral arguments they think favor their side.

ANSWERS: MAP STUDY   (page 354)
Virginia, Arkansas, Tennessee, and North Carolina; Maryland, Missouri, and Kentucky.

ANSWERS: SECTION 1 REVIEW   (page 357)
1. National Bank Act—p. 356. **2.** bounty, bounty jumping—p. 355. **3.** A larger population from which to recruit soldiers and greater industrial strength. **4.** Because on both sides it was possible for a rich person to buy his way out of the army; as a result, poorer people did most of the actual fighting. **5. (a)** The Union levied an income tax. It also imposed new sales taxes, taxes on manufactured goods, and a direct tax on the states. In addition, it sold bonds and issued paper money. **(b)** The Confederacy sold bonds and printed currency. **6.** Possible answer: Its location on the border between the Union and the Confederate states made Kentucky's hopes for neutrality impossible to achieve.

SECTION 2   (pages 357–362)
War Begins

ACTIVITIES
○ **Name Game**   Read these clues or duplicate and distribute copies. Ask students to use the clues to identify each person, place, or thing: (1) last Confederate stronghold on the Mississippi in the spring of 1862; (2) leader of Confederate forces at first battle of Bull Run; (3) Union ironclad ship; (4) fort on the Cumberland River, which surrendered to Grant; (5) general who brought order and discipline

_____
*See "To the Teacher" for an explanation of the symbols.

to Union troops after Bull Run; (6) name given to Union war strategy; (7) earned his nickname for his bravery at Bull Run; (8) battle at which the Union stopped Lee's advance into Maryland.

Answers: **1.** Vicksburg **2.** Beauregard **3.** Monitor **4.** Donelson **5.** McClellan **6.** anaconda **7.** Jackson **8.** Antietam

☆ **Using Visual Evidence**   Tell students that the Civil War was the first American war in which photographers accompanied the armies. Have students look at photographs taken during the war in books such as *The American Heritage Picture History of the Civil War*. Ask them to write a report in which they analyze one or more photographs as a source of evidence about the war. They should emphasize what they can learn about the war through photographs that they cannot learn by reading alone. If possible, ask students to bring the books containing the photographs to class.

☐ **Writing a Report**   The development of ironclad ships was one of the major technological advances of the Civil War. Ask students to write a report in which they describe that development. They might concentrate on either the building of the *Merrimac* (renamed *Virginia*) or the *Monitor*. Students might consult *By Sea and by River: The Naval History of the Civil War* by Bern Anderson.

ANSWER: MAP STUDY   (page 358)

Because almost every major battle was fought on southern soil.

ANSWERS: MAP STUDY   (page 360)

New Orleans and Memphis; Vicksburg.

ANSWER: MAP STUDY   (page 361)

The South won more battles.

ANSWERS: SECTION 2 REVIEW   (page 362)

1. Stonewall Jackson, the *Virginia*—p. 359; the *Monitor,* Ulysses S. Grant, George B. McClellan—p. 360; Robert E. Lee—p. 361. **2.** In the Civil War, larger numbers of soldiers were involved in each battle than in the battles of previous wars. Also, weapons were more efficient. **3. (a)** Blockade Confederate ports, divide the Confederacy into three theaters of war, and use the Union's superior naval strength to strangle each weakened section. **(b)** The far west (west of the Mississippi River), the west (between the Mississippi and the Appalachian Mountains), and the east (area around Virginia and Maryland). **4.** Lee sent Stonewall Jackson's army on a series of diversionary attacks that kept McClellan from getting the reinforcements he

needed to lead an attack on the city. A second Union attack on Richmond under General John Pope also failed when Lee and Jackson surrounded Pope's forces and made him retreat. **5.** Possible answer: The South's advantage in military leadership paid off in the early days; it would take a while before the North could mobilize its industry and larger population to advantage.

SECTION 3   (pages 362–364)
Freedom

ACTIVITIES

○ **Supporting Generalizations**   Ask students to write one or two factual statements to support each of the following generalizations: (1) As the war continued, there was growing pressure for emancipation of the slaves. (2) The Emancipation Proclamation contributed indirectly to greater rights for free blacks. (3) Black Americans made important contributions to the Union war effort.

☆ **Making an Oral Report**   Divide the class into small groups. Ask each group of students to imagine that they are one of the following groups of people living in January 1863: free blacks in the Union; slaves in border states loyal to the Union; slaves in the Confederacy. Tell each group to prepare an oral report about their reaction to the Emancipation Proclamation considering these points: (1) their immediate reaction when they hear of the proclamation; (2) the direct effect the proclamation could have on their lives; (3) the indirect effect the proclamation could have on their lives. Have groups make their report. Then compare the effect of the proclamation on the three groups.

☐ **Analyzing a Primary Source**   Ask students to read the text of the Emancipation Proclamation and answer these questions: (1) By what authority did Lincoln issue the proclamation? (2) Which states were covered by the proclamation? (3) What did Lincoln urge the freed slaves to do? (4) What statement did Lincoln make about the relationship of freed slaves to the armed services?

ANSWERS: SECTION 3 REVIEW   (page 364)

1. contraband—p. 363. **2. (a)** To preserve the Union. **(b)** Pressure came from abolitionists, fugitive slaves, and radical Republicans in Congress. **3.** Confederate states still at war. Slaves in areas occupied by Union troops or slaves in border states still loyal to the Union were not affected. **4.** 180,000 fought in the Union army; 29,000 in the navy. Many showed great courage. **5.** Possible answer: It changed the nature of the war and made it seem that the North was engaged in a moral crusade against slavery. This might have led many southerners to fight harder.

SECTION 4   (pages 365–368)
Behind the Lines

ACTIVITIES

○ **Summarizing**   Ask students to reread the special feature, *Diary of a Confederate Nurse* (text page 367). Have them look up in a dictionary any words they do not know. Then ask them to write a short summary describing Cummings's experience.

☆ **Defending an Opinion**   Have students make a chart with two columns headed Reasons for Opposition and Reaction of Government, and two rows headed Union and Confederacy. Instruct them to fill in the chart based on their text. Lead a class discussion comparing dissent and government responses. Then ask these questions calling for student opinions. (1) Does the Constitution guarantee the right to dissent during a war? Cite specific portions of the Constitution to support your answer. (2) What are the potential dangers of allowing dissent during wartime? What are the potential dangers of not allowing dissent during wartime? (3) What is treason? At what point do you think dissent becomes treason? (4) Do you agree with Davis's and Lincoln's decisions to suspend habeas corpus during the Civil War? Why or why not?

□ **Comparing**   Ask students to write an essay in which they compare the impact of the war on the economy of the North and the South. They should include specific information from the text and conclude by stating which region's economy was affected most positively and which was affected most negatively.

ANSWERS: VOICES OF FREEDOM   (page 367)

1. Poor weather that made transportation of the wounded difficult; crowded conditions in the hospital. **2.** A slave would not want the South to be left alone to resume its old way of life, based on slavery.

ANSWERS: SECTION 4 REVIEW   (page 368)

1. Homestead Act, Morrill Act—p. 366; Clara Barton—p. 367. **2.** copperhead—p. 365. **3.** Industry and agriculture were stimulated. **4.** Most of the fighting took place in the South. **5.** By forming aid societies to collect supplies. They gave food, drink, and medical care to soldiers passing through their towns. Some raised money to purchase military hardware. In the South, women harvested crops and supervised farms. They worked as clerks and secretaries in the North. In both sections, women became nurses. **6.** Possible answer: In wartime, security might seem more urgent than people's civil rights.

SECTION 5   (pages 368–373)
An End to the War

ACTIVITIES

○ **Locating Places**   Read the following clues or duplicate and distribute copies. Ask students to identify each place and then locate and label it on a blank map. (1) Mississippi stronghold that fell to the Union on July 4, 1863; (2) its fall gave the Union complete control of the Mississippi River; (3) marked the beginning of the end for the Confederacy; (4) siege here lasted from the summer of 1864 through the winter of 1865; (5) Lee's army finally forced to retreat from here in the summer of 1864; (6) site of final surrender of General Lee; (7) Confederate victory in May 1863; (8) state where Sherman's march to the sea took place. *Answers:* **1.** Vicksburg **2.** Port Hudson **3.** Gettysburg **4.** Petersburg **5.** Wilderness **6.** Appomattox **7.** Chancellorsville **8.** Georgia

☆ **Applying Information**   Tell students to imagine that they are either northern or southern war correspondents during the Civil War. Ask them to write a newspaper article about one of the battles described on text pages 368–373. They should include a headline as well as the text of the story. Some students may want to do additional research to add details to their story.

□ **Ranking**   Have students list the major Civil War battles after Antietam and rank them from the most significant to the least. Ask them to use specific facts to support their ranking. Some students might want to do additional research.

ANSWER: MAP STUDY (page 369)

Control of Little Round Top would have given Confederate troops a good position from which to fire on Union troops.

ANSWER: MAP STUDY (page 370)

It gave the North control of the Mississippi River, thereby cutting off the western part of the Confederacy.

ANSWERS: MAP STUDY (page 371)

Chattanooga; Savannah.

ANSWER: MAP STUDY (page 372)

Union troops moved southeast from the Wilderness to Petersburg, then swung westward. Lee's troops retreated before the Union advance.

ANSWERS: SECTION 5 REVIEW (page 373)

1. William Tecumseh Sherman—p. 371. **2. (a)** Fredericksburg, Virginia and Chancellorsville, Virginia. **(b)** He hoped that a Confederate victory in Pennsylvania would break the Union's resolve to continue the war. **3.** It placed the entire Mississippi River under Union control, which completely cut off the far western region from the rest of the Confederacy. **4.** Sherman waged total war, destroying farmland, homes, railroads, and cities, and leaving the civilian population unable to contribute to the war effort. **5.** Cut off from his lines of supply and with no reinforcements, Lee realized that resistance was futile. **6.** Possible answer: The South might have expected fair and generous treatment.

ANSWERS: CHAPTER 17 REVIEW (pages 374–375)

Vocabulary 1. bounty **2.** Bounty jumping **3.** ironclad **4.** contraband **5.** copperheads

Chapter Checkup 1. (a) Advantages: The Confederates were strongly motivated to defend their homeland. They were experienced in using firearms and horses and had better military leaders. Disadvantages: The Confederate government had strong constitutional limits to its authority, so it had a limited ability to direct the course of the war. As the South was defending slavery, it had trouble attracting European aid. **(b)** Advantages: greater manpower, more plentiful supplies, a larger railroad network, a larger merchant marine, and a larger navy. Disadvantages: Northern industry needed time to convert from peacetime to wartime production. **2. (a)** Not enough people volunteered. **(b)** First through the offering of bounties; later through a draft. **3. (a)** Because of Britain's strong navy and large industrial capacity. **(b)** Reformers and many ordinary citizens favored the North. Landed nobility favored the South. **(c)** Britain remained neutral. **4. (a)** Blockade the southern coast, divide the Confederacy into three regions, and then attack and strangle each region separately. **(b)** After the South American snake that encircles its prey and then crushes it. **(c)** The East, which was dependent on northern and European sources for manufactured supplies. **(d)** It gradually eliminated imported goods, especially manufactured products such as clothing and spare parts. **5. (a)** He hoped to have a victory that would sap the North's will to continue the fight. **(b)** Each time the southern forces had to retreat. **6. (a)** As the war progressed, the demand for abolition grew. The Union victory at Antietam spawned enough support to allow the President to issue the Emancipation Proclamation, which he hoped would frighten southern slaveholders into ending the war in order to keep their slaves. **(b)** Slaves in Confederate States still at war with the Union. **7.** They enjoyed greater rights in areas such as education and use of public transportation. New government rules stated that blacks were entitled to be citizens. **8. (a)** It was a three-part plan. One army would march through the Shenandoah Valley, defeating the enemy and laying waste the land; one would march across Georgia to Atlanta; the third would march from Washington to Richmond. **(b)** The defeat of Richmond. Because Confederate troops dug trenches and built fortifications.

Critical Thinking 1. Accept answers that point out the North's strengths—such as superior numbers, industry, and transportation network—that made it possible to wear down the South. **2.** Accept answers that emphasize that there were more soldiers involved in this war than in previous wars and that weaponry was more sophisticated.

Connecting Past and Present 1. Possible answer: Probably not; during the Vietnam War a lottery system evolved where few people were exempted, and usually for reasons of health, not wealth. **2. (a)** Many advances in medical technology and training for medical personnel. **(b)** Doctors are now better equipped to patch up wounded soldiers so they can go back and fight some more.

Developing Basic Skills 1. (a) and **(b)** Encourage students to prepare a worksheet with two columns headed Leadership Strengths and Leadership Weaknesses. Under each heading they should note the characteristics that apply to each of the leaders listed. **2. (a)** Union. **(b)** Students might suggest that the chart explains the outcome of the war because it describes the progression of the battles. **(c)** Without all the information, it is impossible to know which side won the most battles. It is still possible, however, to draw some conclusions about the war.

Chapter 18   (pages 376–393)

A Difficult Reunion ——

OVERVIEW

Chapter 18 focuses on the period after the Civil War known as Reconstruction. Students read about various plans for reuniting the nation, including the plan put into effect by the Radical Republicans in 1867. They also examine life in the South during the period and the end of Reconstruction.

HISTORICAL SIDELIGHTS

The following pieces of historical information can serve as notes of interest during the study of Chapter 18. The page numbers in parentheses indicate the points in the student text at which you may wish to introduce the information.

A Valued Opportunity (p. 379)   So eager were many former slaves to learn to read and write that the Freedmen's Bureau schools were not limited to young people. Observers visiting such schools found six-year-olds sitting side by side with sixty-year-olds, both learning from the same book. Remarked one very old man to a teacher who asked him his age, "I'm near on to a hundred, and this is my first chance to get a start."

A Determined Assassin (p. 380)   John Wilkes Booth, the brilliant but erratic actor who assassinated Abraham Lincoln, had been a member of the Virginia militia company that helped arrest John Brown in 1859. In 1864, Booth organized an attempt to kidnap President Lincoln in hopes of ending the war. When that effort failed, he began to plan the assassination attempt. Lincoln, for his part, knew the risks in a time of crisis. When Lincoln was riding alone late one night, a shot rang out, and the President's stovepipe hat flew off his head. He galloped home, shaken but unhurt.

SECTION 1   (pages 377–381)
Beginning of Reunion

ACTIVITIES*

○ **Summarizing**   Tell students to imagine that they have been asked to set up an office of the Freedmen's Bureau. Have them write a

memo in which they describe the goals of the bureau and the types of activities the bureau will engage in. Students should also describe the various types of people needed to staff the office.

☆ **Analyzing a Primary Source**   Have students reread the special feature, *Lincoln's Second Inaugural Address* (text page 380). Then ask these questions: (1) When was the speech given? (2) What was the status of the war at the time? (3) How would you describe Lincoln's attitude toward the war based on the speech? (4) Does the speech reflect the same attitude toward the Confederate states as Lincoln's 10-percent plan for Reconstruction? Explain.

☐ **Biographical Sketch**   Have students write a biographical sketch of Andrew Johnson in which they describe his background before becoming President. Ask them to explain why Johnson was chosen as Lincoln's Vice President in 1864. They might consult *The First President Johnson: The Three Lives of the Seventeenth President of the United States* by Thomas Lately.

ANSWERS: VOICES OF FREEDOM   (page 380)

1. To bring about a just and lasting peace, to bind up the nation's wounds. **2.** He favored conciliation with the South; he chose this opportunity to make that clear to everyone so that later the nation could be reunited with a minimum of discord.

ANSWERS: SECTION 1 REVIEW   (page 381)

1. Freedmen's Bureau—p. 379; Wade-Davis Bill, John Wilkes Booth—p. 380; Joint Committee on Reconstruction—p. 381. **2.** freedmen—p. 378. **3.** Widespread unemployment in the North as factories shut down. Veterans had difficulty finding work. In the South, factories, railroads, and farmlands had been devastated, cities burned out, banks closed, and businesses disrupted. The South also experienced widespread unemployment. And in both regions thousands of veterans were permanently disabled. **4.** Issued surplus army food, distributed clothing, organized schools, provided medical care, and sought work and job protection for former slaves and poverty-stricken whites. **5.** Enabled a state to reorganize and rejoin the Union after it abolished slavery and after 10 percent of its voters subscribed to an oath to support the Constitution and the Union. **6.** Possible answer: President Johnson was anxious to restore the Union; the Radical Republicans wanted to punish the South.

*See "To the Teacher" for an explanation of the symbols.

SECTION 2   (pages 381–385)
Congress Takes Over

ACTIVITIES

○ **Relating Cause and Effect** Write the following statements on the chalkboard and ask students to describe the effects of each event: (1) Immediately after the Civil War many white southerners feared a revolt by former slaves. (2) Southern legislatures passed Black Codes. (3) Republicans in Congress worried that the Supreme Court might declare the Civil Rights Act unconstitutional. (4) Republicans won control of both houses of Congress in the 1866 elections. (5) The House of Representatives impeached President Johnson.

☆ **Analyzing a Quotation** Tell students that many northerners reacted strongly to enactment of the Black Codes. As an illustration read the following statement from the Chicago *Tribune*, which appeared after Mississippi passed the first Black Code: "We tell the white men of Mississippi that the men of the North will convert the state of Mississippi into a frog pond before they will allow any such laws to disgrace one foot of soil over which the flag of freedom waves." Then ask students to answer the following questions: (1) Why do you think the newspaper reacted so strongly to Mississippi's Black Code in the fall of 1865? (2) How might Mississippi legislators have responded to the *Tribune*'s statement? (3) How might Radical Republicans have reacted? (4) What can you learn about the mood of the time from the statement?

☐ **Analyzing** Ask students to read the text of the Thirteenth, Fourteenth, and Fifteenth Amendments to the Constitution (text pages 889–891). Have them write an essay in which they summarize the three amendments and explain why each was significant during Reconstruction.

ANSWERS: SECTION 2 REVIEW   (page 385)
1. Thaddeus Stevens, Black Codes, Civil Rights Act—p. 382; Reconstruction Act, Tenure of Office Act—p. 384. **2.** Radical Republicans believed these states had forfeited their statehood and were now no more than territories, subject to the control of Congress; they wanted to protect their majority in Congress by preventing newly elected southern Democrats from being seated. **3. (a)** The rights to sue and be sued, buy and sell property, marry legally, and receive certain protections when working as apprentices. **(b)** The rights to bear arms, meet together after sunset, and marry whites. They faced fines or imprisonment for being idle or unemployed. **4.** The Fourteenth Amendment guaranteed citizenship to black Americans. The Fifteenth Amendment gave black Americans the right to vote. **5.** Because he dismissed Secretary of War Stanton despite the Tenure of Office Act. **6.** Possible answer: It put the South under military rule.

SECTION 3   (pages 385–388)
The Reconstruction South

ACTIVITIES

○ **Using Visual Evidence** Tell students that political cartoons are used by artists to express their point of view about an issue of the day. Ask students to draw a political cartoon about Reconstruction. It can be from the point of view of a southerner or northerner. It should concentrate on one aspect of Reconstruction. Have them give the cartoon a title. Then ask them to write a caption summarizing the main idea of the cartoon.

☆ **Finding the Main Idea** Divide the class into six groups and assign each group one of the subsections in Section 3. Two groups will be working on each subsection. Tell each group to write one statement that reflects the main idea of the subsection and two other statements about the subsection that are true but not the main idea. When the groups have completed the assignment, have each group read their statements, and ask the other students to decide which is the main idea. Compare the class choices with the groups' choices and have students defend their answers if the answers differ.

☐ **Expressing an Opinion** Lead a classroom debate around the following statement: The South would have been better off if there had been more scalawags like James Longstreet. (Refer students to text page 386.) Make sure they understand what a scalawag was and who James Longstreet was. You might ask students to do further research about Longstreet or the activities of scalawags.

ANSWERS: SECTION 3 REVIEW   (page 388)
1. Hiram R. Revels, Blanche K. Bruce—p. 386. **2.** tenants, sharecroppers—p. 385; carpetbagger, scalawag—p. 386. **3.** U.S. currency was scarce in the South and Confederate money was worthless. **4.** Carpetbaggers, scalawags, and blacks. **5.** Inex-

perienced and incompetent leadership and corruption. **6.** Possible answer: Problems plagued the southern states after the war and southerners blamed the governments—sometimes controlled by former slaves—for their troubles.

SECTION 4   (pages 388–391)
Unfinished Business

ACTIVITIES

○ **Map, Chart, and Graph Reading** Have students study the map, chart, and graph on text page 391 and answer these questions: (1) Which candidate won the largest percentage of popular votes? (2) Which candidate won the largest percentage of electoral votes? (3) In what regions was the Republican candidate the strongest? (4) Which southern states did Hayes win? How might you explain that?

☆ **Ranking** Divide the class into groups of five or six students. Tell each group to review the entire chapter and choose five events from the period that they think were the most significant. Ask them to rank those five events from one to five with one being the most important and five being the least important and to be prepared to explain the reasons for their choices. Have each group report their rankings and lead a discussion of the reasons given. Try to arrive at one list with which most students agree.

□ **Biographical Sketch** Have students read about Horace Greeley, Grant's opponent in the 1872 presidential election. Then ask them to write a biographical sketch emphasizing Greeley's experiences before that election. They might consult *Horace Greeley: Nineteenth Century Crusader* by Glyndon G. Van Deusen.

ANSWER: MAP STUDY   (page 391)
Samuel Tilden.

ANSWERS: SECTION 4 REVIEW   (page 391)
1. Ku Klux Klan, Force Act, Ku Klux Klan Act—p. 389; Rutherford B. Hayes, Samuel Tilden—p. 390. **2.** These events weakened the influence of Radical Reconstruction. **3.** Northern business leaders concluded that the Radical Republican governments were preventing the South from expanding economically. They wanted to invest in the South, but only if they could count on stable governments.

4. Yes. The campaign of intimidation kept many blacks and potential Republicans away from the polls. **5.** Hayes promised federal aid to construct new railroads and to control floods along the Mississippi River, as well as the removal of all federal troops from the South and a speedy end to Reconstruction. **6.** Possible answer: Stubbornness might benefit a general, but an inability to compromise is a serious weakness in a President.

ANSWERS: CHAPTER 18 REVIEW
                                (pages 392–393)
Vocabulary 1. b **2.** c **3.** d **4.** a **5.** e
Chapter Checkup 1. (a) To pardon Confederates who swore an oath to support the Constitution and the Union. When 10 percent of a state's voters subscribed to the oath and the state abolished slavery, the state would be readmitted. **(b)** Lincoln believed that the process of Reconstruction had to work gradually. **2. (a)** The former Confederate states had to renounce their acts of secession, refuse to pay their war debts, and approve the Thirteenth Amendment. **(b)** Because many of the representatives had been war leaders in the Confederacy. **3.** Believing that the former Confederate states had forfeited their statehood and returned to the status of territories, the Radical Republicans thought Congress should have exclusive jurisdiction over the territories. Also, they wanted to retain their majority in Congress by refusing to seat Democrats elected by the South. Some simply felt Johnson's plan was too lenient; they felt the South deserved to be punished. Some Radical Republicans were deeply concerned about the treatment of blacks in the South. **4. (a)** Congress feared that the Supreme Court might declare the Civil Rights Act unconstitutional. **(b)** Guaranteed citizenship to blacks. **(c)** Guaranteed blacks the right to vote. **5. (a)** Republicans won majorities in every northern state legislature as well as all of the northern governorships. They won a two-thirds majority in Congress. **(b)** Every former Confederate state (except Tennessee) had to adopt a new constitution that banned former Confederate leaders from office and guaranteed blacks the right to vote. The states had to ratify the Fourteenth Amendment. **6. (a)** Increased civil rights for blacks, established free public schools, and improved prisons and institutions for the mentally and physically handicapped. **(b)** Inexperienced and incompetent leadership, corruption, and resentment by the South's former ruling class. **7.** Republican Rutherford B. Hayes ran against Democrat Samuel Tilden. Tilden received more popular votes, but was short by one vote from winning a majority of the electoral votes. The votes

of three states were in dispute. A commission was set up to decide the election, and Hayes was chosen. He promised to help the South by giving federal aid for railroad construction and flood control and by removing the last of the federal troops. **8. (a)** When the leaders who had led the radical movement left office, the momentum was lost. **(b)** Republicans' reputation was hurt when corruption was discovered in their administration. **(c)** Corruption made it appear that it was time for a change in government leadership. **(d)** Northern business people wanted to end Reconstruction so they could securely invest in the South. **(e)** Violence prevented many blacks from voting, so more opponents to Reconstruction were elected. **(f)** Removed the troops from the South and officially called an end to Reconstruction.

Critical Thinking 1. Loose interpretation. Students could suggest that the Constitution did not specifically empower the Congress to establish racial equality, yet the Radical Republicans worked for the passage of the Civil Rights Act of 1866, which tried to secure equal rights for blacks. **2.** Accept answers that acknowledge Lincoln's skills as a leader, his experience dealing with Congress, and his belief in moderate treatment of the South.

Connecting Past and Present 1. (a) Possible answers: military aid to the Contras; Star Wars technology; how to cut the federal budget. **(b)** Military aid to the contras was cut off; Star Wars was initiated, later curtailed; compromises were made in how to cut the budget. **2. (a)** Today's farmers often have to borrow against their future crops in order to pay expenses. If the future crop does not earn them enough, they sink further into debt and risk losing their land. **(b)** Today the federal government is involved in helping farmers through price supports and other programs.

Developing Basic Skills 1. (a) Lincoln's policy. **(b)** Radical Republicans' policy. **(c)** Johnson's southern roots may have softened his policy toward the former Confederate states. The Radicals, on the other hand, were northerners who wanted to punish the South. **2. (a)** Tilden. **(b)** Hayes. **(c)** Tilden, probably because the South felt it had been mistreated by the Republican party and so did not support it.

SPIRIT OF AMERICA (pages 394–397)

Equality in America 1. Lincoln defined equality as an ideal, a goal to work toward. **2.** Possible answer: As during Reconstruction, steps were taken toward greater equality, not only in law but in fact.

Notable Americans 1. She became active after hearing an abolitionist speaker. **2.** Because they saw that women were not afforded the rights they deserved, even within the abolitionist movement. Women began to see that their actions could help bring about change.

Voices of Freedom 1. It was a celebration of the Emancipation Proclamation. **2.** He considered the spontaneous singing of "My country, 'tis of thee" by the newly freed men and women to be the highlight of the day. **3.** Possible answer: Because the moment belonged in a special way to the blacks who were for the first time really part of the country they were singing about.

Unit Six
Transforming a Nation

roof. Even worse, when the roof was saturated, it would drip for days, even after the sun had returned. One pioneer woman remembered frying pancakes while someone held an umbrella over her and the stove.

Chapter 19   (pages 400–419)
The Western Frontier ___

OVERVIEW

Chapter 19 focuses on the issues and events that opened the West to settlement and sparked bitter Indian wars. Mining, railroads, cattle ranching, and farming brought about an end to the Native American's traditional way of life. As settlers adapted to the semiarid conditions of the West, they often developed ingenious solutions to the problems of daily living. By the end of the 1800s, railroads linked East and West, and the American frontier was disappearing.

HISTORICAL SIDELIGHTS

The following pieces of historical information can serve as notes of interest during the study of Chapter 19. The page numbers in parentheses indicate the points in the student text at which you may wish to introduce the information.

The Stampede (p. 412) The stampede was the dread of cowhands on the annual long drive. Especially during the first days of the drive, every hand was on the alert. A cowboy would sleep on the ground with one end of a rope tied to his wrist and the other end tied to his horse, which remained saddled and bridled at all times. The greatest danger came on dark and stormy nights when a flash of lightning or clap of thunder might start the herd moving. Then the wranglers would have to work quickly and effectively to prevent the herd from running across the open plains, or even worse, over bluffs, into canyons, or into rivers.

A Leaky Roof (p. 415) Sod houses had certain defects, not the least of which was their leaky roofs. The houses might stay dry at the onset of a rainstorm, but as the sod absorbed the rain, rivulets of muddy water would begin to stream from the

---

SECTION 1	(pages 401–403)
Visions of the West	

ACTIVITIES*

○ **Comparing** Ask students to make a chart with two columns. Tell them to list in the first column the ways Native Americans made use of the buffalo. Then have them list in the other column the materials used today for each purpose. Ask students to write a paragraph comparing the two lists.

☆ **Writing a Report** Divide the class into groups and have each group use the information on text pages 401–403 to prepare a report on the Great Plains. Reports should describe the physical features of the plains and then analyze how the vision of each of the following would affect the natural environment there: Native Americans, William Gilpin, John Wesley Powell. Encourage students to use additional sources.

□ **Researching** Ask students to research John Wesley Powell's trip down the Colorado River through the Grand Canyon and write a report describing the trip. They might consult articles in *National Geographic,* May 1969 and July 1978, or Powell's journal, *The Exploration of the Colorado River and Its Canyons.*

ANSWERS: SECTION 1 REVIEW   (page 403)
1. William Gilpin—p. 402; John Wesley Powell—p. 403. **2.** Treeless areas with an annual rainfall of less than 20 inches. **3. (a)** For food, shelter, clothing, thread, bowstrings, tools, eating implements, and fuel. **(b)** Plains Indians disturbed the land as little as possible, revered nature, and believed it was important to remain in harmony with it.

---

*See "To the Teacher" for an explanation of the symbols.

4. (a) Native Americans believed the land and its creatures should exist in harmony with the spiritual world. They sought to maintain a balance between nature and the spirits that governed it. **(b)** Gilpin believed the West's resources were unlimited, this region would eventually support over a billion people, and the climate would become more humid after crops were planted. **(c)** Powell realized water was scarce and needed to be conserved. He foresaw the need for western settlers to regulate and share the West's water. **5.** Possible answer: Each was influenced by a different background— the Indians by a reverence for nature, Gilpin by his beliefs about vegetation, Powell by his training in geology.

SECTION 2 (pages 403–407)
Opening of the West

ACTIVITIES

○ **Using Visual Evidence** Have students study the painting on text page 402. Then ask them to write a paragraph describing how the coming of the railroad affected the lives of the Indian buffalo hunters and their families such as those shown in the painting.

☆ **Generalizing** Ask students to write one or two factual statements supporting each of the following generalizations: (1) Discoveries of gold and silver contributed to the growth of the West. (2) Transportation and communication between East and West improved during the 1850s and 1860s. (3) Many different peoples contributed to the building of the first transcontinental railroad. (4) Railroads were a major factor in opening up the West.

□ **Researching** Ask students to read about frontier days in Colorado, Nevada, Arizona, the Dakotas, or Montana. Have them write a report describing what life was like. They might consult *The American Heritage History of the Great West* by David S. Lavender.

ANSWERS: SECTION 2 REVIEW (page 407)
1. Comstock Lode—p. 404; Pony Express, Union Pacific Railroad, Central Pacific Railroad—p. 405; Promontory Point, Utah—p. 406. **2.** vigilante— p. 404; public domain—p. 405. **3. (a)** California and western Nevada, in the Columbia and Fraser river valleys, in Idaho and Montana along the Bitter Root and Salmon River mountain ranges, and in Colorado. **(b)** Mineral deposits played out quickly, people moved on, leaving ghost towns behind.

4. Advantages: Regular service, not many other options to choose from, probably safer than going alone. Disadvantages: expensive, dirty, exhausting, bumpy, poor accommodations along the way. **5.** Offered the railroads 20 square miles plus a 400-foot right-of-way for every mile of track the company laid. Agreed to lend the railroads money for every mile of track completed. **6.** Possible answer: No. Additional means of transportation and communication have lessened the importance of the railroad.

SECTION 3 (pages 407–410)
Tragedy for the Plains Indians

ACTIVITIES

○ **Placing Events in Time** Copy the time line that follows on the chalkboard. Then read aloud the list of events. Ask students to write on a sheet of paper the letter of the correct time period for each event.

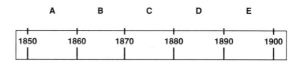

(1) Geronimo surrenders, (2) Dawes Act passed, (3) Fort Laramie agreement, (4) reservation policy begun, (5) massacre at Wounded Knee, (6) Chief Joseph surrenders, (7) *A Century of Dishonor* published, (8) gold discovered in the Black Hills, (9) battle of Little Big Horn, (10) gold rush in Colorado begins.
Answers: **1.** D **2.** D **3.** A **4.** B **5.** E **6.** C **7.** D **8.** C **9.** C **10.** A

☆ **Analyzing a Quotation** Tell students to reread the statement by General Philip Sheridan on text page 409. Ask them to write an essay explaining the meaning of the statement and whether or not they agree.

□ **Defending a Position** Tell half the students to imagine that they are newspaper editors sympathetic to the Plains Indians and the other half to imagine that they are newspaper editors sympathetic to settlers and miners. Ask them to write an editorial about whether the Indian lands in the Black Hills should be open to mining and settlement in 1874.

ANSWERS: MAP STUDY (page 408)

Apache reservations: southern part; Sioux reservations: northern part

ANSWERS: SECTION 3 REVIEW (page 414)

1. Little Big Horn, Chief Joseph—p. 409; Susette La Flesche, Helen Hunt Jackson, Ghost Dance, Wounded Knee—p. 410. **2.** reservation—p. 409. **3. (a)** The gold rush of 1859 brought thousands of miners into Colorado and led to war as government agents forced Indians to give up more land. In 1876 gold was discovered in the Black Hills and thousands of miners moved onto land given as a permanent home to the Sioux. **(b)** The conflicts convinced the government that a new Indian policy was needed. Government agents forced Plains Indians to move to reservations. **4.** Railroad crews took buffalo for food, wealthy easterners hunted them for sport, and merchants used their hides for robes or belts for machinery. **5. (a)** To bring Indians into the mainstream of American life by breaking up old tribal organizations. **(b)** Reservation land was parceled out to families and individuals in 160-acre lots. Those who accepted land became full citizens of the United States. Congress gave funds to support schools that would teach Indian children the "American" way of life. **6.** Possible answer: Each would have reasons to distrust the other.

SECTION 4 (pages 411–414)
The Cattle Frontier

ACTIVITIES

○ **Writing a Diary** Tell students to imagine that they are cowhands on a long drive. Have them write several diary entries describing life on the trail.

☆ **Recognizing Fact and Opinion** Before students begin the section, have them list on the chalkboard everything they know about cowboys. Prompt students by asking what work cowboys did, who became cowboys, and how they settled disputes. After students have read Section 4, have them decide which of the statements on the chalkboard are probably facts and which are myths. Ask: How were myths about cowboys created? Why?

□ **Relating Past to Present** Ask students to research methods of raising cattle today. Have them write a report comparing modern techniques with the method used during the mid-1800s.

ANSWERS: THE AMERICAN EXPERIENCE

(page 411)

1. sombrero; words like buckeroo, lariat, lasso; pointed-toe boots, chaps; ballads. **2.** Possible answer: games such as jai alai; numerous outstanding athletes, especially in baseball; political figures, labor leaders, actors, singers, writers.

ANSWER: MAP STUDY (page 412)

Denver, Dodge City, Abilene, Kansas City.

ANSWERS: SECTION 4 REVIEW (page 414)

1. Texas longhorn—p. 411; long drives—p. 413. **2. (a)** By opening new markets for Texas beef. **(b)** By long drives. **3.** Overgrazing, quarrels over water rights and land boundaries, and the fencing in of land all helped end the cattle bonanza. **4.** Possible answer: There is a natural tendency in many cultures to romanticize the past. In addition, the cowboy experience had adventure, challenge, personal courage, and individualism—all traits that Americans have admired throughout the country's history.

SECTION 5 (pages 414–417)
The Sodbusters' Frontier

ACTIVITIES

○ **Classifying** Ask students to make a chart with two columns. Have them list in the first column the problems facing farmers in adapting to life on the plains. In the second column, ask them to describe how farmers tried to meet those problems. When their charts are complete, ask students to write a paragraph discussing which problems seemed most difficult.

☆ **Analyzing** Ask students to write an essay in which they describe what they think was the farmer's vision of the West. Then ask them to compare that vision with the visions described in Section 1 of Chapter 19 (text pages 402–403).

□ **Analyzing Fiction** Pioneer life on the Great Plains has been the subject of many stories and novels, such as *O Pioneers!* by Willa Cather. Have students read a story or novel about pioneer life and write a report in which they describe life on the plains.

ANSWERS: GEOGRAPHIC CONNECTION

(page 415)

1. Not enough rain, irregular rain, difficult weather such as hail storms, frost, blizzards, strong winds.

2. Possible answer: Weather is important in occupations such as fishing, logging, aeronautics, seamanship, railroading, trucking because there are limits to the extent to which the effects of the weather can be dealt with.

ANSWERS: **SECTION 5 REVIEW**   (page 417)
1. James Hill—p. 415, "sooners"—p. 417 **2. (a)** To encourage farmers to settle the West. **(b)** It provided that any citizen or immigrant who intended to become a citizen could purchase 160 acres of public land to be used as a farm or homestead for a small fee. **3. (a)** Deep wells, windmills, dry farming, steel-tipped plows, mechanical binders, and threshing machines. **(b)** Floods in spring; high temperatures, hot winds, grasshopper plagues, grass fires in summer; ice, dust, and snow storms in winter. **4.** They provided education for children and served as community centers where farm families could find relief from the isolation and hard work of life on the plains. **5.** Possible answer: It would provide a sense of purpose—something for a society to try to achieve.

ANSWERS: **CHAPTER 19 REVIEW**
                                 (pages 418–419)
Vocabulary 1. d. **2.** c. **3.** b. **4.** e. **5.** a.
Chapter Checkup 1. (a) They viewed the plains as the "Great American Desert." **(b)** Attitudes were changed by the visions of men such as William Gilpin. He and others believed that limited rainfall could be overcome with wells. Then through the planting of crops, the climate would be changed and rainfall would increase. **2. (a)** Buffalo provided the Indians with all the necessities of life: meat, shelter, clothing, thread, tools, eating implements. **(b)** Indians became expert riders, traveling hundreds of miles on their nomadic hunts. Their population tripled. **3.** Thousands of people came into the region, causing towns to spring up overnight. **4. (a)** Too costly for most private companies, especially since builders would have to cut through the Sierra Nevadas and the Rocky Mountains. **(b)** Government offered railroad companies land in the West as an incentive to build a transcontinental line. Railroads received 20 square miles of land plus a 400-foot-wide right of way. Congress also lent money to the railroads for every mile of track completed. **(c)** Chinese and Irish Americans. **5. (a)** The conflicts between Indians and settlers in the West during the 1860s. **(b)** Efforts at resistance failed. After the destruction of the buffalo herds on the plains, many Indians could no longer support themselves. **(c)** No, even the Indians who moved to the reservations were not left in peace. Discovery of gold in the Black Hills led to conflict between settlers and the Sioux. **6. (a)** Reservation

lands were parceled out to individual Indians rather than to tribes as a whole. Those who accepted land became full citizens. Congress funded schools to teach Indian children the "American" way of life. **(b)** The intention of the Dawes Act was to put an end to the injustices that had been inflicted on the Indians. **(c)** The changes violated Indian traditions. Whites tricked Indians into selling their land for cheap prices, and the Indians resisted giving up their religion. **7. (a)** Cattle were allowed to roam freely on the grassy plains, grazing at will. **(b)** Every spring a crew of cowboys would be selected by a rancher to drive a herd of cattle to the railhead where the cattle were sold. The long drive took two or three months with the cowboys sitting in the saddle for 16 to 18 hours a day. The long drive enabled ranchers to find new and greatly expanded markets for their cattle since the railheads at the end of the drive linked the ranchers with markets in the East through the railroads. **8. (a)** Led to overgrazing and quarrels over land. **(b)** Allowed ranchers to fence in ranges and created conflict between cattlemen and sheep ranchers, especially over water rights. **(c)** Sheep cropped the grass so close that cattle could not eat it; range wars erupted between cattlemen and sheep ranchers. **(d)** When farmers fenced in former grazing land, conflict developed with cattlemen. **(e)** Two harsh winters followed by dry summers killed 80 to 90 percent of all cattle.

Critical Thinking 1. The Plains Indians depended on the buffalo for many of their needs. **2.** Both stimulated population growth and the growth of towns in the West. Also, both the cattle and mining industries depended on transportation, especially railroads.

Connecting Past and Present 1. (a) From the Indians we can learn a respect for the environment and how to treat it so that its resources are preserved; from Gilpin we can learn about both the benefits and the limits of technology as it serves human purposes; from Powell we can learn the importance of sharing and planning for the wise use of our water resources. **(b)** A romantic, not necessarily accurate view of this time in history as one that was filled with adventure, excitement, violence, and lawlessness in which courageous pioneers and cowboys tamed the natural environment. Increasingly there is also an awareness that this period in the West was one of suffering for, and unfair treatment of, the Indian peoples. **2. (a)** In recent years, the federal government has offered assistance to the automobile industry and the savings and loan industry, guaranteed price supports to farmers, provided scientists with funds for medical research and the development of alternative energy sources, and has supported some railroads and interstate highway construction. **(b)** For: To be competitive in international markets, the government should assist private industry by funding research and development projects. Against: In a free enterprise system, government intervention is unnecessary and unwanted. Such aid may give an unfair advantage to some companies and inhibit the competition of the marketplace.

Developing Basic Skills **1. (a)** Abilene, Dodge City, San Antonio, Los Angeles, San Francisco, Seattle, Butte, Duluth, St. Paul, Omaha, Kansas City, St. Louis, New Orleans, Chicago, and Santa Fe. **(b)** Denver, Abilene, Kansas City, and Dodge City. These cities are located at the end point or along the route of major trails used by cowboys on the long drive to bring their cattle to the railheads. **2. (a)** Lands in the far western, northern, central, and southern sections of the territory west of the Mississippi River; the remaining land west of the Mississippi River; reservations in present-day Arizona, Oklahoma, South Dakota, Montana, New Mexico, Utah, Wyoming. **(b)** The Indians lost their native land to the United States government, and they were moved onto reservations.

Chapter 20   (pages 420–443)
An Age of Industry _____

OVERVIEW
Chapter 20 focuses on the rapid industrialization of the last half of the nineteenth century. Students read about numerous inventions and developments that contributed to rapid economic growth. They also examine the growth of industry in the South and the impact of industrialization on workers.

HISTORICAL SIDELIGHTS
The following pieces of historical information can serve as notes of interest during the study of Chapter 20. The page numbers in parentheses indicate the points in the student text at which you may wish to introduce the information.

Traveling in Style (p. 426)   George Pullman's newly developed sleeping car spared no luxuries. Drapes embellished the windows. French plate mirrors hung on the walls, Brussels carpeting spread across the floor, and elaborate chandeliers hung from the ceiling. Pullman's first model, called the Pioneer, was so large it would not fit under many railroad bridges or next to station platforms. But railroads began to widen the clearances, es-

pecially after a Pioneer was used in Lincoln's funeral train from Chicago to Springfield, Illinois, in 1865.

Condensed Milk (p. 426)   Among the inventors whose enterprise changed American industry was Gail Borden, a man who had been a land surveyor in Stephen Austin's settlement in Texas. Borden devised dozens of inventions, including a dining room table whose center revolved to bring food to diners while the dinner plates around the edge remained stationary. After unsuccessfully experimenting with a condensed meat biscuit, Borden developed a method for condensing milk so it did not need to be refrigerated. Borden's condensed milk quickly caught on in large cities where the demand for sanitary milk was high.

SECTION 1   (pages 421–424)
The Ties That Bind

ACTIVITIES*
○ **Analyzing Cartoons**   Ask students to study the cartoon on text page 423 and answer the following questions: (1) What is the topic of the cartoon? (2) What does Vanderbilt represent in the cartoon? (3) Why do you think the cartoonist chose him? (4) What practices are referred to by the sign in the lower left corner? (5) Do you think the cartoonist approved of Vanderbilt's activities? Explain.

☆ **Summarizing**   Point out to students that the titles of subsections often provide capsule summaries of text content. Ask students whether the titles on text pages 421–424 are good summaries. Have students propose alternative titles and then write a one-paragraph summary of Section 1 using their new titles as an outline.

☐ **Relating Past to Present**   Ask students to write a report in which they compare the role of railroads in the United States today with their role in the economy of the late 1800s. They might use *The Readers' Guide to Periodical Literature* to find newspaper and news magazine articles on railroads today.

ANSWERS: SECTION 1 REVIEW   (page 424)
1. Samuel Morse—p. 421; Alexander Graham Bell—p. 422; Cornelius Vanderbilt—p.423. **2.** consolidate

_____
*See "To the Teacher" for an explanation of the symbols.

—p. 423; bond, stock certificate, asset, watered stock, rebate, pooling—p. 424. **3.** Accelerated the pace of American business by speeding up the communication of orders and messages and also provided employment opportunities for women. **4.** Railroads adopted a standard gauge, decreased rates, allowed freight cars of one line to use another line's tracks, replaced iron rails with steel rails, installed a second set of tracks so that traffic could move in two directions, and consolidated. **5. (a)** By issuing bonds, selling stock certificates, and watering stock. **(b)** By offering rebates, pooling, and reducing rates for long hauls. **6.** Possible answer: Efficiency and scheduling for the railroads necessitated a uniform system of telling time within each time zone.

SECTION 2   (pages 425–428)
Innovations and Inventions

ACTIVITIES

○ **Making a Crossword Puzzle**   Divide the class into small groups. Have each group select seven or eight of the inventors discussed in this section and create a crossword puzzle using the inventors' last names. You may want to bring to class several examples of crossword puzzles for groups to use as models. After all groups have finished work, ask groups to exchange puzzles and solve them.

☆ **Using Statistics**   Copy the following statistics on the chalkboard or duplicate and distribute copies. Ask students to study the statistics and answer the following questions: (1) How many tons of steel ingots and castings were produced in 1880? (2) How did the production of steel change between 1870 and 1875? (3) How many more tons of steel were produced in 1900 than in 1895? (4) How would you describe the change in steel production between 1870 and 1900?

Tons of Steel Ingots and Castings Produced

1870	68,750
1875	389,799
1880	1,247,335
1885	1,711,920
1890	4,277,071
1895	6,114,834
1900	12,188,329

Source: *Historical Statistics of the United States*

□ **Finding the Main Idea**   Read students the following quotation from Andrew Carnegie or duplicate and distribute copies. Have students write an essay in which they explain in their own words Carnegie's solution to poverty. Ask students whether they agree or disagree with Carnegie.

Here's how to solve the problem of poverty: Don't pass any laws controlling either how businessmen make money or what they do with it. Most of the community's money will end up in the hands of a few men, but this is all right if these men consider themselves not as owners of the money but merely as temporary keepers of it. Because these men are wise (or they wouldn't be rich) they will be able to make good decisions about how to spend the money to help the community. In fact, their decisions will be better than those of the people of the community themselves.

ANSWER: CHART STUDY   (page 426)
1886–1890.

ANSWERS: NOTABLE AMERICANS   (page 427)
1. To produce a large number of inventions in a wide variety of fields. **2.** Possible answers: The incandescent lamp made it possible for homes to be lighted at all times of the day or night without subjecting them to the danger of fire from candles or kerosene lamps. The phonograph provided an inexpensive, durable means of entertainment for millions of people. Edison's system of distributing electric power made it possible for factories to run their machines on electricity rather than steam power, increasing factory output at low cost.

ANSWERS: SECTION 2 REVIEW   (page 428)
1. Gustavus Swift, George Pullman, George Westinghouse, Thomas Edison—p. 426; Gospel of Wealth, social Darwinism—p. 428. **2.** Bessemer process—p. 423; laissez–faire economics—p. 428. **3.** Reduced amount of coal needed to produce steel and speeded up the manufacture of steel. **4.** Made possible the efficient and inexpensive marketing of meat to places far from the point of origin. **5.** Refrigeration, sleeping car, air brake, typewriter, elevator, light bulb, generator, electric car, and trolley. **6.** Possible answer: That the poor were incapable of improving their condition and had to depend on charity.

SECTION 3   (pages 428–433)
New Ways of Doing Business

ACTIVITIES
○ **Writing a Diary**   Tell students to imagine that they own a small oil refinery during the 1870s and that John D. Rockefeller is trying to gain control of their refinery. Ask them to write several diary entries in which they describe Rockefeller's tactics and their reactions to what is happening.

☆ **Using Diagrams**   Tell students to review the discussion of vertical and horizontal integration on text pages 431–432. Divide the class into small groups and have each group draw and label two diagrams—one to illustrate Carnegie's vertical integration of the steel industry and one to illustrate Rockefeller's horizontal integration of the oil industry. Ask groups to discuss whether these changes in business had a good or bad effect on consumers, workers, and the national economy.

□ **Biographical Sketch**   Ask students to read about the last ten years of the life of John D. Rockefeller or Andrew Carnegie and to write a biographical sketch. They should concentrate on the philanthropic activities of the two men.

ANSWERS: AMERICAN ENTERPRISE   (page 429)
1. Publicly showing the amount to be collected and providing a paper roll on which to record each day's transactions. **2.** Cash registers now show the amount of change to give customers, record the price of an item through the use of lasers, provide paper receipts with the amount of a sale. A major innovation is the use of credit cards. Orders can now be placed through the use of fax machines.

ANSWERS: SECTION 3 REVIEW   (page 433)
1. Andrew Carnegie—p. 430; John D. Rockefeller—p. 431. **2.** vertical integration, horizontal integration—p. 431; trust, dividend, monopoly, free enterprise—p. 432. **3.** Limited liability, legally permanent, can act as a person in its own right, and usually is able to attract capital more easily. **4.** Businesspeople could obtain capital from commercial and savings banks, life insurance companies, and the sale of stock. **5.** Rockefeller demanded rebates from railroad companies and cut prices to capture competitors' customers. Then he raised prices again after the competition had been driven out of business. **6.** Possible answer: Build a strong

monopolistic industry or business and then maintain your control of this industry by whatever means are required.

SECTION 4   (pages 433–435)
The Growth of Industry in the South

ACTIVITIES
○ **Generalizing**   Ask students to write one or two factual statements to support each of the following generalizations: (1) The southern railroad system improved after the Civil War. (2) Many southern industries developed around agricultural products. (3) In many ways the southern economy remained dependent on the North after the Civil War.

☆ **Map Reading**   Ask students to study the maps on text pages 846–849. Then have them use the maps and the information from text pages 433–435 to answer the following questions: (1) What is the main natural vegetation of the southern states? (2) What mineral resources are found in Alabama? (3) What mineral resources are found in other southern states? (4) What relationship can you identify between natural vegetation and industry in the South? (5) What relationship can you identify between mineral resources and industry in the South?

□ **Applying Information**   Ask students to imagine that they worked for the Freedmen's Bureau during Reconstruction and have returned to visit the South in 1898. Have them write a letter to friends in the North in which they describe their impressions of the South and how the area has changed.

ANSWERS: SECTION 4 REVIEW   (page 435)
1. Henry Grady—p. 433; Washington Duke—p. 435. **2.** Some wanted the South to industrialize. **3.** Southern states encouraged northern financiers by offering free land as well as access to the South's natural resources. As a result, southern railroads grew quickly. **4.** Cotton was used to manufacture thread, cottonseed oil for soap and cosmetics, tobacco for cigarettes, and timber for shingles and furniture. **5.** Possible answer: The South provided raw materials to northern factories and was dependent on the North for manufactured goods.

SECTION 5   (pages 436–441)
Workers Organize

ACTIVITIES

○ **Placing Events in Time** Write the list of events that follows on the chalkboard or duplicate and distribute copies. Ask students to arrange the events in correct chronological order: (1) Homestead strike; (2) Socialist Labor party formed; (3) Knights of Labor formed; (4) Haymarket riot; (5) American Federation of Labor formed; (6) Terence Powderly elected leader of Knights of Labor.
Answers: 3, 2, 6, 5, 4, 1

☆ **Relating Past to Present** Have students make a list of the original goals of the Knights of Labor and the American Federation of Labor. Ask them to decide which of the goals have since been met. Students may have to do additional research.

□ **Interviewing** Tell students to imagine that they are newspaper reporters in the late 1800s who have been assigned to interview an industrial leader about the organization of labor unions. Have students select one of the industrial leaders discussed in this chapter and write a list of questions they would like to ask. They should concentrate on the person's goals, activities, and views about labor unions.

ANSWERS: CHART STUDY   (page 437)
Servants and waiters. Dressmakers. Women served women. They required little training and paid so little that few men were willing to work at these jobs.

ANSWERS: GRAPH STUDY   (page 438)
Most prosperous years: 1872, 1880–1881, 1886–1887, 1889–1890, 1891–1892.
Severe depression years: 1865, 1875–1878, 1885–1886, 1892–1894, 1895–1896.

ANSWERS: SECTION 5 REVIEW   (page 441)
1. Knights of Labor, Terence Powderly—p. 439; American Federation of Labor, Samuel Gompers—p. 440. **2.** anarchist—p. 439; craft union, collective bargaining—p. 440; injunction—p. 441. **3. (a)** Eight-hour workday, improved safety in factories, compensation for on-the-job injuries, and equal pay for men and women. **(b)** Any worker. **4.** Turned the public against labor organizations; membership in the Knights dropped sharply. **5. (a)** Eight-hour workday and collective bargaining. **(b)** Skilled white male workers. **6.** In the late 1880s, much of the public opposed unions. They were considered radical organizations by many people. **7.** Possible

answer: It depersonalized the relationship, causing employers to take little interest in their employees as individuals.

ANSWERS: CHAPTER 20 REVIEW(pages 442–443)
Vocabulary   1. e **2.** a **3.** f **4.** d **5.** b **6.** c
Chapter Checkup   1. Telegraph and telephone **2. (a)** Constructing railroads was costly and most railroads were heavily in debt. Intense competition among railroads for customers. **(b)** To raise money, railroad owners issued bonds and sold stock certificates. Some owners sold watered stock. To reduce competition, owners engaged in rate wars or resorted to such illegal practices as pooling and rebating. **3. (a)** Carnegie's Gospel of Wealth directed the wealthy to donate money to worthy causes. **(b)** Social Darwinism applied the idea of the survival of the fittest to the business world; government regulation was viewed as interference with a natural process and thus as wrong. **(c)** Laissez-faire economics rejected government intervention in the economy. **(d)** Alger's stories reinforced the rags-to-riches theme that through talent and hard work an American could rise to the top. **4. (a)** Because the investors incur limited liability when investing in a corporation. In addition, a corporation has a special permanent legal status, and its survival does not hinge on the life of its owner. **(b)** By borrowing from commercial banks, savings institutions, and insurance companies, and by selling stocks. **5. (a)** A system in which key economic decisions are made by private investors. **(b)** Some pointed to ruthless competitive practices and unsatisfactory labor conditions. **6.** Southern industry remained dependent on the North. Northern bankers exerted control over southern industries, and northern railroad owners charged southerners high rates. Southern factories were discouraged from producing final goods. **7. (a)** Long hours and hazardous working conditions. **(b)** The Knights of Labor in 1869 and the American Federation of Labor in 1881. **(c)** The Knights of Labor achieved gains in the mid-1800s. Its success was weakened, however, by the Haymarket riot and violence during a railroad strike. The AFL achieved longer-lasting success, despite setbacks and negative public attitudes. **8. (a)** Owners reacted with open hostility because they felt they had a right to bargain with each worker individually. **(b)** The courts were generally hostile; many issued injunctions against the unions or held that strikers could be held liable to the company for losses incurred because of a strike. **(c)** The public associated labor unions with radicalism, and they were suspicious of collective bargaining. The tradition of individualism was strong, and people believed that individual effort was the way to advancement.

Critical Thinking 1. Answers will vary. Students can consider both the benefits to the nation of the industrial growth these leaders helped to generate and the methods they used to achieve their goals. **2.** Answers will vary. Students should be aware of the tremendous impact of the railroad. It facilitated trade and the settlement and growth of the western territories and helped unify the growing country.

Connecting Past and Present 1. Benefits: They eliminate companies that are inefficient from the marketplace. They may lead to more efficient management and better product by reducing duplication of services. Disadvantages: Often lead to unemployment and reduced competition. They are often costly and result in the increased indebtedness of companies that must divert funds to participate in or ward off takeover bids. These funds might otherwise be used to buy machinery or modernize factories. **2.** Advances in electronics such as the transistor have brought about the "information revolution." Such advances are continuing to change the way people do business, monitor and use data, and conduct medical and scientific research. Superconductors may one day provide cheaper and more efficient uses of energy.

Developing Basic Skills 1. Check charts for accuracy. **(a)** The Knights admitted all workers; the American Federation of Labor admitted only skilled workers, not blacks, women, or recent immigrants. **(b)** An eight-hour workday. **(c)** The AFL opposed social reform as a union goal. **(d)** The AFL's moderate policy on labor relations and social reform probably appealed to many workers and led it to be regarded with less hostility than the Knights of Labor by owners. **2. (a)** Controls all steps in the process required to turn a raw material into a finished product that it sells. **(b)** Controls many businesses in one area of production. **(c)** A vertically integrated firm can control its costs more easily than a firm using a wide range of independent suppliers. A horizontally integrated firm is often able to buy supplies at a lower price than its smaller competitors.

Chapter 21 (pages 444–465)

Politics and Reform _____

OVERVIEW
Chapter 21 focuses on political developments in the last half of the nineteenth century. Students examine corruption in government and industry and the efforts to curb that corruption. They also read about the development of Jim Crow laws and practices in the South and about the rise and decline of Populism.

HISTORICAL SIDELIGHTS
The following pieces of historical information can serve as notes of interest during the study of Chapter 21. The page numbers in parentheses indicate the points in the student text at which you may wish to introduce the information.

Nast vs. Tweed (p. 448) Thomas Nast, the well-known political cartoonist, made life difficult for Boss Tweed of New York. Tweed was especially enraged when Nast's drawing showed Tweed in a convict's uniform. "I don't care so much what the papers write about me," he remarked, "my constituents can't read; but . . . they can see pictures." Later Tweed fled to Spain to escape being thrown in jail for his corrupt practices. To his surprise, the Spanish police in a small village arrested him. They had recognized Tweed after seeing one of Nast's accurately drawn cartoons.

Waiting for the Cross of Gold (p. 462) Although William Jennings Bryan was young and not well known, the dramatic speech that brought him the nomination at the Democratic convention in 1896 was not just a lucky stroke. Bryan recognized the strategic importance of the speech and had been saving his striking "cross of gold" metaphor for just such an occasion. As he waited for the convention speaker to announce him, a friend passed a note scribbled on an envelope, "This is a great opportunity." Bryan scribbled the reply: "You will not be disappointed."

SECTION 1	(pages 445–447)

Political Corruption in a Gilded Age

ACTIVITIES*

○ **Writing a Diary** Tell students to imagine that they are political advisers to President Grant. Have them write several diary entries in which they describe their thoughts about the various scandals that marred the Grant administration.

☆ **Expressing an Opinion** Ask students to write a paragraph in which they comment on Mark

_____

*See "To the Teacher" for an explanation of the symbols.

Twain's labeling of the late 1800s as the Gilded Age (text page 446). Students should state whether they agree or disagree with the statement and support their opinion.

☐ **Biographical Sketch** Have students write a biographical sketch of President Ulysses S. Grant in which they discuss how the Crédit Mobilier and Whiskey Ring scandals affected him. They might begin with the *Dictionary of American Biography*.

ANSWERS: SECTION 1 REVIEW   (page 447)

1. Gilded Age—p. 446; Crédit Mobilier, Whiskey Ring—p. 447. **2.** Bribed members of Congress to pass favorable legislation. **3. (a)** To propose and make the laws. **(b)** To enforce laws passed by the legislative branch. **4.** Tarnished and weakened the presidency but also inspired some people to work for political reform. **5.** Possible answer: Congressional and presidential elections can cause power to shift depending on party affiliation, leadership qualities of the President, and attitude of the electorate.

SECTION 2   (pages 447–452)
Attempts at Reform

ACTIVITIES

○ **Relating Cause and Effect** Ask students to write one "effect" statement for each of the following "cause" statements: (1) President Garfield died after being shot by an embittered office seeker. (2) The states established commissions to regulate the railroads. (3) Congress passed the Interstate Commerce Act. (4) Congress passed the Sherman Antitrust Act.

☆ **Relating Past to Present** To help students understand the problems caused by the spoils system, have them imagine that a high school football team is holding tryouts. Instead of accepting players based on their athletic ability, they are chosen on the basis of gifts that they bring to the coaches. Ask: (1) How would this affect the quality of the football team? (2) Who would benefit most from the new system? Who would benefit least?

☐ **Writing a Speech** Have students imagine that they are members of Congress during the debate on the Sherman Antitrust Bill. Have them write a speech in which they support or oppose passage of the bill. Ask volunteers to give their speeches in class and have the

class vote on which arguments were most persuasive.

ANSWERS: VOICES OF FREEDOM   (page 450)

1. Morton: Civil service workers form a privileged class whose jobs would be protected for life. Schurz: Civil service workers hold their jobs on the basis of merit. **2.** Possible answers: Agrees with Morton: Workers' interest and performance diminishes if they know they hold a job for life. Agrees with Schurz: An examination system is the only fair way to fill jobs with the government; it also assures that the most qualified people will be chosen.

ANSWERS: SECTION 2 REVIEW   (page 452)

1. Chester A. Arthur—p. 447; Mugwumps—p. 448; Grover Cleveland—p. 449; Interstate Commerce Act, Sherman Antitrust Act, *United States* v. *E.C. Knight Company*—p. 451. **2.** patronage system—p. 446; holding company—p. 449. **3.** Hayes appointed a noted reformer to the cabinet as secretary of the interior and investigated the New York customs house, dismissing two senior customs house employees as a result of the investigation. Garfield's assassination dramatized the need to reform the patronage system. Arthur signed the Civil Service Act passed by the Congress in 1883. **4.** Gave rebates and practiced pooling. Larger shippers got cheaper rates. Short-haul shippers were charged higher rates for hauling freight short distances than they were for hauling freight long distances. **5.** Henry George proposed that Congress enact a single tax as a means of ending "unearned" profits for landowners. Edward Bellamy wanted the government to run all industry. **6.** Possible answer: As interstate industries grew, the need arose for federal legislation and federal agencies to oversee and regulate them.

SECTION 3   (pages 453–457)
Politics in the New South

ACTIVITIES

○ **Making Generalizations** Ask students to write one or two factual statements that support each of the following generalizations: (1) During the 1880s, southern blacks had some political rights. (2) After 1890, the southern states moved to deprive blacks of the right to vote. (3) The Supreme Court did not interfere with segregation.

☆ **Expressing an Opinion** Ask students to write an essay in response to President Hayes's statement that the "rights and interests [of black Americans] would be safer" if southern whites were "let alone by the general government." Tell students when writing their essays to consider both the moderate racial policies of the 1880s and the Jim Crow era that began in the 1890s.

☐ **Analyzing Quotations** Write the following quotations on the chalkboard or duplicate and distribute copies to the class. Tell students that one excerpt is from Booker T. Washington's Atlanta Compromise speech, and the other is from W.E.B. Du Bois's *The Souls of Black Folk*.

Booker T. Washington

The wisest among my race understand that the agitation of questions of social equality is the extremest folly. . . . It is important and right that all privileges of the law be ours, but it is vastly more important that we be prepared for the exercises of these privileges. The opportunity to earn a dollar in a factory just now is worth infinitely more than the opportunity to spend a dollar in an opera-house.

W.E.B. Du Bois

So far as Mr. Washington preaches Thrift, Patience, and Industrial Training for the masses, we must hold up his hands and strive with him. . . . But so far as Mr. Washington apologizes for injustice, North or South, does not rightly value the privilege and duty of voting, belittles the emasculating effects of caste distinctions, and opposes the higher training and ambition of our brighter minds. . . . we must unceasingly and firmly oppose them.

Ask students to read the excerpts and to look up any unfamiliar words in a dictionary. Then have them write an essay in which they compare Washington's views and Du Bois's views about how black Americans should react to discrimination and inequality.

ANSWERS: SECTION 3 REVIEW   (page 457)
1. "solid South"—p. 453; Jim Crow laws, *Plessy* v. *Ferguson*—p. 454; Booker T. Washington—p. 455; W.E.B. Du Bois—p. 456. **2.** disenfranchise—p. 453; poll tax, grandfather clause—p. 454. **3.** Rigid residency requirements, literacy tests, and poll taxes. **4.** Vocational training. **5.** Protest against Jim Crow laws and fight for the right to vote and enjoy equal opportunity. **6.** Possible answer: Many people would object to them because they accept an inferior political and social status for blacks.

SECTION 4	(pages 457–460)

The Populist Crusade

ACTIVITIES

○ **Analyzing a Quotation** Have students review the quotation by Mary Lease on text page 457. Ask them to describe what they think she meant. Have students suggest reforms that might solve the problem mentioned by Lease.

☆ **Applying Information** Tell students to draw on a sheet of paper a chart with two columns entitled Grievance and Proposed Reform. Ask them to review text pages 457–459 and complete the chart. In the left column they should list the grievances of farmers. In the right column they should list the solution for each problem proposed in the Ocala Platform. When students have completed their individual charts, review their answers and construct a class chart on the chalkboard. Then ask: (1) Which of the farmers' grievances was most serious? Why? (2) Why was the National Farmers' Alliance successful in electing local officials and members of Congress?

☐ **Analyzing a Chart** Copy the following chart on the chalkboard or duplicate and distribute copies.

Price of Selected Farm Products, 1890–1895

Year	Corn Price per Bushel in Cents	Wheat Price per Bushel in Cents
1890	.50	.84
1891	.40	.83
1892	.39	.62
1893	.39	.53
1894	.45	.49
1895	.25	.50

Source: *Historical Statistics of the United States*

Ask students to study the chart and then write a paragraph in which they explain how changes in farm prices may have contributed to the growth of the Populist movement.

ANSWERS: SECTION 4 REVIEW   (page 460)
1. Grange—p. 458; National Farmers' Alliance, Ocala Platform, Populist party—p. 459. **2.** deflation—p. 458; graduated personal income tax—p. 459. **3. (a)** Prices for their goods were declining, goods were being overproduced, credit was hard to get, farmers were paying back debts with deflated currency, railroads were charging unfair prices for shipping, and farmers were hit by a series of natural disasters in the 1880s. **(b)** Government policies to

make it easier for farmers to obtain credit; minting of silver coins to increase the money supply and fight deflation; reduction of high tariffs; and creation of a graduated personal income tax. **4. (a)** The Populists received over a million popular votes and 22 electoral votes for their national ticket. **(b)** It raised hopes for further reforms. **5.** Possible answer: Both involved the banding together of people who as individuals would be powerless to effect change.

SECTION 5 (pages 460–463)
The Decline of Populism

ACTIVITIES

○ **Placing Events in Time** Copy the following list of events on the chalkboard. Then ask students to arrange the events in correct chronological order. (1) Sherman Silver Purchase Act passed. (2) Coinage Act passed. (3) Sherman Silver Purchase Act repealed. (4) William McKinley elected President. (5) William Jennings Bryan delivers "cross of gold" speech at the Democratic party convention. (6) Populist party nominates William Jennings Bryan as its presidential candidate. *Answers:* 2, 1, 3, 5, 6, 4

☆ **Analyzing Cartoons** Ask students to study the cartoon on text page 461 and then answer the following questions: (1) What is the subject of the cartoon? (2) Who is leading the group in this cartoon? (3) Why is Bryan riding a donkey? (4) Who are some of the members of the group following Bryan? (5) What party do these people belong to? Why are they following Bryan? (6) What is unusual about the way Bryan is dressed? (7) Judging by this cartoon, what did the cartoonist think Bryan's chances of success were? Explain.

□ **Writing a Speech** Ask students to imagine that they have been invited to address a crowd of Jacob Coxey's followers in Massillon, Ohio, before they set out for Washington, D.C., in 1894. Have them include in the speech the economic problems of the time and the reasons why Coxey and his followers were marching to Washington.

ANSWERS: SECTION 5 REVIEW (page 463)
1. Coinage Act, Bland-Allison Act, Sherman Silver Purchase Act, Coxey's Army—p. 461; William Jen-

nings Bryan, William McKinley—p. 462. **2.** gold standard—p. 461. **3.** Allowing silver to circulate as part of the currency. **4.** Southern and western Democrats favored Bryan; eastern Democrats favored Cleveland. **5.** The Populist party lost morale and declined. Improved economic conditions hurt the movement. **6.** Possible answer: Victory went to the candidate who represented industry, owners, and large banks and not to the candidate of the common people.

ANSWERS: CHAPTER 21 REVIEW

(pages 464–465)

Vocabulary **1.** patronage system **2.** holding company **3.** disenfranchised **4.** poll tax **5.** deflation

Chapter Checkup **1.** Wealthy industrialists used their money to bribe members of Congress to pass legislation favorable to them. **2. (a)** The reputation of the Senate and House of Representatives reached a low point. Congress was thought to be corrupt and interested only in enjoying the spoils of victory. **(b)** Many legislators had been in office for several decades and had accumulated much power and influence. Many Senators were wealthy as well. Congress used the impeachment of Andrew Johnson to exert its authority over the executive branch. After Reconstruction, the presidency remained weak and the Congress became stronger. In addition, the President lacked a sufficient executive staff. **3. (a)** States created regulatory commissions to regulate the railroads. **(b)** In 1877, the Supreme Court ruled in *Munn* v. *Illinois* that the states could regulate railroads; in 1886, it ruled in *Wabash, St. Louis, & Pacific Railway Company* v. *Illinois* that only Congress had the power to regulate commerce between the states. **(c)** Outlawed rebating and polling; ordered railroads to establish just rates and stop charging short-haul customers higher rates than long-haul customers; and set up the ICC to investigate complaints. **4. (a)** By setting up strict residency requirements, literacy tests, poll taxes, and the grandfather clause. **(b)** Laws that provided for segregation of the races in public transportation and other public facilities. **(c)** Allowed "separate but equal" facilities for blacks and whites. **5. (a)** He urged abandoning political and social equality as a cause and concentrating on achieving economic success. He believed conditions in the South made social and political equality impossible. **(b)** Blacks should demand the right to vote and the right to enjoy equality of opportunity. The right to vote was necessary for human dignity, color discrimination was barbaric, and black children needed education as well as white children. **6. (a)** Declining prices, crop overproduction, difficult credit conditions, deflation, and unfair railroad rates. **(b)** Grange and Farmers' Alliance. **(c)** Formed cooperatives to purchase equipment and market crops; set up stores to buy farm machinery and sell it to members at low prices; lectured or published pamphlets on farm problems; and engaged in political action. **7. (a)** Supporters believed that the silver mines would prosper and the money supply would grow. They thought silver coinage would put money in their pockets and help them repay their debts. **(b)** Congress passed the Bland-Allison Act in 1878, requiring the government to buy a set amount of silver each year for minting into coins, and passed the Sherman Silver Purchase Act in 1890, increasing the amount of silver to be purchased and allowing paper money backed by silver. **(c)** He believed that the gold standard would strengthen the economy, restore the confidence of the business community, encourage new investment and reduce unemployment. **8. (a)** Favored unlimited coinage of silver, a lower tariff, and an income tax. **(b)** Defeat of Bryan undermined Populist morale. Then as economic conditions improved, people lost interest in the reforms favored by the Populists.

   Critical Thinking   1. (a) The political corruption of the era was like the brass under a thin layer of gold. **(b)** Answers will vary. Students should mention the political corruption at all levels of government and the abuse of power. **2.** Washington's views would cause little social disruption and were no threat to white power.

   Connecting Past and Present   1. Answers will vary. **(a)** Students might note that there will always be people attracted by the possibilities of wealth and/or power. **(b)** Through the legal system and exposure in the media. **2. (a)** Students might mention the Libertarian, Prohibition, Socialist, and Communist parties. **(b)** Answers will vary. Students should identify the goals and then make a judgment about whether they have been realized.

   Developing Basic Skills   1. (a) The development of corporate trusts. **(b)** People are losing liberty and control of the country. **(c)** Opposes, because he shows the people and the American flag sinking. The cartoon suggests that government has been taken over by the business interests in the country. **2.** Check charts for accuracy. **(a)** Political corruption and economic injustice. **(b)** Reformers were able to weaken the spoils system and pass legislation that curbed some economic abuses. **(c)** Muckraking journalists helped to root out political corruption. Organized pressure groups, such as the farmers, contributed to the movement for economic reform.

Chapter 22   (pages 466–489)
Toward an Urban Age ___

OVERVIEW

Chapter 22 focuses on the growth of cities during the late 1800s and early 1900s, and the problems and prospects that growth created. Students read about the "new" immigration that helped to give cities their unique character. They also read about the reformers who tried to solve some of the problems that beset the cities.

HISTORICAL SIDELIGHTS

The following pieces of historical information can serve as notes of interest during the study of Chapter 22. The page numbers in parentheses indicate the points in the student text at which you may wish to introduce the information.

   Urban "Growth" (p. 467)   European travelers were no strangers to urban life, but American cities amazed many of them because of their astonishing growth. An Italian poet marveled at the efficiency he saw in Chicago: "The day of my arrival, I saw rubbish—still smoking—from a house burned the night before. The day of my departure (and I stayed but a single week), I saw on this same site, the iron framework of a new building, already erected to the height of a third story and already the scaffolding of each story completed."

   Odd Matches (p. 478)   In the early days of baseball, which first flourished in many cities after the Civil War, little distinction was made between amateur and professional teams. When the Harvard University squad went on its western tour in 1870, it played matches against two professional teams—the Chicago White Stockings and the Cincinnati Red Stockings. Harvard won the first game but lost the second.

SECTION 1   (pages 467–471)
Beginning of an Urban Age

ACTIVITIES*
○   **Comparing**   Tell half of the students to imagine that they are wealthy people living in

---

   *See "To the Teacher" for an explanation of the symbols.

Chicago in the late 1800s, and tell the other half to imagine that they are poor people living in Chicago in the late 1800s. Ask students to write a letter to a friend in which they describe life in Chicago. When they are finished, ask volunteers to read their letters. Lead a class discussion comparing the impressions of the city among the "wealthy" residents and among the "poor" residents.

☆ **Graph Reading** Ask students to study the graph on text page 470 and answer the following questions: (1) What is the topic of the graph? (2) What was the total population of the U.S. in 1880? (3) What was the rural population in 1870? (4) What was the urban population in 1870? (5) How much larger was the rural population in 1900 than in 1850? (6) How much larger was the urban population in 1900 than in 1850? (7) Write one generalization based on information from the graph.

☐ **Map Reading** Have students locate a current map of Chicago in an encyclopedia and compare it to the map on text page 471. Ask students to write a paragraph in which they describe how the city has changed based on the maps.

ANSWERS: SKILL LESSON (pages 468–469)
1. **(a)** The growth of industries and cities. **(b)** Populations in urban areas. **(c)** Major industrial areas. 2. **(a)** Eight cities. **(b)** Thirty-one cities. **(c)** New York. **(d)** Chicago, New York, and Philadelphia. **(e)** Chicago, Philadelphia, Boston, and St. Louis. **(f)** The Northeast coast. **(g)** Great Lakes region and St. Louis. **(h)** San Francisco, Minneapolis, St. Paul, Omaha, Kansas City, St. Louis, Chicago, Milwaukee, Louisville, Memphis, New Orleans, Detroit, Toledo, Cincinnati, Buffalo, Rochester. Boston, New York, Baltimore 3. **(a)** Industrial development and urban growth occur together. **(b)** Cities develop around waterways. **(c)** Great Lakes region and Midwest.

ANSWER: GRAPH STUDY (page 470)
1890–1900.

ANSWER: MAP STUDY (page 471)
Many railroad lines led into Chicago, from which goods could be shipped and received via Lake Michigan and the other Great Lakes.

ANSWERS: SECTION 1 REVIEW (page 471)
1. Large numbers of workers and availability of transportation facilities. 2. **(a)** Large numbers of people left rural areas to live in cities, with this trend being most pronounced in the Northeast.

(b) The new jobs created by the industrial expansion taking place in the cities attracted people to these places. 3. Center of industrial growth, job opportunities for workers, slums, overcrowding, absence of basic services in rapidly growing areas, poor sanitation, pollution. 4. Rail and ship transportation. 5. Possible answers: Slums, overcrowding, insufficient basic facilities, filth, and pollution were problems in the nineteenth century and still exist today.

SECTION 2 (pages 471–475)
Immigrants and Cities

ACTIVITIES
○ **Collecting Evidence** Have students list examples of how immigrations to the United States have affected the nation's culture. They might note names, foods, and other items that reflect ethnic diversity.

☆ **Analyzing a Poem** Have students reread the poem in the special feature, Emma Lazarus and "The New Colossus" (text page 473). Ask them to look up any words they do not know in the poem and then write a paragraph in their own words explaining its meaning. Ask: Do the words of the poem apply to the United States today? Explain.

☐ **Researching** Tell students to choose one of the groups of people that immigrated to the United States during the late 1800s and early 1900s. Ask them to do additional research and write a report about the reasons those people had for immigrating. Some students may want to read first-hand accounts of immigrant experiences, such as those found in *Immigration as a Factor in American History,* edited by Oscar Handlin.

ANSWERS: THE AMERICAN EXPERIENCE
(page 473)
1. To help raise money for a pedestal for the Statue of Liberty. 2. Possible answer: The Colossus of Rhodes represented ancient conquest and pomp, while the Statue of Liberty symbolized a welcome to the tired, poor, homeless immigrants.

ANSWER: GRAPH STUDY (page 474)
A smaller percentage came from northern and western Europe, while the percentage from eastern and southern Europe and the Americas increased substantially.

ANSWERS: SECTION 2 REVIEW (page 475)

1. pogrom—p. 474. **2.** Wars, famines, religious persecution, overpopulation, and a lack of jobs and land. **3. (a)** Italy; Jews from eastern Europe, mainly Russia; Slavs from Russia, the Ukraine, Poland, Croatia, Serbia, Bulgaria, and Bohemia. **(b)** In cities, especially in industrial centers and ports such as Boston, New York, and Chicago. **4.** Some Americans resented foreigners because the new immigrants were often willing to accept lower wages and inferior working conditions. The languages, religions, and customs of immigrants seemed strange to many Americans. **5.** Immigrants contributed by helping to build the new industrial society and by contributing the traditions of their homelands to the new urban culture. **6.** Answers will vary. Students might think of ways immigrants and their descendants have shared their cultural heritage with the community through ethnic festivals, celebrations, and foods, and through community members who have contributed to the cultural, political, or social life of the community in important ways.

SECTION 3 (pages 476–479)
An Urban Way of Life

ACTIVITIES

○ **Scrambled Names** Write the following scrambled names and clues on the chalkboard or duplicate and distribute copies. Ask students to use the clues to unscramble the names.

1. AKSENI	**1.** painted realistic portraits and landscapes
2. HIISNAMT	**2.** invented game of basketball
3. LEPZITUR	**3.** publisher of New York World
4. NASLIUVL	**4.** designed first all-steel skeleton building
5. WOTOHOLWR	**5.** developed idea of "five and tens"

Answers: **1.** Eakins **2.** Naismith **3.** Pulitzer **4.** Sullivan **5.** Woolworth

☆ **Applying Information** Ask students to review text pages 476–479 and identify the characteristics of urban life. List their responses on the chalkboard. For each characteristic on the list, ask the class the following questions: (1) Why is this characteristic an example of city life rather than rural life? (2) Do you think this characteristic attracted people to the city?

Why or why not? (3) Do you think this characteristic would have attracted you to the city? Why or why not? (4) Is this characteristic still evident in city life today?

☐ **Relating Past to Present** Ask students to reread the special feature *The Streetcar and the American Dream* (text page 477). Then have them compare the type of public transportation described in the feature to the type available in their community today. You may want to limit comparisons to the modes of transportation. More advanced students, however, may want to investigate other aspects, such as the quantity and quality of public transportation.

ANSWERS: AMERICAN ENTERPRISE (page 477)

1. They were slow and could not manage steep hills. **2.** Possible answer: In many cities, subways, commuter trains, and buses made it possible to live at considerable distances from their workplaces.

ANSWERS: SECTION 3 REVIEW (page 479)

1. F. W. Woolworth—p. 476; Joseph Pulitzer, Louis Sullivan—p. 477; Winslow Homer; American Realists—p. 478. **2.** Helped cities expand and allowed settlement farther from the center of town. **3.** Department stores offered a wide variety of merchandise under one roof, prices clearly marked, free delivery, and credit. **4.** By emphasizing news of crime, sports, and gossip and by devising stunts. **5.** Watching and participating in such sports as baseball, basketball, and football. **6.** Possible answer: Economic and educational opportunities and the chance to attend symphonies, operas, the theater, museums, and sporting events.

SECTION 4 (pages 479–483)
A Changing Society: Problems and Prospects

ACTIVITIES

○ **Identification** Ask students to identify who is being referred to by each of the following clues: (1) helped establish the Red Cross in the United States; (2) believed students should participate actively in their education; (3) author of *How the Other Half Lives;* (4) founded Hull House in Chicago; (5) notorious political boss of New York City; (6) founded 70 hospitals in North and South America.
Answers: **1.** Barton **2.** Dewey **3.** Riis **4.** Addams **5.** Tweed **6.** Cabrini

☆ **Making Generalizations** Have students write one or two factual statements that support each of the following generalizations: (1) Hull House in Chicago served many needs for local residents. (2) In the last half of the nineteenth century, more opportunities opened for women to work outside of the home. (3) Corruption existed in some American cities during the late 1800s and early 1900s. (4) City reformers successfully defeated boss rule in some cities.

☐ **Biographical Sketch** Have students read about Jane Addams's life and write a biographical sketch of her. They should concentrate on her background and note the experiences and characteristics that may have contributed to her success as a reformer. They might consult *American Heroine: The Life and Legend of Jane Addams* by Allen Davis.

ANSWERS: SECTION 4 REVIEW   (page 483)

1. Jacob Riis, Jane Addams—p. 480; John Dewey, Social Gospel, Frances Xavier Cabrini—p. 482; William Marcy Tweed—p. 483. **2.** A nursery and kindergarten for children, adult education classes, a gymnasium, theater group, and medical services. **3. (a)** Many women moved into teaching, social work, clerical and sales jobs. **(b)** Wyoming, Colorado, Utah, and Idaho. **4.** To include teaching about health, jobs, and family and community life; to apply new discoveries in science and psychology to classroom teaching; and to adapt teaching techniques to suit the needs of children being taught. **5. (a)** Aid in finding a job, a loan to pay the rent, free English lessons, legal advice, and baskets of free food on holidays. **(b)** Political reforms to reduce corruption in local government and eliminate the political machine. Reform mayors undertook such projects as forcing the transit companies to cut streetcar fares, the building of public parks and schools, and relief programs for the unemployed. **6.** Possible answer: Police and fire protection, education, sanitation facilities, facilities for the poor and homeless.

ANSWERS: CHAPTER 22 REVIEW (page 484–485)

Vocabulary 1. b **2.** a **3.** c **4.** a **5.** a **6.** b

Chapter Checkup 1. The growth of industry created jobs, which drew people to the cities. This attracted more industries to the cities, and the growth spiral continued, aided by the influx of immigrants. **2. (a)** Chicago's central geographic location, its importance as a center of transportation for railroads and water traffic, its proximity to sources of raw materials, and its growing population. **(b)** Overcrowding, slums, lack of sanitation, polluted water, and corruption in politics.

3. The prospect of finding employment and the chance to escape wars, famine, and religious persecution and leading a better life. **4. (a)** The "new" immigrants were mostly from southern and eastern Europe, especially Italy, Poland, Russia, Hungary, and Bohemia; earlier immigrants had been from Canada and northern Europe. **(b)** Many new immigrants did not speak English; their customs and languages seemed strange to some Americans, fueling antiforeign feeling. **5. (a)** Trolleys allowed people greater mobility and helped cities grow outward. **(b)** Sold goods at lower prices than smaller shops, so people could buy more things and spend less time shopping for them. **(c)** Architects began to build upwards to gain more usable space from small parcels of land. This practice led to the design of the skyscraper by Louis Sullivan in 1889. **6. (a)** Illiteracy, unsanitary conditions, crime, fire hazards, high infant mortality, and overcrowding. **(b)** By offering services such as education, medical help, and recreation and by crusading for health and child-labor laws. **7.** The need for clerical workers, teachers, social workers, and salespeople created new opportunities for women. **8.** Machines controlled cities and offered city jobs and contracts to those who had the right connections. The machines often paid for their activities with city funds.

Critical Thinking 1. Rapid growth led to slums, overcrowding, inadequate housing, poor sanitation and other basic services. It also contributed to the diversity of city life and provided greater opportunities for employment. **2. (a)** By helping feed and house the poor and by offering medical and social services. **(b)** Earlier in American history volunteer groups of citizens and philanthropic organizations worked for social betterment when government was not expected to take on such responsibility.

Connecting Past and Present 1. Answers will vary. Students might consider such issues as influence peddling in politics and related political issues; need for improvements in environmental safety or regulation; services in education, child care, public health, housing, or mass transit. **2.** Answers will vary. Students might consider the work of religious groups such as Habitat for Humanity, which has worked to build housing for the homeless, protests by church groups regarding American policies in Latin America, stands taken by church groups on such issues as nuclear disarmament and human rights violations.

Developing Basic Skills 1. (a) Population distribution has changed. **(b)** There has been a general movement of population from the eastern portion of the country to the South, Southwest, and West. **2. (a–c)** Answers will vary.

SPIRIT OF AMERICA   (pages 486–489)

ANSWERS: **MOBILITY IN AMERICA**
(pages 486–488)

1. The three kinds of physical mobility identified by Lerner are physical, social, and economic. **2.** Possible answer: The availability of land and the wealth of resources provided many opportunities for many people.

ANSWERS: **NOTABLE AMERICANS**
(pages 488–489)

1. Her goals were to achieve a more comfortable life for herself and her family and to use her money to benefit others. **2.** Sarah Breedlove Walker moved to different parts of the country in her search for success.

ANSWERS: **VOICES OF FREEDOM**
(page 489)

1. She spent days and nights in a wagon with all the family's possessions. They had no furniture, stove, or other comforts when they arrived. The family had to deal with illness and fear. **2.** In search of the American Dream, they uprooted their family and worked to make a better life for themselves in America.

Unit Seven
Entering a Modern Age

Chapter 23   (pages 492–519)
The Progressive Era _____

OVERVIEW

Chapter 23 focuses on the progressive movement from 1900 to 1917. Students explore the development, goals, and accomplishments of the movement on both the local and national levels and learn how it fared under Presidents Theodore Roosevelt, William Howard Taft, and Woodrow Wilson. Students also read about reforms of the railroads and of the food and drug industry and about the conservation of natural resources.

HISTORICAL SIDELIGHTS

The following pieces of historical information can serve as notes of interest during the study of Chapter 23. The page numbers in parentheses indicate the points in the student text at which you may wish to introduce the information.

An Uncomfortable President (p. 505)   William Howard Taft's modest, unassuming manner made it difficult for him to be at ease as President. He once admitted that whenever someone said "Mr. President" in his presence, he instinctively looked around for Teddy Roosevelt.

Protecting Wildlife (p. 507)   The push for conservation included a drive to protect birds hunted for their feathers. In the 1800s, more than 5 million birds were killed each year to provide feathers for fashionable hats. One conservationist walking through New York City identified the feathers of 20 different species of birds on hats.

SECTION 1   (pages 493–498)
Voices for Change

ACTIVITIES*

○   **Constructing a Graph**   Have students construct a line graph based on the data in the following table. The vertical axis should show union membership in thousands from 0 to 2,200 in increments of 200. The horizontal axis should represent two-year periods from 1900 to 1910. Have students use the completed graph to write a generalization about union membership in the early 1900s and two factual statements supporting that generalization.

Year	Number of Union Members (in thousands)
1900	791
1902	1,376
1904	2,067
1906	1,892
1908	2,092
1910	2,116

Source: *Historical Statistics of the United States*

☆   **Applying Information**   Divide the class into small groups. Give each group the following instructions: (1) List the reforms sought by the progressives in the early 1900s. (2) In Chapters 20–22, review the major social, economic, and political developments of the late 1800s. (3) Compare the reform issues on your list with the developments of the 1800s. Which had their roots in one of these developments? Briefly describe the relationship. You might want to suggest development such as urbanization, industrialization, or Jim Crow laws to students. When the groups have finished work, compile a list on the chalkboard. Then lead a class discussion about the relationships that students noted.

☐   **Comparing**   Ask students to reread the special feature *Notable Americans, Carrie Chapman*

---

*See "To the "Teacher" for an explanation of the symbols.

Catt (text page 497). Then have them prepare a short biography of Carrie Chapman Catt or of Alice Paul. Have them indicate the goals each favored, and the tactics each used.

ANSWER: **MAP STUDY** (page 496)

Alabama.

ANSWERS: **NOTABLE AMERICANS** (page 497)

1. Firm patriotism and lobbying. **2.** People were attuned to reform.

ANSWERS: **SECTION 1 REVIEW** (page 498)

1. Lincoln Steffens, Ida Tarbell—p. 494; NAACP, W.E.B. DuBois—p. 495. **2.** muckraker—p. 494; women's suffrage—p. 497. **3.** Corruption in government, making local government more responsive, unsafe working conditions, health hazards, slum housing, and regulation of monopolies. **4.** Provided legal aid to black citizens, fought for passage of a federal antilynching law, and investigated race riots and lynchings. **5.** Minimum wage laws for women, state-sponsored industrial accident insurance plans, laws prohibiting children from working at night, and improved factory safety regulations. **6.** Organized parades, picketed the White House for 18 months, went to jail, and went on a hunger strike. **7.** Possible answer: Similarities: Both sought to curb abuses by the wealthy and the corrupt and help the poor. Differences: Muckrakers used their articles and books to draw attention to the need for change. Progressives often sought legislation to effect political reforms.

SECTION 2 (pages 498–500)
Reform in Government

ACTIVITIES

○ **Word Puzzle** Draw the puzzle below on the chalkboard or duplicate it and distribute copies. Read the clues aloud and ask students to fill in the blanks with the missing letters.

1.
—
1. _ _ F _ _ _ E _ D _ _
2. _ I _ _ _ _ A _ _ _ G _ _
—
3. _ _ _ C _ _ _ _
4. _ _ _ _ M _ _ Y
5. _ _ _ I _ _ _ A _ _ _ V _
—
—

Down **1.** When Robert La Follette was governor of Wisconsin, the state became known as a "laboratory for _____."
Across **1.** process by which people vote directly on a proposal **2.** professional hired to run a city **3.** election in which voters can remove officials **4.** election in which voters select party candidates **5.** process by which citizens propose legislation
Answers: Down **1.** democracy *Across* **1.** referendum **2.** city manager **3.** recall **4.** primary **5.** initiative

☆ **Supporting Generalizations** To review the ways progressives hoped to increase the people's role in government, ask students to write five factual statements that support each of the following generalizations: (1) Progressives tried to make government more democratic and more efficient. (2) Governor Robert La Follette of Wisconsin introduced many progressive reforms in that state. (3) Progressive reformers were active in every section of the country. When students have completed the assignment, review and compare their answers in a class discussion.

☐ **Analyzing Quotations** Read students the following statement about the initiative and referendum made by William Howard Taft, President from 1909 to 1913. Ask students whether they agree with Taft's opinion.

I am not complaining of the movement that brings about this initiative and referendum, for that is prompted by a desire to clinch the movement against corruption, on the theory that you cannot corrupt the whole people and that the initiative and referendum mean detailed and direct government by the whole people. But the theory is erroneous. The whole people will not vote at an election, much less at a primary. When the people are thus represented at the polls by a small minority, there is nothing that the politicians will not be able to do with that minority.

ANSWERS: **SECTION 2 REVIEW** (page 500)

1. Robert La Follette, Wisconsin Idea—p. 500. **2.** primary election, initiative, referendum—p. 498; recall election, city manager—p. 499. **3.** Greater efficiency and democracy. **4.** Required direct election of senators in all states instead of having state legislatures elect senators. **5.** Possible answer: Like Jackson, the progressives promoted the cause of the common people and sought to broaden participation in the government.

SECTION 3   (pages 501–505)
Theodore Roosevelt and the Square Deal

ACTIVITIES

○ **Analyzing Cartoons**   Ask students to study the cartoon on text page 502 and answer the following questions: (1) Whom does the man dressed as Uncle Sam represent? (2) Who is the man with the axe? (3) What does the tree stand for? (4) What is Roosevelt's attitude toward regulation of the trusts? (5) Does the cartoonist think Roosevelt has acted properly concerning trusts? Explain.

☆ **Making a Chart**   Draw a chart on the chalkboard with the following headings: Problem, Government Action, Significance. Ask students to review text pages 503–505. Then have them fill in the chart with problems Theodore Roosevelt addressed during his second term, the actions the government took in response, and the significance of each of the actions listed in column 2. Conclude the lesson with a class discussion organized around the following questions: (1) Which action do you think was most significant at the time? Why? (2) From the perspective of today, which action do you think was most important? Why?

□ **Relating Past to Present**   Ask interested students to investigate the role of the federal government in the conservation of natural resources today. Then have them prepare an oral report comparing that role with the role of the government in the conservation of natural resources during Roosevelt's administration.

ANSWERS: AMERICAN ENTERPRISE   (page 504)

1. The contamination and adulteration of food. **2.** Possible answers: For: Without pure-food laws the food industry would revert to the practices it followed before the pure-food laws were enacted. Against: Competition among food suppliers is so intense that any company that tampered with its product would soon be found out by the buying public and be forced out of business, making governmental regulation unnecessary.

ANSWERS: SECTION 3 REVIEW   (page 505)

1. Northern Securities Company—p. 501; Meat Inspection Act, Pure Food and Drug Act, Hepburn Act—p. 503; William Howard Taft—p. 505. **2. (a)** He welcomed the growth of industry, but wanted government to have the authority to regulate the practices of giant corporations. **(b)** He wanted to dissolve trusts that used ruthless competitive tactics. He opposed trusts that endangered public safety or failed to accept negotiation. **3.** He prodded Congress to pass the Pure Food and Drug Act, the Meat Inspection Act of 1906, and the Hepburn Act. **4.** Slowed the destruction of American forests by barring the cutting of trees on 150 million acres of government timberland and created five national wilderness areas. **5.** It endangered Roosevelt's reform program, because conservatives blamed the panic on Roosevelt's antibusiness speeches and actions. **6.** Possible answer: **(a)** He supports people who take action on a problem rather than those who plan and debate about the future but don't act. **(b)** During his administration, Roosevelt acted aggressively on a number of issues from regulation of the trusts to consumer protection and conservation.

SECTION 4   (pages 505–510)
The Ordeal of William Howard Taft

ACTIVITIES

○ **Identification**   Ask students who or what is referred to by each of the following clues: (1) secretary of the interior under President Taft, (2) 1909 act that disappointed progressives in their goal to lower tariffs, (3) act that gave the Interstate Commerce Commission power to regulate telegraph companies, (4) powerful speaker of the house early in the twentieth century, (5) progressive reform program proposed by Theodore Roosevelt in 1910.
Answers: **1.** Ballinger **2.** Payne-Aldrich Tariff Act **3.** Mann-Elkins Act **4.** Cannon **5.** New Nationalism

☆ **Analyzing Cartoons**   Ask students to study the cartoon on text page 506 and answer the following questions: (1) Whom do the two figures represent? (2) What do the cats and balls of yarn stand for? (3) How would you describe the reaction of each of the two men to the situation being illustrated? (4) What would be a good caption for the cartoon?

□ **Applying Information**   Have students read about the 1912 Republican national nominating convention. They might consult *TR and Will:*

A Friendship That Split the Republican Party by William Manners. Ask students to use what they learned from their reading to write an imaginary dialogue between a Taft supporter and a Roosevelt supporter at the convention.

ANSWER: MAP STUDY (page 509)

Taft.

ANSWERS: SECTION 4 REVIEW (page 510)

1. Payne-Aldrich tariff—p. 506; Gifford Pinchot—p. 507; Progressive party—p. 508; New Freedom—p. 509; Eugene V. Debs—p. 510. **2.** Progressives believed such tariffs were unfair to American consumers. **3.** Taft set aside public lands for conservation and supported new conservation laws; continued prosecution of the trusts; supported the Mann-Elkins Act; created a new Children's Bureau; approved new safety regulations for mines and railroads; established an eight-hour workday for government workers; and increased the number of civil service positions. **4.** Roosevelt's disappointment with Taft's performance in office and his own failure to gain the Republican nomination for President. **5.** Wilson believed that trusts should be broken up because they could not be regulated successfully by government. Roosevelt disagreed, believing the federal government could use its power to regulate trusts. Debs wanted government ownership of all large-scale businesses. **6.** Answers will vary. Students should present facts that support their answers.

SECTION 5 (pages 510–513)
Woodrow Wilson and the New Freedom

ACTIVITIES

○ **Generalizing** Have students write one or two factual statements to support each of the following generalizations: (1) The goal of lowering tariffs was important to Woodrow Wilson. (2) Wilson supported legislation aimed at controlling monopolies. (3) Wilson's administration had a mixed record on social issues.

☆ **Using Diagrams** Ask students to make a diagram illustrating the process by which the Federal Reserve Board could regulate the national money supply. Have students display their diagrams and lead a discussion about the various methods students used to illustrate the process.

□ **Researching** Have students investigate state and local laws protecting young workers. They can begin their search for information at the local library. Ask volunteers to report their findings to the class.

ANSWERS: SECTION 5 REVIEW (page 513)

1. Underwood-Simmons Tariff Act, Federal Reserve Act—p. 511; Clayton Antitrust Act—p. 512; Federal Trade Commission—p. 513. **2.** interlocking directorate—p. 512. **3. (a)** The system divided the nation into 12 districts and set up a federal reserve bank for each district. Individual banks deposited a percentage of their monetary reserves in the federal reserve banks in their district. The Federal Reserve Board controlled the system by setting interest rates on loans made by the federal reserve banks to member banks. **(b)** Lower interest rates, making loans easier to obtain. **4.** Forbade large corporations to have interlocking directorates. Prohibited pricing policies that might destroy competition. **5.** Seamen's Act of 1915, establishing minimum standards for the treatment of merchant sailors; the Adamson Act of 1916, establishing an eight-hour workday for railroad workers; Workingmen's Compensation Act of 1916, providing financial aid to disabled federal civil service employees; Child Labor Act of 1916, banning interstate commerce of goods produced by child labor; Farm Loan Act, making it easier for farmers to get loans. **6.** Possible answers: Many of his reforms concerned improving working conditions for factory workers and laborers.

ANSWERS: CHAPTER 23 REVIEW

(pages 514–515)

Vocabulary 1. b **2.** a **3.** c **4.** a **5.** c

Chapter Checkup 1. (a) The belief that the United States needed to be reformed and the confidence that it could be. **(b)** No. Some fought government corruption; others sought regulation of powerful monopolies or legislation against unsafe working conditions and slum housing. **2. (a)** Journalists who sought to reform society by exposing unsafe or unfair practices in government and industry. **(b)** By raising public awareness of urgent problems. **3. (a)** Some progressives ignored segregation and discrimination or worked to strengthen Jim Crow laws. Others, shocked by racial discrimination, felt the rights of blacks should be protected. **(b)** They formed the NAACP to protect the rights of blacks through legal services and through investigation of race riots and lynchings. **4. (a)** Upton Sinclair's *The Jungle* generated public support for federal inspection of meatpacking plants. Government investigators found canned foods that were contaminated with dangerous chemical additives and showed how drug companies exaggerated the curative powers of their products. **(b)** The Meat Inspection Act and the Pure Food and Drug Act were passed. **5.** By initiating 90 antitrust suits, by fighting for a graduated income tax, by pushing for the Sixteenth Amendment, by supporting the Mann-Elkins Act, by creating a Children's Bureau, and by approving legislation to improve conditions for workers. **6.** Divided the nation into 12 districts, with a federal reserve bank for each district. The national banks in each district deposited their monetary reserves in the district federal reserve bank. The Federal Reserve Board controlled this system.

Critical Thinking 1. (a) Roosevelt's trust-busting activities; his creation of the Departments of Commerce and Labor; and his fight for passage of laws on food, drugs, and railroad rates all increased the role of the federal government in the national economy. His threat to use force against the coal owners during the coal strike of 1902 demonstrated the power the federal government could exercise over business. **(b)** Answers will vary. **2.** As women entered the work force, gaining economic independence, they fought for their political rights. Increased interest in reform during the progressive era also helped the suffrage movement succeed. The acceptance of women's suffrage at the state and local levels in the West and Midwest also helped win passage of a constitutional amendment. **3.** Supporters of the New Freedom wanted to break up trusts, while supporters of the New Nationalism wanted to put them under government supervision. Students might argue that the New Freedom approach was impractical in that the breakup of trusts would disrupt the economy.

Connecting Past and Present 1. (a) Minimum wage and hour laws. Child labor laws. **(b)** Answers will vary. Some may argue that without such laws teenagers would be required to work long hours for low pay. Others might argue that such laws make it harder for teenagers to find work, because employers are unwilling or unable to pay young people the same wages as adults. **2. (a)** Reform issues include influence-peddling and other abuses of power and privileges by politicians, environmental pollution issues such as waste disposal, educational reform issues such as how to pay for and improve quality of public schools, taxation and debt reduction. **(b)** Answers will vary.

Developing Basic Skills 1. Research will vary. **2.** Check students' charts for accuracy. Answers may differ concerning which President best represented the progressive era.

SPIRIT OF AMERICA   (pages 516–519)

ANSWERS: SELF-IMPROVEMENT (pages 516–517)

1. Two reasons were the increasing number of educated adults who were seeking to improve themselves and the inability of most people to afford to buy books. **2.** The movement provided a well-rounded program for self-improvement combining ongoing education and physical training. **3.** Possible answer: Yes, effort (pain) is required to achieve most things worth striving for (gain).

ANSWERS: NOTABLE AMERICANS
                                (pages 518–519)

1. He had to overcome the obstacles presented by a move from the farm to the city and his father's objections to his plans. **2.** He taught youngsters to love the outdoors and appreciate nature.

ANSWERS: VOICES OF FREEDOM   (page 519)

1. He required the boys to earn their feathers as the Indians had done. **2.** Possible answer: They were made to sense that they set goals for themselves and in reaching them they were able to feel pride in their achievements.

Chapter 24   (pages 520–543)

Becoming a World Power

OVERVIEW
Chapter 24 traces United States involvement in world affairs from 1865 to 1914. Students examine various rationales for American expansion during the period. They also read about the interest of the United States in Asia and the Caribbean and about the causes and consequences of the Spanish-American War. Students read about United States involvement in Latin America and Asia under two presidents—Theodore Roosevelt and William Howard Taft. Students also examine how the role of the United States in world affairs expanded in the late 1800s and continued to grow during the first decades of the twentieth century.

HISTORICAL SIDELIGHTS
The following pieces of historical information can serve as notes of interest during the study of Chapter 24. The page numbers in parentheses indicate the points in the student text at which you may wish to introduce the information.

A Close Call (p. 523)   Alfred Thayer Mahan, the strategist who advocated a strong United States navy in the Pacific, came close to never having the chance to air his theories. As a midshipman in 1859, Mahan requested transfer to a ship named the *Levant*. Superiors denied the request, however, much to Mahan's later relief. After the *Levant* sailed off into the Pacific, it disappeared mysteriously, leaving no clue of its ultimate fate.

The Origins of Jingoism (p. 526)   The term "jingoism" has come to be associated with extreme patriotism. The phrase was first coined in Britain in 1878 when that country appeared to be on the verge of entering a war that was raging between Russia and Turkey. There was a popular music-hall tune in Britain at the same time that went, "We don't want to fight; but, by Jingo, if we do, we've got the ships, we've got the men, and got the money too." Americans later updated and adapted the lyrics to fit their own situation.

SECTION 1   (pages 521–527)
The Dream of Expansion

ACTIVITIES*

○   **Identifying**   Ask students who is referred to by each of the following clues: (1) secretary of state who purchased Alaska from Russia; (2) naval officer who believed that the United States needed new markets abroad; (3) minister who believed that the United States had a mission to civilize the rest of the world; (4) President who threatened war if the British seized new territory.
  Answers: **1.** William H. Seward **2.** Alfred Thayer Mahan **3.** Josiah Strong **4.** Grover Cleveland

☆   **Analyzing Cartoons**   Ask students to study the cartoon on text page 523 and answer the following questions: (1) Whom does the man with hat represent? (2) What is he doing? (3) How are Hawaii, Canada, Cuba, and Central America shown? (4) What do these countries have in common? (5) What is the cartoonist's opinion of U.S. policy in the western hemisphere? How can you tell? (6) What title might be appropriate for the cartoon?

□   **Analyzing a Quotation**   Write the following statement by Alfred Mahan on the chalkboard or duplicate and distribute copies to students:

Americans must now begin to look outward. The growing production of the country demands it. An increasing volume of public sentiment demands it. The position of the United States, between the two Old Worlds and the two great oceans, makes the same claim. . . .

Have students write a short essay discussing whether they think that United States actions in Hawaii were consistent with Mahan's ideas.

ANSWERS: SECTION 1 REVIEW   (page 525)
1. William H. Seward—p. 522; Frederick Jackson Turner, Alfred Thayer Mahan—p. 523; Josiah Strong, Queen Liliuokalani—p. 524. **2.** imperialism—p. 521. **3. (a)** By demanding that France withdraw its troops from Mexico, which led to the overthrow and execution of Archduke Maximilian and the end of his puppet government. **(b)** By buying Alaska from Russia in 1867 for $7.2 million. **4. (a)** Turner believed that expansion was necessary to avoid domestic unrest caused by the lack of economic opportunities. **(b)** Mahan argued that expansion was necessary to obtain new markets abroad. **(c)** Strong believed expansion was a way to civilize the rest of the world, a mission for which the United States had been divinely chosen. **5. (a)** Germany, Great Britain, and the United States agreed to share control of Samoa, with the United States obtaining the harbor at Pago Pago. **(b)** Americans valued Hawaii as a stopover for their growing trade with China. American sugar growers dominated Hawaii's government and economy. **6.** Britain refused a request from the United States to submit a dispute between Venezuela and its colony of British Guiana to arbitration. **7.** Possible answer: The need for raw materials and markets created by industrialization led to U.S. expansionism.

SECTION 2   (pages 526–531)
The Spanish-American War

ACTIVITIES

○   **Finding the Main Idea**   Have students re-read the verses in the special feature, *Lola Rodríguez de Tió: Poet and Patriot* (text page 527). Ask them to explain the meaning of each verse in their own words and why the poem might have had special importance for a Cuban woman in the 1870s.

☆   **Relating Cause and Effect**   Ask students to write one or two "effect" statements for each

*See "To the Teacher" for an explanation of the symbols.

of the following "cause" statements: (1) General Weyler established the policy of reconcentration in Cuba. (2) The *Maine* sank in Havana Harbor. (3) Admiral Dewey sank the entire Spanish fleet in Manila Bay. (4) The Senate ratified the treaty that ended the war between Spain and the United States.

☐ **Analyzing**   Tell students that in his war message to Congress in April 1898, President McKinley outlined the following grounds for declaring war on Spain: (1) to end Spanish "barbarities" in Cuba; (2) to protect American lives and property in Cuba; (3) to protect American trade; (4) to end the threat to peace presented by conditions in Cuba. He also mentioned the sinking of the *Maine*. Ask students to write an essay in which they explain which reasons they think were most significant in the decision to go to war.

ANSWERS: ARTS IN AMERICA   (page 527)
1. National liberation **2.** They might have aroused the emotions of the people for independence from Spanish rule.

ANSWER: MAP STUDY   (page 528)
Because the United States Navy pushed around both the east and west ends of Cuba.

ANSWERS: SKILL LESSON   (page 530)
1. (a) The *Maine* exploded in Havana Harbor and was destroyed. Many people were killed. The injured were put aboard a Spanish warship and a Ward Line steamer. Representatives of the Spanish armed forces expressed their sympathy to Captain Sigsbee. **(b)** The *Maine* was "blown up." Public opinion should be suspended. **(c)** There is doubt as to the cause of the explosion. The *World* is conducting an inquiry. **(d)** Yes. It is the opinion of the *World* that the explosion was caused by a bomb or torpedo. **2. (a)** The *Maine* was blown up. **(b)** Implies that he does not know whether bomb or torpedo caused explosion. **3. (a)** No. He wants to restrain public opinion until the facts are discovered. **(b)** The picture would arouse the public because it clearly indicates the damage and loss of life that resulted from the explosion. **(c)** It might stir up public opinion against Spain. **(d)** Suspicions, plot, and torpedo. The first two would generate suspicion of Spain while the third would heighten the public's sense of horror. **4. (a)** The *Maine* was deliberately blown up and Spain is probably to blame. **(b)** To heighten reader interest in the story to increase newspaper sales. **(c)** Encouraged prowar feeling in the United States.

ANSWERS: SECTION 2 REVIEW   (page 531)
1. Valeriano Weyler, William Randolph Hearst—p. 526; the *Maine*—p. 527; George Dewey; Theodore Roosevelt—p. 528. **2.** jingoism, reconcentration—p. 526; yellow journalism—p. 527. **3.** Screaming headlines and sensational stories that pictured Spain as a villain. **4.** Thrilled expansionists, who believed they were seeing the dawn of a new age of American expansion. **5. (a)** Puerto Rico, Guam, and the Philippines. **(b)** In theory independent, but temporarily a protectorate of the United States. **6.** Possible answer: The yellow press, expansionists, and industrialists.

SECTION 3   (pages 531–536)
Responsibilities of Empire

ACTIVITIES

○ **Making Generalizations**   Ask students to write one or two factual statements that support each of the following generalizations: (1) The Platt Amendment placed conditions on Cuban independence. (2) During the late 1800s, European nations and the United States were interested in China. (3) The United States benefited from overseas expansion following the Spanish-American War. (4) President Roosevelt took an active role in foreign affairs.

☆ **Analyzing a Quotation**   Write the following statement from the platform of the Anti-Imperialist League on the chalkboard or duplicate it and distribute copies to students:

We earnestly condemn the policy of the present national administration in the Philippines. It seeks to extinguish the spirit of 1776 in those islands. The United States have always protested against the doctrine of international law which permits the subjugation of the weak by the strong. A self-governing state cannot accept sovereignty over an unwilling people.

Have volunteers restate the quotation in their own words. Then have one half of the class argue for and the other half against the position of the Anti-Imperialist League.

☐ **Comparing**   Ask students to review what they learned about Aguinaldo's rebellion in the Philippines and the Boxer Rebellion. Then ask them to compare the goals of the two rebellions and how each rebellion affected the interests of the United States.

T 97

ANSWER: **MAP STUDY**   (page 535)

Nicaragua, Panama, Cuba, Haiti, Dominican Republic, Honduras under American influence; Canal Zone and Puerto Rico owned by the United States.

ANSWERS: **SECTION 3 REVIEW**   (page 536)

1. Teller Amendment, Platt Amendment, Emilio Aguinaldo—p. 532; Open Door notes, Boxer Rebellion—p. 533; Roosevelt Corollary—p. 535. **2.** protectorate—p. 532; sphere of influence—p. 533. **3. (a)** Through the Platt Amendment, under which Cuba recognized the right of the United States to send troops to Cuba in order to preserve law and order. **(b)** American troops occupied the Philippines, and the Senate ratified the peace treaty that ended the Spanish-American War. **4. (a)** Russia, Japan, Britain, and Germany. **(b)** To try to open China to all nations, including the United States, on an equal basis and maintain its independence. **5. (a)** It gave new strength to the Monroe Doctrine since Great Britain, Germany, and Italy had followed the wishes of the United States. **(b)** It asserted the right of the United States to exercise "international police power" in Latin America. **6.** Possible answer: The Open Door Policy indicated the interest of the United States in trade with China, and the Roosevelt Corollary indicated the intention of the United States to intervene in the Americas as it saw fit.

SECTION 4   (pages 536–538)
The Panama Canal

ACTIVITIES

○ **Scrambled Names** Write the following scrambled names and clues on the chalkboard or duplicate them and distribute copies. Ask the students to use the clues to unscramble the names.

1. NUUBA-RALAIVL	**1.**	French leader of a revolt by the Panamanians
2. MOLBOCIA	**2.**	nation that controlled Panama before 1903
3. RAGGOS	**3.**	physician who attacked disease in Panama
4. SOVORLETE	**4.**	President who negotiated the Hay-Pauncefote Treaty
5. HOGATLES	**5.**	engineer in charge of the Panama Canal

Answers: 1. Bunau-Varilla 2. Colombia 3. Gorgas 4. Roosevelt 5. Goethals

☆ **Making a Time Chart** Write the following list of randomly ordered events on the chalkboard or duplicate it and distribute copies: (1) Hay-Pauncefote Treaty, (2) French attempt to build a canal, (3) first passenger ship sails through the canal, (4) Spanish-American War, (5) Panama declares its independence, (6) United States begins work on the canal, (7) French give up trying to build a canal, (8) Clayton-Bulwer Treaty, (9) Panama grants the Canal Zone to the United States. Ask students to find the correct date of each event. Then have students construct a horizontal time line like the one on text page 520. When students have completed their time line, ask the following questions: (1) How many years passed between the beginning of the French attempt to build a canal and the beginning of the United States attempt? (2) How many years did the United States take to complete the canal? (3) How long after Panama declared independence did the United States begin to build a canal? (4) How did the independence of Panama contribute to the ability of the United States to build a canal?

☐ **Applying Information** Tell students to imagine that they are working at building the Panama Canal. Ask them to write a letter to their families at home in which they describe their experiences. Some students may want to do further research.

ANSWER: **MAP STUDY**   (page 538)

It cut thousand of miles off the sea journey between the east and west coasts of the United States, cutting down on the time and cost of the voyage.

ANSWERS: **SECTION 4 REVIEW**   (page 538)

1. Clayton-Bulwer Treaty—p. 536; Hay-Pauncefote Treaty—p. 537; William C. Gorgas—p. 538. **2.** The canal shortened the trip from New York to San Francisco by more than 7,500 miles. It reduced shipping costs and allowed the U.S. to maintain a single navy rather than two separate navies. **3. (a)** The Colombian government asked for more money than President Roosevelt was willing to pay. **(b)** Roosevelt encouraged a revolt by the Panamanians and blocked Colombian efforts to stop the revolt. The United States recognized the new Panama nation almost at once. Two weeks later, Panama granted the United States a larger canal zone than the Colombians had proposed. **4.** Possible answer: The narrow isthmus of Panama was important to Roosevelt's policies. He saw it as a costly obstacle to trade and to defense. His policy in Latin America was aimed at making sure a canal was built across this isthmus.

SECTION 5   (pages 538–541)
The United States and Asia

ACTIVITIES

○ **Relating Past to Present** In 1906, Theodore Roosevelt was awarded the Nobel Peace Prize. Have students write a paragraph explaining why he won this honor. Students can also use a world almanac to make a list of other world leaders who have won this award.

☆ **Applying Information** Tell students to imagine that they are foreign policy advisers to Theodore Roosevelt in 1905. Have them write a short position paper for the President in which they explain the reasons for the outbreak of the Russo-Japanese War. They should also describe the degree of involvement they recommend for the United States.

☐ **Analyzing** Ask students to read about United States foreign policy under President Taft. Refer them to a diplomatic history such as *American Diplomacy* by Robert H. Ferrell or *American Diplomacy, 1900–1950* by George F. Kennan. Have students describe one event during Taft's administration that illustrates Taft's idea of "dollar diplomacy."

ANSWERS: MAP STUDY   (page 540)
France; Britain

ANSWERS: SECTION 5 REVIEW   (page 541)
1. Treaty of Portsmouth—p. 539; "dollar diplomacy"—p. 541. **2. (a)** At Roosevelt's invitation, Russian and Japanese representatives attended a peace conference in Portsmouth, New Hampshire, where they negotiated the Treaty of Portsmouth. **(b)** The Russians blamed Roosevelt for their losses under the Treaty of Portsmouth. The Japanese wanted Manchurian resources and feared that less of those raw materials would flow into Japanese factories as more nations took advantage of the Open Door policy. **3.** Immigration led to a wave of anti-Japanese sentiment on the West Coast. Hostility led to the segregation of San Francisco's Asian students in a special school. Immigration from Japan was restricted. **4.** To show the military strength of the United States. **5.** Short term: New York bankers replaced European financiers as major lenders in

the area; military intervention to protect U.S. economic interests continued. Long term: a growing distrust of the U. S. among Latin Americans. **6.** Possible answer: Realism; he took whatever actions he deemed necessary to protect or to promote U.S. interests.

ANSWERS: CHAPTER 24 REVIEW
                            (pages 542–543)
Vocabulary **1.** imperialism **2.** jingoism **3.** Reconcentration **4.** yellow journalism **5.** protectorate **6.** dollar diplomacy.

Chapter Checkup **1. (a)** Few Americans had interest in foreign affairs. **(b)** Influential Americans had begun to discuss the need for overseas expansion. **2. (a)** Americans organized the overthrow of Queen Liliuokalani in January 1893. Then with the help of the U.S. Marines, they set up a new government and sent a delegation to Washington, D.C., to negotiate a treaty. **(b)** He was outraged at the actions of American sugar growers and the role of the marines in the revolt. **3. (a)** Created popular support for a warlike foreign policy. **(b)** Stirred up reader emotions and encouraged the clamor for war. **(c)** Outraged the American public and created a call for war. **4. (a)** Missionaries were interested in converting the Chinese to Christianity, and merchants wanted to take part in the China trade. **(b)** Sent the Open Door notes calling on the Western nations in China to respect three principles: no power would prevent others from trading in its sphere of influence; tariffs in China would be collected only by the Chinese; no power would charge duties in its sphere that discriminated against other powers. **5. (a)** Asserted the right of the U.S. to intervene in Latin American affairs. **(b)** Sent American troops to stop a Cuban rebellion and set up a new government. **(c)** After Nicaragua defaulted on foreign debts and opposed the takeover of its customs service by the U.S., Taft sent marines to protect American interests there. **6.** Roosevelt offered to purchase the land for the canal from Colombia. When his offer was rejected, he supported a Panamanian revolt against Colombia. **7. (a)** The U.S. invited Russia and Japan to a peace conference in Portsmouth, New Hampshire. Through President Roosevelt's efforts, the two nations agreed to the Treaty of Portsmouth, which ended the war. **(b)** The U.S. was assured that China would be kept open to trade with all nations. **8.** Latin America, because in Latin America, U.S. bankers and investors replaced Europeans in economic affairs. No doubt the nearness of the U.S. to this area helped to account for its success in Latin America.

Critical Thinking   1. Confirm. The United States faced a Filipino rebellion led by Aguinaldo after it took control of the territory from Spain. President McKinley sent American troops to crush the revolt. The war against Aguinaldo's nationalists cost more money and lasted longer than the Spanish-American War. **2.** Answers will vary, but students might point to examples of military, political, and economic intervention of the United States in the affairs of Latin American nations as evidence of agreement with this appraisal.

Connecting Past and Present   1. In both periods Americans wanted to trade with China. In the 1800s, however, the U.S. did not regard China as an equal. It saw as its rivals for Chinese trade other Western powers. Today the U.S. seeks both economic and political ties with China as its equal and as one of the leaders of the Third World, or developing nations. In the late twentieth century Americans also see China as a counterbalance to the Soviet Union, the other communist giant. Superpower politics were not a concern in the 1800s. **2.** The U.S. is less dependent now than in the past, particularly in the area of military defense. Air travel has made the canal less important.

Developing Basic Skills   1. Actions to include in time line: purchase of Alaska (1867); U.S. shares control of Samoa with Great Britain and Germany (1889); Spanish-American War begins (1898); annexation of Hawaii (1898); Hay-Pauncefote Treaty (1901); U.S. granted Canal Zone (1903); Roosevelt Corollary to Monroe Doctrine (1904); U.S. supervises finances of Dominican Republic, initiates Treaty of Portsmouth (1905); U.S. restores order in Cuba (1906); U.S. Marines sent to Haiti (1915); U.S. troops sent to Nicaragua (1912). **(a)** The U.S. acquired new territory in the 1860s, 1880s, and 1890s. **(b)** The U.S. intervened militarily in other nations in the 1900s and 1910s. **2. (a)** Russia, Japan, Germany, France, and Great Britain. **(b)** Great Britain, France, the Netherlands, the U.S., and Japan.

Chapter 25   (pages 544–565)

The World at War ———

OVERVIEW
Chapter 25 focuses on United States entry into World War I and its contribution to final victory. Students explore the developments that led to the decision to enter the war and American support

of the war effort. They also read about President Wilson's role in formulating the peace treaty and the eventual defeat of that treaty.

HISTORICAL SIDELIGHTS
The following pieces of historical information can serve as notes of interest during the study of Chapter 25. The page numbers in parentheses indicate the points in the student text at which you may wish to introduce the information.

The Rough Rider (p. 551)   Theodore Roosevelt played the "Rough Rider" to the end of his life. When the United States entered World War I, Roosevelt proposed that he be made commanding general of a division of "horse riflemen," whom he would recruit from among his friends, just as he had done in the Spanish-American War. Although President Wilson was willing to grant the request, General Hugh Scott, army chief of staff, flatly vetoed the proposal. Scott argued that trench warfare made the use of cavalry obsolete and that Roosevelt, almost 60, was too old for a field command.

Stretching the Food Supply (p. 555)   In an effort to supply Britain with badly needed beef and other food supplies, Herbert Hoover encouraged Americans to eat less. "Wheatless Mondays" and "Meatless Tuesdays" were introduced. Restaurants served whale meat, shark steaks, and horse chops. One magazine admonished parents to watch their children: "Do not permit your child to take a bite or two from an apple and throw the rest away; nowadays even children must be taught to be patriotic to the core."

SECTION 1   (pages 545–548)
Woodrow Wilson and Moral Diplomacy

ACTIVITIES*
○ **Identification**   Ask students who or what is being referred to by each of the following clues: (1) secretary of state under President Wilson; (2) U.S. ship whose crew was held for a short time by Mexican soldiers; (3) Mexican dictator who was overthrown by Carranza; (4) Mexican revolutionary who led

---
*See "To the Teacher" for an explanation of the symbols.

a revolt against Carranza; (5) brigadier general who led United States troops into Mexico. *Answers:* **1.** Bryan **2.** Dolphin **3.** Huerta **4.** Villa **5.** Pershing

☆ **Comparing** Have students construct a chart with columns titled Moral Diplomacy and Big Stick Diplomacy and rows titled Incident, Nations Involved, and Effect. Have students use the material in this section and in Chapter 24, Section 3, to fill in the chart. Then lead a discussion on the merits of the two approaches to foreign policy.

☐ **Writing a Speech** Tell students to imagine that they are speech writers for Secretary of State William Jennings Bryan. Ask them to write a speech for Bryan in which he attempts to convince California officials to change their policy toward ownership of land by Japanese immigrants. Encourage students to do further research about the topic.

ANSWERS: SECTION 1 REVIEW (page 548)

1. moral diplomacy—p. 545; Victoriano Huerta, Venustiano Carranza, Francisco "Pancho" Villa, John Pershing—p. 547. **2.** To foster world peace by encouraging disputants to refrain from acts of war for one year while an international committee investigated their disputes. **3.** Haiti and the Dominican Republic. **4.** Huerta proclaimed himself military dictator. **5.** Possible answer: It intervened in military and economic affairs and assumed a dominant role in the Western Hemisphere.

SECTION 2 (pages 548–552)
War in Europe

ACTIVITIES

○ **Map Reading** Ask students to study the map on text page 549. Have them use the map to make a list of the European Allies, the Central Powers, and the neutral nations during the war.

☆ **Ranking** Review what students have learned about multiple causation. Have them identify all the events or developments that led to the U.S. decision to declare war on Germany. List the answers on the chalkboard. When finished, the list should include the following causes: (1) cultural ties of many Americans to the British, (2) anti-German propaganda,

(3) German use of poison gas and submarines, (4) profitable sale of munitions, food, and other supplies to the Allies, (5) British purchase of cotton, (6) submarine attacks on neutral shipping, (7) Zimmerman Telegram, (8) overthrow of the czar in Russia. Divide the class into small groups and have each group rank the developments from most to least significant in the decision to declare war. When the groups have completed their ranking, ask representatives to explain their conclusions.

☐ **Recognizing Propaganda** Anti-German propaganda appeared on many posters in the U.S. during World War I. Have students locate an example of an anti-German poster from World War I and write a paragraph describing what impact it might have had on American opinion. Students can bring copies of the posters they found to class and present their conclusions as oral reports. Possible sources include *Words That Won the War: The Story of the Committee on Public Information* by James R. Mock and Cedric Larson.

ANSWERS: MAP STUDY (page 549)

Norway, Sweden, Denmark, Netherlands, Switzerland, Albania, Spain; about 10 miles (16 kilometers), in 1914.

ANSWERS: SECTION 2 REVIEW (page 552)

1. Central Powers—p. 549; Allies—p. 550, *Lusitania*—p. 551; Charles Evans Hughes, Zimmermann Telegram—p. 552. **2.** The assassination of Archduke Ferdinand. Strong nationalist feelings in the Balkans, imperialist rivalries, and competing alliances were underlying causes. **3. (a)** Through propaganda in American newspapers. **(b)** Allied effort. **4. (a)** By protesting to the German government. **(b)** Germany agreed to suspend unannounced attacks. **5.** The sinking of ships by submarines, the publication of the Zimmermann Telegram, and the Russian Revolution. **6.** Possible answer: His actions during the Spanish-American War had shown his desire for immediate action.

SECTION 3 (pages 553–556)
The Home Front

ACTIVITIES

○ **Identifying** Ask students who or what is being referred to in each of the following clues:

(1) head of the War Industries Board, (2) head of the Food Administration, (3) established controls over scarce materials, (4) planted in back yards to stretch the food supply, (5) head of the Committee on Public Information.

Answers: **1.** Baruch **2.** Hoover **3.** War Industries Board **4.** victory gardens **5.** Creel

☆ **Making a Chart** Draw the outline of a chart on the chalkboard with two columns, headed Action and Effect. Ask students what actions the government took to organize the U.S. war effort. List their responses in the first column. Then ask students to describe the effect of each of the actions listed and write their responses in the second column. When the chart is completed, lead a class discussion by asking the following three questions: (1) In what areas did government activity increase? (2) Why did increased government activity seem necessary in wartime? (3) Do you think the government's actions were necessary in each case?

☐ **Analyzing a Primary Source** Songs often play an important role in stimulating patriotism during a war. In World War I, songs such as "Over There" by George M. Cohan were enormously popular. Have students study the words of "Over There" or another patriotic song from the war and write an essay in which they describe what effect they think the song had on the public. The words to "Over There" and other World War I songs can be found in *Legion Airs: Songs of the Armed Forces* edited by Lee O. Smith.

ANSWERS: AMERICAN ENTERPRISE (page 554)

1. To impose order on the chaos of American industry by forcing cooperation between the business community and the government in the interest of the war effort. **2.** During a wartime situation, the narrow needs of business may have to give way to the broader interests of the nation as a whole.

ANSWERS: SECTION 3 REVIEW (page 556)

1. War Industries Board, Bernard Baruch, William Gibbs McAdoo—p. 554; National War Labor Board, Herbert Hoover—p. 555. **2.** Through voluntary enlistments and the draft. **3.** By establishing an eight-hour workday in some industries, standards for employment of women and children, and fair wages for workers. **4.** By observing meatless and breadless days and by planting "victory" gardens in their back yards. **5.** To increase public support for the war. **6.** Possible answer: Treating dissent as treason violates the First Amendment guarantee of free speech, thereby limiting a basic constitutional right.

SECTION 4 (pages 557–560)
The United States in the War

ACTIVITIES

○ **Vocabulary Building** Have students define the following words or phrases and use each in a sentence (the numbers in parentheses refer to the text pages on which the words first appear): convoy (p. 558), armistice (p. 559), reparations (p. 559), territorial integrity (p. 559), self-determination (p. 559).

☆ **Using Visual Evidence** Ask students to study photographs of World War I military action in books such as *The Story of World War I* by Robert Leckie. Have them write an essay describing what they learned about the war through this study of visual evidence.

☐ **Relating Past to Present** Have students review coverage of Lincoln's plan for Reconstruction (text page 379). Ask students to write an essay in which they answer the following questions: (1) Why were the post-Civil War and post-World War I periods difficult and sensitive times? (2) Why do you think Lincoln and Wilson urged leniency toward the defeated forces? (3) Do you agree or disagree with the approach to peace taken by Lincoln and Wilson?

ANSWERS: SKILL LESSON (page 557)

1. (a) Excerpt from a novel. **(b)** John Dos Passos. **(c)** 1919. **2. (a)** An American soldier. **(b)** Walking down the side of a hill or mountain onto a battlefield. **(c)** Frightened. **3. (a)** Disillusioned. **(b)** Yes. His account of the war suggests a sense of futility and impending doom. **4. (a)** The war was a terrifying experience for those who fought in it. **(b)** The excerpt is not based on a study of large numbers of combat troops.

ANSWERS: VOICES OF FREEDOM (page 560)

1. Self-determination, avoidance of entangling alliances, government by the consent of the governed, freedom of the seas, moderation of armaments. **2.** Possible answers: treaties limiting arms production and deployment, attempts at free elections in Latin America, establishment of independent nations in former colonies.

ANSWERS: SECTION 4 REVIEW (page 560)

1. Fourteen Points—p. 560. **2.** convoy—p. 558; reparations, territorial integrity, self-determination —p. 559. **3.** The arrival of American troops and supplies in 1918. **4.** Kaiser Wilhelm II gave up his throne and the Germans set up a democratic government. **5.** Wilson's "liberal" peace would have guaranteed the territorial integrity of nations and the right of nations to self-determination, freedom of the seas, and protection from aggression. Wilson called for disarmament and public diplomacy. He urged rejection of reparations. **6.** Possible answer: With hindsight, it would seem that more lenient terms might have led to less bitterness and friction in the postwar period and to a more lasting peace.

SECTION 5   (pages 561–563)
Search for a "Just Peace"

ACTIVITIES

○ **Map Reading**   Have students study the map on text page 562. Ask: (1) Which nations were created from or gained land from Austria-Hungary? (2) Which nations were created from or gained land from Germany? (3) From Russia?

☆ **Analyzing a Primary Source**   Have students study the text of Article 10 of the Covenant of the League of Nations that follows. Ask them to write a paragraph in which they explain why they think Senator Lodge and others considered the article a threat to the United States.

The Members of the League undertake to respect and preserve, as against external aggression, the territorial integrity and existing political independence of all Members of the League. In case of any such aggression, or in case of any threat or danger of such aggression, the Council shall advise upon the means by which this obligation shall be fulfilled.

☐ **Researching**   Ask students to research the positions of France, Great Britain, and Italy at the Versailles peace conference. Have them write a report summarizing the goals of each country and explaining why those goals made President Wilson's task at the conference more difficult. Students could begin by consulting a textbook of European history.

ANSWER: MAP STUDY   (page 562)
Czechoslovakia.

ANSWERS: SECTION 5 REVIEW   (page 563)
1. Treaty of Versailles, League of Nations—p. 562; Henry Cabot Lodge, Article 10—p. 563. **2.** The

Republicans did not want the Democrats to use the peace to win votes; many Americans questioned whether the U.S. should join a world organization; Wilson's attempt to make the 1918 congressional elections a referendum on his policies backfired; he failed to appoint any influential Republicans to the Paris negotiating team; his decision to personally lead the delegation to Paris provoked criticism; the secrecy of the negotiations angered American reporters. **3. (a)** The treaty was negotiated in secret, violated the principles of national self-determination and impartial adjustment of claims, called for huge reparations to be paid by Germany, and contained a clause blaming Germany for the war. **(b)** The covenant allowed for withdrawal from the League, made participation in sanctions optional, and recognized the importance of the Monroe Doctrine in the Western Hemisphere. **4.** Some senators saw the League of Nations as a threat to American sovereignty and also wanted to avoid U.S. involvement in the internal affairs of other nations. Wilson refused to accept any but the mildest changes in the treaty. **5.** Possible answer: Members of the Senate, conscious of a growing isolationist sentiment, were unwilling to jeopardize their chances for reelection by ratifying the treaty.

ANSWERS: CHAPTER 25 REVIEW (page 564–565)
   Vocabulary   1. e **2.** c **3.** d **4.** b **5.** a
   Chapter Checkup   1. (a) Wilson supported a treaty that gave the U. S. a permanent option to build a second canal across Nicaragua. **(b)** Wilson sent marines into Haiti to restore order and protect American property. The Haitian government agreed to a U.S. protectorate over Haiti. **(c)** Wilson sent marines into the Dominican Republic. **2. (a)** He banned arms shipments to Mexico, then offered to mediate the dispute between Huerta and Carranza. He also offered to support the Carranza faction if it would guarantee the establishment of a constitutional government. **(b)** To pursue "Pancho" Villa, who had crossed the border to mount anti-American raids and had killed 19 Americans. **3. (a)** Neutrality. **(b)** The U.S. was a nation of immigrants and many people had strong emotional ties to distant homelands. **4. (a)** German submarines failed to provide warning that they were about to sink an enemy vessel so that the crew might escape. **(b)** Germany did not want to push the U.S. into war on the side of the Allies. **5. (a)** It created the War Industries Board to spur industrial production and coordinate war industries, attempted to organize all rail lines into a single national network, and built a merchant marine. **(b)** It created the National War Labor Board

to arbitrate between management and labor and supported improvements in conditions for American workers. **6.** American troops and supplies gave the Allies a numerical advantage and raised the morale of the British and French troops. **7. (a)** The first five points called for open treaties, freedom of the seas, free trade, arms reductions, and impartial adjustment of colonial claims. Points six through thirteen called for national self-determination and the realignment of borders changed during or before the war. Point fourteen called for the establishment of the League of Nations. **(b)** The Treaty of Versailles was negotiated secretly, recognized new nations created out of the old Austria-Hungary empire, awarded France Alsace-Lorraine and other territories, demanded the payment of reparations by Germany, and blamed Germany for the war. These aspects of the treaty violated the spirit as well as the stated goals of the Fourteen Points. **(c)** Because it provided for the establishment of the League of Nations. **8. (a)** By trying to make the 1918 congressional elections a referendum on his policies, by failing to appoint influential Republicans to the negotiating team, and by personally taking part in the negotiations. **(b)** They did not want an international body making decisions for the U.S.; they feared U.S. involvement in the affairs of other nations; they did not want the Democrats to use the peace to win votes. **(c)** To avoid U.S. involvement in the internal affairs of other nations; to protect Congress's authority to declare war.

Critical Thinking 1. (a) "Big stick" policy: Roosevelt believed a powerful military force was the best means of protecting American interests and security abroad. "Dollar diplomacy": Taft sought to avoid military conflicts, believing American investments abroad would do more to further American foreign policy. "Moral diplomacy": Wilson believed in the use of negotiation and arbitration rather than force or finance as the basis of foreign policy. **(b)** Answers may vary. Students should recognize that each President did become militarily involved in the affairs of other countries, whether he planned to or not. **2. (a)** While during the war it was women's patriotic duty to leave their homes to work for the good of the nation, once the war was over, it was their patriotic duty to give up their jobs to the returning soldiers. **(b)** Answers may vary, but students may suggest that some women needed jobs to support their families, or that women, like men, enjoyed working outside the home.

Connecting Past and Present 1. (a) In general, Mexico and Nicaragua are close neighbors, and events in those countries are bound to affect the United States. In recent years, concerns about Mexico have centered on illegal immigration, drug trafficking, and Mexico's large foreign debt. Concern about Nicaragua has centered on fears that the Sandinista government may be pro-Communist. **(b)** The long history of U.S. military, political, and economic intervention in Latin American affairs has made the countries of this region distrustful of U.S. intentions in the region. **2.** World War II and the events of the postwar period have made Americans more aware of the interdependence of the nations of the world and the need for global cooperation.

Developing Basic Skills 1. (a) Estonia, Latvia, Lithuania, Poland, Czechoslovakia, Yugoslavia, Austria, and Hungary. **(b)** Austria-Hungary. **(c)** Russia, Austria-Hungary, Germany, Bulgaria. **(d)** France. **2. (a)** The speech was written and delivered during World War I by a person directly involved. **(b)** Wilson's goal was a just and nonpunitive peace. **(c)** A diary account is a personal record; Wilson's speech is a public statement.

Unit Eight
The Years Between the Wars

Chapter 26   (pages 568–593)

Life in the 1920s _____

OVERVIEW

Chapter 26 tells about the political, economic, social, and cultural life of the 1920s. The turmoil of the immediate postwar period was followed by a time of calm and prosperity. Students examine the problems of farmers, blacks, and other minority groups. Students also read about material growth and about developments in the arts and in the popular culture of the Roaring Twenties.

HISTORICAL SIDELIGHTS

The following pieces of historical information can serve as notes of interest during the study of Chapter 26. The page numbers in parentheses indicate the points in the student text at which you may wish to introduce the information.

The Fear of Revolution (p. 571)   The remarkably swift success of the Russian Revolution, in which the Bolsheviks took over the government, led American conservatives to overestimate the power of radicals at home. One senator advocated sending American citizens with radical beliefs to a penal colony in Guam. In Indiana, a jury deliberated for only two minutes before acquitting a man who had shot and killed a radical for yelling, "To hell with the United States!"

New Products (p. 579)   During the 1920s, consumers were offered everything from cigarette lighters to wristwatches to book matches, dry ice, and Pyrex glass cooking ware. Synthetics such as rayon and cellophane revolutionized whole industries. George Washington Carver discovered a multitude of uses for the humble peanut, ranging from shaving lotion to axle grease. He made shoe polish and library paste from sweet potatoes.

A Fair Warning (p. 580)   The dramatic change brought by the automobile is perhaps best gauged by the fact that as late as 1900 Vermont had a law on its books requiring every automobile driver to hire "a person of mature age" to walk an eighth of a mile ahead of the auto, bearing a red flag. By 1928, such laws had long become obsolete, and the construction of highways had proceeded so rapidly that a motorist could drive from New York to Kansas on paved roads.

SECTION 1   (pages 569–573)
The Rocky Road to Peacetime

ACTIVITIES*

○ **Analyzing Cartoons**   Ask students to study the cartoon on text page 571 and answer the following questions: (1) Describe the Bolshevik shown in the cartoon. (2) Why do you think he is shown that way? (3) Give the cartoon a title. (4) Write a paragraph disagreeing with the cartoon.

☆ **Graph Reading**   Have students study the graphs on text page 572 and review the subsection Restrictions on Immigration. Then ask them to write answers to the following questions: (1) About what percentage of immigrants came from northern and western Europe between 1900 and 1920? (2) About what percentage came from eastern and southern Europe? How had that percentage changed by the 1920s and 1930s? (3) Write one generalization based on the graphs. (4) How do the graphs reflect laws passed by Congress during the 1920s?

□ **Expressing an Opinion**   Have students do additional research about the trial of Sacco

---

*See "To the Teacher" for an explanation of the symbols.

and Vanzetti. Possible sources include *Sacco and Vanzetti* by Fernando Quesada and *Sacco and Vanzetti* by Osmond Fraenkel. Then ask students to write an essay in which they state whether they think the two men received a fair trial. They should provide factual information to support their opinion.

ANSWER: GRAPH STUDY   (page 572)

The percentage of immigrants from the Americas increased markedly from the 1900–1920 period to the 1920–1940 period.

ANSWERS: SECTION 1 REVIEW   (page 573)

1. Calvin Coolidge—p. 570; Bolsheviks, A. Mitchell Palmer, Sacco and Vanzetti—p. 571. **2.** general strike—p. 570; quota system—p. 572. **3. (a)** During the war, labor unions had cooperated with employers to produce goods for the war effort. After the war, with prices rising and an overabundance of workers, many unions went on strike. **(b)** To many people, the strikes and other labor activities were no different from the actions of the Bolsheviks. **4.** Southern and eastern Europeans and Japanese. **5.** During the war, job opportunities had raised blacks' expectations. After the war, there was more competition for jobs and blacks often suffered discrimination. They could see that things had not changed so much after all. **6.** Possible answer: As people compete for jobs, distrust of "outsiders" often develops.

SECTION 2   (pages 574–578)
The Politics of Normalcy

ACTIVITIES

○ **Summarizing** Ask students to reread The Farm Problem on text page 577. Have them write a one-paragraph summary of the subsection and then work in groups to think of slogans that could have been used by farmers in the 1920s.

☆ **Using Statistics** Have students study the statistics shown in the following table. Then ask them to write a paragraph in which they explain whether the statistics support the conclusion that Andrew Mellon brought greater economy to the federal government. Have them cite specific information.

Government Finances, 1919–1924

Year	Income in $ Billions	Expenditures in $ Billions
1919	5.2	18.5
1920	6.7	6.4
1921	5.6	5.1
1922	4.1	3.4
1923	4.0	3.3
1924	4.0	3.0

Source: *Historical Statistics of the United States*

☐ **Analyzing a Quotation** Ask students to reread Senator George Norris's remark about Coolidge's appointments (see text page 576). Then have them answer the following questions: (1) Did Norris approve of Coolidge's appointments? (2) To what "congressional enactments" and "federal laws" do you think Norris is referring? (3) Do you think the fact that Norris was a progressive was related to his reaction? Explain.

ANSWERS: AMERICAN ENTERPRISE (page 577)

1. That it is good in every respect. **2.** Answers will vary.

ANSWER: GRAPH STUDY   (page 578)

1920–1930.

ANSWERS: SECTION 2 REVIEW   (page 578)

1. Warren G. Harding, Andrew Mellon, Fordney-McCumber Act—p. 574; McNary-Haugen bill—p. 577. **2.** normalcy—p. 574; parity—p. 577; migrant worker—p. 578. **3.** High tariffs; reduced taxes on higher incomes; a budgeting process for government departments that would promote efficiency and economy in government. **4.** The attorney general and a friend sold government favors; Charles Forbes, head of the Veterans Bureau sold supplies and kept the money; Teapot Dome scandal in which Secretary of the Interior Albert Fall leased government oil reserves in exchange for $400,000. **5.** Cut taxes on high incomes; appointed business people to government boards whose job was to regulate business. **6.** Farmers were hurt as farm prices fell while prices for goods farmers needed did not. Blacks also did not share in the prosperity; black sharecroppers in the South and black city dwellers in the North faced discrimination and poverty. Indians and Mexican-Americans, many of whom were migrant workers, also faced poverty and inadequate housing and poor health. **7.** Possible answer: worldwide overproduction; prices of goods needed by farmers; boll weevil and other pests; introduction of new synthetic fabrics.

SECTION 3 (pages 579–581)
A Decade of Material Progress

ACTIVITIES

○ **Drawing Conclusions** Have students choose an everyday activity, such as fixing their hair or preparing breakfast or collecting homework papers in class. Then ask them to do a time-and-motion study of the task—to analyze closely the steps that have to be followed to complete the task. Have them identify at least one step that could be eliminated or shortened. Ask students to demonstrate their improved method of doing the task. As a result of this exercise, do students think scientific management is a valid way of improving worker productivity?

☆ **Generalizing** Ask students to write one or two factual statements that support each of the following generalizations: (1) Electrical power was important to American society in the 1920s. (2) Frederick Taylor's research increased efficiency in industry. (3) Henry Ford contributed to the rapid growth of the automobile industry during the 1920s. (4) The automobile industry had a major impact on the nation's economy.

□ **Interviewing** Ask students to imagine that they are newspaper reporters in the early 1920s. Have them prepare a list of questions they would like to ask Henry Ford about his techniques of producing and selling automobiles. Then have students research the answers that Ford might have given to their questions.

ANSWERS: SECTION 3 REVIEW (page 581)

1. Frederick W. Taylor—p. 579; Henry Ford—p. 580. **2.** scientific management—p. 579; assembly line—p. 580. **3.** By teaching workers how to do their jobs more efficiently, Taylor's studies led to an increase in output of 300 percent. **4.** By employing the assembly line method of production, Henry Ford was able to produce cars inexpensively. **5.** Possible answers: improvement of highways; growth of suburbs; growth of related industries, such as construction, rubber, steel, glass, roadside conveniences for motorists. **6.** Possible answer: Airline industry; has made rapid travel over long distances available to large segments of the population.

SECTION 4 (pages 581–583)
The Jazz Age

ACTIVITIES

○ **Analyzing Art** Have students look closely at the work by Picasso on page 582. Ask them to share their reactions to it. Then suggest they contrast it to the work by Grant Wood on page 583. Ask which they find more pleasing or interesting and have them explain why.

☆ **Using a Primary Source** Have students read "The Diamond as Big as the Ritz" or another story from F. Scott Fitzgerald's collection *Six Tales of the Jazz Age.* Interested students might read parts aloud. Then have the class write a short essay explaining what Fitzgerald's story tells them about the 1920s.

□ **Making an Oral Report** Ask students to research one poet of the Harlem Renaissance. In addition to learning about the poet's life, they should read some examples of his or her poetry. Have them prepare an oral report on the poet that includes a reading from the person's work.

ANSWERS: SECTION 4 REVIEW (page 583)

1. Harlem Renaissance, Langston Hughes—p. 581; Marcus Garvey—p. 582; Gertrude Stein, Ernest Hemingway, F. Scott Fitzgerald, Sinclair Lewis, T. S. Eliot—p. 583. **2.** expatriate—p. 583. **3. (a)** West African rhythms, black work songs and spirituals, minstrel songs, the harmonies of European music, ragtime, and the blues. **(b)** Because it was a music that was alive and experimental, as was the era. **4.** Largely through music and literature. **5. (a)** Artists of the 1920s broke with many traditions and tried new forms. **(b)** They found it meaningless and empty. **6.** Accept any answer that shows a logical connection between the arts and today's values and ideals.

SECTION 5 (pages 584–587)
Changing Times

ACTIVITIES

○ **Relating Past to Present** Have students list persons they consider heroes today. Ask them to compare the kind of people who are heroes today with heroes of the 1920s.

☆ **Finding the Main Idea**   Divide the class into six groups and assign each group one of the subsections in Section 5. Tell each group to write a statement that reflects the main idea of the subsection. Then have them write two other statements about the subsection that are true but are not the main idea. Have each group write the three statements on the chalkboard in random order. Ask the other students to decide which of the statements is the main idea.

☐ **Making an Oral Report**   Ask students to research early silent films and prepare an oral report. Possible topics include the technology used, film stars, public response to the subjects of the movies.

ANSWERS: THE AMERICAN EXPERIENCE

(page 586)

1. They were able to blend into city neighborhoods because of their use of disguises and Izzy's knowledge of languages. **2.** It means that it might be noble for Americans to stop drinking alcohol, but it was unrealistic to pass a law forcing them to do so.

ANSWERS: SECTION 5 REVIEW   (page 587)

1. *The Jazz Singer,* Gertrude Ederle, Charles A. Lindbergh—p. 584; Eighteenth Amendment—p. 585; League of Women Voters—p. 587. **2.** flapper—p. 587. **3.** It made the world smaller by speeding the dissemination of information; it changed family life by introducing a new leisure-time activity. **4.** Some, such as the flappers, embraced the changes. Others tried to find reassurance in old values and a return to religion. **5.** They received the vote and became more active in political issues; many more women began to work outside the home; they experienced more social freedom. **6.** Possible answer: It could improve the quality of people's lives by making more goods available to more people. It could harm society by stressing materialistic values.

ANSWERS: CHAPTER 26 REVIEW

(pages 588–589)

Vocabulary   **1.** c   **2.** b   **3.** e   **4.** d   **5.** a

Chapter Checkup   **1. (a)** Unemployment caused by demobilization and rising prices as consumers demanded products unavailable during the war. **(b)** Workers demanded higher wages to meet the increasing cost of living; their demands were often rejected by employers. **2. (a)** Many foreigners immigrated to the United States and competed for jobs. In addition, terrorist activities were blamed on foreigners. **(b)** The laws decreased the flow of immigrants. They reduced the number of immigrants from southern and eastern Europe. **3. (a)** Mellon favored a high tariff to protect American business; Congress passed the Fordney-McCumber Act in 1922, which raised tariffs to a new high. Mellon also believed that taxes on large incomes should be reduced. The Revenue Act of 1921 was one law that cut taxes on higher incomes. **(b)** Cut taxes on high incomes; appointed business people to head agencies that were meant to regulate business. **(c)** They felt that the policies undermined Congress's intention to regulate business. **4. (a)** Farmers suffered from a reduction in farm prices after the war, which cut their earnings at the same time that other products were costing more. **(b)** Congress passed the McNary-Haugen bill, a law designed to give farmers parity, but Coolidge vetoed it. He said, "Farmers have never made money." **5. (a)** It made home life more enjoyable. Americans could use such consumer goods as refrigerators, vacuum cleaners, and radios. **(b)** Electricity increased industrial production. Factory output increased by 25 percent from 1921 to 1928, and output per work hour increased by 35 percent from 1920 to 1929. **6.** Black pride and the problems of prejudice and discrimination faced by blacks in American society. **7. (a)** American writers and others who felt disillusioned. **(b)** They saw only meaninglessness and uncertainty in the world. They expressed this hopeless feeling in their writings. **8. (a)** Radio speeded communication and introduced a new type of leisure-time activity. **(b)** Introduced a new popular pastime and made heroes of screen entertainers. **(c)** Led to widespread lawbreaking by people who opposed the law; the violation of the law caused a backlash that led many people back toward traditional values.

Critical Thinking   **1. (a–b)** Answers may vary. Students should recognize that Harding and Coolidge appointed people who favored business to head regulatory agencies; this meant that businesses would be regulated in a way that would help businesses. They turned a blind eye to business operations that bordered on the illegal; this helped some people get rich. They favored high tariffs to protect American goods. They favored cuts in taxes on the wealthy, which would make possible more investment. **2. (a)** The writers of the Lost Generation were critical of the obsession Americans had with material wealth and conformity. **(b)** Answers may vary. Students might point to the idolizing of sports and screen heroes as examples of conformity. **3. (a)** Possible answers: People had more money to spend on luxuries; radio was an activity families could share, an idea that appealed to many people at the time. **(b)** In 1922, only two years after the first radio broadcast, sales of radios reached $60 million. By 1929, people had spent $843 million on radios.

Connecting Past and Present **1. (a)** Unions provide a measure of job security, as well as other benefits to members. When union members have jobs, they will have money to spend on goods, thus giving jobs to others as well. **(b)** Unions have not been able to guarantee large raises every few years for their employees; they have had to make concessions in order to keep some companies afloat, as in the automobile and airline industries; also, some states have laws that discourage union membership. **2. (a)** It was similar in that families often listened together and spent a good deal of time listening. **(b)** Answers may vary. Students should recognize that listening to the radio is no longer likely to be a family activity. It is no longer the principal form of entertainment in people's homes. With the development of the Walkman type of radio, it is to a great extent portable entertainment.

Developing Basic Skills **1. (a)** Southern and eastern Europe. **(b)** Northern and western Europe experienced a percentage decrease in immigration to the United States, whereas southern and eastern Europe and Asia experienced an increase. **2.** Research will vary.

SPIRIT OF AMERICA   (pages 590–593)

ANSWERS: SPORTS IN AMERICA   (page 591)
1. With less demanding labor, people needed some form of physical activity. **2.** It can benefit society by teaching teamwork, fair play, and the importance of working hard to reach a goal, but too much emphasis on sports and competition can harm a society.

ANSWERS: NOTABLE AMERICANS   (page 593)
1. Its heroes and their amazing performances in winning the World Series in four straight games captured the imagination of the public. **2.** The feats of the 1927 Yankees—both as individuals and as a team—demonstrated strength, self-reliance, courage, and determination.

ANSWERS: VOICES OF FREEDOM   (page 593)
1. Grange has an alert mind, thinks quickly, runs like a flash, and can topple the opposition seemingly without effort. **2.** Possible answer: Television makes it possible for viewers to "see" the details of a sports event, often better than a spectator at the event. Students may feel that it still does not convey the same sense of excitement provided by reports like the one by Harry Cross.

Chapter 27   (pages 594–609)
From Prosperity to Despair _____

OVERVIEW
Chapter 27 focuses on the developments in the United States economy from 1928 to 1932. Students read about the onset of the Great Depression and the effect it had on millions of Americans. They examine President Hoover's attempts to deal with the depression and his eventual reelection defeat by Franklin D. Roosevelt.

HISTORICAL SIDELIGHT
The following piece of historical information can serve as a note of interest during the study of Chapter 27. The page number in parentheses indicates the point in the student text at which you may wish to introduce the information.

Labor-Saving Devices (p. 604) During the depression, many cities stopped using labor-saving devices such as snow-removal machines and steam shovels because the machines took jobs away from workers. They reverted to the pick and shovel in order to give jobs to unemployed laborers. One member of Congress even urged that the patent office refuse to grant patents on labor-saving devices.

SECTION 1   (pages 595–599)
The Bubble Bursts

ACTIVITIES*
○ **Analyzing a Quotation** Ask students to think about Herbert Hoover's 1928 statement, "We in America are nearer to the final triumph over poverty than ever before in the history of any land." Have them make a list of conditions that might have led people to question Hoover's conclusion.

☆ **Applying Information** Have students review the subsections titled Get-Rich-Quick Fever and The Crash on text pages 597 and 598.

_____

*See "To the Teacher" for an explanation of the symbols.

Then have volunteers play the following roles: a land speculator, a stockbroker, an on-margin investor, a conservative investor, and a banker. Have students reenact the process that led to the stock market crash in October 1929.

☐ **Comparing** Have students write an essay comparing the two major presidential candidates in the election of 1928. They should evaluate the strengths and weaknesses of each candidate from the perspective of 1928. Have them conclude by indicating whom they think they would have voted for at the time.

ANSWERS: AMERICAN ENTERPRISE (page 596)

1. In a bull market there are many buyers and prices go up. In a bear market, prices fall. **2.** Possible answers: Strong economy where it appears that businesses are doing well. Situation where people have enough money to buy what they need with enough left over to invest in stocks.

ANSWERS: SECTION 1 REVIEW (page 599)

1. Herbert Hoover, Al Smith—pp. 596–597. **2.** on margin, margin calls—p. 598. **3.** Because the nation appeared to be so prosperous. **4.** Hoover believed that farmers should cooperate to solve their problems. Smith urged government action. **5.** Land and stocks. **6.** Possible answer: The public ignored the signs of the coming depression, and some people gambled on the stock market. Business favored the high tariffs that contributed to the worldwide economic slowdown and continued to produce large quantities of goods in excess of demand. Many banks made risky loans to speculators in the stock market. Government adopted a laissez-faire attitude toward business and so took no steps to regulate stock market practices.

SECTION 2   (pages 599–603)
The Grim Years Begin

ACTIVITIES

○ **Using Visual Evidence** Ask students to study the photograph and drawing on text page 600. Have them write a paragraph in which they explain how the two illustrations show the human impact of the depression.

☆ **Constructing a Graph** Ask students to use the statistics that follow to construct a bar graph showing the number of bank failures between 1928 and 1933. When they have completed their graphs, have them write a para-

graph in which they summarize the conclusions they can draw from the graph.

Year	1928	1929	1930	1931	1932	1933
Number of Failures	499	656	1,352	2,294	1,146	4,004

Source: *Historical Statistics of the United States*

☐ **Researching** Have students do additional research about the international repercussions of the onset of the depression in the United States and write a report about their findings. They might begin by consulting a textbook on European history.

ANSWERS: SKILL LESSON   (page 601)

1. (a) 11. **(b)** It rose to about 23 in 1929. **(c)** The average yearly income of farmers increased from about $550 in 1922 to about $650 in 1929. **(d)** Manufacturing workers. **(e)** The results of wild speculation in Florida land. **(f)** He believed that changes in the business cycle were a thing of the past. **2. (a)** The economy was becoming more prosperous. **(b)** Confirm. **(c)** No. The quotation represented an optimistic view of the economy, while the picture presents a more depressing assessment. **3. (a)** Yes. During most of the decade, wages in farming, manufacturing, and government service increased. Stock market prices reached new highs. **(b)** Although on the average workers' wages rose, they were still not high enough to buy all the consumer goods that were being produced. In addition, farm wages were indicative of the low state of the farm economy. **(c)** In this paragraph students should refer to the increased use of new products, new techniques of production and management, the stock market boom and collapse, and the groups that did not share in the general prosperity.

ANSWERS: GRAPH STUDY   (page 602)

(left) 1926–1929; 1929–1932; (right) stock prices.

ANSWERS: GRAPH STUDY   (page 603)

1921–1922.

ANSWERS: SECTION 2 REVIEW   (page 603)

1. durable goods, business inventory—p. 599. **2.** Supply greatly exceeded demand by the late 1920s. Workers were not making enough money to buy the products industry was making. **3.** Banks that had loaned large sums to speculators tried to collect on their loans. Speculators were unable to repay the banks, and many banks then went bankrupt. **4.** Because each part of the economy affected another part. Businesses failed; then workers were laid off; then people had little money to spend, which caused more layoffs and bankruptcies, and so on. **5.** In the past, more people lived on farms and could at least feed themselves. With most of the people living in the cities and working in the depressed industries, this was no longer true. Also, this depression was worldwide. **6.** Possible answer: There seems to be an inverse relationship between the two—when GNP is high, unemployment is low; when GNP is low, unemployment is high.

SECTION 3   (pages 603–607)
Failure of Traditional Remedies

ACTIVITIES

○ **Relating Cause and Effect** Ask students to write one "effect" statement for each of the following events: (1) Pressure for more government action mounted during 1931. (2) Demands on private and local relief agencies grew. (3) The Senate failed to pass the Bonus Bill.

☆ **Summarizing** Ask students to write an essay in which they summarize the steps that President Hoover thought the government should take to turn the economy around. Have them explain why the President opposed more direct government involvement.

□ **Analyzing a Quotation** Tell students that one of the Republican party's most well-known slogans in the election of 1928 had been "A Chicken in Every Pot, a Car in Every Garage." Then read them the following extract. Have them write an essay in which they discuss how the public mood had changed between 1928 and 1932.

The roads of the West and Southwest teem with hungry hitchhikers. The camp fires of the homeless are seen along every railroad track. I saw men, women, and children walking over the hard roads. Most of them were tenant farmers who had lost their all in the late slump in wheat and cotton. Between Clarksville and Russellville, Ark., I picked up a family. The woman was hugging a dead chicken under a ragged coat. First she told me she had found

it dead in the road, and then added in grim humor, "They promised me a chicken in the pot, and now I got mine."

ANSWER: CHART STUDY   (page 607)
Minor candidates did not poll enough votes to affect the outcome of the election.

ANSWERS: SECTION 3 REVIEW   (page 607)
1. Reconstruction Finance Corporation—p. 605; Bonus Army—p. 606; Franklin Delano Roosevelt—p. 607. **2.** Provide moral leadership during the crisis. **3.** Congress gave the RFC the right to lend money to communities for public works programs. **4.** It lowered their opinion. **5.** That government should try anything that might work in an effort to bring relief to the nation. **6.** Possible answer: Despite their hardship, people did not resort to violence or other extreme measures to improve their condition. Instead, as the Bonus Army march to Washington for relief demonstrated, they continued to have confidence in the government and in its willingness and ability to help.

ANSWERS: CHAPTER 27 REVIEW
                    (pages 608–609)
   Vocabulary 1. b **2.** b **3.** a **4.** c **5.** c
   Chapter Checkup 1. Wages did not keep pace with prices; decline in demand for goods; increasing unemployment; poor state of coal mines, textiles, and agriculture; a slowdown in housing construction and automobile production; large industrial inventories; overspeculation to "get rich quick." **2.** Hoover was wealthy, efficient, and a humanitarian. He believed that economic problems, such as those of the farmers, would correct themselves. He believed in the philosophy of "rugged individualism." Smith was governor of New York, a Catholic, more middle class, and the son of immigrant parents. Smith favored an active role by government in the economy. He advocated government ownership of some electric companies and direct aid to farmers. **3. (a)** By investing money in the Florida land boom and in the stock market. **(b)** Two severe hurricanes in 1926. **(c)** Investors bought stock by using a small down payment and borrowing the remainder on margin from their brokers. **4. (a)** The imbalance slowed production, created layoffs, and lowered wages. **(b)** Because durable goods are expensive, they tend not to be purchased when money is tight. **(c)** Faced with increasing inventories, industries had to reduce production and lay off workers. **(d)** They shook confidence in other banks. As people withdrew their money, the money supply decreased. **5. (a)** Millions of people were out

of work. People bought only the necessities of life. Rents and mortgages went unpaid, and many people became homeless. Life savings were lost through bank closings. Many people became destitute. **(b)** Foreign investors pulled their money out of American banks. A key bank in Vienna failed; European economies collapsed. **6. (a)** Hoover's advisers favored a hands-off policy. **(b)** By making public pronouncements and sponsoring economic conferences. **(c)** Only those public works programs that the government had the cash to pay for. **7. (a)** The RFC was given the power to make loans to troubled banks, railroads, and insurance companies and to communities to fund public works programs. **(b)** It spent the money to solve the problems of business and industry, reasoning that the money would "trickle down" to ordinary people. **8. (a)** Through private, voluntary agencies. **(b)** The strategy was not successful because the number of people who needed relief far exceeded the capacity of the agencies to provide it.

Critical Thinking **1. (a)** The RFC was intended to solve the problems of business and industry, and the benefits were to have "trickled down" to ordinary people. **(b)** Possible answer: Hoover, a self-made man who believed in the laissez-faire theory of government, believed that other people should be able to take care of themselves. **2.** Poor morale, lack of confidence, and despair under Hoover led most people to seek a change.

Connecting Past and Present **1.** Farmers today also have a problem with earnings going down while prices of goods they must buy go up. Some farmers have lost their farms because they could not keep up their mortgage payments to the bank. **2.** The crash in 1929 was more severe because people were so little prepared for it and there were few safeguards. Today there are protections, such as FDIC, and stock market regulations, such as those governing the buying of stock on margin. **3.** During the Hoover administration, the government was involved very little in the economy. There were a few regulatory agencies, but they did not have a large impact on the way business was conducted. Today, partially as a result of the Great Depression, the government is much more involved in regulating business. There are strict rules governing the sale of stock; there are regulations concerning the conduct of businesses; there is government involvement in farm output and farm prices; there are rules against discrimination in hiring; and so on.

Developing Basic Skills **1.** Research will vary. Students should find evidence that the stock market was unstable and that there was a downward movement of stock prices preceding the crash.

2. (a) 472 electoral votes. **(b)** 22,809,638 popular votes. **(c)** 5,633,092 more popular votes in 1928 than in 1932. **(d)** The public had lost its confidence in Hoover's ability to cope with the problems of the Great Depression.

Chapter 28 (pages 610–627)

A New Deal _____

OVERVIEW
Chapter 28 focuses on the early years of the New Deal. Students read about the roots of the New Deal and the flurry of legislation passed during the first hundred days of Franklin D. Roosevelt's first term in office. They also analyze criticism of the New Deal and the reform measures passed in 1935.

HISTORICAL SIDELIGHT
The following piece of historical information can serve as a note of interest during the study of Chapter 28. The page number in parentheses indicates the point in the student text at which you may wish to introduce the information.

A Colorful Figure (p. 621) Senator Huey Long of Louisiana gained wide publicity not only because of his share-the-wealth ideas, but also because of his informal and often controversial style. For example, once when the commander of a German warship requested an audience, Long received the startled officer in lime-green silk pajamas.

SECTION 1 (pages 611–613)
The Roots of the New Deal

ACTIVITIES*
○ **Identification** Ask students to identify who is being referred to by each of the following clues: (1) person who said, "The only thing we have to fear is fear itself," (2) secretary of the interior under Franklin Roosevelt, (3) two leaders of Roosevelt's brain trust, (4) person who said, "We are at the end of our rope,"

---

*See "To the Teacher" for an explanation of the symbols.

(5) first woman to hold a cabinet position.
   Answers: **1.** Franklin Roosevelt **2.** Ickes **3.** Moley and Tugwell **4.** Hoover **5.** Perkins

☆ **Making a Chart** Draw the outline of a chart on the chalkboard with the following three headings: From Personal Experiences, From National Experiences, Others. Ask students to describe the experiences and ideas that formed the roots of the New Deal. Record their responses in the appropriate column of the chart. When the chart is completed, ask students which experiences they think were most important in the formulation of the New Deal. Have students speculate about what actions they think Roosevelt would take based on the ideas that formed the roots of the New Deal.

☐ **Researching** Ask students to read about President Roosevelt's brain trust and make a list of the chief members. Have students write brief biographical sketches of several of them. Then conduct a class discussion about the characteristics those persons had in common.

ANSWERS: SECTION 1 REVIEW   (page 613)

1. brain trust, Harold Ickes, Henry Wallace, Frances Perkins—p. 612. **2.** Roosevelt learned from having lost the use of his legs through polio that through courage and determination he could succeed against adversity. **3.** The progressive movement, lessons learned during the World War, the brain trust, and Roosevelt's cabinet. **4.** Hoover felt he had done all he could do, after taking certain actions to set in motion the "trickle down" of money. Roosevelt was optimistic that many new approaches could be tried and that some of them would work to bring relief from the depression. **5.** Possible answer: They were attracted by his pledge to take bold action to solve the problems the country and its people were facing. Also, some of these Republicans had been allied with President Theodore Roosevelt in his progressive reform efforts.

SECTION 2   (pages 613–620)
The First Hundred Days

ACTIVITIES

○ **Map Reading** Ask students to study the map on text page 618 and answer these questions: (1) How is the area that receives electric power from the TVA shown on the map? (2) What states are included in that area? (3) What are the two main rivers in the TVA system?

(4) Which cities are within the area served by the TVA electric power?

☆ **Writing a Diary** Tell students to imagine that they are working for the Civilian Conservation Corps. Have them write several diary entries in which they describe their work and their opinion of the value of the program. Encourage students to do additional research about the agency.

☐ **Using Fiction as Historical Evidence** Have students read a story or novel about life in the early days of the New Deal. One example is *Dunbar's Cove* by Borden Deal. Have students write a report in which they respond to these questions: (1) What is the topic of the story or novel? (2) What can you learn about life in the early days of the New Deal from the story or novel? (3) In what ways is the story or novel limited as historical evidence? (4) What other types of evidence would also help you understand the human side of the New Deal?

ANSWERS: VOICES OF FREEDOM   (page 616)

1. Hand gestures, smiles, nods. The listeners might cry or laugh; they reacted to the chats as if they were talking with a friend. **2.** If a President communicates well with the public, the people will tell their representatives to give the President a more sympathetic ear.

ANSWER: MAP STUDY   (page 618)

Kentucky.

ANSWERS: SECTION 2 REVIEW   (page 620)

1. fireside chat, Harry Hopkins—p. 614; Blue Eagle—p. 618. **2.** He declared a national "bank holiday," closing all banks to prevent further bank failures, and proposed the Emergency Banking Relief Act, which allowed banks to reopen if they had sufficient funds on hand to meet depositors' withdrawals; permitted sound banks to borrow federal funds; and closed unsound banks. **3. (a)** It gave money to local governments to give to the unemployed. **(b)** The CWA gave people jobs instead of simply handouts. **4. (a)** Permitted trade associations to draft codes that would regulate production, prices, and working conditions. **(b)** To stimulate employment by spending large sums of money on public works projects. **5.** Built dams, constructed hydroelectric power plants, made fertilizer that it sold to farmers at cost, planted trees to stop erosion, and introduced educational and health services. **6.** Possible answer: Roosevelt's policies were aimed at providing jobs, loans, or relief to those most in need. Hoover's policies provided for aid to trickle down to these people.

SECTION 3 (pages 620–622)
Critics of the New Deal

ACTIVITIES

○ **Name Game** Write the following clues on the chalkboard or duplicate and distribute copies. Ask students to use the clues to identify the names. Then have them use each name in a sentence. (1) American _____ League; (2) nickname of person whose motto was "Share the Wealth"; (3) former member of brain trust who became a bitter critic of the New Deal; (4) proposed government payments to older citizens; (5) believed that stronger action should be taken against banking and money interests.
Answers: **1.** Liberty **2.** Kingfish **3.** Moley **4.** Townsend **5.** Coughlin

☆ **Expressing an Opinion** Ask students to write a paragraph in which they state whether they agree with any of the critics of the New Deal discussed on text pages 621–622. They should support their opinion with facts and arguments.

□ **Researching** Have students research the Supreme Court's ruling on the unconstitutionality of either the NRA or the AAA. Ask them to prepare a report on their findings in which they describe the background of the case, why the legislation was declared unconstitutional, and the impact of the decision.

ANSWERS: SECTION 3 REVIEW (page 622)
1. Huey Long, Charles Coughlin, Francis E. Townsend—p. 621; American Liberty League, *Schechter* v. *United States*—p. 622. **2. (a)** Take money away from the very rich and use it to provide every American family with a house, a car, education for children, a pension for the elderly, and an income of $2,000 to $3,000 a year. **(b)** Action against banking and money interests. **(c)** Every person over 60 should receive $200 a month, if he or she would agree to retire and to spend all the money each month. **3.** Because these were not normal times when people would ignore such appeals; he did not want the United States to follow the path of some countries in Europe, where dictators were coming to power and taking extreme steps. **4.** The National Industrial Recovery Act and Agricultural Adjustment Act. **5.** Possible answer: The situation was desperate and called for drastic measures.

SECTION 4 (pages 622–625)
The Second New Deal

ACTIVITIES

○ **Generalizing** Have students write one or two factual statements that support each of the following generalizations: (1) The WPA provided jobs for a variety of workers. (2) The WPA met with limited success. (3) Organized labor benefited from the National Labor Relations Act. (4) Opposition to the Social Security Act was varied.

☆ **Writing an Editorial** Tell students to imagine that they are newspaper writers living in 1935. Have half the class imagine they are supporters of the New Deal and the other half imagine they are critics of the New Deal. Ask students to write editorials about one of the following measures of the second New Deal: Works Progress Administration, Wagner Act, Public Utilities Holding Company Act, Social Security Act. Ask volunteers from both sections to read their editorials. Lead a class discussion about the strengths of the various editorials and ask students which editorials they think are the most persuasive.

□ **Relating Past to Present** Have students read about present-day operation of the Social Security program. Then ask them to write an essay in which they evaluate the program in light of its original goals.

ANSWERS: NOTABLE AMERICANS (page 624)
1. Started a college; was adviser to President Roosevelt; was first black person to head a government agency. **2.** Because as a result of her persuasiveness, the President agreed to continue the NYA programs for minorities.

ANSWERS: SECTION 4 REVIEW (page 625)
1. Robert F. Wagner—p. 623. **2.** utility company—p. 624. **3. (a)** Widespread unemployment, including theater people, writers, and artists. **(b)** By putting people to work on a wide variety of projects in the fields in which the people had been trained. **(c)** Offered part-time jobs to young people so they could stay in school and earn money as well. **4.** The right to organize and bargain collectively. **5. (a)** The elderly, people who had lost their jobs, the handicapped, and certain dependent children. **(b)** Created a national system of pensions for retired people and a system of unemployment

insurance. **6.** Possible answer: Utility companies provide basic essential public services such as gas and electric service and are usually the only companies offering these services in a particular area.

ANSWERS: CHAPTER 28 REVIEW
(pages 626–627)

Vocabulary 1. brain trust **2.** bank holiday **3.** fireside chats **4.** Intrastate **5.** utility company

Chapter Checkup   1. Since childhood he had been taught that his wealth gave him a responsibility to help the less fortunate. His bout with polio had taught him sympathy for the disadvantaged and dedication to purpose. **2. (a)** Stressed conserving natural resources, regulating the way business was conducted, and improving working conditions. **(b)** Demonstrated that government agencies could work with business and agriculture to produce the right goods in the right quantities. **(c)** Provided ideas and plans for experimentation. **3. (a)** To save the banking system. **(b)** Banks could reopen if they had enough funds to meet withdrawal requests. Sound banks could borrow federal funds. Unsound banks would not reopen. **4. (a)** The Civilian Conservation Reforestation Act and the Federal Emergency Relief Act. **(b)** The Civilian Conservation Reforestation Relief Act set up the Civilian Conservation Corps (CCC), which enlisted single men, aged from 18 to 25, and sent them to camps where they planted trees, made reservoirs, built bridges, and developed parks. The FERA made relief payments to the unemployed through local and state welfare agencies. **(c)** To provide the unemployed with jobs rather than relief. **5. (a)** It called for the government to pay farmers not to plant part of their crop. Taxes on food processors would provide the funds to pay the farmers. **(b)** Farmers were asked to plow under crops that had already been planted. **6. (a)** It set up trade associations to draft codes for each industry that would stabilize production and end the price-cut, wage-cut cycle. **(b)** Codes dealt with too many details; some manufacturers ignored the codes. **7. (a)** To control flooding, provide electricity, and limit soil erosion. **(b)** Power companies objected to competing with a government agency. Others felt the government was interfering in local matters. **8. (a)** Long thought it was too conservative. He favored a "Share Our Wealth" program. **(b)** Coughlin believed that Roosevelt did not act strongly enough against "banking and money interests." **(c)** Townsend wanted government to do more for the elderly poor. **(d)** Moley charged that the New Deal was undermining the

free enterprise system. **9. (a)** Because the federal government could not regulate intrastate commerce. **(b)** Because the government could not tax one part of the population (food processors) to aid another part (farmers). **10.** The Emergency Relief Appropriations Act, which created the Works Progress Administration and the National Youth Administration; the Wagner Act; the Public Utilities Holding Company Act; and the Social Security Act.

Critical Thinking   1. (a) Workers were guaranteed the right to organize and to bargain collectively with management under the Wagner Act. **(b)** During the 1920s, unions lost much public support and union membership dropped. **(c)** Accept answers that refer to the New Deal's sympathetic stance toward organized labor. **2. (a)** Many critics of the New Deal believed that the federal government had imposed too many regulations on private industry. **(b)** Students might suggest that the New Deal transformed the federal government's role in the economy and changed the rules under which the free enterprise economy operated.

Connecting Past and Present   1. (a) Rural South, Appalachia, inner cities. **(b)** Possible answer: During the 1960s, large-scale government programs were tried in these areas without lasting success. Today, with massive deficits, the federal government is unlikely to commit the amount of funds that would be necessary for such programs to work. **2.** Measures that still exist today that might protect against hardship include FDIC, Social Security, farm-price supports. Should a depression occur today, Congress might try enacting laws such as the WPA as a way of employing people who had lost their jobs.

Developing Basic Skills   1. (a) Unemployment. **(b)** Industrial workers, employers, farmers, unemployed people, and residents of the Tennessee Valley. **2.** Research will vary.

Chapter 29   (pages 628–645)

The New Deal Continues

OVERVIEW

Chapter 29 focuses on the New Deal following Franklin Roosevelt's reelection in 1936. Students read about the controversy surrounding the President's attempt to reorganize the judiciary and about the recession of 1937–1938. They also examine new reform measures and life during the depression and New Deal.

HISTORICAL SIDELIGHT

The following piece of historical information can serve as a note of interest during the study of Chapter 29. The page number in parentheses indicates the point in the student text at which you may wish to introduce the information.

A Traveler (p. 642) Eleanor Roosevelt had a reputation for unflagging energy and a concern for the poor and neglected of the United States. In the first year of Franklin Roosevelt's administration, she traveled 40,000 miles to visit Americans in factories, at schools, in slums, and in hospitals. Her travels were so extensive that on one occasion in 1935 the Washington *Star* ran a headline announcing, "Mrs. Roosevelt Spends Night at White House."

the executive and judicial branches of government would have been upset.

ANSWER: GRAPH STUDY (page 630)

Business was on an upward swing but was still in a moderate recession.

ANSWERS: GRAPH STUDY (page 632)

Unemployment declined.

ANSWERS: SECTION 1 REVIEW (page 633)

1. Alfred M. Landon—p. 629. **2.** deficit spending—p. 633. **3.** Landon argued that he could manage New Deal programs more efficiently, waste less money, and achieve longer-lasting results. **4.** "Solid South," big-city "machines," organized labor, and blacks. **5.** Suffered a severe recession. **6.** Possible answer: His plan would have upset the separation of powers and the system of checks and balances established in the Constitution.

SECTION 1 (pages 629–633)
New Deal Gains and Losses

ACTIVITIES*

○ **Using Visual Evidence** Have students study the cartoon on text page 631 and answer these questions: (1) What is the topic of the cartoon? (2) What is the President suggesting in the cartoon? (3) Do you think the cartoonist favored the plan? Why?

☆ **Graph Reading** Ask students to study the graph on text page 632 and answer these questions: (1) About what percentage of the work force was out of work in 1932? (2) About what percentage was out of work in 1933? (3) How did the percentage change between 1933 and 1937? (4) What happened to the percentage in 1938? (5) Write one generalization based on the graph.

☐ **Expressing an Opinion** Have students write an essay in which they agree or disagree with the following statement: If Roosevelt's plan to increase the size of the Supreme Court had succeeded, the constitutional balance between

---

*See "To the Teacher" for an explanation of the symbols.

SECTION 2 (pages 634–638)
Further Reform

ACTIVITIES

○ **Placing Events in Time** Copy the following time line below on the chalkboard. Then read aloud the list of events that follows. Ask students to write the letter of the correct time period for each event on a sheet of paper.

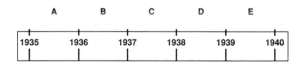

(1) Supreme Court rules first AAA unconstitutional; (2) Fair Labor Standards Act passed; (3) CIO formed; (4) Farm Security Administration organized; (5) Roosevelt reelected to second term; (6) second AAA passed.

Answers: **1.** B **2.** D **3.** A **4.** D **5.** B **6.** D

☆ **Using Fiction as Historical Evidence** Read the following brief extract from John Steinbeck's *The Grapes of Wrath:*

The dawn came, but no day. In the gray sky a red sun appeared, a dim red circle that gave a little light, like dusk; and as that day advanced, the dusk slipped back toward darkness, and the wind cried and whimpered over the fallen corn.

Men and women huddled in their houses, and they tied handkerchiefs over their noses when they went out, and wore goggles to protect their eyes. . . .

All day the dust sifted down from the sky, and the next day it sifted down. An even blanket covered the earth. It settled on the corn, piled up on the tops of the fence posts, piled up on the wires; it settled on roofs, blanketed the weeds and trees.

Ask students to write a paragraph in which they describe what they can learn about the Dust Bowl from the extract.

☐ **Relating Past to Present** In 1939, President Roosevelt created the Executive Office of the President. Since that time, the Executive Office has become an influential part of the federal government. Have students read about the Executive Office of the President in the most recent edition of the *United States Government Manual.* Ask different students to report on the various agencies that are now part of the Executive Office. The reports should include a description of the functions and the size of the agency staffs. You might want to duplicate copies of the organizational chart in order to help students visualize the operation of the office.

ANSWERS: ARTS IN AMERICA (page 636)

1. To create a pictorial record of rural life during the depression. **2.** Possible answer: It demonstrated that the depression was by no means over and that further New Deal actions were needed.

ANSWERS: SECTION 2 REVIEW (page 638)

1. John L. Lewis, Congress of Industrial Organizations—p. 634; Farm Security Administration, second Agricultural Adjustment Act—p. 637. **2.** industrial union, sitdown strike—p. 634. **3.** Every worker in entire industries, not just skilled workers. **4.** Established minimum wages and maximum hours of work in a number of industries and banned child labor. **5. (a)** A disastrous drought, lasting from 1932 to 1936, that eroded the soil in the Midwest and left a film of dust on everything in the region. **(b)** Many left their homes and traveled west in search of work. **6.** Possible answers: **(a)** For: reduces opportunity for abuse of power. **(b)** Against: prevents participation in election campaigns by some highly qualified people.

SECTION 3 (pages 638–643)
Life During the New Deal Years

ACTIVITIES

○ **Identifying** Have students identify each of the following people and explain their contribution to American life during the depression: (1) John Steinbeck, (2) Dorothea Lange, (3) Richard Wright, (4) John Collier, (5) Mary Dewson.

☆ **Using Visual Evidence** Tell students to make a chart with two columns headed Problems and Solutions. Have them review the illustrations that appear on text pages 610–645. Ask them to decide which photographs and paintings represent a problem faced by people during the depression or represent a solution that was attempted. Have them write the page number of the illustration in the appropriate column. When students have completed their individual charts, ask volunteers to list the illustrations they included in each column and explain their reasons for classifying the illustrations in that manner.

☐ **Researching** Have students do additional research and write a report about the effect of the depression and the New Deal on black Americans. Some students might want to report on individual members of the so-called black cabinet. (See the special feature on text page 624, *Mary McLeod Bethune.*) Other students may want to investigate topics such as living conditions, unemployment, or continued discrimination. Students might consult Ralph Ellison's novel *Invisible Man.*

ANSWERS: SKILL LESSON (page 643)

1. (a) David Kennedy. **(b)** The late 1960s. **2. (a)** He stated that Roosevelt saved the nation from complete collapse by giving it hope at the beginning of the Great Depression. **(b)** He grew disenchanted with Roosevelt when he found that the nation was not making as much progress under the New Deal as he had hoped. **3. (a)** Kennedy was a member of the Federal Reserve Board during the New Deal. As a government official, he might have been biased in favor of the Roosevelt administration's policies. **(b)** About 30 years. The intervening years may have changed his perception of events. **(c)** At the time of the interview, Kennedy was the chairman of the board of a major corporation. This experience may have given him an anti-New Deal perspective. **4. (a)** He gave the country hope and saved it from collapse. **(b)** It suggests that while the New Deal generated much hope, it did not always fully implement its programs.

ANSWERS: SECTION 3 REVIEW (page 643)

1. Frank Capra, John Steinbeck, Margaret Bourke-White, Richard Wright—p. 639; Mary Dewson—p. 641. **2.** They provided escape from daily worries. **3.** Employed Indians in soil erosion control, irrigation, and tribal land development programs. **4.** Thousands of Mexican workers were deported, along with their children, to make room for American workers. **5.** Frances Perkins was secretary of labor. Women also held various other posts, including minister to a foreign nation, director of the U.S. Mint, and judge on the Circuit Court of Appeals. Mary Dewson coordinated women's activities. **6.** Possible answer: They provided vivid portrayals of the suffering caused by the depression.

ANSWERS: CHAPTER 29 REVIEW

(pages 644–645)

Vocabulary **1.** Deficit spending **2.** Industrial unions **3.** sitdown strike **4.** Dust Bowl **5.** Okies

Chapter Checkup **1. (a)** The solid South, big-city machines, blacks, and organized labor. **(b)** By giving labor the right to organize and by taking an active interest in living conditions in the black community. **2. (a)** He hoped to change the makeup of the Court so that it would support New Deal measures. **(b)** No; both opponents and supporters of the New Deal opposed the court-packing scheme, arguing that it would upset the balance of power in the government. **3. (a)** The government cut back spending, thinking that the economy could now function on its own; the Federal Reserve Board raised interest rates; Social Security taxes left people with less money to spend. **(b)** He hoped that private business could solve the problem. **4. (a)** All industrial workers, not just skilled workers. **(b)** Sitdown strikes. **(c)** Somewhat; the United Auto Workers were successful at General Motors; the Goodyear Tire workers were successful. Steelworkers were not so successful. **5.** The Resettlement Administration attempted to resettle farmers on more productive land, the Farm Security Administration extended loans, the Forest Service promoted conservation, the Soil Conservation and Domestic Allotment Act encouraged farmers to stop growing soil-depleting crops and stimulated soil restoration, and the second Agricultural Adjustment Act regulated production and provided for storage in granaries. **6. (a)** Blacks were often the first to be fired, black tenant farmers and share-croppers often lost their land when production was reduced, and lynchings increased. **(b)** Moves were made to prevent discrimination in government programs; many blacks learned a trade through the CCC; more blacks held government positions during the New Deal. **7. (a)** Collier extended the benefits of New Deal relief and job programs to Native Americans. He stopped the sale of Indian land. He also saw to it that Indians received jobs as well as help in improving their farms. **(b)** It tried to restore tribal ownership of land, expand tribal land holdings, and encourage tribal self-government. It provided scholarships and funds for Indian-run businesses. **8. (a)** Many women were forced out of jobs, which were given to men. **(b)** She tried to ensure equal treatment for women in government programs. She encouraged the President to appoint more women to important positions.

Critical Thinking **1. (a)** It left the federal government much more actively involved in the economy. **(b)** It left behind certain institutions, such as the Social Security system and FDIC. It left behind airports, bridges, roads, and so on that were built at the time. It also left an attitude that people have had to address ever since about the proper role of government in society. **(c)** Answers will vary. Advocates might point out that the New Deal gave people hope and relieved some of the worst effects of the depression. Opponents might say that it damaged our institutions by allowing government to interfere in people's lives. **(d)** Answers will vary. **2.** Students could note that Roosevelt's plan might have weakened the independence of the Supreme Court. The contrary position could suggest that the Court's independence would be preserved by the constitutional provision granting lifetime tenure to the justices. **3. (a)** Helped Americans temporarily escape the reality of the Great Depression. **(b)** The importance of hard work, honesty, and cooperation among people to overcome life's difficulties.

Connecting Past and Present **1.** Possible answer: Because many workers today are more closely aligned with employers, as the two groups work together to keep companies productive. **2.** Possible answer: Movies are often less hopeful today, offering fewer happy endings. **3.** Possible answers: postal service, highways, taxes, regulations about fuel emissions on cars, regulations about acceptable labeling on consumer goods.

Developing Basic Skills **1. (a)** Commuters on a subway. **(b)** Possible answer: That life goes on, even in hard times. **(c)** That some people still had jobs; that mass transit was available during the depression; that people are absorbed in their own concerns; that, despite the hard times, people had a sense of dignity. **2.** Research will vary.

Unit Nine

War and the Search for Peace

Chapter 30   (pages 648–665)

Prelude to Another World Conflict _____

OVERVIEW

Chapter 30 focuses on U.S. international relations during the 1920s and 1930s. Students read about American isolationist sentiment and about threats to peace in Asia and Europe. The hope of ending aggression without direct U.S. involvement ended at Pearl Harbor in December 1941.

HISTORICAL SIDELIGHTS

The following pieces of historical information can serve as notes of interest during the study of Chapter 30. The page numbers in parentheses indicate the points in the student text at which you may wish to introduce the information.

An Economic Power (p. 650) Despite its posture of isolation during the 1920s, the U.S. had become one of the world's leading nations. The shift in the balance of power was dramatically illustrated in the country's foreign investment figures. Before World War I, U.S. citizens owed European investors $3 billion. By the end of the war, the situation had reversed itself, with foreign investors owing Americans approximately the same sum.

A Small Warning (p. 663) As U.S. ambassador to Japan, Joseph Grew saw the Japanese government's increasingly militant stance reflected in small events as well as large ones. In mid-1938 Grew, an ardent golfer, reported that golf balls with rubber cores had almost entirely disappeared from the Japanese market. Grew concluded that the Japanese government was drawing upon all

available rubber supplies in anticipation of military hostilities. Later, Grew correctly predicted that the Japanese fleet would attack the U.S. in Hawaii—something most military experts believed would not happen.

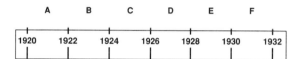

SECTION 1   (pages 649–652)

American Diplomacy From Harding to Hoover

ACTIVITIES*

○ **Placing Events in Time** Copy the time line below on the chalkboard. Then read aloud the following list of events. Ask students to write on a sheet of paper the letter of the correct time period for each event.

```
    A       B       C       D       E       F
 |--+---+---+---+---+---+---+---+---+---+---+--|
 1920    1922    1924    1926    1928    1930    1932
 |       |       |       |       |       |       |
```

(1) Washington Naval Conference held. (2) Japanese begin to occupy Manchuria. (3) U.S. marines withdraw from Nicaragua. (4) Dawes Plan adopted. (5) Five-Power Treaty negotiated. (6) Kellogg-Briand Pact signed.
Answers: **1.** A **2.** F **3.** C **4.** C **5.** A **6.** E

☆ **Making an Oral Report** Divide the class into small groups. Tell each group to prepare an oral report on foreign affairs in the 1920s using the following guidelines: (1) List events and developments of the 1920s. (2) Decide whether each event or development reflected isolation from world affairs or involvement in world affairs. (3) Decide whether U.S. actions in that area in general would be an example of isolation or involvement. When the groups have completed their reports, ask representatives to summarize their conclusions. Have each group defend its position and encourage the groups to reach a consensus.

---

*See "To the Teacher" for an explanation of the symbols.

☐ **Analyzing Primary Sources** Read the following extract or duplicate and distribute copies. Tell students that the extract contains remarks President Hoover made to the cabinet about the Japanese invasion of Manchuria in 1931.

First, this is primarily a controversy between China and Japan. The United States has never set out to preserve peace among other nations by force and so far as this part is concerned we shall confine ourselves to friendly counsel. . . .

Second, our whole policy in connection with controversies is to exhaust the processes of peaceful negotiation. But in contemplating these we must make up our minds whether we consider war as the ultimate if these efforts fail. Neither our obligations to China, nor our own interest, nor our dignity require us to go to war over these questions.

These acts do not imperil the freedom of the American people, the economic or moral future of our people. I do not propose ever to sacrifice American life for anything short of this.

Then ask: (1) What measures does Hoover think the U.S. could use to preserve peace among nations? (2) Does the President think the invasion is reason enough for the U.S. to go to war? Why or why not? (3) Under what conditions does Hoover think the nation should go to war?

ANSWERS: SECTION 1 REVIEW   (page 652)
1. Kellogg-Briand Pact, Dawes Plan—p. 650; Clark Memorandum, Stimson Doctrine—p. 651. **2.** isolationist, internationalist—p. 649. **3.** To discuss ways to ease tensions in the Pacific. **4.** Less emphasis was placed on armed intervention in Latin America. **5.** Possible answer: The Stimson Doctrine did not stop aggression by Japan.

SECTION 2   (pages 652–655)
International Challenges During the 1930s

ACTIVITIES

○ **Name Game** Read the following clues and ask students to identify who or what is being described by each clue: (1) established totalitarian control in Germany; (2) became a figurehead in the Japanese government; (3) leader of fascists in Spain; (4) proclaimed "good neighbor" policy toward Latin America; (5) Roosevelt's secretary of state; (6) dictator of Italy; (7) hoped to be powerful in Mediterranean and Africa; (8) suspended Allied war debts in 1931.
Answers: **1.** Hitler **2.** Hirohito **3.** Franco **4.** Roosevelt **5.** Hull **6.** Mussolini **7.** Italy **8.** Hoover

☆ **Comparing** Ask students to reread the special feature, Voices of Freedom (text page 654). Then have them write an essay in which they compare the attitude toward neutrality expressed by Senator Connally and the attitude expressed by Senator Vandenberg.

☐ **Researching** Have students research the rise to power of Mussolini in Italy or Hitler in Germany. In a written report, they should identify the political, social, and economic conditions that contributed to that rise. Students might consult a European history text.

ANSWERS: VOICES OF FREEDOM   (page 654)
1. Connally: Neutrality favors the aggressor; Vandenberg: Favoring one belligerent might lead to war. **2.** Answers will vary.

ANSWERS: SECTION 2 REVIEW   (page 655)
1. Benito Mussolini, Adolf Hitler—p. 652; Nye committee—p. 654; "good neighbor" policy—p. 655. **2.** totalitarian state—p. 652; devalue—p. 653. **3. (a)** Bitterness over the Treaty of Versailles, proclaiming Germans the "master race. **(b)** On the Jews within Germany. **4.** The civil war in Spain and increasing aggression by Germany, Italy, and Japan. **5.** Possible answer: No, U.S. economic and military ties with Europe today are too strong and too important to the country's well being.

SECTION 3   (pages 656–660)
The Threat of War

ACTIVITIES

○ **Supporting a Main Idea** Have students write two or three sentences supporting each of the following main ideas: (1) Agreements to promote peace and cooperation failed to prevent aggressive acts by Japan in Asia. (2) Roosevelt's efforts in 1937 to change isolationist sentiment did not succeed. (3) The appeasement policy of France and Britain failed.

☆ **Placing Events in Time** Have students arrange the following events in correct chronological order: (1) Germany annexes Austria; (2) Germany invades Poland; (3) German troops occupy Rhineland; (4) U.S. sends 50 destroyers to the British fleet; (5) Germany annexes Czechoslovakia; (6) Britain and France declare war on Germany; (7) Germany annexes the Sudetenland. Then ask them to write a paragraph describing the consequences of the events.
Answers: 3, 1, 7, 5, 2, 6, 4

☐ **Expressing an Opinion** Have students investigate the proposed Ludlow Amendment. Then ask them to write an essay in which they explain whether they think the amendment should have been passed by Congress and ratified by the states.

ANSWERS: MAP STUDY (page 657)

Possible answer: Since he had moved unchecked into the Rhineland, Czechoslovakia, and Austria, there was little reason to think he would not also move into Poland, which divided German territory.

ANSWERS: SECTION 3 REVIEW (page 660)

1. *Panay* incident—p. 656; Munich Conference—p.657; Neville Chamberlain—p.658; Winston Churchill—p. 660. **2.** appeasement—p. 657; blitzkrieg—p. 658. **3.** The U.S. continued to ship arms and war materials to China. **4.** Germany invaded Poland. **5.** Possible answer: Wilson had thought that neutrality might be possible, but Roosevelt saw the necessity of offering aid to the nations combating totalitarianism.

SECTION 4 (pages 660–663)
Between Peace and War

ACTIVITIES

○ **Using Visual Evidence** Ask students to study the photograph on text page 661. Then have them explain the impact such a photograph probably had on American opinion about the war.

☆ **Applying Information** Tell students to imagine that they work on the staff of a newspaper in late November 1941. The newspaper is publishing a special section reviewing the developments in the war since the summer of 1940 and reporting on the current situation in both Europe and Asia. Students are to use information from their text to prepare articles

and illustrations on the following topics: (1) German bombing raids on Britain in the summer of 1940; (2) German submarine attacks on British ships carrying lend-lease supplies; (3) sinking of the *Reuben James* and *Kearny;* (4) German invasion of the Soviet Union; (5) Japanese occupation of areas in French Indochina; (6) meeting between Secretary of State Hull and Japanese diplomats. Have some students write news stories, some write editorials, and some write feature stories. Have others draw cartoons. You may want to ask students to do additional research to supplement text material.

☐ **Reading Graphs** Have students use the following statistics to make a bar graph. Then ask: (1) How did the value of exports to Great Britain change between 1935 and 1939? (2) How did the value change between 1939 and 1940? (3) How much did the value of exports to Great Britain increase between 1940 and 1941? (4) How would you account for the increase of exports to Great Britain in 1940 and 1941?

Exports to Great Britain

Year	Value of Exports (in $ millions)
1935	433
1936	440
1937	536
1938	521
1939	505
1940	1,011
1941	7,637

ANSWERS: SECTION 4 REVIEW (page 663)

1. Wendell Willkie—p. 660; Lend-Lease Act—p. 661; Atlantic Charter—p. 662. **2.** Both supported the Selective Service Act and increased aid to Britain. **3.** Britain was running out of money and could not pay cash for supplies. **4.** Japan reached an agreement with the government of occupied France and took control of military bases in French Indochina and then occupied the area. **5.** Possible answer: Yes. The expansionist plans of the totalitarian governments were sure to involve the U.S. in the war.

ANSWERS: CHAPTER 30 REVIEW (pages 664–665)

Vocabulary **1.** c **2.** e **3.** b **4.** d **5.** a
Chapter Checkup **1.** By sending representatives to conferences, supporting the Kellogg-Briand Pact, instituting the Dawes Plan, and participating in international trade. **2.** The U.S. instituted the Dawes Plan, which was intended to enable Germany to pay reparations to France and the other Allies and to enable the Allies to repay

their wartime debts to the U.S. In the 1920s, the U.S. also experienced tremendous growth in international trade and investments. **3. (a)** Both Presidents refrained from military intervention in Latin America. **(b)** Roosevelt instituted the "good neighbor" policy of nonintervention in Latin America. **4. (a)** Nye told the American people they had been tricked into war by bankers and munitions manufacturers. **(b)** The Neutrality Act of 1935 authorized the President to ban arms sales to nations at war; the Neutrality Act of 1936 prohibited loans to nations at war. The Neutrality Act of 1937 further extended the President's authority to bar shipments to nations at war. **5. (a)** Japan's attacks on China; the sinking of the *Panay*. **(b)** Hoover opposed Japanese aggression but took no actions to preserve China's independence. Roosevelt continued arms shipments to China. In response to the *Panay* incident, the American government accepted a Japanese apology and payment of $2 million for damages. **6. (a)** The policy of appeasement led to passive agreement to Hitler's actions, such as the reoccupation by Germany of the Rhineland, the annexation of Austria, and the takeover of the Sudetenland. Britain and France hoped that through appeasement war could be avoided. **(b)** Germany invaded Poland. **7. (a)** Gave the President authority to sell, exchange, lend, or lease war materials to any country whose defense was deemed vital to the defense of the U.S. **(b)** It allowed the U.S. to lend Britain whatever supplies it needed to resist the Nazis. **8. (a)** The U.S. placed an embargo on the export of scrap metal, oil, and aviation fuel to Japan. Also, all Japanese bank accounts in the U.S. were blocked. **(b)** The Japanese attack on Pearl Harbor.

Critical Thinking **1.** Students might note the self-centered mood, the prosperity, and the wish to avoid another war. **2.** Students should emphasize the tendency to stay with a President in a time of crisis. **3.** During the 1920s, isolationist events included the refusal of the U.S. to join the League of Nations. Internationalist events included the establishment of the Dawes Plan and the signing of the Kellogg-Briand Pact. During the 1930s, isolationist events included the Nye committee investigation, the enactment of neutrality legislation, and the refusal of the U.S. to declare war on Germany when World War II began. Internationalist events included increased military preparedness and legislation that provided for the sale of arms to the Allies on a cash-and-carry basis. Accept factually based answers on the extent of isolationism in the 1920s and 1930s.

Connecting Past and Present **1.** Today, the U.S. takes an active and important role. Americans view themselves as leaders in efforts for international peace. Evidence of increased internationalism include American participation in the UN and the numerous peacekeeping missions State Department officials and presidential advisers take to such places as the Middle East and Latin America. **2.** International condemnation, efforts to get the UN involved in changing policies or condemning aggressive acts, direct and indirect negotiations, force or the threat of force, and terrorism are all ways nations respond to policies with which they disagree.

Developing Basic Skills **1.** Students should discuss the question of neutrality legislation as well as the immediate cause of each war and refer to American reluctance to become entangled in a foreign conflict. The role of America's commitments to its allies should also be examined. **2. (a)** The threat of war in Europe. **(b)** Imminent. **(c)** Isolationist. It presents only the arguments against American intervention in European affairs.

Chapter 31 (pages 666–687)

The Second World War __

OVERVIEW

Chapter 31 focuses on World War II after the entry of the U.S. into the war. Students read about the dark days of 1942 and the allied offensives that began in 1943 and ended with victory in 1945. Students also analyze American efforts on the home front.

HISTORICAL SIDELIGHTS

The following pieces of historical information can serve as notes of interest during the study of Chapter 31. The page numbers in parentheses indicate the points in the student text at which you may wish to introduce the information.

Conserving Wool (p. 670)   The War Production Board, in an effort to increase supplies of wool for the military forces, ordered clothing manufacturers to change fashions. No new suits could be sold with an extra pair of trousers, as had been customary. Jackets were to be shorter, single-breasted instead of double, with narrow lapels. The board estimated that those changes would save 40 to 50 million pounds of wool a year.

The Password (p. 682)   During the Battle of the Bulge, when the advancing American lines in the Ardennes Forest were spread thinly, German forces began to infiltrate, wearing American uniforms. To guard against such tactics, American soldiers devised password exchanges that Germans would not know. "Who is [movie star] Betty Grable's husband?" a sentry might challenge; the American would reply, "Harry James" (a well-known trumpet player). The system was not perfect, however. American General Omar Bradley, it turned out, did not know the name of Betty Grable's husband, but he was still allowed through the lines.

SECTION 1   (pages 667–670)
A World War

ACTIVITIES*
○ **Identification** Ask students to identify who or what is being referred to by each of the following clues: (1) led the defense of Bataan and Corregidor; (2) naval battle near Java that turned back the Japanese fleet; (3) American generals who urged an invasion of France across the English Channel; (4) led the German Afrika Korps; (5) name of Allied strategy to invade North Africa.
   Answers: **1.** MacArthur **2.** Coral Sea **3.** Marshall and Eisenhower **4.** Rommel **5.** Operation Torch
☆ **Making a Report** Divide the class into small groups. Assign each group one of the following theaters of the war: Asia, North Africa, Europe. Tell the groups that they are to prepare a report comparing the military situation in the area in the early months of 1942 and the early months of 1943. They should conclude their reports with an evaluation of whether the Allies had reason for hope in early 1943. When students have completed their reports, draw a chart on the chalkboard with three rows labeled Asia, North Africa, and Europe, and two columns headed Situation in Early 1942 and Situation in Early 1943. Summarize group conclusions on the chart. Ask students which theater of the war seemed most hopeful by early 1943.
□ **Applying Information** Have students research the war in North Africa or in the Pacific in 1942. They might begin with *The United States and World War II* by A. Russell Buchanan. Then tell them to imagine that they are war correspondents for a newspaper in

1942. Ask them to write two or three news reports on the war. They should describe the goals of any battles, the location, the course of the battles, and the outcomes.

ANSWERS: CHART STUDY   (page 668)
Allies: 49; Axis: 9

ANSWERS: SECTION 1 REVIEW   (page 670)
1. Allies, Axis powers—p. 667; Dwight D. Eisenhower, Douglas MacArthur—p. 669. **2.** Europe and Africa and the Pacific. **3.** An invasion of North Africa followed by advances into the Mediterranean area. **4. (a)** Opened the Mediterranean Sea to Allied shipping and made an invasion of southern Europe possible. **(b)** Coral Sea, Midway, Guadalcanal. **5.** Possible answer: A shortage of supplies hampered the Allied response. The U.S., having just entered the war, lacked even the most basic war materials and had little time to train its soldiers.

SECTION 2   (pages 670–675)
On the Home Front

ACTIVITIES
○ **Classifying** Ask students to make a chart with two columns headed Agency and Activities. Have students list in column 1 the government agencies created to coordinate the war effort on the home front. In column 2, ask them to describe the activities of the agency.
☆ **Comparing** Have students write an essay in which they compare improvements in the lives of black Americans during World War II with the ways blacks continued to be subjects of discrimination during the war. Some students might want to do further research.
□ **Using Visual Evidence** Have students do additional research about the internment of Japanese Americans during World War II, concentrating on photographs of the period. A good source would be *Executive Order 9066* by Maisie and Richard Conrat. Then ask students to write a report describing the internment and explaining how the photographs contributed to their understanding.

ANSWERS: SECTION 2 REVIEW   (page 675)
1. War Production Board, Office of War Mobilization—p. 670; Office of Price Administration, War Manpower Commission, National War Labor Board—p. 671; A. Philip Randolph, Executive order 8802—p. 673. **2.** Shirt factories were converted to the

---

*See "To the Teacher" for an explanation of the symbols.

production of mosquito netting; model train producers made bomb fuses; kitchen sink assembly
lines produced ammunition cartridge cases; and
automobile factories manufactured tanks, trucks,
personnel carriers, and aircraft. **3.** Workers' wages
increased and unemployment dropped. **4. (a)** Women piloted airplanes, repaired airplanes and
vehicles, drove trucks, operated radios, did clerical
and technical work of all kinds, and found employment in steel mills, shipyards, and other industries.
(b) Employment opportunities for blacks increased;
blacks enjoyed more social acceptance and made
economic gains in the North and South; lynching
stopped. **5.** Sent to internment camps for most of
the war. **6.** Possible answer: In times of war, people
are more likely to believe that government is the
institution best suited to organizing the massive
commitment of manpower and resources needed
to fight a war.

ANSWER: MAP STUDY   (page 679)

Barely reached the area under control of the
Japanese.

ANSWERS: SECTION 3 REVIEW   (page 679)

1. Joseph Stalin—p. 676; D-Day, Operation Overlord, Cherbourg—p. 677; Chester Nimitz—p. 678.
2. leapfrogging—p. 678. **3.** Allied successes in Sicily
and Italy. **4.** Massive supplies, territorial concessions in eastern Europe, and a second front in
western Europe. **5.** The Allies needed a huge reserve
of supplies, secrecy had to be maintained, and the
weather had to be clear. **6.** Possible answer: The
Soviet Union did not want to divide its strength
for a two-front war.

SECTION 3   (pages 675–679)
The Allies on the Offensive

ACTIVITIES

○ **Identifying** Have students identify each of
the following persons, places, or things and
explain why each was significant during World
War II: (1) Operation Overlord, (2) Leningrad;
(3) Salerno, (4) Tarawa, (5) Douglas MacArthur.

☆ **Map Reading** Have students study the maps
on text pages 676 and 679 and answer these
questions: (1) Which European nations were
controlled by the Axis in 1942? (2) Which parts
of North Africa were locations of Allied advances in 1942 and 1943? (3) Which land areas
were under Japanese control in 1942? (4) What
was the most northern Pacific island controlled
by Japan? (5) What were the starting points
for the Allied advances in the Pacific? (6) In
what year did the Allied advance reach the
Philippine Islands? Then ask: Which Allied
campaigns were most significant in Europe
and North Africa? Which were most significant
in the Pacific?

□ **Researching** Have student research the role
of codes in World War II. Students can write a
report about their findings. Possible sources
include *The Codebreakers* by David Kahn.

ANSWERS: MAP STUDY   (page 676)

From Libya to Tunisia, then to Sicily and up the
spine of Italy; Soviet advance into central and southern Europe.

SECTION 4   (pages 680–682)
Wartime Diplomacy and Politics

ACTIVITIES

○ **Placing Events in Time** Ask students to arrange the following events in correct chronological order: (1) Roosevelt elected to fourth
term; (2) Moscow meeting of foreign ministers;
(3) conference at Yalta, (4) meeting of Roosevelt, Churchill, and Chiang Kai-shek at Cairo;
(5) meeting of the Big Three in Teheran.
Answers: 2, 4, 5, 1, 3

☆ **Making a Chart** Draw the outline of a chart
on the chalkboard with the headings Location,
Date, Who Attended, Agreements Reached. Ask
students for the information necessary to
complete the chart. When the chart is complete, lead a class discussion around the following questions: (1) Which conferences were
concerned with the political situation in Europe
after the war? (2) At which conference were
compromises made in order to bring the Soviet
Union into the war against Japan? (3) Which
conference do you think was most important
for the future of Europe? (4) Which conference
do you think was most important for the future
of Asia?

□ **Researching** Have students read about one
of the wartime conferences and write a report
about the short-term and long-term consequences of decisions reached at the conference.

ANSWERS: **THE AMERICAN EXPERIENCE**
(page 680)

1. It used regular words in the Navajo language. **2.** Possible answer: There were no Navajos in Japan or elsewhere who would break the code for the Japanese.

ANSWERS: **SECTION 4 REVIEW** (page 682)

1. Chiang Kai-shek, Big Three—p. 680; UN, Harry S. Truman, Thomas E. Dewey—p. 681. **2.** A spring offensive to coincide with the cross-channel landing by Britain and the U.S.; to enter the Pacific war once Germany surrendered. **3.** The failure of Democratic economic policies. **4.** To divide Germany into four zones of occupation governed by American, British, French, and Soviet forces. **5.** Possible answer: During World War II the emerging role of the U.S. as a superpower became evident.

SECTION 5 (pages 682-685)
Victory

ACTIVITIES

○ **Name Game** Read the following clues and ask students to use them to identify each person, place, or thing: (1) city where first atomic bomb was dropped; (2) tactic by which Japanese fighter pilots deliberately crashed into ships; (3) general who thought the military goal of defeating Germany was most important; (4) became President when Roosevelt died; (5) location of final meeting of the Big Three. *Answers:* **1.** Hiroshima **2.** kamikaze **3.** Eisenhower **4.** Truman **5.** Potsdam

☆ **Writing a Diary** Tell students to imagine they are advisers to Harry S. Truman in 1945. Have them write diary entries describing their reactions on the following days: (1) the day Roosevelt died; (2) the day Truman learned that scientists had detonated an atomic device; (3) the day Truman decided to use the atomic bomb; (4) the day the Japanese surrendered.

□ **Writing a Report** Ask students to write a research report about the scientific development of the atomic bomb, known as the Manhattan Project. They might consult *Decision of Destiny* by Walter S. Schoenberger.

ANSWERS: **SECTION 5 REVIEW** (page 685)

1. The Holocaust—p. 683; Manhattan Project—p. 684. **2.** kamikaze—p. 684. **3. (a)** Defeat Germany as completely as possible. **(b)** Churchill wanted Eisenhower to push on to Berlin, because he did not trust Stalin's promise for free elections in post-war Europe. He wanted the U.S. and Britain to occupy as much of Germany and eastern Europe as possible before the war ended. **(c)** Moving slowly to defeat the Germans as completely as possible. **4.** The extermination of all Jews in Europe. **5. (a)** Atomic bomb. **(b)** Used to bomb Hiroshima and Nagasaki, Japan. **6.** Possible answer: Even when Japan's eventual defeat became almost a certainty, the Japanese continued to fight.

ANSWERS: **CHAPTER 31 REVIEW**
(pages 686-687)

Vocabulary 1. internment camps **2.** amphibious **3.** leapfrogging **4.** holocaust **5.** kamikaze

Chapter Checkup 1. (a) Japan had conquered many Pacific islands and the nations of eastern and southern Asia. Japan had also crippled China and threatened India and Australia. In addition, Germany had conquered most of eastern and western Europe. **(b)** Capture of North Africa allowed use of the Mediterranean Sea and facilitated the invasion of southern Europe. **(c)** Because of Allied victories in the Pacific. **2. (a)** Helped mobilize American industry by supervising conversion from peacetime to wartime production. **(b)** Coordinated activities of all wartime production agencies. **(c)** Set price ceilings on most items and supervised rationing. **(d)** Determined where in the economy workers were most needed. **(e)** Handled problems between labor and management. **3. (a)** Union membership increased. **(b)** Many job opportunities opened up. **(c)** Job opportunities increased and some gains were made in the fight against discrimination. Racial tension did not disappear, however, and blacks still faced segregation and hostility. **(d)** Faced discrimination and were sometimes attacked. **(e)** Faced some discrimination during the war, but were not treated as severely as Japanese Americans. **(f)** Evacuated from their homes and interned in camps. **4. (a)** Italy appeared to be the weakest point in the Axis empire. **(b)** Yes. The Allies first took Sicily and then Italy. The success of this invasion led to the overthrow of Mussolini. **5. (a)** Operation Overlord, the plan for the Allied invasion of Europe, called for attacking beachheads in northern France. It depended on a buildup of supplies, as well as on secrecy and favorable weather. **(b)** Yes. The beachheads were secured in six weeks, the French port of Cherbourg was captured, and from there the Allies moved into western Europe. **6. (a)** MacArthur wanted to push northward from Australia through New Guinea. Nimitz wanted to advance toward Japan via the islands of the central Pacific. **(b)** They adopted both suggestions, using the strategy known as leapfrogging. **7. (a)** Moscow, Cairo, Teheran, Bretton Woods, Dumbarton Oaks, and Yalta. **(b)** Plans for creating an organization of nations to maintain world peace and security, the strategy for defeating the Axis powers, postwar economic recovery, and the fate of Germany. **8. (a)** Because the Japanese had demonstrated their willingness to fight to the death. **(b)** American leaders were not so hard-pressed to compromise with Stalin in discussions over Poland, Germany, and other difficult postwar problems, because Soviet help was not needed to defeat Japan.

Critical Thinking   1. Student answers should emphasize the number of nations that fought in this war and the many parts of the world in which battles took place. **2. (a)** Japanese Americans were interned at special relocation camps. **(b)** German Americans were harassed by some Americans but they were not placed in detention centers by the federal authorities. **(c)** Students might suggest that race is a factor that explains the kind of treatment received by each group.

Connecting Past and Present   1. The war opened new economic opportunities to women, blacks, and other minorities. However, events such as the civil rights movement of the 1960s have led to legislative changes that have made discrimination based on race or sex illegal. The changes of the postwar years have built on the earlier changes and enlarged the opportunities for minority groups to participate more fully in American society. **2.** The existence of nuclear weapons has made all nations more cautious about becoming involved in an armed conflict. Nuclear weapons are seen by some people as a deterrent to war.

Developing Basic Skills   1. (a) During World War I, the War Industries Board established controls over scarce materials, set prices, and coordinated war production. The War Labor Board supervised labor-management relations. Students should note that during World War II the War Production Board coordinated war production. Another War Labor Board regulated labor-management relations. **(b)** One difference between government's economic role in the two world wars is that only during World War II did the government attempt to control the prices of most items. **(c)** Similarities can be explained by noting the need to coordinate all phases of the economy to support the war effort. Students might suggest that the difference can be explained by the New Deal's redefinition of the government's economic role. **2.** Research will vary.

ANSWERS: SPIRIT OF AMERICA   (page 689)
1. Americans collected scrap rubber, metals, bought large numbers of war bonds. **2.** Women became leaders of temperance, antislavery, and women's

suffrage groups, collected money in wartime, cared for wounded soldiers, became nurses. **3.** Possible answer: Gives volunteers a sense of participation in the nation's time of need.

ANSWERS: NOTABLE AMERICANS   (page 691)
1. Designed a model kitchen for the handicapped, wrote a book suggesting ways for the handicapped to do housework, volunteered for help groups that did physical rehabilitation. **2.** Possible answer: She recognized a need for help in various fields and offered her services without any thought of compensation.

ANSWERS: VOICES OF FREEDOM   (page 691)
1. They are a welcome relief from the grim task of fighting a war. **2.** People felt that there were many tasks to be performed in one of the nation's most critical times and that everyone had to help to get them done.

Chapter 32   (pages 692–711)

The Postwar International Scene

OVERVIEW

Chapter 32 focuses on developments in U.S. foreign policy between 1945 and 1960. Students analyze various challenges to world peace and the outbreak of war in Korea. They also examine relations between the U.S. and the Soviet Union during the cold war.

HISTORICAL SIDELIGHTS

The following pieces of historical information can serve as notes of interest during the study of Chapter 32. The page numbers in parentheses indicate the points in the student text at which you may wish to introduce the information

Inchon (p. 703)   General MacArthur's surprise attack at Inchon, Korea, in September 1950 was a daring gamble that paid off. Many other military officers opposed a landing there because the troops would be required to land both at high tide and in daylight—a combination that occurred only a few days every month. Even worse, there were 30-foot tides, which fell so quickly that in ten minutes troops in landing boats could find themselves stranded on mud flats at the mercy of enemy guns. But the Marine "X" Corps successfully negotiated the landing and quickly captured Seoul, the South Korean capital.

Tour of Disneyland Canceled (p. 706)   When Soviet Premier Nikita Khrushchev toured the United States in 1959, his tentative itinerary included a visit to Disneyland. But local police, worried that they would not be able to guarantee Khrushchev's safety among all of the exhibits and rides, canceled the tour. Khrushchev, who had very much wanted to see this "wonder of the capitalist world," complained vociferously to reporters. "Just imagine, I, a Premier, a Soviet representative . . . told that I could not go. . . . Why not? . . . Do you have rocket-launching pads there? . . . Or have gangsters taken hold of the place?" Khrushchev was given a tour of a Hollywood movie set instead.

SECTION 1   (pages 693–697)
The Postwar World

ACTIVITIES*
○   **Identification**   Ask students to identify who or what is being referred to by each of the following clues: (1) location of a civil war between supporters and opponents of the monarchy; (2) sent to China in 1945 to work for unification of the country; (3) elected president of the southern part of Korea after World War II; (4) leader of communist forces in China; (5) UN body that is directly responsible for maintaining peace.
   Answers: **1.** Greece **2.** George C. Marshall **3.** Syngman Rhee **4.** Mao Zedong **5.** Security Council
☆   **Ranking**   Draw the outline of a chart on the chalkboard with two columns headed Area and Postwar Situation. List the following nations in the first column: Poland, Germany, Iran, Israel, Greece, Japan, Korea, China. Ask students to describe the political situation in each area at the end of World War II. When the chart is complete, ask each student to rank the areas in the first column from the area they think was most likely to become an area of future conflict to the one they think was least likely to become an area of future conflict. Have students defend their choice.

---

*See "To the Teacher" for an explanation of the symbols.

□   **Writing a Report**   Have students do additional research about the U.S. occupation of Japan after World War II. They should concentrate on the efforts to change Japanese politics and society. They might consult *The United States and Japan* by E. O. Reischauer.

ANSWER: MAP STUDY   (page 694)
Great Britain and the Soviet Union.

ANSWER: CHART STUDY   (page 695)
Economic and Social Council.

ANSWERS: SECTION 1 REVIEW   (page 697)
1. United Nations, General Assembly, Security Council—p. 694; Syngman Rhee, Mao Zedong—p. 697. **2.** During the wartime conferences of Allied leaders, Stalin had agreed to free elections in Poland after the war. Instead, however, Soviets installed a communist-dominated government in Poland. A similar fate befell other eastern European nations including Czechoslovakia, Hungary, and Romania. Conflict also arose over the future of Germany and over access to the Soviet zone of Berlin. After the war, the Soviets installed a communist government in their zone of Korea and refused to cooperate in national elections. **3.** It recommended that Palestine be divided into an Arab and a Jewish state. **4.** The nationalist and the communist forces. **5.** Possible answer: The possibility that any small-scale conflict could escalate into a nuclear war makes it no longer safe for nations to engage in global conflicts.

SECTION 2   (pages 696–702)
A Cold War Begins

ACTIVITIES
○   **Locating Places**   Have students label the following places on a blank world map and then explain why each was important after World War II: (1) Greece, (2) Turkey, (3) Berlin, (4) China, (5) Taiwan.
☆   **Biographical Sketch**   Have students research the life of George C. Marshall and write a biographical sketch. They should outline his contributions to U.S. foreign policy. Students might begin by consulting an encyclopedia. More advanced students might want to read a biography of Marshall.
□   **Relating Past to Present**   Ask students to write a report comparing NATO today with

NATO in 1949. They should compare its membership by noting nations that have joined since 1949 and those that have left the alliance. They should also compare its goals. The *Readers' Guide to Periodical Literature* can help students locate current articles about NATO.

ANSWERS: VOICES OF FREEDOM (page 698)
1. misery and want; **2.** It provided for the U.S. to take an active part in supporting people who were resisting subjugation, in contrast to prewar isolationism, which called for the U.S. not to become involved in activities beyond its shores.

ANSWERS: MAP STUDY (page 701)
Estonia, Latvia, Lithuania; taken over by the Soviet Union.

ANSWERS: SECTION 2 REVIEW (page 702)
1. Truman Doctrine—p. 697; Marshall Plan—p. 698; NATO—p. 700; NSC 68—p. 702. **2.** containment—p. 697. **3.** To help bring about a European economic recovery. **4. (a)** To provide for the mutual defense of the nations of western Europe and the U.S. **(b)** NATO was part of the American struggle to prevent the spread of communism. **5.** The communist takeover of mainland China and the announcement that the Soviet Union had atomic power. **6.** Possible answer: An awareness of the potential for conflict resulting from the rising tensions between the communist and noncommunist worlds, awareness that an isolationist policy had not kept the nation out of World War II, and the belief that with possession of nuclear power came the responsibility to exercise world leadership.

SECTION 3 (pages 702–705)
The Korean War

ACTIVITIES
○ **Map Reading** Have students study the map on text page 703 and answer these questions: (1) What symbol is used to indicate the line of the farthest North Korean advance? (2) What symbol is used to indicate the line of the farthest UN advance? (3) In what year did North Korean forces advance the farthest into South Korea? (4) Why is the 38th parallel significant in the history of the Korean War?

☆ **Relating Cause and Effect** Ask students to write one "effect" statement for each of the following events: (1) North Korea invaded South Korea. (2) MacArthur made a surprise

landing at Inchon. (3) UN forces crossed the 38th parallel. (4) MacArthur publicly demanded total North Korean surrender.

☐ **Analyzing a Quotation** Read the following extract or duplicate and distribute copies. Tell students that the quotation is from General MacArthur's address to Congress in April 1951. Ask students to write an essay in which they explain whether they think President Truman would have agreed with the statement and whether they agree with the statement.

It has been said in effect that I was a warmonger. Nothing could be further from the truth. I know war as few other men now living know it, and nothing to me is more revolting. . . .

But once war is forced upon us, there is no other alternative than to apply every available means to bring it to a swift end. War's very object is victory—not prolonged indecision. In war, indeed, there can be no substitute for victory.

ANSWER: MAP STUDY (page 703)
Four times.

ANSWERS: SECTION 3 REVIEW (page 705)
1. 38th parallel—p. 702, General Douglas MacArthur—p. 703. **2.** limited war—p. 704. **3.** The UN Security Council condemned the invasion, demanded withdrawal of North Korean forces, and voted to provide military aid to South Korea. **4.** Truman wanted a limited war with the sole objective of restoring the original boundary between North and South Korea. MacArthur wanted to extend the war into China and urged the use of massive air strikes against targets in that country. **5.** Possible answer: Yes. Civilian control prevents the military from becoming too powerful.

SECTION 4 (pages 705–707)
New Directions in Foreign Policy

ACTIVITIES
○ **Generalizing** Ask students to write one or two factual statements to support each of the following generalizations: (1) John Foster Dulles rejected the policy of containment. (2) There was a thaw in Soviet-American relations after 1953. (3) The U-2 incident ended the thaw in Soviet-American relations.

☆ **Summarizing** Divide the class into three groups. Assign students in each group one of the three subsections in Section 4. Ask each student to write a paragraph summarizing the subsection assigned to his or her group. When students have completed their paragraphs, ask volunteers from each group to read their summaries. Compare the summaries of the subsections and discuss the strong points, arriving at the best summary of each subsection.

☐ **What If?** Ask students to write a paragraph in which they explain what might have happened if the U-2 plane had not been shot down over the Soviet Union in 1960. They should speculate on the effect on the thaw in relations between the Soviet Union and the U.S.

ANSWERS: SECTION 4 REVIEW (page 707)

1. John Foster Dulles—p. 705; Nikita Khrushchev—p. 706. **2.** massive retaliation, arms race—p. 705. **3. (a)** The aim of his policy was to destroy communism. **(b)** He wanted the U. S. to encourage the "liberation of the captive peoples" in eastern Europe through political pressure and propaganda. He favored the strategy known as massive retaliation, which called for the use of nuclear weapons if necessary. **4.** Nikita Khrushchev's two-week visit to the U.S. in the summer of 1959. **5.** Temporarily ended the thaw in Soviet-American relations. **6.** Possible answer: Present policy demonstrates more of a spirit of détente than did policy immediately after World War II.

SECTION 5 (pages 707–709)

The Challenge of Nationalism

ACTIVITIES

○ **Placing Events in Time** Copy the time line on the chalkboard. Then read aloud the list of events. Ask students to write on a sheet of paper the letter of the correct time period for the event.

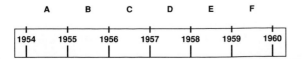

A	B	C	D	E	F
1954	1955	1956	1957	1958	1959	1960

(1) Castro leads successful revolution against Batista; (2) the U.S. begins sending military advisers to South Vietnam; (3) a conference at Geneva divides Vietnam into two regions; (4) U.S. marines land in Lebanon; (5) Hungarians unsuccessfully revolt against the Soviet Union.
Answers: **1.** F **2.** B **3.** A **4.** E **5.** C

☆ **Writing a Report** Divide the class into small groups and assign each group one of the following topics: (1) uprising in Hungary, (2) war in Southeast Asia, (3) Suez crisis, (4) Castro's revolution in Cuba. Tell each group to imagine that it is a committee of foreign policy advisers to President Eisenhower. They are to prepare a background report on the topic assigned to their group, including a description of the situation in the region, an analysis of how that situation threatens the peace, and recommendations for U.S. policy in the region. Have the groups present their recommendations to the class.

☐ **Map Reading** Have students locate the member nations of SEATO on a world map. Then ask: (1) Which noncommunist nations in southern and eastern Asia were not members of SEATO? (2) How do you think that fact might have influenced the effectiveness of the alliance?

ANSWERS: SECTION 5 REVIEW (page 709)

1. Ho Chi Minh, Dien Bien Phu, SEATO, Gamal Abdel Nasser, Eisenhower Doctrine—p. 708; Fidel Castro—p. 709. **2.** domino theory—p. 708. **3.** Soviet tanks and troops moved in to crush the uprising. **4.** With the defeat of France in Indochina, the U.S. became the leading western power in Southeast Asia. Many people justified American presence in the region by citing the domino theory. **5.** The U.S. pressed Britain and France to stop the fighting. It also sponsored a UN resolution condemning the attack. **6.** Possible answer: Hungarian nationalists may have expected U.S. support for their uprising.

ANSWERS: CHAPTER 32 REVIEW

(pages 710–711)

Vocabulary 1. containment **2.** limited war **3.** massive retaliation **4.** arms race **5.** domino theory

Chapter Checkup 1. (a) Soviet resentment over the delay in the cross-channel invasion of Europe and American suspicion that Stalin meant to spread communism throughout Europe contributed to postwar tensions. **(b)** The installation of communist-dominated governments in many eastern European nations. Soviet actions in Berlin.

Refusal of Soviet Union to allow its zone of Korea to participate in national elections. **2. (a)** Peaceful solutions to international conflicts, the prevention of wars, and cooperation to eliminate hunger, disease, and illiteracy. **(b)** Seeking peaceful solutions to international conflicts. **(c)** The Security Council had the power to investigate conflicts between nations and recommend solutions. It could also organize a peacekeeping force composed of troops from member nations. **(d)** The council was not given power to enforce its decisions. Also, any permanent member of the council could veto that body's actions. **(e)** The UN tried to settle a dispute in Iran. In 1947, the UN recommended that Palestine be divided into an Arab and a Jewish state. The UN arranged an armistice in the war that followed Israeli independence. **3. (a)** Called for the U.S. to provide massive economic aid to Europe to finance European economic recovery. **(b)** The designers of the Marshall Plan hoped that the economic recovery of European nations would help western European nations resist domestic communist threats and strengthen their military capacity. **(c)** Yes. Industrial growth in western Europe returned to its prewar level, with the result that the appeal of communist political parties in these countries declined. **4. (a)** The U.S. ordered its planes and ships to back up the South Korean army and sent its own troops into the conflict. **(b)** Because of General MacArthur's successes in overcoming North Korean forces. **(c)** Communist Chinese forces entered the war and forced the UN troops to retreat with heavy losses across the 38th parallel. **5. (a)** New directions in Soviet policy such as concentration on internal affairs and statements that war between the Soviet Union and the West was unnecessary. **(b)** Opened the way for further discussions of disarmament and the banning of nuclear testing. **(c)** The U-2 incident and the collapse of the Paris summit in 1960. **6. (a)** Reacted positively. President Eisenhower recognized the Castro government one week after it took power. **(b)** American businesses there were seized.

Critical Thinking   1. Students might suggest that Vandenberg was right because the explosion of the first Soviet atomic weapon broke the nuclear monopoly of the U.S. **2.** The blockage of Soviet expansion in eastern Europe and the defeat of North Korean aggression indicate the success of the policy of containment between 1947 and 1960.

Connecting Past and Present   1. Answers will vary. Students might consult the *Readers' Guide to Periodical Literature* for the most current articles on summit meetings. **2.** UN peacekeeping forces have served in a variety of international hot spots. UN agency programs to reduce disease, infant

mortality, illiteracy, and malnutrition are other ways of working for peace.

Developing Basic Skills   1. (a) France, Portugal, West Germany, Italy, Great Britain, Norway, Denmark, Netherlands, Belgium, Luxembourg, Greece, Turkey. **(b)** Poland, East Germany, Hungary, Czechoslovakia, Romania, Bulgaria, Albania, USSR. **(c)** Sweden, Finland, Spain, Switzerland, Austria, Yugoslavia, Ireland. **(d)** Most countries felt they would be less vulnerable to attack if they belonged to a military alliance. Soviet bloc nations may also have felt they had no choice. **2. (a)** Berlin airlift. **(b)** Students might say that the mood is expectant, with the Berliners wondering at the "miracle" of the delivery of supplies. **(c)** The Soviets blocked all rail, road, and river traffic to West Berlin. Supplies were cut off to the more than 2 million residents. **(d)** The Soviet Union became convinced of American determination to preserve West Berlin's independence and lifted the blockade after 321 days.

Chapter 33   (pages 712–729)
A Search for Stability ___

OVERVIEW

Chapter 33 focuses on political, economic, social, and cultural developments that took place during the 1950s. Students read about McCarthyism, the growth of the civil rights movement, and domestic politics under Presidents Harry Truman and Dwight D. Eisenhower.

HISTORICAL SIDELIGHTS

The following pieces of historical information can serve as notes of interest during the study of Chapter 33. The page numbers in parentheses indicate the points in the student text at which you may wish to introduce the information.

Greater Leisure (p. 720) With the growth of postwar prosperity, leisure activities increased for many Americans. The 40-hour work week (compared with the 70-hour work week of 100 years earlier) left more time available for play. By 1959, Americans were spending $30 to $40 billion annually on recreation—20 times more per person than in 1900. In 1959, 33 million people went swimming at least once, 32 million went fishing, 32 million dancing, 18 million bowling, and 16 million hunting.

Success in Space (p. 723) The failure of the first U.S. space shot in 1957, compared with the success of the Soviet launching of *Sputnik,* led some members of the foreign press to christen the American satellite as "Flopnik," "Stay-put-nik," and "Sputternik." Even in Washington, officials wisecracked that the satellite ought to be named Civil Servant: "It won't work and you can't fire it." But by the end of 1958, the U.S. had recovered with five successful launches. One satellite broadcast President Eisenhower's Christmas message back to earth, and a visiting Russian scientist admitted, "We haven't thought of anything like that yet."

SECTION 1   (pages 714–729)
From War to Peace

ACTIVITIES*
○ **Ranking**   Have students review text page 716. Ask them to make a list of the ways the civil rights of black Americans were expanded between 1941 and 1952. Then have students rank the items on the list from the most significant to the least significant. Have students compare their rankings and discuss their reasons.

☆ **Comparing**   Ask students to write an essay in which they compare the goals of Franklin Roosevelt's New Deal and Harry Truman's Fair Deal. In their comparison, they should note how the economic and political situation in the country differed.

□ **Recognizing a Point of View**   Have students read a biography of President Truman such as *Harry S. Truman: A Biography* by Leroy Hayman and write a book report in which they describe the author's opinion of Truman.

ANSWERS: SECTION 1 REVIEW   (page 716)
1. Taft-Hartley Act, Thomas E. Dewey—p. 714; States' Rights party—p. 714; Progressive party—p. 715. **2.** closed shop—p. 714. **3.** Workers demanded higher wages to keep up with the rising cost of living. Strikes took place in the steel, automobile, meatpacking, and electrical appliance industries. **4.** Provided a year of unemployment insurance to jobless veterans, gave financial aid to veterans who attended college, and entitled veterans to government loans for home building and business. **5.** National Housing Act of 1949,

---

*See "To the Teacher" for an explanation of the symbols.

Fair Labor Standards Act, Social Security Act of 1935. **6.** Possible answer: He can win the support of the people for his programs and depend on them to influence Congress.

SECTION 2   (pages 717–719)
The Cold War at Home

ACTIVITIES
○ **Finding the Main Idea**   Ask students working in small groups to prepare statements reflecting the main idea of each of the subsections in Section 2. When they have completed the assignment, have students compare their statements and reach a consensus about the main idea of each subsection.

☆ **Making a Chart**   Draw the outline of a chart on the chalkboard with two columns headed Rise of McCarthyism and Decline of McCarthyism. Have students define McCarthyism. Then ask them what events and developments contributed either to the rise or decline of McCarthyism. Summarize responses on the chart. When the chart is completed, ask students to write an essay in which they evaluate the effect of McCarthyism.

□ **Writing a Report**   Television played a major role in the downfall of Senator McCarthy. Have students do additional research and write a report about the Army-McCarthy hearings. They should note especially the effect televising the debates had on the public's perception of McCarthy. Possible sources include *Trial by Television* by Michael Straight or a biography of McCarthy, such as *Senator Joe McCarthy* by R. H. Rovere.

ANSWERS: SECTION 2 REVIEW   (page 719)
1. Committee on Un-American Activities—p. 717. **2.** blacklist—p. 717; McCarthyism—p. 718. **3.** HUAC hearings on alleged communist activity in the movie industry, the Whittaker Chambers–Alger Hiss investigation, and the conviction and execution of Ethel and Julius Rosenberg on spy charges. **4. (a)** By playing on American fears about disloyalty and communist infiltration of government. **(b)** McCarthy's unsupported charge that the army base at Fort Monmouth, New Jersey, was infested with communists and the televised Army-McCarthy hearings, which exposed McCarthy's abrasive manner. **5.** Possible answer: Both were pledged to eliminate the threat of communism. One difference

T 131

was that McCarthy's accusations were aimed at government officials and other public figures.

SECTION 3 (pages 719–721)
Stability Under Eisenhower

ACTIVITIES

○ **Identification** Ask students to identify who or what is being referred to by each of the following clues: (1) popular television program that portrayed women as homemakers; (2) presidential candidate of the Democratic party in 1952; (3) Eisenhower's running mate in 1952 and 1956; (4) author of *The Power of Positive Thinking;* (5) bishop who hosted a popular religious television program.
Answers: **1.** *Father Knows Best* **2.** Adlai E. Stevenson **3.** Richard Nixon **4.** Norman Vincent Peale **5.** Bishop Fulton J. Sheen

☆ **Using Visual Evidence** Have students study the way women were portrayed in advertisements in popular magazines from the 1950s. Local libraries should have bound copies of such magazines. If possible, ask students to photocopy examples. Then have them compare those examples with present-day advertisements. Ask students to summarize their comparisons in a written report. You might have students create a display of advertisements that show the similarities and differences.

□ **Biographical Sketch** Ask students to write a biographical sketch of Edward R. Murrow. They should concentrate on his career as a radio and television reporter. They might want to consult *Edward R. Murrow: Broadcaster of Courage* by Robert Cichello or *Edward R. Murrow: The War Years* by R. Franklin Smith.

ANSWERS: SECTION 3 REVIEW   (page 721)
1. Adlai E. Stevenson—p. 719. **2.** He believed in reducing the government's role in the economy and made it clear that he did not favor additional social welfare programs. **3.** A "baby boom," prosperity, the GI Bill, and a massive road-building program. **4.** Managing a home in the suburbs and raising a family. **5.** Possible answer: Both political parties were looking for a strong candidate who would be popular with the people. General Eisenhower's immense popularity due to his wartime service made his victory seem assured.

SECTION 4 (pages 722–727)
A Deceptive Calm

ACTIVITIES

○ **Placing Events in Time** Ask students to arrange the following events in correct chronological order: (1) quiz show scandal revealed; (2) sit-in movement begins; (3) *Sputnik* launched; (4) Eisenhower sends troops to Little Rock; (5) *Brown* v. *Board of Education of Topeka;* (6) National Defense Education Act passed; (7) Montgomery bus boycott ends; (8) John Kennedy elected President.
Answers: 5, 7, 4, 3, 6, 1, 2, 8

☆ **Using Visual Evidence** Have students study the photographs and paintings in this chapter. Ask them to make a list of the illustrations they think reflect a positive side of life in the 1950s and those that reflect a negative side. Have students compare their lists and defend their choices.

□ **Using Music as Historical Evidence** Point out to students that popular culture such as popular music can be a valuable source of information about a historical period. Ask students to listen to examples of sentimental melodies of "big band" music from the 1940s and of early rock 'n' roll from the 1950s. If possible, play examples of each in class. Then ask students to explain why they think some parents were critical of rock 'n' roll when they first heard it.

ANSWERS: VOICES OF FREEDOM   (page 724)
1. They resented it and threatened Elizabeth Eckford. **2.** Possible answer: They believed strongly that they had the right to attend an integrated school and were willing to face the antagonism of the people and the guards to achieve it.

ANSWERS: SECTION 4 REVIEW   (page 727)
1. Rosa Parks, Martin Luther King, Jr.—p. 722; *Sputnik I,* p. 723; beatniks—p. 725; Richard M. Nixon, John F. Kennedy—p. 726. **2.** civil disobedience—p. 722. **3.** Ruled that "separate educational facilities are inherently unequal," and that the doctrine of "separate but equal" had no place in public education. **4.** Boycotts and sit-ins. **5.** It passed the National Defense Education Act, which provided federal aid for schools and colleges. It also increased the budget of the National Science Foundation, which provided research grants for scientists and curriculum-improvement projects. **6.** Possible answer: Like writers and artists of the

1920s, they were concerned about increasing materialism.

ANSWERS: CHAPTER 33 REVIEW

(pages 728–729)

Vocabulary 1. GI Bill of Rights **2.** closed shop **3.** blacklist **4.** McCarthyism **5.** civil disobedience

Chapter Checkup 1. (a) Inflation and labor unrest. **(b)** The end of wartime price controls, the return of soldiers to civilian life, and the cancellation of government war contracts. **(c)** Congress passed the GI Bill of Rights, a tax cut in 1945, and the Employment Act of 1946. **2. (a)** Many voters blamed President Truman for the inflation, shortages, and strikes that plagued the nation. **(b)** The Eightieth Congress opposed Truman's legislative program and rejected many bills. **(c)** The National Housing Act of 1949, an amendment to the Fair Labor Standards Act, and the Social Security Act of 1950. **(d)** Several parts of the Fair Deal, including bills to provide federal aid to education, to establish federally financed health insurance, and to ban the poll tax and discrimination in employment. Efforts to repeal the Taft-Hartley Act. **3. (a)** In the North, segregation was largely de facto, existing in fact if not in law, while in the South, Jim Crow laws required segregation. **(b)** By placing the weight of the presidency on the side of civil rights. Truman condemned lynchings, created the President's Committee on Civil Rights, issued a directive banning segregation in the armed forces in 1948, and attempted to reduce discrimination in employment. **4.** The investigations of the Loyalty Review Board and the House Un-American Activities Committee, the charges made by Whittaker Chambers against Alger Hiss, the Klaus Fuchs case, and the arrest of Ethel and Julius Rosenberg. **5. (a)** He charged that employees of the federal government were Communist party members or "bad security risks." **(b)** He persuaded thousands of Americans that he was protecting American security, and he ruined the reputations and careers of many scholars and other public figures. **(c)** The televised Army-McCarthy hearings revealed him as a bully, and a 1954 Senate censure resolution further reduced his popular appeal. **6. (a)** Unemployment remained relatively low, factory wages climbed, labor's share of the national income increased, and the rate of inflation was lower than it had been under Truman. **(b)** Eisenhower refused to increase federal spending because he believed government should play a limited role in the economy. **7. (a)** A "baby boom," prosperity, the GI Bill, and a massive road-building program. **(b)** Suburbs of the 1920s depended on the city for entertainment and shopping. The postwar suburbs were more self-contained. Shopping was available nearby in supermarkets. **8. (a)** The 1896 decision said that "separate but equal" facilities for blacks and whites were constitutional. The Court's decision in *Brown* v. *Board of Education of Topeka* ruled that "separate" educational facilities are inherently unequal." **(b)** Argued that public school segregation violated the "equal protection" clause of the Fourteenth Amendment, that it deprived black children of equal educational opportunity, and that it lowered the morale and motivation of black students. **9. (a)** Americans had believed that the U. S. was technologically superior to the Soviet Union. **(b)** Weaknesses in education. **10.** Beatniks felt American society overvalued material possessions and emphasized conformity at the expense of individuality. Others were disillusioned because of television quiz show scandals that were seen as signs of a breakdown of moral values. William Whyte argued that the bureaucracies of big business stifled creativity and individuality, and David Reisman argued that Americans cared too much about other people's opinions of them instead of relying on their own judgment.

Critical Thinking 1. Students should point out that the cold war and fear of Soviet expansion affected domestic politics in many ways. As the cold war intensified, many Americans became less tolerant of any sympathy toward communism or the Soviet Union. **2.** Eisenhower tried to reduce the government's role in the economy, while Truman favored a strong role for government and supported social welfare legislation. Under Eisenhower, Congress limited federal aid for public housing and dropped wage and price controls established by the Truman administration.

Connecting Past and Present 1. Rock music and minimalist music are two newer musical styles. In art, pop art, neorealism, photorealism, and earthworks are newer styles. **2.** The government's role in the economy is an issue of continuing importance. In neither period was unemployment a serious problem. Today, however, major shifts in employment needs from manufacturing to service or high tech jobs and competition from abroad are causing economic dislocations which did not occur in the 1950s.

Developing Basic Skills 1. (a) Yes. **(b)** The picture shows only one suburban development. It does not provide enough information to make generalizations about all suburban housing. **(c)** Answers will vary. **2.** Answers will vary. You may want to encourage students to tape their interviews and prepare a transcript.

Unit Ten
Toward the Next Century

Chapter 34   (pages 732–757)

A Turbulent Decade ____

OVERVIEW
Chapter 34 traces the turbulent events of the 1960s. Students read about John Kennedy's hopes for the future and Lyndon Johnson's plans for a "Great Society." They examine the struggle for greater equality among blacks, Hispanics, American Indians, and women. Students also read about U.S. foreign policy during the period, including the nation's involvement in the war in Vietnam.

HISTORICAL SIDELIGHT
The following piece of historical information can serve as a note of interest during the study of Chapter 34. The page number in parentheses indicates the point in the student text at which you may wish to introduce the information.

Not an Easy Operation (p. 735) Although many of President Kennedy's military advisers supported the Bay of Pigs invasion, not all of them did. General David M. Shoup, Commander of the Marine Corps, illustrated the difficulty of the operation by placing an outline of Cuba over a map of the U.S. Cuba was not a small country, he pointed out; it was over 800 miles long, reaching from New York City to Chicago. Then Shoup placed a tiny red dot over the outline of Cuba. "That, gentlemen, represents the size of the island of Tarawa," noted the general, who had won a Medal of Honor at Tarawa in the central Pacific during World War II, "and it took us three days and 18,000 Marines to take it."

SECTION 1	(pages 733–736)
Increased World Tension	

ACTIVITIES*
○ **Placing Events in Time** Ask students to arrange the following events in correct chronological order: (1) President Kennedy announces presence of Soviet missile launch pads in Cuba; (2) landing at Bay of Pigs fails; (3) treaty banning nuclear tests in the atmosphere concluded; (4) Berlin wall erected; (5) Kennedy and Khrushchev meet in Vienna; (6) Soviet ships turn back rather than challenge the United States blockade of Cuba. *Answers:* 2, 5, 4, 1, 6, 3

☆ **Making a Chart** Divide the class into small groups and assign each group one of the following topics: Bay of Pigs, Berlin crisis, Cuban missile crisis. Ask each group to make a chart with three columns headed Causes of the Crisis, United States Action, Consequences of the Crisis. Have them complete the chart based on text pages 734–736. Have the groups display their charts. Ask: Which crisis do you think brought the United States closest to war?

☐ **Researching** Ask students to do additional research about the activities of the Peace Corps during the 1960s. Some students might want to investigate the types of assignments Peace Corps volunteers received, while others might want to read about the experiences of individual volunteers.

ANSWERS: SECTION 1 REVIEW   (page 736)
1. Robert McNamara, Peace Corps, Alliance for Progress—p. 734. **2.** strategic forces—p.734. **3. (a)** Because he believed that the people of Cuba did not support Castro. **(b)** The Cubans learned of the invasion in advance and captured the American-sponsored invaders. **4.** Either a naval blockade of Cuba or an air strike against the missile sites. **5.** Possible answer: It made an important statement to people in countries where volunteers went that the American people cared about the world.

---

*See "To the Teacher" for an explanation of the symbols.

SECTION 2   (pages 736–740)
The New Frontier

ACTIVITIES

○ **Expressing an Opinion** Ask students to write a paragraph in which they state and defend their opinion about the following statement: President Kennedy acted correctly when he tried to force steel companies to repeal their price increase. Conclude with a class discussion of the question. Encourage students to defend their opinion during the discussion.

☆ **Evaluating** Tell students to imagine that they are newspaper reporters in December 1963. Their editor has asked them to write an article evaluating the administration of President Kennedy in one of the following areas: the space program, economic policies, civil rights. They should summarize the actions or programs and then evaluate them using these criteria: (1) Do you think the programs or actions achieved their goal? (2) Do you think they were beneficial for the group at which they were aimed? (3) Do you think they were beneficial for the country as a whole?

☐ **Analyzing Oral Evidence** Ask students to interview a family member or friend about the day President Kennedy was assassinated. Before they begin, have them read about the day in newspapers or news magazines from the time and prepare a list of questions. Questions should concentrate on the person's recollections of that day. When students have completed their interview, ask them to summarize their findings in a written report.

ANSWERS: VOICES OF FREEDOM   (page 739)
1. We hold these truths to be self-evident; that all men are created equal. **2.** He would have opposed them; he favored a society where everyone lived together as equals.

ANSWERS: SECTION 2 REVIEW   (page 740)
1. Alan Shepard, John Glenn, *Telstar*—p. 737; James Meredith, George Wallace—p. 738. **2.** That an American land on the moon and return safely by 1970. **3. (a)** Established "wage-price guideposts" for business and labor. **(b)** Steel industry. Because so many other industries depend on steel. **4.** Nonviolent protests, such as sit-ins, freedom rides, rent strikes, store boycotts, and rallies such as the march on Washington; lawsuits against people who committed acts of discrimination. **5.** Possible answer: Because the frontier was an important part of U.S. history and it symbolized the hard work and determination of which Americans are proud.

SECTION 3   (pages 741–743)
Building the Great Society

ACTIVITIES

○ **Identifying** Ask students to identify who or what is referred to by each of the following clues: (1) act that provided health insurance for persons over 65, (2) Republican presidential candidate in 1964, (3) the domestic Peace Corps, (4) first secretary of the Department of Housing and Urban Development, (5) keystone of Lyndon Johnson's War on Poverty. *Answers:* **1.** Medicare **2.** Barry Goldwater **3.** VISTA **4.** Robert Weaver **5.** Economic Opportunity Act

☆ **Ranking** Draw on the chalkboard an outline of a chart with three columns headed Legislation, Problems, Actions. Ask students to list Great Society legislation passed between 1963 and 1965 and record their responses. Then ask them to describe what problems each piece of legislation was intended to solve and the actions that could be undertaken as a result of each piece of legislation to solve the problems. When the chart is complete, ask students to rank the Great Society legislation based on its historical significance.

☐ **Relating Past to Present** Have students review the major legislation of President Johnson's Great Society. Ask them to do additional research and find out which Great Society programs still exist today.

ANSWERS: SECTION 3 REVIEW   (page 743)
1. VISTA, Hubert H. Humphrey, Barry Goldwater—p. 741. **2.** Tax cut, Civil Rights Act of 1964. **3. (a)** Because 16 percent of the population lived below the poverty line. **(b)** Provided job training programs for the poor, loans to encourage rural farm cooperatives and urban businesses, and aid to migrant laborers. **4.** Provided hospital coverage for citizens over 65 and allowed them to join a program that helped pay other medical costs. **5.** Civil Rights Act of 1964, Voting Rights Act of 1965. **6.** Possible answer: It attempted to establish a society with equal opportunities for everyone.

SECTION 4 (pages 743–748)
Struggles for Equal Rights

ACTIVITIES

○ **Name Game** Read the following clues and ask students to identify who is described by each: (1) Black Muslim leader; (2) one founder of the American Indian Movement; (3) leader of La Raza Unida; (4) author of *The Feminine Mystique;* (5) leader of movement to organize grape pickers.
Answers: **1.** Malcolm X **2.** Bellecourt or Banks **3.** Gutiérrez **4.** Friedan **5.** Chavez

☆ **Generalizing** Ask students to write one or two factual statements to support each of the following generalizations: (1) After 1963, the civil rights movement for blacks became more militant. (2) Hispanic Americans have a variety of heritages. (3) The policy of the United States government toward American Indians changed several times since the late 1880s. (4) Despite some progress during the 1960s, women who worked outside the home still faced inequalities and continued to be victims of discrimination.

☐ **Relating Past to Present** Have students investigate the current status of women in America. They might look into employment, earnings, or political participation. Ask what issues women's rights organizations focus on today. Ask them to compare women's status today with that of the 1960s.

ANSWER: GRAPH STUDY (page 747)
1962.

ANSWERS: SECTION 4 REVIEW (page 748)
1. Kerner Commission—p. 744; Cesar Chavez—p. 745; Dennis Banks, American Indian Movement—p. 746; Betty Friedan—p. 747. **2.** de facto segregation—p. 743; bracero—p. 745. **3. (a)** They believed nonviolence did not work fast enough. Some black leaders were particularly concerned about the plight of northern blacks and demanded action to overcome the de facto segregation, high unemployment, and low average income that existed for blacks there. **(b)** Some advocated separation of the races; some favored revolution and self-defense. **(c)** Destruction of life and property; white backlash **4. (a)** Hispanics—acceptance of the migrant workers union; more good jobs for Hispanic Americans; improved sensitivity in schools to Hispanics' needs. American Indians—greater pride in Indian heritage. Women—Equal Pay Act of 1963 and the Civil Rights Act of 1964.

(b) Hispanics—poverty, discrimination, conflict within the Hispanic community about assimilation or maintaining ethnic identity. American Indians—failure of AIM at Wounded Knee; conflicting government policies. Women—enforcement of Equal Pay Act and Civil Rights Act. **5.** Possible answer: It encouraged other groups to fight for civil rights, because it created an atmosphere for change in the nation.

SECTION 5 (pages 749–755)
Growing Involvement in World Affairs

ACTIVITIES

○ **Map Reading** Ask students to study the map on text page 750 and answer these questions: (1) Which country is located immediately west of North Vietnam? (2) Which countries border the Gulf of Tonkin? (3) The Mekong River forms a large part of the border between which two countries? (4) Through which countries did the Ho Chi Minh Trail pass? (5) What country is located north of the Gulf of Thailand?

☆ **Using Visual Evidence** Tell students that the war in Vietnam was the topic of many cartoons. Have them study cartoons from the 1960s. They can find examples in news magazines or newspapers from the period, some of which should be available at a local library. Ask students to write a report in which they describe what they learned from the cartoons about public attitude toward the war.

☐ **Interviewing** Ask students to imagine that they are reporters for a television network that is preparing a special program on President Johnson's decision not to run for reelection in 1968. Tell students that they are to interview the President for the program. Have them do additional research about events of that year and then make a list of questions they would like to ask Johnson in the interview.

ANSWER: MAP STUDY (page 750)
Because the trail went through Laos and Cambodia, it encouraged the Americans and South Vietnamese to mount attacks in these countries.

ANSWERS: ARTS IN AMERICA (page 754)
1. war, radioactive fallout, bigotry, injustice. **2.** Music can create an emotional response through rhythms, appealing melodies, and haunting lyrics.

ANSWERS: **SECTION 5 REVIEW**   (page 755)

1. Third World—p. 749; Viet Cong—p. 750; William Westmoreland—p. 752 **2.** apartheid—p. 749. **3.** During an attempt by Juan Bosch to regain power, Johnson sent troops to protect American civilians there and to prevent communists from taking advantage of the unstable situation. **4.** Eisenhower backed Diem by sending military advisers. Kennedy increased the number of advisers and the amount of equipment the U.S. sent to South Vietnam. **5.** To stop North Vietnam from supplying the Viet Cong. **6.** He announced in March 1968 that he was suspending bombing of North Vietnam and that he would not run for reelection. **7.** Possible answer: It led to full-scale U.S. involvement in the war.

ANSWERS: **CHAPTER 34 REVIEW**
                    (pages 756–757)

Vocabulary   1. Strategic forces **2.** poverty line **3.** de facto segregation **4.** bracero **5.** apartheid

Chapter Checkup   1. (a) Bay of Pigs, Soviet threat to sign a separate peace treaty with East Germany, Berlin Wall, Cuban missile crisis. **(b)** Cuban missile crisis, because it made both the United States and the Soviet Union realize the sobering prospect of nuclear war. **2. (a)** He pledged to land a man on the moon by 1970 and supported the NASA space program. **(b)** He urged Congress to pass a tax cut and several programs designed to reduce poverty. To control inflation, he established informal "wage-price guideposts." **(c)** He proposed comprehensive civil rights legislation that would ban discrimination in employment, in public accommodations, in voting, and in state programs receiving federal aid. **3. (a)** To teach and give technical advice to developing countries and thereby convince these nations that democracy is the best system. **(b)** To improve relations with Latin American nations and to convince them to make democratic reforms. **4. (a)** The Great Society "asks not only how much, but how good; not only how to create wealth, but how to use it; not only how fast we are going, but where we are headed." **(b)** The Economic Opportunity Act of 1964 provided job training programs, loans to encourage rural farm cooperatives and urban businesses, and aid to migrant workers. **5. (a)** Sit-ins, "freedom rides," protest marches, and store boycotts. **(b)** Some black leaders believed that nonviolent tactics were not bringing full equality quickly enough. **6. (a)** Hispanic Americans, American Indians, and women. **(b)** Discrimination in education, in employment opportunities, and in wages. **7. (a)** Desire to stop communism in South Vietnam; attacks on two American ships in the Gulf of Tonkin. **(b)** Troop escalation, rising war costs, American deaths,

devastation of the Vietnamese people and countryside. **8. (a)** "Hawks" supported America's role in the Vietnam War. They argued that the U.S., in fighting communism in South Vietnam, was preventing a communist takeover of all of Southeast Asia. **(b)** "Doves" opposed American involvement in the war. They argued that the U.S. had no compelling reason to justify the enormous sacrifice in lives and money and that it was interfering in a civil war.

Critical Thinking   1. The Kerner Commission warned that although African Americans had made significant progress, "our nation is moving toward two societies, one black, one white—separate but unequal." A "commitment to national action," however, could bring equality to all. **2. (a)** During the Korean War, the U.S. fought as part of a UN effort to stop North Korean aggression. In the Vietnam conflict, the U.S. did not fight under the UN banner. **(b)** In World War II, the U.S. declared war on Japan after Japan attacked Pearl Harbor. American involvement in the Vietnam War did not stem from an attack on U.S. territory. **(c)** U.S. efforts in Vietnam did not have active support in the noncommunist world. Many Americans saw little cause or reason for U.S. involvement in the Vietnam War.

Connecting Past and Present   1. Answers will vary. **2.** Women today have more types of jobs open to them, and are freer to choose a career or motherhood or both and to hold high jobs in business and in government.

Developing Basic Skills   1. (a) 1960s. Students might suggest that blacks staged protests against discrimination. **(b)** 1960s. **2. (a)** It went up from $1,500 to $4,500. **(b)** It went up from about $800 to $2,500. **(c)** There was a larger dollar gap between the income of men and women in 1970 than in 1950. **(d)** Women continued to hold lower-paying jobs than men.

Chapter 35   (pages 758–783)

Challenges at Home and Abroad _____

OVERVIEW

Chapter 35 focuses on events between 1969 and 1980. Students read about Richard Nixon's attempts to bring stability and calm to the nation. They also read how the Nixon presidency ended with the President's resignation as a result of the Watergate affair. They examine the domestic and foreign challenges that faced Presidents Gerald Ford and Jimmy Carter.

HISTORICAL SIDELIGHT

The following piece of historical information can serve as a note of interest during the study of Chapter 35. The page number in parentheses indicates the point in the student text at which you may wish to introduce the information.

Quick Thinking (p. 758) As the *Eagle* spacecraft began its final descent to the moon's surface on June 20, 1969, astronaut Neil Armstrong became aware that the computer-controlled landing equipment was directing the vehicle toward a rocky, rough crater. Quickly, Armstrong took over the controls himself and maneuvered the vehicle to a safer spot. During the maneuver, his heartbeat increased to 156 beats per minute—more than twice the normal pulse rate. The *Eagle* landed safely, completing a 200,000-mile flight only one and a half minutes off schedule.

SECTION 1   (pages 759–763)
A Balance of Power

ACTIVITIES*

○ **Identification** Ask students to identify whom or what each of the following clues refers to: (1) agreement that restricted nuclear warheads and missiles, (2) Nixon's national security adviser, (3) act declaring that a President could not send troops into battle for longer than 60 days without congressional authorization, (4) policy according to which the South Vietnamese were to assume more responsibility for fighting the war.
Answers: **1.** SALT **2.** Henry Kissinger **3.** War Powers Act **4.** Vietnamization

☆ **Relating Cause and Effect** Tell students to draw a chart with two rows labeled Vietnamization and Improved Relations with China and the Soviet Union, and two columns headed Causes and Effects. Have them describe the beliefs and developments that contributed to each policy in the first column and list the effects of each policy in the second column. When students have completed their individual charts, ask volunteers to use their charts to

draw a class chart on the chalkboard. Ask students to explain how the effects of each policy are related to one another.

☐ **Relating Past to Present** Have students do additional research and write a report outlining relations between the United States and China since President Nixon's trip to China in 1972. They could consult the *Readers' Guide to Periodical Literature* for possible sources.

ANSWERS: **THE AMERICAN EXPERIENCE**
(page 762)
1. To create a memorial where people could come to think privately about the war and its consequences. **2.** Possible answer: It says publicly that Americans are ready to honor the people who lost their lives in the war.

ANSWERS: **SECTION 1 REVIEW**   (page 763)
1. Henry Kissinger—p. 760; SALT—p. 763. **2.** détente—p. 763. **3. (a)** He believed that in the world there were many centers of power, including Europe, Japan, the People's Republic of China, the Soviet Union, the Middle East, and the U.S. The U.S. should pursue different goals in each one. **(b)** The U.S. will help its allies, but will not take over full planning and execution of policies for their protection. **4.** Both sides signed a cease-fire agreement in January 1973. Over the next few months American troops withdrew from Vietnam. **5.** Nixon and Chinese leaders agreed to allow scientific, cultural, and journalistic exchanges between the two countries. **6.** Possible answer: He was able to take steps to normalize relations with the Soviet Union and with China without seeming to make concessions to communism.

SECTION 2   (pages 764–767)
The Politics of Stability

ACTIVITIES

○ **Placing Events in Time** Ask students to find the dates of these events and put them in chronological order: (1) Arab oil embargo, (2) reelection of Richard Nixon, (3) first landing on the moon, (4) outbreak of the October War.
Answers: 3, 2, 4, 1

☆ **Finding the Main Idea** **1.** Divide the class into five groups and assign each group one of the subsections in Section 2. Tell each group to write one statement that reflects the main idea of the subsection plus two other statements about the subsection that are true but are not the main idea. When the groups have completed their statements, have a representative from each group write the three statements on the chalkboard in random order. Ask the other students to review each subsection and decide which of the three statements is the main idea.

☐ **Biographical Sketch** Have students write a biographical sketch of one of the men President Nixon appointed to the Supreme Court—Warren Burger, Harry Blackmun, Lewis Powell, or William Rehnquist. They should concentrate on the person's legal background.

ANSWER: GRAPH STUDY   (page 765)
1978.

ANSWERS: SECTION 2 REVIEW   (page 767)
1. Earl Warren, Warren Burger—p. 764; OPEC—p. 765; Neil Armstrong—p. 766; George McGovern—p. 767. **2.** impound, stagflation—p. 765. **3.** It ruled that before questioning accused persons, police are required to inform them of their rights to remain silent and to be represented by a lawyer. **4.** Nixon closed the Office of Economic Opportunity, vetoed bills providing funds for social programs, and impounded funds appropriated by Congress. **5.** Successfully negotiated a cease-fire agreement between Egypt and Israel. **6.** Possible answer: He and his views are already well known. Often he can manipulate events to his advantage.

SECTION 3   (pages 768–771)
A Crisis in the Presidency

ACTIVITIES
○ **Name Game** Read the following clues and ask students to identify each person: (1) second special prosecutor appointed to investigate the Watergate affair; (2) reporter who revealed much of the information about the Watergate affair; (3) chairman of the Senate committee investigating the Watergate affair; (4) accused President Nixon of suppressing evidence about the Watergate break-in; (5) attorney general who was indicted in the Watergate affair.
Answers: **1.** Jaworski **2.** Woodward or Bernstein **3.** Ervin **4.** Dean **5.** Mitchell
☆ **Expressing an Opinion** Ask students to state and defend in writing their opinion of the fol-

lowing statement: The House Judiciary Committee was right to pass articles of impeachment against President Nixon.

☐ **Comparing** Many accounts of the Watergate affair have been written since 1974, including *All the President's Men* by Carl Bernstein and Bob Woodward and *Breach of Faith: Fall of Richard Nixon* by Theodore White. Have students read two of the books and write a report comparing their treatment of the event.

ANSWERS: SECTION 3 REVIEW   (page 771)
1. John Mitchell, Sam Ervin, John Dean—p. 768; Archibald Cox, Gerald Ford, Leon Jaworski—p. 769. **2.** Nixon's order to fire special prosecutor Archibald Cox and the consequent resignations of Attorney General Elliot Richardson and his assistant, William Ruckelshaus. **3.** Because they would prove what the President and others knew about the break-in and subsequent cover-up. **4.** That the President had obstructed justice, misused his presidential powers, and refused to comply with the committee's request for evidence. **5.** Possible answer: People have sought the security that a strong President can provide.

SECTION 4   (pages 771–775)
A New Start

ACTIVITIES
○ **Interviewing** Have students speak to relatives or neighbors who remember the bicentennial celebration in your community. After they conduct interviews, ask students to share with the class what they learned. By putting together the information they gathered, have students describe the bicentennial celebration. Ask: Why do you think people made such a fuss about the bicentennial?

☆ **Writing an Editorial** Ask students to imagine that they are writers for a news magazine in January 1977. Their editor has just asked them to write an editorial evaluating Gerald Ford's term as President. Have each student write an editorial addressing the following questions: (1) What were the main achievements of the Ford administration? (2) What were the main failures? (3) On the whole, was the Ford presidency a success or a failure? Students should provide factual information to support their conclusions.

☐ **Identifying a Point of View** Have students read several contemporary reports about

President Ford's pardon of Richard Nixon. Refer them to the *Readers' Guide to Periodical Literature* for sources. Ask them to write a brief summary of each account and to describe the points of view of each of the authors.

ANSWERS: SECTION 4 REVIEW (page 775)

1. Nelson Rockefeller—p. 771; WIN—p. 773; Helsinki Accords—p. 774. **2.** The CIA had violated its charter by keeping files on American citizens, and J. Edgar Hoover, longtime head of the FBI, had kept secret files on prominent Americans. **3. (a)** By convincing Congress to pass a tax cut. **(b)** Sparked a modest recovery, but also caused inflation to worsen. **4.** The Soviet Union had violated nuclear arms pacts, built up its arsenal of weapons, encouraged Egypt to attack Israel in 1973, and was arming other Third World countries. **5.** Possible answer: It might have harmed the nation by further eroding confidence in the office of the presidency.

SECTION 5 (pages 775–781)
The Carter White House

ACTIVITIES

○ **Summarizing** Ask students to write brief summaries of each of the subsections in Section 5. When they have completed their individual summaries, have volunteers read their summaries aloud. Then, through a class discussion, arrive at the best summary of each subsection.

☆ **Comparing** Have students compare U.S. foreign policy under Gerald Ford and Jimmy Carter. They should note regions of crisis and governmental actions. Urge students to do additional research.

□ **Writing a Report** Ask students to research and write a report about the conflict between Israel and the Arab nations in the Middle East. They should describe the causes of the conflict and outline major developments. Possible sources include *The Arab-Israeli Dilemma* by Fred Khouri.

ANSWER: MAP STUDY (page 778)

It serves as a buffer between Israel and the Suez Canal.

ANSWERS: SECTION 5 REVIEW (page 781)

T 140 **1.** Anwar el-Sadat, Menachem Begin—p. 778;

Ayatollah Khomeini—p. 780. **2.** Carter proposed a number of major pieces of legislation and Congress passed versions that were greatly changed. **3.** Carter required the State Department to use a country's human rights activity as a criterion for receiving U.S. aid and suspended military aid to nations guilty of human rights violations. **4.** Iran cut off virtually all oil shipments to the United States, which helped to cause the price of petroleum products to go up; this contributed to a high rate of inflation. **5.** Possible answer: The U.S. might seek to maintain or improve relations with oil-producing nations.

ANSWERS: CHAPTER 35 REVIEW

(pages 782–783)

Vocabulary **1.** Vietnamization **2.** Détente **3.** impounded **4.** Stagflation **5.** shuttle diplomacy **6.** subpoena

Chapter Checkup **1.** Nixon visited China in 1972 and agreed to allow scientific, cultural, and journalistic exchanges between the two countries. He also visited the Soviet Union and signed an arms control agreement with that country. **2. (a)** They resented U.S. aid to Israel during the October War. **(b)** Disrupted American life; caused long lines at gas stations; increased the price of fuel and other petroleum-based products, such as plastics, synthetic fibers, medicines, and fertilizers; and aggravated inflation. **3. (a)** In response to 16 bills calling for the impeachment of the President. **(b)** It passed three articles of impeachment against the President, claiming that he had obstructed justice, misused his presidential powers, and refused to comply with the committee's request for evidence. **(c)** Nixon released transcripts of taped conversations and on August 8, 1974, he resigned. **4. (a)** Inflation, unemployment, and energy shortages. **(b)** Nixon tried freezing prices and then imposing price controls. Ford called for a policy of voluntary restraint. Both Nixon and Ford tried to lower unemployment by cutting taxes. Nixon worked to ease the energy crisis by asking the states to lower speed limits and by signing a bill authorizing the construction of an oil pipeline across Alaska and Canada. **(c)** Nixon's policies restrained price increases in the short run, but after government controls were lifted, inflation again became a serious problem. Although Ford's tax cut reduced unemployment, it also aggravated inflation. Nixon's energy policies made the nation more sensitive to the need to conserve energy. **5. (a)** Critics charged that Carter used a double standard in enforcing his policy on human rights. They said he was lenient with the nation's important allies and strict with those considered less important. **(b)** Critics charged he was giving away American property. **(c)** Conservative Republicans accused Carter of abandoning nationalist China, a longtime ally of the U.S. **(d)** Critics in the Senate argued that the treaty would give the Soviet Union an advantage in nuclear weapons since the Soviets had been outspending the U.S. on defense for ten years.

Critical Thinking   1. Students might note that a person without a strong anticommunist background might have been labeled "soft on communism" by some Americans. **2.** The system worked extremely well, with the legislative and judicial branches carrying out their constitutional authority to check and balance the executive branch. Congress reviewed the President's activities and was thus able to check his abuse of power. The investigations of the Senate and House committees eventually led to Nixon's resignation. The ruling of the Supreme Court forced the President to produce the tapes needed by the special prosecutor and the Judiciary Committee for their investigations.

Connecting Past and Present   1. (a) Congress seems to have taken back some of its power since the 1970s. During the 1970s, Congress passed laws curtailing the President's power to some extent. **(b)** Accept all reasonable answers. **2.** Iran is still a major oil-producing nation. Also, Iran's actions affect the stability of the Middle East, a region in which the United States takes great interest. Also, Iran's suspected role in Middle East terrorism has made the United States reluctant to deal diplomatically with Iran on important questions..

Developing Basic Skills   1. Encourage students to investigate additional products developed as a result of the space program. **2. (a)** It went down dramatically from 112 cents to 40 cents. **(b)** 40 cents worth of goods. **(c)** The average American would have to spend more of his or her money on food and other necessities and would generally feel poorer.

Chapter 36   (pages 784–809)

New Directions ——————

OVERVIEW
Chapter 36 focuses on developments in the U.S. during the late 1970s and the 1980s. Students read about political, economic, and foreign policy developments under President Ronald Reagan and about the early days of the George Bush presidency.

They also examine social issues of the late 1980s and recent developments in the struggle for equality.

HISTORICAL SIDELIGHT
The following piece of historical information can serve as a note of interest during the study of Chapter 36. The page number in parentheses indicates the point in the student text at which you may wish to introduce the information.

How Much Is $850 Billion? (p. 788)   The proposed federal budget for the 1984 fiscal year was almost $850 billion. This figure was so large that it meant little to the average person, so the President and various economists and news reporters devised illustrations to clarify it. For example, if 850 billion dollar bills were placed end to end, they would extend over 80 million miles— almost to the sun. Also, if $1 million had been spent every day for the last 2,000 years, there would still be $120 million left of the $850 billion.

SECTION 1   (pages 785–790)
The Reagan Revolution

ACTIVITIES*
○ **Applying Information**   Tell students to imagine that they are newscasters on the eve of the 1984 presidential election. Have them prepare a newscast that includes a description of the presidential and vice-presidential candidates, an evaluation of the mood of the country, and a prediction of the outcome of the election.

☆ **Analyzing a Quotation**   Ask students to identify Reagan policies that illustrate his belief that "government is not the solution to our problems; government is the problem."

□ **Writing a Report**   Have students research newspaper and magazine articles from 1985 and 1986 for viewpoints about the Gramm-Rudman Act. Students should focus on reactions to passage of the act and to the Supreme Court's decision that a provision of the act was unconstitutional. Ask students to present their findings in a written report.

ANSWER: GRAPH STUDY   (page 787)
1982–1986.

————
*See "To the Teacher" for an explanation of the symbols.

ANSWER: GRAPH STUDY   (page 789)

1980.

ANSWERS: SECTION 1 REVIEW   (page 790)

1. Reaganomics—p. 786; Sandra Day O'Connor—p. 789. **2.** deficit, deregulation—p. 786. **3. (a)** Excessive government spending, which created large deficits that fueled inflation. **(b)** A three-year cut in income taxes and a $35-billion cut in funds budgeted for social programs. **4.** To produce a balanced budget over time. **5.** Possible answer: Decisions might become more conservative.

SECTION 2   (pages 790–796)
Foreign Affairs During the Reagan Years

ACTIVITIES

○ **Map Reading** Have students locate on the map on text pages 842–843 each of the countries referred to in the following clues: (1) where Solidarity organized strikes; (2) where President Reagan and Premier Gorbachev met in 1986 to discuss arms control; (3) where the contras fought the Sandinistas; (4) where 241 American marines were killed by terrorists; (5) where the white government follows a policy of apartheid.

☆ **Supporting Generalizations** Ask students to write one or more factual statements that support each of the following generalizations: (1) Ronald Reagan opposed the policy of détente with the Soviet Union. (2) The Middle East continued to be an area of concern for the United States in the early 1980s. (3) Ronald Reagan viewed problems in Latin America within the framework of the larger struggle with the Soviet Union.

□ **Defending a Position** Have students find newspaper and magazine articles that express opposing viewpoints about SDI. Divide the class into two groups to debate the issue.

ANSWERS: GRAPH STUDY   (page 794)

1980; seven.

ANSWERS: SECTION 2 REVIEW   (page 796)

1. Mikhail Gorbachev—p. 791; INF treaty, contras—p. 792. **2.** glasnost—p. 791; divestiture—p. 795. **3. (a)** He tended to see international situations in

terms of superpower conflicts; however, he also worked to ease tensions with the Soviet Union by negotiating the INF treaty. **(b)** The Soviet Union seemed to be following a less aggressive foreign policy, and the United States took an attitude of watchful waiting. The INF treaty was an example of the easing of tensions. **4. (a)** Anticommunism. **(b)** Some Americans feared that commitment to the contras would eventually lead to the involvement of U.S. troops. Others felt it was illegal to support the overthrow of a government with which the U.S. maintained diplomatic relations. **5.** Ban on new investments in South Africa; prohibition of imports of South African products. **6.** Possible answer: Carter focused on human rights. Reagan focused on a power struggle with the Soviet Union.

SECTION 3   (pages 796–799)
Bush Takes Over

ACTIVITIES

○ **Outlining** Have students write a sentence outline of Section 3. The titles of the subsections can serve as major topics, but suggest that students rephrase them as questions.

☆ **Writing a Letter** Have students write a letter to the President stating what they think should be the most important focus of the antidrug campaign. They should give reasons to support their opinion.

□ **Relating Past and Present** Ask students to choose one issue that faced the Bush administration in its early days. Have them review what they have read about Bush's approach to the issue. Then have them read recent periodicals to see what is now happening in that area. What effects have Bush's actions had? Have them write a short essay summarizing their findings.

ANSWERS: SECTION 3 REVIEW   (page 799)

1. George Bush, Jesse Jackson, Michael Dukakis—p. 796; James A. Baker—p. 798. **2.** Arranged activities so they could be presented in short "sound bites" on the evening news; used extensive paid advertisements. **3.** Increased volunteerism, reduction in federal spending. **4.** Continuation of the "Just Say No" program; appointment of a "drug czar" to coordinate the effort. **5.** Possible answer: A Vice President must be loyal to the programs of the President; thus, the public does not see a Vice

President as "his or her own person." A Vice President must overcome this image in order to appear "presidential."

SECTION 4   (pages 799–803)
Examining Social Issues

ACTIVITIES
○ **Recognizing Trends** Have students review the subsection titled Traditional American Values (p. 799) and outline trends in social behavior and values during the 1960s, 1970s, and 1980s.
☆ **Analyzing a Quotation** Have students discuss the following quotation from "A Nation at Risk," a 1983 report by the U.S. Department of Education on the nation's educational system: "If an unfriendly power had attempted to impose on America the mediocre educational performance that exists today, we might well have viewed it as an act of war." Students should evaluate the emotional content of the quotation, the values it reflects, and its effectiveness in drawing attention to educational needs.
□ **Defending a Position** Have students read newspaper and magazine articles for viewpoints on drug testing. Ask students to write an essay in which they state and defend their opinion of drug testing of the following: government employees, corporation employees, and professional and college athletes.

ANSWERS: NOTABLE AMERICANS   (page 801)
1. It meant determination to work hard and do one's best. **2.** Possible answer: As students gained more confidence through success in calculus, they would feel less need to turn to drugs and gangs.

ANSWERS: SECTION 4 REVIEW   (page 803)
1. As a result of the increased divorce rate and the rising number of women working outside the home, increasing numbers of children are being cared for by someone other than their parent. **2.** Increasing the amount of time spent in school and the number of required courses in basic subjects. **3.** It has resulted in lost employee productivity, in high government expenditures to fight drugs, and in controversy over the question of drug testing. **4.** Possible answer: Many religious groups feel that values are matters for the family and the churches and should not become political issues.

SECTION 5   (pages 803–807)
Striving for Equality

ACTIVITIES
○ **Graph Reading** Have students study the graph on page 805 and answer the following questions: (1) What percentage of black workers were skilled trade workers in 1960? (2) What percentage of black workers were professional and technical workers in 1960? (3) How did the percentage of blacks who were professional and technical workers change between 1960 and 1980? (4) In which occupation did the percentage of black workers decline the most between 1960 and 1980?
☆ **Interviewing** Ask students to interview a female relative or family friend who is working in a job that has traditionally been considered a "man's job." Have students prepare a list of questions they would like to ask before the interview. When students have completed their interviews, have volunteers make oral reports about what they learned.
□ **Evaluating an Opinion** Ask students to research one of the Supreme Court cases relating to affirmative action. Have students write an essay explaining how the decision affected the meaning of affirmative action.

ANSWERS: GRAPH STUDY   (page 804)
Professional and technical workers, managers and administrators, service workers; managers and administrators, craft workers.

ANSWER: GRAPH STUDY   (page 805)
Operatives, nonfarm laborers, household workers, farm laborers.

ANSWERS: SECTION 5 REVIEW   (page 807)
1. Sally Ride—p. 803. **2.** affirmative action—p. 804; mainstream—p. 807. **3.** Careers in the armed forces, police and fire departments, engineering, and management. **4. (a)** Careers in professional, technical, and managements jobs; 1987 legal decision in support of affirmative action. **(b)** High unemployment, especially among youths; elimination of busing as a tool for school integration. **5.** They are the second largest minority group and form high percentages of the populations of many major cities. **6.** Rehabilitation Act of 1973 forbade discrimination against the handicapped in jobs, education, and housing. Special facilities have been designed for public buildings and means of transportation. Education for All Handicapped Children

Act provided for mainstreaming. **7.** Possible answers: American society is pluralistic; its democratic institutions generally allow all qualified people to participate and reach their own level of achievement.

Vocabulary   1. c 2. c **3.** c 4. c **5.** a **6.** b

Chapter Checkup   1. **(a)** Too much government spending, high taxes, high interest rates, inflation, and unemployment. **(b)** Reduction in government spending, cuts in personal income taxes, deregulation of industries. **2. (a)** He proposed to cut taxes, which would leave more money for investment; this would create jobs, which would lead to more income tax revenues and ultimately a balanced budget. The administration also called for reduced government spending. **(b)** Devalued the dollar; negotiated a free trade agreement with Canada. **3.** At first Reagan took a hard stand toward the Soviet Union; later he became more open to Soviet initiatives and negotiated the INF treaty. **4. (a)** Supported anti-communist governments and groups in Nicaragua, El Salvador. **(b)** Promote stability in the area and prevent Soviet gains there; supported the government of Lebanon, but later withdrew U.S. forces from the international peacekeeping force; maintained close relations with Israel while keeping up friendly relations with Arab countries; banned arms shipments to Iran; used its navy to protect the flow of oil through the Persian Gulf. **(c)** Adopted "constructive engagement"—minimum criticism of apartheid and quiet diplomacy—in order to protect U.S. strategic and economic interests. **5.** He said there was a "new breeze"; he called for cooperation between the parties and between the executive branch and Congress. **6. (a)** How far to continue the Reagan revolution; what attitude to take toward the Soviet Union; how to handle foreign policy in other areas, such as the Middle East, Latin America, and Asia; how to handle domestic economic problems, as well as the drug crisis. **(b)** Continued efforts to solve the problems between Israel and the Palestinians; cultivated relations with Japan, China, and South Korea by visiting them in the early days of his administration; supported the sending of humanitarian aid to the contras; called for more attention to education and supported an antidrug campaign. **7.** Increased divorce rate, increase in the number of single-parent families, teenage pregnancy, increased number of women who work outside the home. **8. (a)** Women have entered many careers traditionally reserved for men; however, as a group, women still earn less than men do, because most still work at jobs that do not pay as

well. **(b)** Blacks have benefited from affirmative action laws, although the laws have been limited by the courts; more blacks are receiving high school and college educations, enabling them to get better jobs and enter the middle class. **(c)** Hispanic Americans have become a major percentage of the population in many cities and in the Southwest. They have played an increasingly important role in political and social life. **(d)** Some Indian groups have made gains through court awards of property once owned by their ancestors; Indians now make up more than half of the workers in the Bureau of Indian Affairs; a few Indians have entered the professions; however, many Indians are still very poor. **(e)** The handicapped have benefited from the Rehabilitation Act of 1973 and the Education for All Handicapped Children Act; public buildings now provide easier access for the handicapped; some people, however, oppose mainstreaming.

Critical Thinking   1. **(a)** Roosevelt responded to the Great Depression of the early 1930s by dramatically increasing the involvement of the federal government in all aspects of the American economy in order to provide jobs and to stimulate economic recovery. Reagan felt that the recession of the early 1980s had been caused, in large measure, by excessive involvement of the federal government in the national economy. He proposed measures to decrease such involvement, including reduced government spending and less regulation of business and industry. **(b)** In the period between the beginning of the New Deal in 1933 and the early 1980s, the role of the federal government in American economic life had expanded enormously. In the early 1980s, many people felt that the government's role had become too large and its activities too all-encompassing. **2.** Students might suggest that the nature and extent of federal funding determines the availability of social services.

Connecting Past and Present   1. Students should list problems such as the Vietnam War, human rights, relations with China and the Soviet Union, conflict in the Middle East, arms control, and unrest in Latin America. Many of these areas were also of concern after World War II. After World War II, the United States faced the problems of rebuilding Europe and Japan and the growing conflict with the Soviet Union. In the 1970s and 1980s, western Europe and Japan had become strong economic powers; the superpowers began easing tensions and opened negotiations in important areas of mutual concern. **2.** The 1960s were a period when many people worked to improve American society, through the civil rights movement, women's movement, and participation in the Peace Corps and VISTA and other poverty programs. People spoke out on issues of concern, including the Vietnam War. During the 1980s, people turned inward; there were fitness crazes, self-help programs, and less attention to social issues.

Developing Basic Skills **1.** Research will vary. **2. (a)** 1982. **(b)** 1980. **(c)** Inflation declined between 1980 and 1982, but unemployment rose.

Chapter 37   (pages 810–833)
The United States: Today and Tomorrow ___

OVERVIEW
Chapter 37 provides an overview of major trends and developments in the present-day United States. Students examine government and politics, changing population patterns, science and technology, the economy, and foreign policy.

HISTORICAL SIDELIGHT
The following piece of historical information can serve as a note of interest during the study of Chapter 37. The page number in parentheses indicates the point in the student text at which you may wish to introduce the information.

A Buried Treasure (p. 822) Modern technology is contributing to exploration deep under water as well as far into outer space. In the mid-1970s, two ships were discovered 300 feet under water on the bottom of Lake Ontario. The U.S. Navy schooners *Hamilton* and *Scourge* had sunk in a storm on the way to fight the British in the War of 1812. In 1983, scientists took pictures with a specially designed remote control camera showing that the ships remained in good condition even after 170 years under water.

SECTION 1   (pages 811–814)
Governing a Growing Nation

ACTIVITIES*
O **Generalizing** Ask students to write one or two factual statements to support each of the following generalizations: (1) A growing num-

_____
*See "To the Teacher" for an explanation of the symbols.

ber of people have gained the right to vote since the Constitution was ratified in 1789. (2) Television has become an important feature of political life. (3) The size and functions of the federal government have grown over the course of the nation's history.

☆ **Graph Reading** Have students study the graph on text page 814 and answer the following questions: (1) What percentage of the voting-age population voted in the 1964 election? In the 1988 election? (2) How would you describe the trend in voting in presidential elections from 1964 to 1988? (3) What generalization can you make about voter turnout in off-year elections?

☐ **Defending a Position** Have students do additional research about the debate over the participation of political action committees in elections. Then ask them to write an essay in which they state and defend their position on the issue.

ANSWER: GRAPH STUDY   (page 812)
$300 million.

ANSWER: GRAPH STUDY   (page 814)
The trend in both presidential and congressional elections is for a smaller percentage of the voting-age population to go to the polls.

ANSWERS: SECTION 1 REVIEW   (page 814)
1. PAC—p. 812; Black Caucus—p. 813. **2.** special interest group—p. 812. **3.** It provides a wide range of social programs; it regulates many aspects of people's lives. **4.** Television has been an important factor in the decline of the power of political parties. Television offers coverage of candidates to a large audience; through the use of carefully controlled television coverage. The candidates themselves determine the nature of their campaigns and the issues they will discuss. **5.** Minorities such as blacks and Hispanics and women have won many posts in government on all levels. Blacks have made gains, particularly in state and local government. **6.** Possible answer: Because they concentrate on one issue, they can devote all their resources to getting their viewpoint across.

SECTION 2   (pages 815–820)
A Changing Population

ACTIVITIES
O **Graph Reading** Ask students to study the graph on text page 815 and answer these ques-

tions: (1) Which region was the source of most immigration in the period 1891–1910? (2) Which region was the source of most immigration in the period 1951–1970? (3) In which period did the number of immigrants from the Americas increase the most? (4) How would you describe immigration from northern and western Europe since 1910?

☆ **Studying Charts and Graphs** Have students write answers to the following questions about the graphs on text pages 816 and 818:

Major Religious Groups in the United States: (1) Which religious group is the largest? (2) Approximately how many members does the Roman Catholic church have in the United States? (3) Approximately how many members are there of Jewish congregations?

Distribution of United States Population by Age and Sex: (1) What percentage of the population in 1980 was women between ages 35 and 39? What percentage was women between ages 15 and 19? (2) What percentage of the population was men between ages 35 and 39? What percentage was men between ages 15 and 19? (3) Which two age groups represented the largest percentage of men and women in 1980?

Then ask students how they would describe the American people based on their study of these graphs and charts.

☐ **Identifying Relationships** Have students study the maps on text pages 846 and 847. Then ask them to describe what relationships they can identify between current population distribution and patterns of settlement.

ANSWERS: GRAPH STUDY   (page 815)
The Americas; the Americas and Asia.

ANSWER: GRAPH STUDY   (page 816)
Larger than all the others combined.

ANSWERS: GRAPH STUDY   (page 818)
The "bulge" in the 30–34 and younger group will become slimmer, while that in the 35–39 and older group will become larger; with more people in the older groups, the expenses for Medicare and Medicaid will probably increase.

ANSWERS: GEOGRAPHIC CONNECTION
                                        (page 820)
1. The seven states drained by the river signed a pact allotting the river's water. **2.** Possible answer: Communities have to decide how much development and population growth can be supported by the available water.

ANSWERS: SECTION 2 REVIEW   (page 820)
1. sunbelt, frostbelt—p. 819. **2.** bilingual education—p. 816; zero population growth—p. 818. **3.** People from Latin America, Asia, and the Caribbean Islands. **4.** Older people will make up less of the work force, but will be a higher percentage of the people needing services. **5.** Increase in gasoline prices, making commuting more expensive; the interest of some younger people in renovating old city buildings. **6.** Possible answer: Because an important part of American culture is the use of the English language; some people think that accepting another language would undermine a basic aspect of our culture. Defenders of bilingual education maintain that forcing children to abandon their native language would cut them off from an essential part of the culture of their parents and other forebears.

SECTION 3   (pages 821–824)
Advances in Science and Technology

ACTIVITIES

○ **Graph Reading** Have students study the graph on text page 821 and answer these questions: (1) What was the average life expectancy of Americans born in 1910? (2) How did the average life expectancy change between 1900 and 1950? (3) What was the average life expectancy of Americans born in 1960? (4) How did it change between 1960 and 1980?

☆ **Researching** Divide the class into small groups and assign each group one of the following topics: (1) disease prevention, (2) genetic engineering, (3) transplanting or replacing body parts, (4) home computers, (5) computers in offices, (6) computers in factories, (7) space program, (8) uses of lasers. Ask each group to do research and prepare an oral report.

☐ **Debating** Have students do additional research and then conduct a classroom debate on the following: Resolved that computers have had a negative impact on the quality of life in the U.S.

ANSWER: GRAPH STUDY   (page 821)
75 years.

ANSWERS: SECTION 3 REVIEW   (page 824)
1. genetic engineering—p. 821; modem, artificial

intelligence—p. 822; laser—p. 823. **2.** Students might mention the artificial production of insulin; development of pacemakers and dialysis machines; CAT scanning; use of lasers in surgery; and re-attachment of severed limbs by means of microsurgery. **3.** They have vastly increased the availability of information: VCRs make the storing of television programs possible; library card catalogs are now often on computers. **4.** They have made possible compact disc players, as well as fiber-optic cables. **5.** Whether they agree or disagree, students should give examples of changes to explain their answer. Some students might argue that it is not yet possible to determine the overall effects of computers on people's lives.

ANSWERS: SECTION 4 REVIEW (page 828)
1. sunrise industry—p. 825; dumping—p. 826. **2.** productivity—p. 826; givebacks—p. 827. **3. (a)** Instead of manufacturing, the American economy is now based on professions and service industries. **(b)** It has been one factor in the declining membership in labor unions because unions have traditionally had their largest memberships in the manufacturing industries. **4.** By guaranteeing a minimum price for certain crops; by paying farmers not to plant on some of their land. **5.** Possible answer: Improvement of environmental conditions creates higher operating costs for industry.

SECTION 5   (pages 829–831)
The United States and the World

ACTIVITIES

○ **Applying Information**   Point out to students that many products they use every day were imported into the U.S. Have students make a list of such products. Use individual student lists to compile a list of products on the chalkboard. Ask students why they think people buy the imported products rather than brands made in the U.S.

☆ **Locating Places on a World Map**   Have students make a list of the places mentioned in Section 5. Refer them to the world map on pages 842–843 to locate each of the places. Then ask them to give examples of the way in which the world has become more interdependent.

□ **Making an Oral Report**   Discuss with students the areas of the world that currently concern American policy makers the most. Then ask students to research the issues and present their findings in an oral report.

ANSWERS: SKILL LESSON (page 830)
Answers to questions will depend on the trend selected by students.

ANSWERS: SECTION 5 REVIEW (page 831)
1. default—p. 831. **2.** Until recently, American foreign policy related mainly to the conflict between the Soviet Union and the United States. In recent years, Americans have come to see that international relationships are very complex, not just a question of pro-American or pro-Soviet. **3.** Poverty, illiteracy, poor health conditions, difficulty in repaying debts to other nations. **4.** Food for Peace

SECTION 4   (pages 825–828)
The American Economy Today

ACTIVITIES

○ **Graph Reading**   Ask students to study the graph on text page 826 and answer the following questions: (1) When was the percentage of the work force in labor unions the highest? (2) What was the percentage of the work force in unions in 1988? (3) Based on the graph, what generalization can you make about union membership from 1950 to 1988?

☆ **Constructing a Graph**   Ask students to use the following data to construct a bar graph. Then have them write a paragraph describing what they can learn from the graph.

Percentage of Work Force

	Blue Collar	White Collar	Service	Farm
1952	40.1	35.9	10.2	11.6
1982	30.0	53.6	13.7	2.7
1989	27.1	57.2	13.1	2.6

Source: U.S. Department of Labor

□ **Researching**   Ask students to bring to class current newspaper and magazine articles pertaining to foreign trade competition. Have them prepare an outline of the main ideas and supporting details of the articles.

ANSWER: GRAPH STUDY (page 825)
It increased by about $2,500 billion.

ANSWER: GRAPH STUDY (page 826)
By about 10 percent.

program, which sends surplus food to people in need; Agency for International Development, which gives low-interest loans to worthy projects; Peace Corps; aid programs; private contributions and training programs. **5.** Accept all well-supported answers.

ANSWERS: CHAPTER 37 REVIEW

(pages 832–833)

Vocabulary   1. special interest group **2.** Zero population growth **3.** Genetic engineering **4.** Artificial intelligence **5.** laser **6.** Givebacks

Chapter Checkup   1. Fifty years ago, the federal government played a very minor role in people's lives. Today, the federal government touches all aspects of American life. Besides providing social services, today's federal government regulates a wide variety of things, ranging from the food Americans eat and the clothes they wear to the cars they drive and the safety of their environment. **2. (a)** To reach a large audience, campaigns focus on televised debates, appearances, and commercials. They generate "sound bites" that can fit neatly into the evening news. **(b)** Computerized polling enables candidates to pinpoint interests and views of given audiences and to tailor their messages to those audiences. **3.** Since 1965, most immigrants have come from Asia, Latin America, and the Caribbean Islands, instead of from Europe. **4.** The population is becoming older; the largest growing areas of population are in the Sunbelt. **5.** Possible answers include: alteration of the genetic code of cells to fight disease; use of human genes to produce insulin needed by diabetics; use of nylon thread thinner than a human hair to reattach severed limbs; use of CAT scan to look inside the brain and other organs of the body; use of electronic devices to assist or replace the body's own organs (pacemakers, dialysis machines). **6.** Technology, in the form of computers, modems, fiber-optic cables, VCRs, and other devices have enabled information to flow faster and more clearly. This has led to a veritable explosion of information. **7. (a)** Greater productivity and dumping. **(b)** By building new, more efficient plants; giving workers a greater role in solving on-the-job problems; negotiating international agreements limiting the exporting of certain goods from competing countries. **8. (a)** Possible answers include: air pollution; garbage and industrial wastes; contamination of the public water supply; acid rain; need to provide safe working environment. **(b)** Establishment of safe water and air standards by the federal government, appropriate disposal of garbage and industrial wastes. **9.** The complexity of the world's political and economic balance;

the concerns of America's traditional allies; domestic acceptability. **10.** Aid was given to famine-stricken Ethiopia. The Peace Corps has provided the expertise of trained Americans. The Agency for International Development has given low-interest loans. Food for Peace has shipped surplus food.

Critical Thinking   1. Students should note the ways the media were used in the campaign and explain which they found most effective. **2.** Students should note how computers could affect their homes, work, recreation, and health.

Connecting Past and Present   1. (a) Answers include: welfare programs, farm subsidies, funding of abortions, energy policy, industrial safety regulations. **(b)** Answers will vary. Supporters might argue that some problems can be tackled only by the federal government. Opponents might argue that we can no longer afford the luxury of federal involvement in so many areas. **2.** Possible answer: As the population ages, there will be political pressure to maintain or increase funding of programs such as social security and Medicare; however, with fewer young people to pay the taxes needed to support these programs, the government will have to find areas of expenditure to cut.

Developing Basic Skills   1. Answers may vary. Encourage students to provide specific information to support their ranking. **2. (a)** Distribution of federal government expenditures. **(b)** Income security. **(c)** 27.3%. **(d)** The percentage for interest will increase.

SPIRIT OF AMERICA   (pages 834–837)

ANSWERS: SPEAK AMERICAN   (page 835)

1. Science and technology, local regions, immigrants, and blacks have all contributed words to the language. **2.** It has words drawn from all backgrounds and walks of life and is therefore a democratic language.

ANSWERS: NOTABLE AMERICANS   (page 837)

1. Public awareness of the use and abuse of words. **2.** Possible answers: Agree, because knowledge of English is essential to realizing the opportunities of American life; disagree, because all Americans are well aware that they must know English to improve their economic situation.

ANSWERS: VOICES OF FREEDOM   (page 837)

1. Spanish was the language of home, not of life outside the home. **2.** It provides the ability to communicate outside the home.

THE UNITED STATES

A HISTORY OF THE REPUBLIC

Fort Snelling was built of stone and stood in a commanding
position overlooking the Mississippi River. It was one of a series of
forts built after the War of 1812 to protect settlers and fur traders
on the western frontier. The painting above, *A View of Fort Snelling,*
has been attributed to Seth Eastman, a painter of genre scenes,
who commanded the fort at one time.

Thomas Otter's painting, *On the Road,* symbolizes the final winning of the West by American settlers. Before the Civil War, families trekked westward in covered wagons. Soon after the Civil War, the railroad spanned the continent, speeding the fulfillment of the nation's manifest destiny. By the end of the nineteenth century, the frontier was closed.

THE UNITED STATES

A HISTORY OF THE REPUBLIC

James West Davidson/Mark H. Lytle

Prentice Hall
Englewood Cliffs, New Jersey
Needham, Massachusetts

(continued on page 916)

Contents

Chapter **4**
A Struggle for Empire (1600–1763)

UNIT
TWO   Creating a Republic

Chapter **5**
The Road to Revolution (1763–1775)

Chapter **6**
A War for Independence (1775–1783)

UNIT
FOUR   **An Era of Expansion**   242

UNIT FIVE   A Nation Torn Apart   330

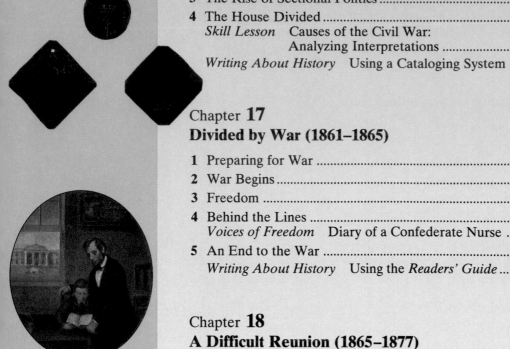

Chapter 20
An Age of Industry (1865–1914)
                                               420

Chapter 21
Politics and Reform (1867–1900)
                                               444

Chapter 22
Toward an Urban Age (1865–1914)
                                               466

Spirit of America

UNIT EIGHT   The Years Between the Wars

UNIT NINE
War and the Search for Peace   646

"above and beyond the call of duty"

UNIT TEN   **Toward the Next Century** 730

REFERENCE SECTION   838

Special Features

Skill Lessons

Writing About History

Maps

Charts and Graphs

A Letter From the Authors

"History is more or less the bunk," auto maker Henry Ford once remarked. "We want to live in the present."

Yet all of us, whether we realize it or not, have to draw on the past in everything we do. Decisions that were made years ago, often by other people, continue to affect us in major ways. That's one reason why science fiction stories about time machines are popular. They give their heroes a chance to go back and change the events that have shaped their lives.

Although we can't physically go back in time—at least, not in a machine—studying history offers a way. It is not as easy as pulling a lever and being instantly transported to long ago. But it can be a good deal of fun.

Try an experiment. Take whatever objects are in your pocket or purse and ask a few questions about the history behind them. We tried it and brought out of one of our pockets a couple of train tickets, a watch, keys, and some spare change. Nothing particularly unusual. But we began looking at each item, asking questions, and thinking about its history.

Take the ticket stubs, for instance. Today anyone can pick up a phone, dial an 800 number, and make train reservations from one city to another. But what sort of history lies behind those simple actions? A traveler of the 1860s would have had a much harder time purchasing tickets. There was no national booking system that sold one ticket for a journey that stretched over several rail lines. There was no telephone system that made it possible to call in reservations. Before a national railway network could be put into place, the United States had to build a highly complex industrial system.

The frontier had a tremendous impact on the course of American history. As a result, whether your ancestors were born in Europe, Asia, Africa, Oceania, or the Americas, the frontier experience is part of your history.

Or think about the pocket watch. Time is something we all take for granted. Clocks and watches sell for only a few dollars. Yet ordinary people could not afford to buy accurate clocks before the mid-1800s. Even when they did, each town set its own official time by taking measurements on the position of the sun. No national system of time existed. (New York and Boston, for example, were 11 minutes and 45 seconds apart.)

By 1882, there were about 50 systems of time—all different. To help passengers, train stations often had several clocks showing the time on different lines. Only in 1883 did the railroads set up four standard time zones across the United States. These time zones correspond to the ones we have today.

For each object in our everyday lives, it would be possible to find similar histories. Taken together, these histories would provide a fairly good picture of how your own life got to be the way it is. But it is the responsibility of a textbook to go further. Along with the stories of Presidents and politicians are the stories of ordinary people—nurses and soldiers, sports heroes and ministers, teachers and farmers. A textbook must synthesize their stories into a bigger picture to show the important themes that have characterized American history.

Despite time machine fantasies, we can never go back and change the past. But by understanding it, we can do something better: profit from its lessons and use them to shape our future.

James West Davidson
Mark H. Lytle

Even the contents of someone's pocket can be historical evidence.

About the Authors

James West Davidson (right) has written on a wide range of American history topics. He and Mark H. Lytle are the authors of *A History of the Republic: The United States From 1865* and *After the Fact: The Art of Historical Detection.* Dr. Davidson also wrote *The American Nation* and *A History of the Republic: The United States to 1877* with John E. Batchelor. With extensive teaching experience, Dr. Davidson consults on curriculum design for American history courses.

In his spare time, Dr. Davidson is an enthusiastic hiker and canoeist. *One River Down* is his own documentary film of a canoe trip in Labrador. *The Complete Wilderness Paddler,* written with John Rugge, is a how-to book for the wilderness canoeist. *Great Heart* is the true story of a 1903 canoe trip.

Mark H. Lytle is chairperson of American Studies at Bard College. Author of numerous articles on the United States and Iran and *Origins of the Iranian-American Alliance, 1941–1953,* Dr. Lytle has taught high school social studies, including black history in the Buffalo public schools. Dr. Lytle wrote *A History of the Republic: The United States From 1865* and *After the Fact: The Art of Historical Detection* with James West Davidson.

Dr. Lytle is an avid sportsman and tennis player. He is co-author of *Shang,* a book about the traditional art of carving duck decoys. Dr. Lytle lives with his wife and two children in Rhinebeck, New York.

The Art of Historical Detection

The following anecdote is from After the Fact, *a book of historical detection by James West Davidson and Mark H. Lytle. It describes an incident that focused the authors' attention on how historians work.*

One day while working on another project, we went outside to watch a neighboring farmer cut down a large old hemlock that had become diseased. As his saw cut deeper into the tree, we joked that it had now bit into history as far back as the Depression. "Depression?" grunted our friend. "I thought you fellows were historians. I'm deep enough now so's Hoover wasn't even born yet."

With the tree down, the three of us examined the stump. Our woodcutter surprised us with what he saw.

"Here's when my folks moved," he said, pointing to a ring. "1922."

"How do you know without counting the rings?" we asked.

"Oh, well," he said, as if the answer were obvious. "Look at the core, here. The rings are all bunched up tight. I bet there's sixty or seventy—and all within a couple of inches. Those came when the place was still forest. Then, you notice, the rings start getting fatter all of a sudden. That's when my dad cleared behind the house—in '22—and the tree started getting a lot more light. And look further out, here—see how the rings set together again for a couple years? That's from loopers."

"Loopers?" we asked cautiously.

"Sure—loopers. You know. The ones with only front legs and back." His hand imitated a looping, hopping crawl across the log. "Inchworms. They nearly killed the tree. That was sometime after the war—'49 or '50." As his fingers traced back and forth among the concentric circles, he spoke of other events from years gone by.

Now, it occurs to us that our neighbor had a pretty good knack for putting together history. The evidence of the past, like the tree rings, comes easily enough to hand. But we still need to be taught how to see it, read it, and explain it before it can be turned into a story. Even more to the point, the explanations and interpretations behind the story often turn out to be as interesting as the story itself. ∎

This book is organized into 10 units and 37 chapters. The Table of Contents (pages v–xx) lists the titles of the units and chapters. It also lists special features, skill lessons, writing lessons, and maps, charts, and graphs in the text. At the back of the book is a reference section with useful maps, charts, and documents.

Many features have been included in this book to assist you during your course of study:

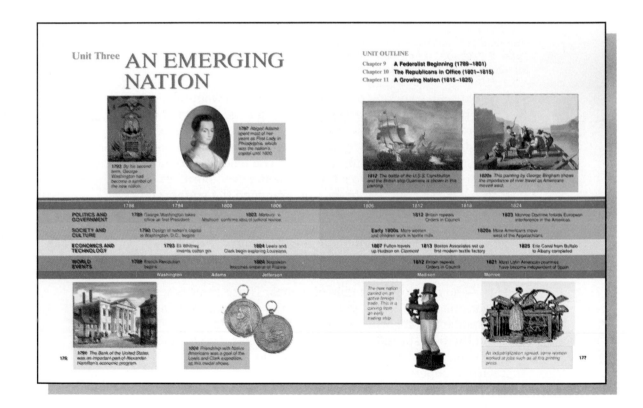

1. **Unit Opener.** Each unit begins with an illustrated time line that correlates major events in politics and government, society and culture, economics and technology, and world history.

2. **Chapter Opener.** Every chapter opens with an outline of the chapter as well as an illustration and an introductory story about a major theme, person, or event in the chapter.

3. **Time Lines.** A time line appears after each chapter introduction. By highlighting major events and developments, it will help you understand how events discussed in the chapter are related in time.

4. **Important Terms.** Historical terms and vocabulary words are boldfaced and clearly defined the first time they appear in the text. You will be asked to define each term in a section review question. Important historical terms also appear in a glossary at the end of the book.

5. **Geography and History.** A special heading calls your attention to the impact of geography on people, events, or ideas.

6. **Great Debate.** A special heading alerts you to controversial issues of both the past and the present. The discussion includes the points of view in the ongoing debate.

7. **Maps, Graphs, Charts.** Numerous maps, graphs, and charts appear throughout the book to help you understand major historical developments and events. Captions provide background information and relate the maps, graphs, and charts to what you are reading.

8. **Illustrations.** The text contains many historic paintings, photographs, cartoons, and posters to enliven the study of each historical period. The captions contain useful information about the illustration and the people or events pictured.

9. **Special Features.** These features give you a close look at people and events in American history. They include biographies, connections with geography, and selections from diaries and other contemporary sources.

10. **Skill Lessons.** These step-by-step lessons help you understand and practice important skills, such as reading maps and graphs, using visual evidence and statistics, recognizing propaganda, and analyzing conflicting sources.

11. **Section Reviews.** Each section ends with a set of review questions including identifications, vocabulary definitions, and a critical thinking question to test your understanding of what you have read.

12. **Chapter Review.** The materials at the end of the chapter help you review and apply what you have learned. They include:

   - **Summary** to outline the main ideas of each section.

   - **Vocabulary** to review definitions of important terms.

   - **Chapter Checkup** to review important ideas.

   - **Critical Thinking Questions** to analyze historical issues and deepen your understanding of history.

   - **Connecting Past and Present** to link what you have learned with current events.

   - **Developing Basic Skills** to apply such basic skills as classifying, comparing, map and graph reading, and interpreting source materials.

   - **Writing About History** to help you develop writing and research skills needed for studying history.

13. **Spirit of America.** Each unit contains a four-page feature that focuses on an important theme in American history. The Spirit of America feature contains an essay that discusses the historical development of a particular theme, the biography of a person who exemplifies it, and a document related to it.

14. **Reference Section.** The Reference Section can be found on pages 838–917. It includes an atlas with both physical and political maps, a chronology, a glossary with pronunciation key, information about the states and the Presidents, the Declaration of Independence, the Constitution of the United States, and an index.

Unit One

THE AMERICAS

Pre–1450 *This early American bowl shows the skill of Indian potters in the Southwest.*

1590 *This view of Roanoke Island shows where the first English colony was established.*

	1450	1500	1550	1600
POLITICS AND GOVERNMENT		**1492** Columbus reaches the Americas	**1500s** Iroquois League formed to end warfare among Indian nations	
SOCIETY AND CULTURE	**1300s–1400s** Aztecs develop precise calendar and system of mathematics		**1500s** Plains peoples become nomads	
ECONOMICS AND TECHNOLOGY	**1400s** Invention of caravel at Sagres spurs exploration			**1573** Laws of the Indies outline economy of New Spain
WORLD EVENTS		**1517** Protestant Reformation begins in Europe		**1588** English defeat Spanish Armada

1400s *The caravel allowed sailors to explore regions far from Europe.*

1500s *Fishing provided abundant food for Native Americans on the Atlantic coast.*

UNIT OUTLINE

1609 The landing of a relief ship at Jamestown is shown in a painting by John Gadsby Chapman.

1700s Colonial cities were bustling centers of economic activity.

1600	1650	1700	1750

1607 Jamestown founded as first successful English colony

1673 Joliet and Marquette explore Mississippi River

1754 French and Indian War breaks out in North America

1647 First public school law passed in Massachusetts

1735 John Peter Zenger found innocent of libel

1660 Navigation Act regulates trade of the American colonies

1740s Eliza Pinckney raises indigo as a cash crop

1660 Charles II restored to throne of England

1756 War spreads to Europe, where it is called the Seven Years' War

1600s Selling oysters was one way settlers in the American colonies made their way in the New World.

1745 New Englanders carried this flag in an early battle between the English and the French in North America.

1

The American Land and Its People
(Prehistory–1492)

1

CHAPTER OUTLINE

1 Geography and History

2 The American Land

3 The First Americans

4 Europe Awakens

CHAPTER OBJECTIVES After completing this chapter, students should be able to
1. define the five major themes of geography.
2. describe the physical regions and climate areas of North America.
3. describe several early cultures of the Americas.
4. explain why Europeans began to explore other parts of the world.

CHAPTER PREVIEW Have students locate these places on the world map on pp. 842–843: North America, South America, Europe, Africa, India, China. Have them calculate the distance by sea from Europe to the other places.

As light glowed in the early morning sky, the villagers crowded into the plaza. Silently, they watched the procession of costumed dancers moving toward them. Everyone knew that at sunset the rainmaking spirits would leave the earth for six months. If today's ceremonies did not win their favor, the spirits would not return as rain for the next season's crops.

As the sun grew brighter, the chief dancer suddenly signaled for the ceremonies to begin. The sounds of rattles, stamping feet, and chanting voices filled the air.

For the Hopi people, the dancing marked the end of a festival celebrating the return of the kachinas, or spirits, to the World Below. It was late June and men dressed as spirits performed the ancient rituals that ensured the arrival of rain in December.

At sunset, a kachina chief addressed the departing spirits:

We may have just a few crops in our fields, but when you bring the rain they will grow and become strong. Then, if you will bring some more rain, we will have more corn, and more beans, and more watermelons, and all the rest of our crops. When harvest time comes, we will have plenty of food for the whole winter.

Over thousands of years, the Indians of the Americas had adapted to a variety of landforms and climates. They had learned to grow corn and dozens of other crops. Among the earliest riches Europe reaped from the New World was the wide variety of Indian foods. To their limited diets, Europeans added maize, or corn, potatoes, squash, melons, pumpkins, kidney beans, lima beans, chili peppers, avocados, pineapples, tomatoes, and peanuts. From the Americas, too, came tobacco, chocolate, quinine, vanilla, and rubber.

In this chapter, you will read about the land and about some of the hundreds of cultures existing in North and South America by the 1400s. You will also read about changes in Europe that would alter the course of human history.

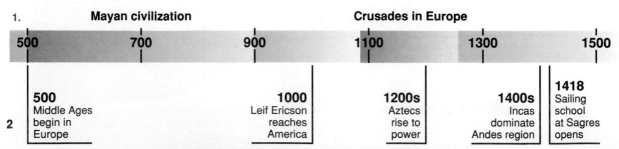

1.

Mayan civilization

Crusades in Europe

| 500 | 700 | 900 | 1100 | 1300 | 1500 |

500 Middle Ages begin in Europe

1000 Leif Ericson reaches America

1200s Aztecs rise to power

1400s Incas dominate Andes region

1418 Sailing school at Sagres opens

1. **TIME LINE QUESTION** How long after Leif Ericson reached America did a sailing school open at Sagres?

The first Americans respected the natural forces that made plants grow. No plant was more precious to them than corn, which they considered sacred. Dances celebrated each stage during the planting, cultivating, and harvesting of corn. The
1. *Green Corn Dance, shown here, marked the appearance of the husks that would grow into corn.*

1. **VISUAL EVIDENCE** This painting is by Joseph Henry Sharp, an American artist famous for his accurate paintings of Indians and Indian life in the Southwest.

1 Geography and History

READ TO UNDERSTAND

■ What the five major themes of geography are.

■ How the themes help you understand history.

2. ■ *Vocabulary:* geography, history, latitude, longitude.

You live in the present, but inevitably your life has been shaped by the dramas and events of the past. If our nation's history sometimes seems like a play, then the stage on which that play takes place is the American land. Throughout this book, connections are drawn between history and geography—that is, between what has happened and where it has happened.

Themes of Geography

Every human action occurs somewhere. The more you know about where things happen, the easier it is to understand why they happened and how they affect you. For this reason, it is important to study the connections between geography and history. **Geography** is the study of people, their environments, and their resources. **History** is an account of what has happened in the life or development of a people, a nation, or a civilization.

To help you understand the connections between geography and history, geographers have developed five themes: location, place, interactions between people and their environment, movement, and regions.

Location

Where are you? The answer to that question pinpoints your location. As you study United States history, there may be times when you

3

2. **VOCABULARY** Have students look up these words in the glossary before they begin reading.

SKILL LESSON

The American Land and Its People: Skimming a Chapter

Skimming is a special way to read that is helpful when you are studying history. To skim a chapter, read it more quickly than usual just to get a general idea of what it is about. Having an overview can help you pick out the main ideas as you read the chapter more carefully. Use these steps to skim Chapter 1.
See p. T1.

1 **Read the chapter title.** (a) What is the topic of the chapter? (b) What years of history does the chapter cover?

2 **Read the chapter outline and introduction.** (a) How many sections are in the chapter? (b) In which section would you expect to find out about the geography of the Americas? (c) What clues does the in-

troductory story give you about the relationship of the early Americans to the land?

3 **Read the main headings and introductory paragraphs.** (a) What is the topic of Section 1? (b) Based on the introduction, why should you be aware of the connections between geography and history?

4 **Read the subheadings within the sections.** List the subheadings for Section 1.

5 **Read the chapter summary.** (a) Based on the summary, in what areas are population density and economic development greater? (b) What two changes in Europe encouraged exploration?

1.

1. **CRITICAL THINKING** Ask: What information would you miss by just skimming this chapter?

want to know the exact location of some place. Where was gold found in California? If you knew the latitude and longitude of Sutter's Mill, you could find its exact location on a map.

Latitude lines on a map or globe measure distance north and south of the Equator. **Longitude** lines measure distance east and west of the Prime Meridian which runs through Greenwich (GREHN ihch), England. You can locate any place on earth exactly by using the grid of longitude and latitude. For example, by using the map on page 840, you can locate Sutter's Mill at 38 N latitude and 2. 121 W longitude.

Sometimes it is more meaningful to know the relative location of some place—where something is in relation to another place and how the two places affect each other. California, Oregon, Washington, Alaska, and Hawaii form part of the Pacific Rim, the area bordering the Pacific Ocean. Several East Asian countries, such as Japan and South Korea, also border the Pacific and have rapidly expanding economies. Understanding the potential for trade in the Pacific Rim will help 4 economists and politicians prepare for the future.

2. **ACTIVITY** Have students find the latitude and longitude of their own community on a map.

Place

When geographers use the term place, they are referring to the physical and human characteristics of a location. For example, New England has a hilly terrain and a rock-bound coast with deep harbors. These physical characteristics encouraged the early European settlers to turn to the sea for their livelihood. Boston, with its fine harbor, became a densely populated area with a lively economy based on fishing, shipbuilding, and trade. The specific physical and human characteristics of Boston distinguish it from other 3. places.

Interactions Between People and Their Environment

People interact with their environment. They adapt to the natural settings and modify them to meet their needs. In the 1500s, the Pueblo Indians adapted to the Southwest by building adobe dwellings that reflected the heat of the searing southwestern sun. The Pueblo timed their crop planting to take advantage of the rain cycles and modified, or changed, the natural environment relatively little.

3. **DISCUSSION** Ask students to describe the specific physical and human characteristics of their community.

1. **DISCUSSION** Ask: What other developments have made movement of people and ideas in the 1900s easier?

See p. T2.

In contrast, modern cities with their cement sidewalks, paved streets, and air-conditioned high-rise buildings represent the greatest modification of the earth's environment. Food is supplied for these cities by farmers who use machinery and chemical fertilizers to alter the environment.

Movement

Perhaps no geographic concept has been so dramatically affected by the development of technology as movement. Movement is the mobility of people, ideas, and goods. In earliest times, movement was gradual—no faster or farther than a person could walk. Later, people used animals and sailing ships for transportation. In the 1800s, rail travel, steam power, the telegraph, and the telephone revolutionized movement. Now, through telecommunications, there is barely a corner of the earth that cannot be reached in an instant.

1.

Movements of every kind have affected the course of United States history. The earliest known inhabitants migrated to the Americas from Asia. Europeans arrived later, then Africans. Along with the movement of people came the movement of ideas. The ideas of European thinkers such as John Locke, Baron de Montesquieu, and Jean Jacques Rousseau helped shape the United States Constitution.

Regions

A region is an area that is united because of its similar characteristics. A region's characteristics may be physical, such as its climate or landforms, or they may be the human characteristics of language, religion, politics, or economics. Every state has recreation areas known for their natural beauty. Many cities have so-called "downtown" regions where businesses and shops abound.

2. **DISCUSSION** Ask students to give examples of physical, social, economic, and ethnic regions in their area.

People's desire to live with others who share the same heritage can make part of a city into a region. In the 1800s, many Chinese immigrants drew together in neighborhoods. The sounds of the Chinese language, smells of the food, and celebrations of traditional holidays made "Chinatowns" distinctive regions of many large cities. This painting shows a celebration in San Francisco's Chinatown in 1888.

SECTION 1 REVIEW

1. **Identify:** (a) location, (b) place, (c) interaction, (d) movement, (e) region.

2. **Define:** (a) geography, (b) history, (c) latitude, (d) longitude.

3. Why is it important to understand the relationship between geography and history?

4. How has movement been affected by technology?

5. **Critical Thinking** How do the themes of geography help you to see the earth as an interrelated system of people and resources?

---

3. **BACKGROUND** San Francisco's Chinatown is the largest Chinese settlement outside Asia.

2 The American Land

READmemory TO UNDERSTAND

- What are the major physical regions of North America.

- What are the major climates of North America.

1. ■ *Vocabulary:* elevation, relief, climate.

North America, South America, and the islands in the Caribbean make up the Western Hemisphere. From the lofty heights of Aconcagua Mountain in Argentina to the depths of Death Valley in California, the Western Hemisphere encompasses a wide variety of landforms and climates.

Different Landforms

North and South America are washed by the waters of the Atlantic Ocean on the east and the Pacific Ocean on the west. North Amer-ica reaches 4,500 miles (7,200 kilometers) from the frigid Arctic Ocean to the narrow Isthmus of Panama. There it meets South America, which stretches 4,750 miles (7,645 kilometers) southward to the Antarctic Ocean.

The landforms of North and South America provide stunning contrasts. Soaring mountains and rolling hills rise above level plains and plateaus. These landforms differ from one another in both elevation and relief. **Elevation** is the height of the land measured from the point where the land meets the sea. People refer to how many feet land rises above sea level. **Relief** refers to the rate of change in the elevation of the land. In areas of high relief, the land rises or falls sharply. In areas of low relief, the change is gradual.

Mountains are rugged land that rises abruptly above the surrounding area. Their elevation is at least 5,000 feet (1,500 meters) above their surroundings. Although few people can live on the steep mountain slopes, people often settle in the valleys formed between mountains where the land is level and the climate generally milder.

3. *Many areas of the rugged California coast, where cliffs seem to rise out of the ocean, have kept their wild beauty. Not far from the birds and seals of the seacoast are forests where bears and mountain lions still roam. Now protected by law, the American wilderness is a reminder of the bountiful land that greeted the European settlers.*

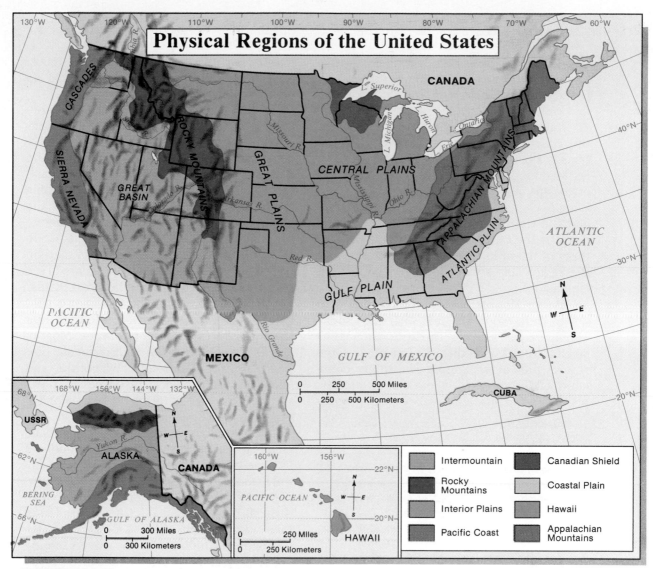

Physical Regions of the United States

Intermountain	Canadian Shield
Rocky Mountains	Coastal Plain
Interior Plains	Hawaii
Pacific Coast	Appalachian Mountains

MAP STUDY *Mountains, hills, plateaus, and plains make up the seven major physical regions that form the varied landscape of the United States. Name the four mountain ranges shown on the map. Where are they located?* See p. T2. 1.

Hills are also areas of raised land. They are generally less than 5,000 feet (1,500 meters) high and have a moderate relief. Many hills were formed by the erosion, or wearing away, of mountains.

Areas of high, level land are plateaus. Plateaus usually rise to at least 2,000 feet (600 meters) above sea level. In the low latitudes near the equator, most people live on the plateaus where the climate is cooler than in the lowlands.

The plains are broad areas of gently rolling land of low elevation. They are generally heavily settled because of the ease of transportation and farming. Large parts of North and South America are plains.

Physical Regions of North America

The mountains, hills, plateaus, and plains form the seven major physical regions of the United States in jigsaw pattern. (See the map above.) 2. The regions differ not only in landforms, but also in economic activities. Vast harvests on the fertile plains have made the United States one of the richest agricultural nations. Widely distributed mineral resources such as iron, coal, and oil have supported unequaled industrial development.

Pacific Coast The beauty of the Pacific Coast region is enhanced by a dramatic sweep of mountains from Alaska to Mexico. Rugged mountains fringe the coastline in the Pacific 7

1. **MAP READING** Ask: Which regions stretch from the northern to the southern borders of the United States?

2. **ACTIVITY** Have students find and bring in photographs illustrating the major regions of the United States.

1. **GEOGRAPHY** Of the 25 largest cities in the United States, only two, Phoenix and El Paso, are in the Intermountain Region. (location, region)

states. The Cascades and the Sierra Nevadas rise a little farther inland. Dense forests add to the beauty of the region while fertile mountain valleys make farming profitable.

Intermountain Region Lying between the coastal mountains and the Rocky Mountains is a broad area of dramatic landscapes. Isolated mountain ridges, high plateaus, desert basins, and deep canyons create a panorama of changing landforms. The Great Basin and the Grand Canyon, carved over a mile deep by the Colorado River, are natural features of the area. The harshness of much of the region has always hindered population
1. expansion.

Rocky Mountains On the eastern edge of the intermountain plateaus, the Rocky Mountains rise sharply. The Rocky Mountains stretch from Alaska through Canada into the rest of the United States. The thinly populated wilderness area is marked by majestic peaks and steep-walled valleys. This moun-

2. **VISUAL EVIDENCE** Have students compare this painting by Thomas Hart Benton to the one on p. 617.

In the heart of the country is a vast plain, which is the "breadbasket" of the nation. Enterprising Americans draw from the rich soil enough wheat to feed much of the world's population. The Great Plains today make up the greatest wheat-growing area on earth. In 1938, the Missouri painter Thomas Hart Benton celebrated the farmers' labor
2. *in this painting called* Cradling Wheat.

3. **GEOGRAPHY** The Appalachian Trail, the longest footpath in the United States, runs for 2,000 miles (3,200 kilometers), from Georgia to Maine. (location)

tain barrier dismayed settlers in the 1800s. Now the rugged beauty and fashionable ski areas attract many tourists.

Interior Plains The large lowland area known as the Interior Plains extends eastward from the Rocky Mountains to the Appalachian Mountains. The western portion is called the Great Plains. The wetter eastern part is called the Central Plains. Farming is an important economic activity on the plains even in the west where the rain supply is undependable. The Central Plains are more highly industrialized (see the map on page 849) and more densely populated (see the map on page 847) than the Great Plains.

Canadian Shield The Canadian Shield extends from the Arctic Ocean to the Great Lakes and the Gulf of St. Lawrence. Most of it is in Canada. But the southernmost portion dips into Minnesota, Wisconsin, and Michigan. Rich mineral resources help offset the lack of good farmland. No major cities occupy this heavily forested region.

Appalachian Mountains The Appalachian Mountains stretch from Newfoundland in Canada to Alabama, separating the Central Plains and the Coastal Plains. Rivers flow-
3.
ing eastward have cut deep valleys, or gaps, through the mountains. Early settlers found their way west through the Delaware Water Gap and the Cumberland Gap. Rivers emptying into the Atlantic Ocean have also carved the broader Hudson Valley in New York and the Shenandoah Valley in Virginia.

Coastal Plains Brushing against the Atlantic Ocean on the east and the Gulf of Mexico in the south are the Coastal Plains. Boston and New York lie in the narrow portion of the Atlantic Plain to the north. Farther south, the plain fans out to include most of Georgia and all of Florida. To the west, the Gulf Plain includes the oil-rich areas of Louisiana and Texas. Houston and New Orleans lie on the Gulf Plain.

Rivers and Lakes

Water means life. Without it, neither plants nor animals could survive. North America has usually had a generous and dependable supply of water, but it cannot be taken for granted.

Several large river systems flow through North America. In the spring, as they follow their course to the oceans, the rivers swell with the runoff from rain and melting snow. The Missouri and the mighty Mississippi rivers make up the longest river system in the United States (4,663 miles, or 7,505 kilometers). Flowing through the Interior Plains, the waters of this river system provide transportation and irrigation before they empty into the Gulf of Mexico at New Orleans. The Ohio, Tennessee, Arkansas, and Platte rivers are part of this system.

The Colorado River system is another vital river system. Originating in the Rocky Mountains, it flows about 1,400 miles (2,250 kilometers) to the Gulf of California and the Pacific Ocean. It provides drinking water, irrigation, and hydroelectric power for much of the Southwest. (See the map on page 7.)

The St. Lawrence River and the Great Lakes form part of the boundary between the United States and Canada as well as an
1. important inland waterway. The Rio Grande River marks part of the border between the United States and Mexico.

Landforms of South America

The towering Andes Mountains form the backbone of South America. They are barely separated from the Pacific Ocean by a narrow coastal plain and, in Chile, by the Atacama Desert. To the east, the river basins of the Orinoco, the Amazon, and the Paraná rivers drain an interior plain. The Amazon, the second longest river in the world, flows 4,000 miles (6,400 kilometers) from the Andes to the Atlantic Ocean. Highlands lie to the north and the southeast of the Amazon basin.

Factors Affecting Climate

People listen to the weather report each morning to learn the condition of the air at a given time and place. They want to know if they need a sweater or an umbrella. **Climate,** on the other hand, is the average weather of a place over a period of 20 or 30 years. It tells whether the winters are cold or the summers are wet, but not what the conditions will be on a particular day.

Climate is affected by several factors. One of these is latitude, how far north or south of the Equator a region is located. Generally, climate is warmer the closer a region is to the Equator and cooler the closer it is to the Poles. Climate is also influenced by altitude, or height above sea level. Highlands tend to be cooler than lowlands.

Prevailing winds, winds that blow almost constantly from one direction, and mountains also affect climate. Winds pick up moisture from the oceans and bring it across land. Mountains deflect the moisture-laden air so that it rises and cools quickly, resulting in rain or snow. The other side of the mountain will be drier since the moisture has already been released from the clouds.

Climates in North America

Like the landscape, the climate of North America is varied. Climates in North America range from the arctic to the tropics. The United States itself has ten climate regions. (See the map on page 10.)

Marine The marine climate is characterized by mild, moist weather. It is found in the Pacific Northwest, the coastal region from southern Alaska to northern California. The Pacific Northwest is warmer and wetter than inland areas of a similar latitude. Heavily forested, it is the center of a busy lumbering industry.

Mediterranean This climate, named after the Mediterranean region in Europe, has mild, moist winters and hot, dry summers. Most of the farm areas of California have a mediterranean climate. These regions provide fresh fruit and vegetables all year.

Steppe The Great Plains have a steppe climate. The climate is dry and does not support the growth of trees. During the 1800s, buffalo roamed the Great Plains, feeding on plentiful, short grasses. Today, the cattle industry is centered on the Great Plains.

Humid Continental About one-quarter of the United States has a humid continental climate. The rainfall on the Central Plains and in the Northeast is fairly evenly spaced throughout the year. Winters are colder and summers are warmer than in most other regions. The Central Plains are an important source of the world's grain crop.

9

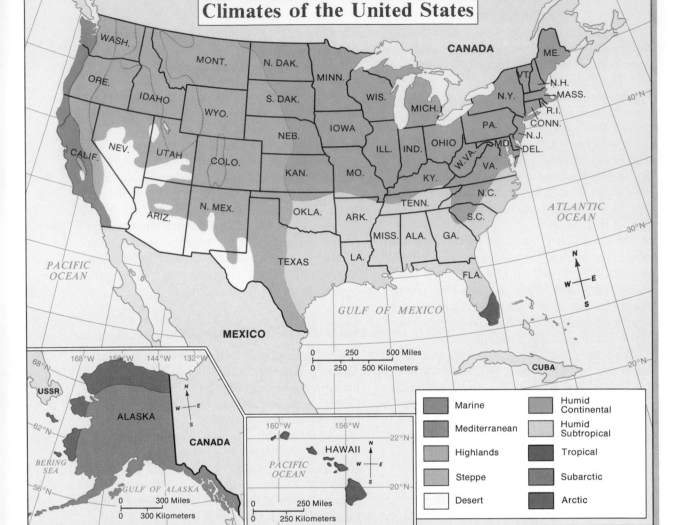

Climates of the United States

MAP Legend:
- Marine
- Mediterranean
- Highlands
- Steppe
- Desert
- Humid Continental
- Humid Subtropical
- Tropical
- Subarctic
- Arctic

MAP STUDY Climates in the United States are as varied as the landscape. Which areas have climates that could make life easier? Which have climates that could make life more difficult? According to the map, which type of climate is found in the state where you live? See p. T2.

2.

1. **GEOGRAPHY** The average annual rainfall in the state of Nevada, which is largely desert, is less than five inches. By contrast, the annual rainfall in Florida is almost 60 inches. (place)

Humid Subtropical The southeastern portion of the United States has a humid subtropical climate. This climate has regular rainfall and warm temperatures. Cotton, tobacco, and peanuts are important crops.

Other Climates The more extreme climates include the arctic and subarctic climates in Alaska. There the winters are long and cold and the summers are very short. In the southwestern desert region, the climate is hot and dry. In contrast, tropical southern

1. Florida has a hot, wet climate. The highland climate in the Rocky Mountains is not as easily defined. The seasons and the rainfall depend on the elevation.

10

Climates in Central and South America

Like North America, South America has a wide variety of climates. Argentina, Uruguay, and Chile have climates similar to those in the United States. But much of southern Mexico, Central America, and South America is a tropical rain forest.

The tropical rain forest in the Amazon River basin in Brazil is an important source of oxygen for the planet. Brazil also has major areas of savannah south and east of the rain forest. The savannah climate has a rainy season followed by a dry season.

2. **MAP READING** Ask: Which state contains the widest variety of climate zones?

See p. T2.

SECTION 2 REVIEW

1. **Identify:** (a) plateau, (b) marine climate, (c) mediterranean climate, (d) humid continental climate, (e) humid subtropical climate.

2. **Define:** (a) elevation, (b) relief, (c) climate.

3. What are the major physical regions of the United States?

4. What contributions have rivers made to life in the United States?

5. **Critical Thinking** How does the major landform and climate in your area affect how people live and work?

1. **VOCABU**LARY Have students look up these words in the glossary before they begin reading.

3 The First Americans

READ TO UNDERSTAND

■ How the Americas were inhabited.

■ How the first Americans developed different cultures.

■ What were the achievements of the first Americans.

1. ■ *Vocabulary:* potlatch, pictogram, adobe, kiva, matrilineal, nomadic, sachem.

Fifty thousand years ago, huge herds of animals roamed across North and South America. Wild horses, bison, and camels grazed in vast fields. Jaguars stalked their prey. Woolly mammoths—large, shaggy-haired elephants with long, sweeping tusks—wandered from present-day Alaska to Texas. Exactly when and how people came to be a part of this landscape is uncertain, though scientists have a general idea.

Peopling a Continent

Most scientists believe that the first humans crossed into America during one of the ice ages in prehistoric times. As vast amounts of water froze into glaciers, the depth of oceans dropped by 200 or 300 feet (60 or 90 meters).

3. **PAST AND PRESENT** Remains of mammoths and other prehistoric animals have been found in the La Brea tar pits of California and elsewhere in the United States.

Underwater ridges were exposed and formed a land bridge from Asia across the Bering Strait into present-day Alaska. Scientists believe that when herds of animals moved eastward across the bridge, Asian hunters followed, tracking them throughout the Americas. They may have come as early as 60,000 years ago, or as recently as 12,000 years.

Although scientists do not agree when the earliest inhabitants arrived, most agree that about 10,000 years ago the environment changed in the Americas. The glaciers retreated, temperatures warmed, lakes dried up, and many animal species became extinct. The oceans rose and the land bridge to Asia closed, isolating American cultures from the rest of the world.

The Rise of Agriculture

The changes in climate forced prehistoric peoples to alter their way of life. As some regions became hot and dry and others warm and wet, people living in different areas had to develop different skills to survive. When the huge game animals disappeared, people hunted smaller game. Groups living near the sea became expert at catching fish.

More important for the development of civilization was the rise of agriculture. Some groups who gathered wild fruits, roots, and vegetables began raising their own crops. As the cultivation of crops spread, different groups began experimenting with varieties of beans, squash, and corn. The first Americans no longer had to move from place to place in an endless search for food. They were able to settle in permanent communities.

By 1400 A.D., sharp contrasts existed between cultures in the Americas. Some groups were still hunting and gathering while others lived in highly organized societies with cities, roads, and taxes. And hundreds of other cultures fell somewhere in between. Each had its own forms of government, religion, and art, reflecting its culture.

Life in the West

Many of the early Americans who lived in the western region extending from the Arctic Circle to the warm Pacific coast of California

11

1. **BACKGROUND** Because they were so important to survival, animals also played a central part in Eskimo religion. Before they could be hunted, animals had to be honored with specific rituals and songs.

lived by hunting, fishing, or gathering plants. Among these groups were the Eskimo, the peoples of the Northwest Coast and the Great Basin region.

Eskimo The Eskimo lived on the plains and seacoasts of the Arctic. Bitter cold and heavy snows tested the skills of these early Americans. Because few plants grow in the frigid climate, the lives of the Eskimo revolved around hunting and fishing. Animals such as the seal, walrus, whale, and caribou were a source not only of food but also of clothing, tools, weapons, boats, and household

implements. The successful use of every bit of these animals often meant the difference between life and death.

Northwest Coast Indians The mild climate of the northwest Pacific coast made life easier for the settlers there. Salmon and other fish thrived in the many streams and rivers. Offshore the seas teemed with seals, whales, and otters, while on land herds of deer, moose, and elk roamed the thick forests. The food supply was plentiful.

Under these favorable conditions, the people of the northwest Pacific had time to

1.

2. **MAP READING** Ask: In which culture area are the Great Lakes located? What are two nations of the southeast culture area?

MAP STUDY

See p. T3.

Hundreds of cultural groups lived in North America in the 1500s. Each had its own form of government, art, and religion. In the map below, color indicates groups with similar styles of living. Compare this map with the map of physical regions on page 7. What conclusions can you draw about the influence of geography on the way people live?

2.

Major North American Cultures in the 1500s

Legend:
- Arctic
- Sub-Arctic
- Northwest Coast
- Plateau
- Great Basin
- California
- Southwest
- Northern Mexico
- Middle America
- Great Plains
- Eastern Woodland
- Southeast

0   500   1000 Miles
0   500   1000 Kilometers

Plentiful food along the northwest Pacific coast allowed early Americans leisure time to develop their crafts. Blankets that adorned their homes became more than useful objects—they were works of art. In this Paul Kane painting, one woman weaves cloth while another spins wool into yarn. Weavers used wool from
1. mountain goats as well as white hair from dogs bred especially for their fine coats.

1. **VISUAL EVIDENCE**
This painting shows the Klallam tribe, who lived in what is now British Columbia, Canada.

2. **CRITICAL THINKING** Ask: Can you think of any present-day customs that are similar in some way to the potlatch ceremony? Do people today gain social status by giving away money or other possessions?

do something other than search for food. They built very big, elaborately decorated houses, fashioned striking copper shields, carved massive totem poles and canoes, and made beautiful wooden masks, furniture, and utensils.

Gradually, they developed a complex society based on wealth. Each person's status depended on his or her possessions. To demonstrate their prosperity, people held feasts called **potlatches** (PAHT latch ehz). At these ceremonies, the host family entertained guests lavishly for several days and gave away valuable possessions. Those who received gifts held their own potlatches in return. Anyone who could not do this lost social
2. standing in the community.

Great Basin Indians The groups living in the Great Basin, between the Sierra Nevadas and the Rocky Mountains, had a more difficult life. The region supports few animals or edible plants. Peoples such as the Ute and Shoshone were forced to move about in small bands, often no larger than a single family, in order to gather what food they could. Men dominated the bands. Women and children held low status.

The Desert Tradition

A harsh environment made survival a struggle in much of the region that is now part of Arizona, New Mexico, southern Utah, and northern Mexico. In the north, rapidly flowing rivers had carved steep-walled canyons into the land or washed away the soil to form huge mesas* thousands of feet high. In the south, foothills and mountains gave way to flat stretches of desert. There, summer temperatures reached over 100° Fahrenheit (38° Celsius) and winter temperatures dropped well below 0° Fahrenheit (–18° Celsius).

Anasazi Despite these extreme conditions, several imposing civilizations emerged in the area. One of the earliest groups was the Anasazi (ah nah SAH zee). Skilled people, they turned the desert into productive farmland with an irrigation system of dams and canals. Within the remote canyons of much of today's Southwest, they built cliff dwellings resembling modern high-rise apartments. 3.

_____

*mesa: "mesa," which means table in Spanish, is a high, flat plateau or tableland with steep sides.

13

3. **PAST AND PRESENT** Cliff dwellings can be seen today at Mesa Verde National Park in Colorado.

1. **BACKGROUND** Early explorers who saw the pueblos called them "cities of gold" because of the way the sun reflected off the adobe.

On the rock walls of the canyons they drew **pictograms,** pictures conveying their ideas about life. The Anasazi were also excellent weavers, basketmakers, and potters.

Pueblo Although the Anasazi disappeared mysteriously, several later groups traced their origins to them. One group, the Pueblo,* lived in the area of present-day Arizona and New Mexico. The Pueblo were farmers who grew beans, cotton, tobacco, squash, and gourds—a difficult task in a region that received so little rain.

Like the Anasazi, the Pueblo often built their dwellings on the mesas or along the sides of steep cliffs. Made of stone and **adobe,** sun-dried clay brick, the structures were several stories high. The Pueblo grouped the buildings around a broad, open space, forming a kind of town with a main square.

At the center of each town was an underground room called a **kiva.** Pueblo men met there to conduct religious ceremonies. Some of their rites were held to bring rain, others to cure the sick, and still others to please the gods. The kiva societies emphasized conformity and the importance of society over the individual. A warrior class enforced the rules of conduct.

The Pueblo were a **matrilineal** society. In other words, they traced descent within a family through the mother's line. Women headed the families and held all property rights. A wife who wanted to divorce her husband merely put his belongings outside her door—a signal that the husband had to return to his mother's house. Pueblo women were exceptionally skilled potters and basketweavers—crafts that were probably passed down to them from the Anasazi.

Navajo During the 1500s, another important southwestern group, the Navajo (NAV uh hoh), migrated into what is now northern New Mexico. There, the Navajo came under the influence of their Pueblo neighbors, from whom they learned farming and weaving.

Navajo religion, heavily influenced by that of the Pueblo, emphasized that a person's

2. **BACKGROUND** Early Navajo made homes by piling logs against three poles joined at the top. Later, they built hogans, dome-shaped mud plaster structures with log frames.

life should be in harmony with the universe. Immortal beings called Holy People, who had to be pleased through strict rituals, could affect the lives of mortals, called Earth Surface People.

On the Great Plains

As you have read, between the Rocky Mountains and the Mississippi River lies a large area of relatively flat grasslands known today as the Great Plains. For thousands of years, most inhabitants of the Great Plains lived near rivers so they could be sure of a water supply for farming. Women were responsible for the farming and plowed their garden plots with digging sticks and hoes made from large animal bones. Maize, squash, beans, and sunflowers were the principal crops.

For most of the year, the Plains people lived in fairly permanent villages. There they built lodges by covering log frames with brush and sod. But during the summer, the men often left for weeks to hunt buffalo.

Sometime in the mid-1500s, most of the Plains people became more **nomadic.** Instead of living in permanent villages, they moved from place to place, building temporary settlements near water and food supplies. Migrations were on foot. Dogs dragged travois* carrying the owners' possessions.

The nomadic settlements relied on farming for much of their food, but the men often hunted. On the hunt, they lived in portable teepees made from buffalo hides. Farther west, Americans who were completely nomadic lived in teepees year-round.

The semiagricultural, seminomadic groups of the Plains included the Osage, Missouri, Omaha, Kansas, Iowa, Wichita, and Mandan, as well as the Pawnee. The Blackfeet achieved the greatest power in the western part of the Great Plains. The Crow hunted the land between the Missouri and Yellowstone rivers, and the Comanche, Kiowa, and Apache dominated the southern plains. 3.

---

*pueblo: "pueblo" (PWEHB loh), which means town in Spanish, is the name given to these people in the 1500s by Spanish explorers, who thought the settlements looked like European towns.

---

*travois (trah VOI): two poles with an animal skin mounted between them. After the Spanish reintroduced horses to the Americas, the Plains people used horses rather than dogs during their migrations.

3. **READING** Students interested in Native American cultures can read *This Country Was Ours: A Documentary History of the American Indian,* by Virgil J. Vogel.

14

1. **READING** Students might like to read parts of *The Song of Hiawatha* by Longfellow. Ask: Is the poem a reliable source of information about Hiawatha?

2. **CITIZENSHIP** According to some historians, the Iroquois League served as a prototype for the federal system created by the U.S. Constitution.

In the Eastern Woodlands

Three major peoples lived in the woodlands east of the Mississippi River: the Algonquin (al GAHN kwihn), the Iroquois (IHR uh kwoi), and the Muskogean (muhs KOH gee ehn).

Algonquin The Algonquin lived in the dense forests that covered the Northeast from present-day Labrador and Quebec as far south as Maryland and Virginia. They lived in small bands, hunting deer and caribou or gathering wild nuts and berries. The Algonquin also used the resources of the forest to build efficient transportation: snowshoes and toboggans in the winter, canoes in the summer.

Algonquin society was relatively simple. Families within the band hunted primarily in one area they regarded as theirs. But they willingly shared their catch with others. Food was often scarce during the harsh winters, and every family knew that one day it might have to depend on another's support.

Iroquois The Iroquois were several related tribes that originally lived in southeastern North America. Around 1300, they migrated north to the area of present-day New York State and drove out the Algonquin. However, not long after the departure of the Algonquin, the Iroquois began to feud among themselves. During the 1500s, the warfare became especially bitter and threatened to undermine the Iroquois people.

According to legend, two reformers, Dekanawidah, a Huron religious leader, and his disciple Hiawatha, a Mohawk chief, began 1. preaching the idea of a political confederation, or alliance, of the Iroquois tribes. They believed that such a union would not only end the bloodshed but would also provide a strong defense against their enemies.

The goal of the two reformers was finally achieved during the 1500s. Five tribes—the Mohawk, the Seneca (SEHN ih kuh), the Cayuga (kay YOO gah), the Oneida (oh NĪ duh), and the Onondaga (ahn uhn DAH guh)—gradually formed a confederation known as the Iroquois League.

The league, whose values were based on those of traditional Iroquois culture, proved successful. A representative council, consisting of the chiefs of each tribe and 50 specially chosen leaders called sachems (SAY chehms), governed the league. The **sachems** were responsible for regulating relations 2. among the tribes.

Iroquois society, like Pueblo society, was matrilineal. All property passed from generation to generation on the female side of the family. Women owned the gardens and the spacious longhouses in which several related families lived. Although they did not serve on the league council, women who headed the clans appointed the male sachems.

Muskogean Other eastern woodlands groups also had complex social and political

3. **VISUAL EVIDENCE** Ask: What does this painting show about the environment of these Native Americans?

In this painting, two young Indians of the eastern woodlands play a game while a third watches. The Indians made good use of the natural resources of the eastern woodlands. They stripped bark from birch trees to make sturdy and light canoes,
3. *such as those shown in the painting.*

1. **CRITICAL THINKING** Ask: How did the Muskogean system differ from the hereditary monarchies of Europe?

systems—the Muskogean, for example. These farming people had a highly structured class system based on worship of the sun. At the top was the chief, called the Great Sun. Just below him in status were the nobles, known as Suns. Below them were the Honored People, and at the very bottom were the Stinkards.

The reigning Great Sun, worshipped as a god, had the power of life and death over the Muskogean. The group's complicated marriage rules insured that membership in each class changed over time so that no one family could hold the position of Great Sun indefinitely. Over several generations, a Great Sun's descendants would become Stinkards.

1.

Empires to the South

Many scholars believe that the Muskogean and other southeastern peoples were influenced by cultures that had developed to the southwest of them, in present-day Mexico. The first of these great civilizations was created by the Maya, who flourished on the Yucatán peninsula of Mexico and in present-day Guatemala from about 300 to 900 A.D.

3. **CRITICAL THINKING** Ask: In what ways did a written language help Mayan civilization to develop?

Maya The largest Mayan cities boasted as many as 40,000 inhabitants. While they were centers of trade, their most important purpose was religious. Towering over all the other buildings in the city were huge temple-pyramids covered with carved pictures. Within these structures, brightly costumed priests conducted religious ceremonies.

2.

Aztec Farther to the north, in the Valley of Mexico, the Aztec rose to power sometime after 1200 A.D. As their power grew, they conquered their neighbors and forced them to pay tribute of food and labor. They erected a spectacular capital city, Tenochtitlán (tay NOHCH tee TLAHN), on an island in the middle of a large saltwater lake. An enormous pyramid, the Pyramid of the Sun, dominated the other structures in the city. Here Aztec priests sacrificed humans to Huitzilopochtli (WEE tsee loh POHCH tlee), the chief god.

Floating artificial islands, made by piling dirt on log rafts, surrounded Tenochtitlán. Some formed the foundations for homes; others were cultivated as vegetable gardens. Fresh water flowed into the city through aqueducts. Several long causeways connected the

2. **BACKGROUND** An important part of a Mayan city was the ball court. Spectators sat around the playing field in rows of stone seats. Players tried to knock a ball through a hoop fixed high above the ground using only their elbows, hips, and legs.

ARTS IN AMERICA

Mayan Ideograms

Mayan scribes recorded important events using a form of pictures called ideograms. Mayan ideograms represented numbers, names, words, sounds, and ideas. Mayan ideograms inscribed on monuments, walls, pottery, and books concern religion, science, and history. The writing, accompanied by illustrations, is a valuable source for historians and archaeologists who study Mayan civilization.

3.

In the picture on the left, Bird Jaguar, a great Mayan leader, is shown triumphantly taking a prisoner. The ideogram caption in the upper left corner reads: "On the day 7 Imix 14 Zec (755 A.D.), Bird Jaguar, lord of Yaxchilan (ee ahk shee LAHN), captured Jeweled Skull." Bird Jaguar is the figure on the right. The prisoners' names are on their thighs.
See p. T3.

1. Find Jeweled Skull's and the other captive's names in the captions in Mayan writing.

2. **Critical Thinking** How might a study of what topics appear in Mayan texts help give insight into Mayan civilization?

Great warriors and builders, the Aztec excelled in many fields. Tenochtitlán was home to many artisans who worked with gold, silver, and feathers. The artisan at right is crafting a royal headdress, such as the one shown above. The headdress, more than four feet high, once
1. belonged to the last ruler of the Aztec nation. It is a very rare example of this fine art.

1. **VISUAL EVIDENCE** This headdress was made from the tail feathers of the quetzal, a colorful bird sacred to the Aztec. The headdress was decorated with gold beads.

2. **BACKGROUND** The Inca accomplished all of this without a system of writing. They used clay models instead of blueprints to plan their buildings.

island-city to the mainland. Inside the city, paved streets led to the elaborate homes of the wealthy, to beautiful temples, and to zoos, orchards, and parks.

Even the few surviving remains make it clear that both the Aztec and Maya were brilliant builders and engineers. The priests of both cultures also excelled in astronomy. Their calendars were more exact than European systems of the day, and Aztec and Maya could predict eclipses of the sun and moon. The Aztec and Mayan religions demanded a precise knowledge of how the stars in the heavens moved.

Inca The engineering feats of another civilization, the Inca, surpassed even those of the Aztec and Maya. By 1400, the Inca dominated settlements stretching along a band 1,500 miles (about 2,400 kilometers) long on the western coast of South America. Incan cities were often constructed on the tops of mountains or along the faces of steep cliffs. Even today, Incan buildings survive earthquakes that demolish modern structures. The carefully fitted stones move apart under
2. stress, then slide back together.

The Maya, the Aztec, and the Inca were among the first Americans to feel the impact of European exploration in the late 1400s. Although their complex civilizations fell to invaders, the remains of their huge stone temples and public buildings have left an indelible imprint on the imagination of the
3. world.

See p. T3.

SECTION 3 REVIEW

1. **Identify:** (a) Iroquois League, (b) Tenochtitlán.

2. **Define:** (a) potlatch, (b) pictogram, (c) adobe, (d) kiva, (e) matrilineal, (f) nomadic, (g) sachem.

3. According to most scientists, how did the first people come to the Americas?

4. How did the travois and the teepee contribute to the lives of the Plains peoples?

5. Describe an accomplishment of the (a) Maya, (b) Aztec, (c) Inca.

6. **Critical Thinking** Why did Indians living in more moderate climates develop more complex social and political systems?

17

3. **READING** Students interested in learning more about the Maya, Aztec, and Inca civilizations can read *Ancient America*, by Jonathan Norton Leonard.

1. **VOCABULARY** Have students look up these words in the glossary before they begin reading.

2. **VOCABULARY** The word *feudal* has the same origin as the word *fief*, the land granted by a lord in return for service.

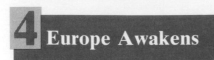

4 Europe Awakens

READ TO UNDERSTAND

■ What were the effects of the Crusades on exploration.

■ How changing politics and economics in Europe sparked exploration.

■ How technological advances affected exploration.

1. ■ *Vocabulary:* serf, vassal, feudalism, manor, astrolabe, quadrant.

Until the late 1400s, people in the Americas remained largely isolated from the rest of the world. One European map showed Europe, Africa, and Asia filling all the space on Earth. Another showed the oceans filled with sea monsters. But much to the surprise of Europe, before long these myths would clear away. Developments that had been underway for many years would soon bring the two worlds together.

Europe in the Middle Ages

During the Middle Ages (500–1500 A.D.), people in Europe focused largely on local affairs. Since the fall of the Roman Empire in the 400s, the continent of Europe had been split into hundreds of small, independent states, each ruled by a lord.

Most of the people were **serfs,** or peasants bound to the lord's land. They gave the lord part of their crop in return for protection against bandits or invaders. Serfs could not leave the land, change jobs, or travel even short distances without the lord's permission.

Theoretically, the lord also owed allegiance and services to a superior: a king, an emperor, or a higher lord. He was the king's **vassal,** or tenant. According to the law of the time, a lord received lands from his superior in return for loyalty. For the most part, however, lords ruled their territories independently of one another. This political and so-

2. cial system is known as **feudalism.**

18   Most medieval states were divided economically into **manors,** or large estates owned by lords. Peasants grew food for everyone on the manor and produced most of life's other necessities. For example, a manor would have a cobbler who made shoes, a blacksmith who forged tools, a brewer who made beverages, and a miller who ground grain into flour. As a result, few goods had to be 3. traded between manors.

The religious ideas of the Middle Ages contributed to a lack of interest in the wider world. Christians learned that life on earth was merely a preparation for life after death. They saw this world as a place of suffering and sadness, or of riches and corruption, but they believed that their station in life was God's will and did not question it.

A New Age Dawns

Around 1100, life in Europe began to change. People's horizons gradually widened, and they became more curious about the world beyond their own community.

The Crusades were a major cause of the new mood in Europe. Beginning in 1099, European Christians conducted a series of crusades, or holy wars, with the aim of recapturing the city of Jerusalem and the Holy Land from the Muslims.*

The Holy Land had fallen into the hands of the Muslims in the 600s. Until around 1000, however, Muslim rulers allowed Christians to come and go as they wished. At that time, the Seljuk (sehl JOOK) Turks conquered the Holy Land. Pilgrims returning from the Holy Land claimed that the Turks were killing and torturing Christians and turning Christian churches into Muslim temples.

The Crusades against the Turks lasted for about 150 years. At first, the Christian armies were successful. But by the end of the 1200s, all the land they had won was regained by the Muslims.

Although the Crusades did not achieve their goal, they did affect life in Europe. For example, Crusaders brought back books written by Arabic scholars. The new ideas

---

*Muslim: a believer in the Muslim religion, in which the supreme deity is Allah and the chief prophet and founder is Mohammed. The Muslim religion is also known as Islam, and the Muslims are sometimes known as Moslems.

Europeans quickly acquired a taste for the spices Crusaders brought back from Asia. At first, only the rich could afford the scarce cinnamon, pepper, and cloves sold by merchants such as the man at right. The search for a less costly route to Asia helped spur sea exploration.

1.

1. **VISUAL EVIDENCE** Have students try to imagine what good or service is being sold at each stall in this market.

2. **READING** Interested students might read excerpts from *The Book of Ser Marco Polo* and share selections with the class.

and knowledge the books contained sparked curiosity about the world beyond local borders. The spices, perfumes, fabrics, and other items the returning Crusaders introduced to Europe also gave people new ideas of food, fashion, and comfort in their homes. Soon, a profitable trade arose between the countries of Europe and Asia.

Expanding Horizons Eastward

At first, Europeans traded only with the countries of the Middle East. But, in time, merchants became curious about what lay beyond. In 1271, Venetian merchants Maffeo and Niccolo Polo and Niccolo's 17-year-old son Marco set off from Venice. They were bound for China, a land celebrated for its fabulous wealth.

The Polos traveled over sea and land for three years, reaching the court of Kublai Khan (koo blī KAHN), China's emperor, around 1275. They remained in China as guests of the Khan for 17 years. During that time, Marco Polo surveyed the vast empire of China. Little escaped his notice, and in 1295, three years after the Polos had returned to Venice, he

told the story of his travels to a scribe.* Marco Polo's account of his travels revealed to Europeans a civilization beyond their wildest dreams. 2.

Polo also provided some very practical information. He revealed that Asian goods were much cheaper in China than they were in Europe. He also noted that China was bordered by oceans, not by huge, impassable 3. swamps as had been thought. Therefore, a sea route to Asia would be possible if one could be found.

Over the next 200 years, Europeans became more interested in trade with China and with India, China's neighbor to the southwest. Fine silks, gold, and jewels mainly attracted the rich, but nearly everyone in Europe wanted to buy Asian spices.

In the years since the Crusades, Europeans had discovered that spices such as cloves, ginger, cinnamon, and pepper added flavor to food. Further, many perishable foods could be preserved only by heavy, often distaste-

---

*In the Middle Ages, few men and women could write, so they hired professional writers called scribes.

19

3. **ECONOMICS** Chinese goods were expensive in Europe because many merchants handled and profited from them as they traveled from the Far East to Europe.

ful, salting. Medieval cooks often had to pick worms out of meat before cooking it. Sauces made with Asian spices covered up the taste

1. of spoiled foods.

Because of the growing demand for products from Asia, merchants and adventurers began to search for faster and cheaper routes to the East. They looked to the sea to avoid the enormous taxes charged by rulers along the land routes.

Exploration and Politics

A changing political scene in Europe sparked greater interest in exploration. During the Middle Ages, kings and queens generally had ruled in name only. It was the feudal lords who held the real power.

As a new middle class grew and prospered, merchants, bankers, and other well-to-do commoners began to crave the kind of power and status held by the nobility. Kings and queens discovered that they could increase their own power by taking advantage of the merchants' ambition. Over a period of 100 years or so, they allied themselves with the merchants and bankers, using these people's wealth to help create strong monarchies and powerful nations.

Merchants and bankers also profited from the alliance. With the backing of a strong nation, merchants could compete with the city-states* of Italy, which had a virtual monopoly on Asian trade. A city-state like Venice, no matter how wealthy, was no match for the might of a united nation.

Changes in Outlook

Change occurred beyond the realm of politics and economics. During the period of intellectual revival known as the Renaissance (REHN uh sahns), which began in the 1300s, attitudes toward life, learning, and religion also were affected.

The work of Arabic scholars brought back by the Crusaders deeply impressed well-educated Europeans. Arabic translations reintroduced European scholars to the writings of many classical Greeks and Romans

whose works had been lost to Europe since the fall of Rome. Europeans also studied Arabic science and advances made by Arab mathematicians.

A new, inquisitive attitude toward the world sparked advances in science and technology, including new inventions in sea travel. For example, a ship's captain could use a compass to tell direction, even when neither land nor the sun was visible. The **astrolabe** (AS truh layb), an instrument used to find the altitude of the stars, helped the captain fix the ship's location. With the **quadrant,** the captain could take bearings from the sun or the stars in order to plot the ship's position on a map.

By making more precise measurements of distance and location possible, new inventions advanced the art of mapmaking. Another invention, the printing press, made the improved maps more widely available. These developments spurred interest in travel and exploration.

GEOGRAPHY AND HISTORY
Portugal Takes the Lead

Portugal was the first European nation to begin systematic exploration of the world beyond Europe and the Mediterranean Sea. No one there was more eager than Prince Henry, known as the Navigator. In 1418, Henry set up a school of navigation in his castle at Sagres (SAH grehs) on the southwestern tip of Portugal. From there, he sent expeditions to Africa.

Henry had several reasons for sending explorers south. Like other European princes, he felt that his nation had the duty to convert people to Christianity. He had heard the popular tale of Prester John, who was said to rule a Christian empire in the heart of Africa, and he hoped to be the first to find this legendary kingdom.

But Henry had commercial goals in mind as well. Gold from the distant kingdoms of western Africa had reached Europe as early as the 900s. However, it had come to Mediterranean ports by a long and costly route across the Sahara. Prince Henry hoped the Portuguese could find a quicker, cheaper route to the source of this gold by sea. Finally, Prince Henry dreamed of finding a sea route

*city-state: a small territory controlled by a thriving, independent city.

to India, a place that symbolized riches, mystery, and power.

For many years, Henry could not convince his sailors to dare a trip beyond Cape Bojador (boh huh DOHR) on the African coast. Below Bojador, the prevailing winds would be at the ships' backs, pushing them south. The sailors feared that they would not be able to sail north into the wind to return safely home. Henry encouraged his shipbuilders to experiment with new types of ships. Eventually, they developed a vessel called the caravel (KAR uh vehl), which could sail into the wind.

Henry also showed his captains how to use the quadrant so that they could sail out of sight of land and still be confident of getting back. In 1434, one of Henry's ships finally ventured south of Cape Bojador. To the crew's relief, they found that they were able to turn around and sail back home.

Prince Henry died in 1460, but Portuguese explorers continued to push farther down the African coast, erecting stone pillars on shore to mark their progress. Gradually, they established a profitable trade with West African kingdoms whose wealth and power impressed the Europeans. The bulk of their trade was in gold, but they also bought some African slaves. The explorers took the slaves back to Portugal to work as domestic servants. Some were eventually freed, took Portuguese names, and within generations became assimilated into the population.

In 1487, Bartolomeu Dias sailed around the Cape of Good Hope, the southernmost tip of Africa. He had planned to go on to India, but his crew mutinied and forced him to return to Portugal. Ten years later, in 1497, Vasco da Gama made the complete trip to India. Europeans had finally reached Asia by water, and Portugal was well on its way to becoming a powerful trading empire.

Early Contacts With the Americas

By 1490, Europeans were on the verge of reaching the Americas. Yet this would not be the first contact between Europeans and the Americas. Sometime around 1000, Scandinavian sailors led by Leif Ericson reached the northern tip of North America, explored briefly, and then went home.

The gold trade originally lured the Portuguese to explore Africa. There, they encountered people with rich cultures and artistic traditions. Bronze-working was a highly developed art in many West African kingdoms. This sculpture of the oba, or divine king, came from the kingdom of Benin, in what is today Nigeria.

2.

2. **VISUAL EVIDENCE** This statue, which stands almost two feet high, shows the full ceremonial costume of the oba. Ask: What qualities of the oba does the statue show?

Twenty years later, another group of Scandinavians arrived and settled for a couple of years before they also went back. The only trace of these early visitors are the half-buried foundations of their abandoned houses and a few stone objects.

According to legend, a few Irish fishermen crossed the Atlantic to North America. But if they did, they left no evidence of it. It was not until the late 1400s that the new spirit of discovery infecting Europe ended its isolation. ■

See p. T3.

See p. T3.

SECTION 4 REVIEW

1. **Identify:** (a) Marco Polo, (b) Henry the Navigator, (c) Vasco da Gama.

2. **Define:** (a) serf, (b) vassal, (c) feudalism, (d) manor, (e) astrolabe, (f) quadrant.

3. (a) What were the Crusades? (b) List two ways the Crusades increased people's interest in a wider world.

4. How did each of the following contribute to an age of discovery: (a) Marco Polo's writings; (b) desire for spices; (c) alliance between monarchs and merchants?

5. What new technology made sea travel safer and easier?

6. **Critical Thinking** Why have the Crusades been called a "successful failure"?

21

Summary

1. **Geographers have developed five major themes to help people understand the relationship between geography and history.** The themes are location, place, interaction between people and their environment, movement, and regions.

2. **North and South America have a wide range of physical regions and climates.** Population density and economic development are greater on the plains and plateaus with milder climates. The waterways provide transportation, irrigation, and hydroelectric power.

3. **The first Americans developed a vast array of different cultures.** Each culture had its own religious traditions, art forms, and way of life. Some groups maintained a simple hunting and gathering society while others developed complex economic and political systems.

4. **Changes in Europe sparked interest in exploration.** The development of nation states and improvements in technology in the 1300s and 1400s made the meeting of Europe and the Americas only a matter of time.

See p. T3.

Vocabulary

On a separate sheet of paper, write the word or words that best complete each of the following sentences.

1. _____ is the study of people, their environments, and their resources.

2. _____ is an account of what has happened in the life or development of a people, a nation, or a civilization.

3. _____ refers to the height of land measured from sea level.

4. _____ is sun-dried clay brick.

5. The _____ was the site of Pueblo religious ceremonies.

6. _____ people move from place to place, living in temporary settlements.

See p. T3.

Chapter Checkup

1. (a) How do location and place differ? (b) What are some different ways to distinguish between regions?

2. (a) How do geographers define movement? (b) How has movement changed from earliest times to the present? (c) How has movement affected the course of United States history?

3. How do different landforms and climates affect the distribution of population and economic activity in the United States?

4. The Eskimo and the people of the Great Basin lived by hunting and fishing, or by gathering plants, but their lives differed. (a) How were they different? (b) How do you explain the differences?

5. How did the Anasazi, the Pueblo, and the Navajo cope with the harsh conditions in the desert?

6. What role did religion play in each of the following cultures: (a) Pueblo, (b) Navajo, (c) Muskogean?

7. How did the change in the intellectual climate of Europe contribute to the age of discovery?

8. (a) Describe the role Portugal played in the exploration of the world beyond Europe. (b) Why were the activities of Prince Henry so important?

See p. T4.

Critical Thinking

1. **Recognizing Relationships** Explain how differing environments and natural resources may have contributed to the diversity of early American cultures.

2. **Projecting** How might the Native Americans be living today if they had never come in contact with Europeans?

See p. T4.

Connecting Past and Present

1. In some ways, the first Americans tried to live in harmony with the environment; in other ways they altered it. (a) How have people in modern times adapted to the environment and how have they altered it? (b) Why have recent alterations of the environment raised concern?

2. During the Middle Ages, advances in technology helped bring about contact between Europe and the Americas. What advances in technology have brought people over the globe in closer contact in the past few decades? Explain.

See p. T4.

Developing Basic Skills

1. **Geography** Relate the five themes of geography to where you live. (a) Find the coordinates of longitude and latitude. (b) Describe the physical and human characteristics of your community. (c) How have people in your community adapted to the environment? (d) How has movement affected the development of your community? (e) In what political region and geographic region do you live?

2. **Skimming** Follow the steps outlined in the Skill Lesson accompanying Section 1 of this chapter to skim Section 4, "Europe Awakens." Then answer the following questions: (a) What is the title of the section? What do you think it means? (b) What clues does the section introduction give about the meaning of the section title? (c) What are the subheadings for Section 4? (d) What is the topic of subsection 1? (e) In which subsection would you expect to find out about early voyages to the East? (f) Based on section 4 of the chapter summary, when did European attitudes toward the outside world begin to change?

WRITING ABOUT HISTORY

Answering Essay Questions

In order to answer an essay question, you must understand what the instruction word is telling you to do. Some of the most common instruction words and the type of answer each calls for are listed below.

Discuss: tell the significance of a person or event

Describe: write a full account of *what* happened

Explain: tell *how* or *why* an action or event affects something else

Identify: give a person's or event's place in time and its relation to other persons or events

Compare: give similarities and differences or only differences

Sometimes an essay question will have a question word. Some of the most common question words and the type of answer each calls for are listed below.

Why: give reasons

How: tell in what way or by what means something was done

What: give specific examples or illustrations

Practice: Analyze each of the Critical Thinking questions in this Chapter Review. Tell which type of response the question calls for.

Europe's Age of Discovery (1492–1650)

2

CHAPTER OUTLINE

1 Spanish Conquest in the Americas

2 Settling New Spain

3 The French and English Look North

4 A Gamble in Virginia

5 The New England Way

CHAPTER OBJECTIVES After completing this chapter, students should be able to
1. describe the impact of the explorations of Columbus.
2. describe the government and economy of New Spain.
3. explain how competition among European nations in the 1500s affected the Americas.
4. identify the goals and problems of early colonists in Jamestown and New England.
5. use visual evidence.

CHAPTER PREVIEW Read this passage by Jonathan Swift: "A European crew lands and finds an harmless People and are entertained with Kindness. The Natives are driven out or destroyed, their Princes tortured to discover their Gold; and this is a modern Colony sent to civilize a barbarous People." Ask: What point is Swift making? Do you agree?

"Desperation drove us to risk our lives in this way," wrote Cabeza de Vaca many years later. Along with hundreds of other Spanish soldiers, young Cabeza de Vaca had hoped to find gold in the Americas. Instead, he and his band found themselves stranded in Florida. Their only hope was to sail across the Gulf of Mexico and locate a Spanish settlement.

The soldiers crafted five rough vessels and set sail. After six weeks, Cabeza de Vaca's parched and starved crew was the first to reach an island off the coast of Texas. They crawled ashore on hands and knees.

Desperate to reach a settlement, they rowed out again into the surf the next day. Suddenly, a huge wave capsized their boat. "We survivors," wrote Cabeza de Vaca, "escaped naked as we were born. . . . Our bodies were so thin that our bones could be counted, and we looked the very images of death."

The date was November 7, 1528. Of the 80 Spanish soldiers who eventually reached the island, only four survived the next months. Three Spanish soldiers and an African slave known as Estevanico (ehs tay vahn EE koh) spent a year on the island and then wandered for years across the scorched Texas plains.

One day, the Spaniards saw an Indian wearing the buckle of a Spanish sword belt and realized their journey was near its end. Cabeza de Vaca wrote later that he and Estevanico tracked a party of Spanish horsemen, who "stood staring at me a length of time, so confounded that they neither greeted me nor drew near to make an inquiry." Back among their own people, Cabeza de Vaca and the others relayed Indian stories about the "seven cities of gold."

In the years after Columbus's voyages, waves of European explorers reached the Americas. Many of them came in search of gold and glory. Still others came to build permanent homes in the rich and varied lands of the New World.

1.

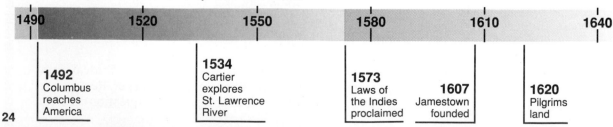

Spanish establish empire in New World

1490	1520	1550	1580	1610	1640

1492 Columbus reaches America

1534 Cartier explores St. Lawrence River

1573 Laws of the Indies proclaimed

1607 Jamestown founded

1620 Pilgrims land

24

1. TIME LINE QUESTION Ask: How long after Columbus reached America was Jamestown founded?

Spain led the way, but both France and England also carved out empires in the New World. Early French traders and fishermen traveled up the St. Lawrence River. Later, explorers ventured into the Great Lakes. The expedition in this
1. painting is setting off from a fort on Lake Ontario.

1. **VISUAL EVIDENCE** This painting was one of a series by American artist George Catlin, depicting the French explorer Sieur de La Salle.

2. **VOCABULARY** Have students look up these words in the glossary before they begin reading.

1 Spanish Conquest in the Americas

READD TO UNDERSTAND

■ How Columbus reached the Americas.

■ How exploration increased the rivalry between Spain and Portugal.

■ What role the conquistadores played in the conquest of the Americas.

2. ■ *Vocabulary:* circumnavigate, conquistador.

As Portuguese ships followed the African coast, other nations sought faster routes to the wealth of Asia. Spain, Portugal's neighbor, set out for the east by sailing west—across the Atlantic. In doing so, the Spanish came upon two continents unknown to Europe and founded their own empire in the Americas.

A Determined Explorer

Spain owes Christopher Columbus credit for its claim to the Americas. A tall, stubborn sailor from the Italian port of Genoa, Columbus had sailed much of the then-known world in the service of Portugal. A curious man, he studied geography and read Marco Polo's story of his travels.

Columbus agreed with scholars of the time that the world was round. However, on the basis of his own calculations, he was sure that the earth was much smaller than people thought. By sailing west, he maintained, a ship could navigate the distance between Europe and China in "a very few days" if winds were favorable.

3.

Failing to persuade King John II of Portugal to support a westward voyage to Asia, Columbus pleaded his case in one European country after another. Finally, after ten years, he turned to Spain as a last resort. Against the advice of cautious counselors, Queen Isabella agreed to back Columbus's venture. **25**

3. **GEOGRAPHY** Columbus estimated that a ship traveling west from Europe would have to sail only 6,000 miles to reach Asia. Ask students to use a globe to calculate the actual distance from Spain to China traveling westward. (movement)

She made him an admiral and outfitted him with three ships, the *Niña,* the *Pinta,* and the *Santa María,* and a crew of 90 sailors.

Arriving in the Americas

Columbus and his crew set sail from Palos, Spain, in August 1492. Two months later, on October 7, sailors spotted great flocks of birds flying southwest. Suspecting that the birds were heading for land, Columbus altered his course to follow them. Four days later, the crew saw tree branches and flowers floating in the water.

Finally, at two o'clock in the morning on October 12, the Pinta's lookout spotted white cliffs on the horizon and raised a shout. Without realizing it, Columbus and his crew had found a world unknown to Europeans. Columbus, certain he had reached an island off the coast of India, called the friendly people who greeted him Indians. (See the map on page 27.)

The Europeans saw no evidence of the fine silks or large buildings Marco Polo had described. The Arawaks (AR uh wahks), who lived on the island, seemed to lead a simple life. But their few gold ornaments convinced Columbus that he was not far from the Asian mainland.

Three months later, after exploring neighboring islands, including present-day Haiti and Cuba, the expedition sailed home to Spain. Queen Isabella and her husband Ferdinand were impressed with the "Indians" Columbus brought back to show that he had found a western route to Asia.

Columbus led three more expeditions funded by Spain. Men and women he brought with him set up outposts on a number of Caribbean islands. Columbus continued to insist that the islands were part of the fabled
1. Indies of the East. When the truth was finally realized, after his death in 1506, the islands were named the West Indies.

In 1501, Amerigo Vespucci (ah may REE goh veh SPOO chee), a merchant from Florence, Italy, scouted the shores of South America. He realized that he was looking at "a very great continent, until hitherto unknown." When a mapmaker in Europe later needed a name for the new and uncharted continents, he labeled the region "America."

GEOGRAPHY AND HISTORY

Rivals for the New World

Word of Columbus's explorations spread rapidly. Portugal's King John refused to believe that Columbus had reached India or China, nor would he recognize Spain's claim to the Caribbean islands. He argued that they were actually part of the Azores, islands in the Atlantic already owned by Portugal, and he claimed them for himself.

Spain and Portugal were suddenly embroiled in a bitter dispute. Worried that a war between these two Catholic nations would weaken the Church, the pope offered to mediate. After months of talks, Spain and Portugal agreed to the Treaty of Tordesillas (taw day SEE yahs). The treaty, signed in 1494, established the Line of Demarcation about 1,100 miles (1,770 kilometers) west of the Azores.

By the terms of the treaty, Spain gained the right to all undiscovered territory west of the line and Portugal the territory east of it. What neither nation knew in 1494 was that the eastern part of South America extended across the line. When a storm blew Portugal's Pedro Álvares Cabral (AHL vah rehz kuh BRAHL) off his course in 1500, he landed in this part of the Americas and promptly claimed it for King John. The territory is now 2. part of Brazil.

A Western Route to Asia

The desire to find a fast route to Asia still overshadowed any Spanish or Portuguese interest in settling what became known as the New World. After Columbus's voyages, many people believed that Asia lay just beyond the western coast of North America. To reach it, a person had only to find a water passage through the continent. Over the next few decades, expeditions eagerly searched the coastlines.

Balboa Vasco Núñez de Balboa (NOO nyehth day bal BOH uh), a Spanish explorer, discovered the shortest overland route across the New World. In 1513, Balboa made a grueling journey across the Isthmus of Panama, the narrow strip of land connecting North and South America. His path cut through rain forest so thick that an explorer who followed

2. **MAIN IDEA** Have students write a few sentences explaining the who, what, and why of the Treaty of Tordesillas.

the same trail 350 years later did not see the sky for 11 days.

When Balboa reached a mountain, he climbed to the top and gazed down on the vast ocean now known as the Pacific. He named it the South Sea, assuming that it was south of Asia. He had no idea of its great size.

Magellan It was Ferdinand Magellan (muh JEHL uhn) who discovered the immensity of the Pacific Ocean by sailing across it. Magellan's expedition set out from Spain in 1519, made its way around the stormy southern tip of South America, and then crossed the Pacific to the Philippine Islands. (See the map below.) There Magellan died in a battle with the island's inhabitants.

The remains of Magellan's fleet continued the hazardous westward journey. In 1522, the one remaining ship limped back to Spain. Of the 237 men who had set sail three years earlier, only 18 wretched survivors returned.

Those 18 sailors were the first to have **circumnavigated,** or sailed around, the globe.

The discoveries of Balboa and Magellan added to Europe's store of knowledge about the world and to Spain's position as a world power. Spain now possessed the key both to the largest ocean on earth and to the lands on the western side of the vast American continent. ■

The Conquistadores

In order to gain a strong foothold in the Americas, Spain relied on **conquistadores** (kohn KEES tah DOH rehs), or conquerors. These bold and ruthless soldiers were lured to the Americas by tales of riches and adventure. But they also had other motives. Many hoped to make Christian converts of the inhabitants. As one conquistador aptly put it: "We came here to serve God, and also to get rich."

MAP STUDY *The hope of discovering a fast route to Asia led European explorers all over the world, as this map shows. Trace the routes these explorers took. How was the route taken by the Portuguese different from that taken by other explorers?*

See p. T5.

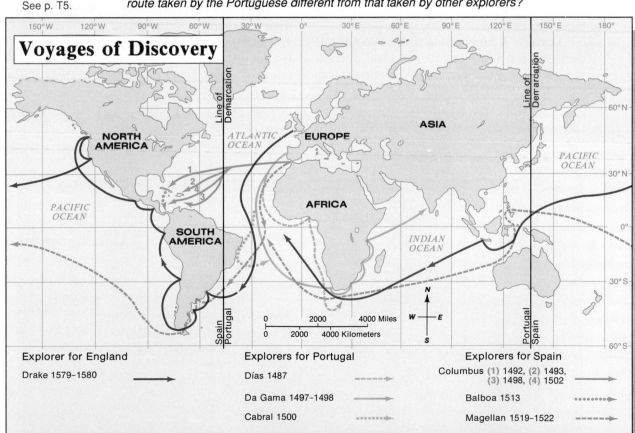

Voyages of Discovery

Explorer for England	Explorers for Portugal	Explorers for Spain
Drake 1579–1580	Días 1487	Columbus (1) 1492, (2) 1493, (3) 1498, (4) 1502
	Da Gama 1497–1498	Balboa 1513
	Cabral 1500	Magellan 1519–1522

1. DISCUSSION Ask: Is there any kind of endeavor today that carries the same kind of risks and potential rewards?

2. BACKGROUND Quetzalcoatl had often been depicted as a white-faced god with a beard. This description fit Cortés.

The Spanish crown gave each conquistador a license to establish outposts and settlements in the Americas. In return, the conquistadores agreed to send one fifth of any gold or silver they mined back to the royal treasury.

The conquistadores recognized the gamble they were taking. They had to equip and finance their expeditions, risking possible shipwreck, huge losses, or even death.
1. But success could mean untold riches.

For many years, the Spanish government was content to leave colonization to these military adventurers. Under this system, Spain risked little to expand its power and authority. In fact, gold and silver from the New World eventually made Spain rich.

Great Empires Fall

Spain gradually gained control of most of South and Central America and parts of North America. Until 1519, however, Spain had no more than a handful of settlements in the West Indies. In that year, Hernando Cortés (kawr TEHZ) gathered a small army and prepared to look for the gold and riches rumored to exist in present-day Mexico.

Cortés A remarkable leader, Cortés understood the value of psychological warfare as well as physical combat. When he discovered the skill of Aztec warriors, he allied himself with other tribes who resented paying tribute to the Aztec.

Cortés also acquired the services of a translator, speechmaker, and negotiator, a Native American woman whom the Spanish named Doña Marina (DOH nyah mah REEN ah). Doña Marina "possessed such manly valor," reported one soldier, "that she never allowed us to see any sign of fear in her."

Cortés then made one of the most daring—some might say foolhardy—moves in military history. He marched his small band of 400 heavily armored soldiers into Tenochtitlán, the Aztec capital, and confronted the Aztec ruler, Montezuma (MAHN tee ZOO muh).

Montezuma could have easily surrounded the Spanish and cut off their retreat. But as Cortés knew, the Aztec ruler believed the Spanish had come to fulfill an ancient Aztec prophecy. According to the prophecy, the Aztec god, Quetzalcoatl (keht SAHL koh AH tuhl), would return to Mexico from the east, the direction of the rising sun. And this, of course, was the direction from which the Spaniards had appeared.
2.

In a tense game of diplomacy lasting more than six months, Cortés held Montezuma a virtual captive in his own city. Then the Spanish fought their way out, losing half their number in the process. Gathering their Na-

3. BIOGRAPHY While she was Cortés's interpreter, Doña Marina heard of an Aztec plot to kill the Spanish. She told Cortés, thus saving his life.

Because of her knowledge of local politics and languages, Doña Marina was a
3. *valuable negotiator for Cortés. She is shown talking to Cortés below. However, the Spanish also took advantage of their superior weapons and armor to conquer the Aztec and other nations of Mexico.*

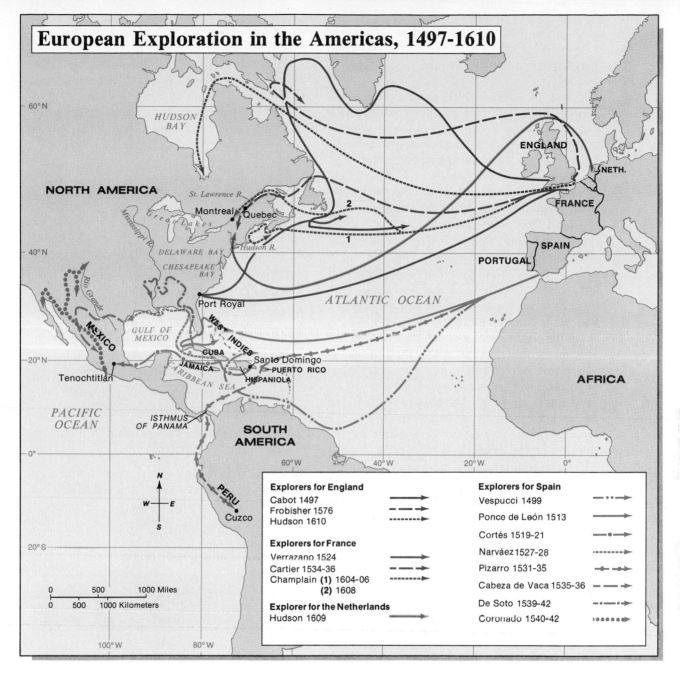

European Exploration in the Americas, 1497-1610

HUDSON BAY

NORTH AMERICA

St. Lawrence R.
Montreal
Quebec

Mississippi R.

Great Lakes

DELAWARE BAY

CHESAPEAKE BAY

Hudson R.

ENGLAND

NETH.

FRANCE

SPAIN

PORTUGAL

ATLANTIC OCEAN

Rio Grande

MEXICO

GULF OF MEXICO

Port Royal

WEST INDIES

CUBA

JAMAICA

Santo Domingo

PUERTO RICO

HISPANIOLA

CARIBBEAN SEA

Tenochtitlán

AFRICA

PACIFIC OCEAN

ISTHMUS OF PANAMA

SOUTH AMERICA

PERU

Cuzco

N
W E
S

0   500   1000 Miles
0   500   1000 Kilometers

Explorers for England
Cabot 1497
Frobisher 1576
Hudson 1610

Explorers for France
Verrazano 1524
Cartier 1534-36
Champlain **(1)** 1604-06
         (2) 1608

Explorer for the Netherlands
Hudson 1609

Explorers for Spain
Vespucci 1499
Ponce de León 1513
Cortés 1519-21
Narváez 1527-28
Pizarro 1531-35
Cabeza de Vaca 1535-36
De Soto 1539-42
Coronado 1540-42

MAP STUDY *Inspired by the voyage of Columbus, English, French, and Dutch adventurers raced to explore the New World. (See page 27.) Which nation had the largest number of explorers? Which areas did they visit?* See p. T5.

1. MAP READING Ask: How is Cortés shown? Which explorer crossed the Mississippi River?

tive American allies, the Spanish returned and surrounded Tenochtitlán, hoping to starve it into submission. The Aztec were weakened further when thousands perished from smallpox. Victorious at last, Cortés entered the city and destroyed it, bringing an end to the Aztec empire.

Pizarro Ten years later, in 1530, Francisco Pizarro (pee ZAHR oh), another conquistador, received permission to conquer the Inca empire of present-day Peru. With 180 metal-clad soldiers—less than half of Cortés's force—Pizarro marched into the Andean kingdom. When he arrived, a civil war was raging among the Incas.

Pizarro launched a surprise attack, imprisoned the Inca leader, Atahualpa (AH tah WAHL pah), and killed most of Atahualpa's attendants. The attack stunned the Inca and weakened their resistance to the Spanish. By 1535, Pizarro had taken the capital and crushed nearly all opposition.

29

2. LOCAL HISTORY Ask: Did any explorers shown on the map come near your local area? If so, do any reminders of their visit exist today?

1.

2.

Exploration to the North

Legends of great wealth drew Spanish adventurers to the northern regions of the Americas as well as to the south. These expeditions, however, were much less profitable to Spain than those of Cortés and Pizarro.

Ponce de León Tales of a miraculous fountain whose water kept people young forever attracted two Spanish expeditions to the land they named Florida. In 1513, Juan Ponce de León (WAHN PAHN say day lay AWN) made a vain attempt to find this "fountain of youth." Pánfilo de Narváez (nahr VAH ehz) tried again in 1527. But he had to contend with the Appalachees (a pah LAH chees), the best archers in the area. They strung their six-foot oak bows so tightly that no Spaniard could pull them. And their precisely aimed arrows could pierce the cracks between the soldiers' armored fittings.

Cabeza de Vaca Unable to withstand the Appalachees, the Spaniards retreated to the coast. In makeshift boats, they sailed across the Gulf of Mexico. As you have read on page 24, only four soldiers survived, including Cabeza de Vaca, a conquistador, and Estevanico, an African.

De Soto From 1539 to 1542, Hernando de Soto (day SOH toh) led a gold-hunting expedition into the Southeast. His army wandered as far north as the Carolinas and as far west as present-day Oklahoma. When de Soto died without finding any treasure, the expedition returned to Mexico.

Coronado Farther west, Francisco Coronado (KOH roh NAH doh) organized another expedition at about the same time as de Soto's. Coronado hoped to find the legendary "seven cities of gold," which were said to be nestled in the hills of present-day New Mexico. He chose Estevanico to lead the scouting party.

When the expedition reached the Zuñi pueblos, the villages named in the tales of the "seven cities," the inhabitants launched an attack. Refusing to retreat, the "Black Mexican," as Zuñi legend later called Estevanico, was killed by a hail of arrows.

The next year, in 1540, Coronado himself took up the search. He found the Zuñi pueblos but not the gold. In the process, however, he explored much of the future southwestern United States.

Coronado, de Soto, and Ponce de León all failed to find gold and conquer new lands in the north. Now the Spanish concentrated on settling the area to the south, in present-day Mexico, the Caribbean, and South America. There, they had much greater success.

See p. T5.

SECTION 1 REVIEW

1. **Identify:** (a) Queen Isabella, (b) Montezuma, (c) Pizarro (d) Ponce de León, (e) Cabeza de Vaca, (f) Estevanico, (g) de Soto, (h) Coronado.

2. **Define:** (a) circumnavigate, (b) conquistador.

3. How did Spain make Columbus's achievements possible?

4. (a) What roles did Balboa and Magellan play in the exploration of the world? (b) How did their discoveries benefit Spain?

5. What did Cortés hope to gain by conquering the Aztec empire?

6. **Critical Thinking** How might Spain's location in Europe have affected the areas it settled in the Americas?

3. **VOCABULARY** Have students look up these words in the glossary before they begin reading.

2 Settling New Spain

READ TO UNDERSTAND

■ How New Spain was organized and governed.

■ How Spanish conquest affected the Native Americans.

■ Why African slaves were introduced to New Spain.

■ *Vocabulary:* presidio, encomienda.

Columbus and his crew were the first to construct a Spanish settlement in the New World. The crude fortress was built from the timbers of the *Santa María,* which had drifted onto a reef on Christmas Eve in 1492 and burst apart at its seams. Columbus dubbed

2. **BIOGRAPHY** For six years, Cabeza de Vaca and his men lived as slaves of the Native Americans. Estavanico learned their captors' language, and so was able to help win freedom for the group.

1. **VOCABULARY** The word viceroy is made up of *vice,* which means someone who acts in the place of someone else, and *roy,* from the Spanish word for king.

2. **BACKGROUND** By the 1530s, the Spanish realized that the islands Columbus had found were not part of Asia. They began to call the islands the West Indies.

the outpost La Navidad, "the birth," in honor of Christmas; but eventually it was abandoned.

The first permanent settlement, Santo Domingo, was built on the Caribbean island of Hispaniola in 1496. Within a few decades, other towns sprang up on the islands and on the mainland of the Americas.

Governing New Spain

Soon the Spanish faced the task of managing a huge empire. While overseeing explorations, they also had to choose sites for towns, transport colonists from Europe, distribute land, and promote farming, mining, and trade.

The informal, one-man rule of the conquistadores could not carry out all these goals. The rapid growth of New Spain, as the North American part of the empire was called, demanded a more formal system of government. In 1535, Emperor Charles V appointed Antonio de Mendoza (mehn DOH sah) the first viceroy* of New Spain. Mendoza was an able administrator, and the Spanish colony prospered, as did the South American part of Spanish America.

———

*viceroy: a person who rules a country or province as the deputy of a king or queen.

3. **VISUAL EVIDENCE** This painting was done by Ferdinand Peppe. Have students compare this picture to the description of a mission on p. 32.

By the mid-1500s, Mexico City, the capital of New Spain, boasted paved and lighted streets, as well as a police department and public water system. By 1551, universities had opened in the West Indies, Mexico, Ecuador, and Peru. Theaters and printing presses were thriving in Spanish America before England began colonizing.

In 1573, Charles's successor, Philip II, proclaimed the Laws of the Indies in an attempt to control Spain's American colonies more tightly. This royal legislation regulated nearly every aspect of life in New Spain, from how much open space a town should have, to what kind of seeds should be planted.

A Plan for Settlement

The Laws of the Indies reveal much about the goals of the Spanish in America. They specified that separate settlements be built: **presidios** (pray SIH dee ohs) for military activities, missions for religious work, and pueblos for farming, trade, and town life.

Presidios The presidios, designed in the shape of a rectangle, were surrounded by high, thick walls. Within the walls were barracks, storehouses, stables, shops, and a few houses for the families of married soldiers.

4. **CITIZENSHIP** Lead a discussion on why the Laws of the Indies —issued by the king in Spain—might not always have been enforced in New Spain.

Many Spanish missions like this one at San Gabriel prospered. Some Indians were forced to farm the land while others worked as ranchers, traders, or artisans for the Spanish. Missions were the foundations of later Spanish settlements in present-day California, Texas, Arizona, and New Mexico.

1. **ACTIVITY** Students might find out more about the architectural styles of New Spain and present their findings to the class in an oral report.

2. **BACKGROUND** Many Native Americans thought the Spanish were divine because they were immune to several of the diseases that were killing the Native Americans.

In time, houses and farms sprouted up outside the walls of the presidio as colonists clustered there for security. Gradually, the military communities developed into towns much like the civilian pueblos.

Missions Roman Catholic priests ran the missions as centers for converting Native Americans to Christianity. Many Native Americans were either persuaded or forced to live there. Usually, the mission also included a few Spanish settlers and a small garrison of soldiers.

Each mission supported itself, mostly by farming. Many also manufactured pottery, woven blankets, leather, wine, or olive oil—all goods that could be exported to Spain or sold to other colonists.

Pueblos Pueblos were usually located in the middle of a huge tract of farmland. The buildings found in the pueblos of New Spain were far from simple "frontier" structures. The Laws of the Indies stated clearly that settlers were to build with "the beauty of the town" in mind. Thus churches, private homes, shops, and other buildings were among the finest examples of Spanish architecture.

Impact on Native Americans

The promise of free or cheap land lured many Spaniards to the Americas. Europeans craved the bananas, rice, melons, and wheat that the settlers raised. The farmers in the Americas also began to cultivate native crops such as potatoes, tomatoes, corn, beans, pumpkins, squash, and tobacco.

Ranching proved even more profitable than farming, so many Spanish settlers turned to raising horses, pigs, cattle, burros, and sheep on the broad expanses of American land. These vast ranches, however, required back-breaking work, usually done by Native Americans.

An early policy of the Spanish government had effectively forced many Native Americans to work on Spanish estates. Conquistadores had been granted **encomiendas** (ehn koh mee EHN dahs), the right to demand a tax from Native Americans living on a given piece of land. Often the conquistador would force the Native Americans to work for him as payment. Under this system, the Native Americans eventually became bound to the land because they had no other way of paying the tax. They were often reduced to a form of slavery. Once caught in the system, there was rarely any way out.

Where the Spanish discovered gold and silver, they put Native Americans to work in the mines. If labor on the ranches was grueling, working in the mines was even more deadly. The dust, dirt, darkness, and disastrous cave-ins combined to produce staggering rates of injury and death.

To make matters worse, many Native Americans caught European diseases from the colonists. Smallpox spread like wildfire, killing millions of people. In Mexico, the population dropped from five million in 1492 to only one million a century later.

A Misguided Proposal

Eventually, word of the brutal treatment of Native Americans reached Spain. Many Spaniards reacted with concern. Bartolomé de Las Casas (BAR toh loh MAY day lahs KAH sahs), a Dominican priest, devoted his life to rescuing the Native Americans. He pleaded with Spanish officials to place Native Americans under the protection of the clergy. De Las Casas and other priests were not able to end enslavement of Indians throughout all the colonies, but they allowed many Indians to own cattle and raise their own crops. They also replaced some Spanish overseers in the mines with Native Americans.

To reduce the reliance on Native American labor, de Las Casas suggested that the Spanish import slaves from Africa. The Africans, he reasoned, had shown on the early voyages of exploration that they could live in the New World and that they had developed immunity to many European diseases. And the Africans were skilled farmers.

When de Las Casas's reform proposals were put into place, an African slave trade to the New World began. The Spanish were soon buying slaves by the shipload from Portuguese traders, who had set up contacts years before with African kingdoms. (See page 21.)

De Las Casas later bitterly regretted that his efforts to free one group from slavery had resulted in the equally cruel bondage of another. To other Spaniards, however, the solution seemed worth the brutal price. Ameri-

3. **BACKGROUND** De Las Casas knew that the Portuguese used captured Africans as slaves. In Portugal, however, Africans worked as butlers and footmen. Only in the New World did slaves toil in mines and on plantations.

An unknown artist sketched this scene around 1584 at the silver mines of Potosí in Bolivia. Llamas brought the ore from the mine to the refinery for processing. The Spanish forced Indians to work long hours in dangerous mines. By 1600, the
1. mines at Potosí were the largest source of silver in the world.

---

1. **ECONOMICS** Because of the rich vein of silver ore in Cerro Potosí, the mountain shown here, Potosí became for a time the largest settlement in the New World.

can gold and silver, mined by both Native Americans and newly enslaved Africans, catapulted Spain to unprecedented riches. By the mid-1500s, Spain had the most powerful over-
2. seas empire in the world.

See p. T6.

SECTION 2 REVIEW

1. **Identify:** (a) Santo Domingo, (b) New Spain, (c) Philip II, (d) Bartolomé de Las Casas.

2. **Define:** (a) presidio, (b) encomienda.

3. How did the activities of the three types of Spanish settlements differ?

4. How did the Spanish use encomiendas to force Native Americans to work for them?

5. **Critical Thinking** What kinds of problems dealt with in the Laws of the Indies still concern town planners today?

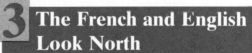

3 The French and English Look North

READ TO UNDERSTAND

■ Why the French were interested in North America.

■ How the "sea dogs" benefited the English.

■ How England first tried to settle North America.

By the mid-1500s, Spain had become the strongest nation in Europe. King Philip II ruled not only Spain but also Portugal, the Netherlands, and parts of Italy. Without colonial competitors, Spain dominated the Americas, and its ships controlled their coastal waters.

The enormous wealth that Spain reaped from the Americas aroused the curiosity and envy of other European nations. The governments of France and England, in particular,

33

---

2. **ACTIVITY** Have students imagine that they are Bartolomé de Las Casas as an old man. Tell them to write a letter or diary entry expressing his feelings about what he accomplished in New Spain.

Gateways to the Continent

Land ho! It was a blessed sound for those who had weathered an Atlantic crossing to America. But sighting land was just the beginning of the challenge. To reach the untapped wealth of North America, the early European explorers and settlers needed easy approaches or entryways into the continent. Controlling one or more of the six navigable waterways that extend inland from the Atlantic Ocean proved vital for empire building. (See the map on page 29.)

In 1492, Columbus came by chance upon the largest of these entryways—the Caribbean Sea and the Gulf of Mexico. The Spanish achieved undisputed control of this western arm of the Atlantic through their grip on Cuba, the Florida Strait, the Yucatán Channel, and the Central American land bridge. Lasting Spanish influences spread along the coast and deep inland along the Mississippi and Rio Grande rivers.

Excluded from this southern region, the English looked to the north. In 1497, John Cabot discovered the entryway to Hudson's Bay for England. Frozen over in winter and ignored for more than a century, this northernmost gateway later offered Hudson's Bay fur traders an easy route into northern Canada.

The French also staked a claim to a North American entryway. Jacques Cartier discovered the route inland to Montreal along the St. Lawrence River–Great Lakes waterway in 1535. By 1606, other French explorers had extended French influence to the Great Lakes, and by 1672, to the Mississippi, as shown at left.

The Chesapeake Bay–Tidewater Virginia entryway, opened with the founding of Jamestown in 1607, gave England its first permanent foothold in North America. In 1664, England gained control of two other gateways from the Dutch—the Hudson River and the Delaware Bay. Soon the British began pushing inland toward the Appalachians and future conflict with others who claimed the continent.

See p. T6.

1. Why did the Europeans seek control of the entryways to North America?

2. **Critical Thinking** How were the patterns of early settlement influenced by the location of navigable waterways?

1. **VISUAL EVIDENCE** This painting depicts the same expedition as the painting on p. 25.

2. **BACKGROUND** Like Columbus, Cabot believed he had reached Asia. His actual landing place was probably on the coast of Newfoundland.

wanted to find gold in the Americas and a quicker sea route to Asia.

During the late 1400s and early 1500s, explorers employed by England and France, including John Cabot, Giovanni da Verrazano, and Martin Frobisher, sailed along the North American coast looking for a waterway to the east. (See the map on page 29.) They gathered valuable geographic information but found no passage to the Pacific.

As their hopes for quick wealth crumbled, both nations embarked on other, more realistic ventures. Each organized colonies in the northern part of North America and began to exploit what the land had to offer.

An Empire of Fish and Fur

In 1504, fishermen from France sailed into what is today known as the Gulf of St. Lawrence looking for cod. After a few years, they realized that they could increase their profits by trading with the Americans they encountered there. In exchange for furs, they supplied the Indians with hatchets, kettles, muskets, and other European goods.

3. **READING** Students interested in the reactions of the first Europeans to the New World can look at *The Discovery of North America* or *The Exploration of North America 1630-1776*, by W. P. Cumming, et al.

1. **GEOGRAPHY** Have students study the map on p. 12. Ask: With which Native American groups might the French fishermen have traded? (location)

2. **BACKGROUND** One sea dog, Sir Humphrey Gilbert, wrote a book for Queen Elizabeth called *How Her Majesty May Annoy the King of Spain.*

In 1534, the French explorer Jacques Cartier (kahr tee YAY) sailed up the St. Lawrence River. Cartier, like other explorers, was looking for the fabled northwest passage to Asia. Local inhabitants told him of great golden cities that lay "just beyond" the horizon. Cartier explored the St. Lawrence as far as present-day Montreal, where he founded an outpost. But the northwest passage and the gold always seemed just out of reach.

Political and religious strife in France prevented the government from paying serious attention to colonizing North America until the end of the century. It was only then that the French government stirred up new interest by granting fur-trading rights. In 1604, Samuel de Champlain (sham PLAYN) set out to explore and to establish a few trading settlements in North America.

Limited French Settlement

Champlain was a knowledgeable sailor, geographer, and superb mapmaker. His maps, most of which have survived to this day, showed not only the features of the areas he explored but also details of the settlements he founded.

In 1608, Champlain sailed up the St. Lawrence River as far as present-day Quebec (kwee BEHK). There, on a shelf of land overlooking the river, he constructed a massive wooden fortress, which he called the Habitation (ah bee tah SYOHN). Slowly, the city of Quebec grew up around the fortress.

Over the next hundred years, settlers did trickle in to what became known as New France. But there were never enough to sustain a thriving colony. The wealth and success of New France lay not in towns and cities but in the packets of furs that French trappers brought down the St. Lawrence from the interior in 36-foot (11-meter) birchbark canoes. Since the French government preferred fur trading to colonizing, that state of affairs continued.

The Sea Dogs

Relations among the nations of Europe during the 1500s were tense. Religious disputes pitted Catholic countries against Protestant countries, as each struggled to win people and lands to its cause.

At the time, Spain was the most powerful Catholic nation in the world. The expansion of its power in the Americas and Europe made it a natural foe of Protestant England.

Gradually, an undeclared war developed between Spain and England. Into the fray stepped the "sea dogs." Eager for plunder and fiercely loyal to England and its queen, Elizabeth I, the sea dogs scoured the Atlantic Ocean pirating Spanish treasure ships. The English government did not officially hire them; nonetheless, Elizabeth turned a blind eye to their exploits and took a share of the booty for her government.

Sir Francis Drake, one of the boldest sea dogs, made an especially daring raid in 1573. Aided by black African slaves who had escaped from the Spanish, he and his crew stole the yearly silver shipment being carried from Peru to Spain over the Isthmus of Panama.

As war between Protestant England and Catholic Spain loomed, Queen Elizabeth I stalled for time while England built ships. In the meantime, English captains known as "sea dogs" preyed on treasure-filled Spanish vessels returning from the New World. Elizabeth, shown here being carried to the wedding of a lady-in-waiting, hoped to gain a generous share of the booty.

3. **BACKGROUND** In 1559, King Philip II of Spain proposed marriage to Queen Elizabeth, but she declined. The two nations contended against each other for years.

SKILL LESSON

A View of the New World: Using Visual Evidence

The pictures in this textbook, which include drawings, paintings, and photographs, all provide valuable historical clues. Such pieces of visual evidence can help you understand the past by giving you a glimpse of what was happening at a particular time and place. However, the people who made the pictures influence what you see. To make the best use of visual evidence, you must analyze it.

Follow the steps below, using the picture to practice using visual evidence.

See p. T6.

1 **Study the visual evidence to decide what you are seeing.** Look both at the details and at the picture as a whole. (a) Which people in the picture probably lived in the territory shown? Which seem to have arrived recently? (b) What does the picture tell you about the territory? About the waters off the coast? (c) What seems unusual about the location of Florida, Canada, and Mexico?

2 **Analyze the reliability of the visual evidence as a source.** (a) Do you think the artist actually saw all the things shown? Why or why not? (b) Can you tell from the picture where the artist was from? Whose viewpoint does this picture help you understand? Why? (c) Is this a reliable source?

3 **Study the visual evidence to learn more about a historical event or period.** Refer to the picture and what you have read to answer the following questions: (a) How did people in the mid-1500s view the voyage to the Americas? (b) Why do you think the picture appears to be upside down? Why might this view seem natural to a French artist? How might a Spaniard have drawn this picture?

1. **READING** Students can find more visual evidence in *The New World: The First Pictures of America,* edited by Stefan Lorant, which contains drawings by John White and other explorers.

1.

Four years later, Drake followed Magellan's route around the world, raiding Spanish settlements along the way on the Pacific coast of South America.

Because no English ship had sailed those waters before, Drake caught the Spaniards by surprise. He would sweep into a harbor and at gunpoint force the Spanish to transfer the silver plate, gold bars, and other treasures from their ships into his ship's hold. Then, in gallant style, he might entertain a Spanish official or two at dinner in his stateroom, complete with violin serenades played by his crew.

Drake returned to England in 1580 with stolen treasure. Queen Elizabeth rewarded Drake by knighting him right on the deck of his ship. King Philip II of Spain responded to this public insult by preparing for war.

In 1588, Philip sent a huge fleet, known as the Armada, against England. The English navy was outnumbered two to one, but Drake and other captains made good use of their smaller, more maneuverable ships. With the help of a storm that scattered the Spanish fleet, the English won a stunning victory. Spain's dominance of Europe was shattered.

The First English Colonies

Once their interest in the New World had been aroused, the English began to think of more permanent ways to exploit the Americas. Sir Walter Raleigh, a royal favorite, sponsored the first English attempt to found a settlement in North America.

Raleigh saw the outpost as more than a way station for pirates and gold seekers. The colonists, he hoped, would raise bananas, sugar, and other crops impossible to grow in England's cold climate. They would ship these products back to England along with valuable raw materials such as lumber.

In 1585, Raleigh's expedition of about 100 men landed on Roanoke (ROH uh nohk) Island, off the coast of present-day North Carolina. The spot was an appealing location for a settlement because it was sheltered from the Atlantic by a chain of long, narrow, sandy islands. The colonists included John White, a surveyor and artist, who painted watercolors of the new land and its inhabitants, and

Thomas Hariot, an English scholar. Hariot may have gone as an interpreter, having had contact with Indians who had journeyed back to England with earlier explorers.

The 1585 expedition did not stay at Roanoke, but another, including 100 men and 17 women, tried again in 1587. Once the colony had been set up and was prospering, John White returned to England for supplies. Unfortunately, he was unable to make it back to America for nearly three years.

To White's dismay, his relief expedition to Roanoke found only deserted buildings, rusty armor, and grass-choked lanes and paths. White's crew searched for the sign of a cross, which the settlers had agreed to leave if they were in distress. But they found only the cryptic word "CROATOAN" carved on the door post of the crumbling fort.

Had the settlers, threatened with hunger and hard times, joined the friendly Croatoan tribe nearby? White never found the answer. A storm prevented him from staying to search for the settlers.

Although Roanoke failed as a permanent settlement, the experience proved valuable. Raleigh and his friends had established a beachhead in America using their own funds. But they saw that future colonies were likely to prosper only with a more formal, better organized way of raising financial support. The solution to raising money for such risky ventures was not long in coming.

See p. T7.

SECTION 3 REVIEW

1. **Identify:** (a) Jacques Cartier, (b) Samuel de Champlain, (c) Sir Francis Drake, (d) Armada, (e) Sir Walter Raleigh.

2. (a) What goals did most of the early French and English explorers have? (b) How did their goals change?

3. What did the sea dogs accomplish?

4. (a) Why did Raleigh found Roanoke? (b) Was the colony sucessful? Explain.

5. **Critical Thinking** Why might the defeat of the Spanish Armada have fueled England's ambitions for the New World?

1. **VOCABULARY** Have students look up this term in the glossary before they begin reading.

2. **BIOGRAPHY** Walter Raleigh (1552?–1618) was granted 12,000 acres in Ireland by Queen Elizabeth. There he grew the first potatoes in the Old World, with American plants.

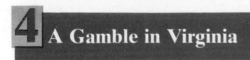

A Gamble in Virginia

READ TO UNDERSTAND

■ How John Smith contributed to the survival of Jamestown.

■ How growing tobacco altered the economy of Virginia.

■ What was the importance of the House of Burgesses.

1. ■ *Vocabulary:* joint stock company.

Sponsoring a colony in an untamed, unknown country thousands of miles from England was a difficult, risky, and expensive business. The sponsor had to buy ships, pay sailors to transport colonists, and persuade settlers—especially laborers and skilled workers—to migrate to America. Raleigh's experience with the colony of Roanoke had shown that individuals, no matter how wealthy, could not do this alone.

Financing the Colonies

The English had devised a form of business organization for trade in Russia, Persia, and the East Indies that helped them solve the problem of financing the American colonies. This organization was known as a **joint stock company.**

A joint stock company pooled the funds of many investors by selling stock, or shares, in the company. The amount of an investor's profit or loss depended on the number of shares owned. If the company went bankrupt, an investor was liable only for the amount of his or her investment. With the joint stock company, creditors could not seize the investor's personal property as payment for a debt, as they could with private individuals or other forms of business organization.

Their ability to raise capital and limit their liability allowed joint stock companies to undertake ventures both expensive and risky. Among these ventures was the founding of colonies in America.

The Fort on the James

In 1606, 15 years after John White had returned from England to the ghostly emptiness of Roanoke, King James I granted a charter to two companies of English investors. The charter authorized the companies to found colonies in the New World.

One group, the Plymouth Company, included merchants from the port of Plymouth, England. For many years they had sponsored expeditions to the rich Atlantic fishing grounds off Newfoundland. The Plymouth Company's charter gave it the exclusive right to settle land from present-day Maine to New York. (See the map on page 39.)

The London Company acquired rights to the territory stretching from the Potomac River south to what is now North Carolina. According to the agreement between the crown and the investors, the land between the two grants could be claimed by the company that settled it first.

In December 1606, 120 men and boys left London with instructions from the London Company to establish a settlement in what is now Virginia. Four months later, after a rough voyage, the colonists landed and began to build a fort along a low, swampy peninsula 30 miles upstream from the mouth of the James River.

The settlement around the fort was named Jamestown, in honor of the king. Its location was easy to defend from any outside attack, but the marshy peninsula provided a breeding ground for malaria-carrying mosquitoes. Furthermore, the drinking water was brackish, and the unusually damp air rotted the wooden buildings. It was a situation made for disaster.

Soon Jamestown residents were beset by disease. To make matters worse, most colonists were soldiers or aristocrats not used to doing hard physical labor. Others could make glass, do brickwork, or make iron tools, but virtually no one had the basic farming skills needed to survive.

Instead of telling this ill-assorted crew of workers to grow corn, the London Company wanted them to search for gold. Most settlers had visions of finding rich mines, as the Spaniards had done, so little important work

38

3. **MAIN IDEA** Have students write a paragraph explaining how a joint stock company worked and what its advantages were.

4. **BACKGROUND** The colonists had also been instructed to search for a northwest passage to China, but soon realized that none existed in that area.

1. **CRITICAL THINKING** Ask students to consider how the splendor of the Spanish empire may have led English settlers to be preoccupied with finding gold.

2. **DISCUSSION** Before they read further, have students discuss what actions they would have proposed to improve conditions in Jamestown.

1. was accomplished. "No talk, no hope, nor work," recalled Captain John Smith, Jamestown's military expert, "but dig gold, wash gold, refine gold, load gold."

2. Conditions deteriorated rapidly. Within a year, nearly half of the original 104 settlers had died. The future of the only English outpost in the Americas looked bleak.

Jamestown Survives

The experiment on the James River might well have ended in its first year if John Smith had not been a member of the colony. Smith, an experienced soldier and a brash, strong-willed man, was appalled by the apathy, selfishness, and disorganization he saw around him.

Smith had been expelled from the colony's governing council for fighting with its aristocratic leaders. When those who remained could not halt the colony's march toward destruction, however, they recalled him—this time as president of the council.

3. Smith responded to the chaos by taking control of what was left of the colony. He stopped the wasteful hunt for gold and refused to allow anyone the privilege of not working. Under Smith's leadership, the men of Jamestown marched to the day's tasks as if they were members of a military battalion. They built shelters, cleared the land, and began planting crops.

From the beginning, Jamestown's residents obtained some food supplies from the original inhabitants of the area in exchange for English beads and copper. But Smith's demand for more food at his price cooled these friendly relations. Moreover, the Indians regarded the settlers' clearing of land and planting crops as an invasion of their hunting grounds. The growing hostility sometimes erupted into violence.

Once, a group of Indians seized Smith and threatened his life. Only the intervention of Pocahontas (poh kuh HAHN tuhs), the chief's young daughter, saved Smith. After this incident, friendly relations between the English and the Native Americans gradually resumed.

John Smith steered the settlement through its first years, but he departed for England in

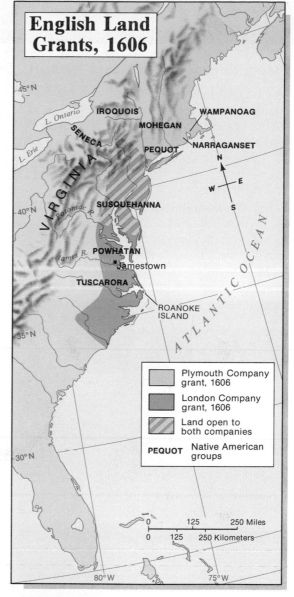

English Land Grants, 1606

L. Ontario
L. Erie
IROQUOIS
MOHEGAN
SENECA
PEQUOT
WAMPANOAG
NARRAGANSET
VIRGINIA
Potomac R.
SUSQUEHANNA
James R.
POWHATAN
Jamestown
TUSCARORA
ROANOKE ISLAND
ATLANTIC OCEAN
45°N
40°N
35°N
30°N
80°W
75°W

Plymouth Company grant, 1606
London Company grant, 1606
Land open to both companies
PEQUOT Native American groups

0   125   250 Miles
0   125   250 Kilometers

MAP STUDY *King James I of England gave two companies of investors the right to found New World colonies. Claims were on a first-come, first-served basis: Whichever company settled the land first gained title to it. According to the map, who else might have had claims to the land?* See p. T7.

1609. The following winter, food became so scarce that the colonists were reduced to eating rats, horses, frogs, roots, and insects. In the years that followed, the unhealthy conditions persisted and settlers continued to die in large numbers. By 1617, only 400 of **39**

Henry Hudson: The Risks of Pressing Too Far

As the tiny ship *Half Moon* slipped away from Holland on a spring day in 1609, it headed north. The English captain, Henry Hudson, had promised his Dutch employers he would seek a northeast passage to the fabled East Indies—north past Norway, then northeast across the North Pole.

In his pocket, however, Hudson carried a letter from his friend John Smith in Virginia. Smith said the way to the Indies lay through North America, via a north*west*—not a north*east*—passage. Despite his pledge "to seek no other route," Hudson followed his instincts and turned west toward America.

After scouting the shore of North America from the Chesapeake Bay to Maine, Hudson guided the *Half Moon* into a wide waterway that seemed promising. He sailed far inland, only to be disappointed when the river, which now bears his name, grew shallow.

Still confident of finding a northwest passage, Hudson returned to America the following year on behalf of the English. This time Hudson sailed farther north—into what is now called Hudson's Bay.

The decision was fateful. As ice trapped the ship for the winter, Hudson and his crew quarreled. In the spring, mutineers threw him, his son, and others into a small boat and sailed off without them. Hudson was never heard from again.

Although Hudson had failed to find the Northwest Passage, his explorations benefited the Dutch. By 1626, they had established New Amsterdam (now New York) on Manhattan Island at the mouth of the Hudson River.

Explorers finally found the Northwest Passage in 1850. Sealed by ice for most of the year, the Arctic waterway across northern Canada can be navigated only by modern icebreakers.

See p. T7.

1. Why did Hudson change the direction of his journey for the Dutch?

2. Critical Thinking What motives other than riches could Hudson have had for his journeys?

---

1. ECONOMICS At the time, the Dutch were on their way to becoming the biggest trading nation in Europe. By 1650, they owned 80 percent of all ships engaged in European trade.

more than 2,000 people who had come to Jamestown survived.

The London Company realized that if the settlement were to last, some family life would have to develop. In 1620 and 1621, two ships brought groups of unmarried women to Jamestown. The company auctioned them off to the eager colonists as wives. The colonists paid for them not with cash, but with tobacco, a new crop that was beginning to provide the economic base the colony needed.

Tobacco: The Key to Survival

Ultimately, Virginia's survival depended on two things: its ability to export something that Europeans wanted and its ability to attract new settlers. In 1612, a settler named John Rolfe found the key to both when he discovered that Jamestown was an ideal place to grow tobacco.

The Spanish had first introduced Europeans to tobacco, a native American plant.

2. DISCUSSION Ask: Why were families necessary to the survival of Jamestown?

In the early 1600s, the market for it grew as the use of snuff and the habit of smoking spread. The West Indian tobacco that Rolfe adapted to Virginia soil became a favorite with Europeans. Within a few years, tobacco farms dotted the banks of the James River, and the settlers began shipping tobacco to England at a handsome profit.

Tobacco not only guaranteed the survival of Jamestown, it also encouraged the growth of slavery in the English colonies. Raising tobacco involved back-breaking, unskilled hand labor, the kind of labor the Jamestown settlers found distasteful.

In 1619, just as tobacco cultivation was expanding rapidly, a Portuguese ship arrived at Jamestown with 20 Africans, who were sold either as servants or slaves. Since the Africans came from farming societies, they proved to be a boon to the colony.

Slavery did not take hold immediately, though. Until 1670, some blacks and whites worked side by side as servants, and some blacks were free laborers. By the close of the 1600s, however, slavery had become entrenched in Virginia.

The First Representative Assembly

Unable to find a leader of Smith's caliber to replace him, the London Company disbanded the council and reformed the colony's government. They appointed a governor with control over military and civilian matters. When the new governor arrived in Virginia in 1619, he instructed the eligible voters to elect 22 burgesses, or representatives, two from each of the 11 areas of the colony. The burgesses, meeting with a council appointed by the governor, would make laws and help administer the colony.

As a representative assembly, the House of Burgesses was part of an English tradition of limiting royal authority and increasing citizens' role in government. In 1215, a group of English nobles had forced King John to guarantee them certain rights and privileges, set down in a document known as the Magna Carta, or Great Charter. These written rights and privileges benefited mainly the nobles, but they set a precedent, or tradition, that the king's power was not absolute.

The daughter of an Indian chief, Pocahontas brought food to hungry Jamestown settlers during "the starving time." Said John Smith, "She was the instrument to preserve this Colony from death, famine, and utter confusion." Later, Pocahontas married John Rolfe, and the two of them took Virginia's first tobacco crop to London, where this portrait of her in English costume was painted.

2.

2. **BACKGROUND** Pocahontas's real name was Matoaka. Pocahontas, her nickname, means "playful one."

In 1265, the English had set up a parliament that further limited the power of the monarchy. Parliament consisted of two groups who presented their interests to the king: the House of Lords, made up of nobles and high church leaders; and the House of Commons, a group of gentlemen* elected to represent English counties and boroughs.

Parliament was far from representative of all English people. Yet its existence guaranteed that monarchs could not rule without obtaining the consent of at least some of their subjects.

3.

The London Company's order establishing Virginia's new government in 1619 also came to be called the Great Charter—and

---

*The title "gentleman" referred to any man who was rich enough to support himself without working. Most often a gentleman's wealth came from land. However, university students, members of the clergy, and army commanders could call themselves gentlemen.

41

1. **ACTIVITY** Have students make a chart comparing early Virginia settlement with early Massachusetts settlement.

2. **TECHNOLOGY** Fencing in farmland was called enclosure. Interested students can research enclosure and other aspects of England's Agricultural Revolution.

with good reason. The House of Burgesses, as the first representative assembly in the New World, established a pattern of government that other colonies would follow.

See p. T7.

SECTION 4 REVIEW

1. **Identify:** (a) Plymouth Company, (b) London Company, (c) Pocahontas, (d) John Rolfe, (e) Magna Carta.

2. **Define:** joint stock company.

3. List three problems faced by the first settlers at Jamestown.

4. What steps did John Smith take to help Jamestown survive?

5. (a) What was the House of Burgesses? (b) What was its importance?

6. **Critical Thinking** How did the London Company's plans for Jamestown reflect ignorance of the area's geography?

5 The New England Way

READ TO UNDERSTAND

■ How the Protestant Reformation affected the Church in England.

■ Why the Pilgrims and the Puritans sought refuge in North America.

■ What steps some settlers took toward democracy.

It was John Smith who first named the area farther north of Virginia "New England." In 1614, he mapped the territory around Massachusetts Bay and recognized its potential for fishing and fur trading. Six years later, a group of English settlers arrived there. The path they followed was different from that of the Jamestown settlers.

Many single men hoped to make their fortunes in Jamestown and return to England. Flimsy wood houses were slapped together quickly in a boom-town atmosphere. Ships served as floating taverns where colonists squandered their profits from tobacco.

On the other hand, more families with children came to settle down in New England and begin new lives. In the dry, healthy New England climate with its plentiful supply of fresh water and game, the colonists were soon outliving the people in Virginia or England.

1.

Search for a More Comfortable Life

In England, a person's social class and place of birth often determined the quality of his or her life. Among the upper classes, the eldest son inherited the family wealth. Younger sons often found themselves without gainful employment. Traditionally, these young men entered the church or the army, or competed for posts at the royal court. With the opening of America, they had other, better prospects.

Lower classes from the rural areas and the cities also had reasons for seeking a better life. As wool became increasingly important for the English economy, acre upon acre of English farmland was fenced in for sheep pastures. Peasants whose families had tilled the land for centuries as tenant farmers suddenly found themselves evicted from their homes.

2.

A middle class of merchants and artisans lived prosperously in England's cities. But cramped housing, filthy streets with open sewers, frequent fires, water shortages, crime, epidemics, and unemployment characterized life for most city dwellers.

These conditions influenced many people's decision to make the long and risky journey across the Atlantic. Even more important to earliest immigrants, however, was the New World's promise of the chance to worship in their own way.

3.

The Protestant Reformation

Throughout the Middle Ages, the Roman Catholic Church united Christian believers under the spiritual leadership of the Pope. On the local level, the church was led by priests, who in turn were responsible to their superiors, the bishops and archbishops.

1. **BACKGROUND** Henry VIII's split with the Catholic Church began when the Pope refused to annul, or cancel, Henry's marriage to his first wife.

Martin Luther In the early 1500s, Martin Luther, a young German monk, became dismayed by the corruption and worldliness that had crept into the church. Too many bishops and priests, he felt, were preoccupied with power and wealth. Luther especially objected when priests taught that Christians could win eternal salvation simply by performing "good works." Good works could never save a Christian, Luther argued. "Faith alone"—a belief in God's willingness to freely forgive sins—had the power to do that. When Pope Leo X condemned Luther's teachings, he left the church in 1517.

Martin Luther's actions started a movement that came to be known as the Protestant Reformation. Soon it spread throughout Europe. John Calvin established a strict version of the new faith in Geneva, Switzerland, and new churches also formed in France and in the Netherlands.

The Reformation in England In England, Henry VIII declared himself, rather than the Pope, head of the Church in England. This
1. provoked a split with Rome. Unlike Luther and Calvin, Henry did not oppose Roman Catholic teachings. He simply wanted to govern his nation's branch of the church himself—without interference from the Pope. 2. After Henry's death, however, Protestantism flourished in England. Elizabeth, who became queen in 1558, was a Protestant, as were many of her subjects.

But what did being a Protestant mean? All Protestants agreed, in one degree or another, with Luther's emphasis on scripture, but they often parted company there. Some felt that the offices of bishop and archbishop should be abolished because the Bible made no mention of them. Still others argued that the only spiritual leaders should be local ministers.

Under Elizabeth, the Church of England felt it was proper to retain the traditional hierarchy of bishops and archbishops. The English church also kept many other Catholic practices.

Some English people believed, however, that the English church had not reformed enough. They objected to church services that included Catholic practices. And they claimed that English priests were still too worldly, superstitious, and ignorant: "Dumme Doggs," one Protestant called them. From these strongly dissenting groups came many of New England's colonists.

2. **PAST AND PRESENT** This church became known as the Church of England, or Anglican Church. Today its descendant in the United States is called the Episcopal Church.

On landing in the New World, the Pilgrims "fell upon their knees & blessed ye God of heaven, who had brought them over ye vast & furious ocean," wrote William Bradford, who would lead the new colony. Their religious faith and determination
3. *gave the Pilgrims strength to survive in a hostile land.*

3. **VISUAL EVIDENCE** Ask: What does the painting show about the Pilgrims' arrival? Do you think it is a realistic depiction of the scene?

1. *The signers of the Mayflower Compact pledged to obey decisions made for the common good. By abiding by majority rule, they set a precedent for the growth of democracy in the colonies.*

1. **BACKGROUND** The Compact was signed November 11, 1620.

The Pilgrims of Plymouth Colony

Some dissenters believed that the Church of England was so impure that true believers should separate from it completely. This radical position was held by Separatists.

When James I succeeded Elizabeth in 1603, the Separatists became alarmed, for the king had vowed to "harry them out of the land." Fearing for their safety and their freedom, many moved to the Netherlands. There the Dutch, known in Europe for their tolerance, allowed the Separatists to worship as they pleased. Yet the Separatists missed their familiar English customs.

Having heard of the London Company's new lands in North America, the Separatists requested permission from the company to start a settlement there. In September 1620, 102 settlers, later called Pilgrims, set sail from Plymouth, England, on a small ship, the *Mayflower*.

When they reached the coast of North America, the Pilgrims realized that their course had taken them north of the London Company's lands and, hence, outside its authority. The colonists were thus responsible for governing themselves.

While still on shipboard, the Pilgrims gathered together and drafted an agreement that formed the basis of their new community. Forty-one colonists signed this agreement, called the Mayflower Compact. The compact was not intended to set up a formal government. Rather it was a simple agreement that the settlers would consult each other about matters affecting the community and would abide by majority rule.

The first winter at the colony was hard, for the Pilgrims had arrived too late to plant crops. By the following spring, almost half the settlers had died. That more did not perish was due partly to the leadership of young William Bradford. He became governor of the Plymouth colony and led it for many years.

The colony also received invaluable aid from Native Americans, who showed them how to raise corn. When the colonists harvested their first crop in October 1621, they gratefully proclaimed a day of thanksgiving. 2.

The Puritans

While the Pilgrims had separated themselves completely from the Church of England, other dissenters, called Puritans, hoped to reform it from within. For a while, the Puritans achieved modest successes. Many English congregations simplified their forms of worship. And quite a few Puritans rose to positions of power in the English government.

When King James's son, Charles I, gained the throne, the Puritans felt themselves threatened. Charles's religious beliefs had more in common with the Catholic church of Rome. Also, Charles believed that if the Puritans objected to church authority, they might soon object to his own power as well.

Charles and his government denied Puritans freedom of worship and deprived them of leadership positions in the government and universities. As a result, some Puritans began to look toward America.

After much negotiation, a group of Puritans won a charter from King Charles to set up a colony in America with the support of the Massachusetts Bay Company, a joint stock company the Puritans had formed. In 1630, 11 ships carrying more than 900 colonists arrived in Massachusetts. Under John Winthrop, the colony soon began to prosper. 3.

44

3. **BIOGRAPHY** John Winthrop (1588–1649), son of a well-to-do family, was a successful lawyer in England. A devout Puritan, he was elected governor of Massachusetts many times between 1630 and 1649.

1. **READING** Winthrop told the settlers, "We shall be as a city upon a hill. The eyes of all people are upon us." Have students explain what they think he meant.

Government at Massachusetts Bay

Meanwhile, persecution of Puritans in England continued. The government's hostility to their beliefs led the members of the Massachusetts Bay Company to take an unusual step. Instead of governing from England, as other joint stock companies had, the company moved its headquarters to Boston, its new American settlement.

Under its royal charter, the Massachusetts Bay Company had the right to govern its settlers as it saw fit. But Winthrop and the other leaders created a true government of the colony by allowing settlers, not just shareholders, to elect the colony's officers.

Voters chose a legislature, called the General Court, and a governor to direct affairs. In order to preserve the religious character of the colony, however, only male church members were allowed to vote.

Even with this requirement, though, many more citizens could vote in Massachusetts than in England, where only men who owned or rented property worth a certain amount could vote. As long as a Massachusetts settler was a free man and a church member, he could vote. Thus, at an early stage, Massachusetts governed itself with a representa-
1. tive assembly.

Despite this advance, Puritans did not believe in democracy. Free men elected leaders, but the leaders' duty was to do God's bidding. Puritans wanted their colony to be run according to their interpretation of the Bible. They did not want other groups taint-
2. ing the settlement with "impure" notions.

GREAT DEBATE

A Search for Tolerance

Not everyone in the Massachusetts Bay colony held those views. One of the most prominent "heretics" was Roger Williams, who came in 1630. Williams, like the Puritans, believed that spiritual leaders of the church should keep themselves separate from the worldly affairs of the state. He agreed that ministers should not hold political office. But Williams went a step further and claimed that the state should neither interfere with church matters nor force people to worship in a particular way, as the Puritans were doing.

3. **CITIZENSHIP** Have students consider which of the three colonies—Massachusetts, Rhode Island, or Connecticut —they would have chosen to live in and why.

In 1635, Massachusetts banished Williams for these opinions, as well as for his belief that the king had no right to grant the settlers Indian lands. Williams fled to live among Native Americans. He later bought land from them, which became the colony of Rhode Island. There he tolerated all forms of religious worship.

Rhode Island soon became a haven for religious dissenters. Among them was Anne Hutchinson, an intelligent, forceful woman who quarreled with Massachusetts leaders over theology and was herself banished. (See page 50.)

Another group of settlers from Massachusetts Bay founded the town of Hartford, Connecticut, in 1636. Their minister and leader, Thomas Hooker, felt strongly that government should rest on "the free consent of the governed." In his eyes, John Winthrop and the other magistrates of Massachusetts had assumed too much power.

Accordingly, in 1639 the settlers in the Hartford area adopted the Fundamental Orders of Connecticut as their new plan of government. It differed significantly from the Massachusetts system in basing colonial authority on self-government by the people rather than on the divine rule of kings.

While neither Rhode Island nor Connecticut was democratic in the modern sense, both established representative governments of some kind. Both also tolerated and respected differing religious beliefs. ■

See p. T8.

3.

SECTION 5 REVIEW

1. **Identify:** (a) Martin Luther, (b) Pilgrims, (c) Mayflower Compact, (d) Puritans, (e) Roger Williams, (f) Fundamental Orders of Connecticut.

2. Why did the Pilgrims decide to settle in the New World?

3. Who was qualified to vote in the Massachusetts Bay colony?

4. In what way was the founding of Rhode Island similar to that of Connecticut?

5. **Critical Thinking** Why did Puritan beliefs not allow for tolerance of other views?

45

2. **BACKGROUND** The General Court said "corrupt and pernicious opinions disturbing the peaceable administration and . . . worship of God are to be . . . punished."

Summary

1. **Columbus's voyage in search of Asia brought two worlds together and laid the groundwork for a Spanish empire.** Spanish conquistadores found great wealth among the Aztecs and Incas.

2. **Spanish soldiers, missionaries, and settlers followed the conquistadores to the New World and began to set up colonies.** Spanish accomplishments, however, came at the expense of Native Americans and African slaves.

3. **During the 1500s, the French and English began to establish a foothold in North America.** The French developed a prosperous trade with the Indians. In the late 1580s, English settlers set up a colony on Roanoke Island in Virginia. The colony failed, but it provided valuable experience for future English settlement.

4. **English settlement in North America began in earnest in the 1600s.** A group of private investors founded a colony at Jamestown. After initial difficulties, the colony began to thrive on profits from tobacco production. The Jamestown colony established the House of Burgesses, the first representative assembly in America.

5. **The Pilgrims and the Puritans, the first settlers in New England, came in search of religious freedom for themselves.** But the founders of Connecticut and Rhode Island fled from persecution in Massachusetts and planted the seeds of religious toleration for all.

See p. T8.

Vocabulary

Choose the answer that best completes each of the following sentences.

1. Magellan's fleet was the first to _____, or sail around, the globe. (a) revolutionize (b) circumnavigate (c) rotate

2. The _____ were the Spanish conquerors of the Aztecs and the Incas. (a) encomiendas (b) pueblos (c) conquistadores

3. Settlements devoted to military activity were the _____. (a) presidios (b) pueblos (c) viceroys

4. The _____ were settlements devoted to farming, trading, and town life. (a) pueblo (b) encomiendas (c) presidios

5. A deputy who represents a monarch in a country or province is a _____. (a) pueblo (b) viceroy (c) provincial

See p. T8.

Chapter Checkup

1. (a) How did Columbus's discoveries affect the relationship between Spain and Portugal? (b) Why did the Pope intervene? (c) What solution did he offer?

2. What role did the conquistadores play in the exploration and colonization of the Americas?

3. How did the Laws of the Indies affect the pattern of settlement and activities of the Spanish settlers in the Americas?

4. How did concern about the treatment of Native Americans lead to the introduction of African slavery into the Americas?

5. What factors shaped the nature of French activity in North America?

6. How did the London Company create problems for the Jamestown colony?

7. How did the attitudes of the Pilgrims and the Puritans differ toward the Church of England?

8. In what ways was Massachusetts better suited for settlement than Jamestown?

See p. T8.

Critical Thinking

1. **Comparing** What traits did people like Columbus, Cortés, Estevanico, Cartier, and Drake have in common?

2. **Comparing** (a) Compare the early experiences of the Spanish, the English, and the French with respect to settling the Americas. (b) How might you explain the similarities and the differences?

See p. T8.

Connecting Past and Present

1. How is the age of space exploration similar to the European age of discovery?

2. Spain was a leading colonial power in southern North America and in South America. What Spanish influences remain in these areas?

See p. T8.

Developing Basic Skills

1. **Classifying** Make a chart with two columns. In the first column, list the groups and individuals you read about in this chapter. In the second column, list the motives of each for coming to the Americas. (a) What similarities and differences do you see? (b) What were the most common reasons why people set sail for the Americas during the late 1400s and early 1500s?

2. **Map Reading** Study the map on page 27. (a) Which two explorers led expeditions that circumnavigated the globe? (b) How did the routes of the Portuguese explorers differ from those of the Spanish and English explorers? (c) Who was the first European explorer to reach Asia by an all-water route?

3. **Map Reading** Study the map on page 29. (a) What general area was explored by the Spanish? (b) What general area was explored by the English? (c) What general area was explored by the French? (d) Where did Henry Hudson explore? (e) Why did the search for a northwest passage to India fail?

WRITING ABOUT HISTORY

Using Question Clues

Before you write the answer to an essay question, study the question for clues. Read the following essay question: How did Spain leave its imprint on the Americas in the 1500s?

1. What does the question word ask you to do? Look for the word that tells you what you are to do with the subject you are writing about. (See Writing About History, page 23.) In the question above, the key word is *how*. The answer requires an explanation of ways Spain influenced or changed the Americas.

2. What is the scope of the essay? Look for limits, such as a time frame or a geographic area. In this question, the discussion is limited to events that took place in the 1500s in the Americas.

3. What information do you have that is related to the topic of the question? Since the essay includes time and geographic limits, consult the time line, maps, and text.

Practice: Ask the questions in this writing lesson about the Critical Thinking questions in this Chapter Review before you write the answers.

47

Religion has played a central role in American life, as the bold and confident Puritans demonstrated in the 1600s. Rejected and persecuted by the English government, the Puritans were lucky to have escaped jail—or worse. Having reached safety in America, they were convinced that they had a mission to fulfill—to form a society based on God's word as a model for the rebuilding of England. "We must consider that we shall be as a city upon a hill," John Winthrop told his fellow settlers. "The eyes of all people are upon us."

The Puritans believed that God would bless them and make them known around the world. Countless others throughout American history have shared that same feeling of a special destiny. When the colonists took up arms to fight for independence in 1775, many saw religious significance in the act. As one minister proclaimed, "God requires a people struggling for their liberties to treat such of the community who will not join them, as open enemies, and to reject them as unworthy of the privileges which others enjoy."

Religious Freedom   Many nations have been guided by religious principles. What made the United States unusual was the importance its citizens placed on religious freedom. Americans came to insist that the government keep itself separate from religious affairs. "Congress shall make no law respecting an establishment of religion," reads the first sentence in the Bill of Rights.

Religious freedom spread partly because it was supported by English political tradition. But practical circumstances in America were also important. The Puritans were not the only group to cross the Atlantic seeking religious freedom. Other Protestants as well as Catholics and Jews also wanted to be free to worship as they pleased. With so many different religious groups in America, it made sense to allow each its own freedom.

Influence on Society   Even though Americans believed strongly that government should stay out of religious affairs, they also held that religion had a legitimate role in shaping society. On the frontier, churches strove to promote order. They disciplined members for fighting, drinking, gambling, and spreading malicious gossip. In the growing cities, churches encouraged hard work and thrift.

During the 1800s, religion spurred believers to social action. Some people campaigned to improve prison conditions or to obtain political rights for women. Some worked to abolish slavery. "Every [church] member must work or quit," said the minister Charles Finney. "No honorary members."

For those who had little power to change society, religion provided guidance and comfort. Christianity was strong among blacks in pre-Civil War slave quarters. Black preachers brought the message of God's love for all, and slave songs looked forward to triumph both in heaven and here on earth. As one religious song put it, "But some of these days my time will come,/I'll hear that bugle, I'll hear that drum,/I'll see them armies, marchin' along/I'll lift my head and join the song." With the coming of the Civil War and freedom, many blacks did just that.

Religion also played an important part in the lives of immigrants. Churches and religious groups helped these newcomers to adjust to their new homeland. Congregations often helped people in times of sickness and unemployment, and many set up insurance programs to aid women whose husbands had died.

The lack of legal restrictions against different religions did not guarantee smooth

1. The Pilgrims put their hope for a safe journey in God's hands. Their faith influenced the history of their colony and the role of religion in American life.

1. **VISUAL EVIDENCE** Ask: What does this painting show about the place of women among the Pilgrims? Why is a suit of armor shown on the deck?

relations between religious groups. Immigrants often found that native-born Americans were hostile to and suspicious of them. It was not until 1960 that a Catholic, John F. Kennedy, was elected President of the United States. The first Jew to hold a position on the Supreme Court, Louis Brandeis, was appointed in 1919.

Role of Religion Today   Religion continues to influence American culture. Churches provide their members with religious worship, support in hard times, and strong moral beliefs. These beliefs have affected American society in many ways. During the 1960s, the Reverend Martin Luther King, Jr., led a nonviolent movement to gain blacks the right to live in a truly integrated society. One leading advocate of the Civil Rights Act of 1964 claimed that it would never have been passed without the support of religious leaders.

Americans have debated how much religion and politics can mix without violating the idea of keeping churches separate from the state. In the 1980s, the Reverend Jerry Falwell spoke for evangelical Christians who hoped to promote their values through the political process. Other religious groups have sought ways to nurture moral values through political action and yet avoid everyday politics.

Society faces several difficult questions. Should religious leaders seek public office? Should prayer be allowed in public schools? Should the government provide funds for religious schools? Where do Americans draw the line between being free to believe as they choose and imposing those beliefs on others? As in the past, these questions are important because religion plays a central role in American life.

See p. T9.

1. What Puritan belief was the basis of religious influence on colonial America?

2. **Critical Thinking**   How do you think diversity of religious beliefs has affected American society?

49

Anne Hutchinson: A Voice of Religious Dissent

Standing before her accusers, the officials and clergy of Massachusetts Bay, the fiery Anne Hutchinson was defiant. In response to one accusation, she shot back, "Prove that!" To another, she snapped, "I did not come hither to answer questions of that sort."

Hutchinson's judges had noted her "bold spirit" even before her 1637 trial. But they were not favorably impressed. To them she was a rebel, and they found her guilty of having "troubled the peace of the commonwealth." Her crime: questioning Puritan doctrines and winning others to her beliefs. Her penalty: exile.

Hutchinson's troubles started innocently enough. The wife of a wealthy merchant and mother of 14 children, she had come from England a few years earlier. Shortly after her arrival, she began inviting her neighbors in to talk over the week's sermon. At first, only women came, and

1. **VISUAL EVIDENCE** This woodcut was engraved by Edwin Austin Abbey in the 1800s.

"I do deliver you up to Satan," pronounced the Reverend John Wilson when he excommunicated
1. *Anne Hutchinson. Hutchinson firmly believed that the individual conscience was the court of last resort. She trusted that God would set aside the Reverend Wilson's judgment.*

Hutchinson would merely relate what minister John Cotton had said.

Soon, however, as many as 80 people at a time, including men of prominence in the colony, were crowding into Hutchinson's home. Even more important, Hutchinson was expounding her own ideas.

Like Cotton, Hutchinson held that people could know, on their own, whether or not they were chosen as God's elect. She also agreed that despite this knowledge, the elect were obliged to lead a godly life. Hutchinson, however, went much further than Cotton. According to her, people who had received the gift of God's grace might not have to follow the laws that bound other people.

Such ideas created a deep rift in Massachusetts Bay. More than 70 men and women sided with Hutchinson against the Puritan authorities. Her followers' refusal to fight in a war against the Pequot Indians seemed to threaten the very existence of the colony.

As dissension spread, the authorities became increasingly alarmed. When Hutchinson's followers signed a petition implying that the government was doing Satan's work, Puritan officials cracked down. They banished Hutchinson and several of her followers.

Hutchinson fled with her family, first to Rhode Island and later to Dutch territory, in what is now New York. There, she and five of her children died in an Indian attack in 1643. The idea of religious freedom, however, continued to grow in the American colonies.

Anne Hutchinson had seen herself as a seeker of God's truth. Today, we see her as a proud figure in the long struggle for religious freedom.
See p. T9.

1. For what crime was Anne Hutchinson sent into exile?

2. **Critical Thinking** Why do you think Puritan leaders thought it was necessary to exile Hutchinson?

Liberty of Conscience

Roger Williams, a Puritan preacher, earned a special place in American history as a courageous advocate of religious freedom. Unlike Anne Hutchinson, who merely tried to spread her own beliefs, Williams sought liberty of conscience for all. Expelled from Massachusetts Bay in 1635, Williams and a tiny band of followers bought land from the Indians and founded Providence, the first settlement in Rhode Island. In January 1655, Williams was absent from Providence while the colony was experiencing difficulties. He wrote the following letter supporting religious freedom but defining the rights of government to maintain order.

Because Roger Williams was friendly with the Narragansett, he was able to gain their help for the Massachusetts colonists during the Pequot War. (See page 85.)

1.

1. **BACKGROUND** Williams paid the Narragansetts for the land on which he and his followers settled, because he believed that it rightfully belonged to them.

To the town of Providence:

I would never speak or write the slightest bit that suggests an infinite liberty of conscience, which I have always disclaimed and hated. To prevent such mistakes, I shall . . . only propose this case: Many a ship goes to sea, with many hundred souls in one ship, whose welfare and woe is common. The ship's company is a true picture of a commonwealth, or a human combination or society. . . .

Sometimes both Catholics and Protestants, Jews, and Turks may be embarked in one ship. . . . All the liberty of conscience that ever I pleaded for, turns upon these two hinges—that none of the Catholics, Protestants, Jews, or Turks be forced to come to the ship's prayers or worship, nor denied their own particular prayers or worship, if they practice any.

I further add . . . that notwithstanding this liberty, the commander of this ship ought to command the ship's course. He should also command that justice, peace, and sobriety be kept and practiced, both among the seamen and all the passengers. If any of the seamen refuse to perform their duties, or passengers to pay their freight; if any refuse to help; . . . if any refuse to obey the common laws and orders of the ship concerning the peace or safety; if any . . . mutiny and rise up against their commanders and officers; if any . . . preach or write that there ought to be no commanders or officers . . . in such cases, whatever is pretended, the commander or commanders may judge, resist, compel, and punish such transgressors.

I remain studious of your common peace and liberty.

Roger Williams

Adapted from a letter from Roger Williams to the town of Providence, January 1655. From Narragansett Club, *Publications*.

See p. T9.

1. What are the two areas of freedom of conscience sought by Williams?

2. **Critical Thinking** How do Williams's views support the idea of separation of church and state?

Life in Colonial America (1650–1750)

3

CHAPTER OUTLINE

1 **Developing a Colonial System**

2 **The New England Colonies**

3 **The Middle Colonies**

4 **The Southern Colonies**

5 **Colonial Culture**

CHAPTER OBJECTIVES After completing this chapter, students should be able to

1. describe and give examples of the various types of governments in the colonies.
2. describe life in the New England, Middle, and Southern colonies.
3. describe the situation of slaves in the colonies.
4. explain how children were educated in the colonies.
5. read a line graph.

CHAPTER PREVIEW Before they begin the chapter, have students look at the time line. Ask: Which event on the time line signals a growing interest in education? Which events show increasing religious tolerance? Which event suggests that some colonists responded violently to challenges they faced?

The late fall day was drawing to a close at a typical farmhouse outside Lynn, Massachusetts. On this chilly evening, the family gathered in the main room that served as kitchen, living room, and bedroom. Logs blazed in the huge fireplace. Within the fireplace was a bench where the children sat in winter to get warm. A large kettle, bubbling with the next day's noon meal, hung from a heavy pole of green wood.

As supper time approached, the children placed a thick oak plank across trestles near the fire. Along this makeshift table, they set gourds for drinking, wooden spoons, and a half dozen trenchers, or round wooden bowls. Supper, as usual, was a light meal—corn pudding, bread and butter, and milk or cider. The adults sat on hard benches as the children stood by the side of the table. The fire cast a gentle glow across the drafty room. The precious supply of tallow candles was not for daily use.

Soon winter would be closing in. After 50 years in the New England wilderness, the set-tlers had learned to adjust to the harsh climate, building their homes to meet the demands of icy winters. Despite such precautions, the family knew that soon water would freeze on the hearth. Why, a visiting minister even complained that the ink froze on his pen as he wrote his sermon.

By using a warming pan to heat the feather beds, the family might just be able to sleep in comfort. But comfort was out of the question on Sundays. Then the parents and children shivered in an unheated church as they sat on hard benches and listened to sermons for hours on end.

For New Englanders, the challenge was the cold, but people in other colonies faced other trials—grueling summer heat, perhaps, or rugged terrain, or fierce hurricanes. People in each region adapted as best they could. In the process, three distinct styles of life emerged in the New England, Middle, and Southern colonies between 1650 and 1750.

1.
Royal colonies develop

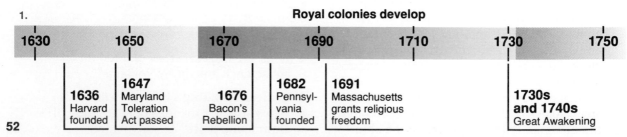

| 1630 | 1650 | 1670 | 1690 | 1710 | 1730 | 1750 |

1636 Harvard founded

1647 Maryland Toleration Act passed

1676 Bacon's Rebellion

1682 Pennsylvania founded

1691 Massachusetts grants religious freedom

1730s and 1740s Great Awakening

52

1. **TIME LINE QUESTION** Ask: How long after the founding of Harvard did Massachusetts grant religious freedom?

Despite hardships, settlers in the English colonies adapted to their new life. Towns and villages grew and soon dotted the Atlantic seaboard. In 1752, Baltimore,
1. Maryland, shown here, was a thriving village of 100 people and 25 houses.

1. **VISUAL EVIDENCE** Ask: What does this painting suggest about the layout of some colonial villages?

2. **VOCABULARY** Have students look up this word in the glossary before they begin reading.

1 Developing a Colonial System

READ TO UNDERSTAND

■ Why England adopted new approaches to organizing its colonies.

■ How proprietary and royal colonies differed.

■ How representative government was strengthened in the colonies.

2. ■ *Vocabulary:* proprietor.

By the 1620s, James I of England could not help but draw a comparison between the wealth that Spain had gathered from its colonies and the problems he was facing. James was convinced that England's first colonies in North America were being mismanaged. Virginia was not profitable, and the religious dissenters in Massachusetts were too independent.

English officials began to experiment with new ways of organizing the colonial system. The original method—placing control in the hands of joint stock companies—had not worked out. In its place, England created two new types of colonies. For a time, several colonies were governed by English nobles who were friends of the king. By 1700, most colonies were ruled directly by the crown. This latter system remained in place until the colonies won their independence.

A New Approach to Colonization

Although the colony of Virginia thrived once planters there began to cultivate tobacco, the London Company failed to make a profit. In 1624, James I withdrew the company's charter and placed Virginia directly under royal control. Massachusetts posed different prob- 3. lems for England. After a few uncertain years, the colony made a profit for the Massachusetts Bay Company. But it acted with too much independence to suit the king.

Believing that their authority came directly from God, the leaders of Massachusetts ran the colony's churches and its government with little regard for the king. The king, in turn, found it nearly impossible to   **53**

3. **BIOGRAPHY** James I was a willful king. "He . . . thought that a king had a right to make and unmake what laws he pleased, and ought to be accountable to nobody on earth," wrote Charles Dickens.

1. **MAIN IDEA** Have students write a paragraph describing the main features of a proprietary colony.

2. **GEOGRAPHY** As they read about each of the colonies on the next few pages, have students locate them on the map on p. 59. (location)

impose his will on a settlement of religious dissenters 3,000 miles away.

With the lessons of Virginia and Massachusetts in mind, the English government began a more systematic approach to colonization. To organize the settlement of the colonies and to establish uniform rules for them, the crown created a new form of colonial organization, the proprietary colony.

Under the new system, the king granted territory to a person or small group of persons called **proprietors.** Like feudal lords, proprietors were the sole owners of their domains, acknowledging the king's authority by making an annual payment of some sort. Proprietors had the right to parcel out their land to other individuals. These tenants could use the land only as long as the proprietor wished. Their rent and taxes were an important source of income for the proprietors.

The king limited most proprietors' powers. They could make laws, but the laws could not violate the laws of England. Nor could the laws usually go into effect without the consent of the free men of the colony or their
1. chosen representatives.

2. Maryland: A Proprietary Colony

George Calvert, Lord Baltimore, established the first proprietary colony. Originally, he hoped to begin a colony along the shores of Newfoundland. But when the cold, rough territory proved unsuited for settlement, Calvert set his sights farther south. From Charles I, he acquired the rights to 10 million acres of Virginia territory around the Chesapeake Bay.

George Calvert died before the grant could be issued, but his son Cecilius accepted it in 1632. The Calverts named the new colony Maryland in honor of King Charles's wife, Queen Henrietta Maria. The first 200 settlers arrived in March 1634. Calvert, who was a Roman Catholic, saw his colony both as a refuge for Catholics and as a money-making real estate venture.

If their colony was to be profitable, the Calverts had to attract thousands of settlers. Thus they welcomed Protestants as well as Roman Catholics. In 1649, the colonial assembly passed the Maryland Toleration Act, affirming religious freedom for all Christians.

Land Grants Under Charles II

Charles I did little more to settle America because he found himself in trouble at home. A revolution in England, directed by Puritans and other Protestant dissenters, led to civil war in 1642. Charles was executed in 1649 and, for a time, the monarchy was abolished. Charles's son spent 11 years in exile in France until he regained the throne in 1660, as King Charles II.

New York An easygoing and pleasure-loving king, Charles II granted land in America primarily to reward nobles who had remained loyal to the monarchy during the civil war. One recipient was his brother James, the Duke of York. In 1664, Charles gave James a huge grant, stretching from Connecticut to the Delaware Bay. This was a bold move on the part of the king because the territory had been settled by the Dutch, who called it New Netherlands. But the people living in New 3. Netherlands, many of them New England farmers who had moved south, were dissatisfied with Dutch rule.

When a well-armed English fleet appeared at the mouth of the Hudson River, the Dutch governor surrendered, and the colony was renamed New York. The Dutch declared war on England and harassed English shipping, but New York remained in English hands.

The Duke of York, who had absolute political power in the colony, appointed a governor and council to administer it rather than go to America himself. He allowed wealthy Dutch landowners to keep their huge estates and gave away equally large tracts of land to his English followers. At first, he denied the colony a representative assembly, but the settlers protested so much that he was forced to give in. In matters of religion, James was broad-minded. A Roman Catholic himself, he allowed colonists to worship as they pleased.

New Jersey The area to the south of New York, renamed New Jersey, originally belonged to the Duke of York. He turned over the rights to this land to his friends, Sir George Carteret and Lord John Berkeley. Unfortunately, before the governor of New York heard about the new owners, he had given a group of Puritans the authority to govern the area. The resulting legal tangle lasted almost 50

3. **BIOGRAPHY** One famous governor of New Netherlands, Peter Stuyvesant, was known for his temper. When a colonist criticized him, he replied, "I will make him a foot shorter and send the pieces to Holland."

Founding of the Colonies

Colony/Date Founded	Leader	Reasons Founded	Type of Government
New England Colonies			
Massachusetts Plymouth/1620 Massachusetts Bay/1630	William Bradford John Winthrop	Religious freedom Religious freedom	Corporate 1620–1691 Corporate 1630–1691 Both colonies merged 1691; royal 1691–1776
New Hampshire/1622	Ferdinando Gorges John Mason	Profit from trade and fishing	Proprietary 1622–1641; corporate (part of Mass.) 1641–1680; royal 1680–1776
Connecticut Hartford/1636 New Haven/1639	Thomas Hooker	Extend trade; religious and political freedom	Self-governing 1636–1662 Self-governing 1639–1662 royal 1662–1665 Both colonies merged 1665; royal 1665–1776
Rhode Island/1636	Roger Williams	Religious freedom	Self-governing 1636–1644; corporate 1644–1776
Middle Colonies			
*New York/1624	Peter Minuet	Expand trade	Colony of Dutch West India Co. 1624–1664; proprietary (Eng.) 1664–1685; royal 1685–1776
**Delaware/1638	Swedish settlers	Expand trade	Proprietary 1638–1682; part of Pa. (proprietary) 1682–1704; royal 1704–1776
New Jersey/1664	John Berkeley George Carteret	Profit for founders from land sales; religious and political freedom	Proprietary 1664–1702; royal 1702–1776
Pennsylvania/1682	William Penn	Profit for founders from land sales; religious and political freedom	Proprietary 1682–1776
Southern Colonies			
Virginia/1607	John Smith	Trade and agriculture	Corporate 1607–1624; royal 1624–1776
Maryland/1632	Lord Baltimore	Profit for founders from land sales; religious and political freedom	Proprietary 1632–1691; royal 1691–1715; proprietary 1715–1776
The Carolinas/1663 North Carolina/1712 South Carolina/1712	Group of eight proprietors	Profit from trade and agriculture; religious freedom	Proprietary 1663–1712; self-governing until 1719; king buys back North 1719; king buys back South 1729; both royal 1730–1776
Georgia/1732	James Oglethorpe	Profit; haven for debtors; buffer against Spanish Florida	Proprietary 1732–1752; royal 1752–1776

* New York was settled by the Dutch in 1624 and named New Netherlands. It surrendered to the English in 1664.
** Delaware was settled by the Swedes in 1638 and named New Sweden. It was captured and incorporated into New Netherlands by the Dutch in 1655. It was then captured by the English in 1664.

CHART STUDY *The American colonies were founded for a variety of reasons. Which colonies were founded to take advantage of the resources of the New World?* See p. T10.

years. The territory split into two separate colonies in 1676 and was not united as New Jersey until 1702.

The Carolinas and Georgia

In 1663, the generous Charles II bestowed land on a group of eight nobles including Sir William Berkeley, the governor of Virginia. The gift included all the land lying between present-day Virginia and Florida, bordered on the east by the Atlantic Ocean and on the west by the Pacific. The delighted proprietors named the territory Carolina (Latin for "Charles"), after the king and his father.

The Carolinas Colonists settled at first around Albemarle Sound, the mouth of the Cape Fear River, in the area that soon came to be known as Charles Towne. Although the lord proprietors, as they become known, were members of the Church of England, they welcomed colonists of all religions.

Like the Calverts in Maryland, the proprietors of Carolina had the powers of feudal lords. They kept huge estates for themselves and rented out other parcels of land to tenants. The proprietors nearly ruined their chances for profit by organizing their colony in a highly unusual way.

Their plan, known as the Fundamental Constitutions of Carolina, was drawn up by
1. the English political philosopher John Locke. The constitution stated that Carolina's society was to be set up along rigid class lines with hereditary nobles at the top. The proprietors themselves would have titles like Lord Palatine and Lord High Chamberlain. When frustrated colonists complained about the rigid regulations, immigration dropped dramatically. Eventually, a more democratic
2. and realistic colonial society developed.

In 1712, the proprietors divided Carolina into two parts and gave each its own government. While most settlers in North Carolina had moved there from other colonies, especially New England and Virginia, the first colonists of South Carolina came largely from England or from the plantations of the West Indies. A few were Protestant refugees from France.

Georgia A third part of the original Carolina grant, Georgia, was separated from South Carolina in 1732. Unique among the colonies, it was founded neither as a money-making venture nor as a refuge for religious dissenters. A group of proprietors, led by James Oglethorpe (OH gehl thorp), wanted to provide a place where people imprisoned for debt could make a new start. Oglethorpe also hoped to provide a barrier against the Spanish in Florida.

Only a few debtors actually migrated to Georgia. But the colony did become a haven for poor shopkeepers and artisans from England and Scotland. Protestant refugees from Switzerland and Germany also settled there, but Roman Catholics were barred. The proprietors feared that they would aid neighboring Catholic Florida in the event of a war.

A Haven in Penn's Woods

When Charles II was in exile, Admiral William Penn loaned him a lot of money. After Penn died, the king, short of cash as ever, repaid the debt to Penn's son William by granting him land.

As a young man, Penn had joined a religious sect called the Society of Friends. Members of the Society were known as Quakers because their founder, George Fox, directed them to "tremble at the name of the Lord."

The Quakers were a thorn in the side of English authorities. They had no hierarchy of church officers, no regular church building, and no paid clergy. Furthermore, they showed their contempt for the English class system by treating everyone as an equal, and they
3. refused either to take oaths or to fight in wars.

With the Church of England stepping up its persecution of dissenting religious groups, Penn sought a refuge for Quakers. Pennsylvania, or "Penn's woods," seemed the ideal place. Penn added more land by buying neighboring territory that would become Delaware. William Penn, unlike most proprietors, lived in America himself for a time and administered the colony. When he had to be away, he appointed a deputy governor to take charge.

Pennsylvania's system of government was the most democratic in the colonies. Until 1701, it consisted of a legislature with upper and lower houses elected by the freemen of

James Oglethorpe envisioned his colony of Georgia as a "calm retreat" for those who had suffered the horrors of London's debtor prisons. He promoted his colony with a shrewd sense of advertising. In 1734, Oglethorpe took Tomo-Chi-Chi, chief of the Yamacraw Indians, the chief's wife, and other members of the tribe to
1. London, where they were received by King George II, as shown here. This trip won increased support in England for Georgia.

the colony. The upper house proposed laws, and the lower house accepted or rejected them. Every man who owned a small amount of land or paid taxes was entitled to vote, so a large number of colonists took part in choos-
2. ing the government.

Movement Toward Royal Colonies

As the colonies grew and prospered, the English crown wanted a share of the profits. Gradually, the king assumed control, creating royal colonies. By 1730, only Pennsylvania and Maryland were still proprietary colonies.

Colonists usually preferred royal control to government by the proprietors. For one thing, the English army and navy seemed to protect royal colonies better. And colonists often had more political power in a royal colony than in a proprietary one.

In a royal colony, the king appointed the governor and council, and the eligible voters elected the lower house of the assembly. The governor controlled trade, appointed judges and other officials, and served as the colony's chief executive.

The council, usually composed of prominent colonists, advised the governor and approved official appointments. The governor had to consult the council before he called the assembly into session, issued paper money, or declared martial law. The council functioned as the highest court and as the upper house of the assembly.

The colonial assembly considered itself the guardian of colonists' interests. The assembly had to consent to any laws before they could go into effect. This continued the tradition of representative government that was common to all colonies.

Gradually, the people's right to consent to laws through their representatives grew into the right to propose laws, a trend that continued in the royal colonies. Colonial assemblies gained further influence because they had to approve the salaries of the governor 3. and other officials. The assemblies consid-   **57**

2. **PAST AND PRESENT** Have students compare voting rights in the various colonies. Ask: How do they compare with voting rights today?

3. **CITIZENSHIP** Ask: Why do you think this "power of the purse" was so important to the colonists?

1. **READING** Students interested in political developments in the colonies might consult *Struggle and Survival in Colonial America,* edited by David Sweet and Gary Nash.

2. **VOCABULARY** Have students look up these terms in the glossary before they begin reading.

ered this an especially important power, as you will see in Chapter 5.

The "Glorious Revolution" in America and England

The growth of this representative tradition did not come without a struggle. As you have seen, when James, the Duke of York, was proprietor of New York, he tried to eliminate representative government. It was only pressure from the settlers that caused him to back down.

Two decades later, James again demonstrated his dislike of representative government. Only now, as a result of Charles's death in 1685, he was King James II. James took a series of steps to tighten royal control. He revoked Massachusetts's original charter and disbanded the representative assemblies in all colonies north of New Jersey. He renamed the area the Dominion of New England.

Resentment flared in the American colonies. They might even have rebelled, but the English beat them to it. In 1688, the English ousted James II in a revolt called the Glorious Revolution. The New England colonies promptly reinstated the assemblies, an act that showed their deep commitment to representative government.

See p. T10.

SECTION 1 REVIEW

1. **Identify:** (a) Maryland Toleration Act, (b) Charles II, (c) James Oglethorpe, (d) Glorious Revolution.

2. **Define:** proprietor.

3. (a) Why was Maryland established? (b) Who settled there?

4. (a) Why did William Penn found Pennsylvania? (b) What kind of government did it have?

5. What value did royal colonies have over proprietary colonies for the colonists and the king?

6. **Critical Thinking** Why do you think the American colonists valued representative government so highly?

2 The New England Colonies

READ TO UNDERSTAND

■ How religion and government were related in New England.

■ How the people of New England earned their living.

■ Why the lines of social class began to blur in New England.

■ *Vocabulary:* subsistence farming, self-sufficient, town meeting.

New England was not an easy land from which to gain a living. The topsoil was thin, and rocks strewn by ice-age glaciers constantly snared the farmers' plows. As one frustrated settler wrote home to England, Massachusetts was "builded upon rocks, sand, and salt marshes."

Yet most New Englanders came to love their region. They took pride in their ability to withstand the harsh winters and howling storms. They grew attached even to those annoying rocks. When fellow settlers learned of the remark quoted above, they were so angry that they sued the writer for slandering their promised land.

Farms and Towns in New England

Most people in New England earned a living by **subsistence farming.** That is, they raised just enough to feed their families but little more. A few had slaves, but most farms were too small to make slave labor pay.

The Self-Sufficient Farm Running a farm in New England was largely a cooperative effort. Survival depended on the labor of each member of the family, including the children. Men were largely responsible for cultivating crops and raising animals; the women made clothes, utensils, candles, and other necessities. Thus, the New England farm was largely **self-sufficient.** In other words, a farm family had the resources to get along without outside help. In spite of this self-sufficiency, fami-

3. **BACKGROUND** New Englanders frowned on bachelors. They often were required to live with a family, chosen by town leaders, until they married.

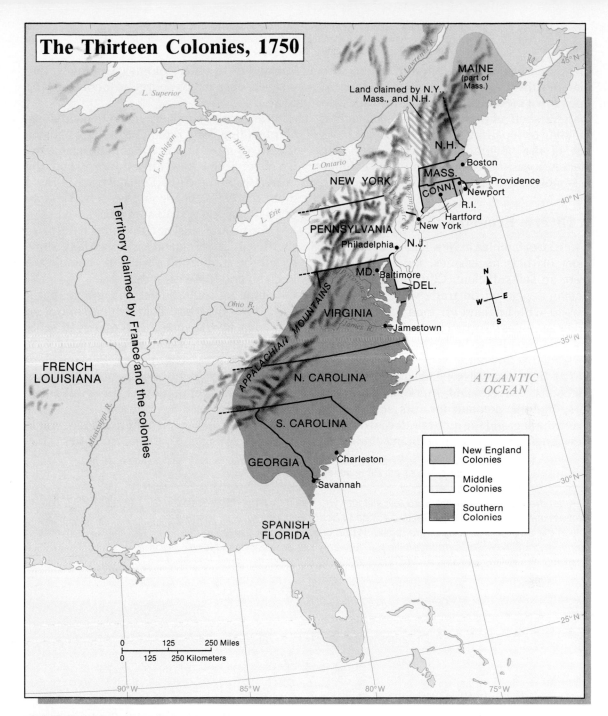

The Thirteen Colonies, 1750

Land claimed by N.Y., Mass., and N.H.

MAINE (part of Mass.)

L. Superior

L. Michigan

L. Huron

L. Ontario

L. Erie

St. Lawrence R.

N.H.

NEW YORK

MASS.
• Boston
CONN.
•Providence
•Newport
R.I.
•Hartford
New York

Territory claimed by France and the colonies

Ohio R.

PENNSYLVANIA
Philadelphia•
N.J.

MD.•Baltimore
DEL.

FRENCH LOUISIANA

Mississippi R.

APPALACHIAN MOUNTAINS

Potomac R.

VIRGINIA

James R.
•Jamestown

N. CAROLINA

ATLANTIC OCEAN

S. CAROLINA

GEORGIA
•Charleston
Savannah•

SPANISH FLORIDA

N
W E
S

New England Colonies
Middle Colonies
Southern Colonies

0   125   250 Miles
0   125   250 Kilometers

45° N
40° N
35° N
30° N
25° N

90° W   85° W   80° W   75° W

MAP STUDY *Between 1650 and 1750, English colonies developed in three regions along the Atlantic coast. Which colonies made up each region? How many miles were there between the most southern and the most northern of the colonies?*   See p. T10.   1.

1. MAP READING Ask: Which two rivers on the map formed borders between colonies? Which colonies?

lies did not live in isolation. Farmers settled in clusters around a town.

Towns and Town Government Because religion was so important to the people of New England, many early towns were founded by church congregations. The elders of a congregation received a tract of land from the colonial legislature. They surveyed the

land and divided it into lots. Each family in the community received land on which to build a house, to pasture animals, and to grow crops. In addition, families had the right to cut wood in the communal forest land.

At the center of the settlement stood the meeting house, a plain building used for town meetings as well as worship. During a settle-

2.

59

2. BACKGROUND In the center of town was also the town common, or green. This was a patch of grass that the townspeople used in common to graze their cattle.

ment's early years, the church elders who planned the town served as its leaders. At

1. open **town meetings,** the residents discussed matters such as hiring a new schoolteacher, building or repairing streets, or keeping cows out of the neighbors' gardens. They also elected local representatives to the colonial assembly.

A Diverse Economy

While farm families in New England produced most of their necessities, not all residents were so self-sufficient. City dwellers in particular depended on trade with other colonies or with England for food, clothing, and other supplies. To pay for such purchases,

2. colonists needed to find a product that could be traded at a profit.

At first, many New Englanders trapped raccoons, beavers, and otters and sold their furs. But the demand for furs soon led to overtrapping, and the fur trade declined. Other New Englanders began shipping timber to

England or to other colonies. Gradually, timber became a major source of income for the region.

Timber also supplied lumber to build ships. Shipbuilding grew rapidly as fishing became the area's most important commercial activity. Over 5,000 New Englanders fished the coastal waters, and New England ports boasted more than 900 oceangoing vessels. The city of Boston alone had 12 shipyards.

Yet fishing was not the only enterprise that used New England's ships. Many ships sailed the trade routes from the colonies to England and the West Indies.

Shipping could be very profitable, but it was a risky business. Communication was so slow that by the time a cargo arrived at its destination, the product might no longer be needed. The success of New England merchants in this highly competitive business earned them a reputation as shrewd "Yankee traders."

Women played an important economic role in New England's towns and cities. They

2. **ECONOMICS** Have students research the economy of New England today to find out if any of the colonial industries are still important there.

"Let not the meanness of the word fish distaste you," said Captain John Smith. Settlers in New England took Smith's advice to heart. Fishing played a leading
3. *role in the diverse economy of the region. When dried, as shown at left in this painting, codfish would keep indefinitely. Thus, they became not only a food source in the colony but also an important export to Europe.*

3. **ECONOMICS** The fishing industry affected every aspect of life in New England. In the 1670s, Plymouth enacted a law earmarking profits from Cape Cod fisheries for the building of schools.

1. **CRITICAL THINKING** Ask: Are there social classes in the U.S. today? Does the government encourage or discourage class differences? Explain.

2. **MAIN IDEA** Have students restate the quotation in their own words and then express its main idea in a sentence.

worked as shopkeepers, printers, innkeepers, merchants, tinkers, midwives, and shipbuilders. Colonial women often learned new occupations from a male relative, since most colonial businesses operated out of the home. Frequently, women would take over the family business when a male relative died.

Social Classes in New England

A rigid class system existed in England, as in the rest of Europe. The royal family and the aristocracy were at the top, followed by landowners and merchants. Beneath them were shopkeepers, artisans, and small landowners. Lowest on the social scale stood city workers, tenant farmers, and agricultural laborers. These class lines were firm, and movement from one class to another was virtually impossible.

At first, New England's society seemed almost as rigid as England's. In 1651, the Massachusetts General Court divided the colony's people into three classes: "the better class," "those above the ordinary degree," and "those of mean [low] condition." Members of each class were expected to behave
1. as befitted their station.

As the New England colonies grew, however, a more democratic spirit began to appear. Members of the lower and middle classes, especially skilled artisans, grew increasingly prosperous. And with their prosperity came a desire to imitate the upper classes.

Since a person's clothing showed his or her rank in society, dressing like the upper classes was a common form of imitation. Alarmed by such behavior, the Massachusetts General Court expressed horror

> . . . that men and women of mean condition should take upon them the garb of gentlemen, by wearing gold or silver lace, or buttons . . . or to walk in great boots, or women of the same rank to wear silk or tiffany hoods or scarves which, though allowable to persons of greater estates . . . yet we cannot but judge it intolerable in persons of such like
2. condition.

The court passed a law specifying how much property a family had to own in order to wear "any gold or silver lace, or gold and silver buttons, or any bone lace above two shillings per yard, or silk hoods, or scarfs." 3.

Despite such attitudes, social mobility soon became the norm rather than the exception in New England. Everyone except a slave could hope for and perhaps gain a place in society higher than the one into which he or she had 4. been born.

See p. T10.

SECTION 2 REVIEW

1. **Define:** (a) subsistence farming, (b) self-sufficient, (c) town meeting.

2. How were New England farms largely self-sufficient?

3. How did church congregations set up towns in New England?

4. Why was the social system in New England more democratic than in Europe?

5. **Critical Thinking** How did geography influence the New England economy?

3. **CITIZENSHIP** Anyone breaking this law not only had to pay a fine, but his or her property would then be taxed at the rate of the social level being imitated.

3. The Middle Colonies

READ TO UNDERSTAND

- Where the settlers of the Middle Colonies originated.

- Why New York farms differed from farms in the other Middle Colonies.

- What life was like for blacks and backcountry families in the North.

- *Vocabulary:* patroon, fall line. 5.

A traveler in Pennsylvania in the 1700s asked a frontier farmer how life was going. "We have a belly full of victuals [food] every day," the farmer replied, "our cows run about, and come home full of milk, our hogs get fat of themselves in the woods. Oh, this is a good country!" **61**

4. **CRITICAL THINKING** Ask: Why do you think social mobility became the norm in New England? What aspects of colonial life encouraged social mobility?

5. **VOCABULARY** Have students look up these terms in the glossary before they begin reading.

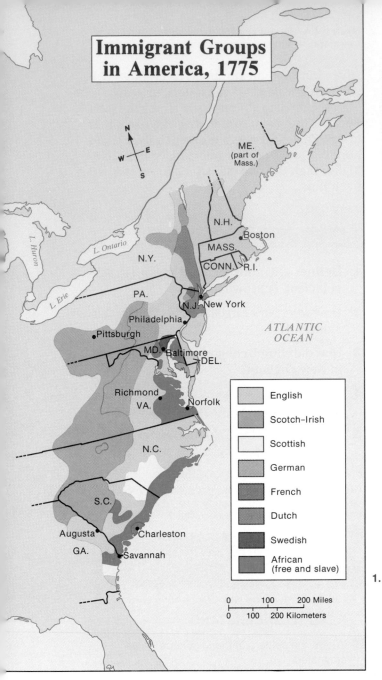

Immigrant Groups in America, 1775

ME. (part of Mass.)

N.H.

Boston

MASS.

CONN. R.I.

N.Y.

New York

PA.

Philadelphia

Pittsburgh

MD. Baltimore

DEL.

Richmond

VA.

Norfolk

N.C.

S.C.

Augusta

Charleston

GA.

Savannah

L. Huron

L. Ontario

L. Erie

ATLANTIC OCEAN

- English
- Scotch-Irish
- Scottish
- German
- French
- Dutch
- Swedish
- African (free and slave)

0   100   200 Miles

0   100   200 Kilometers

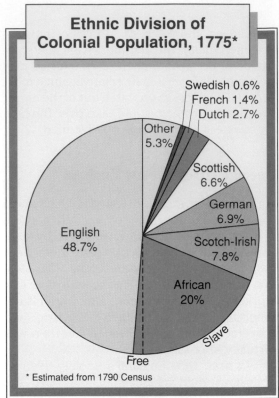

Ethnic Division of Colonial Population, 1775*

- Swedish 0.6%
- French 1.4%
- Dutch 2.7%
- Other 5.3%
- Scottish 6.6%
- German 6.9%
- Scotch-Irish 7.8%
- African 20% — Slave / Free
- English 48.7%

* Estimated from 1790 Census

MAP AND GRAPH STUDY

New immigrants from Europe, as well as black slaves from Africa, brought their own cultures to the New World. According to the map, where did the Scottish mainly settle? Where were most Africans located? By 1775, what percentage of the colonists had English roots? See p. T11.

1. **MAP READING** Ask: Which group of colonies had the smallest number of different immigrant groups? Why?

1.

2.

The settlers took pride in their new land. In the Middle Colonies, people came from Ireland, Scotland, and mainland Europe, as well as from England. The flood of settlers did not begin to pour in until the 1700s, somewhat later than in New England.

A Diverse Population

The largest number of non-English settlers in the Middle Colonies came from northern Ireland and Germany. The Scotch-Irish, whose families had moved from Scotland to north-

ern Ireland in the 1500s, were the most numerous of the new wave of immigrants.

During the 1700s, about 250,000 Scotch-Irish migrated to the Middle Colonies, especially to Pennsylvania. They left northern Ireland because the British Parliament was setting high taxes on their cattle and wool, which competed with the products of English farmers. Furthermore, their Presbyterian religion had been virtually outlawed. As a result, the Scotch-Irish developed a hatred for England that was to have a profound influence on the future of the colonies.

The second largest group of settlers were Germans from the Rhineland region in western Germany. They were fleeing from a series of brutal religious wars between Protestants and Catholics that had devastated their homeland. They were also seeking refuge from

2. **GEOGRAPHY** Using the world map on pp. 842–843, have students locate the places of origin of the immigrant groups shown on the map above. (movement)

1. **READING** Students might read Washington Irving's *Rip Van Winkle* for a satirical look at Dutch settlements on the Hudson.

2. **READING** Interested students can learn more about the life of blacks from *The Black Family in Slavery and Freedom, 1750–1925,* by Herbert Gutman.

the dire poverty and famine that a series of crop failures had brought to the Rhineland.

Pennsylvania, with its rich lands, low rents, and religious toleration, seemed a haven to these immigrants. Eventually, the Rhineland Germans came to be known as Pennsylvania Dutch, from a misuse of the word "Deutsch" (doich), meaning German. The arrival of the Scotch-Irish and the Germans, when combined with the few Swedish colonists who had settled in Delaware in the 1640s and the Dutch in New York, made the population of the Middle Colonies the most diverse among the English territories in America.

An Agricultural Economy

The Middle Colonies contained rich farmland. Still, the land would not yield up its harvest without a good deal of backbreaking work. Farmers tilled the soil with crude wooden plows drawn by teams of oxen, or they just hoed it by hand. Harvesting was a grueling task performed by hand with sickle or scythe.

On the rich farmlands of the Delaware River Valley, German farmers turned farming into a thriving business. Their farms produced such large surpluses of wheat, rye, and corn that they were able to feed not only their own people but many people in New England and the Southern Colonies as well. They even exported food to Europe and the West Indies.

New York's soil was as rich as that of Pennsylvania, but few European settlers would put up with the oppressive land system established by the original Dutch settlers. Landowners called **patroons** owned huge feudal-style manors. The patroons divided the lands among tenant farmers, who worked their farms but could never own them. Farmers had to pay the patroon rent and taxes as well as work his lands. With land abundant in other colonies, relatively few immigrants headed for New York.

Blacks in the North

Although slavery was legal in the Middle Colonies and New England, there were fewer slaves in those colonies than in the South. Farms were smaller and required much less labor. Thus, most northern slaves worked as household servants, and a few worked in trades in the towns.

Some northern masters treated their slaves with a degree of respect, evoking criticism from other slaveholders who favored stricter treatment. A French traveler remarked that slaves in Pennsylvania "were regarded as being part of the family. They are assiduously cared for when they are sick. They are well fed and clothed."

Free blacks lived mostly in the Middle Colonies and New England. But in some colonies, laws limited the number of free black residents. In others, free blacks were allowed to work only at certain occupations. Many free blacks headed for the frontier, where they found more equality and freedom than anywhere else in colonial America.

GEOGRAPHY AND HISTORY
The Backcountry Frontier

The population of the Middle Colonies grew rapidly and soon expanded westward, into the backcountry. Pioneers moved beyond the **fall line,** the area in which inland rivers begin dropping toward sea level. (See the map on page 64.) They carved new farms out of the raw wilderness. Expansion continued westward through Pennsylvania until the rutted paths bumped up against the Appalachian Mountains. Settlers then turned south, following a wide Indian trail that became known as the Great Wagon Road.

In the backcountry, nearly all farming was on a subsistence level. Farmers planted crops in small patches between the stumps of newly felled trees rather than on broad, well-plowed fields. When the fertility of one patch was exhausted, farmers simply cleared another. Far from the coastal towns, backcountry settlers lived free of many restraints. They paid no taxes, were subject to few laws, and seldom mixed with others.

Under such conditions, family members depended on one another for survival. Although the men generally did most of the hunting, trapping, and farming, the women developed frontier skills, too. Philip Ludwell, one of the first colonists to leave a full record of rural life, had great admiration for the frontier woman in 1710:

3. **BACKGROUND** Frontier families often worked together to complete a difficult task such as building a barn or removing fibers from flax plants. These group activities also served as social events.

Colonial Settlement 1650-1770

Map labels: L. Huron, L. Erie, L. Ontario, L. Champlain, Montreal, ME. (part of Mass.), Falmouth, N.H., Oswego, Salem, Ft. Niagara, MASS., Boston, Mohawk R., N.Y., Hartford, Newport, R.I., New Haven, CONN., Ft. Detroit, N.J., New York, PA., Pittsburgh, Philadelphia, Ft. Cumberland, Baltimore, Ohio R., Alexandria, MD., DEL., VA., Richmond, Norfolk, Ft. Chiswell, Roanoke R., APPALACHIAN MTS., N.C., Charlotte, Wilmington, Augusta, S.C., Charleston, GA., Savannah, ATLANTIC OCEAN, St. Lawrence R., Hudson R., Connecticut R., Delaware R.

Legend:
- Settled before 1650
- Settled between 1650 and 1700
- Settled between 1700 and 1770
- Fall line

Scale: 0 — 125 — 250 Miles / 0 — 125 — 250 Kilometers

40° N, 35° N, 30° N, 25° N, 85° W, 80° W, 75° W

MAP STUDY *The 13 colonies grew steadily during the 1600s and 1700s. By 1770, the colonies had spread west to the Appalachians and beyond. They stretched nearly the full length of the Atlantic coast from Maine to Florida. Where were the first settlements located? What role do you think rivers played in determining the areas of new settlement?* See p. T11.

64

1. MAP READING Ask: Where had settlement gone farthest inland? Why might this have been so?

2. MAIN IDEA Ask students to state the main idea of the quotation in their own words.

> She is a very civil woman and shews nothing of ruggedness or Immodesty in her carriage, yett she will carry a gunn in the woods and kill deer, turkeys &c., shoot down wild cattle, catch and tye hoggs, knock down beeves [domestic cattle] with an ax, and perform the most manfull Exercises as well as most men in those parts.

2.

Politically, the backcountry settlers were among the most independent in the colonies. They deeply resented the colonial governments, which seemed to be dominated by easterners who ignored their interests. Frustrated by their lack of political influence, these pioneers occasionally resorted to violent revolt in order to have their grievances heard.

In time, social conditions came more and more to resemble those in the coastal regions. As the pioneers became more prosperous, neat farmhouses replaced rough log cabins. Yet the pioneers did not give up the independence imposed on them by geography. They remained self-sufficient and repeatedly demonstrated their willingness to take matters into their own hands if necessary. ■ 3.

See p. T11.

SECTION 3 REVIEW

1. **Identify:** (a) Scotch-Irish, (b) Pennsylvania Dutch.

2. **Define:** (a) patroon, (b) fall line.

3. (a) What were the two largest groups of non-English settlers in the Middle Colonies? (b) Why did each choose to come to America?

4. (a) Which colony had the most productive farms? (b) Which colony had the least productive farms? Why? (c) How did settlers make a living in the backcountry?

5. (a) In what areas did most free blacks live? (b) Did they have the same freedom as whites? Explain.

6. **Critical Thinking** Why did a tradition of self-sufficiency and independence develop in the backcountry?

3. DISCUSSION Ask students to consider why people might choose the difficult frontier life.

1. **GEOGRAPHY** Have students locate the Southern Colonies on the map on page 59. (location)

2. **VOCABULARY** Have students look up these terms in the glossary before they begin reading.

4 The Southern Colonies

1.

READt TO UNDERSTAND

- Why backcountry farmers resented landowners on the coast.

- What life was like on a southern plantation.

- How slavery became an important source of labor in the South.

2. ■ *Vocabulary:* piedmont region, tidewater region, planter, cash crop, indigo, indentured servant, slave code.

The South was a region of sharp contrasts—in geography, in people, and in culture. The wealthy landowner, proudly surveying his estates, had little in common with his own poor slaves or with the struggling farmer in the backcountry. Yet the life of the one was intricately tied in with the lives of the others.

GEOGRAPHY AND HISTORY

Southern Backcountry Farmers

Geographically, the South has three distinct areas: the mountainous highlands that form the western boundary; the rolling hills of the **piedmont region** at the base of the highlands; and the **tidewater region,** a flat coastal plain with land so low in places that the rivers crossing it flow backward with the incoming tides.

The people and ways of life in the South contrasted almost as sharply as its physical features. While mostly English settlers inhabited the coastal plain, many Germans and Scotch-Irish, a few English, and some French Protestants settled the interior.

In many ways, the southern backcountry was an extension of the backcountry of the Middle Colonies. In spite of the rich soil, dense forest that had to be cleared by hand made farming a demanding task. Farms tended to be small, and families usually produced what they needed to live, with just enough left to trade at the local market for tools and other necessities.

Many farmers, chronically in debt, bitterly resented the wealthy landowners along the coast. As in the Middle Colonies, such resentment occasionally erupted into violence. For example, in 1771, a group of Carolina settlers calling themselves the Regulators revolted against taxes and their general lack of representation in the colonial legislature. The revolt was put down, but bitterness only increased. 3.

Growth of the Plantation System

The aristocratic landowners, called **planters,** controlled the colonial governments of the South. The objects of backcountry anger, these powerful planters owned the huge plantations that became the region's distinctive type of farm.

The roots of the plantation system went back to the Virginia tobacco boom of the 1620s. Settlers had scrambled to control large tracts of land and raise as much tobacco as possible. To tend the crop, planters hired work crews of up to 30 people each.

In different regions, planters experimented with other **cash crops,** those grown to be sold at a profit. Along the coasts of Georgia and South Carolina, planters grew rice.

In the 1740s, a woman named Eliza Lucas Pinckney successfully grew **indigo,** a West Indian plant used to make blue dye. Planters soon began to cultivate this valuable crop. Those with the largest plantations made the largest profits. ■

Life on the Plantation

Plantations usually could develop into self-sufficient communities as a result of their large size. They produced one or more cash crops and food for the residents of the plantation. Skilled artisans produced many tools and other necessities. A well-equipped plantation might include stables and a blacksmith's shop, a dairy, bakehouse, brickworks, and smokehouse.

A planter's family life centered around the "great house." Besides elegant quarters for the family, this mansion usually contained guest rooms, a wine cellar, a dining room, and perhaps even a library and music room. **65**

3. **CITIZENSHIP** In the South Carolina backcountry, settlers were angry because the colony did not provide courts or schools. In North Carolina, they complained that tax collectors kept tax money for themselves.

1. **DISCUSSION** Have students agree or disagree with the following statement: The job of a planter was a cross between that of a mayor and a company president.

The landowner himself presided over the many plantation activities. He decided what lands would be planted each season and what crops would be grown. He arranged for the sale of harvested crops. Together with his wife, the planter supervised the staff and slaves.

Although women's legal rights to land ownership were limited, the planter's wife, who was called the plantation mistress, often played a key role on the estate. She organized household activities and supervised the people who worked in the house. Some women also assumed more direct control of plantations. Eliza Lucas Pinckney, for example, managed both her father's and her husband's planta- tions in South Carolina when the men were away on business.

Indentured Servants

Because cash crops such as tobacco, rice, indigo, and cotton had to be cultivated on a large scale to be profitable, a plantation's success depended on a big supply of labor. At first, planters depended on men, women, and children who came to the colonies as indentured servants. **Indentured servants** agreed to work from four to seven years in return for the cost of passage to America. When they completed their term of service,

2. **VISUAL EVIDENCE** Point out that many luxury items—such as paintings, carpets, and furniture—were imported from England.

Hospitality and gracious living were hallmarks of life in the "great house." The social life of the plantation owners included elaborate parties and extended visits from neighbors and relatives. Dancing was an important social grace, as this painting shows.

the servants received "freedom dues": clothing, tools, a rifle, and occasionally a parcel of land.

Although the life of the indentured servant was hard, the system had its advantages. It often gave men and women the chance to learn a trade or get an education. Indentured servitude also provided an opportunity for a poor person to eventually acquire land and become independent.

In the South, however, large planters had claimed most of the good land along the coast. Thus, when an indentured servant became free, the only available land lay in the backcountry. Like other backcountry farmers, the former indentured servants resented the wealth and political power of the planters.

Bacon's Rebellion In 1676, the friction between backcountry farmers and coastal planters exploded into open warfare in Virginia. A group of farmers felt that the colonial government controlled by planters had not protected them from local Indians, so they marched on the capital, Jamestown. Led by Nathaniel Bacon, a wealthy landowner who sympathized with their cause, the rebels burned Jamestown and tried to redistribute large tracts of land. In the middle of the revolt, Bacon died. The uprising, known as Bacon's Rebellion, fell apart, and the governor hanged its leaders. But the friction between planters and farmers remained.

The Growth of Slavery

As plantations expanded, planters found it difficult to meet their labor needs with indentured servants. Every few years, when servants received their freedom, a new group of workers had to be taught the skills needed to run the estate efficiently. Furthermore, the presence of bitter former servants in the backcountry constantly posed a threat.

Under these conditions, the demand for slave labor grew. As you read in Chapter 2, the first Africans arrived in Jamestown in 1619. Some were probably bought by the local planters as indentured servants, not as slaves. And like white servants, they were freed when their term of servitude had ended.

Gradually, however, temporary servitude became permanent slavery for blacks. There were several reasons for this change. First,

Slave Population in the Colonies, 1650–1770

Year	North	South	Total
1650	880	720	1,600
1660	1,162	1,758	2,920
1670	1,125	3,410	4,535
1680	1,895	5,076	6,971
1690	3,340	13,389	16,729
1700	5,206	22,611	27,817
1710	8,303	36,563	44,866
1720	14,091	54,748	68,839
1730	17,323	73,698	91,021
1740	23,958	126,066	150,024
1750	30,222	206,198	236,420
1760	40,033	285,773	325,806
1770	48,460	411,362	459,822

Source: *Historical Statistics of the United States*

CHART STUDY As the chart above shows, both northerners and southerners kept slaves. Use the chart to make a generalization about the growth of slavery in the North and South. See p. T11.

3. **CHART READING** Ask: In which year did the North have more slaves than the South?

slaves provided a constant supply of workers. Second, the owner had complete control over this labor force. Finally, because of their color, black slaves could not run away and blend easily into the free population.

Slaves did not pose the same threat of class conflict as indentured servants because they could never rise out of their bondage and compete with their former masters for wealth and power. Although the cost of buying a slave was higher than that of purchasing a servant's contract, in the long run, slaves were cheaper than servants. A slave's bondage to the master was lifelong.

The English government responded quickly to the colonial planters' demand for more slaves. In 1672, it established the Royal African Company to conduct the slave trade. Soon, slave trading developed into a profitable colonial business. Colonists continued to import black Africans as slaves throughout the 1600s and 1700s.

67

Millions of Africans were shipped unwillingly to the Americas in slave ships. The "loading plan" for the slave ships tried to jam as many chained people as possible
1. into the limited area of the ship's hold. This painting, by a British naval officer, is the only surviving sketch from life of the inhuman conditions aboard slave ships.

1. **VISUAL EVIDENCE** Have students describe what they can conclude from the painting about crossing the Atlantic in a slave ship.

The Life of a Slave

2. The life of bondage for an African slave began on the cruel "middle passage" from Africa to America. On the slave ships, men, women, and children were crammed below deck in spaces sometimes less than five feet (1.5 meters) high. One observer said they were packed together "like books upon a shelf . . . so close that the shelf would not easily contain one more."

For most of the trip, they were chained to each other, making it difficult to turn or move easily. When the hatches were shut, closing off air circulation, the heat below deck became intolerable. Some slaves died from the

2. **READING** Students interested in finding out more about slavery can read *Roll, Jordan, Roll: The World the Slaves Made,* by Eugene Genovese.

heat or disease; others tried to kill themselves.
3.

Once in America, most new slaves worked in the fields, where they performed the tiring, repetitious tasks involved in growing tobacco, rice, indigo, and cotton. Some were trained as carpenters, blacksmiths, sailors, barrelmakers, or millers. A few slaves worked in the great house as cooks, maids, butlers, and nursemaids.

Few slave owners were intentionally brutal to their slaves, but brutality was basic to the slave system. Even with the most humane 4. treatment, life as a slave was oppressive and dehumanizing. This was especially true for Africans who suddenly found themselves

68

3. **BACKGROUND** So many bodies of dead or dying Africans were thrown into the ocean that sharks regularly followed the slave ships across the Atlantic.

4. **READING** Interested students might read a slave narrative from *Great Slave Narratives,* edited by Arna Bontemps.

wrenched from familiar surroundings, deprived of their freedom, thrown onto a cramped ship, and thrust into a totally foreign environment.

Whether born in Africa or the colonies, slaves lacked all legal rights, since to most colonists they were merely property—no different from a horse or a plow. Owners had immense power over the lives of slaves. They could break up a family, selling the members to other planters, or they could force slaves to perform life-threatening work.

Slave Codes As the number of slaves in the South grew, colonial assemblies passed laws to regulate relations between slaves and their owners. Eventually, each colony had its own **slave code.** Regulations differed from place to place, but their purpose and effect were the same: to control slaves and prevent uprisings.

Slave codes typically prohibited slaves from leaving a plantation without written permission. A slave accused of a crime could be arrested, tried, and condemned on the testimony of only one witness. While slaves could testify against one another, they could not testify against whites. A slave who killed his or her owner—even if the owner had a reputation for exceptional brutality—was hanged, beheaded, or drawn and quartered. But the killing of a slave by a white person

1. was not always a punishable offense.

Resistance to Slavery The slave codes made it difficult for slaves to resist their condition. Some tried to run away, but few succeeded. Slaves who organized rebellions—and some did—were treated as dangerous criminals and executed. A safer course was to engage in passive resistance—for example, by purposely working slowly to spite the owner or by secretly damaging tools.

To make life more bearable, slaves preserved elements of their African culture, such as names, songs, and religious traditions. They proudly passed this culture on to their children.

Quakers and a few others protested against
2. slavery and the slave trade. For example, a New England merchant named Samuel Sewall deplored the "horrible . . . Uncleanness, Mortality, if not Murder, that the Ships are guilty of that bring great crowds of these miserable Men and women." But antislavery protests

had little effect. The vast majority of whites accepted slavery, and thus it remained a central part of the colonial experience.

See p. T11.

SECTION 4 REVIEW

1. **Identify:** (a) Regulators, (b) Eliza Lucas Pinckney, (c) Nathaniel Bacon, (d) "middle passage."

2. **Define:** (a) piedmont region, (b) tidewater region, (c) planter, (d) cash crop, (e) indigo, (f) indentured servant, (g) slave code.

3. Why did farmers in the southern backcountry resent the planters?

4. What was the advantage of growing crops such as indigo and rice on a large plantation?

5. (a) What did indentured servants hope to gain by coming to America? (b) List three reasons for the demand for slave labor.

6. **Critical Thinking** Why do you think antislavery protests had little effect on the growth of slavery?

3. **VOCABULARY** Have students look up these terms in the glossary before they begin reading.

5 Colonial Culture

READ TO UNDERSTAND

■ Why limited religious tolerance developed in the colonies.

■ How schooling differed from one region to another.

■ What kinds of culture flourished in colonial cities.

■ *Vocabulary:* established church, primer, dame school, literacy rate.

3.

The people who came to the American colonies had not wiped the slate clean when they crossed the ocean. They brought traditions **69** as well as tools. They brought their own ways of worshiping, of cooking, of dressing, of having fun. They brought their own beliefs and values—European or African, as the case might be.

To make themselves feel at home in their new land, the newcomers tried to recreate as much as possible the ways they had known in the old. But America was neither Europe nor Africa. In the face of widely differing challenges and opportunities, people began to adapt their ways to their new environments. By the mid-1700s, they were developing a distinctively American culture.

Religious Tolerance and Intolerance

The religious faiths of the colonies originated in Europe, but they varied widely. Each European nation had an **established church,** an official, state-supported church to which responsible citizens were expected to belong. Other churches, if not officially outlawed, were considered undesirable, and their members often faced discrimination. Toleration of religious diversity in Europe was the exception, not the rule.

No one church dominated all the colonies. The Puritans' Congregational church was the established church in most of New England. The Church of England, or Anglican church, was the established church in Virginia, Maryland, New York, the Carolinas, and Georgia. Regardless of their personal beliefs, citizens paid taxes to support the established church. Dissenters could sometimes worship freely in these colonies, but they still had to support the established church with their taxes.

On the other hand, colonies like Pennsylvania and Rhode Island had originated as havens for religious dissenters. Their policies of toleration meant that no church became officially established.

Great Awakening   In the 1730s and 1740s, a series of religious revivals spread through the colonies. The revivals began when an English minister, George Whitefield (WHIHT feeld), traveling from New England to Georgia, held more than 100 rousing open air serv-

ices. Thousands flocked from cities, small towns, and farms to hear Whitefield preach.

Local ministers also encouraged churchgoers to examine their spiritual state. One such preacher was Jonathan Edwards of Northampton, Massachusetts. In a powerful sermon, "Sinners in the Hands of an Angry God," Edwards warned of the fiery torments of hell that awaited sinners. He spoke with equal power of the joys of heaven and a holy, pure life.

1.

The religious movement, which became known as the Great Awakening, immediately sparked controversy. Supporters of the Awakening often split away from their old churches to form new ones. Opponents criticized the revival meetings as being too emotional.

Although the disputes over the Awakening continued for decades, they had the practical effect of increasing toleration. With so many different religious denominations living side by side, mutual toleration seemed preferable to persecuting each other.

Although colonial legislatures gradually extended toleration to most Protestant groups, they continued to discriminate against Roman Catholics as well as against Jewish immigrants. For example, most colonies did not allow Jews to vote. Still, when compared to Europe at the time, the American colonies practiced a relatively high degree of toler- 2. ance.

The Importance of Education

Education was often closely connected with religion in colonial America, especially in New England. The early Puritans had emphasized the importance of schooling, for they believed that all should be able to read the Bible for themselves. To achieve this goal, the Puritans created a **primer,** a small textbook which 3. taught children how to read and spell while they memorized the tenets of the Puritan faith.

In 1647, Massachusetts passed America's first public school law. It required towns of 50 or more families to maintain a grammar school to prepare young men for college by instructing them in Latin and other classical subjects. Other New England colonies passed similar laws.

2. **MAIN IDEA** Have students write a paragraph summarizing the extent to which religious toleration existed in the English colonies in America.

3. **VOCABULARY** *Primer* is pronounced PRIHM er.

1. **TECHNOLOGY** Have interested students find out about some of Franklin's inventions and report on them to the class, noting which are still used today.

NOTABLE AMERICANS

Benjamin Franklin: Inquiring Into Medicine

Benjamin Franklin had a questioning mind, so when he read at the age of 16 that a vegetarian diet was the way to good health, he tried it. This could have been inconvenient, since Franklin had his meals at a boarding house where everyone else ate meat. But it was no problem for someone as resourceful as Franklin. He arranged to buy simple fare, such as bread and raisins, for himself. He took to eating his meals at the print shop where he was an apprentice, finishing quickly to save time for reading books.

Franklin developed a lifelong interest in medicine and health. This was not unusual in colonial America, where people often treated themselves. In later years, Franklin printed a popular medical guide called *Every Man His Own Doctor; or, the Poor Planter's Physician.*

As in his other endeavors, Franklin used the experimental method to explore medical questions. He did not mind admitting when experiments proved one of his theories unsound. For example, he tried applying electricity to stiff or paralyzed joints. When he found little or no improvement, he stopped the treatment.

Franklin also practiced what we now call preventive medicine. As a young printer in London, he convinced his fellow workers that it was unhealthy to drink beer with breakfast. (And water was cheaper.)

In an age when the need for personal cleanliness did not even occur to most people, Franklin urged regular nude bathing in a tub of water. The idea shocked many. Franklin designed and built his own bathtub, with a rack on which to rest a book for bathtime reading.

In *Poor Richard's Almanac,* he counseled moderation. "He that drinks fast pays slow." And "Early to bed and early to rise makes a man healthy, wealthy, and wise." He championed exercise, especially swimming, for health, and also inoculation against smallpox. Franklin maintained his health practices throughout his life.

But when he fell ill at age 84, he recognized the seriousness of his condition. His daughter, sitting by his bed, wished him many more years of life. "I hope not," commented Franklin. As usual, he was right.

See p. T12.

1. Which of Franklin's health measures are still recommended today?

2. **Critical Thinking** If Benjamin Franklin were alive today, what do you think he would do for a living?

Although the Middle Colonies had no tax-supported schools, religious groups founded schools for poor children. Some private schools, mainly for boys, existed for those who could afford them. In the Southern Colonies, tutors who lived with the planters' families often taught their children. Others had little access to education.

Although most colonial education was limited to boys, women frequently held classes

2. **BACKGROUND** Few doctors had formal training in the colonies. Some served apprenticeships under doctors, but many just declared themselves to be physicians.

3. **READING** Have students read other excerpts from *Poor Richard's Almanac* and share their favorites with the class.

Few black men and women were able to get a formal education in colonial America, but some managed to do so. Phillis Wheatley was brought from Africa as a slave at age eight. She taught herself English and Latin and began writing poetry, which was widely admired.

1. **VISUAL EVIDENCE** This portrait first appeared in a book of verse by Wheatley published in London in 1773.

in their homes for girls and the younger children. At these so-called **"dame schools,"** pupils learned reading and writing, as well as skills like sewing and embroidery. In some colonial cities, moreover, artisans set up evening schools for their workers.

As a result of such efforts, the **literacy rate,** or the proportion of people who could read and write, in the colonies was relatively high, especially in towns and in New England in general. In frontier areas, fewer people could read. People who could not write signed legal documents with an *X.*

Soon after their arrival in the New World, colonists had also turned their attention to higher education for young men, primarily to educate ministers and preachers. Settlers in Massachusetts established the first colonial college in 1636, naming it Harvard after a wealthy colonist who donated land and money to build it. The College of William and Mary was founded in Virginia in 1693, and in 1701 a group of Congregationalists founded Yale.

2. **CRITICAL THINKING** Lead a discussion on the purpose of schools in colonial America. Ask: How does that purpose compare with the purpose of schools today?

Cities: Centers of Culture

Although the towns and cities contained less than 10 percent of the population of America in the mid-1700s, they strongly influenced colonial life. Through the great ports of Philadelphia, New York, Boston, and Charleston, merchants shipped the products of America to England and the West Indies. Towns and cities also served as the focus of a busy trade between the coast and the rapidly growing backcountry.

Cities were the exchange points not only for goods but also for ideas. John Campbell founded the *Boston News-Letter,* the first regular weekly newspaper in the colonies, in 1704. Fifty years later, each of the 13 colonies except New Jersey and Delaware had at least one weekly paper.

The growth of colonial newspapers led to a dispute over freedom of the press. In 1734, John Peter Zenger, publisher of the *Weekly Journal* in New York City, was arrested for libel.* Zenger, who often criticized government officials in his paper, had attacked the governor of New York. Zenger's lawyer argued that his client had not libeled the governor because what he printed had been the truth. The jury agreed and freed Zenger.

At the time, this seemed like a revolutionary idea, since criticism of the government was generally considered a crime. The principle of freedom of the press was upheld in this case, but years would pass before it became firmly established in America.

Culture also flourished in the cities. By the mid-1700s, all the major colonial cities had their own theaters. City dwellers also found entertainment at singing societies, traveling circuses, carnivals, and horse races. Here and there, communities established libraries and stocked them with books imported from abroad or printed on new colonial presses.

The lives of city dwellers were not typical of most colonists' lives. But the cities served as a center for new products and ideas that eventually spread throughout the colonies.

---

*libel: the act of publishing a statement that unjustly damages a person's reputation.

3. **BACKGROUND** The first printing press in the English colonies was set up in 1639 and was owned by Mrs. Jose Glover. The first magazine in North America, *The American Magazine,* began publication in 1746.

4. **BACKGROUND** Benjamin Franklin organized the first lending library in America in Philadelphia in 1732.

1. **GRAPH READING** Ask: Which city grew the least between 1700 and 1710? During which ten-year period did New York experience its greatest growth?

SKILL LESSON

The Growth of Colonial Cities: Reading Graphs

Graphs are one way to present information visually and to condense a large amount of data. Graphs allow you to see the relationship between two or more sets of data. A line or bar graph can show changes over time. A circle graph points up the relationship of parts to a whole. The steps outlined below will help you learn how to read a graph.

See p. T12.

1 **Identify the type of information presented on the graph.** Ask yourself: (a) What do the numbers on the vertical axis represent? (b) What do the numbers on the horizontal axis represent? (c) Describe the type of information the graph gives.

2 **Practice reading the data shown on the graph.** (a) What was the population of New York in 1690? (b) In what decade did the population of Boston decline? (c) How much did the population of Philadelphia grow between 1710 and 1720?

1.

3 **Look for relationships among the data presented.** (a) Which city had the largest population in 1690? (b) Which city grew most rapidly between 1700 and 1710? (c) How many more people lived in Boston than in Philadelphia in 1720?

4 **Use the graph to draw conclusions about a topic.** Use the line graph and this chapter to answer these questions: (a) What statement can you make about the population of all four cities between 1690 and 1730? (b) Why do you think port cities were the largest cities in the 1700s?

2.

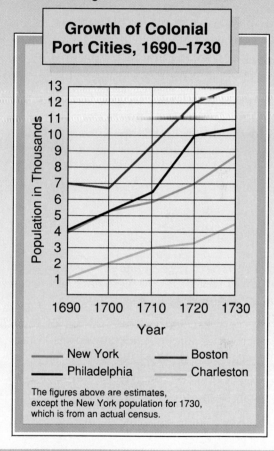

Growth of Colonial Port Cities, 1690–1730

The figures above are estimates, except the New York population for 1730, which is from an actual census.

See p. T12.

SECTION 5 REVIEW

1. **Define:** (a) established church, (b) primer, (c) dame school, (d) literacy rate.

2. (a) How did having many religions in the colonies make for religious toleration? (b) Which religions were often not tolerated?

3. (a) Which colony passed the first public school law? (b) Why did the people of this colony think education was important?

4. Compare the education offered to boys with that offered to girls in the colonies.

5. **Critical Thinking** Why do you think religion was such an important part of colonial life?

73

2. **ACTIVITY** To practice creating graphs, have students translate the information on the chart on p. 67 into a line graph.

CHAPTER 3 REVIEW

Summary

1. **All but the first colonies were either proprietary or royal colonies.** In time, the colonies developed their own forms of representative government.

2. **In New England, a harsh environment conditioned the lives of settlers.** Most people were subsistence farmers, but shipping and fishing industries thrived. Social barriers gradually began to disappear.

3. **Settlers of diverse origins came to the fertile farmland of the Middle Colonies.** New York continued the oppressive Dutch system that kept farmers permanently as tenants, but elsewhere farmers were freer.

4. **The plantation system flourished in the South.** Wealthy planters grew cash crops and came to rely on slaves rather than indentured servants for labor. Friction developed between the small farmers in the backcountry and the powerful planters on the coast.

5. **The colonists came to differ more from Europeans than from one another.** Religious toleration was more common in America than in Europe and education easier to get. In the growing cities, people shared ideas and values that provided the basis for greater unity, as you will read in the chapters to come.

See p. T12.

Vocabulary

On a separate sheet of paper, write the word or words that best complete each of the following sentences.

1. _____ were granted ownership of territory by the king but acknowledged his authority by making annual payments.

2. A farm family that had the resources to get along without outside help was _____.

3. In New York, feudal-style manors were owned by _____.

4. _____ were crops grown to be sold at a profit.

5. _____ were laws passed to regulate the relations between slave owners and slaves.

See p. T12.

Chapter Checkup

1. Describe the role of each of the following in the government of a royal colony: (a) the king, (b) the governor, (c) the council, (d) the assembly.

2. How did representative government begin to develop in the colonies?

3. (a) What was the basis of the economy in New England? In the Middle Colonies? In the Southern Colonies? (b) What factors account for different economic patterns?

4. (a) Describe the social class system in New England. (b) Why did it gradually become less rigid?

5. How did life in the backcountry differ from life along the coast?

6. Why did slavery replace the use of indentured servants on southern plantations?

7. Why were there fewer slaves in the Middle Colonies and New England than in the South?

8. List the limitations placed on slaves by the slave codes.

9. (a) Describe the Great Awakening. (b) How did it help to increase religious tolerance in the colonies?

10. (a) Why did the American colonies have a relatively high literacy rate? (b) In which areas was the literacy rate lower? How would you account for this difference?

See p. T13.

Critical Thinking

1. **Comparing** How did the proprietary governments differ from the governments organized under royal charters?

2. **Analyzing** Why was slavery a dehumanizing experience regardless of how a slave was treated?

3. **Reasoning** How did the decision of planters to replace indentured servants with slaves reflect their own self-interest?

4. **Analyzing** How did the difference in education for boys and girls reflect the values of colonial society?

See p. T13.

Connecting Past and Present

1. (a) Is social class more or less important in American society today than in colonial times? (b) Would you say it is easy or difficult for someone today to rise to a higher station? Explain.

2. In the United States today, newspapers have almost unlimited freedom to criticize public officials in editorials. On the whole, would you say that this freedom serves the public interest or harms it? Explain.

See p. T13.

Developing Basic Skills

1. **Reading a Chart** Use the chart on page 55 to answer these questions: (a) Which colonies were started by people from nations other than England? (b) Which colonies were founded as proprietary colonies? (c) What were the two most common reasons for founding a colony?

2. **Ranking** Rank the social systems of the following regions from the most rigid to the least rigid: New England towns, Middle Colonies coastal area, Middle Colonies backcountry, Southern Colonies backcountry, Southern Colonies coastal area. (a) Why did you rank the social systems of the different regions in the order you did? (b) How would you account for the different patterns?

3. **Reading a Graph** Use the steps you learned in the Skill Lesson on page 73 to read the circle graph on page 62. Study the graph and answer the following questions: (a) What information is shown on this graph? (b) Which were the three largest and three smallest ethnic groups? (c) Based on the graph, what general statements would you make about the ethnic composition of the American colonies?

WRITING ABOUT HISTORY

Writing a Topic Sentence

The topic sentence expresses the central idea of a paragraph. When it opens a paragraph, it gives the reader a preview of what will follow. You might consider the topic sentence to be a special kind of generalization. It shows how a number of specific facts or ideas in the paragraph are related, by including them in one general statement.

Consider a paragraph that discusses the roles of women in colonial America. It will mention how women lived in many places—on New England farms, in cities, on the frontier, on southern plantations. A possible topic sentence is "Women played important but varying roles, depending on where they lived in the colonies."

Practice: Write a generalization to serve as a topic sentence for each Critical Thinking question in this Chapter Review. Follow it with specific support.

A Struggle for Empire 4

(1600–1763)

CHAPTER OUTLINE

1 Colonies: A Vital Part of the British Empire

2 Rivalry in North America

3 The French and Indian War

CHAPTER OBJECTIVES After completing this chapter, students should be able to
1. explain the effect of British mercantilism on the colonies in America.
2. describe how conflicting European claims affected the American colonies.
3. describe the causes and effects of the French and Indian War.
4. read a map.

Optimism and high spirits marked the start of the British effort to seize Quebec—the heart of New France. But there was also urgency. The St. Lawrence River was free of ice for only a brief time. British troop ships arrived near Quebec by late June. By the end of September, ice could block their route home.

The battle for Quebec (and hence control of North America) became a duel between two generals—the sickly but ambitious British general James Wolfe and the dashing, determined French general Louis de Montcalm. All summer, Wolfe struggled to draw Montcalm into battle. But Montcalm would not be lured from his secure position high above the cliffs that protected the town at Quebec. All summer, the French general held his defensive position.

Becoming restless, Wolfe ordered a bold attack on July 31, 1759. Then he watched helplessly from shipboard as 450 of his best troops died in vain. The British troops trying to scale the daunting cliffs were mowed down by French gunfire from above. A sudden summer storm sent mudslides cascading down the cliffs. The soldiers who could, retreated; those who could not died in the mud, out of reach of their comrades.

Aware that his health was failing, Wolfe was desperate by early September. How could he draw out the wily fox, as he called Montcalm? At last, he decided to send his men up a small break in the cliffs that Montcalm had failed to guard. Under cover of dark, troops scrambled up the breach. It was a gamble, but it worked.

Wolfe was mortally wounded as the ensuing battle unfolded on the Plains of Abraham. He gasped, "Now, God be praised, I can die in peace." Montcalm, conspicuous on his large black horse, was also shot. When told he was dying, he replied, "Good, then I will not have to witness the surrender of Quebec."

The battle for Quebec was a closing chapter in the struggle between Britain and France for control of North America. By the 1700s, the Americas had come to the forefront in European designs for empire. As you will read, three nations—Spain, France, and Britain—competed for power in the Americas. Their rivalry extended from land to sea, as they competed for control of the world's growing trade.

CHAPTER PREVIEW Ask students to study the map on p. 83. Tell them that it shows the territory in North America claimed by Europeans in 1753. Ask students to look at the United States map on pp. 840–841 and find place names that show the influence of British, French, and Spanish settlement.

1.

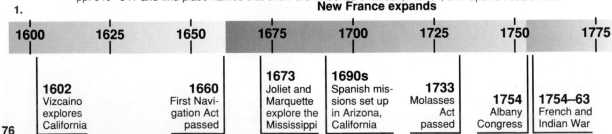

New France expands

1600	1625	1650	1675	1700	1725	1750	1775

1602 Vizcaino explores California

1660 First Navigation Act passed

1673 Joliet and Marquette explore the Mississippi

1690s Spanish missions set up in Arizona, California

1733 Molasses Act passed

1754 Albany Congress

1754–63 French and Indian War

76

1. TIME LINE QUESTION Ask: In what decade did the Spanish set up missions in California and Arizona?

The turning point of the French and Indian War was the British victory at Quebec. The British secretly scaled the cliffs by a little-known path, shown at left in this painting by Sigmund Samuel. The surprised French troops were soundly defeated and an empire was lost.

1. **VISUAL EVIDENCE** Ask: Based on this painting, how did geography affect the outcome of the Battle of Quebec?

1 Colonies: A Vital Part of the British Empire

READ TO UNDERSTAND

■ What role colonies played in the mercantilist system.

■ Why Parliament passed the Navigation Acts.

■ How the Navigation Acts affected the colonies.

2. ■ *Vocabulary:* mercantilism, enumerated commodities, triangular trade.

Early in the age of exploration, Sir Walter Raleigh had foreseen the value of commerce to a nation. "Whoever commands the trade of the world," he said, "commands the riches of the world and consequently the world itself." Fierce commercial rivalry would mark the European struggle for control of far-flung empires. In the late 1600s and 1700s, colonies became increasingly important in this competition, especially for the British Empire.*

Mercantilism

Behind this sharp contest for colonies lay an economic theory that has come to be called **mercantilism**, from the word merchant. Under the mercantilist system, each nation tried to sell more than it bought in order to preserve or increase its precious hoard of gold. By providing its own needs, a nation would be less vulnerable in time of war.

Colonies and trading posts were an important source of this economic indepen-

---

*One part of England's transformation into a world power was the unification of England and Scotland into the nation of Great Britain in 1707. After that date, "Great Britain" and "British" were the official terms used to describe the new nation and its residents. Throughout the 1700s, however, these new terms were used interchangeably with "England" and "English."

77

2. **VOCABULARY** Have students look up these terms in the glossary before they begin reading.

3. **DISCUSSION** Have students restate Raleigh's comment in their own words. Then discuss whether they agree with Raleigh and, if so, whether his idea is valid today.

dence. They would increase a nation's self-sufficiency by providing vital raw materials such as precious metals, lumber, farm products, cotton, and wool. Without the colonies, a nation would have to buy these essential raw materials from a rival power.

Colonies played a second vital role in the mercantilist system—markets for goods produced at home. Without colonies, a nation could manufacture only what it could expect to sell at home and to a few foreign customers. Goods stacked in warehouses were a loss. But a colony might buy these surpluses, raising manufacturers' profits.

In the late 1600s, the British began to see the value of colonies. First, as you learned earlier, the government tightened its political control over the colonies. Next, it strengthened its hold on colonial trade. Charles II worked with his ministers to design a strong mercantilist colonial policy that would allow the empire to "command the riches of the
1. world" and possibly "the world itself."

Regulating Trade

Before the mid-1600s, colonial merchants enjoyed a measure of economic independence. They reaped tidy profits from trade with England. Goods were also traded in the English, French, Dutch, and Spanish islands of the Caribbean, often for even greater gain.

From the British point of view, such practices were dangerous. Trade between a colonial merchant and other nations and their colonies deprived the British of valuable revenues. On a large scale, such trade could threaten England's status as a world power.

Unless the American colonies were forced to play their appointed role in the mercantilist system, England's power would be threatened. In 1660 and 1663, Parliament passed the Navigation Acts to make sure the colonists traded only with England.

First, colonial merchants were allowed to ship goods only on colonial or English-owned vessels. Three quarters of the crew had to be colonial or English sailors.

This regulation was aimed primarily at the Netherlands, England's chief commercial competitor. With the world's largest merchant fleet, the Dutch regularly transported products to and from the English colonies. Every Dutch ship in a colonial harbor meant profits for the Dutch and losses for the British. Charles II intended to stop this drain on England's economy.

Next, Parliament made a list of colonial products, called **enumerated commodities,** that could be shipped only to England. Sugar, cotton, indigo, ginger, tobacco, and woods used for dye had to pass through England before they could be sent elsewhere. Later, Parliament added rice, furs, and naval supplies to the list.

2.
3. *Trade with colonies was at the heart of mercantilism. Ships carried goods between England and its colonies in America. Because of New York City's excellent harbor, shown here, the city grew into a major center of trade. In 1760, when this painting was made, New York had about 16,000 residents.*

78

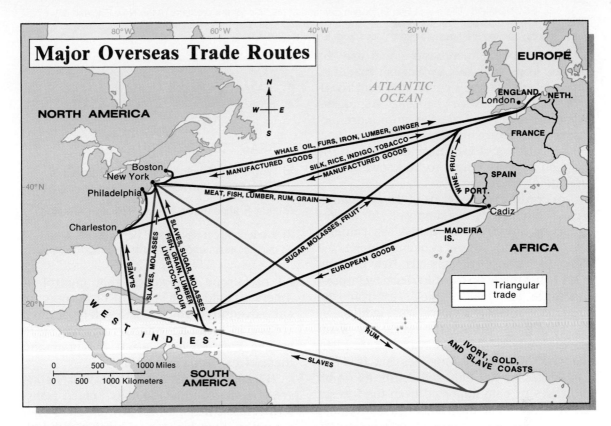

Major Overseas Trade Routes

ATLANTIC OCEAN

EUROPE

NORTH AMERICA

ENGLAND NETH.
London

FRANCE

WHALE OIL, FURS, IRON, LUMBER, GINGER
MANUFACTURED GOODS
SILK, RICE, INDIGO, TOBACCO
MANUFACTURED GOODS

SPAIN

WINE, FRUIT

PORT.

Boston
New York
Philadelphia

MEAT, FISH, LUMBER, RUM, GRAIN

Cadiz

Charleston

SLAVES, MOLASSES
FISH, GRAIN, LUMBER
LIVESTOCK, FLOUR
SLAVES, SUGAR, MOLASSES

SLAVES

SUGAR, MOLASSES, FRUIT

MADEIRA IS.

AFRICA

EUROPEAN GOODS

Triangular trade

W E S T

I N D I E S

RUM

IVORY, GOLD, AND SLAVE COASTS

0   500   1000 Miles
0   500   1000 Kilometers

SOUTH AMERICA

SLAVES

MAP STUDY *The colonists carried on an extensive trade with Europe, Africa, and the West Indies. The slave trade was part of a triangular route (shown on the map in red) between the colonies, the West Indies, and the west coast of Africa. What goods were traded at each point of that route?* See p. T14.

1.

1. **MAP READING** Ask: What products did England sell to the colonies? What products went from New York to England? What products did the Southern Colonies ship to England?

The Navigation Acts also prohibited the colonies from importing most products from other European nations unless those products passed through England first. The only exceptions to this rule were slaves, wines, horses, and salt.

This provision guaranteed that the English could tax colonial imports and exports no matter where in Europe they were coming from or going to. The taxes on European products raised their prices in the colonies, thus protecting English industries from cheap competition. Furthermore, processing imports and exports created jobs in England.

Impact on England and the Colonies

For the most part, the mercantile system benefited both England and the American colonies. To make up for any lost profits, the English government granted the colonial manufacturers bonuses for producing certain essential goods. American merchants welcomed the exclusion of foreigners from colonial trade and the protection provided by British forces.

Although most colonists took the trade laws in stride, others resisted. Some merchants resented the law requiring that goods they imported and exported pass through England. They claimed that it cut into their profits and used up precious shipping time.

Others opposed the regulation forcing them to sell enumerated articles only to England. They knew that they could get higher prices for their products in other European countries. Merchants found that it was sometimes cheaper to bribe customs officials than to pay duties on goods.

Triangular Trade The Navigation Acts posed bigger problems for colonial merchants in the 1700s. New England had come to rely on the production of rum, made from molasses, to support its trade. Merchants would ship grain, barrel staves, horses, and fish to the West Indies and bring back molasses.

2. **ACTIVITY** Have students make a chart listing the provisions and purposes of the Navigation Acts.

3. **PAST AND PRESENT** Ask students to suggest similarities between protection under the Navigation Acts and that advocated by protectionists today.

79

ECONOMICS There was little European demand at the time for the products of the New England or Middle colonies. The triangular trade was thus an important way for these colonies to raise money to pay for imported manufactured goods from England.

New England merchants could use the profits from rum to buy English manufactured goods. Or they could ship rum to Africa, buy slaves with the rum, sail to the West Indies and sell the slaves for more molasses, then return home and make more rum. These patterns of exchange, outlined on the map on page 79, came to be known as the **triangular trade.**

According to the terms of the Navigation Acts, colonists were supposed to import molasses only from the British West Indies. But the islands there could not meet the demand. To meet their needs, New England merchants made up the difference by importing large amounts of molasses from the French, Spanish, and Dutch West Indies.

Facing lost profits, the rich sugar planters of the British West Indies pressured Parliament to pass the Molasses Act in 1733. The Molasses Act imposed a stiff tax on all molasses or rum imported from the foreign West Indies. If the duty had been enforced, it would have ruined New England's economy. But the wily New England merchants ignored the law or bribed customs officials to overlook the foreign molasses. As a result, the triangular trade routes flourished as much
1. as ever.

By and large, the mercantile system worked well—so well, in fact, that, as you will read in the next section, it brought the prospering English colonies into conflict with the two rival empires, Spain and France.
See p. T14.

SECTION 1 REVIEW

1. **Identify:** Molasses Act.

2. **Define:** (a) mercantilism, (b) enumerated commodity, (c) triangular trade.

3. How were colonies an important part of the mercantilist system?

4. Why were the Navigation Acts passed?

5. (a) Did the trade laws work? (b) In what way could colonists benefit from them?

6. **Critical Thinking** Why was naval power important to any nation trying to maintain a mercantilist system?

CRITICAL THINKING Ask: Which British policies encouraged settlement in the New World?

2 Rivalry in North America

READp TO UNDERSTAND

- Why rivalry developed between Britain and Spain in the Americas.

- How France made its mark in North America.

- What conflicts developed between the American colonists and the North American Indians.

All of Europe recognized that control of America could mean control of Europe. As one adventurer put it, "The safety of monarchs and commonwealths rests chiefly in making their enemies weak and poor and themselves strong and rich."

England learned the lesson well. Its aggressive mercantilist policies helped transform it into a major world power in less than a century. Step by step, it strengthened its hold on lands from India to North America.

In America, the British presence grew
2. rapidly. At the end of the seventeenth century, 200,000 people lived in British America. By the mid-1700s, the population reached 1,500,000 and was still growing. At the same time, barely 70,000 colonists lived in New France, a territory more than twice the size
3. of the British colonies.

As English settlements expanded, they ran the risk of encroaching on French or Spanish territory. From the start, friction seemed inevitable.

The Spanish Empire

Spain, as you will recall, had established its American colonies years before either France or England and had realized a far greater profit from them. By the 1700s, the Spanish empire in America included most of Central and South America, plus what is now Mexico, Florida, the southwestern United States, and California.

The defeat of the Armada in 1588 weakened Spanish power. As a result, the amount of money invested in the Americas dwindled,

BACKGROUND Remind students that France had concentrated on the fur trade in North America and had not encouraged families to settle in New France.

and Spanish control of the colonies weakened. Soon the Spanish colonies were left to develop largely on their own. As fewer soldiers, missionaries, and settlers came, settlers born in New Spain began to replace officials sent over from Spain.

Still, the Spanish continued to explore the Southwest and the Pacific coast during the 1600s and early 1700s. Sebastian Vizcaino (VEES kah EE noh) explored the northern coast of California as early as 1602. He paved the way for later Spanish settlement of the area and gave many places their present names, including San Diego, Santa Barbara, Monterey, and Carmel.

The Spanish founded Santa Fe in present-day New Mexico in 1609, and almost 50 years later established several missions near El Paso. During the 1600s, Father Eusebio Francisco Kino helped establish missions in present-ent-day Arizona and California.

Conflict With the British Spanish settlement was concentrated in the Southwest and West, and British settlement was confined to the east coast of North America. Therefore, contacts between the two empires were limited to skirmishes between trading vessels at sea and to friction between Spanish Florida and British settlers in Georgia.

Settlers in Georgia accused Spain of allowing outlaws to cross the Florida border and harass them. Their fears were raised in 1738 when the Spanish governor declared that slaves who escaped from the British colonies could live in freedom in Florida. This step confirmed long-held British suspicions that Spain planned to expand its empire in the area.

New France

Friction with Spain was a minor irritation compared to the threat of a major conflict with France. This had not always been so. During its first years, New France had grown slowly. Few French men and women wanted to face the dangers and uncertainties of a wilderness far from home. Protestants, who wanted to leave France to escape religious persecution, were forbidden to settle in New France.

By the 1700s, Spanish civilization was firmly established in large parts of the New World. This painting, gilded with gold and silver, shows the sophistication of Spanish art in the Americas. Called *Our Lady of Victory, it was done to celebrate a great Spanish victory.*

2. **VISUAL EVIDENCE** The painting was done by Luis Niño, who lived in the Spanish silver-mining settlement of Potosí (see p. 33).

French settlers in North America endured long, harsh winters. Everyday life challenged the determination of families living on the frontier. This painting shows one way they survived. When the rivers froze, they broke holes in the ice to catch fish.

3. **VISUAL EVIDENCE** The painting was done by Peter Rindisbacher, a Swiss immigrant to Canada, at the age of 15.

SKILL LESSON

Rival Claims in North America: Reading Maps

Maps can provide geographic, social, political, and economic information. Knowing how to interpret maps can help you understand American history. Most maps include a title, legend, scale, directional indicator, and topographical features. Follow the steps below, using the map on page 83, to practice reading maps.

See p. T15.

1 **Decide what is shown on the map.** The *title* tells you the subject of the map. The *legend,* or key, tells you what the symbols and colors on the map represent. (a) What is the title of the map? (b) What is the date of the information? (c) What information is shown on the map?

2 **Practice reading the information on the map.** The scale, directional indicator, and topographical features also help you read a map. The *scale* tells you the actual distances that are represented on the map.

Direction is usually shown by an arrow or compass needle indicating which way is north. *Topographical features* are surface land characteristics such as mountains or rivers. (a) What is the distance in kilometers between Quebec and Charleston? Between Quebec and New York? (b) Which country claimed the territory north and east of French territory? (c) Which mountains bordered British claims? (d) Which major river was part of New France?

3 **Use the information on the map to draw conclusions about the historical period being studied.** (a) How far west did British settlement extend in what later became the United States? Why do you think it stopped there? (b) Where would conflict between the Spanish and British be most likely to occur? (c) Where would conflict between the French and British be most likely?

1.

2. **ECONOMICS** France also competed with Portugal for the spice trade in Asia and, along with England and Portugal, set up trading stations in India.

After 1661, the situation changed. Louis XIV assumed complete control of the French government and launched an ambitious program of empire building. He hoped to make New France into a market for French exports and a source of food for the French West Indies.

2. Indies.

Without more French colonists, however, the plans for empire would not work. So, for the first time, the French government took steps to encourage people to migrate to North America. It granted large tracts of the best

3. land in New France to army officers and other gentlemen, who in turn rented parts of their land to merchants or peasants.

The land grants somewhat increased the number of people who came to North America. But the gentlemen-landlords were not going to soil their hands by working the land.

Although some of their tenants made farming pay, most resented working land they did not own.

As a result, New France never became the cornerstone of empire that Louis XIV had envisioned. New France not only failed to grow food for the West Indies, it did not even produce enough to feed its own population. Food for the people of New France had to be imported either from France or from neighboring New England.

GEOGRAPHY AND HISTORY

Expanding French Claims

Since farming failed in New France, the French had to look elsewhere for success. They found it in two other enterprises: exploration and fur trading.

82

3. **BACKGROUND** The development of New France was encouraged by Louis XIV's powerful finance minister, Jean Baptiste Colbert. A mercantilist, Colbert believed that the development of French colonies would strengthen the French economy and the power of the French monarchy.

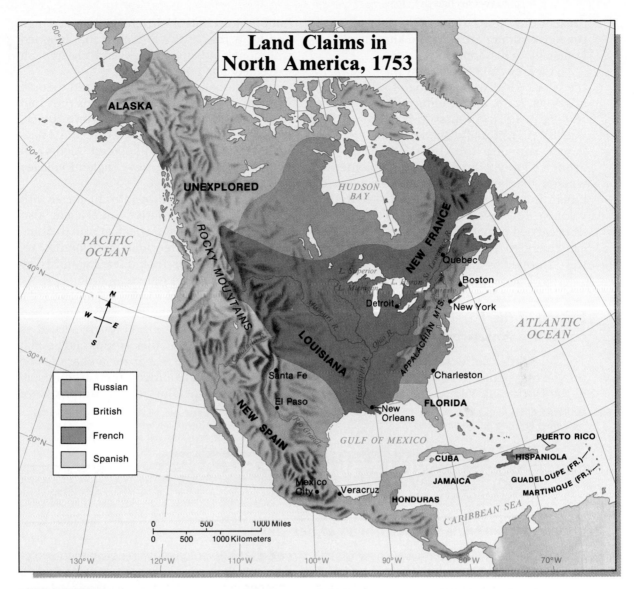

Land Claims in North America, 1753

ALASKA

UNEXPLORED

HUDSON BAY

ROCKY MOUNTAINS

PACIFIC OCEAN

NEW FRANCE

Quebec

L. Superior

L. Michigan

L. Huron

Boston

Detroit

New York

ATLANTIC OCEAN

LOUISIANA

APPALACHIAN MTS.

Missouri R.

Ohio R.

Charleston

Santa Fe

Mississippi R.

El Paso

New Orleans

FLORIDA

NEW SPAIN

Rio Grande

GULF OF MEXICO

PUERTO RICO

HISPANIOLA

CUBA

GUADELOUPE (FR.)

JAMAICA

MARTINIQUE (FR.)

Mexico City

Veracruz

HONDURAS

CARIBBEAN SEA

Russian
British
French
Spanish

0   500   1000 Miles
0   500   1000 Kilometers

130°W   120°W   110°W   100°W   90°W   80°W   70°W

60°N   50°N   40°N   30°N   20°N

MAP STUDY *France, Spain, Russia, and Great Britain all claimed parts of North America. As English colonists moved westward, conflict with other European nations was inevitable. Based on the map, with which nation do you think conflict was likely to arise first? Why?* See p. T15.

1.

1. **MAP READING** Ask: Why might control of New Orleans be important to a country?

In 1673, Louis Joliet (zhoh LYEH) and
2. Jacques Marquette (mahr KEHT), a Jesuit priest, journeyed by canoe down the Fox, Wisconsin, and Mississippi rivers, as far south as the mouth of the Arkansas River. Indians they met there told them that the Mississippi emptied into the Gulf of Mexico, not into the Gulf of California to the west or the Atlantic Ocean to the east as the explorers thought. Armed with this information,

Joliet and Marquette decided to turn back rather than to risk capture by the Spanish, who controlled the territory to the south.

Later, René-Robert Cavelier, Sieur de La Salle (suhr duh lah SAHL), resumed explorations of the region. By 1682, he reached the delta* of the Mississippi, just north of

―――――――――

*delta: a deposit of soil at the mouth of some rivers, usually forming a triangular shape.

83

2. **BIOGRAPHY** Marquette came to New France in 1666. After studying Indian languages, he founded two missions before embarking on his journey with Joliet. After this trip, Marquette continued his missionary work until his death in 1675. Joliet went on to lead expeditions to Hudson Bay and Labrador.

present-day New Orleans. There he claimed the surrounding area for the king, naming it Louisiana in his honor.

The French consolidated their claims in the New World with a string of settlements, missions, forts, and trading posts. From the trading posts, coureurs de bois (koo RUHR duh BWAH), literally "runners of the woods," fanned out into the thick forests of New France. They traded metal implements, woolen blankets, textiles, and weapons to Indian hunters in exchange for the furs so

1. valuable to French merchants. Fleets of canoes carried heavy loads of fur over the northern rivers to Quebec. From there, the furs were shipped to Europe. ■

Impact of the Fur Trade on Native Americans

The fur trade, so lucrative for the French, proved disastrous to many Native Americans in the Northeast. Fierce competition among

hunters for control of rich hunting grounds and for a role in the French trade inflamed traditional Indian rivalries and created an extremely unstable situation.

As the balance of power shifted, people were forced out of hunting grounds they had held for centuries. The Iroquois, for instance, drove the Algonquin eastward to the Atlantic coast. There the displaced Algonquin vented their anger on New England villages and settlements.

As they were drawn into alliances with European powers, Native Americans also became involved in European efforts to dominate the North American continent. Frequently, Europeans took advantage of rivalries between Native American groups. 2.

The Huron and the Iroquois, for example, were traditional rivals. The Huron, who had friendly relations with the French, served as middlemen between other groups and French traders. The Dutch, eager for a share of the rich fur trade, encouraged their Iroquois allies to attack the Huron. The Hurons were

2. **MAIN IDEA** Have students explain how Native Americans were affected by the fur trade.

3. **ECONOMICS** Women played an important role in the Creek economy. Most of the farming was done by the women while the men were on hunting trips or at war.

NOTABLE AMERICANS

Coosaponakeesa: A Woman Ahead of Her Time

Coosaponakeesa (coo suh PAHN uh KEE suh) was a woman who had to struggle to be taken seriously. With one foot in Creek society and one foot in colonial society, she played a unique role in the America of the 1700s.

Coosaponakeesa was born around 1700 to a Creek mother and an English father. She married a South Carolina fur trader named John Musgrove and took the name Mary Musgrove. Yet she kept her links with the Creek nation. As a leader of a ruling clan, she called herself a "queen" and ran a trading business

3. in the independent tradition of Creek women.

Colonial leaders, seeking friendly relations with the Creek, saw her as a vital link. To James Oglethorpe and the founders of Georgia, the Creek were useful trading partners and a vital buffer against the Spanish in Florida. As Mary Musgrove, Coosaponakeesa

helped to cement friendship between the colonists and the Creek. She promoted the trading interests of the Creek, and she rallied the Creek in support of Oglethorpe against the Spanish.

But when Coosaponakeesa sought recognition as a Creek leader in 1749, the colonials scorned her. They dismissed her as "only a woman," put her in jail briefly, and dealt with the Creek's male leaders.

Despite this, Coosaponakeesa promoted strong English-Creek friendship when the French made efforts to woo the Creek. By supporting British interests, she played an important part in history.

See p. T15.

1. What was Coosaponakeesa's unique role?

2. **Critical Thinking** Why do you suppose English settlers resisted the idea that a woman could be a leader?

1. **BIOGRAPHY** William Johnson, an English trader who married the daughter of a Mohawk chief, arranged an alliance between the Iroquois and the English.

3. **CRITICAL THINKING** Ask: How do you think European nobles reacted to Native Americans who visited Europe?

outmatched by the more numerous and better-armed Iroquois. The Iroquois drove the surviving Hurons westward toward the Mississippi.

The English who replaced the Dutch in New Amsterdam (renamed New York) also profited from the warfare. By pitting the Iroquois against Indian nations that allied with the French, they struck a blow at French power in North America. Native Americans would eventually be drawn in on both sides when war broke out between the French and the British in 1754.

The British and Native Americans

The few French fur traders and trappers did not encroach heavily on Indian lands in New France. By contrast, British settlements were permanent and far more numerous. More often than not, the British farmers' hunger for land pushed the Native Americans out of their territory. Sometimes this was done by
1. treaty, but often settlers simply moved into Indian lands and began clearing the forest for planting. Indian opposition produced repeated violence along the frontier.

In 1636, the Pequot (PEE kwaht) resisted English settlement in the Connecticut Valley. In the Pequot War that followed, colonists attacked and burned a major Pequot town, killing 600 men, women, and children.

Almost 40 years later, in 1675, another war, known as King Philip's War, broke out between Native Americans and colonists in New England. The Indians imposed heavy losses on the New England militia and destroyed 13 frontier towns, but the Indians were ultimately defeated. After that, settlers in New England generally met little resistance.

Some early English settlers had established harmonious relations with the Indians. Roger Williams and William Penn were known for negotiating fair treaties and paying for their land. But, in general, the competition for land between Native Americans and
2. English settlers led to conflict.

Although some Indian groups were able to resist English expansion for a while, rivalries among the groups made a united effort difficult. As a result, the settlers steadily pushed the Indians farther west.

Iroquois chief Ho Nee Yeath Taw No Row, also called John Wolf Clan, visited London in 1710. The Dutch artist John Verelst painted this portrait during the visit. 3.

See p. T15.

SECTION 2 REVIEW

1. **Identify:** (a) Louis XIV, (b) Joliet, (c) Marquette, (d) La Salle, (e) coureur de bois, (f) Pequot War.

2. Where and why did the English and Spanish compete in North America?

3. (a) What was Louis XIV's design for New France? (b) Why did it fail? (c) What two French activities in North America were successful?

4. **Critical Thinking** Considering the size of the land and the relatively small populations involved, why did the arrival of Europeans disrupt Indian society?

2. **BACKGROUND** French relations with the Indians were not all peaceful either. The French waged an ongoing war against the Iroquois, Sauk, and Fox.

3 The French and Indian War

READ TO UNDERSTAND

■ What circumstances led to the French and Indian War.

■ How William Pitt helped turn the tide of the war.

■ How the Treaty of Paris of 1763 redrew land boundaries.

By the mid-1700s, land speculation was reaching a fever pitch in Virginia. Tobacco had already exhausted the land in the tidewater region, and planters looked for land west of the Appalachians for themselves and their heirs. Meanwhile, a French military expedition in the Ohio Valley was placing engraved lead plates along the shores of the waterways in the valley to make clear their claim to the area. The scene was being set for a heated conflict that would decide once and for all whether Britain or France would control much of North America.

European Conflict in America

Competition for North American territory was part of a larger struggle between Great Britain, France, and Spain for dominance of Europe. As Spain's power waned after the defeat of the Armada in 1588, the power of Britain and France steadily increased. A showdown between the two was simply a matter of time.

France and Britain had gone to war in Europe three times since the late 1680s. Beyond some border skirmishes, colonists were little affected by these wars. But this was destined to change. A fourth war, known as 1. the French and Indian War, began in the lush Ohio Valley.

France claimed the region, but the British colonies had been expanding toward the valley for more than a decade. In fact, some prominent Virginians had formed the Ohio Company to encourage settlers to move into 86 the valley. As the pace of British settlement

increased, the French expanded a line of forts to defend the territory.

The Albany Congress

In June 1754, representatives from New Hampshire, Massachusetts, Connecticut, Rhode Island, Pennsylvania, Maryland, and New York met in Albany, New York, with representatives from the Iroquois League. The colonists wanted to solidify their friendship with the Iroquois and plan a common defense against the French and their Indian allies.

Discussion centered on the best way to defend the colonies, but also included the possibility of a union of the colonies. The delegates drew up a plan, called the Albany Plan of Union, which was designed to unite the 13 colonies under a single government.

When the Plan of Union was submitted to the individual colonial governments, however, not one approved it. Most colonial legislators thought it called for too much control by a central government. Benjamin Franklin, author of the original plan, lamented, "Everyone cries a union is necessary, but when they come to the manner and form of the union, their weak noodles are perfectly distracted."   2.

Early French Victories

While the representatives argued at Albany, the French finished building their line of forts along the Ohio River. At the same time, George Washington, a 22-year-old officer in the Virginia militia, led 150 soldiers into western Pennsylvania to construct forts for the British.

On March 28, 1754, Washington's troops fired on a small party of French soldiers and took them prisoner. Learning that a larger French force was about to move against them, the colonists hastily built a stockade and called it Fort Necessity.   3.

The fort was quickly attacked by a combined force of almost 1,000 French soldiers and their Indian allies. Washington and his small party could not withstand the siege and surrendered on July 3. This was the first of a series of French victories.

2. **CRITICAL THINKING** Ask: Although the colonies did not approve the Plan of Union, why was the meeting at Albany considered significant?

3. **GEOGRAPHY** As they read, have students locate each fort on the map on p. 87. (location)

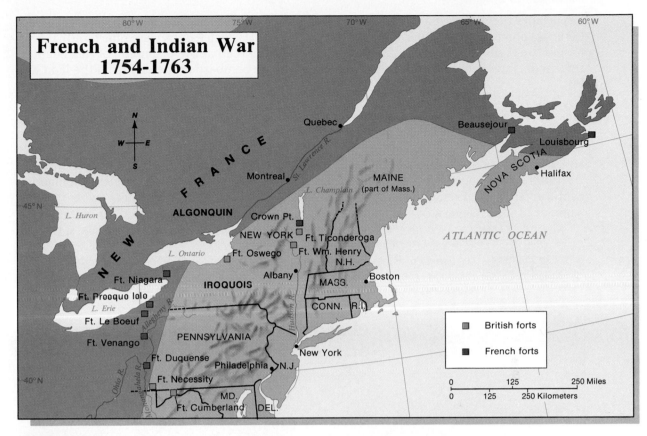

French and Indian War
1754-1763

British forts
French forts

0   125   250 Miles
0   125   250 Kilometers

MAP STUDY In the French and Indian War, both sides fought for control of key western forts. Locate the French forts on the map. What effect would the capture of these forts have had on the French effort to protect its rights in Canada, or New France, as it was called? See p. T15.

1.

1. **MAP READING** Have students identify the French forts that were nearest to British forts.

The following year, General Edward Braddock took command of British colonial forces. With 2,500 soldiers, Braddock began cutting a road through the wilderness of western Pennsylvania to Fort Duquesne (doo KAYN), a French stronghold at the junction of the Allegheny and Monongahela (muh NANH guh HEE luh) rivers.

When Braddock was within ten miles of the fort, the French and their Indian allies launched an ambush. On July 9, just after the red-coated British soldiers had crossed the Monongahela, they were mowed down by musket fire. Braddock and 900 soldiers perished. The surviving British troops fled to the safety of Philadelphia.

That same year, the British tried and failed to capture Fort Niagara. A campaign against Crown Point, led by William Johnson, ended in a virtual draw. The British, however, desperately in need of success, proclaimed Johnson the victor and knighted him.

2.

Pitt and British Victories

In 1756, William Pitt became the British secretary of state. He moved quickly to reverse the string of British defeats. Pitt was a vigorous, uncompromising man, brimming with confidence. "I am sure that I can save the country, and that no one else can," he remarked, and he promptly set out to do just that.

Pitt united the previously divided colonies by guaranteeing the colonists payments for military service and supplies. He also dismissed older military commanders and installed more capable young officers. Two of these, General Jeffrey Amherst and General James Wolfe, captured Louisbourg, the most

87

2. **DISCUSSION** Ask: Why would it be advantageous for a country at war to claim a victory when no victory actually occurred?

1. PAST AND PRESENT Fort Pitt became the city of Pittsburgh, Pennsylvania.

important French Canadian fortress, in 1758. General John Forbes, another Pitt appointee, forced the French to abandon and burn Fort Duquesne, later rebuilt by the British as Fort
1. Pitt.

In 1759, Pitt planned a three-pronged attack on the French: first, capture Fort Niagara to cut off the Great Lakes from the east; second, clear Lake Champlain of French forts; and, third, strike at Quebec itself.

Pitt's plan succeeded. British troops captured strategic French forts. In the early summer of 1759, General Wolfe and his fleet

2. VISUAL EVIDENCE Refer students to the painting on p. 77.

sailed up the St. Lawrence to Quebec, where 15,000 French troops were quartered. At first, as you read at the beginning of this chapter, 2. Wolfe bombarded the city from the land and the water but failed to draw the French into open battle. Then he ordered his troops to mount a surprise attack by scaling the cliffs below Quebec during the dead of night. Wolfe hoped to draw Montcalm out of his fortress by coming between him and his supplies.

On September 13, the French commander, Louis Joseph de Montcalm, awoke to find 5,000 British troops arrayed for battle on the

3. MAP READING Have students compare this map to the United States map on pp. 840–841. Ask: In 1763, what nation controlled the area where you now live? Is there any evidence of that control remaining today?

MAP STUDY *The Treaty of Paris drastically changed the map of North America. Compare this map to the map on page 83. How was North America in 1763 different from North America in 1753?* See p. T15.   3.

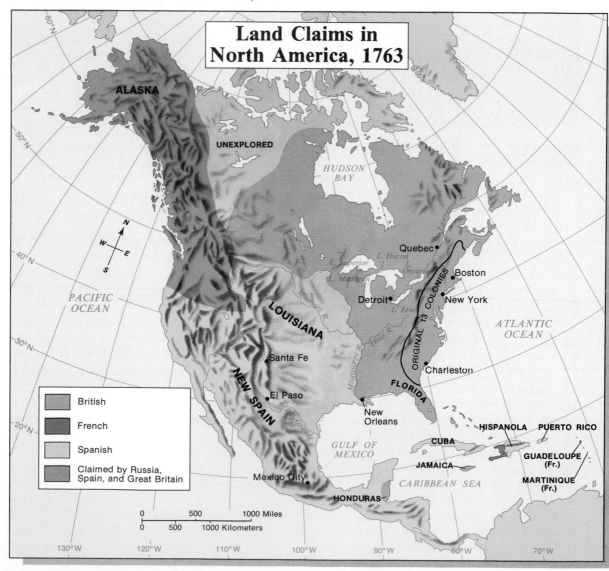

Land Claims in North America, 1763

Legend:
- British
- French
- Spanish
- Claimed by Russia, Spain, and Great Britain

ALASKA

UNEXPLORED

HUDSON BAY

PACIFIC OCEAN

LOUISIANA

NEW SPAIN

Santa Fe

El Paso

Quebec

Detroit

Boston

New York

ORIGINAL 13 COLONIES

Charleston

FLORIDA

New Orleans

ATLANTIC OCEAN

GULF OF MEXICO

CUBA

JAMAICA

HISPANOLA

PUERTO RICO

GUADELOUPE (Fr.)

MARTINIQUE (Fr.)

CARIBBEAN SEA

Mexico City

HONDURAS

0 500 1000 Miles
0 500 1000 Kilometers

General Braddock tried to seize Fort Duquesne during the French and Indian War, but his red-coated forces were an easy target for an ambush. After Braddock was
1. *killed, Lt. Colonel George Washington led the survivors back to Fort Cumberland.*

1. PAST AND PRESENT Ask: What color are most soldiers' uniforms today? Is this color better-suited for battle conditions than the red worn by the British in the picture? Explain.

Plains of Abraham outside the city. With only a scant supply of food in his camp, Montcalm knew he would have to fight. In the bloody battle that followed, both Montcalm and Wolfe were killed. On September 17, Quebec surrendered to the British.

Return of Peace

Although fighting continued between the major powers and their allies in Europe, the fall of Quebec signaled the fall of France's
2. American empire.

According to the Treaty of Paris of 1763, France granted Canada and lands east of the Mississippi River to Great Britain. Spain, which had entered the war against England in 1762 in alarm at British success, gave up Florida to Britain. In return, Spain received French lands west of the Mississippi. France kept two islands in the Gulf of St. Lawrence and the prosperous sugar-producing islands of Guadeloupe and Martinique in the Caribbean.

The English colonies, which had been confined to the Atlantic coast, now stretched as far west as the Mississippi River. With the French and the Spanish removed from their flanks, the colonists looked toward a new frontier. Wagons were soon rolling westward.

See p. T16.

See p. T16.

SECTION 3 REVIEW

1. **Identify:** (a) Plan of Union, (b) Benjamin Franklin, (c) William Pitt.

2. What incident led to the French and Indian War?

3. Why was the Albany Conference held?

4. How did William Pitt help turn the tide of war in Britain's favor?

5. What were the terms of the Treaty of Paris?

6. **Critical Thinking** Why was control of Quebec critical to the outcome of the French and Indian War?

2. CITIZENSHIP Have students imagine that they are French Canadians in 1763. Ask them to write a letter describing their feelings about the British victory.

CHAPTER 4 REVIEW

Summary

1. **During the 1600s, European nations competed for power in Europe and throughout the world.** Behind the fierce competition for colonies was the mercantilist theory. Both England and the American colonies benefited from this system, but the colonists resisted efforts to control the triangular trade.

2. **As England strengthened its hold on land in North America, it came into conflict with France and Spain.** The only serious area of conflict with Spain was in the region around Spanish Florida. France provided more of a threat because Britain and France had more extensive conflicting claims to territory in the Northeast.

3. **Problems with France erupted into a major war in 1754.** Both Great Britain and France allied with Native Americans by exploiting longstanding rivalries. The combined efforts of the British and the colonists defeated the French. As a result of the Treaty of Paris of 1763, France was all but eliminated from North America.

See p. T16.

Vocabulary

On a separate sheet of paper, write the word or words that best complete each of the following sentences.

1. An economic system in which each nation attempted to sell more than it bought was called _____.

2. _____ were colonial products that could be shipped only to England.

3. The pattern of exchange of goods between New England, the West Indies, and England was known as the _____.

4. French fur trappers and traders were called _____.

5. An early plan to unite the 13 colonies under a single government was the _____.

See p. T16.

Chapter Checkup

1. Why did the English government want to control trade in the colonies?

2. Describe the major provisions of the Navigation Acts.

3. Explain the effects of the Navigation Acts and the Molasses Act on trade in the 1770s.

4. (a) In what areas in the Americas did the British Empire compete with the Spanish? (b) In what areas did the British Empire compete with the French?

5. (a) What impact did the French fur trade have on the Indians? (b) What impact did English settlement have? (c) Which was most likely to lead to violent conflict? Why?

6. What developments helped Britain and the colonists win the French and Indian War?

See p. T16.

Critical Thinking

1. **Evaluating Information**   Sir Walter Raleigh said, "Whoever commands the trade of the world commands the riches of the world and consequently the world itself." Does this seem to have been true for Great Britain in 1763?

2. **Analyzing**   Some people have argued that conflict in North America between the English and the French and Spanish was inevitable. Do you agree? Explain.

See p. T16.

Connecting Past and Present

1. Under the mercantilist system, exporting more than one imported was important for the economic health of a country. Is the United States today concerned with how much it imports and how much it exports? Why or why not?

2. Part of the friction between the Indians and the Europeans was caused by a clash of cultures. How do differences in values lead to misunderstandings between nations today?

See p. T16.

Developing Basic Skills

1. **Map Reading**   Study the map on page 88. (a) Where is British territory? (b) Spanish territory? (c) French territory? (d) Which nation would probably be Britain's main territorial rival after 1763?

2. **Map Reading**   If you compare maps, you can often gain insight into historical developments. Compare the maps on pages 83 and 88. (a) Which nation gained the most territory east of the Mississippi River? (b) Which lost the most?

WRITING ABOUT HISTORY

Developing a Topic

Support your topic sentence with specific, related information. Supporting information can include examples, details, facts, reasons, and incidents. A paragraph may include one kind or several kinds of support.

■ **Examples**   Specific instances that provide evidence to support a generalization.

Topic: The British government passed many measures to tighten its control over colonial trade. *Supporting examples:* For example, the Navigation Acts forbade colonial merchants from shipping goods on any but colonial or English-owned vessels. Most goods could be shipped to England only. The Molasses Act required the colonists to import rum only from the British West Indies.

■ **Details**   Descriptive pieces of additional information.

Topic: John Verelst's painting of the Iroquois chief Ho Nee Yeath Taw No Row was not unlike a painting of a European monarch. *Supporting details:* The painter used the same kinds of symbols of power and majesty. The chief's red blanket was draped across his shoulders like a royal robe. In his hand he held a bow—a symbol of his power.

■ **Facts**   Verifiable information.

Topic: The population of the British colonies increased rapidly. *Supporting facts:* By the late 1600s, there were 200,000 people living in the British colonies. By the mid-1700s, the population had reached 1,500,000. At the same time, the much larger territory of New France had only 70,000 colonists.

■ **Reasons**   Causes for the main idea.

Topic: Colonies were important to a nation's independence. *Supporting reasons:* Colonies provided raw materials and markets for manufactured goods so that a nation could be self-sufficient.

■ **Incidents**   Related events or a story that illustrates the main idea.

Topic: The British needed luck to win the French and Indian War. *Supporting incidents:* British troops bombarded Quebec but could not draw the French out of their fortress. Then the British spotted a soldier walking along a hidden path to the water. By climbing that path in the dark, the British surprised the French and engaged them in battle.

Practice: For each Critical Thinking question you answer, underline the topic sentence once and supporting information twice.

Unit Two CREATING A REPUBLIC

As the split between Britain and the colonies grew, some colonists directed their anger at King George III. This painting shows New Yorkers tearing down a statue of him.

1775 At the battle of Bunker Hill, American troops showed they could hold their own against the British.

	1760	1765	1770	1775
POLITICS AND GOVERNMENT		**1763** Proclamation limits westward expansion by colonists	**1770** Boston Massacre	
SOCIETY AND CULTURE		**1765** Daughters of Liberty protest the Stamp Act	**1772** Committees of Correspondence formed	
ECONOMICS AND TECHNOLOGY		**1764** Sugar Act passes to raise revenue	**1773** Boston Tea Party held to protest Tea Act	
WORLD EVENTS		**1763** War between France and Britain ends	**1770** Lord North becomes prime minister of Britain	

1765 The Stamp Act required stamps on items such as legal documents, newspapers, and pamphlets.

1775 John Paul Jones was a commander in the Continental Navy, which was formed in 1775.

1788 By ratifying the Constitution, the American states created a nation based on law.

Many Native Americans, including Joseph Brant, a Mohawk Chief, fought with the British against the colonists.

1775   1780   1785   1790

1776 Colonies declare independence from Britain

1783 War for Independence ends

1788 Constitution of the United States is ratified

1777 Vermont abolishes slavery

1786 Virginia law separates church and state

1780s Trade begins with China

1787 Northwest Ordinance controls settlement of western lands

1778 French become allies of the Americans

1789 Revolution breaks out in France

The economy of the new nation would be built on its agriculture and manufacturing, such as glassmaking.

Early in the nation's history, the eagle came to symbolize the United States.

The Road to Revolution (1763–1775)

5

CHAPTER OUTLINE

1 Problems of Britain's New Empire

2 The Quarrel Widens

3 The Roots of Independence

4 From Protest to Revolution

CHAPTER OBJECTIVES After completing this chapter, students should be able to
1. list events that increased tensions between Britain and the colonies.
2. explain why fighting began.
3. describe the trend toward unity in the colonies.
4. analyze a primary source.

CHAPTER PREVIEW Before they begin reading the chapter, students should scan it, reading the section titles and subtitles. Ask: What is the chapter about? How can you tell?

A light breeze rustled the trees outside the Warren farmhouse. Inside, Mercy Otis Warren put down her needlework to adjust the oil lamp. Its light reflected off the faces of her husband and a visitor from Boston, her brother James. Upstairs, the Warrens' five sons slept soundly.

All seemed peaceful on that spring evening in 1765 except for the angry tones of James Otis as he reported the latest news. Once more the British were trying to tax the colonists in order to pay off their huge national debt. Part of the debt came from the cost of defending the colonies. But Otis, a successful lawyer, resented how Parliament imposed laws on the colonies without consulting them. This time it was the Stamp Act.

"The people despise the Stamp Act," Otis told the Warrens. "We must meet with committees from the assemblies of each colony and discuss how to get it repealed." Otis's plan resulted in the Stamp Act Congress that you will read about later. But James Otis paid heavily for his efforts, becoming a target of the

king's supporters. One evening in 1770, he was so brutally beaten that from then on he suffered periods of insanity.

Growing political tensions and her brother's sad condition strengthened Mercy Warren's commitment to the cause of liberty. Encouraged by friends such as John and Abigail Adams, she began writing letters, plays, and pamphlets that promoted the cause of self-government. "And be it known to Britain," she warned, "even American daughters are politicians and patriots and will aid the good work with their female efforts."

In 1772, Warren published the first of her five popular plays. Her characters, such as Hum Humbug, Judge Meagre, and Sir Spend-all, poked fun at well-known allies of the king.

Warren was one of many writers drawn into an angry war of words between the colonies and Britain. By 1775, American colonists and British troops were exchanging bullets as well. Some colonists were even considering independence.

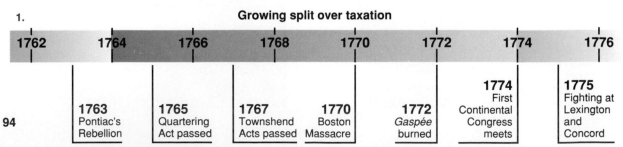

1. **Growing split over taxation**

1762	1764	1766	1768	1770	1772	1774	1776
	1763 Pontiac's Rebellion	**1765** Quartering Act passed	**1767** Townshend Acts passed	**1770** Boston Massacre	**1772** *Gaspée* burned	**1774** First Continental Congress meets	**1775** Fighting at Lexington and Concord

94

1. **TIME LINE QUESTION** Ask: How long after the Townshend Acts were passed did the Boston Massacre take place?

Tensions rose as the British imposed taxes to pay off their huge national debt.
Gradually, more and more colonists favored independence. In some towns, they
1. raised liberty poles, like the one shown here, to demonstrate their support of freedom.

1. **VISUAL EVIDENCE** Liberty poles were also known as liberty trees. The first liberty tree
was a Boston elm. A group called the Sons of Liberty met under the tree to denounce
British treatment of the colonies.

Problems of Britain's New Empire

READ TO UNDERSTAND

■ What problems faced Britain after the French and Indian War.

■ How Britain tried to ease its burden of debt.

■ How the colonies reacted to the Stamp Act.

The French and Indian War left Britain master of North America east of the Mississippi River. But this domain was only part of the war's legacy. Britain's victory brought with it a host of problems. How should the Native Americans be dealt with? Should settlers be allowed in the fertile Ohio Valley west of the Appalachians? How could the staggering war debt be paid? 2.

Ironically, British attempts to answer these questions created new and even more disturbing problems. The strain drove a wedge between Britain and its American colonies that would eventually split the two apart.

An Uneasy Frontier

The unsettled situation in the lands west of the 13 British colonies demanded immediate action. As the lure of the frontier drew American colonists into the area, the newcomers came into conflict with the Indian nations and the few French farmers and traders who lived there. And if this were not enough, several colonies stubbornly claimed that their boundaries extended all the way to the Pacific. To reinforce their claims, they promptly

95

2. **ACTIVITY** Have students propose possible solutions to Britain's problems in America.
After they have read the section, ask them to compare their ideas with what happened.

1. **MAP READING** Ask: Which colonies were affected by the Proclamation of 1763? Which were not affected?

2. **DISCUSSION** Remind students that Amherst led the British to victory at Louisbourg (p. 87). Ask: Why do you think Amherst governed the area in the way described here?

built a road over the Appalachian Mountains into the Ohio Valley.

Britain tried to head off open conflict by stationing troops in the frontier territory under the command of General Jeffrey Amherst. But Amherst bungled the efforts to maintain peace. He not only allowed settlers to

build forts in western New York and present-day Ohio in violation of treaties with the local Indian nations, he also refused to pay the Indians for their land. The French had long cultivated friendly relations with Native Americans by trading supplies and offering gifts and credit. The arrogant Amherst, in contrast, was determined to force the Indians into submission.

2.

In spring 1763, Amherst harvested the bitter fruits of his efforts. Pontiac, an Ottawa chief, led the combined forces of the Seneca, the Delaware, the Shawnee, and other western nations in a rebellion against the British. As Pontiac's forces swept through the Ohio Valley, Amherst struggled to hold on to Fort Pitt, Fort Detroit, and Fort Niagara.

For nearly a year, war seared the western frontier. But Pontiac's tribal union collapsed when the Native Americans learned they could no longer expect help from the French. By December, peace had been restored.

MAP STUDY *To reduce friction with Native Americans, the British issued the Proclamation of 1763, forbidding settlement west of an imaginary line along the crest of the Appalachians. Settlers already living in the area*
1. *were ordered to leave "forthwith." Do you think the Proclamation line would be easy to enforce? Why or why not?* See p. T18.

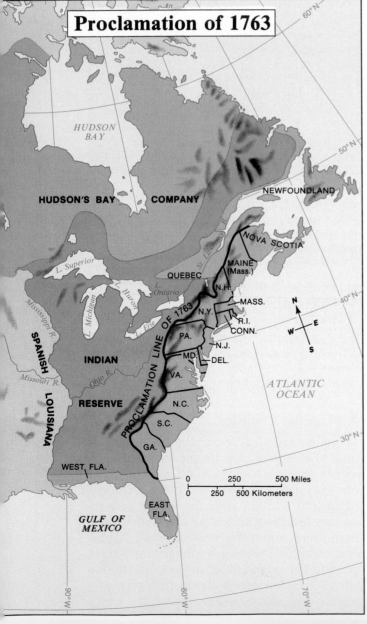

Proclamation of 1763

HUDSON BAY

HUDSON'S BAY COMPANY

NEWFOUNDLAND

L. Superior

NOVA SCOTIA

QUEBEC

MAINE (Mass.)

N.H.

L. Ontario

MASS.

N.Y.

R.I.

CONN.

PROCLAMATION LINE OF 1763

PA.

N.J.

MD.

DEL.

SPANISH

L. Michigan

L. Huron

L. Erie

INDIAN

Mississippi R.

Missouri R.

Ohio R.

VA.

ATLANTIC OCEAN

RESERVE

N.C.

LOUISIANA

S.C.

GA.

WEST FLA.

0   250   500 Miles

0   250   500 Kilometers

EAST FLA.

GULF OF MEXICO

The Proclamation of 1763

The fear of Indian unrest forced the British to review their western land policy. The new plan, unveiled in the Proclamation of 1763, established a boundary between Native American and colonial lands. According to the proclamation, no colonists could enter the area west of the Appalachians without permission from British authorities. Those colonists already living there were ordered "forthwith to remove themselves."

The British government wanted to reduce the cost of protecting settlers by limiting their contact with the Indians. But with the French gone, many colonists had hoped for unchecked expansion of the frontier. Now the colonists saw that they were to be tightly controlled and that revenues from the western fur trade and land speculation would be out of their reach.

The colonists resented the British troops stationed west of the Appalachians. After their 3. successes in the French and Indian War, most Americans were convinced that they could do with less, not more, supervision by the British government. And they bristled at the suggestion that they pay more taxes to ease the empire's finances.

3. **BACKGROUND** To enforce the Proclamation, the British stationed 6,000 troops in the western region.

Goods headed for the American colonies had to pass through a British port, where duties were imposed. Port towns, such as Bristol, shown here, thrived **1.** because of this trade. Colonists, however, resented the customs duties and often tried to evade them.

---

1. VISUAL EVIDENCE Ask: What evidence can you find in the picture of an active trade?

The Empire's Empty Treasury

When George Grenville became the British chancellor of the exchequer in April 1763, he faced a staggering national debt. The wars Britain had just concluded in Europe, America, and India had created budgets running 20 times their prewar size. Moreover, Grenville discovered that by smuggling, bribery, or both, the colonists were evading British customs duties. Salaries for British customs officials were four times greater than the duties they collected. Grenville was determined that the colonies would yield profits for the king and shoulder some of the burden of Britain's war debt. With Parliament, he designed a series of measures to bring **2.** this about.

In April 1764, Parliament passed the Sugar Act. This law lowered the molasses duty and levied new taxes on sugar and other commodities. The cut in rates set by the Molasses Act (see page 80) did not benefit the colonists, however, because Grenville planned to enforce the Sugar Act. Almost no one had actually paid the old duties on molasses.

The Sugar Act represented an important departure from previous British policy. Its purpose was not only to regulate colonial

2. MAIN IDEA Have students explain Grenville's goals as chancellor of the exchequer.

trade, a power of Parliament the colonists accepted, but also to raise revenue. The colonists saw this as a form of taxation, which they opposed even though their taxes were much lower than those in England. (For example, the people in Massachusetts were taxed at about 4 percent of the rate charged in England.)

Most Americans firmly believed that, as British subjects, they should not be taxed without the consent of their representatives, who sat in colonial legislatures, not Parliament. If Britain wanted money, it should ask the colonial legislatures to raise it. Revenue taxes levied directly by Parliament threatened the tradition of "no taxation without representation." If such actions went unchallenged, the colonists realized that taking part in colonial government might become meaningless. **3.**

Growing Pressure

The Currency Act of 1764 and the Quartering Act of 1765 angered the colonists even more. The Currency Act struck yet another blow at American control of their own finances. It **97** prohibited the colonial governments from is-

3. PAST AND PRESENT Have students compare Britain's national debt problem in 1763 with that of the U.S. today. Ask: How did Britain try to pay the debt? What is the U.S. doing to pay its debt?

1. **ECONOMICS** Have students explain in their own words the provisions and purpose of the Currency Act.

suing any more paper money and demanded that they immediately recall all the paper money in circulation. Furthermore, the act stated that taxes and debts owed to British merchants be paid in British silver currency. In the colonies, silver currency was in short supply.

Instead, the colonists depended on paper money. Great Britain, in keeping with mercantilist theory, had drained silver from the colonies by restricting trade and selling the colonists manufactured goods. The colonists had reacted by printing colonial currency and paying taxes and debts with it, but the paper money had less value than silver. In effect, the colonists were getting a discount on goods, debts, and taxes, while the British were losing money. The Currency Act stopped this practice.

The Quartering Act required that the colonists help support the several thousand British troops stationed in the colonies. Upon demand, Americans were to provide barracks, candles, bedding, and beverages to soldiers stationed in their area. That burden intensified the general ill will the colonists felt toward Britain.

The Stamp Act

The Sugar Act, Currency Act, and Quartering Act were just a beginning. In 1765, Grenville introduced the Stamp Act. This law required that a tax stamp be attached to a wide variety of items. It taxed all legal documents, as well as almanacs, newspapers, pamphlets, playing cards, and dice.

The tax stamps were not particularly costly. They sparked intense anger, however, because they were highly visible. Unlike the duties levied by the Sugar and Molasses acts, the stamps could not be overlooked. There seemed to be no way to avoid paying for them.

Of even greater concern was the fact that violators of the Stamp Act would not face a jury of sympathetic colonists in regular colonial courts. To ensure compliance, Grenville planned to try them in the Vice-Admiralty Courts. In the past, Vice-Admiralty Courts had been used only for laws broken at sea. Using the Admiralty Courts for domestic cases threatened the colonists' cherished liberties.

The Stamp Act produced a storm of protest throughout the colonies. The Pennsylvania Journal mocked the act and published this cartoon of "the fatal stamp."

2. **VISUAL EVIDENCE** Have students look at the picture of the real stamp on page 92.

A Question of Representation

Perhaps most important, the Stamp Act again raised the issue of "taxation without representation." Unlike the Sugar Act, which at least claimed to regulate trade, the Stamp Act was an outright tax. The British government had assumed powers that the colonists felt belonged to their representative assemblies, not Parliament.

British officials countered the colonists' complaints by arguing that all members of Parliament represented all British subjects. Even though the colonists had not elected specific members of Parliament, their interests were represented there. Thus Parliament could tax them.

Although Americans complained loudly, they did not really want to be represented in Parliament. They knew that at a distance of 3,000 miles (4,800 kilometers), communication with representatives would be impossible. Americans wanted colonial legislatures to continue to be responsible for tax laws, as they always had been. An editorial in the Providence, Rhode Island, *Gazette* summed up the American position.

> It is really a piece of mockery to tell us that a country, detached from Britain by an ocean of immense breadth, and which is so extensive and populous, should be represented by the British members, or that we can have any interest in the House of Commons.

American Reaction

Before the Stamp Act took effect, colonists demonstrated that they would back their principles with action. From Massachusetts

98

3. **ACTIVITY** Have students complete this editorial as they continue reading. Tell them to include the colonists' other complaints, as explained later.

1. **CRITICAL THINKING** Ask: How did the Stamp Act Congress show that British policies were welding the colonies together? What did this mean for Britain?

2. **ACTIVITY** Have students, working in groups, write petitions that might have been sent to the king and Parliament by the Stamp Act Congress.

to South Carolina, mobs, often calling themselves the Sons of Liberty, stopped attempts to unload stamped papers. Stamp tax collectors all over the colonies became uneasy as they weighed the value of their jobs against the threat of hot tar and feathers. Many chose to resign.

On the morning of August 14, 1765, a Boston mob hanged the Massachusetts stamp distributor in effigy. Later, they destroyed the stamp tax collector's warehouse, tearing it apart board by board. They chopped off the effigy's head, "stamped" its body, and burned the remains in a bonfire made from the timbers of the collector's building. Next, they attacked the stamp collector's house and ransacked the rooms. When the Massachusetts lieutenant governor tried to disperse the crowd, they stoned him and chased him off into the night. Satisfied, the mob finally dispersed at midnight.

Colonists also took political action against the Stamp Act. In October 1765, representatives from nine colonies called a Stamp Act
1. Congress to convene in New York. They drew up a petition to King George and Parliament,

stating their position on Parliament's recent actions.

The petition granted that the colonies were legally under the control of Parliament and that the British government had the power to regulate colonial trade. But it denied that Britain's legislature had the right to tax the colonists; only the colonial assemblies could rightfully do that. Finally, it asked the king and Parliament to repeal the Stamp 2. and Sugar acts.

Colonial merchants backed up the appeal by boycotting British goods. The Daughters of Liberty, a protest group formed by colonial women, supported the boycott and urged colonists to use "homespun" instead of British manufactured cloth.

The boycott did disrupt the British economy, producing the desired effect. In March 1766, Parliament repealed the Stamp Act. Yet, stung by colonial defiance and fearful that repeal might be interpreted as weakness, Parliament passed the Declaratory Act. This legislation denied the claims of the Stamp Act Congress and, in effect, reasserted Parliament's authority to tax the colonies.

3. **GRAPH READING** Ask: In what period was there a surge in imports? What does that indicate about relations between Britain and the colonies during that period?

GRAPH STUDY Colonists boycotted British goods in 1765 and 1766 to protest the Stamp Act, in late 1768 and 1769 to protest the Townshend Acts (see page 100), and again in 1775 and 1776. How does the graph reflect the effect of these boycotts? See p. T18. 3.

Imports From Great Britain 1763–1776

Value of Goods Imported to America From Great Britain

Thousands of Pounds Sterling

Year

Source: *Historical Statistics of the United States*

1. **BIOGRAPHY** Have interested students research the earlier life of one of the men mentioned here and report their findings to the class.

2. **VOCABULARY** Have students look up these terms in the glossary before they begin reading.

Consequences of the Stamp Act

The Stamp Act had far-reaching consequences. It created colonial unity where disagreement had been the rule. The same colonists who had been unable to agree to a plan of union at the Albany Congress in the 1750s stood together in the 1760s. While accepting Parliament's right to regulate trade, they firmly rejected its right to tax them.

Perhaps even more important, colonial opposition to the Stamp Act brought to the public arena men whose names would haunt the British in the years to come. Among them were Patrick Henry and George Washington in Virginia and cousins Samuel Adams and 1. John Adams in Massachusetts.

One other Virginian would not emerge into the public eye for some time, but he was present during the Stamp Act debates in the Virginia House of Burgesses. A law student, aged 22, stood outside the legislature, thrilled at what he called Patrick Henry's "torrents of sublime eloquence." Although he was too young in 1765 to sit in the House of Burgesses, 11 years later his own words would stir the people to revolution. His name was Thomas Jefferson.

See p. T18.

SECTION 1 REVIEW

1. **Identify:** (a) Pontiac, (b) Proclamation of 1763, (c) George Grenville, (d) Sons of Liberty, (e) Stamp Act Congress, (f) Daughters of Liberty.

2. What problems confronted the British after the French and Indian War?

3. What events led to Pontiac's Rebellion?

4. In what way was the Sugar Act a departure from Britain's former colonial policy?

5. (a) What were the provisions of the Currency Act? (b) Of the Quartering Act? (c) Of the Stamp Act?

6. **Critical Thinking** How did some colonists' view of representative government differ from that of Parliament?

2 The Quarrel Widens

READ TO UNDERSTAND

■ What were the purpose and provisions of the Townshend Acts.

■ How Townshend tried to reassert British authority over the colonies.

■ Why Parliament repealed the Townshend Acts.

■ *Vocabulary:* nonimportation agreement, writs of 2. assistance.

As the colonists rejoiced over the repeal of 3. the Stamp Act, British nobles grumbled that the government had "sacrificed gentlemen to the interests of traders and colonists." In 1767, the newly appointed chancellor of the exchequer, Charles Townshend, faced the same problems that George Grenville had faced in 1763: making the colonies more profitable and reducing the national debt.

The Townshend Acts

By 1767, a sharp depression that led to outbursts of violence in Britain limited Townshend's choices. Parliament was forced to cut taxes at home. This made Townshend even more determined to gain additional revenue from the colonies.

The revenue measures passed by Parliament in 1767 soon became known as the Townshend Acts. In the end, they met the same fate as Grenville's legislation—disastrous failure and repeal.

The Townshend Acts placed small customs duties on glass, tea, paper, paint, and lead, all items that the colonists imported from Britain. The revenues from these duties would pay the cost of colonial administration, including governors' and judges' salaries. Because the colonial assemblies traditionally paid these expenses, Townshend's measures seemed to be another attack on their authority.

Townshend thought he could convince opponents of the measures that the duties were merely regulations of trade. After all,

3. **DISCUSSION** Ask: Do you think the colonists had good reason to rejoice, even though Britain had passed the Declaratory Act? Explain.

he argued, the colonists agreed that Parliament had the right to control trade. But no one was convinced. Americans saw the acts for what they were: taxes to raise money, not duties to encourage trade. In fact, the measures even hurt British trade. They encouraged the colonists to manufacture goods rather than to import them from England.

Protest welled up in the colonies. In 1768, merchants from Philadelphia, New York, and Boston reacted to the Townshend Acts with a **nonimportation agreement,** vowing not to import certain articles rather than pay the tax. Later, they were joined by southern merchants and planters. Suddenly, it became more fashionable to use colonial-made goods than English luxury items.

Asserting British Authority

Responsibility for collecting the duties fell to the customs collectors. Townshend tried to strengthen the enforcement of his measures by firing customs collectors who had been taking bribes. But to no one's surprise, the new officials turned out to be as corrupt as the old. Customs officials could seize ships and cargo, sell them, and take one third of the selling price. The governor and British government split the remainder.

John Hancock, one of Boston's richest merchants, experienced typical treatment at the hands of customs officials. The incident began when two customs officials boarded one of his ships illegally. Hancock threw them off, and they looked for a way to get back at him. It did not take them long.

The law required that a bond, or deposit of money, be posted when a ship was being loaded, as a guarantee that taxes on the goods would be paid. In practice, officials had allowed payment of the bond when a ship sailed. Customs officials armed themselves with one of the hated **writs of assistance,** documents authorizing unrestricted searches, and customs officials boarded Hancock's ship, the *Liberty*. They searched the holds, discovered a cargo of whale oil and tar, and then ordered ship and cargo seized because the bond had not been posted. The incident showed many colonists the kind of justice Americans could expect from the British government.

A violent reception awaited the tax collectors in some parts of the colonies. This print shows a customs official, Johnny Malcolm, who was tarred and feathered both in Maine and in Boston. In Maine, he was allowed to keep his clothes, but in Boston, the mob stripped him naked for the ordeal. Notice the upside-down Stamp Act on the tree and the ominous noose dangling from its branch.

4. VISUAL EVIDENCE This print was titled *Paying the Exciseman.* Ask: Do you think the artist was a supporter of the colonies or of the crown? Why?

Townshend also tried to enforce the irritating Quartering Act, which colonial legislatures had largely ignored. Since New York was one of the chief offenders, Townshend singled it out as an example to the rest of the colonies. He called a halt to all meetings of the New York assembly until the Quartering Act was obeyed there.

The rest of the colonies rallied immediately to the support of New York by drafting letters announcing that they would resist every tax imposed by Parliament. Faced with such hostility, Townshend modified the Quartering Act. Instead of making the colonists open their homes to soldiers, he let them provide barracks, unoccupied dwellings, or barns. Even a weakened Quartering Act, however, demanded a greater British presence than the colonists would tolerate.

101

2. CRITICAL THINKING Ask: How does this show that the Townshend Acts angered upper-class colonists?

3. CITIZENSHIP Writs of assistance allowed searches in any place at any time. Such searches were illegal in Britain.

1. **BIOGRAPHY** Crispus Attucks's father was black; his mother an American Indian. Attucks, meaning deer, was a common Indian name in New England.

2. **CRITICAL THINKING** Samuel Adams convinced many people that the massacre was a British plot. Ask students to compare the responses of John Adams and Samuel Adams to the massacre. .

The Boston Massacre

In response to repeated pleas from Boston customs commissioners for help, the British government sent two regiments of troops to Boston. In September 1768, a sullen crowd watched as the troops came ashore and set up camp on the Boston common. For the next year and a half, the colonists did all in their power short of violence to make the soldiers' lives miserable. They shunned them and taunted them behind their backs.

On March 5, 1770, the friction turned to open conflict. A crowd of several hundred colonists gathered in front of the Boston customs house, where ten British soldiers stood guard. The crowd began jeering and cursing the soldiers, pelting them with oyster shells, snowballs, sticks, and slivers of ice. At least one member of the mob had a cutlass, and another carried a pistol.

Captain Thomas Preston, the commander of the guard, ordered his men to hold steady and not to fire. Unfortunately, someone— whether a soldier or a member of the crowd is unknown—fired a gun, and a volley of shots from British muskets followed. When the shooting stopped, five of the crowd lay dead or mortally wounded on the street. The first to die was Crispus Attucks, a black sailor active in the Sons of Liberty. His wounds killed him almost immediately. The colonial press called the incident the Boston Massacre.

Preston and his troops stood trial in Boston later that year. John Adams accepted the unpopular duty of defending them in court. He believed that British soldiers had the right to a legal defense. Just as important was his feeling that the American cause would lose its moral advantage if the soldiers could not get a fair trial in Boston.

Adams obtained deathbed testimony from one of the mortally wounded colonists. The dying man swore that the crowd, not the troops, had been to blame for the Boston Massacre. As a result of this testimony, the worst penalty any of the soldiers received was a branding on the hand.

Repeal at Last

News of the Boston Massacre contributed to growing concern in Britain about the colonies. Clearly, the Townshend Acts were failing. Little tax money flowed to British cof-

3. **VISUAL EVIDENCE** Point out to students that Preston's headquarters is labeled "Butcher's Hall." Ask: Why do you think Revere put this in his engraving?

Boston silversmith Paul Revere made this widely circulated propaganda engraving of the Boston Massacre. The first colonist to be killed was Crispus Attucks, a black sailor, who is not shown in Revere's engraving.

1. **ECONOMICS** Ask: Why would American economic independence threaten Britain's mercantile system? Refer students to pp. 77–78.

2. **DISCUSSION** Ask students to compare Parliament's reason for keeping the tax on tea with its rationale for passing the Declaratory Act in 1766.

fers, and by 1769 the nonimportation agreements had reduced trade to some degree. Americans had begun to manufacture paint, glass, paper, and lead products. For the British, this new American economic independence represented one of the least desirable developments possible.

Ironically, Charles Townshend had died in 1767 and never saw the problems his taxes had created. In 1770, George III appointed Lord North as prime minister. Both men agreed completely about how to run the colonies. Thus, for the next 12 years, King George would firmly support his prime minister.

Once in office, Lord North persuaded Parliament to allow the unpopular Quartering Act to expire. Parliament also repealed all the Townshend taxes, except the one on tea, leading to an end of the American boycott of British goods. The remaining tax on tea guaranteed some revenue and also served as a reminder that Parliament claimed the right to tax the colonists.

Resistance to Parliamentary measures broke down in America. On the surface, the colonies were calmer than they had been at any time since 1764. Nevertheless, the colonists had been shaken. They had begun, for the first time, to think more clearly about their political rights.

See p. T18.

SECTION 2 REVIEW

1. **Identify:** (a) Charles Townshend, (b) Boston Massacre, (c) John Adams, (d) Lord North.

2. **Define:** (a) nonimportation agreement, (b) writs of assistance.

3. Did the Townshend Acts raise revenue? Explain.

4. How did the colonists react to enforcement of the Quartering Act?

5. Why did the British repeal the Townshend Acts but keep the tax on tea?

6. **Critical Thinking** Why was it difficult to obtain reliable testimony about the Boston Massacre?

3 The Roots of Independence

READ TO UNDERSTAND

■ How the British challenged colonial self-rule.

■ Why the colonists resisted the tax on tea.

■ Why the colonists opposed the Intolerable Acts.

The 1770s began in an atmosphere of deceptive calm. The repeal of the Townshend Acts had taken the edge off colonial anger, but a series of events would soon bring colonial suspicion and mistrust to the surface. Looking back on these events years later, George Washington would conclude that the evidence of British tyranny had been "as clear as the sun in its meridian brightness."

Tensions Renewed

Early in 1772, the British government renewed its challenge to colonial self-rule. Parliament passed a law that made the king, and not the colonial assemblies, responsible for paying the salaries of royal governors and judges. For the past decade, the colonies had strongly resisted such attempts to infringe on their responsibilities. What control could the assemblies have over governors and judges if the assemblies no longer paid their salaries? The announcement of the new law provoked a swift, unfavorable reaction.

Another incident soon revived tensions. The British warship *Gaspée,* which patrolled the Rhode Island coast to enforce customs regulations, also harassed the local inhabitants. Its crew frequently seized small boats engaged in local trade, cut down orchards for firewood, and stole farmers' livestock. One day, while on a patrol mission near Providence, the *Gaspée* ran aground. That night, the people of Providence burned the ship.

The British government realized that the Rhode Island officials would do nothing to round up the offenders, so it appointed a special investigative commission of its own. But the Rhode Islanders claimed to recall

103

1. **BACKGROUND** The commission was empowered to send offenders to England for trial.

1. nothing about that night, and the investigation failed. The very existence of such a commission made the colonists edgy. They feared that if Britain could bypass the colonial courts, it might shut them down permanently.

These and other incidents, such as the tarring and feathering of a customs officer on Boston's streets and the seizing of a revenue ship on the Delaware River, increased friction between the British and the colonists. Until 1773, however, there was no clear-cut renewal of old hostilities. In that year, the lull broke once and for all.

The Tea Act

The British East India Company managed British interests in India and handled the exporting and marketing of Indian tea. During the 1760s, a depression of the European economy hurt the East India Company's profits. To recover, the company wanted to sell its unsold stock of tea to the colonies.

2. **CRITICAL THINKING** Ask: Why do you think the colonists wore Indian disguises?

2. *British warships like the* Gaspée *patrolled the coastal waters to prevent smuggling. When the* Gaspée *went aground off Providence, Rhode Island, gleeful colonists in Indian disguises rowed out and burned it.*

3. **ECONOMICS** Parliament thought the Tea Act would help everyone and cause little controversy. Ask: Why do you think colonists might oppose the Tea Act?

Americans drank Dutch tea, not because they liked it better but because it was cheaper than English tea. Dutch tea was smuggled into the colonies directly from the East Indies. It bypassed wholesalers and customs officials. On the other hand, the East India Company could sell its tea only to British wholesalers. The wholesalers, in turn, sold the tea to American distributors who then resold it to retail merchants. By the time the tea had reached the colonial market, it had been marked up four times.

In 1773, Parliament tried to save the East India Company from bankruptcy by passing the Tea Act. The measure allowed the East India Company to sell tea directly to American retailers. In addition, the act removed Britain's own import tax on tea. The small tax remaining from the original Townshend Acts was the only duty remaining on the tea. (See page 103.) As a result, the East India Company could undersell its competition. 3.

A Tempest Over Tea

The solution looked good to Parliament. Although Americans would be paying a small tax on English tea, they would now buy it because it would be cheaper than Dutch tea. But American merchants faced the loss of their profitable business in smuggled tea. They warned that once they were driven out of business, the East India Company would raise the price of tea. All over the colonies, the tea tax became a symbol of British oppression. The American spirit of independence had been aroused again.

The angry colonists acted quickly. For the third time since 1763, they set up a boycott. East India tea rotted on the waterfronts along the American coast. Women brewed "liberty teas" from local plants, signed anti-tea declarations, and formed anti-tea leagues. 4.

In Boston, Governor Thomas Hutchinson decided that British control over the American colonies hinged on the issue of the tax on tea. In December 1773, he ordered East India tea ships in Boston harbor to tie up along the wharves and unload their cargoes.

The Sons of Liberty responded swiftly. On the night of December 16, a gang of 30 to 60 men thinly disguised as Indians boarded

4. **READING** One colonist said, "Do not suffer yourself to sip the accursed, dutied STUFF. For if you do . . . you will instantly become a traitor to your country."

British officials were outraged by the Boston Tea Party, shown here. One called it "the most wanton and unprovoked insult offered to the civil power that is recorded in history." John Adams believed, however, that many colonists wished that "as many dead Carcasses were floating in the Harbour, as there are Chests of Tea."

1.

1. **BACKGROUND** A popular song of the 1770s, *Revolutionary Tea,* ended with the colonies calling out to England, "Your tea you may have when 'tis steeped [soaked] enough/But never a tax from me."

the East India ships and dumped the tea into the harbor. The incident became known as the Boston Tea Party.

The Intolerable Acts

When Lord North received news of Boston's defiance, he lost all patience. He felt these "New England fanatics" were undermining all British authority in the colonies. Both North and George III agreed that the time had come to force the colonists to obey.

Since Boston was the center of colonial resistance, Lord North and the king decided to make an example of Massachusetts. In 1774, they struck back with the Coercive Acts, hoping to spread fear throughout the colonies and force them into submission.

To begin with, the acts closed the port of Boston to all trade. Next, they revoked the Massachusetts charter, prohibiting the Massachusetts legislature and courts from holding sessions. Military rule was imposed on the colony, and General Thomas Gage, commander of all British troops in North America, became governor of the colony. The acts also forbade town meetings, placing even local government under military control.

More troops arrived in Boston to reinforce the existing garrison. By the time the new arrivals stopped coming, there were 4,000 British soldiers in Boston—one for every four Bostonians.

Finally, the Coercive Acts revived the old Quartering Act, giving General Gage the authority to house all his troops in Boston, in private residences if need be. Even worse, any British officials who committed crimes while enforcing the acts would be tried in Britain, not in America. The colonists felt that this gave the British a free hand to use any sort of violence against them and be acquitted in a London court.

The Quebec Act, an attempt to secure the loyalty of French-Canadians to Britain, soon followed. This act gave French-Canadians freedom to practice their Catholic faith and expanded the boundaries of Quebec west and south to the Mississippi and Ohio rivers.

The act was not intended to punish the colonies, but the colonists regarded the expansion of Quebec's borders as an insult. They felt that Britain had deliberately created an obstacle to westward expansion.

2.

In the end, the Intolerable Acts, as the colonists labeled the Coercive Acts and the **105**

2. **DISCUSSION** The king declared, "We must master them or totally leave them to themselves and treat them as aliens." Ask: Why do you think the king and North chose the course they did?

VOICES OF FREEDOM

The Local Tavern: A Communication Center

Handbills, pamphlets, and local newspapers were important ammunition in the war of words that developed between Great Britain and the colonies. But casual gatherings at local taverns often were even more critical. There people also could discuss events and plan possible actions. Below, John Adams describes one conversation he heard at a tavern in Massachusetts in 1774.

Within the course of the year, before the meeting of Congress in 1774, on a journey to some of our circuit courts in Massachusetts, I stopped one night at a tavern in Shrewsbury about forty miles from Boston, and as I was cold and wet, I sat down at a good fire in the bar-room to dry

my great-coat and saddle-bags, till a fire could be made in my chamber. There presently came in, one after another, half a dozen, or half a score substantial yeomen of the neighborhood, who, sitting down to the fire after lighting their pipes, began a lively conversation on politics. As I believed I was unknown to all of them, I sat in total silence to hear them.

One said, "The people of Boston are distracted." Another answered, "No wonder the people of Boston are distracted. Oppression will make wise men mad." A third said, "What would you say if a fellow should come to your house and tell you he was come to take a list of your cattle, that Parliament might tax you for them at so much a head? And how should you feel if he was to go and break open your barn or take down your oxen, cows, horses, and sheep?" "What should I say?" replied the first. "I would knock him in the head." "Well," said a fourth, "if Parliament can take away Mr. Hancock's wharf and Mr. Rowe's wharf, they can take away your barn and my house." After much more reasoning in this style, a fifth broke out: "Well, it's high time for us to rebel."

See p. T19.

1. What seemed to be the concern of the five speakers?

2. Critical Thinking Why would the feelings of the general public be of interest to John Adams?

1.

2.

3.

---

1. **VOCABULARY** A *yeoman* in Britain was a small landowner who worked his own farm.

2. **VOCABULARY** *Distracted* in this sense means crazed or insane.

Quebec Act, helped the colonies forge a united front. Before they could fully come together, however, 13 separate governments had to overcome their differences.

To Submit or Unite?

Thirteen separate and often disparate governments found it difficult to work together, as the Albany Congress of 1754 had demonstrated. Furthermore, the colonies occupied a vast region with varied climate and geography. The economies and social systems of

the colonies differed, too, ranging from the sprawling plantations of the South to the compact farms of New Engand.

Yet, the forces for unity were stronger than the differences that set the colonies apart. Up and down a territory 1,500 miles long and several hundred miles wide, most colonists spoke a common language and shared common traditions of government. When Parliament and the crown acted to deny what the colonists saw as their "English liberties," Americans began to recognize how much the 13 colonies had in common.

106

3. **PAST AND PRESENT** Ask: Are there any institutions or meeting places today that perform the same function as the tavern in colonial America?

This sense of unity grew as colonists learned more about the issues of the day. Communication increased as newspapers spead reports of events from colony to colony. In pamphlets, writers examined vital issues in depth and called for greater resistance to British tyranny.

Committees of Correspondence

The most effective means of developing a united colonial front proved to be the Committees of Correspondence. First organized by Samuel Adams in 1772 to connect Boston to the rural towns of Massachusetts, committees existed in every colony by 1774.

The Committees of Correspondence kept colonists from north to south and east to west continuously informed of developments in the struggle with Britain. For instance, when the Committees of Correspondence spread the word that the Coercive Acts had closed the port of Boston, other colonies promptly sent food supplies: Bostonians baked bread with Pennsylvania flour and made pudding with South Carolina rice.

In reporting news, the committees made sure that every incident was portrayed as an attack on American liberty. One British sympathizer called the committees "the foulest, subtlest, and most venomous serpent ever issued from the egg of sedition."

A decisive step toward unity came in 1774. After the royal governor of Virginia dissolved the House of Burgesses, members of the assembly met in a Williamsburg tavern. There they decided to call for a meeting to discuss "those measures which the united interests of America may from time to time require." The Committees of Correspondence spread the word to the other colonies. Soon, colonial assemblies were at work electing delegates to the First Continental Congress.

When the meeting convened in Carpenters' Hall at Philadelphia in September 1774, all 13 colonies except Georgia were represented. As the delegates assembled, they knew their first task was to decide on a response to the Intolerable Acts. Yet, another question probably lingered in the back of their minds. At some future date, would there be only one choice left—independence?

Mercy Otis Warren of Plymouth, Massachusetts, was an effective American propagandist who wrote and published many political satires and plays. Her plays were too inflammatory to be performed publicly, but they were read aloud in meetings at private homes. This painting of her is by John Singleton Copley.

See p. T19.

SECTION 3 REVIEW

1. **Identify:** (a) *Gaspée,* (b) British East India Company, (c) Intolerable Acts, (d) Committees of Correspondence, (e) Samuel Adams.

2. (a) What was the purpose of the Tea Act? (b) How did the colonists react?

3. What was the purpose of the Coercive Acts?

4. How did effective communication contribute to colonial unity?

5. Why did the First Continental Congress meet?

6. **Critical Thinking** Why do you think that the issue of the authority of colonial courts was so important to the colonists?

107

4 From Protest to Revolution

READ TO UNDERSTAND

- How the views of the delegates to the Continental Congress differed.

- What actions were taken by the Continental Congress.

- Why fighting broke out at Lexington and Concord.

1. ■ *Vocabulary:* minutemen.

The delegates from Massachusetts had misgivings when they left their homes and families to attend the Continental Congress. There was trouble in the air, and British troops

2. **VISUAL EVIDENCE** This portrait was painted by the same artist as was the portrait of Mercy Otis Warren on p. 107.

2. *Samuel Adams of Boston was a fiery leader of the cause of American independence. He helped form the Sons of Liberty and the first Committee of Correspondence. According to his cousin, John Adams, Samuel Adams was one of the first colonists to argue that independence should be their goal.*

were roaming the countryside. But something had to be done about the Intolerable Acts.

In Philadelphia, John and Samuel Adams of Massachusetts sided with other radicals such as Charles Thomson of Pennsylvania and Patrick Henry of Virginia. They felt the time had come either to force Britain to accept all their demands or to take a stronger stand. The moderates, led by Joseph Galloway and John Dickinson of Pennsylvania, wanted to patch up the quarrel with Great Britain.

Defining Relations With Britain

At first, the moderates seemed to take the lead at the Congress. Under Galloway's direction, they proposed a union of the colonies under British authority. Parliament would still pass laws affecting the colonies, but a "grand council" of American representatives could also veto them.

Samuel Adams managed to defeat Galloway's plan—by one vote. Adams, complained Galloway, was a man who "eats little, sleeps little, thinks much, and is most decisive . . . in the pursuit of his objects." He would accept no halfway measures.

With the defeat of Galloway's plan, the radicals increasingly dominated the Congress. In *A Summary View of the Rights of British America,* Thomas Jefferson tried to define the relationship between the colonies and Parliament. He argued that just as Parliament had no right to tax the colonies, it could not make laws for them either. For Jefferson and the radicals, the British empire was not a single, undivided whole. Rather it was a loose union of more or less independent states. Each had its own legislature, which acted as a little parliament, and all were united by a shared loyalty to the king. 3.

The Congress's most significant document, *Declaration and Resolves,* strongly attacked the Coercive Acts and the Quebec Act as well as all revenue measures passed by Parliament since 1763. Citing "the immutable laws of nature," "the principles of the English constitution," and the original colonial charters, the *Declaration and Resolves* demanded that Britain repeal all oppressive legislation.

3. **MAIN IDEA** Have students explain Jefferson's view of the relationship between the colonies and Great Britain.

Give Me Liberty or Give Me Death

On March 28, 1775, Patrick Henry delivered a fiery speech to the Virginia Convention of Delegates. For almost ten years, he had opposed Britain's attempts to impose taxation without representation. As this excerpt shows, he now felt words were not enough.

Let us not deceive ourselves, sir. These are the implements of war and subjugation; the last arguments to which kings resort. I ask gentlemen, sir, what means this martial array, if its purpose be not to force us to submission? Has Great Britain any enemy, in this quarter of the world, to call for all this accumulation of navies and armies? No, sir, she has none. They are meant for us; they can be meant for no other. And what have we to oppose them? Shall we try argument? Sir, we have been trying that for the last ten years. Sir, we have done everything that could be done and we have been spurned, with contempt, from the foot of the throne. . . . We must fight! I repeat it, sir, we must fight!

Gentlemen may cry peace, peace—but there is no peace. The war is actually begun! The next gale that sweeps from the north will bring to our ears the clash of resounding arms! Our brethren are already in the field. Why stand we here idle? Is life so dear, or peace so sweet, as to be purchased at the price of chains and slavery? Forbid it, Almighty God! I know not what course others may take; but as for me, give me liberty, or give me death!

See p. T19.

1. Why does Patrick Henry think the king plans to force the colonies to submit to his will?

2. **Critical Thinking** Patrick Henry has been described as a "fiery orator." What words or techniques does he use in this speech to arouse his listeners' emotions?

1. **BACKGROUND** According to one witness, Patrick Henry delivered the final words of this speech "with both his arms extended aloft, his brows knit, every feature marked with the resolute purpose of his soul, and his voice swelled to its boldest note of exclamation."

Other Actions

The First Continental Congress also took other decisive action. Urged on by Samuel Adams, the delegates voted for an immediate and complete end to trade with Great Britain. To carry out their resolution, delegates formed a Continental Association to set up committees in every town, city, and county. The committees would ensure that no colony imported or consumed British goods or exported American goods to Britain. By April 1775, "the Association" was operating in 12 colonies.

Before adjourning on October 26, 1774, the delegates agreed to meet again the following spring. Little did they know that by then an incident in Massachusetts would set forces in motion that would sever the colonies from Great Britain forever.

2. **ECONOMICS** The boycott by the Continental Association was the first to be organized by representatives of the people rather than by merchants in the colonies.

SKILL LESSON

Lexington and Concord: Analyzing a Primary Source

Two types of written sources can be used to learn about historical events: primary sources and secondary sources. Primary Sources are first-hand accounts usually written by a person who was closely involved in the event. They include government documents, letters, diaries, and eyewitness newspaper accounts. Secondary sources are second-hand accounts of historical events.

Both types of sources provide factual information, but primary sources also provide insight into the feelings, attitudes, and motives of people. Because the author is closely involved in the event, however, the account may not be accurate. Thus, when using a primary source, it is important to analyze its reliability.

Carefully read the document at right. Then use the steps described below to analyze it.

See p. T19.

1 **Identify the nature of the document by asking yourself the following questions.** (a) What type of document is it? (b) Who wrote the document? Was he or she closely involved in the event? (c) When was it written?

2 **Describe how reliable the source is.** (a) Why did the author write it? (b) What was the author's role in the event described? (c) Was the author British or American? How can you tell? How could that have affected what was reported? (d) Would you say this is a reliable source?

3 **Study the source to learn more about a historical event.** Distinguish between facts and opinions. A *fact* is something that is true and that can be proven. An *opinion* is a judgment that reflects a person's feelings, beliefs, or attitudes. (a) What facts about the fighting at Lexington and Concord can you learn from this document? (b) What was the author's opinion of the colonists' actions at Lexington? What was the author's opinion of British intentions?

(c) How would you describe the British feelings toward the fighting?

Report of Lieutenant-Colonel Smith to Governor Gage, April 22, 1775

SIR,—I marched on the evening of the 18th with the corps of grenadiers and light infantry for Concord, to execute your Excellency's orders with respect to destroying all ammunition, artillery, tents, &c, collected there. When I had got some miles on the march from Boston, I detached six light infantry companies. On these companies' arrival at Lexington, they found on a green close to the road a body of the country people drawn up in military order, with arms. Our troops advanced towards them, without any intention of injuring them, further than to inquire the reason of their being thus assembled, and, if not satisfactory, to have secured their arms; but they in confusion went off, principally to the left, only one of them fired before he went off, and three or four more jumped over a wall and fired from behind it among the soldiers; on which the troops returned it, and killed several of them.

While at Concord we saw vast numbers assembling in many parts; at one of the bridges they marched down, with a very considerable body, on the light infantry posted there. On their coming pretty near, one of our men fired on them, which they returned; on which an action ensued and some few were killed.

On our leaving Concord to return to Boston, they began to fire on us from behind the walls, ditches, trees, and continued for, I believe, upwards of eighteen miles; so that I can't think but it must have been a preconcerted scheme in them, to attack the King's troops the first favorable opportunity that offered, otherwise, I think they could not, in so short a time from our marching out, have raised such a numerous body, and for so great a space of ground.

I have the honor, &c,
F. Smith, Lieutenant-Colonel 10th Foot.

1.

1. **READING** Interested students might present a dramatic reading of the poem *Paul Revere's Ride* by Henry Wadsworth Longfellow to the rest of the class.

Lexington and Concord

Over the winter of 1774–1775, Massachusetts protestors formed a militia, calling themselves **minutemen** because they would be ready to fight on a moment's notice. The minutemen, seriously committed to colonial self-defense, did not have long to wait for a hostile move by the British.

As winter turned into spring, General Thomas Gage, commander of the British forces in Boston, received orders to round up the leaders of the colonial resistance. At first he hesitated to provoke open conflict, but the news that the colonists had an arsenal of weapons and powder at Concord prompted him to act. On April 18, Gage sent nearly 1,000 soldiers under Major John Pitcairn to seize the arsenal. Pitcairn believed that resistance could be smothered easily with a "small action" and the burning of a few towns.

British forces set out from Boston at night, hoping to surprise the colonists at daybreak. But as they tramped over the countryside, William Dawes and Paul Revere galloped to villages and farms to warn the minutemen. At sunrise, when the British reached Lexington, 70 minutemen commanded by Captain John Parker waited on the village green. Pitcairn ordered the minutemen to disperse, and Parker gave the order to retreat. Then someone—no one knows who—fired a shot. After a brief skirmish, eight Americans were dead and ten more lay wounded on the new spring grass. Only one British soldier received a wound, and that was slight.

Delayed no more than 15 minutes, Pitcairn pushed on to Concord. He entered the village without resistance at eight o'clock but found few of the military supplies he sought. To protect his main body of troops while they searched, Pitcairn ordered a covering party to North Bridge, just outside the village. There, the British met 300 minutemen, and a British trooper fired "the shot heard 'round the world."

After a five-minute exchange of fire, Pitcairn began his retreat. By then, over 3,000 minutemen lined the woods, fields, and stone fences along the road to Boston. Pitcairn's troops barely made it back to Lexington, where 1,200 British reinforcements rescued

Minuteman Amos Doolittle made this detailed engraving of two British commanders scouting the terrain around the Concord cemetery. Their brilliantly clad troops are marching toward the village to face colonial minutemen

2. **VISUAL EVIDENCE** Ask: Would a formation of soldiers like this one be at an advantage or at a disadvantage?

them. By the time the British ran the entire "bloody chute" back to Boston, 73 of their men had been killed, with another 200 wounded or missing. In contrast, the Americans had only 93 casualties.

On April 22, the Massachusetts provincial congress voted to raise 13,600 troops. Within a week, Boston was a city under siege. When the Continental Congress gathered again in Philadelphia on May 10, 1775, it had a fight on its hands.

See p. T20.

SECTION 4 REVIEW

1. **Identify:** (a) Joseph Galloway, (b) Thomas Jefferson, (c) *Declaration and Resolves,* (d) Continental Association.

2. **Define:** minutemen.

3. (a) Describe the moderates' proposal to the Continental Congress. (b) How did the radicals' attitude toward Parliament differ from the attitude of most colonists?

4. What action was taken by the Continental Congress?

5. What information convinced General Gage to act against the colonists?

6. **Critical Thinking** Why was economic independence nearly as important for the colonists as political independence?

111

3. **PAST AND PRESENT** Massachusetts still celebrates Patriot's Day on April 19 to commemorate these events. The Boston Marathon more or less follows the route of the British retreat.

CHAPTER 5 REVIEW

Summary

1. **In 1763, after the French and Indian War, Great Britain faced problems governing its new empire.** Britain's land policy prohibiting settlement in the West angered many colonists, as did the attempts by the British to raise revenue by taxation.

2. **In the early 1770s, the quarrel widened as British efforts to make the colonies profitable resulted in more taxes.** The Townshend Acts provoked a colonial boycott of British goods. The Boston Massacre caused unrest, but the repeal of the Townshend Acts temporarily eased matters.

3. **Before long, a protest over a tax on tea renewed hard feelings.** Angry colonists threw a shipment of tea overboard into Boston harbor. In reaction to the Boston Tea Party, Parliament passed the Coercive Acts. The Committees of Correspondence kept colonists informed of developments in the struggle with Britain.

4. **In September 1774, colonial representatives met at the First Continental Congress.** The Congress adopted a resolution protesting the Intolerable Acts and voted for an immediate end to all trade with Great Britain. The first military clash between the British and the colonists took place soon afterward at Lexington and Concord, in Massachusetts.

See p. T20.

Vocabulary

Choose the answer that best completes each of the following sentences.

1. The _____ was an agreement among merchants not to import certain goods. (a) tariff (b) nonimportation agreement (c) Stamp Act

2. A _____ is a document authorizing unrestricted searches. (a) writ of assistance (b) bill of rights (c) boycott

3. Groups of colonists who wrote to one another concerning the struggle with Britain were the _____. (a) minutemen (b) Vice-Admiralty Courts (c) Committees of Correspondence

4. The First Continental Congress set up a Continental _____ to carry out a boycott of British goods. (a) Resolution (b) Legislature (c) Association

5. Massachusetts protestors formed a militia and called themselves the _____. (a) Sons of Liberty (b) minutemen (c) delegates

See p. T20.

Chapter Checkup

1. (a) Why did Pontiac lead the western Indian nations in a rebellion against the British? (b) What impact did the rebellion have on British policy?

2. (a) Describe the measures George Grenville and Parliament took to ease Britain's national debt. (b) How did the colonists react to them?

3. (a) What were the Townshend Acts? (b) How did the British try to enforce them? (c) How did the colonists react?

4. (a) Describe the Coercive Acts. (b) Why did the colonists consider the Quebec Act a threat?

5. (a) How did the position of the moderates at the First Continental Congress differ from the position of the radicals? (b) Which position seemed to dominate by the end of the Congress?

6. How did events at Lexington and Concord heighten tension between the British and the colonists?

See p. T20.

Critical Thinking

1. **Analyzing** (a) Why did the colonists consider the Sugar Act (1764) and the Stamp Act (1765) to be taxation without representation? (b) How did these acts differ from the Molasses Act (1733)? (c) What body did the colonists think had authority to tax them? Why?

2. **Recognizing a Point of View** Look up a definition of "massacre" in a dictionary. Why do you think the incident in Boston was called a massacre in the colonial press when only five people were killed?

See p. T20.

Connecting Past and Present

1. Some minorities and women today may feel that they are underrepresented in state and national legislatures much as the colonists were in Parliament. What means have these groups used to promote their views?

2. The issue of justice for the colonies stirred some people to participate actively in protest. What issues today stir active protest?

See p. T20.

Developing Basic Skills

1. **Map Reading** Study the map on page 96. (a) What served as a natural boundary for the Proclamation Line of 1763? (b) For whom was the land west of the Proclamation Line intended? (c) What country claimed the land west of the Mississippi ?

2. **Placing Events in Time** Construct a time line with 1763 as the starting date and 1775 as the ending date. Write in the events that led up to the American Revolution. Then answer the following questions: (a) How long was the Stamp Act in effect? (b) How long were the Townshend Acts in effect? (c) Does the time line support the idea that the colonies were on the road to revolution? Explain.

WRITING ABOUT HISTORY

Organizing Supporting Detail

Once you have written a topic sentence and gathered supporting information, you must arrange the information in some logical order, or sequence. The most common sequences are chronological order, order of importance, comparison and contrast, spatial order, and cause-and-effect order.

- **Chronological order** Events are arranged in the time order in which they occurred. Chronological order is useful for relating circumstances leading up to an event.
- **Order of importance** Ideas are organized from the least significant to the most significant, or vice versa. This order is helpful for developing an argument for or against some action or issue.
- **Comparison and contrast** Ideas or details are organized according to similarities or differences. The ideas can be contrasted item by item, or all of the items of one kind can be compared with all of the items of another kind. This pattern would be useful to show how things were the same or different.
- **Spatial order** Items are organized according to the place they occupy in space, from inside to outside, near to far, left to right, and so on. This pattern is useful for writing a word picture.
- **Cause-and-effect order** Events are organized to show that an event that occurs first is directly or indirectly responsible for an event that follows. An event can be the result of one thing and the cause of something else. This pattern is useful for discussing results of actions or events.

Practice: For each of the Critical Thinking questions in this Chapter Review, indicate the order of organization of your answer.

A War for Independence (1775–1783)

CHAPTER OUTLINE

1 The Revolution Begins

2 The Road to Independence

3 The Balance of Forces

4 Fighting a Colonial War

5 Victory for the Americans

CHAPTER OBJECTIVES After completing this chapter, students should be able to
1. explain what the Second Continental Congress did.
2. list the main ideas in the Declaration of Independence.
3. describe the major battles of the Revolution.
4. list the provisions of the Treaty of Paris.

CHAPTER PREVIEW Have the class brainstorm all the information they know about the Declaration of Independence. Save the list and go over it when students have finished the chapter.

Boston, August 1, 1786

These may certify that Robert Shurtleff was a soldier in my regiment in the Continental Army, for the Commonwealth of Massachusetts, and was enlisted for the term of three years; that he had the confidence of his officers, did his duty as a faithful and good soldier, and was honorably discharged from the army of the United States.

Henry Jackson, late Colonel
in the American Army

Robert Shurtleff needed that statement in later years to prove his record of service. Shurtleff had signed up as a raw recruit in May 1782 seeking, like many others, adventure and excitement. What no one knew was that Robert Shurtleff was, in reality, Deborah Sampson, a strong-willed, independent-minded young wo-

man who was eager to take part in the stirring events of the day.

Sampson's disguise worked for three years. She saw action, was wounded, and was sent to survey land near the Ohio River. When her disguise was discovered, she received an honorable discharge and returned to Massachusetts. There she married Benjamin Gannett and had three children.

Between 1775 and 1783, many women took part in the nation's struggle for independence. Few took the extreme measures of Deborah Sampson Gannett, but they planted, harvested, tended the wounded, and defended their homes during the difficult war years.

In April 1775, most Americans had not expected the skirmishes at Lexington and Concord to lead to war. But in July 1776, delegates at the Second Continental Congress voted for independence. The struggle to make it a reality was long and bitter.

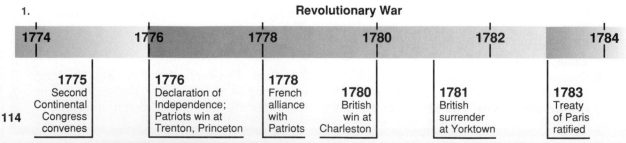

1.   **Revolutionary War**

1774	1776	1778	1780	1782	1784

1775 Second Continental Congress convenes

1776 Declaration of Independence; Patriots win at Trenton, Princeton

1778 French alliance with Patriots

1780 British win at Charleston

1781 British surrender at Yorktown

1783 Treaty of Paris ratified

1. TIME LINE QUESTION Ask: What events took place the same year that the colonies declared independence?

British General John Burgoyne called the colonial troops an "untrained rabble."
Yet from this "rabble" an army was created. The Continental army took on the
1. most powerful nation in the world and won.

1. **VISUAL EVIDENCE** This painting is *The Battle of Bunker Hill* by Alonze Chappel. Have students compare it to the picture on p. 117.

1 The Revolution Begins

READ TO UNDERSTAND

■ How the goals of the moderates and radicals differed at the Second Continental Congress.

■ What steps the colonists took to oppose the British.

■ Why the Congress chose George Washington as commander in chief of the Continental Army.

On May 10, 1775, less than a month after the fighting at Lexington and Concord, the Second Continental Congress convened in Philadelphia. Delegates met at the Pennsylvania statehouse, a simple brick building with a white steeple.

On the steeple's bell, later known as the Liberty Bell, was inscribed: "Proclaim liberty throughout all the land unto all the inhabitants thereof." But above the building's entrance hung King George III's coat of arms. On entering the statehouse, few delegates could avoid noticing this reminder of the colonies' past loyalty to the king.

The Liberty Bell and the king's coat of arms symbolized the two choices facing the delegates. They could break all ties with Britain, or they could try to work out their differences through negotiation. But if independence was declared, the colonies would have to fight.

2.

115

2. **ACTIVITY** Have interested students research the history, legend, and symbolism of the Liberty Bell and present their findings to the class.

1. **CRITICAL THINKING** Have students explain Adams's comment. Ask: Are debates in Congress lengthy and slow today? Is this inevitable in a democracy? Why?

2. **BACKGROUND** Among the American officers was Benedict Arnold, who had been authorized by the Massachusetts legislature to seize the fort.

The Opening of the Second Continental Congress

A vital question faced the delegates assembled at the Second Continental Congress: Where did their loyalties lie? The moderates, led by John Dickinson of Pennsylvania, still favored negotiating an agreement with Britain. The radicals, with John and Samuel Adams as leaders, clamored for independence.

The public seemed to be squarely behind the radicals. Throughout the colonies, citizens formed Committees of Safety to recruit and train local militia, collect funds and supplies, gather information, and disrupt the activities of the king's representatives. One traveler reported, "Wherever you go, you see the inhabitants training, making firelocks, [and] casting mortars, shells and shot."

The radical cause was strengthened further by the superb political skills of Samuel and John Adams. Both worked tirelessly as they prodded the moderates to support independence. In private, John Adams complained about the Congress's lengthy debates, but in public he was more than willing to argue, cajole, and then wait. At one point, he described America as "a great unwieldy body. It is like a large fleet sailing under convoy. The fleetest sailors must wait for the dullest 1. and the slowest."

The Colonists Take Action

Adams did not have to wait long. Events rapidly drove most of the delegates toward a decision for independence. On the morning of May 10, the same day that the Second Continental Congress assembled, Ethan Allen and his band of Green Mountain Boys surprised and captured a sleepy British garrison at Fort Ticonderoga in New York.

A little over a month later, fighting broke out again—this time in Boston, the center of radical agitation. Armed conflict became unavoidable when the British declared that the city and surrounding area were under military command. To prevent the British from occupying the heights overlooking the city, the local Committee of Safety decided on a countermove. American forces under the direction of General Israel Putnam took up a fortified position on Breed's Hill.

On the morning of June 17, more than 1,500 British troops launched a frontal attack on the heights, with each soldier carrying a full pack of almost 125 pounds. Putnam cautioned his inexperienced and poorly supplied troops to conserve their ammunition. "Don't fire until you see the whites of their eyes!" he warned them.

Withering fire from American guns forced the British back twice. Reinforced with fresh troops, the British prepared for a third attack. They threw off their heavy packs, fitted their bayonets, and stormed the heights. But this time they met only scattered fire. The Americans, with dwindling supplies of powder and no bayonets, had held their ground as long as they could. They retreated before the third British attack.

The British took Breed's Hill and Bunker Hill in a battle that was a technical victory for them but a moral victory for the Americans. Colonial forces proved they could hold their own against better-trained and better-equipped troops. Now they could enter the struggle in earnest—and with some hope of winning.

Beginnings of a Continental Army

Two weeks after the battle, Massachusetts asked the Continental Congress to assume responsibility for the army that had formed in the Boston area. Congress unanimously voted to appoint George Washington commander in chief.

Although the 43-year-old Washington had limited military experience, he brought valuable qualities to the job. As a southerner, he broadened colonial support for what had been a New England war. As a natural leader, he commanded the respect of the officers and soldiers in the army. And as an early supporter of independence, he had the trust of the delegates to the Continental Congress.

Shortly after his appointment, Washington left for Cambridge, Massachusetts, to take command of an undisciplined force of about 14,000 men. From this motley group, Washington had to build a national army. Fortunately, the heavy British losses at Bunker

3. **GEOGRAPHY** Have students study the map on p. 118 and explain why seizing Fort Ticonderoga might have been an important goal for the Americans. (location)

4. **BACKGROUND** After running out of ammunition, the Americans stood and fought with their rifle butts.

1. Hill forced the redcoats to remain inactive. That gave Washington time he badly needed.

Indeed, the new American commander knew little about directing large groups of soldiers, less about military strategy, and virtually nothing about the use of artillery. Furthermore, Washington's staff, appointed by the Continental Congress, consisted of a few well-meaning but poorly qualified officers. Israel Putnam had Bunker Hill behind him as well as some combat experience during the French and Indian War. But another officer, Artemas Ward, reportedly "had no acquaintance whatever with military affairs." In time, Washington developed a corps of capable officers: Nathanael Green, Anthony Wayne, Daniel Morgan, and Henry Knox, among others. At the start, however, inexperience hampered American efforts.

Military Action in Canada

The British stayed in their Boston quarters during the summer of 1775, awaiting reinforcements from across the Atlantic. During this lull, Washington mounted a siege, placing cannons on Dorchester Heights, strategically located above Boston's harbor. Realizing that he could no longer defend Boston, General William Howe, the new British commander, withdrew British troops north to Halifax, Nova Scotia, in March 1776.

Meanwhile, the Continental Congress learned that Canada's governor, Guy Carleton, was preparing to invade the colonies. Rather than wait for the attack, the Congress ordered American troops to invade Canada.

2. Colonel Benedict Arnold marched his troops north, reaching Quebec in November

3. This contemporary painting by Winthrop Chandler shows a bird's-eye view of the battle of Bunker Hill, the first formal engagement of the war. The Americans had a good defensive position, and twice they stopped frontal assaults by the redcoats. On the third try, the British took the hill. But they lost more men in this one battle than they would in any other battle of the war.

1. **MAP READING** The cannons captured at Fort Ticonderoga were hauled to Boston by the Green Mountain Boys and used to fortify Dorchester Heights. Ask: About how far were the cannons transported? What difficulties would the Green Mountain Boys have encountered?

1775. Weakened by the two-month trek, Arnold's troops waited for reinforcements before waging a full-scale attack on the walled city in mid-December. Hunger, smallpox, and

MAP STUDY *The first clashes of the Revolution took place even before the colonies declared independence. As shown on the map, these early skirmishes occurred in the northern colonies and in Canada. Which of these were American victories? Which were American defeats?* See p. T21.

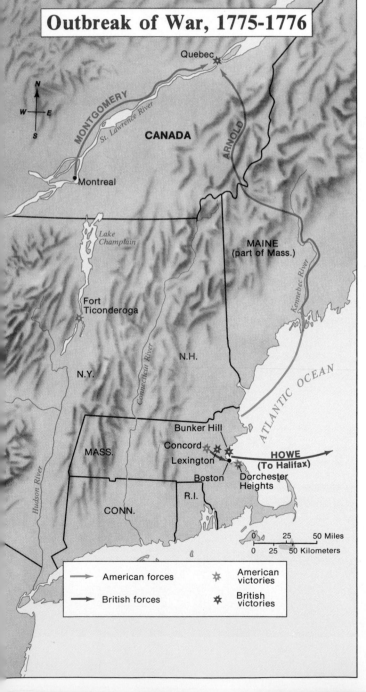

Outbreak of War, 1775-1776

American forces →
British forces →

American victories ✶
British victories ✶

bitter Canadian weather took their toll. The Canadians, who were well-equipped, simply bided their time. The siege, a desperate gamble from the outset, ended in failure and frustration.
See p. T21.

SECTION 1 REVIEW

1. **Identify:** (a) John Dickinson, (b) Committees of Safety, (c) Israel Putnam, (d) Bunker Hill, (e) William Howe, (f) Benedict Arnold.

2. What was the basic difference between the goal of the moderates and that of the radicals at the Second Continental Congress?

3. What three qualities made George Washington a good commander in chief?

4. What news convinced the Continental Congress to order an invasion of Canada?

5. **Critical Thinking** Why were the early battles of the American Revolution fought in and around Massachusetts?

2 The Road to Independence

READl TO UNDERSTAND

■ How King George III reacted to the Olive Branch Petition.

■ Why the Americans considered a formal declaration of independence important.

■ How the three parts of the Declaration of Independence were used to justify the steps taken by the colonists.

"Blows must decide whether they [the colonies] are to be subject to the Country or Independent," claimed King George as early as November 1774. The Americans' attempt to capture Canada confirmed the worst fears of this troubled ruler: that the colonists would not come around unless they felt the effect of force.

2.

2. **CRITICAL THINKING** Ask students to agree or disagree with this statement: If Britain had used milder policies, the colonists would never have rebelled.

1. **VOCABULARY** Have students research the origin of the olive branch as a symbol of peace. Ask: Why was this petition called the Olive Branch Petition?

2. **BACKGROUND** Between January and July 1776, 500,000 copies of *Common Sense* were sold.

The British were determined to punish the rebels, but such tactics only served to swell their ranks. The final break came on July 4, 1776. At that time, what had been thought of as only a limited military action became a war for independence.

A Harsher British Position

Colonial radicals, favoring independence, found unexpected allies in King George and his ministers. Enraged by colonial resistance, George III repeatedly refused to make concessions that might have strengthened the position of the moderates.

In a final attempt to mend the split, the Continental Congress adopted the Olive Branch Petition on July 8, 1775. Written by John Dickinson, the resolution urged the repeal of the Coercive Acts to bring about "a happy and permanent reconciliation." Six weeks later, George III responded with the Prohibitory Act. In it, the king and Parliament proclaimed that a general rebellion existed in the colonies and authorized steps "to bring the traitors to justice." These measures included cutting off all American trade, seizing American ships, and demanding that the rebels formally and publicly repent.

To make matters worse, the Continental Congress learned that the king had hired 10,000 Hessian mercenaries* to suppress the rebellion. Such troops usually looted, burned, and ravaged the countryside. Such a hostile step stunned the delegates.

Thomas Paine's *Common Sense*

If George III's statements inflamed Americans, another Briton's words kindled their patriotism even more. Thomas Paine, in his pamphlet *Common Sense,* helped colonists see the issue more sharply than ever.

Paine was the son of a poor English corset maker. Although he lacked formal schooling, Paine had educated himself and learned to write better than most university-trained

---

*mercenary: a soldier who fights for pay in a foreign army. The Hessians were from the German state of Hesse.

scholars of the day. In 1774, he immigrated to America. In *Common Sense,* Paine used direct, forceful language to persuade Americans that they owed no loyalty to the king of Great Britain because *all* monarchies were evil.

> For all men being originally equals, no one by birth could have a right to set up his own family in perpetual preference to all others for ever. . . . [A monarch is] nothing better than the principal ruffian of some restless gang. Of more worth is one honest man to society and in the sight of God, than all the crowned ruffians that ever lived.

3.

Declaring Independence

By the spring of 1776, the Continental Congress was adopting openly anti-British resolutions. Although the Middle Colonies still leaned toward compromise, New England and the South had already made a decisive break. As a result, the Continental Congress approved privateering against British ships, entered into relations with foreign nations, and cut off all trade with Great Britain.

Congress also organized a committee to draft a formal declaration of independence. Declaring independence seemed a good idea for several reasons. As citizens of an independent nation, captured Americans could demand to be treated as prisoners of war rather than as traitors, subject to the death penalty. Moreover, an independent nation would probably be able to obtain aid from Britain's enemies. Eventually, arguments like these won over all but the most reluctant moderates.

Supported by a congressional resolution stating that "these United States are, and of right ought to be, Independent States," John Adams, Benjamin Franklin, Robert Livingston, Roger Sherman, and Thomas Jefferson set to work on the declaration. Jefferson, who was responsible for most of the draft, later commented, "I turned to neither book nor pamphlet while writing the Declaration."

On July 2, 1776, the committee presented the completed declaration to the Congress. Two days later, the delegates adopted it. No opposing votes were cast. Three delegates from Pennsylvania, however, absented them-

119

3. **READING** Have students restate the quotation in their own words. Ask: How did Paine's view of the king differ from that of Jefferson in his *Summary View* (p. 108)?

Signing the Declaration of Independence marked a point of no return for the delegates to the Continental Congress. It made them traitors to the British crown and put their lives in danger. When the Declaration was published, other colonists, too, had to decide where they stood. The ringing words of the Declaration of Independence inspired many then and have continued to be an inspiration to people around the world.

---

1. VISUAL EVIDENCE The committee that drafted the Declaration of Independence is shown at the center of this painting. Have students identify Jefferson.

selves, and the New York delegation abstained. Congress then sent the document to the printer.

The Declaration

The Declaration of Independence contained three major sections. The preamble explained the principles behind the act of declaring independence. The middle section listed specific grievances against the king. The Declaration concluded by stating that the United States of America had severed its ties to the crown and had formed an independent government. (See the Declaration of Independence, pages 865–866.)

The preamble had the greatest impact on American society because it proclaimed general principles of human rights that applied to all people, not just to the colonists. The beliefs about human rights set forth in

2. BACKGROUND Congress considered using Hebrew, the language of the Bible, instead of English, the language of Great Britain, for the Declaration.

the Declaration of Independence were ideals rather than realities in America in the late 1700s. Yet they helped lay the foundation for a future society based on equal rights for all.

The preamble also justified colonial resistance to Britain in a new way. Earlier, colonists had emphasized the rights they possessed as British subjects, rights guaranteed them by the unwritten British constitution. Now they spoke of natural rights that no human power could take away. Jefferson wrote that people were "endowed by their Creator with certain unalienable rights" and that "among these are life, liberty, and the pursuit of happiness."

People "secure these rights" by forming governments for their protection. Jefferson's thoughts on this subject were influenced by John Locke, an English political philosopher of the 1600s. Like Locke, Jefferson believed that "governments . . . [derive] their just powers from the consent of the governed."

120

3. ACTIVITY Have students, working in small groups, make a list of the rights they think colonists would have demanded based on America's experience from 1763 to 1776.

1. **MAIN IDEA** Have students read the preamble to the Declaration of Independence on p. 865. Then ask them to list its main points in their own words.

2. **VOCABULARY** Have students look up these words in the glossary before they begin reading.

Thus, he argued, the people are the fundamental source of power in any state. This claim ran directly counter to the European theory that kings had a God-given right to rule.

If the people were always the final source of a government's power, it followed that the people also had the right "to alter or to abolish it." However, such a change should be made only when the circumstances truly warranted it, Jefferson wrote, not for "light and transient causes."

The second section of the Declaration then listed the reasons why separation from Britain was necessary. To make the argument as forceful as possible, Jefferson blamed everything on the king. The king, he stated, had refused to allow laws "necessary for the public good" unless the people gave up their "right of representation in the legislature."

The third section of the Declaration officially established a new independent nation. It said that the states had the power to make war, establish alliances, trade with whomever they wanted, and sever all connections with Great Britain. With the adoption of the Declaration of Independence on July 4, 1776, the 13 British colonies ceased to exist. The United States of America were at war.

See p. T22.

SECTION 2 REVIEW

1. **Identify:** (a) Olive Branch Petition, (b) Prohibitory Act, (c) Thomas Paine, (d) *Common Sense.*

2. What two actions by King George helped make the colonists more radical?

3. What argument did Thomas Paine use to convince Americans that they owed no allegiance to the king?

4. Why was the Declaration of Independence important?

5. Describe the three major sections of the Declaration of Independence.

6. **Critical Thinking** Compare the attitudes of Thomas Paine and John Locke toward royalty.

3 The Balance of Forces

READ TO UNDERSTAND

■ What role American blacks and women played in the Revolutionary War.

■ What were the advantages and problems of British and American forces.

■ How localism affected colonial efforts during the Revolutionary War.

■ *Vocabulary:* pacifism, localism.

Early in 1776, John Adams had predicted that Americans would "have a long, obstinate, and bloody war to go through." But few believed that the fighting that had erupted at Lexington in April 1775 would continue for six and a half years. Even fewer realized that it would be the first of more than 80 major battles.

Choosing Sides

Many Americans rejoiced at the news of the Declaration of Independence. In Philadelphia, people rang bells and lighted bonfires. In New York City, an enthusiastic crowd threw ropes around a statue of King George and pulled it to the ground.

But not all Americans felt this way. A significant number—about 10 to 20 percent—remained loyal to the crown. These Loyalists, as they called themselves, included wealthy merchants, former officials of the royal government, and ministers of the Church of England. Many farmers and artisans remained "loyal" too. Often, local rivalries motivated people's decisions. In the Carolina backcountry, for example, many settlers were Loyalists because they distrusted the plantation owners along the eastern coast who were Patriots. Harassed by Patriots, many Loyalists fled to Canada or Britain. Others found shelter in cities controlled by the British, such as New York. Most, however, remained in their homes as inconspicuously as possible.

An even larger number of Americans—perhaps about 30 to 50 percent—remained neutral. Among them were the members of

121

---

3. **VOCABULARY** Patriots referred to the Loyalists as Tories. The Tory party was a conservative political party in England that upheld the power of the king.

religious groups such as the Moravians, Quakers, and Mennonites, whose belief in **pacifism** led them to oppose the use of force for any reason. On occasion, however, the tide of battle sometimes forced them to lend a hand.

America was thus a nation of divided loyalties. Many families had members on opposing sides. For example, Benjamin Franklin's son, the governor of New Jersey, sided with the British, causing his father much anguish.

The British population itself was split on the American question. Some members of Parliament publicly supported the Patriot cause. Several generals refused to fight in the war and resigned their commissions.

Many Native Americans saw the war as an opportunity to oust colonial intruders. The Iroquois in the North, the Shawnee and Delaware in the western part of the Middle Colonies, and the Cherokee in the South formed key alliances with the British.

The Role of African Americans

Blacks, both slave and free, tended to support the Patriot cause. In fact, some black veterans of the French and Indian War en-

NOTABLE AMERICANS

Paul Cuffe: Fighter for Equal Rights

A Massachusetts shipowner named Paul Cuffe noticed something that many other Americans had overlooked: "taxation without representation" did not end with the American Revolution. As a landowner and business person (he owned a farm in Westport and had started his own shipping business), Cuffe had to pay taxes to his town and state. But as a black, Cuffe could not vote for the representatives who levied those taxes.

Cuffe and seven other free blacks decided to fight for their rights. In 1780, they sent a petition to the Massachusetts legislature. "We are not allowed the privilege of freemen of the state, having no vote or influence in the election of those that tax us," the men wrote. They

also pointed out that many blacks had "entered the field of battle and fought against a similar situation in regard to taxation."

Unmoved by this reference to the American Revolution, the white male legislators rejected the blacks' petition. Cuffe and his brother, who had been captured off a whaling ship by the British during the Revolutionary War, were not people to give up easily. To protest, they stopped paying taxes. The authorities threw them in jail. But in the end, the Cuffes won. In 1783, a Massachusetts court ruled that black male taxpayers had a right to vote.

Cuffe, a tall, energetic Quaker, continued to struggle for black rights for the rest of his life. In 1797, he bought a farm at New Bedford, south of Boston, where he lived with his Indian wife, Alice Pequit. When he realized that there was no school for free black children, Cuffe started one. He built a schoolhouse and paid a teacher out of his own funds. He also used his ships to take black Americans to Sierra Leone, in Africa, where he hoped they would start colonies and spread Christianity.

See p. T22.

1. What argument did Cuffe and other blacks use to support their petition for the right to vote?

2. **Critical Thinking** How did Cuffe's life reflect the peaceful principles of the Quaker religion?

3.

1. **CITIZENSHIP** James Otis, who favored freedom for slaves, wrote, "The colonists are by the law of nature free born as indeed all men are, white or black."

rolled as minutemen. Black soldiers also fought at Fort Ticonderoga, Bunker Hill, and Lexington and Concord.

As much as the support of able-bodied soldiers was welcomed, the participation of blacks posed problems for the members of the Continental Congress. They worried that blacks would take the idea of freedom too seriously and wondered if such thinking might encourage slaves to revolt.

In November 1775, George Washington, acting with the advice of other generals, recommended that black soldiers be barred from enlisting in the Continental army. The Continental Congress agreed. In the same month, the British stepped up their efforts to recruit blacks, offering freedom to any slave or indentured servant who would join the British Army.

The British action forced the Americans to reconsider their position, and in January 1777, the Continental army began enlisting free blacks. A year later, Rhode Island raised an entirely black battalion, made up of soldiers both slave and free. In all, about 5,000 black soldiers fought for the Patriot cause.

Women's Contribution to the War Effort

Although men were expected to do the fighting, women fought too. Sally St. Clair of South Carolina, like Deborah Sampson of Massachusetts, disguised herself as a man and enlisted in the Continental army. When Molly Pitcher's husband fell next to his artillery piece, legend has it that she took his place. Women were also among the most skilled spies in the colonial intelligence network.

Wives often accompanied their husbands' regiments. They cooked, laundered, or sewed during lulls in combat. They collected or prepared medicines and nursed sick and wounded soldiers. Benjamin Franklin's daughter, Sara Franklin Bache, organized a Daughters of Liberty chapter to make clothing and handle hospital shipments. With many men away fighting, women took over traditionally male jobs. They maintained farms, ran businesses, and worked as blacksmiths, producing the cannons, guns, and shot needed to keep the Continental army going.

Some women went to war with their Patriot husbands and shared in the battle. Among them was Mary Ludwig Hays, nicknamed Molly Pitcher. She became a legend in the battle of Monmouth when she took her fallen husband's place to keep a Patriot cannon firing.

3. **BIOGRAPHY** Mary Hays earned the nickname Molly Pitcher when she carried a pitcher of water to her husband and other soldiers during the battle.

The British Position

Great Britain began the war with several distinct advantages. Many British generals had wide-ranging experience in large-scale European wars. They understood military strategy, and they knew how to transport and deploy regiments effectively.

Redcoats, as British soldiers were called because of their bright red uniforms, were well-trained and highly disciplined. They followed the orders of superior officers unquestioningly, unlike the freewheeling amateur colonial militia. Moreover, the redcoats were well-supplied with artillery, firearms, powder, and the many other necessities of war.

The British regulars were supported by a strong navy. The Royal Navy placed 28 warships in ports from New York to Halifax, Nova Scotia. Vessels transported fresh troops from

123

2. **BACKGROUND** New Yorkers tore down a statue of King George III in July 1776. The lead scraps were sent to Litchfield, Connecticut, where women made them into cartridges for the Continental army.

1. **CRITICAL THINKING** Have students consider how Britain might have reacted to American "guerrilla" tactics. Ask: Are guerrilla tactics effective today? Explain.

2. **BIOGRAPHY** Haym Salomon, a Polish-Jewish immigrant who worked with the New York Sons of Liberty, devoted his efforts to raising money for food and military gear.

Europe, usually without interference, and shifted armies in the colonies by sea, a method far more efficient than marching men along dangerous country roads.

The British faced disadvantages too, and these contributed to their undoing. Chief among them was the problem of supply. Fighting in a hostile country that was 3,000 miles (4,800 kilometers) from ports in England meant that it could take weeks and sometimes months for needed materials and reinforcements to arrive. Campaigns often stalled while generals waited for supplies. As British troops pushed farther into the interior, the supply problem grew worse. The British also found it difficult to adapt to the new kind of war being fought in America. The British army could conquer, occupy, and hold cities like Boston, New York, or Philadelphia without difficulty, but in the countryside it was at the mercy of colonial forces. Colonial militias would attack and then vanish into the woods, only to reappear in unexpected locations to ambush British soldiers and supply units. American officers used this hit-and-run tactic often.

The American Position

The colonies had several advantages of their own when the war began. As a besieged nation, Americans responded to the threat to their land with a fervor that often inspired heroism. Most Americans also knew how to use guns, and their hunting rifles proved more accurate than British muskets. Furthermore, George Washington turned out to be a superb leader. Finally, several foreign countries, especially France, provided valuable aid, as did private citizens from other nations.

But the American cause was not without its problems. Few soldiers had regular army experience, and volunteers enlisted for short terms. The Continental and state navies gave the British navy little to fear. And, while Americans did not have to send supplies across an ocean, the Continental Congress lacked the authority to require states or citizens to provide funds or military service. Thus, the Continental army could never get enough food, ammunition, or clothing. And most of all, the Americans had to overcome the problem of **localism,** 13 states going their separate ways instead of acting as one nation.

Maintaining the Military Forces

The lack of a strong navy posed a serious problem for the Americans. Six states owned ships suitable for patrolling inland waterways, but none had vessels like the seagoing British men-of-war. On October 13, 1775, the Continental Congress authorized the construction of a Continental navy, but one hardship after another befell the effort. For instance, four frigates had to be destroyed before they were finished to prevent them from falling into British hands.

3. **VISUAL EVIDENCE** Ask students to describe the mood of this painting.

Offers of land were made to encourage men to enlist in the Continental army. However, the fishermen of Marblehead, Massachusetts, willingly responded to the call for Patriots to join. In this painting, they are being drilled before setting out to join the action around Boston.

1. **TECHNOLOGY** Have interested students find out more about the types of ships used during the war. They might prepare an illustrated oral report.

2. **ECONOMICS** Have interested students research the causes and effects of inflation. Ask them to compare present-day causes with those during the Revolution.

Despite all its problems, the United States Navy did win a few battles. In 1779, Captain John Paul Jones, commanding the *Bonhomme Richard,* engaged the British ship *Serapis* in a savage fight. During the heat of battle, the British captain called on Jones to surrender his leaking ship, but Jones retorted, "I have not yet begun to fight." Two hours later, the British captain surrendered. Jones's feat, however, was the exception, not the rule. At the end of the war, the American navy consisted of only one or two ships larger than a schooner.

Creating a national army was also difficult. Most soldiers' loyalties were to their own states, not to the nation as a whole. If war threatened their home ground, they flocked to its defense. But as soon as the scene of battle shifted, the war became someone else's problem. Soldiers returned immediately to their farms, shops, and families. Those who remained often refused to serve under officers from other colonies.

This narrow view of each state's military responsibilities extended to the area of supplies. State governments provided powder, tents, uniforms, and blankets to their own soldiers, but failed to contribute such supplies to the Continental army. It was not unusual for one state militia to refuse to share its provisions and equipment with another— even when it had a surplus.

Washington did everything in his power to discourage the individual colonies from operating as though they were fighting private wars with Britain, but he was not very successful. "I have laboured," he wrote, "to discourage all kinds of local attachments and distinctions of country . . . but I have found it impossible to overcome prejudices."

Political and Financial Localism

Congress's problems were similar to those facing Washington. With the approval of the Declaration of Independence, the Continental Congress assumed the role of the new nation's government. But what powers did it have? How could it enforce its decisions?

The individual states were not very cooperative. Their concern with local matters made them indifferent to national issues as a whole. For example, only states had the power to draft men into the army. When the Continental Congress asked the states to provide more troops, few states filled their quotas. Early in the war, several states even seemed willing to negotiate separate treaties with foreign nations.

Raising money to finance the war created the worst problems. The states would not grant the Continental Congress authority to tax. The Congress assessed each state a certain sum, but the states either refused to pay or refused to levy the necessary taxes for fear of alienating their people.

The only course of action left to Congress was to authorize the creation of a national currency, known as the Continental dollar. With the crank of a printing press, plain paper was turned into money. But without any gold or silver to back up the currency, it had little value. The resulting inflation made it difficult for people to buy the necessities of life. As more money was printed, its value declined further.

Eventually, even Patriots objected to being paid for supplies in Continental dollars; to say that something was "not worth a Continental" meant it was worthless. To make matters worse, each of the 13 states continued to print its own paper money. With 14 different currencies circulating during the war, public finance became chaotic.

See p. T22.

SECTION 3 REVIEW

1. **Identify:** (a) Loyalists, (b) Patriots, (c) redcoats, (d) John Paul Jones.

2. **Define:** (a) pacifism, (b) localism.

3. Describe the policies of the Continental Congress toward the enlistment of American blacks in the army.

4. How did women contribute to the war effort?

5. (a) List the advantages and disadvantages of the British forces. (b) List the advantages and disadvantages of the Americans.

6. **Critical Thinking** Why do you think that the states found it difficult to submit to a central authority?

4 Fighting a Colonial War

READ TO UNDERSTAND

■ Why American morale was low near the end of 1776.

■ Why American victories at Trenton and Princeton were important.

■ What hindered the British plan to conquer New York and isolate New England.

As the late summer sun beat down on New York City in 1776, the Continental army faced its first real test. Washington, with a ragtag band of hastily trained and poorly armed Patriots, faced a force of 32,000 professional British soldiers.

The British won skirmish after skirmish. But in a pattern that would be repeated, a decisive military victory remained out of their reach. As the drama of these encounters unfolded, Washington and his staff began to realize that the British were not the invincible war machine that the Americans had feared they would be.

The New York Campaign

In deciding to strike at New York City, General Sir William Howe assumed that the mere sight of his troops sailing into New York Harbor would terrify the rebels into surrender. As one witness described the scene from his window, "I spied as I peeped out something resembling a wood of pine trees trimmed. The whole bay was [as] full of shipping as it could be. I thought all London was afloat." But Howe, who was sympathetic to the Americans, hoped to avoid a battle. He even went so far as to offer the Continental Congress a royal pardon if it would surrender.

To Howe's regret, the Congress chose to fight rather than submit. Though Washington mustered a force only half as large as Howe's, he marched resolutely into battle. War, even with the threat of a crushing defeat, seemed preferable to a humiliating surrender.

Despite courageous fighting and skillful maneuvering, Washington's troops could not hold New York. The British chased them out of Long Island and forced them to abandon strategic positions on Manhattan Island. 1. Pushed across the Hudson River into New

2. **VISUAL EVIDENCE**
Though the Americans had built two heavily armed forts on either side of the river, the British warships sailed northward right past their fire, as shown here.

2. *At the start of the war, Washington's poorly equipped and untrained army was no match for the well-drilled British forces. A British officer painted this watercolor of British ships forcing their way up the Hudson River. Washington's forces were on Manhattan Island, to the right, and Fort Lee, New Jersey, on the left. Soon Washington abandoned the positions and retreated.*

1. BACKGROUND Washington and his troops were ferried across the Delaware by the Marine Regiment, a group of skilled boatmen from Marblehead, Massachusetts.

Jersey, Washington was then pursued by Lord Cornwallis. He beat a hasty retreat southward over the New Jersey plains, finally crossing the Delaware River into Pennsylvania.

By year's end, American morale was very low. Thousands of militiamen began to desert Washington's army. Others, whose one-year enlistments were about to expire, counted the days before they could rejoin their families. For Washington, the situation could not have been bleaker.

Success at Trenton and Princeton

As was customary in warfare at the time, the British had settled into their encampments for the winter. Their troops occupied various New Jersey towns, including Trenton, just across the river from Pennsylvania. In that desperate hour, Washington conceived a bold plan: The hunted prey would become the hunter. On the night of December 25, just days before his soldiers' enlistments expired, Washington recrossed the ice-choked Delaware into New Jersey with 2,400 men. His target was Trenton.

Battling a nasty combination of rain, snow, and sleet, Washington marched his band through the night. Early the next morning, he surprised a contingent of Hessian mercenaries who were groggy with holiday drink. Within 45 minutes, the Hessians were beaten. Washington recrossed the river with 900 prisoners in tow.

Four days later, American troops forged across the river again with an army of 5,000. Although the British blocked their path, the Americans managed to outflank Cornwallis and capture Princeton. Had Washington possessed the necessary supplies and equipment, he would have been able to hold the town. Without them, and with an exhausted army, he was forced to give up Princeton and take refuge for the rest of the winter in the Morristown hills.

As 1776 drew to a close, the Americans felt renewed hope. They had suffered defeat, but they had also accomplished one of their principal objectives: to push the British 60 miles (96 kilometers) back from Philadelphia. An Englishman took note of the fact, commenting, "A few days ago they had given up the cause for lost. Their late successes have

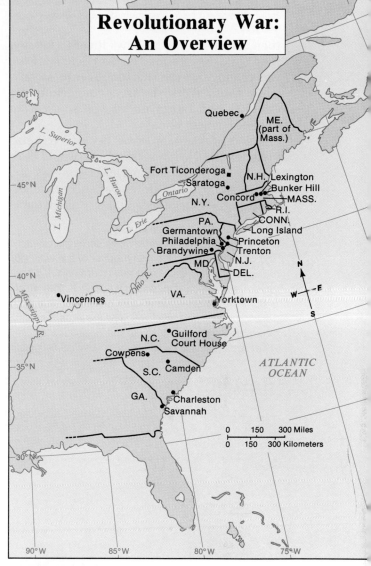

Revolutionary War: An Overview

MAP STUDY *The Revolutionary War was fought over an enormous land area. This map shows the location of the major battles of the war. In which colonies did most of the battles shown on the map take place?* See p. T23.

2.

3.

turned the scale and now they are all liberty mad again."

Saratoga and Philadelphia

During the winter of 1777, the British secretary of war approved a plan to conquer New York and isolate New England. If the strategy had succeeded, it might have split the United States in two and paved the way for a British victory.

According to the plan, Lieutenant Colonel Barry St. Leger (sahn lay ZHAIR) was to lead a force down the St. Lawrence River and

127

2. MAP READING As students read, have them locate the site of each battle on the map.

3. ACTIVITY Have students who have visited the site of a Revolutionary War battle report on what they saw there.

1. **BIOGRAPHY** Burgoyne's troops called him "Gentleman Johnny" because he treated them decently. Burgoyne was also an actor and playwright.

2. **MAP READING** Ask: According to the map, which British general fought the most successful campaign?

then east along the Mohawk River to Albany, New York. (See the map below.) General Howe was to move up the Hudson River to Albany, while another British force, commanded by

1. General John Burgoyne, moved south from Canada to meet him.

Instead, General Howe decided to seize Philadelphia. He hoped the move would both demoralize the Americans and encourage the dispirited Loyalists. Howe was successful, occupying the Patriots' capital city and trounc-

See p. T23.

2. **MAP STUDY** After serious setbacks during the first months of the war, victories at Trenton and Princeton at the end of 1776 gave the Americans new heart. In 1777, they won a stunning victory at Saratoga, marking a major turning point in the war. Who led the American forces at Saratoga? Who led the British forces? What route did the British take to reach Saratoga?

ing Washington at the Battle of Brandywine. In the long run, however, his maneuver proved disastrous to the British cause.

St. Leger's forces reached Fort Stanwix, in the Mohawk River Valley, but they retreated when they received word that a large American army led by Benedict Arnold was approaching. General Burgoyne got off to a more promising start. He captured Fort Ticonderoga, with its huge arsenal of gunpowder and supplies. But without help from Howe, Burgoyne could not keep up the pace, and a string of crushing defeats followed. Marching south from Ticonderoga, Burgoyne's large, unwieldy army was constantly harassed by the hit-and-run guerrilla tactics of the smaller, more agile American forces. Short of supplies and with no reinforcements in sight, Burgoyne finally withdrew to Saratoga.

The move was ill-advised and Burgoyne knew it, but he had no choice. At Saratoga, he was besieged by a crack force under the command of General Horatio Gates and some of the finest officers of the Continental army. 3. Realizing that he had no alternative but to surrender, Burgoyne ordered his entire army of 6,000 men to lay down their arms on October 17, 1777.

Thus, through a combination of chance, poor coordination by British generals, and American persistence, the British plan failed. With this failure, the tide of the war turned firmly in the Patriots' favor.

See p. T23.

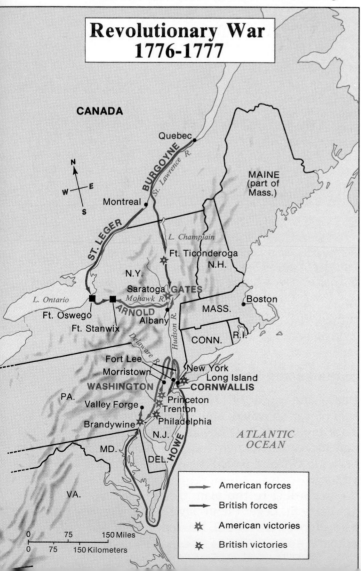

Revolutionary War 1776-1777

CANADA

Quebec

MAINE (part of Mass.)

Montreal

BURGOYNE

St. Lawrence R.

ST. LEGER

L. Champlain

Ft. Ticonderoga

N.H.

N.Y.

Saratoga GATES

Mohawk R.

L. Ontario

ARNOLD

Ft. Oswego

Albany

Ft. Stanwix

Delaware R.

Hudson R.

Boston

MASS.

CONN. R.I.

Fort Lee

Morristown

New York

Long Island

WASHINGTON

CORNWALLIS

PA.

Princeton

Valley Forge

Trenton

Brandywine

Philadelphia

N.J.

HOWE

ATLANTIC OCEAN

MD.

DEL.

VA.

→	American forces
→	British forces
✷	American victories
✷	British victories

0   75   150 Miles
0   75   150 Kilometers

SECTION 4 REVIEW

1. **Identify:** (a) Lord Cornwallis, (b) Barry St. Leger, (c) John Burgoyne, (d) Horatio Gates.

2. What impact did the defeat in New York have on American morale?

3. (a) What new plan did the British devise during the winter of 1777? (b) How did General Howe thwart the plan?

4. Why was the outcome of the battle of Saratoga critical?

5. **Critical Thinking** Why was the issue of morale important to the American cause?

3. **BACKGROUND** The Green Mountain Boys were among those supporting Gates against the British at Saratoga.

1. **BACKGROUND** The French government did send money and weapons secretly before it began to support the United States openly.

2. **MAP READING** Point out to students that the region known as the West in the 1700s is the Midwest today.

5 Victory for the Americans

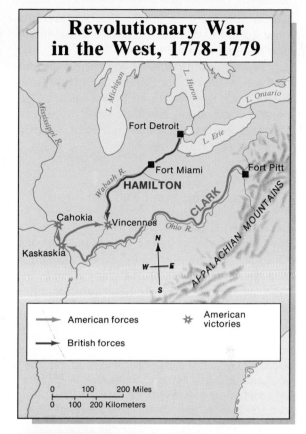

Revolutionary War in the West, 1778-1779

READ TO UNDERSTAND

■ How foreign assistance helped the United States win its independence.

■ Why Britain was unable to conquer the South.

■ What agreements were reached in the Treaty of Paris in 1783.

Despite the Patriots' success at Saratoga, General George Washington suffered from moments of frustration. He wrote to a cousin, "New scenes are beginning to unfold themselves, which will by no means lessen my present trouble.—You ask how I am to be rewarded for all this?—There is one reward that nothing can deprive me of, and that is the certain knowledge that if we should—ultimately—fail in the present contest, it is not owing to the want of exertion in me."

But the victory at Saratoga proved to be a major turning point of the war. It eliminated the British threat from the north and removed an entire British army from action. Even more important, it brought France into the war on the American side.

MAP STUDY *The Revolutionary War was also fought in the West. A small band of frontiersmen led by George Rogers Clark took on the British and broke their control in the region. Near which rivers did the fighting take place? Why was control of the Ohio River probably important in the outcome of the fighting?* 2. See p. T23.

The French Alliance

As a long-standing rival of Britain, France decided early in the struggle that support for the Americans was in its own best interest. Before making a commitment, however, French leaders wanted to be assured that 1. the Americans could win. Saratoga gave them that assurance.

In February 1778, Benjamin Franklin negotiated two treaties with France. The first recognized the United States as an independent nation and granted France special trading privileges with it. The second agreement, which would go into effect only if France and Great Britain went to war, announced that France would give up claims to land in North America east of the Mississippi. The Americans, in turn, agreed to recognize the French right to any lands in the West Indies captured during the war.

The French alliance offered the United States substantial benefits, which undoubtedly changed the course of the war. French naval vessels soon patrolled the American coast, and France dispatched money, military experts, and large quantities of supplies. Even more important, the alliance reduced British pressure on America. When Britain went to war with France in June 1778, and later with Spain, the British could no longer devote all their military strength to putting down the American revolution.

Individuals from foreign nations also aided the Patriot cause. After spending a bitter, 3. hungry, and demoralizing winter (1777–1778) camped at Valley Forge, Pennsylvania, Washington's ragged troops were whipped into fighting shape by Friedrich von Steuben. An experienced veteran of the Prussian army, **129**

3. **CITIZENSHIP** The Spanish governor of Louisiana, Bernardo de Gálvez, supplied cattle to the Americans from herds in Texas. He also attacked the British in Florida. Galveston, Texas, is named after him.

1. Baron von Steuben taught the Continentals how to drill, maneuver, and use bayonets like professional soldiers.

From Poland came Thaddeus Kosciusko (kahs ee UHS koh) and Casimir Pulaski (poo LAHS kee). Kosciusko, an able engineer, designed forts along the Delaware River and the first fortifications at West Point. Pulaski served as a cavalry officer.

The War in the West and the South

Several significant battles of the war were fought in the West, in the area of present-day Ohio, Illinois, and Kentucky. American troops
2. engaged the Shawnee and other western tribes who, as allies of the British, attacked frontier settlements. In 1778–1779, George Rogers

Clark, a Virginian, led 175 volunteer frontiersmen on a soggy march against the British and their Indian allies. Clark won over many of the French inhabitants of the area with promises of religious freedom. He and his party captured major British supply bases at Cahokia, Kaskaskia, and Vincennes, thus breaking British power in the West.

In the meantime, the main battleground of the war had shifted to the South. After their plan to conquer New York and New England failed in 1777, the British developed a new strategy. This time the target was the South rather than the North. The goal, however, remained the same: to crush American resistance once and for all.

3. The British based their hope of success on two factors. First, they believed that they could use troop ships to move soldiers from

4. *General Francis Marion, better known as the "Swamp Fox," harassed the British in South Carolina. Marion and his roughly dressed men launched surprise attacks and then disappeared into the swamps. This painting by William Ranney, done in the 1800s, shows Marion's men crossing the Pee Dee River by raft to attack the British forces.*

1. **BACKGROUND** The blow was struck by General
Daniel Morgan, who led Morgan's Rifles, a brigade
of crack riflemen.

place to place in the South. In this way, they
would be able to travel more rapidly and
efficiently than the Americans, who had to
march overland. Second, the British counted
on wide support from southern Loyalists.

On both points, the British guessed wrong.
They wildly overestimated the number of
Loyalists in the South. Most southerners ar-
dently supported the Patriot cause and provided American forces with constant aid as
they trekked over the countryside. The southerners supplied the army not only with food,
but also with vital intelligence about British
maneuvers. Furthermore, the British had not
anticipated the presence of French warships.
Although the French could not patrol every
inch of the coast, they prevented the British
navy from having a completely free hand.

The British captured Savannah, Georgia,
in December 1778, and for a year American
forces tried to regain it without success. In
May 1780, the British won a stunning victory
at Charleston, South Carolina. Then, working
their way inland, they crushed a Continental
force under Horatio Gates at Camden, South
Carolina. (See the map at the right.)

Although the British won three major
victories in the South, they saw few more.
Washington replaced the blundering Gates
with General Nathanael Greene, a far abler
leader. By the time Greene assumed command of the Continental forces, the British
had begun to make mistakes that would cost
them the war.

Final Victory

The capable but hot-headed British general,
Lord Cornwallis, persisted in using European
battle tactics that did not work. He would
mass his troops for a showdown in open
battle, only to have them harassed by Greene
with small units. As Greene described it: "We
fight, get beat, rise, and fight again." The redcoats often found themselves standing in
battle as stationary targets.

As a result of his devotion to such tactics, Cornwallis received a "very unexpected
1. and severe blow" at Cowpens, South Carolina, on January 17, 1781. There the rebels
inflicted heavy casualties on his troops. Three
months later, Greene's forces destroyed more

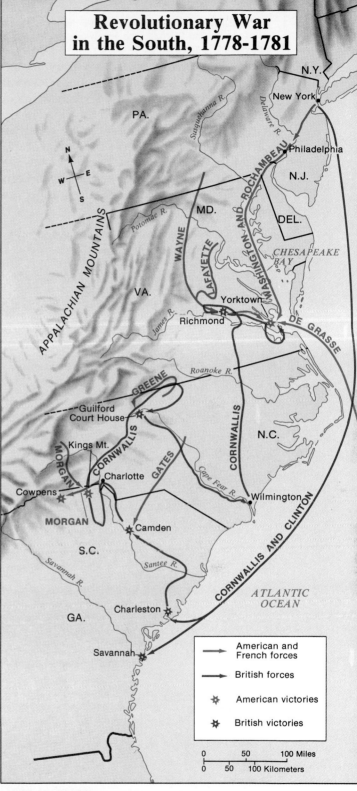

Revolutionary War in the South, 1778–1781

MAP STUDY *The final stages of the
Revolutionary War were fought*
in the South. The British won impressive victories
at Savannah, Charleston, and Camden, but the
Patriots soon had them on the run. Finally, trapped
at Yorktown, Cornwallis surrendered in October
1781. Why was Cornwallis unable to retreat from
Yorktown? See p. T23.

2.

131

2. **MAP READING** Have students trace the movement of Cornwallis and his troops
from New York to Yorktown.

1. **VOCABULARY** Such a victory is a "Pyrrhic victory," a reference to King Pyrrhus, who won two battles against the ancient Romans but suffered very heavy losses.

2. **ACTIVITY** Have interested students research the career of Benedict Arnold and the reasons for his defection, and present their findings to the class.

than a quarter of Cornwallis's army at Guilford Court House, North Carolina. Cornwallis claimed victory at Guilford because Greene withdrew his troops before the close of the battle, but a British observer noted, "Another
1. such victory would destroy the British army."

After Guilford Court House, Cornwallis withdrew to Wilmington, on the North Carolina coast. Battle-weary and discouraged, he wrote to a friend:

My present undertaking sits heavy on my mind. I have experienced the distresses and

dangers of marching some hundreds of miles, in a country chiefly hostile, without one active or useful friend; without intelligence, and without communication with any part of the country.

For a while, Cornwallis's situation seemed to improve. Benedict Arnold, who had deserted to the side of the British, captured 2. and burned Richmond, Virginia. Other areas of the state fell prey to isolated British raids, and reinforcements brought Cornwallis's army up to 7,000 men.

3. **MAP READING** Ask: What territory in North America was still under British control?

MAP STUDY *The Treaty of Paris (1783) ceded to the United States all British land from the Atlantic to the Mississippi and from the Great Lakes to Florida. What European nation claimed territory west of the new nation?* See p. T23. 3.

North America, 1783

Legend:
- Claimed by U.S. and Spain
- Claimed by U.S. and Great Britain
- British
- French
- Spanish
- United States

0 250 500 Miles
0 250 500 Kilometers

1. **BACKGROUND** Lafayette, a French noble, had been fighting with the Patriots since 1777. He was only 20 years old when he arrived in America.

2. **BACKGROUND** The British preferred to have the territory west of the Appalachians controlled by the relatively weak United States rather than by France or Spain.

Once again, however, Cornwallis erred disastrously. He refused an order by Sir Henry Clinton to send part of his army to New York. Instead, he retreated to the Yorktown peninsula in Virginia and began building fortifications.

Washington, who had just received 5,000 French reinforcements led by the Comte de Rochambeau (roh shahm BOH), immediately recognized Cornwallis's mistake. The British general had given him the chance he had been waiting for: an opportunity to stage a combined land and sea attack on the major British force. The picks and shovels being used to fortify Yorktown were digging British graves.

Rochambeau and Washington marched a French and American force overland from New York to join the Marquis de Lafayette (lah fay EHT) in Virginia. At the same time, Admiral de Grasse sailed with 30 ships and 3,000 French marines to Chesapeake Bay. Cut off by land and sea, Cornwallis held out for three weeks. Then, realizing that rescue was impossible, he surrendered his entire army on October 17, 1781, ending all serious fighting in America.

The battlefield at Yorktown presented an imposing spectacle. The French and the Americans lined up in two facing columns a half mile long. As the British army marched between the victorious troops, the British band played "The World Turned Upside Down." Cornwallis, unwilling to appear, sent his deputy, General Charles O'Hara, who turned his sword over to Washington's deputy, General Benjamin Lincoln. The British soldiers then marched to an open field, where they stacked their muskets.

Clinton still had 16,000 troops in New York, but Yorktown and several French victories in the West Indies brought the war to a close. The defeated British sued for peace.

The Peace Treaty

Although Congress ordered Benjamin Franklin not to hold peace talks without the French, he began informal, secret talks with the British anyway. Formal talks began when the other peace commissioners, John Adams, John Jay, and Henry Laurens, arrived in Paris. The British agreed to recognize American independence and granted the Americans all the land from the Atlantic coast to the Mississippi River between the Great Lakes and Florida. Britain also agreed to evacuate military posts in several areas, and the United States won fishing rights off Newfoundland. The terms were considered generous.

Both sides signed the Treaty of Paris on November 30, 1782. It went into effect two months later and was approved by Congress on April 19, 1783, eight years to the day after the first shot at Lexington.

How did it all happen? Washington later marveled at the achievement. Who would believe, he said, "that such a force as Great Britain has employed for eight years in this country could be baffled in their plans of subjugating it by numbers infinitely less, composed of men sometimes half-starved, always in rags, without pay, and experiencing every species of distress, which human nature is capable of undergoing." But happen it did!

The Patriots straggled home, one way or another, to neglected farms and happy families. Now there were 13 free states. What kind of nation would they form? Would they be able to work together for the common good of all?

See p. T23.

SECTION 5 REVIEW

1. **Identify:** (a) Baron von Steuben, (b) Thaddeus Kosciusko, (c) Casimir Pulaski, (d) George Rogers Clark, (e) Nathanael Greene, (f) Marquis de Lafayette.

2. In what three ways did the French alliance help the American cause?

3. Why did the British think they would succeed in the South?

4. What were the terms of the peace treaty ratified in 1783?

5. **Critical Thinking** How was victory at Saratoga a turning point in world history?

3. **ACTIVITY** Have students write a short essay in which they rank the factors that helped the Americans win the Revolution.

Summary

1. **After the Second Continental Congress convened in May 1775, fighting broke out between the British and the colonists.** Colonial forces at Fort Ticonderoga and Boston showed that they could hold their own against the British. The Continental Congress appointed George Washington as commander in chief of the Continental army.

2. **The British responded harshly to colonial resistance.** As a result, Congress adopted the Declaration of Independence on July 4, 1776, and the United States went to war with Great Britain.

3. **The American war effort was hampered by the fact that many colonists were neutral or remained loyal to Great Britain.** Localism also made it difficult to maintain and support a national army. The British advantages of a large, well-trained army and navy were offset in part by the leadership of Washington and the contributions of many women and black Americans.

4. **After an early setback in New York, the Continental army enjoyed victories at Trenton and Princeton.** Other successes followed, at Philadelphia and Saratoga. By the end of 1777, the tide of the war had turned in the Patriots' favor.

5. **Aid from France and other European nations helped the colonists counter British strength.** Tactical errors by British commanders led to final American victory at Yorktown in 1781. When the peace treaty was ratified in 1783, the states faced the challenge of surviving as a new republic.

See p. T24.

Vocabulary

On a separate sheet of paper, write the word or words that best complete each of the following sentences.

1. Groups of citizens who recruited and trained local militia, collected funds, and gathered information were the _____.

2. A request by the Continental Congress urging the repeal of the Coercive Acts was the _____.

3. _____ is the belief that the use of force for any reason is wrong.

4. _____ is the tendency of states to act in their own interests instead of in the interests of the nation as a whole.

5. Colonists who wanted independence called themselves _____.

6. Colonists who supported the king called themselves _____.

See p. T24.

Chapter Checkup

1. What was the significance of the battle of Bunker Hill?

2. What effect did Britain's harsh position toward the colonies have on the movement for independence?

3. (a) What important principle was contained in the preamble to the Declaration of Independence? (b) Why has this continued to be significant? (c) What justifications did the Declaration give for independence?

4. (a) Why did the participation of black soldiers in the war pose serious problems for American leaders? (b) What role did American blacks play in the war?

5. (a) How did localism handicap George Washington in building and maintaining the Continental army? (b) Was he able to overcome this problem? Explain. (c) How did localism handicap the Continental Congress during the war?

6. Describe the significance of each of the following battles: (a) Trenton; (b) Saratoga; (c) Yorktown.

7. (a) What were the terms of the treaties Benjamin Franklin negotiated with the French? (b) Why did the French wait to form a formal alliance?

8. How did miscalculations on the part of the British in the South contribute to an American victory?

See p. T24.

Critical Thinking

1. **Analyzing** (a) According to Thomas Jefferson, what are natural rights? (b) Explain how the theory of natural rights could be used to justify a demand for national independence.

2. **Supporting an Opinion** British statesman Sir Edmund Burke urged a reconciliation with the American colonies. "The use of force alone," declared Burke, "is but temporary. It may subdue for a moment; but it does not remove the necessity of subduing again: and a nation is not governed, which is perpetually to be conquered." Do you agree with Burke's position on the use of force? Give examples of recent events that support your opinion.

See p. T24.

Connecting Past and Present

1. During the Revolutionary War, France provided America with money, military experts, and military supplies. (a) Identify three countries to which the United States provides military assistance today. (b) Why does the United States help other nations in this way?

2. In what ways would your life be different today if America had not won its independence from Great Britain?

See p. T24.

Developing Basic Skills

1. **Comparing** Make a chart with four columns. In column 1, list the advantages of the British at the start of the war. In column 2, list Britain's disadvantages. In columns 3 and 4, do the same for the Americans. (a) Who would seem to have the most advantages? (b) Who would seem to have the most disadvantages? (c) Which advantages or disadvantages do you think were the most important to the outcome of the war? Explain.

2. **Map Reading** Compare the map on page 132 with the map on page 88. Describe how the boundary lines of the United States changed between 1763 and 1783.

WRITING ABOUT HISTORY

Chronological Order

As you have learned, events that are arranged in the order in which they occurred are in chronological order. Supporting information can be arranged in time order when you are describing a series of events. For example, you should use chronological order to organize the supporting details for the answer to this essay question: What events led up to the issuance of the Declaration of Independence?

Some words used to show time relationships are: *when, first, later, soon, immediately, then, at last, afterward, as soon as, while,* and *next.*

Practice: (a) Read the subsection "The Colonists Take Action" on page 116. Copy the words and phrases that show the chronological order of the events being described. (b) Write the answer to the essay question in the first paragraph of this lesson. Organize the supporting facts in chronological order.

American Individualism

"What, then, is the American, this new man?" asked Hector St. John de Crèvecoeur (krehv KOR), a Frenchman who visited America around the time of the revolution. Like most Europeans, Crèvecour quickly recognized that Americans behaved differently from the people of Europe. One trait that set them apart from other people was their individualism.

What is individualism? To many Americans, it means self-reliance. They feel that people should count on themselves to get things done. The rough conditions of early American life encouraged such an attitude. To survive, a backcountry farm family had to master many skills: clearing land, harvesting crops, building furniture, hunting animals, skinning hides, weaving cloth. . . . The list went on and on.

People who rely on themselves also tend to think for themselves. Individualism also means the ability to accept the consequences of one's decisions, no matter how dangerous or unpopular they are. The colonists, after much consideration, decided that the colonies should be free of British rule. They declared independence. They had made their decision; now they had to fight for it.

Even before the skirmish at Lexington and Concord in 1775, Governor Gage of Massachusetts discovered a new spirit among the colonists. He sent someone into the countryside to find out what the people were thinking. The agent stopped at a house where an old man was cleaning his rifle. "I asked him what he was going to kill," the agent reported. "As he was so old, I should not think he could take sight at any game; he said there was a flock of redcoats at Boston, which he expected would be here soon; he meant to try and hit some of them. . . . I asked him how old he was; he said, 'Seventy-seven, and never was killed yet.'" Here was an individualist, indeed—thinking for himself and willing to fight for his principles.

As the United States expanded westward, the frontier experience enhanced the spirit of individualism. People reveled in the exploits of the likes of Mike Fink—a real-life keelboater along the Ohio and Mississippi rivers. "I can out-run, out-jump, throw down, drag out, and lick any man in the country," he boasted. "I'm a Salt-River roarer an' I'm chock full of fight." Similarly, the American cowboy came to be admired as a rugged individualist in the 1870s and 1880s.

Limits on Individualism   How far can individualism be pushed? In the 1840s, Henry David Thoreau built a cabin along the shores of Walden Pond in the Massachusetts woods. He lived there alone for two years. His goal was to simplify his life and be on his own. "I would say to my fellows, once and for all, as long as possible live free and uncommitted. . . ." *Walden,* Thoreau's book about his experiences, describes individualism taken to its limits. Even Thoreau, however, realized that he could not exist forever without others. He planned only a temporary stay at Walden Pond.

The pioneers, too, valued the friendship of good neighbors. They may have been individualists, but they also gathered regularly for barn-raisings and quilting bees. Being an individual did not mean shutting out the rest of the world.

While tolerant of individualists, American society has put limits on them. The

1. The hardy frontier hunters formed the backbone of George Rogers Clark's forces during the Revolutionary War. When the war was over, these rugged individualists once more led the way west.

1. **BACKGROUND** During one campaign in the war, Clark's hardy frontier volunteers covered 180 miles in 18 days, often marching knee-deep in icy water without food.

right to do as one pleases ends where it will infringe on the personal freedoms of others. Some of the best-known Western heroes were people who enforced the law, such as Wyatt Earp and Bill Hickok.

As the population of the country has increased and as people have become more dependent on one another, establishing limits has become more complicated. An inventor with an idea for a new product has the freedom to try to make a fortune from it. But the manufacturer of the product cannot pollute public waterways or produce the product with total disregard for the safety of the people who will use it.

Individualism Today How much freedom to be individualists do we have today? The balance between individual rights and society's need for protection is still a subject of debate. Most states have laws preventing citizens from driving cars that

have bad brakes or are unsafe in other ways. But should people be free not to wear seat belts in a car—even if seat belts reduce the consequences of accidents? Some states say yes, others no. Do "individualists" have the right to play radios loudly on a downtown street? Should sightseeing planes be free to fly low over national parks like the Grand Canyon? These questions are not easily answered, because Americans, in their individualistic ways, will no doubt continue to disagree on issues that are important to them.

See p. T24.

1. How did the need to rely on oneself encourage the development of individualism in early Americans?

2. **Critical Thinking** Why do you think the rights of the individual must be balanced against the needs of society?

137

Ethan Allen

What was there about Ethan Allen that earned him a place in history? Of course, he defeated the British at Fort Ticonderoga. But why was he there? The answer lies in the fact that Allen was a person who did things his own way.

Allen was born in 1738 in Litchfield, Connecticut. By the late 1760s, he had moved to the New Hampshire Grants. At the time, New York and New Hampshire disputed ownership of the Grants, which later became the state of Vermont. Allen joined many of the Grants settlers in refusing to recognize the jurisdiction of New York. The settlers wanted to reorganize the area into a separate province. In 1770, Allen formed a militia—the Green Mountain Boys—to press the case by force, if necessary.

In 1771, the new royal governor of New York decided to enforce the colony's claims to the Grants. He offered generous rewards for the capture of the Grants outlaws and a particularly high price for their popular leader, Ethan Allen.

Although Allen stepped up his attacks on the Yorkers, by the spring of 1775, the Vermont landholders were clearly losing the battle of the Grants. Just then, however, the Revolutionary War broke out, and everyone's attention turned elsewhere. Throwing his lot in with the revolutionaries, Ethan Allan led the Grants settlers into open rebellion against the British.

At the time of the revolution, the British had a fort at Ticonderoga. Situated astride the major north-south water route from Canada into the 13 colonies, it was a strategic stronghold. To isolate Canada and cut off British supplies to the western colonies, the Committees of Correspondence sent troops from Massachusetts and Connecticut led by Benedict Arnold to capture the fort. In a bold undertaking, 200 militiamen led by Ethan Allen spearheaded the fight. Arnold's troops and Allen's Green Mountain Boys combined forces on May 8, 1775. By May 10, they had secured the fort. Later, they captured Crown Point to the north.

1. *Ethan Allen (1738–1789) was known for doing things his own way. His exploits and legendary strength won him the admiration of many people. Allen, at right, waves his sword at the British commander as the colonists seize Fort Ticonderoga.*

1. **VISUAL EVIDENCE** This painting of Ethan Allen's capture of Fort Ticonderoga now hangs in the Fort Ticonderoga museum.

Shortly afterward, the Green Mountain Boys were attached to the Continental army under their own officers. The Americans planned to attack Montreal. When expected troops failed to join the invaders, Allen, perhaps rashly, led a raid with his own men. The British took him prisoner and threatened to hang him in London. But after a brief stay in a British prison, he was returned to America and held until General Washington himself secured his release.

In the meantime, the Grants had declared independence, but the Continental Congress refused to recognize them. Upon regaining his freedom, Allen returned to take up the cause. He died in 1789. Two years later, New York gave up its claim and Vermont became the fourteenth state.

Ethan Allen was a colorful leader, a strong supporter of individual liberty, and a fiery defender of the Vermont country. During his lifetime, his strong streak of individualism won him the admiration of his fellow Americans.

See p. T24.

1. What was the basis of the conflict over the New Hampshire Grants?

2. **Critical Thinking** How does the story of Ethan Allen's adventures resemble a folk talc?

Voices of Freedom

A New Breed of People

French-born Hector St. John de Crèvecoeur traveled widely in the American colonies. He married an American and in 1769 bought a farm in New York. A series of 12 essays that he wrote describing life in America was published in 1782 as Letters From an American Farmer. *The following reading is taken from the third of these "letters," entitled "What Is an American?"*

What, then, is the American, this new man? He is either a European, or the descendant of a European. . . . He is an American, who, leaving behind him all his ancient prejudices and manners, receives new ones from the new mode of life he has embraced, the new government he obeys, and the new rank he holds. . . . Here the rewards of his industry follow with equal steps the progress of his labor. . . .

Europe contains hardly any other distinctions but lords and tenants. This fair country alone is settled by freeholders, the possessors of the soil they cultivate, members of the government they obey, and the framers of their own laws, by means of their representatives. . . . It is here that the idle may be employed, the useless become useful, and the poor become rich. But by riches I do not mean gold and silver; we have but little of those metals. I mean a better sort of wealth: cleared lands, cattle, good houses, good clothes, and an increase of people to enjoy them. . . .

But how is this accomplished in that crowd of . . . people who flock here every year? . . . Let me select one [newcomer] as an example of the rest. He is hired, he goes to work. Instead of being employed by a haughty person, he finds himself with his equal, placed at the table of the farmer. His wages are high, his bed is not like that bed of sorrow on which he used to lie. If he behaves with propriety, and is faithful, he . . . becomes almost a member of the family. . . .

Judge what an alteration there must arise in the mind and thoughts of this man. He begins to forget his former servitude and dependence; his heart involuntarily swells and glows. This first swell inspires him with those new thoughts which constitute an American.

Adapted from *Letters From an American Farmer*, 1782.
See p. T24.

---

1. What did Crèvecoeur believe the newcomers could achieve in America?

2. **Critical Thinking** How would you account for Crèvecoeur's optimistic view of life in America?

An Experimental Era

(1777–1787)

CHAPTER OUTLINE

1 Making a New Start

2 The New American States

3 The First National Government

4 A Need for Further Experimentation

CHAPTER OBJECTIVES After completing this chapter, students should be able to

1. describe the advances made by women and blacks after the Revolution.
2. describe the state governments set up after the Revolution.
3. list the provisions of the Articles of Confederation and the Northwest Ordinance.
4. discuss the problems under the Articles of Confederation.

CHAPTER PREVIEW Tell students that some historians call the period discussed in this chapter the "critical period." Ask them what they think the term means and why they think it might be appropriate for the years covered.

By any standards, the Peale household was unusual. The house on Lombard Street in Philadelphia was bursting with Charles Willson Peale's 17 children, countless relatives, and various live bears, snakes, and birds. From its windows came the sounds of a xylophone under construction and clouds of steam from a portable steam bath Peale had invented.

Peale was a skilled artist who painted portraits of George Washington, the Marquis de Lafayette, and other revolutionary heroes. He turned his hand to anything and everything. A bold experimenter, he invented a machine to pare apples, another to duplicate letters, and a third to chase away flies. His collection of plants, animals, and rocks constituted the first museum of natural history in North America.

"You must visit the Peale house," Philadelphians told out-of-town guests. There, visitors might be greeted by one of the painter's sons— Raphaelle, Rembrandt, Reubens, Titian, or Vandyke, named for great European artists.

The boys would show guests around. One might point to the huge mastodon that their father had helped excavate on a New York farm. (See page 141.) Another might tell how his father had tried to preserve Benjamin Franklin's dead angora cat for his collection. A third might recall that when Lafayette sent Washington several French pheasants, their father wrote the general requesting the body of any bird that died. Washington soon replied, "Sir: You will receive by the stage the body of my gold pheasant, packed up in wool agreeable to your directions."

Like Franklin, Jefferson, and others interested in scientific inquiry, Peale was an optimist. He was sure that all problems had a solution. In that sense, he reflected the mood of the new nation. He reflected, too, the nation's willingness to try new ideas.

The country needed that bold approach to its affairs. Even as Americans were winning their revolution, they faced many challenges. Foremost was the need to create a stable government. The 13 states wrote their own constitutions and then designed a central government under the Articles of Confederation. When that government faltered, Americans tried a new experiment.

1.

Articles of Confederation

1776	1778	1780	1782	1784	1786	1788

1777 Vermont abolishes slavery

1779 Massachusetts convention drafts a constitution

1781 Articles of Confederation ratified

1783 Treaty of Paris ratified

1786 Shays' Rebellion begins

1787 Northwest Ordinance passed

1. **TIME LINE QUESTION** Ask: What rebellion took place while the nation was governed under the Articles of Confederation?

Science intrigued many Americans in the new republic. Charles Willson Peale, who founded a museum to "create a world in miniature," painted this scene of the

1. unearthing of mastodon bones in New York. Spectators could take part in the project by walking inside the huge wheel, which turned a chain of buckets bringing water out of the hole.

---

1. **VISUAL EVIDENCE** Both this painting and the mastodon skeletons were exhibited at Peale's museum.

1 Making a New Start

READ TO UNDERSTAND

■ How the nation moved to broaden political and social equality after the Revolutionary War.

■ What gains were made by women and free blacks after independence.

■ What actions were taken against slavery and to establish separation of church and state.

2. ■ *Vocabulary:* segregated, manumission.

The Revolutionary War jolted Americans out of their everyday habits. By the 1780s, Americans were ready to accept sweeping social

and political change. As Benjamin Franklin observed, "We are, I think, on the right road to improvement, for we are making experiments." Not only in politics, he might have 3. added, but in all aspects of life, people's expectations had been raised.

Moving Toward Political and Social Equality

Political equality became a major goal in the young republic. The new state constitutions seemed to echo Jefferson's words in the Declaration of Independence, that "all men are created equal." Some states extended the right to vote by lowering or eliminating property requirements.

But the advance of political equality was **141** less than perfect. To qualify to vote, a per-

2. **VOCABULARY** Have students look up these words in the glossary before they begin reading.

3. **CITIZENSHIP** Ask: How does this statement show his belief that experimentation could lead to progress in the social and political world?

1. **CITIZENSHIP** During the colonial period, a few wealthy women had been permitted to vote in local elections.

*Women did not share in the growing political
1. equality. Only in New Jersey could women vote.
And after a political scandal in 1806, they lost the
right to vote even there.*

2. **BACKGROUND** The society was named after Lucius Quinctius Cincinnatus, a Roman soldier and statesman.

son typically had to be male, white, Christian, and a property owner. Despite some criticism of these qualifications, most state governments did little to change them in the early years.

A reaction set in against organizations that set up some people as superior to others. In 1783, a group of former Continental army officers founded the Society of the Cincinnati to promote the views of veterans. Membership was hereditary; only officers and their descendants could belong. Even though George Washington himself was a member, the society was roundly attacked as being dangerously aristocratic.

In the new nation, land was widely available, and poorer Americans felt they had the chance to become the social equal of their richer neighbors. One observer later noted how a farmer knew that "every stroke of the axe and the hoe made him a capitalist, and made gentlemen of his children." Changes in inheritance laws broke up many large landholdings. In addition, the government sold property taken from Loyalists during the revolution and gave soldiers western land as bonuses. The creation of equality of opportunity through land ownership tended to break down social barriers.

3. **ACTIVITY** Have students research the European philosophical movement known as the Enlightenment, one subject of interest at the time.

Experiments in Education

With changes in society came a demand for reform in education. Most schools concentrated on instruction in Latin and Greek to prepare students for entrance into a university. People in the expanding middle class began to question this emphasis on the classics. They clamored for practical education to prepare their children for careers in crafts or business. Soon, too, the first coeducational schools appeared.

Heightened interest in learning encouraged the publication of newspapers, magazines, and a flood of new, American textbooks. Scientific societies such as the newly founded American Academy of Arts and Sciences and the older American Philosophical Society encouraged communication between scientists at home and abroad.

Limited Opportunities for Women

Although new ideas about equality abounded in the United States, the status of women remained unequal. Abigail Adams, among others, denounced the lack of female equality. While her husband John was attending the Continental Congress, she warned him: "Do not put such unlimited power in the hands of husbands. Remember all men would be tyrants if they could."

Abigail Adams was not alone in her belief that the phrase "all men are created equal" should mean "all humans are created equal." Nonetheless, the laws did not provide for such equality. Women had few property rights and no voting rights, except for a brief period in New Jersey when they were allowed to vote. The political system was in men's hands and remained there until the 1900s.

Women fared a little better in the realm of education. In the late 1700s, a number of New England academies began to admit female students. Some even let women take the same courses as men. But women still faced discrimination. Lucinda Foote's experience is just one example.

At age 12, Lucinda Foote proved to a board of examiners that she could do college work. The report came back saying that she appeared "fully qualified except in her sex, to

4. **BACKGROUND** She continued, "If particular care and attention is not paid to the ladies, we are determined to foment rebellion, and will not be bound by any laws in which we have no voice or representation."

be received as a pupil of the freshman class of Yale University." And so her application
1. was rejected.

Limited Advances for Free Blacks

The revolutionary idea that "all men are created equal" appealed to black as well as white Americans. More than 50,000 free blacks lived in the United States in the 1780s, mostly in the Middle Atlantic states.

In several states, courts began to look more favorably on lawsuits filed by slaves seeking freedom. North Carolina, Maryland, Kentucky, and Tennessee gave free blacks the right to trial by jury, the right to compel the appearance of witnesses, and the right to legal counsel. Furthermore, the first state

constitutions in the Northeast did not generally limit voting rights by race.

After the revolution, the demand for workers in the North improved the standard of living of many free blacks. Meanwhile, some formerly all-white churches admitted blacks, although not always with equal membership rights.

Still, blacks suffered far-reaching discrimination. Most northern states discouraged black immigration, and areas where free blacks could live were **segregated,** or separated on the basis of race. In the northern part of the South, free blacks might at any moment be kidnapped back into slavery. And states in the deep South, if they allowed free blacks at all, usually denied them most civil rights.
2.

Folk artists captured many vignettes from American life, like the scene on this tea tray. It shows Congregational minister Lemuel Haynes, a Revolutionary War
3. *veteran, addressing one of his congregations.*

Early Actions Against Slavery

Try to picture Thomas Jefferson, sitting in his plantation at Monticello, reviewing the words he had written in the Declaration of Independence. As his eyes once again scan the words "all men are created equal," he turns and looks out the window at some of the people working on his estate. These people are his slaves. The moral dilemma did not escape him. Jefferson struggled with the prob-
1. lem of slavery all his life.

Jefferson was not alone in his dilemma. The Continental Congress had banned the slave trade during the Revolutionary War, and all states except Georgia and South Carolina outlawed it by the war's end. Yet such actions did not end the slave trade, which was protected by the Constitution until 1808. (See pages 162–163.)

Vermont's constitution, written in 1777, was the first to abolish slavery itself. Over the next 20 years, all the northern states either outlawed slavery or made plans for gradually freeing slaves within their borders.

In the South, the institution of slavery grew stronger. Slave labor was vital to southern agriculture. Jefferson, Washington, and Madison opposed slavery in principle; in practice, they could not run their plantations without the help of slaves. While the Virginia legislature allowed **manumission,** or the freeing of slaves, sentiment for the abolition of slavery was not widespread in the South.

In states like New York and Pennsylvania, citizens formed societies to oppose slavery and promote equality. Together with the Quakers, who steadfastly opposed slavery, such societies formed the base from which a strong movement to abolish slavery would eventually grow. (See Chapter 15.)

Separation of Church and State

Slavery was just one institution that came under attack. As you have learned, before the Revolutionary War, most colonies supported an official church. All citizens, whether members or not, had to support this established church with taxes. The Congregational Church was the established church in much

144

of the Northeast, and the Church of England, renamed the Episcopal Church after the war, was the established church in the South.

Thomas Jefferson, among others, thought that such partnerships of church and state restricted religious freedom and gave the established church an unfair advantage. "Almighty God hath created the mind free," argued Jefferson.

In 1786, Virginia adopted a law, first proposed by Jefferson, that effectively separated church and state. The law stated that "no man shall be compelled to frequent or support any religious worship, place, or ministry whatsoever." Other southern states also 2. disestablished the Episcopal Church, but in 3. New England, some states maintained a favored status for the Congregational Church until 1817.

New National Consciousness

After the revolution, former British subjects began to think of themselves proudly as citizens of a new nation. Politicians and philosophers predicted that the United States would become "a great and mighty empire." According to one New Englander, it would be "the largest the World ever saw, to be founded on such principles of Liberty and Freedom, both civil and religious, as never before took place in the world." 4.

Claims of American inferiority by European philosophers brought quick responses from proud Americans. Benjamin Franklin, for example, gave a dinner party in Paris at which a Frenchman, the Abbé Raynal (ray NAHL), argued that the American environment caused plants, animals, and even humans to grow smaller than those found in Europe. Franklin, noticing the height of his dinner guests, asked everyone to stand. The Abbé, who had been so eager to make his point, stood nearly a head shorter than the American guests.

Noah Webster, who would later gain fame for his dictionary, contributed to the new national awareness by experimenting with the American language. (See page 145.) Efforts by individuals like Webster helped Americans forge a national spirit.

Noah Webster: Creating an American Language

Imagine a small New England town in the late 1700s. A printer stands in his shop, arranging type. He looks up and sees a tall, earnest stranger holding out a sheet of paper.

"My good man," says the stranger, "take this sheet. Study the words and their spellings. We Americans must rid our language of the oddities we inherited from our former British masters. I should be much obliged if you would use these American spellings in your work." And, with a polite nod, the stranger—Noah Webster—was gone.

Webster was a man with a mission. He could not rest until he broke the hold of "the king's English," as Americans had broken the hold of the king's rule. To this end, Webster published a series of textbooks: a speller in 1783, a grammar in 1784, and a reader in 1785.

Webster claimed that borrowings from other languages had turned English spelling into a senseless hash. Letters sometimes seemed to have been tossed into words by chance. Many letters were not pronounced the way they looked; others were not pronounced at all.

Webster urged Americans to simplify their spelling. He thought "friend" should be spelled "frend"; "head" should be "hed"; and "laugh" should be "laf." Although the change from "theatre" to "theater" caught on, most of Webster's suggestions did not. Despite this, Webster's books sold by the millions.

Webster continued to work for a national language, publishing the respected *An American Dictionary of the English Language* in 1828. "A national language," he wrote, "is a band of national union. Every engine [means] should be employed to render the people of this country national; . . . and to inspire them with the pride of national character."

See p. T25.

1. What was Noah Webster's mission?

2. Critical Thinking How does a common language help to form a people's identity?

---

1. **ECONOMICS** Webster's "blue-backed speller" was a best seller for years after his death, selling more than 60 million copies in 50 years.
See p. T25.

SECTION 1 REVIEW

1. **Identify:** (a) Society of the Cincinnati, (b) Abigail Adams, (c) Noah Webster.

2. **Define:** (a) segregated, (b) manumission.

3. (a) What were the typical qualifications for voting in state elections? (b) How was the opportunity for land ownership extended?

2. **VOCABULARY** Many English words retain the spelling of Old English, a medieval Germanic language in which consonants and vowels that are silent today were pronounced.

4. What limits on equality did women face?

5. (a) In what ways did the position of free blacks improve after the Revolutionary War? (b) What limitations remained?

6. **Critical Thinking** Why do you think social change accompanied the political change brought about by the American Revolution?

3. **BACKGROUND** Webster's *Dictionary* was also popular in England, although many English scholars criticized the inclusion of "Americanisms" and slang words.

1. **VOCABULARY** Have students look up these terms in the glossary before they begin reading.

2 The New American States

READ TO UNDERSTAND

■ Why Americans modeled their new state governments on the existing colonial governments.

■ What safeguards for liberty were included in state constitutions.

■ How the process of writing state constitutions served as a model for the writing of a national constitution.

1. ■ *Vocabulary:* veto, bicameral legislature, inalienable rights.

The band of soldiers marched onto the parade ground. Off to one side, a new recruit nervously shifted his feet and pledged an oath: "I do solemnly swear to bear true allegiance to the United States of America and to serve *them* honestly and faithfully"—them, not it.

The United States of the 1770s and 1780s differed greatly from the United States today. Soldiers served *them*—the states that had united. They did not think of the United States as a unit. Not until the Civil War would
2. people stop referring to "these" United States.

When Thomas Jefferson said "my country," he meant Virginia. In most people's minds, the new national government had only limited importance. People felt loyalty first of all to their states.

Preserving Traditions

The English philosopher John Locke supposed that when a people decided to overthrow one government, they would have to start from scratch and design a new one. Yet nothing of the sort happened in America in 1776. Instead, Americans built on British traditions and their own experiences.

Colonial assemblies became state legislatures, and many prewar laws remained in
3. effect. In a few cases, the old royal charters became the new state constitutions. By the end of 1776, independent governments were functioning in every state except Georgia and New York.

3. **CITIZENSHIP** The Fundamental Orders of Connecticut, the first written constitution in the English colonies, had been adopted in 1639. (See p. 45.)

Why were so few changes made? In general, Americans were satisfied with the unwritten British constitution or with the local colonial governments. Their anger had been directed at the king, his representatives, and Parliament for what they saw as violations of British political traditions. The changes they did make were usually to insure that power could not be abused as it had been in the past.

State Governments

Each new state government had three branches: an executive branch, a legislature, and a court system. Colonial governors had been the symbol of British monarchy, and Americans remained suspicious of the office. That being the case, state constitutions limited the governors' powers.

In most states, the governor was elected by the legislature, often for only a one-year term. Usually, the governor could not **veto,** or reject, a bill passed by the legislature. Pennsylvania eliminated the position of governor entirely and substituted a council of 12 men. State judges, like governors, had limited authority. On the other hand, people trusted the legislatures. They held wide powers, including the power to declare war and conduct foreign affairs.

This faith in representative assemblies had deep roots. Americans had depended on colonial assemblies to represent their interests since the establishment of the Virginia House of Burgesses in 1619.

Yet the former colonists did not grant unlimited power to the state legislatures. Except for Pennsylvania, each state had a **bicameral legislature**—a legislature with two houses, lower and upper. In this way, lawmaking power was split between two groups that balanced each other.

The lower house was the larger one, and voters elected its members directly, usually every year. It generally possessed the greater power because people believed it was more responsive to their wishes. By tradition, the upper house was designed to be a more cautious body, tempering the more extreme ideas that the lower house, pressured by the people, might entertain. Thus, its members were elected for longer terms, two to four years.

2. **VOCABULARY** Even the choice of the word *state,* which implies a sovereign entity, rather than *county* or *province,* to designate the former colonies indicates how Americans felt about their localities.

The forms of government that developed during colonial times became the basis for state and local governments after independence. New England towns like Essex, New Hampshire, shown here, traditionally had strong town governments in which citizens took an active part.

1.

1. VISUAL EVIDENCE This painting is one of the earliest surviving American landscapes. Ask: What buildings dominated the town?

Most state constitutions sought to protect the people against an abuse of governmental powers by including a bill of rights. This guaranteed certain **inalienable rights**—rights that governments could never take away. A bill of rights typically protected freedom of the press, freedom of religion, and the right to trial by jury.

A Constitution Drawn From the People

During the colonial period, American rights had been based on the English constitution. That, however, was not a written document. It consisted of centuries of accumulated laws, judicial decisions, and traditions, subject to many interpretations. Americans wanted to guarantee their freedoms by putting them in writing.

In most states, legislatures elected during the Revolutionary War simply wrote a constitution and passed it. Although there was vague dissatisfaction with this method, no one faced the problem squarely until 1778. That year, the people of Massachusetts rejected the constitution written by their state legislature. Massachusetts citizens argued that if a legislature could write a constitution, it could also change it whenever it pleased. As a result, nothing could stop a legislature from being as tyrannical as a king.

In 1779, Massachusetts voters elected delegates to a constitutional convention to create a constitution that came directly from the people. The document the delegates drafted was approved the next year by a vote of the people. This method gave the constitution extra strength, because the state legislature could not change the constitution without the consent of the people it represented.

2.

Thus Massachusetts helped set an important rule of American government: constitutions were to be written by special conventions. The rule gained wide acceptance and was followed in 1787, when a special convention wrote the present United States Constitution.

See p. T26.

SECTION 2 REVIEW

1. Define: (a) veto, (b) bicameral legislature, (c) inalienable rights.

2. How did the new state governments build on British traditions and their own experiences?

3. (a) What were the three branches of the new state governments? (b) Why was the power of the governor limited?

4. How did Massachusetts protect its constitution from changes by the state legislature?

5. Critical Thinking Why might it be harder to violate a written constitution than an unwritten one?

2. READING In the Massachusetts Bill of Rights of 1780, John Adams wrote that "the people alone have an incontestable, unalienable . . . right to institute government; and to reform, alter, or totally change the same . . . ."

3 The First National Government

READlTO UNDERSTAND

- How our first national government operated.

- Why speculators cared about a national land policy.

- What changes the Revolutionary War brought to the American economy.

1. ■ *Vocabulary:* confederation, ratify, squatter.

When the delegates to the Continental Congress declared independence in 1776, an uncertain future loomed. What if the colonies did defeat the British? Could they build a nation? Earlier observers had warned that an independent America would be "a mere shambles of blood and confusion," and that civil war would rage from "one end of the continent to the other."

Quick action was needed. The Continental Congress named a committee to draft a national constitution. Everyone realized that the new government had to please 13 strong-minded states.

The Articles of Confederation

The committee completed a draft in a month. But the pressure of the ongoing war, as well as squabbling among delegates who wanted to protect the rights of their individual states, held up agreement on a final draft of the nation's first constitution. This constitution, known as the Articles of Confederation, took effect in 1781. (See page 150.)

The Articles of Confederation proposed a **confederation,** or alliance of independent states. The confederation would have a central government—a congress, much like the existing Continental Congress. On paper, it appeared to be a powerful government. Congress could declare war and appoint military officers. It could receive and send ambassadors, sign treaties and alliances, and regulate dealings with Indians. In the domestic sphere, it could set up post offices, borrow money, and fix weights and measures.

Yet the Articles of Confederation placed strict limits on Congress. For example, Congress could not collect taxes or draft men into the army. It could only request the states to provide it with money or soldiers. 2.

With abuses by the British Parliament fresh in mind, the states were wary of giving too much power to a central authority. Thus,

2. **DISCUSSION** Remind students of the problems faced by the Continental Congress. Ask: Why might this provision cause a problem?

CHART STUDY *Under the Articles of Confederation, the national government had very limited powers. Important powers, such as the right to tax, were kept by the states. How* 3. *would this make it difficult for Congress to exercise the powers it did have?* See p. T26.

The Articles of Confederation

No chief executive
No national court system
Laws need approval of 9 of the 13 states
All other powers reserved to the states

Congress could	Congress could not
Declare war and make peace	Levy taxes
Raise an army and navy	Regulate foreign or domestic trade
Make foreign treaties and alliances	Settle disputes among states
Coin and borrow money	Collect state debts owed the central government
Regulate weights and measures	Enforce any of its powers
Establish a post office	
Regulate Indian affairs	

148

3. **CHART STUDY** Ask students which power of Congress they consider to be most important and explain why. Then ask them to think of problems that might arise as a result of limitations on the power of Congress.

1. **DISCUSSION** Have students, taking the part of large and small states, debate the issue of representation.

a clause in the Articles guaranteed that each state would retain its "sovereignty, freedom, and independence" and keep "every power, jurisdiction, and right" not given directly to Congress. This clause made it more likely that the states would approve the document.

A Question of Fair Representation

The question of representation in the new Congress had caused heated debate in the Continental Congress. There, each state had one vote regardless of its area or population. The proposed Articles of Confederation contained the same provision. Delegates from states with larger populations protested. They insisted that states with more people deserved more influence and hence more votes. Delegates from less populous states, on the other hand, favored one vote per state, since it gave them equal power.

The majority at last accepted the principle of equal representation, with every state

1. having one vote. Nine of the 13 states had to approve a measure before it became law. Although the representatives of the larger states were not satisfied, they saw an urgent need for a national government because of the ongoing war with Great Britain.

Before the Articles of Confederation could take effect, the legislatures of all 13 states had to **ratify,** or approve, them. The Continental Congress submitted the document to the states in late 1777, expecting rapid ratification. However, disputes over conflicting state claims to western territories delayed approval until March 1781.

Dispute Over Western Lands

The boundaries of the new states were not clearly defined. Two or more states often claimed the same territory, and a few states claimed land all the way to the Pacific. Some states refused to ratify the Articles of Con-

2. federation until their claims were settled.

States that had no claim to lands in the West also balked at ratifying the new constitution until the land issue was resolved. Maryland legislators, for example, thought the vast claims of states like Virginia were unfair. What if Virginia sold its western lands

As settlers moved onto the lands of Native Americans, Indian leaders had to decide how to keep the settlers out. The Iroquois chief Ki-on-twog-ky, called Cornplanter, wrote several letters to General Washington complaining about the intruders.

3.

3. **ACTIVITY** Have students find out more about Cornplanter. Then have them write a letter such as Cornplanter might have sent to General Washington.

to gain income? Then Virginia would not need to tax its citizens. What would prevent people and businesses in Maryland from flocking to Virginia to escape taxes? Other states with definite boundaries, particularly Pennsylvania and New Jersey, urged that all western lands be ceded, or turned over, to the national government. Then, as Americans bought and settled the land, the revenue would benefit the entire nation.

Such general arguments, however, were not the only reasons some people wanted the western lands ceded to the national government. A group of individuals, mostly from Maryland, Pennsylvania, and New Jersey, had purchased vast stretches of western territory from Native Americans, often illegally.

These land speculators hoped to sell the land to settlers at a large profit. But first they wanted to make sure that their claims would not be challenged. The speculators believed

149

2. **GEOGRAPHY** Have students find out more about the conflicting land claims and prepare a map showing them. (location)

1. that a national congress would be more co-operative than legislatures from states other than their own. Therefore, they pressured their state legislators to refuse to ratify the Articles until the states ceded all western territory to the national government.

Recognizing the need for a national government, Thomas Jefferson and other Virginians urged their legislature to cede Virginia's claims to the United States government. They argued that with vast western lands, Virginia would be too large to govern properly. Virginia agreed to cede its claims, but the agreement would take effect only when the government voided all purchases of Native American land. In effect, this action destroyed the speculators' hopes for profits. In March 1781, Maryland finally approved the Articles of Confederation. It was the last state to do so.

2.

New Land Policies

After the Revolutionary War ended in 1783, Congress had to decide how to settle and govern the western lands. Representatives were particularly worried about the vast area ceded by Virginia known as the Northwest Territory. (See the map on page 151.)

The Land Ordinance of 1785 Congress passed the Land Ordinance of 1785 in the hopes of raising money. The ordinance provided for the survey and sale of public land. The land was to be divided into townships. Each township would be subdivided into 36 sections, each measuring one square mile

GEOGRAPHIC CONNECTION

The Land Ordinance of 1785: A Neat Plan

If you look down from a plane flying over the mid-portion of the United States today, you see a pattern of neat squares and rectangles. Why so neat? Why aren't fields shaped by wandering streams and ridges as they are in Europe and in the parts of the country that were settled first?

The fact is, what you are seeing from a plane is a cultural landscape, one shaped by human decisions. Congress set the pattern in 1785 when it voted to use the rectangular land survey system for all new lands. This was to be an orderly system, based on a grid of straight lines. Everything would be neat. Calculating area would be a simple matter of multiplying one side by another. Of course, the system had its drawbacks—as when a farmer's straight fence crossed and recrossed a wiggly creek. But, by and large, the system has worked well.

Congress ordered land surveys to be based on the earth's grid of east-west latitude lines (parallels) and north-south longitude lines (meridians). It provided for a three-step division of land. The biggest parcel was to be the township, divided into sections, which in turn were divided into quarters. (See the chart below.)

Surveyors set to work, and soon people were buying lots and starting farms. Over time, the original lines have been modified in places. But the square gridwork has marked the landscape for all to see.

3.

See p. T27.

1. What were the three divisions of land established by Congress?

2. **Critical Thinking** Why was the system of land division in the original 13 colonies similar to the system followed in Europe?

Township	Section	Quarter
6 miles x 6 miles = 9.6 km x 9.6 km = 23,040 acres = 9,324 hectares	1 mile x 1 mile = 1.6 km x 1.6 km = 640 acres = 260 hectares	0.5 mile x 0.5 mile = 0.8 km x 0.8 km = 160 acres = 65 hectares

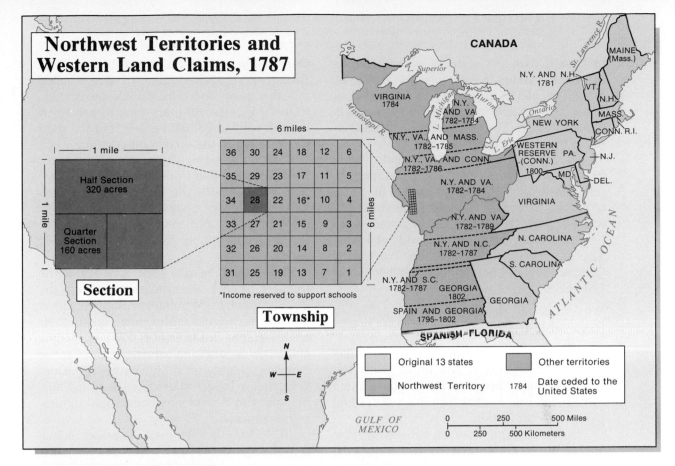

Northwest Territories and Western Land Claims, 1787

1 mile

Half Section
320 acres

Quarter Section
160 acres

1 mile

Section

6 miles

36	30	24	18	12	6
35	29	23	17	11	5
34	28	22	16*	10	4
33	27	21	15	9	3
32	26	20	14	8	2
31	25	19	13	7	1

6 miles

*Income reserved to support schools

Township

CANADA

MAINE (Mass.)

L. Superior

N.Y. AND N.H. 1781

VIRGINIA 1784

VT.

N.H.

N.Y. AND VA. 1782–1784

NEW YORK

MASS.

CONN. R.I.

N.Y., VA., AND MASS. 1782–1785

WESTERN RESERVE (CONN.) 1800

PA.

N.J.

N.Y., VA., AND CONN. 1782–1786

MD.

DEL.

N.Y. AND VA. 1782–1784

VIRGINIA

N.Y. AND VA. 1782–1789

N.Y. AND N.C. 1782–1787

N. CAROLINA

S. CAROLINA

N.Y. AND S.C. 1782–1787

GEORGIA 1802

GEORGIA

SPAIN AND GEORGIA 1795–1802

SPANISH FLORIDA

ATLANTIC OCEAN

Mississippi R.

L. Michigan

L. Huron

Ontario

L. Erie

St. Lawrence R.

N

W E

S

Original 13 states

Other territories

Northwest Territory

1784 Date ceded to the United States

GULF OF MEXICO

0   250   500 Miles
0   250   500 Kilometers

MAP AND GRAPH STUDY *Western land claims created friction among the states. One dispute was resolved when Virginia ceded the land that became known as the Northwest Territory to the national government. In 1785, Congress*
1. *devised a plan for settling the vast area. What provision was made for supporting schools in the Northwest Territory?* See p. T27.

1. **MAP READING** Have students use the map on pp. 840–841 to find out which states were carved out of the Northwest Territory.

(2.6 square kilometers), with one lot set aside to support a school. One provision called for honoring Indian claims, but it was largely ignored.

On paper, the plan seemed sound, but surveyors faced many problems. The terrain was basically uncharted wilderness, with rivers, mountains, and swamps that did not lend themselves to perfect squares. Thus, the work moved slowly. Land speculators had time to revive their efforts to buy large tracts of unsurveyed land. Because Congress desperately needed the revenue, it sold more than a million acres to one group of New England specu-
2. lators for less than ten cents per acre.

The plan was further complicated by **squatters,** people who had moved into the new territory and established homesteads without complying with the ordinance. Congress tried unsuccessfully to clear them out.

Land speculators, worried that squatters would take over their lands, too, urged Congress to pass new legislation dealing with the territory. Other eastern interests, viewing the squatters as violent and dangerous, supported the speculators' urgings. As a result, Congress passed a second land bill, the Northwest Ordinance of 1787.

The Northwest Ordinance Under the new law, Congress would appoint a governor, secretary, and three judges to govern the Northwest Territory. Residents could elect a legislature when the adult male population reached 5,000, but the governor had the power to veto legislation.

The ordinance gave Congress the authority to divide the entire area into three to five separate territories based on settlement patterns. Once a territory had a population of 3. 60,000 free inhabitants, it could be admitted **151**

2. **BACKGROUND** This influential group of New England land speculators was called the Ohio Company.

3. **MAIN IDEA** Have students explain why the Northwest Ordinance was important in American history.

1. **CITIZENSHIP** The Northwest Ordinance also contained a clause saying, "The utmost good faith shall always be observed toward the Indians; their lands and property shall never be taken from them without their consent." Ask: Do you think this policy was always followed?

as a state, with all the rights and obligations of existing states. Meanwhile, the law guaranteed residents' property rights as well as other rights such as trial by jury and religious freedom. The law also prohibited slavery throughout the territory.

Despite continued wheeling and dealing by land speculators, the land ordinance experiment worked. Congress had set up a system that extended republican government westward with the settlers. New states would be admitted as equals of the original states. The pattern established by the Northwest Ordinance continued to work well for over 100 years.

Economic Recovery

Like all wars, the War for Independence disrupted the economy. The impact was the more dramatic because the United States waged this war against its principal trading partner, Great Britain.

In New England, business suffered greatly. Massachusetts shipyards, turning out 125 ships per year before the war, built only 25 ships per year after the war. The whaling industry was reduced from 150 whaling ships to just 24. Some shippers took to privateering and robbed British vessels, but the risks were great and the income uncertain.

After the war, foreign trade built up slowly. France had hoped to exploit its wartime alliance with the United States to develop a lucrative postwar trade, but it was disappointed. Americans still had a taste for the British products they had traditionally used.

Independence did give Americans the freedom to seek world markets outside the British empire. Merchants pursued these markets with great enthusiasm, taking their trade as far as China. In May 1785, the sailing ship *Empress of China* returned from Canton carrying a highly profitable cargo of tea and silks. Before long, traders from Boston, Philadelphia, and Providence began plotting new routes to Asia.

The war also boosted American industry. The fighting created a demand for muni-

2. **GEOGRAPHY** To reach China, the *Empress* sailed south from New York, around the southern tip of South America, and across the Pacific Ocean. The voyage took over six months. (movement)

Freed of British trade restrictions, American merchants opened up markets in Asia. In this scene, traders deal with tea merchants in Canton, China. All trading there took place inside warehouses called hongs. The workers at left are trampling the tea into crates. Yankee captains also brought back fine porcelains and silks.

3. **BACKGROUND** The Chinese considered westerners barbarians and restricted western traders to a small area of Canton.

tions, guns, clothing, and other supplies. In addition, during the war, Americans created new industries to manufacture goods they formerly had imported from Great Britain.

Southern planters survived the war, but suffered great losses. Exports of tobacco and indigo dropped sharply, while Britain's high import duty prevented South Carolina from selling as much rice as before. Furthermore, Loyalists and the British had taken many slaves during the war (almost 25,000 in South Carolina). That meant that many southern plantations lacked the labor they needed.

Small farmers were in a better position. Many grew wealthy providing food for the armies. Farmers who had borrowed large sums of money before the war—and there were many of them—also benefitted from the inflation of the war years. The same was true of debtors who, after the war, paid back their debts with nearly worthless Continental dollars. These economic dislocations caused a 1. depression in the years following the war, but by 1787 economic recovery was clearly evident. Americans were beginning to build a sound economy.

See p. T27.

SECTION 3 REVIEW

1. **Identify:** (a) Articles of Confederation, (b) Northwest Territory, (c) Land Ordinance of 1785, (d) Northwest Ordinance.

2. **Define:** (a) confederation, (b) ratify, (c) squatter.

3. (a) List the powers given to Congress under the Articles of Confederation. (b) What two crucial powers did Congress lack?

4. (a) What two problems made enforcing the Land Ordinance of 1785 difficult? (b) When could a territory become a state, according to the Northwest Ordinance?

5. How did the revolution affect the American economy?

6. **Critical Thinking** What did Philadelphia Patriot Benjamin Rush mean when he said, "The American war is over, but this is far from being the case with the American Revolution"?

4 A Need for Further Experimentation

READ TO UNDERSTAND

■ How money troubles plagued the first national government.

■ What other problems confronted the new government.

■ Why national leaders blamed the Articles of Confederation for the problems of the nation.

As year followed year, Americans gained more experience at running a national government. Some liked the system created by the Articles of Confederation. In 1783, a Virginia county declared bitter opposition to "any attempts" to strengthen the powers of Congress. But others saw a desperate need to make changes. As early as 1780, Alexander Hamilton wrote, "'Tis a universal sentiment that our present system is a bad one." People agreed on only one thing—that problems were mounting.

Raising Revenue for the New Government

Since "taxation without representation" had been the major charge against the British Parliament, the authors of the Articles of Confederation tried to make sure that only popularly elected bodies had the right to tax people. Consequently, raising money proved to be one of the most serious problems that the new national government faced.

Under the Articles, state legislatures, not the people, elected members of Congress. Congress did not directly represent the people and therefore could not tax them. It could ask the states for money, but only the representatives of the people—the state legislatures—could grant such requests. If the states turned down the requests, as they usually did, Congress could do nothing.

Thus, the young government desperately needed money. Without the power to tax, 2. Congress began looking elsewhere. It could continue printing paper money as it had done **153** to help finance the war, although inflation had made the paper Continentals almost worthless. It could borrow, and Dutch bankers did lend money to the new nation. Finally, the best source of revenue turned out to be the sale of western lands.

But these sources of income were not nearly enough. On two occasions, Congress tried to levy tariffs but failed. Both times, the vote was just one short of the number needed for passage. Congress seemed powerless to
1. raise the money it needed.

Economic Disunity

Congress also had little authority to promote economic cooperation among the states. State legislatures guarded their economic independence as strongly as they protected their political independence.

2. GEOGRAPHY This trail became known as the Wilderness Road. One of the first settlements in Kentucky was named Boonesborough in Daniel Boone's honor. (movement)

Of all the backwoodsmen who helped open the frontier, none was more famous or more likely to spin tall tales about his exploits than Daniel Boone. In 1775, Boone led the first white settlers through the Cumberland Gap into Kentucky along a trail he
2. *had blazed himself. In 1799, he moved farther west to Missouri, where he lived until his death at age 86.*

As the Continental dollar, the only national currency, declined in value, states issued their own money. Businesses and individuals preferred their own state currency to others. Furthermore, states often refused to accept other states' currencies at face value. The resulting confusion made trade between states difficult.

Economic rivalry among the states further compounded the difficulty. State legislatures sought to regulate trade with other states, often imposing tariffs. Sometimes, one state tried to profit from trade between two other states. New York, for example, taxed goods passing through from New Jersey to Connecticut.

Since the Articles of Confederation denied Congress the power to regulate trade or settle disputes between states, the central government could do little about such problems. The continuing state rivalries blocked economic cooperation and stifled unity in the new nation.

Foreign Pressures and Western Intrigues

The lack of unity also hurt the new nation's reputation among Europeans. Aware of the problems, foreign countries refused at first to enter into trade agreements with the United States. They also saw the nation as weak because, according to the Articles, Congress could only "request troops" from the states.

Even though the colonists had defeated Great Britain, King George III saw that he could take advantage of the Congress's inability to raise an army. He ordered troops to remain at military posts in the Northwest Territory, in violation of the peace treaty. Ambassador John Adams's heated protests moved neither the monarch nor the troops.

Spain renewed its interest in western American lands after the war. In the areas that would eventually become Tennessee and Kentucky, groups of western settlers organized a new state called Franklin, in honor of Benjamin Franklin. They petitioned Congress 3. to admit the state to the Union but were refused. At the same time, Spain tried to bring Franklin under Spanish rule by paying secret agents to promote its interests. Among the

3. BIOGRAPHY The governor was John Sevier (1745–1815). After Franklin became part of Tennessee, Sevier served six times as Tennessee's governor.

1. **GEOGRAPHY** Ask: Why was the Mississippi River the only practical route for trade? (movement)

3. **BACKGROUND** Shays' men closed courthouses because judges had been foreclosing on many farms in the area.

agents was the famous frontiersman Daniel Boone, who apparently took the money but did nothing.

Spain found still another way to pressure the westerners. In 1784, it barred American navigators from the lower Mississippi River, the only practical route for western settlers to ship products to New Orleans and
1. points east. If westerners wanted to use the river, the Spanish declared, they had only to agree to become part of New Spain. Such foreign challenges underscored the weakness of the national government.

Weakness at the Center

In the years following the war, the prestige of Congress among Americans steadily declined. The most experienced leaders of the war years were busy elsewhere. George Washington had returned to his Mount Vernon plantation. Thomas Jefferson served as ambassador to France and John Adams as ambassador to Britain. Others, such as Patrick Henry, remained active in state government. States that bothered sending representatives to Congress sent poor substitutes for the leaders of the Revolutionary War. It was not unusual for representatives of fewer than nine states to be present in Congress, too few to act on important matters.

George Washington peered into the future and warned in 1780, "I see one head gradually changing into thirteen. . . . I see the powers of Congress declining too fast for the consequence and respect which is due to them as a grand representative body of America." Others such as James Madison, Alexander Hamilton, and John Adams shared Washington's fears and his desire for a stronger
2. central government.

They saw Congress becoming a subject of ridicule in the world community and being scorned by state legislatures. They saw a central government so weak that it could not even dislodge troops of the country that the Americans had defeated in war.

They saw speculators, whose concern was money and not the national welfare, influencing land policies. They saw the possibility of losing land in the West to Spain because of jealousy among states. These lead-

ers needed little prompting to experiment again.

Toward a Constitutional Convention

The opportunity came in the fall of 1786. Convinced that the nation was falling into economic anarchy, leaders in Virginia called on the other states to meet in Annapolis, Maryland, to discuss new ways of regulating commerce. Representatives from only five states showed up, but they decided to call another meeting the next year to discuss the broader problem of government under the Articles of Confederation.

If leaders in other states doubted that action was needed, they became convinced during the winter of 1787, when a group of disgruntled farmers from western Massachusetts rebelled against the state government. The farmers had been suffering from a combination of low farm prices and high state taxes. Under the leadership of Daniel Shays, they closed many county courthouses and 3. nearly captured an arsenal at Springfield.

The Massachusetts militia finally quelled Shays' rebellion, but many Americans now believed that the country needed a stronger, more effective government. With the reality of rebellion and fears of anarchy in mind, state delegates began arriving in Philadelphia in the spring of 1787. A new experiment was about to begin.

See p. T27.

SECTION 4 REVIEW

1. **Identify:** Shays' Rebellion.

2. (a) According to the Articles of Confederation, who had the power to tax? (b) How could Congress raise money?

3. List two factors that made trade between states difficult.

4. (a) What action did George III take that showed contempt for the new nation? (b) What disrespectful action did Spain take?

5. **Critical Thinking** Which weakness of the Articles of Confederation do you think was most serious? Why?

CHAPTER 7 REVIEW

Summary

1. **After the revolution, America entered an experimental age.** The country moved toward broader political and social equality, but much inequality remained.

2. **Once Americans declared independence from Great Britain in 1776, they had to govern themselves.** The new states quickly adopted state constitutions with safeguards against the abuse of power. British rule had left Americans deeply suspicious of strong government.

3. **Creating a national government proved difficult.** Throughout most of the Revolutionary War, the nation had no official government, because some state legislatures had not ratified the Articles of Confederation. The major stumbling block was a dispute over control of land in the West. The Articles of Confederation were finally ratified in 1781.

4. **The central government was too weak to be effective.** Major economic, political, and foreign-policy problems could not be resolved. State leaders called a meeting for 1787 to discuss the need for a new form of government. Many Americans were ready to experiment again.

See p. T27.

Vocabulary

Match each term at left with its definition or description at right.

1. segregated
2. manumission
3. veto
4. bicameral legislature
5. inalienable rights
6. confederation
7. ratify
8. squatter

a. an alliance of independent states

b. rights of citizens that government cannot take away

c. separated on the basis of race

d. the rejection of a bill by a governor

e. a person who illegally settles on land

f. a two-house legislature

g. the freeing of a slave

h. to approve

See p. T27.

Chapter Checkup

1. How was the period after the Revolutionary War an experimental era?

2. (a) Describe a typical state government. (b) What branch had the most power? Why?

3. (a) How were states' rights protected under the Articles of Confederation? (b) Why did the delegates want this protection?

4. (a) Describe the central government under the Articles of Confederation. (b) How were representatives allocated? (c) Did everyone agree with this system? Explain.

5. What effect did state claims to land in the West have on the ratification of the Articles of Confederation? Why?

6. (a) What were the provisions of the Land Ordinance of 1785? (b) Of the Northwest Ordinance?

7. Why was economic unity difficult to achieve under the Articles of Confederation?

8. How did foreign nations react to signs of weakness in the United States?

See p. T28.

Critical Thinking

1. **Evaluating** Why would a period of social and political experimentation be likely to follow an event such as the revolution?

2. **Using Relevant Information** Did Americans during the 1770s and 1780s consider their state government or the United States government more important? What evidence can you give to support your answer?

See p. T28.

Connecting Past and Present

1. (a) What rights do women and blacks have today that they generally lacked in the 1780s? (b) Are you satisfied with the level of political and social equality in the United States today? Why or why not?

2. Think about the ways state governments are organized and the tasks they perform. (a) In what ways are state governments today similar to those of the 1780s? (b) How are they different?

See p. T28.

Developing Basic Skills

1. **Using Diagrams** Study the diagram on page 148. (a) Under the Articles of Confederation, what powers did Congress have? (b) What powers were denied to Congress? (c) What was required for Congress to pass laws? (d) What powers were held by the states?

2. **Map Reading** Study the map on page 151. (a) Which states claimed territory beyond their own borders? (b) What country owned Florida and Louisiana? (c) Why was it important that the United States settle the conflicting land claims?

WRITING ABOUT HISTORY

Order of Importance

One natural way to arrange reasons or facts is in order of importance. You may emphasize the event that had the greatest effect on later events or that led to the most important results. The order of importance is useful for presenting arguments in favor of or opposed to a point of view. When organizing information in order of importance, you have to think about which ideas are essential and should be developed and which ideas are minor and could be merely mentioned.

Transition words are used to show the relationship between ideas and to make the order of ideas clear. Some transition words used to show order of importance include: *first, second, third, even more, even greater, most significant, greatest, more important,* and *most important.*

Practice: Decide which item in each pair you think was more important to the development of democracy in the new nation. Then write a sentence explaining your choice.

1. a. Some states extended voting rights by lowering or eliminating property requirements.
   b. Americans organized a large number of volunteer fire departments.

2. a. Most states had a bicameral legislature.
   b. The idea that constitutions were to be written by special conventions gained acceptance.

3. a. Virginia gave up its claims to land in the West.
   b. A territory with 60,000 inhabitants could be admitted as a state equal to others.

4. a. In 1786, the Virginia legislature passed a bill that effectively separated church and state.
   b. Noah Webster promoted the adoption of an American language.

A More Perfect Union 8

(1787–1791)

CHAPTER OUTLINE

1 Producing a New Constitution

2 The Principle of Federalism

3 Limits to Power

4 Ratifying the Constitution

5 Ensuring Individual Rights

CHAPTER OBJECTIVES After completing this chapter, students should be able to
1. explain the compromises worked out at the Constitutional Convention.
2. define federalism, separation of powers, and checks and balances.
3. describe the ratification of the Constitution.
4. list the main provisions of the Bill of Rights.

CHAPTER PREVIEW As the Constitutional Convention met to change the Articles, Thomas Jefferson observed: "This example of changing [them] by assembling the wise men of the state, instead of assembling armies, will be worth as much to the world as the former examples we have given it." Ask: What did Jefferson mean?

The stiff and weary passengers climbed down from the *Philadelphia Flier*. The coach earned its name for speed, not comfort. Jammed on a hard, backless bench, the travelers had endured a bruising ride from New York. One passenger, a slight young man a friend once described as "no bigger than a half piece of soap," picked up his bags and headed to a nearby boarding house. His mind was on the convention due to begin on May 14, 1787— only 11 days away.

At 36, James Madison was among the youngest delegates to the convention called to revise the Articles of Confederation. He was undoubtedly also the best prepared. For months, Madison had holed up at his father's plantation in Virginia to read stacks of books on history, politics, and commerce. Since Madison rarely slept more than three or four hours a night, he would get up at odd times to read more or write some notes. He arrived in Philadelphia with a bulging briefcase.

On May 14, the eager Madison walked the few blocks along rain-slicked streets to Penn-

sylvania's State House. He joined George Washington, who had arrived with great fanfare the day before, and several other delegates. But without delegates from at least seven states, the work could not begin. Disappointed, Madison waited as the days slipped by and others braved spring rains and muddy roads to reach the city. Finally, on May 25, in yet another downpour, enough delegates arrived.

Madison kept a record of the proceedings of the convention so that others could know how the delegates arrived at their decisions. Sitting front and center in the hall, he scribbled notes as the delegates spoke. Each night, by candlelight, he filled in the gaps.

Madison, being a discreet politician, decided that the frank and often controversial debates should not be made public in his lifetime. Not until 1840, a few years after his death, were Madison's careful notes published. From them, the nation learned of the momentous discussions that shaped the new Constitution of the United States and provided the nation with a solid, enduring government.

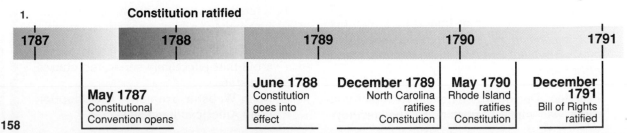

1.
Constitution ratified

1787	1788	1789	1790	1791

May 1787 Constitutional Convention opens

June 1788 Constitution goes into effect

December 1789 North Carolina ratifies Constitution

May 1790 Rhode Island ratifies Constitution

December 1791 Bill of Rights ratified

1. **TIME LINE QUESTION** How long after the Constitution went into effect was the Bill of Rights ratified?

The delegates to the Constitutional Convention wrote a document that has stood
1. the test of time. Among those at the convention were George Washington, presiding, and Benjamin Franklin, seated, second from left.

1. **VISUAL EVIDENCE** Ask: Why did the artist paint the sun behind Washington?

2. **BIOGRAPHY** Alexander Hamilton (1757–1804) was Washington's private secretary during the Revolution.

1 Producing a New Constitution

READ TO UNDERSTAND

■ Why the delegates at the Constitutional Convention rejected the Virginia and New Jersey plans.

■ How the delegates settled the issue of representation.

■ What other compromises were reached.

By February 1787, the weaknesses of the Articles of Confederation could no longer be ignored. Congress sent out an urgent call to all the states to send delegates to a convention in Philadelphia for "the sole and express purpose of revising the Articles of Confederation." Only Rhode Island, called Rogue Island by some, stayed away. The smallest of the states, it did not trust what the large states might do.

Once gathered, the delegates realized that their work involved more than simple revision of the existing government. What was needed was a new government that would bring the country back from the brink of disaster and secure a peaceful future.

The Delegates

The 55 men who came to Philadelphia were a relatively young but politically experienced group. The convention's elder statesmen included George Washington and the 81-year-old Benjamin Franklin. Other familiar names belonged to much younger men, such as Alexander Hamilton of New York and James 2. Madison of Virginia. Five delegates were only in their twenties; another five were in their early or mid-thirties. But their youth belied their experience: The delegates included two college presidents, three professors, and twenty-eight men who had served in the Continental Congress. 3.

Several well-known Americans were absent. Patrick Henry, a strong advocate of states' rights, refused to come because he "smelt a rat." Samuel Adams, who shared Henry's suspicions, also stayed away. John Adams and Thomas Jefferson did not attend because both were serving as American ambassadors, Adams in Great Britain and Jefferson in France.

159

3. **CITIZENSHIP** The delegates had experience in business, plantation management, and politics. Most were property owners. Over one third were college graduates—a rare attainment in colonial times.

The Convention Opens

Convening on May 25, 1787, the delegates' first order of business was to choose a president to lead the convention. The choice was obvious: George Washington gave the proceedings a "national complexion."

Areas of Agreement   Before getting down to work, the delegates agreed that all debates and discussion should be kept secret so that they could speak their minds freely, without pressure from outside.*

For the next six weeks, through a hot and humid summer in Philadelphia, the delegates discussed ways of dealing with the disrupted state of national affairs. Nearly all present agreed that the nation was heading for disaster under the Articles of Confederation. "Something should be done immediately," argued Gunning Bedford of Delaware. Caleb Strong of Massachusetts agreed that under the Articles, Congress was "nearly at an end. If no Accommodation takes place the Union itself must be dissolved."

The delegates also agreed that the new government must be given clear power to raise taxes, enforce laws, and provide for national defense. It should be a republic, in which citizens elected representatives to make and enforce laws. Finally, the delegates believed that the government of the United States should be based on a written
1. constitution, which they set about drafting.

Issues for Debate   Within the framework of these principles, however, the delegates faced seemingly countless choices about the nature of the new government. For example, when the debates began, few delegates had a clear idea of what the office of chief executive would be like, although nearly everyone agreed that the nation needed one.

Should the chief executive be an elected president or a monarch chosen for life? The decision that the nation should have an elected president only raised more questions. Who should elect the President—the people, the state legislatures, or the Congress? How long should the term of office be? Delegates debated dozens of detailed questions like these.

*The record of the Constitutional Convention is based on notes taken by delegates. Extracts from James Madison's notes appear on page 162.

GREAT DEBATE

Plans for a National Legislature

One of the sharpest debates concerned the plans for a congress, or national legislature. The desire of each state to protect itself from the tyranny of others complicated settlement of this issue.

The Virginia Plan   The Virginia Plan, written by James Madison, proposed a national legislature that would be divided into two houses, the House of Representatives and the Senate. The number of representatives allotted to each state would be proportional to the size of its population. Thus, larger states would have more representatives than smaller ones.
2.

According to the Virginia Plan, the voters in each state would elect members to the House of Representatives. Senators were to be chosen by House members from a list of candidates suggested by state legislatures. The House would also choose members of the judiciary and a President, who would serve for seven years. Congress would have the power to override state laws and, when necessary, make laws for the states.
3.

Some delegates objected to the Virginia Plan because they felt it gave the national government too much power. The main subject of debate, however, was proportional representation. Delegates from small states like New Jersey protested that such a system would give larger states all the power in the national government. Pennsylvania delegate James Wilson only aggravated the small states' fears when he exclaimed with annoyance, "Shall New Jersey have the same right or influence in the councils of the nation with Pennsylvania? I say no. It is unjust."

The New Jersey Plan   After two weeks of debate, William Paterson of New Jersey proposed an alternative plan. The New Jersey Plan suggested that each state, large or small, have an equal voice in Congress. Congress would consist of only one house, to be elected by the state legislatures, not directly by the people.

The New Jersey Plan granted the central government the power to raise taxes, regulate commerce, and enforce national laws. But the plan also specified that the states would retain powers not expressly given to

The Constitutional Convention took place at the Pennsylvania State House, shown here. It had already been the site of crucial steps in the creation of the United States. There, the Declaration of Independence had been signed and General Washington had taken command of the Continental army. In the 1820s,
1. the building began to be called Independence Hall, as it is known today.

the national legislature. This plan, in effect, maintained the major features of the Articles
2. of Confederation, making only minor revisions.

The Great Compromise

The delegates rejected both the New Jersey and Virginia plans. The convention was deadlocked when Roger Sherman of Connecticut stepped forward and offered his proposal. It became known as the Great Compromise.

The compromise, like the Virginia Plan, called for a Congress made up of two houses. Representatives to the House would be elected by the voters for two-year terms. The number of representatives each state would have would be proportional to its population. This satisfied the larger states. To accommodate the smaller states, each state, regardless of size, would have two senators.

As in the New Jersey Plan, this gave all states an equal voice, in at least one house. Senators were to be chosen by state legislatures for six-year terms.

The Great Compromise tried to satisfy both sides in the dispute over representation. Its acceptance by the delegates marked a turning point. Had each side refused to budge, the convention might have broken up. Willingness to compromise on this crucial issue opened the door for still other compromises.

Northern and Southern States Compromise

Although the Great Compromise settled one debate, it fueled another. In determining the number of representatives each state would have in the House, should slaves be counted

161

Slavery and the Constitution

Delegates to the Constitutional Convention hotly debated whether the Constitution should abolish the importation of slaves. This excerpt is from James Madison's Journal of the Constitutional Convention *from August 21, 1787.*

Mr. L. Martin [of Md.] proposed to vary article 7, sect. 4 so as to allow a prohibition or tax on the importation of slaves. First, as five slaves are to be counted as three freemen in the appointment of representatives, such a clause would leave an encouragement to this traffic. Second, slaves [through danger of insurrection] weakened one part of the Union, which the other parts were bound to protect; the privilege of importing them was therefore unreasonable. Third, it was inconsistent with the principles of the Revolution, and dishonorable to the American character, to have such a feature in the Constitution.

Mr. Sherman [of Conn.] . . . disapproved of the slave trade; yet, as the states were now possessed of the right to import slaves, as the

public good did not require it to be taken from them, and as it was expedient to have as few objections as possible to the proposed plan of government, he thought it best to leave the matter as we find it.

Col. Mason [of Va.] This infernal traffic originated in the avarice of British merchants. The British government constantly checked the attempts of Virginia to put a stop to it. Maryland and Virginia, he said, had already prohibited the importation of slaves. All this would be in vain if South Carolina and Georgia be at liberty to import. The Western people are already calling out for slaves for their new lands, and will fill that country with slaves, if they can be got through South Carolina and Georgia. He held it essential, in every point of view, that the general government should have power to prevent the increase of slavery.

Gen. [Charles C.] Pinckney [of S.C.] declared it to be his firm opinion that if himself and all his colleagues were to sign the Constitution, and use their personal influence, it would be of no avail towards obtaining the assent of their constituents [to a slave-trade prohibition]. South Carolina and Georgia cannot do without slaves. He contended that the importation of slaves would be for the interest of the whole Union. The more slaves, the more produce to employ the carrying trade; the more consumption also; and the more of this, the more of revenue for the common treasury.

1. How did each delegate stand on the issue of the slave trade?

2. **Critical Thinking** General Pinckney "contended that the importation of slaves would be for the interest of the whole Union." What do these words show about his attitude toward slaves?

1.

1. **CRITICAL THINKING** Ask: Who is Sherman excluding from his definition of "the public"?

as part of the population? This question divided northern and southern states.

The Three-Fifths Compromise Southern delegates, who wanted to increase their representation in the House, answered yes. Northerners, however, argued that because slaves were considered property they should not

be counted. Again the delegates compromised. They agreed that only three fifths of the slaves in a state would count toward determining its representation in the House.

The Slave Trade Compromise Another conflict between northern and southern states involved the slave trade. Many northerners

2.

2. **DISCUSSION** This debate saw northerners arguing that slaves were property while southerners maintained that slaves were people. Ask: Why did both sides reverse their usual positions on this issue?

wished to abolish it completely. Southerners objected, claiming that slavery was necessary for their economic survival. The delegates finally agreed that Congress would not interfere with the slave trade for 20 years after the Constitution went into effect.

Other Sectional Compromises Southern delegates also wanted to protect their foreign trade. The South's economy depended more on agricultural exports than that of the North. Southern delegates wanted to be sure that northern congressmen would not band together to tax southern exports. Such taxes would place their crops at a disadvantage in world trade.

In the end, the delegates agreed to prohibit export taxes. They also required that two thirds of the Senate ratify treaties, which meant that southern states would have enough power to block unfavorable trade agreements made with foreign coun-
1. tries. ■

The Convention Ends

By August 6, the delegates placed the fruits of their labor in the hands of a five-member Committee of Detail. This group produced a document of 23 clauses. Finally, on September 12, the Committee on Style went to work to polish the language.

Five days later, 39 of 42 delegates remaining in Philadelphia signed the document. Two Virginians, Edmund Randolph and George Mason, along with Elbridge Gerry of Massachusetts, abstained. They felt that the new Constitution vested too much power in the national government. Alexander Hamilton left the convention early for the opposite reason. He thought the states had retained too much power.

The Constitution required each state to hold a special state convention to decide whether the plan for the new government should be accepted. Once nine out of the thirteen states endorsed it, the Constitution would go into effect. But before that occurred, the new Constitution was eagerly discussed throughout the 13 states. It is worth looking in detail at the features of the new government that the convention proposed. (See the Constitution, pages 867–897.)

SECTION 1 REVIEW

1. **Identify:** (a) Virginia Plan, (b) New Jersey Plan, (c) the Great Compromise.

2. List three principles of government agreed upon by the convention delegates.

3. (a) What was the main objection to the Virginia Plan? (b) What was the major weakness of the New Jersey Plan?

4. What compromises were made between the northern and southern states?

5. **Critical Thinking** How does the name of the United States reflect its early history?

2. **VOCABULARY** Have students look up these terms in the glossary before they begin reading.

2 The Principle of Federalism

READ TO UNDERSTAND

■ What sovereignty meant to the framers of the Constitution.

■ How the Constitution divided powers between the states and the national government.

■ How federalism changed the relationship between the people and the national government.

■ *Vocabulary:* popular sovereignty, federalism, delegated powers, reserved powers, concurrent powers. 2.

Out of the accumulated knowledge and experience of the delegates to the Constitutional Convention emerged a government based on certain rules, or principles. The Constitution begins with an affirmation of the principle of **popular sovereignty,** that is, that the people 3. are the source of the government's power or authority. But did this mean the people of the individual states or the people of the nation as a whole? Did ultimate power rest with the states or the national government?

Debate Over Sovereignty

Many delegates to the Philadelphia convention considered sovereignty, or the government's power, indivisible. It must, they be- **163**

System of Federalism

Examples of Delegated Powers

Regulate laws of immigration and naturalization
Regulate interstate and foreign commerce
Set standard weights and measures
Create and maintain armed forces
Make copyright and patent laws
Establish postal system
Establish foreign policy
Create lower courts
Print money
Declare war

Examples of Concurrent Powers

Borrow money
Provide for health, safety, and welfare
Administer criminal justice
Set minimum wage
Charter banks
Levy taxes

Examples of Reserved Powers

Create corporation laws
Regulate intrastate commerce
Establish and maintain schools
Establish and maintain local governments
Determine eligibility requirements for elected state officials
Determine and regulate laws of marriage, divorce, and professional licenses

CHART STUDY *The federal system created by the Constitution delegated some powers to the federal government and reserved others to the states. Some powers were to be concurrent, or shared by both the states and the federal government. Compare this chart with the chart on page 148. How would experiences under the Articles of Confederation have influenced the way powers were divided under the Constitution?* See p. T30.

1. CHART READING Ask: Which of the following are powers of the federal government, state governments, or both: raising a navy, appointing judges, granting a dentist a license to practice.

lieved, lie completely with the states or with the national government.

The Virginia Plan delegated power to the national government, which could veto state legislation. This arrangement appealed to men like Gouverneur Morris of Pennsylvania, who favored the establishment of "a supreme Legislative, Executive, and Judiciary." He warned the delegates, "We had better take a supreme government now than a despot twenty years hence, for come he must."

Under the New Jersey Plan, on the other hand, the states remained sovereign, as they had been under the Articles of Confederation. Although the Articles provided for a national legislature, that body was not sovereign. It had to depend on state governments to carry out national laws, raise money through taxation, and regulate trade.

2. VOCABULARY The word *federalism* is derived from the Latin root *fides*, meaning confidence or faith.

A Division of Power

The Constitution solved the conflict over whether sovereignty belonged to the national government or to the states by creating a system of dual, or shared, sovereignty. Un-

der this system, known as **federalism,** governmental authority was divided between national and state governments.

The Constitution gave certain powers exclusively to the national government. These **delegated powers** included the right to coin money, to regulate foreign and interstate trade, to declare war on another country, and to establish a postal system. States were forbidden by the Constitution to do any of these things.

Powers that the Constitution did not specifically grant to the national government were reserved for the states. These **reserved powers** included the right to control trade within a state, to create local governments, and to establish qualifications for voting.

The Constitution granted a third set of powers to both the national and the state governments. These **concurrent powers** included the right to support education, to enforce laws, and to spend money on internal improvements, such as roads, dams, and parks. Finally, the Constitution stated that when disputes over authority arose between states and the national government, federal courts would resolve the conflict.

3. LOCAL HISTORY One concurrent power is the power to build and maintain roads. Ask students to identify roads in your area built by the state government and those built with federal funds.

164

1. **PAST AND PRESENT** Have students list federal laws or institutions that affect them directly.

See p. T30.

A True Union

The system of federalism established a new relationship among the states, the people, and the national government. The Constitution and any national laws passed under it were now the supreme laws of the land. State legislatures could not change them, and the people had to abide by them.

The Constitution also established a direct link between the people and the national government. Members of the House of Representatives were elected by the people, and laws passed by the national government affected the people directly. No longer did state legislatures serve as intermediaries.

Federalism is at the heart of the American political system. The delegates at Philadelphia created a stronger national government because they saw that a true union was necessary. At the same time, they retained significant powers for the state governments, to guarantee that the national government would not become too strong.

2. **CITIZENSHIP** Have students list the features of federalism that satisfied advocates of (1) strong central government; (2) strong state governments.

SECTION 2 REVIEW

1. **Define:** (a) popular sovereignty, (b) federalism, (c) delegated powers, (d) reserved powers, (e) concurrent powers.

2. (a) Would the central or state governments have been sovereign under the Virginia Plan? (b) Under the New Jersey Plan?

3. How did the Constitution solve the conflict over sovereignty?

4. Give one example each of a delegated, a reserved, and a concurrent power.

5. How did the system of federalism change the relationship of the people to the national government?

6. **Critical Thinking** How has federalism protected the right of states to some individuality?

The right to spend money on road building was a concurrent power of the national and state governments. In the early days of the republic, however, roads outside the cities were primitive, with huge potholes and even tree stumps. When it rained, horses could sink up to their bellies in mud. Passengers who traveled by stagecoach on the nation's roads took it for granted that they would be "crushed, shaken, thrown about . . . and bumped."

3. **VISUAL EVIDENCE** Ask: What hazards of stagecoach travel are shown in this picture? What does it show about the passengers?

3 Limits to Power

READ TO UNDERSTAND

- Why the delegates separated the powers given to each branch of the national government.

- How the system of checks and balances operates.

- How the Constitution limited the direct power of the people.

1. *Vocabulary:* separation of powers, checks and balances, impeach, unconstitutional, electoral college.

In drafting plans for the new government, the framers of the Constitution were steering a narrow and treacherous course. They had to avoid dangers that lurked on either side of them—one was tyranny and the other was ineffectiveness.

If they granted the government too much power, they might be no better off than they had been with a monarch. If the government had too little power, affairs could become as disordered as they had been under the Articles of Confederation. Popular sovereignty upheld the people's authority. Federalism prevented both the states and the central government from becoming too powerful. But the delegates went one step further. As believers in the principle of limited government, they defined and limited the power of each branch of the national government.

Separation of Powers

The idea of separating the government into branches, each with well-defined and limited powers, was not new to Americans. For many years, colonial legislatures shared power with judges and governors appointed by the king. Later, state constitutions specified separate executive, legislative, and judicial branches. But these constitutions usually gave the legislative branch more authority than the executive.

The Articles of Confederation had created a legislature but no court system or executive. After living with this form of government for four years, Americans saw that it was not effective. Consequently, the delegates to the Constitutional Convention revived the principle of **separation of powers.**

In so doing, the delegates drew on the ideas of the French Baron de Montesquieu (mahn tuhs KYOO). In *The Spirit of the Laws* (1748), Montesquieu argued that to function properly a government had to possess legislative, executive, and judicial authority. In other words, the government had to be able to make, to enforce, and to interpret the laws of the land. To prevent tyranny, Montesquieu recommended dividing these functions among three separate branches of government.

The delegates incorporated Montesquieu's ideas into the Constitution. The government was separated into legislative, executive, and judicial branches. The main function of the legislature, Congress, was to make laws. The executive branch, headed by the President, was to enforce them. The judiciary, or the courts, were to interpret the laws and ensure that they were applied fairly.

Checks and Balances

To prevent any one branch from exceeding its specified powers, the Constitution set up a system of **checks and balances.** Each branch of government was given the means to check the power of the others. This principle was based on another of Montesquieu's ideas.

The Executive Branch Remembering their quarrels with the king, the delegates in Philadelphia worried about the possible abuse of power by the chief executive. Some delegates considered distributing executive authority among several Presidents from different parts of the country. Although this plan was quickly abandoned, the delegates built checks on presidential power into the new government.

The President's appointment of cabinet officers, federal judges, and ambassadors was subject to approval by the Senate. Any treaties the President negotiated with foreign governments had to be approved by the Senate before they could go into effect. Congress's sole authority to declare war limited the President's power as commander in chief of the armed forces.

3. **DISCUSSION** Ask: Why is it important that Congress, rather than the President, has the power to declare war?

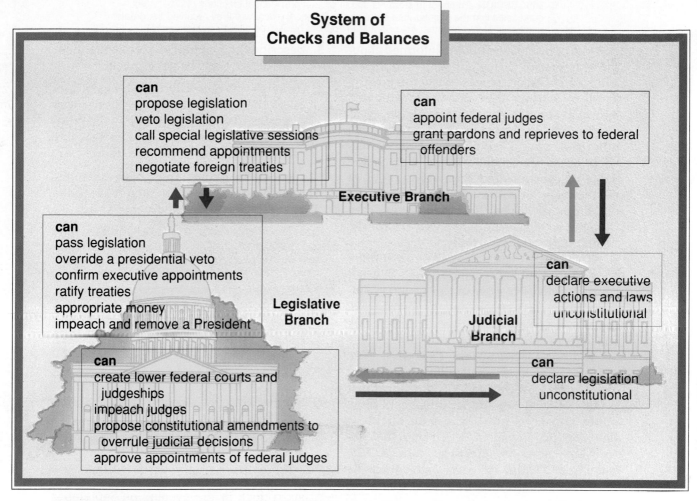

System of Checks and Balances

Executive Branch

can
propose legislation
veto legislation
call special legislative sessions
recommend appointments
negotiate foreign treaties

can
appoint federal judges
grant pardons and reprieves to federal offenders

Legislative Branch

can
pass legislation
override a presidential veto
confirm executive appointments
ratify treaties
appropriate money
impeach and remove a President

can
create lower federal courts and judgeships
impeach judges
propose constitutional amendments to overrule judicial decisions
approve appointments of federal judges

Judicial Branch

can
declare executive actions and laws unconstitutional

can
declare legislation unconstitutional

CHART STUDY *The framers of the Constitution wanted to prevent government tyranny. To do so, they set up a system of checks and balances among the three branches of government. Give three examples of how this system prevents any one branch from becoming too powerful.* See p. T30.

2.

1. PRESIDENTS Andrew Johnson was the only President ever impeached.

Congress could also check presidential authority by its power to remove a President from office. The House of Representatives could **impeach,** or accuse, a President of "treason, bribery, or other high crimes and misdemeanors." The Senate could then try the President and, upon conviction by a two-thirds majority, remove him or her from office.

The Legislature and the Judiciary Congressional powers were also limited by the other branches of government. The President could check Congress by vetoing, or rejecting, measures it passed. Congress could override a veto, but both houses had to pass the bill again by a two-thirds majority.

The Supreme Court, with its authority to interpret the laws of the land, could check both the President and Congress by ruling their actions **unconstitutional,** that is, in vio-

2. CHART READING Ask: Can you think of recent examples of one branch checking the power of another branch?

lation of the Constitution. Congress, in turn, could impeach and remove judges from office, since the Constitution specified that they "hold their offices during good behavior."

The system of checks and balances resulted from compromises among the delegates. In the end, they were satisfied that the combination of federalism, separation of powers, and checks and balances would prevent tyranny by the national government. However, many delegates also feared tyranny by the people. The Constitution addressed this concern as well.

3.

Limiting Direct Power of the People

Why did the delegates believe that direct participation in the national government should be limited? Some argued that, in gen-

167

3. CRITICAL THINKING The Constitution set up different terms of office for members of Congress, the President, and federal judges. Ask: Why do you think the framers devised this system?

eral, the public tended to be ill-informed about the issues facing the nation. Representatives, whose main business was to run the government, were likely to be better educated and informed about issues than the people.

In addition, communication at the time was slow and unreliable. Rarely could voters know all of the candidates and their views. Some delegates feared that large groups of people might be inflamed by rabble rousers or emotional issues. Representatives, they thought, would be more likely to act slowly, deliberately, and impartially.

To address these issues, the Constitution created a republic in which voters elected representatives to govern the country. Furthermore, voters chose only the members of the House of Representatives directly. State legislatures selected members of the Senate.*

Indirect Election of the Executive The delegates also devised an indirect method of electing the President and Vice-President that is still in effect today. Under the Constitution, states choose electors who vote for President and Vice-President. As a group, the electors are called the **electoral college.** The number of electors for each state equals the total number of the state's representatives

1. in Congress.

When the convention adjourned, most delegates felt they had created a document that balanced the powers of the national government properly. Based on the principles of popular sovereignty, federalism, limited government, separation of powers, and checks and balances, the new government could act with firmness and vigor when needed, but it

2. would be unable to abuse its power.

---

*The Seventeenth Amendment to the Constitution (1913) changed the method of electing senators. After that date, they were elected by popular vote rather than by state legislatures. (See page 891.)

See p. T30.

SECTION 3 REVIEW

1. **Identify:** Baron de Montesquieu.

2. **Define:** (a) separation of powers, (b) checks and balances, (c) impeach, (d) unconstitutional, (e) electoral college.

3. Describe the function of each of the three branches of the new government.

4. Describe (a) one way the President can check the power of Congress, (b) one way Congress can check the power of the President, and (c) one way the Supreme Court can check the power of Congress.

5. **Critical Thinking** How have attitudes toward popular participation in elections changed over the past 200 years?

4 Ratifying the Constitution

READnTO UNDERSTAND

■ Why the Federalists supported ratification of the Constitution.

■ Why the Antifederalists opposed ratification.

■ How the Constitution was ratified.

At six o'clock in the evening on September 15, the delegates' work was done. After almost four months of argument and debate, the convention overwhelmingly approved the Constitution. In encouraging fellow delegates to sign it, Benjamin Franklin said, "Mr. President: I confess that there are several parts of this Constitution which I do not at present approve, but I am not sure I shall never ap-
3. prove them. I doubt, too, whether any other convention may be able to make a better constitution. Thus I consent, Sir, to this Constitution, because I expect no better and because I am not sure that it is not the best."

The Constitutional Debate

Before the Constitution became law, it had to be ratified by at least nine states. As copies of the Constitution spread across the country, supporters and opponents of the proposed Constitution marshaled their arguments for the debates in state conventions that lay ahead.

168

1. **BACKGROUND** When they first appeared as letters in a New York newspaper, the *Federalist Papers* were signed with the name Publius, from the Latin word for *public*. Most of them were actually written by Hamilton.

Arguments in Favor Supporters of the Constitution, known as Federalists, argued that the Articles of Confederation produced a government that was frighteningly weak. It had placed the nation in grave danger largely because individual states could reject national policy. According to the Federalists, the Constitution gave the national government the authority to function effectively. Yet, it still protected the rights of the individual states.

Three of the most articulate Federalists were Alexander Hamilton, James Madison, and John Jay. These men wrote a series of newspaper articles summarizing the advantages of a federal union under the Constitution. Published as the *Federalist Papers,* they remain one of the best discussions of the political theory behind the American system of government.

Arguments in Opposition The chief concern of the Antifederalists, or opponents of ratification, was that the new government would be too powerful. Most thought the states should have retained more authority.

The Antifederalists rejected the indirect method of electing the President and the Senate on the grounds that it removed government too far from the people. They also were suspicious of the long terms of office

1.

2.

2. **READING** Have interested students read excerpts from the *Federalist Papers* and present summaries of them to the class.

VOICES OF FREEDOM

A Farmer Argues for the Constitution

Many Antifederalists were concerned that the proposed Constitution would not protect the country from tyranny. However, farmer Jonathan Smith urged the Massachusetts convention to ratify the Constitution because he believed it was the only way to prevent the development of tyranny.

Mr. President, I am a plain man, and get my living by the plough. I am not used to speak in public, but I beg your leave to say a few words in this house.

I have lived in a part of the country where I have known the worth of good government by the want [lack] of it. There was a black cloud [Shays' Rebellion] that rose in the east last winter, and spread over the west. . . . It brought on a state of anarchy and that led to tyranny. People that used to live peaceably, and were before good neighbors, got distracted, and took up arms against government.

Our distress was so great that we should have been glad to snatch at anything that looked like a government. Had any person that was able to protect us come and set up his standard, we should all have flocked to it, even if it had been a monarch, and that monarch might have proved a tyrant. So that you see that anarchy leads to tyranny; and better have one tyrant than so many at once.

Now, Mr. President, when I saw this Constitution, I found that it was a cure for these disorders. I had been a member of the convention to form our state constitution, and had learnt something of the checks and balances of power; and I found them all here.

Some gentlemen say, don't be in a hurry; take time to consider; and don't take a leap in the dark. I say, take things in time—gather fruit when it is ripe. There is a time to sow, and a time to reap. We sowed our seed when we sent men to the federal convention. Now is the harvest; now is the time to reap the fruit of our labor. And if we won't do it now, I am afraid we never shall have another opportunity.

See p. T31.

1. According to the farmer, why had Shays' Rebellion increased the chance that people would accept a tyrant?

2. **Critical Thinking** If you had been a member of the Massachusetts convention, what about the farmer's argument would have impressed you most? Why?

3.

3. **DISCUSSION** Ask: How would you describe Jonathan Smith as a person and as a citizen? Would you agree that he was a "plain man"?

1. **CITIZENSHIP** On December 7, 1787, Delaware became the first state to ratify the Constitution. The vote was unanimous.

2. **BACKGROUND** The Federalists, who had a majority near Philadelphia, wanted to organize the convention before Antifederalists on the frontier could send delegates.

proposed in the Constitution, since many local officials were normally elected for terms of only one year. Long terms of office, argued the Antifederalists, would make representatives less responsive to the voters.

Even more serious was the lack of a bill of rights to protect individual liberties. The Antifederalists feared that the new government might become tyrannical, destroying everything Americans had won through the revolution. They urged delegates to state conventions to reject the Constitution.

Battles Over Ratification

1. Because the Constitution seemed to protect their interests, smaller states such as Delaware, New Jersey, and Connecticut quickly ratified the Constitution. The hotly contested battles came in more populous states: Penn-

sylvania, Massachusetts, Virginia, and New York.

In Pennsylvania, the Federalists resorted to tough political tactics. On November 30, 1787, Federalist legislators in the Pennsylvania assembly moved to form a ratifying convention, but before business could be completed, the assembly broke for lunch. Antifederalist legislators tried to force an adjournment by refusing to return.

The speaker sent the sergeant-at-arms out into the streets to find at least two more members so that a quorum, or the minimum number needed to conduct business, could be assembled. Two members, "white with rage," were dragged protesting from their lodgings. With the doors barred to prevent anyone from escaping, the assembly passed the motion for a convention, which ratified the Constitution on December 12.

2.

3.

3. **BACKGROUND** One account said, "[A Federalist crowd] . . . broke into their lodgings, seized them, dragged them through the streets to the State House, and thrust them into the assembly room. . . . The quorum was now complete."

4. *The Society of Pewterers carried this banner in a parade celebrating the ratification of the Constitution. The pewterers associated their "Solid and Pure" products with patriotic sentiments. The banner at top right reads: "The Federal Plan Most Solid and Secure, Americans Their Freedom Will Endure. All Art Shall Flourish in Columbia's Land, And All Her Sons Join as One Social Band."*

4. **VISUAL EVIDENCE** Point out the flag shown on the banner. The "Stars and Stripes" had been adopted by the Continental Congress in 1777.

1. **BACKGROUND** Randolph, a delegate to the Constitutional Convention, had refused to sign the final draft because he felt it did not protect states' rights.

The Federalists in Massachusetts avoided the political shenanigans used in Pennsylvania. Instead, they hinted to John Hancock, an influential delegate, that he might win the post of Vice President in the new government. Hancock's subsequent support led Massachusetts to ratify by a narrow margin in February 1788.

Maryland and South Carolina ratified later that spring. Then all eyes turned toward Virginia. Virginia delegates included prestigious figures such as George Washington and James Madison, who supported the Constitution. On the Antifederalist side, however, stood Patrick Henry, George Mason, and Edmund Randolph, all respected names in Virginia politics.

A real battle loomed until Randolph suddenly announced he would support ratification. His move weakened opposition, and Virginia ratified the Constitution at the end of June. Once news of the Virginia vote reached the New York convention, that state also ratified. New Hampshire's approval had already come in.

With more than the nine votes needed for ratification, Congress, in its last act under the Articles, ordered national elections to be held in January 1789. North Carolina did not ratify the Constitution until December 1789 and Rhode Island not until 1790. But by then, the new government was already at work.

See p. T31.

SECTION 4 REVIEW

1. **Identify:** (a) Federalists, (b) *Federalist Papers,* (c) Antifederalists.

2. What arguments did the Federalists make in favor of the Constitution?

3. What arguments did the Antifederalists make against the Constitution?

4. In which of the states did the key ratification battles take place?

5. **Critical Thinking** How could you have answered the Antifederalist argument that the Constitution was opposed to the interests of state governments?

2. **VOCABULARY** Have students look up these terms in the glossary before they begin reading.

5 Ensuring Individual Rights

READ TO UNDERSTAND

■ How amendments are added to the Constitution.

■ Why some Americans objected to adding a bill of rights to the Constitution.

■ What rights are protected by the Bill of Rights.

■ *Vocabulary:* amend, writ of habeas corpus, bill of attainder, ex post facto law, due process.

On April 1, 1789, the first Congress of the United States assembled in New York. Amazingly enough, one of its first orders of business involved changing the Constitution. Hard as the framers had worked to create a perfect document, they knew that situations might arise that required the Constitution to be changed. In fact, such a situation developed during the ratification process. Fortunately, the delegates had incorporated an amendment process into the final document.

Amending the Constitution

The delegates realized that a method of **amending,** or altering, the Constitution was necessary. The document had to be flexible enough to adjust to changing times. At the same time, they wanted any changes to be well considered. Thus, the amendment process they devised was a difficult one.

Under the Constitution, an amendment could be proposed by either a two-thirds majority vote of Congress or by a special convention called by two thirds of the state legislatures. That amendment would become part of the Constitution when it had been ratified by three fourths of the states.

The farsightedness of the framers is evidenced by the fact that in two centuries, the Constitution has been amended only 26 times. The first ten amendments were adopted in 1791, and only 16 changes have been made since that time.

171

3. **ACTIVITY** Have students create a diagram illustrating the amendment process.

4. **PAST AND PRESENT** Have students research and report on any currently proposed amendments to the Constitution.

1. **DISCUSSION** Ask: How might the colonists' experience with the unwritten constitution of England have affected support for a written bill of rights?

2. **BACKGROUND** Although Massachusetts was one of the states to propose the addition of amendments, it did not ratify the Bill of Rights until 1937.

The Debate Over a Bill of Rights

The question of whether the Constitution should guarantee specific rights of citizens surfaced many times during the Constitutional Convention. Several delegates wanted them listed so that they could never be violated by the government.

Opposition Other delegates, led by Alexander Hamilton and James Madison, felt that the Constitution already protected individual liberties. One such protection was the right of citizens to obtain a **writ of habeas corpus** (HAY bee uhs KOR puhs), a court order releasing a person arrested without specific charges. Habeas corpus prevented arbitrary imprisonment.

In addition, the Constitution prohibited state and national governments from passing a **bill of attainder,** a law allowing a person charged with treason or other serious crime to be fined or imprisoned without trial. The Constitution also outlawed **ex post facto laws,** or laws that made an act a crime after it had been committed. Finally, the document provided for jury trials in criminal cases.

Madison also argued that listing specific rights could prove restrictive. It might imply that only those rights and no others deserved protection. Madison agreed that a bill of rights might be necessary in a government ruled by a king but not in one in which sovereignty lay with the people.

Support Despite these arguments, pressure for a bill of rights persisted throughout the ratification struggle. Several states, including Massachusetts and Virginia, ratified the Constitution with the understanding that the new Congress would adopt a bill of rights. Some Antifederalists had even demanded that a second constitutional convention be called to prepare a bill of rights to the Constitution before it was ratified.

Yielding to political pressure in his home state, Madison, now a congressman from Virginia, sponsored a series of amendments constituting a bill of rights in the House. Madison made sure that none of these amendments would weaken the power of the national government.

Congress actually approved twelve amendments, which it submitted to the states for ratification. Over the next two years, the required number of states ratified ten of the amendments, which became part of the Constitution in December 1791.

The Bill of Rights

The ten amendments that make up the Bill of Rights ensure the basic freedoms of American citizens. The First Amendment guarantees individual liberties, including freedom of speech and of religion, the right to peaceful assembly, and the right to petition the government. It also protects freedom of the press.

The next three amendments grew out of experiences with British rule. The Second Amendment guarantees the right of people to keep and bear arms. The Third Amendment prohibits the quartering of troops in private homes during peacetime without the owner's consent. The Fourth Amendment, recalling the hated writs of assistance used by British customs officials, protects citizens from "unreasonable" searches and seizures.

The Fifth Amendment guarantees **due process** of law. This means that the government cannot act arbitrarily against a person. It must follow a specific open process in which the accused is notified of the charge and is given the opportunity to present a defense in court. Under the Fifth Amendment, the government cannot require self-incriminating testimony nor may it try a defendant twice for the same crime.

The Sixth Amendment guarantees a jury trial in criminal cases and the right to be represented by a lawyer. Jury trials in civil cases are required by the Seventh Amendment. The Eighth Amendment forbids judges to set "excessive bail" or to prescribe "cruel and unusual punishments."

The Ninth Amendment assures citizens that the rights listed in the Constitution are not the only ones that exist. This answered the Federalist argument that such a list might restrict individual rights.

The Tenth Amendment was designed to reassure Antifederalists that the power of the national government would be limited. It states that all powers not given to the national government nor denied to the states are reserved for the states or for the people.

172

Americans took full advantage of the rights to free speech and assembly, guaranteed by the Bill of Rights. This painting, Stump Speaking, *by George Caleb*

1. *Bingham, captures a typically American event, the campaign speech. Attending such speeches was a popular form of entertainment, and speakers often spoke for hours.*

1. **VISUAL EVIDENCE** Ask: What conclusions can you draw from your observations of the audience?
See p. T31.

A Rising Sun

With the addition of the Bill of Rights, the framework of the new government was complete. But this was a beginning, not an ending. No one, perhaps, knew this better than Benjamin Franklin. In his 81 years, he had seen the colonies grow from little more than local settlements along the coast into a nation.

As the delegates signed the final draft of the new Constitution, Franklin called attention to the high-backed chair of the convention president. On it was carved a sun.

Artists, he observed, often found it difficult to distinguish a rising from a setting sun in their work. "I have often in the course of the Session . . . looked at that sun behind the President without being able to tell whether it was rising or setting. But now at length I have the happiness to know that it is a rising

2. and not a setting sun."

SECTION 5 REVIEW

1. **Define:** (a) amend, (b) writ of habeas corpus, (c) bill of attainder, (d) ex post facto law, (e) due process.

2. (a) What are the two ways a constitutional amendment can be proposed? (b) What proportion of the states must ratify an amendment?

3. Why did Madison object at first to the idea of a bill of rights?

4. List five rights guaranteed by the Bill of Rights.

5. **Critical Thinking** Describe one way in which you personally have benefited from the Bill of Rights.

173

2. **CRITICAL THINKING** Have students suggest interpretations of Franklin's statement.

Summary

1. **In May 1787, delegates from 12 states came to Philadelphia to revise the Articles of Confederation.** Few realized they would draft a new constitution instead. The delegates reached compromises between the large and small states and between northern and southern states.

2. **The new Constitution provided for a government based on the principle of federalism.** Power was balanced between the national government and the state governments. The Constitution also established a direct link between the people and the national government.

3. **The delegates divided the powers of the national government among three separate branches.** They also set up a system of checks and balances and limited the direct power of the people.

4. **To become law, the Constitution had to be ratified by three fourths of the states.** In some states, ratification was hotly contested. But by 1788, the necessary nine states had given their approval and the Constitution went into effect. National elections were held in January 1789.

5. **A Bill of Rights was added to the Constitution soon after the members of the new government took office.** These amendments guaranteed individual liberties, while at the same time assuring opponents of the Constitution that the powers of the national government would be limited.

See p. T31.

Vocabulary

On a separate sheet of paper, write the word or words that best complete each of the following sentences.

1. _____ is the principle that the people are the source of a government's power.

2. Powers shared by the states and the national government are _____.

3. _____ exists in a government where each branch has defined and limited powers.

4. To prevent any one branch of government from attaining too much power, Congress set up a system of _____ .

5. The delegates provided a method to _____, or change, the Constitution.

6. A (An) _____ is a law that permits a person charged with treason or other serious crime to be fined or imprisoned without trial.

See p. T31.

Chapter Checkup

1. (a) Why was the method of allocating representation in the national government such a hotly debated question? (b) How did the Virginia Plan propose to solve the question? (c) How did the New Jersey Plan propose to solve it? (d) What compromise was finally reached?

2. (a) What issues particularly concerned the southern states during the Constitutional Convention? (b) How were these issues resolved?

3. How was each of the following designed to prevent the abuse of power in the new republic: (a) federalism; (b) separation of powers; (c) checks and balances?

4. (a) What checks were to be placed on presidential power in the new government? (b) Why were the delegates especially concerned about the authority of the President?

5. (a) What checks were to be placed on the powers of Congress? (b) What checks do the legislative and executive branches have on the judicial branch?

6. Describe the arguments for and against ratification of the Constitution.

7. (a) Why did the delegates believe that a process for amending the Constitution was necessary? (b) Describe the amendment process that was included in the Constitution.

8. (a) How were individual liberties protected in the Constitution? (b) Why did many Antifederalists believe that this was not enough protection?

See p. T32.

Critical Thinking

1. **Making Judgments** (a) Why do you think the delegates to the Constitutional Convention decided to make the chief executive a President elected for a limited term of office rather than a monarch chosen for life? (b) What arguments could be made in favor of a monarch chosen for life?

2. **Analyzing** How might the popularity of a President have an effect on his or her influence on Congress and the nation?

See p. T32.

Connecting Past and Present

1. Review the limits on the direct power of the people in the Constitution. (a) Why did the delegates want to limit the direct power of the people? (b) Do you think their reasons are still valid?

2. Under what circumstances has one branch of the federal government used its power of checks and balances recently?

See p. T32.

Developing Basic Skills

1. **Classifying** Make a chart with three columns. Title the columns Delegated Powers, Reserved Powers, and Concurrent Powers. Using the Constitution, your textbook, and other sources you may have, place each of the following in its appropriate column: voting age, education, an army, fishing regulations, off-shore drilling rights, income tax, police protection, motor-vehicle regulations, postal service.

2. **Researching** Research the background of any two of the delegates to the Constitutional Convention: (a) What similarities do you see in their lives? (b) What differences? (c) Was each a Federalist or an Antifederalist? Why?

WRITING ABOUT HISTORY

Comparison and Contrast

When you *compare* events or items, you show how they are the same. When you *contrast* elements, you show how they are different. One way to prepare a comparison and contrast is to arrange your information in chart form. For example, if you were comparing and contrasting the Virginia Plan, the New Jersey Plan, and the Great Compromise, you would have a chart with three horizontal columns: Virginia Plan, New Jersey Plan, and Great Compromise. The headings for the vertical columns would be: Number of Houses, Method of Selection of Lower House, Basis of Representation. You could then tell at a glance how the plans were the same and how they were different. Some words used to compare and contrast include: *but, besides, in addition, however, but . . . also, too, as well as.*

Practice: Make a chart comparing and contrasting the powers of Congress under the Articles of Confederation and under the United States Constitution. Then write the information in paragraph form.

175

Unit Three
AN EMERGING NATION

1793 *By his second term, George Washington had become a symbol of the new nation.*

1797 *Abigail Adams spent most of her years as First Lady in Philadelphia, which was the nation's capital until 1800.*

	1788	1794	1800	1806
POLITICS AND GOVERNMENT	**1789** George Washington takes office as first President		**1803** *Marbury* v. *Madison* confirms idea of judicial review	
SOCIETY AND CULTURE	**1790** Design of nation's capital at Washington, D.C., begins			
ECONOMICS AND TECHNOLOGY		**1793** Eli Whitney invents cotton gin	**1804** Lewis and Clark begin exploring Louisiana	
WORLD EVENTS	**1789** French Revolution begins		**1804** Napoleon becomes emperor of France	
	Washington		Adams	Jefferson

1791 *The Bank of the United States was an important part of Alexander Hamilton's economic program.*

1804 *Friendship with Native Americans was a goal of the Lewis and Clark expedition, as this medal shows.*

UNIT OUTLINE

1812 *The battle of the U.S.S.* Constitution *and the British ship* Guerriere *is shown in this painting.*

1820s *This painting by George Bingham shows the importance of river travel as Americans moved west.*

1806	1812	1818	1824

1812 War of 1812 with Britain begins

1823 Monroe Doctrine forbids European interference in the Americas

Early 1800s More women and children work in textile mills

1820s More Americans move west of the Appalachians

1807 Fulton travels up Hudson on *Clermont*

1813 Boston Associates set up first modern textile factory

1825 Erie Canal from Buffalo to Albany completed

1812 Britain repeals Orders in Council

1821 Most Latin American countries have become independent of Spain

Madison   **Monroe**

The new nation carried on an active foreign trade. This is a carving from an early trading ship.

As industrialization spread, some women worked at jobs such as at this printing press.

A Federalist Beginning 9

(1789–1801)

CHAPTER OUTLINE

1 Challenges of the New Government

2 A Question of Entangling Alliances

3 The Birth of Political Parties

4 John Adams's Sacrifice

CHAPTER OBJECTIVES After completing this chapter, students should be able to
1. describe Alexander Hamilton's economic policy.
2. describe the new nation's foreign policy.
3. explain why two political parties formed and what each stood for.
4. discuss the Alien and Sedition acts.

As soon as the sun climbed over the horizon, New York City was awakened by the roar of 13 cannons. Their thunder was followed by the peal of church bells and the gathering of excited crowds around the house on Cherry Street. Inside was a man revered as few others have been in history, the man an entire nation relied upon. It was April 30, 1789, and George Washington would soon be inaugurated as the first President of the United States.

Washington would have preferred less fuss. He wore a plain brown suit of Connecticut cloth, and, after laboring over a 73-page speech, discarded it for one lasting under 20 minutes. Yet the crowd was thrilled. After Washington took the oath of office on the balcony of Federal Hall, a great shout went up. "Long live George Washington, President of the United States!"

The President was 57, but felt older. His eyesight was weak and his hearing poor. As one witness said, "Time has made havoc upon his face." Washington would rather have been at his Mount Vernon plantation experimenting with plants, riding across the meadows, and sharing in the harvesting. But instead, he was the new nation's President and felt like "a culprit who is going to the place of his execution." He had borne the burden of leading the Continental army. Now, to him fell once again the task of uniting 13 independently minded states.

The United States was a great experiment—the first nation to create itself by writing a constitution and building a government from the ground up. If the United States failed, republics anywhere might be doomed.

Unexpected challenges faced President Washington and his successor John Adams. Among them were the development of political parties and the threat of war with France. Even with the Constitution as a guide, many details of government remained to be worked out. The officials of the new government knew that the decisions they made and the actions they took would set precedents, or examples, for the future.

CHAPTER PREVIEW Ask students to name the two major political parties today and to list differences between them. Point out that the Constitution says nothing about political parties. Ask: Why do you think political parties first developed? Are they good or bad for the nation? Why?

1.

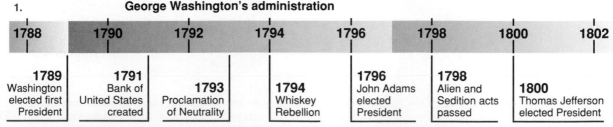

George Washington's administration

1788	1790	1792	1794	1796	1798	1800	1802
1789 Washington elected first President	**1791** Bank of United States created	**1793** Proclamation of Neutrality	**1794** Whiskey Rebellion	**1796** John Adams elected President	**1798** Alien and Sedition acts passed	**1800** Thomas Jefferson elected President	

1. TIME LINE QUESTION Ask: Who served as President between Washington and Jefferson?

George Washington was a symbol of the patriotism Americans felt for the young republic. This painting shows the enthusiastic reception Washington received when he arrived in New York City to be inaugurated as the first President of
1. *the republic.*

1. **VISUAL EVIDENCE** Washington said, "Integrity and firmness is all I can promise." Ask: What qualities of Washington are shown in this picture?

2. **VOCABULARY** Have students look up these terms in the glossary before they begin reading.

Challenges of the New Government

READ TO UNDERSTAND

■ How the national government was set up.

■ How Hamilton planned to restore confidence in the credit of the United States.

■ How Washington demonstrated the power of the federal government during the Whiskey Rebellion.

2. ■ *Vocabulary:* funding, assumption, strict construction, loose construction, protective tariff.

It is small wonder that George Washington would rather have stayed at Mount Vernon. The problems facing the nation in 1789 were staggering. Huge war debts and worthless paper money threatened the financial secu-

rity of the nation. With only the barest of outlines of government provided by the Constitution, Washington was setting out, as he put it, on "untrodden ground."

The First President

The electoral college voted unanimously for George Washington as the nation's first President. There had been no question ever since Washington had presided over the Constitutional Convention in 1787 that he would be called on to lead the government.

As President, Washington was a leader who stood above political conflict and intrigue. He saw himself as an arbiter, or a person who decides disputes, among the various interests within the government and within the nation. To fulfill the role, the President held himself aloof from others and did not allow his air of dignity to be broken by familiarity. Once when Gouverneur Morris, **3.179**

3. **BIOGRAPHY** Gouverneur Morris (1752–1816), as minister to France, 1792–1794, left in his diary an important record of the French Revolution. Note that Gouverneur was Morris's first name, not his title.

acting on a dare, slapped the President on the back, Washington's icy stare froze Morris in his tracks.

Setting Up the National Government

To launch the newly created national government, the President and Congress had to organize the judiciary and find qualified people to serve in the executive department.

Shaping the Judiciary The Constitution stated that there would be a Supreme Court, but it did not describe how such a court should be organized. Congress amplified the Constitution by passing the Judiciary Act of 1789. The law created a court with a chief justice and five associate justices. President Washington appointed John Jay, a veteran of the government under the Articles of Confederation, as the first Chief Justice.

The Judiciary Act gave the Supreme Court final jurisdiction over disputes involving the Constitution, federal law, and treaties. It also created 13 district courts, one in each state,
1. and three federal circuit courts.

Creating the Cabinet No one person could possibly handle all of the administrative duties of the government. But the Constitution was silent on the specific details of how to set up the executive branch. According to Article 2 of the Constitution, the President could "require the Opinion, in writing, of the principal Officer in each of the executive Departments." The Constitution went on to allow the creation of several unspecified executive departments.

By 1789, a presidential cabinet began to take form. Congress established the positions of attorney general, postmaster general, and
2. the secretaries of state, treasury, and war. Washington chose experienced advisers to head these departments. He selected Thomas Jefferson, author of the Declaration of Independence, as secretary of state. His secretary of war was Henry Knox, chief of artillery during the Revolutionary War.

Washington's most important appointment was his secretary of the treasury, Alexander Hamilton. Hamilton was an expert in finance and as one of Washington's staff during the revolution had won his personal trust.

He greatly influenced the President's views on important financial questions.

Only 34 at the time he accepted the treasury position, Hamilton was a man of rare genius and ambition. Born in the British West Indies, Hamilton never developed any intense loyalty to a particular state. Thus he found it easier to think in national terms.

Yet Hamilton held some strange opinions for a leader in a democratic republic. He had little faith in the principle of equality, as he 3. had demonstrated at the Constitutional Convention in Philadelphia.

"All communities," he argued there, "divide themselves into the few and the many. The first are the rich and well-born; the other the mass of the people. . . . The people are turbulent and changing; they seldom judge or determine right. Give therefore to the first class a distinct, permanent share in government." Hamilton's aristocratic leanings influenced his proposals for solving the economic problems of the new nation.

Restoring Public Credit

A key problem facing Hamilton was how to settle the national debt. To finance the revolution, the government had borrowed millions from foreign investors and American citizens. In exchange, the government gave them bonds. With the war long over, bondholders wanted their bonds redeemed.

Most people agreed that the debt owed to foreigners had to be paid, but they disagreed over what to do about bonds sold to Americans. Most of the people who originally bought the bonds had sold them to speculators, in many cases for only 10 to 15 cents on the dollar. Was it fair, some asked, for the speculators to make such a huge profit?

Repaying the National Debt Hamilton proposed funding the national debt at its full value of approximately $40 million. **Funding** is a process by which a government raises or borrows money to pay off a debt. Hamilton planned to raise the money by issuing new bonds. He believed that any speculators 4. deserved to profit because they had supported the government in its darkest times. Besides, the purpose of funding was to restore the nation's credit and reputation. The

180

1. **ACTIVITY** Have students write and act out a conversation between Hamilton and Madison about the funding measure.

2. **BACKGROUND** Thomas Jefferson, a bitter opponent of full funding, called Hamilton's economic system "a machine for the corruption of the legislature."

United States could do so only if it paid its debts in full. Furthermore, Hamilton argued, many of the speculators were wealthy individuals upon whom the nation would depend for future credit.

James Madison, for one, objected to full funding. He felt the bonds should be paid off at full value only to the original holders. Speculators should be paid at a reduced rate. Madison's position in part reflected the sectional strain that was developing between the North and the South. Most of the debt was owed to northerners. Full funding seemed to reward northern interests at the expense of southerners.

1.

Congress passed Hamilton's proposal in February 1790. Some members may have been influenced by their own speculation in war bonds. They stood to make a profit if the bonds were funded in full.

2.

Assuming State Debts The states also had an outstanding $25 million debt from the war. Hamilton proposed that the federal government assume, or take over, all state debts. The **assumption** of state debts, he argued, would equalize the financial burden of the

3. **CRITICAL THINKING** Ask: Why do you think delegates to the Constitutional Convention decided to create a brand new capital for the United States?

THE AMERICAN EXPERIENCE

Building a Worthy Capital

When the delegates met in Philadelphia in 1787 to draft a new constitution, they included a provision to set aside an area "10 miles square" (16 kilometers square) to serve as the permanent capital of the republic. Never before had any nation created a totally new capital city.

3.

Pierre L'Enfant, a French architect and engineer who had served with distinction in the Continental army, begged for "a share of the undertaking." Commissioned by his friend President Washington to plan the new city, L'Enfant set to work.

4.

With an eye to the federal nature of the American government, L'Enfant planned beautiful squares to represent each of the states. He planned a hilltop site for the "Congress House" and set the "Presidential Palace" some distance away, to allow room in between for a grand avenue for public processions. As L'Enfant looked over the site of this "federal city," flanking the Potomac River, he envisioned a magnificent capital worthy of a great republic like the United States.

Completing the grand design was not easy. L'Enfant quickly made enemies. When a landowner began to build a new home blocking the future New Jersey Avenue, L'Enfant had the house torn down. Finally, L'Enfant's temper got the better of him and he left angrily with his plans in hand. Work might have stopped had

L'Enfant's assistant, Benjamin Banneker, not memorized the original plans.

In 1800, when the government arrived, only part of L'Enfant's plan had been realized. But later generations carried the plan forward, and Washington, D.C., became a capital of distinction.

See p. T34.

1. What was L'Enfant's vision for the national capital?

2. **Critical Thinking** Did Washington, D.C., fulfill L'Enfant's prediction that it would "leave to posterity a grand idea of the patriotic interest which promoted it"?

4. **BIOGRAPHY** Pierre L'Enfant (1754–1825) also designed the medal of the Society of the Cincinnati (see p. 142) and renovated Federal Hall in New York, where George Washington was inaugurated. After designing Washington, D.C., he asked Congress for payment of $95,500. Congress voted to give him $3,800.

Mathematician and astronomer Benjamin
Banneker published highly popular almanacs
1. in the 1790s. He was also a member of the
commission that helped design the new capital
city of Washington, D.C.

---

1. **BACKGROUND** Banneker was largely self-taught. He
built a clock after merely reading about clocks.

war and put the new nation on a sound economic foundation. The plan would strengthen
national unity by binding the states more
firmly to the national government.

Opposition came from some southern
states that had already paid off their debts.
Citizens in these states did not want to be
taxed to pay the debts of another state when
they had already paid their own.

Hamilton, Madison, and Jefferson finally
worked out a compromise. Hamilton offered
to move the nation's capital from New York
to a site on the Potomac River donated by
Virginia and Maryland. The prestige and advantages of having the capital in the South
appealed to Madison and Jefferson. Thus,
2. Congress agreed to full funding of the na-

182 tional debt and the assumption of state debts.

3. **READING** Have students look up this clause and the
Tenth Amendment on pp. 874 and 888 and restate them
in their own words.

---

2. **CRITICAL THINKING** Ask: Do you think the South was
right or wrong in opposing assumption of the state debt?
Explain.

GREAT DEBATE

Strict or Loose Construction

Not every issue lent itself readily to compromise. Conflicts arose from basic differences
in interpretation of the role of the government. One such conflict centered on the establishment of a national bank.

A National Bank As the second part of
his program to build a sound economy, Hamilton proposed the creation of a national bank.
The bank would issue United States currency
and be a collecting point for all federal taxes.
The bank's directors, in turn, could invest
that money.

The government would own one fifth of
the stock in the bank, and private citizens
could buy the rest. Since stockholders would
elect the bank officers, the management of
the national bank would be in private hands.
Hamilton's goal was to cement the loyalty of
wealthy investors to the national government.

In February 1791, Congress passed a bill
creating the Bank of the United States. Opponents of the bill fervently urged the President to veto it. Madison and Jefferson strongly
objected to the bank because they feared
that the bank's directors would have too much
power over the nation's economy. Along with
Attorney General Edmund Randolph, they
tried to convince the President that a national bank was unconstitutional.

The Issue of Constitutionality Jefferson
argued that the national government did not
have the authority to create a bank because
the Constitution did not specifically authorize it. He cited the Tenth Amendment to the
Constitution, which states that "all powers
not delegated to the United States . . . are
reserved to the states or to the people." The
government, he concluded, had only those
powers specifically listed in the Constitution.
This literal interpretation of the Constitution
has become known as **strict construction.**

Alexander Hamilton, on the other hand,
favored a **loose construction** of the Constitution. He argued that the government
had more powers than were actually listed.
He cited Article 1, Section 8, Clause 18, of the 3.
Constitution, which gives Congress the power
to make all laws "necessary and proper" to 4.
carry out the specific powers listed in the

4. **BACKGROUND** Jefferson replied that a law could not
be considered "necessary" unless there was no other
possible way for Congress to carry out its powers.

1. **TECHNOLOGY** Hamilton, in his *Report on Manufactures,* urged: "1. The division of labor. 2. An extension of the use of machinery. 3. Additional employment to classes of the community not ordinarily engaged in the business. 4. The promoting of emigration from foreign countries."

Constitution.* Since the United States had the power to tax, according to Hamilton, it also had the power to create a bank to receive the taxes it collected. Hamilton's arguments won the support of the President, who signed the bill into law. ■

Protecting the Nation's Industries

The third part of Hamilton's economic plan was rejected by Congress. To give American manufacturing a boost, Hamilton proposed that Congress pass a **protective tariff.** This would place a tax on imported products, making them more expensive than products made in the United States. Such a tariff would protect American manufacturers from European competition.

Much of the opposition to Hamilton's tariff proposals came from the South. With a largely

_____
*This clause is often called the "elastic clause."

agricultural economy, southerners bought more imported manufactured goods than northerners did. They felt a protective tariff would be unfair to them.

Congress did pass a tariff bill in 1792. However, it was meant to raise money for operating the government, and not to protect American industry. Consequently, it was much lower than the protective tariff called for by Hamilton would have been.

The Whiskey Rebellion

Finally, to raise money, Hamilton proposed an excise tax on distilled liquors. Congress adopted it in 1791, but the measure was so unpopular it incited a rebellion that threatened the stability of the new nation.

Distilling grain into whiskey made economic sense for many farmers in the Pennsylvania backcountry. Whiskey was easier to transport by wagon and brought a higher

2. **VOCABULARY** A tax on certain goods, such as whiskey, made and sold within a country is called an excise tax.

3. When Pennsylvania farmers rioted against the whiskey tax, President Washington called up the militia to put down the rebellion. Washington personally rode out to review the troops at Fort Cumberland, Maryland, as depicted in this painting by James Peale.

3. **PRESIDENTS** Washington was the only President ever to lead troops into battle while in office.

1. **CRITICAL THINKING** Have students compare the farmers' response to the excise tax to the colonists' response to taxes imposed by England.

2. **DISCUSSION** Ask: Why might the U.S. have wanted to avoid a European war?

price than grain. It was also used as a form of payment, since no stable currency existed yet.

As the excise tax cut into the farmers' profits, resentment flared. Finally, in 1794, the farmers rebelled. They refused to pay any further tax, and some even tarred and

1. feathered revenue officials.

Pennsylvania's governor thought that the state could handle the unrest, but Alexander Hamilton saw a chance to demonstrate the power of the federal government. Taking Hamilton's advice, President Washington summoned a troop of state militia. This overpowering show of federal force ended the rebellion without the need to fire a shot. Though Hamilton wanted to punish the leaders, the coolheaded Washington pardoned them.

Washington had used his personal prestige and constitutional authority to strengthen the nation. Hamilton's economic program restored the confidence of both foreign and domestic investors and built a firm foundation for future economic growth. The vigorous response to the Whiskey Rebellion demonstrated that the new government would act decisively in times of crisis.

See p. T34.

SECTION 1 REVIEW

1. **Identify:** (a) John Jay, (b) Thomas Jefferson, (c) Alexander Hamilton.

2. **Define:** (a) funding, (b) assumption, (c) strict construction, (d) loose construction, (e) protective tariff.

3. (a) What was the Constitutional basis for the original cabinet? (b) What precedents did Congress and Washington establish in setting up the cabinet?

4. What were the major elements of Hamilton's financial plan?

5. (a) What sparked the Whiskey Rebellion? (b) What action did Washington take?

6. **Critical Thinking** How was operating the new government like sailing an uncharted sea?

2 A Question of Entangling Alliances

READ TO UNDERSTAND

■ How United States neutrality was threatened by France and Britain.

■ How treaties affected American relations with Britain and Spain.

■ Why Washington favored a policy of neutrality.

While calm prevailed at home, the nations of Europe were embroiled in war and revolution. Even though the conflicts were far across the Atlantic, the United States faced difficult questions: Should the nation help old allies? 2. Should it fight old enemies? How could it protect its ships from becoming casualties of war? The answers were not clear-cut.

Divisions Over Foreign Policy

In 1789, the same year that the United States adopted the Constitution, the French people rose up against their king. Most Americans rejoiced at the news of the French Revolu- 3. tion.

Four years later, however, the revolution took a startling turn. King Louis XVI and many other French nobles were beheaded in what became known as the Reign of Terror. In an attack on the power of the Catholic church, the revolutionaries replaced Catholicism with the worship of what they called the Supreme Being. This rejection of Christianity outraged many Americans. Much of the early admiration Americans felt for the French revolutionaries turned into bitter opposition.

Alexander Hamilton particularly hated the course of the French Revolution. In his opinion, the attack on the upper classes threatened the foundations of society. In addition, American support for the revolution could mean war with Britain and economic disaster for the United States.* About 90 percent

---

*By 1793, Great Britain had joined other European nations in a war against France. The British government considered the revolution in France a threat to all monarchies.

3. **BACKGROUND** The American Revolution influenced events in France in several ways: the Declaration of Independence and Bill of Rights inspired the French Declaration of the Rights of Man, and French financial support of the Patriots helped bankrupt the crown, thus prompting rebellion.

1. **VOCABULARY** Have students define neutrality. Ask: What specific actions would a nation take or not take to remain neutral?

2. **ACTIVITY** Have students draw a political cartoon supporting an alliance with France against Great Britain.

of the government's revenue came from customs duties, and 75 percent of its imports came from Britain. War with Britain would wipe out a major source of income.

Other Americans were less disturbed by the course of France's revolution. Thomas Jefferson, for one, regretted the violence but sympathized with the rebels' goals. Indeed, the French revolutionaries themselves had used Jefferson's ideas in their Declaration of the Rights of Man.

Hamilton and Jefferson each tried to persuade President Washington to take sides in the war between France and Great Britain. But Washington decided on a more moderate course of action. In April 1793, he issued the Proclamation of Neutrality. 1.

Citizen Genêt

About the same time Washington issued his proclamation, a new French ambassador, Citizen Edmond Genêt (zhuh NAY), arrived in Charleston, South Carolina. Genêt wanted the United States to honor the Treaty of 1778 with France, in which the United States promised to defend the French West Indies if France went to war with Britain.

Without even meeting first with the American government, the Frenchman began his intrigues. He outfitted American ships as privateers against England and set up courts to deal with the ships they captured. Genêt also organized an attack by American frontiersmen on Spanish New Orleans. His warm reception by the people persuaded the arrogant Genêt that he was better liked than the President. He told his government, "I live in a round of parties. Old Man Washington can't forgive my success."

When Genêt began organizing pro-French clubs that loudly criticized American neutrality, Washington decided the ambassador had gone too far. Even Jefferson agreed that Genêt's conduct had become intolerable. President Washington demanded that France recall its ambassador immediately. Genêt might have protested, but another revolution in France removed his friends from power. The new French government ordered his arrest. Rather than face the guillotine at home,

Genêt retired from public life and lived quietly in New York until his death in 1836.

The Jay Treaty

The British government also tested the American commitment to neutrality. Britain's navy stopped American ships bound for the West Indies and seized sailors who they claimed had deserted British ships. Many were American citizens. The British forced them into service in the Royal Navy. Angered by the violation of their neutral rights, many Americans clamored for war with Great Britain. 2.

Washington sent Chief Justice John Jay, an experienced diplomat, to London in 1794

John Jay, below, had many years of diplomatic experience. He had served in Spain and France and had been secretary of foreign affairs under the Articles of Confederation. However, many people regarded the Jay Treaty as a failure. Jay was widely criticized and burned in effigy. 3.

1. **ECONOMICS** Britain also wanted the U.S. to honor its commitment to pay Loyalists for property confiscated during the Revolution.

to try to work out the dispute. Conditions did not favor successful negotiations. The British felt they were winning their war with France, so they were not in a mood to compromise. Jay himself could not negotiate from a position of strength because the United States lacked any real military power. Alexander Hamilton had further weakened the American diplomat's position by telling the British minister about Washington's decision not to enter into an alliance with other European nations.

After learning that it did not have to worry about an American-French alliance, Britain drove a harder bargain. As a result, the Jay Treaty was disappointing to the United States.

2. **BACKGROUND** Robert Livingston, an opponent of the Jay Treaty, wrote: "And what is our submission to these terms . . . but the lowest political degradation?"

The British did promise to evacuate their posts on United States soil and to pay damages for the ships they had recently seized. But they made no promises about future seizures. In return, Jay had to pledge payment of debts owed to British merchants before the Revolutionary War.

1.

Although the Jay Treaty avoided war, many Americans saw the pact as a surrender to Great Britain. The treaty especially offended 2. southern planters, who owed most of the debts. They would have to pay, but northern shipowners would collect compensation for ships and cargoes that had been seized.

President Washington recognized that the terms were probably the best Jay could ne-

VOICES OF FREEDOM

Washington's Farewell Address

President Washington's Farewell Address is probably best known for its warning against permanent foreign alliances. However, as you can see in the extracts below, Washington spoke about many challenges facing the young 3. *republic.*

National Unity

The unity of government which constitutes you one people is also now dear to you. It is justly so, for it is a main pillar. . . of your real independence, the support of your tranquility at home, your peace abroad, of your safety, of your prosperity, of that very liberty which you so highly prize. . . . it is of infinite moment [importance] that you properly estimate the immense value of your national union. . . . You have, in a common cause, fought and triumphed together; the independence and liberty you possess are the work of joint councils and joint efforts, of common dangers, sufferings, and successes.

The Constitution

The basis of our political system is the right of the people to make and to alter the constitutions of government. . . . The very idea of the

power and the right of the people to establish a government presupposes the duty of every individual to obey the established government.

Political Parties

I have already intimated to you the danger of parties in the State. . . . Let me now warn you, in the most solemn manner, against the baneful effects of the spirit of party generally. . . . It serves always to distract the public councils, and enfeeble [weaken] the public administration. It agitates the community with ill-founded jealousies and false alarms; kindles the animosity of one part against another.

4.

The National Government

And remember especially, that for the efficient management of your common interests, in a country so extensive as ours, a government of as much vigor as is consistent with the perfect security of liberty, is indispensable.

See p. T34.

1. What issues affecting the future of the nation were of concern to Washington as he left office?

2. **Critical Thinking** Do you agree or disagree with Washington's views? Explain.

3. **MAIN IDEA** Divide the class into four groups and have each group summarize Washington's advice on one of the topics in this special feature.

4. **CRITICAL THINKING** Ask: Why did Washington think political parties were dangerous?

gotiate. He reluctantly recommended that the Senate ratify the treaty. Exactly the two-thirds majority of senators required by the Constitution voted for it.

A Treaty With Spain

The United States had better luck in its negotiations with Spain the following year. Spain had fared badly in its war with France. Furthermore, the Spanish feared that the Jay Treaty might foreshadow a British-American alliance aimed at them one day. So American diplomat Thomas Pinckney found Spain willing to negotiate.

The United States had two long-standing disputes it wanted settled. The first was over the border between the United States and Spanish Florida. The second involved the right to deposit American cargo from the Mississippi Valley in Spanish-controlled New Orleans until it could be picked up by larger, oceangoing ships.

Pinckney negotiated solutions to both problems. Spain allowed the United States access to the Mississippi River as well as the right to deposit cargo in New Orleans. It further agreed to fix the boundary between the United States and Florida at the thirty-first parallel, exactly what Pinckney had been in-
1. structed to seek.

Warning About Permanent Alliances

President Washington was convinced that his policy of neutrality had been best for the nation. So important was the policy, in fact, that he devoted a lengthy portion of his Farewell Address to it when he left office in 1796. Washington warned the nation not to form "permanent alliances." The United States as a young nation would be better off, he said, if
2. allowed to develop on its own.

Washington's warning referred to long-term political alliances that might embroil the United States in European conflicts. He did not oppose economic agreements that would build trade and promote economic growth. His successors would try to maintain his policy of neutrality, but they would find it difficult to do so.

3. **PAST AND PRESENT** Have students suggest several benefits and drawbacks of modern political parties.

3 The Birth of Political Parties

READ TO UNDERSTAND

■ How Hamilton's and Jefferson's views differed on who should control the government.

■ What steps Madison and Jefferson took to establish an opposition political party.

■ How the development of political parties affected the outcome of the election of 1796.

Campaign buttons, lawn signs, bumper stickers—political symbols are such a familiar part of American life that people often assume that political parties have always existed. In the early years of the United States government, however, parties did not exist. In fact, people regarded them as evils to be avoided. 3.

Thomas Jefferson expressed the general American attitude toward parties when he said, "If I could not go to heaven but with a party, I would not go at all." Even though most Americans shared Jefferson's views, the seeds of political parties were planted during Washington's presidency.

187

2. **BACKGROUND** Washington said, "Europe has interests which to us have a very remote relation. Hence she must be engaged in frequent controversies, the causes of which are foreign to our concerns. Therefore, it must be unwise to implicate ourselves in combinations and collisions of her friendships or enmities."

Contrasting Figures

As symbols of the two opposing views that emerged in the new government, Thomas Jefferson and Alexander Hamilton were a study in contrasts. Hamilton was a short, well-dressed, energetic, and charming man. He was married to a woman from a wealthy New York family, and her aristocratic attitudes influenced his thinking. Hamilton was knowledgeable and had a well-disciplined mind, yet he wrote in a heavy style that most people could not understand.

The tall and lanky Jefferson, on the other hand, seemed awkward and shy. His clothes seldom fit well. When he talked, he did not look people in the eye. His mind seemed less organized than Hamilton's, but it was active and curious. His writing stirred people's emotions.

GREAT DEBATE
An Agricultural or Industrial Economy

Hamilton's and Jefferson's political differences were even more striking than their personal ones. As the details of Hamilton's economic program emerged, Jefferson found himself opposed to the course being charted for the nation.

Hamilton supported a strong central government with power concentrated in the hands of wealthy, well-educated men. For the government to have sufficient power to govern, Hamilton believed that the Constitution had to be interpreted loosely. As he showed during the debate over the national bank, he felt the Constitution gave the government implied powers that it did not list. In another area, Hamilton believed, the nation's economy should depend less on farming and more on manufacturing, shipping, and commerce.

Jefferson believed that power should be dispersed. He thought the safest and most virtuous storehouse for power was with the people. Jefferson supported the idea of universal education because it would increase the people's ability to govern. While Hamilton emphasized a strong central government, Jefferson thought the states should retain authority. As a result, Jefferson was a strict constructionist. He believed the Constitution

granted the government only those powers that it specifically listed. Jefferson thought the nation's economy should be based on agriculture. ■

Creation of a Party Machinery

In 1791, Jefferson and James Madison went to New York, claiming they were going to study botany. The claim was not entirely an exaggeration, since Jefferson was a well-known naturalist. But their real purpose was to meet with people who opposed Hamilton's views. Control of New York politics was in the hands of a small number of families. Governor George Clinton and Aaron Burr led one side. The Schuylers, who were related to Hamilton by marriage, controlled the other.

While Jefferson and Madison were in New York, they agreed to work together with the Clinton-Burr faction to achieve their goals. This action marked a turning point in American politics. Previously, Jefferson and Madison had opposed Hamilton only on specific issues. Now they were taking a step toward setting up a national party of opposition.

The next step was to find a way of informing the public of their party's point of view. In 1791, the United States had only one influential newspaper, John Fenno's *Gazette of the United States.* The paper consistently praised Hamilton and his economic program. Furthermore, Fenno received profitable printing contracts from the Treasury Department and personal loans from Hamilton himself.

Jefferson had a plan to counteract Fenno's newspaper. He appointed Philip Freneau, a popular poet, to a clerk's position in the State Department. The job, which paid $250 per year, required little work. But Freneau knew how he was expected to fill his time. He started a newspaper, the *National Gazette,* which published biting attacks on Hamilton. Its praise of Jefferson outdid Fenno's praise of Hamilton.

Madison, Jefferson, and their followers had not originally intended to start a political party, but by 1792 they were openly referring to themselves as "the Republican party." When the Hamiltonians took the name "Federalists," the two-party system in American politics had begun.

Choosing a New President

The split between Hamilton and Jefferson, two trusted advisers, greatly distressed President Washington. In 1792, he decided to seek reelection to prevent the rift from widening further. Washington's popularity discouraged party activity in that election.

Four years later, when Washington announced his decision not to run for a third term, the two parties became more visible and active.

The Candidates Although both Hamilton and Madison were well known among members of the government, neither man had enough popular support to make a serious run for the presidency. The Federalists chose John Adams as their candidate; the Republicans chose Thomas Jefferson.

Hamilton was unhappy with his party's selection. He wanted to remain influential in the government, and he feared that John Adams would be too independent. So Hamilton devised a scheme to defeat Adams by arranging for Thomas Pinckney of South Carolina to be the Federalist candidate for Vice President.

In the 1796 election, each of the two parties designated one candidate for President and one for Vice President. The Constitution, however, did not recognize this distinction. It provided that each elector in the electoral college simply vote for two persons. The candidate receiving the largest number of electoral votes would become President; the one receiving the second largest number would become Vice President.

Hamilton thus tried to persuade electors from both parties to cast one of their votes for Pinckney for Vice President. If all went as planned, Pinckney would receive more electoral votes than either Adams or Jefferson and would become President.

The Results Adams's supporters outfoxed Hamilton and cast their votes for Vice President almost at random. As a result, Pinckney received only 59 votes. The Federalist John Adams became the second President of the United States with 71 electoral votes. Thomas Jefferson, a Republican, was elected Vice President with 68 votes.

The outcome of the election disclosed a flaw in the election process as originally de-

The youngest member of the first Cabinet, Alexander Hamilton was held in the highest regard by Washington and was called the "evil genius of America" by Jefferson. Hamilton called for a strong central government with power resting in the hands of the wealthy and well-educated. His reputation for elegance and style is reflected in this portrait by John Trumbull.

2.

2. **VISUAL EVIDENCE** Like his subject, Trumbull was a believer in an American aristocracy.

fined in the Constitution. Candidates with opposing views could be elected President and Vice President. This fact became more important now that the opposing views were represented by distinct political parties.

3.

See p. T35.

SECTION 3 REVIEW

1. **Identify:** (a) Republican party, (b) Federalist party.

2. Contrast Hamilton's and Jefferson's views on government and the economy.

3. How did Madison and Jefferson help create the Republican party?

4. What major flaw in the election process did the 1796 election reveal?

5. **Critical Thinking** Why have political parties been called "the lengthening shadows of two great men"?

189

4 John Adams's Sacrifice

READ TO UNDERSTAND

■ What events worsened relations between France and the United States.

■ How Adams avoided war between the United States and France.

■ Why the Federalists lost the election of 1800.

1. ■ *Vocabulary:* nullify.

In many ways, John Adams was a reluctant President. He loved his country dearly and felt both proud and duty-bound to serve it. Yet he loathed the trappings and rituals of political office. Before he was inaugurated, he told his wife, Abigail, "I hate to live in Philadelphia in summer,* and I hate still more to relinquish my farm. I hate speeches, messages, addresses and answers, proclamations, and such things. I hate to speak to a thousand people to whom I have nothing to say. Yet all this I can do." And so he did, during one of the most turbulent presidencies in American history.

Assuming the Presidency

2. The 61-year-old Adams knew an arduous task lay before him. First, he followed in the shadow of the revered George Washington. Second, he inherited Washington's neutral foreign policy, which was becoming increasing difficult to uphold. But Adams was not without political assets. He had been a lawyer, a patriot, a delegate to the Continental Congress, and Vice President under Washington. He was also both fair and honest.

Yet, honesty did not always serve Adams well in politics. Carried to the point of bluntness, it cost him the personal loyalty of his subordinates and limited his close political friendships. This tendency to speak his mind,

*Philadelphia served as the nation's capital from 1790 until 1800, when Washington, D.C., became the capital.

combined with Adams's frequent, extended trips home to Quincy, Massachusetts, prevented him from controlling the Federalist party as closely as he might have.

As President, John Adams kept Washington's cabinet. There were two reasons: He did not want to slight the former President, and it was hard to find people who were willing to serve in government. The pay was low, the jobs were hard, and government officials were increasingly subject to personal criticism.

Unfortunately for Adams, Washington's cabinet members were loyal to Alexander Hamilton, the very man who had tried to sabotage Adams's election. The split between President Adams and Hamilton's followers, known as High Federalists, grew as relations with France worsened.

Pressure for War

The French government deeply resented the Jay Treaty. (See pages 185–186.) To the French, it seemed that the United States favored Great Britain. In reaction, France began to seize American merchant vessels sailing for England—300 by the middle of 1797. President Adams sent a mission of three men 3. to France to negotiate an end to this piracy.

The XYZ Affair When the Americans arrived, they were contacted by three secret representatives of the French government, called *X, Y,* and *Z* in published reports. *X, Y,* and *Z* demanded a loan of several million dollars to the French government, plus a bribe of $250,000 merely for allowing the Americans to talk to the French foreign minister. "Not a sixpence!" cried one of the Americans.

A war fever erupted in the United States at the news of the so-called XYZ Affair. "Millions for defense, but not one cent for tribute!" was the cry. The High Federalists saw 4. the crisis with France as an opportunity to crush their Republican opponents. Arguing that the country had to prepare in case of war, they proposed that the United States raise a navy and an army—this despite the fact that all the fighting had been at sea.

Adams Reacts The President was under tremendous pressure to declare war, but

3. **BACKGROUND** They were Elbridge Gerry, John Marshall, and Charles Pinckney.

4. **VOCABULARY** Ask students to look up the definition of *tribute.* Then have them rewrite the slogan in their own words.

1. **TECHNOLOGY** Since colonial days, New England shipyards were known for producing some of the world's finest vessels.

2. **BACKGROUND** In addition, the Navy Department and the Marine Corps were established.

Adams had an independent streak. He acted in a way that surprised many people, not least the members of his own Federalist party.

Adams believed he should avoid war if possible but be prepared in case it came. He resisted the pleas of the High Federalists for an army because concentrating on land forces would leave the American merchant fleet defenseless. Instead, he proposed the creation of an American navy.

As of March 1798, the United States had no warships. The small navy of the Revolutionary War ceased to exist once the war ended. Congress now appropriated money

1. to complete work on three frigates, and in July it issued bonds to pay for 24 more. During the summer, the first three—the *Constitution,* the *United States,* and the *Constellation*—set sail. The new American ships, larger than comparable vessels in the British and French navies, performed well in skir-
2. mishes over the next two years.

Avoiding War With France

In the meantime, the High Federalists continued to press for an army and a declaration of war. Adams realized that a declaration of war would increase the Federalists' popularity and perhaps win him a second term. But recognizing the country's weakness, he refused to gamble with its survival.

After receiving reports that the French might be willing to reopen negotiations, the President decided to make one more attempt to smooth out differences. He appointed a new ambassador to France and, as the Constitution required, submitted the nomination to the Senate.

The High Federalists, who wanted war, not negotiation, threatened to block approval of Adams's nominee. Adams countered by telling his own party that he would resign and leave the presidency to the Republican Vice President, Thomas Jefferson, if they thwarted him. The High Federalist senators then agreed to compromise on a three-man delegation to France.

When the delegation arrived in Paris, it found a new French government, headed by Napoleon Bonaparte. Napoleon was more interested in European conquest than in

conflict with the United States, so he was willing to compromise. In the Convention of 1800, the French promised that they would not harass American shipping. They refused, however, to pay for the American ships and cargoes they had already seized. Still, John Adams had saved the country from war.

3.

4. **VISUAL EVIDENCE** Ask: Why is Miss Liberty shown with her foot on a crown?

American artists tried to find symbols for the patriotism of the new nation. This painting contains several such symbols, including the laurel leaf of victory being placed on George Washington's head, the new flag, the American eagle, and Miss Liberty. Washington's position as a symbol of the new nation made it difficult for his successor, John Adams, to establish his own independence.

4.

FIRST in WAR,
FIRST in PEACE,
&
FIRST in the HEARTS
OF HIS
COUNTRYMEN.

3. **ACTIVITY** Have students write a letter that John Adams might have written to explain his feelings about events leading to the Convention of 1800.

As the United States and France neared war in the 1790s, the United States built warships. This print by William Birch shows construction of the 36-gun frigate,
1. Philadelphia.

1. CRITICAL THINKING Ask: Why was the Northeast well-suited to shipbuilding?

The Alien and Sedition Acts

Back home, the High Federalists were provoking another crisis. They introduced a series of acts in Congress, supposedly to protect the nation from foreign treachery. But in actuality, these laws were among the most repressive ever adopted in the United States.

The Alien Act authorized the President to deport or imprison foreigners during wartime and lengthened the residency requirement for citizenship from 5 to 14 years. Most immigrants voted Republican when they became citizens. By delaying their citizenship, the Federalists hoped to weaken the Republican party.

The Sedition Act was even more political. It called for the fining or imprisonment of anyone who impeded the progress of the government or defamed its officials. To many **192** people, especially the Republicans, this seemed to be a direct violation of the right of free speech guaranteed in the First Amendment to the Constitution. **2.**

The expiration date of the Sedition Act was further evidence of its political nature—March 3, 1801, the day of the next presidential inauguration. The High Federalists hoped that the law would curb Republican criticism over the next three years and thereby guarantee a Federalist victory in the election of 1800. If the Federalists still lost the election, the law would expire, thus allowing them to attack the new Republican President. While the Sedition Act was in effect, the government indicted 15 Republican newspaper editors and convicted 10.

Republican Resistance

To the Republicans, the Alien and Sedition acts were a clear abuse of governmental **3.** power. Since Federalists controlled the fed-

2. BACKGROUND One Republican warned that soon it would be a crime "to give dinner to a Frenchman."

3. CITIZENSHIP The Supreme Court unanimously held that the Sedition Act was constitutional.

1. **ACTIVITY** Have students draw political cartoons either supporting or criticizing the Alien and Sedition acts.

3. **READING** Adams corresponded with Jefferson after leaving the White House. *The Adams-Jefferson Letters,* edited by Lester J. Cappon, make fascinating reading.

eral courts, Republicans turned to state governments in an attempt to repeal the laws.

In 1798, the Kentucky legislature adopted a series of resolutions written by Thomas Jefferson which stated that since the states had created the federal government, they could **nullify,** or declare invalid, any law it passed. The Virginia legislature passed similar resolutions.

These resolutions revived the debate over whether the federal government or the states were sovereign. At the time, they had little effect because no other states were willing to adopt such measures. The Alien and Sedition acts eventually expired. But the idea of state nullification of federal laws would surface again.

1.

The Federalist Defeat in 1800

The Federalists faced an uphill battle as the election of 1800 neared. Resentment ran deep among American voters over the Alien and Sedition acts. Voters were also angry about high taxes the "Federalists warmongers" had levied in preparation for a war with France that never happened.

The taxes sparked violent resistance. In Pennsylvania, federal tax assessors were attacked, and an armed band set two tax dodgers free. President Adams sent federal troops and state militia into Pennsylvania to restore order. Although Adams later pardoned all those arrested, the use of federal troops increased resentment.

The Federalists knew the election would be difficult to win. They tried to persuade George Washington to reenter public life, but he refused. The party finally decided to support John Adams for reelection. The Republicans nominated Thomas Jefferson for President and Aaron Burr for Vice President.

2.

During the campaign, wild charges flowed from both sides. Federalists charged that Jefferson was an agent of French revolutionaries and atheists. Republicans, in turn, claimed that John Adams was a monarchist who wanted his daughter to marry Britain's King George III.

When the electoral votes were counted, Jefferson and his running mate, Burr, were tied with the most votes. As you recall, the Constitution required each elector to cast

two ballots; the candidate with the highest number of votes would be President, the candidate with the next highest number would be Vice President. Every Republican elector had cast one of his two votes for Jefferson and the other for Burr. In such an event, the Constitution stated that the House of Representatives would choose the President. With a majority in the House, the Federalists tried to prevent Jefferson's election by voting for Burr. After casting 35 ballots over more than a week's time, the House finally elected Jefferson.*

The last major act of the Adams administration was passage of the Judiciary Act of 1801. It created a new system of 16 circuit courts and reduced the number of justices on the Supreme Court from six to five. President Adams quickly appointed circuit judges to fill the new posts, rather than allow the incoming Republican President to select them. Adams also appointed a Federalist, John Marshall, as the new Chief Justice of the Supreme Court. Marshall was to become one of the most influential persons ever to hold that office.

3.

---

*Congress later took steps to prevent the situation from recurring. In 1804, the states ratified the Twelfth Amendment, which required electors to cast their ballots separately for President and Vice President.

See p. T35.

SECTION 4 REVIEW

1. **Identify:** (a) High Federalists, (b) XYZ Affair, (c) Convention of 1800, (d) Judiciary Act of 1801.

2. **Define:** nullify.

3. (a) What two French actions led to demands for war by many Americans? (b) What did Adams do to avoid war?

4. (a) Compare the stated purpose of the Alien and Sedition acts with the real purpose. (b) How did the Republicans try to repeal the two laws?

5. **Critical Thinking** Why did Jefferson refer to his election as "The Revolution of 1800"?

Summary

1. **President Washington and the first Congress established a national government.** Washington chose able advisers and tackled important domestic and foreign issues. Alexander Hamilton, his secretary of state, put forward a plan to create a solid economic foundation for the new nation.

2. **A revolution in France and war in Europe threatened to involve the United States.** While debating what course of action to follow, the government negotiated treaties to keep out of war. When Washington left office, he advised the nation to avoid permanent alliances.

3. **Hamilton and Jefferson represented differing views that became the basis for the creation of political parties.** In 1796, for the first time, each party ran its own candidate for the presidency. John Adams, a Federalist, was elected President, and Jefferson, a Republican, was elected Vice President.

4. **Adams was pressured by his own party to declare war on France.** Adams avoided war, but the Alien and Sedition acts and increases in taxes proved disastrous to the Federalist party's chances in the election of 1800.

See p. T36.

Vocabulary

Match each term at left with its definition or description at right.

1. funding

2. assumption

3. strict construction

4. protective tariff

5. nullify

a. literal interpretation of the Constitution

b. to declare invalid

c. raising or borrowing money to pay a debt

d. tax designed to reduce imports

e. taking over the debts of states by the national government

See p. T36.

Chapter Checkup

1. How did each of the following contribute to a strong beginning for the new government: (a) election of George Washington as President; (b) Judiciary Act of 1789; (c) creation of a cabinet?

2. (a) What measures did Alexander Hamilton propose to build a sound economy? (b) Which of these measures were adopted? (c) How did one of Hamilton's proposals lead to the Whiskey Rebellion?

3. (a) Why did James Madison object to full funding of war bonds? (b) What was Hamilton's position on this issue?

4. (a) Why did Hamilton think the creation of a national bank was important? (b) Why did Thomas Jefferson believe that such a bank was unconstitutional? (c) How did Hamilton justify his proposal?

5. (a) What positions did Jefferson and Hamilton advocate in America's policy toward France and Great Britain? Why? (b) What position did Washington take? Why?

6. (a) What actions of the British government alienated Americans? (b) How did many Americans react to the Jay Treaty?

7. (a) Why were the Republican and Federalist parties formed? (b) Who were the leaders of each? (c) Why is it correct to say that the United States system of political parties developed by accident?

8. (a) What developments made it difficult for President Adams to continue Washington's foreign policy of neutrality? (b) What steps did Adams take to avoid war?

9. (a) What were the Alien Act and the Sedition Act? (b) Why did the Federalists propose these acts? (c) Why did the Republicans oppose them?

10. (a) What circumstances led to the defeat of the Federalists in the election of 1800? (b) How did the Constitution's provisions for electing a President and Vice President complicate the election?

See p. T36.

Critical Thinking

1. **Recognizing a Point of View** (a) Why do you think Washington chose Alexander Hamilton to be secretary of the treasury? (b) How did Hamilton's economic program reflect his political and social views?

2. **Applying Information** (a) What was the purpose of the Kentucky and Virginia resolutions? (b) How did they reflect Jefferson's attitude toward government? (c) Under what circumstances might they have had a greater impact than they did in 1798?

See p. T36.

Connecting Past and Present

1. (a) Which American industries would favor protective tariffs today? Why? (b) Who are our greatest competitors today?

2. (a) How do the Republican and the Democratic parties of today differ? (b) Would Jefferson be a Democrat or a Republican today? Why? (c) Which party would Hamilton most likely join? Why?

3. (a) What role did newspapers play in the origin of the first two political parties? (b) What role do newspapers play in politics today?

See p. T37.

Developing Basic Skills

1. **Comparing** Make a chart with three columns. In column 1, list the following issues: creation of a national bank, interpretation of the Constitution, the French Revolution, powers of the national and state governments, trust in the people, manufacturing versus farming. In column 2, describe Hamilton's view on each issue. In column 3, describe Jefferson's view on each issue. How might you explain the differences between them?

2. **Using a Primary Source** Study the extracts from Washington's Farewell Address on page 186. (a) What type of document is it? (b) What does it tell you about Washington's concerns for the new nation? (c) What can you learn from the document about the United States in 1796?

WRITING ABOUT HISTORY

Spatial Order

Spatial order is the sensible order to use when describing how something looks. Details are arranged by their location. Usually, you would organize the various items in some pattern, such as left to right, near to far, front to back, and so on. The readers should be able to follow the description in a logical manner as though their eyes were traveling across a scene. Spatial order is helpful when writing an account of a gathering of people, the strategy of a battle, or the visual results of warfare.

Some words to use to show spatial order include: *above, near, beside, in front of, in the distance, beyond, overhead,* and *outside.*

Practice: Look at the picture on page 183 of George Washington reviewing his troops. Write a word picture of the scene.

The Republicans in Office (1801–1815)

10

CHAPTER OUTLINE

1. **Jefferson and the National Government**
2. **Expanding the Nation's Boundaries**
3. **The Coming of Another War**
4. **A Complex War**

CHAPTER OBJECTIVES After completing this chapter, students should be able to
1. explain Thomas Jefferson's views on government.
2. describe the purchase and exploration of Louisiana.
3. list the causes of the War of 1812.
4. describe the course of the war.

CHAPTER PREVIEW Have students look at the map on p. 203, which shows the Louisiana Purchase. Ask them to compare the size of the nation before and after the purchase. Ask: Which present-day states were part of the Louisiana Purchase? Who controlled the territory north of the United States? Who controlled Florida? Who controlled Texas, New Mexico, and California? Who claimed Oregon?

There was no moon that February night in 1804. The Barbary pirates aboard the captured American frigate, the *Philadelphia,* could barely see the ship sailing into Tripoli harbor. When the mysterious vessel drew close, a pirate called out and ordered it to drop anchor. The reply came that the ship had lost its anchors in a storm. Could they tie up alongside for the night? Hardly were the ropes in place when the pirates realized it was a trick.

An outcry went up as armed men boarded the *Philadelphia.* In confusion and fear, some Barbary sailors dove overboard; others grabbed weapons. But within minutes, 20 lay dead and the fight was over. The daring American sailors from the *Intrepid* loaded the decks of the *Philadelphia* with combustibles. Once the ship was ablaze, they made their escape to the open sea.

What were American sailors doing 5,000 miles from home, launching a sea raid in a North African pirate stronghold? For years, the United States had been paying what amounted to blackmail to the rulers of the Barbary States to buy protection for American ships. When President Jefferson decided the practice would stop, the Pasha of Tripoli declared war on the young nation. The *Philadelphia* was an early casualty of that war. The bold captain of the *Intrepid,* Stephen Decatur, and his crew had volunteered to destroy the captured ship so that it could never be used against the United States Navy.

Jefferson's decision to go to war with the Barbary States revealed once more the practical side of a man many considered to be a dreamer. During his administration, Jefferson also presided over the most significant territorial expansion in United States history and kept the country out of a war raging in Europe. His successor, James Madison, would not be able to avoid involvement. But in the end, the war that followed served to confirm the vitality and independence of the young nation.

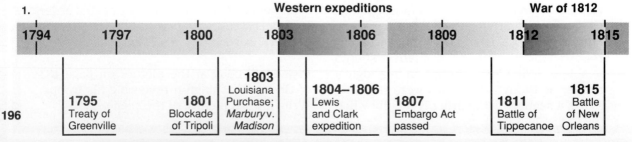

1. Western expeditions — War of 1812

1794	1797	1800	1803	1806	1809	1812	1815

1795 Treaty of Greenville
1801 Blockade of Tripoli
1803 Louisiana Purchase; *Marbury* v. *Madison*
1804–1806 Lewis and Clark expedition
1807 Embargo Act passed
1811 Battle of Tippecanoe
1815 Battle of New Orleans

1. TIME LINE QUESTION Ask: How long after the Louisiana Purchase did the Lewis and Clark expedition end?

UNDER MY WINGS EVERY THING PROSPERS

President Thomas Jefferson presided over a growing, bustling nation. A vigorous President, he challenged the blackmail of the Barbary pirates and doubled the size of the nation by buying the Louisiana Territory. The city of New Orleans, 1. shown in this 1803 watercolor, became the chief trading port for the new territory.

1. **VISUAL EVIDENCE** Ask students to explain the meaning of the eagle and banner at the top of the painting.

2. **VOCABULARY** Have students look up these terms in the glossary before they begin reading.

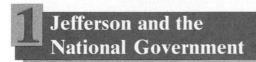

Jefferson and the National Government

READ TO UNDERSTAND

- Why a conflict developed between Jefferson and the judiciary.

- How Jefferson tried to limit the role of government.

- Why the United States fought the Barbary States.

2. *Vocabulary:* judicial review, laissez-faire, secede.

Thomas Jefferson's inauguration was the first to take place in the new capital, Washington, D.C. Despite this distinction, Jefferson deliberately made it an almost casual affair. Rather than use the presidential coach, he walked from the boardinghouse where he had been living to the still unfinished Capitol building.

After taking the oath of office, Jefferson read his inaugural speech in a voice so low that hardly anyone in the chamber could hear

him. Then, the new President of the United States walked back to his boardinghouse for a quiet dinner. When he entered the room, only one of his fellow diners even rose to offer him a chair.

People soon grew accustomed to seeing the President walking or riding an old horse about town. Instead of delivering rousing speeches to Congress, he had a clerk read his messages. Instead of holding formal meet- 3. ings, he conducted as much business as he could at small dinners. Jefferson consistently made informality his approach to government. The presidency, he felt, should not glorify the person who held the office. 4.

A Policy of Conciliation

Printed copies of Jefferson's inaugural speech quickly found their way into newspapers around the country, and most people liked what they read. It showed that Jefferson was determined to unite the country, not divide it further. In particular, Jefferson assured his opponents that his administration would not follow a wild course like becoming involved **197** in the turbulent French Revolution. To the

3. **BACKGROUND** Jefferson was more eloquent in writing, so he found ways to avoid public speaking.

4. **CRITICAL THINKING** Have students discuss whether Jefferson's personal style was in keeping with his political philosophy.

"God forbid that we should ever be twenty years without a rebellion," said Thomas Jefferson, as a young man. *"The tree of liberty must be refreshed from time to time with the blood of patriots and tyrants."* Despite these sentiments, as President, Jefferson followed a policy of reconciliation with
1. his opponents.

---

1. **VISUAL EVIDENCE** Have students find other portraits of Jefferson painted at different stages of his career.

embittered and defeated Federalists, Jefferson offered hope, noting, "We are all Repub-
2. licans, we are all Federalists."

Jefferson went to work right away to ease Federalist fears of an abrupt change in government. The new cabinet appointees, including James Madison as secretary of state and Albert Gallatin as secretary of the treasury, were Republicans. But Jefferson did not automatically dismiss all Federalists in government positions.

The new administration also kept in place some key Federalist policies. For example, the national government continued to pay off the states' war debts. And Jefferson allowed the Bank of the United States to remain in operation.

After these early gestures of conciliation, however, Jefferson quickly took advantage of his party's majority in Congress to implement Republican principles. He allowed the Alien and Sedition acts to expire, and he re-
198 funded all fines collected under those acts.

2. **MAIN IDEA** Have students explain what Jefferson meant by "We are all Republicans, we are all Federalists."

3. **BACKGROUND** Adams had worked late his last night as President signing commissions for 16 new federal judges.

Congress also restored the original requirements for naturalization, allowing immigrants to become citizens after only five years of residence.

Conflict With the Judicial Branch

President Jefferson next took aim at the Federalist party's control of the judicial branch. As you remember, as one of his last acts as President, John Adams had appointed a number of judges. He hoped to secure Federalist control of the judiciary during the new Republican administration.

Jefferson refused to be bound by these "midnight appointments," as he called them. Adams, who had made the appointments in the final hours of his presidency, was not 3. able to deliver the official letters of appointment to the new judges. Jefferson decided to fight the appointments: He told Secretary of State James Madison not to deliver the letters to any of the new judges. In response, William Marbury, one of the Federalist "midnight judges," sued Madison.

Marbury v. *Madison* In the case of *Marbury* v. *Madison,* the Supreme Court ruled that the section of the Judiciary Act of 1789 under which Marbury was appointed was unconstitutional. Chief Justice John Marshall, a Federalist appointed by John Adams, stated that Congress had exceeded its constitutional authority when it passed the bill. In his decision, the Chief Justice firmly established the Supreme Court's power to review all laws passed by Congress and reject those it considered unconstitutional. This authority is referred to as the power of **judicial review.** 4.

Even though the court's decision voided the "midnight appointments," it enraged the Republicans. They thought Marshall was assuming too much power for the judiciary. The justices were turning the Constitution into "a mere thing of wax," Jefferson grumbled, which they could shape any way they pleased. He opposed this not only because the Federalists controlled the judiciary but also because he feared that Marshall had upset the constitutional balance between the three branches of government, by giving the judiciary too much power.

4. **CITIZENSHIP** This idea was implied in Art. 3, Sec. 2 of the Constitution (p. 880). The case clarified and confirmed the Court's power of judicial review.

1. **BIOGRAPHY** Samuel Chase (1741–1811) had been a Maryland representative at the Continental Congress, where he signed the Declaration of Independence.

Checks and Balances Jefferson and the Republicans in Congress moved to counteract the judiciary's power. Under the Constitution, Congress could use its own power of impeachment to limit judicial clout.* Jefferson urged the House of Representatives to impeach certain judges he believed were unfit. The House impeached one federal judge for drunkenness, and the Senate convicted him.

The House of Representatives also began impeachment proceedings against Samuel Chase, a Supreme Court justice. Chase, a Federalist who openly denounced Jefferson's administration in court sessions, was accused of misconduct in office. The Senate, however, refused to convict Chase, arguing that his actions were not within the constitutional meaning of misconduct. In spite of Jefferson's efforts, the Federalists remained strong in the federal judiciary.

Jefferson Advocates Laissez-Faire

In his inaugural speech, Thomas Jefferson had suggested that the key to a "happy and a prosperous" future for America lay in a "wise and frugal [thrifty] government." According to Jefferson, the role of government should be confined to preventing people "from injuring one another" and "shall leave them otherwise free to regulate their own pursuits of industry and improvement." The philosophy that Jefferson described has become known by the French term **laissez-faire** (LEHS ay FEHR), meaning noninterference.

As President, Jefferson tried to reduce the role of government in people's lives. He decreased the size of the Department of State and Department of the Treasury and cut the federal budget. Congress also repealed the unpopular excise tax on whiskey.

Jefferson took special aim at the military budget, partly because of his belief in laissez-faire, and partly because he believed that a large peacetime army or navy posed a threat

---

*According to the Constitution, the House of Representatives can impeach, or accuse, federal judges of "treason, bribery, or other high crimes." If a two-thirds majority of the Senate votes to convict the judge, he or she is removed from office.

3. **BACKGROUND** Refer students to the picture of the building of the *Philadelphia* on p.192.

2. **VOCABULARY** The word *Barbary* comes from the Latin *barbari* and originally meant foreigners, as in *barbarians*.

to liberty. Consequently, he slashed the armed forces budget by half and confined the navy to coastal defense, using small, inexpensive gunboats. The government canceled contracts to build several large oceangoing warships.

Conflict on the Barbary Coast

Cutting the navy proved too hasty an action, however, for its sailors and ships were soon needed against pirates off the coast of North Africa. For years, the rulers of the Barbary Coast states of Morocco, Algiers, Tunis, and Tripoli had forced many nations, including the United States, to pay them an annual tribute, or risk the capture of their merchant ships in the Mediterranean Sea.

Paying tribute was not only offensive, it was also costly because of the extent of American trade in the area. When the pirates increased their demands in 1801, President Jefferson struck back. He sent a squadron of eight naval vessels to the Mediterranean to blockade Tripoli harbor. When one of the ships, the *Philadelphia,* ran aground, the pirates threw its crew into prison and seized the ship. As you have read, Lieutenant Stephen

4. **MAP READING** Have students use the map on pp. 842–843 to find out which countries are in this area today.

MAP STUDY *Determined to put an end to attacks on United States shipping by the Barbary pirates, President Jefferson sent a naval squadron to blockade the port of Tripoli. On what body of water is Tripoli located? Why was its location strategic?* See p. T37.

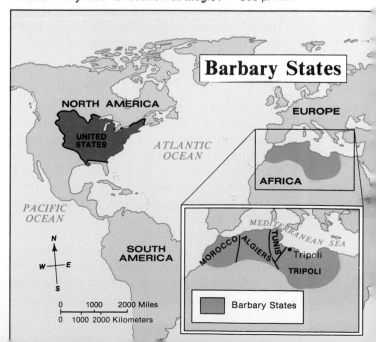

Barbary States

The daring exploits of the new American navy on the Barbary Coast aroused pride in the United States. When Stephen Decatur and his men boarded an enemy
1. gunboat, an American sailor saved Decatur's life by blocking a pirate's scimitar with his head.

Decatur later sailed another American ship into the harbor and burned the *Philadelphia*.

Meanwhile, a small force of American marines landed in Tripoli and forced the Barbary States to make peace. In 1805, the United States negotiated a favorable treaty with Tripoli. The Barbary Coast action demonstrated the importance of maintaining a reasonably sized navy to protect American shipping.

Threats to the Nation's Unity

Throughout his first term, Jefferson worked to smooth over disputes with Federalists and among Republican party members. He built Republican strength in the former Federalist strongholds of New York and New England. As a result, Jefferson was reelected in 1804, with George Clinton replacing Aaron Burr as Vice-President.

Dissension Not everyone had been willing to make peace with Jefferson during his first administration. Embittered by the re-sounding defeat of their party in 1800, a small group of Federalists devised a plan to unite New England and New York in an independent confederation and **secede,** or withdraw, from the Union. They approached Vice President Aaron Burr with their plan. Burr, who had lost Republican support after he allowed the Federalists to back him for President in 1800, agreed to join forces with the High Federalists. (See page 193.) In return, he expected the Federalists to support him as a candidate for governor of New York.

Before the plan could get very far, Alexander Hamilton exposed Burr's role and called him unfit for public office. Burr responded 2. by challenging Hamilton to a duel. Dueling was illegal, and Alexander Hamilton was publicly opposed to the practice, but this time he decided to fight. He paid for his decision with his life. In Weehawken, New Jersey, at dawn on July 11, 1804, Aaron Burr shot and killed Hamilton. 3.

The Burr Conspiracy Soundly defeated for the New York governorship and liable for arrest on murder charges as a result of the

200

2. **BACKGROUND** Hamilton was quoted as having called Burr "a dangerous man, and one who ought not to be trusted with the reins of government."

3. **READING** Students might be interested in reading a fictionalized account of Burr's life in *Burr*, by Gore Vidal.

duel, Burr next became involved in a wild conspiracy. In 1806, Burr plotted with General James Wilkinson, the commander of American troops in the Louisiana territory, to carve their own country out of Spanish territory in the Southwest.

The details of their scheme were probably no clearer in 1806 than they are to historians today. After a year of plotting, Wilkinson suddenly betrayed Burr and informed Jefferson of the scheme. Burr was arrested, charged with treason, and brought to Virginia to stand trial. But Chief Justice John Marshall, who presided, insisted there was not enough evidence of treason to convict Burr, so he was freed.

1. In spite of such dramatic dissension, the overall mood of the early years of Jefferson's presidency was one of cooperation and conciliation. His efforts to bring Federalists into his following paid off. But what was perhaps Jefferson's most popular move came to him more by chance than by design. In 1803, with one stroke of his pen, President Jefferson almost doubled the size of the United States.

See p. T37.

SECTION 1 REVIEW

1. **Identify:** (a) "midnight appointments," (b) *Marbury* v. *Madison* (c) Aaron Burr.

2. **Define:** (a) judicial review, (b) laissez-faire, (c) secede.

3. (a) How did Jefferson try to gain the good will of the Federalists? (b) What measures reflected Jefferson's Republican principles?

4. What two reasons did Jefferson have for objecting to the Supreme Court's decision in *Marbury* v. *Madison?*

5. (a) Why did the United States pay tribute to the Barbary Coast states? (b) How did the government finally resolve the problem?

6. **Critical Thinking** What did Jefferson mean when he said, "We are all Republicans, we are all Federalists"?

2 Expanding the Nation's Boundaries

READ TO UNDERSTAND

■ How the United States acquired the Louisiana territory.

■ What constitutional issue was raised by the purchase of Louisiana.

■ Why the Lewis and Clark expedition was important.

Since his youth, Thomas Jefferson had been fascinated with the desire to learn about and explore the unknown lands west of the Mississippi River. When the opportunity arose for the United States to purchase this vast tract, Jefferson jumped at the chance. He then assigned his young private secretary, Meriwether Lewis, to make preparations for a "voyage of discovery" to explore this exciting territory.

The Louisiana Purchase

The area known as the Louisiana territory was an enormous expanse of land that extended from the Mississippi River to the Rocky Mountains and from Louisiana to Canada. The territory was largely unexplored, and its ownership had changed hands several times by the early 1800s. France, which had originally claimed the area, gave it to Spain as part of the treaty ending the French and Indian War. Then, in 1800, Napoleon Bonaparte* secretly arranged for the territory to be transferred back to France.

The Importance of the Territory When President Jefferson learned of the secret transfer, he worried that Napoleon might try to use the territory as a base to build a colonial empire in the West. Moreover, the French were at war with Great Britain again. If Napoleon closed New Orleans to American shipping, Jefferson feared that the United States would be forced into an alliance with Britain. 2. Jefferson decided to try to gain control of New Orleans for the United States.

---

*At this time Napoleon was known as the first consul of France. In 1804, he became emperor.

2. **BACKGROUND** Jefferson wrote, "There is on the globe one single spot, the possessor of which is our natural and habitual enemy. It is New Orleans, through which the produce of three-eighths of our territory must pass to market. . . . France, placing herself in that door, assumes to us the attitude of defiance."

1. **LOCAL HISTORY** Refer students to the population chart on p. 227.

2. **GEOGRAPHY** Have students define *tributary*. Then ask them to locate and identify the major tributaries of the Mississippi on the map on p. 844. (location)

A desire to avoid an entangling alliance was not Jefferson's sole reason for interest in the Louisiana territory, however. New settlements were sprouting up in the area of present-day Ohio, Indiana, Kentucky, and Tennessee. The security of settlers in these areas depended on who owned the territories around the Mississippi. Furthermore, since there were no roads beyond the Appalachians, the Mississippi River and its tributaries were the main trade route into and out of the West. Furthermore, the port of New Orleans at the mouth of the river was especially important and, as you will recall, in 1795 Spain had granted American traders the right to use the port for overseas shipment. (See page 187.).

Buying Louisiana President Jefferson sent James Monroe to France in April 1803 to help Robert Livingston negotiate the purchase of New Orleans and western Florida. Congress appropriated $2 million for the purchase. When Livingston and Monroe made their offer, the French representative, Talleyrand, unexpectedly asked how much the United States would be willing to pay for the entire Louisiana territory.

Although the American ambassadors had instructions to purchase only New Orleans, they quickly decided that this was an opportunity they could not pass up. They agreed to buy this immense territory for about $15 million, or less than three cents an acre.

Napoleon decided to sell the whole territory for several reasons. He needed money to finance his military campaigns in Europe. Furthermore, his dream of building an American empire had been shattered.

Napoleon had wanted to build this empire around a secure sea base in the Caribbean and had chosen the island of Haiti, a former French possession, for that purpose. In 1791, during the French Revolution, Toussaint L'Ouverture (too SAN loo vehr TYOOR) had led a successful slave rebellion and won Haiti's independence. Napoleon's attempt to reconquer Haiti in 1800 failed. Once he had given up his goal of an American empire, Napoleon had little interest in keeping Louisiana.

Throughout the dealings, neither the French nor the United States government considered the rights of the Native Americans living in the territory. Jefferson assumed the problem could be resolved later.

A Constitutional Dispute

The purchase of Louisiana presented the President with a dilemma. The Constitution did not specify how the country could acquire new territory or who had the authority to do it. As you know, Jefferson had long argued for a strict construction of the Constitution, while his Federalist opponents endorsed a loose construction. (See page 182.)

The President first thought about adding an amendment to the Constitution that would specify how new territory was to be purchased. But the amendment process would take time, and he was afraid that in the meantime Napoleon might change his mind about the sale. Jefferson finally decided he could base the purchase on his constitutional power to make treaties with foreign nations. With this reasoning in mind, he sent the agreement to the Senate for ratification.

Federalists opposed the purchase, arguing that it was a waste of money and would add unreasonably to the national debt. Ironically, the Federalists reversed their position on interpreting the Constitution. They asserted that because the Constitution did not specifically authorize the President to buy land, he could not do so. Nevertheless, after a brief debate, the Senate overwhelmingly approved the treaty. In December 1803, the United States took possession of its vast new territory in the west.

GEOGRAPHY AND HISTORY
Exploring the New Frontier

Even before the purchase, Jefferson had secretly planned an expedition to explore the Louisiana territory. After the Senate approved the treaty, he authorized the expedition to begin. Jefferson chose his private secretary, Meriwether Lewis, and William Clark, younger brother of Revolutionary War General George Rogers Clark, to lead the expedition.

The President instructed Lewis and Clark to gather information about the flow of rivers and the availability of natural resources,

3. **BACKGROUND** L'Ouverture (1743–1803) had helped the French drive the Spanish and British from Hispaniola. He died in France after being imprisoned for conspiracy.

4. **CITIZENSHIP** The United States guaranteed Napoleon that French Catholics living in the territory would be given citizenship and the right to worship freely.

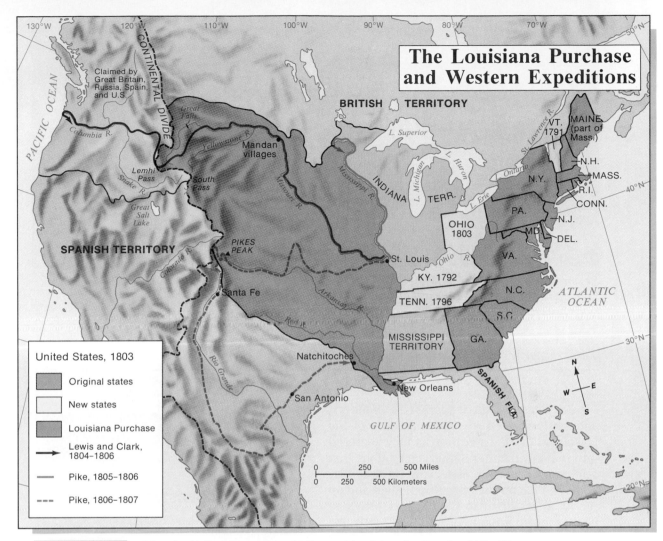

The Louisiana Purchase and Western Expeditions

Claimed by Great Britain, Russia, Spain, and U.S.

PACIFIC OCEAN

Columbia R.

Great Falls

Lemhi Pass

Snake R.

South Pass

Great Salt Lake

SPANISH TERRITORY

Colorado R.

PIKES PEAK

Santa Fe

Rio Grande

San Antonio

Yellowstone R.

Mandan villages

Missouri R.

CONTINENTAL DIVIDE

BRITISH TERRITORY

L. Superior

L. Michigan

L. Huron

Mississippi R.

INDIANA TERR.

L. Erie

L. Ontario

St. Lawrence R.

VT. 1791

MAINE (part of Mass.)

N.H.

MASS.

R.I.

CONN.

N.Y.

PA.

OHIO 1803

MD.

N.J.

DEL.

VA.

St. Louis

Ohio R.

KY. 1792

TENN. 1796

Arkansas R.

Red R.

N.C.

S.C.

GA.

ATLANTIC OCEAN

MISSISSIPPI TERRITORY

Natchitoches

New Orleans

SPANISH FLA.

GULF OF MEXICO

United States, 1803

- Original states
- New states
- Louisiana Purchase
- → Lewis and Clark, 1804–1806
- — Pike, 1805–1806
- --- Pike, 1806–1807

0   250   500 Miles
0   250   500 Kilometers

N E S W

MAP STUDY *After the United States bought the vast Louisiana territory for $15 million, Jefferson was eager to have it thoroughly explored and mapped. Who explored the northern part of the territory? Who explored its southern portion?* See p. T38.

1.

1. MAP READING Ask: In what direction did Pike travel from St. Louis in 1805? For how many miles did Lewis and Clark follow the Missouri River?

information that could be used to plan the future commercial development of the region. But Jefferson's natural curiosity and interest in science inspired additional instructions to study the climate, plant growth, and geology of the area. One critical issue Lewis and Clark had to resolve was whether or not a Northwest Passage existed. (See the map above.) Could people travel by navigable rivers from one coast of North America to the other?

The Lewis and Clark expedition, consisting of about 30 soldiers and 10 civilians, left St. Louis in May 1804. They journeyed up the Missouri River to the Great Falls and spent the winter of 1804–1805 in a Mandan Indian village near what is now Bismarck, North Dakota. In the spring, they crossed the Rocky Mountains with difficulty and canoed down

the Snake and Columbia rivers toward the Pacific. Their trip showed there was no easy water route across North America. In November 1805, the expedition reached the Pacific Ocean, where Clark carved on a tree, "By land from the U. States in 1804 & 5."

2.

Along the route, Sacajawea (SAKH uh juh WEE uh), a Shoshone woman married to a French-Canadian explorer, assisted Lewis and Clark as a translator and guide. Sacajawea proved especially helpful when the expedition reached what is now Idaho, the region of the Shoshone nation.

The group returned to St. Louis by the same route in 1806. Their expedition was an enormous success, and the publication of their journals several years later provided detailed knowledge about the territory.

203

2. READING Lewis wrote in his journal, "Great joy in camp. We are in view of the ocean, this great Pacific Ocean which we have been so long anxious to see." Students interested in learning more about the Lewis and Clark expedition can read further selections from *The Journals of Lewis and Clark.*

Seventeen-year-old Sacajawea knew the languages of several Indian nations. Born a Shoshone, she had been kidnapped by another Indian nation as a girl. Her knowledge of languages and the geography of the region was of great value

1. to the Lewis and Clark expedition. When the party reached Shoshone territory, Sacajawea was reunited with her people. Her reaction at the meeting was "to dance and show every mark of the most extravagant joy."

1. **BIOGRAPHY** Just before Sacajawea and her husband, Charbonneau, embarked on the expedition, she gave birth to a son. Throughout the difficult journey, Sacajawea carried the infant with her.

For decades, fur traders, road builders, and settlers referred to the records of the Lewis and Clark expedition as they ventured into the new frontier. Other expeditions that Jefferson organized, especially those led by Zebulon Pike up the Mississippi River and up the Arkansas River to the Rockies, provided

2. further information about the new lands. ■

See p. T38.

SECTION 2 REVIEW

1. **Identify:** (a) Meriwether Lewis, (b) Napoleon Bonaparte, (c) William Clark, (d) Sacajawea.

2. (a) Why did Jefferson want to buy Louisiana? (b) Why did Napoleon want to sell it?

3. (a) What provisions did the Constitution make for acquiring new territory? (b) How did Jefferson justify the purchase of Louisiana?

4. (a) What instructions did Jefferson give the Lewis and Clark expedition? (b) What did they find out about the long-sought Northwest Passage through America?

5. **Critical Thinking** How did the Lewis and Clark expedition strengthen the role of the United States on the continent?

204

3 The Coming of Another War

READ TO UNDERSTAND

■ How the United States responded to violations of its neutrality.

■ Why the United States went to war with Great Britain in 1812.

■ How the American Indians reacted to the westward migration of settlers.

■ *Vocabulary:* impressment, naturalized citizen, embargo.   3.

During his eight years as President, Jefferson feared entanglements with Europe that could lead the nation into war. He spent much of his second term in office trying to maintain American neutrality. But he was not willing to avoid war at any cost. In 1808, he warned that America's peaceful posture was making European nations think that the United States was weak. By 1811, from his retirement, he said that the policy of peace was "more losing than war." And by 1812, he wrote, "Every hope . . . is exhausted, and war or abject submission are the only alternatives left us." His successor, James Madison, tried to forestall war, but his efforts were in vain.

2. **LOCAL HISTORY** Ask: Was your state part of the Louisiana Purchase? Did Lewis and Clark pass through it?

3. **VOCABULARY** Have students look up these terms in the glossary before they begin reading.

1. **BACKGROUND** Remind students that Napoleon had sold Louisiana in 1803 in order to free France to fight in Europe.

2. **VOCABULARY** The U.S. considered such actions to be violations of "freedom of the seas." From their reading, have students define this term.

Challenges to Neutrality

During the early 1800s, Europe was the stage for yet another war. Between 1803 and 1807, Napoleon Bonaparte conquered nearly all of the continent. The French emperor then turned his sights toward Great Britain.

Both nations used economic as well as military tactics to win the war. In 1806 and 1807, Napoleon devised the so-called Continental System. He closed all European ports to goods from Great Britain and ordered the seizure of all ships carrying such goods, even if they were the ships of neutral nations. The British government responded by issuing the Orders in Council, which prohibited neutral nations from trading with France or its allies. Violators of the orders risked seizure by the British navy.

The United States found itself caught in the middle. France would not allow American ships to trade with Britain, and Great Britain objected to American trade with France. After 1806, ships bound for European ports were often stopped by the French or the British navies, or sometimes by both navies and searched for cargoes destined for the enemy.

By 1807, France had seized 500 American ships and Britain had seized nearly 1,000. Such seizures were costly because the United States was the largest neutral carrier of goods in the world.

To make matters worse, the British began to search American ships for deserters from its navy. Since conditions in the British navy were notoriously bad, the British resorted to **impressment,** the practice of forcing sailors to serve in the Royal Navy. Many sailors deserted and began serving on American ships, where conditions were better. The British enraged the Americans by claiming the right to search American ships for these deserters.

As the war continued, British searches became increasingly belligerent. Often, the sailors they seized were former British subjects who had become **naturalized citizens** of the United States. A naturalized citizen is a person who gives up citizenship in one country to become a citizen of another country. By 1811, nearly 10,000 American sailors had been illegally "pressed" into service for Great Britain.

American ships that resisted search and seizure risked attack. In 1807, for example,

3. **VISUAL EVIDENCE** Ask: What part of the world is Napoleon's share? King George's? What seems to be the cartoonist's point of view? How can you tell?

In this 1805 cartoon, King George III of Great Britain and the Emperor Napoleon of France carve up the world between their two nations. Napoleon's army controlled much of Europe, but England's navy dominated the seas.

1. **ECONOMICS** Ask: When had the U.S. previously used embargoes as a political weapon? How effective were they? How was the situation in 1807 different?

2. **ECONOMICS** The surplus of wheat grew so large that the price fell from $2.00 to $.75 a bushel.

the British warship *Leopard* fired on the *Chesapeake,* an American warship, when it refused to allow an impressment gang to board. The *Chesapeake* suffered 21 casualties and extensive damage.

The Embargo

Despite these violations of American rights, President Jefferson tried to find a peaceful way to show France and Great Britain that the United States insisted on having its neutrality respected. He decided to impose an **embargo,** or a complete halt to trade.

Britain and France each wanted to retain American trade, but only for itself. Thus, Jefferson thought that he could pressure the two governments into recognizing the new nation's neutrality by withholding trade benefits from both. Congress agreed and in 1807 passed the Embargo Act, which prohibited virtually all commerce with foreign nations.

The embargo did hurt both Britain and France. Unfortunately, it hurt American merchants, too, especially in New England. The combination of the Embargo Act and the earlier French and British seizures of American ships had a devastating impact on American
1. exports. (See the graph on page 207.)

President Jefferson hoped to rely largely on voluntary cooperation from merchants to enforce the embargo, and some merchants did cooperate. Many, however, sought to evade the law. This evasion was most widespread in New England, where economic survival depended on commerce. The West and South did not feel the effects of the embargo as much since they relied more on domestic trade. Yet, some farmers had unsold grain because they could not export their prod-
2. ucts.

Many merchants who upheld the embargo were ruined, and pressure mounted for its repeal. In 1809, Congress voted to end the embargo, and Jefferson reluctantly agreed that it had been a failure.

One positive effect of the embargo was not immediately apparent. While the United States was cut off from Europe, American manufacturers began to produce goods that had formerly been imported. The embargo had helped stimulate the development of American industry.

Outbreak of War

Thomas Jefferson decided not to run for a third term in 1808. He chose instead to return to the quiet life of Monticello. His secretary of state, James Madison, easily won election as President over Charles Pinckney, the Federalist candidate. Madison wanted to continue Jefferson's firm policy of American neutrality.

Americans regarded the British practice of impressment as an insult to their independence. Although the British claimed they were looking for deserters, their captains were desperate for men. They often took sailors off American ships with
3. *little proof that they were deserters. Other Americans were grabbed by press gangs in British ports. As many as 10,000 Americans may have been abducted into the British navy.*

1. **BACKGROUND** When France had seized American merchant ships, Napoleon claimed that he was merely helping Jefferson enforce the Embargo Act.

In 1809, Congress passed the Nonintercourse Act. Less severe than the embargo, this act prohibited trade with Great Britain and France, but allowed Americans to trade with all other nations. The Nonintercourse Act proved to be as unpopular as the embargo because most American trade was with Britain and France.

Shortly after the Nonintercourse Act expired in 1810, Madison announced that if either Britain or France would remove its restrictions on neutral shipping, the United States would halt its trade with the other nation. Napoleon seized this opportunity to trap the United States into siding with France. In November 1810, he announced that France would repeal its decrees against American trade with the British.

Napoleon probably had no intention of holding to his promise, but Madison believed him and did exactly what Napoleon hoped. In February 1811, the President declared that the United States would continue trading with France but would stop all shipments to Great Britain.

The loss of trade with the United States severely damaged the British economy. In June 1812, Britain suspended the Orders in Council, but it was too late. Irate over continued British seizures of American ships, President Madison already had asked Congress to declare war on Great Britain.

The South and West overwhelmingly supported the declaration of war. Federalists, whose sympathies were with the British, strongly opposed it. Representatives from New England and other trading centers—New York, New Jersey, and Delaware—also voted against the war. Many merchants thought a war would further damage trade. Despite the opposition, however, the United States was at war with Great Britain for the second time in 30 years.

Why War With Britain?

Historians have long debated why the United States went to war with Great Britain in 1812. The question is a difficult one since no single incident touched off hostilities. The attack on the *Chesapeake* was the sort of incident that could have started a war, but that hap-

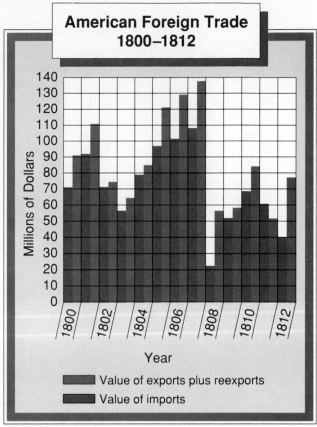

American Foreign Trade 1800–1812

Millions of Dollars (y-axis: 0 to 140)

Year (x-axis: 1800, 1802, 1804, 1806, 1808, 1810, 1812)

■ Value of exports plus reexports
■ Value of imports

Source: *Historical Statistics of the United States*

GRAPH STUDY *Trade was important to the new nation. Based on this graph, describe American foreign trade between 1800 and 1812. How can you explain the fluctuations shown on the graph?* See p. T39.

3. **GRAPH READING** Ask: What was the value of exports plus reexports in 1807? In 1808?

pened in 1807, and war was not declared until 1812.

In his war message to Congress, President Madison stated that the United States was fighting to maintain freedom of the seas. Undoubtedly, Great Britain had violated that freedom, but so had France.

American seamen languished in French prisons, yet impressment seemed a more immediate insult to many Americans. In the end, the traditional sympathy of Madison and a majority of the Republican members of Congress toward France probably played a role in the decision.

Another factor that contributed to the demand for war with Great Britain was a growing sense of national pride, particularly among westerners. Although impressment and the seizure of American ships had little direct impact on them, they considered such actions an attack on all Americans, and they clamored for war.

207

2. **PRESIDENTS** Madison had said, "British cruisers have been violating the American flag. . . . Our attention is also drawn to the warfare just renewed by savages. . . . It is difficult to explain this without linking their hostility with British influence."

1. **ACTIVITY** Ask half the class to prepare a leaflet taking the side of the War Hawks. Have the other half create a leaflet reflecting the point of view of Federalists who opposed the war.

Senator Henry Clay of Kentucky led an especially belligerent group of Republican congressmen from the West, called the War Hawks because of their agitation for war. As intense nationalists, they saw war with Great Britain as an opportunity to expand the territory of the United States. They made no secret of their desire to win Canada from Britain and, as one of them put it, "to drive the British from our Continent." The War Hawks also wanted to end British support of Native Americans who resisted the influx of settlers into the Northwest Territory.

Western Conflicts

Native Americans had tried to stop American settlers from encroaching on their lands in the West since the mid-1700s. As you read in Chapter 5, in 1763 the British tried to prevent conflict by outlawing settlement beyond the Appalachian Mountains. After independence, settlers poured into the West. Attempts to control settlement, such as the Northwest Ordinance, had little effect.

In theory, the government should have obtained Indian land by treaty and then allowed settlement. In reality, settlers ignored Indian rights and pushed into whatever region they wanted. When the best land was taken, they simply moved farther west. Furthermore, many invalid treaties were negotiated. Native Americans who signed them often did not represent their nations or own the land in question.

Indian resistance to settlement increased in the late 1780s, especially in the area north of the Ohio River. In 1791, the Shawnee overcame a force led by General Arthur St. Clair, but the triumph did not last. Three years later, an army force under General Anthony Wayne defeated the Indians at the Battle of Fallen Timbers. In 1795, in the Treaty of Greenville, Indian leaders ceded a large part of present-day Ohio to the United States. This opened up the Northwest Territory to more settlement. As a result, between 1795 and 1809, the United States acquired a total of about 48 million acres (about 20 million hectares) of Native American land.

2. **MAP READING** Ask: When was the land just south of the Ohio River taken over?

MAP STUDY *As the map shows, settlers moving westward gradually took over more and more Indian land. What does the inset map show? Why do you think the mapmaker included the inset map?* See p. T39.

Land Acquired From Native Americans by 1810

ABNAKI
PENOBSCOT
WAMPANOAG
NARRAGANSET
PEQUOT
IROQUOIS
MOHEGAN
KICKAPOO
SUSQUEHANNA
ERIE
MIAMI
DELAWARE
ILLINOIS
MISSOURI
POWHATAN
KANSAS
SHAWNEE
OSAGE
CHEROKEE
CHICKASAW
CHOCTAW
CREEK
NATCHEZ
SEMINOLE
ATLANTIC OCEAN

L. Michigan
L. Erie
Fallen Timbers, 1794
Wabash R.
St. Clair's Defeat, 1791
Vincennes
Ohio R.

— Greenville Treaty Line
✸ Battle sites

Land acquired prior to 1750 or without cession
Land acquired 1750–1783
Land acquired 1784–1810
Boundary of United States, 1810

0   250   500 Miles
0   250   500 Kilometers

Tecumseh: Who Has a Right to the Land?

Tecumseh was a complex figure who studied the Bible, Shakespeare, and history in order to understand his opponents better. His overwhelming desire was to keep white settlers off Indian land. He tried to convince individual tribes to stop selling land to the United States government, arguing that all Indians had to give their permission for any sale to occur. In the following speech, he protests the Treaty of Fort Wayne (1809), in which two Indian nations sold 3 million acres (1.2 million hectares) of land for a small amount of money.

The Being within, communing with past ages, tells me that . . . until lately there was no white man on this continent; that it then all belonged to red men, children of the same parents, placed on it by the Great Spirit that made them, to keep it, to traverse it, to enjoy its productions, and to fill it with the same race—once a happy race, since made miserable by the white people, who are never contented, but always encroaching. The way—and the only way—to check and to stop this evil is for all red men to unite in claiming a common equal right in the land, as it was at first, and should be yet.

The white people have no right to take the land from the Indians, because they had it first. It is theirs. They may sell, but all must join. Any sale not made by all is not valid. All red men have equal rights to the unoccupied land. The right of occupancy is as good in one place as in another. There cannot be two occupations in the same place. The first excludes all others. It is not so in hunting or traveling; for there the same ground will serve many, as they may follow each other all day. But the camp is stationary, and that is occupancy. It belongs to the first who sits down on his blanket or skins which he has thrown upon the ground; and till he leaves it no other has a right.

Source: Chauncey M. Depew, ed., *The Library of Oratory: Ancient and Modern* (New York: Globe, 1902).

See p. T39.

1. Why did Tecumseh feel that the Indians had a valid claim to the land and the settlers did not?

2. **Critical Thinking** Was war between Tecumseh and the settlers inevitable? Explain.

1. **BIOGRAPHY** When Tecumseh (1768–1813) was six years old, his father was killed by whites. He grew up with a desire for vengeance and a deep mistrust of whites, although he had several white foster brothers.

Tecumseh and the Prophet

As settlers continued to move into the Northwest Territory, the Native American inhabitants faced not only the loss of their land but also the loss of their culture. Out of the Indians' anger and frustration emerged two powerful Shawnee leaders, Tecumseh (tih KUHM suh) and his brother, who was called the Prophet. Their goal was to unite all Indian nations east of the Mississippi to resist further settlement. The Prophet also urged the Indians to revive their own culture by giving up customs adopted from the new settlers.

By 1811, Tecumseh, a skilled orator, had organized a confederation that stretched from the Northwest Territory to Florida. In November, General William Henry Harrison, the governor of Indiana Territory, led a force of 1,000 soldiers against Tecumseh's headquarters at Tippecanoe Creek. The battle was, in fact, a draw. However Harrison's forces destroyed the Indian camp, and westerners celebrated the Battle of Tippecanoe as a great victory. Many Indians became disillusioned with the confederation.

When the War of 1812 broke out, Tecumseh continued his fight against the Americans by supporting the British. The alliance of the British and the Indians, however, did not dim the War Hawks' enthusiasm. Senator Henry Clay of Kentucky boasted that "the militia of Kentucky alone" could beat the British. Clay would discover that winning the war was not that easy.

See p. T39.

SECTION 3 REVIEW

1. **Identify:** (a) Nonintercourse Act, (b) Henry Clay, (c) Treaty of Greenville, (d) William Henry Harrison.

2. **Define:** (a) impressment, (b) naturalized citizen, (c) embargo.

3. (a) What action did Jefferson take to pressure France and Great Britain into recognizing American neutrality? (b) How did this affect American merchants?

4. What did the War Hawks hope to gain from a war with Great Britain?

5. **Critical Thinking** How might an alliance between the British and the Indians have benefited each?

4 A Complex War

READ TO UNDERSTAND

■ Why the United States found itself unprepared at the start of the War of 1812.

■ Why New England opposed the war.

■ What were the terms of the Treaty of Ghent.

The War of 1812 was an unusual conflict. Although it lasted for two and a half years, it was never more than a series of skirmishes that took place at widely scattered locations. Full-scale battles were few and far between.

The British, preoccupied with their fight against Napoleon, tended to view the war in the United States as a sideshow to events in Europe. The United States had to deal with opposition to the war, particularly in the Federalist stronghold of New England. By the time the war was over and a peace treaty was signed, neither side had won a clear-cut victory.

A Slow Start

When the nation declared war, the regular army of the United States numbered fewer than 7,000 soldiers. Although many more were in uniform in state militias, the militias were still under state and local control, and many soldiers were reluctant to leave their home states. Congress acted very slowly to bring these units under federal authority.

In addition, the army could boast few competent leaders. Most generals had not seen action since the Revolutionary War more than 30 years earlier. It took time and several defeats in battle to identify promising junior officers and appoint them to command positions.

The navy was in slightly better shape; a number of its officers had fought in battles on the Barbary Coast. Still, the American fleet remained pitifully small. Congress wasted valuable months arguing before it approved the construction of warships. And, by the time these were completed, the war had ended.

For the United States to win the war quickly, it had to conquer Canada, the center of British power in North America. An attack on Montreal would have cut off British access to the sea and brought victory. However, American leaders, especially War Hawks, were preoccupied with western Canada and Indian activity on the frontier. As a result, a full-scale attack on Canada was never launched.

Not surprisingly, the war began with a series of reverses for the United States. In August 1812, General William Hull moved his American forces to Detroit. At Detroit, the British tricked Hull into believing that he faced a much larger force than was actually the case. Hull abruptly surrendered his army without firing a shot.

210

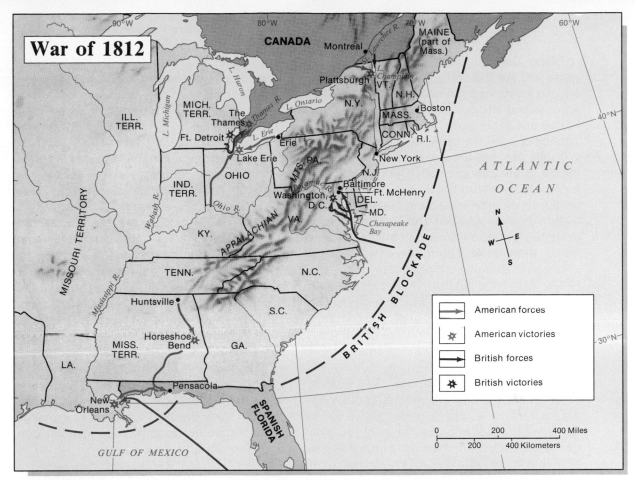

War of 1812

CANADA

Montreal
Plattsburgh
MAINE (part of Mass.)

MICH. TERR.
The Thames
Ft. Detroit
Lake Erie
Erie
L. Michigan
L. Huron
L. Ontario
L. Erie
Thames R.

VT.
N.H.
N.Y.
MASS.
Boston
CONN.
R.I.
New York

ILL. TERR.
IND. TERR.
OHIO
PA.
N.J.
Baltimore
Ft. McHenry
Washington, D.C.
DEL.
MD.
VA.
Chesapeake Bay

MISSOURI TERRITORY
Wabash R.
Ohio R.
Mississippi R.

KY.
APPALACHIAN MTS.
Potomac R.

TENN.
N.C.
S.C.

Huntsville
Horseshoe Bend
MISS. TERR.
GA.
LA.
Pensacola
New Orleans
SPANISH FLORIDA

ATLANTIC OCEAN

BRITISH BLOCKADE

GULF OF MEXICO

→	American forces
☆	American victories
▶	British forces
✸	British victories

0   200   400 Miles
0   200   400 Kilometers

90°W   80°W   70°W   60°W
40°N
30°N

MAP STUDY *The War of 1812 was fought on several fronts. What clues does the map give that the British navy played an important part in the fighting?* See p. T39. **1.**

1. **MAP READING** Ask: What were two U.S. victories? Where did fighting take place?

Closer to Montreal, another American campaign failed when the New York state militia refused to cross into Canada to fight. Only at sea were the Americans victorious, when the USS *Constitution* sank the British 2. ship *Guerrière*.

Opposition to the War

New England was the center of opposition to the war. The early defeats provided further evidence to Federalists in New England that the war could not be won. Moreover, the British blockaded the Atlantic coast, seriously disrupting American trade. By 1814, foreign trade had fallen over 90 percent from its peak in 1807. Shipbuilding, a major industry, dropped 80 percent during the war.

New Englanders, who depended a good deal on trade, were also uneasy about the growing power of the West. Territorial expansion would mean additional western states, and a lessening of New England's influence in national affairs.

Opposition to the war reached a peak in the fall of 1814. Twenty-six delegates from the New England states gathered in Hartford, Connecticut, to protest President Madison's conduct of the war. The delegates issued a long series of demands designed to protect the interests of New Englanders. The delegates at the Hartford Convention threatened to secede and form an independent federation if their demands were not met. However, by the time their demands reached Washington, the war was over. Their protest had become irrelevant.

The Tide Begins to Turn

By 1813, American fortunes had improved. In September, a squadron of naval ships led by Captain Oliver Hazard Perry defeated a British fleet on Lake Erie. "We have met the enemy and they are ours," Perry reported to General Harrison. Perry's victory gave the United States control of Lake Erie.

211

2. **BACKGROUND** When the *Guerrière's* captain was asked if he had struck his flag, or surrendered, he said, "Well, our mizzenmast is gone, our mainmast is gone. Upon the whole, you may say we *have* struck our flag."

1. **VOCABULARY** Samuel Wilson, called Uncle Sam, supplied meat to the American army. The barrels containing the meat were marked *U.S.* for United States, but many assumed it stood for Uncle Sam. Soon, Uncle Sam became a nickname for the United States government.

Next, General Harrison moved his troops north of Lake Erie into Canada. A month after Perry's victory, Harrison's troops defeated a combined British and Indian force at the Battle of the Thames. The Shawnee leader Tecumseh died while urging on his warriors. Without his extraordinary leadership, the Indian confederation collapsed, as did the Indian alliance with the British.

Early the following year, Napoleon's defeat in Europe allowed the British to turn their full attention to war with the United States. But Captain Thomas Macdonough and a force of Vermont shipbuilders upset the British plan to invade the United States from Canada. Constructing 10 ships in just 30 days, Macdonough's men won a decisive victory against 16 British ships on Lake Champlain. The British were forced to abandon their invasion from the north.

An Attack on the Capital The British, however, had already launched another invasion farther south. A large British force landed at the mouth of the Patuxent River on Chesapeake Bay and marched toward Wash-ington, D.C. American defenders put up little resistance, and the British entered the city. Dolley Madison, the President's wife, was forced to flee the White House, with dinner still on the table. President Madison, who had ridden to the battlefront to evaluate the British position, soon followed his wife and the cabinet members to safety in Virginia. British troops burned most of the city. Only the quick thinking of Dolley Madison and the efforts of White House servants saved a portrait of George Washington and several important government documents.

The Defense of Baltimore The British then moved up Chesapeake Bay toward Baltimore. They met strong resistance from a force of volunteers at Fort McHenry in Baltimore harbor. Despite a three-day bombardment, the British could not take the city.

The heroic defense of Baltimore instilled pride and confidence in the Americans. Francis Scott Key was inspired to write "The Star-Spangled Banner" when he saw that after the bombardment the American flag continued to wave.

2. **CITIZENSHIP** The flag was 42 feet x 30 feet, with the 15 stars each measuring 2 feet across.

3. **BACKGROUND** Among the other buildings burned were the Capitol, the Treasury, and the War Office.

British troops attacked Washington, D.C., in retaliation for the American burning of York (what is today Toronto) in 1813. On entering the White House, the British found a cooked meal and the table set for 40. The British admiral took a cocked hat that belonged to President Madison and the cushion from Dolley Madison's favorite chair. As the White House burned, the admiral rode through the streets of Washington with the cushion swinging from his saddle.

1. BACKGROUND A British officer wrote, "Of all the sights I ever witnessed, that was the most shocking . . . nearly a thousand bodies, all . . . in British uniforms."

2. BACKGROUND Capt. Chauncey said that black sailors "are not surpassed by any seamen . . . and I have yet to learn that the color of the skin . . . can affect a man's qualifications. . . ."

Battle of New Orleans

General Andrew Jackson was in command of American forces at New Orleans. Jackson's reputation as a talented soldier was well-earned. As major general of the Tennessee militia, he had successfully fought the Creek in the Southwest. The so-called Creek War ended in March 1814 when Jackson's militia won a decisive victory at Horseshoe Bend. In the resulting Treaty of Fort Jackson, the Creek ceded two thirds of their land to the United States.

Anticipating a British invasion at New Orleans, Jackson's men dug trenches for defense. In January 1815, British forces landed and marched forward, expecting Jackson's soldiers to leave their defenses and run. Although outnumbered, the Americans held their ground and slaughtered the advancing army, inflicting more than 2,000 casualties while losing only 21 of their own troops.

It was a great victory for Jackson and his forces, which included the local militia, Kentucky riflemen, the militia from Jackson's home state of Tennessee, some pirates, and two battalions of black soldiers. Many of the latter were veterans of L'Ouverture's revolt in Haiti. (See page 202.) After the battle, Jackson congratulated his troops, singling out the black soldiers for special praise.

> I expected much from you but you have surpassed my hopes. . . . Soldiers, the President of the United States shall be informed of your conduct on the present occasion; and the voice of the Representatives of the American nation shall applaud your valor, as your General now praises your ardor.

Free blacks contributed to the war effort in other parts of the country as well. Two thousand black men constructed fortifications for the defense of Philadelphia. Free black sailors fought in the Great Lakes battles, and two regiments of black volunteers from New York served in the army.

Many slaves also fought for the United States in the war. Others fought for the British, who promised them freedom after the war. Some did win their freedom, but many were returned to their owners or sold in the West Indies.

A Tentative Victory

Jackson's victory at New Orleans actually came after the signing of a peace treaty in December 1814. But word of the treaty did not arrive in time to prevent the battle.

The Treaty of Ghent itself did little more than restore prewar conditions. By late 1814, the British dropped earlier demands, including the creation of a self-governing Indian nation in Ohio. American demands for an end to impressment and the search of American ships were no longer important because the war between Britain and France was over. The negotiations left other issues, such as border disputes, to be settled later.

Even though the treaty changed little, many Americans considered the War of 1812 a victory. The new nation had held its own against a major European power. The victory at New Orleans fueled national pride and convinced many Americans that they had won the war.

The war also contributed to the nation's territorial and economic growth. The defeat of powerful Indian nations in the Northwest Territory and the South opened new land for settlement. And the British blockade of American ports helped encourage many American manufacturers to begin producing items that formerly had been imported.

See p. T39.

SECTION 4 REVIEW

1. **Identify:** (a) Hartford Convention, (b) Andrew Jackson, (c) Creek War, (d) Treaty of Ghent.

2. List three disadvantages the United States faced at the beginning of the war.

3. Why was opposition to the war centered in New England?

4. What two events in 1813 marked a turning point in the war for the Americans?

5. **Critical Thinking** Based on the definition of treason in the United States Constitution (see Article 3, Section 3, page 879), were the members of the Hartford Convention treasonous? Why or why not?

3. GEOGRAPHY In 1817, the Rush-Bagot Agreement forbade U.S. or British warships from sailing the Great Lakes. In 1818, the U.S. and Britain set the boundary between Canada and the U.S. at 49° N latitude. (location)

CHAPTER 10 REVIEW

Summary

1. **President Jefferson tried to unite the nation.** He retained some Federalist programs while carrying out his own Republican ideas. He also used military force to put an end to piracy of American ships by the Barbary States.

2. **Jefferson nearly doubled the size of the nation by the purchase of Louisiana.** He dispatched Meriwether Lewis and William Clark to gather information about the new land. The Lewis and Clark expedition determined that there was no easy water route across North America.

3. **The threat of war plagued Jefferson's presidency.** He imposed an embargo on trade to try to force Britain and France to recognize American neutrality. James Madison also tried to maintain American neutrality, but by 1812, the United States went to war with Britain.

4. **At first, the United States fared poorly in the War of 1812.** But victories on the Great Lakes and in Canada later turned the tide. The Treaty of Ghent changed little, but success at the Battle of New Orleans raised Americans' pride in their nation.

See p. T39.

Vocabulary

Match each term at left with its definition or description at right.

1. judicial review
2. laissez-faire
3. secede
4. embargo
5. impressment
6. naturalized citizen

a. forcing a sailor to serve in the British navy

b. person from one country who becomes a citizen of another

c. policy of government noninterference

d. complete trade halt

e. to withdraw from the Union

f. power of the Supreme Court to declare a law unconstitutional

See p. T39.

Chapter Checkup

1. How did President Jefferson benefit from having his own party in power in Congress?

2. (a) What steps did Jefferson take to reduce the Federalist influence over the judicial branch of the government? (b) Why did he object to the principle of judicial review?

3. (a) Why did Jefferson reduce the military budget? (b) Why did his decision prove to be premature?

4. (a) Why was the United States interested in buying land near the Mississippi, particularly New Orleans? (b) Why were the Americans able to buy all of Louisiana?

5. (a) How did the purchase of the Louisiana territory conflict with Jefferson's interpretation of the Constitution? (b) On what presidential power did he ultimately base his action?

6. (a) What was the purpose of the Lewis and Clark expedition? (b) How was the information they gathered used?

7. (a) How did the British and French challenge American neutrality after 1806? (b) How did President Jefferson react to the challenge? (c) What were the results of his actions?

8. (a) What actions did President Madison take to maintain neutrality? (b) Was he successful? Explain.

9. (a) How did conflicts between American settlers and Indian nations in the Northwest Territory contribute to the begin-

ning of the War or 1812? (b) What role did Tecumseh and the Prophet play in this conflict?

10. (a) Why did the War of 1812 begin poorly for the United States? (b) What circumstances caused Americans to become more hopeful by 1813?

11. (a) What impact did the battle of New Orleans have on the outcome of the War of 1812? (b) What role did black Americans play in that battle?

12. (a) What were the provisions of the Treaty of Ghent? (b) What issues were not included in the treaty? Why? (c) Why did many Americans feel that the United States had won the war?

See p. T40.

Critical Thinking

1. **Analyzing** How did the principle of checks and balances operate during the dispute between President Jefferson and the Federalists in the judiciary?

2. **Drawing Conclusions** (a) Who favored war with Great Britain in 1812? (b) Who opposed the war? Why? (c) Which group had a right to think it had been right in 1812? Explain.

See p. T40.

Connecting Past and Present

1. List three ways in which the government involves itself in the daily lives of American citizens today. What would Thomas Jefferson have thought about the degree to which the federal government involves itself in people's lives today? Why?

2. (a) When in recent years has the United States used an embargo? (b) What caused the United States to institute the embargo? (c) Was it successful?

See p. T40.

Developing Basic Skills

1. **Map Reading** Study the map of the Louisiana Purchase on page 203 and the maps of the United States on pages 848 and 849. (a) What mineral resources have been found in the Louisiana territory? (b) How is that land used today?

2. **Graph Reading** Study the graph on page 207: (a) In what year was the value of American exports highest? (b) In what year was the value of imports highest? (c) Explain the change in American foreign trade between 1807 and 1812.

WRITING ABOUT HISTORY

Cause-and-Effect Order

Events in history do not just happen. Every event or development has a least one *cause*, or reason why it happened. And every event or development has at least one *effect*, or result. In writing about such a chain reaction, you should arrange your information in cause-and-effect order, making clear that a given cause or causes led to certain effects. You may find it helpful to prepare a cause-and-effect chart before writing about a series of events. For example, if you were writing about events leading up to the War of 1812, you could prepare a chart like the one shown at the right.

Cause	Britain impressed American sailors.
Cause	France removed restrictions on neutral shipping.
Effect	Congress declared war on Britain.

Some words that are used to show cause-and-effect order are: *because, as a result, consequently,* and *thus.*

Practice: Prepare a cause-and-effect chart about Jefferson's conflict with the judiciary branch. Then write a paragraph based on the chart.

A Growing Nation

11

(1815–1825)

CHAPTER OUTLINE

1 A Sense of National Unity

2 The Industrial Revolution

3 Henry Clay's American System

4 Building Pathways to the West

5 James Monroe and Foreign Affairs

The first shot went off at 10 A.M. Then down the line a cannon, and yet another farther east set off a blast. And so it continued, until cannons had roared across New York State, from Buffalo to New York City. It took 81 minutes. In those days before the telegraph, it was probably the fastest message that had ever been sent.

What was that message? The great Erie Canal, the pride of New York's governor De Witt Clinton, was open for business. The packet boat *Seneca Chief,* laden with potash, flour, butter, fish, dignitaries, and Clinton himself, was on its way from Buffalo. It was October 26, 1825, little more than eight years after the first shovelful of dirt was thrown on the most magnificent engineering project of its day.

The flotilla began with just five boats, but its numbers swelled as well-wishers joined in. When it reached Albany a week later, the boats numbered in the hundreds. At each town along the route, people recited poems, made speeches, and set off fireworks.

The procession arrived in New York Harbor on November 4. There, Clinton poured a keg of fresh Lake Erie water into the salt sea—a ritual that symbolized the "wedding" of the Great Lakes with the Atlantic Ocean. A great ball at City Hall capped days of celebration. In 1812, when Clinton had proposed what was laughingly called the "Big Ditch," even Thomas Jefferson called the idea "little short of madness." Now, it was done.

Before the Erie Canal, the cost of shipping freight across New York was $100 a ton. After it, the cost was $5 a ton! The treasures of the American interior—grain, timber, fur—were now available to the entire world. Traffic moved in the opposite direction, too, as waves of settlers headed to the Midwest.

No wonder that the Erie Canal was opened with such fanfare. The country felt that a new era was dawning. At a time when the United States was developing a sense of itself as a nation, the Erie Canal served as a physical link bringing regions together.

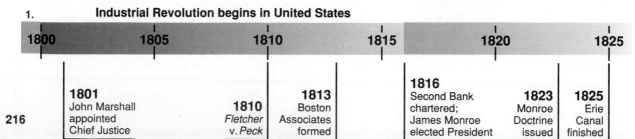

1.

Industrial Revolution begins in United States

| 1800 | 1805 | 1810 | 1815 | 1820 | 1825 |

1801 John Marshall appointed Chief Justice

1810 *Fletcher v. Peck*

1813 Boston Associates formed

1816 Second Bank chartered; James Monroe elected President

1823 Monroe Doctrine issued

1825 Erie Canal finished

216

1. TIME LINE QUESTION Ask: How long after the charting of the second Bank was the Erie Canal finished?

Some people called the Erie Canal "Clinton's Ditch" after DeWitt Clinton, the governor of New York. The State of New York paid for building the canal, partially with money raised by lotteries and by a $1 tax on steamboat rides. Canal building throughout the nation increased trade and travel in the growing nation.

1.

---

1. **GEOGRAPHY** The canal had to cross over two rivers—the Mohawk River at Cohoes and the Genessee River at Rochester. Workers built stone aqueducts to carry the canal over the rivers. (Interaction)

1 A Sense of National Unity

READ TO UNDERSTAND

■ How the Era of Good Feelings got its name.

■ How President Monroe represented the ideas of an earlier age.

■ How John Marshall's Supreme Court contributed to national unity.

Americans had entered the War of 1812 in a spirit of discord, with Republicans and Federalists quarreling over neutral rights and trade. But the coming of peace smoothed over many differences and sparked a new sense of unity. "The people . . . are more Americans; they feel and act more as a nation," observed statesman Albert Gallatin at war's end.

For a brief period, Americans would forget the competition of political parties. Disagreement, however, still lay beneath the surface.

An Era of Good Feelings

As James Madison neared the end of his second term, he took great care to see that the Republicans nominated James Monroe, his secretary of state and fellow Virginian, to succeed him. Despite the objections of some Republican representatives and much grumbling about the "Virginia Dynasty" controlling the presidency, the party chose Monroe. With the Federalist party now weak and breaking apart, he easily defeated his opponent, Rufus King of New York.

2.

When Monroe was inaugurated in 1817, the nation seemed more united and optimistic than it had ever been. A presidential goodwill tour, which took Monroe to the former

217

---

2. **BIOGRAPHY** Rufus King (1755–1827), while a delegate to the Continental Congress, had urged the outlawing of slavery in the Northwest Territory.

Federalist stronghold of New England, demonstrated this change in the American mood. Citizens of Boston warmly received him. One newspaper, the *Columbian Sentinel,* referring to the way in which old political foes greeted each other, called the times the "Era of Good Feelings."

Good feelings seemed to prevail all over the country. In 1820, when President Monroe ran for reelection, he faced no opposition and received all but one of the electoral votes. The Federalists, in decline since 1800, had lost most of their remaining support with the American victory in the War of 1812. The country seemed firmly united under the Republicans.

James Monroe: Symbol of Unity

As President, James Monroe became a symbol of the nation's political unity. Over 60 years old when he took office, Monroe was the last President of the Revolutionary War generation. To be sure, men such as Andrew Jackson and John Quincy Adams had been born before 1776, but they were still children during the war. Monroe, in contrast, was already a young man.

Monroe shared the views of the earlier generation, as his quaint attire showed. He dressed in the fashion of decades past, from white-topped boots and knee-length pantaloons to cocked hat. He even powdered his hair and tied it in a queue at the back. To the postwar generation he was, as one historian observed, "a last nostalgic look at the eighteenth century."

Monroe's point of view was equally rooted in the past. Except in the area of foreign affairs, he believed the President had little responsibility for policy making. Monroe believed that the Congress should interpret the public will and the President should follow.

Nor had he ever fully accepted the idea of political parties, which he called "the curse of the country." "The existence of parties," Monroe declared "is not necessary to free government." But political unity turned out to be only an illusion. A new and stronger opposition party would eventually grow out of the ruins of the Federalists.

Marshall and the Supreme Court

Even while the Federalist party was in decline, a leading Federalist, John Marshall, was contributing to the growing sense of national unity.

President John Adams had appointed Marshall as Chief Justice of the Supreme Court just before he left office in 1801. (See page 193.) When Marshall assumed his duties, the Supreme Court lacked both power and prestige. Indeed, John Jay, the first Chief Justice, had resigned because he felt that he had too little to do.

The Supreme Court rarely met for longer than six weeks a year, and its proceedings attracted little attention. For part of the year, Marshall, like the other justices, presided over a lower federal district court.

The justices met in the basement of the Capitol, lived in the same boarding house, and rarely went out socially. In fact, Justice William Paterson once traveled a full day on the same stagecoach as Thomas Jefferson without either recognizing the other.

Although Chief Justice John Marshall was not a legal scholar, his keen mind helped him get to the heart of legal problems and write clear, forceful decisions. Seldom has a person so dominated the nation's highest court. During 35 years as Chief Justice, he wrote almost half of the Court's decisions and dissented from the majority opinion only eight times. Even Republican justices came under the sway of his forceful personality.

The Court and National Unity

John Marshall was a moderate Federalist who favored strengthening the power of the national government. As Chief Justice from 1801 to 1835, he was able to influence the nation's developing political system.

As early as 1803, in *Marbury* v. *Madison,* the Supreme Court had confirmed the principle of judicial review, the Court's power to decide whether or not a federal law violated the Constitution. (See page 198.)

In *Fletcher* v. *Peck* (1810), the Court ruled a state law unconstitutional for the first time. The case involved land grants that the Georgia legislature had made to the Yazoo Land

Company. When legislators at a later session realized that the grants had been obtained by bribery and fraud, it tried to invalidate them. In his decision, Marshall ruled that the grants were legally binding contracts. The state could not refuse to honor them because the Constitution forbade states to "impair the obligation of contracts."

In *Dartmouth College* v. *Woodward* (1819), the Supreme Court again upheld the sanctity of contracts. This time, it overturned an attempt by the New Hampshire legislature to revise Dartmouth's charter. Marshall said that a contract could not be changed without the consent of both parties, even if one of the parties was a state government. Through these rulings, the Court made legal contracts nearly unbreakable.

In two rulings that increased the authority of the national government, Marshall based his decisions on a loose construction of the Constitution. In the case of *McCulloch* v. *Maryland* (1819), the Court upheld the constitutionality of the second Bank of the United States, which Congress had chartered in 1816. The state of Maryland had tried to force the Bank out of the state by taxing it. Marshall claimed no state had the right to hinder or control any national institution established within its borders. "The power to tax involves the power to destroy," Marshall stated.

While admitting that the Constitution did not specifically authorize a national bank, Marshall asserted that Congress had to have some leeway in exercising its powers.

> Let the end be legitimate, let it be within the scope of the Constitution, and all means which are appropriate, which are plainly adapted to that end, which are not prohibited, but consistent with the letter and spirit of the Constitution, are constitutional.

In *Gibbons* v. *Ogden* (1824), the Supreme Court struck down a New York State law that had awarded a steamboat company a monopoly on passenger service across the Hudson River between New Jersey and New York. The ruling held that a state can regulate commerce only within its borders and 1. that only Congress could control interstate commerce. In this case, the Court guaranteed that the nation would have a unified

Tall, gangly John Marshall grew up in frontier Virginia and served with distinction in the Revolutionary War. Under his strong leadership as Chief Justice, the Supreme Court gained prestige and power.

2.

interstate trade policy. Individual states would not be able to interfere with interstate trade as they had under the Articles of Confederation.

The Supreme Court under John Marshall clarified and affirmed important national powers, especially those of the Supreme Court and Congress. In that way, it contributed to a growing sense of national unity.

See p. T41.

SECTION 1 REVIEW

1. **Identify:** Era of Good Feelings.

2. How was James Monroe "rooted in the past"?

3. How did John Marshall leave his imprint on the national government?

4. (a) What two Supreme Court rulings upheld contracts? (b) What two rulings strengthened the national government?

5. **Critical Thinking** How did the decision in *McCulloch* v. *Maryland* strengthen the federal government?

1. **VOCABULARY** Have students look up these terms in the glossary before they begin reading.

2. **CRITICAL THINKING** Have students compare and contrast the meaning of the word *revolution* in the terms Industrial Revolution and American Revolution.

2 The Industrial Revolution

READ TO UNDERSTAND

■ How changes in technology, labor, and capital led to industrialization in the United States.

■ How the factory system developed in the United States.

■ Why the growth of industry created both unity and division.

1. ■ *Vocabulary:* factory system, capital, limited liability, interchangeable parts.

With little industry of their own, the American colonies depended on British manufacturers for many of their needs. When the colonists wanted a cooking pot or a tool, they often had to buy one made in Britain. After the revolution, British industry made even more advances because of new techniques developed in the 1700s. Could the Americans ever catch up? The War of 1812 provided an answer. By cutting the United States off from foreign supplies, it launched an era of American industrial development.

The Needs of Industry

2. Historians use the term "Industrial Revolution" to describe the economic shift from farming and commerce to manufacturing. The term "revolution" suggests that the changes were so far-reaching that they seemed like a complete overthrow of the old way of life.

In fact, however, the growth of industry was neither violent nor abrupt. It involved many gradual changes. These changes were most evident in three areas crucial to the development of industry: technology, labor, and capital.

Technology The development of the steam engine is an important example of how changes in technology fostered industrialization. For centuries, gristmills had been turned by water. Then in 1769, James Watt of Scotland patented a steam engine. By the 1790s, millers had begun using more efficient steam engines to turn their mills.

A number of other major inventions came out of Great Britain in the same era. James

Hargreaves devised the spinning jenny, which replaced a woman sitting at each spinning wheel. The new jenny connected several spinning wheels together so that they spun eight threads at a time. Improvements on his design soon enabled spinners to produce a hundred threads at once. Other inventions mechanized the process of weaving cloth. The net result was a manufacturing process that produced more goods at lower cost.

Labor By the 1700s, the organization of labor itself had undergone change in Great Britain. Rather than spreading the manufacturing process out in several locations, the newly developed **factory system** brought workers together under one roof. In textiles, for example, early producers had farmed out wool for women to spin in their homes. Weaving took place in another place and sewing in still another. Under the new system, these steps of production all happened in one place, a textile factory.

Capital This industrial growth required **capital,** or money for investment. As early as the 1500s, joint stock companies had worked out fairly simple ways to pool money and lessen the risks of commercial ventures. (See page 38.) But the high cost of new machinery required much larger sums of money.

In Europe, corporations had developed to obtain the needed capital. Corporations could raise the large amounts of money from many small investors. Each investor's personal responsibility for the debt of the corporation was limited to the amount of money invested. This **limited liability** made corporations more attractive, since under the old system, investors risked losing their personal savings or even their homes if a business venture went too far into debt.

3.

But Americans were wary of corporations, at first permitting them only for public projects like bridges and canals. Only after the Civil War did the corporation become a dominant business form in the United States. Until then, most American businesses were family-owned firms or partnerships.

Americans at Work

In the late 1700s, the excitement of the Industrial Revolution began to spread to the United States. Improved versions of the steam

3. **ECONOMICS** Many Americans distrusted corporations. Before the 1850s, corporations could be formed only by a special act of a state legislature.

Steamboats cut the traveling time for passengers and cargo and made river travel upstream as easy as downstream. Robert Fulton's boat, the Clermont, *provided*
1. *the first regular steamship service. The* Paragon, *shown here, went into service in 1808 and had a luxurious paneled dining room. Before long, riverboat builders tried to outdo each other. Expensive furnishings became commonplace, although passengers unaccustomed to luxuries were warned not to sleep in their shoes.*

1. **VISUAL EVIDENCE**
Ask: Why do you think the *Paragon* was equipped with a mast?

2. **ECONOMICS** Fitch started a ferry service, but it failed because few people used it. Fulton's steamboats, however, quickly began making profitable runs on the Hudson.

engine appeared. In 1787, John Fitch launched the first steam-powered boat on the Delaware River in Philadelphia. Twenty years later, in August 1807, Robert Fulton traveled up the Hudson River from New York City to Albany in 32 hours aboard the steam-powered *Clermont,* proving the practical value of us-
2. ing steam to power a boat.

Another American, Eli Whitney, revolutionized cotton processing by inventing the cotton gin in 1793. By hand, the average worker could clean the seeds out of one to three pounds of cotton per day. Using Whitney's power-driven cotton gin, the same worker could clean 1,000 pounds a day.

Whitney also invented **interchangeable parts,** which he used in the production of
3. firearms. Traditionally, gunsmiths made each gun by hand, slowly honing the various parts until they fit. If a part broke later, a new one had to be custom made. Whitney built a large number of each component part, all exactly alike. The various interchangeable parts could be rapidly assembled to make a gun. Repairs could be made just as quickly. The use of interchangeable parts spread to other industries, further boosting industrial development in the United States.

The Spread of New Ideas from Britain

As the first country to industrialize, Great Britain was eager to protect the competitive advantage British goods enjoyed. For this reason, it banned the export of industrial secrets and prohibited skilled mechanics from moving to other nations.

Britain could not long prevent this knowledge from spreading beyond its borders. For one thing, as you have read, American inventors were at work themselves. Furthermore, some British mechanics managed to slip away to the United States, carrying plans in their heads for factory machinery.

Twenty-one-year-old Samuel Slater, an apprentice in a British cotton-spinning mill, heard that several states offered large rewards for technical information. When he came to the United States in 1789, a wealthy manufacturer, Moses Brown of Rhode Island, hired Slater to set up a factory. Slater built several improved versions of the machinery he had used in Britain, and in a year he had a factory producing cotton thread. Seven similar mills were operating by 1800, and by 1815 there were 213 in operation.

221

3. **ECONOMICS** Whitney tried his system on guns first because he knew the government wanted to buy large numbers of muskets for the army.

1. **GEOGRAPHY** Have students locate Lowell on a map. Then ask: What river probably was used to power the mill? (location, interaction)

2. **BACKGROUND** Point out that in the early 1800s, there were no child-labor laws or safety regulations: children worked 12 hours a day, 6 days a week.

In 1813, a group of merchants called the Boston Associates, led by Francis Cabot Lowell, set up the first American textile factory that combined all the tasks required to turn raw cotton into finished cloth. Like Slater, they relied to a large extent on British technology, for Lowell had smuggled the plans for a power loom into the country. The Boston Associates later set up other centers of textile manufacturing in New England. A factory in Lowell, Massachusetts, became the center of their operations.

Labor for the New Factories

Scarcity of labor had been a feature of the United States economy from its beginning. Because the nation's vast territory made it relatively easy for Americans to acquire farm land, few Americans were at first interested in factory work. Artisans were not a likely source of factory labor either. They could make good money working at home or in small shops, turning out products by hand. Thus, early factory owners had to look elsewhere for workers.

In the textile industry, especially, factory owners found most of their workers among women and children. Children had a special appeal because they were small and could move nimbly around dangerous machinery. Both women and children, lacking the skills of well-trained artisans, worked for low wages.

The Boston Associates recruited many young, unmarried women from farm families to work in their textile factories. The women usually worked for a few years before they married. Because the company wanted to attract hard-working women from respectable families, it closely supervised their lives. The company provided boardinghouses, educational and recreational facilities, religious instruction, and land for gardening. The workers even published their own monthly magazine.

The women in the Lowell mills worked long hours, but at least in the early years, they were fairly well treated because the company needed to attract workers. Although some observers reported that the Lowell workers were oppressed or unhappy, the women themselves denied it. As their magazine, the *Lowell Offering,* declared, "We are

3. **BACKGROUND** In 1791, Alexander Hamilton wrote: "Women and children are rendered more useful . . . by manufacturing establishments, than they would otherwise be."

The swift-moving streams of New England were an ideal source of power for early factories. The tall building in this painting of Pawtucket Falls in Rhode Island is thought to be the first American textile mill to use water-powered machinery. By the 1830s, textile manufacturing had become a major American industry.

4. **VISUAL EVIDENCE** This factory, built by Moses Brown and Samuel Slater, still stands today.

Most workers in early textile mills were women and children, as shown in this print. Mill owners assured the parents of young women that they would receive proper supervision while working at the mill. In New England, the mill owners even offered foreign language classes after hours. Such jobs often gave young women the chance to be independent and self-supporting.

1. VISUAL EVIDENCE On the basis of this lithograph, what conclusions can you reach about conditions in the early textile mills?

not generally miserable, either in point of fact, or in the prospect of a dreadful future."

As the factory system spread, life for factory workers became increasingly harsh. When the arrival of large numbers of immigrants provided a cheap labor supply, wages dropped. Those who needed jobs had to take what they could get. Such changes, however, were in the future.

A Force for Unity and Division

The growth of industry enabled the United States to free itself from some of its Old World ties. The nation had grown up with an economy based on agriculture and exports. The colonies had exported raw materials to Britain, which in turn had produced manufactured goods and sold them back to the colonies. But by the early 1800s, the United States relied increasingly on local industries to supply manufactured goods. The development of domestic industry enhanced Americans' pride and sense of national identity.

Industrialization produced divisions as well. Most manufacturing developed in the North, especially New England, boosting northern prosperity and fostering new ways of life. The South and the sparsely populated West lagged behind. Thus, the development

of industry acted as a force for both unity and sectional division.

See p. T41.

SECTION 2 REVIEW

1. **Identify:** (a) James Watt, (b) Robert Fulton, (c) Eli Whitney, (d) Samuel Slater, (e) Francis Cabot Lowell.

2. **Define:** (a) factory system, (b) capital, (c) limited liability, (d) interchangeable parts.

3. (a) Describe how two inventions of the late 1700s affected manufacturing. (b) How did British technology become available in the United States?

4. List two reasons why owners of textile factories were eager to hire women and children as workers.

5. (a) Give one example of how industrialization brought the people of the United States closer together. (b) Give one example of how it also created divisions.

6. **Critical Thinking** How did technological change bring about social change in the United States in the 1800s?

223

2. BACKGROUND One historian notes, however, "From the beginning young women complained of overcrowded sleeping rooms and rigid supervision. They were vulnerable to arbitrary wage cuts."

1. **VOCABULARY** Have students look up this term in the glossary before they begin reading.

3 Henry Clay's American System

READ TO UNDERSTAND

■ How a generation of leaders expanded the scope of the federal government.

■ How Henry Clay's American System fostered greater self-sufficiency.

■ How changes in tariffs and banking practices affected American life.

1. ■ *Vocabulary:* bank note.

When "Gallant Harry of the West" rode into the nation's capital, politicians braced themselves for action. "Gallant Harry" was Henry Clay, one of the new young leaders in Congress who rose to prominence during the War of 1812. Impatient with the "old-fashioned" ideas of Jefferson and Madison, they spurred the federal government to take more responsibility for developing the nation's economy after the war. With their limitless faith in the country's future, they became the advocates of an economic program for the nation that put national rather than sectional interests first.

2. **BIOGRAPHY** Henry Clay (1777–1850) was the seventh of 20 children. He practiced oratory on his own and studied with a lawyer who had trained Jefferson and Marshall.

Three Dominant Political Figures

Clay and two other young politicians among the new generation became powerful figures in American politics. Clay, from Kentucky, and John C. Calhoun, from South Carolina, were Republicans. The pair first attracted notice as War Hawks during the crisis that led to war with Britain in 1812. Daniel Webster, the third leader, was a Federalist from New Hampshire.

Despite their differences, all three championed nationalism at one time or another in their careers. Of the three, Clay was the most consistently nationalistic in his outlook. Webster and Calhoun spoke for nationalism when it benefited their section of the country but opposed it when it did not.

Henry Clay was a tall, dashing Kentuckian, full of charm and swagger. His powerful personality enabled him to influence people and mold them into loyal political followers. At times pushy and overbearing, at other times cheerful and accommodating, he quickly set himself up as one of the nation's most influential political leaders. **2.**

Slim and handsome, John C. Calhoun was an intelligent and eloquent speaker. His knowledge of political theory served him well as a nationalist and, later, as a champion of the South. **3.**

3. **BIOGRAPHY** John Caldwell Calhoun (1782–1850), born in Abbeville County, South Carolina, attended Yale College, and later studied at Tapping Reeve's famous law school in Litchfield, Connecticut.

---

4. *The War of 1812 brought to the forefront three politicians who would dominate American politics for the next four decades. The young Daniel Webster, at left, had refused to vote taxes for the war. Henry Clay, center, and John Calhoun, at right, were ardent supporters of the war. After the war, all three urged the government to take a larger role in developing the national economy.*

4. **VISUAL EVIDENCE** Point out that appearance can often add to a speaker's effectiveness. Ask: Which of these men might have been aided by his striking appearance?

1. Daniel Webster's dark hair and brows had earned him the nickname "Black Dan." His stocky build helped lend forcefulness to a speaking style that was among the most powerful in the land.

Henry Clay's Design

As the party of Thomas Jefferson, the Republicans had traditionally opposed strengthening the national government at the expense of state or local governments. In fact, the party had developed out of opposition to Alexander Hamilton's economic policies of promoting an active government role in the nation's economic development. Furthermore, Republicans had favored a rural economy rather than an industrial one. But the British blockade during the War of 1812 reduced America's supply of manufactured goods and revealed the danger of relying too heavily on foreign imports. Thus, many Republicans began to change their thinking and to accept some of Hamilton's original economic policies.

Henry Clay brought these ideas together in what he called his American System. Coming from the isolated and less developed West, Clay strongly supported government programs for economic development. He believed that the American economy had to become more self-sufficient.

For a start, Clay called for a protective tariff to keep American manufacturing growing. Second, Clay proposed that the government charter a new national bank to provide a sound and uniform currency, necessary for the smooth operation of business and trade. Finally, he urged a federal program of internal improvements such as better canals and

2. roadways that would aid interstate commerce.

GREAT DEBATE
Protectionism Versus Free Trade

Once peace returned in 1815, many industries that grew during the war felt threatened. American manufacturers, lacking the capital and skill of those in Britain, could not compete with cheaper imported goods.

Clay, like Hamilton earlier, proposed a protective tariff to guard these new indus-

tries from foreign competition. By raising the price of imported goods, a protective tariff would make the more expensive American-made products competitive. In the Tariff of 1816, Congress raised the tax on foreign imports by an average of 20 percent. This did the trick. Americans had to pay higher prices, but American industries sold more goods and grew stronger.

Clay's followers in the Middle Atlantic and western states favored the tariff. They believed that flourishing commerce as well as tariff revenues would help pay for the roads and canals they needed for trade with the Northeast and the South.

Calhoun also spoke eloquently in favor of the tariff. He thought it was necessary to protect the South's growing cotton industry, and he believed that the South would soon develop its own industrial strength.

Of the three young leaders, only Daniel Webster spoke against the tariff. Although some New Englanders wanted it, Webster staunchly opposed it. His constituents in New Hampshire still relied on shipping from Great Britain, which the tariff would hurt. Ironically, over the years, Calhoun and Webster would reverse their views on the tariff. ■

Second Bank of the United States

Republicans in Congress had long been suspicious of the first Bank of the United States, which Hamilton had created, so they let its charter expire in 1811. After that, only state banks could issue paper money. Each bank issued its own **bank notes,** supposedly backed by gold or silver held by the bank.

The bank notes did not remain a stable currency, however. The number of state banks issuing them increased greatly. Since each bank issued its own notes, a wide variety of notes circulated at all times. Whenever farmers needed to buy land or manufacturers wanted to buy equipment for new factories, the demand for credit grew and the situation got worse. Banks often issued more paper money than they could redeem, or buy back, with the amount of gold or silver on deposit. During the War of 1812, few state banks redeemed their bank notes for gold and silver.

1. **ECONOMICS** Have students compare the arguments in favor of the second Bank with those used in support of the first Bank (pp. 182–183).

See p. T42.

No one could be sure, therefore, exactly how much the various bank notes were worth. Businesses often took a big risk by accepting paper money for their goods. The lack of a uniform national currency made interstate commerce extremely difficult.

Clay and others called for the creation of a new national bank. It would provide a uniform national currency and would offer a safe place for the federal government to deposit its funds. In 1816, Congress chartered the second Bank of the United States for a 20-year period. The Bank soon had a chance to

1. show whether or not it could do its job.

The Panic of 1819

The Bank's charter gave it enough power to regulate the state banking and currency system. During the economic boom after the war, such regulation was badly needed as speculation in western land became more popular. But, instead of restraining land speculators, the Bank recklessly encouraged them by eagerly extending credit.

In 1819, the Bank, under a more conservative management, began to call in its loans and to demand gold or silver from state banks in exchange for their notes. State banks, in turn, called in their loans. Since prospective buyers could no longer obtain loans to buy land, speculators could not sell the land in which they had invested. Western land prices plunged. Speculators could not repay their loans to the banks, and as a result, many banks failed.

At the same time, European demand for American farm products and textiles began to decline. Southern cotton prices fell. Not only did many southern farmers suffer from lower cotton prices, they also lost money from speculating in western land.

These events brought on an economic crisis. During the Panic of 1819, banks foreclosed on mortgaged farms, business firms went bankrupt, and people lost their jobs, especially in the South and West.

Americans tried to figure out what had caused their troubles, and many blamed the badly managed Bank of the United States.

2. Right or wrong, their anger threatened the

226 Bank's future.

SECTION 3 REVIEW

1. **Identify:** (a) Henry Clay, (b) Daniel Webster, (c) John C. Calhoun.

2. **Define:** bank note.

3. What did Henry Clay, Daniel Webster, and John C. Calhoun have in common?

4. Describe Henry Clay's American System.

5. Why did Daniel Webster oppose the Tariff of 1816?

6. What two purposes did Clay think a national bank would serve?

7. **Critical Thinking** How might the Industrial Revolution in the United States have affected people's attitude toward the role of the federal government?

3. **VOCABULARY** Have students look up this term in the glossary before they begin reading.

4 Building Pathways to the West

READ TO UNDERSTAND

■ Why many Americans moved west of the Appalachians after the War of 1812.

■ How a government policy of road building encouraged westward migration.

■ How canals and steamboats improved transportation and commerce.

■ *Vocabulary:* corduroy roads.

3.

Travelers muttered about roads pitted by mudholes and strewn with tree stumps. Migrants struggled to squeeze their wagons through roads too narrow for passage. In the West, especially, farmers grumbled that they needed more roads for getting crops to market. Responding to such complaints, Clay's American System called for building a network of roads and canals paid for by the federal government.

His supporters saw such internal improvements as vital to promoting national unity and pride. John C. Calhoun argued that

2. **DISCUSSION** Have students support or refute the contention that the Bank of the United States caused the Panic of 1819. They may want to do more research first.

SKILL LESSON

Westward Movement: Using Statistics

Statistics, or numbers, provide factual information that helps you understand past events. They can reveal important patterns or trends. Yet, statistics present only a partial picture. For example, the table below tells about population growth but leaves out Native Americans who lived in those states during the period. If you had not learned previously about the Indian nations in the region, you might assume that the lands were uninhabited before white settlers arrived. Interpret the statistics using these steps:

See p. T43

1 Identify the type of information presented in the table. Begin by asking yourself questions about the different categories of information and how they relate to one another. (a) What time period is covered? (b) What is the interval between the beginning and ending years? (c) What do the numbers represent?

2 Practice reading the statistics. (a) What was the population of Mississippi in 1820?

(b) What was the population of Ohio in 1800? (c) By what year did the population of Indiana total more than 100,000 people?

3 Look for relationships among the numbers. (a) How did Kentucky's population change between 1810 and 1820? (b) How much did Louisiana's population grow between 1810 and 1820? (c) Which state had the largest population in 1810? In 1830? (d) Compare the population growth of Ohio and Tennessee from 1810 to 1830.

4 Draw conclusions about an historical event or period by applying what you have learned from statistics. (a) How would you describe the population change in the West between 1790 and 1830? (b) How might you explain the reasons for the change? (c) Why do you think Ohio, Kentucky, and Tennessee had the largest populations? (d) When did each state join the Union? (See page 863.) (e) What is the relationship between statehood and population growth?

1.

2.

Population Growth in the West 1790–1830

	1790	1800	1810	1820	1830
Ohio	73,600	145,300	230,700	581,400	937,900
Kentucky	35,690	220,900	406,500	564,300	687,400
Tennessee	*	105,600	261,700	422,800	681,900
Mississippi	*	8,800	40,300	75,400	136,600
Indiana	*	5,600	24,500	148,100	343,000
Michigan	*	*	4,760	8,900	31,600
Louisiana	*	*	76,500	153,400	215,700
Illinois	*	*	12,200	55,200	157,400
Missouri	*	*	19,700	66,500	140,400
Arkansas	*	*	1,060	14,200	30,300
Alabama	*	*	*	127,900	309,500

*no data available

1. **BACKGROUND** By 1820, all but 2 of the 13 original states had lost population.

2. **READING** Students might enjoy reading some of the works of James Fenimore Cooper, which describe contacts between Indians and whites in this period.

better transportation would strengthen the nation. He called on Congress to "bind the republic together with a perfect system of roads and canals."

Westward Expansion

After the War of 1812, a wave of migration swept across the Appalachian Mountains into territory yielded by the Indian nations. "Old America seems to be breaking up and moving westwards," an English visitor observed
1. in 1817. While the pace of westward movement slackened during the Panic of 1819, it picked up again in the economic recovery that followed and reached a peak in the 1830s. By 1840, more than a third of the United States population lived west of the Appalachians. In 1810, only one seventh had.

High food prices in the East and the availability of rich western farmlands attracted new settlers from the older eastern states. Families from New England and the Middle Atlantic region settled around the Great Lakes.

Settlers from Kentucky and Tennessee turned to the lands of the old Northwest and the old Southwest. From the southern seaboard states, pioneers poured into the old Southwest and the Ohio River Valley.

The frequent admission of new states to the nation reflected the steady westward expansion. Ohio became a state in 1803 and Louisiana in 1812. Indiana (1816), Mississippi (1817), Illinois (1818), Alabama (1819), Missouri (1821), Arkansas (1836), and Michigan (1837) followed.

Demand for Better Transportation

As people moved westward, they felt an urgent need for better connections with the East and access to its markets. In most areas, there were no roads at all. Often, travelers had to go on horseback or on foot.   2.

Where roads did exist, they were crude, at best. Following old Indian trails, many roads were too narrow for wagon passage. From winter through spring, the hard-packed dirt

3. **VISUAL EVIDENCE** Have students write a paragraph describing what life might be like in the cabin pictured.

Life on the frontier could be lonely and hard, and many skills were necessary to survive. The pioneer of the early 1800s had to be a farmer, carpenter, and hunter.
3. *This isolated log cabin on the Missouri frontier was sketched by French artist Charles Lesueur.*

1. **LOCAL HISTORY** Today the National Road is part of U.S. Highway 40. Ask: What U.S. highways are located near your community? When were they built?

turned to mud, and stumps and ruts stood ready to break a wagon's axles.

Corduroy roads, made by laying tree trunks side by side, offered the best overland route. Yet even on good roads, travel was uncomfortable. One angry traveler complained about "the noise of the wheels, the rumble of a coach . . . the jerking of the bad roads," and "the most detestable stagecoach that ever a Christian built to dislocate the joints of his fellow man."

Most existing transportation simply did not meet western needs. Settlers needed a way to send their farm products to the East and bring manufactured goods back to the West. In many cases, the cheapest way for residents of western towns to ship their products to eastern buyers was to float the goods down the Ohio and Mississippi rivers, around the Florida peninsula, and up the coast. Eager to travel in a direct route, settlers clamored for improved canals and roads.

The National Road

Either state governments or private investors paid for the earliest roads. They then charged a toll to get back their investment. The federal government did not pay for a major road until 1806, when Congress authorized the building of a "National Road." Eventually, that road stretched westward from Cumberland, Maryland, to Wheeling, Virginia, and then through Ohio and Indiana to Van-
1. dalia, Illinois.

By the standards of the time, the National Road was very good. It could withstand the weight of wagons jammed with people without caving in. Wagons loaded with 20 passengers were not unheard of. One traveler counted 42 children in three wagons during one day's journey. Yet, by modern standards, the National Road was barely a road at all. In Indiana, for example, where the route ran through dense forest, plans permitted "rounded and trimmed" tree stumps 9 to 15 inches high to remain on the road.

Although President Madison expressed doubts about the constitutionality of roads paid for by the federal government, he continued the construction of the National Road. But, when Congress tried to distribute money to the states for their own internal improve-

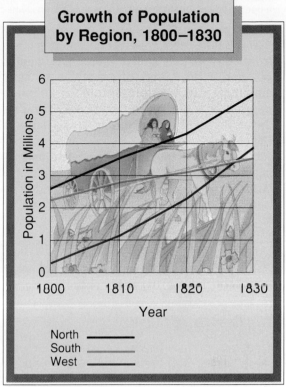

Growth of Population by Region, 1800–1830

North ——————
South ——————
West ——————

Source: *Historical Statistics of the United States*

GRAPH STUDY *The lure of rich farmland drew increasing numbers of pioneers westward. When did the population of the West become larger than the population of the South?* See p. T42.   2.

ments, Madison vetoed the measure. Thereafter, local roads and other local improvements would remain the responsibility of the individual states.

Canals and Steamboats

As you read in the beginning of this chapter, the completion of the Erie Canal in 1825 opened a new era in transportation. Built by the state of New York with public funds, the Erie Canal stretched about 350 miles (560 kilometers) from Buffalo to Albany. From Albany, boats could travel down the Hudson River to New York City.

The canal allowed New York City to tap the markets of the Ohio River Valley and the Great Lakes region. By using the canal, shippers could cut the cost of transportation from nearly $100 to $5 a ton. Travel time was reduced from 20 days to 8. The success of the Erie Canal made New York City the country's **229** major commercial center.

2. **GRAPH READING** Ask: About how many people lived in the South in 1800? In the West in 1810? In the North in 1820? Which grew most slowly? Why?

1. **GEOGRAPHY** Have students use the map on p. 231 to follow the water route from Cleveland to N.Y.C. Ask: How might the trip have been made before the Erie Canal was built? (movement)

2. **BACKGROUND** Shreveport, Louisiana, is named after Henry M. Shreve. In the 1830s, Shreve cleared the Red River of a massive logjam.

Shippers used the Erie Canal so heavily that the state recovered its construction costs from tolls in just seven years. The canal's popularity prompted other states to start ambitious canal-building projects, although none matched the Erie's success. The Erie Canal heralded the beginning of the nation's Canal Age.

1.

Meanwhile, inventors had been improving on James Watt's early steam engine. In 1811, Robert Fulton and Robert Livingston built a steamboat in Pittsburgh and sent it down the Ohio and Mississippi rivers to New Orleans. This trip demonstrated that steamboats could be used in western waters.

Five years later, Henry M. Shreve built a steamboat specifically designed to meet the needs of western commerce. Despite its towering decks, Shreve's boat could operate in shallow water. Thus, it could navigate the numerous sandbars and snags of the Mississippi, Missouri, and Ohio rivers. Shreve's boat could also travel at great speeds and carry heavy loads of cargo. When several of his

2.

GEOGRAPHIC CONNECTION

The Growth of Cities

What makes a city thrive? Why is one place so much larger and richer than other places nearby? Geographic conditions can make the difference.

In colonial times, while settlement was restricted to the eastern coast, Boston was the most prosperous American city. It benefited from a large, protected harbor located closer to Europe than any other port on the Eastern Seaboard. Fortunes could be made importing goods from England and reshipping them to other colonial ports farther south.

When westward expansion followed the end of British rule, however, other ports challenged Boston's lead. By 1800, the Mississippi River and New Orleans had become the easiest, cheapest route for shipping goods from the West. Soon an intense rivalry developed

3.

between New York, Baltimore, and Philadelphia to capture western trade. The construction of the National Road, the first road across the mountains, gave an early advantage to Baltimore. But it could not hold it for long.

In 1825, the completion of the Erie Canal tipped the scales in favor of New York. The Erie Canal crossed the only lowland route through the Appalachian Mountains along the Mohawk River. The Erie Canal, by following a lowland route, proved far cheaper to build and operate than competing canals built over far more difficult terrain west of Baltimore and Philadelphia.

The railroad era added a new dimension to the rivalry of the three coastal cities. In 1828, Baltimore began building the Baltimore and Ohio Railroad to the West. Philadelphia responded with the Pennsylvania Railroad and New York with the New York Central and lesser lines. The two southern routes were shorter, but New York's route, following lowlands along the Hudson River and Erie Canal, required less leveling, and was finished first. Once New York established its leadership, the city grew with increasing momentum.

See p. T42.

1. Why did rivalry develop between Baltimore, Philadelphia, and New York?

2. **Critical Thinking** How did geography and technology affect the ability of New York City to increase its trade with the West?

3. **VISUAL EVIDENCE** This picture shows wagons setting out on the National Road near Baltimore. These wagons, developed in the Conestoga Valley of Pennsylvania, became known as Conestoga wagons.

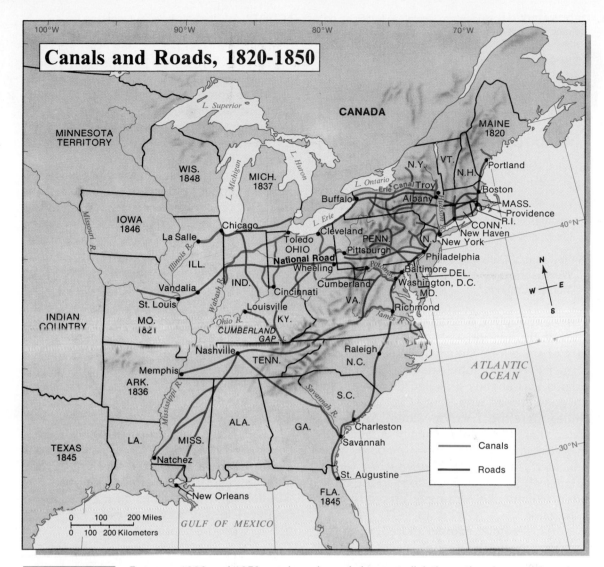

Canals and Roads, 1820-1850

MAP STUDY

See p. T43.

Between 1820 and 1850, roads and canals began to link the nation. Improved roads made it easier for settlers to reach the West, and canals created a network of inland waterways for shipping goods. Find one inland water route from the northeastern Atlantic coast to New Orleans. What canals, rivers, and lakes make up the route?

1.

1. **MAP READING** Ask: In which area of the country were most of the canals built? Why do you think this was the case?
See p. T43.

vessels successfully made upstream journeys to Pittsburgh, all doubts about the practicality of his design ended. Steamboats that cut western freight and passenger rates in half soon crowded the waters.

2.

Improvements in technology quickened the flow of trade in all directions. Farm products could move eastward along the canals. Manufactured goods bound for the West could come up the Mississippi in steamboats instead of taking the slower route over the mountains. As Calhoun had predicted, internal improvements led to better communications, helping to bind the republic together. This phase of Clay's American System seemed to be working.

SECTION 4 REVIEW

1. **Identify:** (a) National Road, (b) Erie Canal.

2. **Define:** corduroy roads.

3. Why was westward expansion attractive?

4. Why were roads important to western settlers?

5. (a) How did the Erie Canal improve trade? (b) Why was the development of the steamboat important?

6. **Critical Thinking** How was the American System an example of nationalism?

231

2. **READING** Although it describes a somewhat later era, students might be interested in reading *Life on the Mississippi* by Mark Twain, a book about Twain's experiences on a steamboat.

5 James Monroe and Foreign Affairs

READ TO UNDERSTAND

■ What international agreements opened the way for national expansion.

■ How the independence of Spain's American colonies created opportunities and concerns for the United States.

■ How fear of European intervention in the Western Hemisphere led to the issuing of the Monroe Doctrine.

President Monroe delegated much of the responsibility for foreign policy to his secretary of state John Quincy Adams, the son of former President John Adams. The younger Adams was already a skilled diplomat, having gone abroad with Henry Clay and others to negotiate the Treaty of Ghent. Ten years older than Clay, John Quincy Adams was everything Clay was not—well-born, well-educated, reserved, and devout. At Ghent, Adams would rise at 5 A.M. to read the Bible, often to find Clay wrapping up an all-night card game.

Adams's quiet manner did not keep him from being a hard bargainer, eager to extend the country's boundaries. His shrewd grasp of diplomacy helped him to accomplish many of his goals for the nation.

Foreign Affairs After 1816

Before Adams's appointment, Richard Rush, the acting secretary of state, negotiated an important accord with the British. In the Rush-Bagot Agreement of 1817, the two nations agreed not to use military ships on the Great Lakes. Later, in the Convention of 1818, they
1. agreed on the 49th parallel as the boundary line between the Louisiana Purchase and Canada.

Spanish-owned Florida posed another border problem for the United States. Outlaws frequently used Florida as a haven. Slaves escaping from southern plantations also sought refuge there. In addition, some groups of Native Americans in Florida raided United States settlements.

In 1818, President Monroe sent troops under the command of Andrew Jackson into Florida to fight the Seminoles, who had made 2. raids into Georgia. Jackson, exceeding his instructions, captured two towns, hanged two British subjects for helping the Spanish, and arrested the Spanish governor.

Although John Quincy Adams knew Jackson had no authority for his actions, the secretary recognized that Jackson's raid bolstered the bargaining position of the United States. When Spain protested the raid, Adams 3. replied that Florida had turned into "a derelict, open to the occupancy of every enemy . . . of the United States, and serving no other earthly purpose than as a post of annoyance."

Plagued by revolts among their own colonies, the Spanish wanted a way out of a difficult situation. In the Adams-Onís Treaty of 1819, Spain agreed to cede Florida to the United States. (See the map on page 233.) In return, the United States dropped a claim to Texas.

The treaty also formally established the boundary between the Louisiana Purchase and Spanish territory. The western portion of the boundary would extend along the 42nd parallel from the Rockies all the way to the Pacific. The way was now clear for the nation to span the continent.

Other Concerns in the Western Hemisphere

Between 1810 and 1821, most of Spain's colonies in the Western Hemisphere revolted and declared their independence. Henry Clay had grand visions of trade with these new countries. He pressed Congress to recognize the revolutionary governments. President Monroe and Secretary of State Adams resisted Clay's efforts, however, fearing that such a rash move would endanger negotiations about Florida with Spain. The United States finally granted official recognition to the Latin American republics in 1822, when it was clear that they would remain independent.

Most Americans sympathized with the new nations, but most European governments did not. After the defeat of Napoleon in 1812, the governments of Russia, Prussia, Austria, and France formed an alliance. Fearing that revolutions abroad might inspire rebellions

3. **BACKGROUND** Although Adams and Jackson were on the same side of the Florida issue, they became bitter rivals for the presidency in 1824 and 1828.

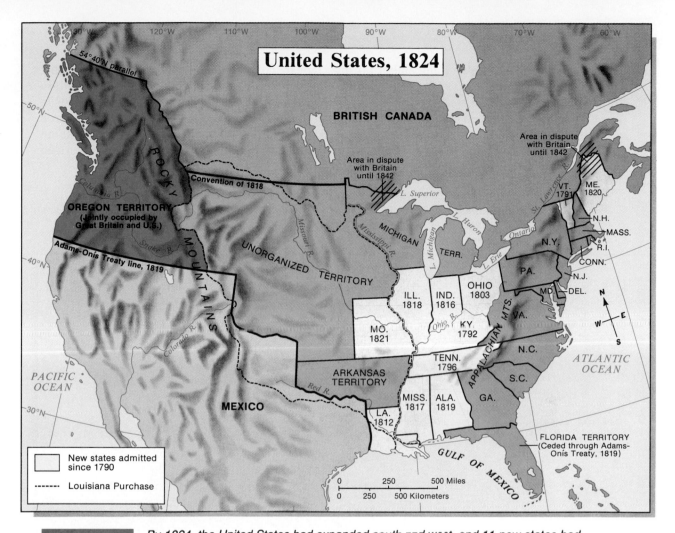

United States, 1824

BRITISH CANADA

54°40'N parallel

ROCKY MOUNTAINS

Convention of 1818

OREGON TERRITORY
(Jointly occupied by
Great Britain and U.S.)

Area in dispute
with Britain
until 1842

Area in dispute
with Britain
until 1842

Adams-Onís Treaty line, 1819

UNORGANIZED TERRITORY

MICHIGAN

TERR.

VT. ME.
1791 1820

N.H.

MASS.

N.Y.

R.I.

CONN.

PA.

N.J.

OHIO
1803

MD. DEL.

ILL. IND.
1818 1816

VA.

MO.
1821

KY
1792

N.C.

PACIFIC
OCEAN

MEXICO

ARKANSAS
TERRITORY

TENN.
1796

S.C.

APPALACHIAN MTS.

ATLANTIC
OCEAN

MISS. ALA.
1817 1819

GA.

LA.
1812

Red R.

GULF OF MEXICO

FLORIDA TERRITORY
(Ceded through Adams-
Onís Treaty, 1819)

New states admitted
since 1790

------- Louisiana Purchase

0   250   500 Miles
0   250   500 Kilometers

MAP STUDY   *By 1824, the United States had expanded south and west, and 11 new states had joined the original 13. What treaty resolved a boundary dispute with British Canada? How was Florida acquired? What territory might be the source of a future dispute? Explain.*   See p. T43.

1.

1. **MAP READING** Ask: By 1824, which states had been carved from the Louisiana Purchase? Which states entered the Union after 1800?

in their own countries, they pledged to suppress any revolutionary movements in Europe. Americans were concerned that the alliance might look beyond Europe and try to restore Spanish control over its former colonies in Latin America.

American diplomats also worried about Russian expansion down the coast of Alaska toward Spanish California. Secretary Adams told Russia "that the American continents are no longer subjects for any new European colonial establishments." Russia agreed to drop any territorial claims south of the 54°40' line.

Britain shared the concern of the United States that other European countries might try to seize Spain's former American colo-
2. nies. In 1823, the British foreign minister proposed that the two countries issue a joint

declaration opposing intervention by the European alliance in the Americas. But Secretary of State Adams strongly objected. He feared that such a declaration might prevent the United States from annexing new territory, such as Texas, California, or Cuba.

Instead, the intensely patriotic Adams wanted the United States to make a declaration of its own. A joint statement with Britain, he explained, would make the United States appear "to come in as a cockboat in the wake of the British man-of-war." The cabinet finally agreed.

The Monroe Doctrine

With his advisers in agreement, Monroe issued a statement of United States policy concerning European influence in the New World.

233

2. **CRITICAL THINKING** Ask: Why might Britain have been concerned about other European countries gaining control of Spain's former colonies?

He chose to make the announcement during his annual message to Congress in December 1823.

Monroe proclaimed that the United States would not interfere in the internal concerns of European countries or in existing European colonies in the New World. It would, however, oppose all European intervention in the affairs of the independent countries in the Americas. The United States, Monroe warned, would view any intervention as an unfriendly act toward itself. "The American

MAP STUDY *Between 1800 and 1822, many new countries won independence in Latin America. Look at the map of the world on pages 842–843. Why do you think the United States felt the need to issue the Monroe Doctrine warning European powers not to intervene in the new nations?*

See p. T43.

2.

New Nations in Latin America

1821 Date of independence

Under foreign control

James Monroe was the "Last of the Cocked Hats"—the last Revolutionary War officer to become President. This painting shows him studying a map of the Louisiana Purchase. Just as Jefferson had made a bold move purchasing Louisiana, Monroe marked his place in history by issuing the Monroe Doctrine, a cornerstone of United States foreign policy.

1. **VISUAL EVIDENCE** Many public buildings in Washington are decorated with scenes from American history. This painting is found on a panel near one of the ceilings in the Capitol Building.

continents," Monroe declared, ". . . are henceforth not to be considered as subjects for future colonization by any European powers."

Monroe's message marked a milestone in United States diplomacy. Beginning with George Washington, Presidents had followed a policy of nonintervention in European affairs. In addition, Americans had always viewed European designs on the New World with suspicion. Monroe, in effect, united these principles in a single declaration that Europe and the New World should refrain from interfering in each other's internal affairs.

Impact of the Doctrine

Monroe's independent actions naturally annoyed the British government. Nevertheless, the British quietly informed other European governments that they agreed with Monroe's policy. Without British support, the American declaration would have meant little. The young nation lacked the might to back up its strong words. The British navy, as the European nations well knew, made Monroe's doctrine a reality.

Monroe's message was in tune with the strong nationalist feeling of the time. It showed once again America's pride as a nation. Americans throughout the country warmly applauded and endorsed it. Yet, the people soon forgot about the Monroe Doctrine. Its greatest significance lay in the future, when a new generation of leaders would unearth it and reestablish it as the country's most basic diplomatic policy.

See p. T43.

SECTION 5 REVIEW

1. **Identify:** (a) John Quincy Adams, (b) Rush-Bagot Agreement, (c) Convention of 1818.

2. (a) What three problems did Spanish-owned Florida pose for the United States? (b) How did the Adams-Onís treaty solve the problems? (c) What other boundary dispute was settled by the treaty?

3. (a) Why did the United States wait until 1822 to recognize the newly independent Latin American nations? (b) Why were Americans concerned about the new alliance in Europe?

4. What principles were set forth in the Monroe Doctrine?

5. **Critical Thinking** How did the Monroe Doctrine reflect American nationalism?

235

2. **MAIN IDEA** Have students identify the main points in Monroe's message to Congress.

3. **CRITICAL THINKING** What benefits do you think the U.S. expected to gain from the Monroe Doctrine?

CHAPTER 11 REVIEW

Summary

1. **After the War of 1812, Americans enjoyed an Era of Good Feelings.** Decisions by the Supreme Court under John Marshall added to the sense of unity by strengthening the national government.

2. **The Industrial Revolution spread to the United States from Great Britain.** New inventions, the factory system, and new means of raising capital contributed to the growth of industry. The changes enhanced national pride but created divisions as well.

3. **Henry Clay's American System reflected the nationalism of the period.** It called for a protective tariff, a new national bank, and federal aid to transportation. The people's reaction to the American System was mixed.

4. **Westward migration sparked a demand for improvements in transportation.** New roads and canals, as well as the invention of the steamboat, strengthened the ties between regions and promoted economic growth.

5. **President Monroe and his secretary of state, John Quincy Adams, followed a policy of national expansion.** They gained title to Florida and settled borders with British and Spanish territories. The Monroe Doctrine provided the basis for American foreign policy in later years.

See p. T43.

Vocabulary

Match each term at left with its definition or description at right.

1. factory system
2. capital
3. limited liability
4. interchangeable parts
5. bank notes

a. reduced responsibility for debts
b. paper money
c. method of organizing labor
d. money for investment
e. identical components

See p. T43.

Chapter Checkup

1. (a) How did President James Monroe symbolize the Era of Good Feelings? (b) In what ways was he a part of the Revolutionary War generation?

2. (a) How did the status of the Supreme Court change while John Marshall was Chief Justice? (b) How did the Marshall Court increase the authority of the national government? (c) Why did this Court's decisions contribute to the spirit of national unity?

3. (a) Why was labor scarce in the United States in the early 1800s? (b) What groups of people did manufacturers rely on as a result? (c) How did the Boston Associates treat their workers at the Lowell mills?

4. How was industrialization both a force for unity and a force for division in the United States?

5. (a) Explain how, according to Henry Clay, the Tariff of 1816 would help the United States become more self-sufficient. (b) Why did representatives from the West, the South, and the Middle Atlantic states tend to support the tariff?

6. (a) Why did a national bank seem necessary in 1816? (b) How did the second Bank of the United States contribute to the onset of panic in 1819? (c) What other factors contributed to the panic?

7. (a) Why did westward movement lead to demands for better transportation? (b) How did better roads, canals, and steamboats help bind the nation together?

236

8. (a) Why did President Monroe issue the Monroe Doctrine? (b) How did the doctrine reflect the nationalism of the period?

See p. T44.

Critical Thinking

1. **Recognizing Relationships** Which political, social, and economic developments contributed to the growing sense of nationalism and national unity between 1816 and 1824?

2. **Analyzing a Quotation** President Monroe stated, "The existence of parties is not necessary to free government." How did his statement reflect American political traditions of an earlier era?

See p. T44.

Connecting Past and Present

1. Federal aid to transportation has greatly expanded since Henry Clay introduced his American System. How does the federal government aid transportation today?

2. Henry Clay and other supporters of a protective tariff argued that it would help infant American industries get a start. Do you think the country's industries need a protective tariff today? Why or why not?

3. The Erie Canal has largely fallen into disuse, but the St. Lawrence Seaway and other canals do a brisk business even today. Why might canals be useful in a day of fast planes and superhighways?

4. When President Monroe issued the Monroe Doctrine, his chief concern was the prospect of Spain's regaining control over its former American colonies. What concerns affect United States policy toward Latin America today? Do you think the Monroe Doctrine is still useful? Why or why not?

See p. T44.

Developing Basic Skills

1. **Inferring** Reread the section on the Marshall Supreme Court described on pages 218–219. Study the Constitution and decide which clause or clauses the Court might have used to defend its actions.

2. **Map Reading** Study the map on page 233. (a) What is the topic of the map? (b) What treaty established the northern boundary of the Louisiana Purchase? (c) What treaty established the southern boundary of the Louisiana Purchase? (d) How did the Adams-Onís Treaty change the status of Florida?

3. **Researching** Using library resources, list the government offices held by Henry Clay, John C. Calhoun, and Daniel Webster. Based on what you learn, why do you think these three men had such a great impact on American politics in the years during and after the war of 1812?

WRITING ABOUT HISTORY

Writing a Summary

A summary is a short report for which you use only one source of information. The source may be an article, a speech, or a book. A summary contains only the main ideas. To help pinpoint the main ideas of the source, read the material and then ask yourself the following questions: *Who? What? When? Where? Why?* and *How?* After you have written the summary, review the original source to make sure you have not left out anything important.

Practice: Choose a subsection of this chapter such as "The Monroe Doctrine" and write a summary of it.

When the American republic was launched in the 1790s, it was young in more ways than one. Not only had it existed as a nation for only a few years, but also its people themselves were youthful. According to the first census in 1790, nearly half of the white men living in the United States were under age 16. The 1790 census collected much less information about free blacks, slaves, and women, but they too were relatively young.

Why was the American population so youthful? In part, this youth resulted from an extremely high birthrate. The average American woman bore about seven children during her lifetime, compared with an average today of fewer than two children. Disease took such a high toll that only about half the population lived beyond age 45. Today many people live into their seventies or eighties.

Differences From Europe   The young nation was different from the older countries in Europe. In those early days, visitors commented on the obvious freedom enjoyed by American children. American youngsters seemed more independent and less respectful than European children.

Relations between parent and child became even more informal as Americans moved west. A German visitor in the mid-1800s observed a father and his 14-year-old son riding together on a train. "They had long been talking on a footing of equality," he noted. "At last, to while away the time, they began to sing together. . . . There was no attempt at keeping up the dignity of a parent, as might have been considered necessary and proper with us." In 1905, another traveler noted, "Daughters are much with their mothers, and they become their companions younger than they do in Europe."

In fact, youth has always been celebrated in American culture. As a result of the American belief in democracy, the young and old are on a more equal footing than they are in other parts of the world. "Have you reverence enough among your people?" one worried Englishman asked the poet Walt Whitman. "Do the American children respect and obey their parents sufficiently . . . ?" Whitman replied, "Your old world has been soaked and saturated in reverence. We are laying here in America the basements and foundation rooms of a new era."

1. **VISUAL EVIDENCE** Ask: How many generations are presented in this family portrait?

1. *In the early 1800s, large extended families were common. The new nation had a high proportion of young people, which added to its vigor and growth. On farms, children worked from an early age to help support the family.*

238

A Young Nation Politically, younger leaders have often played a key role in directing the nation. Delegates to the Constitutional Convention were remarkably young. Five of them were under 30; Alexander Hamilton was 32; and James Madison, 36. Only four members were over 60. It was the youthful "War Hawks" like John Calhoun and Henry Clay who led the charge into the War of 1812. Teddy Roosevelt, one of the most active Presidents, took office at the age of 42. John F. Kennedy was 43 when he took office.

When the tide of immigrants to the United States swelled in the late 1800s, the youngest newcomers often led the way in adjusting to American life. Jane Addams, who worked with immigrants in Chicago during the 1890s, noted that parents "count upon the fact that their children learn the English language and American customs before they themselves do and act not only as interpreters of the language . . . but as buffers between them and Chicago. . . ."

In the twentieth century, young people have continued to set the pace in American culture. The 1920s celebrated bold young fliers like Charles Lindbergh and Amelia Earhart, who flew solo across the Atlantic. College campuses were the setting for fads, fashions, and popular literature. The 1960s, too, were a time when youth was prominent. President Kennedy's Peace Corps sent young volunteers all over the world. The young were also at the center of movements seeking greater civil rights for blacks, Hispanics, and women. Their tastes and lifestyles altered the habits of adults as well.

Enthusiasm and Experience Inevitably, people will question whether Americans have struck the right balance between youth and age. The young favor new styles, new faces, new experiments. "What old people say you cannot do, you try and find that you can. Old deeds for old people, and new deeds for new," proclaimed Henry David Thoreau in *Walden*. But youthful enthusiasm can lead to excess. Those who rush to take up the new and the untried are likely to make the same mistakes their parents did during their own youth.

This detail of a watercolor shows young women attending an evening school where they learned reading, writing, and homemaking skills.

1.

1. **VISUAL EVIDENCE** Ask: To what social or economic class do these young girls seem to belong?

Indeed, the study of history is one way that young people can temper their enthusiasm for the new with a knowledge of the past. As the philosopher George Santayana once said, "Those who cannot remember the past are condemned to repeat it." Without the guidance of age and tradition, some people worry that youth will have no jumping-off point from which to launch its experiments.

In coming years, the relation of youth to age will become even more crucial. After World War II, a baby boom among young couples made the population of the United States again more youthful. But those who were children in the 1950s will be the older Americans of the 2000s. With advances in medicine increasing longevity, the percentage of older Americans will increase steadily.

What responsibilities do the youth of America have to their parents and grandparents? How will society balance the vigor of youth with the experience of age? These are important questions that new generations of Americans will have to answer. Yet a nation that encourages new ideas and new directions will always hold the energy and boldness of youth in high regard.

See p. T44.
1. How have Europeans seen the place of youth in American society?

2. **Critical Thinking** Do you think that people can learn from the experience of others? Why or why not?

Notable Americans

Catharine Beecher

Catharine Beecher was born in Long Island, New York, in 1800. Like many other families of the time, the Beechers were a large family. Their talents and accomplishments, however, made them one of the most extraordinary of the 1800s.

Catharine was the oldest child of Lyman and Roxana Beecher. Besides Catharine,

1. **VISUAL EVIDENCE** Ask: Why do you think Catharine Beecher was photographed holding a pen and paper?

Catharine Beecher (1800–1872), shown later in
1. *life, grew up in a large, exceptionally talented family. She founded a school for women in Hartford, Connecticut, in 1824 and later set up several others in the Midwest. In her seventies, she entered Cornell University, ignoring the fact that no facilities were available for women.*

Lyman and Roxana had seven other children who survived infancy. After Roxana died, Lyman remarried and had three more children who lived to adulthood.

In the early years, Lyman was the pastor of the local Presbyterian church. The young family struggled along on his wages of $300 a year and firewood supplied by the congregation.

To supplement their income, Lyman and Roxana opened a school. There Roxana and her sister Mary, who lived with them, taught English, French, painting, embroidery, and the latest rage—chemistry.

Catharine herself was a somewhat reluctant student. She recalled later, "Oh, the mournful, despairing hours when I saw the children at their sports, and was confined till I had picked out the bad stitches, or remedied other carelessnesses. . . ."

Lyman Beecher was attached to his children and devoted a great deal of time not only to their spiritual upbringing but also to entertaining them. As the oldest child, Catharine occupied a special place in the household. Later she wrote: "I remember [my father] . . . as a playmate. . . . He taught me to catch fish and I was his constant companion, riding . . . to the villages around, where he went to hold meetings."

Catharine also recalled, "There was a free and easy way of living, more congenial to liberty and society than to conventional rules." This is not to say there was no discipline. Lyman expected immediate obedience from his children and did not "spare the rod." Any harshness, however, was softened by his obvious affection.

When Catharine was nine, the family moved to Litchfield, Connecticut. Here Lyman Beecher was spiritual adviser to Miss Sarah Pierce's School for "young ladies." Allowed to attend the school free of charge, his daughters received an education superior to that of most women of the time.

Catharine's relatively carefree childhood ended in 1816 when her mother died of consumption. Because she was the oldest, many of the responsibilities for the younger children fell to Catharine. It was with both resentment and relief that she welcomed her stepmother Harriet Porter the next year.

In the years that followed, the Beecher children continued to grow and develop. Of Lyman Beecher's eleven children, ten pursued professional careers. Catharine Beecher became a noted educational reformer, a writer on morality and religion, an avid promoter of education for women, and the author of a best-selling book, *The Treatise on Domestic Economy*. Edward Beecher was the first president of Illinois College. Harriet Beecher Stowe was the author of *Uncle Tom's Cabin*. Henry Ward Beecher was a famous preacher. Isabella Beecher Hooker was an advocate of women's rights. James Beecher was a missionary in China and a Civil War general. Lyman Beecher, said a contemporary, was "the father of more brains than any man in America."

See p. T44.

1. What advantages and disadvantages did Catharine have as the oldest child?

2. **Critical Thinking** How would you account for the unusually high level of achievement of the Beechers?

Abraham Lincoln's Education

Children who grew up with the young nation learned by "doing." One of the most remarkable examples of this upbringing was Abraham Lincoln. Born in Kentucky in 1809, Lincoln attended a one-room log schoolhouse with a dirt floor and no windows. By the time the family had moved to Indiana, young Abe's formal education was mostly behind him. But Lincoln took every opportunity to satisfy his thirst for learning. His famous biographer, Carl Sandburg, quotes Lincoln: "The things I want to know are in books; my best friend is the man who'll get me a book I ain't read." The reading below is from Lincoln's own account of his childhood, published in 1859.

My father, at the death of his father, was but six years of age, and he grew up literally without education. He removed from Kentucky to what is now Spencer County, Indiana, in my eighth year. We reached our new home about the time the state came into the Union. It was a wild region, with many bears and other wild animals still in the woods. There I grew up. There were some schools, so called, but no qualification was ever required of a teacher beyond readin', writin', and cipherin'. If a straggler supposed to understand Latin happened to sojourn in the neighborhood, he was looked upon as a wizard. There was absolutely nothing to excite ambition for education. Of course, when I came of age I did not know much. Still, somehow, I could read, write, and cipher, but that was all. I have not been to school since. The little advance I now have upon this store of education, I have picked up from time to time under the pressure of necessity.

Adapted from Abraham Lincoln, *Autobiography*, 1859.

See p. T44.

1. How did Lincoln seem to have gotten his education?

2. **Critical Thinking** Writing about his youthful experiences, what character traits does Lincoln reveal?

Unit Four AN ERA OF EXPANSION

During the early 1800s, Americans became more interested in politics.

1835 Osceola led the Seminoles when they resisted being moved from Florida to Oklahoma.

	1820	1830	1840
POLITICS AND GOVERNMENT	**1821** Stephen Austin founds American colony in Texas		**1838** Southern Indians follow "Trail of Tears" to Oklahoma
SOCIETY AND CULTURE	**1821** Cherokee adopt Sequoyah's alphabet	**1831** *The Liberator* founded to fight for abolition of slavery	
ECONOMICS AND TECHNOLOGY	**1820** Stevens steam engine is used to pull a train	**1834** Mechanical reaper makes harvesting wheat easier	
WORLD EVENTS	**1821** Mexico wins independence from Spain	**1832** Santa Anna comes to power in Mexico	
	Monroe	Adams	Jackson	Van Buren

The cotton gin, invented by Eli Whitney, helped create the Cotton Kingdom in the South.

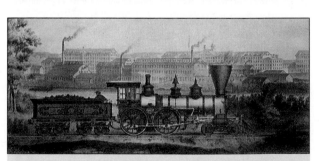

1830s The first commercial railroads went into operation in the 1830s.

242

UNIT OUTLINE

1844 The telegraph, perfected by Samuel Morse, made communication faster.

Spanish and Mexican influence remained in the Southwest even after the United States had annexed the area.

1840	1850	1860

1848 United States acquires the Southwest
and California from Mexico

1848 Convention for   **1856** Wilberforce College
women's rights held at Seneca Falls   founded for black students

1846 Howe   **1851** *Flying Cloud* sails to
invents sewing machine   California in record time

1845 Famine in Ireland   **1854** Japan allows trade
brings immigrants to America   with United States

| Tyler | Polk | Fillmore | Pierce | Buchanan | Lincoln |

Harrison   **Taylor**

1848 The discovery of gold at Sutter's Mill led to a gold rush in California.

Slaves feared auctions, such as this one, because families were often broken up.

243

A Democracy for the People

12

(1824–1844)

CHAPTER OUTLINE

1 Emergence of a New Party System

2 Rise of the Common People

3 Strengthening the National Government

4 Hard Times

CHAPTER OBJECTIVES After completing this chapter, students should be able to
1. describe how democracy grew in the 1820s.
2. describe Jackson's handling of domestic issues.
3. list causes and results of the Panic of 1837.

CHAPTER PREVIEW Read students this comment, made by Alexis de Tocqueville in 1830: "It is difficult to say what place is taken up in the life of an American by his concern for politics. To take a hand in the regulation of society and to discuss it is his biggest concern. . . . Even the women frequently attend public meetings. . . ." Ask: Why would a European find it unusual for ordinary people to take part in politics?

The boy was only 13, but he was sure that he was old enough to fight in the American Revolution. The British officer who captured the young rebel thought otherwise. To give the lad a lesson in respect, the arrogant officer ordered him to clean his boots. History has not recorded exactly what the boy replied, but it must have been defiant. Angered, the officer unsheathed his saber and slashed the youngster, who raised his arms in defense. His left hand was sliced to the bone and a deep wound cut into his forehead, leaving a white scar that remained visible for the rest of his life.

It would take 34 years for the boy to exact his revenge. But when he repaid the British for the blow, it was for keeps. The boy's name was Andrew Jackson. He grew up to lead the Americans to victory over the British at the battle of New Orleans in 1815. Later, he became President of the United States.

The scar Jackson received that day in 1781 was the first of many he would receive in his 78 years. Born in the backwoods of South Carolina, Jackson spent his adult life in Tennessee, where he lived an adventurous frontier life. No stranger to brawls, gambling, and duels, he had a violent temper, little sense of humor, and a poor education. One childhood acquaintance, on hearing the news that Jackson was running for President, exclaimed, "If Andrew Jackson can be President, anybody can!"

But Jackson's virtues more than overcame his shortcomings. A loving husband, he was fearless, principled, and strong. His troops, marveling at his endurance, nicknamed him "Old Hickory," after the toughest wood they knew. The general public also thought well of him. As the first President elected from a state outside the original 13, he represented America's frontier and, to many, its future.

President Jackson was not exactly a common man, for he had become a wealthy landowner who owned more than 150 slaves. But he always thought of himself as the champion of the common people. Of the four Presidents who served from 1824 to 1844, he did the most to increase the prestige and power of the presidency and the national government.

1.

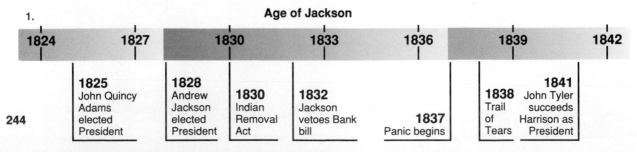

Age of Jackson

| 1824 | 1827 | 1830 | 1833 | 1836 | 1839 | 1842 |

1825 John Quincy Adams elected President

1828 Andrew Jackson elected President

1830 Indian Removal Act

1832 Jackson vetoes Bank bill

1837 Panic begins

1838 Trail of Tears

1841 John Tyler succeeds Harrison as President

1. TIME LINE QUESTION Ask: Who was President when the Indian Removal Act was passed?

Election day in the 1800s had a holiday spirit, as shown in this detail from a
1. painting of Independence Square in Philadelphia. As voting requirements were
eased, most white men gained the right to vote. Leaders like Andrew Jackson
urged their supporters to make their influence felt in government.

1. **VISUAL EVIDENCE** The painting was by John L. Krimmel, a German immigrant who arrived in Philadelphia in 1810. Ask: Why would an immigrant be especially attracted to a scene like this one?

Emergence of a New Party System

READ TO UNDERSTAND

■ Why John Quincy Adams had difficulty carrying out his policies.

■ Why the Republicans split into two parties in the election of 1828.

■ How sectional differences influenced the elections of 1824 and 1828.

2. ■ *Vocabulary:* party platform.

In 1820, James Monroe's supporters had reveled in the Era of Good Feelings. Madison observed that Americans seemed to be "one great family with a common interest." Who could dispute him? The Federalist party was all but dead, and Jeffersonian Republicans were presiding over the westward expansion of their young nation.

Americans did not yet realize that their interests remained too diverse to be fully represented by one party. But by the end of Monroe's second term, a new party system

had begun to take shape. And before long, democratic reforms enabled more people to participate in the government of their nation than ever before.

The Election of 1824

As the presidential election of 1824 approached, the large number of presidential hopefuls revealed the sectional divisions in Thomas Jefferson's old Republican party. Four major candidates emerged, and each tended to draw strength from a different section of the country.

Henry Clay, the Kentuckian who was speaker of the House, had the support of many westerners. William Crawford, Monroe's secretary of the treasury, attracted followers from his native Georgia and other southeastern states. John Quincy Adams, Monroe's able secretary of state, was popular in New England. Andrew Jackson, hero of the battle 3. of New Orleans, had strong support in the states of the old Southwest.

The four-way race between the candidates resulted in a deadlock. Jackson won more popular votes than any other presidential **245** candidate, but no one received a majority of

2. **VOCABULARY** Have students look up this term in the glossary before they begin reading.

3. **PRESIDENTS** Adams wrote his father at age 9: "I wish, Sir, you would . . . advise me how to proportion my studies and my play."

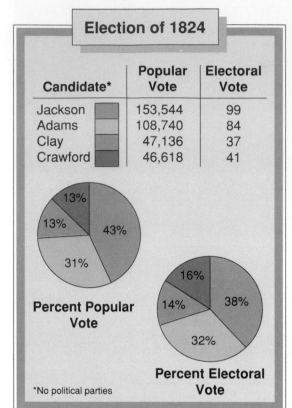

Election of 1824

Candidate*	Popular Vote	Electoral Vote
Jackson	153,544	99
Adams	108,740	84
Clay	47,136	37
Crawford	46,618	41

Percent Popular Vote

13%
13%
43%
31%

Percent Electoral Vote

16%
14%
38%
32%

*No political parties

Source: *Historical Statistics of the United States*

GRAPH STUDY *In the 1824 presidential election, no candidate won*
1. *a majority of the electoral vote, and, as required by the Constitution, the House of Representatives chose the President. Based on the graphs above, why did the House's choice of John Quincy Adams seem unfair to Andrew Jackson?* See p. T46.

1. **GRAPH READING** Ask: How many electoral votes short of a majority was Jackson?

the 261 electoral college votes. Jackson had 99 electoral votes; Adams, 84; Crawford, 41; and Clay, 37. According to the Constitution, the election would have to be decided by the House of Representatives, whose members would choose from among the top three candidates. (See pages 859–860.)

Since Henry Clay had come in fourth, he was eliminated. But he had enough power and influence in the House to determine the outcome of the election. Clay endorsed Adams, whose principles were closest to his own, allowing Adams to win on the first ballot. Adams then appointed Clay his secretary of state, a position that had often been a stepping stone to the presidency.

Cries of "corrupt bargain" rang out. Jackson and his supporters felt that Clay had helped Adams into the White House in re-

turn for a powerful position from which to launch his own next presidential campaign. In fact, no deal had been struck, but the accusation would prove quite damaging to both Adams and Clay.

Indignant at the result of the House vote, Jackson returned to Tennessee. Determined not to be cheated again, he and his supporters immediately started planning for the next election. The 1828 campaign thus began almost with Adams's inauguration.

John Quincy Adams

John Quincy Adams's presidency never recovered from the cloud of suspicion surrounding his election. This was unfortunate, for President Adams was a man of considerable talent and vision. A nationalist, he took a broad view of the powers of the national government. He wanted the federal government to take an active role in promoting economic growth. He also proposed a national university and a national observatory to foster the arts, literature, and science.

Those who insisted on a limited role for the federal government were aghast at the President's nationalist agenda. Jefferson accused him of trying to establish an aristocracy, a government run by a privileged few. Even Adams's friends considered him impractical. In the end, he lacked the personal skills to strengthen his party, promote his program, and overcome mistrust on all sides.

Parties in the Campaign of 1828

By 1828, the split within the Republican party had widened. Four years earlier, all four candidates had called themselves Republicans. But now Adams's supporters labeled themselves *National* Republicans, to emphasize the President's nationalist program. Andrew Jackson and his followers wanted to stress their opposition to the "aristocratic" Adams, so they called themselves *Democratic-Republicans*.

In the next few years, these party names would undergo further change as the split among Republicans widened. National Republicans renamed themselves the Whigs. And Democratic-Republicans became the Democrats, forerunners of the present-day Democratic party.

246

2. **PRESIDENTS** Jackson met a friend who said, "Well, General, we did all we could for you here, but the rascals at Washington cheated you out of it." Replied Jackson, "There was *cheating* and *corruption*, and *bribery*, too."

1. **PAST AND PRESENT** Have students research a recent political party platform and list the issues it covers.

2. **VOCABULARY** Jackson's troops nicknamed him Old Hickory, but Indian opponents during the Creek War (p. 213) called him Sharp Knife.

Party principles, like party names, were also still changing in 1828. **Party platforms**, or declarations of principles and programs, remained quite vague, and a wide range of opinion existed within each party. Jackson's advisers, for example, made few specific promises about what their candidate would do if
1. elected. They emphasized his personality instead of his policies.

All across the country, campaign managers used new methods to interest Americans in the election. They held barbecues, served roast ox, organized torchlight parades and bonfires, and provided fireworks displays.
2. Old Hickory, "man of the people," was celebrated everywhere.

Mudslinging was also part of this campaign. Jackson's supporters accused Adams of buying "gaming tables and gambling furniture" with government funds. (Actually, Adams had used his own money to buy a chess set and install a billiard table in the White House basement.) The Adams forces

claimed Jackson was an ignoramus from the backwoods who could not spell "more than about one word in four." Even worse, they accused Jackson of murder. Handbills were distributed, with pictures of the coffins of 12 men he supposedly executed.

3.

Jackson Triumphant

The 1828 campaign was rough, but it excited Americans as no other presidential election had. Jackson received 56 percent of the popular vote and won the presidency with 178 electoral votes to 83 for Adams. In part, this election demonstrated the major role that sectional differences continued to play in American politics. Adams won all the New England states but, outside of New England, he captured only Delaware and New Jersey. Jackson took the entire South and West.

Although Jackson ran as the candidate of the "common people," he attracted voters at every economic level. As expected, he

3. **ACTIVITY** Have students research the election campaign of 1828. If possible, they should bring to class examples of newspaper articles and handbills directed against both Jackson and Adams.

MAP AND GRAPH STUDY *In 1828, Andrew Jackson swept both the popular vote and the electoral vote. In what section of the country was the National Republican party strongest? Which areas of the country were gaining political power?* See p. T46.

4.

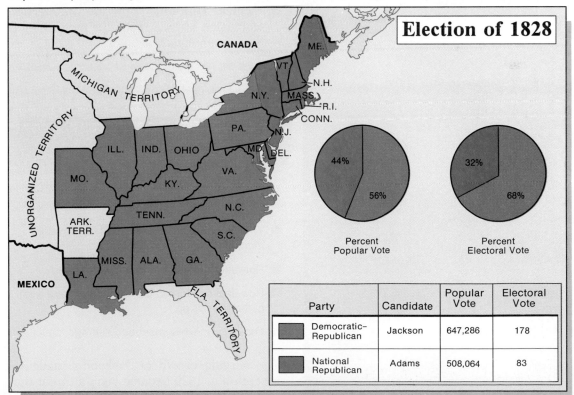

Election of 1828

Party	Candidate	Popular Vote	Electoral Vote
Democratic–Republican	Jackson	647,286	178
National Republican	Adams	508,064	83

Percent Popular Vote: 44% / 56%

Percent Electoral Vote: 32% / 68%

4. **GRAPH READING** Ask: Were Jackson and Adams closer in the popular or electoral vote? Can you explain why there is a difference between the two?

1. **READINGS** "Such a scene had never before been witnessed at the White House, and the aristocratic old Federalists saw, to their disgust, men whose boots were covered with the red mud of the unpaved streets standing on the satin-covered chairs to get a sight of the President of their choice," wrote one witness. Ask: How was Jackson different from the "aristocratic old Federalists"?

picked up strong support from southern planters and small farmers in the South and West, people who shared his background. But Jackson also captured the votes of small business leaders, factory workers, and urban artisans, or skilled craft workers. He won Pennsylvania's electoral votes and a majority of New York's. As it turned out, he was not simply the candidate of the rural South and West.

Andrew Jackson's inauguration turned into an event unlike anything the nation had ever seen. Great crowds cheered the general as he journeyed to Washington. Days before the ceremony, people from all over the country began pouring into the capital.

A roaring throng watched their hero being sworn in, then rushed to greet him at the White House. Ann Royall, a journalist, commented on the wild disorder that followed.

Andrew Jackson was an imposing figure. A handsome man with white, flowing hair, he stood
2. *tall and lean. As a former military man, Jackson was used to giving orders and being obeyed. His quick temper and self-confidence sometimes led to impulsive actions, and he tended to take political disputes personally.*

2. VISUAL EVIDENCE This portrait of Jackson is by Thomas Sully, who came to the United States from England at the age of nine.

They clambered upon the satin furniture with their muddy boots. . . . Only after disgraceful scenes in the parlors, in which even women got bloody noses, was the situation relieved by the device of setting tubs of punch on the lawn to lure the new "democracy" out of the house.

1.

To a horrified Supreme Court justice who was present, it seemed to be the beginning of "the reign of 'King Mob.'" To Jackson's admirers, democracy reigned in the White House.

See p. T46.

SECTION 1 REVIEW

1. **Identify:** (a) National Republicans, (b) Democratic-Republicans, (c) Old Hickory.

2. **Define:** party platform.

3. (a) How did John Quincy Adams win the presidency? (b) Why did some claim that his election was the result of a "corrupt bargain"?

4. How did the results of the election of 1828 reveal sectional differences in the United States?

5. **Critical Thinking** How did the election campaign of 1828 resemble modern election campaigns?

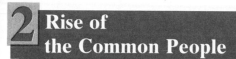

2 Rise of the Common People

READ TO UNDERSTAND

- What political changes marked the development of Jacksonian democracy.

- How Jacksonian democracy was limited.

- How Jackson forced the Indians to move west of the Mississippi.

- *Vocabulary:* white manhood suffrage, caucus. 3.

The surging crowd at Jackson's inaugural reception in 1829 became such a threat that aides had to help him slip out a rear exit. No

3. **VOCABULARY** Have students look up these terms in the glossary before they begin reading.

Many painters during Jackson's administration celebrated the life of the common people. William Sidney Mount originally used a formal style in his paintings—choosing classical and religious subjects. But he later turned to what he called "a
1. closer observation of nature." The setting for this painting, The Rustic Dance, is thought to be a tavern owned by his father.

1. **VISUAL EVIDENCE** Mount wrote in his journal, "Never paint for the few, but for the many." His style of painting scenes of everyday life with close attention to realistic detail is called *genre painting*.

matter: His followers stayed behind to celebrate the triumph of democracy. But did Jackson's victory mean that ordinary citizens would have more power? To what extent would the new President's democratic leanings leave their mark on the political system? To what extent would the system remain unchanged?

Political Reform

Even before Jackson's administration, popular enthusiasm for democracy had resulted in political changes. For one thing, the right to vote had been extended to more Americans. During colonial years, most political thinkers believed that the right to vote should be given only to property owners. It was assumed that such people had a vested interest in making society work. But most states had eliminated property requirements by 1828. They now permitted **white manhood suffrage,** that is, voting by all white males.

Popularly Chosen Electors Democratic developments continued throughout the Jacksonian era. They included changes in the method of selecting the President. The Constitution's framers had championed the idea of an electoral college in which each state cast its votes for a presidential candidate. They believed that the people themselves would not know enough about the candidates to make a wise choice. (See page 168.)

At first, most states left the choice of presidential electors to their own legislatures. But states gradually moved toward having the voters choose electors directly. By 1832, electors in all states except South Carolina were being picked by the voters.

1. **LOCAL HISTORY** Have students find out how delegates to the national party conventions are chosen in your state.

2. **ACTIVITY** Have students make a line graph from this data: percentage of adult white males voting—1824, 26%; 1828, 56%; 1832, 55%; 1836, 55%; 1840, 78%; 1844, 75%.

Nominating Conventions Political parties, too, became more democratic. Formerly, most presidential candidates were chosen by a secret party **caucus,** a meeting in which only a few members of Congress took part. By the mid-1830s, however, political parties were holding national conventions, at which delegates from all states had a voice in choosing their nominee. Party leaders might still dominate a particular convention, but the nominating process was becoming subject to the will of the people.

1.

These reforms had an important impact on American politics. The voter turnout in presidential election years rose from 26 percent of eligible voters in 1824, to 56 percent in 1828, to 78 percent in 1840. Such widespread voter participation was new in national politics.

2.

Limits to Jacksonian Democracy

Although white males had a greater voice in government under Jackson, other groups did not. Neither women nor most black Americans had any power to choose their leaders. Some states had allowed free blacks to vote, but a number of those states repealed that right during the 1820s and 1830s. Slaves continued to be denied all political rights.

The idea of political equality would evolve slowly. For black men, it would gain wider acceptance as a result of the movement to abolish slavery in the mid-1800s. (You will read about these developments later in this unit.) For women, it would gain momentum as a result of changes in the workplace and increased educational opportunities. But to most white Americans in the first half of the nineteenth century, limiting political activity to white men seemed normal and proper.

A Policy of Indian Removal

Native Americans also had no part in Jacksonian democracy. Under the Jackson administration, thousands of Indians were forcibly removed from their homes in the East and relocated west of the Mississippi River. Their tragic plight was rooted in a long-simmering conflict over land rights.

For generations, American settlers had eyed the fertile land owned by Indians in western Georgia and parts of North Carolina, Tennessee, Florida, Alabama, and Mississippi. Organized attempts by Indians to resist the encroachment of such settlers generally had failed.

As you read earlier, Tecumseh's confederation of Indian nations collapsed after his death in the War of 1812. (See pages 209–210.) In the Treaty of Ghent ending that war, the British insisted that the United States "restore to such tribes . . . all possessions . . . which they have enjoyed or been entitled to . . . previous to such hostilities." The federal government ignored the provision, and American settlers continued to push Indians westward.

By the mid-1820s, about 125,000 Native Americans still lived east of the Mississippi. Chief among them were five southern nations, the Cherokee, Creek, Choctaw, Chicasaw, and Seminole. The people of these nations, known as the "civilized tribes," had adopted many customs of white Americans. Some Indians were prosperous farmers; others owned large plantations. But President Jackson sympathized with the settlers who wanted the land for themselves.

President Jackson was determined to complete the forced removal of Indian nations living east of the Mississippi. His first opportunity to act came soon after he took office. In 1828, the Cherokee in Georgia had tried to safeguard their land by writing a constitution establishing an independent state within the boundaries of Georgia. But the state of Georgia, saying that the Cherokee were subject to its laws, refused to recognize the Indians' constitution.

3.

The Cherokee then appealed to the Supreme Court, which ruled in their favor. Chief Justice Marshall held that the "laws of Georgia can have no force" in Cherokee lands. The Indian nations, he ruled, were "distinct political communities, having political boundaries, within which their authority is exclusive."

Jackson, in keeping with the theory of states' rights, held that the federal government could not interfere with the right of the state of Georgia to remove the Indians.

3. **BACKGROUND** Jackson instructed army officials negotiating with the Indians: "Say to my red Choctaw children . . . my white children of Mississippi have extended their law over their country. . . . Where they are now, say to them, their father cannot prevent them from being subject to the laws of the state."

Sequoyah: Creator of a Written Language

Like other Cherokees, Sequoyah feared that white people would overpower his nation. But he had an idea. If the Cherokee people only had a way of writing their language, they could learn about events far and wide and, most important, be independent of white people. But who would create this writing system? At that time, Cherokees did not know how to read and write in any language.

Sequoyah, who had been a skilled hunter and trapper before being crippled in an acci-

dent, took up the task himself. He rejected the idea of pictographs—pictures to represent words—because too many would be necessary. He recognized, however, after careful study of the Cherokee language, that the entire vocabulary of the language was based on only 86 syllables.

Sequoyah then devised a symbol for each syllable of the Cherokee language. He used letters from the English, Greek, and Hebrew alphabets, as well as other symbols he invented himself. In 1821, 12 years after he began his work, Sequoyah had completed a writing system. It was known as a syllabary.

Sequoyah's syllabary was easy to learn, and before long, the Cherokees adopted the system. They used it to create a written translation of the Bible and to publish a weekly newspaper, the *Cherokee Phoenix.*

1.

The Cherokee people see Sequoyah as one of their giants and honor his memory. Some want to revive his syllabary. Other Americans have paid him tribute by naming the mighty redwood tree of the Pacific coast, the sequoia, after him.

See p. T46.

1. Why did Sequoyah want his people to have a writing system?

2. Critical Thinking   How is Sequoyah's syllabary different from the English alphabet?

---

1. **DISCUSSION** The phoenix was a mythical bird that rose out of its own ashes after death. Ask: Why might the Cherokee have chosen this name for their newspaper?

2. **CRITICAL THINKING** Ask: What does this incident reveal about the balance of power among the branches of government?

Jackson is reported to have said, "John Marshall has made his decision. Now let him enforce it." The Cherokee were left without 2. legal protection.

The Trail of Tears

3. In 1830, Congress passed the Removal Act. The effect of the act was to force eastern Indians to sell their lands at unfair prices and then to move to barren territory in what is now Oklahoma. With the scales of justice

tipped against them, thousands of Indians were forced to embark on a "Trail of Tears."

In 1838, soldiers drove more than 15,000 Cherokee, plus remnants of the Choctaw, Creek, and other tribes, on a westward march to Oklahoma. Provided with little or no cloth- 4. ing or shelter, sick, and suffering emotionally after being wrenched from their homes, thousands of Indians died along the way. An eyewitness, the Reverend Evan Jones, described the scene in the *Baptist Missionary Magazine.*

3. **BACKGROUND** Some Congressmen, including Daniel Webster, fought the Removal Act.

4. **GEOGRAPHY** The act did not consider the rights of Indian nations already inhabiting territory allocated to eastern Indians. (movement)

251

1. **READINGS** One Creek said: "Brothers! I have listened to many talks from our great white father. When he first came over the wide waters, he was but a little man. . . . But when the white man had warmed himself before the Indians' fire and filled himself with their hominy, he became very large . . . and he said, 'Get a little further, lest I tread on thee.'"

The Cherokee are nearly all prisoners. They had been dragged from their homes and encamped at the forts and military places, all over the nation. In Georgia, especially, multitudes were allowed no time to take anything with them except the clothes they had on. . . . It is a painful sight. The property of many has been taken and sold before their eyes for almost nothing—the sellers and buyers, in many cases, having combined to

1. cheat the poor Indians.

Some Indian nations resisted removal with force. The Sac and the Fox, unhappy with their new lands, recrossed the Mississippi River in 1832 to return to Illinois. Led by Chief Blackhawk, they launched a series of attacks to regain their homelands. United States Army troops and state militia defeated the Sac and Fox in the Blackhawk War that followed.

A larger war broke out in Florida, where the Seminole people under Chief Osceola refused to leave their homeland. Fugitive slaves who had taken refuge with the Seminole supported their stand. The resulting war lasted from 1835 until 1838, when the United States Army finally defeated and removed the Seminole. By 1844, only a few scattered groups of Native Americans remained east of the Mississippi River.

2. **BACKGROUND** Osceola was captured while meeting with U.S. officers under a flag of truce. He was put in prison, where he later died.

MAP STUDY *Under the Removal Act of 1830, some 100,000 southern Indians were forced to march under military guard to a reservation in the West. How many miles did the Cherokee have to walk on this "Trail of Tears"?* See p. T46.

Indian Removal, 1830-1842

3. **MAP READING** Ask: In which states did the Chickasaw live? How far were the Creek Indians forced to travel?

Native Americans who resisted government efforts to force them westward were driven out by the army. This painting by Mary Ann Thompson shows a group of Cherokee moving along what they called the Nuna-da-ut-sun'y—"The Trail Where They Cried," or Trail of Tears. On the 116-day journey, more than one out of every four Indians died from illness and exhaustion.

1.

See p. T46. **1. READING** Ralph Waldo Emerson said, "Such a denial of justice, and such deafness to screams for mercy were never heard in time of peace since the earth was made."

SECTION 2 REVIEW

1. **Identify:** (a) Removal Act, (b) Trail of Tears, (c) Blackhawk, (d) Osceola.

2. **Define:** (a) white manhood suffrage, (b) caucus.

3. (a) What group of Americans gained the vote during the early 1800s? (b) How had the selection of presidential electors changed by 1832?

4. What groups were denied political participation under Jacksonian democracy?

5. (a) What was the ruling of the Supreme Court on the forced removal of the Cherokee from Georgia? (b) What was Jackson's reaction?

6. **Critical Thinking** Jackson called Indians "subjects" of the government and whites "citizens." What do you think he meant by this distinction?

3 Strengthening the National Government

READ TO UNDERSTAND

■ Why Jackson adopted the spoils system.

■ How Jackson handled the controversy over states' rights.

■ Why Jackson wanted to destroy the second Bank of the United States.

■ *Vocabulary:* spoils system.

2.

Because Jackson had made no specific campaign promises, no one was quite sure what policies he meant to pursue as President. Daniel Webster wrote, "No one knows what he will do when he comes. My opinion is . . . that he will bring a breeze with him. Which way it will blow I cannot tell." Before long, however, it was clear that Old Hickory in-

253

---

1. **VISUAL EVIDENCE** Have students compare this painting to the one on p. 245. Ask: Do the painters seem to have similar views of American democracy in the 1800s?

2. **DISCUSSION** Organize a class debate on the spoils system. Ask: Does the spoils system exist today? Explain.

tended to command the nation as firmly as he had led troops in battle.

Jackson's policies had far-reaching consequences in two areas. First, because Jackson saw himself as the protector of the common people, he strongly opposed government policies that protected privileged groups. Second, seeing himself as the leader of a truly united nation, he asserted federal authority whenever he believed it was needed. Although he believed in states' rights, Old Hickory was also a strong defender of the federal union.

A Democratic Approach

Jackson's democratic leanings affected how he organized his administration. Like other Presidents, he appointed cabinet members. But Jackson often did not see eye to eye with them. For advice, he turned instead to a small group of editors, officeholders, and old Tennessee associates. This group came to be known as his "Kitchen Cabinet."

In filling lower government positions, President Jackson removed officeholders who opposed him politically and replaced them with faithful supporters. As one Jacksonian leader explained, "To the victors belong the spoils." The policy of treating political jobs

as rewards for loyalty became known as the **spoils system.**

The spoils system made good political sense because it strengthened Jackson's party by rewarding party workers. But the President initiated the spoils system for another reason as well. He believed that it furthered the ideals of democracy. Jackson thought that long-time officeholders saw their jobs as personal property, rather than as a public trust. Rotation in office would prevent such thinking. He also was convinced that most government jobs were simple enough that any intelligent person could perform them without special training. Thus Jackson attacked the idea that government workers were a special group set apart from the people.

All in all, Jackson replaced only about one fifth of those holding federal office in 1828. And some of those replacements were for misbehavior rather than for political reasons. Still, his actions set an unfortunate precedent for the future. Too often, government offices would be handed out to political cronies who would contribute little or nothing to public service. As you will read in Chapter 21, the spoils system frequently led to outright government corruption.   2.

The Tariff of Abominations

Ever since the nation's founding, Congress had levied tariffs on imported goods. Originally, the purpose of such taxes was to raise revenue. But tariffs also had a "protective" value, raising the price of inexpensive European products higher than American manufactured goods. Over the years, American manufacturers had repeatedly influenced Congress to raise tariffs.

In 1828, before Jackson's election, Congress enacted a new tariff. It was favored by New England manufacturers because it raised the prices of European imports that competed with their products. Southern planters, who regularly imported European goods in exchange for the cotton and other raw materials they exported, objected bitterly. Because the 1828 tariff inflated the price of imports, southerners argued that the tariff was, in effect, an indirect tax on their region. They called it the Tariff of Abominations.   3.

Personal campaigning was common in the early 1800s. Voters often made their choice based on a candidate's promises and appearance. George Caleb Bingham, who made this painting of a
1. *candidate trying to win undecided voters, had first-hand experience. He had run successfully for the Missouri legislature in 1846.*

3. **ACTIVITY** Have students draw a political cartoon about the tariff from the perspective of a southerner.

GREAT DEBATE

The Controversy Over States' Rights

John C. Calhoun of South Carolina, Jackson's Vice President, was the country's leading opponent of the Tariff of Abominations. At one time, Calhoun had been a nationalist. But by 1828, he was vigorously defending a state's right to free itself from unwanted control by the national government.

In an unsigned essay called the "South Carolina Exposition and Protest," Calhoun argued that the people of any state could nullify any federal law they believed to be unconstitutional. If a state convention declared a federal law null and void within that state, he said, its citizens did not have to obey it. Calhoun and his supporters had important reasons for taking this position: They were aware that the doctrine of states' rights could also be used to defend slavery from federal interference.

Calhoun raised an issue that had been debated since the Revolutionary War. Was the United States one indivisible nation with a supreme federal government? Or did the states have final say on how much national authority they would accept, as Jefferson and Madison had suggested in the Virginia and Kentucky resolutions of 1798? (See page 193.) The Constitution was not specific on the question of sovereignty.

In 1830, Senator Daniel Webster of Massachusetts and Senator Robert Hayne of South Carolina debated whether the states or the federal government held ultimate authority. Hayne defended the argument that states had the right to nullify federal laws. Webster rose to reply for the nationalists. An impressive man with booming voice and piercing black eyes, he brought all his debating skills to bear against Hayne.

Webster argued that the federal government, not the states, held final authority under the Constitution and that Calhoun's theory of nullification was illegal and unconstitutional. If any state could disregard a law whenever it wished, chaos would reign and the nation would collapse. The federal government was not the agent of the states, Webster continued, but the direct agent of the people.

"It is the people's Constitution," Webster affirmed, "the people's government, made for the people, made by the people, and answerable to the people." His final, ringing plea was "Liberty *and* Union, now and forever, one and inseparable!"

The Nullification Crisis

The dispute over nullification simmered for two more years, until Congress enacted another tariff law in 1832. The new law kept rates high and granted southerners little relief. Voters in South Carolina reacted angrily. A popularly elected state convention met in November 1832 and declared the tariff null and void in South Carolina.

This was too much for Jackson. He lashed out at such a rejection of federal authority. "If one drop of blood be shed there in defiance of the laws of the United States," he warned privately, "I will hang the first man of them I can get my hands on to the first tree I can find." Publicly, he vowed to uphold the law. In 1833, he asked Congress to pass a "force bill" allowing him, if need be, to call on the military to enforce the new tariff.

Despite his threats, Jackson moved cautiously. Eager to avoid pushing South Carolina into open rebellion, the President welcomed a compromise suggested by Henry Clay. Clay proposed a gradual reduction of tariff rates over a nine-year period to 20 percent. Would South Carolina accept the compromise? Since Clay's bill would lower tariff rates and since no other southern state sided with South Carolina in the dispute, the state legislature agreed to the compromise.

On March 1, 1833, Congress passed Clay's tariff bill, and Jackson signed it. The South Carolina convention then repealed its nullification of the earlier tariff law. South Carolina's challenge to the national government had failed, and the crisis passed. Jackson's bold stand—and his uncharacteristic restraint—had strengthened the role of the federal government and the presidency. ■

Jackson Against the Bank

When Andrew Jackson came into office, the second Bank of the United States was remarkably powerful. The federal government

255

2. DISCUSSION For years afterward, schoolchildren in many areas had to memorize Webster's speech. Ask: Where do you think this occurred?

3. MAIN IDEA Have students write a paragraph explaining the meaning of Webster's statement.

1. **VISUAL EVIDENCE** Ask: Do you think the artist approved of Jackson's veto? Explain.

2. **BIOGRAPHY** Nicholas Biddle (1786–1844) had been editor of a literary magazine. A wellborn, refined Philadelphian, Biddle stood for everything Jackson disliked.

Race over Uncle Sam's Course.
4th March 1833.

President Jackson believed the Bank of the United States was undemocratic. This cartoon shows the President trying to wield a presidential veto against
1. *plans to renew the Bank. Nicholas Biddle, the Bank's director, thought Jackson was an ignorant backwoodsman. "As to mere power," Biddle said, "I have been for years in the daily exercise of more personal authority than any President."*

the Bank. A wide variety of Americans also wanted to see it destroyed, although their reasons differed.

Many business leaders, state bankers, and speculators opposed the Bank because it did not issue enough currency in the form of paper money. For these groups, a large supply of money was vital to making quick investments and seizing economic opportunities as they arose.

By contrast, farmers in the South and West and factory workers in the East thought the Bank issued too much paper money. They preferred a "hard" currency of gold and silver coins, currency whose value did not easily change. The farmers argued that ordinary citizens had no way of knowing whether the bank notes they received for wages were really worth the amount printed on them. Like Jackson, both groups wanted to see the Bank destroyed.

Victory for the President

Controversy swirled around the Bank issue. And Henry Clay, who had his eye on the presidency, thought that he could manipulate it to his advantage.

The Bank's charter was due to expire in 1836, but Clay encouraged Nicholas Biddle, the Bank's director, to seek its renewal before the presidential election in 1832. Clay and Daniel Webster felt sure they could get the renewal bill through Congress. They were also sure that most Americans supported the Bank. If Jackson vetoed it, they reasoned, the National Republicans would have a ready-made issue for the approaching presidential campaign.

Congress passed the renewal bill in March 1832. President Jackson, sick in bed at the time, vetoed it, affirming, "The Bank is trying to kill me, but I will kill it!" His veto message attacked the Bank's constitutionality, its size and power, and its tendency to aid "the rich and powerful."

A few months later, the National Republican party nominated Henry Clay for President. As planned, Clay campaigned against Jackson's veto of the Bank. The voters, however, decisively backed Jackson for a second term. He won by an electoral vote of 219 to 49. Taking his victory as a mandate against

deposited all its revenue in the Bank, which was allowed to use this money without paying interest. The Bank also issued the only
2. national currency, in the form of bank notes. This gave it control of how much paper money was in circulation. If, for example, the Bank issued large numbers of notes, loans were
3. easier to obtain.

No one was more hostile to the Bank than President Andrew Jackson. As a private business, the Bank was responsible not to the government but to a small group of stockholders. Jackson condemned these men as agents of "special privilege" who grew rich with public funds. Jackson also argued that the Bank's power made it a corrupting influence in politics. Indeed, the Bank had distributed favors to government officials, some of whom were even on its payroll.

Was a national bank constitutional? The Supreme Court had ruled in *McCulloch* v. *Maryland* (1819) that it was. Jackson disagreed. He argued that Congress had no constitutional power to charter such a bank. The President was not alone in his opposition to

256

1. **TECHNOLOGY** Ask: How might modern public opinion polls have affected the Republican attempt to defeat Jackson?

2. **ECONOMICS** Have students debate the question of who was more responsible for this economic downturn—Biddle or Jackson.

the Bank, he resolved to destroy it immediately rather than wait until its charter expired in 1836.

1.

The President soon ordered all government deposits removed from the Bank. When the secretary of the treasury refused, Jackson fired him and appointed an old supporter, Attorney General Roger B. Taney (TAW nee), to the office. Taney began depositing federal revenues in state banks controlled by fellow Democrats. Opponents called them "pet banks."

Biddle counterattacked by refusing to extend new loans to customers and by demanding that existing loans be paid back immediately. With credit unavailable, businesses began to fail, and unemployment rose. Shocked business leaders begged Jackson to end his opposition to the Bank, just as Biddle had expected. Jackson refused, blaming the economic downturn on Biddle, who had clearly shown how powerful the Bank actually was.

2.

President Jackson eventually won this economic war of nerves. After the Bank's federal charter expired in 1836, the Bank continued to operate under a charter from Pennsylvania. But the Panic of 1837 (see page 258) weakened it further, and in 1841 it went out of business.

See p. T47.

SECTION 3 REVIEW

1. **Identify:** (a) Kitchen Cabinet, (b) Tariff of Abominations, (c) Robert Hayne, (d) Nicholas Biddle, (e) pet banks.

2. **Define:** spoils system.

3. What arguments did Jackson give to justify the spoils system?

4. (a) How did the Tariff of 1828 spark a controversy over states' rights? (b) Why was the issue of states' rights particularly important to southerners?

5. Why did Jackson oppose the second Bank of the United States?

6. **Critical Thinking** Does the spoils system further democracy? Why or why not?

4 Hard Times

READ TO UNDERSTAND

■ What strategy the Whigs pursued in the election of 1836.

■ What caused the Panic of 1837 and the depression that followed.

■ How the Whigs captured the presidency in the election of 1840.

Andrew Jackson, democrat, was remembered fondly by Americans long after he left public office. In *Moby Dick* (1851), Herman Melville would write that the "great democratic God . . . didst pick up Andrew Jackson from the pebbles" and place him "higher than a throne." Even though the first signs of an economic depression appeared during his second administration, Old Hickory left office as popular as ever. One of his last moves was to engineer the choice of his party's next presidential candidate.

The Election of 1836

The Democrats held their first national nominating convention in 1836. Jackson took great pains to ensure that Martin Van Buren, his Vice President, became the nominee. Van Buren faced bitter opposition from the National Republicans, who now called themselves the Whigs.*

3.

The Whigs were able to agree on their opposition to Jackson's policies, but they found it difficult to agree on what they were for. In general, they shared John Quincy Adams's faith that the United States could become a great nation on the basis of its wealth and growing industry. Many Whigs, supporting the goals of Henry Clay's American System, wanted the federal and state governments to take a more active role in encouraging the construction of canals, roads, and other internal improvements.

---

*The Whigs took their name from the British Whigs who had opposed King George III during the Revolutionary War. The Whig party in 1836 claimed that Jackson, or "King Andrew I," was acting like George III.

3. **BIOGRAPHY** Van Buren (1782–1862) was the first President born in the U.S. rather than the English colonies. He had served as a state senator, U.S. senator, governor of New York, and secretary of state under Jackson.

1. **CRITICAL THINKING** Ask: Do you think the Whigs controlled a majority of the votes in the House of Representatives in 1836? Why or why not?

2. **VOCABULARY** Tell students that *specie* means hard currency—that is, gold or silver.

In the North, a number of merchants and manufacturers supported the Whigs, as did educators, reformers, and commercial farmers. Southern bankers and planters, who felt that their region's prosperity was linked with the North's expanding commerce, also joined the Whig party.

Despite such support, the Whigs did not believe they were strong enough to run a single candidate for President. Instead, they decided to run three separate candidates, one popular in each section of the country: William Henry Harrison in the West, Daniel Webster in New England, and Hugh Lawson White in the South.

The Whigs hoped to prevent Van Buren from winning a majority in the electoral college. They wanted to throw the election into 1. the House of Representatives. But their strategy failed. Van Buren won a small majority of both the popular and the electoral vote. Unfortunately for the Democrats, Van Buren soon encountered an economic storm.

Depression Strikes

As President, Van Buren intended to follow the policies of his popular predecessor. But two months after his inauguration, a severe financial panic gripped the nation.

Land Speculation The Panic of 1837 had its roots in land speculation. A decade of prosperity had stimulated the purchase of western land on a greater scale than ever before. The federal government, which owned most of this land, offered it for sale to farmers and investors. Over 12 million acres (4.8 million hectares) were put on the block in 1835; over 20 million acres (8 million hectares) in 1836. The offers attracted speculators, who grabbed up huge tracts with hopes of reselling them at a high profit.

The effects of the massive land grab rippled through the economy. Many new landowners in the Southwest put their land into cotton. For a time, this expanded cotton supply found eager purchasers in eastern merchants and manufacturers. The large amount of money in circulation encouraged state governments to back extensive canal and railroad-building projects. Meanwhile, state banks eased credit terms.

Without a national bank to control the money supply, state bank notes flooded the country. But many of these notes were not backed by gold or silver. The approaching crisis began to take shape: What would happen if holders of large debts demanded that they be repaid in hard currency?

Specie Circular Shortly before Van Buren's election, President Jackson had become aware that an economic storm was brewing. He tried to slow land speculation and its effects by issuing a Specie Circular. The circu- 2. lar stated that public land could be paid for only in gold or silver. Jackson's move convinced prospective land buyers that the boom economy would not last forever. Land sales began to fall off.

Then, early in 1837, the price of cotton on the international market dropped sharply. For farmers who had mortgaged their farms to buy more land, this drop in prices spelled disaster. Without adequate profits from cotton sales, farmers could not repay their loans. The sagging land market collapsed.

Depression The depression that soon resulted was one of the most severe in the nation's history. Unable to reclaim outstanding loans, banks failed by the hundreds. Even a few state governments went bankrupt. As the consumer market shrank, factories closed and unemployment climbed. 3.

Many Americans blamed the Democratic administration for the economic hard times. But the administration was not directly responsible for the speculation that had caused the panic. President Van Buren attributed the crisis to current banking practices and urged Congress to restructure the United States Treasury. Congress complied in 1840, but the government did little else to combat the depression.

A Missed Opportunity for the Whigs

The Democrats renominated President Van Buren in 1840, but the continuing economic depression filled the party with gloom. The Whigs, on the other hand, saw their opportunity. The country was in the grip of hard times—due partly to the Democrats' "hard money" policies. With a popular candidate, they would surely seize victory.

3. **READING** One witness recorded the effects of the panic in his diary: "Matters worse and worse. . . . Workmen thrown out of employ by the hundred daily. Business at a stand; the coal mines in Pennsylvania stopped, and no fuel in prospect for next winter—delightful prospects, these."

1. **ACTIVITY** Have students imagine that they are moderating a debate between Van Buren and Harrison. Ask what questions they would ask both candidates.

The Whigs nominated General William Henry Harrison of Ohio, a military hero well known for his victory over Tecumseh at the Battle of Tippecanoe in 1811. To balance the ticket, they chose John Tyler, a conservative Virginian who favored states' rights, for Vice President.

The campaign of 1840 was one of the most colorful in the nation's history. With the slogan "Tippecanoe and Tyler Too," the Whigs set out to capture the presidency from Martin Van "Ruin." Taking a lesson in campaign tactics from the Democrats, who bemoaned, "We have taught them to conquer us," the Whigs portrayed Harrison as a western farmer, a man of the people who lived in a log cabin and loved hard cider. (Actually, he came from a distinguished Virginia family and lived rather elegantly.) People flocked to political rallies, parades, bonfires, and barbecues, where bands and other entertainers whipped up their enthusiasm.

The Whigs carefully avoided discussing any real issues and made sure that Harrison said nothing of substance. "Let him say not one single word about his principles, or his creed," Nicholas Biddle advised. "Let him say nothing, promise nothing."

The Democrats sarcastically dubbed Harrison "General Mum," but the Whig strategy paid off. In a large turnout of voters, Harrison won 234 electoral votes to Van Buren's 60. The popular vote was much closer, but the Whigs had elected their first President, after 12 years of Democratic control.

The Whigs looked forward to carrying out a bold program of economic growth and development based on Clay's American System. But only a month after taking office, the 68-year-old Harrison died of pneumonia contracted at his inauguration. For the first time, a Vice President would succeed to the presidency. The Whigs were thunderstruck.

As President, Tyler caused the Whigs further grief. He blocked legislation that would have strengthened the national government at the expense of the states. He vetoed a new national bank, and he opposed federal funds for internal improvement projects.

The Whigs quickly realized that choosing a vice presidential candidate who was so out of sympathy with their policies had been

Not only banks suffered during the depression. In the era of general prosperity, people had bought on credit, trusting that they could pay their bills later. Now that hard times had hit the nation, many people faced a "Long Bill," like this general-store customer contemplating the amount of money he owes the shopkeeper.

3. **VISUAL EVIDENCE** The painting is by James H. Beard.

a major mistake. For the last years of his term of office, Tyler was literally a President without a party. The Whigs had won an empty victory.

See p. T48.

SECTION 4 REVIEW

1. **Identify:** (a) Whigs, (b) Specie Circular, (c) John Tyler.

2. (a) Why did the Whigs run three candidates for President in 1836? (b) Was their strategy successful? Explain.

3. How did the drop in cotton prices in 1837 contribute to the economic depression that followed?

4. What campaign strategies did the Whigs learn from the Democrats?

5. **Critical Thinking** Could the techniques of the campaign of 1840 be used today? Explain.

259

2. **BIOGRAPHY** John Tyler (1790–1862), born in Greenway, Virginia, was an ardent states' rightist who supported Jackson in 1828 and 1832. In 1861, Tyler took a seat in the Confederate Congress.

Summary

1. **During the 1820s, the Republican party split into two new parties: the Democrats and the Whigs.** Andrew Jackson, a Democrat, won the presidential election of 1828. His election was seen as a triumph for the "common people."

2. **Andrew Jackson's election ushered in an era of greater democracy for some people.** Most states allowed white male suffrage, but women and most black Americans had no direct political role. Under Jackson's administration, thousands of Native Americans were forcibly removed from their homelands.

3. **Jackson worked to end special treatment for privileged groups and to strengthen the Union.** He instituted the spoils system for both political and idealistic reasons. His strong position in the nullification crisis and in the dispute over the national bank strengthened federal authority.

4. **The economic depression following the Panic of 1837 severely handicapped Martin Van Buren.** In 1840, William Henry Harrison captured the presidency for the Whigs. His untimely death left the presidency in the hands of John Tyler, who had little sympathy for Whig policies.

See p. T48.

Vocabulary

On a separate sheet of paper, write the word or words that best complete each of the following sentences.

1. A (An) _____ is the declaration of the principles and programs of a political party.

2. A (An) _____ is a government run by the privileged few.

3. _____ is voting by all white males.

4. A (An) _____ was a secret meeting at which presidential candidates were chosen.

5. Under the _____, an elected official's loyal supporters are given government jobs.

See p. T48.

Chapter Checkup

1. What factors contributed to the weakness of John Quincy Adams's presidency?

2. (a) How did the two parties that emerged during the late 1820s differ? (b) What role did they play in the election of 1828?

3. (a) What reforms increased the political participation of some Americans? (b) Which groups were not included in these reforms?

4. (a) Describe the methods used to force Native Americans to move west. (b) How did some Indian nations try to resist removal?

5. Explain how each of the following reflected Jackson's democratic approach to government: (a) the Kitchen Cabinet; (b) the spoils system; (c) his opposition to the second Bank of the United States.

6. (a) What arguments did John C. Calhoun use to support a state's right to nullify a federal law? (b) What arguments did Daniel Webster use against the principle of nullification?

7. (a) Why was South Carolina opposed to the tariff law of 1832? (b) What action did it take to oppose the law? (c) What was Jackson's reaction? (d) Why were Jackson and South Carolina willing to accept Clay's compromise?

8. (a) Why was the second Bank of the United States a powerful institution? (b)

What steps did President Jackson take to try to "kill" the Bank? (c) Was he successful? Explain.

9. Explain how each of the following contributed to the Panic of 1837: (a) land speculation; (b) the availability of large amounts of money; (c) Jackson's Specie Circular; (d) the drop in cotton prices.

10. (a) Why did the Whigs nominate William Henry Harrison for President? (b) Why did they nominate John Tyler for Vice President? (c) How did their choices backfire?

See p. T40.

Critical Thinking

1. **Making a Judgment** Do you think that Jackson's presidency was democratic? Or was it "the reign of King Andrew I"? Explain.

2. **Drawing a Conclusion** From what you have learned about Andrew Jackson, why do you think he agreed with the settlers who wanted the Native Americans removed?

See p. T49.

Connecting Past and Present

1. Andrew Jackson's presidency was celebrated as a new age for democracy in America. At the same time that popular participation in government was increasing, many groups were left out of the political process. What contradictions, if any, do you see between the ideal of democracy and its practice in the United States today?

2. The economic downturn following Martin Van Buren's election had its roots in the Jackson administration. What unresolved problems have recent Presidents left for their successors to deal with?

See p. T49.

Developing Basic Skills

1. **Map Reading** Study the map on page 252. (a) What information is shown on this map? (b) In what states did the southern Indian nations hold land before 1830? (c) How many miles did each nation have to travel from its homeland to the Indian reservation in the West?

2. **Graph Reading** Study the circle graphs of the 1824 and 1828 presidential elections on pages 246 and 247. (a) Which two candidates ran in both elections? (b) What percentage of the electoral vote did each candidate receive in 1824? In 1828? (c) As you review the election results for 1824, do you think Andrew Jackson had reason to object when John Quincy Adams was elected by the House of Representatives? Why or why not?

WRITING ABOUT HISTORY

Choosing a Research Topic

When you write a research paper, choose a topic that holds your interest and that you can readily research. Select a number of possible topics, then check what resources your library has available. If you discover that there is very little information on a topic, it will probably be wise to eliminate it. If there is a great deal of information on a topic, it is possible that the topic is too broad.

Practice: Choose two of the topics from the following list and write a sentence describing what aspect of each subject you would like to research.

1. Sectionalism and the Election of 1828
2. Andrew Jackson and the National Bank
3. The "Trail of Tears"
4. The "Civilized Tribes"
5. The Role of Women in the 1820s
6. The Panic of 1837

From Sea to Sea

13

(1820–1860)

CHAPTER OBJECTIVES After completing this chapter, students should be able to
1. describe Spanish settlements in the West.
2. explain how settlers from the U.S. moved into Oregon, Texas, Utah, and California.
3. describe how Texas won its independence.
4. list the causes and results of the Mexican War.

CHAPTER PREVIEW Ask students if they know who lived west of the Mississippi River in 1820. Ask: Why do you think settlers began moving west between 1820 and 1860? Where did they settle first? How did the western lands become part of the U.S.? Write down the answers and refer back to them when the class has finished the chapter.

CHAPTER OUTLINE

1 The View From West to East

2 Oregon and the Fur Trade

3 The Republic of Texas

4 Surge to the Pacific

5 The Challenge of Greater Diversity

The young bride wrote in her diary:

> A cool breeze made our ride very pleasant. Husband & myself were alone entirely behind the dust of camp & enjoyed a sweet repast in conversing about home & dear friends. . . . Was much cheered with a view of the Fort at a considerable distance. Anything that looks like a house makes us glad. . . . Our dinner consisted of dry buffalo meat, turnips & fried bread, which was a luxury. . . . To one who has had nothing but meat for a long time this relishes very well.

The bride's name was Narcissa Whitman, and she was on a most unusual honeymoon—a 2,000-mile journey across the wilderness to Oregon country. A few years before, as a schoolteacher outside Albany, New York, Narcissa had pleaded with Presbyterian officials to send her out west as a missionary. They refused because they considered the trip too dangerous for a woman traveling alone.

One Sunday, Marcus Whitman, a doctor and minister, showed up at Narcissa's church to tell of his missionary work on the frontier. To Narcissa, it seemed that fate had intervened. She and the doctor were married, and Narcissa was soon headed where no white woman had gone before—across the Rockies to the Pacific.

After an exhausting 156-day trek, the Whitmans arrived in Oregon on September 1, 1836. There they founded their outpost, Waiilatpu Mission. The Whitman homestead became a welcome sight for the pioneers who soon followed the Oregon Trail. These settlers were not only trappers and traders but also farmers, lured by tales of land so rich that wheat grew taller than a man and turnips reached five feet around.

American expansion to the Pacific was under way. Beginning in 1843, wagon trains bound for Oregon would set off every spring from Missouri. The dream of land, wealth, and opportunity had already begun to draw American settlers to Texas, California, and other parts of the West. By 1850, the United States had fulfilled a sense of destiny—a mission to extend its borders from sea to sea.

1.

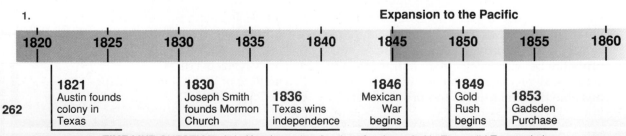

Expansion to the Pacific

| 1820 | 1825 | 1830 | 1835 | 1840 | 1845 | 1850 | 1855 | 1860 |

1821 Austin founds colony in Texas

1830 Joseph Smith founds Mormon Church

1836 Texas wins independence

1846 Mexican War begins

1849 Gold Rush begins

1853 Gadsden Purchase

262

1. TIME LINE QUESTION Ask: How long after Stephen Austin settled in Texas did Texas win its independence?

The pioneers who followed after the Whitmans often traveled in cloth-covered wagons called Conestoga wagons or prairie schooners. Children, women, and the sick could ride inside to escape the rain and the hot sun. Experienced trappers and traders, who knew the country, sometimes led the wagons west. In this
1. painting, The Old Scout's Tale, a guide tells a group of "tenderfeet" what lies
2. ahead on the trail.

1. **BIOGRAPHY** The painting is by William T. Ranney (1813–1857). Ranney was born in Connecticut and studied art in Brooklyn before joining the trek westward. He became a soldier in the Texas army in 1836.

2. **VISUAL EVIDENCE** The scout in this painting is most likely Jim Bridger, a trapper and frontiersman known as the "Daniel Boone of the Rocky Mountains."

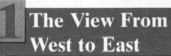

The View From West to East

READ TO UNDERSTAND

■ How Spanish missions influenced the early development of the West.

■ How Mexican independence altered the economic and political organization of California and hastened the settlement of Texas and New Mexico.

■ How the United States and Britain agreed to a joint occupation of the Oregon Country.

3. ■ *Vocabulary:* ranchero, mortality rate.

The Spanish had established a claim to vast areas of North America almost 100 years before the first English settlers arrived in Jamestown. By the time settlers from the former English colonies became interested in the western part of North America, Spanish culture and institutions flourished in many areas. Indeed, the "native wild animals" spotted by adventurers from the United States in the 1800s were long-horned cattle descended from animals brought by the Spanish nearly 300 years before.

The Spanish in California

Between 1640 and 1770, New Spain expanded as far north as present-day Montana and as far east as the Mississippi River. The Spanish generally ignored the area north and east of present-day Mexico. For the most part, they set up only small settlements to prevent other European nations from claiming territory near Mexico.

263

3. **VOCABULARY** Have students look up these terms in the glossary before they begin reading.

1. **GEOGRAPHY** Portolá built his first stockade at San Diego. He then continued north to Monterey. In 1769, he discovered San Francisco Bay. (movement)

2. **ACTIVITY** Have students research the traditional life of California Indians before the Spanish arrived.

All this changed in the late 1700s. At that time, Spanish authorities became aware that Russian seal hunters and traders were moving south from Alaska. In 1769, they dispatched an expedition under Don Gaspar de Portolá (por toh LAH) to assert their authority in Upper California, north of the California peninsula. Portolá was to build stockades at critical points along the coast.

A group of Franciscan friars led by Father Junípero Serra (SEHR rah) accompanied Portolá's expedition. Serra planned to set up missions in California to convert the Indians to Christianity. Between 1769 and 1782, a chain of missions and stockades reached northward from San Diego. As the British colonies in the East were gaining their independence from Britain, Spain was building its empire in the West.

The Mission System

The missions claimed virtually all the land in California. The friars either convinced or compelled a large number of local Indians to live on mission lands. Within 60 years, about one tenth of California's 300,000 Indians were working under Franciscan supervision.

The missions greatly influenced the economic and cultural life of the Indians. The Indians raised cattle and sheep, grew grapes and wheat, and built irrigation facilities. In return for their labor, they received food, clothing, and shelter. To the Spaniards, the greatest gift the missions could offer Indians was Christianity. Many Indians accepted conversion, and over the years, their own customs and traditions faded. Even though the missionaries started with good intentions,

3. **VISUAL EVIDENCE** Have students compare this picture of Mission Francisco Solano to the picture of Mission San Gabriel on p. 31.

Most West Coast Indians were nomadic food-gatherers. The Spanish wanted to teach them to grow crops, tend farm animals, and live much as Spanish peasants did. To the Indians, however, this meant backbreaking labor in the fields, often enforced by an overseer with a whip. Indians sometimes tried to revolt or escape, but Spanish soldiers kept many of them on the mission lands.

1. **DISCUSSION** Have students compare what happened to the Indians in California with what had happened when the Spanish first arrived in the Americas.

1. however, some came to view the Indians as a pool of cheap labor. The Indians' working conditions then became harsher.

The missions had a political impact as well. Since the Spanish set up few forts in California, the missions symbolized Spanish control in the region until 1821. In that year, revolutionaries in New Spain rejected Spanish rule and declared Mexico an independent nation. Although isolated from the fighting, California accepted the authority of the new Mexican government.

Impact of Mexican Independence

In 1833, the Mexican government passed a law that greatly altered the existing economic and political organization of California. The Secularization Act opened church lands to settlement by Mexican citizens and decreed that Indians were no longer under the protection or control of the church.

The Mexican government granted large portions of valuable mission land to Mexican citizens. Vast ranches quickly replaced the missions as the main economic unit in California. The new **rancheros,** or ranch owners, needed laborers, just as the missionaries had. Although the Indians were technically free, most rancheros forced them to work and hunted them down if they tried to escape.

Such abuse was deadly. The **mortality rate,** or death rate, among Indians on California ranches was four times as high as that of Mexicans in the region, and twice as high as the mortality rate among slaves in the United States. By 1848, about 20 percent of California's Indians had died.

Mexican independence had another dramatic consequence. Mexico's new government opened up markets on the west coast to traders from the United States for the first time. Yankee merchants soon dominated California's profitable cattle hide trade. In 20 years, one Boston-based firm alone exported half a million hides. Still, until the mid-1840s, development on the east coast of North America had little impact on life in California.

Arizona and New Mexico

During the 1700s, the Spanish had made several attempts to establish settlements in the area of present-day Arizona. The Yuma and

Wealthy landowners in New Spain often controlled vast tracts of land. They built grand haciendas, or mansions, in which they lived according to Spanish custom. Dancing on the veranda, or summer porch, shown in top picture, was popular among many Spanish settlers. Their architecture, music, clothing, and food influenced the culture of the American Southwest. Spanish vaqueros, or horsemen, like those shown in bottom picture, developed many of the skills later adopted by American cowboys.

4. **VISUAL EVIDENCE** These pictures were painted by Alexander Harmer (top) and James Walker (bottom).

Apache Indians of the area, however, fiercely defended their homelands and forced the Spanish to withdraw from the silver mines and missions they had established. By 1830, the Spanish presence was limited to a few outposts.

Farther east, in New Mexico, the Pueblo and Zuñi offered less open resistance. The Spanish were able to set up more permanent outposts. About 44,000 sheep ranchers settled along the Rio Grande from El Paso to Taos. As in California, a few rich families owned vast herds, tended by local Indians.

265

2. **LOCAL HISTORY** Some early presidios and missions can still be seen in California today.

3. **PAST AND PRESENT** Have students find out how important ranching and farming are in California's economy today.

1. **BACKGROUND** Mexico hoped settlers would develop the land, increasing Mexico's revenues and helping to control the Indians.

2. **PAST AND PRESENT** Austin is the name of the present-day capital of Texas. Have students locate the city on the map on pp. 840–841.

Fearing that it would lose control of its territory, Spain wanted to discourage foreign contact. When, as early as 1804, traders from the United States appeared in Santa Fe, the capital of New Mexico, the Spanish threw them in jail and confiscated their goods. But when Mexico declared its independence in 1821, the new government welcomed traders as a way of increasing its own prosperity. Traders from Missouri reached Santa Fe that same year and returned home triumphant; they dumped bags of Spanish dollars on the sidewalks before amazed onlookers.

Texas

The settlement of Texas in the 1800s took a somewhat different course from that of California and New Mexico. For one thing, Spain had never effectively dominated Texas. Although the Catholic church set up a few missions there, the local Indians, such as the Comanche and Apache, were nomadic and resisted attempts to force them to adopt Spanish ways.

At the time Mexico gained its independence, only about 4,000 Spanish settlers lived in Texas. The government of the new Republic of Mexico recognized that it had to attract more people if its sparsely inhabited north-
1. ern province were to prosper.

In 1820, an American named Moses Austin had requested and received permission from the Spanish authorities to found a colony in Texas. Austin died before he could begin the trip, but the new government of Mexico extended the permission to his son Stephen.

Sensitive and well-educated, Stephen Austin seemed ill-suited to life on the frontier. But Austin was tolerant, fair, and honest, and demonstrated the kind of judgment and diplomatic skills needed for his task.

Austin founded his Texas colony in December 1821. Each family that joined the colony received about 250 acres (about 100 hectares) for farming and stock raising. The colony thrived in large part because of Austin's skill in choosing people to settle it. By 1824, he had 2,021 residents in his colony, the cen-
2. ter of which was the little town of Austin. His success marked the beginning of an ever-increasing flood of American settlers to Texas.

266

Oregon

The land north of Upper California, extending to Vancouver Island and the coast of present-day British Columbia had been claimed not only by Spain but also by Russia, Great Britain, and the United States.

In 1818, the United States and Great Britain agreed to a joint occupation of the Oregon country, the area north of the 42nd parallel and south of latitude 54°40'. The British and the Americans would be free to settle and trade there. Both, however, generally ignored the rights of Indians living in the territory. By 1825, Spain and Russia withdrew their claims to these lands.

3.

4.

For many years, the few Europeans or Americans who settled in Oregon were mainly fur traders. Since furs bought from the Indians could be sold at tremendous profit in China, Yankee traders from New England stopped along the Oregon coast frequently—so frequently, in fact, that in many areas the Indian name for a white man was "Boston."

The Yankee traders in Oregon were among a small number of Americans who lived in the West. Until the mid-1820s, if you had viewed the history of North America from the west coast looking east, the conflicts and trials of the United States would have played a minor role. Very soon, that situation would change.
See p. T50.

See p. T50.

SECTION 1 REVIEW

1. **Identify** (a) Don Gaspar de Portolá, (b) Father Junípero Serra, (c) Secularization Act, (d) Stephen Austin.

2. **Define:** (a) ranchero, (b) mortality rate.

3. What political function did the missions serve for the Spanish in California?

4. What role did California Indians have on mission lands and on the ranches that succeeded them?

5. Why were settlers welcomed to Texas by the government of Mexico?

6. **Critical Thinking** Some Mexican leaders were opposed to American settlement in Texas. Why do you think that was so?

3. **BACKGROUND** Refer students to pp. 12–13, where the culture of the Northwest Coast Indians is described.

4. **CRITICAL THINKING** Remind students of the Monroe Doctrine. Ask: How might it have contributed to the decision of Russia and Spain to drop their claims?

1. **BACKGROUND** One mountain man recalled fending off starvation: "I have held my hands in an anthill until they were covered with ants, then greedily licked them off."

2 Oregon and the Fur Trade

READ TO UNDERSTAND

■ How the fur trade helped open Oregon to settlement.

■ Why various groups of Americans moved to Oregon in the early 1800s.

■ Why the Oregon settlers set up their own framework of government.

During the early 1800s, what little most Americans knew about Oregon was based on the Lewis and Clark expeditions. Gradually, however, word began to trickle eastward that Oregon was blessed with rich resources. Enterprising fur trappers known as "mountain men" first spread the word and blazed trails for later pioneers. Their efforts greatly influenced the role of the United States in the far West.

The Mountain Men

Resourceful and hardy adventurers could make a small fortune trapping beavers in Rocky Mountain streams. Yet the "mountain men" led an often perilous existence. Grizzly bears, wildcats, and poisonous snakes populated the forests. Furthermore, many Indians, such as the Blackfeet, attacked the outsiders who trapped on their hunting grounds. Help was often far away.

The mountain man's way of life tested and shaped character. Louis Vasquez, a mountain man of French and Spanish descent, later became one of the founders of Denver, Colorado. James Beckwourth, a black mountain man, was accepted as a chief among the Crow Indians. At least one mountain "man" was a woman. Marie Dorion, an Iowa Indian, won fame across the nation for her survival skills.

There was money to be made from the fur trade. But the trappers received only a small share of the profits. The traders who bought the furs and shipped them all over the world gained most.

2. **LOCAL HISTORY** Astor Place, in Manhattan, is named after the fur trader. Its subway station is adorned with plaques that show beavers gnawing wood.

Two of the largest trading companies were the Rocky Mountain Fur Company and John Jacob Astor's American Fur Company. In its 12 years of operation, the former purchased furs worth nearly $500,000, an enormous sum at that time. Other smaller companies eagerly joined the search for furs, competed with each other, and recruited their own mountain men.

The competition among such companies led to a drastic overtrapping of streams and rivers. By 1832, the sharp decline in the beaver population doomed the Northwest fur trade and the traders' way of life.

4. **VISUAL EVIDENCE** Ask: What qualities of the trapper are shown in this picture?

To survive the dangerous and lonely life on the frontier, a trapper had to have strong self-reliance. After months of this solitary life, trappers would gather at forts that doubled as trading posts in the Northwest. Dances were a favorite form of entertainment at the trading posts. Anyone who could play a musical instrument would be recruited for the fort's "orchestra."

3. **ECONOMICS** In addition, beaver hats went out of fashion as silk hats became popular, so demand for beaver fur declined.

1. **BACKGROUND** According to one popular rumor, an Indian from Oregon had walked all the way to St. Louis in search of a Bible.

Early Settlers in Oregon

As the heyday of the mountain man ended, the day of the pioneer began. Many settlers were lured west by tales of beautiful, rich land. Others wanted to spread the word of God. They had heard rumors that the Indians wanted to learn about Christianity and the Bible. Oregon Indians actually had their own religious traditions, and few had even heard of Christianity. But churches in the East sent willing missionaries to Oregon in response to the reports.

Among the best-known missionaries were Jason Lee, sent by the Methodists in 1834; Marcus and Narcissa Whitman, Presbyterians who led a band of settlers west in 1836 (see page 262); and Henry and Eliza Spalding, who traveled with the Whitmans. Al-

2. **BACKGROUND** One tall tale said that in Oregon "pigs run about under the great acorn trees, already cooked, with knives and forks in them."

though the missionaries had little success, they nevertheless wrote home urging friends to join them.

Gradually, more and more Americans settled in the Willamette Valley, near the missionaries' homes. Settlers sent descriptive letters back East, which newspapers often published. A farmer's plea to his family to leave hard times in Missouri and join him on the trek westward reveals the place that Oregon had won in Americans' dreams.

Out in Oregon I can get me a square mile of land. And a quarter section for each of you all. . . . I am done with this country. Winters its frost and snow freeze the body; summers the overflow from Old Muddy drowns half my acres; taxes take the yield of them that's left. What say, Maw, it's God's country.

GEOGRAPHIC CONNECTION

Crossing the Continental Divide

A large wooden sign greets present-day motorists when they reach the crest of a pass through the Rocky Mountains. It announces that they have reached the Continental Divide, an imaginary north-south line that runs along the ridge of the Rocky Mountains. From this point, waters to the east flow into the Atlantic Ocean or the Gulf of Mexico and waters to the west flow into the Pacific. For the modern traveler riding on an interstate highway, it may be of only momentary interest.

But there was a time when crossing the Continental Divide was a challenge of heroic proportion. Setting out in canoes from the area of present-day Bismarck, North Dakota, in the spring of 1805, the Lewis and Clark expedition (see page 202) followed the Missouri River— an eastward-flowing stream—high into the Rockies. From there, guided by a Shoshone woman, Sacajawea, the explorers struck out overland on horseback. In August, they rode up and over the lofty mountains—across the Continental Divide. On the other side of the mountains, they came upon westward-flowing rivers—the Clearwater, the Snake, and the Columbia, that led them to the Pacific Ocean.

Lewis and Clark's journey provided both inspiration and information for the thousands of pioneers who followed them west. However, while the two explorers had crossed the Continental Divide at Lemhi Pass, 8,000 feet (2,348 meters) above sea level, other, less difficult, routes were soon discovered. The most popular was South Pass, a broad gentle valley at 7,550 feet (2,300 meters) above sea level, in present-day Wyoming. The Mormon Trail, the Oregon Trail, and the California Trail all crossed the divide through South Pass. (Today, Interstate 80 also follows near this pass.)

Why did the early pioneers take these northern passes rather than those in the South where the Rockies are lower? At the time, southern routes lay in territory ruled by Spain and then by Mexico. Not until 1848 would the United States gain control of the southern portion of the Continental Divide.

See p. T50.

1. What is the Continental Divide?

2. **Critical Thinking** How do you think the Continental Divide influenced how pioneers could migrate westward?

3. **GEOGRAPHY** The Continental Divide runs from Canada through Central America. In the United States, it passes through Montana, Wyoming, Colorado, and New Mexico. (location)

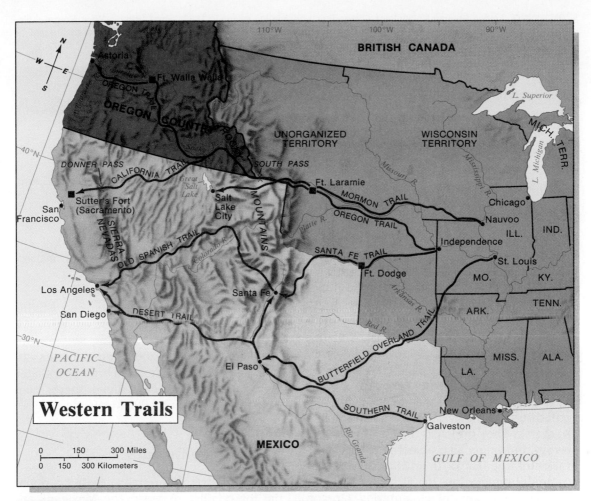

Western Trails

See p. T50.

MAP STUDY *Travelers to the far west had to follow rough trails across dry, often barren, country for nearly 2,000 miles (3,200 kilometers). What route would a pioneer family bound from Independence, Missouri, to San Francisco take? In what towns and forts might they seek shelter along the way? How would they get across the Rocky Mountains?*

1.

1. MAP READING Ask: Why do you think the Oregon Trail often followed the course of a river?

GEOGRAPHY AND HISTORY

The Way West

The Oregon Trail, developed by earlier traders and trappers, became the most famous route to the Northwest in the early 1800s. It began easily enough at Independence, Missouri, followed the Missouri and Platte rivers to southern Wyoming across gradually rougher terrain, and then crossed the Rockies at South Pass. From there, the trail swung north to the Columbia River, which it followed to the Willamette Valley. In all, the Oregon Trail stretched for about 2,000 miles (about 3,200 kilometers), a journey of four to six months.

In the early 1840s, growing numbers of people responded to news about Oregon. Pioneers traveled along the trails to Oregon in caravans of covered wagons. Safety and

prudence required such organization. Although Indians did not often attack the wagon trains that crossed their lands, most settlers wanted to be prepared.

Another problem for Oregon pioneers was the nature of the land they had to cross. West of central Nebraska, streams ran dry in the summer, and the grass grew thin where it grew at all. Poisonous alkali springs endangered livestock. Easterners who were used to wooded, well-watered country were uneasy. When a wagon train drew into a circle for the night, it was as much to keep livestock from wandering to find more grass as it was for mutual protection.

Each wagon train winding westward established its own government, complete with a code of laws and officials to enforce them. This experience of forming their own government proved to be a valuable prepara-

269

2. PAST AND PRESENT Settlers bypassed the plains, calling them the Great American Desert. Today, with irrigation, the plains are known as the nation's breadbasket.

1. tion for the pioneers once they arrived in Oregon. There government was limited, at times even nonexistent. ∎

Self-Government: The First Organic Law

The joint occupation of Oregon agreed to by the United States and Great Britain did not result in any form of regional government. When the first American settlers arrived in the Willamette Valley, the only authority was an outpost of the British Hudson's Bay Company, a trading organization. It was hardly equipped to deal with a flood of settlers.

After 1842, when Americans began to outnumber the British in Oregon, they drew up their own framework of government. The First Organic Law, an outline for a temporary

2. government for the Oregon Territory, remained in force for the next few years.

Most of the 5,000 Americans who had settled in Oregon by 1845 were from northern states. They opposed the introduction of slavery, but many also objected to the immigration of free blacks. In an effort to discourage such immigration, the First Organic Law provided that any black entering Oregon would be whipped.

Even in the face of such threats, a few blacks did arrive and some prospered. George Washington Bush, for one, led a company of black settlers to Oregon. He and his family became wealthy wheat farmers, known for their kindness toward poorer white settlers.

See p. T50.

SECTION 2 REVIEW

1. **Identify:** Oregon Trail.

2. How did the mountain men contribute to the settlement of Oregon?

3. What attracted pioneers to Oregon?

4. (a) What was the First Organic Law? (b) What purpose was it to serve?

5. **Critical Thinking** Why do you think the Oregon settlers, while opposing slavery, were at the same time opposed to immigration of free blacks into the territory?

3 The Republic of Texas

READ TO UNDERSTAND

■ How the interests of American settlers in Texas clashed with those of Mexicans.

■ How Texas gained its independence from Mexico.

■ Why Americans disagreed over the annexation of Texas.

In 1829, a Mexican general warned, "Either the government occupies Texas now, or it is lost forever." But the warning was already too late. By 1827, 10,000 United States citizens had settled in Texas. Three years later, about 20,000 Americans lived there, compared to only about 4,000 Mexicans.

Clash of Two Cultures

Strong cultural differences created a potential for conflict between the Mexicans and the Americans. Most Mexicans spoke Spanish; most Americans spoke English. The American settlers were overwhelmingly Protestant; most Mexicans were Catholic. And the Mexican government banned public worship by Protestants.

Political differences also contributed to the tension. Settlers from the United States had strong democratic traditions. Mexicans in Texas were used to the ways of the old Spanish empire, in which local officials were appointed by the crown, not elected by the people. When Mexico became independent, its government did adopt a constitution. Texans, however, had little voice in the government of Mexico.

Americans found it difficult to adapt to the Mexican judicial system. A single judge sitting in the state capital ruled on court cases. Neither the plaintiff nor the defendant could testify personally before the judge, nor was a jury present. A system of justice that depended so heavily on one person's opinion seemed unfair to Americans.

2. **CITIZENSHIP** The First Organic Law was designed to govern the territory "until such time as the United States of America extend their jurisdiction over us."

3. **PAST AND PRESENT** Although Spanish is Mexico's official language, 8 percent of the population speak one of many Indian languages.

1. **PRESIDENTS** Until 1819, the U.S. claimed that Texas was part of the Louisiana Purchase. In the 1820s, both Presidents Adams and Jackson tried to buy Texas.

Another point of friction was the issue of slavery. Most Americans who settled in Texas were southerners. Some had brought slaves, and others expected to acquire them. But the Mexican government had abolished slavery in Texas in 1827. Since enforcement was lax, American settlers continued to bring in slaves. But they feared that slavery would not be secure so long as Texas remained under Mexican rule.

Beginning of Conflict

The Mexican government had its own reasons for distrusting the American colonists. It suspected that most American settlers wanted to hand Texas over to the United States. The United States government, after all, had already tried twice to purchase Texas, once in 1826 and again in 1829.

To strengthen its hold on Texas, Mexico established new military garrisons in the region and fortified posts already there. To American-born Texans, that looked like the beginning of military rule. Then, in the summer of 1832, another revolution occurred in Mexico. A new leader, General Antonio de Santa Anna, came to power. American settlers who had supported Santa Anna were pleased. They believed he would grant them a greater role in the government of Texas.

Santa Anna, however, proved less liberal than he had first appeared. In October 1834, he abolished the Mexican constitution and set himself up as a dictator. Rumors spread wildly. Santa Anna, some said, intended to abolish local governments and drive all Americans out of Texas. Santa Anna was sending troops north, said others.

Hearing of discontent in Texas, Santa Anna actually did send reinforcements to the area. At this, a group of Americans led by William B. Travis decided to strike for independence from Mexico. On June 30, 1835, they captured the Mexican garrison at Anahuac (AHN ah wahk).

Struggle for Texan Independence

Independence for Texas! Stephen Austin rallied American settlers to this cause. When a Mexican force reached Gonzales, Americans

3. **BIOGRAPHY** At 15, Houston (1793–1863) ran away to live with the Cherokees. Before going to Texas, he served in the House and as governor of Tennessee.

2. **BACKGROUND** Gonzales is called "the Lexington of Texas," after the battle that began the American Revolution.

from all over the countryside rushed to the town, fiercely attacked the Mexicans, and forced them to withdraw.

A convention representing all American settlements met in November 1835 at Austin. The delegates issued a Declaration of Causes justifying their decision to take up arms. They appointed Sam Houston, a popular figure in Texas, as commander of their forces and established a provisional government. On March 2, 1836, Texas declared its independence as the Republic of Texas and prepared to fight.

At the same time, the Mexican army was pushing northward. During February and March 1836, it laid siege to a garrison of fewer

4. **MAP READING** Ask: What battle was a victory for the forces led by Santa Anna?

MAP STUDY Texas won independence from Mexico in a short but bitter war. Where were the major battles of the war fought? Which were won by the Texans? See p. T51.

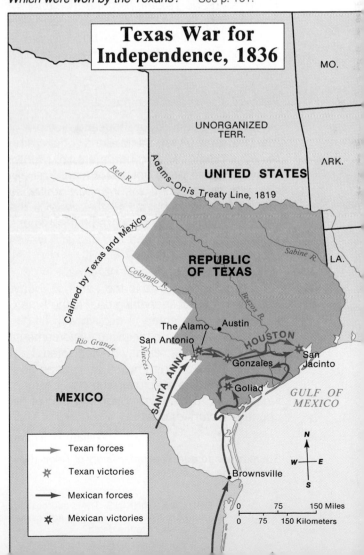

Texas War for Independence, 1836

- → Texan forces
- ✶ Texan victories
- → Mexican forces
- ✶ Mexican victories

than 200 Texans in the Alamo, an abandoned mission in San Antonio. The defenders of the Alamo included William B. Travis, commander; Jim Bowie, second in command; and

1. Davy Crockett, the best known of a large number of American volunteers who had raced to Texas to join the fight.

All the defenders were killed when the fort fell to the Mexicans on March 6. But their heroic efforts had given the Texas revolutionaries time to arm and had provided a

2. rallying cry, "Remember the Alamo!"

With the Americans now aroused and united, volunteers flocked to Sam Houston's army. Houston realized that his new recruits were too inexperienced to fight. Despite the criticism of rasher men, he retreated to whip his army into fighting shape before challenging Santa Anna.

On April 21, 1836, Houston led a surprise attack on Santa Anna's army near the San Jacinto (SAHN jah SEEN toh) River. The Texans routed their foes in 15 minutes and captured Santa Anna himself. While a prisoner,

2. **PAST AND PRESENT** The Alamo was restored by the U.S. government in 1849 and today stands as a memorial to the slain defenders.

THE AMERICAN EXPERIENCE

The Siege at the Alamo

Fewer than 200 Texans held the Alamo for 12 days against almost 4,000 Mexican troops. The heroism of this defense can be seen in the following message from Commander William B. Travis.

Fellow Citizens and Compatriots:

I am besieged by a thousand or more of the Mexicans under Santa Anna. I have sustained a continued bombardment for twenty-four hours and have not lost a man. The enemy have demanded a surrender; otherwise the garrison is to be put to the sword if the place is taken. I have answered the summons with a cannon shot, and our flag still waves proudly from the walls.

I shall never surrender or retreat.

Then, I call on you in the name of liberty, patriotism, and of everything dear to the American character to come to our aid with all dispatch. The enemy are receiving reinforcements daily. Though this call may be neglected, I am determined to sustain myself as long as possible and die like a soldier who never forgets what is due to his own honor and that of his country. *Victory or death.*

William B. Travis

See p. T51.

1. What was the purpose of Commander Travis's message?

2. **Critical Thinking** How do you think the Americans' belief in their cause strengthened their defense?

3.

Source: Henderson Yoakum, *History of Texas* (New York: 1856).

3. **CRITICAL THINKING** Travis addressed the letter "To the People of Texas and all Americans in the world." Ask: Why did he address it this way? Why do you think the defenders of the Alamo fought to the death?

1. **BACKGROUND** The Texas flag had a single white star; Texans called their new country the Lone Star Republic.

Santa Anna signed two treaties. One granted Texas its independence. The other set the Rio Grande as the boundary between Texas and Mexico.

Texas: An Independent Republic

In the fall of 1836, the Republic of Texas held 1. its first presidential election. Sam Houston was chosen by an overwhelming majority. In 2. the same election, Texans voted 100 to 1 in favor of seeking annexation by the United States.

In Washington, however, feelings about annexation were mixed. President Andrew Jackson favored it but recognized that it might bring war with Mexico. It would surely strain relations between the North and South. Texas had been settled mostly by southerners. If it were admitted as a slave state, northerners argued, the South would be strengthened. In the end, Jackson refused to support the annexation of Texas, but he did formally recognize its independence.

Heavy American migrations to Texas during the late 1830s continued to swell its population. The new Texas government encouraged immigration by offering free land to settlers. The timing of this offer was good. The economic depression of 1837 was bringing hard times to the United States. (See page 258.) For many people, it was the right moment to pull up stakes and move west.

Although most of the settlers were white southerners, others also moved to Texas. Among them were free blacks who were attracted by the offer of land. Between 1836 and 1846, the population of Texas soared from 30,000 to 142,000.

The city of Houston typified the growth of most of Texas. In 1839, it was a small village with tree stumps blocking the main streets. A year later, it had a courthouse, a jail, two theaters, a statehouse, 12 stores, and 47 saloons. Five years later, it had 40 stores, three hotels, several newspapers, schools, four churches, a cotton press, an iron foundry, sawmills, and two packing houses.

Throughout those years of vigorous growth, Texans continued to press for annexation. But the United States government 3. remained reluctant to take the step until 1845.

See p. T51.

SECTION 3 REVIEW

1. **Identify:** (a) Antonio de Santa Anna, (b) Declaration of Causes, (c) Sam Houston, (d) "Remember the Alamo!"

2. (a) What were two cultural differences between Mexicans and Americans in Texas? (b) List two political differences.

3. What action by Santa Anna led to military conflict between Mexicans and Americans?

4. What were the provisions of the two treaties signed by Santa Anna in 1836?

5. (a) Why was President Jackson reluctant to annex Texas? (b) What action did he take?

6. **Critical Thinking** In 1836, Mexico's population outnumbered that of Texas by 120 to 1. What, then, explains the Texans' victory over Mexico?

4 Surge to the Pacific

READ TO UNDERSTAND

■ What Americans meant by their "manifest destiny" to expand westward.

■ How the United States acquired Texas and California.

■ What terms were set forth in the Treaty of Guadalupe-Hidalgo.

Americans who took up ranching in the Southwest in the 1800s had to learn an important spring ritual: cattle branding. The red-hot iron that burned a "Lazy Z" or "Running A" onto a young calf's hide created the only proof that the calf was a rancher's property.

In a way, Americans who lived in the far West in the 1840s wanted their nation's "brand" to be stamped on the lands they now called home. The thousands who had recently moved to Oregon, California, and Texas felt, **273**

2. **BIOGRAPHY** They elected Lorenzo de Zavala (1788–1836) as vice president. From southeastern Mexico, he had gone to Texas to fight Santa Anna.

3. **BACKGROUND** Northerners argued against annexation. "To annex Texas is to declare perpetual war with Mexico," wrote William Ellery Channing, an influential New England author and clergyman.

in fact, that it was the "destiny" of the United States to govern the far West.

Manifest Destiny

From the days of the first English settlements, many Americans had felt a deep sense of mission about their society and its future. The New England Puritans, for example, had come to America to establish a society that would be an example for the world. In Pennsylvania, the Quakers had called their colony the Holy Experiment. Early settlers were sustained by a strong sense of the righteousness of their actions.

The American Revolution added a political element to this sense of mission. The United States, many of its new citizens believed, had become the torchbearer of liberty in the world. Its system of government was a shining example of how a republic ought to conduct its affairs. As time went by, events strengthened Americans' belief in the superiority of their way of life. When they heard tales of mountain men or listened to accounts of Yankee merchants in California or read letters from pioneers in Texas, they assumed that one day those frontier lands 1. would become part of the United States.

In 1845, a New York editor, John O'Sullivan, used a phrase that summed up such attitudes. He wrote that it was America's "manifest destiny to overspread the continent allotted by Providence for the free development of our yearly multiplying millions." Americans quickly took up the phrase "mani- 2. fest destiny" as a slogan for expansion.

Under Presidents Tyler and Polk, the United States government endorsed the will of Americans in Texas, California, and Oregon. In at least one instance, the price of this endorsement was war.

Annexation of Texas

Texas president Sam Houston worked hard to have the independent republic of Texas annexed by the United States because he realized that Mexico still posed a danger. President John Tyler favored annexation. He hoped that he could win popular favor by expanding the nation's boundaries. He also feared that Texas might turn to Britain for

protection. But when Tyler signed a treaty of annexation with the Texans in April 1844, the Senate refused to ratify it. It was uncertain of public support for the treaty and feared that war with Mexico would result.

In November 1844, the Democrats nominated James K. Polk of Tennessee, an enthusiastic expansionist, as their candidate. Polk soundly defeated Henry Clay, his Whig opponent. Interpreting Polk's election as a victory for expansionist sympathies, President Tyler decided to try one last time to annex Texas during his own term. He urged Congress to admit Texas to the Union by a joint resolution rather than through a treaty.*

The Democrats mustered enough votes in both houses of Congress to approve annexation, and Tyler signed the joint resolution on March 1, 1845, three days before he left office. In December 1845, after Texas voters approved the proposal, Texas joined the United States as the twenty-eighth state.

The annexation brought new problems. Texas claimed that its borders extended south to the Rio Grande, as specified in the treaty that Santa Anna had signed in 1836. The Mexican government argued that its border with Texas should be the Nueces (noo AY says) River, some 200 miles (320 kilometers) north of the Rio Grande. Santa Anna, they claimed, had been forced to sign the treaty when he was a prisoner of the Americans. The United States supported Texan claims. In March 1845, Mexico broke off diplomatic relations with the United States. Further troubles seemed likely.

The Division of Oregon

For a time, war threatened in Oregon as well. Since 1818, the United States and Great Britain had agreed to occupy the territory jointly. (See page 266.) But the expansionists who wrote the Democratic party platform of 1844 brushed Britain's claims aside. "Our title to the whole of the Territory of Oregon is clear and unquestionable," they proclaimed. They demanded exclusive rights for the United

---

*A joint resolution would require only a simple majority vote in both houses of Congress. Ratification of a treaty would have required a two-thirds vote of approval by the reluctant Senate.

2. **CITIZENSHIP** Often a sense of racial superiority went along with feelings of political superiority. Also, many white Americans felt that God was on their side and that this justified taking over land held by Mexicans and Indians.

Sarah Hardinge, who came to Texas from New York, kept a record in pictures of her life as a pioneer. This picture shows an early plantation in the Republic of Texas. Although smaller than plantations in the Old South, it has slave cabins in the back. The household furnishings included a piano that had been shipped from New York.

1. **VISUAL EVIDENCE** The plantation shown in this picture was built in 1854.

States as far north as latitude 54° 40'. "Fifty-four Forty or Fight!" became a rousing slogan for many Americans.

The British government's alarm over that slogan increased when Polk, whose expansionist views were well known, won the election. The British knew that in Oregon itself the 5,000 American settlers greatly outnumbered the 750 British. Furthermore, following a depletion of the local fur stock, the British Hudson's Bay Company had moved its headquarters away from the heart of Oregon Territory.

Despite his expansionist beliefs and his party's slogan, President Polk did not want to fight Great Britain. He secretly renewed an earlier American offer to divide the territory. The British government decided that the disputed land was not worth a war and agreed to a division along the 49th parallel. The United States Senate approved a treaty confirming this agreement in June 1846.

Attempts to Acquire California

Like many other ardent expansionists, President Polk had a vision of the United States stretching from sea to sea. From the beginning, his aim had been to acquire California.

By 1845, only about 700 United States citizens lived in California, mostly in the Sacramento and San Joaquin river valleys. Nevertheless, President Polk decided to try to buy California from Mexico.

Slidell's Mission As you have read, Mexico broke off diplomatic relations with the United States in 1845 over a Texas boundary dispute. When Polk sent diplomat John Slidell to Mexico to reopen discussions about the border, he also authorized Slidell to offer to buy California for $25 million and New Mexico for $5 million. The Mexicans, however, were strongly opposed to any further loss of territory. They refused to meet with Slidell, and he returned home.

Having failed to buy California, President Polk tried another approach. He encouraged Thomas Larkin, the American consul at Monterey, California, to support Californians who wanted annexation by the United States. Before Larkin could act, a swashbuckling American named John C. Frémont arrived in California with plans of his own.

Frémont, a United States Army captain, had become famous as the "Pathfinder" for his explorations of the Sierra Nevada mountains. He now claimed to be in California on a mission of scientific exploration for the United States. He had, however, brought with him a band of 60 frontiersmen. The Mexican government was suspicious.

The Bear Flag Revolt Before Frémont could take any action, another group of Americans impulsively attacked the town of Sonoma. On June 15, 1846, the rebels proclaimed the formation of the California Republic and raised their new flag, featuring a grizzly bear and a lone star, over the town. The Bear Flag

2.

2. **ACTIVITY** Have students do research on John C. Frémont and prepare a biographical sketch about him.

275

1. **CRITICAL THINKING** Ask: At this point, could war with Mexico have been avoided? If so, how?

2. **PRESIDENTS** Abraham Lincoln, a Whig congressman, charged that Taylor's troops may not have been on American soil when the attack took place.

Revolt, as it came to be called, signaled the beginning of an open struggle to break California away from Mexican control.

Frémont rushed to support the revolt. Taking command of the rebel forces, he drove the Mexican governor's troops out of northern California. He then learned a startling piece of news: War had already been declared between the United States and Mexico.

The War With Mexico

The spark that had finally touched off war between the United States and Mexico was ignited by the continuing dispute over the southern border of Texas. After the Slidell mission failed, President Polk ordered General Zachary Taylor and 1,500 troops to cross the Nueces River and take up a position to the south, along the Rio Grande. The Mexi-

can authorities viewed Taylor's action as nothing less than an invasion of their country. Tensions were high.

Convinced that war with Mexico was inevitable, Polk decided to make the first move. As he was working on a war message to Congress, he received word that Mexican troops had crossed the Rio Grande on April 25, 1846, and clashed with Taylor's force. Sixteen American soldiers were killed or wounded in the skirmish. Polk revised his message. Asserting that Mexico had "shed American blood on American soil," he asked for a declaration of war, which Congress quickly passed.

Mexico eagerly accepted war. It was confident that its army could defeat the Americans and end what it considered aggressive designs on its territory. Sentiment among Americans was mixed. Most Americans in the

1.

2.

3.

3. **MAP READING** Ask: Which American commanders fought in the Mexican War? What were three major battles of the war? Who won the battles?

MAP STUDY *A dispute between the United States and Mexico over land claimed by Texas helped trigger the Mexican War in 1846. To what areas did the fighting spread? Based on the map, what use did the United States make of sea power in the war?*

See p. T52.

Mexican War, 1846-1848

United States forces
United States victories
Mexican forces

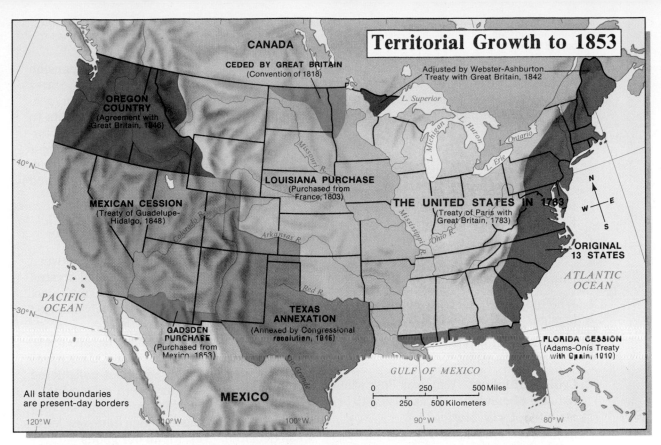

Territorial Growth to 1853

CANADA

CEDED BY GREAT BRITAIN
(Convention of 1818)

Adjusted by Webster-Ashburton
Treaty with Great Britain, 1842

L. Superior

OREGON
COUNTRY
(Agreement with
Great Britain, 1846)

40°N

LOUISIANA PURCHASE
(Purchased from
France, 1803)

THE UNITED STATES IN 1783
(Treaty of Paris with
Great Britain, 1783)

MEXICAN CESSION
(Treaty of Guadalupe-
Hidalgo, 1848)

Colorado R.

Arkansas R.

ORIGINAL
13 STATES

ATLANTIC
OCEAN

PACIFIC
OCEAN

30°N

Red R.

GADSDEN
PURCHASE
(Purchased from
Mexico 1853)

TEXAS
ANNEXATION
(Annexed by Congressional
resolution, 1845)

FLORIDA CESSION
(Adams-Onís Treaty
with Spain, 1819)

Rio Grande

GULF OF MEXICO

All state boundaries
are present-day borders

MEXICO

0   250   500 Miles
0 250 500 Kilometers

120°W   110°W   100°W   90°W   80°W

MAP STUDY *This map shows the growth of the United States from sea to sea. State boundaries are shown, but in 1853, Missouri, Louisiana, Iowa, Texas, and California were the only states west of the Mississippi River. Look at the map of the United States on pages 840–841. What states were later created from the Oregon Country? The Mexican Cession? The Gadsden Purchase?* See p. T52.

1.

1. **MAP READING** Ask: Which lands were acquired by treaty? By purchase?

southern and western states enthusiastically supported the war. Northeasterners, on the other hand, tended to view the conflict as just another way for southerners to extend slavery westward.

President Polk's war plan was to attack on several fronts at the same time in hopes of a quick victory. In the summer of 1846, General Stephen W. Kearny marched from Fort Leavenworth, Kansas, to Santa Fe, which he captured without firing a shot. Leaving part of his army behind, he then marched to California. There, with the aid of American naval forces, he subdued pockets of Mexican resistance. By January 1847, the United States had control over New Mexico and California.

General Taylor, in the meantime, crossed the Rio Grande and won a series of victories in Mexico. The last one, at Buena Vista, ended the war in northern Mexico.

The final offensive was led by Major General Winfield Scott. Under Scott, American forces landed near Veracruz, Mexico, and

began a slow and difficult march toward the nation's capital. On September 14, 1847, they successfully captured Mexico City, thus ending the conflict.

The Treaty of Guadalupe-Hidalgo

With their armies defeated and their capital occupied, Mexico's leaders had no choice but to agree to American terms. Under the Treaty of Guadalupe-Hidalgo (GWAH duh LOOP ay ih DAHL goh), ratified in 1848, Mexico recognized the Rio Grande as its border with Texas. The United States acquired California and the territory of New Mexico. In return, the United States paid Mexico $15 million and assumed responsibility for existing Mexican debts to United States citizens.

2.

The treaty almost completed American expansion across the continent. In 1853, the United States paid Mexico $10 million for a strip of land south of the Gila River in Arizona and New Mexico. Known as the Gadsden

277

2. **BACKGROUND** Only a year after the treaty was signed, gold was discovered in California. To some, this proved that God favored U.S. possession of the West.

1. Purchase, this land would provide Americans with a route for a southern transcontinental
2. railroad. With the Gadsden Purchase, the struggle to realize manifest destiny seemed to be over.

See p. T52.

SECTION 4 REVIEW

1. **Identify:** (a) manifest destiny, (b) James K. Polk, (c) "Fifty-four Forty or Fight," (d) John C. Frémont, (e) Zachary Taylor, (f) Gadsden Purchase.

2. How did the United States acquire Texas?

3. Why did the United States go to war with Mexico?

4. What were the terms of the Treaty of Guadalupe-Hidalgo?

5. **Critical Thinking** Why was Polk willing to make a boundary compromise with Britain but not with Mexico?

5 The Challenge of Greater Diversity

READ TO UNDERSTAND

■ How cultural conflicts created tension and led to discrimination in newly acquired United States territory.

■ How the discovery of gold affected life in California.

■ How the Mormons found a way to live without interference from others.

When word traveled eastward in 1848 that there was gold in California's hills, people raced to stake out claims. In 1849, thousands made their way to California. The flood of newcomers intensified a challenge faced by the new American territories: Would people representing so many diverse cultures be able to get along?

In the short term, many did not. The 1840s and 1850s were decades of cultural misun- derstanding and conflict. With the expansion of the nation to the Pacific, the United States acquired not only new territory but also hundreds of thousands of new residents to whom English culture and customs were for- eign. These residents formed two major groups: Indians with a wide variety of cul- tures, and Mexicans who shared a combined Spanish and Indian heritage.

Roots of Continuing Tensions

As you read earlier, differences between Mexicans and American settlers had created friction while Texas was still part of Mexico. This friction continued in the newly annexed areas.

In New Mexico and California, Mexicans, without moving an inch, found themselves living under a government that considered them "foreigners." They were suspicious of American intentions. "The Americans say they have come for our good," one irate New Mexi- can declared. "Yes, for all our goods."

In California, the wealthier Mexican land- owners, desiring order and stability, gener- ally welcomed United States rule. Other resi- dents, however, shared the resentment of the New Mexicans and organized a rebellion. American forces defeated the rebels and of- fered generous terms of surrender, which were accepted.

The situation for the Indians remained complex. The Mexican government had re- garded California Indians as Mexican citizens. When it surrendered California to the United States, Mexico insisted on guarantees for the land rights of all Indians living there. The United States agreed to those guarantees in the Treaty of Guadalupe-Hidalgo. But there were no provisions to allow Indians full rights as citizens, and the nation's previous record of keeping promises to Indians was poor.

Gold in California

Cultural conflicts in California were intensi- fied after the discovery of gold in the foot- hills of the Sierra Nevadas. The California "gold rush" provided an early test of the na- tion's ability to accommodate different cul- tures and rapid change.

3.

Gold was discovered first at Sutter's Mill, near Sacramento, in January 1848. Within a short time, the rush was on. Men and women from all parts of the United States, as well as from Europe, Australia, South America, and China, poured into California's gold fields. About 80,000 people journeyed to California
1. in 1849.

The first miners to arrive found considerable deposits of gold. They found these deposits in dry gulches, creek beds, shallow streams, and other places that were easy to mine. But before long, all the deposits that could be worked easily had been picked clean. To get at the remaining gold, heavy machinery was necessary. Since this machinery required a large capital investment and a large labor force, individual prospectors were replaced by large mining companies. The once individualistic miners became simply hired hands, toiling long hours for a wage.

Gold Rush Society

Society in the early mining camps had a special flavor. Towns sprang up overnight with names like Wildcat Bar, Skunk Gulch, Git-up-and-Git, and Ground Hog Glory. Without accepted rules of public conduct, life was rather unrestrained. Drinking and gambling were common, along with singing, dancing, and racing.

Although the population of the mining camps consisted chiefly of young men, women filled critical needs as workers and shopkeepers. They laundered, cooked, entertained in saloons, ran boardinghouses, and sold food supplies. Women who became landladies and merchants often prospered. Supplies were scarce, and demand was so great that shopkeepers in San Francisco could charge 50 to 75 cents for a loaf of bread that cost 5 cents in New York.

The "Conquered" Californians

The mining towns and camps governed themselves informally. The miners made laws, held trials, and carried out punishments that included whipping, branding, and even ear cropping. Such crude justice was perhaps unavoidable, since the camps and towns were growing so quickly. But it often had undesirable consequences. In a rough-and-tumble world, where fortunes were at stake, California miners ignored the rights of Indians, rights

2. **VISUAL EVIDENCE** Lone prospectors often used pans to separate gold ore from gravel, as shown at right. Sluices, as shown at left, required several partners to share in the work, but were much more efficient.

"Gold! Gold from the American River!" yelled Sam Brannan, who hoped to make a fortune with a store near Sutter's Mill. Brandishing a bottle full of gold dust, he electrified crowds in San Francisco. The word soon spread, and the timeless lure
2. of gold drew thousands of prospectors to California from all over the world.

1. **ACTIVITY** In 1770, there were 310,000 Indians in California. Have students use this and statistics for 1848 and 1870 to make a line graph.

2. **READING** Interested students can read *Mountain of Gold: The Chinese in America* by B. L. Sung.

that had been spelled out in the Treaty of Guadalupe-Hidalgo. Indians whose land claims stood in the way of ambitious miners were forcibly removed.

The social organization of local Indians made such removals easy. The Indians were generally peaceful and lived in small groups, often numbering only a few dozen people. Consequently, they could offer little resistance. When driven off their lands, many fell ill or starved to death. Individual Indians were casually murdered; whole villages were sometimes massacred. The California Indian population, which numbered over 200,000 in 1848, plunged to roughly 17,000 by 1870.

The Mexicans, who were regarded as a conquered people, were not treated any better. If a dispute arose over land rights, miners' courts customarily ruled against Mexican claims. To enforce the court rulings, vigilante groups drove Mexicans from the gold fields. In 1850, a law was passed taxing foreign miners. Foreigners, according to the law, included Mexicans—no matter how long they had lived in California.

Chinese Arrive in California

Like many other immigrants, Chinese prospectors arrived in California expecting to make their fortune and then return to their native land. The first Chinese immigrants were treated with respect. California needed laborers. But as their numbers increased, they encountered bitter hostility.

English-speaking miners abused and mocked the Chinese, whose customs they found strange. Perhaps more significant, they resented the economic success of the Chinese. By patience and hard work, Chinese immigrants were often able to make a success of mining claims that other, less industrious, miners had abandoned.

Faced with prejudice and hostility, the Chinese relied on one another for aid and protection. They regulated their own affairs and often transferred traditional Chinese institutions to America. Frequently forced out of the mines, the Chinese did back-breaking work scorned by other groups. Overall, their contributions to the developing California economy were vitally important. They farmed,

irrigated, and reclaimed vast stretches of land. In cities, they opened restaurants and did laundry. Others fished in the bays off the California coast.

Black Americans in California

During the late 1840s, many settlers brought slaves to California with them. Some of those slaves earned their freedom by working in the gold fields. Free blacks also migrated to California's gold fields to make their fortunes. By 1850, California's blacks numbered about 1,000 and formed the wealthiest black community in the country. At that time, it was decided that slavery would not be permitted in California, as you will read later.

Like blacks in other parts of the country, black Americans in California faced prejudice and discrimination. One law, for example, denied free blacks the right to testify in trials involving whites. California's black citizens would organize against that law and win its repeal in 1863.

By 1850, the peak of the California gold rush had passed. The rapid influx of people had swelled the territory's population, and California looked forward to becoming a state.

A Sanctuary for the Mormons

While people from different cultures were struggling with the problems of living side by side in California and New Mexico, the Mormons, a religious group from the East, were also seeking a way to ease the tensions of diversity. After years of rejection, the Mormons finally moved to unsettled lands where, isolated from others, they could pursue their way of life without interference.

In 1830, in the village of Palmyra in western New York, a farmer named Joseph Smith had founded a new religion. He based its teachings on writings he claimed had been revealed to him by an angel. Smith published these writings as the *Book of Mormon*, and his followers became known as Mormons. The church Smith organized is called the Church of Jesus Christ of Latter-Day Saints.

Joseph Smith was an energetic man who convinced many people to follow his teachings. But some of the religion's doctrines, such as the communal ownership of prop-

280

"This is the place," said Mormon leader Brigham Young when he saw the Great Salt
1. Lake in July 1847. With him were about 170 other Mormons. The settlement
thrived under Young's leadership, despite drought and hordes of crickets that
destroyed crops. Larger groups of Mormons, like the one shown here in winter
quarters, followed Young's party. By 1849, Salt Lake City had a population of 5,000.

1. **VISUAL EVIDENCE** One Mormon wrote, "We were happy and contented, and the songs of Zion resounded from wagon to wagon, reverberating through the woods while the echo returned from the distant hill."

erty, angered many Americans. Smith and his followers were forced to move frequently, first to Ohio, then to Missouri, then to Illinois.

In Illinois, the Mormons built a model city at Nauvoo, where Smith ruled over thousands of followers. But as Smith's power grew, his non-Mormon neighbors grew uneasy, especially after Smith revealed a teaching that permitted men to marry more than one 2. woman. Jailed for ordering the destruction of a printing press owned by their opponents, Joseph Smith and his brother were killed in 1844 by a lynch mob.

Leadership of the Mormons fell to Brigham Young. He decided that his flock should move to the Great Salt Lake Basin, a sparsely populated region in Utah. The final migration began in the summer of 1847. Wave after wave of recruits followed, swelling the population of Utah.

In the isolation of frontier Utah, the Mormons flourished. They established a church-centered government, which emphasized community values and cooperation more than individual achievement. Families were assigned land they were not permitted to abandon. With hard work and a remark-

able system of irrigation, the Mormons made the desert bloom. By moving to a remote location in Utah, the Mormons had found a way to avoid conflict with other Americans and to live according to their own vision.

See p. T52.

SECTION 5 REVIEW

1. **Identify:** (a) Sutter's Mill, (b) Joseph Smith, (c) Brigham Young.

2. (a) What impact did the gold rush have on California Indians? (b) On Mexicans in California?

3. How did English-speaking miners react to the Chinese gold seekers?

4. What problems did black Americans face in California?

5. How were the Mormons able to set up a successful community in Utah?

6. **Critical Thinking** Did the discovery of gold help or harm California? Explain.

281

2. **VOCABULARY** This practice is called polygamy. Smith believed that in heaven a widower who had remarried would find himself with two wives. His teaching thus permitted on earth what he felt existed in heaven.

Summary

1. **In the late 1700s, Spain was building its empire in the West.** Missions were the center of economic and political life and the symbol of Spanish control. After Mexico gained its independence from Spain in 1821, vast ranches replaced the missions as the main economic unit.

2. **Fur trappers known as "mountain men" blazed the trail to Oregon.** By the 1840s, large numbers of settlers were arriving from the United States. In 1842, the pioneers drew up a plan of government called the First Organic Law.

3. **Cultural and political differences created tensions between Mexicans and American settlers in Texas.** The Americans revolted and, in 1836, won their independence. Texas then sought annexation by the United States.

4. **In the 1840s, the United States fulfilled its "manifest destiny" by extending its territory to the Pacific Ocean.** In 1845, it annexed Texas, and in 1846, a compromise with Great Britain confirmed its control over Oregon. A war with Mexico in 1846–1847 won it the territories of California and New Mexico.

5. **Territorial acquisitions brought a diverse population under United States control.** Cultural differences led to conflict, especially in California, where thousands of people flocked to make their fortunes in the gold rush of 1849. In Utah, the Mormons avoided conflict by living in isolation.

See p. T52.

Vocabulary

On a separate sheet of paper, write the word or words that best complete each of the following sentences.

1. Mexican ranch owners, or _____, used Indians as laborers on their land.

2. The _____, or death rate, among the Indian workers was very high.

3. Enterprising fur trappers who explored the Oregon country were known as _____.

4. The _____ is an imaginary north-south line along the ridge of the Rocky Mountains that separates rivers flowing eastward from rivers flowing westward.

5. _____ was the belief that it was the mission of the United States to extend its territory to the Pacific Ocean.

6. An agreement reached by both houses of Congress that requires only a majority vote is a (an) _____.

See p. T52.

Chapter Checkup

1. (a) Describe the Spanish mission system in California. (b) How did mission life affect the California Indians?

2. Describe the role of the following in the settlement of Oregon: (a) mountain men; (b) fur trading companies; (c) missionaries.

3. (a) Why did tensions exist between Mexican and American settlers in Texas? (b) How did Santa Anna's revolution affect the American settlers there?

4. (a) What is the meaning of the phrase "manifest destiny"? (b) Was the attitude behind the principle of manifest destiny new in America? Explain.

5. (a) Why did the United States want to acquire California? (b) What methods did it try? (c) How did it succeed?

6. (a) Describe the impact of the discovery of gold in California. (b) How was gold rush society unique?

7. Describe the status and any problems of each of the following during the California gold rush: (a) California Indians; (b) Californians of Mexican origin; (c) Chinese immigrants; (d) black Americans.

8. (a) How did the Mormons anger other Americans? (b) Where did the Mormons finally settle? (c) Describe their way of life in their new home.

See p. T53.

Critical Thinking

1. **Analyzing** (a) What challenges did mountain men face that most other people in the early 1800s did not? (b) What personal characteristics might have helped in the type of life they lived?

2. **Comparing** (a) In what ways were the American Revolution and the struggle of Texas for independence similar? (b) In what ways were they different?

See p. T53.

Connecting Past and Present

1. In the mid-1800s, the United States went to war with Mexico to settle a boundary dispute. How do you think the United States would settle a dispute with Mexico today? Explain?

WRITING ABOUT HISTORY

Determining Your Purpose

Before you decide on the exact topic of a research paper, you should consider your purpose for writing the paper. The most common purposes for a history research paper are to inform or to persuade your audience. Possible topics for a paper designed to inform are: The Effect of the Mission System on the Indians of California; or The Events Leading to the Independence of Texas. Possible topics for a paper designed to persuade are: Why the United States Had/Did Not Have

2. The sudden increase in population in California in the mid-1800s created problems. What areas of the country are developing quickly now? Why is rapid expansion a mixed blessing?

See p. T53.

Developing Basic Skills

1. **Map Reading** Study the map on page 269. (a) Why was the journey to Oregon and California difficult? (b) How might you explain the route of the Oregon Trail?

2. **Comparing** Make a chart with four columns. In column 1, list: Louisiana, Florida, Texas, Oregon, California, New Mexico, Gadsden Purchase. In column 2, write the date each territory was acquired. In column 3, write the name of the country or countries from which each territory was acquired. In column 4, describe how each territory was acquired. To complete this chart, refer to earlier chapters in this book.

Use your chart and the map on page 277 to answer these questions: (a) Which method of acquiring territory was most common? (b) From which country did the United States acquire the most territory? (c) Explain why you agree or disagree with this statement: The greatest expansion of the United States took place between 1845 and 1848.

the Best Claim to Oregon; or Why the United States Was/Was Not Justified in Annexing Texas. If you choose a controversial topic, it is important that you present the topic in a balanced and fair manner.

Practice: Choose a topic from the lesson above or any other topic covered in Chapter 13. Write a one-paragraph essay to inform your reader about the topic or a one-paragraph essay to persuade your reader to accept your view.

283

The Different Worlds of North and South 14 (1820–1860)

CHAPTER OBJECTIVES After completing this chapter, students should be able to

1. explain how industry affected the economy and people of the North.
2. describe how cotton became king in the South and how whites, free blacks, and slaves lived.
3. analyze conflicting sources.

CHAPTER PREVIEW Ask students to study the maps, graphs, and pictures in this chapter. Then have them make two lists: one of words and phrases describing life in the North, and another for the South. Ask: What differences do you see between the two sections? What similarities?

The passengers waited nervously as the locomotive built up a head of steam. Boilers, after all, had been known to explode. But then the engine pulled away. Finally, they were off! It was August 1831, and the *De Witt Clinton,* one of America's earliest steam locomotives, had begun a 17-mile trial run from Albany to Schenectady, New York.

The passengers had good reason to be uneasy. Early train travel was not for the timid. As the engine picked up speed, the black smoke thickened, and a cloud of sparks shot into the air. The riders who were perched atop the coaches raised umbrellas to shield themselves, but the glowing cinders ignited the fabric. Chaos broke out as the passengers began jumping up and down and pummeling each other to put out the flames.

On one trip a flying coach lamp alerted a traveler to impending disaster. Within moments, the train turned over, leaving the disheveled riders to crawl from the wreckage. Most amazingly of all, they took it in stride, as if accidents were merely an inconvenience. Such scenes were common on early American railroads.

Clearly, no one would have called the earliest locomotives reliable. But just as clearly, railroads were the transportation of the future. Railroads were cheaper to build than canals, they could cross mountains, and they were fast. A journalist noted the time saved on one train trip, from Ballston to Troy, New York, in the 1830s. On a steep grade, the passengers, aided by a borrowed team of oxen, had to get out and push. Even so, it took only six hours to go 26 miles, compared to two days by boat on the Erie Canal.

As you will read in this chapter, despite the early problems, a railroad network developed in the North by the middle of the 1800s. Commercial railroads, and an influx of immigrant labor, helped to boost industrial expansion. In the South, however, the invention of the cotton gin encouraged a very different economy—one based on cotton production and slavery.

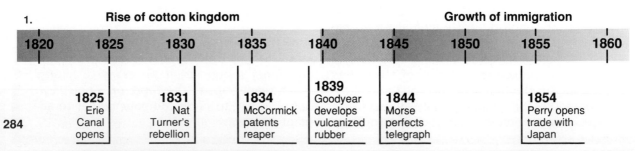

1.

Rise of cotton kingdom | Growth of immigration

| 1820 | 1825 | 1830 | 1835 | 1840 | 1845 | 1850 | 1855 | 1860 |

1825 Erie Canal opens

1831 Nat Turner's rebellion

1834 McCormick patents reaper

1839 Goodyear develops vulcanized rubber

1844 Morse perfects telegraph

1854 Perry opens trade with Japan

284

1. **TIME LINE QUESTION** Ask: How many events on the time line took place in the decade of the 1830s?

1. *Passengers on the new "iron horse" faced hazardous and uncomfortable conditions. Still, railroads won the day because of their speed. By 1840, almost 3,000 miles (4,800 kilometers) of track linked cities from New England to Georgia.*

1. **VISUAL EVIDENCE** This painting shows the "Atlas," a locomotive of the B&O railroad line, arriving at Frederick, Maryland, in 1838.

1 The Growth of Industry in the North

READ TO UNDERSTAND

■ How inventions in the early 1800s spurred industry and agriculture in the North.

■ How the North developed a major railroad network.

■ What role the merchant marine played in America's foreign trade.

2. ■ *Vocabulary:* feeder line, trunk line, clipper ship.

In 1835, Henry Burden of Troy, New York, patented a machine that could turn out 60 horseshoes a minute. Burden's horseshoe machine symbolized what was happening in the North between 1820 and 1860. New industries and new forms of agriculture, propelled by remarkable inventions, expanded goods and services. Improved forms of transportation carried these goods across the country and overseas to foreign ports. The Industrial Revolution was spreading to more and more places in the North.

The Spread of Industry

During the early 1800s, American industry expanded rapidly. Records of the textile industry reveal the pace. In 1800, the United States had seven textile mills, operating about 2,000 cotton spindles. By 1830, the industry had more than 2 million spindles. By 1860, there were more than 5 million spindles, most of them in New England.

285

2. **VOCABULARY** Have students look up these terms in the glossary before they begin reading.

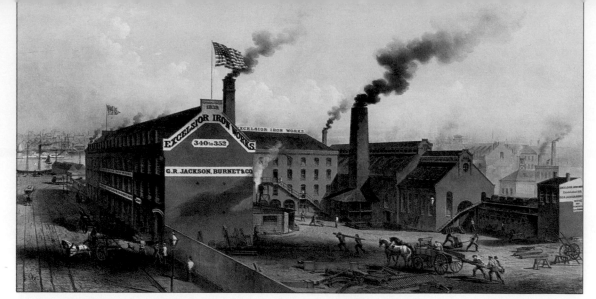

The demand for iron stimulated mining in Pennsylvania, where the ore was
1. plentiful. Great furnaces produced iron in foundries like the one here. The iron was
made into finished products by blacksmiths throughout the country.

1. **VISUAL EVIDENCE** Have students imagine that they are rural Americans of the 1800s seeing this factory or the railroad on p. 285 for the first time. Ask: What words might you use to describe the sights?

Growth in one area of manufacturing promoted growth in other industries. For example, the machinery for textile mills and other factories was made from iron; as the demand for machinery increased, the iron industry expanded. Then, in the 1820s, foundries in Pittsburgh introduced new techniques to remove the impurities from iron ore. After 1840, the switch from charcoal to anthracite coal for fuel also improved the production of iron. As the demand for anthracite grew, so did mining operations in Pennsylvania and elsewhere.

Technology developed in other areas as well. In 1839, Charles Goodyear found a way to vulcanize rubber, so it could withstand extreme heat and cold. This allowed the manufacture of heavy-duty drive belts to help run machinery. In 1844, Samuel F. B. Morse perfected the telegraph. Messages that had
2. taken days to deliver now took seconds, and the speed of American life increased to meet the change. Elias Howe's sewing machine, invented in 1846, made the mass production of "ready-made" clothing possible.

The impact of these changes was substantial. By 1860, more than 74,000 factories in the North were employing almost one million people—about nine times the number employed in the South. In 1859, for the first time ever, the value of the nation's industrial products exceeded the value of its agricul-

tural output. Manufacturing continued to grow most rapidly in the North, and it affected the quality and style of life there.

Improved Transportation

The increased production of goods created pressure for faster ways to ship them. As you have read in Chapter 11, the development of the steamboat and the construction of canals encouraged the internal growth of American trade and industry in the early 1800s. By 1837, however, a depression forced many northern states to reduce their support for internal improvements, including canals. By that time also, railroads were becoming an important alternative to water transportation.

The principles of railroad technology—the steam engine and carts drawn on rails—had been available since the beginning of the nineteenth century. Experiments in which steam engines towed cars mounted on rails began soon after 1800 in both Great Britain and the United States. In 1820, a steam locomotive invented by John Stevens of New Jersey successfully pulled five cars over a short stretch of track.

But early drawbacks delayed acceptance of rail transport. The first rails, made of wood covered with a strip of iron, broke frequently under heavy carloads. Soft roadbeds and weak

2. **BACKGROUND** Morse's first telegraph line went from Washington, D.C., to Baltimore. The first message was a quotation from the Bible, "What hath God wrought!"

bridges added to the hazards. Still, promoters believed in the future of train travel. "The time will come," one boasted, "when people will travel in stages moved by steam engines . . . almost as fast as birds fly, fifteen or twenty miles an hour."

Gradually, engineering skills caught up with this optimism. Engineers learned to construct sturdier bridges and solid roadbeds. They replaced the wooden rail with a T-shaped cast-iron rail. Such improvements made railroad travel safer, faster, and more efficient. Soon, Americans looked as hopefully to the railroad as they once had to the
1. canal.

Expanding the Railroad Network

The first commercial railroads in the United States went into service in the 1830s. Early railroads were short **feeder lines** that linked inland depots to docks or ports along the nation's water routes. Feeder trains hauled freight to a river or canal. There the load was transferred to a boat and then transported by water to its final destination.

As railroads expanded, **trunk lines** developed. These were longer, more heavily traveled rail lines, which linked major cities. Trunk lines had their own feeders, short railroad lines that merged with the trunk at points along its route. The feeders served the same function for the trunk lines as they had for canals and rivers.

Merging rail lines into a trunk system was difficult. Varying track widths and equipment created technical problems for consolidation. Rivalry between competing lines further complicated the situation. But once established, trunk lines cut shipping costs and time.

By 1860, a series of major railroads and associated branch lines crisscrossed the nation. However, while the South had made enormous strides in building railroads in the 1850s, the major lines were concentrated in
2. the North and West. New York and Chicago were major rail centers, and all the principal northern cities were linked by rail. The South, which had much less track and far fewer trunk lines (see the map at right), tended to remain isolated.

In less than two decades, the railroad had gone from being a novelty to a major means of transportation. American railroads had expanded dramatically from 2,818 miles (4,509 kilometers) of track in 1840 to 30,626 miles (49,003 kilometers) in 1860. Although water transport still served many shippers, railroads were making it easier to move raw materials and products cheaply and quickly.

Impact on Northern Agriculture

Farmers in the West benefited from the expansion of railroads. New rail links made it profitable for them to ship their crops to markets in the East. With the added income from the eastern sales, farmers could afford to buy more manufactured goods, expanding northeastern industry.

MAP STUDY *A flurry of railroad building in the 1850s greatly expanded train service. As the map shows, many rail lines connected the older port cities on the Atlantic coast with new cities west of the Appalachians. What cities along the Mississippi were becoming rail centers?* See p. T54.   3.

Growth of Railroads, 1850-1860

1. **ACTIVITY** Students might research the life of one of the inventors mentioned in this chapter and present their findings in an oral report.

2. **TECHNOLOGY** When exhibited in London, McCormick's reaper was called a "cross between an Astley chariot, a wheelbarrow, and a flying machine."

As had happened in manufacturing, new
1. inventions revolutionized the way that farm work was done. Cyrus McCormick, who invented the mechanical reaper in 1834, and John Deere, who perfected the steel plow three years later, made possible more efficient farm work. Using McCormick's reaper, a farmer could harvest many more acres with
2. much less labor than before. (See page 310.) Deere's plow enabled farmers to slice through the root-choked soil of the midwestern prairies. (See page 308.)

Farmers only gradually adopted these inventions. At first, many could not afford the expensive machinery. McCormick patented his reaper in 1834, yet more than 15 years passed before it came into general use.

The opportunity for greater profit provided by the new machines could not be realized until farmers had the money to buy them. As a result, farmers in the North and West switched from subsistence farming to cultivating cash crops. In the West, farmers planted great quantities of wheat. Farmers in eastern states such as New York concentrated on raising fruits and vegetables, which could be shipped swiftly to nearby cities. As you

will read later in this chapter, southern agriculture was also affected by technology, but with far different results.

America's Merchant Marine

Steam engines, providing power for railroads and steamboats, came to dominate both land and river transportation. They would come to dominate ocean commerce as well, but not before Yankee ingenuity had enjoyed a triumphant "golden age" of sail.

As you have read, American merchants in the early 1800s bought hides in Spanish California and furs in Oregon, then traded these items all over the world. New England merchants had controlled colonial trade in the 1700s, and the northern section of the country continued to dominate foreign trade in the 1800s.

Trade with China grew in the 1840s and 1850s. When the British forced China to grant them special trading privileges in 1844, the
3. United States was able to win the same guarantees. By 1860, Americans carried more than half the trade going to and from Shanghai.

3. **BACKGROUND** Trade with China expanded after Britain won the Opium War, which began when the Chinese government refused to allow Britain to sell opium to the Chinese.

Commodore Matthew Perry sailed to Japan with a fleet of United States warships in 1853 to open trade with the Japanese. Here the commodore presents gifts
4. *(including a miniature train) to the Japanese government.*

4. **VISUAL EVIDENCE** Perry also brought a telescope, cases of firearms, and clocks. In return, the Japanese gave silk, brocades, and lacquerware.

1. **VOCABULARY** Clipper ships got their name because they could move along the water at such a fast clip.

2. **VOCABULARY** Have students look up these terms in the glossary before they begin reading.

For a few decades, America's merchant marine boasted sleek sailing vessels known as **clipper ships.** The clippers were long and narrow, with tall masts that towered almost 200 feet (60 meters) over the decks and great canvas sails that strained to catch every gust of wind. Clipper ships set amazing records for their time. In 1851, Donald McKay's *Flying Cloud* sailed from New York to San Francisco in 89 days. Another clipper sailed from Boston to Liverpool, England, in 12 days.

By the mid-1850s, however, clipper ships were already becoming obsolete. The construction of a railroad across Panama, which could carry goods between the Atlantic and the Pacific oceans, reduced the need for clipper routes around South America. The introduction of steam power in ocean vessels dealt the final blow. By 1860, English steamships were outstripping the clippers in speed and cargo capacity.

It was the steamship, too, that helped open Japanese markets to American traders. In 1853, President Millard Fillmore sent Commodore Matthew Perry to win access to Japanese ports, which had long been closed to American merchants. When Japanese officials saw the black smoke belching from the stacks of Perry's warships, they were impressed and concluded that the United States was a power to respect. In 1854, through a combination of vague threats and diplomatic skill, Perry was able to persuade the Japanese to grant commercial privileges to the United States.

See p. T54.

SECTION 1 REVIEW

1. **Identify:** (a) Charles Goodyear, (b) Samuel F. B. Morse, (c) Cyrus McCormick, (d) Matthew Perry.

2. **Define:** (a) feeder line, (b) trunk line, (c) clipper ship.

3. What problems had to be overcome in order to develop a major railroad network?

4. What was the major contribution of the merchant marine in the 1800s?

5. **Critical Thinking** Why would the expansion of the United States have increased its interest in Asia?

2 Life in the Industrializing North

READ TO UNDERSTAND

■ Why workers formed unions and political parties in the mid-1800s.

■ Why immigrants flooded into the North after 1845.

■ How nativist Americans reacted to new immigrants in the mid-1800s.

■ *Vocabulary:* strike, union, workingmen's party, nativist, assimilate.

The increasing industrialization of the United States after 1820 changed the way people lived and worked. The expansion of industry brought increased demand for labor, and immigrants who flooded into the nation from Europe in the mid-1800s quickly found their way into the factories of the North. Their labor was as important to the North's industrial development as any new technology.

The New Factory as a Work Place

As you have read earlier, the American factory system developed in the 1820s. (See page 221.) To many Americans, especially in New England where the soil was thin and rocky, factory work seemed a welcome escape from the toils of farm life. Women and children frequently sought factory work to add to the family income.

At first, New England factory owners tried to provide good conditions for their workers. But as competition from new factories increased during the 1830s, manufacturers lowered workers' wages in an effort to cut costs.

Gradually, employers' attitudes toward workers changed, too. One factory manager remarked, "I regard my workpeople just as I regard my machinery. So long as they can do my work for what I choose to pay them, I keep them, getting out of them all I can."

When the reputation for bad working conditions spread around a New England

289

1. In small towns and rural areas across the nation, one of the most welcome visitors was the traveling peddler. A peddler brought not only goods but also news and gossip. Many peddlers eventually established shops or warehouses as factories began turning out more and more products.

1. **VISUAL EVIDENCE** Have students list the peddler's products. Ask: Why would such goods be difficult to buy in rural areas?

2. **BACKGROUND** In the 1850s, songs extolled life in the mills: "Oh, sing me a song of the Factory Girl! So merry and glad and free! / The bloom in her cheeks, of health how it speaks, / Oh! a happy creature is she!"

2. town, mill owners had to try to recruit more workers from the countryside. Recruiters painted an idyllic but false picture of factory life to farm women, promising "that the work is so very neat, and the wages such, that they can dress in silks and spend half their time in reading." "Now is this true?" fumed one angry woman. "Let those girls who have been thus grossly . . . deceived answer."

Attempts to Organize

Seeking better working conditions, carpenters, shoemakers, and other skilled artisans led the effort to organize labor. Pressing their demands was risky. In the 1790s, the courts had ruled that **strikes,** or work stoppages, were illegal conspiracies that harmed manufacturers and the public. Nevertheless, in the 1820s, workers in major cities of the North-

east began to join together in associations that became known as **unions.**

First and foremost, unions objected to the long work hours that were standard in the factories of the time. They proposed reducing the workday to ten hours, from 6:00 A.M. to 6:00 P.M., with two hours off for meals. In several cities, workers called strikes to demand such changes, but only in New York City were they successful. Elsewhere, employers either took court action to force strikers back to work, or hired nonunion workers to take their places.

Still, the movement gradually spread. Workers' groups from different cities realized the value of coordinating their efforts. In 1834, several groups joined to form the National Trades Union. By this time, about 300,000 workers belonged to some sort of labor organization.

3. **ACTIVITY** Have interested students research the growth of labor unions in Europe, particularly Britain and Germany, and report their findings to the class.

4. **PAST AND PRESENT** Have students research a recent strike, then prepare a report comparing the reasons for that strike with the reasons people struck in the early 1800s.

1. **PAST AND PRESENT** Have students use the *Readers' Guide* to find out the types of political activities carried on by workers' organizations today.

2. **BACKGROUND** By 1860, less than one percent of the nation's labor force was organized.

Early Political Action

Workers also began to seek reforms through political action. Beginning in the late 1820s, local **workingmen's parties** campaigned to improve the status of workers. They demanded an end to property qualifications for voting. To provide their children with better opportunities, they called for free public education.

Workers had economic grievances, too. In most states in the 1820s, over 80 percent of the persons in the jails of northern states were debtors, most of whom owed less than $20. Workingmen's parties campaigned to
1. abolish all laws that put debtors in prison.

For all their enthusiasm, the first unions and workingmen's parties were unable to make much headway. The Panic of 1837, in particular, seriously weakened the workers' cause. The depression threw thousands of people out of work. The jobs that remained were fought over by workers desperate to make a living. Under such conditions, employers were free to keep wages as low as they wanted. The workingmen's parties disappeared and the unions were practically destroyed.

Still, many of the reforms that early workers had sought were written into law. By the mid-1840s, nearly all states had abolished debtor imprisonment laws. All white males had won the right to vote whether they owned property or not. And other reformers were picking up the crusade to create or improve state public school systems, as you will read in Chapter 15.

Workers also won an important legal victory in 1842, in the case of *Commonwealth* v. *Hunt*. That case arose when a group of bootmakers in Boston tried to keep nonunion workers from being hired. Their employers accused the bootmakers of having formed a "criminal conspiracy." But the Massachusetts supreme court ruled that trade unions were lawful, as were strikes to keep out nonunion workers. Despite this victory, the union movement grew slowly. 2.

Other Workers

Only a small number of American workers, mostly skilled artisans, were actively involved in the labor movement before 1860. Factory workers, including women textile workers, were slow to get involved. And when they did attempt to organize, they were seldom successful.

In 1834, when the owners of the Lowell factories cut women's wages by 15 percent, nearly 1,000 women walked off the job. One of the leaders "mounted a stump, and made a flaming . . . speech on the rights of women." But the strike failed, and the women returned 3. to work.

3. **BACKGROUND** During the 1840s, Sarah Bagley organized the women at Lowell into the Female Labor Reform Association. She was the first American woman labor organizer.

4. Working conditions in early factories and foundries, like the one here, were dangerous and unhealthy. The average work day was 12 to 15 hours, and the pay was around $5 a week. Early unions tried, usually without success, to persuade state legislatures to set standards for better labor conditions. Even where such laws were passed, employers could get around them by making new employees sign agreements to work longer hours.

4. **VISUAL EVIDENCE** Ask: Can you see any evidence of dangerous or unhealthy conditions in this picture?

1. **BIOGRAPHY** Ira Aldridge (1807–1867) won worldwide acclaim as a Shakespearean actor, but prejudice kept him from getting serious roles in America.

2. **ECONOMICS** Immigration was briskly promoted by steamship companies, who could profitably load their vessels with immigrants.

Another group of laborers who remained outside the early labor movement were free blacks. Northern states had eliminated virtually all slavery by 1820,* but prejudice against free blacks remained. Frederick Douglass, who had escaped from slavery in Maryland, was a skilled ship's caulker. Nevertheless, he could not find work at his trade in the shipyards of New Bedford, Massachusetts. He was told that, if hired, he would drive away white workers.

Under such circumstances, free blacks were compelled to work at unskilled jobs for very low wages. Consequently, white workers feared that blacks would undercut wages and take their jobs. In many cases, blacks, unable to find employment any other way, worked as strikebreakers.

Although most black workers were unskilled, some became doctors, lawyers, and ministers who served the needs of the black community. Frederick Douglass, who eventually gained world renown as a writer, once observed that his son could more easily find work in a lawyer's office than in a blacksmith's shop.

1.

An Increase in Immigration

Between 1845 and 1854, almost 3 million people from northwestern Europe migrated to the United States. Roughly three fourths of them were from Germany and Ireland.

2.

The immigrants came for many reasons. In 1848, revolutionaries throughout Europe wanted to replace the ruling monarchies with democratic governments. In Germany, the revolution failed and its supporters were forced to flee. Many of them were attracted to the United States because of its traditions of freedom and republican government.

In a number of cases, German immigrants brought money they had been able to save in Europe. When they arrived in the United States, they could move west and buy good farm land. German immigrants also included merchants and artisans, many of whom settled in midwestern cities such as Cincinnati, St. Paul, St. Louis, Chicago, and Milwaukee.

3.

---

*All northern states had passed emancipation laws by 1804. But since some of those laws called for gradual emancipation, there were still slaves in the North after 1804.

3. **BACKGROUND** The ideas of kindergarten (German for *children's garden*) and decorated Christmas trees were brought to the U.S. by German immigrants.

GRAPH STUDY *Immigration increased sharply after 1830. From what country did the greatest number of immigrants arrive between 1841 and 1850? What have you learned that would account for this?* See p. T54.

4.

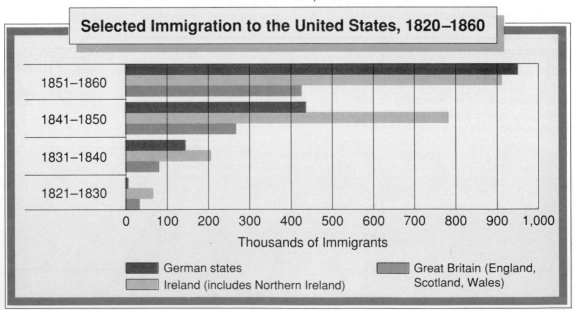

Selected Immigration to the United States, 1820–1860

German states
Ireland (includes Northern Ireland)
Great Britain (England, Scotland, Wales)

Thousands of Immigrants

Source: *Historical Statistics of the United States*

4. **GRAPH READING** Ask: In which decade was immigration from Ireland nearly three times that from Britain? In which decade did German immigration exceed immigration from Ireland?

NOTABLE AMERICANS

Carl Schurz: Crusader for Democracy

Thousands of immigrants came to the United States from Germany to seek freedom and justice. But few fought harder for those ideals on both sides of the Atlantic than Carl Schurz.

While a student at the University of Bonn, Schurz emerged as a leader in Germany's student movement and as a champion of political democracy. During the Revolution of 1848, Schurz fought as an officer in the revolutionary army.

When this struggle met with defeat, Schurz sought political asylum in Switzerland. He might

have remained there but for his loyalty to an old friend and university professor, imprisoned in Germany. Risking his own life, Schurz returned and rescued his friend from prison. From Germany, he fled to France and then to England. Finally, in 1852, he emigrated to the United States.

Once in the United States, Schurz continued to champion the cause of democracy. He took an active role against slavery, both as a speaker and as a brigadier general in the Civil War. After the war, he dared to advise the President that former slaves should be given the right to vote before Confederate states were permitted to rejoin the Union.

Schurz's passion for justice found other avenues. Elected a United States senator in 1868, he fought corruption in the government. Later, as secretary of the interior, he urged a fairer policy toward the Indians. Civil service reform was yet another concern. (See page 448.)

The passion that Carl Schurz brought to his life stands as a reminder of the deep feelings that drove many immigrants to the United States in search of freedom.
See p. T54.

1. In what ways did Carl Schurz take a stand against slavery?

2. Critical Thinking What causes do you think Carl Schurz would support today?

1.

1. **CRITICAL THINKING** Ask: Why do you think Schurz decided to settle in the U.S.?

A famine that resulted from the failure of the Irish potato crop between 1845 and 1850 sparked Irish immigration. For the two thirds of the Irish population affected by the famine, the choice was stark: move or starve. Many began the trip to America in poor health, and hundreds died en route. Almost all who arrived were penniless.

Although most Irish had been farm workers, few could afford to buy land in America. Instead, they tended to take manual jobs, working on canals or railroads or in New England factories. Many wound up in Boston simply because the fare from Ireland to that city was cheaper than to any other city in America.

Indirectly, immigrant workers from Europe helped sharpen the differences that already existed between life in the North and life in the South. The South, with its system of slave labor, was generally unattractive to immigrants. The North, with its expanding economy and need for workers, seemed truly a land of opportunity.

2.

3.

2. **READING** The editor of a Boston Catholic newspaper wrote, "God made Ireland need America and he made America an asylum for Ireland."

3. **PAST AND PRESENT** Have students research what percentage of the population of Boston is of Irish descent today.

293

1. **BACKGROUND** Employers would often discriminate openly against immigrants. It was not unusual for want ads to include the phrase "No Irish Need Apply."

2. **BACKGROUND** Nativists mistakenly feared that the pope would try to control the U.S. by telling Catholic immigrants how to vote.

Negative Reaction to Immigrants

Some Americans viewed the arrival of immigrants with alarm. They began to campaign against what they considered the harmful effects of immigration. Active anti-immigrant groups became known as **nativists,** because they championed the virtues of native-born Americans and their way of life.

Much of the nativist dissatisfaction sprang from economic causes. Immigrants competed with other workers for jobs and, as they expanded the country's labor supply, wages 1. dropped. Furthermore, when native-born workers went on strike for higher pay, immigrants were often hired as strikebreakers.

Social, religious, and political differences contributed to tensions between new immigrants and people born in the United States. Most Irish immigrants and many Germans were Catholic. Since the United States had been a mainly Protestant country since its founding, the appearance of large numbers of people who followed a different religion 2. alarmed many Americans.

Immigrants tended to settle in the same neighborhood as other people from their homeland. In ethnic neighborhoods, they worshiped in their own churches, formed their own social institutions, and spoke their native language. As a result, many immigrants did not **assimilate** quickly into the mainstream of American society. That is, they did not merge into American society by adopting its cultural standards and values. To nativists, they seemed "foreign."

Nativists also pointed with alarm to the high rate of poverty and crime that existed among new immigrants, especially in eastern cities. They claimed these conditions were the result of character faults in the immigrants. In fact, poor housing and other difficulties were at the root of crime and other related problems.

After five years in the country, many immigrants became naturalized citizens and began to vote in significant numbers. By the 1850s, immigrants outnumbered native-born Americans in New York, Chicago, Milwaukee, St. Louis, and several other cities. As both major political parties courted these new voters, nativists began to put forward their own political candidates.

The Know-Nothings

During the 1840s in many areas of the North, nativists organized secret societies. Members pledged to vote for candidates who were sympathetic to nativist beliefs and never to vote for an immigrant or a Catholic candidate. In a few cities, these secret societies enjoyed some success.

In 1845, one of these societies, the Supreme Order of the Star-Spangled Banner, made nativism a national movement. The group was nicknamed the Know-Nothings because its members were sworn to answer inquiries about the order by saying, "I know nothing." The order rapidly spread through the North and showed considerable strength in the South. Soon, it dropped its secrecy 3. and became a political party.

Calling themselves the American party, the former Know-Nothings nominated Millard Fillmore for President in 1856. As you will read in Chapter 16, the issue of slavery in the territories flared in the 1850s. The Know-Nothings in the North split over whether to take an antislavery stand, and the party rapidly lost support.

Nativism was soon overshadowed by the growing conflict between the North and the South. However, the hostility toward immigrants, which had fueled the Know-Nothing party, would surface again after the Civil War. Immigration, and tensions between immigrants and the native-born, had become significant features of American society.

See p. T54.

SECTION 2 REVIEW

1. **Identify:** (a) National Trades Union, (b) *Commonwealth* v. *Hunt*, (c) Know-Nothing party.

2. **Define:** (a) strike, (b) union, (c) workingmen's party, (d) nativist, (e) assimilate.

3. List three goals of workingmen's parties.

4. Why were immigrants attracted to the North?

5. **Critical Thinking** Why did new immigrants try to preserve their traditional way of life?

3. **CITIZENSHIP** Know-Nothing election victories included: 1854—governor and majority of legislature in Massachusetts, 40 state legislators in New York; 1855—governors in Rhode Island, New Hampshire, Connecticut, California, and Kentucky.

1. BACKGROUND Whitney worked on a plantation owned by Catherine Greene. One day in 1793, some planters were complaining about the problems of cleaning cotton. Greene said, "Gentlemen, apply to my young friend Mr. Whitney—he can make anything." Within 10 days, Whitney had built his first cotton gin.

3 Economic Growth in the South

READ TO UNDERSTAND

■ How the invention of the cotton gin changed the South.

■ What crops other than cotton were important in the southern economy.

■ What industries developed in the South.

Cotton Is King was the triumphant title of a book by David Cristy in 1855. If the title sounded boastful, there was reason to justify it. Cotton accounted for over half of all United States exports between 1815 and 1860. Its sale abroad brought in hundreds of millions of dollars a year.

In the South before 1860, the Industrial Revolution had the greatest impact on farming, not manufacturing. A few new factories did open in the South during this period, but cotton production was the heart of the South's economy and cotton the major export. And it was so largely because of one invention.

GEOGRAPHY AND HISTORY

Changes in Southern Agriculture

The most significant development for the southern economy before 1860 was the invention of the cotton gin by Eli Whitney in 1793. The gin, which mechanically separated cotton fibers from the plant's seeds, hull, and leaves, completely transformed cotton production.

Before the introduction of the cotton gin, field workers had to remove cotton seeds from each boll, or pod, by hand. A worker often required a whole day to produce a single pound of raw cotton. For efficiency in this task, the best strain of cotton was one that had long fibers that could be separated fairly easily from the seeds. This type of cotton would grow only on the Sea Islands, off the coast of Georgia and South Carolina. So cotton agriculture tended to be concentrated along the Atlantic coastline.

The cotton gin made it much easier to separate the seeds from the fiber, whether the fibers were long or short. Introduction of this machine meant that cotton production could spread inland, where a short-fiber variety, called short-staple cotton, was able to grow.

2. VOCABULARY The word *gin* was short for *engine,* which meant a machine in the 1800s.

A British visitor to New Orleans wrote, "The most animated and bustling part of all the city is the levee or raised bank running along immediately in front of the river . . . from one end of the city to the other." At New Orleans's wharves, shown in
3. *this painting, he saw a greater number of ships than in any other port he had visited. Ships carried cotton up the Mississippi or across the Atlantic to Europe.*

3. VISUAL EVIDENCE This painting was by William A. Walker, a South Carolinian who portrayed many aspects of life in the South.

1. **TECHNOLOGY** Whitney's early models were operated by one person. Later gins could be turned by water or horses.

2. **ECONOMICS** Remind students that white settlers seeking additional land in the South were the main advocates of the Indian removal policy of the 1820s and 1830s (see p. 250).

The economic impact of the cotton gin was incredible. Using improved gins in the early 1800s, a single worker could clean up to 1,000 pounds (about 450 kilograms) of cotton a day. The improvement occurred at just the time when the expanding textile industry in the North and in Great Britain created enormous demands for raw cotton. Southern farmers rushed to fill these demands by putting more land into cotton production.

plant cotton.* After the War of 1812, many of these farmers flocked to large tracts of unused fertile land in Alabama, Mississippi, and Louisiana. By 1860, cotton production had expanded as far west as Texas. The map below shows the westward expansion of the "cotton kingdom."

The cotton boom of the early 1800s had a human dimension, too. Cotton could now be cleaned mechanically, but it was still picked

Rise of the Cotton Kingdom

Gradually, the soil along the Atlantic coast became depleted, and southern farmers looked westward for new land on which to

*With land plentiful and cheap, Americans in both the North and the South had traditionally used land wastefully. Instead of replacing minerals in depleted soil, they simply moved to new land.

3. **MAP READING** Ask: What products were grown along the Atlantic coast in 1860?

MAP STUDY Although cotton was "king," rice, tobacco, and sugar cane were also important to the economy of the South. In what general area was cotton grown? To what areas did cotton growing spread between 1840 and 1860? See p. T55.

Southern Agriculture

Legend:
- Cotton, 1840
- Cotton, 1860
- Corn and wheat, 1860
- Tobacco and hemp, 1860
- Rice and sugar cane, 1860

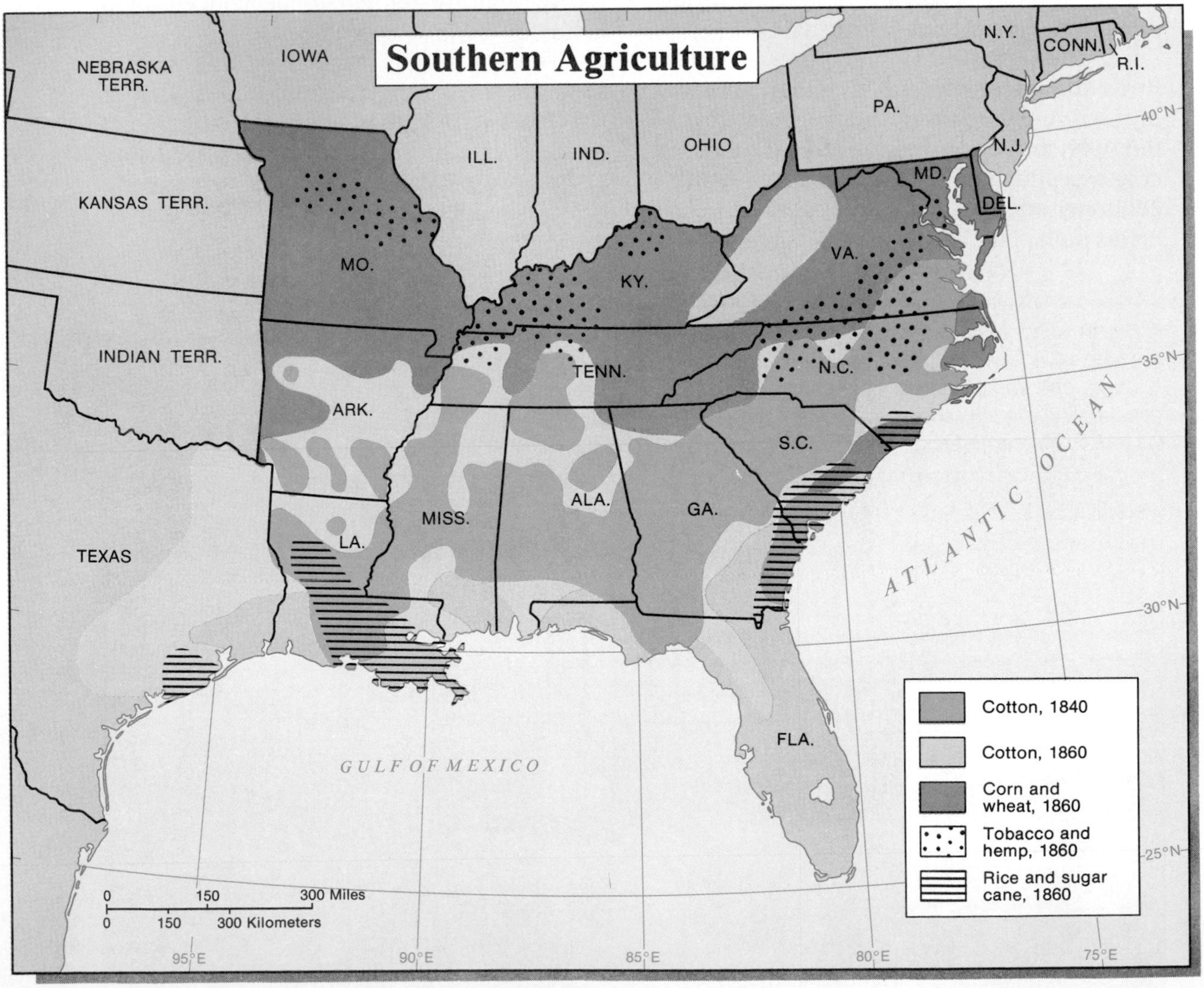

1. **CRITICAL THINKING** Ask: How might the economic importance of cotton affect efforts to end slavery in the South?

1. by hand. To make a large profit, a planter needed a large labor force. Most planters saw no reason to hire workers if they could use slaves. As a result, the institution of slavery spread westward along with the cultivation of cotton.

By the 1840s, 1.5 million bales of American cotton were being produced each year, compared with only 10,000 in the late 1790s. By the mid-1800s, over 60 percent of all the cotton produced in the world grew in the South, and cotton accounted for over 60 per-
2. cent of the value of all United States exports. Clearly cotton had become king.

Other Southern Crops

Since cotton requires a growing season of at least 200 frost-free days a year, it was limited to the South's southernmost portion. In the northern sections of the South, farmers depended on other cash crops. (See the map on page 296.) Tobacco had been an export of the region since 1619, and it continued to be planted in Virginia, North Carolina, and Kentucky. However, in the early 1800s, the large tobacco plantations of colonial days had given way to small tobacco farms, where a few field hands tended five or six acres of tobacco.

Other southern crops required large plantations to be profitable. Growing rice, important along the coasts of South Carolina and Georgia, and sugar cane, important in Louisiana and Texas, required expensive irrigation and drainage systems. Cane growers needed machinery to grind their harvest. Since small-scale farmers could not afford such expensive equipment, the plantation system dominated areas of sugar and rice production.

In addition to the major cash crops of cotton, rice, and sugar, the South also led the nation in livestock production. Southern livestock owners profited from hogs, oxen, horses, mules, and beef cattle. Much of this livestock was raised in areas that were unsuitable for growing crops, such as the pine woods of North Carolina. ∎

Early Industry in the South

As cotton grew increasingly important to the economy of the South, southerners became concerned about their dependence on banks

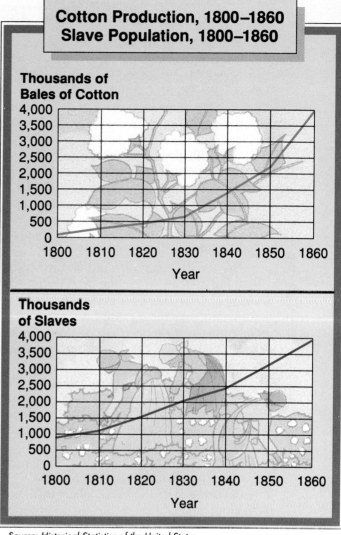

Cotton Production, 1800–1860
Slave Population, 1800–1860

Thousands of Bales of Cotton

Year

Thousands of Slaves

Year

Source: *Historical Statistics of the United States*

GRAPH STUDY *These two graphs show cotton production and the slave population in the United States between 1800 and 1860. Based on the graphs, what generalization can you make about the relationship of cotton to the growth of slavery?* See p. T55.

3.

3. **GRAPH READING** Ask: About how much cotton was produced in 1820? In 1860? What was the slave population in 1820? In 1860?

and factories in the North. Southern planters often borrowed money from northern banks to expand their plantations, and many of their farm tools and machines came from northern factories. Northern shippers transported raw cotton from the South to New England, where northern textile firms wove it into cloth. The very price of cotton was influenced by buyers from the North and from Europe. When the price fell in the 1840s, some southerners decided to establish factories and other industries in their own region, to make the South more independent.

297

2. **ECONOMICS** The actual value of the cotton exported from the South grew from $5,000,000 in 1800 to $191,000,000 in 1860.

William Gregg of South Carolina led the movement to bring the textile industry to the South. He built a successful mill in Graniteville, South Carolina, and operated it in the same humane manner that had characterized the owners of the early Lowell mills in New England. Gregg landscaped his mill grounds with shrubbery and flowers and set up garden cottages for working families. He began the first compulsory school in the South and punished any boy or girl he caught playing hooky. Wages for his workers were low, but they compared favorably with wages in northern mills.

The South also developed other successful industries. In Richmond, Virginia, the Tredegar Iron Works turned out railroad equipment, machinery for Louisiana sugar plantations, and cannons for the United States Navy. Flour milling was another important southern industry.

Southern transportation also grew. The South has an extensive system of navigable rivers, and farmers in the interior were able to ship their crops by water to the coast. After 1850, railroads developed, but, as you read earlier, rail networks expanded more slowly in the South than in the North.

Despite efforts to industrialize, the South remained dependent on the North for industrial goods. The Industrial Revolution had changed the South in the first half of the 1800s, but it did so chiefly by making cotton king.

1.

See p. T55.

SECTION 3 REVIEW

1. **Identify:** (a) Eli Whitney, (b) William Gregg.

2. What single event transformed the southern economy in the early 1800s? Explain.

3. How did the cotton boom encourage the spread of slavery?

4. What attempts were made to diversify the economy of the South?

5. **Critical Thinking** Did the early success of cotton in the South help or hinder the region's economic development? Explain.

4 Life in the South

READ TO UNDERSTAND

■ What social groups made up free southern society in the South before 1860.

■ How southerners earned their living.

■ What daily life was like for each of the South's social groups.

Life in the South was heavily governed by tradition in the early 1800s. For those who were not slaves, most days were spent in hard work and simple joys. The forms of work and recreation varied from place to place and from group to group.

Life on Small Farms

The great majority of white southerners, perhaps 75 percent, lived on small, independent family farms. They owned their own land and possibly a few slaves. Said one southerner, "If we have very few rich men, we have, on the other hand, not many that are poor: the great mass is composed of the 'middle interest,' the bone and sinew of every country."

Independent farmers could be found throughout the South. But their biggest concentration was in the hilly regions of eastern Tennessee; in northern Georgia, Alabama, and Mississippi; and on the poorer soil of the coastal regions. Most were subsistence farmers who raised corn, oats, wheat, and sweet potatoes for food. Occasionally, they planted an acre or two of cotton or tobacco to sell for cash.

In many ways, these men and women were like frontier people. Proud and hardworking, they lived simply. They learned to overcome their isolation by gathering together whenever they could, and they had a genius for turning work into play. Routine, time-consuming chores such as corn shucking, quilting, and house raising became occasions for a party. Neighboring farmers and their 2. families would join together to turn the job into a contest, followed by a cookout and a square dance.

2. **BACKGROUND** Log rolling involved lifting logs off fields that were to be planted in the spring. A farmer's neighbors would gather from nearby farms and turn the job into a weightlifting contest.

Most southerners had small farms, not rich plantations. But hospitality and amusements were important in their life. This painting, Virginia Wedding, is by a 1. contemporary artist, William Ranney. In the joyful scene, nine couples dressed in their finery parade on horseback.

1. **VISUAL EVIDENCE** Remind students that Ranney also painted *The Old Scout's Tale* on p. 263.

Poor Whites

About 10 percent of the southern population were "poor whites," so-called because they occupied land that would not profitably support the planting of crops. Poor whites lived in the backwoods, on the sides of hills and mountains, and in the depths of sandy-soiled pine barrens.

The occasional traveler passing a backwoods cabin might see a few rows of corn, a patch of sweet potatoes, and a few domestic animals, such as cows, horses, or hounds. Such a view might well conceal the family's greatest source of income: a herd of wild cattle or razorback hogs that foraged in the nearby forest. Some poor whites were content to manage a herd only large enough to feed their family. Others tended several hundred head of cattle or hogs, which they periodically drove to market and sold for a profit.

Herdsmen in such settings usually considered it beneath their dignity to farm. As a result, women had the hardest life. They not only had to perform such household chores as weaving and making lye soap, they also had to tend the vegetable patch and, perhaps, a small field of tobacco as well. The backwoods diet was monotonous, and many poor whites suffered from malnutrition. 2.

Free Blacks

By 1860, about 260,000 free blacks lived in the South. Many were the descendants of slaves who had been freed during the revolutionary era. Most free blacks lived in or around the cities and towns in the northern sections of the South. Over one third resided in Maryland alone.

Most free blacks worked as domestic servants or hired themselves out as farm laborers. Some were skilled workers—shoemakers and blacksmiths, for example. Others were barbers, a trade in which free blacks had a virtual monopoly. A handful were merchants, hotel keepers, and planters who owned their 3. own black slaves.

299

2. **MAIN IDEA** Have students write a paragraph summarizing the life of poor whites in the South.

3. **READING** Students who want to learn more about free blacks in the South can read *Slaves Without Masters: The Free Negro in the Antebellum South,* by Ira Berlin.

1. **ACTIVITY** Have students make a pyramid diagram illustrating the social classes of the South.

2. **DISCUSSION** Ask: If so few southerners were planters, why do you suppose planters have been shown as typical of the Old South by so many books, films, and television programs?

The life of a free black in the South was not easy. In the towns and cities, white workers and artisans resented them for competing for jobs, just as white laborers did in the North. Plantation owners generally suspected free blacks of being potential leaders of slave rebellions. Moreover, many white southerners saw the mere presence of blacks who were free and prospering as a threat to the institution of slavery.

As a result of such fears, southern legislatures severely restricted the rights of free blacks. Although they had to pay taxes, as did other free persons, free blacks could not vote.* Blacks normally could not testify in court. They were sometimes required to have a white guardian and were subject to curfew laws. Their rights of movement and assembly were severely limited, and they lived in constant danger of being illegally kidnapped and sold into slavery.

Yet, in many cases, the harsh laws against free blacks were not enforced. In fact, the status of free blacks in the South before 1860 was little worse than it was in the North.

---

*Free blacks were restricted from voting in the North, too. After 1822, they could vote only in Massachusetts, New Hampshire, and Vermont.

The Planters

At the top of southern society were the planters. With their gracious manners, elegant homes, and huge landholdings worked by slaves, southern planters set the social style of the region and dominated its politics as well. Small farmers usually envied the planters. Sometimes, they resented their power. Almost always, they hoped to gain enough land and slaves to join their ranks. **1.**

To be considered a member of the planter class, a landholder generally had to own at least 20 slaves, employ an overseer to supervise the slaves, and possess a cotton gin. Not many achieved this goal. Out of 8 million southerners, fewer than 50,000 families had more than 20 slaves. Only 10,000 families had more than 50 slaves. **2.**

Many planters in the established areas of the South tried to live in the style of the English country gentry, or land-owning upper class. They built spacious brick mansions faced with white columns. They imported elegant furniture, silver tea sets, and other luxuries from Great Britain. Usually, they hired tutors to teach their children. The wealthiest planters also maintained town houses in Charleston and other southern cities. Far-

3. **VISUAL EVIDENCE** Ask: Why do you think the painting does not show the slave quarters?

---

3. *Wealthy southern planters built elaborate country homes such as this one in Louisiana. The red building at right is the sugar refinery on the Olivier Plantation. The elegant clothing shown typified the lives of many plantation owners.*

ther to the west, in the newer farming regions, plantation life was less refined.

Planters had to work hard in order to succeed. A plantation was a large and complex enterprise. Planters had to stay informed about the current world demand for their crop, whether it was cotton, sugar, or rice. They had to make critical decisions about planting, harvesting, and marketing. A planter's wife often helped in the management of the plantation. She supervised the household servants, directing those who wove the cloth, made the soap, and sewed the clothes. And she cared for the sick, both black and white.

Planters with large landholdings preferred to break them into small plantations, since it was impractical for a field to be more than an hour's walk from the slave quarters. Overseers supervised the day-to-day operations of the individual plantations. Most of the overseers were either the younger sons of planters or ambitious farmers who hoped to earn enough money to enter the planter class themselves. Occasionally, a trusted slave was made the overseer, but this was the exception rather than the rule.

Although planters remained a minority among white southerners, they left an indelible stamp on the sectional character of the
1. South. They resisted social change, especially any threat to the preservation of slavery. And they created a grand lifestyle that was extraordinary in a democratic society.

See p. T55.

SECTION 4 REVIEW

1. How did most white southerners make a living?

2. (a) Who were the "poor whites"? (b) Describe their daily life.

3. List three legal restrictions on the rights of free blacks in the South.

4. (a) What distinguished a planter from other farmers? (b) What role did the planters play in southern society?

5. **Critical Thinking** Why would white slave owners see the existence of free blacks as a threat to the institution of slavery?

5 | The Slaves' World

READ TO UNDERSTAND

■ What slaves had to endure in their living and working conditions.

■ How enslaved blacks preserved their dignity.

■ How blacks resisted slavery before 1860.

■ *Vocabulary:* task system, gang system.   2.

"Sold down the river" became a popular expression in the 1850s. It implied—often, in fun—that a person had been double-crossed. But for slaves along the Mississippi, where the expression originated, it symbolized being taken from family and friends and sold to someone far away.

A slave working in a planter's home might have less grief than one working in a rice field. The pace of life on one plantation might differ greatly from life on another. Yet all slaves were united by the fact that they were considered another person's property. They were denied even the most basic human rights.

Work

As of 1860, slaves made up over one third of the population of the South. The vast majority of them—both men and women—worked in fields, where they planted, cultivated, and harvested crops. Slaves also worked as servants in plantation houses and as skilled artisans in small shops. If a slave worked for a landowner who had just a few acres, the two might be in close daily contact, sharing the same tasks and often the same food. Most slaves, however, worked on large plantations.

On these plantations, a slave's work day was usually organized in one of two ways. On rice and hemp plantations and on the Sea Islands cotton plantations, slaves worked under the **task system.** They had specific jobs, or tasks, to complete each day. If they finished their jobs before the day's end, they had free time for personal pursuits.

The **gang system,** which was used on tobacco, sugar, and inland cotton plantations,   **301**

HAULING THE WHOLE WEEKS PICKING

For slaves on a plantation, life was a constant round of hard work. Children started work young, with light chores. A grown slave could expect to work from dawn to
1. *dusk. This picture shows a slave family "hauling the whole week's picking" of cotton.*

1. **VISUAL EVIDENCE** Ask: What does the picture show about the division of labor in this slave family?

2. **CRITICAL THINKING** Ask: Why do you think the journals gave this advice?

was more common. Under this system, field slaves were assigned to work together in gangs, supervised by an overseer. These slaves normally worked from sunrise to sunset, with a two-hour rest period in the middle of the day.

The physical treatment a slave received could be brutal or relatively mild. It depended on the plantation and especially on the temperament of the owner. But regardless of temperament, most planters used the threat of physical punishment to force slaves to work long hours for limited rewards.

Living Conditions

Large-scale planters typically grouped their slaves' quarters together, not far from the main house. Southern farm magazines frequently advised planters to provide slaves
2. with good housing. Some planters did build decent brick or frame cabins for their slaves and even provided ample firewood for fuel. Typically, however, slave cabins had one room with a dirt floor and were crudely built.

Clothing and food were hardly better. Slaves commonly received a regular allotment of clothing that was too scanty to carry them through the year. Cases of frostbitten feet were fairly common among slaves in the colder areas of the South. Despite an occasional holiday feast, the usual slave diet was "hog and hominy," or pork and corn. Seafood, dairy products, and other meats were rarely available to them, although they often had fruits and vegetables.

Importance of Family Life

Nothing provided critics with a more compelling case against slavery than the practice of breaking up slave families. Although some planters tried to keep slave families together, it was by no means uncommon for a slave's husband or wife to be sold to a planter hundreds of miles away. State laws in the South were no help in this matter. The South did not recognize the legality of slave marriages.

But family life was of great importance to slaves. By providing needed emotional support, a slave's family could help make life bearable. On some plantations, slaves used their garden plots to promote family contacts. By growing their own vegetables or hunting their own food, slave families quietly but firmly asserted their competence. By providing for their children's needs without the planter's direction, slave parents showed themselves worthy of their children's respect.

Preserving Human Dignity

Cultural bonds were also very important to the slaves' sense of dignity. Religious practices, holiday celebrations, and the remnants of African culture that slaves had managed to preserve became part of their family traditions in America. Ironically, Christianity proved to be sometimes a comfort to slaves, and sometimes a hindrance.

1. **BACKGROUND** Frederick Douglass described the songs of slaves: "They were tones loud, long, and deep; they breathed the prayer and complaint of souls boiling over with the bitterest anguish. Every tone was a testimony against slavery, and a prayer to God for deliverance from chains."

On the one hand, planters often supervised the slaves' religious life, making sure the sermons emphasized meekness and obedience. On the other hand, slaves stressed the importance Jesus attached to marriage, the family, and people's human obligations to one another. In addition, slaves developed spirituals, an important body of religious music, that provided great comfort. At Christmas, most slaves had some free time, which they used in celebrating together.

Many slaves relied on traditions from their African homelands to shape their culture in America. Because slave importation had been prohibited in the United States since 1808, few slaves in the mid-1800s had direct ties or contacts with Africa. Yet some African customs were faithfully passed down by word of

2. **ACTIVITY** Play recordings of some spirituals in class. Ask: How do you think the words and mood of the songs helped people cope with slavery?

3. **CRITICAL THINKING** Ask: Is it significant that Lyell is describing a plantation in Georgia while Northrup is describing a plantation in Louisiana?

SKILL LESSON

Two Views of Slavery: Analyzing Conflicting Sources

Historians who want to investigate a past event or trend must deal with primary sources. Often, such sources present conflicting information. Read the two descriptions of slavery below. One was written by Sir Charles Lyell, a British aristocrat who visited a Georgia plantation in the 1840s. The other was written by Solomon Northrup, a free black who was kidnapped and sold into slavery on a Louisiana plantation.

See p. T56.

1 **Compare the contents of your sources.** Do both writers agree about (a) the working conditions of slaves, (b) the type of food slaves were given, or (c) the use of whippings by slave owners?

2 **Evaluate the reliability of each source.** (a) How might Lyell's background have affected his attitude toward southern planters and slavery? (b) How might the fact that Northrup was kidnapped and sold into slavery have affected his views?

3 **Use the sources to help you draw conclusions.** (a) Would you accept either account as an accurate description of slavery? Explain. (b) What conclusions about slavery can you draw from both accounts?

Sir Charles Lyell

The laborers begin work at six o'clock in the morning, have an hour's rest at nine for breakfast, and many have finished their assigned task by two. In summer they go to bed in the middle of the day, then rise to finish their task, and afterward spend a great part of the night in chatting, preaching, and psalm-singing. The laborers are allowed Indian meal, rice, and milk, and occasionally pork and soup. As their rations are more than they can eat, they either return part of it at the end of the week, or they keep it to feed their fowls. . . . The sight of the whip was painful to me as a mark of degradation, reminding me that the lower orders of slaves are kept to their work by bodily fear. That the whip is rarely used, . . . is no doubt true on all well-governed estates.

Solomon Northrup

An hour before day light the horn is blown. Then the slaves arouse, prepare their breakfast, fill a gourd with water, in another deposit their dinner of cold bacon and corn cake, and hurry to the field again. It is an offense invariably followed by a flogging to be found at the quarters after daybreak. Then the fears and labors of another day begin; and until its close there is no such thing as rest. With the exception of ten or fifteen minutes, which is given them at noon to swallow their allowance of cold bacon, they are not permitted to be a moment idle until it is too dark to see, and when the moon is full, they often times labor till the middle of the night. . . . Each one receives, as his weekly allowance, three and a half pounds of bacon, and corn enough to make a peck of meal.

4. **BIOGRAPHY** Charles Lyell (1797–1875) was the leading English geologist of the 1800s. He visited the U.S. on lecture tours three times during the 1840s and 1850s.

mouth from older slaves to their children and grandchildren.

Slaves, for example, often followed the West African custom of naming children after their grandparents. The slave tradition of maintaining extended families, in which parents, grandparents, aunts, uncles, and other relatives were considered part of the immediate family, also had roots in Africa. Most important, oral traditions kept alive the memory of a time when their ancestors had been free. This memory fueled their will to resist slavery and to believe that someday it would end.

The Slaves' Reaction to Slavery

Trying to preserve human dignity through family life, religion, holidays, and cultural traditions helped many slaves to live in a society that denied them their most basic rights. But they dealt with slavery in other ways, too.

Many slaves adopted an outwardly cheerful and carefree manner, professing loyalty to the landholder. For some, especially for house servants who were treated kindly, such loyalty may have been sincere. But many slaves adopted a carefree expression to mask or hide their resentment. While pretending to be happy, they developed countless ways to exasperate their masters and still escape punishment.

Some slaves became adept at a sort of day-to-day resistance to slavery. They slowed down their pace of work, stole extra food, broke tools, destroyed crops, and pretended sickness or disability. Slaves aptly called this type of resistance "puttin' on old Massa."

Running away was a more extreme reaction to slavery. The chances of a successful escape were slim. Runaways were tracked with dogs, and most slaves did not know the countryside outside the plantation they lived on. Yet in the 1850s, about 1,000 slaves tried to run away each year. Sometimes, slaves would run away as a temporary protest. They would hide in swamps or woods for months and then return. This was one of the few means of active protest available in the deep South, where the distance from free states made permanent escape impossible.

At a slave market, such as the one below, an auctioneer described the strength and skills of the men, women, and children he had for sale. Members of a slave family could be sold to different owners and thus separated forever. The worst fate was to be "sold down the river," to a rice or sugar plantation in the Deep South, where slaves faced the harshest working conditions of all.

Slave Revolts

The slave's ultimate protest was violent revolt, something white southerners constantly feared. Yet, in reality, few slaves revolted. This is hardly surprising, since the odds were always overwhelmingly against the slaves. Slaves had few weapons and were under constant guard. The threat of discovery by whites or betrayal by slaves loyal to their masters was always present. As a result, only a handful of slaves ever participated in a revolt.

1.

Nevertheless, there were several important slave revolts before 1860. In 1791, Toussaint L'Ouverture successfully led a revolt in Haiti, where he established a black republic. (See page 202.) His success served as an inspiration for slaves on the mainland.

In 1800, Gabriel Prosser was caught stirring up a conspiracy to make Virginia a black republic. In 1811, between 300 and 500 slaves marched on New Orleans in a well-organized rebellion, but they were easily defeated by a militia. Denmark Vesey, a free black carpenter in Charleston, was plotting a major uprising when he and his associates were betrayed by a slave and arrested in 1822.

In 1831, Nat Turner, a slave preacher, led a full-scale revolt in Southampton County, Virginia. Inspired by reading the Bible and by his vision of black and white angels in combat, Turner led a group of about 70 armed slaves in a bloody revolt. By the time authorities crushed the uprising, the rebels had killed more than 60 whites. The Virginia militia responded by killing scores of blacks, including many who had played no part at all in the revolt. Turner himself was captured and executed.

The Defense of Slavery

The Turner revolt sent shock waves of fear throughout the South. That anxiety, as well as the rise of abolitionist activities in the North, led many white southerners to harden their attitudes toward slaves.

At the time of the Revolutionary War, many southerners had considered slavery a "necessary evil." They felt guilty about owning slaves and sometimes freed them in their wills. But, following Nat Turner's rebellion in 1831, southern legislatures began to enact harsher slave codes, limiting the actions of free blacks as well as of slaves. The codes also made it more difficult for planters to free their slaves.

These attempts to strengthen the institution of slavery accompanied a growing attitude among many southerners that slavery was a positive good. They noted that the ancient civilizations of Greece and Rome had been based on slavery. They claimed that, since slaves were property, the Constitution's protection of property applied to their "ownership" of slaves. A few even insisted that slavery benefited the enslaved.

2.

Some writers defended slavery by comparing the treatment of slaves with the treatment of workers in northern factories. George Fitzhugh, a Virginia planter, wrote that slave owners formed a genuine bond of affection with their slaves—much like that between parents and children. A plantation, Fitzhugh asserted, was like a little community, in which each person performed certain duties that contributed to the good of all. Northern factory owners, Fitzhugh said, took no responsibility for workers who became sick, disabled, or aged.

Besides the insult of comparing slaves to children, Fitzhugh and writers like him simply failed to recognize the basic abuse in allowing one person to enslave another. That so many slaves managed to retain their dignity and humanity in the face of such an institution is a tribute to their remarkable strength and heritage.

See p. T55.

SECTION 5 REVIEW

1. **Identify:** (a) "puttin' on old Massa," (b) Nat Turner.

2. **Define:** (a) task system, (b) gang system.

3. (a) Which plantations used the task system? (b) Which used the gang system?

4. What Christian teachings were most important to slaves?

5. What effect did Nat Turner's revolt have on southerners' attitudes toward slavery?

6. **Critical Thinking** How was the poorest northern worker better off than the best-treated slave?

Summary

1. **Between 1820 and 1860, industry expanded rapidly in the North.** Industrial growth was the result of important inventions in manufacturing, agriculture, and transportation. Factories multiplied, farmers began to specialize, and new railroad networks linked West to East.

2. **As industry spread, working conditions worsened in the industrialized North.** Skilled workers tried to organize to improve conditions but met with limited success. Immigrants from Europe expanded the labor supply, but despite their contributions, the newcomers were resented by many Americans.

3. **In the South, invention of the cotton gin and increased demand for cotton caused a boom in cotton production.** Southern farmers also raised rice, sugar cane, tobacco, and livestock. The South also began to industrialize on a modest scale.

4. **The daily lives of white southerners varied, but in one way or another all made their living from the soil.** Most free blacks in the South lived in its coastal and northernmost cities.

5. **Enslaved blacks made up more than one third of the South's population before 1860.** Many relied on family bonds, religion, and memories of their African heritage to maintain their dignity and strength. Slaves found a variety of subtle and open ways to show their resistance to their condition.

See p. T56.

Vocabulary

On a separate sheet of paper, write the word or words that best complete each of the following sentences.

1. _____ are heavily traveled railroads that link major cities.

2. A (an) _____ is a work stoppage.

3. Workers form _____ in order to bargain for better conditions.

4. _____ were groups opposed to unlimited immigration.

5. The _____ was a means of assigning slave labor according to the jobs to be done.

See p. T56.

Chapter Checkup

1. (a) How were early problems in the development of the railroads overcome? (b) What impact did the railroads have on the economy of the North?

2. (a) How did America's trade expand during the 1840s and 1850s? (b) What was the role of the clipper ships? (c) Why were they replaced by steamships?

3. (a) How did industrialization affect northern agriculture? (b) How did farming in the North differ from farming in the South in the years before 1860?

4. (a) How did factory work change during the 1830s? (b) How did workers try to improve conditions? (c) Were they successful? Explain.

5. (a) After 1840, where did new immigrants to the United States come from? (b) Where did they settle? (c) Why did some Americans protest the influx of immigrants at this time?

6. (a) How did the invention of the cotton gin affect the nature of cotton growing in the South? (b) What impact did textile mills in the North and Great Britain have on the cotton industry? (c) What impact did the expansion of the cotton kingdom have on slavery?

7. (a) How did the life of southern farmers with small landholdings differ from that of "poor whites"? (b) How did the life of the planters differ from that of other southern farmers?

8. (a) How did most slaves struggle to maintain their sense of human dignity? (b) In what ways did some show resistance to slavery? (c) In the long run, which strategies were best? Explain.

See p. T57.

Critical Thinking

1. Analyzing (a) Why do you think most railroads in the early 1800s ran from east to west rather than from north to south? (b) What effect do you think this had on the settlement of the West?

2. Comparing (a) What problems did free blacks face in the North? (b) What problems did they face in the South? (c) In what ways were their problems similar? (d) In what ways were they different?

3. Inferring Planters with large landholdings formed a very small part of the southern population. Why do you think they had such a major impact on the society, politics, and economy of the South?

See p. T57.

Connecting Past and Present

1. In the period between 1820 and 1840, skilled crafts workers organized unions to resist changes being made by industrialization. (a) Should workers today rely on unions for job security? (b) What other possible solutions are there for job security in a changing economy?

2. How does prejudice against any group damage the fabric of society?

See p. T57.

Developing Basic Skills

1. Map Reading Study the map on page 296: (a) What information is shown on this map? (b) In what areas was cotton growing most prevalent in 1840? (c) In what part of the South was cotton not grown? (d) How might the absence of cotton growing in a region be explained?

2. Researching Find out more about the life of one of the inventors you read about in this chapter. Study the person's personal background and the circumstances surrounding his invention(s). Did his invention(s) bring him success?

WRITING ABOUT HISTORY

Considering Areas for Research

A major part of your success in writing a research paper will depend on your ability to find the information you need. Often, you will be able to find your information listed under more than one topic. For example, suppose your paper is on the effect of the cotton gin on southern agriculture. After you have exhausted sources listed under the topic *cotton gin,* you should try to think of topics that deal with the period of time you are studying, the geographic location involved, and other related subjects. For example, you might look into the topics *Eli Whitney, Tech-nological history,* and *Slave labor.* Books about the history of agriculture in the South might also help.

If you cannot think of any related topics, look in an encyclopedia for an article on your original topic. Often, such an article will include a bibliography as well as a list of related topics.

Practice: List two related areas of research for each of these topics: The Expansion of Industry in the 1800s; The Labor Movement in the 1800s; American Reaction to Immigrants, 1840–1860; Slave Revolts.

In the 1830s, John Deere's neighbors in Illinois knew him as a blacksmith with an inventive mind. If they had a practical problem, they took it to Deere. One problem they had was plowing the soil. The Illinois prairie was covered with thick grass that broke the cast iron blade of the farmers' plows.

Deere was sure that hardened steel would do the job, so he reshaped the blade of an old steel saw and attached it to a plow. Hitching his plow to a team of horses, Deere cut 12 smooth, straight furrows. Not once did he have to stop to clean the plow blade!

1. **VISUAL EVIDENCE** Ask: How similar is Singer's original sewing machine to sewing machines of today?

Isaac Singer is seen here at a demonstration of his
1. *sewing machine. Singer made improvements on the original machine, invented by Elias Howe. Singer's business partner increased sales of the machine by allowing families to purchase it on the installment plan, in which people agreed to pay a small sum each month, with interest, until the purchase price was paid off.*

Word of Deere's success spread quickly. Soon he was selling so many steel plows that his backyard business grew into a major industry. Deere's ingenuity made him rich.

Inventive Americans Simple ingenuity—the knack for figuring things out—seems to have been part of the American character from the nation's beginning. Long before Deere built a plow for prairie sod, Thomas Jefferson had adapted the English plow to the Virginia soil. By 1855, the Patent Office in Washington, D.C., had issued 372 patents—just for improvements to the plow!

Why were Americans so adept at inventing and improving? For one thing, there was so much to do in the New World. In Europe, houses, churches, and streets had existed for hundreds of years. But Americans had to build everything from scratch. And while the new nation was rich in natural resources, it was always short of labor. Americans had to find ways to get a job done as quickly and easily as possible.

When Alexis de Tocqueville visited America in the 1830s, he commented on how well Americans understood "the purely practical." De Tocqueville noted that Americans saved their highest praise for practical inventions. "Every new method that leads to a shorter road to wealth, every machine that spares labor . . . seems the grandest effort of the human intellect."

Age of Invention By the mid-1800s, Americans were producing one invention after another. In the 1840s alone, Yankee ingenuity created the telegraph, the sewing machine, vulcanized rubber, and an improved printing press. Most of the inventors were ordinary people who improved the tools and machines they worked with ten hours a day, six days a week. For every well-known inventor like John Deere, there were thousands like Walter Hunt whom few people remember. Yet anyone who has used a safety pin owes Hunt thanks for his 1849 invention.

Walter Hunt may not be famous, but at least he profited from his invention. Not all inventors were so lucky. In the Old South, for example, slaves could not get credit for inventions. It was only after the Civil War that black inventors finally received protection of the law. In 1872, a freed slave named Elijah McCoy created a device that oiled engines automatically. The saying "the real McCoy" may have come from customers who would buy only McCoy's invention, not a copy.

The industrial boom after the Civil War nearly doubled the rate of patents being issued. At the same time, Americans began to approach technology in a more systematic way. In 1861, the Massachusetts Institute of Technology began to train students in engineering and other practical sciences. The Morrill Land Grant Act of 1862 helped states create new universities that specialized in improving agriculture.

As industry became more scientific, businesses began to take research and development seriously. Thomas Edison's "invention factory," which he built in Menlo Park, New Jersey, in 1876, served as a model. When industrialists saw hundreds of useful and profitable inventions pouring out of Menlo Park, they began to establish similar workshops.

A Practical Philosophy In the late 1800s, an American philosopher, William James, pioneered a new philosophy based on practicality. He called his philosophy pragmatism. To James, most philosophers had wasted their time debating whether abstract ideas were true or false. James believed that an idea had to be judged on the basis of its practical results—the truth of an idea could be tested by experience.

Pragmatism had a wide influence. In the 1890s, John Dewey set out to reform public schools, which he felt were teaching ab-

According to Thomas Edison, genius was "1 percent inspiration and 99 percent perspiration." Edison's favorite invention was the phonograph. Partially deaf from childhood, Edison could enjoy music that was electronically magnified by his invention. In his lifetime, he acquired more than 1,300 United States and foreign patents for his inventions.

1.

1. **VISUAL EVIDENCE** Ask: What point is being made by this advertisement? To whom would it appeal?

stract ideas that had little to do with real life. Dewey believed students should learn by doing. While studying colonial America, for example, students at Dewey's "laboratory school" in Chicago cleaned cotton, spun wool, and built a weaving loom. "You can concentrate the history of all mankind into the evolution of the flax, cotton, and wool fibers into clothing," Dewey said. Dewey's ideas had a lasting impact on American education.

Today, much research is carried on in gleaming laboratories at universities or corporate research-and-development departments. Yet the individual inventor is not obsolete. Not long ago, a computer "hacker" named Steven Jobs along with two or three other computer experts built a small electronic machine in a garage. A few years later, that machine—the Apple II personal computer—was in use in millions of homes, schools, and businesses.

Is it possible that Americans are too practical? De Tocqueville worried, 150 years ago, that Americans were so practical they would ignore important issues. But a blend of the practical and the ideal holds promise for society today.

See p. T57.

1. How did the American approach to technology become more systematic after the Civil War?

2. **Critical Thinking** How do the ideas of William James and John Dewey reflect American practicality?

Notable Americans

Cyrus McCormick

Cyrus Hall McCormick was a leader among the industrialists of his era. He developed a machine that revolutionized farming in the 1800s. He also introduced to American industry some business practices that have remained important to this day.

Cyrus McCormick was born in 1809 on a farm in Virginia. His father, Robert McCormick, was a part-time inventor who had developed a new type of mill to grind wheat. But his efforts to build a horse-drawn reaper had failed. Robert McCormick encouraged his son to take up the project.

Cyrus worked on a mechanical reaper enthusiastically. In 1831, he and his father tested the new machine successfully in a Virginia wheat field. For a fee of $30, Cyrus patented the McCormick reaper and set out to make his fortune manufacturing it for local farmers.

Although his invention was a great advance, McCormick sold only a few reapers in Virginia, where there was still a slave economy. Deeply in debt, he decided to go west. Labor was scarce on the vast prairies of Illinois and beyond, and the gently rolling terrain was ideally suited to the mechanical reaper.

McCormick needed to build a factory near his potential customers. At the time, Chicago was little more than a way station on Lake Michigan. But McCormick saw that the town lay between the opening West and the commercial East. With a $25,000 loan from the mayor of Chicago, he set up his factory. Rail lines fanning out from Chicago carried McCormick's reapers to farmers, and wheat poured back to Chicago to be

With $60 in his pocket, Cyrus McCormick (1809-1884) arrived in Chicago to start manufacturing his reaper. Two years later, he was a millionaire. His father, a blacksmith, had worked for 20 years without success to develop a machine that would harvest wheat. The son's invention increased crop yields in the Midwest and throughout the world.

1.

1. **BACKGROUND** In France, McCormick was honored for "having done more for . . . agriculture than any living man."

shipped east. Both Chicago and Cyrus McCormick prospered.

McCormick was clearly a practical man. He stayed ahead of the competition by constantly improving his reaper. At the same time, he was a brilliant entrepreneur. For example, he let cash-poor farmers buy his reaper by putting a little money down and paying the rest in installments. If times were hard, McCormick let customers

310

stretch out their payments. At the time, most companies insisted on payment in full.

Unlike other manufacturers, McCormick also gave a written guarantee with his product. He refunded the money of dissatisfied customers. McCormick showed that integrity was indeed practical. By 1880, the McCormick reaper works in Chicago was shipping 50,000 reapers a year to farmers all over the world.

When McCormick died in 1884, he was a rich man. Unlike many wealthy industrialists of the Gilded Age, however, McCormick was mourned by farmers and working people. They admired him for his business ethics as well as for his success.

See p. T57.
1. How were McCormick's marketing methods unusual for his time?

2. **Critical Thinking** How did McCormick show that "integrity was indeed practical"?

Celebration of the Railroad

American ingenuity answered the need for improvements in travel. In 1847, Whig Senator Daniel Webster spoke at a celebration marking the completion of the Northern Railroad in his native New Hampshire. Webster described the changes that had transformed rural New Hampshire.

In my youth and early manhood, I crossed these mountains along all the roads or passes which lead through or over them. . . . At that day, one must have traversed this wilderness on horseback or on foot. . . .

It was difficult to persuade men that it was possible to have a passable carriage road over these mountains. . . . As far as I now remember, my first speech after I left college was in favor of what was then regarded as a great and almost impractical internal improvement, to wit, the making of a smooth, though hilly, road from [the] Connecticut River to the Merrimack River.

But a vastly greater [achievement] was now approaching, the era of steam. This is the invention which distinguishes this age. The application of steam to the moving of heavy bodies, on the water and on the land, towers above all other inventions of this or the preceding age. . . .

Fellow citizens, can we without wonder consider where we are and what has brought us here? Several of this company left Boston and Salem this morning. . . . They have threaded all the valleys and gorges, and here they now are, at 2 o'clock at the foot of the Cardigan Hills. . . . By the way, if they had thought fit, they might have brought us a few fish taken out of the sea at sunrise this morning, and we might here enjoy . . . a fish dinner. . . .

Fellow citizens, this railroad may be said to bring the sea to your doors. You cannot, indeed, snuff its salt water, but you will taste its best products, as fresh as those who live on its shores. I cannot conceive of any policy more useful to the great mass of the community than the policy which established these public improvements. Let me say that in the history of human inventions there is hardly one so well calculated as that of railroads to equalize the conditions of men. The richest must travel in the cars, for there they travel fastest. The poorest can travel in the cars, while they could not travel otherwise, because this mode of conveyance costs but little time or money. . . .

Adapted from *The Works of Daniel Webster,* 16th edition, Boston, 1872, Vol. II. Reprinted in *Annals of America.*

See p. T57.
1. What did Webster consider the greatest achievement of the age?

2. **Critical Thinking** According to Webster, how did this development encourage the growth of democracy?

A Land of Idealism 15

(1820–1860)

CHAPTER OUTLINE

1 The Reforming Impulse

2 Social Reform

3 A Campaign for Women's Rights

4 The Battle Against Slavery

5 Flowering of an American Culture

CHAPTER OBJECTIVES After completing this chapter, students should be able to

1. describe the roots of reform in the early 1800s.
2. describe reforms in education, prisons, and care for the mentally ill.
3. list the demands of the women's rights movement.
4. describe the goals and methods of the abolitionist movement.
5. discuss themes used by American writers and artists.

CHAPTER PREVIEW Have students think of some problem at school or in the local community that they would like to solve. Ask them to work in small groups to plan a strategy to achieve their goal. After they have read the chapter, discuss whether any of the reformers of the early 1800s used strategies similar to the ones suggested by the students.

There were eleven of them—all slaves, all running away, all heading north. They were freezing, hungry, and so tired that their bones ached. But they plodded on through the night, one weary step after another. Finally, one of the fugitives could stand it no more. "Let me go back," he cried. "It is better to be a slave than to suffer like this in order to be free."

The woman leading the group glared at the man and then slowly leveled her rifle. "Go on with us or die," she said. She knew that anyone who turned back would be forced to reveal the hiding places used by the escaping slaves and the names of the people who provided them. A secret network of escape, the "underground railroad," was at risk. For thousands of slaves, the "railroad" represented the only hope of freedom. The eleven went on.

The woman's name was Harriet Tubman. Called the "Black Moses," she had dedicated her life to helping her people escape from bondage. An escaped slave herself, she understood well the sentiments of slaves who chose to run away. "I had reasoned this out," she explained. "There was one of two things I had a right to—liberty or death. If I could not have one, I would have the other."

After her own escape, Tubman became a "conductor" on the underground railroad. Risking her freedom and even her life, she returned to the South nineteen times. She led more than 300 slaves, including her parents and her sister, to freedom in the North.

Harriet Tubman and others who worked for the underground railroad were among the many reformers who set out to change America in the mid-1800s. Besides abolition of slavery, these reformers worked for women's rights, better education for all Americans, prison reform, and humane treatment of the mentally ill.

1.

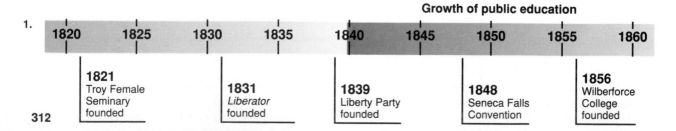

Growth of public education

| 1820 | 1825 | 1830 | 1835 | 1840 | 1845 | 1850 | 1855 | 1860 |

1821 Troy Female Seminary founded

1831 *Liberator* founded

1839 Liberty Party founded

1848 Seneca Falls Convention

1856 Wilberforce College founded

312

1. TIME LINE QUESTION Ask: Which developments on the time line were improvements in education?

1. *These weary slaves have reached the safety of Levi Coffin's Indiana farm. Coffin, a prominent abolitionist, offered his property as a station on the "underground railroad" that led to freedom in Canada.*

1. **VISUAL EVIDENCE** This painting is by Charles T. Webber. Ask: What details in the painting would arouse sympathy for runaway slaves?

The Reforming Impulse

READODO TO UNDERSTAND

■ What kinds of political ideals motivated American reformers in the early 1800s.

■ What role churches and preachers played in the reform movement.

■ How the temperance movement gained strength in the United States.

2. ■ *Vocabulary:* revival, temperance movement, abstinence.

In 1843, John Bartholomew Gough traveled
3. almost 7,000 miles and gave more than 350 speeches. His topic was always the same: the evils of alcohol. At the end of each lecture, he led his audience in an emotional pledge to renounce liquor.

Gough was only one of thousands of reformers who were active in the United States between 1815 and 1860. Reformers believed that people could be better and do better. This belief grew out of both the political and the religious heritage of the nation.

Political Ideals

The United States began its history with a revolution that proclaimed that all men were created equal. The Constitution, especially its first ten amendments, established that individuals had certain rights under the law and that these rights could not be violated.

Reformers of the 1820s and 1830s believed that the ideals of liberty and equality had not been fulfilled. If all people were created equal, they argued, why did slavery exist? And why did women have fewer rights than men? Why were prisoners and the mentally ill treated poorly? Hundreds of reform movements sprang up to deal with these and **313**

2. **VOCABULARY** Have students look up these terms in the glossary before they begin reading.

3. **DISCUSSION** Remind students of what they have learned about transportation and travel during this period. Ask them to speculate on what it might have been like to travel 7,000 miles in 1843.

1. **PAST AND PRESENT** Ask: Are churches and religious groups still active in reform movements today? Give examples.

2. **BACKGROUND** Many Americans at the time thought that individuals and, thus, society as a whole could be perfected.

other troubling issues. Reformers believed that by working for change, they were moving the American nation closer to the ideals of the revolution.

Religious Influence

Religious ideals were also at the root of the reform movement. When the first Puritans arrived in Massachusetts Bay in the 1630s, their leader, John Winthrop, challenged them to be "as a city upon a hill." The new colony had a mission, Winthrop said, to show how a "godly community" ought to live.

This religious vision of America persisted as the nation grew. Many Revolutionary War leaders believed that the young republic would be a moral as well as a political example to the rest of the world.

In the 1800s, as Americans moved westward, different denominations, like the Congregationalists, Presbyterians, Baptists, and Methodists, founded churches in the new settlements. All shared the dream that the United States would one day be a Christian nation, where sin was unknown and goodness ruled. Along with the political ideals of equality, liberty, and democracy, this religious conviction spurred many reformers.

Reforming Personal Lives

Reform movements are often associated with calls for sweeping changes in laws and institutions. But some reformers in the 1800s called for changes in personal conduct. If individuals led holy and upright lives, they believed, the nation would be improved. To renew people's religious faith, these reformers held meetings known as **revivals.**

Revivals took place under open skies. Thousands of people came from miles around to a clearing in the woods. Gathered under enormous tents, they listened to stirring sermons for several days. Six or seven ministers might preach at the same time to different groups. "The noise was like the roar of Niagara," recalled one revivalist preacher. "Some people were singing, others praying, some crying for mercy. . . ."

3. **VISUAL EVIDENCE** Ask: What does this painting show you about the people who attended revival meetings? What social classes seem to be represented?

3. *A revival meeting was an eagerly awaited event, particularly in rural areas. It was not only a religious experience, but also an important social occasion. Days in advance, people came and pitched their tents to await the revival. They were awakened by the blast of a trumpet on the starting day. One Maryland revivalist expressed the joy of the occasion: "O! Glorious day! They went home singing and shouting."*

314

1. **ECONOMICS** Many factory owners supported temperance, believing that workers would be more productive if
they did not drink.

Revivals were not the only method used by religious reformers. Various Protestant denominations put aside their differences and joined in organizations to promote Christianity. One such group, the American Bible Society, distributed Bibles at a low cost. Other groups published inexpensive religious pamphlets that encouraged readers to reform their lives. In 1836 alone, one religious society sold more than 3 million copies of its publications.

The Temperance Movement

One of the most widespread movements to improve individual lives was the **temperance movement,** as the campaign against alcoholic beverages was called. The inspiration for this movement was clear to everyone—even those who opposed it. For many Americans during the early 1800s, no social event—dance, house raising, wedding, or funeral—was complete without ample quantities of liquor.

At first, reformers in the temperance movement urged only that Americans reduce
1. the amount of liquor they drank. But beginning in the late 1820s, more and more reformers demanded **abstinence**—that people give up all alcohol.

The temperance movement reached its height in the early 1850s. At that time, several states passed laws banning the sale of
2. all alcoholic beverages. Many citizens opposed such drastic measures, however, and most states soon repealed them. But setbacks did not stop reformers from extending their efforts to other areas.

See p. T58.

SECTION 1 REVIEW

1. **Define:** (a) revival, (b) temperance movement, (c) abstinence.

2. What did reformers believe about individual liberties and equality?

3. What was one goal of religious reformers in the 1800s?

4. **Critical Thinking** How do people's religious beliefs affect their idea of what constitutes an ideal society?

2 Social Reform

READ TO UNDERSTAND

■ What reforms were made in education in the early 1800s.

■ How reformers sought to help prisoners and the mentally ill.

■ What utopians hoped to accomplish in their communities.

■ *Vocabulary:* compulsory education, utopian.   3.

The pressures of growing industrialization and immigration helped spark a demand for social reform. As more people gained the right to vote, attention focused on the need for improved education. As one workingmen's committee in Philadelphia pointed out: "In a republic, the people constitute the government. . . . They frame the laws and create the institutions that promote their happiness or produce their destruction." If Americans were 4. to perform this job well, they needed to be educated.

Educating the Young

Public education had a low priority in the early 1800s. The quality of teachers varied from place to place, but almost all were poorly educated, overworked, and ill-paid. Students of different ages and grades crowded into one-room schools. On any day, some children would be reading, others doing arithmetic, and still others reciting a history lesson—all at the same time. The reasons for such conditions varied from region to region.

The first New England settlers had placed great emphasis on educating the young. Those influenced by Puritan beliefs thought a person should be able to read the Bible, and they required each town to maintain a public school. Over the years, however, interest in public education waned.

In other areas of the country, the situation was no better. Free education existed in the Middle Atlantic states only for those who declared themselves paupers. In the South, geography contributed to educational problems. People living on farms isolated by poor roads found it difficult to muster the community effort needed to support public schools. Wealthy plantation owners hired private tutors for their children and so had little interest in public education. And in many places in the South, it was illegal to teach slaves to read.

In the West, new settlements were slow to establish good schools. Even when towns set up schoolhouses, they were often crude, poorly ventilated, poorly heated buildings, located on the most worthless site for miles around. "For the sheepfold and cow-house, sheltered situations are carefully selected," complained one reformer, "but a bleak hilltop, swept by the winter blast . . . will do for a school."

Beginnings of Educational Reform

Horace Mann was perhaps the most vigorous supporter of good public education. He gave up a promising career as a lawyer to become Massachusetts's first superintendent of education in 1837.

1.

For 12 years, Mann pleaded and argued with the state government. With the zeal of a missionary, he demanded better school buildings, better textbooks, and less physical punishment of students. Working through his summer vacation, he visited schools and delivered his message: "If we do not prepare children to become good citizens, then our republic must go down to destruction as others have gone before it."

Mann's enthusiastic efforts paid off. During his term as superintendent, state spending for education doubled, teachers' salaries increased, and the school year was lengthened. In addition, Massachusetts set up three schools for training teachers.

In other states, the fight for free public schools met strong resistance. Some taxpayers asked, "Why should we have to pay school taxes even if we have no children?" Parents who paid to send their children to private

2.

3. *The schoolroom in this painting by William Tolman Carlton was much better equipped than most early schools, which usually had few books and limited supplies. Since paper and ink were sometimes scarce, children used small slates and slate pencils. Still, learning took place. Foreign visitors to the United States commented on the exceptional number of people who could read.*

1. **DISCUSSION** Ask: What response could be made to these arguments against compulsory public education?

schools—a common practice at the time—complained about paying taxes to support a public school.

Many parents objected to the proposal for **compulsory education,** that is, that all children be required to attend school until a certain age. Parents argued that compulsory education deprived them of control over their own children. In addition, many farm families and families in mill towns complained that compulsory education would prevent children from putting in a full day's work; these people depended on their children's labor to help support the family. In spite of opposition, by the 1850s most northern states set up free public elementary schools.

Education for Some

Educational reform was uneven. Most towns either ignored the education of black Americans or openly barred them from public schools. Some public school systems did admit blacks—New York City and Boston, for example. But the schools that blacks attended were segregated and less well-financed than schools for whites.

Women were also denied equal educational opportunity. Few were taught more than reading and writing. "We don't pretend to teach the female part of the town anything more than dancing, or a little music perhaps," commented one New Hampshire resident. Colleges, like most elementary and high schools, were primarily for white males.

Catholics had their own problems. Although the Constitution guaranteed the separation of church and state, many public schools promoted Protestantism and used textbooks with an anti-Catholic bias. Many Catholics, including new immigrants, supported the idea of parochial schools, where their children would also be instructed in the Catholic faith.

Reforming the Prisons

Reforming the prison system proved to be a difficult task. Prisons were a recent institution in America. In colonial times, states generally imposed the death penalty for serious offenses; minor offenses were punished by public flogging or some other form of pain or humiliation.

Oberlin College became the first coeducational college in 1837, when four women joined thirty young men in the freshman class. One woman wrote, "Our advantages here are great, very great." Oberlin also pioneered in the education of black women. In 1862, Mary Jane Patterson, shown here, became the first black woman to receive a college degree.

4.

4. **BACKGROUND** Earlier, a Female Department at Oberlin had considered Latin and Greek too difficult for women.

In the early 1800s, imprisonment for crimes gradually replaced physical punishment. The first prisons were makeshift. Men, women, and children were crowded together in small rooms and and often served inadequate food. Some prisons even charged inmates fees for their stay in jail, and jailers made extra money by selling them rum.

In the 1820s, a prison in Auburn, New York, became the model for a new system based on work and isolation. Prisoners performed hard labor in groups during the day and were kept in solitary confinement at night. Talking or even exchanging glances was prohibited at all times. Reformers hoped that a regular occupation and a strict schedule, combined with removal from bad influences, would help prisoners develop good habits. The main effect, however, was to place a se-

317

2. **LOCAL HISTORY** Ask students to find out when public schools were first set up in their state and prepare a report.

3. **BACKGROUND** In 1815, Thomas Gallaudet set up a school for the deaf.

2. **ACTIVITY** Have interested students find out about prison reforms being attempted today and compare them with those of the 1840s.

rest of the country. In response to her appeals, 15 states established special hospitals for the mentally ill.

Creating an Ideal Society

Some reformers were not content to reorganize or improve just one institution—prisons, for example, or schools. Instead, they wanted to remake society entirely. Such reformers founded **utopian,** or ideal, communities. In these, they hoped to show how a new social system might work.

Some utopian communities were founded on religious principles. The members of one such community, the Shakers, supported themselves by farming while working to gain perfection. Other communities, such as that set up by Robert Owen in New Harmony, Indiana, were more concerned with economic ideals. It was Owen's dream to escape the harsh conditions of industrial society and to build a community based on cooperation.

Most utopian communities enjoyed some early success, then failed. Often, they split into competing groups or broke up after the original founders died.

3.

The utopians and other reformers of the 1800s had bigger dreams than they were able to realize. Yet even if they did not "perfect" American society, their efforts at reform reminded Americans of their heritage and challenged them to extend liberty and equality to all.

4.

See p. T59.

The sight of so-called "harmless lunatics" locked in a small, dark, cold room touched Dorothea Dix's heart and goaded her to action. She crusaded for better medical care and proper facilities for the mentally ill. Her campaign led 15 states to
1. establish hospitals for their care.

1. **BACKGROUND** In 1843, the nation had 13 mental hospitals; by 1880, shortly before Dorothea Dix retired, there were 123.

vere psychological strain on prisoners. For all the changes, the new system produced
2. little evidence of rehabilitation or "reform."

Helping the Mentally Ill

Efforts on behalf of the mentally ill lagged behind other reforms until the 1840s, when a Boston schoolteacher named Dorothea Lynde Dix launched a campaign. Dix first became acquainted with the problems of the mentally ill when she was invited to teach a Sunday School class at a jail in Cambridge, Massachusetts. Among the inmates, dressed in filthy rags, were people whose only crime was mental illness. Deeply shocked, Dix visited every institution in the state where mentally ill men, women, and children were held. In a report, she detailed their mistreatment vividly and urged that the mentally ill be treated as patients who were sick, not as criminals.

Dix convinced Massachusetts lawmakers to raise the standards of care for the mentally ill. She also carried her crusade to the

318

SECTION 2 REVIEW

1. **Identify:** (a) Horace Mann, (b) Dorothea Dix.

2. **Define:** (a) compulsory education, (b) utopian.

3. List three reforms made in public education in the early 1800s.

4. What steps were taken to reform the treatment of prisoners and the mentally ill?

5. **Critical Thinking** Why is the success of self-government dependent on the education of all citizens?

3. **ACTIVITY** Have students find out more about utopian communities such as New Harmony or Brook Farm and consider why it was difficult for them to survive.

4. **READING** Students might like to read an example of utopian literature, such as *Looking Backward* by Edward Bellamy.

3 A Campaign for Women's Rights

READ TO UNDERSTAND

■ How women gained access to higher education.

■ Why women held a political convention in Seneca Falls, New York.

■ What professions women were entering by the 1840s and 1850s.

The swirl of reform to improve schools, revive religion, and reduce drinking attracted women. Yet women themselves suffered many forms of discrimination. Nowhere could they vote, and in many states they could not own property, make a will, or file a lawsuit. In time, reformers turned their attention to rights for women.

Early Strides in Education

As you have read earlier, American women rarely received an education that included more than reading and writing. It was widely believed that women could not master more advanced subjects. In 1821, Emma Willard attacked that notion when she set up the Troy Female Seminary in New York State. Here young women successfully learned "men's subjects," such as mathematics, physics, and philosophy.

In 1836, Mary Lyon founded Mount Holyoke Female Seminary in South Hadley, Massachusetts. Mount Holyoke was the first women's college in the United States. Lyon knew that many men would object to having a college for women, so she called it a "seminary," until the idea became accepted. In 1837, Oberlin College in Ohio began to admit women, thus becoming the nation's first coeducational institution.

Resistance to Women Reformers

Often, women who tried to join in the general reform spirit of the age found that even male reformers opposed their participation. A group of Massachusetts ministers warned that any woman who gave up her "dependence" on men to speak out for reform would yield "the power God has given her for her protection," and would run the risk of becoming "unnatural."

Courageous women reformers vigorously rejected such ideas. Sarah and Angelina Grimké, for example, led the fight for a place for women in the antislavery movement. The two sisters had left the South Carolina home of their father, a slave owner, because of their own opposition to slavery. At first, they lectured only to women, but soon they began speaking to mixed audiences. The boos and shouts of men in the crowd did not stop them.

4. **VISUAL EVIDENCE** This portrait of Mary Lyon was painted by Joseph Goodhue Chandler.

As a young woman, Mary Lyon taught school for 75 cents a week. In 1828, she and another woman started their own school for girls in Buckland, Massachusetts. But Lyon was determined to establish a college "consecrated to the training of young women for usefulness." She reached her goal in 1836, when she founded Mount Holyoke Female Seminary.

2. **PAST AND PRESENT** The Troy Female Seminary continues to operate in Troy, New York. It is now called the Emma Willard School.

3. **BACKGROUND** When the school opened there were 80 students; today there are about 2,000. Mary Lyon was later elected to the Hall of Fame for Great Americans.

1. **CRITICAL THINKING** Ask: Based on what you have read, how do you think most Americans at the time would have reacted to this statement?

1. "To me," said Sarah, "it is perfectly clear that whatsoever it is morally right for a man to do, it is morally right for a woman to do."

GREAT DEBATE
The Seneca Falls Convention

Frustrated by limits on their actions, women reformers began to campaign for their own rights. In 1848, Lucretia Mott and Elizabeth Cady Stanton boldly called for a convention
2. on women's rights at Seneca Falls, New York.

For the convention, Stanton drafted a proclamation modeled after the Declaration of Independence. "We hold these truths to

2. **BACKGROUND** In 1840, the World Anti-Slavery Convention in London voted to bar female delegates from the U.S., including Mott and Stanton.

be self-evident: that all men and women are created equal," it began. Then, referring to women's grievances, it went on: "The history of mankind is a history of repeated injuries . . . on the part of man toward woman." Stanton accused men of wanting to establish "an absolute tyranny" over women.

3. More than 250 women and 40 men attended the meeting. Stanton introduced nine resolutions, including two that called for improved education and job opportunities for women. The convention approved eight of the resolutions unanimously, wavering only on the call for women's suffrage, which barely passed.

3. **READING** Have students read a copy of the Declaration of Sentiments. Then ask: Which demand do you think was most important? Why?

VOICES OF FREEDOM

Sojourner Truth: Equality for Women

Sojourner Truth was born a slave in New York State in 1797. She ran away in 1826. Originally named Isabelle Baumfree, she took the name Sojourner Truth because she believed she had a mission to journey across the country, speaking the truth about slavery and women's rights. In 1851, she responded with these powerful words to a man who claimed
4. *that women were inferior to men.*

That man over there says that women need to be helped into carriages, and lifted over ditches, and to have the best place everywhere. Nobody ever helps me into carriages, or over

mudpuddles, or gives me any best place! And ain't I a woman? Look at me! Look at my arm! I have ploughed, and planted, and gathered into barns, and no man could head me! And ain't I a woman? I could work as much and eat as much as a man—when I could get it—and bear the lash as well! And ain't I a woman? I have borne thirteen children, and seen them most all sold off to slavery, and when I cried out with my mother's grief, none but Jesus heard me! And ain't I a woman?

Then they talk about this thing in the head: what's this they call it? That's it, honey [intellect]. What's that got to do with women's rights? If my cup won't hold but a pint and yours hold a quart, wouldn't you be mean not to let me have my little half? . . . If the first woman God ever made was strong enough to turn the world upside down all alone, these women together [here] ought to be able to turn it back, and get it right side up again! And now they are asking to do it, the men better let 'em.

See p. T59.

1. What argument does Sojourner Truth offer in favor of women's rights?

2. **Critical Thinking** Why do you think the abolitionist and women's rights movements were linked in people's minds?

4. **ACTIVITY** Have a student read Truth's speech aloud to help the class feel the impact of her words. Ask: Does the unpolished language of the speech add to its effectiveness?

1. BIOGRAPHY Blackwell was turned down by 29 medical schools because she was a woman. She said, "The idea of winning a doctor's degree gradually assumed the aspect of a great moral struggle."

In the years after the Seneca Falls Convention, advocates of women's rights held meetings and petitioned state legislatures for laws to end discrimination. Among the most important of the movement's leaders was Susan B. Anthony, whose great energy and organizational skills gained support for the cause. However, the surge of feminist activity was dampened by the Civil War. ■

Advances of American Women

Slowly, women's role in American life expanded. The Troy Female Seminary, Mount Holyoke, and similar schools turned out highly qualified graduates, many of whom became teachers.

1. Elizabeth Blackwell expanded women's horizons even farther. Blackwell applied to medical school at Geneva College, New York, and was accepted—almost as a joke. But Blackwell surprised her male classmates and graduated at the head of her class. In 1850, she began practicing medicine in New York City—the first woman doctor in America. Blackwell founded the first school of nursing in the United States in 1857, opening the doors to a profession that women would enter in increasing numbers.

Women writers also gained acceptance. Margaret Fuller edited a noted philosophical magazine and wrote several books. One of these, *Woman in the Nineteenth Century,* was an important influence in the movement for women's rights. Fuller argued that women were able to do the same type of work as men.

Despite the accomplishments of individuals, the legal status of most women changed very little before 1860. Women, still without the vote, remained outside the political process. In some states, however, they did gain the right to control their own property after marriage. And advocates of women's rights made certain that the issue of women's rights

2. could never again be ignored.

See p. T59.

See p. T59.

SECTION 3 REVIEW

1. **Identify:** (a) Sarah and Angelina Grimké, (b) Elizabeth Cady Stanton, (c) Seneca Falls Convention, (d) Elizabeth Blackwell.

2. **ACTIVITY** Have students prepare oral reports on Lucretia Mott, Elizabeth Cady Stanton, Susan B. Anthony, Lucy Stone, or Margaret Fuller.

2. Why did some women reformers in the early 1800s decide to campaign for women's rights?

3. In what areas did women make progress in the early 1800s?

4. **Critical Thinking** How did the small advances by women in the early 1800s make it easier for women to make large advances later?

3. **VOCABULARY** Have students look up these words in the glossary before they begin reading.

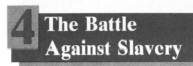

4 The Battle Against Slavery

READ TO UNDERSTAND

■ Why the African colonization program was unsuccessful.

■ What differences led to a split among abolitionists before 1860.

■ How Americans reacted to the proposals of radical abolitionists.

■ *Vocabulary:* emancipation, abolitionist. 3.

When Angelina Grimké published a pamphlet calling for an end to slavery in 1836, the mayor of Charleston, South Carolina, was furious. He told her father that she would never be allowed in her home town again.

That a southern mayor disagreed with an antislavery crusader in the 1830s was not surprising. But even those who wished to end slavery could not agree on when and how to achieve their common goal.

A Gradual Approach

Even in colonial days, there had been some Americans who had opposed slavery. When the United States abolished the slave trade in 1808, many believed that slavery would soon die out. Others, not fully convinced, worked actively to abolish it. Newspapers committed to ending slavery sprang up in the North and in parts of the South, too—in 4. Tennessee and North Carolina, for example. **321**

4. **BACKGROUND** The abolitionist newspaper *Freedom's Journal* was published by two free blacks, Samuel Cornish and John Russwurm.

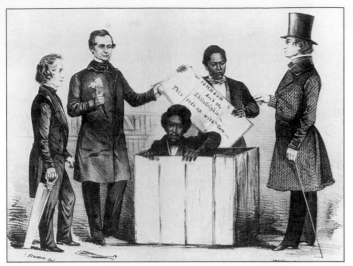

1. *In 1849, abolitionists rescued a Richmond, Virginia, slave by sending him to Philadelphia in a crate. After a 25-hour trip, he emerged with the greeting, "How do you do, gentlemen." He became known as Henry "Box" Brown.*

1. **VISUAL EVIDENCE** Ask: How would the circulation of pictures like this help the antislavery movement?

One such antislavery newspaper was the *Genius of Universal Emancipation,* published by Benjamin Lundy in Ohio in the 1820s. In his paper, Lundy proposed a gradual **emancipation,** or freeing, of slaves. He called for the nation to stop the spread of slavery to new states, to abolish the slave trade within the borders of the United States, and to urge slave states to free their slaves gradually. In 1829, Lundy hired an assistant editor, William Lloyd Garrison, a man who held more radical views and would eventually become a leader in the drive to abolish slavery.

The Colonization Movement

The American Colonization Society, established in 1817, proposed to end slavery by returning blacks to Africa, and in 1822 founded the country of Liberia in West Africa for that
2. purpose. White supporters of colonization believed that blacks could never find a full and equal role in American society. Black supporters argued that blacks would have a better chance of making a good life for themselves if they lived where they did not face discrimination.

The society ran into enormous problems. Its funds were limited, and by 1830 it had sent only about 1,400 free blacks to Liberia. Furthermore, society members had little success in persuading plantation owners to free
322 their slaves and send them to Africa.

2. **VOCABULARY** The name *Liberia* comes from the Latin word for *free*. The capital was named Monrovia in honor of President James Monroe, who supported colonization.

But it was opposition from free blacks that eventually doomed the colonization movement. In 1831, a convention of free blacks meeting in New York City declared that they had no interest in going to Africa, a continent most of them had never visited. America "is our home," they declared, "and this is our country. Beneath its sod lie the bones of our fathers; for it, some of them fought, bled, and died. Here we are born, and here we will die."

Radical Abolitionism

By the 1830s, some American reformers argued that gradual abolition was impractical. Eli Whitney's cotton gin had enlarged the cotton kingdom in the South (see page 295), and the planters' dependence on slave labor was greater than ever. **Abolitionists,** reformers who worked for an immediate end to slavery, saw little hope that slave owners would ever give up their slaves.

William Lloyd Garrison symbolized the shift of mood in the abolitionist movement. In 1831, in Boston, Garrison established his own antislavery newspaper, *The Liberator.* Its pages proclaimed that slavery was a sin of which the nation must be purged immediately. The first page of the first issue revealed Garrison's fierce sense of commitment: "I *will be* as harsh as truth, and as uncompromising as justice. . . . I will not equivocate—I will not excuse—I will not retreat a single inch—AND I WILL BE HEARD."
3.

Garrison was not alone in his radical approach. Theodore Weld, an intensely religious young man, spoke fervently against the evils of slavery. In 1834, Weld led a revival among the students at Lane Seminary in Cincinnati. When the school trustees saw that the students eagerly adopted Weld's views, they banned all antislavery activity from the campus. Weld and many of his students left the seminary and traveled from town to town to stir up abolitionist sentiment.

Division Among Abolitionists

Although abolitionists were united in their desire to end slavery immediately, they did not agree on tactics. One dispute was over whether women should be allowed to participate in the movement. William Lloyd Gar-

3. **BACKGROUND** Garrison realized that immediate abolition of slavery was unlikely. "We have never said that slavery would be overthrown by a single blow," he admitted privately. "That it ought to be, we shall always contend."

1. **READING** Interested students can read *Journey Toward Freedom: The Story of Sojourner Truth* by Jacqueline Bernard.

2. **BACKGROUND** Douglass wrote: "Slavery is one of those monsters of darkness to whom the light of truth is death. . . . All the slaveholder asks of me is silence."

rison's outspoken support for an active role for women alienated many of the movement's supporters. In 1840 the abolitionists split into two groups over this and other issues.

Garrison's views on political action were another subject of disagreement. Garrison believed that political activity, such as working for antislavery laws, was useless. He claimed that the Constitution itself protected slavery, and urged antislavery supporters to refuse to vote or hold public office. At the same time, he opposed the use of violence to end slavery. The American public must be roused against slavery's moral evil, Garrison contended, and only then would abolition be achieved. He favored newspaper articles, lectures, and letter-writing campaigns.

Many abolitionists supported this approach, including the Grimké sisters, Theo-
1. dore Weld, Sojourner Truth, and Frederick

Douglass. Sojourner Truth, a former slave, greatly aided the abolitionist movement with her impassioned speeches in favor of equality. Frederick Douglass emerged as the most important black leader of the movement. During the 1840s and 1850s, Douglass lectured in the United States and Great Britain against American slavery. In 1847, he began 2. publishing an antislavery paper, the *North Star*, in Rochester, New York.

Political Activity

Unlike Garrison and his allies, some abolitionists favored taking the issue of slavery to the voters. Arthur and Lewis Tappan, two wealthy New York City merchants, became leaders in this camp. In 1839, the Tappans and James Birney, a former Kentucky slave owner, joined forces to found the Liberty

VOICES OF FREEDOM

Frederick Douglass: A Denunciation of the Slave Trade

Although the slave trade was banned in America after 1808, smuggling of slaves continued. Frederick Douglass was a slave for 21 years. After his escape in 1838, he became a noted abolitionist speaker. Below is an excerpt from a speech Douglass made in New York in 1852.

To me the American slave trade is a terrible reality. When a child, my soul was often pierced with a sense of its horrors.

The flesh-mongers gather up their victims by dozens, and drive them chained, to the general depot at Baltimore. When a sufficient number has been collected here, a ship is chartered to convey the forlorn crew to Mobile, or to New Orleans.

In the deep, still darkness of midnight, I have been often aroused by the dead, heavy footsteps, and the piteous cries of the chained gangs that passed our door.

Fellow-citizens, this murderous traffic is, today, in active operation in this boasted republic. I see the bleeding footsteps; I hear the doleful wail of fettered humanity on the way to the slave-markets where the victims are to be

sold like horses, sheep, and swine. . . . My soul sickens at the sight.
See p. T60.

1. What memories of childhood slavery still bothered Frederick Douglass?

2. **Critical Thinking** Why do you think Douglass was an influential opponent of slavery?

3.

3. **CRITICAL THINKING** Ask: Why does Douglass address his listeners as "fellow-citizens?" Would many white Americans have agreed with him? What does he mean when he calls the United States a "boasted republic"?

party. In 1840 and again in 1844, Birney ran for President on the Liberty party ticket.

In 1848, the Free Soil party replaced the Liberty party as the nation's leading antislavery political party. The support enjoyed by the Free Soil party among both politicians and voters resulted largely from its more moderate platform. Instead of demanding the abolition of slavery in the South, Free Soilers wanted to stop the expansion of slavery into the western territories. Most Free Soilers actually had little concern for the rights of blacks. Many, in fact, wanted to keep all blacks, free as well as slave, out of the territories.

Reactions Among Whites

More than anything, radical abolitionists tended to divide the country along regional lines. Their fiery attacks on the South stirred white southerners to defend slavery even more strongly. Southerners who had once leaned toward ending slavery now began to defend it. Southern postmasters refused to deliver abolitionist pamphlets being sent through the mail. The state of Georgia even offered a reward of $5,000 to anyone who would bring abolitionist leader William Lloyd Garrison to the state for trial.

Even in the North, moderates feared the consequence of the "immediate emancipation" advocated by Garrison. Moreover, while white northerners might detest the institution of slavery, most did not want free blacks living in their communities. Many white workers feared that free blacks would take their jobs by agreeing to work for lower pay.

When abolitionists spoke throughout the North, they were frequently booed and treated roughly. In 1835, a Boston mob dragged Garrison through the streets, at the
1. end of a rope. Authorities probably saved his life by throwing him in jail.

Reactions Among Blacks

Black Americans had actively opposed slavery long before most white reformers became involved. By 1830, 50 black antislavery groups existed.

For a while, most black abolitionists supported Garrison's approach, although they were dismayed to realize that even the most ardent white abolitionists were frequently condescending. "Too many," noted one black reformer, ". . . best love the colored man at a distance." Despite the antislavery agitation of the 1830s and 1840s, blacks felt little hope that they would soon be set free.

More and more, black leaders began to pay attention to men like David Walker, a free black in Boston. In 1829, Walker had published *An Appeal to the Colored Citizens of the World,* in which he challenged blacks to rise up and free themselves. Henry Highland Garnet, a former Maryland slave, renewed Walker's appeal in 1843: "Brethren, Arise, Arise! . . . Rather die like free men than live as slaves." In 1854, a group of blacks announced, "The time is come . . . when our people must assume . . . the battle against caste and Slavery; . . . no one else can fight it for us. . . ."

The Underground Railroad

While most abolitionists pursued their goals through politics, the press, and public debate, some took direct action by working for the "underground railroad." This was not an actual railroad but rather a network of men and women who helped southern slaves escape to the North or to Canada. The "conductors" on this railroad led slaves, or "passengers," along backcountry roads called "tracks." Farm wagons often served as "trains." Homes along the way where slaves could find food and shelter were called "stations."

The success of the railroad depended on the cooperation of many blacks and whites in both the North and South and on such heroic individuals as Harriet Tubman. An escaped slave herself, the "Black Moses" 2. repeatedly risked capture to return to help others. (See page 312.) Slave owners offered a reward of $40,000 for her capture.

Despite decades of speeches, pamphlets, and political action, the abolition movement failed to find an acceptable way to end slavery. During the 1850s, divisions over the slavery issue became increasingly sharp. Americans would soon find themselves engulfed in a conflict that would test not only the strength of their ideals but their unity as a nation.

Even though the underground railroad probably rescued only 1,000 slaves a year, it caused great excitement in the nation. Abolitionists found it an active way to oppose slavery, and southerners denounced it with hatred. This painting, On to Liberty, by
1. Theodor Kaufmann, shows slave women leading their children to freedom.

See p. T60. **1. VISUAL EVIDENCE** Have students compare this painting to the one on p. 313. Ask: Do the two paintings present a similar picture of the underground railroad? Of slaves?

SECTION 4 REVIEW

1. **Identify:** (a) William Lloyd Garrison, (b) Sojourner Truth, (c) Frederick Douglass, (d) underground railroad.

2. **Define:** (a) emancipation, (b) abolitionist.

3. What steps did Benjamin Lundy propose for the gradual emancipation of slaves?

4. What differences split the radical abolitionists?

5. (a) What were the goals of the Liberty party? (b) Of the Free Soil party?

6. **Critical Thinking** What was the possible psychological impact of the underground railroad on slaves and slave owners?

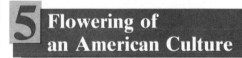
5 Flowering of an American Culture

READ TO UNDERSTAND

■ How American culture in the early 1800s mirrored the reform movement.

■ Who the notable writers and artists of this period were.

■ How writers and artists in the 1800s reflected American nationalism.

As a young nation, the United States lacked the ancient ruins, history, and myth that inspired painters, writers, and poets in Europe. But Americans were beginning to discover that their land and its values set their society apart from the Old World. "American 2.

325

2. GEOGRAPHY Ask: How might the distance between the U.S. and Europe have encouraged the development of a uniquely American culture? (location)

Thomas Cole came to the United States from England as a teenager. A founder of the Hudson River School of painting, he stressed the importance of sketching outdoors. Cole spent much time exploring the Catskill region, shown here in his
1. painting *Catskill Creek.* The majesty of nature in the painting totally overpowers the small human figure in the rowboat.

1. **VISUAL EVIDENCE**
Cole wrote, "The Hudson for natural magnificence is unsurpassed. . . . The lofty Catskills stand afar—the green hills gently rising from the flood, recede like steps by which we may ascend to a great temple . . ."

scenery . . . has features, and glorious ones unknown to Europe," insisted the American landscape painter Thomas Cole, in 1836. He and a host of other creative people contributed to the flourishing of American arts from the 1830s through the 1850s.

The American Landscape

Until the early 1800s, many American painters and artists looked to Europe for their inspiration. They imitated European tastes, scenes, and values. By the 1830s, however, American artists began to discover the grandeur of American landscapes that rivaled and even surpassed those of Europe.

George Caleb Bingham was one such artist who found a new vision in his native land.
2. Having lived in Missouri in the early days of its settlement by whites, Bingham had learned to appreciate a land of wild forests, hills, and rivers. In his painting *Fur Traders Descending the Missouri,* he portrayed both the beauty of the river as a wilderness landscape and the resourceful fur trappers who traveled it.

Back east, the frontier had long since disappeared. Now, villages and farms dotted the landscape. Still, painters like Thomas Cole and Asher Durand developed a romantic view of nature. In their paintings of rugged Hudson River and Catskill Mountain scenes, nature, not humans, dominated. The artists of the so-called Hudson River School glorified the American wilderness.

Reflections on American Life in the Era of Reform

"The reason why the world lacks unity and lies broken in heaps, is because man is disunited with himself." The philosopher Ralph Waldo Emerson, like the Hudson River painters, believed that the human spirit was reflected in nature. Emerson also thought that modern civilization might provide material wealth, but it was nature that held the spiritual values and higher laws that came from God.

Emerson was among a group of New England writers known as Transcendentalists.

2. **VISUAL EVIDENCE** Refer students to the pictures on pp. 173 and 177 for examples of Bingham's work. Ask: What details in the painting show Bingham's interest in everyday life?

They believed human beings could improve their world by establishing a closer spiritual tie to nature. In a series of essays and lectures on subjects such as self-reliance, character, nature, and politics, Emerson encouraged his fellow citizens to concentrate on improving themselves and society.

Emerson's friend and neighbor, Henry David Thoreau, thought more radical steps were needed to reform a corrupt society. To get even closer to nature and away from civilization, he spent two years alone in a remote cabin on Walden Pond (although he did visit his mother for supper every Sunday).

Both Emerson and Thoreau focused on the importance of individuals reforming their own lives. Thoreau concluded that in the face of unjust laws, an individual had the obligation to commit acts of "civil disobedience."

1. In 1846, such an act landed Thoreau briefly in jail; he refused to pay taxes to support a war with Mexico (see page 276), because he saw the war as a government scheme to extend slavery.

A Flourishing American Literature

The tension between wilderness and civilization inspired a generation of American writ-
2. ers. In his "Leatherstocking Tales," James Fenimore Cooper created a resourceful frontier hero known as Natty Bumppo. Natty Bumppo was Cooper's ideal American. He lacked the manners and refinements of eastern gentlemen, but he had nobility, common sense, and the skill to survive in an untamed wilderness.

Washington Irving popularized stories he set in American locales. His tales of a headless horseman in "The Legend of Sleepy Hollow" and of the lazy Dutch farmer "Rip Van Winkle" showed how much America had changed. These stories of a simple rural past contrasted with a nation filled with cities, commerce, and new manufacturing centers. Similarly, Nathaniel Hawthorne drew upon the history of Puritan New England to create his novels *The Scarlet Letter* and *The House of the Seven Gables*. Both criticized what Hawthorne saw as the excessive individualism of his own age.

Herman Melville's epic tale of New England's whaling industry, *Moby Dick,* also used a distinctly American setting. Captain Ahab sought his personal liberation as he hunted the great white whale Moby Dick across the trackless ocean wilderness. But blinded by his obsession with the whale, Ahab sailed to his destruction.

The nation's poets also developed an American voice. The tormented Edgar Allan Poe was often inspired by visions of pain and horror. His most famous poem, "The Raven," explored the darker worlds of spirit and emotion.

By contrast, Walt Whitman became the poet of American democracy. His first thin 3. volume of poems, *Leaves of Grass,* was published in 1855. In both style and content, Whitman was uniquely American. He celebrated the freedom of the individual, the dignity of the common people, and the pleasures of the spirit and the flesh. Just as American society was plunging toward a bloody Civil War, Whitman wrote of a common national feeling:

> A southerner soon as a northerner, a planter nonchalant and hospitable
> A Yankee bound my own way . . . ready for trade . . . my joints the limberest joints on earth and the sternest joints on earth,
> A Kentuckian walking the vale of the Elkhorn in my deerskin leggings
> A boatman over the bays or along coasts . . . a Hoosier, a Badger, a Buckeye . . .
> In all people I see myself, none more and not one barleycorn less,
> And the good or bad I say of myself I say of them.

See p. T60.

SECTION 5 REVIEW

1. **Identify:** (a) Hudson River School, (b) Nathaniel Hawthorne, (c) Walt Whitman.

2. What was the subject of most American painting in the 1800s?

3. What were important themes of the works of Ralph Waldo Emerson and Henry David Thoreau?

4. **Critical Thinking** How do artists and writers influence society?

2. **BACKGROUND** The "Leatherstocking Tales" include five novels: *The Last of the Mohicans, The Deerslayer, The Pathfinder, The Pioneers,* and *The Prairie.*

3. **READING** Have students read selections from the works of one of these writers and prepare book reviews.

Summary

1. **Between 1820 and 1860, reform movements motivated by religious and political ideals swept the nation.** The first efforts at reform were directed toward improving personal conduct. The temperance movement, for example, urged Americans to abstain from liquor.

2. **Reformers soon turned to social reform.** Horace Mann led the fight for compulsory education and improved educational standards. Dorothea Dix crusaded for protection for the mentally ill. Utopians tried to improve society as a whole.

3. **Efforts to gain rights for women met with mixed results.** Opportunities for education became available, but prejudice against women in public life was strong. When women were excluded from the antislav-

ery movement, they recognized the need to launch a campaign for women's rights.

4. **The movement to end slavery split after the 1830s.** Radical abolitionists such as William Lloyd Garrison and Frederick Douglass demanded immediate freedom for slaves. But abolitionist members of the Liberty and Free Soil parties sought a political solution to the problem of slavery.

5. **In the decades after 1820, the nation's artists and writers created a distinctly American culture.** Painters of the Hudson River School and other landscape artists portrayed the glory of America's natural environment. Writers such as Emerson and Thoreau challenged Americans to be self-reliant, and poet Walt Whitman celebrated the variety in the young nation.

See p. T60.

Vocabulary

On a separate sheet of paper, write the word or words that best complete each of the following sentences.

1. _____ were spirited religious meetings to renew people's faith.

2. The _____ was a campaign against the use of alcoholic beverages.

3. _____ is the act of refraining from all alcoholic beverages.

4. Under a system of _____, children are required to attend school until a certain age.

5. A (An) _____ community is one that seeks to be ideal or perfect.

See p. T60.

Chapter Checkup

1. Describe the political and religious roots of the reform spirit of the early 1800s.

2. (a) How did reformers try to change the personal lives of Americans? (b) How successful were they?

3. Describe education in New England, the South, and the West in the early 1800s.

4. (a) Why did some Americans oppose free public education? (b) Why did some oppose compulsory education?

5. (a) What type of education existed for black Americans in the early 1800s? (b) What type of education existed for women?

6. How successful were women's efforts to gain equal rights during the 1840s and 1850s?

7. What tactics did each of the following propose for the abolition of slavery: (a) Benjamin Lundy; (b) William Lloyd Garrison; (c) David Walker; (d) Arthur and Lewis Tappan?

8. How did literature and painting assume a unique American character in the early 1800s?

See p. T61.

Critical Thinking

1. **Evaluating** Why do you think it was effective for individuals like Sojourner Truth and Frederick Douglass to speak out against slavery?

2. **Analyzing** Reread the extract from Walt Whitman's poem on page 327. How does the poem reflect the idealism and optimism of many Americans of the time?

3. **Making Applications** (a) What modern-day examples of the "reforming impulse" can you identify? (b) Do current reform efforts seem to be motivated by religious, or by political, ideals? Explain.

See p. T61.

Connecting Past and Present

1. (a) Describe the legal position of women in the early 1800s. (b) How does the legal position of women today differ from what it was in the 1800s?

2. The writings of Washington Irving, Ralph Waldo Emerson, and Walt Whitman entertained and inspired Americans in the 1800s. Select a writer or television program whose ideas appeal in the same way to Americans today. Explain the writer's or program's philosophy, or "message."

See p. T61.

Developing Basic Skills

1. **Using a Primary Source** Reread Frederick Douglass's speech about the slave trade on page 323. (a) What type of document is it? (b) Was the author closely involved with the events described? Explain. (c) Why did Douglass make this speech? (d) What can you learn about the slave trade from this document?

2. **Comparing** Make a chart with three columns: Area of Reform; Reformers; Results. Use what you have learned in the chapter to fill in the chart. (a) What were the major areas of reform? (b) Which areas enjoyed the most success? Why?

3. **Analyzing Literature** Choose a work or passage from the work of one of the authors of the early 1800s discussed in this chapter. Show how the work reflects the idealism or nationalism of the time.

WRITING ABOUT HISTORY

Sources of Information

Some of the most common research aids are the library card catalog, the *Readers' Guide to Periodic Literature,* newspaper indexes, and specialized reference books. The card catalog is an alphabetical list of books in the library arranged by subject, title, and author. The *Readers' Guide to Periodic Literature* is an index to articles in 170 different magazines. It is particularly helpful in finding information on current events. A newspaper index lists articles according to subject. Since news events are usually covered by many newspapers on the same day, any newspaper index can be a guide to finding articles in other newspapers. The index for *The New York Times* begins in 1851. Specialized reference books include in-depth information on such topics as definitions of terms, biographies, and statistics. You will learn more about these reference tools in later Chapter Reviews.

Practice: List one possible source of information for each of the following: Horace Mann; the women's rights movement in the 1840s; current educational reforms; the complete works of Walt Whitman; the number of slaves in 1850; prison reform in the 1800s. Explain each choice.

Unit Five
A NATION TORN APART

1852 Southerners were enraged by the portrayal of slavery in the novel and play Uncle Tom's Cabin.

Abraham Lincoln is shown here with his young son Tad.

	1850	1855	1860
POLITICS AND GOVERNMENT	**1850** North and South reach compromise over slavery in territories		**1857** Dred Scott decision by Supreme Court shocks northerners
SOCIETY AND CULTURE		**1854** Pro- and antislavery groups rush to settle Kansas	
ECONOMICS AND TECHNOLOGY		**1850s** Cotton becomes critical to southern economy	
WORLD EVENTS		**1854** United States begins trade with Japan	**1858** United States and China sign friendship treaty
	Fillmore	Pierce	Buchanan

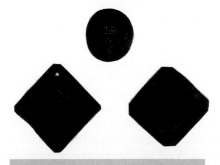

Slaveowners used tags such as these to identify their slaves.

330

The Fugitive Slave Law of 1850 required all citizens to help recover runaway slaves.

Drummer boys were the youngest "soldiers" on both sides of the Civil War.

So much Confederate money was printed during the war that the South suffered terrible inflation.

1860	1865	1870	1875

1860 Southern states begin to secede from the Union

1865 General Lee surrenders at Appomattox

1871 Congress outlaws the Ku Klux Klan

1863 President Lincoln issues the Emancipation Proclamation

1870 Fifteenth Amendment guarantees the right to vote

1862 Ironclad ships battle at Hampton Roads

1869 Transcontinental railroad complete

1861 Czar of Russia abolishes serfdom

1871 A unified German state is created

Lincoln   Johnson   Grant

The diary kept by Mary Boykin Chesnut of South Carolina revealed the horrors of the war for southern women.

1872 These seven black men were elected to Congress by southern Reconstruction governments in 1872.

The Cords of Union Broken (1820–1861)

16

CHAPTER OUTLINE

1 Differences Over Slavery

2 A Faltering Compromise

3 Rise of Sectional Politics

4 The House Divided

CHAPTER OBJECTIVES After completing this chapter, students should be able to
1. discuss how slavery sharpened sectional differences.
2. describe compromises over slavery from 1820 to 1860.
3. explain events that led to the South's secession.
4. describe the rise of the Republican party.
5. analyze interpretations.

CHAPTER PREVIEW Discuss with students the meaning of the word *compromise*. Review the importance of compromises at the Constitutional Convention, especially compromises over slavery. Ask: Why do politicians seek compromise? Are compromises good for the general public? In this chapter, students will study how Congress continued to pursue compromise on the slavery issue.

It wasn't the nippy February air that caused Senator Daniel Webster of New Hampshire to shiver. Rather it was his southern colleagues' chilling account of their private meeting with the President. Webster listened in dismay as they told how angry threats of "secession" and accusations of "traitor" had turned the meeting into a stormy confrontation.

Of course, disputes between the North and the South were nothing new. But by 1850, sectional differences over slavery had created a crisis. Many northerners wanted to prohibit slavery in the new western territories. Southerners saw such attacks on slavery as a threat to their way of life. If slavery could not expand, they insisted, they would leave the Union.

Alarmed by this latest confrontation, Webster resolved to make a plea for moderation on the Senate floor. News of his intention spread quickly. On the appointed day, March 7, 1850, spectators filled every seat in the Senate galleries. They even squeezed into odd corners of the Senate floor, some sitting on stacks of documents, many standing. Webster began:

Mr. President, I wish to speak today, not as a Massachusetts man, nor as a northern man, but as an American. . . . I speak today for the preservation of the Union. Hear me for my cause.

For three hours, the senator pleaded for compromise. Both the South and North had legitimate grievances, he admitted. But they must settle their differences and learn to live together. The only alternative would be unthinkable. Webster warned:

Secession! Peaceable secession! Sir, your eyes and mine are never destined to see that miracle. . . . Peaceable secession is an utter impossibility. . . . I see that it must produce war, and such a war as I will not describe.

Webster's dramatic speech helped to buy time. The North and the South managed to live together for ten more years. In the end, however, secession came. And just as Webster had predicted, war came, too.

1. **Attempts to balance slave and free states**

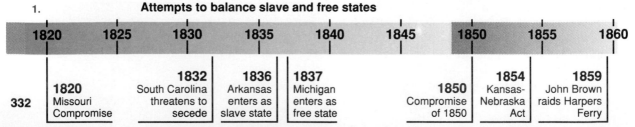

| 1820 | 1825 | 1830 | 1835 | 1840 | 1845 | 1850 | 1855 | 1860 |

1820 Missouri Compromise

1832 South Carolina threatens to secede

1836 Arkansas enters as slave state

1837 Michigan enters as free state

1850 Compromise of 1850

1854 Kansas-Nebraska Act

1859 John Brown raids Harpers Ferry

332

1. **TIME LINE QUESTION** Ask: What two compromises are shown on the time line? How many years passed between them?

The conflict over slavery had heated up by 1850. Spirited debate in the Senate led to the Compromise of 1850, but the seeds of conflict remained. In the mid-1850s, Kansas became a battleground between proslavery and antislavery forces, as this
1. drawing of the battle of Hickory Point shows.

1. **VISUAL EVIDENCE** Ask: What does this drawing show you about who took part in the fighting in Kansas?

2. **VOCABULARY** Have students look up these terms in the glossary before they begin reading.

Differences Over Slavery

READ TO UNDERSTAND

■ Why the slavery issue strained relations between North and South.

■ What solutions were proposed by moderates and by extremists.

■ How leaders in Congress tried to settle the slavery issue through compromises.

2. ■ *Vocabulary:* free state, slave state.

Slavery caused a growing strain between the North and the South. As settlers continued to push west, Congress faced an agonizing decision: Should it prohibit slavery within the territories and later admit them as **free states,** states that barred slavery? Or should it permit slavery within the territories and later admit them as **slave states,** states that allowed slavery? As President Monroe wrote, "I have never known a question so menacing to the tranquility and even the continuance of our Union as the present one."

How Congress decided this vital issue would determine the balance of political power between North and South. The more populous North had more votes in the House of Representatives, since population determined the number of representatives from each state. In the Senate, however, each state had two senators. By 1819, there were 11 free states and 11 slave states. Thus, either side could usually block legislation unfavorable to its region. Neither the South nor the North wanted the balance in the Senate to tip in favor of the other.

3.

The Missouri Compromise

In December 1818, Missouri, which had been part of the Louisiana Purchase, asked to enter the Union as a slave state. Fearing this threat to the balance of power in the Senate, northern members of Congress offered a counterproposal. Missouri could enter as a slave state if no more slaves were brought into the state and all children of slaves were freed at age 25. That way, Missouri would eventually become a free state.

333

3. **CITIZENSHIP** Passing a bill in Congress required a majority vote—one more than half the members present. Since the South controlled half the Senate votes, it could keep the North from getting a majority. Ask: In the case of a tie, what would happen?

Missouri Compromise, 1820

OREGON COUNTRY

CANADA

UNORGANIZED TERRITORY

Missouri Compromise line 36° 30'

ARKANSAS TERR.

NEW SPAIN

MICH. TERR.
ILL. IND. OHIO
MO. KY.
TENN.
MISS. ALA. GA.
LA.
FLA. TERR.

ME.
VT.
N.H.
MASS.
N.Y.
PA.
R.I.
CONN.
N.J.
MD. DEL.
VA.
N.C.
S.C.

PACIFIC OCEAN

ATLANTIC OCEAN

GULF OF MEXICO

Free states and territories

Slave states and territories

0   250   500 Miles
0 250   500 Kilometers

N
W   E
S

MAP STUDY *The Missouri Compromise maintained a balance between slave and free states. What was the significance of the Missouri Compromise line? Based on the map, why was the Missouri Compromise likely to be only a temporary solution to the problem of slavery in the nation?* See p. T63.

1. **MAP READING** Ask: What slave states east of Missouri were above 36°30'?

2. **CRITICAL THINKING** Ask: Based on your reading, who was probably not satisfied with the Missouri Compromise? What problems would you foresee?

Debate raged as northerners and southerners accused each other of trying to seize additional power and influence. Seventy-six-year-old Thomas Jefferson, observing the crisis from his plantation in Virginia, foresaw great danger to the Union: "This momentous question, like a firebell in the night, awakened and filled me with terror."

Henry Clay tackled the problem and, after much negotiation, persuaded Congress to adopt a measure known as the Missouri Compromise. To preserve the balance between free and slave states, Missouri would be admitted as a a slave state and Maine, formerly part of Massachusetts, as a free state. The compromise also provided that in the remaining part of the Louisiana Purchase slavery would be prohibited forever north of latitude 36°30', the southern boundary of Missouri, and would be permitted south of that line. Southerners accepted the limitation, believing that plantation agriculture would

not develop north of the line. (See the map above.)

Most Americans breathed a sigh of relief when Congress adopted the Missouri Compromise in 1820. Leaders hoped that the slavery question had been settled for good. But the issue persisted.

A Delicate Balance

Whenever a new state requested admission to the Union, the problem of maintaining a balance between the North and the South resurfaced. In 1836 and 1837, Arkansas and Michigan, respectively, joined the Union, the former a slave state, the latter a free state. Then in 1845, Florida and Texas both entered as slave states. Additional free states—Iowa in 1846 and Wisconsin in 1848—soon restored the balance.

The outbreak of war with Mexico in 1846 raised a new problem, however. A victory

334

3. **READING** John Quincy Adams wrote in his diary, "Take it for granted that the present is a mere preamble—a title page to a great, tragic volume."

1. **CITIZENSHIP** The Wilmot Proviso was the first important rider to a routine congressional bill. Ask: Why do you think the measure passed the House but not the Senate?

2. **ACTIVITY** Have students write a paragraph presenting arguments against Calhoun's position.

over Mexico might add extensive territory to the United States. Since the Missouri Compromise applied only to territories in the Louisiana Purchase, a disturbing question arose: Would Congress ban slavery or allow it in the new territories?

On a steamy Washington night in August 1846, Representative David Wilmot of Pennsylvania proposed an answer. Congress was debating an appropriation to purchase land in the Southwest from Mexico. In a surprise move, Wilmot added a provision that would forbid slavery forever in any territory acquired from Mexico.

Suddenly the members of Congress, who had been wearily fanning themselves, plunged into a heated debate that revived all the old emotions. The House passed the amendment, known as the Wilmot Proviso, but two days later the Senate defeated the measure. When the United States finally acquired the southwestern territory from Mexico in 1848, the peace treaty said nothing about slavery. But the question of slavery in the new territories did not go away.

GREAT DEBATE
Positions on the Slavery Issue

As the debate over slavery in the territories continued, various groups proposed solutions. Wilmot's proposal, which had sought to ban slavery in all territory gained from Mexico, represented the extreme northern position. Supporters included northern moderates who had once argued that slavery would eventually die out. Seeing that slavery was spreading instead, they wanted firm legislation to control it.

John C. Calhoun, now a grizzled and gaunt old man, represented the extreme southern position. Slaves were personal property, he declared. The Fifth Amendment to the Constitution specified that no person could be deprived of "life, liberty, or property without due process of law." Yet under current law, a slave owner could be deprived of his property upon moving to a territory where slavery was forbidden. Therefore, Calhoun concluded, slavery should be permitted in all territories.

Between the extreme positions lay two moderate solutions. One group of moderates, supported by President James Polk, proposed that the Missouri Compromise line of 36°30' be extended west to the Pacific Ocean. Slavery would be prohibited north of the line but allowed south of it. Senator Stephen Douglas of Illinois championed the idea of popular sovereignty, the principle that the power of government rests with the people. He proposed that the voters of each territory decide whether or not to allow slavery within the territory, regardless of where it was located.

Over the years, the two moderate solutions lost support. By the end of the 1850s, the two extreme positions dominated. ■

Emergence of the Free Soil Party

During the election campaign of 1848, both the Democratic and Whig parties wanted to avoid the question of slavery in the territories. But many Democrats and Whigs in the North demanded a strong stand against the expansion of slavery. Abandoning their parties, they joined with members of the Liberty party (see page 323) to form the Free Soil party. As you have read in Chapter 15, the Free Soil party opposed slavery in the territories. It did not, however, advocate the abolition of slavery in existing states, North or South.

In 1848, the Free Soilers nominated former President Martin Van Buren for President. Lewis Cass, a Michigan senator who favored popular sovereignty, was the choice of the Democrats. The Whig nominee was Zachary Taylor, a hero of the Mexican War and a wealthy slave owner from Louisiana. Although Taylor had not taken a stand on the slavery question, many assumed that he would support the South's position.

In the end, Taylor won with electoral votes from both the North and the South. The Free Soiler vote, however, was ominous. Winning nearly 10 percent of the popular vote, the Free Soilers received all their support from the North. The emergence of a political party with strength in only one section showed that the North-South split was widening.

335

The Compromise of 1850

As the news spread in 1848 of gold in California, thousands headed west to seek their fortunes. In 1849, California requested admission as a free state. If admitted, California would tip the balance to 16 free states and 15 slave states. No longer could the Whigs and Democrats evade the question of slavery in the territories.

Clay's Proposal When Congress met in December 1849, the question of California statehood was the subject of angry debate. Other issues fueled the bitter mood. Many northerners wanted to end the selling and buying of slaves in the nation's capital. Southerners, on the other hand, demanded a more effective fugitive slave law to prevent abolitionists from helping slaves escape.

The very existence of the Union seemed to be at stake. Henry Clay, who had earned the nickname "The Great Compromiser" during his long career, stepped forward to offer a solution that he hoped would satisfy both sides. Clay proposed that California be admitted as a free state but that the rest of the southwestern territory be open to slavery by popular sovereignty. The slave trade would be abolished in the District of Columbia, but Congress would officially declare that it had no power to abolish the slave trade between existing slave states. Finally, Congress would pass a strong fugitive slave law.

For six months, Clay used all his eloquence and powers of persuasion to win support for the compromise. He received crucial backing from Daniel Webster, his longtime rival, who warned that without compromise the United States would be torn apart. (See page 332.) 1.

Calhoun's Warning But John C. Calhoun, who strongly upheld the South's position, made the most dramatic warning about

MAP STUDY *The Compromise of 1850 tried a new approach to the question of slavery in the territories. California was admitted as a free state. How was the status of Utah and New Mexico to be decided?* See p. T63.   2.

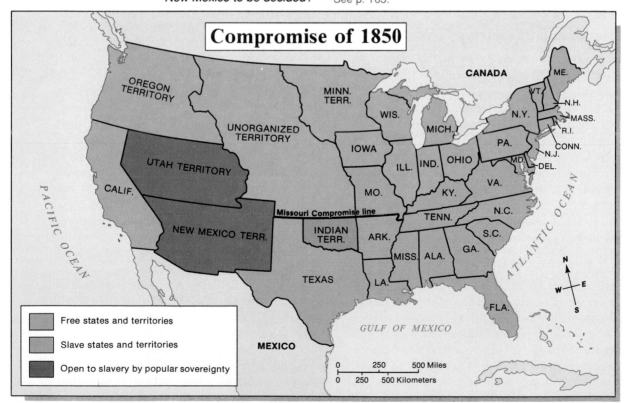

The Republic

Politicians were not the only Americans who feared for the fate of the United States in 1850. Poet Henry Wadsworth Longfellow expressed his faith in the republic in his poem "The Building of the Ship," an excerpt of which appears below.

Thou, too, sail on, O Ship of State!
Sail on, O Union, strong and great!
Humanity with all its fears,
With all the hopes of future years,
Is hanging breathless on thy fate!
We know what Master laid thy keel,
What Workmen wrought thy ribs of steel,
Who made each mast, and sail, and rope,
What anvils rang, what hammers beat,
In what a forge and what a heat
Were shaped the anchors of thy hope!
Fear not each sudden sound and shock,

'Tis of the wave and not the rock;
'Tis but the flapping of the sail,
And not a rent made by the gale!
In spite of rock and tempest's roar,
In spite of false lights on the shore,
Sail on, nor fear to breast the sea!
Our hearts, our hopes, are all with thee,
Our hearts, our hopes, our prayers, our tears,
Our faith triumphant o'er our fears,
Are all with thee—are all with thee.

Source: Henry Wadsworth Longfellow, *Complete Poetical Works* (Boston, 1893).

See p. T63.

1. What encouragement does Henry Wadsworth Longfellow offer in his poem?

2. **Critical Thinking** What may have been "each sudden sound and shock" to which Longfellow referred?

---

1. **CRITICAL THINKING** Ask students why Longfellow says of the U.S. that "Humanity . . . Is hanging breathless on thy fate!"

danger to the Union. Too ill to deliver his speech, Calhoun sat one last time in his Senate seat, staring fiercely ahead, while Senator James Mason of Virginia read the speech for him.

"It is a great mistake to suppose that disunion can be effected at a single blow," Calhoun argued. "The cords which bind these states together in one common Union are far too numerous and powerful for that." Yet one by one, he noted, these cords were being cut. "Already the agitation of the slavery question has snapped some of the most important, and has greatly weakened all the others. . . ." If controversy continued, he warned, the United States would break apart.

Calhoun's stern warning and the pleas of Webster and Clay pushed Congress toward compromise. Opposition to the compromise, led by President Taylor, faded upon his death in the summer of 1850. With the support of the new President, Millard Fillmore, Congress accepted all the terms of Clay's compromise

by an overwhelming majority. Once again, it appeared that crisis had been averted.

See p. T63.

SECTION 1 REVIEW

1. **Identify:** (a) David Wilmot, (b) Stephen Douglas, (c) Zachary Taylor.

2. **Define:** (a) free state, (b) slave state.

3. What were the two major provisions of the Missouri Compromise?

4. (a) What were the extreme northern and southern positions on slavery in the new territories? (b) What were the two moderate positions?

5. Compare the ways that northerners and southerners would benefit from the Compromise of 1850.

6. **Critical Thinking** What do you think Calhoun meant by "the cords which bind these states together"?

---

2. **BACKGROUND** John C. Calhoun died only 27 days later. His last words were "The South! The South! God knows what will become of her!"

3. **DISCUSSION** Have students discuss how the following might have felt about the Compromise of 1850: David Wilmot; a free black in California; a wealthy planter in Georgia.

1. **VISUAL EVIDENCE** Point out that southerners proudly referred to slavery as their "peculiar institution." "Peculiar" in this case meant unique or special.

2. **CITIZENSHIP** Have students review the Bill of Rights and identify the amendments violated by these procedures.

2 A Faltering Compromise

READ TO UNDERSTAND

■ Why the Compromise of 1850 caused tensions.

■ How the Kansas-Nebraska Act differed from the Missouri Compromise.

■ How Kansas came to be called "Bleeding Kansas."

To the dismay of many, the Compromise of 1850 did not quench the flames of controversy; it fanned them. Soon, developments in the territory of Kansas revived people's fears. Americans again felt the terror of that "firebell in the night."

Abolitionists glorified the exploits of fugitive slaves like Frederick Douglass. The Hutchinsons, a family singing group, popularized "The Fugitive's Song,"
1. *which was about Douglass. Douglass, who spoke often at abolitionist rallies, told his audience, "I stole this head, these limbs, this body from my master, and ran off with them."*

The Fugitive Slave Law

To southern slave owners, the strong Fugitive Slave Law that was part of the Compromise of 1850 represented only what was due them. They claimed that the Constitution permitted them to hold slaves as property and that fugitive slaves were either runaways or stolen property and should be returned.

Northern Resentment Many northerners, however, considered the Fugitive Slave Law too harsh. For example, any black accused of being a fugitive slave had to stand trial before a special commissioner, not a judge. No jury heard the case, and the accused could not testify. Furthermore, the com- 2. missioner received a $10 fee if he sent the accused back to slavery and only $5 if he freed the person. This, angry northerners argued, amounted to little less than a bribe to insure that the accused was declared a runaway slave. Finally, the law required all citizens to assist in capturing a fugitive slave.

The new law left free blacks in the North both angered and frightened. It permitted the capture not only of newly escaped slaves but of anyone who had ever fled from slavery. Thus, a person who had escaped many years earlier could be thrown in jail and returned to a former master in the South. Furthermore, protection against false identification was so flimsy that slave owners could easily claim free blacks as fugitives.

Many northern newspapers denounced the Fugitive Slave Law as "an outrage to humanity," "a hateful statute" that should be "disobeyed at all hazards." When slave owners sent agents north in search of escaped slaves, abolitionists organized resistance. Free blacks set up vigilance committees as protection against kidnappers.

Uncle Tom's Cabin Hatred of the Fugitive Slave Law was one reason for the immense popularity of Harriet Beecher Stowe's novel *Uncle Tom's Cabin,* published in 1852. Stowe created scenes and images that haunted the imagination: the desperate flight to freedom of fugitive slaves, the breakup of slave families and marriages, and the cruel effects of slavery on blacks and whites alike. Although 3. southern leaders protested that slaves were treated much better than *Uncle Tom's Cabin*

3. **VOCABULARY** Abolitionists used the term *Uncle Tom* for a patiently suffering slave. The modern sense—a submissive black—emerged in the 1940s.

suggested, thousands of northerners who read the book or saw the play came away determined to oppose the Fugitive Slave Law.

The Fugitive Slave Law increased sectional tensions because it affected northerners directly. Confronted with the plight of a slave seeking freedom, more and more northerners, even those once immune to abolitionist appeals, sympathized with the fugitive.

Growing Political Division

Despite controversy over the Fugitive Slave Law, political leaders tried to minimize tensions during the election year of 1852. Both Whigs and Democrats accepted the Compromise of 1850. Yet sectional tensions pulled at each party.

Northern and southern Whigs quarreled among themselves before northern Whigs pushed through the nomination of another war hero, General Winfield Scott, for President. Although southern and northern Democrats also argued, they avoided a split by nominating a little-known New Hampshire politician, Franklin Pierce. With the Whigs divided, Pierce won the election easily.

Uncle Tom's Cabin *was the first American novel to sell over one million copies. Stage readings of it were also very popular. The Webb family, shown here, gave dramatic readings of the novel throughout the North and in England.*

2.

2. ACTIVITY Suggest students read parts of *Uncle Tom's Cabin* and prepare skits or readings of important scenes.

VOICES OF FREEDOM

A Conspiracy of Silence

Many northerners defied the Fugitive Slave Law and helped runaway slaves. Levi Coffin, an abolitionist, describes how a conspiracy of silence in an Ohio courtroom enabled the defendant Louis, a captured runaway, to evade the clutches of the law.

The court-room was crowded with interested listeners, white and black. . . . To gain more room, [Louis] slipped his chair back a little way. Neither his master nor the marshal noticed . . . and he slipped in his chair again, until he was back of them. Next he rose to his feet and took a step backward. Some abolitionists . . . gave him an encouraging touch on the foot, and he stepped farther back. Then a good hat was placed on his head by some one be-

hind, and he quietly and cautiously made his way . . . toward the door. I and several other abolitionists had our eyes on him, and our hearts throbbed. . . . About five minutes after he left the court-room his absence was discovered. . . . A vigorous search was made for Louis by the marshal and the proslavery party, but he could not be found.

3.

Source: *Reminiscences of Levi Coffin* (Cincinnati, 1876), pp. 550–552.

See p. T63.

1. Why were tensions high in the courtroom?

2. **Critical Thinking** How was the behavior of the abolitionists an example of civil disobedience?

3. CRITICAL THINKING Ask: Do you think the escape of Louis was part of a deliberate plan? Why or why not? How do you think Louis's owner would respond to Coffin's account?

1. **BACKGROUND** Douglas cared more about territorial expansion than the moral issue of slavery. He once said, "I do not care whether slavery is voted up or voted down."

2. **CRITICAL THINKING** Ask: Which people were included within Douglas's concept of "popular sovereignty"? Which were not?

Northerners soon discovered, however, that President Pierce sympathized with many southern goals. In particular, Pierce hoped to obtain Cuba from Spain. If Cuba joined the United States, it would surely be as a slave territory and ultimately as a slave state.

In 1854, three of Pierce's diplomats met in Ostend, Belgium, and issued a manifesto, or declaration. In it, they suggested that the United States try to buy Cuba from Spain. If that failed, the so-called Ostend Manifesto boldly proclaimed, Americans might be justified in seizing the island by force. Although Pierce rejected the statement, northerners branded the act another attempt to expand slavery.

The Kansas-Nebraska Act

The question of slavery in the territories became an issue again in 1854 when Senator Stephen Douglas of Illinois introduced a bill to organize the vast Nebraska territory west of Iowa and Missouri. Douglas wanted to establish a transcontinental railroad by extending the existing lines from Chicago to the Pacific. He felt that the route would be possible only if the Nebraska territory were organized.

The Missouri Compromise of 1820 had prohibited slavery in the Nebraska lands. But by 1854, a number of prominent southern senators backed John C. Calhoun's position that slavery ought to be permitted in all territories. Those senators refused to support Douglas's bill unless it allowed slavery within the Nebraska territory.

Douglas then proposed, and Congress
1. passed, a compromise bill that divided the area into a Nebraska and a Kansas territory. The Kansas-Nebraska Act repealed the Missouri Compromise and in its place applied the doctrine of popular sovereignty. The people of each territory, rather than Congress, would decide whether to permit slav-
2. ery in the territory.

Senator Douglas believed that popular sovereignty was the only democratic solution to the slavery question. Many northerners, however, protested the repeal of the long-respected Missouri Compromise. They argued

that the Kansas-Nebraska Act made it possible for slavery to spread to any territory.

Conflict Over Kansas

Most Americans assumed that Nebraska would be "free" because it was too far north for plantation agriculture. Kansas, they expected, would be "slave" because it was located directly west of Missouri, a slave state. But since the voters in each territory would decide the question, the final outcome was still uncertain.

The Battle for Political Control Some abolitionist groups encouraged supporters of the antislavery cause to move to Kansas, hoping to influence the vote against slavery there. The New England Emigrant Aid Society, for example, sent about 650 settlers to Kansas in 1854. Hearing that "mobs" of abolitionists were moving to Kansas, Missourians became alarmed. They feared that if slavery were not allowed in Kansas, their own slaves could easily escape to freedom across the border. Consequently, proslavery elements began to encourage settlers from Missouri to move to Kansas.

When the first elections to the territorial legislature were held in March 1855, about 8,000 settlers lived in Kansas. Proslavery voters were a majority and could have won the election fairly. But several thousand Missouri "border ruffians" crossed into Kansas and voted illegally, giving the proslavery forces a lopsided victory.

Northerners protested that the election had been stolen. They became even more incensed when the new territorial legislature passed harsh proslavery laws. One law made it a crime to agitate against slavery; another ordered the death penalty for anyone who helped an escaped slave. In response to these actions, antislavery settlers established a rival free-state government at Lawrence, Kansas. Chaos soon reigned, with two separate governments proclaiming authority and armed bands roaming the territory.

"Bleeding Kansas" In May 1856, three events thrust Kansas into the national limelight. On May 21, a mob of Missourians acting as a sheriff's posse charged into Lawrence, looted and burned several houses,

340

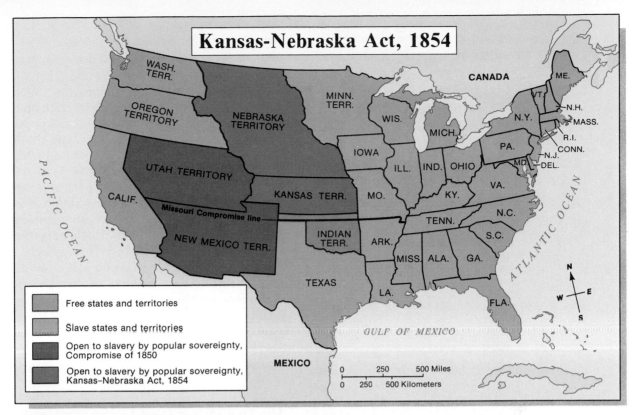

Kansas-Nebraska Act, 1854

WASH. TERR.
OREGON TERRITORY
NEBRASKA TERRITORY
MINN. TERR.
CANADA
ME.
VT.
N.H.
WIS.
N.Y.
MASS.
R.I.
MICH.
CONN.
IOWA
PA.
N.J.
UTAH TERRITORY
ILL. IND. OHIO
MD. DEL.
CALIF.
Missouri Compromise line
KANSAS TERR.
MO.
KY.
VA.
N.C.
NEW MEXICO TERR.
INDIAN TERR.
TENN.
S.C.
ARK.
MISS. ALA. GA.
TEXAS
LA.
FLA.
PACIFIC OCEAN
ATLANTIC OCEAN
GULF OF MEXICO
MEXICO

Free states and territories

Slave states and territories

Open to slavery by popular sovereignty, Compromise of 1850

Open to slavery by popular sovereignty, Kansas–Nebraska Act, 1854

0   250   500 Miles
0   250   500 Kilometers

N E S W

MAP STUDY *The Kansas-Nebraska Act organized the Kansas and Nebraska territories. Compare this map with the map on page 334. How did the Kansas-Nebraska Act "repeal" the Missouri Compromise?* See p. T63.

1.

1. **MAP READING** Ask: How many slave states were there in 1854? How many free states? In which areas was the question of slavery not yet decided?

threw two printing presses into the river, and bombarded the Free State Hotel with cannon.

On May 22, Senator Charles Sumner of Massachusetts delivered an angry speech denouncing the violence in Kansas. Sumner blamed slave owners, including some of his fellow senators. The next day, Congressman Preston Brooks of South Carolina, the cousin of a South Carolina senator, attacked Sumner with a cane as he sat at his Senate desk. The injured Massachusetts senator was unable to resume his duties in the Senate for three years, and he never fully recovered.

On the night of May 24, a little-known antislavery agitator named John Brown took vengeance for the Lawrence attack. Brown and a group of followers murdered five proslavery settlers at Pottawatomie Creek, Kansas, even though the victims had noth-
2. ing to do with the Lawrence raid.

These three violent events, following one another so closely, demonstrated how badly the Compromise of 1850 had failed. One of its major elements, the Fugitive Slave Law,

had outraged the North. The question of slavery in the territories, which the compromise was supposed to settle, had erupted more violently than ever on the battleground of "Bleeding Kansas."

3.

See p. T63.

SECTION 2 REVIEW

1. **Identify:** (a) *Uncle Tom's Cabin,* (b) Franklin Pierce, (c) Ostend Manifesto, (d) Kansas-Nebraska Act, (e) John Brown.

2. (a) How did southerners justify the Fugitive Slave Law? (b) What aspects of the law especially angered northerners?

3. (a) What was the outcome of the first territorial elections in Kansas? (b) What led to the establishment of a free-state government?

4. **Critical Thinking** Why was the Compromise of 1850 less successful than the Missouri Compromise?

341

2. **BACKGROUND** Violence led to more violence. By late 1856, more than 200 people had been killed in Kansas.

3. **CRITICAL THINKING** The struggle in Kansas was later called a "mini civil war." Ask: Why do you think this term was used?

3 The Rise of Sectional Politics

READ TO UNDERSTAND

■ Why the new Republican party was called a "sectional" party.

■ How the Dred Scott decision caused a new crisis in 1857.

■ Why Senator Douglas's Freeport Doctrine of 1858 split the Democrats.

Since the mid-1830s, the Whigs and the Democrats had been important "cords" binding the Union together. Receiving support from both the North and the South, they were truly national parties. But growing sectional bitterness snapped those cords too, dividing both parties and giving rise to a new political party that was sectional rather than national.

Birth of the Republican Party

As you have read, a growing number of northerners opposed the spread of slavery into the territories. These antislavery forces had little faith in either the Whig or Democratic party. The Whigs had been weakened by disputes between northern and southern factions; and the Democratic President, Franklin Pierce, seemed sympathetic to the South. Two earlier antislavery groups, the Liberty and Free Soil parties, had faded.

Hoping to form a new party, Free Soilers held conventions in several northern states during the summer of 1854. At one such convention in Jackson, Michigan, the delegates for the first time called themselves Republicans to show their connection to Jefferson's Democratic-Republican Party. During 1855, many former Whigs, Democrats, and Free Soilers joined the Republicans, who were sure they could become a major party opposing slavery in the new territories.

The Republican party grew rapidly. By 1856, it had elected many representatives to Congress and had won several state elections. That same year, Republicans made their first bid for the presidency, nominating John Frémont, the impulsive, swashbuckling military leader who had encouraged the Bear Flag Revolt in California.

The Democrats chose James Buchanan of Pennsylvania as their candidate. Buchanan supported the Kansas-Nebraska Act and popular sovereignty. Yet he remained vague about how or when the people of Kansas and Nebraska would decide on slavery. The remnants of the Whig and Know-Nothing parties nominated former President Millard Fillmore in separate conventions. The contest, however, was between Frémont and Buchanan. Buchanan won—but only by a narrow margin.

The 1856 election showed just how divided the nation had become. Buchanan carried every southern state except Maryland. Frémont carried every free state except Pennsylvania, Indiana, Illinois, New Jersey, and California. Increasingly, the Democrats spoke for the South, the Republicans for the North.

The Dred Scott Decision

A few months after Buchanan's victory, in early 1857, the Supreme Court rocked the nation with a major proslavery decision in the case of *Dred Scott* v. S*andford*. Dred Scott had been a slave in Missouri. His owner served in the army for several years and took Scott with him to Illinois, a free state, and to Minnesota, a free territory. Eventually, Scott's owner returned to Missouri.

When Scott's owner died, some abolitionists aided Scott in suing for his freedom, claiming that he was free because he had lived for a time in Illinois and Minnesota. After conflicting judgments in the lower courts, the case reached the United States Supreme Court.

The Supreme Court faced two major questions. First, was Scott a Missouri citizen with the right to bring suit in a federal court? Second, had Scott's residence in a free state and a free territory made him a free man?

The Supreme Court Ruling The Court answered "no" to both questions. It ruled that blacks who were slaves or descendants of slaves could not be citizens of the United States. Scott, therefore, could not sue in a federal court. Missouri law, the court concluded, should determine Scott's status, and according to Missouri law, Scott was a slave.

3. **CRITICAL THINKING** Ask: How does the rapid rise of the Republican party show that the slavery issue was dissolving old political loyalties?

But the Dred Scott decision went even further. It ruled that the Missouri Compromise was unconstitutional because it had prohibited slavery north of 36°30'. Under the Fifth Amendment, the Court declared, Congress had no power to deprive anyone of property without due process of law. Because slaves were property, Congress could not forbid owners to take them into free territories—as, in effect, the Missouri Compromise had done.

Northern Reactions The Dred Scott decision shocked many northerners, even moderates. First, it affirmed the extreme southern position, that slavery could not be outlawed in any territory. Second, the decision marked the first time the Supreme Court had ruled a major piece of federal legislation unconstitutional. Only once before (*Marbury v. Madison,* see page 198) had it ruled a law unconstitutional.

Republicans were especially incensed. Above all, their party stood for the principle that Congress had the right to keep slavery out of the territories. And now the Supreme Court had, in effect, ruled that the party's goals were unconstitutional.

Northern Democrats, led by Stephen Douglas, also felt the shock. The Court, by implication, had ruled against the doctrine of popular sovereignty. If Congress did not have the power to ban slavery in a territory, then it could not delegate that power to a territorial legislature.

A Senate Race With National Implications

As controversy spread, national attention turned to the 1858 Senate race in Illinois. There, the Democratic and Republican candidates skillfully debated the issues that divided the country.

The Democratic candidate, Senator Stephen Douglas, was better known. Douglas was just over five feet tall, with a large head and broad shoulders. A scrapper who loved an argument, he had a burning, energetic drive. Few could match his debating skills on the Senate floor, where he had helped Henry Clay push through the Compromise of 1850 and had vigorously defended the doctrine of popular sovereignty.

Douglas's Republican opponent was a respected lawyer named Abraham Lincoln. Born in Kentucky, Lincoln had moved with his family to Indiana and then to Illinois. There, he combined his law practice with a career in politics, first as a Whig and then as a Republican.

At six feet four inches, Lincoln was as tall and lanky as Douglas was short and stocky. The self-educated Republican combined a folksy, backwoods manner with a keen legal mind that sought out the logic of a situation in its clearest, simplest terms. Lincoln appeared awkward and homely and lacked a polished speaking style, but he had a sharp sense of humor, an easy manner, and a compelling eloquence.

Lincoln had sounded his campaign theme in his speech accepting the nomination for senator. Beginning with the biblical observation that "a house divided against itself cannot stand," Lincoln stated his case:

3. **VISUAL EVIDENCE** Ask: What effect might the physical contrast between Lincoln and Douglas have had at a debate?

Stephen Douglas (left) was a leader of the Democratic party in 1856. His opponent for a seat in the Senate, Abraham Lincoln, became nationally known after debating Douglas. 3.

2. **CRITICAL THINKING** Ask: Why do you think abolitionists were especially incensed that the Court used the Fifth Amendment to open the territories to slavery?

> I believe this government cannot endure, permanently, half slave and half free. I do not expect the Union to be dissolved; I do not expect the house to fall; but I do expect it will cease to be divided. It will become all one thing, or all the other.

1.

The Lincoln-Douglas Debates

As the lesser-known candidate, Lincoln challenged Douglas to a series of debates during the campaign. In seven memorable appearances, "Honest Abe" squared off against the "Little Giant," as people called Douglas. Despite the hoopla of cheering crowds, bands, and torchlight parades, the debaters faced head-on the very serious issue of slavery. Newspapers across the country reprinted the candidates' words, and citizens argued over who was more persuasive.

2.

Lincoln argued that the major philosophical difference between Republicans and northern Democrats like Douglas was the Republican belief that the institution of slavery was morally wrong. Douglas, Lincoln pointed out, had said that he did not care whether slavery was accepted or rejected in the territories. Although Lincoln believed that blacks and whites might not be equal, he maintained that blacks were entitled to "all the natural rights enumerated in the Declaration of Independence, the right to life, liberty, and the pursuit of happiness."

Douglas defended the doctrine of popular sovereignty as fair and workable. At Freeport, Illinois, Lincoln pressed Douglas to reconcile popular sovereignty with the Dred Scott decision. The Court had ruled that slavery must be allowed in every territory. Was there a legal way, Lincoln asked, that the people of a territory could exercise popular sovereignty and prohibit slavery?

Douglas replied that since slavery could not exist without a slave code to protect it, the people of a territory could simply refuse to enact a slave code. Douglas's solution, soon known as the Freeport Doctrine, was convincing to many voters. The Illinois legislature elected Douglas by 54 to 41.

3.

The senator's victory cost his party dearly, however. Southerners considered the Freeport Doctrine an act of treachery. As

344

they saw it, Douglas was encouraging settlers in the territories to stop slavery from spreading. These suspicions deepened the wedge between northern and southern Democrats, further weakening the Democrats as a national party.

4.

See p. T64.

SECTION 3 REVIEW

1. **Identify:** (a) Dred Scott, (b) Freeport Doctrine.

2. What issue led to the creation of the Republican party?

3. How did the election of 1856 reveal divisions in the nation?

4. In the Supreme Court's opinion, why was Dred Scott still a slave?

5. **Critical Thinking** Why does a lesser-known candidate stand to gain more by participating in a campaign debate?

4 The House Divided

READ TO UNDERSTAND

- Why John Brown's raid at Harpers Ferry caused a sensation.

- How the 1860 election drove a new wedge between the sections of the nation.

- What steps led to the formation of the Confederacy and to war.

- *Vocabulary:* lame duck.

5.

Constant haggling over slavery in the territories rubbed the nerves of northerners and southerners raw. The nation's leaders struggled to soothe tensions, but their compromises could not paper over basic strains between the northern and southern regions of the country. As the presidential election of 1860 approached, the nation was on edge.

1. **BACKGROUND** Abolitionist Henry Ward Beecher said, "Let Virginia make him a martyr! . . . His soul was noble; his work miserable. But a cord and a gibbet would redeem all that, and round up Brown's failure with a heroic success." Ask the class to explain Beecher's words.

Harpers Ferry

John Brown tipped the balance. Brown, a Kansas abolitionist, had stunned the South and much of the rest of the nation by leading the 1856 massacre at Pottawatomie Creek. (See page 341.) After his raid in Kansas, Brown traveled east and began raising money for a mysterious mission. Even to his abolitionist contributors, he revealed few details of his intentions.

Brown's plan was to stockpile weapons and lead southern slaves in an uprising. When Frederick Douglass heard about the plan, he warned that it would fail. As an escaped slave, Douglass saw that the plan was impractical. Still Brown persisted.

On the night of October 16, 1859, Brown led a band of 18 men to the federal arsenal at Harpers Ferry, Virginia, seized its weapons, and waited for slaves to rise in rebellion and join him. But he had made several mistakes. Few slaves lived in the area of Harpers Ferry,

and those who did were unlikely to stake their lives on the leadership of a man they had never heard of. Furthermore, Brown lingered at Harpers Ferry until all avenues of escape were cut off. Two days after the attack, United States troops led by Colonel Robert E. Lee easily subdued the raiders.

Although Brown's military conduct had been amateurish, his demeanor as he stood trial for treason was impressive. Even his southern jailers admired his dignity and calm. Many northerners saw Brown as a martyr. On December 2, following his conviction, state authorities hanged Brown from a scaffold in Charles Town, Virginia.

A Charged Atmosphere

John Brown's death proved more effective in mobilizing antislavery opinion than had his actions in life. In the North, church bells tolled in mourning. Black bunting hung on

2. **BACKGROUND** Before he was hanged, Brown handed his guard this note: "I John Brown am now quite certain that the crimes of this guilty land will never be purged away but with blood."

3. In this painting by the black artist Horace Pippin, the abolitionist John Brown is hauled to his execution in 1859. At right, a black woman turns away in despair as Brown rides in his own coffin to the gallows. Pippin's mother told him she had watched Brown's execution.

3. **VISUAL EVIDENCE** Horace Pippin was born in 1888. This painting was one of a series Pippin did in the 1940s on the life of John Brown.

1. windows, and sympathizers held mass prayer meetings in New York, Boston, and Philadelphia. Despite the show of sympathy, however, many northern leaders, including Republican party members, repudiated Brown's actions and dismissed him as a lunatic.

In the South, however, such words had little effect. Southerners heard about the church bells and prayer meetings and read of abolitionist speeches calling for slave insurrections. Increasingly, they came to believe that they could remain secure only by seceding from the Union. One Virginia newspaper noted that there were "thousands of men in our midst who, a month ago, scoffed at the idea of a dissolution of the Union as a madman's dream, but who now hold the opinion that its days are numbered."

In Washington, nerves were so taut that senators and representatives often went to legislative sessions armed. Some claimed that spectators in the galleries carried weapons, too. When a pistol accidentally fell from the pocket of a New York congressman during one heated debate, a shooting fray nearly erupted. "The only persons who do not have a revolver and a knife," reported one South Carolina senator, "are those who have two revolvers."

The 1860 Conventions

In this explosive atmosphere, the presidential nominating conventions of 1860 assembled. The Democrats met in Charleston, South Carolina. Some southerners demanded that the party endorse a federal code to protect slavery in all territories. When the convention rejected this platform, those delegates walked out.

Unable to agree on a nominee, the convention finally adjourned, reassembling six weeks later in Baltimore, Maryland. There, the delegates nominated Stephen Douglas. A group of southern Democrats then held their own convention, adopted the original southern platform, and nominated John Breckinridge of Kentucky to head their ticket.

A new party, the Constitutional Union party, also held a convention and nominated John Bell of Tennessee. The Constitutional Unionists hoped to rally conservatives in both the North and South around a vague platform that supported the Constitution and the Union.

The Republican convention met in Chicago in the Wigwam, a building specially constructed for the event. Enthusiastic Republicans squeezed inside while as many as 20,000 people cheered outside. When the convention opened, the leading contender was William H. Seward of New York. However, party leaders worried that Seward was too radical to win and looked to Abraham Lincoln as a more moderate candidate. Besides being acceptable to all factions of the party, Lincoln came from Illinois, a state Republicans needed to carry. He received the nomination on the third ballot.

The Republicans sought to broaden their platform. They endorsed a protective tariff, which was popular in the industrial Northeast. They also supported a homestead law granting free land to settlers, which was popular in the West. Moreover, their state- 2. ments about slavery were less shrill than in 1856, although they continued to insist that Congress ban slavery from all territories.

2. CRITICAL THINKING Ask: How did the other planks of the Republican platform reinforce the sectional character of the party?

The Election of 1860

The presidential campaign of 1860 dramatized the great rift between North and South. Lincoln's supporters did not campaign in the South, and his name was not even on the ballot in ten southern states. Breckinridge, on the other hand, had virtually no support in the North. Only Douglas, weary but determined, campaigned actively in both northern and southern states, warning of the dire consequences of disunion.

In the end, Lincoln carried every northern state except New Jersey, receiving 39 percent of the popular vote. Breckinridge swept the deep South and divided the border states with Bell and Douglas. Although Douglas finished last in the electoral college, he received more popular votes than anyone except Lincoln. (See the map on page 347.) 3.

Lincoln's election marked a startling change in American politics. He was the first President to be elected by a sectional party with its strength entirely in the North. To southerners, the future seemed bleak. Northerners had simply outvoted them. Since the South now had only one third of the total

3. LOCAL HISTORY Have students use the map on p. 347 to determine which party probably received the most support in your area in 1860.

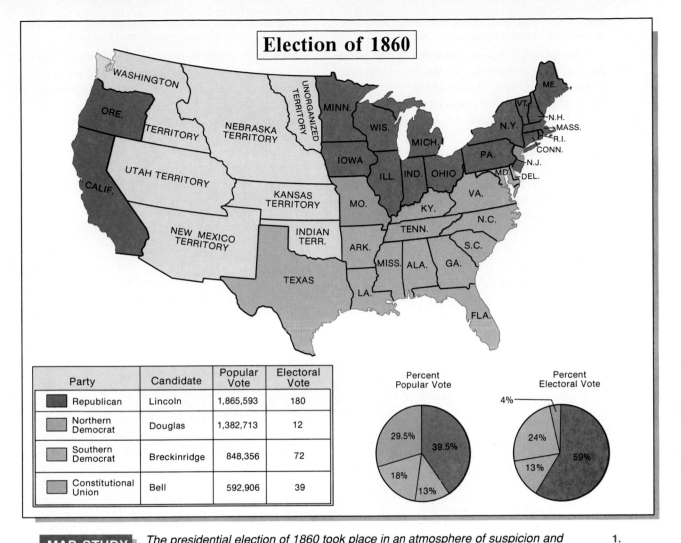

Election of 1860

Party	Candidate	Popular Vote	Electoral Vote
Republican	Lincoln	1,865,593	180
Northern Democrat	Douglas	1,382,713	12
Southern Democrat	Breckinridge	848,356	72
Constitutional Union	Bell	592,906	39

Percent Popular Vote: 39.5%, 29.5%, 18%, 13%

Percent Electoral Vote: 59%, 24%, 13%, 4%

MAP STUDY *The presidential election of 1860 took place in an atmosphere of suspicion and distrust. How does the map reveal the deep sectionalism that divided the nation?*

1.

See p. T64.

1. **MAP READING** Ask: How can you account for the difference between Douglas's standing in the popular vote and in the electoral college?

2. white male population of the United States, many southerners concluded that the only way they could play a role in any national government was to secede and form a government of their own.

2. **GEOGRAPHY** The 1860 census showed that the center of the U.S. population had moved from Parkersburg, Va., northwest to Chillicothe, Ohio. (movement)

The Secession Crisis

South Carolina, which had threatened to secede during the nullification crisis of 1832 (see page 255), led the way. On December 20, 1860, a convention called by the state legislature adopted an ordinance of secession stating that South Carolina was no longer part of the Union but was now a free and

3. independent state. By the end of February 1861, the six states of the deep South—Alabama, Florida, Georgia, Louisiana, Mis-

sissippi, and Texas—had followed South Carolina's lead.

In February, delegates from the seceded states met in Montgomery, Alabama, and formed the Confederate States of America. As their frame of government, they adopted most features of the United States Constitution, making only a few changes. They stressed the "sovereign and independent character" of each individual state, and they made it clear that slaves could be held as property.

On February 18, the Confederate States inaugurated Jefferson Davis of Mississippi as their president. Davis, a former United States senator, read his inaugural address while new military companies clad in red, green, and gray battle jackets paraded with bayonets on their rifles.

347

3. **DISCUSSION** Have students compare the events that led American colonists to declare independence from Britain in 1776 to the events that led the South to secede in 1860.

1. **PRESIDENTS** Buchanan predicted that he would go down in history as "the last President of the United States." Ask students to explain this remark.

2. **BIOGRAPHY** John Crittenden (1787–1863) also served as U.S. Attorney General. Though his compromise failed, he did help persuade Kentucky to remain in the Union.

In the North, meanwhile, President James Buchanan watched these developments with a sense of powerlessness. He was a **lame duck** President, serving only until his successor, Abraham Lincoln, was inaugurated. So he did little.

In December 1860, Congress made one last attempt to hold the Union together. Senator John Crittenden of Kentucky proposed restoring the old Missouri Compromise line as a way of permanently settling the slavery issue. He also suggested adding an "unamendable" amendment to the Constitution to forever guarantee the right to hold slaves in states south of the compromise line. Republicans, however, refused to support these or any other compromise proposals. The breach between North and South was now too wide.

3. **DISCUSSION** Ask: Do you think that either the economic differences alone or the slavery issue alone could have caused the Civil War?

SKILL LESSON

Causes of the Civil War: Analyzing Interpretations

Historians may interpret events differently even if they study the same sources. Their frame of reference affects the way they view a historical event. Two views of the causes of the Civil War are printed here. The first was written by Frank Owsley in 1930, the second by Arthur Schlesinger, Jr., in 1949.

See p. T64.

1 Identify the interpretation. (a) What was the basic cause of the Civil War according to Owsley? (b) According to Schlesinger?

2 Decide how a person's frame of reference affects his or her interpretation. Consider the time in which the historian wrote. In 1929, the United States plunged into economic depression. In 1945, shocked Americans learned about Nazi concentration camps. (a) Can you find evidence that economic worries influenced Owsley? (b) How might Nazi atrocities have affected Schlesinger's interpretation?

3 Decide which interpretation you think is most accurate. (a) What role did the economies of the North and South play in bringing about war? (b) How did people's response to the moral aspects of slavery help cause the war? (c) What other factors were important?

Frank Owsley

[S]lavery as a moral issue is too simple an explanation. . . . Complex though the factors were which finally caused war, they all grew out of two fundamental differences which existed between the two sections: the North was commercial and industrial, and the South was agrarian. . . . Herein lies the irrepressible conflict . . . between the agrarian South and the commercial and industrial North to control the government either in its own interest or, negatively, to prevent the other section from controlling it in its interests. . . . The irrepressible conflict, then, was not between slavery and freedom, but between the industrial and commercial civilization of the North and the agrarian civilization of the South.

Arthur Schlesinger, Jr.

It was the moral issue of slavery, for example, that gave the struggles over slavery in the territories . . . their significance. . . . To say that the Civil War was fought over the "unreal" issue of slavery in the territories is like saying that the Second World War was fought over the "unreal" issue of the invasion of Poland. The democracies could not challenge fascism inside Germany any more than opponents of slavery could challenge slavery inside the South; but the extension of slavery, like the extension of fascism, was an act of aggression which made a moral choice inescapable. . . . Human slavery is certainly one of the few issues of whose evil we can be sure. It is not just "a very ancient labor system," it is also a betrayal of the basic values of our Christian and democratic tradition. No historian can understand the circumstances which led to its abolition until he writes about it in its fundamental moral context.

1. PRESIDENTS There was a news blackout for 24 hours before Lincoln reached Washington because of fears that he would be killed by proslavery mobs in Baltimore.

Fort Sumter

1. When Abraham Lincoln became President in March 1861, the seceded states hoped that the North would allow them to depart in peace. However, across the South, Confederate forces had seized forts and federal arsenals, places where weapons are stored. Only Fort Sumter, on an island outside Charleston Harbor in South Carolina, and three forts in Florida remained in federal hands.

Lincoln was determined to hold the Union together, but he faced a delicate situation. The northern part of the South, including the key state of Virginia, had rejected secession and had chosen to remain in the Union. If Lincoln used force rashly, he would risk losing the border states.

The Ultimatum Events finally forced Lincoln to act. Major Robert Anderson, the commander of Fort Sumter, reported that his supplies were running low. With Confederate forces threatening, he could not hold out much longer unless resupplied. Lincoln was determined not to surrender federal authority without a fight, yet he did not want the North to be guilty of starting a civil war. After much deliberation, he notified Confederate officials that he would not reinforce the fort with either arms or men. He promised to send only food.

In Charleston, Confederate General P.G.T. Beauregard demanded that Major Anderson surrender Fort Sumter. Anderson told the Confederates that he would withdraw on April 15 if he did not receive supplies or other orders. But southern suspicion of northern intentions ran high.

The Attack At 4:30 A.M., April 12, Confederate batteries opened fire on the fort. All day long, the Confederates kept up the bombardment while fashionable ladies and gentlemen of Charleston watched from the shore. On April 13, his ammunition gone, Anderson accepted Beauregard's terms of evacuation and marched out of the fort.

The tension of waiting was broken; the decision for war was taken. The attack on Fort Sumter boosted morale in the South. At the same time, because Lincoln's cautious diplomacy had forced the South to fire the first shot, the North rallied behind the cause

2. of union with a sense of moral outrage.

2. DISCUSSION Ask: Did the bombardment of Fort Sumter make a major war inevitable? Explain.

The attack on Fort Sumter was a point of no return for the nation. Although the only life lost in the battle was due to an accident, it marked the beginning of the bloodiest war in American history. The tattered Confederate flag shown in this painting of Fort Sumter flew over the fort until February 1865. It became the symbol of the Confederacy's struggle for independence.

3.

See p. T65.

SECTION 4 REVIEW

1. **Identify:** (a) Harpers Ferry, (b) Confederate States of America, (c) Jefferson Davis, (d) Fort Sumter.

2. **Define:** lame duck.

3. (a) What effect did John Brown's death have in the North? (b) What effect did it have in the South?

4. Why did Republican party leaders favor Abraham Lincoln as their presidential candidate in 1860?

5. How did the election of 1860 convince many southerners that the South should secede from the Union?

6. **Critical Thinking** Was there any way that war might have been avoided?

349

3. **VISUAL EVIDENCE** This painting was done by southern artist Conrad Wise Chapman in the midst of the Civil War.

Summary

1. **For 30 years, Congress struggled to resolve conflicts between the North and the South.** Congress worked out the Missouri Compromise and the Compromise of 1850 to address the issues of slavery in the territories and the balance of power between free and slave states.

2. **The Fugitive Slave Law and the Kansas-Nebraska Act of 1854 heightened sectional tensions.** Violence in "Bleeding Kansas" was stark proof that compromise had failed.

3. **Sectional tensions divided the Whigs and Democrats and led to the emergence of the Republican party.** Opposed to slavery in the new territories, the Republicans received all their support from the North.

4. **When Lincoln was elected President in 1860, seven southern states seceded from the Union.** They declared independence and formed the Confederate States of America. Civil war began with the bombardment of Fort Sumter in April 1861.

See p. T65.

Vocabulary

On a separate sheet of paper, write the word or words that best complete each of the following sentences.

1. In a (an) _____ state, slavery was not allowed.

2. In a (an) _____ state, slavery was legal.

3. According to the doctrine of _____, the decision about whether or not to allow slavery in a territory should be made by the voters of that territory.

4. A (An) _____ is an official who is serving until a successor takes office.

5. A (An) _____ is a place where weapons are stored.

See p. T65.

Chapter Checkup

1. (a) Why did the issue of the extension of slavery strain relations between the North and the South? (b) How was the balance between the North and South maintained in the Senate between 1820 and 1848?

2. (a) Why did the acquisition of territory from Mexico in 1848 complicate the problem of slavery in the territories? (b) What solution was proposed in the Wilmot Proviso? (c) Describe the other three proposed solutions.

3. (a) Why did California's request for statehood cause heated debate in Congress? (b) How did the Compromise of 1850 try to solve the problem?

4. (a) Why did the Fugitive Slave Law increase sectional tensions? (b) How did it threaten free blacks?

5. (a) How was the question of slavery to be decided in the Kansas and Nebraska territories? (b) How did that method differ from the one established by the Missouri Compromise?

6. (a) How did the Dred Scott decision affect the status of slavery in the territories? (b) Why were Republicans especially shocked by the decision?

7. (a) Why were the Lincoln-Douglas debates important? (b) What was Douglas's Freeport Doctrine? (c) How did the doctrine affect the Democratic party?

8. How did John Brown's raid at Harpers Ferry contribute to the tense atmosphere of 1860?

9. (a) Why were there two Democratic candidates for President in 1860? (b) How did the election results show the sectional split?

10. Why did Lincoln's election lead southerners to seriously consider secession?
See p. T65.

Critical Thinking

1. **Applying Information** Why was the term "Bleeding Kansas" used to describe the territory after passage of the Kansas-Nebraska Act?

2. **Analyzing** Why did John Brown's death create more sympathy for abolitionism than did his actions at Harpers Ferry?
See p. T65.

Connecting Past and Present

1. Many critics of slavery found it hard to compromise on what they felt to be an issue of basic morality. What issues today have led some Americans to take an uncompromising stand?

2. Within six years of its formation in 1854, the Republican party had won the presidency. Could a new political party be as successful today? Explain.
See p. T65.

Developing Basic Skills

1. **Map Reading** Based on the maps on pages 334, 336, and 341, how did each of the following pieces of legislation affect the status of slavery in the territory west of Iowa and Missouri: (a) Missouri Compromise; (b) Compromise of 1850; (c) Kansas-Nebraska Act?

2. **Placing Events in Time** On a time line, write the events that led to the split between South and North. (Review Chapters 12 through 16.) Does the completed time line support the belief that a division of the nation was becoming increasingly likely?

WRITING ABOUT HISTORY

Using a Cataloging System

A library card catalog has subject, title, and author cards. The call number classifies a book according to the Dewey Decimal System or the Library of Congress System. Under the more commonly used Dewey Decimal System, history and geography fall in the 900s.

Practice: Study the catalog subject card and answer the following questions:

1. What is the title of the book?
2. When was the book published?
3. Does the book include a bibliography?
4. What is the call number of the book?
5. Is the book illustrated?

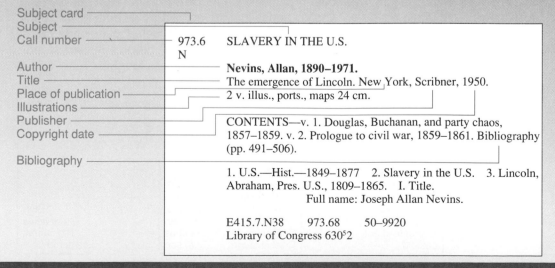

Subject card
Subject
Call number → 973.6   SLAVERY IN THE U.S.
           N

Author — **Nevins, Allan, 1890–1971.**
Title — The emergence of Lincoln. New York, Scribner, 1950.
Place of publication — 2 v. illus., ports., maps 24 cm.
Illustrations
Publisher
Copyright date

         CONTENTS—v. 1. Douglas, Buchanan, and party chaos, 1857–1859. v. 2. Prologue to civil war, 1859–1861. Bibliography
Bibliography — (pp. 491–506).

         1. U.S.—Hist.—1849–1877   2. Slavery in the U.S.   3. Lincoln, Abraham, Pres. U.S., 1809–1865.   I. Title.
             Full name: Joseph Allan Nevins.

         E415.7.N38   973.68   50–9920
         Library of Congress 630^{5}2

Divided by War

17

(1861–1865)

CHAPTER OBJECTIVES After completing this chapter, students should be able to
1. list strengths and weaknesses of each side in the Civil War.
2. identify major Civil War battles.
3. explain the impact of the Emancipation Proclamation.
4. discuss the effect of war on soldiers and civilians.

CHAPTER PREVIEW Read students the following statement by Henry Adams, "Tell your war-like friends that we want no blood-thirsty men here. If the time comes when men are wanted, it will be men who fight because there is no other way, not because they are angry; men who will come with their Bibles as well as their rifles and who will pray God to forgive them for every life they take." Ask: How are civil wars different from other wars?

"The cavalry is upon us! Get along! Get along!" Great clouds of dust rose into the late afternoon sky as thousands of Union soldiers took flight. When the dust cleared, all that remained of the hasty retreat were the guns, blankets, and provisions strewn along the roadside.

"A cruel, crazy, mad hopeless panic possessed them [the troops]," wrote a northern member of Congress who had observed the scene. "Their mouths gaped, their lips cracked and blackened with the powder of the cartridges they had bitten off, . . . their eyes staring in frenzy; no mortal ever saw such a mass of ghastly wretches."

"Retreat is a weak term to use when speaking of this disgraceful rout," reported another eyewitness. "Those who had been fortunate enough to get places in the baggage-wagons thrust back others with their bayonets and musket-stocks."

This frantic retreat of the Union army on July 21, 1861, marked the end of the first ma-jor battle of the Civil War, the battle of Bull Run. The untried troops of North and South had met on the banks of a Virginia creek. The Union forces attacked, but the Confederate soldiers held them off. Then, giving a terrifying yell, the rebels scattered their enemy in a ferocious counterattack.

The North had entered the war with impatience and optimism. Barely a month before, northern newspapers had clamored for President Lincoln to send the army into battle. "Forward to Richmond!" was the cry. Many Union soldiers had enlisted for 90 days, sure that they could whip the upstart rebels in no time. Some northern politicians even thought that after one glimpse of the mighty Union army the South would fold its tents and fade away.

The battle of Bull Run, however, dashed hopes that the conflict would be brief and decisive. The war, in fact, lasted four bloody years, and more Americans died in it than in any other war the nation has fought.

1.

Confederate victories in East			Union moves toward victory	
1861	**1862**	**1863**	**1864**	**1865**

1861
Firing on
Fort Sumter;
Battle of
Bull Run

1862
Battles of
Fort Henry,
Fort Donelson,
Shiloh, Antietam;
Homestead Act
passed

1863
Emancipation
Proclamation;
Battles of
Vicksburg,
Gettysburg,
Chickamauga

1864
Lincoln
reelected;
Sherman
marches
to sea

1865
Grant takes
Richmond;
Lee surrenders

352

1. TIME LINE QUESTION Ask: How long after the firing on Fort Sumter was the Emancipation Proclamation made?

The Union army that marched out of Washington, D.C., in July 1861 was the largest ever assembled on American soil. Its defeat by Confederate troops at Bull Run, just 30 miles from the White House, was a hint of costly battles to come. The

1. bloodiest of them all was the battle of Antietam, shown here. In a single day, more than 24,000 men from both sides lost their lives.

1. **VISUAL EVIDENCE** Have students study this picture to find reasons why this battle was particularly bloody. Ask: How clear-cut were the battle lines?

1 Preparing for War

READ TO UNDERSTAND

■ What strengths and weaknesses each side possessed.

■ How the Union and the Confederacy mobilized for war.

■ Why many northerners and southerners objected to draft laws.

2. ■ *Vocabulary:* bounty, bounty jumping.

At the outset of the Civil War, each side boasted future victory. "Just throw three or four shells among those blue-bellied Yankees and they'll scatter like sheep," one southerner predicted.

2. **VOCABULARY** Have students look up these terms in the glossary before they begin reading.

Soon political leaders in both the North and South realized, however, that victory would not come easily. How would they raise troops? Where would they get supplies? How would they pay for it all?

Both governments had untested leaders. The North had just inaugurated a new President, Abraham Lincoln, who held responsibility for pursuing the war. Jefferson Davis, the president of the month-old Confederacy, had to organize not only an army but also a government.

The Border States

As the two sides prepared for war, one major issue overshadowed all others. On whose side would the uncommitted states fight? Seven states had not yet thrown in their lot 3. with either the Union or the Confederacy.

3. **CRITICAL THINKING** Ask: What problems might have been created for Lincoln by having slave states in the Union during the Civil War?

353

1. **BACKGROUND** This rock-throwing crowd in Baltimore killed four Union soldiers. They were the first troops to die in the war.

2. **DISCUSSION** Ask: Do you think Lincoln was justified in suspending habeas corpus and other rights in Maryland during this crisis?

President Lincoln forced a decision three days after the attack on Fort Sumter. He sent out a call to the state governors for 75,000 militia. Would those seven states that had not seceded fight the Confederacy or join it? Virginia, Arkansas, Tennessee, and North Carolina seceded; Maryland, Missouri, and Kentucky wavered.

The situation in Maryland was tense. If Maryland joined the Confederacy, Confederate territory would surround Washington, D.C., the Union capital. Lincoln sensed the danger. When Confederate sympathizers attacked Union soldiers in Baltimore, the President decided to act quickly.

On April 27, Lincoln sent federal troops to occupy the city. Then he proclaimed martial law in Maryland and suspended habeas corpus, the right not to be imprisoned unless charged with, or convicted of, a crime. Before Confederate supporters had time to react, he jailed them, including some state legislators. With the major opposition in prison, the Maryland legislature defeated a resolution to secede.

Kentucky tried to remain neutral at first. However, Lincoln's personal diplomacy toward the state where he had been born fostered sympathy for the federal government. A Confederate invasion of the state in September 1861 prompted the Kentucky legislature to throw its support to the Union, ending the state's neutrality.

In Missouri, sharp guerrilla fighting between groups favoring opposing sides disrupted the state for several months. Finally, a decisive battle in August 1861 secured the state for the Union. When the dust had settled, three critical states had sided with the Union. (See the map below.)

The South's Position

Southerners believed that they were fighting a war for independence, similar to the Revolutionary War. They aimed to defend their

3. **MAP READING** Ask: Which of the seven undecided states was not on the border between North and South?

MAP STUDY *In early 1861, seven states had not yet chosen sides in the struggle. Which border states eventually seceded? Which remained in the Union?* See p. T66.

On the Eve of War, 1861

Legend:
- Free states
- Slave states loyal to Union *Separated from Va. 1861, admitted to Union 1863
- The Confederate States of America
- Seceded after April 14, 1861
- Seceded before April 14, 1861

1. **ACTIVITY** Have students begin a chart showing the advantages and disadvantages of the North and South at the beginning of the war.

2. **ECONOMICS** Have students list items that factories would have to produce in wartime, for example, blankets, boots, bandages, weapons, and ammunition.

homeland, not carry the war to the North. The North, on the other hand, had the difficult task of invading enemy territory. Its lines of supply would be much longer than those of the Confederates and thus more open to attack.

The South had other advantages. Soldiers from the rural South were experienced in the use of firearms and horses. Also, Confederate military leaders were among the nation's best. Many had been trained at the United States Military Academy at West Point, including talented leaders such as Robert E. Lee, Thomas "Stonewall" Jackson, and Joseph Johnston.

But the South was not without its problems. The Confederate constitution limited the authority of the central government over individual states. For example, Governor Joseph Brown of Georgia insisted that only Georgia officers be in command of Georgia troops. Moreover, the South carried the burden of defending slavery, which made it more
1. difficult to enlist European nations as allies.

The North's Position

The North counted among its advantages a larger population that gave it potentially four times as many soldiers as the South. The North also had many more factories. Massachusetts alone produced more manufactured goods than the entire Confederacy. A good railroad network and control of the country's navy and almost all its merchant marine added to its strength. The North wasted some of its advantage, however, because it was slow to put its superior resources
2. to use.

Military leadership proved to be a problem. President Lincoln had offered the command of the Union army to Robert E. Lee, a Virginian, but Lee chose to serve the Confed-
3. eracy. Lincoln and his advisers appointed several commanders before they discovered the most able military men and a winning general.

Civil Leadership

The quality of civil leadership also played a vital role in the war effort. When the fighting began, few people in Washington knew Abra-

ham Lincoln well. Many thought him an unlikely commander-in-chief. Lincoln's own attorney general wrote that the President "lacks will and purpose, and, I greatly fear, he has not the power to command."

But Lincoln proved his critics wrong. He got the most from his cabinet and demonstrated rare political skills. For example, he kept up morale through regular contact with citizens. Several days a week, he opened the White House to the public and talked with anyone who wanted to see him. He called these sessions his "public opinion baths."

Jefferson Davis, the Confederate president, appeared more distinguished and more experienced than Lincoln. He had served in the House of Representatives, in the Senate, and as secretary of war under President Pierce. He was hard-working and dedicated. As a graduate of West Point and a veteran officer of the Mexican War, he seemed well equipped to lead the Confederacy.

Yet President Davis tried to do too much. He labored over details of military strategy best left to others. He quarreled with the Confederate Congress and vetoed 38 bills. (Lawmakers overrode 37 of the 38 vetoes.) Lincoln, in contrast, vetoed only three bills.

Mobilizing for War

Each side tried to raise an army of volunteers, but failed to reach its goals. The Union army encouraged enlistment by offering **bounties,** sums paid to new recruits. Bounties appealed especially to the poor, but some unscrupulous men took advantage of the system by **bounty jumping.** They would enlist, collect a bounty, then desert and reenlist somewhere else, collecting another bounty.

In 1863, the United States passed its first national draft law, requiring military service of males between the ages of 20 and 45. A person with money, however, could hire a substitute or pay a fee of $300 to exempt himself from military service.

The Confederacy had passed its draft law earlier, in 1862. At first, the draft took men between the ages of 18 and 35; later, the upper limit was extended to age 45. The Confederacy allowed paid substitutes until 1863. The most hated provision of the Confederate **355**

3. **BACKGROUND** When Lincoln asked Lee to command the Union army, Lee said, "With all my devotion to the Union, I have not been able to make up my mind to raise my hand against my relatives, my children, my home."

In the first days of the war, enthusiasm ran high. Recruiters in the North used posters such as this one to attract volunteers to fight for the Stars and
1. *Stripes. As the war dragged on, however, the Union had to offer bounties. Eventually, both sides resorted to a draft system.*

1. **VISUAL EVIDENCE** Point out that the Union flag still included a star for each state that had seceded.

draft exempted one man from each plantation that had 20 or more slaves.

Disillusioned soldiers on both sides came to feel that the Civil War was "a rich man's war and a poor man's fight." That feeling was one cause of desertion, a problem that plagued both the Union and the Confederacy.

Paying for the War

Southern leaders did not levy taxes to pay for the war, because they feared that heavy taxation would erode popular support. Instead, they raised 40 percent of their income by selling bonds to be cashed in after the war. The remaining source of Confederate income was the printing press. The government simply printed money, with little gold or silver to back it. In time, that practice led to runaway inflation.

356 Like the South, the North hesitated to raise taxes. In August 1861, however, it im-

2. **ECONOMICS** The tax was 3 percent on yearly incomes over $8,000—a very high income in the 1860s. The tax raised about 20 percent of the Union's revenues.

posed new taxes on manufactured goods and new sales taxes. It also levied the first income tax in the nation's history. Only the tax 2. on manufactured goods raised much money, but the sales and income taxes set precedents. The North also raised money by selling bonds.

By 1862, the war was costing the North almost $1.75 million a day. To raise further funds, Congress passed the Legal Tender Act, which authorized the government to issue paper money. Since the new bills were printed in green ink, people called them greenbacks.

The most significant change in northern finance came with the passage of the National Bank Act in 1863. The act raised extra income by requiring new national banks to invest one third of their deposits in federal bonds. It also prohibited state banks from printing their own notes, allowing only national banks to issue paper money.

For the first time, the nation had a truly centralized banking system. In order to continue issuing bank notes, more than 800 state banks became national banks and invested in United States war bonds.

Diplomacy During the War

When the war began, both the Union and the Confederacy hoped for foreign assistance. Because of Great Britain's strong navy and large industrial capacity, each side was especially eager to win its support. 3.

British opinion was divided over the war. Many English reformers and ordinary citizens supported the North because they opposed slavery. On the other hand, many others believed the Confederacy had the right to become an independent nation. The landed nobility, especially, identified more with southern planters and their way of life.

Early in the war, Jefferson Davis banned cotton shipments to England, hoping that shortages would force the British to recognize the Confederacy. British textile mills, however, had a surplus of cotton, and the scheme failed. In the end, Great Britain refused to commit itself to either South or North.

As the war continued and neither side gained a clear upper hand, Europeans generally stayed neutral. The war between North and South remained a civil war.

3. **ACTIVITY** Have students imagine that they live in 1861 and support either the Union or the Confederacy. Tell them to write a letter to the Prime Minister of Britain explaining why Britain should support their side.

See p. T66.

SECTION 1 REVIEW

1. **Identify:** National Bank Act.

2. **Define:** (a) bounty, (b) bounty jumping.

3. What two major advantages did the North have over the South as the war began?

4. Why did soldiers on both sides feel that the Civil War was "a rich man's war and a poor man's fight"?

5. (a) What methods did the Union use to raise funds? (b) What methods did the Confederacy use?

6. **Critical Thinking** Why has the declaration of neutrality by the Kentucky legislature been termed a "vain dream"?

2 War Begins

READ TO UNDERSTAND

■ How the Civil War differed from earlier wars.

■ How northern and southern strategy affected the conduct of the war.

■ Why the early battles were inconclusive.

The soldiers marched off to war with flags flying and drums rolling. Few realized the devastation that was to come. Northerners thought that victory would be theirs once they captured Richmond, Virginia, the Confederate capital. Southerners thought that victory was simply a matter of beating back Union invaders until they gave up.

In fact, the struggle marked a turning point in military history, a transition from an era of relatively small battles to an era of mass slaughter. The war proved long and bloody.

The New Shape of War

Compared to earlier American wars, Civil War battles were huge in scope. Even the biggest battles of the War of 1812 and the Mexican War never involved more than 15,000 sol-

diers. By contrast, more than 100,000 might participate in a single battle of the Civil War, with grim consequences. At least 540,000 soldiers lost their lives during the war.

More efficient weaponry caused many of the deaths. Old rifle balls gave way to cone-shaped Minié bullets, which were twice as accurate. Thus, trenches became necessary for defense. Bayonets lost much of their usefulness because a soldier would be shot from a distance long before he could get close enough for hand-to-hand combat. The Union made cannons that could fire shells weighing up to 300 pounds (135 kilograms). With few factories, the Confederacy had to import or capture most of its field artillery.

Battlefield medical practices also contributed to suffering and death. Doctors were scarce, and they had to combat poor sanitation, often caused by dirty water. Effective painkillers were rarely available. Moreover, doctors lacked antiseptics. One Confederate officer wrote that his men had as much to fear from doctors as from Union troops.

Northern Strategy

At the outbreak of war, General Winfield Scott, a hero of the Mexican War, supervised all Union forces. Old and ill, Scott still had a keen mind. Unlike most people, he realized that the war could not be won in 90 days.

Scott suggested a grand war strategy to President Lincoln. The navy should block off Confederate ports from Virginia to Texas. Union forces should split the Confederacy into three parts at the Appalachian Mountains and the Mississippi River and then use Union naval superiority to isolate and strangle each weakened section.

People ridiculed Scott's scheme, calling it the "anaconda," after a huge South American snake that kills its prey by crushing it. But the course of events would prove Scott right. The Appalachians and the Mississippi did divide the Confederate states into three regions, which became the theaters of the war. (See the map on page 358.)

West of the Mississippi, in Louisiana, Arkansas, and Texas, Confederate defenders under the command of Edmund Kirby-Smith kept northern forces at bay. But this far western theater had little influence on the final

1. **BACKGROUND** Early on, Henry Adams wrote: "We shall blockade and starve them out. The cotton states can be finished in 9 months or I'm a beggar."

2. **BACKGROUND** Jefferson Davis said, "All we ask is to be left alone."

3. **BACKGROUND** For every Union soldier killed in battle, two died from disease.

4. **READING** Stephen Crane's short story "An Incident of War" tells of a Union soldier's fear of medical care.

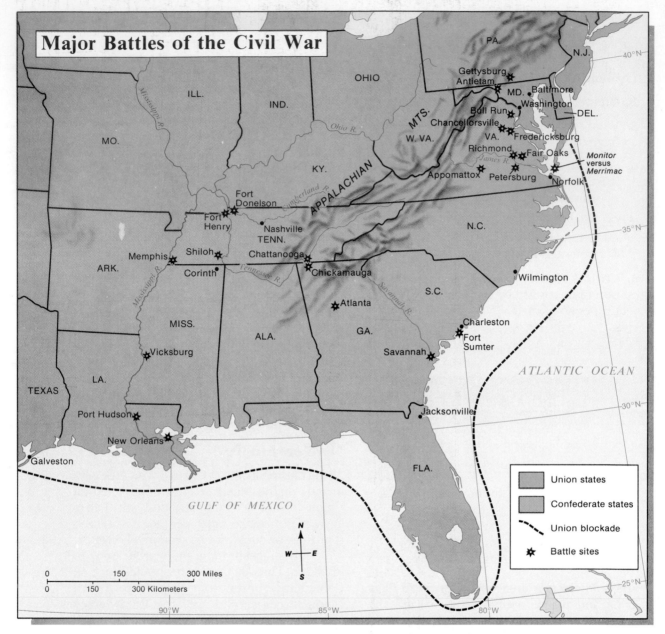

Major Battles of the Civil War

OHIO
PA.
N.J.
40°N
ILL.
IND.
Gettysburg
Antietam
MD. Baltimore
Washington
DEL.
Bull Run
Chancellorsville
Fredericksburg
W. VA.
VA.
Richmond
Fair Oaks
Monitor
versus
Merrimac
Appomattox
Petersburg
Norfolk
MO.
Ohio R.
KY.
APPALACHIAN
MTS.
Fort
Donelson
Fort
Henry
Nashville
TENN.
N.C.
35°N
Memphis
Shiloh
Chattanooga
ARK.
Corinth
Chickamauga
Wilmington
MISS.
Atlanta
S.C.
ALA.
GA.
Charleston
Fort
Sumter
Vicksburg
Savannah
LA.
TEXAS
ATLANTIC OCEAN
Port Hudson
New Orleans
Jacksonville
30°N
Galveston
FLA.
GULF OF MEXICO

Union states
Confederate states
Union blockade
Battle sites

N
W — E
S

| 0 | 150 | 300 Miles |
| 0 | 150 | 300 Kilometers |

90°W   85°W   80°W   25°N

MAP STUDY

See p. T67.

This map shows the broad extent of the Civil War, while the smaller maps on the following pages show details of individual campaigns. Based on the map, why would the South be more devastated after the war than the North, no matter who won?

1.

2.

1. **MAP READING** Ask: In which state were the most battles fought? Why might that have been true?

outcome of the war. Most of the action centered in the western theater (the area between the Appalachians and the Mississippi) and in the eastern theater (the area around Virginia and Maryland).

The First Battle of Bull Run

Scott's plan would take time, and northerners insisted on bold action to end the war quickly. To satisfy their demands, President

Lincoln sent Union troops to fight a Confederate army camped in northern Virginia near Washington. On a pleasant afternoon on July 21, 1861, northern picnickers and newspaper reporters settled on a grassy hill overlooking a small stream called Bull Run. They waited for Union troops to advance, expecting a decisive Union victory. But they were disappointed.

Soldiers on both sides were poorly prepared. Moreover, neither Union General Irvin

2. **LOCAL HISTORY** If there is a Civil War battle site in your area, have students research what took place there. You also might plan a trip to the site.

1. **DISCUSSION** Lead a discussion on the question: How would everyday life in the South be changed by an effective Union blockade?

2. **BACKGROUND** The *Merrimac* was named after a stream that flows from New Hampshire to Massachusetts.

McDowell nor Confederate General P.G.T. Beauregard was accustomed to commanding large forces.

At first, Union troops fought well. But their advance was blocked by the forces of General Thomas J. Jackson, who stood "like a stone wall" awaiting relief. (Thus, Jackson earned the nickname "Stonewall.") When Confederate reinforcements arrived, General McDowell tried an orderly retreat, but his men bolted and ran. The inexperienced southern troops, in turn, were too surprised to press their advantage.

As word of the Union failure spread, dismayed northerners realized that victory would not come easily. Southerners rejoiced.

War at Sea

Because the South was primarily an agricultural region, it depended on northern and European sources for manufactured goods. With the start of the war, trade with Europe became crucial because the North was no longer a source of supply. Under Scott's anaconda strategy, the Union navy tried to cut off southern imports by blockading, or wherever possible capturing, the South's ports.

Before the war, some 6,000 ships a year entered southern ports; in the first year of the blockade, the number dropped to 800. As the war continued, the Union blockade became even more effective. Still, enterprising southerners sometimes used fast, maneuverable ships to "run" the blockade.

The small Confederate fleet of seagoing cruisers also damaged Union trade. In less than four years, the *Alabama* and the *Florida,* built for the Confederacy in Great Britain, destroyed 257 northern ships.

Both sides saw the importance of navies and worked to produce the strongest ships possible. This led to the use of armor-plating to strengthen ship hulls. The Confederacy was first to put a fully ironclad ship into service. This was the reconditioned *Merrimac,* a 40-gun warship abandoned by Union forces near Portsmouth, Virginia.

Armed with iron plate four inches (ten centimeters) thick and renamed the *Virginia,* the ironclad *Merrimac,* while barely seaworthy, proved superior to wooden warships in battle. On March 8, 1862, it sank one Union ship at Hampton Roads, drove another aground, and forced a third to surrender. The *Virginia* seemed capable of defeating the entire Union navy.

1.

2.

3. **BACKGROUND** The *Merrimac* destroyed one of the two ships with its iron ram and the other by shelling.

3.

When the Merrimac, *shown here, left dry dock, it was one of only three ironclads in the world. Renamed the* Virginia, *the Confederate ship destroyed two of the Union's wooden warships on its first day out. But the Union countered quickly with its own ironclad, the* Monitor, *which engaged the* Virginia *on its second day at sea.*

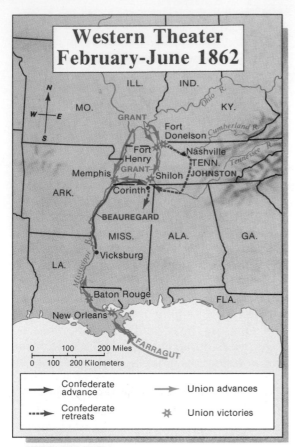

Western Theater
February–June 1862

ILL. IND.
MO.
KY.
GRANT
Ohio R.
Fort Donelson
Cumberland R.
Fort Henry
Nashville
TENN.
GRANT
JOHNSTON
Memphis
Shiloh
Tennessee R.
ARK.
Corinth
BEAUREGARD
MISS. ALA. GA.
Vicksburg
LA.
Baton Rouge
FLA.
New Orleans
FARRAGUT

0   100   200 Miles
0   100   200 Kilometers

→ Confederate advance
----▶ Confederate retreats
→ Union advances
✳ Union victories

MAP STUDY *Part of the Union's strategy was to gain control of the*
1. *Mississippi River. What strategic points fortifying the river did Union forces capture in 1862? What city remained in Confederate hands?* See p. T67.
1. **MAP READING** Have students use the text and the map to describe Grant's western campaign.

The Union countered with its own iron-clad, the *Monitor.* A battle between the *Virginia* and the *Monitor* on March 9 ended in a draw. Eventually, Confederates destroyed the *Virginia* to keep it from falling into enemy hands. The *Monitor* later sank in heavy seas off the North Carolina coast.

General Grant in the West

While the Union blockade pressured the southern coast, a little-known Union general, Ulysses S. Grant, carried out another part of Scott's anaconda strategy in the western theater. The plan called for Union forces to take control of the Mississippi River. Since the Confederates had fortified the Mississippi well, Grant aimed to reach the heart of the Confederacy by pushing south along the Cumberland and Tennessee rivers.

360   Two Confederate forts stood in Grant's way: Fort Henry on the Tennessee and Fort

2. **BACKGROUND** Almost 23,000 were killed or wounded at Shiloh. More Americans died there than in the Revolution, War of 1812, and Mexican War together.

Donelson on the Cumberland. President Jefferson Davis, recognizing Grant's aim, sent General Albert Johnston to coordinate southern defenses. In early February 1862, Grant captured Fort Henry with a flotilla of Union gunboats. Johnston withdrew to Nashville, leaving 15,000 troops to guard Fort Donelson. Within ten days, Grant had captured the fort and all its defenders.

General Grant next pushed south but was surprised on April 6 by Confederate forces under Generals Johnston and Beauregard. The ensuing melee, near a country meetinghouse called Shiloh, was the largest battle to date in North America. Johnston and Beauregard 2. nearly routed the Union forces, but Grant stoutly held on until reinforcements arrived on April 7. The weakened Confederates, who 3. had lost General Albert Johnston in the battle, retreated to Corinth, Mississippi, and then south.

The anaconda plan was having its effect in the West. Flag Officer David Farragut took New Orleans in April and continued up the Mississippi. Union gunboats also captured Memphis, leaving Vicksburg the only remaining Confederate stronghold on the river.

The Eastern Peninsular Campaign

The Union's campaign in the East did not go as well. After Bull Run, Lincoln named the young, popular General George B. McClellan to command the Army of the Potomac. McClellan's first task was to transform raw recruits into able soldiers. This he did well. But the general seemed reluctant to wage war. "If McClellan does not want to use the army," said a frustrated President Lincoln, "I would like to *borrow* it."

In March 1862, after almost a year of training, McClellan decided that his men were ready, and he set out to attack Richmond. He intended to move most of his army by steamboat down the Potomac River to the Chesapeake Bay, put them ashore on the peninsula between the York and James rivers, and attack the Confederate capital from the southeast. (See the map on page 361.) The success of the operation depended on surprise and speed. But after he landed, McClellan moved cautiously, giving Confederate forces ample time to prepare.

3. **BACKGROUND** One Confederate wrote: "It was an awful thing to hear the sing of grape shot, the hum of cannon balls, and the roaring of the bomb shell. . . . O keep me out of such another fight!"

1. **GEOGRAPHY** In May 1861, the Confederacy had moved its capital from Montgomery to Richmond—110 miles from Washington, D.C. (location)

On May 31, General Joseph E. Johnston attacked McClellan at Fair Oaks Station. When Johnston was wounded in the indecisive battle, Jefferson Davis ordered Robert E. Lee to take command of Johnston's forces, the Army of Northern Virginia. Lee would keep that command until the end of the war.

As Davis's military adviser, Lee already had devised a brilliant plan to keep Union forces from pressing too quickly toward Richmond. Lee and McClellan had attended West Point together. Remembering McClellan's caution, Lee sent Stonewall Jackson on a series of rapid marches against Union troops in the Shenandoah Valley of Virginia. Jackson's diversions were so successful that President Lincoln believed that Washington, D.C., was threatened. As a result, troops earmarked for McClellan were sent instead to deal with Jackson.

Between June 26 and July 2, 1862, Lee and Jackson kept McClellan off balance in a series of encounters known as the Seven Days' Battles. With the help of the dashing cavalry of J.E.B. "Jeb" Stuart, the Confederates not only prevented McClellan from taking Richmond, but forced him to withdraw to the James River. By taking the offensive, Lee had saved Richmond. Disgusted by McClellan's failure to take the Confederate capital, President Lincoln ordered him back to Washington and temporarily relieved him of his command.

Union generals planned another attack on Richmond in August, but once again Lee and Jackson outwitted them, at the Second Battle of Bull Run on August 28 and 29. Union General John Pope found his forces surrounded, and he retreated in defeat. Reluctantly, Lincoln allowed McClellan to resume his command.

Antietam

President Lincoln had reason to be concerned. In September, General Lee crossed the Potomac on a bold offensive into Maryland. The Confederates knew that a successful campaign in enemy territory would be a great blow to northern morale.

Expecting McClellan to move slowly, as before, Lee divided his army. He sent Stonewall Jackson to capture the federal arsenal

2. **BACKGROUND** McClellan failed to pursue Lee after the Battle of Antietam. Lincoln then gave command of Union forces to Gen. Ambrose Burnside (see p. 369).

at Harpers Ferry, Virginia, while he marched into western Maryland. But McClellan had an incredible stroke of luck. One of his men stumbled upon three cigars dropped by an unknown Confederate messenger. They were wrapped in a dispatch containing Lee's battle plan.

This time McClellan did not delay. He attacked Lee at Antietam Creek on September 17, before Jackson returned. Reinforcements arrived in time to prevent a complete Confederate rout, but Lee had to retreat across the Potomac into Virginia.

3. **MAP READING** Ask: How far was McClellan forced to retreat during the course of the Seven Days' Battle?

MAP STUDY *The eastern theater was the scene of some of the bloodiest battles of the Civil War. Which side enjoyed greater success in the early campaigns shown on the map? Explain.* See p. T67.

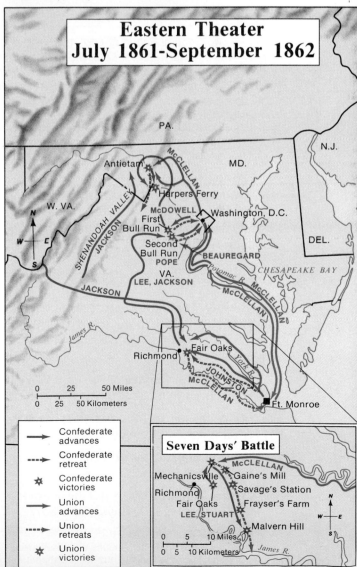

Eastern Theater July 1861–September 1862

PA.

N.J.

Antietam

MD.

W. VA.

Harpers Ferry

McDOWELL   Washington, D.C.

First Bull Run

DEL.

SHENANDOAH VALLEY   JACKSON

Second Bull Run   POPE

BEAUREGARD   CHESAPEAKE BAY

VA.   LEE, JACKSON

JACKSON

Potomac R.   McCLELLAN

James R.

Fair Oaks

Richmond

JOHNSTON   McCLELLAN

Ft. Monroe

0   25   50 Miles
0   25   50 Kilometers

— Confederate advances
--- Confederate retreat
☆ Confederate victories
— Union advances
--- Union retreats
☆ Union victories

Seven Days' Battle

McCLELLAN

Mechanicsville   Gaine's Mill
Richmond   Savage's Station
Fair Oaks   Frayser's Farm
LEE, STUART   Malvern Hill

0   5   10 Miles
0   5   10 Kilometers   James R.

1. *Confederate General Robert E. Lee (right), in a photograph taken by Mathew*
2. *Brady, was a military genius. Lee, who grew up in a wealthy Virginia family, had freed his slaves before the Civil War. General Ulysses S. Grant (left), with his stubby beard and casual dress, seemed the opposite of the aristocratic Lee. Yet he was a brilliant choice to lead the faltering Union armies. He understood the nature of modern warfare more completely than any other general of his time.*

1. **VISUAL EVIDENCE** Brady and his assistants traveled with Union troops, taking more than 3,500 pictures.

2. **ACTIVITY** Have students research the Civil War photography of Mathew Brady and bring examples to class.

The battle of Antietam may have marked the bloodiest single day of the war. Lee lost 11,000 men; McClellan, 13,000. Limited though it was, the Union victory had more than just military importance, as you will read later. See p. T67.

SECTION 2 REVIEW

1. **Identify:** (a) Stonewall Jackson, (b) the *Virginia,* (c) the *Monitor,* (d) Ulysses S. Grant, (e) George B. McClellan, (f) Robert E. Lee.

2. How was the warfare of the Civil War different from that of earlier wars?

3. (a) What was Scott's war strategy? (b) What were the three theaters of the war?

4. How did General Lee prevent Union forces from taking Richmond?

5. **Critical Thinking** Why did the South take the lead in the early days of the war?

3 Freedom

3. **VOCABULARY** Have students look up this word in the glossary before they begin reading.

READ TO UNDERSTAND

■ How northern attitudes toward slavery changed during the war.

■ Why President Lincoln issued the Emancipation Proclamation.

■ How blacks contributed to the Union war effort.

■ *Vocabulary:* contraband.   3.

Even as soldiers died in battle, abolitionist Julia Ward Howe pleaded the cause of war in *The Battle Hymn of the Republic.* In a powerful blend of Christian and antislavery fervor, she wrote, "As He [Jesus] died to make men holy, let us die to make men free."   4.

At first, however, most northerners did not view the Civil War as a war to end slav-

362

4. **BACKGROUND** Julia Ward Howe wrote *The Battle Hymn of the Republic* in one night after visiting a Union army camp. When it was published in 1862, she received a fee of $4.

ery. Unlike southerners, who had the clear goal of independence, northerners had mixed feelings. They were sure that they wanted to preserve the Union. But they were not sure whether the Union should continue with slavery or without slavery.

Pressure for Emancipation

President Lincoln argued that union, not slavery, was the war's primary issue. "If I could save the Union without freeing any slave I would do it," he wrote in August 1862, "and if I could save it by freeing all the slaves I would do it; and if I could save it by freeing some and leaving others alone I would also do that."

Eager to keep the support of the border slave states, Lincoln handled the slavery issue cautiously at first. But more and more northerners favored an end to slavery. Pressure for emancipation came from abolitionists, fugitive slaves, and radical Republicans in Congress.

Abolitionists found increasing support. "It is hard to realize the wondrous change which has befallen us abolitionists," wrote a reformer named Mary Grew. "After thirty years of persecution . . . abolitionists read with wonder . . . respectful tributes to men whose names had hitherto been used as a cry wherewith to rally a mob."

With the change in the nation's mood, President Lincoln reconsidered his policy toward fugitive slaves. At first, Lincoln had urged military commanders to return runaway slaves to their masters. But in the spring of 1861, General Benjamin Butler declared fugitive slaves in his camp not returnable to their masters; these slaves became known as **contraband,** after the term used to describe merchandise that is smuggled across enemy lines. Thereafter, Lincoln gave Union generals the power to deal with fugitive slaves as they saw fit.

Congress passed antislavery measures in the spring and summer of 1862. One law abolished slavery in Washington, D.C., and the territories. Another forbade Union officers to return fugitive slaves to their owners. It also allowed the President to recruit blacks for the army. The most vocal support for these laws came from a group of radicals in the Republican party led by Senator Charles

Sumner of Massachusetts and Congressman Thaddeus Stevens of Pennsylvania.

The Emancipation Proclamation

Lincoln recognized the growing call for abolition. But he would not act, he decided, until Union forces had won a victory. That way, emancipation would have the impact of a bold, new policy. The battle of Antietam gave Lincoln his opportunity. On September 22, 1862, he issued a preliminary proclamation that all slaves in territories still in a state of rebellion on January 1, 1863, would be freed.

On January 1, 1863, Lincoln issued the Emancipation Proclamation. It applied only to Confederate states still at war. It did not affect slaves in areas occupied by Union troops or slaves in border states still loyal to the Union. In effect, it did not apply to any slaves under Union jurisdiction.*

The President had hoped that the threat of emancipation would pressure southern slave owners to surrender in order to safeguard slavery. Although that did not happen, the proclamation dramatically changed the character of the war. The war now became a war for freedom as well as for union.

Rights of Black Americans

Despite its narrow scope, the Emancipation Proclamation did advance the struggle for equal rights for black Americans. When war began in 1861, free blacks suffered severe discrimination in northern states. Only in New York and most of New England could black males vote, and in New York they had to meet a property requirement not applied to whites. Only in New England could black and white children attend the same schools. In many major northern cities, blacks rode on segregated public transportation, if they were allowed to ride at all. Black Americans everywhere faced discrimination in housing and employment.

During the Civil War, reformers helped win new rights for northern blacks. In many places, they succeeded in opening public

---

*Slavery was abolished completely by the Thirteenth Amendment to the Constitution, ratified in December 1865.

363

1. **TECHNOLOGY** After the war, Robbins patented a cotton cultivator and a saw sharpener.

A carpenter before the war, Parker Robbins served as a sergeant-major of a Union cavalry regiment. Later, he became a representative from North
1. *Carolina and an inventor.*

schools to black children. In New York City, they secured the right of blacks to use public transportation.

After the war, several actions in effect reversed the Dred Scott decision denying citizenship to black Americans. (See Chapter 16.) For example, in 1865 John Rock, a black attorney from Boston, was admitted to practice before the Supreme Court. Both the State and Justice departments established rules clearly stating that blacks were entitled to
2. citizenship.

Black Soldiers

The movement for black rights was strengthened by black contributions during the war. Many blacks volunteered as cooks, drivers, carpenters, and scouts for the Union army. They were motivated not only by patriotism but also by a desire to be recognized as full partners in the nation and the war effort. At first, federal law prohibited blacks from serving as soldiers, but when Congress repealed
364 that law in 1862, blacks enlisted in the Union army.

2. **CITIZENSHIP** Illinois repealed a law that punished blacks for entering the state. Congress voted to let blacks testify in federal courts.

Frederick Douglass explained why blacks were eager to participate: "Once let the black man get upon his person the brass letters, *U.S.;* let him get an eagle on his button, and a musket on his shoulder and bullets in his pocket, and there is no power on earth that can deny that he has earned the right to citizenship in the United States." By the end of the war, 180,000 blacks had fought in the Union army and 29,000 in the navy.

Black soldiers suffered discrimination, nonetheless. Their term of enlistment was longer than whites', and they earned less. The army assigned them to all-black regiments, mostly under the command of white officers. Medical care, bad enough for white soldiers, was even worse in the black units. The weapons blacks carried had often been discarded by whites. If taken prisoner by the Confederates, black soldiers faced enslavement or execution.

In spite of such difficult conditions, black soldiers earned recognition for bravery under fire. In 1863, for example, the all-black 54th Massachusetts Regiment led an assault on Fort Wagner in Charleston Harbor. Under heavy artillery barrage, nearly 100 soldiers forced their way into the fort and engaged the Confederate troops in hand-to-hand combat. Such displays of courage won black sol- 3. diers a degree of acceptance among many white Americans.

See p. T67.

SECTION 3 REVIEW

1. **Define:** contraband.

2. (a) What did President Lincoln believe was the main reason to fight the Civil War? (b) Why did his attitude toward freeing the slaves change?

3. Which areas of the nation were affected by the Emancipation Proclamation?

4. How did blacks help the Union during the war?

5. **Critical Thinking** President Lincoln hoped the Emancipation Proclamation would pressure the South to surrender. Why might it have had the opposite effect?

3. **BACKGROUND** In a letter to President Lincoln, Secretary of War Stanton said that blacks "have proved themselves among the bravest of the brave, performing deeds of daring and shedding their blood with a heroism unsurpassed by soldiers of any other race."

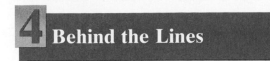

4 Behind the Lines

READ TO UNDERSTAND

■ How the war caused divisions in both the North and the South.

■ How the war affected the economic life of the North and the South.

■ What role women played in the war.

■ *Vocabulary:* copperhead.

"The gaunt form of wretched famine still approaches with rapid strides. . . . I am spading up my little garden, and hope to raise a few vegetables to eke out a miserable subsistence for my family." So wrote a hungry clerk in beleaguered Richmond in March 1864. The war caused hardships not only for soldiers but for civilians, especially in the South.

On both sides, civilians worked on farms and labored in factories to back the war effort. They used their mules to move troops and supplies. They tended the wounded. This suffering and sacrifice spurred their opposition to the war.

Discord in the North

The government of a nation at war counts on the loyalty and support of its citizens. Yet the Constitution of the United States guarantees the right of free speech and open dissent. Did northerners who opposed Lincoln's handling of the war, then, have the right to speak out? At what point would political opposition to the war become treason?

A few northerners openly supported the Confederacy. This was especially true in the border states and in sections of the Old Northwest originally settled by southerners. Other northerners simply demanded an immediate armistice and peace talks. Loyal Republicans called those people who opposed the war **copperheads,** after the poisonous snake.

Lincoln believed that in time of war a President had special powers not available in peacetime. He felt that, to preserve the Union, he was justified in suspending rights

guaranteed by the Constitution. As you read earlier, in 1861, to prevent Maryland from seceding, he had denied habeas corpus in that state. In 1863, he denied habeas corpus to all persons who resisted the draft, discouraged enlistment, or were suspected of being "guilty of any disloyal practice affording aid and comfort to rebels."

Resistance to the draft was especially strong in large cities like New York, where many immigrant workers belonged to the Democratic party and so had little sympathy for Republicans. Workers resented being drafted for a "rich man's war" when those who could afford to pay the exemption fee remained home. Also, white workers who already felt threatened by job competition from free blacks had little interest in fighting a war to free the slaves.

Resentment boiled over in July 1863, when a mob in New York City attacked army recruiters. The mob looted the homes of several wealthy citizens, burned a black orphanage, and lynched several blacks.

Opposition to the draft and to the war continued until the war ended. Between 1863

For four days in July 1863, a mob of 50,000 people rioted against the draft in New York City. The police battled the rioters, but it took troops returning from the battle of Gettysburg to restore order. About 75 people were killed during the riot.

and 1865, military authorities arrested more
1. than 13,000 people for alleged disloyalty.

The Northern Economy

The Civil War prompted economic growth in the North and accelerated the industrialization that had begun before the war. Between 1860 and 1865, for example, woolen mills producing uniforms for Union troops almost tripled their profits.

The war also spurred the growth of agriculture in the North. To meet the army's demands, farmers stepped up food production. Grain farmers purchased more than 165,000 mechanical reapers during the war, increasing grain supplies and freeing farm workers for fighting.

Congress also came to the aid of farmers in 1862. The Homestead Act gave 160 acres (64 hectares) of western land to any citizen who agreed to occupy and improve it for five years. The Morrill Act gave states land grants to endow colleges of agriculture. To increase their support among farmers, Republicans persuaded Congress to establish a cabinet level Department of Agriculture.

Inflation accompanied the expansion of industry and agriculture. Wartime demand for goods increased prices by 50 percent between 1860 and 1862. Wages, however, failed to keep pace, increasing by only 10 percent. People could buy fewer goods with their weekly earnings than before the war. Thus, although the war spurred the North's economy, individuals faced economic hardship.

Hardships in the South

Although the war disrupted life behind the lines in the North, suffering in the South was far worse. Most of the fighting took place in the Confederacy, which endured tremendous destruction of property and crops. As time passed, the Union blockade became increasingly effective, and many southerners were forced to do without basic manufactured goods, such as new clothing.

Unlike the North, the South lacked the industrial capacity to carry on a long war. When locomotives broke down, parts were

not available to repair them. When track was destroyed, it could be replaced only by borrowing track from other lines.

Shortages like these seriously hurt the war effort. The Confederacy could not move enough troops and supplies, nor could it distribute enough food. In 1863, although Confederate farmers in the Shenandoah Valley had reaped good harvests, famine threatened Richmond and mobs rioted for bread.

Since Confederate currency lacked a firm backing, the South experienced astronomical inflation. In 1863, a Confederate official 2. noted that boots cost $200, a coat $350, and shoes $125. Food was expensive, too, when it was available. A chicken cost $15, potatoes $25 per bushel, and butter $15 per pound. In 1863, flour sold for $275 a barrel; by the end of the war, the price had reached $1,000.

Divisions in the Confederacy

The Confederacy faced political as well as economic problems. Not all southerners supported the war. The draft, for example, was as unpopular in the Confederacy as in the Union. Small farmers, especially, objected to the exemptions for planters.

Pro-Union sentiment flourished in border areas, the mountains, and poorer sections of the Confederacy. In 1861, residents 3. in western Virginia, who had long felt estranged from the wealthier and more established eastern part of the state, organized a pro-Union government. In 1863, the area formally joined the Union as the state of West Virginia.

President Davis, like President Lincoln, tried to suspend habeas corpus, and some southerners denounced him as a dictator. Others thought he was not decisive enough. Davis's most outspoken critic was his own vice president, Alexander H. Stephens. 4.

The unwillingness of some state governors to give up authority to the central government also handicapped President Davis. For example, the governor of Alabama would not allow the central government to collect taxes in his state. Governor Joseph Brown of Georgia even considered making a separate peace with the Union.

Diary of a Confederate Nurse

Kate Cummings served the Confederate cause as a nurse. In the excerpt below, she describes her first encounter with wounded soldiers after the battle of Shiloh.

April 11—Miss Booth and myself arrived at Corinth to-day. As I had never been where there was a large army, and had never seen a wounded man, except in the cars, as they passed, I could not help feeling a little nervous at the prospect of now seeing both. When within a few miles of the place, we could realize the condition of an army immediately after a battle. As it had been raining for days, water and mud abounded. Here and there were wagons hopelessly left to their fate, and men on horseback trying to wade through it. As far as the eye could reach, in the midst of all this slop and mud, the white tents of our brave army could be seen through the trees, making a picture suggestive of any thing but comfort. . . .

The crowd of men at the depot was so great that we found it impossible to get to our place of destination by ourselves. . . . I met Mr. George Redwood of Mobile, who kindly offered to pilot us. . . . We are at the Tishomingo Hotel, which, like every other large building, has been taken for a hospital. The yellow flag is flying from the top of each. Mrs. Ogden tried to prepare me for the scenes which I should witness upon entering the wards. But alas! nothing that I had ever heard or read had given me the faintest idea of the horrors witnessed here. . . . Certainly, none of the glories of the war were presented here. Gray-haired men—men in the pride of manhood—beardless boys—Federals and all, mutilated in every imaginable way, lying on the floor, just as they were taken from the battlefield; so close together that it was almost impossible to walk without stepping on them. I could not command my feelings enough to speak, but thoughts crowded upon me. O, if the authors of this cruel and unnatural war could but see what I saw there, they would try to put a stop to it! . . . What can be in the minds of our enemies, who are now arrayed against us, who have never harmed them in any way, but simply claim our own, and nothing more!

See p. T68.

1. What problems limited the care available for the victims of a major battle?

2. Critical Thinking How might a slave disagree with Kate Cumming's lament?

1.

1. CRITICAL THINKING Ask: Whom do you think Cummings is referring to when she mentions "the authors of this cruel and unnatural war"?

Women in the War

Although women were not allowed to fight, they contributed greatly to the war effort. In both the North and the South, women formed aid societies as soon as the war began. These organizations collected millions of dollars worth of supplies to improve the troops' living conditions. More informally, volunteer women operated "refreshment saloons" and "wayside homes" that offered food, drink, and medical care to soldiers who were passing through. Women also aided in the purchase of military hardware. "Ladies Gunboat Funds" were common in the Confederate states.

Women played an increasing role in the work force, especially in the South where labor was short. They often harvested crops and supervised the day-to-day operation of farms and plantations. Many women took jobs as clerical workers in government offices.

Nursing became an important activity for women in both the South and the North. At first, people did not consider nursing male soldiers proper work for women. Despite arguments that such work was "too unpleasant" or "too difficult," women met the challenge.

In 1861, the Union government named Dorothea Dix superintendent of women nurses. She was efficient and warmhearted, but some men found her toughness as an administrator hard to accept. Clara Barton, a schoolteacher, held no official post, but she

2.

2. READING Interested students might read Louisa May Alcott's *Hospital Sketches,* based on her experiences as a Union nurse.

367

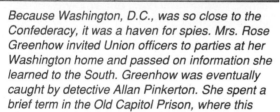

Because Washington, D.C., was so close to the Confederacy, it was a haven for spies. Mrs. Rose Greenhow invited Union officers to parties at her Washington home and passed on information she learned to the South. Greenhow was eventually caught by detective Allan Pinkerton. She spent a brief term in the Old Capitol Prison, where this

1. *photograph of her and her daughter was taken. Then she was sent to Richmond, where she was greeted as a hero.*

---

1. **VISUAL EVIDENCE** Ask: Judging from this picture, how do you think Mrs. Greenhow was treated in prison?

organized care for the sick and wounded behind Union lines and on the battlefields of

2. some of the fiercest conflicts of the war.

Black women also took an active role in the northern war effort. They worked in hos-

3. pitals and in the field, and they helped resettle former slaves who had fled from the South. Sojourner Truth continued to speak out, turning her oratory against all those who wished to conclude peace without abolishing slavery. Charlotte Forten and Mary Peake taught former slaves to read and write. Harriet Tubman, in addition to helping slaves to escape, acted as a spy behind Confederate

368 lines.

3. **BIOGRAPHY** Susie King Taylor was a former slave who had learned to read and write in a secret slave school in Georgia. During the Civil War, she married a Union soldier and served the Union army as a nurse and teacher.

See p. T68.

SECTION 4 REVIEW

1. **Identify:** (a) Homestead Act, (b) Morrill Act, (c) Clara Barton.

2. **Define:** copperhead.

3. What effect did the war have on the northern economy?

4. Why was there greater destruction of property in the South than in the North?

5. How did women contribute to the war effort?

6. **Critical Thinking** How does a war create a strain on civil rights?

---

2. **READING** Interested students can read *Angel of the Battlefield: The Life of Clara Barton* by Ishbel Ross.

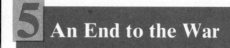

5 An End to the War

READ TO UNDERSTAND

■ What strategies the two sides followed from 1863 to 1865.

■ How the Union gained a new commander and won the war.

■ What factors contributed to the defeat of the South.

The war dragged on. At the end of two hard years of fighting, the Union's naval blockade continued to squeeze tightly, and the North's superior resources began to make a difference on the battlefield. In his diary, a Confederate official wrote: "Steadfastness is yielding to a sense of hopelessness." With each passing day, the likelihood of southern victory became more remote.

Confederate Victories

After the battle of Antietam, General Lee's forces retreated through the Shenandoah Valley. Once again, General McClellan failed

1. **VOCABULARY** Burnside wore whiskers that reached from each ear to his chin. The term *sideburns,* from his name, became a popular term for such whiskers.

to pursue or attack; instead, he encamped and sent requests for supplies. On November 7, 1862, an irritated President Lincoln removed McClellan from command.

1. Lincoln's new commander, General Ambrose E. Burnside, set his sights on Richmond. On December 13, Confederates under Lee turned back the advancing Union troops near
2. Fredericksburg, Virginia.

The following spring, Confederate generals outwitted Union General Joseph Hooker at Chancellorsville, Virginia. On May 3, 1863,
3. Hooker tried to outflank the Confederate forces. But Lee and Jackson routed the Union troops in ten minutes. Although they won the battle, the South suffered a severe loss. An edgy Confederate sentry fired into the night, hitting Stonewall Jackson twice in the arm. One of the Confederacy's ablest generals died soon after from complications related to the wound.

Gettysburg

Victories at Fredericksburg and Chancellorsville inspired the Confederacy, but the Union showed no sign of giving up. General Lee and President Davis hoped that another Confederate drive into the North would break the Union's resolve. Lee led his army into Pennsylvania and the battle that would be a turning point of the war.

At Gettysburg, Pennsylvania, advance detachments of Lee's army unexpectedly met a Union division commanded by General George Meade. On July 1, Confederates won an opening skirmish, but Meade's army managed to occupy the strategically located Cemetery Ridge. Lee's forces took up a position across the way, on Seminary Ridge. (See the map at right.)

Lee hoped to attack around both ends of Cemetery Ridge and trap the Union forces from behind. On July 2, Confederates led by General Richard S. Ewell took the northern slope of Culp's Hill. But Union forces repelled the attack on the southern end at Little Round Top. If Confederates had occupied that hill, they could have directed their artillery fire up and down the main Union line. The next day, Union forces drove Ewell off Culp's Hill.

4. **MAP READING** Ask: Which Union generals fought in the eastern theater? Which Confederate generals? How far did Lee march his troops from Fredericksburg to Gettysburg?

2. **BACKGROUND** Confederates could hardly believe the bravery of the doomed Union troops: "We forgot they were fighting us, and cheer after cheer at their fearlessness went up all along our lines."

Lee then decided to attack the Union forces head-on. When 15,000 Confederates in three lines began their march across three quarters of a mile of open ground, Union troops were ready and opened up a devastating fire. Still, the Confederates pushed on. Through clouds of gunsmoke, General George Pickett led one last valiant attempt to storm the lines. About 100 Confederates actually 3. breached the Union lines temporarily, but Meade's forces held the ridge.

3. **BACKGROUND** This heroic attempt is known as Pickett's Charge.

MAP STUDY *After two years of Confederate victories in the East, the tide of* 4. *war began to turn in the Union's favor at the battle of Gettysburg. Study the inset map. Why was control of the hill called Little Round Top crucial to the outcome of the battle?* See p. T69.

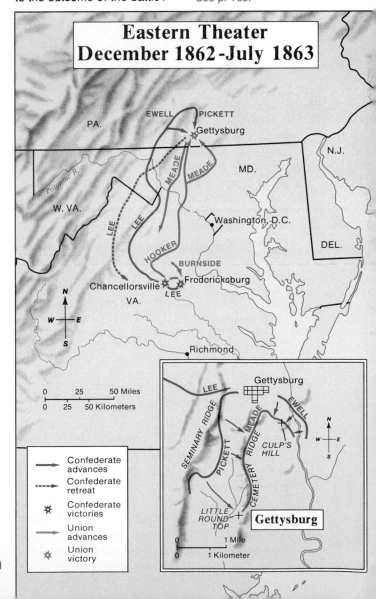

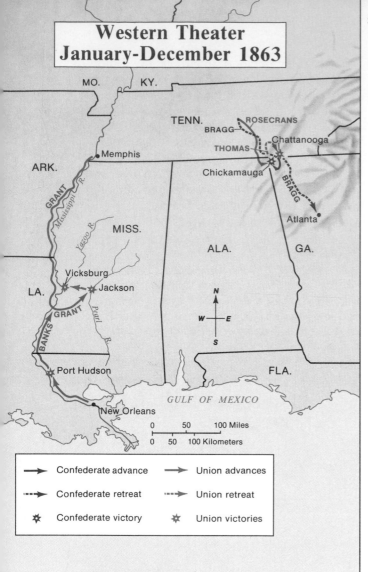

Western Theater
January-December 1863

MO.   KY.

TENN.   ROSECRANS
BRAGG
THOMAS   Chattanooga

Memphis

ARK.
Chickamauga

BRAGG

MISS.
Atlanta

ALA.   GA.

Vicksburg
Jackson
LA.
GRANT
Pearl R.
BANKS

Port Hudson   FLA.

GULF OF MEXICO

New Orleans

0   50   100 Miles
0   50   100 Kilometers

N
W   E
S

→ Confederate advance   → Union advances
▸▸▸ Confederate retreat   ▸▸▸ Union retreat
✸ Confederate victory   ✸ Union victories

MAP STUDY 1. *In a swiftly executed maneuver, General Grant sent ships and troops to surround Vicksburg. How did the Union victories at Vicksburg and Port Hudson complete one part of the North's "anaconda" strategy?* See p. T69.

1. **MAP READING** Ask: Which battle on this map represented a Confederate victory?

Lee had no choice but to take his exhausted and weakened army back to Virginia. The battle of Gettysburg was the beginning of the end for the Confederacy.

2. **PRESIDENTS** Interested students should read Lincoln's Gettysburg Address, given in November 1863.

Vicksburg and Port Hudson

Meanwhile, General Ulysses S. Grant had begun a campaign to secure Union control of the Mississippi River by seizing Vicksburg, Mississippi. Vicksburg sat on a heavily fortified bluff overlooking the Mississippi and the

3. **READING** Students interested in learning how the Civil War affected Native Americans in the West can read *Lincoln and the Indians: Civil War Policy and Politics* by David A. Nicholas.

swamplands of the Yazoo River. Grant spent the first three months of 1863 trying to outflank Confederate General John Pemberton in the Yazoo swamps. Failing to do so, Grant adopted a bolder strategy.

In April, a fleet of Union gunboats floated silently downstream past Vicksburg, their engines and lights turned off. The gunboats then ferried Union troops from the west bank (Louisiana) to the east bank (Mississippi) of the Mississippi River.

Carrying only four days' rations and living off the land as they marched, Grant's men moved eastward. After a series of small victories, they captured the Mississippi capital of Jackson on May 14. Grant then headed back to Vicksburg, arriving only 18 days after he had left. Union forces now surrounded Vicksburg. After a six-week siege, the Confederates surrendered Vicksburg on July 4, 1863—the day after the Battle of Gettysburg ended.

On July 9, Union forces captured Port Hudson, Louisiana. Two black regiments, spurred on by the heroism of Captain Andre Callious, were instrumental in the victory. The Union now held the entire Mississippi River. The western grip of the anaconda was 3. tightened. The Confederacy's position was becoming steadily more desperate.

Grant Takes Command

With the western front largely secure, Union troops pushed eastward. In September, 4. Union armies under General William Rosecrans secured the strategic railroad center at Chattanooga, Tennessee. Thinking that Confederate General Braxton Bragg's force was retreating, Rosecrans proceeded to march eastward. He almost lost his entire army when Bragg's force counterattacked at Chickamauga on September 19 and 20. However, General George Thomas held off the Confederates long enough to allow Rosecrans to retreat to Chattanooga.

The next spring, Lincoln placed Grant in charge of all Union armies. Grant devised a three-pronged attack. One Union army would march into the fertile Shenandoah Valley of Virginia, defeat enemy forces, and lay waste the land so that no crops would grow until

4. **ACTIVITY** Have students report on a Civil War battle. They should discuss major troop movements and the outcome and include a battle map.

1. "The Father of Waters again goes unvexed to the sea," said Lincoln when he heard about Grant's victory at Vicksburg. Taking the town cut the Confederacy in two and allowed supplies to come down the Mississippi to Union forces in the South. For the people of Vicksburg, defeat was made more bitter by the date of surrender—July 4. The city did not celebrate Independence Day again until 1945.

1. **VISUAL EVIDENCE**
This picture depicts Grant's first attack on Vicksburg on May 19, 1863.

2. **MAP READING** Ask: How many miles did Sherman's army travel after capturing Atlanta?

after the war. General Philip Sheridan completed this mission in October 1864.

The two other armies that were to make up Grant's three-pronged attack would be led by Grant himself and by General William Tecumseh Sherman. Sherman's army was to march from Chattanooga to Atlanta, and Grant's was to march from Washington to Richmond.

Grant and Sherman were alike in several ways. Both men wore stubby, short-cropped beards, dressed sloppily, and possessed an indomitable will to win. Both were willing to take any steps necessary to achieve victory. They intended to wage total war, defeating not only the opposing military forces but the
3. civilian will to resist as well.

Sherman's March to the Sea

General Sherman assembled 100,000 soldiers. On May 6, 1864, they left Chattanooga. As the Union army proceeded, it lived off the land, leaving destruction behind. General Sherman described the march: "We have devoured the land, and our animals eat up the wheat and corn fields close. All the people retire before us and desolation is behind. To realize what war is one should follow our tracks."

Confederate forces under General Joseph Johnston and General John Hood opposed
3. **DISCUSSION** Ask students to discuss the implications of Grant's "total war."

2.

MAP STUDY *General Sherman's march to the sea left a path of destruction. From what inland city did he begin his march? In what coastal city did his march end?* See p. T69.

Sherman's March to the Sea
May–December 1864

TENN.   N.C.

Chattanooga

SHERMAN
JOHNSTON
HOOD

Atlanta

GA.   S.C.

SHERMAN

ALA.

Savannah

ATLANTIC
OCEAN

FLA.

→ Union advances
★ Union victories
⇢ Confederate retreat

0   50   100 Miles
0   50   100 Kilometers

Sherman at every turn. But Sherman's men marched on, finally occupying Atlanta on

1. September 1.

Until the capture of Atlanta, Lincoln had expected that public frustration over the war would result in his defeat in the 1864 election. The Democrats had adopted a platform calling for an armistice and had nominated General McClellan to oppose Lincoln. Even some Republicans had been urging immedi-

2. ate peace with the South. News of the fall of Atlanta rallied popular support for Lincoln and insured his reelection.

In mid-November, General Sherman prepared to set out for Savannah, on the coast. Before leaving, he ordered his troops to set

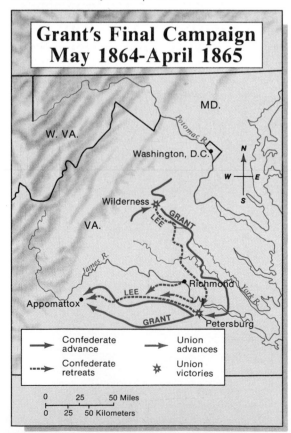

Grant's Final Campaign May 1864-April 1865

MD.

W. VA.

Potomac R.

Washington, D.C.

N
W   E
S

Wilderness

GRANT
LEE

VA.

James R.

Richmond

LEE

York R.

Appomattox

GRANT

Petersburg

→ Confederate advance
⇢ Confederate retreats
→ Union advances
★ Union victories

0   25   50 Miles
0   25   50 Kilometers

fire to Atlanta, destroying much of the city. Sherman's army arrived at Savannah on December 10, having left a path of devastation 60 miles (96 kilometers) wide all across Georgia. On December 21, Savannah fell.

Throughout the campaign, Sherman's army had destroyed any supplies that might have fed Confederate soldiers. It had wrecked railroad lines and ruined cotton gins. A bitter South would not soon forget Sherman's march through Georgia.

Capturing Richmond

Grant led the third prong of the attack himself. Early in May 1864, troops under his command arrived in the Wilderness, a wild area near Fredericksburg, Virginia. There, Grant initiated the first of three unsuccessful efforts to defeat Lee's much smaller army.

Both sides suffered heavy casualties over the next two months. Grant lost nearly 60,000 men, Lee nearly 30,000. Although Grant's casualties were greater, the Union had reserves to replace them. The Confederacy had no reserves. Lee's army retreated to Petersburg, a few miles south of Richmond, where the Confederates dug a network of trenches, built heavy fortifications, and prepared for a siege.

The siege of Petersburg lasted from June 1864 through the winter of 1865. Finally, cut off from his lines of supply, Lee withdrew on the night of April 2, 1865, abandoning both Petersburg and the Confederate capital of Richmond. Grant pursued.

4.

Appomattox: A Sad Peace

One week later, Union troops trapped Lee's army near the small town of Appomattox Court House. Realizing that further resistance was

5.

futile, Lee sent a soldier carrying a white towel as a flag of truce.

On April 9, 1865, Lee met with Grant to discuss the terms of surrender. Robert E. Lee wore a full-dress uniform with ceremonial sash and sword. Ulysses S. Grant, characteristically untidy, appeared in a private's shirt, his collar unbuttoned. The two generals talked about the days before the Civil War, when they had both served in the United

At the end of the war, General Lee's troops had one final duty—to furl the "Stars
and Bars," the Confederate flag, for the last time. The soldiers in Richard Brooke's
painting of the scene show the weariness of war and the sorrow of defeat.

1. **BACKGROUND** Some Confederate units buried or
burned their flags rather than surrender them.

See p. T69.

States Army. Then Grant suggested generous terms of surrender:

> Officers and men paroled . . . arms and ma-
> terials surrendered . . . officers to keep their
> side arms, and let all the men who claim to
> own a horse or mule take the animals home
> with them to work their little farms.

One of Grant's aides recalled that General Lee "gazed sadly in the direction . . .
where his army lay—now an army of prisoners. He thrice smote the palm of his left hand
slowly with his right fist in an absent sort of
way." As the Union soldiers saw Lee mount
and ride away toward his men, they began
cheering their victory. Grant immediately
ordered them to stop. "The war is over," he
told them; "the rebels are our countrymen
again."

2. **READING** Students interested in the Civil War can read
The New York Times Book of the Civil War, edited by
Arlene Keylin and Douglas J. Bowen.

SECTION 5 REVIEW

1. **Identify:** William Tecumseh Sherman.

2. (a) What victories in late 1862 and early
   1863 encouraged the Confederates? (b)
   Why did Lee invade Pennsylvania?

3. What did the capture of Vicksburg and
   Port Hudson mean for the Union?

4. How did General Sherman try to destroy
   the Confederates' ability to resist?

5. What convinced Lee to surrender?

6. **Critical Thinking** Based on the terms
   of surrender, what kind of treatment might
   the South have expected after the war?

373

3. **DISCUSSION** Have students anticipate what problems
the newly reunited nation would have to face after the
Civil War.

Summary

1. **After hostilities began, the Union and the Confederacy had to prepare for war.** The Union had important material advantages, but both sides had to build up and finance their armies. Neither side gained European allies.

2. **Illusions of an early end to the war quickly faded.** In this first "modern" war, battles were big and bloody and the loss of life tremendous. General Winfield Scott's "anaconda" strategy proved in the long run to be successful.

3. **The Emancipation Proclamation changed the purpose of the war for many northerners.** Although the proclamation did not directly affect free blacks or slaves in the Union, it did contribute to the struggle for greater rights.

4. **The war affected all aspects of life, including the role played by women in society.** Both sides experienced divisions over the war, resentment over the draft, and inflation. Yet the war stimulated economic growth in the North, while it caused increasing hardships in the South.

5. **The superior numbers and supplies of the Union army gradually wore the South down.** Robert E. Lee finally surrendered to Ulysses S. Grant in April 1865 at Appomattox Court House. The war was over, but the difficult task of reuniting the nation lay ahead.

See p. T69.

Vocabulary

On a separate sheet of paper, write the word or words that best complete each of the following sentences.

1. A sum paid to a recruit who signed up for military service was a (an) _____.

2. _____ was the act of enlisting, collecting a fee, deserting, reenlisting, and collecting another fee.

3. A (An) _____ is a ship strengthened with armor plates.

4. During the Civil War, the term _____ referred to a slave who had fled behind Union lines.

5. Loyal Republicans called opponents of the Civil War _____.

See p. T69.

Chapter Checkup

1. (a) List the advantages and disadvantages of the Confederacy as war began. (b) List the advantages and disadvantages of the Union.

2. (a) Why did neither side rely completely on volunteers for their armies? (b) How were soldiers recruited?

3. (a) Why were both the North and the South eager to win British support? (b) Which groups in Britain favored the North? Which favored the South? (c) What was Britain's official policy?

4. (a) Describe General Scott's war strategy. (b) Why was it called the anaconda? (c) Was the strategy most successful in the west or in the east? (d) What impact did the blockade have on the South?

5. (a) What did General Lee hope to accomplish by invading the North in September 1862 and again in June 1863? (b) What was the result of each invasion?

6. (a) Why did Lincoln finally decide to issue the Emancipation Proclamation? (b) Whom did it affect directly?

7. How did the status of black Americans in the North change during the Civil War?

8. (a) Describe Grant's plan for defeating the Confederacy. (b) Which part of his plan proved most difficult to achieve? Why?

See p. T69.

Critical Thinking

1. **Analyzing** Why did the North win the war? Give examples to support your answer.

2. **Determining Cause and Effect** Why were there more casualties in the Civil War than in previous American wars?

See p. T69.

Connecting Past and Present

1. During the Civil War, a person could hire a substitute or pay a fee to exempt himself from military service. If the nation had a draft today, do you think a person would be permitted to buy an exemption? Why or why not?

2. Inadequate medical knowledge contributed to many deaths during the Civil War. (a) What changes since the Civil War would contribute to better medical care in a future war? (b) What might cause new problems?

See p. T69.

Developing Basic Skills

1. **Comparing** Compare Abraham Lincoln, Jefferson Davis, Ulysses S. Grant, George B. McClellan, Robert E. Lee, and Stonewall Jackson. (a) What characteristics did each have that may have helped make him a good leader? (b) What characteristics did each have that may have weakened his leadership ability?

2. **Classifying** Make a chart with two columns, titled Western Theater and Eastern Theater; and three rows, titled Confederate Victory, Union Victory, and Neither. Write the name of each battle you have read about in the appropriate box. Then answer the following questions: (a) Which side won the largest number of battles? (b) How does the chart help explain the outcome of the Civil War? (c) Your history text did not discuss all encounters between Confederate troops and Union troops. How does that affect the accuracy of your analysis?

WRITING ABOUT HISTORY

Using the *Readers' Guide*

To find information in magazines and journals, you will need to consult an index to periodicals. The *Readers' Guide to Periodical Literature* lists subjects and authors alphabetically according to date.

Practice: Use the sample entry from the *Readers' Guide* to answer the following questions. The labels will help you interpret the entries.

1. What is the title of the article by J. Skow?
2. Under what subject heading does it appear?
3. In what magazine was it published?
4. What is the date of the magazine?
5. On what pages does the article appear?

Subject heading

United States—History

Civil War, 1861–1865—Campaigns and battles
Bang, bang! You're history, buddy [battle reenactments]
J. Skow, il *Time* 128:58–9 Ag Il '86

Civil War, 1861–1865—Literature and the war
The scribe of the Civil War [S. Foote] W. C. Carter. il por *South Living* 21:147–8 Je'86
Civil War, 1861–1865—Personal narratives
Enlisted for life [O. W. Holmes's experiences]
H. B. Zobel, il pors *Am Herit* 37:56–64 Je/Jl '86

Illustration — Title of magazine
Author — Volume and pages
Title of article — Date
Subheading

A Difficult Reunion

18

(1865–1877)

CHAPTER OBJECTIVES After completing this chapter, students should be able to
1. discuss different Reconstruction plans.
2. explain the conflict between President Johnson and Congress.
3. describe changes in the South during Reconstruction.
4. discuss the end of Reconstruction.

CHAPTER PREVIEW Have students think about problems facing the South after the Civil War. Ask them to read the excerpt from Lincoln's Second Inaugural Address on p. 380. Then ask: In what specific ways could Lincoln's views have been implemented?

CHAPTER OUTLINE

1 Beginning of Reunion

2 Congress Takes Over

3 The Reconstruction South

4 Unfinished Business

He was an actor—he could come and go as he pleased in Ford's Theater. Few people paid much attention when he dropped by three times that night of April 14, 1865.

On the first visit, the theater was empty. He proceeded to Box 7, the one reserved for the President of the United States. It had two doors: the first opening into an antechamber, the second leading to the box itself. Once inside, he cut a two-inch opening in the brick wall next to the outer door. Then he bored a small hole through the inner door. His preparations made, he left.

By the time the man returned to the theater a second time, the play, *Our American Cousin,* was in progress. He walked around backstage, smiled at the actors, and checked to see how far the comedy had progressed. It had about 40 minutes to go. He wanted to wait until there were very few people on stage.

To while away the time, he went to the tavern next door for refreshment. It was a few minutes before 10 P.M. when the lone actor returned to the theater and chatted a minute with the ticket taker. Then, he walked softly up

the steps and entered the antechamber. He took a slender iron bar, put one end into the prepared opening and jammed the other end against the door panel. No one could enter.

Peering through the peephole, he saw four people: the President, the President's wife, Major Henry Rathbone, and Clara Harris, the major's fiancée. From his pocket, the actor took an eight-ounce, one-shot derringer pistol. He opened the second door and extended his right arm until the pistol was less than five feet from the President.

And then John Wilkes Booth pulled the trigger, firing a lead ball into Abraham Lincoln's head, three inches from the left ear. Jumping to the stage, the assailant yelled, "Sic semper tyrannis!"—Thus always to tyrants—and fled before the shocked audience knew what had happened. But they—and the rest of the country—would soon find out.

The death of Lincoln was but one more agony the nation would endure as it struggled to recover from the Civil War. Although the Union had been preserved, the scars of war would be slow to heal.

1.

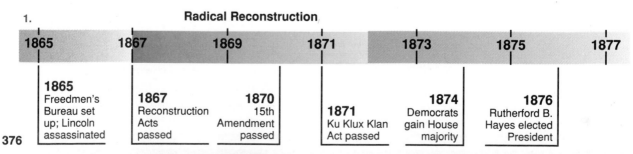

Radical Reconstruction

| 1865 | 1867 | 1869 | 1871 | 1873 | 1875 | 1877 |

1865
Freedmen's Bureau set up; Lincoln assassinated

1867
Reconstruction Acts passed

1870
15th Amendment passed

1871
Ku Klux Klan Act passed

1874
Democrats gain House majority

1876
Rutherford B. Hayes elected President

376

1. **TIME LINE QUESTION** How many years did Radical Reconstruction last?

1. *For two days, President Lincoln's body lay in state in the Capitol. Then it was carried to Illinois on a funeral train, which retraced his route to the White House five years earlier. Along the route, people waited in the rain to pay their last respects. "Oh, Abraham Lincoln, are you dead? Are you dead?" cried a black woman in Philadelphia, summing up the grief of a nation.*

1. **VISUAL EVIDENCE** This print was made by Nathaniel Currier and James Ives. Inexpensive Currier and Ives lithographs were found in many homes in the 1800s and are still popular today.

1 Beginning of Reunion

READ TO UNDERSTAND

■ What hardships faced the South and the North after the Civil War.

■ How former slaves began their new lives of freedom.

■ Why congressional leaders objected to presidential plans for bringing the South back into the Union.

2. ■ *Vocabulary:* freedmen.

When Union soldier Leander Stillwell returned to his farm in Illinois after the Civil War, he found his father shucking corn. Stillwell set to work. "It almost seemed . . . as if I had been away only a day or two, and had just taken up the farm work where I had left off," wrote Stillwell. Try as they might, however, most Americans could not just take up life

where they had left off. The war had brought too many changes—political, social, and economic. Reunion would be a difficult task.

Effects of War

The human consequences of the war would haunt the nation for many years. More than 360,000 Union soldiers and 258,000 Confederate soldiers had lost their lives, as had many civilians. Thousands of veterans were permanently disabled. A legacy of bitterness 3. and resentment lingered. Confederates had lost their struggle for independence and seen much of their land laid waste by Union armies. Furthermore, many southerners feared retribution by the victors.

It was not easy to begin life anew. In the North, some 800,000 former soldiers needed jobs. Yet the government was canceling its war orders, and factories were laying off workers, not hiring them. But the North's economic disruption was only temporary. After a brief recession, boom times quickly returned.

2. **VOCABULARY** Have students look up this word in the glossary before they begin reading.

3. **BACKGROUND** In Mississippi, one third of military-age whites had been killed or disabled. One fifth of the state's revenue went for artificial limbs.

377

At war's end, the once bustling city of Richmond was a desolate sight, as you can see here. During the last days of the war, the Union army had advanced on Richmond. As the Confederate government prepared to evacuate, it ordered
1. factories and arsenals to be destroyed. Soon fires raged throughout the city. "The old war-scarred city seemed to prefer annihilation to conquest," noted one Confederate soldier who witnessed the destruction.

1. **VISUAL EVIDENCE** One retreating soldier described the scene as "a tidal wave of destruction . . . miles on miles of fire; mountain piled on mountain of black smoke . . . one mighty pandemonium of woe."

The South faced more serious problems. Union armies had destroyed factories and railroads and ravaged plantations and farms. The once-thriving cities of Atlanta, Charleston, Columbia, and Richmond were burned-out shells. Everywhere, business was at a standstill. Small farmers and poor whites were especially hard hit. One traveler in Alabama reported, "I visited four families, within fifteen minutes' ride of town, who were living in the woods, with no shelter but pine boughs, and this in mid-winter."

Freedmen

The Civil War had begun as a war over the right of secession, but in the end it freed about 4 million slaves. To former slave owners, emancipation meant property losses totaling billions of dollars. Emancipation also had a great impact on social relationships. In both the North and the South, most white Americans refused to accept blacks as equals. 2. Although the Thirteenth Amendment to the Constitution, ratified in December 1865, abolished slavery, it did not change the attitude of whites. Few southern whites thought of blacks as other than slaves. And generous behavior on the part of most blacks did little to relieve the fear that the blacks might seek revenge.

Severe problems beset the former slaves, known as **freedmen.** Since teaching slaves to read and write had been illegal in most states, few freedmen were literate. Although most were skilled farmers, they owned no land and had no money to buy any. Impoverished by the war, few people could afford to hire them; besides, working for a former master seemed too much like slavery.

378

2. **BACKGROUND** The governor of Mississippi noted: "The Negro is free, whether we like it or not; we must realize that fact now and forever. To be free, however, does not make him a citizen or entitle him to social or political equality with the white man."

1. **BACKGROUND** One former Confederate was amazed to see "a government which was lately fighting us . . . now generously feeding our poor and distressed."

2. **BACKGROUND** The Bureau set up over 4,300 elementary schools in the South and four universities—Howard, Morehouse, Fisk, and Hampton Institute.

In March 1865, Congress set up the Freedmen's Bureau to aid freedmen and refugees. The bureau provided medical care, clothing, and surplus army food for freed slaves and poor whites. It sent agents to set up schools for black children and adults. The agents sought work for the freedmen and tried to prevent their exploitation by employers.

GREAT DEBATE

Rival Plans for Reconstruction

Even before the end of the war, President Lincoln had considered how to bring the seceded states back into the Union. From the beginning, the President had believed that states had no legal right to secede from the Union. When he first summoned troops after the fall of Fort Sumter, Lincoln treated the southern rebellion as an insurrection. The Confederacy, he argued, was only a group of individuals who were resisting federal authority, not states that had seceded. The Constitution gave the President, as commander-in-chief, power to put down insurrections; thus

Lincoln believed it was his responsibility to restore harmonious relations with the South as soon as possible.

Lincoln's Plan As early as December 1863, Lincoln had proclaimed a plan of Reconstruction for those areas of the South that had come under Union control. He offered a pardon to Confederates if they would swear an oath to support the Constitution and the Union. When a former Confederate state abolished slavery and 10 percent of its voters subscribed to the oath and formed a loyal government, the President promised to readmit it to the Union.

Lincoln believed that Reconstruction should be gradual. "We shall sooner have the fowl by hatching the egg," he argued, "than by smashing it." By the spring of 1864, Louisiana and Arkansas had reorganized their governments under Lincoln's 10 percent plan.

The Radicals' Plan A group of Republicans in Congress, known as Radicals, rejected the President's plan as too lenient. Even moderate Republicans argued that Lincoln had overstepped his authority by acting with-

3. **CITIZENSHIP** One bureau agent said freedmen "will starve themselves, and go without clothes, in order to send their children to school."

Even before the war ended, the federal government set up the Freedmen's Bureau to help freed slaves adjust to their new lives. One activity of the bureau was to open schools for former slaves. Idealistic women flocked south to teach in the schools. One of them, Charlotte Forten, was the granddaughter of a black Philadelphia merchant. She said she "never before saw children so eager to learn. . . . Coming to school is a constant delight and recreation to them."

VOICES OF FREEDOM

Lincoln's Second Inaugural Address

When President Abraham Lincoln delivered his second inaugural address on March 4, 1865, Confederate armies were still holding out. (See Chapter 17.) But Lincoln was looking ahead to reuniting the nation, as you can see from the excerpt below.

. . . Fondly do we hope, fervently do we pray, that this mighty scourge of war may speedily pass away.

Yet, if God wills that it continue until all the wealth piled by the bondsman's 250 years of unrequited toil shall be sunk, and until every drop of blood drawn with the lash shall be paid by another drawn with the sword, as was said 3,000 years ago, so still it must be said, "The judgments of the Lord are true and righteous altogether."

With malice toward none, with charity for all, with firmness in the right as God gives us to see the right, let us strive on to finish the work we are in, to bind up the nation's wounds, to care for him who shall have borne the battle and for his widow and his orphan—to do all which may achieve and cherish a just and lasting peace among ourselves and with all nations.

Source: John G. Nicolay and John Hay, eds., *Complete Works of Abraham Lincoln* (New York: 1905), vol. 11, p. 47.
See p. T70.

1.

1. What did Lincoln see as his responsibility?

2. Critical Thinking Why do you think Lincoln chose this tone for his second inaugural address?

out seeking the advice and consent of Congress.

In July 1864, moderate Republicans joined with the Radicals to pass a rival version of Reconstruction. The Wade-Davis Bill stipulated that a majority of white males had to take an oath of allegiance before a state could be reorganized. Those who wished to vote or take part in the new government would have to swear that they had never willingly supported the Confederacy. The bill also required southern states to refuse to honor Confederate debts, to abolish slavery, and to cancel their acts of secession. Lincoln re-
2. fused to sign the bill. ■

The President Assassinated

Could Lincoln make his moderate plan for reconstruction work? He never had a chance to try. On April 14, 1865, little more than a month after his second inauguration, the President attended a play at Ford's Theater in Washington, D.C. During the performance, an unstable actor, John Wilkes Booth, crept into the President's box and fired a bullet

into the back of his head. The President died the next day.

Federal troops tracked Booth to a barn near Bowling Green, Virginia. When Booth refused to surrender, his pursuers set the barn on fire. Booth was shot to death, probably by his own hand. Four alleged accomplices were hung and four others imprisoned. But nothing could make up for the loss of Lincoln. Without his firm leadership and abil- 3. ity to bring together the different elements within the Union, Reconstruction would arouse violent passions.

A New President, A New Plan

The assassination thrust Vice President Andrew Johnson into the presidency. He bore little love for southern aristocratic planters. 4. A southern Democrat in the mold of Andrew Jackson, he had served as governor of Tennessee and had represented that state in both houses of Congress.

When Tennessee had seceded in 1861, Johnson had bitterly opposed the move. As a reward for his loyalty, President Lincoln appointed him military governor of the occupied areas of the state. In 1864, the Republicans offered Johnson the vice presidential nomination. As a Democrat, he attracted badly needed votes to help Lincoln win reelection.

As President, Johnson appeared ready to take a firm stand against the South. He promptly offered rewards for the capture of Jefferson Davis and other Confederate officials. He proclaimed that "treason must be made infamous and traitors must be impoverished." Senator Benjamin Wade, a Radical Republican, rejoiced, "By the gods, there will be no trouble now in running the government."

But Johnson soon angered the Radical Republicans. He recognized the governments that had organized under Lincoln's plan. For the remaining Confederate states, he announced new requirements for readmission. Although these were stiffer than those set up by Lincoln, they fell far short of what was demanded by the Radical Republicans.

1.   Johnson required that former Confederate states renounce their acts of secession, refuse to pay their war debts, and ratify the Thirteenth Amendment. By winter, all the former Confederate states except Texas had moved to obtain recognition. But some states were reluctant to fulfill the President's terms. For example, South Carolina refused to cancel its war debt, and Mississippi refused to ratify the Thirteenth Amendment.

Many Republicans were even more troubled by the refusal of the southern states to give freedmen equal rights. One state convention voiced the feelings of many white southerners when it declared that it was establishing a "Government of White People, made and to be perpetuated for the exclusive political benefit of the White Race"; blacks, said the convention delegates, were not to be considered citizens.

President Johnson was eager to restore the Union, however, so he recognized the new southern governments. The readmitted states immediately elected representatives to Congress.

When Congress convened in December 1865, it refused to seat the southerners, many of whom had led the Confederacy in war. Instead, a Republican majority, made up of moderates and Radicals, set up a Joint Committee on Reconstruction to determine if the southern states were truly "reconstructed." 2.

See p. T70.

SECTION 1 REVIEW

1. **Identify:** (a) Freedmen's Bureau, (b) Wade-Davis Bill, (c) John Wilkes Booth, (d) Joint Committee on Reconstruction.

2. **Define:** freedmen.

3. Identify one problem faced by the North and one problem faced by the South after the Civil War.

4. What did the Freedmen's Bureau do?

5. What was Lincoln's 10 percent plan?

6. **Critical Thinking** How did the priorities of President Johnson and the Radical Republicans differ?

2 Congress Takes Over

READ TO UNDERSTAND

■ Why Radical Republicans wanted control of Reconstruction.

■ What Congress did to protect freedmen.

■ Why Congress tried to remove President Johnson from office.

Who would control Reconstruction: Andrew Johnson or the Radical Republicans in Congress? As long as the Radicals lacked the two-thirds majority needed to override a veto, Johnson could prevail. But by early 1866, even many moderates were becoming disillusioned with Johnson. The President and Congress had squared off for a critical battle.

The Radical Position

The Radical Republicans had important reasons for opposing Johnson's Reconstruction plan. First, they argued that the seceded states had given up their statehood and returned

381

to the status of territories. Like new territories, the Radicals insisted, the southern states should be "under the exclusive jurisdiction of Congress." Congress, not the President, should decide when the states could return to the Union.

Many Radicals felt Johnson's plan was too lenient. Representative Thaddeus Stevens, an outspoken Radical, strongly protested presidential pardons of former Confederates. "Did any respectable Government ever before allow such high criminals to escape with such shameful impunity? . . . No sir; they have not been punished as they deserve. They have exchanged forgiveness with the President, and been sent on their way rejoicing." Stevens urged confiscation of all plantations and division of the land among the freedmen.

The Radicals also had political motives for demanding a harsh policy toward the South. The South was sending mostly Democrats to Congress. If they were seated, the Republicans risked losing their majority and with it their power.

Some Radical Republicans, who had long fought for the freedom of slaves, had higher motives. These Radicals believed that unless black Americans received their full rights as citizens, the war would have been fought in vain. "We must see to it that the man made free by the Constitution . . . is a freeman indeed," explained one Radical, "that he can go where he pleases; work when and for whom he pleases . . . and that he walks the earth, proud and erect in the conscious dignity of a free man."

The Black Codes

When the Joint Committee on Reconstruction (see page 381) met early in 1866, its members heard testimony about conditions in the South. Disturbing reports about laws called Black Codes convinced even moderate Republicans that a more severe Reconstruction plan was needed.

Although modeled on the old slave codes (see page 69), the Black Codes did provide freedmen with certain basic rights. They allowed blacks to sue and be sued and to buy and sell property. Former slaves who had been married informally could now make their

marriages legal. And while the Black Codes required young blacks to work as apprentices, they did provide guidelines to protect them from abuse.

But the granting of a few select rights could not alter the fact that the Black Codes explicitly denied black citizens some of their most important civil rights. Blacks were not permitted to bear arms or to meet together after sunset. They were not permitted to marry whites. A black found idle or unemployed could be fined for vagrancy and imprisoned or sentenced to hard labor for a year.

Southern state legislatures passed most of the Black Codes in the fall and winter of 1865 and 1866. Many southerners were convinced that former slaves might rise in revolt or that, at best, they would be unable to deal with their sudden freedom.

Congress was determined to protect the rights of blacks. In February 1866, it passed a bill to increase the authority of the Freedmen's Bureau and to extend its life for an indefinite period. President Johnson vetoed the bill. Later in the year, Congress passed a second Freedmen's Bureau bill over Johnson's veto.

Meanwhile, in April, Congress overrode the President's veto of the Civil Rights Act. The act gave blacks United States citizenship and guaranteed various other rights (although not the right to vote). With this legislation, Radicals hoped to secure for blacks the rights denied them by the southern states.

A Guarantee of Citizenship

As you read in Chapter 16, the Supreme Court had ruled in the Dred Scott case in 1857 that blacks were not citizens. Now Republicans feared that the Court might declare the Civil Rights Act unconstitutional. Congress therefore proposed a constitutional amendment guaranteeing citizenship to black Americans.

The heart of the Fourteenth Amendment was a simple statement: "All persons born or naturalized in the United States . . . are citizens." In addition, the amendment provided that a person who had held a federal or state government position before the Civil War and who had given aid and comfort to the Confederate cause could not hold public office without first being pardoned by Congress.

Under the Black Codes, freedmen could be fined if they had no visible means of support. If they did not pay the fines, their services could be sold, as shown in this
1. *engraving. Republicans in Congress pointed to such actions in their argument for a more severe Reconstruction plan.*

1. **VISUAL EVIDENCE** Have students compare this picture to the picture of a slave auction on p. 304.

2. **BACKGROUND** Between 1865 and 1868, voters in Wisconsin, Minnesota, Connecticut, Nebraska, New Jersey, Ohio, Michigan, and Pennsylvania denied suffrage to blacks.

The amendment also canceled all Confederate debts and forbade any government to repay former slave owners for slaves lost by the act of emancipation.

Some Radicals wanted to include a provision guaranteeing all males, black or white, the right to vote. Only a few northern states
2. permitted blacks to vote, however, and moderate Republicans, fearing a public outcry, rejected this proposal. A compromise clause did provide for a reduction in congressional representation of any state that did not allow black males to vote.

Congress passed the Fourteenth Amendment in June 1866 and sent it to the states for ratification. By July 1868, enough states had approved the measure to make it part of the Constitution. Two years later, in 1870, the Fifteenth Amendment gave black Americans the right to vote in all states. The Fifteenth Amendment stated that no citizen could be denied the right to vote "on account of race, color, or previous condition of servitude." Efforts by women to gain the vote
3. at this time were rejected.

The Beginning of Radical Reconstruction

When Republicans in Congress first proposed the Fourteenth Amendment in 1866, they split with President Johnson. Johnson detested the Fourteenth Amendment and urged southern legislatures to reject it as a violation of states' rights.* To counter Radical influence, the President campaigned for candidates who supported his policies in the fall congressional elections. His speeches were a failure. Often, when pro-Radical audiences heckled him, he lost his temper and responded with remarks that many people considered unsuitable to a President.

Mob violence against blacks in Memphis and New Orleans caused new troubles for the President. The riots convinced many northerners that Johnson's lenient policies

*Every state government Johnson had recognized, except for the government of Tennessee, did reject the Fourteenth Amendment the first time it was considered.

383

3. **CRITICAL THINKING** Susan B. Anthony and Elizabeth Cady Stanton campaigned against the amendment because it did not give women the vote. Ask: Do you agree with this position?

had not worked and that stronger measures were needed to protect the freedmen.

The election results were a disaster for Johnson. The Republicans won majorities in every northern state legislature and captured every northern governorship. They also won more than a two-thirds majority in Congress, giving them enough votes to override any presidential veto.

The triumphant Radical Republicans now passed their own program, the Reconstruction Act of 1867. All seceded states except Tennessee, which had been readmitted in July 1866, had to meet a new set of requirements for readmission to the Union. Each state had to adopt a state constitution that barred former Confederate officials from office and granted black men the right to vote. The states also had to ratify the Fourteenth Amendment.

Until they were readmitted, the former Confederate states would be under military control. The Reconstruction Act divided the South into five military districts, each commanded by an army general. The commanders were responsible for organizing the state constitutional conventions and for registering blacks and loyal whites to vote for convention delegates. In this way, Congress hoped to prevent state conventions from rejecting parts of the plan, as Johnson had originally encouraged them to do. The President vetoed the Reconstruction Act and several other acts. But Congress easily overrode the vetoes, and Radical Reconstruction went into
1. effect.

A ticket to the impeachment trial of President Johnson was a popular item. At the beginning of the trial, the sergeant-at-arms called, "Hear ye! Hear ye! Andrew Johnson, Andrew Johnson!" But Johnson disappointed both ticket-holders and senators. He never attended any of the sessions in which the Senate debated his fate.

A Showdown Between the President and Congress

Would the President sabotage Radical Reconstruction? Congress tried to make sure he could not by passing several laws limiting the President's freedom to act. The Tenure of Office Act was aimed at protecting Radical sympathizers in the Administration. According to the law, the President would need Senate approval to dismiss an officeholder he had appointed with the advice and consent of the Senate.

2.

President Johnson decided to test the constitutionality of the Tenure of Office Act by removing Secretary of War Edwin Stanton from office. The Senate took up the challenge and the same day, February 21, 1868, passed a resolution for impeachment.

By then, many Radical Republicans had reached the conclusion that the success of Reconstruction hinged on the removal of Johnson from office. The only way to remove a President was to impeach and convict him for "high crimes and misdemeanors" committed while in office.* A congressional committee appointed to investigate the President's actions had searched in vain for evidence of such crimes. Johnson's dismissal of Stanton provided the Radical Republicans with what they considered adequate justification.

On February 24, 1868, the House voted to impeach. President Andrew Johnson stood trial in the Senate from March 25 to May 26.

Much was at stake beyond the immediate issue of Reconstruction. There was no specific evidence to back up the charge of "high crimes and misdemeanors." Members of Congress were really trying to dismiss a President because he disagreed with them.

In the final tally, 35 senators voted for conviction and 19 voted against, one vote short of removing the President from office. Johnson served out his term, but the impeachment effort had undermined his power. Although Congress had not convicted him, it

---

*As you learned in Chapter 8, the House of Representatives can impeach, or accuse, a President of committing "high crimes and misdemeanors." If a two-thirds majority of the Senate votes to convict, the President is removed from office.

came close enough to show its determination to maintain control of Reconstruction.

See p. T71.

SECTION 2 REVIEW

1. **Identify:** (a) Thaddeus Stevens, (b) Black Codes, (c) Civil Rights Act, (d) Reconstruction Act, (e) Tenure of Office Act.

2. Why did Radical Republicans pursue a harsh policy toward former Confederate states?

3. (a) What rights did the Black Codes extend to black Americans? (b) What rights did they deny black Americans?

4. What were the major provisions of the Fourteenth and Fifteenth Amendments?

5. Why did Congress try to impeach President Johnson?

6. **Critical Thinking** President Johnson considered the Reconstruction Act of 1867 unconstitutional. On what grounds do you think he based his opinion?

2. **VOCABULARY** Have students look up these words in the glossary before they begin reading.

3 The Reconstruction South

READ TO UNDERSTAND

■ Why most southerners faced economic hardship after the war.

■ How Radical Reconstruction changed political life in the South.

■ What were the achievements and shortcomings of the Reconstruction governments.

2. ■ *Vocabulary:* tenant, sharecropper, carpetbagger, scalawag.

"The Christmas holidays here are cold, rainy, cheerless. The heart of the South is beginning to sink in despair." So wrote a white Alabamian in 1866 as the South struggled to rise from the ashes of war. Other southerners had different feelings. The blacks who voted for the first time under Radical Reconstruction looked forward to electing new governments. By July 1868, most of the South was back in the Union; all states had returned by 1871. The new governments turned to rebuilding the South's tattered economy.

The Difficulty of Rebuilding

The devastation caused by the war made southern economic recovery extremely difficult. United States currency was scarce in the South, and Confederate dollars were worthless.

Deeply in debt, the South's planters and small farmers looked for a way to begin again. Many planters and farmers were forced to sell their land in order to survive. Others bought supplies on credit at high prices and high interest rates. They promised to repay the loans when the crops were harvested, but each year, more planters and farmers found themselves going deeper into debt. 3.

Poor white farmers and poor black farmers who owned no land of their own had to work on other people's land either as tenants or as sharecroppers. **Tenants** rented land and supplied their own seed and supplies. Some tenants sold their crops and paid their rent in cash, but many paid "in kind," by giving the landowner a portion of the crop.

Sharecroppers gave a portion of the crops they raised to the landowner. Usually, one third of the crop went to the landowner, one third to the sharecropper, and one third to whoever provided seeds, fertilizer, and other supplies. The system gave blacks unwilling to work for their former masters a semblance of independence.

Many freedmen became sharecroppers with the idea of one day buying their own land. But few realized that dream. Instead, like many white southerners, they became locked into a system of debt that promised little more than year-to-year survival. 4.

New Forces in Southern Politics

Radical Reconstruction brought a revolution in southern politics. Black citizens could now take part in political life, while former Confederate officials could not. Two groups, whom

385

3. **PAST AND PRESENT** Have students compare the situation of the South in 1865 with that of developing countries burdened with large debts today.

4. **CRITICAL THINKING** Ask: What do you think kept poor whites and poor blacks from working together to better their position?

conservative southerners called carpetbaggers and scalawags, assumed a prominent role.

Carpetbaggers were northerners who settled in the South after the war and supported Radical Reconstruction. Southern whites viewed them as unscrupulous intruders from the North, seeking only personal gain. All carpetbaggers, however, did not fit that description. Some were Union soldiers who had remained in the South after the war. Others were teachers or ministers who had come to help the freedmen adjust to their new life.

Scalawags were white southerners who supported Radical Reconstruction. Many had been Unionists during the war. Although some southerners supported the Radicals in hopes of political or financial favor, many did so because they thought it was in the best interest of the South. James Longstreet, who had been one of Lee's most able generals, argued that the South needed to cooperate with the Radicals in order to regain economic stability.

The influence of carpetbaggers and scalawags varied from state to state. In Mississippi, the carpetbaggers controlled politics. In Tennessee, the scalawags did.

Black Americans held offices previously denied them, but their influence was far less than conservative whites claimed. Only in South Carolina did blacks win a majority in one house of the legislature, and in no state did they succeed in winning the governorship. Hiram R. Revels and Blanche K. Bruce, 1. both college-educated Mississippians, were the only blacks elected to the United States Senate during Reconstruction.

Actions of the Reconstruction Governments

The Radical Reconstruction government achieved some genuine improvements. Legislatures passed laws giving African-American citizens equal civil and political rights. For the first time, southern states established free public education for all children, although it was segregated in fact if not

2. **VISUAL EVIDENCE** Ask: How do you suppose these dispossessed southerners felt toward the government?

2. With the southern economy in ruins, fields unplanted, and many homes burned to the ground, many southern families moved west to rebuild their lives. Ironically, former Confederate soldiers and former slaves worked together as cowboys on western ranches.

A lawyer and a scholar, Representative Robert Brown Elliot of South Carolina was a southern black leader. Here he argues for a civil rights bill in the House of
1. Representatives in 1874. In a speech that lasted two days, Elliot said that African Americans had "never failed to lift their earnest prayers for the success of this government when the [Confederacy] was seeking to break up the Union . . . and to blot the American Republic from the galaxy of nations."

1. **VISUAL EVIDENCE** The words on the flag in the painting are from a speech of Elliot's. Have students discuss their meaning.

by law. New laws improved conditions in prisons and provided centers for the care of mentally and physically handicapped persons.

2. But the governments faced many problems. Since most of the South's experienced political leaders had been Confederates, the Reconstruction governments sometimes suffered from inexperience. New officeholders often found it difficult to handle their jobs, since they had little preparation for public service.*

———

*In the years before the war, southern legislatures were dominated by wealthy planters who had denied educational and political opportunities to lower- and middle-class whites and to all blacks.

Corruption also plagued the Reconstruction governments. One state legislature, for example, voted $1,000 to cover a member's bet on a horse race. Other items billed to the state included hams, perfume, clothing, champagne, and a coffin. (As you will read in Chapter 21, political corruption was common throughout the nation after the Civil War.)

Most white southerners bitterly opposed Radical Reconstruction. They resented northerners who came to the South and prospered while many southerners lost their land. As former Confederates, they hated to see southern Unionists in positions of power. And they feared and resented former slaves, who now 3. voted and held office in governments once controlled by wealthy whites.

387

2. **CITIZENSHIP** Have students think about the problems faced by freedmen. Ask: How did slave codes leave freedmen poorly prepared to cope after the war?

3. **VOCABULARY** *Solid South* first meant that blacks voted Republican and whites, Democratic. Later it meant the solid Democratic vote of the South.

Some southerners used satire to attack what they saw as the abuses of Reconstruction. This sheet
1. *music is for an 1869 song that poked fun at the carpetbagger. A Yankee figure walks into a southern town with his carpet bag labeled "Reconstruction."*

See p. T71.

SECTION 3 REVIEW

1. **Identify:** (a) Hiram R. Revels, (b) Blanche K. Bruce.

2. **Define:** (a) tenant, (b) sharecropper, (c) carpetbagger, (d) scalawag.

3. What factors made it difficult to rebuild the southern economy after the war?

4. What new groups entered southern politics after the war?

5. List two problems that plagued Reconstruction governments in the South.

6. **Critical Thinking** Why were southern governments after the war likely to become scapegoats?

4 Unfinished Business

READ TO UNDERSTAND

■ Why northerners lost interest in Reconstruction.

■ What tactics southern whites used to oust Radical Republicans.

■ How the 1876 election hastened the end of Reconstruction.

It is hard to say just when the Radical Republicans lost their momentum. Their power peaked when they first seized control of Reconstruction in 1867. In the years that followed, their power gradually eroded. All the while, southern conservatives worked diligently to "redeem" the South for the Democratic, or, as they called it, the "white man's," party. Finally, ten years after it had begun, Radical Reconstruction collapsed.

A Changing Political Climate

Radical Reconstruction faltered partly because the leadership of the Republican party changed. Thaddeus Stevens died in 1868; a 2. few Radicals lost their seats in the Senate, and others retired.

Radical Republicans hoped to restore their failing influence by nominating General Ulysses S. Grant for President in 1868. In a close election, Grant defeated the Democratic nominee, Governor Horatio Seymour of New York. Once in office, however, President Grant proved much less sympathetic to the Radicals' cause than they had hoped. He was also ill-prepared for the presidency.

As a military leader, Grant had been hard driving, stubborn, and thorough. As a political leader, he lacked experience, and often depended on the advice of others. Thus Grant rewarded many of his friends with public appointments. Several members of his cabinet swindled the government of millions of dollars.

By 1872, one group of Republicans, disillusioned with the corruption, had split with the Grant administration. Calling themselves Liberal Republicans, they ran their own candidate for President. But Grant won by an even greater margin than he had in 1868.

The North's Declining Interest in Reconstruction

The war still divided Americans in 1868 and even in 1872. But as the 1870s progressed, passions cooled. Northerners were increasingly inclined to forget the past and let southerners run their own governments—even if that meant blacks might lose the rights they had so recently gained.

Reports of corruption among carpetbaggers and scalawags shocked many Republicans who had supported Radical Reconstruction. They were also disheartened when some black officials, often through inexperience, became tainted by corruption.

Many northern business leaders argued for an end to Reconstruction. They believed that the Radical governments were preventing the South's economic expansion. Northern manufacturers wanted to invest in the South, but only if they could count on stable governments there. "We have tried this Reconstruction long enough," concluded one business leader. "Now let the South alone."

Ending Radical Rule

How could conservative southern whites regain control of the state governments from the Republicans? Some, particularly among the upper classes, believed that the best way to return to power was to accept the Radicals' changes, gain the goodwill of the new black voters, and woo them away from the Republicans into the Democratic party.

When Wade Hampton, a wealthy South Carolinian, ran for governor in 1876, he campaigned among blacks, telling them, "We want your votes; we don't want you to be deprived of them. . . . if we are elected, as far as in us lies, we will observe, protect, and defend the rights of the colored man as quickly as any man in South Carolina."

But a large number of white southerners rejected this strategy. Poor white farmers,

who were having trouble making a living, feared economic competition from blacks. Moreover, many white southerners, both rich and poor, resented the freedmen's right to vote and hold office. Groups of whites were determined to end the influence of carpetbaggers, scalawags, and blacks.

Pressure and intimidation were among the tactics used. Neighbors might snub southern whites sympathetic to Reconstruction. Landowners could pressure black tenant farmers to vote Democratic or not at all.

Other people resorted to force or the threat of it. In some areas, groups banded together in informal military groups or rifle clubs. They drilled openly in areas where blacks lived or sent armed pickets to prevent blacks from registering to vote.

Groups like the Ku Klux Klan, the Knights of the White Camellia, and the Society of the White Rose used floggings, hangings, and other acts of violence to frighten blacks and their white supporters. In this 1874 cartoon, Thomas Nast shows the plight of blacks. The Ku Klux Klan and the White League join together to keep blacks in a state "worse than slavery."

389

1. **VOCABULARY** The name *Ku Klux Klan* comes from the Greek word *kiklos,* meaning circle.

2. **BACKGROUND** Tilden had been an outspoken critic of Radical Reconstruction. As governor of New York, he won renown for attacking political corruption in the state.

Whites formed secret organizations such
1. as the Ku Klux Klan and the Knights of the White Camellia with the goal of ending Radical Republican rule in the South. The Klan burned houses of Republicans and whipped, shot, or hung blacks and sympathetic whites. Dressed in white robes and hoods, the Klan often rode at night, breaking up Republican meetings. Moderate southerners condemned such violence, and even some leaders of the Klan felt it had gone too far. But the Klan's campaign of intimidation kept many potential Republican voters away from the polls.

In 1870 and 1871, Congress passed the Force Act and Ku Klux Klan Act, outlawing the use of force to prevent people from voting and authorizing President Grant to use federal troops to enforce the laws. The Klan's activities diminished, but the threat of violence lingered. One by one, the southern states voted out the Radical Republican governments and replaced them with conservative ones. By 1876, only Louisiana, Florida, and South Carolina retained their Radical governments.

The Hayes-Tilden Compromise

The election year of 1876 found the Republicans in disarray. In 1874, southerners elected enough Democrats to Congress to give that party a majority in the House of Representatives and a near-majority in the Senate. Scandal after scandal had marred the Grant administration. With the issue of corruption so prominent, both parties nominated for President men with reputations as reformers. The Republicans chose Rutherford B. Hayes, an Ohio lawyer, and the Democrats selected
2. Governor Samuel Tilden of New York.

Tilden got 250,000 more popular votes than Hayes but was one vote short of the necessary 185 electoral votes. Hayes had 165 electoral votes. Both sides claimed the remaining 20 electoral votes, from Florida, Louisiana, and South Carolina, plus one from Oregon.

The Oregon vote eventually went to Hayes, but the decision in the other states was not easy. Florida, Louisiana, and South Carolina were the only southern states still
390 dominated by Republicans. Tilden had won

a majority of the popular vote in each state, but the Republican-controlled state election boards ruled that he had received his majority through fraud and intimidation of black voters. The Republicans claimed that many people, especially blacks, had been kept from voting for Hayes. Rival Republican and Democratic electors both claimed victory, voted for their candidate, and sent in a set of electoral votes.*

The nation now faced a terrible dilemma. Which electoral votes should be counted? Congress appointed a commission, consisting of seven Republicans, seven Democrats, and one independent, to decide the issue. At the last minute, however, a Republican replaced the independent, and Hayes had the votes to win the election.

Democrats were outraged, especially in the South. It seemed as if Hayes had stolen the election. Although hotheads talked of a new civil war, conservative southerners in Congress negotiated a compromise with the Republicans. In return for their support, Hayes promised federal aid to construct new railroads and to control floods along the Mississippi River. Most important, he pledged to remove the last federal troops still in the South and to end Reconstruction.

The End of Reconstruction

Rutherford B. Hayes took office on March 5, 3.
1877. In April, the last federal troops withdrew from South Carolina and Louisiana. Democrats now controlled state governments throughout the South.

Although Reconstruction was over, much remained to be done. The South had not recovered economically. Neither in the South 4. nor in the North had African Americans won true equality. As you will read in Chapter 21, in the years to come, blacks would lose many of the gains they had made.

Nonetheless, the postwar events had laid the foundation for change. The states had ratified two amendments, granting black

---

*According to the Constitution, the electors of each state send a list of their votes to the President of the Senate, who counts the votes in the presence of both the House and the Senate.

3. **PRESIDENTS** Hayes ended sex discrimination in proceedings of the Supreme Court. The first woman to practice before the Court was Belva Ann Lockwood.

4. **TECHNOLOGY** Students will read about the development of industry and recovery of agriculture in the South in Chapter 20.

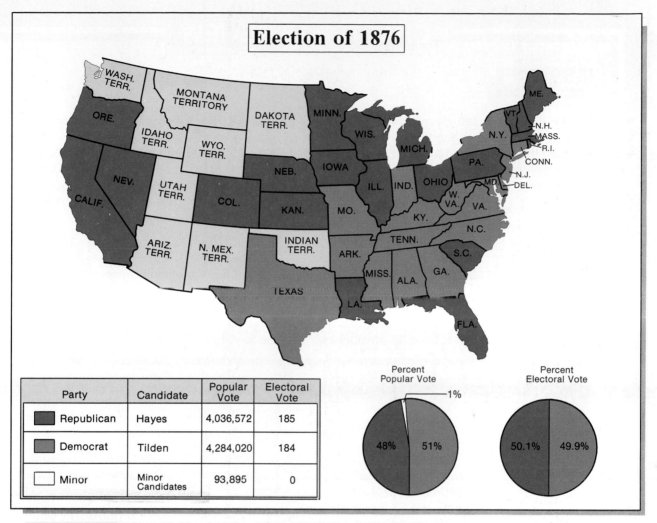

Election of 1876

Party	Candidate	Popular Vote	Electoral Vote
Republican	Hayes	4,036,572	185
Democrat	Tilden	4,284,020	184
Minor	Minor Candidates	93,895	0

Percent Popular Vote: 1%, 48%, 51%

Percent Electoral Vote: 50.1%, 49.9%

MAP STUDY *The election of 1876 was one of the closest—and most controversial—in American history. Rutherford B. Hayes eventually became President when a congressional commission awarded him the disputed electoral votes of Florida, Louisiana, and South Carolina. Which candidate had won the other southern states?* See p. T72.

1.

1. **MAP READING** Have students compare this map to the map on p. 347. Ask: In which election did more states vote for the Republican candidate?

Americans full rights of citizenship and the right to vote. Many years would pass before these rights would become a reality, but the amendments set standards toward which the country could aim. In later years, they would 2. become levers for freedom.

See p. T72.

SECTION 4 REVIEW

1. **Identify:** (a) Ku Klux Klan, (b) Force Act, (c) Ku Klux Klan Act, (d) Rutherford B. Hayes, (e) Samuel Tilden.

2. How did the death of Thaddeus Stevens and the defeat and retirement of other Radical Republicans affect Reconstruction?

3. Why were northern business leaders among those who sought an end to Radical Reconstruction?

4. Did the tactics used in the South to discourage blacks from voting succeed? Explain.

5. How did Rutherford B. Hayes gain support for his election from conservative southerners?

6. **Critical Thinking** How might qualities that benefited Ulysses S. Grant as an army general have limited his success as a President?

2. **ACTIVITY** Have students construct a time line showing the major events and stages of Reconstruction, from the end of the Civil War to the Hayes administration.

Summary

1. **The Civil War left deep scars.** Lincoln's moderate plan for reuniting the Union died when he was assassinated. Congress challenged President Andrew Johnson for control of Reconstruction.

2. **Alarmed by the Black Codes, Congress passed laws to protect blacks.** It also proposed the Fourteenth Amendment, guaranteeing their citizenship. After Radical Republicans won a two-thirds majority in Congress in 1866, they were able to override any presidential veto. Their attempt to remove President Johnson by impeachment failed, but it weakened his presidency.

3. **Under Radical Reconstruction, southern black men voted for the first time.** They helped to elect new state governments that Congress then readmitted to the Union. Although handicapped by inexperience and corruption, the new governments did institute important reforms.

4. **In the 1870's, support for the Radical Republicans faded.** More conservative state governments replaced those set up under Radical Reconstruction. Reconstruction ended in 1877 when President Hayes ordered the withdrawal of federal troops from the South.

See p. T72.

Vocabulary

Match each term on the left with its definition or description at right.

1. freedmen
2. tenants
3. share-croppers
4. carpet-baggers
5. scalawags

a. northerners who settled in the South after the Civil War and supported Radical Reconstruction

b. former slaves

c. people who rented farmland

d. people who shared with the landowner the crops they raised

e. white southerners who supported Radical Reconstruction

See p. T72.

Chapter Checkup

1. (a) Describe Lincoln's Reconstruction plan. (b) Why did he favor a moderate approach to restoring the southern states?

2. (a) What conditions did Johnson establish for readmission of the seceded states? (b) Why did Congress refuse to seat the southern representatives?

3. List three reasons why the Radical Republicans favored a harsh policy toward the South.

4. (a) Why did Congress propose the Fourteenth Amendment to the Constitution? (b) What was the major provision of this amendment? (c) What was the major provision of the Fifteenth Amendment?

5. (a) What were the results of the 1866 congressional elections? (b) Describe the program of Reconstruction adopted by the new Congress.

6. (a) What were the achievements of the Reconstruction governments in the South? (b) What problems did they have?

7. Describe the presidential election of 1876.

8. How did each of the following contribute to the collapse of Radical Reconstruction: (a) retirement of Radical leaders; (b) corruption in the Grant administration; (c) corruption in southern states; (d) desire for business expansion; (e) violence; (f) the Hayes-Tilden compromise.

See p. T73.

Critical Thinking

1. **Analyzing**   Do you think the Radical Republicans believed in a strict or loose interpretation of the Constitution? Give specific examples to support your answer.

2. **Predicting**   How might the history of Reconstruction have been different if Lincoln had not been assassinated?

See p. T73.

Connecting Past and Present

1. Disputes between the President and Congress are still common today. (a) What issues have divided the executive and legislative branches of the federal government in recent years? (b) How have they been resolved?

2. Like sharecroppers and tenant farmers of the Reconstruction South, many farmers today are deeply in debt. (a) How does the modern farmer's plight resemble that of the Reconstruction-era farmer? (b) How does it differ?

See p. T73.

Developing Basic Skills

1. **Comparing**   Make a chart with three columns. In column 1, list the provisions of Lincoln's Reconstruction policy. In column 2, list the provisions of Johnson's policy. In column 3, list the provisions imposed by the Radical Republicans. (a) Which policy was least severe? (b) Which policy was most severe? (c) Based on what you have read, how would you explain the differences?

2. **Map Reading**   Study the election map and graphs on page 391. (a) Which candidate received the most popular votes? (b) Which candidate received the most electoral votes? (c) Which candidate received most of the southern votes? How would you account for this?

WRITING ABOUT HISTORY

Using an Index for Old Newspapers

Newspapers provide up-to-the-minute information about current affairs. Most libraries have the index to *The New York Times* and back copies of the newspaper on microfilm. Larger libraries may have a complete collection of *The New York Times* on microfilm since it began publication in 1851.

The New York Times index has changed over the years. The sample below is from 1876. A sample of the current index is in the Chapter 19 Review. (See page 417.)

Practice: Use the sample index to answer the following questions. The labels will help you understand how to use the index.

1. What is the subject of the first article?

2. What is the date, page, and column of the article about Hayes's record as governor?

3. What is the subject of the article about R. B. Hayes in the December 10, 1876, issue of *The New York Times?*

Subject heading

Hayes, R. B., Governor of Ohio and President-Elect of the United States.
Acceptance: Letter of ...July   10–4-2
American Alliance
  and ....Oct.   5–6-1
Secretary L.S. Tyler's
  Letter ....Oct.   7–4-1
Character Sketch ....Dec.   10–6-3
Civil Service Reform,
  Record on ....Oct.   22–6-3
Governor; Record as ...Nov.   4-4-3

Article   Column
            Page
            Date

393

SPIRIT OF AMERICA
Equality in America

"We hold these truths to be self-evident, that all men are created equal . . ." That phrase from the Declaration of Independence is breathtakingly simple, yet at the same time extremely complex. Certainly, it was complex when the nation was embroiled in the conflict over slavery.

The Debate Over Equality   In their debates over slavery in 1858, Abraham Lincoln and Stephen Douglas struggled to define the "equality" referred to in the Declaration. Douglas argued that equality could not apply to blacks because the writers of the Constitution had permitted slavery to continue. The phrase "all men are created equal" must include only white men, Douglas concluded.

Lincoln replied that the Declaration's notion of equality was not a statement of fact. It was a goal—an ideal to work toward. As an example, he recalled a saying of Jesus: *As your Father in Heaven is perfect, be ye also perfect.* "The Savior, I suppose, did not expect that any human creature could be perfect as the Father in Heaven," said Lincoln, "but He . . . set that up as a standard, and he who did most towards reaching that standard, attained the highest degree of moral perfection. So I say in relation to the principle that all men are created equal, let it be as nearly reached as we can."

Lincoln and Douglas were neither the first nor the last to argue the meaning of equality. The debate has long been a central part of American history. For many years after the Declaration was written, the phrase "all men are created equal" did not mean that women, blacks, or Indians had the same rights as white men. In fact, in the years after the Revolution, only white, property-holding adult males had full equality before the law. And, even for those who had the same legal rights, factors such as education and wealth could limit the realization of equality.

What should be done about those conditions? How much should they be changed to make all Americans equal? James Fenimore Cooper, the novelist of the early 1800s, readily accepted the Declaration's guarantee of the right to "life, liberty, and the pursuit of happiness." But in his view, in practice, equality "can only mean a common misery."

The Continuing Struggle   But what if people could not compete equally because of past discrimination? Unlike Cooper, some Americans argued that society should step in to alter such situations. After the Civil War, for example, Radical Republicans claimed that it was not enough to free blacks from slavery. If blacks had been deprived of property for years, how could they be expected to compete with whites who had long owned property?

To solve this problem, Thaddeus Stevens proposed that the government break up rebel estates. "Give, if you please, 40 acres to each adult freedman," he urged. "This subdivision of the lands will yield ten bales of cotton to one that is made now, and he who produced it will own it and feel himself a man."

In the end, Congress failed to provide land for the freedman. As Frederick Douglass lamented, "The government . . . felt it had done enough for him. . . . He was free from the old plantation, but he had nothing but the dusty road under his feet."

Women, too, challenged notions of equality in the 1860s. In its Declaration of Sentiments, the Seneca Falls Convention of 1848 rephrased the principle of equality in

The career of Hiram Revels reflected the impact of the Civil War on the issue of equality. He was the first black member of the Senate and the first black lawyer admitted to try cases before the United States Supreme Court. He was also president of Alcorn College.

1. **VISUAL EVIDENCE** Ask: How does the artist show that Revels was the equal of the other lawyers in this picture?

the Declaration of Independence: "We hold these truths to be self-evident; that all men and women are created equal." Women's rights crusaders concentrated their efforts on the right to vote. Even after women finally were granted that right in 1920, however, the debate over equality for women did not end. For women, as well as for blacks, immigrants, and other minority ethnic groups, equality was still a goal—not a reality.

A New View of Equality The civil rights movement of the 1960s, sometimes referred to as the "second Reconstruction," opened a new chapter in the ongoing debate over the meaning of equality. President John F. Kennedy reminded Americans, "This nation . . . was founded on the principle that all men are created equal. . . . Every Ameri-

can ought to have the right to be treated as he would wish to be treated."

The civil rights movement resulted in legislation designed to end the discrimination that had threatened equality for so many years. In particular, the Civil Rights Act of 1964 prohibited discrimination on the basis of race, sex, or ethnic origin.

Yet the civil rights movement of the 1960s raised the same question as Reconstruction had in the 1860s: Was it enough simply to grant equal rights? Should society step in and guarantee equal opportunity as well? As President Lyndon Johnson argued, "You do not bring a person who for years has been hobbled by chains and liberate him, bring him to the starting line of a race and then say, 'You are free to compete with all the others,' and still justly believe you have been completely fair."

In effect, the debate over civil rights during the 1960s brought into focus a new view of equality. This view went beyond granting everyone the right to run in the race *(equal rights)*. It went beyond giving the disadvantaged a head start in the race *(equal opportunity)*. Indeed, it went so far as to suggest that everyone should have the chance to finish the race at the same time *(equal results)*. Equality of results has proven to be the most controversial view of equality.

The emphasis on equality in the Declaration of Independence ensured that Americans would never stop seeking to define its meaning as broadly as possible. Like the nation's founders, Americans today are committed to the principle of equality. They will continue to debate the meaning of equality and seek it for years to come.

See p. T73.

1. How did Abraham Lincoln define equality?

2. **Critical Thinking** Why do you think the civil rights movement of the 1960s has been called the "second Reconstruction"?

Notable Americans

Josephine White Griffing

In the 1800s, most American women were confined to traditional roles—daughter, wife, mother. For most of her life, Josephine White Griffing fit this pattern. But at age 36, she started on a course that turned her into one of the leading figures in the struggle for equality in America.

Born in 1814, the daughter of a Connecticut state legislator, Josephine White received her education at home. At age 21, she married Charles Griffing, a machinist. They later had five daughters. Seven years after their marriage, the Griffings moved to Litchfield, Ohio. It was there, around 1850, that Josephine Griffing heard the speech that changed her life.

A group of abolitionists were touring the Midwest, and Griffing attended one of their lectures. Inspired by their cause, she joined the Western Anti-Slavery Society and began to write for an antislavery newspaper. The Griffing home became a stop on the underground railroad, offering rest and safety to slaves on their way north to freedom.

At a time when women rarely spoke in public, Griffing became a powerful speaker. She addressed hundreds of antislavery meetings, moving audiences with her accounts of the cruel separation of slave families. She also learned how to lobby Congress for her cause. Toward the end of the Civil War, she moved to Washington, D.C., with her daughters.

As the war ended, Griffing turned to the task of helping newly freed slaves build new lives. She convinced influential senators to set up the Freedmen's Bureau to aid former slaves. But Griffing soon grew impatient with the bureau's inefficiency. She asked private charitable groups for more help.

Griffing personally led groups of blacks to northern cities to help them find jobs. When all else failed, she opened her own home to ex-slaves who were too old or sick

1. **VISUAL EVIDENCE** Ask: What skills are the women in this picture learning?

1. *Josephine Griffing was one of many white women who taught young black women basic skills at freedmen's schools like this one.*

to care for themselves. Some critics said that she was encouraging "laziness" among the blacks. She replied that the nation had to set right its past treatment of blacks. Just freeing the slaves was not enough.

Busy as she was, Griffing also became active in the fight for women's rights. She helped found the Ohio Woman's Rights Association and became its president in 1853. Like other women in the antislavery movement, she saw that she could influence political affairs. As a result, she turned her efforts to winning women the right to vote.

Her endless labors cost her dearly. She and her husband separated, and her health began to fail. When Josephine Griffing died at age 57, the fight for equality was still just beginning.

See p. T73.

1. How did Josephine Griffing become active in the antislavery cause?

2. **Critical Thinking** Why do you think many women abolitionists became leaders of the women's rights movement?

Voices of Freedom

Celebrating Emancipation

Emancipation marked the first meaningful step for blacks in their search for equality. On the day the Emancipation Proclamation was issued—January 1, 1863—Union Colonel Thomas Higginson held a formal celebration at his headquarters on the Sea Islands of Georgia. In this account of the celebration, Higginson reveals the joy and hope of the newly freed slaves present at the event.

The colors were presented to us by the Rev. Mr. French, a chaplain who brought them from the donors in New York. Then followed an incident so simple, so touching, so utterly unexpected and startling, that I can scarcely believe it on recalling, though it gave the keynote to the whole day. The very moment the speaker had ceased, and just as I took and waved the flag, which now for the first time meant anything to these poor people, there suddenly arose, close beside the platform, a strong male voice (but rather cracked and elderly), into which two women's voices instantly blended, singing, as if by an impulse that could no more be repressed than the morning note of the songsparrow, "My Country, 'tis of thee, / Sweet land of liberty, / Of thee I sing!"

People looked at each other, and then at us on the platform, to see whence came this interruption, not set down in the bills. Firmly and irrepressibly the quavering voices sang on, verse after verse; others of the colored people joined in; some whites on the platform began, but I motioned them to silence. I never saw anything so electric; it made all other words cheap; it seemed the choked voice of a race at last unloosed. Nothing could be more wonderfully unconscious; art could not have dreamed of a tribute to the day of jubilee that should be so affecting; history will not believe it; and when I came to speak of it, after it was ended, tears were everywhere. . . . Just think of it!—the first day they had ever had a country, the first flag they had ever seen which promised anything to their people, and here, while mere spectators stood in silence, waiting for my stupid words, these . . . souls burst out in their song, as if they were by their own hearths at home! When they stopped, there was nothing to do for it but to speak, and I went on; but the life of the whole day was in those unknown people's song.

Adapted from Thomas Wentworth Higginson, *Army Life in a Black Regiment* (Boston, 1882).
See p. T73.

1. What was the occasion for the celebration?

2. What incident did Higginson consider the highlight of the celebration?

3. **Critical Thinking** Why did Higginson motion to whites on the platform to stop singing?

Unit Six TRANSFORMING A NATION

The Homestead Act, which offered land to settlers, encouraged many Americans to move onto the Great Plains.

By the late 1800s, more immigrants to the United States were arriving from eastern and southern Europe.

	1865	1870	1875	1880	1885
POLITICS AND GOVERNMENT			**1872** Crédit Mobilier scandal is first one of Grant presidency		**1883** Civil Service Act passed
SOCIETY AND CULTURE		**1869** Wyoming grants women right to vote		**1881** Tuskegee Institute founded for black students	
ECONOMICS AND TECHNOLOGY			**1870** Rockefeller founds Standard Oil	**1876** Invention of telephone revolutionizes communication	
WORLD EVENTS	**1866** Atlantic cable provides rapid communication with Europe			**1882** United States bars Chinese immigration	

| Johnson | Grant | Hayes | Arthur |

Garfield

398

The Plains Indians respected nature and believed that the arrival of settlers from the East threatened their way of life.

1878 Thomas Edison invented the phonograph, which was patented in 1878.

UNIT OUTLINE

During the Gilded Age, wealthy people indulged in elaborate decorations, such as this Tiffany lamp.

Late 1800s Museums were among the attractions of the expanding cities.

1885	1890	1895	1900	1905

1887 Dawes Act tries to bring Indians into American mainstream

1895 More than half of federal employees are in the civil service

1889 Addams founds Hull House

1893 Columbian Exposition celebrates American progress and industry

1887 ICC set up to regulate railroads

1894 Coxey's Army protests the government's silver policy

1897 Wheat crop failure in Europe creates demand for American farm exports

| Cleveland | Harrison | Cleveland | McKinley | Roosevelt |

The steel industry grew rapidly in the late 1800s. This painting shows steelworkers at lunch time.

As railroads expanded, they offered more comforts to passengers, including a reclining chair seat.

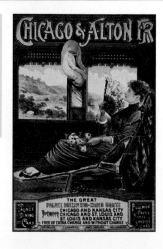

The Western Frontier (1865–1914)

19

CHAPTER OUTLINE

1 Visions of the West

2 Opening of the West

3 Tragedy for the Plains Indians

4 The Cattle Frontier

5 The Sodbusters' Frontier

CHAPTER OBJECTIVES After completing this chapter, students should be able to
1. explain how mines and railroads spurred settlement of the West.
2. describe causes and results of conflicts between settlers and Indians.
3. explain the rise and fall of the Cattle Kingdom.
4. list ways that plains farmers adapted to severe hardships.

CHAPTER PREVIEW Have students list the different peoples and occupations described in the chapter. Ask: How might different groups have contributed to the ways of life in the West? What possible conflicts might have developed among these groups? Why?

"I have heard that you intend to settle us on a reservation near the mountains. I don't want to settle. . . . A long time ago this land belonged to our fathers. But when I go up the river I see the camps of soldiers on its banks. These soldiers cut down my timber. They kill my buffalo. . . . I feel as though my heart will burst with sorrow."

The speaker was the Kiowa chief Satanta, or "White Bear." The occasion was a peace council at Medicine Creek Lodge in Kansas. On one side were more than 5,000 Indians—Kiowa, Comanche, Cheyenne, Arapaho. On the other side were commissioners of the United States government.

It was October 1867, and one of the thorniest problems facing Washington policy makers was how to deal with the western Indians. Land-hungry settlers were pouring into Indian territory. They were eager to carve out farms and ranches. But these were Indian lands. At Medicine Creek Lodge, the commissioners presented Congress's plan. If the Indians would sign treaties giving up their hunting grounds, they would receive tracts of land and be supplied with tools and livestock. They would settle down to become farmers and ranchers.

Such a prospect filled warriors like Satanta with grief. But the treaties promised peace and freedom, and the Indians signed them. In the words of another Kiowa chief, Setangya: "We thank the Great Spirit that . . . the old days of peace and friendship [are] to come again. . . . The green grass will not be stained with the blood of the whites."

But the grass was to be stained—with both white and Indian blood. When promises to supply the Indians with provisions and clothing were not kept, some warriors raided white settlements for food and ammunition. By the time the fighting was over, Satanta was dead, his heart broken by being denied the freedom to ride the plains.

Treaties and peace councils did little to protect the Indians from the steady advance of white settlers. It was only a matter of time before farms and ranches replaced the great open range of the West.

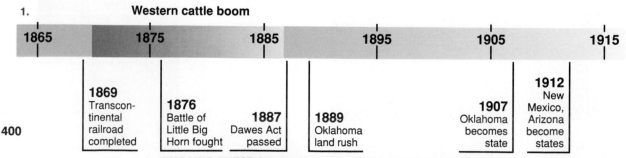

1.

Western cattle boom

1865	1875	1885	1895	1905	1915

1869 Transcontinental railroad completed

1876 Battle of Little Big Horn fought

1887 Dawes Act passed

1889 Oklahoma land rush

1907 Oklahoma becomes state

1912 New Mexico, Arizona become states

400

1. **TIME LINE QUESTION** Ask: How long after the Oklahoma land rush did Oklahoma become a state?

The arrival of white settlers on the Great Plains meant the end of a way of life for the Indians living there. This clash of cultures often led to bloodshed. In this painting by Frederic Remington, Indian scouts help United States Army troops find a trail.

1. **VISUAL EVIDENCE** Frederic Remington (1861–1909) was the most popular of many artists who depicted life in the American West. He prided himself on his skill at drawing horses.

2. **GEOGRAPHY** Have students locate the Great Plains on the map on pp. 840–841. Ask: Which states were carved out of the Great Plains? (regions)

1 Visions of the West

READ TO UNDERSTAND

■ What conditions were like on the Great Plains.

■ How the American Indians lived on the Great Plains.

■ How different groups viewed the land of the West.

In the early 1800s, explorers who visited the region of the Great Plains reported enormous tracts "where the wind has thrown up the sand in all the fanciful forms of the ocean's rolling waves, and on which not a speck of vegetable matter existed." They dubbed the area the "Great American Desert," and for many years settlers were quite content to leave the region to the Indians. After the Civil War, however, settlers began to push into the plains, and their vision of the area quickly came into conflict with that of the Indians who already lived there.

GEOGRAPHY AND HISTORY

Life of the Plains Indians

The Great Plains, stretching from about the 100th meridian to the Rocky Mountains, are a vast semiarid grassland. Far from moist ocean winds, most of the plains get under 20 inches (50 centimeters) of rainfall a year, less than half the amount received by most eastern areas. When the first settlers arrived, the plains were covered with grass and scrub, with occasional trees in a river bottom.

As you have read in Chapter 1, before the arrival of the Europeans, many Plains peoples were nomadic hunters. At that time there were no horses in North America, so the Indians hunted buffalo and other game on foot. Later, Spanish explorers brought European horses to the Americas. Over the years, some horses strayed. Herds of wild horses gradually migrated north from Mexico onto the Great Plains. In the 1700s, Plains Indians began to tame the horses, and by the 1780s, most groups had become accomplished riders.

On horseback, the Kiowa, Sioux, Crow, Comanche, Cheyenne, Arapaho, Blackfeet, and

3. **ECONOMICS** The horse also became a major commodity for trade among Plains Indians. Families with many horses to trade or give away attained a high social status in some tribes.

401

1. **ECONOMICS** One historian wrote that, to the Plains Indians, the buffalo was a "galloping department store." Have students comment on the statement.

2. **GEOGRAPHY** The *artesian springs* formed by these types of wells have become a major source of water in many arid areas. (interactions)

other Indian nations could ride hundreds of miles to hunt buffalo. The Plains Indians prospered and their population tripled, reaching about 150,000 by the mid-1800s. Yet, because the plains were so vast, they remained sparsely settled.

Buffalo supplied the Plains Indians with most of the necessities of life. The carcass provided meat, and what could not be eaten right away was dried for use during winter. Buffalo hides were used to make teepees and clothing, sinew was made into thread and bowstrings, bones into tools, and horns into eating utensils. Dried buffalo dung became fuel, and the rough side of the tongue served

1. as a hairbrush. Most of the Indians hunted only enough buffalo to supply their needs, and so did not threaten the survival of the herds. ■

GREAT DEBATE

American Indian Vision of the West

The Indians of the West believed that the natural world was in close harmony with the spirits who governed it. Only by maintaining

a proper relationship with the many spirit-gods would the Indians be rewarded with success in hunting and in war. Accordingly, the purpose of Indian religious rituals was to achieve harmony with the spiritual world.

The Plains Indians disturbed the land and its creatures as little as possible. Any wasteful or harmful use of the environment upset their vision of a balanced world. But all this changed drastically with the arrival of settlers from the East, whose ideas about the relationship of people to the land were very different from those of the Indians.

Settlers' Visions of the West

On the Fourth of July, 1868, William Gilpin, the first territorial governor of Colorado, delivered an enthusiastic speech on the future of the Great Plains. Limited rainfall would be overcome by wells drilled deep into the ground, he declared. Crops would be planted 2. in the newly fertile soil. As a result of the new vegetation—and here Gilpin was expressing a belief shared by many at the time—the climate would change and rainfall would in-

3. **VISUAL EVIDENCE** Like Frederic Remington, Charles Russell (1864–1926) specialized in paintings of the West. He spent eleven years as a cowboy in Montana.

During buffalo hunts, Indian women were responsible for moving the camp from one hunting site to the next. They broke down the old camp and packed everything on a travois. Then, with the children, they traveled to the new site.

3. *Charles M. Russell captures this activity in his painting* Following the Buffalo Run.

1. *For the Kiowa, as for other Plains people, vast buffalo herds provided food, clothing, and shelter. Kiowa warrior Two Hatchets, shown here, typifies the dignity of the Plains Indians.*

1. **ACTIVITY** Have interested students research the Kiowa Indians and report their findings to the class.

crease. The "Great American Desert" would become a fertile garden.

A year later, a young man who was to reject Gilpin's vision began his own trek westward. John Wesley Powell was a striking figure and a magnetic leader. Fighting as a volunteer in the Civil War battle of Shiloh, he had lost his right arm at the elbow. Undaunted, he returned to active service and rose to become a major. Additionally, Powell was a trained geologist.

In 1869, Powell set out on a scientific expedition down the Colorado River through the Grand Canyon. As he mapped the Grand Canyon and studied the surrounding areas, Powell developed his own vision of how the land should be used. Settlement of the West, Powell claimed, was subject to one overriding fact: water was scarce throughout. In the rainy East, a farmer could make an adequate living on 160 acres (64 hectares). In the arid West, Powell said, a farmer would need 1,200 acres (480 hectares) of unirrigated land.

With water so scarce, Powell saw a need for cooperation among western settlers. In the East, a farmer could do whatever he wanted with a river flowing through his prop-

erty. In the West, Powell warned, the use of water would somehow have to be regulated and shared. 2.

Powell's warning went largely unheeded. Beginning in the 1860s, the relationship of the Plains Indians to the land would be challenged by miners, railroad builders, ranchers, and farmers who came west with their own dreams and hopes. Many of the earliest settlers shared Gilpin's vision of a land of unlimited resources. Gradually, however, the majority of them discovered the hardships 3. posed by the harsh climate. ■

See p. T74.

SECTION 1 REVIEW

1. **Identify:** (a) William Gilpin, (b) John Wesley Powell.

2. List one climatic and one topographical feature of the Great Plains.

3. (a) How did the Plains Indians make use of the buffalo? (b) How did the Plains Indians treat the land?

4. (a) What was the Native American view of the West? (b) What was Gilpin's vision? (c) What was Powell's vision?

5. **Critical Thinking** How would you account for the different views of the West held by the Indians, Gilpin, and Powell?

4. **VOCABULARY** Have students look up these terms in the glossary before they begin reading.

2 Opening of the West

READ TO UNDERSTAND

■ How the discovery of rich mineral deposits brought thousands of people to the West.

■ What life was like in the mining towns of the West.

■ How new means of transportation helped to open the West to settlement.

■ *Vocabulary:* vigilante, public domain. 4.

Why would anyone want to settle the vast empty middle of America? People who crossed the Great Plains on the journey to Oregon or **403**

3. **DISCUSSION** Have students compare the visions of the West offered by Gilpin and Powell. Ask: On what points do they disagree? Do they have any points of agreement?

ECONOMICS Henry Comstock struck gold in the Sierras in 1859. He often complained that blue mud made the gold hard to reach. When a Mexican miner told him that blue mud was loaded with silver, Comstock realized he had one of the richest silver mines in the world.

California told of the "dreary monotony of sun-scorched plains," an unpleasant landscape to be crossed as quickly as possible and then forgotten. But the hunger for land changed people's minds. The completion of the first transcontinental railroad tied the resources of the West to urban markets in the East and in Europe. By the 1860s, settlers were flooding into the plains region.

The New Mining Frontier

When the gold fields in California's first Gold Rush in the late 1840s were played out, prospectors set out to find new strikes. From California, they pushed east into the Sierra Nevadas and the Rockies.

New strikes came in the late 1850s, in western Nevada. Over the next 20 years, the Comstock Lode near Virginia City yielded more than $300 million in gold and silver, the richest mining strike to that time.

To the north, miners discovered valuable mineral deposits in the Columbia and Fraser river valleys. They also made strikes in Idaho and Montana along the Bitter Root and Salmon River mountain ranges. Farther east in Colorado, mining towns such as Denver, Boulder, and Colorado Springs grew up near gold strikes. (See the map on page 412.)

Even more than in the earlier California mines, extraction of the mineral riches from these deposits required large enterprises. In
1. strikes like the Comstock Lode, the richest deposits lay well underground and could not be mined without costly tools. Organized investors with large sums of money for rock-crushing machinery and drills that could bore down 1,000 (300 meters) or more had a great
2. advantage in exploiting the new finds.

From Mining Camps to Towns and Cities

Gold and silver strikes brought thousands of people to the West. They built towns and settled down. Often, however, mineral deposits played out quickly and people moved on, leaving empty ghost towns behind.

Sometimes mining towns were built even before a big strike had been made. In 1858, prospectors found a few ounces of gold in Colorado streams. Farsighted planners bought up the surrounding land and began laying out the streets of Denver and erecting cabins. When rich deposits were found the next year, Denver prospered. By 1860, it had a lending library, two newspapers, a theater, a schoolteacher, and a barber who encouraged miners to "get your beards mowed."

Although most miners were men, enterprising women also profited in the new boom towns. With only a few dollars, a woman could open a boardinghouse and make a tidy fortune. Cooking and baking paid well, too. One ambitious woman reported that in less than a year she had baked and sold $18,000 worth of pies.

Although makeshift governments tried to keep the peace, disorder and lawlessness often accompanied this rapid growth of towns. Miners resorted to organizing groups of **vigilantes.** These self-appointed law enforcers tracked down outlaws and sometimes hung them.

Informal methods of government gradually gave way to more formal arrangements. In 1861, Colorado, Dakota, and Nevada were organized as territories; Idaho and Arizona followed in 1863 and Montana in 1864. Although wild mining towns would continue to spring up in the West through the mid-1870s, the process of more permanent settlement had begun.

Transportation Opens the West

When news of gold strikes in Colorado first reached the East in 1859, transportation between the two regions was limited. Few railroads extended west of the Mississippi River. The coming years would see a rapid extension of transportation. (See the map on page 412.)

In the 1850s, the first stagecoach lines began linking East and West. Travelers who could afford the $200 fee and were willing to wait 10 days for a seat on the stage could travel from Missouri to California in about 20 days. Passengers rode three abreast in an elegant coach complete with broad iron "tire" wheels that did not sink in the sand. The bumpy ride was grimy and exhausting.

Yet few passengers cared to take advantage of the lodging available at the way sta-

3.

2. **READING** Students who want to find out more about the effect of mining on western settlement can read *Mining Frontiers of the Far West, 1848–1880* by Rodman W. Paul.

3. **READING** Both Bret Harte and Mark Twain wrote about life in western mining camps. Interested students might read short stories by these authors.

For two years, the riders of the Pony Express galloped across the West. Stations were located every 10 to 20 miles along the route. A rider would stop at a station just long enough to exchange his exhausted horse for a fresh mount. This painting by Frederic Remington is titled The Coming and Going of the Pony Express.

1.

1. **VISUAL EVIDENCE** Have students compare this painting by Remington to the one on p. 401.

tions where stage drivers changed horses. The accommodations were a few bunks covered with old rags and buffalo robes. The floors, grumbled one traveler, were "much like the ground outside, only not nearly so clean."

Improved mail service could also be had, at a price. Started in 1860, the Pony Express delivered a letter from St. Joseph, Missouri, to Sacramento, California, in ten days. Eighty riders sped east and west along a route almost 2,000 miles (3,200 kilometers) long,
2. working in relays to deliver the mail. The Pony Express lasted less than two years, and even at $5 per letter was never profitable. By 1862, wires crossed the plains, and messages could be transmitted instantly using the telegraph, invented by Samuel Morse in 1844.

Linking East and West by Rail

As eastern railroads expanded in the 1850s, westerners began to demand rail service to the Pacific. But building a transcontinental railroad posed major problems. Most lines in the East were run by small companies.

The funds needed to build a railroad to the Pacific were beyond the means of most private investors, especially since builders would have to cut through both the Sierra Nevadas and the Rocky Mountains.

Government's Role   In 1862, the government stepped in. It offered railroad companies land in the West as an incentive to build a transcontinental line. The government had acquired the land through treaties or by buying it from the Indians. (See the map on page 408.) Land that belongs to the nation and not to individuals is called **public domain.** For every mile (1.6 kilometers) of track laid, Congress granted the railroads 20 square miles (52 square kilometers) of land plus a 400-foot-wide (120-meter) right of way. In addition, Congress agreed to lend the railroads money for every mile of track completed.

Race to the Finish   In 1863, the laying of the first section of track for the transcontinental railroad started one of the greatest races in American history. Two companies competed for the government grants and loans. Union Pacific crews laid their first tracks in Nebraska and began to move westward. The workers of the Central Pacific   **405**

2. **BACKGROUND** One exhausted Pony Express rider, on reaching his last station, found that the rider who was to relieve him had died. "I did not hesitate to undertake an extra ride of 85 miles and I arrived on time," boasted the young rider. He later won fame as Buffalo Bill Cody.

1. **BACKGROUND** Entire crews were sometimes buried by avalanches—the bodies, frozen solid with picks and shovels in hand, often not found until spring.

2. **TECHNOLOGY** The Union Pacific laid 1,085 miles of track and the Central Pacific laid 689 miles to reach Promontory Point.

started in Sacramento, California, and moved eastward.

The workers of the Central Pacific had to break through the high Sierra Nevadas. In the first four years, they laid only about 100 miles (160 kilometers) of track. Charles Crocker, in charge of the Central Pacific crews, was determined to conquer the difficult route.

Crocker supervised about 10,000 Chinese laborers who had been hired when other workers were unwilling to take on the dangerous task of bridging the mountains. The Chinese had to break through solid granite walls and cart away tons of rubble in baskets and wheelbarrows. The work was so difficult that their progress sometimes dwindled to a mere 8 inches a day. When winter came, Crocker ordered his workers to dig tunnels through 40-foot snowdrifts in order to lay

1. track on the frozen ground. The strength and endurance of the Chinese workers contributed much to the completion of the transcontinental railroad.

To the east, the Union Pacific relied largely on Irish Americans, many of whom were Union veterans of the Civil War. Crossing the flat plains from Omaha, the work went quickly. As much as 3 miles (5 kilometers) of track might be laid between sunrise and sunset.

Every 60 miles (about 100 kilometers), the workers threw up a temporary town. As soon as the next stretch of track was complete, they pulled the buildings down, loaded the wood on a flatcar, and built a new town farther down the line. The towns included shacks for the men to live in as well as saloons, dance halls, and gambling tents.

By 1868, both crews had reached the flat Utah plains, and the pace of laying track increased. Since each company was eager to lay more track than the other, and thereby receive more government land and loans, the crews raced past each other without meeting. They continued putting down track until Congress ordered them to join at Promontory Point, Utah. On May 10, 1869, the sym- 2.

3. **DISCUSSION** Some 300 blacks also helped build the Union Pacific. Ask: Why do you think minorities and immigrants made up the majority of the work crews?

By 1869, railroad tracks connected the West Coast with the Midwest. Much of the backbreaking work of hacking out a railbed through the Sierra Nevadas was done
3. *by crews of Chinese workers. The workers in this painting cheer one of the first trains along a track they have built.*

1. **PAST AND PRESENT** The original golden spike is now at Stanford University, which was founded by Leland Stanford, president of the Central Pacific.

2. **VOCABULARY** Have students look up this word in the glossary before they begin reading.

1. bolic gold spike was driven into the ground with a silver hammer, and the nation celebrated the completion of its first transcontinental railroad.

Settlement Follows the Rails

In time, several major railroads linked West and East. By 1893, the Southern Pacific ran from New Orleans across Texas and along the Mexican border into California. The Santa Fe connected Missouri with southern California. The Northern Pacific and the Great Northern spanned the north, from the Great Lakes to Washington.

The railroad routes greatly influenced the course of development in the West. Towns grew quickly along the tracks. Railroads brought new settlers and ensured them of supplies and a way to send their products to eastern markets. The largest towns and cities—for example, Los Angeles—developed where major railroad lines met.

All across the West, the railroad brought growth and prosperity. With travel and transportation of goods made easier, it was not long before miners were followed by farmers and ranchers.

See p. T75.

SECTION 2 REVIEW

1. **Identify:** (a) Comstock Lode, (b) Pony Express, (c) Union Pacific Railroad, (d) Central Pacific Railroad, (e) Promontory Point, Utah.

2. **Define:** (a) vigilante, (b) public domain.

3. (a) Where were discoveries of gold and silver made in the 1850s and 1860s? (b) Why did ghost towns develop?

4. List the advantages and disadvantages of stagecoach travel.

5. What did the federal government do to encourage railroad companies to lay track in the West?

6. **Critical Thinking** Are railroads as important for transportation and communication today as they were in the 1800s? Explain.

3 Tragedy for the Plains Indians

READ TO UNDERSTAND

■ Why the Plains Indians felt bitterness toward settlers and miners.

■ How the government responded to the fighting on the Plains.

■ What efforts were made to improve the treatment of the Indians.

■ *Vocabulary:* reservation.   2.

Could Indians and whites live together in peace? When Andrew Jackson implemented his policy of removing all Indians to lands west of the Mississippi River in 1830, he ex- 3. pected conflict between the two cultures to end. But after 1840, the United States extended its boundaries to the Pacific. With foreboding, Indians watched the wagon trains snaking across the plains and heard the railroad whistles echoing in the distance. As the miners closed in from the West and more settlers arrived from the East, the Indians fought back to save their way of life.

Warfare on the Plains

In 1851, representatives of the United States government and the major Plains Indian nations met near Fort Laramie in Wyoming. In exchange for yearly payments, the Indians agreed to confine their hunting to specified regions. By containing the Indians in certain areas, the government hoped to limit conflict among Indian nations and between Indians and settlers.   4.

The agreement of 1851 quickly broke down because neither the government nor the Indian leaders could enforce it. The chiefs could not prevent members of their nations from hunting where they wished, and miners and settlers ignored Indian land claims.

During the Colorado gold rush of 1859, miners claimed land that less than a decade before had been promised "forever" to the Cheyenne and Arapaho nations. When United States agents forced Indian leaders to give up their land, many Indian nations declared **407**

3. **BACKGROUND** You may wish to review with students the Indian Removal Act that uprooted the southeastern Indian nations, discussed on pp. 250–253.

4. **BACKGROUND** In battle, Plains Indians valued "counting coup" more than killing. A warrior tried to ride close enough to an enemy to touch him with a coup stick.

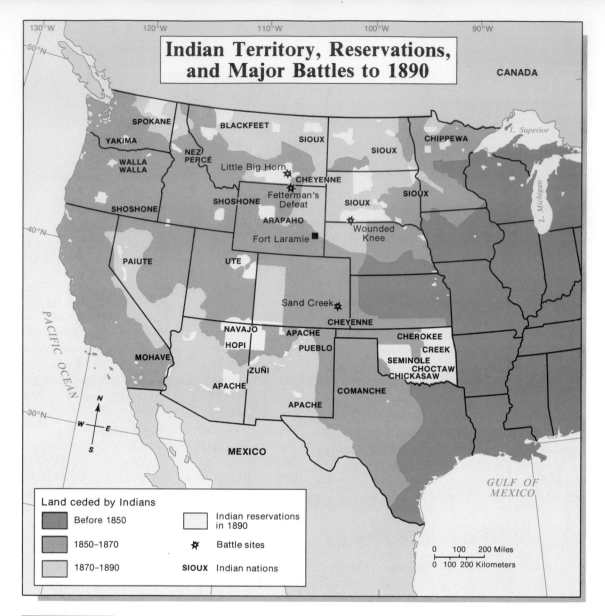

Indian Territory, Reservations, and Major Battles to 1890

CANADA

SPOKANE
YAKIMA
BLACKFEET
SIOUX
CHIPPEWA
L. Superior
NEZ PERCÉ
WALLA WALLA
Little Big Horn
CHEYENNE
SIOUX
SHOSHONE
Fetterman's Defeat
SIOUX
SIOUX
L. Michigan
SHOSHONE
ARAPAHO
Wounded Knee
Fort Laramie
PAIUTE
UTE
NAVAJO
HOPI
APACHE
PUEBLO
Sand Creek
CHEYENNE
CHEROKEE
CREEK
SEMINOLE
CHOCTAW
CHICKASAW
MOHAVE
ZUÑI
APACHE
COMANCHE
APACHE
MEXICO

PACIFIC OCEAN

GULF OF MEXICO

N
W   E
S

Land ceded by Indians

- Before 1850
- 1850–1870
- 1870–1890

- Indian reservations in 1890
- � Battle sites
- **SIOUX** Indian nations

0   100   200 Miles
0 100 200 Kilometers

See p. T76.

MAP STUDY   *The United States government had promised large tracts of western land to American Indians. However, most of that land was ceded back to the government. By 1890, Indians were restricted to the reservations shown on this map. In which area of the West were Apache reservations located? Where were the Sioux reservations?*

1.

1. **MAP READING**   Had Indians given up more land in California or in Nevada before 1870? Why?

war. In 1865, the Sioux went to war when the United States government announced its plan to build a road through Sioux hunting grounds to mining towns in Idaho and Montana.

The warfare was bitter. The Plains Indians were fighting for their homeland and their way of life against people who had consistently broken promises to them. Indians attacked many settlements. In 1866, Sioux in the Big Horn Mountains ambushed a detachment of troops led by Captain W. J. Fetterman, killing all 82 soldiers.

The miners and settlers believed they had a right to the land. Most felt they would make better use of it than the Indians had. Easterners were outraged by tales of Indian ambushes and torture.

United States troops often struck mercilessly at the Indians. In 1864, for example, Colonel John Chivington ordered his soldiers to slaughter 450 Cheyenne men, women, and children at Sand Creek, Colorado, after the Cheyenne had been guaranteed protection. "I have come to kill Indians," Chivington de-

2.

408

2. **BACKGROUND**   Sioux chief Red Cloud, who led several raids on U.S. forts in the 1860s, recalled one broken treaty: "We kept this treaty . . . we never committed any murder or depredation until afterward the troops were sent into that country, and the troops killed our people and ill-treated them. . . ."

1. **CRITICAL THINKING** Have students discuss Chivington's statement. Ask: Is his attitude correct in a time of war? Do civilians have the right to protection?

2. **ECONOMICS** The discovery of gold on their land began the Nez Percé's troubles. Ask: How did economic factors contribute to the problems of other Plains Indians?

clared, "and believe it is right and honorable to use any means under God's heaven to kill them."

Outcome of the Wars

The conflicts in the West convinced the government that a new Indian policy was needed. In 1867 and 1868, government agents demanded that the Plains nations move to **reservations,** areas specifically set aside for them. The Indians of the southern plains were to be relocated on a poor, unproductive tract in Oklahoma. The northern nations were to be confined to the Black Hills area of the Dakota Territory. Major Indian leaders agreed to the demands but many Indians did not, and warfare on the plains continued.

Even the Indians who moved to the reservations were not left in peace. In 1874, rumors of gold drew miners to the Black Hills. Thousands of prospectors rushed to stake claims despite the fact that the land had been given as a permanent home to the Sioux.

In June 1876, Colonel George Custer led a detachment of 265 men into the heart of Sioux country against the Indians. But he found himself outmaneuvered. Crazy Horse, Sitting Bull, and Rain-in-the-Face led a Sioux force of 2,500 that killed Custer and all his men in fierce fighting along the Little Big Horn River.

Victory was short-lived, however. United States troops continued to pursue the Sioux, and in the autumn of 1876, Crazy Horse was captured and most of the Sioux surrendered.

In the years that followed, a few nations continued to resist, but in vain. In 1877, Chief Joseph led the Nez Percé (NEHZ puhr SAY) of Oregon and Idaho in a skillful, defensive campaign across 1,000 miles (1,600 kilometers) before he was forced to surrender near the Canadian border. The Apache of Arizona, led by their determined chief, Geronimo, held out until 1886.

Individuals on both sides deplored the tragedy. Chief Joseph put aside his weapons. "I am tired of fighting," he declared sadly.

> Our chiefs are killed. . . . The little children are freezing to death. My people, some of them, have run away to the hills and have no blankets, no food. . . . Hear me, my chiefs,

I am tired; my heart is sick and sad. From where the sun now stands, I will fight no more forever.

General Philip Sheridan, the Civil War veteran who led many campaigns against the Indians, was also aware of the injustice of the conflict. "We took away their country and their means of support, broke up their mode of living, their habits of life, introduced disease and decay among them, and it was for this and against this that they made war. Could anyone expect less?"

A Vanishing Way of Life

The Indians lost more than battles and land. One of the most devastating blows was the destruction of the buffalo herds that had been central to Plains Indian culture. Beginning in the 1860s, the herds dwindled. Thousands of animals were slaughtered to provide food for railroad crews laying tracks across the prairie. Buffalo hunting became a fashionable sport, with trainloads of easterners shooting at the animals from the comfort of railroad cars.

The final blow came in the 1870s, when merchants discovered a thriving market for buffalo hides in the East. Commercial hunters shot animals by the thousands. The number of buffalo on the plains decreased from 13 million in 1860 to a few hundred in 1900.

4. **VISUAL EVIDENCE** Ask: Do you think this artist sympathized with the Indians? Why?

Hunting buffalo was central to the life of Plains Indians. When commercial hunters from the East destroyed the buffalo herds, they also destroyed a way of life.

3. **BIOGRAPHY** Buffalo Bill Cody (1846–1917) got his nickname by slaughtering some 4,000 buffalo in 18 months while working for the Kansas Pacific Railroad. He later exhibited live buffalo as a rarity in his famous Wild West Show.

1. **READING** In 1884, Jackson wrote *Ramona*, a novel dealing with the plight of the Plains Indians. It was hailed as the *Uncle Tom's Cabin* of Indian policy. Interested students might read it and report to the class.

With the buffalo nearly gone, the Plains Indians could no longer support themselves as they always had. Driven onto reservations, they were forced to depend on the government for food.

Unfortunately, the corruption that became widespread in government after the Civil War also affected Indian policy. Money meant to purchase food supplies often went directly into the pockets of government agents. Food that did find its destination was often spoiled. "No branch of the national government is so spotted with fraud, so tainted with corruption . . . as this Indian Bureau," concluded one member of the House of Representatives in 1869.

Calls for Reform

Many people, Indian and white, spoke out against the mistreatment of the Indians. Susette La Flesche, an Omaha Indian, campaigned vigorously on behalf of the Indians. Her father had been chief of the Omaha when that nation's hunting grounds had been reduced to a small reservation on the Missouri River. In the 1870s, La Flesche drew attention to Indian grievances through her writing and lecture tours.

One of the people La Flesche influenced was Helen Hunt Jackson. Incensed by the Indians' plight, Jackson wrote a book, *A Century of Dishonor* (1881), which vividly outlined the history of broken treaties between

1. the United States and the Indians.

Dawes Act Partly in response to public outcry, Congress passed the Dawes Act in 1887. The act aimed to break up the traditional tribal structure and bring Indians into the mainstream of American life. Reservation land, formerly held by the tribe in common, was parceled out to families and individuals in 160-acre (64-hectare) lots . Those who accepted land became full citizens of the United States. Congress also provided funds to support schools that would teach Indian children the "American" way of life.

The creators of the Dawes Act failed to

2. appreciate the strength of Indian traditions. Furthermore, settlers eager for additional land often tricked Indians into selling their lots

410 for a small price. Once again, Indian land ended up in the hands of others.

Wounded Knee Supporters of the Dawes Act hoped that, as part of their "Americanization," the Indians would give up their traditional religion. The Indians resisted, however. Looking back to their days of freedom, some of the Sioux began to practice a religious ritual that became known as the Ghost Dance. The Ghost Dance celebrated the sacred customs of the past and hailed the time when the Sioux would regain their independence.

Settlers near the Sioux reservations incorrectly interpreted the Ghost Dance as a call to war, and in 1890 they summoned troops to put an end to this activity. At Wounded Knee, South Dakota, the soldiers arrested a group of several hundred Indians and disarmed the men among them. In a moment of confusion a shot rang out, and the troops turned their machine guns on the defenseless Sioux. By the time the firing had ceased, nearly 300 men, women, and children had been killed or wounded.

For many Indians, the massacre at Wounded Knee symbolized the sad fate of their people. Although some made the transition to the "American" way of life, many others clung with determination to the Indian vision of what the West should be. Not able to return to the life they had known and unable or unwilling to adapt to a new culture, they had neither hope nor opportunity.

See p. T76.

SECTION 3 REVIEW

1. **Identify:** (a) Little Big Horn, (b) Chief Joseph, (c) Susette La Flesche, (d) Helen Hunt Jackson, (e) Ghost Dance, (f) Wounded Knee.

2. **Define:** reservation.

3. (a) Why did most of the Indians of the West go to war in the 1860s and 1870s? (b) What was the outcome of these wars?

4. How were the buffalo herds destroyed?

5. (a) What was the purpose of the Dawes Act? (b) List the provisions of the act.

6. **Critical Thinking** Based on their experiences, how would the settlers and the Indians view one another?

2. **ECONOMICS** Indians and whites had different ideas about the land. Most Indian cultures did not hold the belief that land could be owned.

1. **BACKGROUND** The Spanish had learned about horsemanship from the Moors, who lived in Spain for hundreds of years.

2. **VOCABULARY** Other words the cowboys borrowed from Spanish include *rodeo, bronco, stampede,* and *hoosegow.*

4 The Cattle Frontier

READ TO UNDERSTAND

■ What attractions lured cattle ranchers to the Great Plains.

■ What were the long drives.

■ Why the western cattle boom came to an end.

As the miners moved in from the West, another, quite different, group began pushing up from the South. Whoops of cowboys and the thundering hooves of cattle announced the arrival of this new wave of settlers. Drawn mainly from Texas by the prospect of unlimited grasslands, the new arrivals hoped to make their fortunes not by panning gold in the mountains but by raising cattle on the plains.

The New Cattle Country

As you have read in Chapter 13, the Spanish and then the Mexicans had established cattle ranches in the Southwest. The land there was so hospitable, in fact, that many cattle had thrived untended. By 1860, some 5 million head of wild cattle, known as longhorns, roamed freely across the grassy plains of Texas.

Despite the abundance of cattle, ranching developed slowly in Texas. The longhorn

THE AMERICAN EXPERIENCE

Spanish Heritage of the American Cowboy

The American cowboy, sitting tall in the saddle, hat over his eyes, is a legendary figure. Yet there could have been no cowboys without the Spanish settlers of the Southwest.

1. Between 1600 and 1845, Spaniards brought both cattle and horses to the New World. On the grassy plains of present-day Texas, New Mexico, Arizona, and southern California, they built large *ranchos,* or ranches, where *vacas* (VAH cahz), or cows, were tended by men known as *vaqueros* (vah KEHR ohz).

After the Civil War, American veterans of both sides, including many blacks, moved west. There they became "cowboys," adopting many Spanish words and customs from Mexican American settlers. The American cowboy wore a wide-brimmed *sombrero* (sahm BREHR oh), in Spanish "a hat that provides shade," to protect him from the sun and rain. He called other cowboys buckeroos, a corruption of vaquero.

The vaquero's special horned saddle became the western saddle of the cowboy. The cowboy draped his *riata* (ree AHT ah), or lariat, over the saddle horn and, after throwing his *lazo,* or lasso, around a calf, tied it to the horn so that the weight of his horse held the calf still. The cowboy's pointed-toe boots slipped easily into the stirrups of his saddle, and the boots' high heels kept him from slipping. The cowboy wrapped leather *chaparreras* (CHAP a RAY ras), or chaps, around his legs to protect them from thorny chaparral bushes.

Vaqueros often sang and played the guitar in the evenings on the open trail. English-speaking cowboys adopted this custom and created their own ballads, many of which are still popular today.

See p. T76.

1. What items and customs did the American cowboy adopt from the Spanish vaquero?

2. **Critical Thinking** In what other ways have Hispanic Americans contributed to American culture?

1. **LOCAL HISTORY** If your school is in the West, ask students to find out whether raising cattle contributed to the growth of the region.

2. **CRITICAL THINKING** Ask: Why do you think black Americans were attracted to the life of a cowboy?

was a tough and ill-tempered creature, its wiry frame providing very little tender meat. Besides, few buyers existed locally. And Texans had no way of transporting the beef to distant markets.

With the arrival of the railroads on the Great Plains, all that changed. The demand for beef was enormous in the rapidly growing cities of the East. Cattle purchased for $3 to $5 a head in Texas could be sold at a railhead, or shipping point, for $30 to $50 each. A rancher who marketed a herd of 3,000 steers could make a profit of $100,000 in one year.

In 1866, the closest railheads lay more than 1,000 miles (1,600 kilometers) to the north. Enterprising Texans took their cattle north on "long drives" across prairie country. The first herds reached the new depot of

Abilene, Kansas, in 1867. As the railroads pushed west during the next decade, new cattle centers sprang up at Ellsworth and Dodge City, Kansas. The cattle boom was on. **1.** (See the map below.)

The Long Drive

The men who drove the cattle north became heroes of American folklore. These cowboys, as they are called, owed much of their skill and many of their customs to the earlier Spanish vaqueros who had raised cattle on the open range in Mexico. (See page 411.) Large numbers of blacks and Mexican Americans joined the cattle drives. On the long drives, one out of every seven cowboys was black, and nearly one in five was of Mexican **2.** ancestry.

3. **MAP READING** Ask: Which cattle trail ended in Abilene? Which trail went farthest north? In what present-day state did it end?

MAP STUDY   *Railroads, mining, and cattle grazing helped open the Great Plains for later*   **3.**
settlement, as indicated on this map. Which cities were probably major centers
See p. T76.   *for shipping cattle east by rail?*

Western Railroads, Cattle Trails, and Mining Centers

1. **ACTIVITY** Have students find and bring in recordings of old cowboy songs like "The Old Chisholm Trail," "The Dying Cowboy," or "Goodbye, Old Paint."

Every spring, ranchers would select the crews for the long drive. A rancher with 3,000 cattle would need about 18 men, one for every 175 animals. A chuck wagon would follow with a cook and a wrangler to look after the extra horses. Each cowboy had about eight mounts. The horses had distinctive names like Gold Dollar, Julius Caesar, or Pop Corn.

1.

The long drive took two or three months to complete. Cattle walked in a long thin line. Moving the men and animals at a pace of 20 to 25 miles (32 to 40 kilometers) a day, the herd manager signaled his crew using arm motions borrowed from Plains Indian sign language. Such work was hard indeed. Cowboys often sat in the saddle for 16 to 18 hours a day.

2.

The Cattle Boom

The cattle business boomed, and railheads became busy cities. In 1867, Abilene, Kansas, consisted of only a dozen log huts with dirt roofs. The town was so poor that to survive the saloonkeeper raised prairie dogs that he sold to the occasional tourist. By 1870, Abilene was shipping out 300,000 cattle a year, and the sleepy town had become a bustling business center.

Before long, cattle ranchers decided to expand their grazing range. As the buffalo vanished from the plains, ranchers began grazing cattle there. Ranchers let their cattle run wild, identifying them with a distinctive mark, or brand. Twice a year, the cattle were rounded up, and new calves were branded with a hot iron.

3.

By 1880, nearly 5 million cattle grazed from Kansas to Montana. The profits were so handsome that ranching became a field for speculation. Investors came from the East and from as far away as Europe. The cattle business was the latest bonanza, the newest way to get rich quick. But the bonanza was not to last.

From Boom to Bust

Several developments contributed to the end of the cattle bonanza. As the number of cattle multiplied, the plains were overgrazed and the grasses died. Ranchers quarreled over

Many of the cowhands on the long drives were blacks or Mexican Americans. Yet in the folklore of the West, those cowboys were often ignored or forgotten.

4.

4. **VISUAL EVIDENCE** Ask: In what ways does the cowboy in this picture fit the popular image of a cowboy?

land and water rights, often violently, and cattle rustlers, or thieves, proved to be a nagging problem.

Competition for grazing land led to other problems. Fencing had been limited on the plains as long as fencing materials—wood or stone—were scarce. When barbed wire was marketed in 1874, ranchers began stringing up fences to keep their cattle in. But ranchers were not the only people who found a use for barbed wire.

Conflict also arose with other groups who wanted to use the land. Sheep ranchers wanted to graze their herds on the prairie, but the cattlemen complained that the sheep cropped the grass so close to the ground that it would not grow again. Farmers moved onto the plains and began fencing the land. Bitter range wars erupted over who had the right to use the land or control valuable water holes.

413

2. **READING** Students interested in a contemporary novel set during a long cattle drive in the 1870s can read *Lonesome Dove* by Larry McMurtry.

3. **VOCABULARY** The word *maverick*, meaning an independent person, comes from Samuel Maverick, a Texas rancher who refused to brand his calves.

1. The detail of the painting above by Clara Williamson shows a cattle drive at the height of the cattle boom. The days of the trail drives were numbered, however, as harsh weather forced many ranchers out of business.

1. **VISUAL EVIDENCE** This painting was done by Clara McDonald Williamson.

The weather delivered the cruelest blow to the cattle ranchers, however. Two terrible winters, in 1885–1886 and 1886–1887, whipped the plains with blizzards and subzero temperatures. In between, a drought had wiped out the grasses. By the time warmth and moisture returned to the land, 80 to 90 percent of the cattle lay dead.

Many ranchers and speculators were ruined. Those who were not soon discovered that the cattle business had changed. With the spread of barbed wire, animals no longer roamed free. Ranchers purchased and fenced land, drilled wells to guard against dry weather, and provided hay for cattle during difficult winter months. One by one, individually owned ranches were taken over by large corporations.

The cattle frontier went the way of the other boom economies. Ranching remained an important activity in the West, but it had

2. become big business.

See p. T76.

SECTION 4 REVIEW

1. **Identify:** (a) Texas longhorn, (b) long drives.

2. (a) How did railroads contribute to the growth of cattle ranching? (b) How did ranchers move cattle to the railhead?

414

2. **PRESIDENTS** Theodore Roosevelt, who owned two ranches, noted: "The cattlemen are soon to be overtaken. The great defenseless ranges will be divided into corn land."

3. List the factors that contributed to an end of the cattle bonanza.

4. **Critical Thinking** Why do you think folklore has romanticized life on the cattle frontier?

5 The Sodbusters' Frontier

READ TO UNDERSTAND

■ How the government encouraged settlement in the West.

■ How new techniques and inventions made farming possible on the plains.

■ What hardships western farmers faced.

Miners and ranchers were the first to stake out claims to the West, but farmers followed close behind. They arrived full of hope and fired by dreams of prosperity. But most barely scraped by. Only the early arrivals got the rich river valleys; latecomers toiled on the parched plains of the Dakotas, Nebraska, Kansas, and western Texas. It was not an easy life.

Encouraging Settlement

In 1862, Congress passed the Homestead Act to encourage farmers to settle the West. In return for a small registration fee, any citizen or immigrant planning to become a citizen was granted 160 acres (64 hectares) of public land to be used as a farm, or homestead.

Only about 20 percent of the homestead land went directly to small farmers. Speculators purchased large parcels of land, which they then divided and resold to farmers at higher prices. Nonetheless, by 1900, 600,000 farmers had claimed homesteads.

The Homestead Act was impractical in many areas. As John Wesley Powell had foreseen, a 160-acre (64-hectare) farm might be fine in the East, but in the drier West, crop yields were smaller and risks greater; much larger tracts of land were needed. Nonetheless, many farmers came west in response to the Homestead Act. Others came in response to appeals from the railroads.

As you read earlier, the government had given the railroads large areas of land along their western routes. Railroad executives were eager to attract settlers to these lands to increase railroad usage. The railroads advertised in the East, painting glowing pictures of

1. life on the plains. As an added incentive, people who bought the railroad's land received a free train ride west.

The railroads advertised in Europe also. From the Scandinavian countries especially, thousands of families emigrated to Minnesota and the Dakotas. Many German and Irish immigrants joined American settlers in Nebraska and the Dakotas.

When railroads worked together with settlers to develop an area, both the region

and the railroad prospered. One of the most successful efforts was led by James J. Hill, president of the Great Northern Railway. Hill saw that his railway could reach the Pacific only by developing the country as it progressed. So he introduced scientific farming, distributed livestock free to farmers, supported churches and schools, and assisted in countless others ways the development of the communities of "Hill country." Towns and farms grew up quickly along his rail line.

GEOGRAPHY AND HISTORY

Adapting to the Plains

Life on the plains differed greatly from what the settlers had known before. They had to 2. learn many new skills.

Little wood was available on the dry, nearly treeless plains, and families had to rely on other materials to build houses. At first, they used the land itself, tough sod held

GEOGRAPHIC CONNECTION

Hazards of the Great Plains

The hopeful settlers who homesteaded the Great Plains were pitched in a duel with nature. The region straddling the 100th meridian (100° W longitude) often has less than the 20 inches of average rainfall needed for normal farming. And the term "average" rainfall is deceiving. Periods of plentiful rain are followed by periods of drought. Hail, frost, blizzards, strong winds, and a glaring sun add to farmers' woes.

After the Civil War, pioneers poured into this region. Many people came from neighboring states on the more hospitable Central Plains. The new farmers prospered in the rainy period between 1875 and 1880, only to be driven from their lands in the drought of the 1890s. Plants withered and died, and the blazing sun drove every living creature to seek shelter. But the long awaited relief was sometimes as devastating as the drought had been. A rumble of distant thunder and gathering black clouds could signal a torrent of rain and hail that would leave destruction in its wake.

Specialized dry-farming methods were a weapon in the battle against drought, but most farms were too small to profit from them. In 1909, Congress raised the size of the homestead from 160 acres to 320 acres and raised it again in 1916 to 640 acres, or one square mile. A succession of rainy years in 1914–1916 and high wheat prices caused by World War I lured tens of thousands of hopeful settlers onto the Great Plains.

By 1930, most of the land had been settled and plowed. Then one of the worst droughts of all struck. On a larger scale than ever before, people were forced to abandon their land. Soon, all that moved in many parts of the Great Plains were the strong winds sweeping away forever the once fertile soil.

See p. T76.

1. Why was farming on the Great Plains unpredictable?

2. **Critical Thinking** In what other occupations does weather have an important impact? Why?

together by the tight weave of prairie-grass roots. Settlers cut bricks of sod, then arranged them into walls three feet (one meter) thick. The roof was tarpaper, if available, covered with a layer of sod. Eventually, grass and flowers might grow from the roof of the sod house.

The settlers developed new techniques and inventions or adapted old ones to farm the plains. By drilling deep wells, farmers were able to reach water several hundred feet below the dry surface of the land. A new kind of windmill harnessed the high, changeable winds of the plains to pump out the water. Most wells, however, supplied only enough water to irrigate an acre near the house where the family could raise its own vegetables. To farm large areas, farmers used a technique known as dry farming. Farmers 1. loosened the topsoil with steel-tipped plows that enabled them to cut through the dense root networks that would have broken earlier iron or wooden plows. In this way, the farmers created a blanket of dust that kept the moisture below from evaporating too quickly. Dry farming made it possible to grow cash crops such as wheat over large areas of the plains.

Improved machinery allowed the farmers of the plains to cultivate more land. Mechanical binders tied the wheat into bundles, and threshing machines separated the grain from the stalk. With machinery, a wheat farmer could harvest in three hours what originally took 61 hours to do. The time spent harvest- 2. ing corn, oats, and hay also dropped sharply.

Farm Life on the Plains

New farming techniques and labor-saving inventions made it possible for farmers of the plains to survive, but life still posed severe trials. Each season of the year held its special threat to the farmer.

Spring brought welcome warmth, but along with melting snow came floods that washed away houses and drowned livestock. In the summer, sweltering temperatures of over 100° F (39° C) and hot winds blasted the plains for weeks. Summer also meant grasshopper plagues: Swarms of grasshoppers **416** swooped from the sky, eating everything in

their path—crops, food, tree bark, even clothing. The summer heat finally broke in September or October, but by then the grasses were so dry that one spark could ignite thousands of acres.

The pioneers dreaded winter most. Cruel winds swept ice, dust, and snow across the plains. Settlers might awaken on a January morning to find their food frozen and snow on their bed. Animals suffered even more.

Many of those who came to the plains buckled under the strain of farm life. Some proceeded westward; others retreated back East. "From Kansas, where it rains grasshoppers, fire, and destruction," read the sign on one returning wagon.

Of course, life was not always so harsh, and many prairie farmers prospered. Women 3. worked alongside men. Some, like Elinore Stewart from Wyoming, homesteaded their own farms. Women's contribution to life in 4. the West is made evident by the fact that 11 western states and territories, led by Wyoming in 1869 and Utah in 1870, granted women the vote before any states east of the Mississippi.

Almost from the start, churches and schools played an important part in western settlement. Church members joined together to recreate the patterns of community life left behind in the East or in Europe. At first, most rural families relied on the churches and Bible reading to educate their children.

Gradually, communities erected schools. These were usually one-room buildings with rows of hard benches where a teacher taught six to eight grades together. Both the church and the school were centers of community life where families found relief from isolation and toil. ■

The Closing Frontier

As farmers spread across the plains, fewer and fewer areas remained to be settled. The last major land rush took place in central Oklahoma in 1889. This area had belonged to Cherokees, Creeks, Seminoles, and other southeastern nations since the 1830s, when Andrew Jackson's removal policy had forced them from their eastern homes. In 1885, the

It took backbreaking work for pioneers to "plow under the buffalo bones" and make a life for themselves on the plains. With few trees for wood, early settlers cut squares of sod from the ground and used them like bricks to build sod houses.

1. Harvey Dunn, born on a South Dakota homestead, captures both the beauty and the isolation of prairie life in this painting, The Prairie Is My Garden.

1. **VISUAL EVIDENCE** Ask: What qualities of a prairie woman does Dunn illustrate in his painting? How are the children portrayed?

United States, pressured by settlers, bought back the land.

The government announced that free homesteads would be available to citizens, but these could be claimed only after 12 o'clock noon on April 22, 1889. About 100,000 land seekers lined up on the border on horseback or in wagons. Soldiers fired a signal, and the settlers charged in. They discovered, however, that others had slipped by the border patrols and gotten there sooner. Because of these "sooners," the entire district was parceled out in the space of a few hours.

2. In 1890, the superintendent of the census announced that, for the first time in the history of the United States, settlements had spread so far that "there can hardly be said to be a frontier line." One by one, the western territories became states: Nebraska in 1867; Colorado in 1876; North Dakota, South Dakota, Montana, and Washington in 1889; Idaho and Wyoming in 1890; Utah in 1896;

Idaho and Wyoming in 1890; Utah in 1896; Oklahoma in 1907; and New Mexico and Arizona in 1912.

See p. T77.

SECTION 5 REVIEW

1. **Identify:** (a) James J. Hill, (b) "sooners."

2. (a) Why did the government enact the Homestead Act? (b) What were its provisions?

3. (a) List three inventions or techniques that made farming on the plains easier and more profitable. (b) What hardships drove some people from the plains?

4. How did churches and schools contribute to community life on the plains?

5. **Critical Thinking** How might the existence of a frontier affect a society?

2. **BACKGROUND** One journalist who took part in the land rush wrote, "On the morning of April 23, a city of 10,000 people, 500 houses, and innumerable tents existed where twelve hours before was nothing but a broad expanse of prairie."

CHAPTER 19 REVIEW

Summary

1. **Indian nations on the Great Plains developed a vision of life based on a reverence for the balance of nature.** Settlers had rival visions of the plains. Some saw the West as a place of unlimited resources. Others stressed the challenges of the environment and called for cooperation.

2. **After the Civil War, settlers encroached on the Indians' land on the Great Plains.** Discoveries of gold and silver lured miners eastward from California. The transcontinental railroads increased the pace of settlement from the East.

3. **The influx of settlers marked the end of the Indians' way of life.** Overwhelmed by the United States army and weakened by the destruction of the buffalo herds, the Indians were finally forced onto reservations.

4. **Cattle raising spread to the Great Plains as railroads opened up eastern markets.** But by 1890, bitter weather and range wars between cattle ranchers, sheep ranchers, and farmers over land and water rights put an end to the cattle boom.

5. **New techniques and inventions enabled farmers to adapt to the harsh environment of the Great Plains.** Although farm life on the plains was a struggle, many settlers prospered. In 1889, "sooners" and other homesteaders took advantage of the offer of free land and settled Oklahoma.

See p. T77.

Vocabulary

Match each term at left with its definition or description at right.

1. vigilante
2. public domain
3. reservation
4. vaquero
5. long drive

a. cattle drive
b. land set aside for the Indians
c. land that belongs to the nation
d. self-appointed law enforcer
e. Spanish cowboy

See p. T77.

Chapter Checkup

1. (a) How did settlers view the Great Plains before 1860? (b) What caused settlers to change their view after 1860?

2. (a) What role did the buffalo play in the lives of the Plains Indians? (b) How did the introduction of horses in the 1700s affect the Indians?

3. How did the mining boom contribute to the growth of western towns and cities?

4. (a) Why was it difficult for private companies to begin construction of a transcontinental railroad? (b) How did the government help to resolve this problem? (c) What ethnic groups played a major role in the building of the railroad?

5. (a) What reasons did the United States government give for wanting to confine the Indians to reservations? (b) Why did the Indians agree to move to reservations? (c) Was this effort to make peace with the Indians successful? Explain.

6. (a) What were the provisions of the Dawes Act? (b) What was the act intended to do? (c) What was its effect?

7. (a) How were cattle raised on the open range? (b) Describe the "long drive" and its role in the cattle boom.

8. Describe how each of the following contributed to the end of the cattle bonanza:

418

(a) increased numbers of cattle; (b) barbed wire; (c) sheep ranches; (d) farmers; (e) climate.

See p. T77.

Critical Thinking

1. **Analyzing** How did the disappearance of the buffalo symbolize the end of a way of life for the Plains Indians?

2. **Comparing** How were the mining bonanzas and cattle bonanzas similar?

See p. T77.

Connecting Past and Present

1. (a) What meaning do the three visions of the West—those of the Indians, Gilpin, and Powell—have for us today? (b) How would you describe the vision of the West held by contemporary Americans?

2. The first transcontinental railroad was built by private companies with help from the federal government. (a) What types of projects run by private industry does the federal government support today? (b) Make a list of arguments for and against such federal aid to private industry.

See p. T78.

Developing Basic Skills

1. **Map Reading** Use the map on page 412 to answer the following questions. (a) What cities developed along railroad lines in the West? (b) Which of these cities do you think were cattle centers? Explain.

2. **Map Reading** (a) Locate the following on the map on page 408: the land ceded by Indians to the United States between 1850 and 1870; the land ceded by Indians to the United States between 1870 and 1890; Indian reservations in 1890. (b) Make a generalization about what happened to American Indians between 1850 and 1890.

WRITING ABOUT HISTORY

Using an Index for Current Newspapers

The New York Times index for current newspapers is more complex than the index for older newspapers you learned about on page 393. To become acquainted with how to use a current index, study the labeled sample below.

Date, section, page, column

"See also" references

Subject heading   Abstract on article

INDIANS, American. See also
Agr, N 25
Archeology, My 5, Je 9, 14, O 3,6
Art, F 28, Mr 24, O 6
Astronautics, My 4
Bolivia, Jl 15
Brazil, Ap 9
  White Mountain Apaches in east central Arizona are among handful of Indian tribes in US that have achieved high degree of self-sufficiency in part because of enterprises they have created on their reservation; despite their successes, problems remain; illustrations (M), Ja 9,I,14:3

American Indian tribal leaders, meeting in Reno, vote, 84-18, to reject proposals by Presidential Commission on Indian Reservation Economies to direct development efforts on reservations away from social goals and toward private ownership and profit motive; report to Pres Reagan also suggests abolishing Indian Affairs Bureau, waiving tribes; immunity from certain legal actions and subordinating tribal courts to Federal judiciary on questions of legal interpretation and Constitution; proposes creating Indian Trust Services Administration to protect Indians' natural resources; tribal assn leader Elmer Savilla charges misinterpretation of Indian communal tradition; photo of US funded fish hatchery (M), Ja 13,I,1:6

Article of particular   (M) for medium length
importance   (S) for short
(boldfaced)   (L) for long

Practice: Answer the following questions based on the information in the labeled sample.

1. What is the date, section, page, and column of the article about the meeting of American Indian tribal leaders?

2. What is the length of the article?

3. How is the information in this article related to the subject matter in Chapter 19?

An Age of Industry

20

(1865–1914)

CHAPTER OBJECTIVES After completing this chapter, students should be able to
1. describe technological advances in the late 1800s.
2. explain how new ways of doing business spurred the economy.
3. describe the growth of industry in the South.
4. discuss how workers responded to changing conditions.

CHAPTER PREVIEW Have students make a list of major American corporations today and their products or services. Then ask: What is a corporation? When were the first corporations organized? Which of the corporations on the list might have begun doing business in the 1800s? Which grew up more recently? What industries do you think were important in the 1800s? Why?

Isaac Lewis stared at the handwritten message in disbelief. "Does he take me for a fool? I can't chance doing this," he muttered. The message was an order to get his westbound express train moving.

The order was a clear violation of the rules. In the 1850s, railroads ran on single tracks. To limit the risk of head-on collisions, all Erie locomotive engineers observed a hard-and-fast rule: A westbound train would pull onto a siding to wait for a due eastbound to pass. But on this particular occasion, the eastbound was very late.

It so happened that the railroad superintendent himself, Charles Minot, was a passenger on Lewis's westbound train. Impatient with the delay, Minot hopped off the train and at a nearby telegraph office wired the next station to see if the eastbound had arrived. When the answer came that it had not, Minot wired back a message to hold the eastbound. Then he wrote the order for Lewis to move on.

Lewis refused to obey the order, even when Minot repeated it to him in person. To Lewis,

the telegraph was not a reliable means of running a railroad. The frustrated Minot seized the throttle himself and set off while the terrified engineer rushed to the last car to better his chances of surviving a crash.

The safe arrival of the westbound train at its destination marked a giant step in transportation and communication. As an eyewitness reported, "An hour and more in time had been saved to the westbound train, and the question of running trains on the Erie by telegraph was once and forever settled." In fact, most railroads soon had telegraph operators at each station to monitor the passing trains.

The telegraph had been in use for seven years, but until Minot, it had not been used to keep the traffic on the nation's burgeoning railroads moving smoothly. Minot's combining of two new technologies was an example of the innovations that would spur American industrial growth. The increased efficiency of the railroad helped transform the United States from a largely rural nation in 1865 to a leading industrial world power in 1914.

1.

Growth of union movement

1865	1875	1885	1895	1905	1915

1869 Knights of Labor founded

1872 Westinghouse invents air brake

1876 Bell invents telephone

1881 AFL founded

1886 Haymarket riot

1892 Homestead strike

1904 AFL grows to 1 million members

1. TIME LINE QUESTION Ask: What two inventions are shown on the time line?

1. By the late 1800s, a complex railroad system spanned the continent, connecting cities throughout the nation. By speeding the movement of raw materials and finished products, the railroads made great economic growth possible.

1. **VISUAL EVIDENCE** Have students compare this picture to the one on p. 285. Ask: What changes in the railroad can you see?

1 The Ties That Bind

READ TO UNDERSTAND

■ How the telegraph and telephone revolutionized communications.

■ Why rail transportation became more efficient.

■ What problems resulted from railroad consolidations.

2. ■ *Vocabulary:* consolidate, bond, stock certificate, asset, watered stock, rebate, pooling.

Out on the prairies, farmers leaned on their hoes and listened to the haunting whistles of the railroad trains. Overhead, telegraph lines stretched for miles. A new age had come, one in which advances in transportation and communication would stimulate the nation's industrial growth.

2. **VOCABULARY** Have students look up these terms in the glossary before they begin reading.

Communication by Wire

In 1844, for the first time, Samuel Morse sent a message over an electrical wire. He signaled "What hath God wrought!" At the time, no one could have predicted how much Morse's invention would revolutionize communication. But by 1861, the Western Union Telegraph Company was operating a nationwide telegraph network.

The telegraph hastened the pace of business, allowing companies to order supplies almost instantly. It provided new jobs for women, as telegraphers. And it allowed railroad stationmasters to coordinate the movement of trains, making rail transportation safer and more efficient. (The railroads allowed Western Union to string telegraph wires parallel to their tracks in exchange for free telegraph service.)

One person's success fueled another's ambition. In 1858, financier Cyrus Field and other investors spent $1.5 million to lay an 3.

3. **BIOGRAPHY** Cyrus Field (1819–1892), son of a famous Congregational minister, made his first fortune by age 33. He lost it twice and died deep in debt.

421

underwater telegraph cable across the Atlantic. Although the cable broke within three weeks, Field did not give up. In 1866, he laid a new and improved cable that provided almost instant communication across the Atlantic.

In 1876, Alexander Graham Bell, a Scotsman who taught speech to the deaf in Boston, transmitted the human voice over wires with his new "speaking telegraph." One year later, the first intercity phone conversation took place between Boston and New York.

That same year, Bell organized the Bell Telephone Company after Western Union refused to buy his invention for $100,000. In 1885, the company's directors set up American Telephone and Telegraph, which combined local telephone companies and provided long-distance service. Bell's "electrical toys" soon became vital to many businesses,

with more than 300,000 telephones in use by the mid-1880s. Not until rates dropped in the early 1900s, however, did many homes acquire telephones.

1.

Transportation by Rail

Although advances in communication were important, they took a back seat to the achievements of railroad builders. Transportation was the key to industrialization. The nation needed a vast transportation network in order to move raw materials to factories, products to markets, and passengers quickly across the country.

2.

In 1860, the rail network was still fragmented. Most of the 30,000 miles (48,000 kilometers) of track were in the East. No railroad bridge yet crossed the Mississippi, Ohio, or Hudson rivers. Furthermore, a large number

With the rapid growth of the railroad network, the building of railroad cars and equipment became a major new industry. Factories like this one in Springfield,
3. *Massachusetts, did a thriving business.*

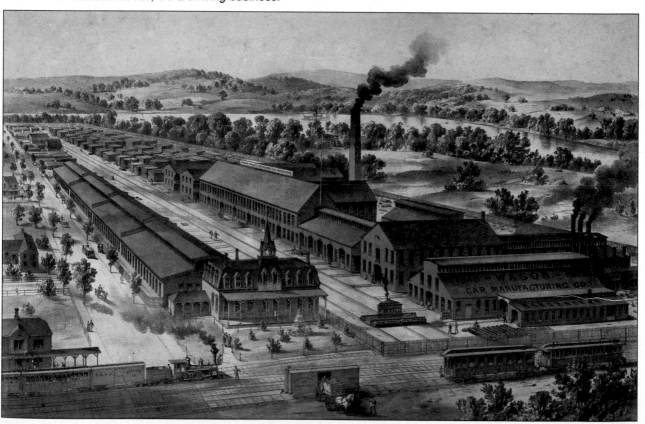

of small companies controlled various sections of track, which were frequently not interconnected. The city of Richmond, Virginia, for example, was the last stop for six separate rail lines.

Even if local rail lines had been connected, one company's cars often would not have been able to travel on another company's track. The wheels might have been too far apart or too close together, since railroads had not agreed upon a standard gauge, the

1. distance between rails. Long-distance freight, consequently, required unloading and reloading along the way. Each link in the journey added to shipping costs, paperwork, and delay.

Consolidation of Railroads

After the Civil War, railroad builders created a more efficient rail system by **consolidating,** or combining, small lines. Owners of large lines often bought smaller lines or tried to drive them out of business.

The development of the New York Central illustrates one method of consolidation. In 1866, the New York Central connected Albany and Buffalo. Other railroad lines ran east and south from Albany (to Boston and New York City), and west from Buffalo (to

2. Chicago). Commodore Cornelius Vanderbilt hoped to unite these lines into one company. He had already made a fortune with a steamship line, hence his nautical title.

Vanderbilt quickly bought up most of the railroad lines linking New York and Chicago, but the strategically located New York Central held out. In 1867, to end the stalemate, Vanderbilt suddenly refused to let passengers and freight transfer from the New York Central to his lines. With freight and passengers stranded, the New York Central asked the New York State legislature for protection, but to no avail.

The New York Central finally surrendered, and Vanderbilt promptly went to work acquiring the feeder lines that joined his New York-to-Chicago trunk line. At the time of his death in 1877, he controlled 4,500 miles (7,200 kilometers) of integrated railroad connecting New York City and the Great Lakes region.

Railroad tycoon Cornelius Vanderbilt is pictured in 3. *this cartoon as a modern colossus towering over his domain. As the cartoon indicates, Vanderbilt was only one of several men who held the reins of the rapidly expanding rail network.*

3. **VISUAL EVIDENCE** Ask: Did the cartoonist approve of these railroad tycoons? How did he think they used their tremendous power?

Progress Along the Rails

Consolidating small railroads led to more efficient rail service. The rail system also improved in other ways. By 1886, the railroads had adopted a standard gauge. Since trains were able to run longer distances without stopping, passengers and freight were moved faster.

At the same time, rates decreased. By the end of the century, passenger fares had dropped by half, and freight rates had dropped even more. Shippers also benefited because rail companies often arranged for freight cars on one line to use the tracks of another. For example, goods loaded in Chicago stayed on the same car all the way to **423**

2. **BIOGRAPHY** Cornelius Vanderbilt (1794–1877) was not a naval officer; he was called "Commodore" because he made his fortune in shipping. When he died, he left over $105 million, the largest estate in U.S. history up to that time.

New York, and the shipper paid only one fare for the whole distance.

Railroad companies also invested in new materials and devices to improve efficiency. Many lines replaced iron rails with steel rails that could support the weight of more powerful locomotives. New signals along the tracks helped to prevent accidents. Major lines began to install a second set of tracks so that traffic could move in both directions at the same time.

In 1883, the American Railway Association created a system of standard time to improve efficiency and simplify scheduling. It divided the country into four time zones: Eastern, Central, Mountain, and Pacific. Every point within each zone would observe the same time. Previously, each town had kept its own time, based on local sun time. Often people set their watches by the time on the clock in the local jeweler's window. The variations from town to town made scheduling difficult.

Persistent Problems

With progress came problems. Constructing railroads required huge amounts of money, so most railroads were heavily in debt. To raise money, owners of railroad lines issued **bonds,** certificates that earn interest and are redeemed on a given date. They also sold **stock certificates,** shares of ownership in a company.

Some of the stock certificates sold, however, had little value. To make the stock attractive to buyers, companies exaggerated their **assets,** that is, their property, equipment, and cash. Such worthless certificates were known as **watered stock,** a reference to the rancher's trick of having cattle drink a lot of water before being weighed for sale. Furthermore, railroad owners often did not have the money to pay the interest on bonds or to redeem them.

Cutthroat Competition The burden of large debt was complicated by intense competition. Despite efforts to consolidate, in some areas many lines continued to vie for the same customers. A manufacturer wanting to ship freight from Atlanta to St. Louis, for example, could choose from 20 different carriers.

Rival railroad lines engaged in rate wars, even if they had to operate at a loss. Since owners had already paid for tracks, engines, and freight cars, running at a loss cost less than not running at all.

Illegal Practices As competition intensified, some companies resorted to illegal practices. To attract more business, railroads secretly offered rebates to their best customers. A **rebate** was a discount on the normal shipping charge. Because reductions were not offered to all shippers, rebating was illegal. The practice hurt mainly small shippers.

Sometimes the managers of several competing railroads entered a **pooling** arrangement. Under this system, they agreed that each line would carry a certain portion of the freight, thus assuring that they all could stay in business. They also pledged not to cut prices.

Pooling, rebates, and other questionable practices, such as charging more for a short haul than for a long haul, led state and federal governments to regulate railroads, as you will read in Chapter 21. In spite of the abuses, however, a nationwide rail system developed and became an essential part of the national economy. Improved communication and transportation strengthened the ties that bound the nation together.

See p. T78.

SECTION 1 REVIEW

1. **Identify** (a) Samuel Morse, (b) Alexander Graham Bell, (c) Cornelius Vanderbilt.

2. **Define:** (a) consolidate, (b) bond, (c) stock certificate, (d) asset, (e) watered stock, (f) rebate, (g) pooling.

3. What impact did the telegraph have on business in the United States?

4. List four ways railroads improved after the Civil War.

5. (a) How did the railroad companies raise money? (b) What methods did they use to attract more business?

6. **Critical Thinking** Why did the spread of railroads lead to a system of time zones?

Innovations and Inventions

READ TO UNDERSTAND

- Why new ways of making steel boosted economic developments.

- What inventions gave rise to new industries.

- How industrial growth encouraged pro-business philosophies.

1. ■ *Vocabulary:* Bessemer process, laissez-faire economics.

Americans of the late 1800s loved to tinker. They watched the wheels and chains of farm machines go round, then thought up better ways to do the same job. Some inventions, such as Bell's telephone, radically changed American life. Others that seemed less substantial—for example, manufacturer Levi Strauss's use of rivets to strengthen the stress points of blue jeans—proved surprisingly significant.

2. **TECHNOLOGY** This was more than ten times the yearly average number during the 1850s.

By the 1890s, Americans were patenting 21,000 new inventions a year. The commissioner of the patent office observed: "America has become known the world around as the home of invention."

2.

3.

Steel: A Foundation for Industry

No development contributed more to the growth of American industry than the discovery of how to make large quantities of steel cheaply and easily. Steel is stronger than the iron from which it is made. Before the 1860s, steel was made by heating iron to high temperatures that could be created only in small furnaces. Besides being slow, the process required a large amount of coal and produced only a small amount of steel.

In 1859, Henry Bessemer, in England, and William Kelly, in the United States, independently discovered a cheaper and quicker way to make steel. The **Bessemer process,** as it came to be known, began by heating iron in a large furnace. Blasts of cold air were then blown through the heated iron, causing impurities to burn.

3. **TECHNOLOGY** The U.S. showed off its progress at the 1876 Philadelphia Exhibition. One German visitor applauded "the diligence, energy, and inventive gift of the North Americans."

4. *The invention of the Bessemer process for refining iron into steel revolutionized industry. The use of Bessemer converters, shown below in a Pennsylvania plant, permitted the development of a large-scale steel industry. Because steel was stronger and more durable than iron, it spurred many other technical advances, such as the construction of steel bridges and steel-frame buildings.*

4. **VISUAL EVIDENCE** Steel workers risked injury and death working close to white-hot vats of melted steel. Students will read about these hazards on p. 438.

425

1. **LOCAL HISTORY** Have students find out if steel production was an early industry in your area. Ask: What environmental factors favor steel production?

This "air boiling" technique produced strong and durable steel. At the same time, the new process reduced from seven tons to one ton the amount of coal needed to produce one ton of steel.

The Bessemer process revolutionized industry. Before 1867, when the first Bessemer steel was produced, United States manufacturers were turning out fewer than 2,000 tons (1,820 metric tons) of steel a year. By the end of the 1800s, they were producing 7 million tons (6.4 million metric tons) a year.

Railroads used much of the earliest Bessemer steel. Steel rails were found to last ten times longer than the old iron rails. Soon other industries found uses for the cheap steel. New "skyscrapers," soaring 20 stories and more into the air, required steel girders to support their great weight. In 1879, plans for the Brooklyn Bridge called for steel beams. Nails, screws, needles, pins, bolts, barrel hoops, and barbed wire were only a few of the everyday uses of steel.

Inventions Create New Industries

While the Bessemer process reshaped many existing industries, other inventions made entirely new businesses possible. Gustavus Swift and Philip Armour introduced refrigeration to the meatpacking* industry. They set up firms in Chicago, a railroad hub midway between the farms on the Great Plains and the cities of the East. Cattle were shipped to the Chicago plants, where they were slaughtered and cut into sides of beef. The beef was stored in refrigerated warehouses and shipped east on refrigerated railroad cars, even in warm weather. This procedure turned the meatpacking industry from a local $65 million-a-year business in 1870 to a national $500 million-a-year business by the 1890s.

Refrigeration helped change eating habits and the national economy. Stores offered a greater variety of fresh meats. And the new packing plants provided thousands of jobs. "Through the wages I disburse and the provi-

---

*The term "meatpacking" dates from the days when beef was salted and packed in wooden barrels. Today, meatpacking refers to the processing and distribution of fresh and frozen meat.

United States Patents Issued, 1861–1900

Five-Year Periods	Number of Patents
1861–1865	20,725
1866–1870	58,734
1871–1875	60,976
1876–1880	64,462
1881–1885	97,156
1886–1890	110,358
1891–1895	108,420
1896–1900	112,188

Source: *Historical Statistics of the United States*

CHART STUDY Americans—both native-born and immigrant—used what they called Yankee ingenuity to devise better ways of making things. This chart shows the number of inventions filed with the United States Patent Office in the decades before 1900. In which five-year period did the average number of patents per year exceed 20,000 for the first time?
See p. T79.

sions I supply," boasted Armour, "I give more people food than any man living." As meatpacking became a national business, many small, local meatpackers went bankrupt.

Inventions to improve rail travel helped spark other new industries. In 1864, George Pullman designed a railroad sleeping car. In 1868, George Westinghouse began marketing his new air brake. The locomotive engineer could now stop all the railroad cars himself; a brakeman on each car was no longer necessary. The new brake both increased passenger safety and comfort and allowed for longer, faster trains.

Thomas Edison's electrical inventions, especially the incandescent light bulb, created a demand for electrification. Electricity had far more flexibility than earlier sources of power such as wind or water. By 1882, the Edison Illuminating Company already brightened the skyline of New York City at night. New generating plants, forests of electrical poles, and George Westinghouse's electrical transformer all made it possible. By the turn of the century, electric-powered trolleys had replaced horse-drawn carriages in the cities. In many heavy industries, electrical machinery began to replace steam engines.

2. **CHART READING** Ask: Between which two five-year periods was there the greatest jump in the number of patents issued?

3. **CITIZENSHIP** Edison believed the key to success was hard work. "Genius," he said, "is one percent inspiration and ninety-nine percent perspiration."

Other inventions helped business to prosper. Christopher Sholes, a printer, developed a typewriter that was first sold by the Remington Arms Company in 1875. Secretaries no longer had to write letters by hand. In 1852, Elishu Otis developed the first passenger elevator. Frank Sprague, an engineer, helped to improve the elevator, a necessary feature of the new skyscrapers.

A New Philosophy for Business

Innovation spurred industrial growth that in turn created huge fortunes for many business leaders. By 1900, more than 4,000 Americans could claim to be millionaires, compared with only a few before the Civil War.

The rich were not shy about displaying their wealth. Many of the new millionaires built large mansions and competed to see who could ride in the fanciest private railroad cars or buy the fastest racehorses. Newspaper social pages featured reports of spectacular parties. At one such affair, the lobby of a hotel was turned into a small lake complete with gondolas. Theories to explain and justify the success of rich industrialists soon emerged.

Carnegie's Social Gospel Andrew Carnegie, a millionaire steel mill owner (see page

NOTABLE AMERICANS

Thomas Alva Edison: The Wizard of Menlo Park

The small audience sat stunned that day in 1877 as Thomas Alva Edison demonstrated his invention. "Mary had a little lamb / Its fleece was white as snow," Edison recited. As he spoke, a needle made grooves in a sheet of tinfoil covering a spinning cylinder. When he had finished, Edison started the needle over the tinfoil again. Those present gasped as they heard his voice, high-pitched but recognizable, reciting the lines again.

What kind of wizard was Edison, that he could reproduce the sound of the human voice? Basically self-taught, Edison showed his genius at a very young age. When he was 10 years old, he set up a chemistry laboratory in the cellar. At age 22, he received his first patent—for an electric vote recorder.

Edison's inventions numbered in the hundreds. At least three of them revolutionized American life—the phonograph, an improved incandescent lamp (the ordinary household light bulb), and a system for producing and distributing electric power.

Perhaps Edison's most important contribution to technology, however, was the idea of a research laboratory. In 1876, Edison built what he called "an invention factory" in Menlo Park, New Jersey. He hired physicists and engineers and put them to work inventing things. Together the group devised the storage battery, an electric safety lantern, the mimeo-graph machine, the electric dynamo, and an experimental electric railroad. Edison boasted that his "factory" could turn out a minor invention every ten days.

In the 1890s, large companies such as Bell Telephone and General Electric followed Edison's lead and set up their own research laboratories. Today, Edison's "invention factory" has become the norm, as teams of inventors work together to generate technological advances.

See p. T79.

1. What was the purpose of Edison's "invention factory"?

2. **Critical Thinking** How did some of Edison's inventions revolutionize American life?

1. **CITIZENSHIP** Carnegie also advocated larger taxes on huge estates. He hoped that this would encourage the rich to spread their wealth more generously while they were alive. He condemned millionaires who hoarded their wealth, saying, "The man who dies thus rich, dies disgraced."

430), vigorously defended the accumulation of wealth. In a magazine article written in 1889, Carnegie claimed that the wealthy had a right to make money and a responsibility to spend it properly. The millionaire, he argued, should be a "trustee for his poorer brethren, bringing to their service his superior wisdom, experience, and ability to administer, doing for them better than they would or could do for themselves." This Gospel of Wealth, as Carnegie called it, commanded the wealthy to donate their money

1. to worthy causes.

Social Darwinism Some philosophers applied the theories of English biologist Charles Darwin to defend the accumulation of wealth. Darwin believed there was a constant struggle in nature in which only the fittest members of a species survive. Thinkers who applied Darwin's concept of survival of the fittest to society became known as social Darwinists. Most influential among the American social Darwinists was William Graham Sumner, a professor of political and social science at Yale University, who claimed, "Millionaires are a product of natural selection."

Sumner and others argued that the struggle for survival occurred in the business world and should be free of government regulation. Firms led by the "fittest" would drive their weak competitors out of business. With the strongest, wisest, and most able citizens as its leaders, society as a whole would benefit.

Laissez-faire Economics Related to social Darwinism was **laissez-faire economics,** a school of thought that rejected government involvement in the economy. According to

2. Herbert Spencer, an English social Darwinist whose ideas were well known in the United States, the economy worked best when it was free of government regulation. Government regulation, the supporters of laissez-faire argued, would only upset the free operation of the marketplace.

Most Americans, whether rich or poor, accepted the pro-business philosophy. Millions of Americans became avid readers of

3. Horátio Alger's dime novels. In these rags-to-riches stories, young men worked hard and then by "pluck and luck" got the breaks that

428 brought them fame and fortune.

The ideas of the late 1800s and early 1900s reflected the spirit of the age. Bessemer steel, electric devices, and other inventions changed daily life. The ideas of Carnegie, Sumner, Spencer, Alger, and others offered a philosophy that justified the change.

See p. T79.

SECTION 2 REVIEW

1. **Identify:** (a) Gustavus Swift, (b) George Pullman, (c) George Westinghouse, (d) Thomas Edison, (e) Gospel of Wealth, (f) social Darwinism.

2. **Define:** (a) Bessemer process, (b) laissez-faire economics.

3. How did the Bessemer process affect the production of steel?

4. What impact did refrigeration have on the meatpacking industry?

5. List four inventions that helped create new industries in the 1800s.

6. **Critical Thinking** What is the underlying assumption about the poor in Carnegie's Gospel of Wealth?

4. **VOCABULARY** Have students look up these terms in the glossary before they begin reading.

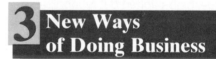

3 New Ways of Doing Business

READ TO UNDERSTAND

■ Why many business people turned their firms into corporations.

■ How new methods of expansion made businesses more efficient.

■ Why business leaders were called both "robber barons" and "industrial statesmen."

■ *Vocabulary:* vertical integration, horizontal integration, trust, dividend, monopoly, free enterprise.

4.

As industries grew, they had to adopt new and more efficient forms of organization. If they did not, they would lose the fierce com-

2. **BIOGRAPHY** Spencer (1820–1903) tried to apply the principle of evolution to many areas of knowledge, including philosophy, psychology, and ethics.

3. **READING** Interested students could read a Horatio Alger story and report on it to the class. Ask them to identify the values Alger seems to support.

The Incorruptible Cashier

James Ritty ran a cafe in Dayton, Ohio, in the 1870s.

Watching the steady stream of customers through the shop, Ritty assumed he was making a tidy profit. Much to his surprise and disappointment, however, he was not. Ritty suspected that his "losses" were his employees' "gains," that clerks were helping themselves from the open cash box.

Such were the pitfalls of doing business in the 1870s. Merchants did not keep detailed records of sales and receipts. Clerks made change from their own pockets or from a cash box. Some owners required clerks to record cash transactions in an account book, but carelessness and dishonesty often resulted in inaccuracies.

Worry over business losses ruined Ritty's health, and he took an ocean voyage to Europe to recover. In the engine room one day, he spotted a machine automatically recording each revolution of the ship's propeller shaft. Maybe he could devise a similar machine to record each sale in his cafe, he mused. He rushed back home to work on his idea.

In 1879, Ritty patented a simple cash register based on the principles he had discovered in the ship's engine room. He soon improved his invention to display the amount to be collected so both clerk and customer could see it. Publicly showing the amount, he hoped, would reduce the temptation to steal. So pleased was Ritty with having invented a machine that would keep clerks honest, he dubbed it "the incorruptible cashier."

Later developments included a mechanism to record each day's transactions on a paper

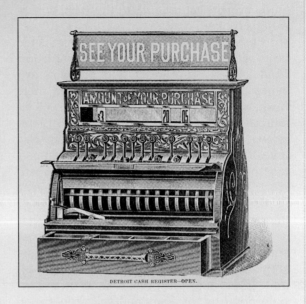

DETROIT CASH REGISTER—OPEN.

roll. Now the owner could check the amount of money in the cash box as well as the number of transactions that had been made. A still further refinement was a device that added the day's transactions and recorded the total. Finally, a cash drawer was added, along with a bell that rang every time the drawer was opened. Now, the clerk had to record the sale in order to have access to the cash drawer. And the bell announced to the world that a brisk business was being done. Indeed, James Ritty's simple invention was a major step in the development of modern merchandising methods.
See p. T80.

1. What were two improvements to Ritty's cash register?

2. Critical Thinking How have inventors continued to meet the needs of expanded retail selling?

---

1. ECONOMICS Ritty sold his patent for $1,000 to John Henry Patterson, a Dayton coal merchant. In 1884, Patterson founded the National Cash Register Company, which still exists today.

petition for customers. But was competition good for business? Alarmed by price wars that slashed profits and made planning impossible, business leaders looked about for ways to make business more orderly by reducing destructive competition.

The Rise of the Corporation

Before the Civil War, individual proprietors or partners owned and ran most businesses. Proprietorships and partnerships were well suited to small-scale operations in which a

429

2. TECHNOLOGY Have interested students find out what improvements have been made on the cash register since the 1800s.

few employees produced simple goods or services. After the war, however, a movement got under way to expand and consolidate businesses. As proprietorships and partnerships proved inadequate to the task, corporations took hold. (See page 220.)

Corporations provide certain benefits for large-scale industry. The first is protection from losses. Proprietors and partners are generally responsible for the debts of their business. A business failure could spell financial ruin for them. The corporate organization shields the investor. A person who invests, or buys stock, in a corporation can lose no more than he or she paid for the stock. The liability of the investor in the event of the failure of the corporation is thus limited.

Second, the corporation has a special legal status and permanence. Unlike proprietorships and partnerships, the corporation is, for legal purposes, a "person" in its own right. A corporation may buy and sell property or sign contracts without any personal risk to its owners, the stockholders. Furthermore, a corporation, unlike a proprietorship or partnership, can survive even when its owners die. A corporation can "live" forever.

The characteristics of the corporation make it easier to attract investors and raise capital—as you recall, money used in a business. Thus, after the Civil War, the manufacturers of iron, steel, brass, aluminum, textiles, and chemicals, among others, decided to incorporate.

New Sources of Capital

To pay for its rapid expansion, industry needed capital. It found three major sources.

One was commercial and savings banks. Such banks had existed before the Civil War, and from 1860 to 1900 their number multiplied many times over. Banks made loans to businesses, using the money that people had deposited. Banks could even expand the amount of money in circulation by extending credit even when they did not have deposits on hand to cover all their loans.

Life insurance companies provided a second source of capital. They invested millions of dollars in railroad construction. They

also supplied mortgages to farmers and business people.

Finally, corporations raised additional capital by selling more stock to the public. Although a corporation might be worth millions of dollars, one share of its stock was relatively inexpensive. Thus even the average person could afford to invest in stocks. The widespread ownership of corporate stock increased the amount of investment capital available to business.

Seeking Better Organization

As corporations grew larger, the need for better internal organization became clear. Before the Civil War, large factories employing hundreds of workers had only a few executives to manage the bookkeeping and direct operations.

Gradually, corporations began to set up separate departments to handle each major activity: purchasing raw materials, manufacturing, marketing the finished product, and coordinating finances. An executive headed each department. As the business grew, the corporate "ladder" gained new rungs.

Corporations continued to search for ways to get ahead of their competitors. Andrew Carnegie and John D. Rockefeller were two business leaders who pioneered effective new forms of organization.

Andrew Carnegie and the Vertical Integration of Steel

The career of Andrew Carnegie closely resembled a Horatio Alger rags-to-riches story. Born in Scotland in 1835, Carnegie came to America at age 13. He began working in a textile mill for $1.20 a week. Then he took a job as a telegram messenger. Carnegie worked long hours and studied Morse code at night. Soon he became a skilled telegrapher.

Luck favored Carnegie when Thomas Scott, superintendent of the Pennsylvania Railroad, hired the young man as his assistant. Scott introduced Carnegie to other industrial leaders and helped him invest the savings from his salary. Although Carnegie's annual salary was only $2,400, shrewd investments quickly made him a millionaire.

1. **ECONOMICS** Carnegie kept up friendly relations with railroad owners. He named one steel mill after the president of the Pennsylvania Railroad.

2. **ECONOMICS** To help students understand vertical integration, ask what subsidiary industries they would buy to integrate the oil industry vertically.

While traveling in England, Carnegie became familiar with the revolutionary Bessemer process for making steel and realized its potential. Although the United States was in the midst of an economic depression in 1873, Carnegie began building the nation's largest steel plant at Homestead, Pennsylvania, near Pittsburgh. Using the Bessemer process, Carnegie was able to produce steel rails inexpensively and sell them for half the price charged by his competitors.

But Carnegie was not satisfied with this initial success. In 1880, there were more than 1,000 separate producers in the highly competitive steel and iron business. Carnegie realized that his steel plant was dependent on people and forces he could not control. Mining companies removed the iron ore from the ground. Ships and rail lines transported the ore to a plant to be converted to pig iron. Other railroads then brought the pig iron to the Homestead plant for the production of steel.

To insure a steady supply of raw materials and dependable transportation, Carnegie bought mining companies, rail lines, ore ships, and pig iron plants until he had a hand in each industry critical to steel making. The control of all the steps required to turn a raw material into a finished product is known as **vertical integration.** Through vertical integration, Carnegie gained an advantage over other steel companies.

"Watch the costs," said Andrew Carnegie, "and the profits will take care of themselves." As his profits increased, Carnegie plowed them back into his company. He became a multimillionaire, but he gave millions of dollars to charity, believing that great wealth was a "sacred trust."

3. **VISUAL EVIDENCE** Although photography was gaining popularity in the late 1800s, many prominent people still chose to sit for painters. Ask: How does this portrait present Carnegie?

John D. Rockefeller and the Standard Oil Trust

As Carnegie expanded his control of the steel industry, John D. Rockefeller took aim at the oil industry. The first major oil drilling in the United States took place in 1859 near Titusville, Pennsylvania. Oil then had limited use as a patent medicine and for kerosene, an efficient and cheap fuel for lamps. When news of the first successful wells spread, a boom in oil drilling began. Scenes reminiscent of the gold rush in California were played out in rural Pennsylvania.

Rockefeller knew that oil had little value until it was refined, or purified. During the Civil War, Rockefeller entered the oil-refining business. In 1870, he formed the Standard Oil Company.

Rockefeller believed that the savage competition of his era was wasteful and destructive. Unlike Andrew Carnegie, however, Rockefeller at first chose not to expand his business vertically. Instead of buying drilling companies, rail lines, and warehouses, Rockefeller concentrated on acquiring other refineries. Expansion in one area of production is known as **horizontal integration.** Rockefeller realized that horizontal control of refining gave him control over production and prices.

John D. Rockefeller often used ruthless methods to get rid of competition. Because

431

4. **BIOGRAPHY** When Rockefeller looked for his first job at age 16, he showed the thoroughness and persistence that made him a success. He made a list of companies that interested him and visited each one. When no job was forthcoming, he went back a second time, then a third. At last, a produce company hired him as a clerk.

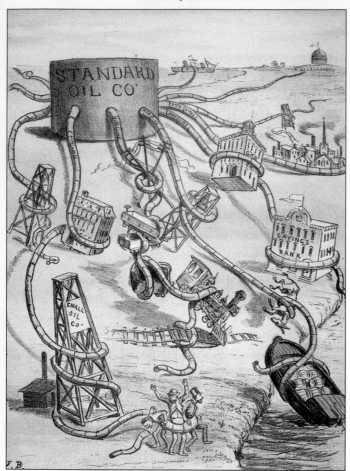

After eliminating most of the competition in the oil industry, John D. Rockefeller said, "Individualism has gone, never to return." The stronger Standard Oil became, the less likely it was that anyone could
1. *compete with it. In this cartoon, Standard Oil is portrayed as an octopus whose tentacles have a stranglehold on everything it can reach.*

2. **READING** In 1903, Ida Tarbell's *History of the Standard Oil Company* exposed Rockefeller's ruthless tactics. Students will read about Tarbell and other muckrakers on p. 494.

the railroads needed Rockefeller's business, railroad executives agreed to give rebates to Standard Oil freight. Weakened by higher freight rates, rivals of Standard Oil suffered further from Rockefeller's relentless price cutting. Standard Oil would lower oil prices to capture a competitor's customers and then raise prices after driving the competitor out
2. of business. As a result of Rockefeller's tough methods, Standard Oil controlled over 90 percent of American oil refining capacity by 1879.

3. **ECONOMICS** Carnegie, though an admirer of Rockefeller, did not approve of trusts. He felt that, because trusts violated the laws of competition, they would quickly die out as a form of business.

To tighten his control over the industry, Rockefeller also accumulated the stock of other oil companies under trust agreements. In a **trust,** stockholders of independent companies agree to exchange their shares of stock for trust certificates issued by a giant firm such as Standard Oil. The holders of trust certificates receive **dividends,** or shares of the company's profit, but lose the right to take part in the management of the firm. 3.

In time, Standard Oil turned to vertical integration. It bought barrel companies and railroads and began to manufacture and install its own pipelines. By such methods, Standard Oil acquired a near **monopoly** of the oil industry. That is, the company had almost total control of the market until new oil fields were discovered in Texas and Louisiana.

Other large businesses soon imitated the success of Standard Oil. In the 1880s, trusts appeared in such areas as sugar refining, whiskey distilling, and the manufacture of cottonseed and linseed oils.

Free Enterprise in an Age of Growth

Free enterprise is a system in which private individuals make economic decisions about what products to make, how much to produce, where to sell products, and what prices to charge. Since the founding of the nation, free enterprise has been the cornerstone of the American economy.

In the late 1800s, some people believed that leaders of the giant corporations were abusing the free enterprise system. These 4. critics argued that the creation of monopolies eliminated competition, a central part of free enterprise. To end the abuses, critics began to demand government regulations, as you will read in Chapter 21.

Historians and economists still debate the economic changes of the late 1800s. One area of debate is the character and aims of the business leaders of the period. Some historians call men like Carnegie and Rockefeller robber barons. They charge that the business leaders ruthlessly drove small companies out of business and exploited workers.

4. **ECONOMICS** When British Prime Minister William Gladstone heard that one American had $100 million, he said, "The government ought to take it away from him, as it is too dangerous a power for any one man to have."

1. **PAST AND PRESENT** Rockefeller set up the Rockefeller Foundation in 1913. It continues to be one of the country's most important philanthropies.

2. **READING** Students interested in learning more about the business giants of this period can read *Captains of Industry* by Bernard Weisberger and Allan Nevins.

Other historians refer to these same business leaders as industrial statesmen. In their view, men like Carnegie and Rockefeller deserve praise for their innovative methods and for bringing greater order and efficiency to the economy.

Still, it is not clear just how efficient the giant corporations were. Critics claim that big firms discouraged technological change because they did not want to buy new equipment. Big businesses polluted the environment, exposed workers to injury, and wasted raw materials.

Defenders of big business argue that large corporations invented and perfected technologies that revolutionized American life. They maintain that the growth of giant corporations brought lower production costs and prices, higher wages, and a better quality of life for millions of Americans.

There is no question that the business practices of the 1800s transformed American life, taking the nation from the "horse and buggy" to the automobile age. By 1900, Americans had the highest standard of living in the world.

See p. T80.

SECTION 3 REVIEW

1. **Identify:** (a) Andrew Carnegie, (b) John D. Rockefeller.

2. **Define:** (a) vertical integration, (b) horizontal integration, (c) trust, (d) dividend, (e) monopoly, (f) free enterprise.

3. List three advantages of corporations over proprietorships and partnerships.

4. What sources of capital were available to business people in the last half of the 1800s?

5. What methods did John D. Rockefeller use to eliminate competition in the oil industry?

6. **Critical Thinking** What do you think Carnegie meant when he said "Put your good eggs in one basket and then watch the basket"?

4 The Growth of Industry in the South

READ TO UNDERSTAND

■ What southerners meant when they called for a "New South."

■ How new industries sprang up in the South.

■ Why the South continued to lag behind the North and the West.

After the Civil War, a new generation of southern leaders resolved not only to repair the devastation of their region but also to build a new economy. Agriculture was part of the past, these southerners agreed. The future would lie in industry. In one community after another, citizens gathered in mass meetings to pray and sing—and to contribute their pennies and dollars to start textile mills. Southerners were determined to use their region's rich natural resources to create a "New South," an industrial South.

The Rise of the "New South"

No one expressed the idea of the "New South" better than Henry Grady, editor of the Atlanta *Constitution*. In spreading the idea of southern industrialization, Grady liked to tell the story of a poor Georgia cotton farmer's funeral.

The farmer had been buried in a pine forest in Georgia. His pine coffin, however, was made in Cincinnati. Although an iron mine stood not far from the cemetery, the coffin's iron nails were made in Pittsburgh. The cotton coat the farmer was buried in came from New York, his trousers from Chicago. Concluded Grady, the "South didn't furnish a thing on earth for that funeral but the corpse and the hole in the ground!" Grady's story pinpointed the South's dilemma. Though rich in natural resources, the South produced few of the manufactured goods it consumed.

With other southerners, Grady argued that an important first step toward attracting industry was to improve the southern rail-

3. **VOCABULARY** The era of the "Old South" is also called the *antebellum* period, from the Latin for "before the war."

4. **BACKGROUND** Grady made several lecture tours of large northern cities, trying to drum up support from industrialists and merchants. His lectures on the "New South" became quite popular.

433

road network. Southern states encouraged northern financiers to invest in southern lines, offering free land as well as access to the natural resources of the region. As a result, southern railroads grew at a faster rate than the national average.

The South also changed the gauge of its track to conform to the national standard. In one day, at a prearranged signal, 8,000 workers for the Louisville and Nashville railroad moved the rails of over 2,000 miles (3,200 kilometers) of track 3 inches (7.5 centimeters) closer together. Now rail freight could move directly between North and South.

Agricultural Industries

The best way to begin industrialization, southerners agreed, was to build plants to process the region's agricultural goods, such as cotton and tobacco. Among the new plants were textile mills that wove cotton thread.

Like the plantation owner of the past, the owner of the textile mill provided the workers with housing, stores, churches, and schools, as well as jobs. Most mill towns were segregated and most of the textile workers were white women and children. Wages were low, 75-hour work weeks were common, and decent housing was rare. But a small garden plot and a steady cash income put mill workers slightly ahead of most southern agricultural workers.

By 1880, the entire South was still producing fewer textiles than the state of Massachusetts. In the next decade, however, southern industry grew, as more and more communities started textile factories and purchased the latest machinery. "Every little town wanted a mill," noted one observer. "If it couldn't get a big one, it would take a small one."

The American Cotton Oil Trust built factories in the South to extract oil from cotton seeds. Cottonseed oil was the essential in-

By the 1880s, many cities in the South had regained their prewar vitality. As the hub of a busy rail network, Atlanta, Georgia, shown here, attracted many investors and became a thriving manufacturing center. In 1895, the Cotton States Exposition in Atlanta gave the city a chance to show off the progress it had made.

1. **BIOGRAPHY** James Duke (1856–1925) gave a major endowment to Trinity College in Durham, N.C., in 1924. Later, the school was renamed Duke University.

2. **ACTIVITY** Interested students could research and report on how data about the hazards of smoking have affected the tobacco industry.

gredient in soap and cosmetics and served as a substitute for butter. The remaining cotton pulp was used for fertilizer and cattle feed.

The southern tobacco industry also grew rapidly after the Civil War. In 1865, Washington Duke returned from General Lee's army to his North Carolina farm to find only one tobacco barn remaining. Undaunted, he and his son James soon began to market Duke's Mixture. Using innovative advertising techniques, James Duke persuaded many people to switch from pipes, cigars, and snuff to cigarettes. He also purchased exclusive rights to the cigarette-rolling machine invented by James Bonsack, also a southerner.

With each machine turning out 100,000 cigarettes a day, Duke revolutionized the tobacco industry. He pioneered new forms of advertising and sales promotion. With his profits, he bought out several competitors and in 1890 formed the American Tobacco Company. Like John D. Rockefeller, who served as his model, Duke established a mammoth trust that eventually controlled 90 percent of the nation's tobacco industry. But he was the exception rather than the rule in the South.

Mining and Lumbering

Southern industry was not limited to the processing of agricultural products. The South also tapped its mineral resources. Local deposits of iron ore and coal made steel production cheaper in Alabama than in Pennsylvania. Pig iron production began in Birmingham, Alabama, in 1876 and steel production in 1880. Oil refining developed in Texas and West Virginia. Coal mining grew in West Virginia and Alabama, copper mining and granite and marble quarrying in Georgia and Tennessee.

Forest-related industries also flourished. Many forests in the North had been depleted, and by 1895 the southern yellow pine was competing with the northwestern white pine as a lumber source. Some southern factories began to manufacture cypress shingles and hardwood furniture. As one sign of changing times, more and more products were being carried by railroads rather than being shipped

on "swimming volcanoes," as the steamboats were called.

A Dependent Economy

By 1900, the South had developed a more balanced economy. It had its own textile factories, consolidated railroads, and giant companies such as the tobacco trust. But the growth of the North and West had been even more spectacular. The South continued to lag behind. In fact, it had a lower percentage of the nation's factories in 1900 than in 1860.

Many factors contributed to this lag. To raise money, southerners often borrowed from large northern banks. Consequently, northern bankers controlled many southern industries and reaped much of the profits. Furthermore, many industries in the South produced only raw materials. These were sent to factories in the North for final processing—and from final processing came the greatest profits.

When southern factories did produce finished goods, northern railroad owners charged them higher rates to ship their products to the North. In addition, cotton remained king. Southerners devoted their greatest energies to farming. Although industry expanded, the farm population grew even faster, keeping wages low and most of the South poor.

See p. T80.

SECTION 4 REVIEW

1. **Identify:** (a) Henry Grady, (b) Washington Duke.

2. How did some southerners want to change the economy of the South after the Civil War?

3. How did southern railroads improve after the Civil War?

4. List three ways southern industries used the South's agricultural products.

5. **Critical Thinking** How was the economic policy of the North toward the South similar to mercantilism?

3. **ECONOMICS** In 1911, the American Tobacco Company was reorganized after being prosecuted for restraint of trade under the Sherman Antitrust Act (see p. 451).

4. **LOCAL HISTORY** Direct students to the map on p. 848. Ask: What is the major mineral resource of Louisiana? Which southern states have no coal reserves?

1. **VOCABULARY** Have students look up these terms in the glossary before they begin reading.

2. **DISCUSSION** Have students discuss how cheap immigrant labor helped the country grow.

5 Workers Organize

READ TO UNDERSTAND

■ What American workers hoped to gain by forming labor unions.

■ How the Knights of Labor and the American Federation of Labor differed in their goals and philosophies.

■ Why labor unions faced opposition.

1. ■ *Vocabulary:* anarchist, craft union, collective bargaining, injunction.

Economic expansion created new jobs for factory workers. Leaving farm and family behind, many young men and women migrated from rural areas to cities like Chicago, Buffalo, and Pittsburgh. Immigrants from Europe joined them. Struggling to make a living, workers spent ten hours a day amid the clanks and hisses of dangerously whirring machinery. To fight for better wages and safer working conditions, workers found it necessary to organize.

The Work Force

People from a variety of backgrounds made up the industrial work force. The majority of workers were white American men, many of whom had left the farm for the city hoping to better their lot. A small number of factory workers were black. Many factories, however, either turned away black applicants or gave them the hardest and lowest-paying jobs.

Women played an increasingly important role. By 1890, some one million women were working in factories. They made up at least half of the work force in textile mills and tobacco factories and outnumbered men in garment factories. Women also worked in shoemaking, food processing, packaging, and other industries that did not require heavy physical labor. Even a few businesses requiring heavy labor occasionally hired women. No matter what the work, a woman generally received less than half the wage of a man for the same job.

Between 1865 and 1900, more than 13.5 million immigrants came to the United States. (See page 471.) Without their contribution, the national economy would never have expanded at such a rapid pace. In 1870, about 2.

3. **CRITICAL THINKING** Ask: What do you think happened to the average wage of office clerks when the profession came to be dominated by women? Why?

New inventions often created new types of jobs, including jobs for women. Office clerks had traditionally been men. With the introduction of the typewriter, however,
3. *women began to replace men on office staffs. These typists worked for an insurance company.*

Common Occupations in the Late 1800s

Occupation	Number of Males	Number of Females	Total
Farmers (self-employed, managerial)	5,055,130	226,427	5,281,557
Hired hands (farm)	2,556,958	447,104	3,004,062
Servants, waiters	238,152	1,216,639	1,454,791
Carpenters	618,044	198	618,242
Railroad workers	460,771	1,442	462,213
Miners	386,862	376	387,238
Wagon drivers, teamsters	368,265	234	368,499
Teachers, college professors	101,278	246,066	347,344
Dressmakers	836	292,668	293,504
Salespeople	205,943	58,451	264,394
Blacksmiths	209,521	60	209,581
Tailors	123,516	64,509	188,025
Bookkeepers, accountants	131,602	27,772	159,374
Physicians, surgeons	100,248	4,557	104,805
Lawyers	89,422	208	89,630
Clergy	87,060	1,143	88,203
Barbers, hairdressers	82,157	2,825	84,982
Sailors	76,823	51	76,874
Guards, police, detectives	74,350	279	74,629
Nursery workers, gardeners, florists	70,186	2,415	72,601

CHART STUDY

See p. T81.

Women who joined the labor force in the late 1800s were concentrated in certain occupations, as can be seen in this table. Which jobs were most commonly performed by women? Why do you think that was the case?

1.

1. **CHART READING** Have students study the table. Ask: What were the three most common occupations for men? For women? How did women's employment compare to men's in law and medicine? Can you suggest why?

one third of all factory workers in America were foreign-born. The immigrants tended to specialize in specific industries. Many Slavs, for example, took jobs in the steel mills of Gary, Indiana; Jews often worked in New York City's garment industry.

Immigrants were new to the country, and in many cases their standard of living in Europe had been low. Thus they often accepted unpleasant, dangerous, and low-paying jobs that Americans preferred to turn down. With immigrants so eager for work, employers could hire them for low wages. In the steel industry, for example, immigrants might earn $12 a week, while white native-born workers earned $22 a week.

Working Conditions in Industry

Working conditions varied, but most factories were badly lighted, poorly ventilated, and hazardous. Facing stiff competition, owners refused to pay for expensive safety features that would raise the price of their products. Textile workers inhaled the dust and fibers that filled the air in the mills. Workers in cigarette factories endured tremendous heat and the stench of tobacco. Coal miners inhaled coal dust and faced the additional perils of explosions and cave-ins. Garment workers, who often worked at home, crouched over tables in dimly lit apartments, straining their eyes to see that seams were properly sewn.

437

2. **BACKGROUND** Students will read more about patterns of settlement among immigrants on p. 474.

3. **DISCUSSION** Have students discuss these wage differences. Ask: Should factory owners have the right to pay whatever wage workers will accept?

Jobs in the steel mills were especially dangerous. At Andrew Carnegie's Homestead plant, men toiled 12 hours a day, 6 days a week. In the furnace room, Bessemer converters belched fire and sparks. The metal floors were so hot that they sizzled when water fell on them. Men sometimes worked within inches of molten steel. Inevitably, such conditions took a toll. In one year during the late 1800s, accidents killed 195 workers in Pittsburgh's steel factories.

Wages and the Economy

Despite difficult working conditions, the economic situation of the average worker improved between 1870 and 1900. Average wages rose more than 10 percent. Buying power increased because consumer prices declined. The statistical averages, however, hid variations in pay among workers in different occupations and different areas. Even workers whose wages had increased found it hard to support a family.

"A family of workers can always live well," commented a man familiar with the textile industry in Massachusetts, "but the man with a family of small children to support, unless his wife works also, has a small chance of living properly." With no food in the house or coal for the stove, some families were forced to send their children to work in mines or factories. At the turn of the century, almost 2 million American children between the ages of 10 and 15 were at work.

Furthermore, workers' gains were subject to economic uncertainties. Competition was often fierce, and many companies went out of business suddenly, leaving workers without jobs. Depressions in 1873, 1882, and 1893 threw many people out of work. During 1873 and 1874 in New York City, for example, between one fourth and one third of the workers were jobless. National unemployment figures soared from 4 percent in 1890 to 11.7 percent during the depression of 1893. Because there was no system of unemployment insurance, depressions were times of great distress.

The Knights of Labor

Low wages, periodic unemployment, illness, and accident threatened a worker's well-being. Some workers escaped misfortune by mov-

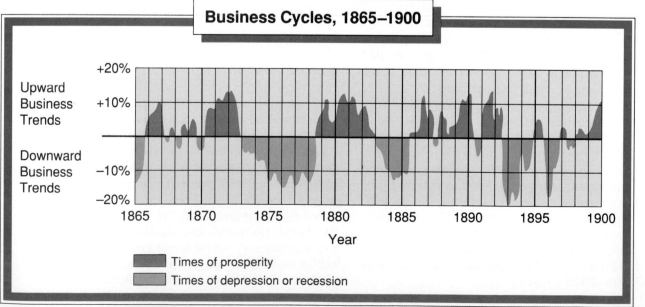

GRAPH STUDY *The ups and downs of the economy were felt more sharply as the nation industrialized and more people worked for wages. Which years were most prosperous? In which years did severe depressions strike?*

See p. T81.

Business Cycles, 1865–1900

Upward Business Trends

Downward Business Trends

+20%
+10%
−10%
−20%

1865   1870   1875   1880   1885   1890   1895   1900

Year

■ Times of prosperity
■ Times of depression or recession

1. **BIOGRAPHY** Powderly (1849–1924) was mayor of Scranton, Pennsylvania, for three terms. In 1894, he became a lawyer and later practiced before the Supreme Court.

2. **VISUAL EVIDENCE** One journalist wrote of the prim Powderly, "No one ever drew such a looking man as the leader of a million of the horny-fisted sons of toil."

ing on to better jobs. Others tried to band together to achieve common goals.

The Knights of Labor was formed in 1869 as a secret brotherhood of skilled workers. Under the leadership of Uriah Stephens, a garment cutter, the society supported idealistic goals. The chief goal was the unity of all laborers within "one big brotherhood." Other goals included an eight-hour day for workers and equal pay for men and women.

1. In 1879, the Knights elected Terence V. Powderly as their leader. To strengthen the union, Powderly removed its veil of secrecy and opened its ranks to women, blacks, immigrants, and unskilled laborers. This was the first attempt to organize all workers.*

Powderly opposed the use of strikes, or work stoppages. He believed that the Knights of Labor should campaign for social and economic reforms: the eight-hour day, improved safety in factories, and compensation for on-the-job injury. Under Powderly's leadership, membership increased from 9,000 in 1879 to 115,000 in 1884.

The Knights' greatest gains came in 1885. Despite Powderly's no-strike policy, railroad workers belonging to the Knights went on strike to protest a pay cut at tycoon Jay Gould's southwestern railroads. They forced Gould to restore their wages. Thousands of laborers, impressed by the successful strike, joined the Knights of Labor. By mid-1886, membership had soared to a peak of 700,000.

The Haymarket Riot and the Decline of the Knights

Worker discontent, more than the Knights' appeal, had swelled the union's ranks. Strangely enough, however, discontent also contributed to the downfall of the organization. In 1886, 80,000 Chicago workers went on strike in support of an eight-hour day. During the strike, police killed several workers near the McCormick Harvester Works. To protest these deaths, a group of **anarchists**,

*Earlier unions had been restricted to skilled workers, as you have read in Chapter 14. (See page 291.)

Terence Powderly opened the Knights of Labor to unskilled workers, blacks, immigrants, and women. In this drawing, Powderly (center) is introduced to 2. the Knights' annual convention at Richmond, Virginia, by delegate Frank Farrell (left).

people who oppose all organized government, planned a rally for May 4.

On that day, rain fell, and a little more than 1,000 people gathered in Haymarket Square to hear anarchist speakers denounce the police and the industrialists. When police moved in swiftly to break up the meeting, someone threw a bomb, killing one 3. police officer and six other people. In the violent riot that followed, seven police officers and four civilians died.

Eight anarchists were convicted of conspiracy to commit murder in the Haymarket incident. Four were hanged, and one committed suicide. In 1893, a newly elected governor pardoned the three others, claiming that the trial had been unfair.

The Haymarket riot turned the public sharply against labor organizations. Because the Knights and the anarchists both supported **439**

3. **BACKGROUND** For years, scholars have debated who threw the bomb. Recent findings by Paul Avrich point to George Meng, a German-born anarchist who was indicted but not brought to trial. Meng later died in a saloon fire.

1. **BACKGROUND** Except for one year (1895), Gompers remained president of the AFL until his death in 1924.

2. **PAST AND PRESENT** The AFL, now part of the AFL–CIO, is still organized in this way.

the eight-hour day, the public had linked the two groups. Even though Terence Powderly and other Knights officials deplored the Haymarket bombing, their reputations suffered.

Weakened by the Haymarket incident and by violence during an unsuccessful railroad strike in 1886, the Knights of Labor declined. By 1890, membership had dropped to 100,000. Many members either left the labor movement or joined the rising American Federation of Labor.

The American Federation of Labor

The American Federation of Labor (AFL) was founded in 1881. Its first president was a London-born cigarmaker named Samuel Gompers. Gompers believed that the Knights of Labor should not have tried to include unskilled workers. Membership in the AFL was open only to skilled workers. Unskilled workers, blacks, women, and recent immigrants, particularly those from Asia, were excluded.

Workers did not join the American Federation of Labor directly. Rather, they joined a local **craft union,** a union of persons working at the same occupation. Each local union was an affiliate of a state and national organization. The AFL itself was a federation of self-governing, independent national unions.

The American Federation of Labor set limited goals. "Our organization does not consist of idealists," insisted one AFL leader. "We are going on from day to day. We are fighting only for immediate objects—objects that can be realized in a few years." The AFL favored the eight-hour day and **collective bargaining,** the right of unions to represent workers as a group.

Unlike the Knights of Labor, the AFL regarded strikes as an acceptable tactic. And unlike anarchists, the AFL rejected schemes to reorganize society. Its moderate philosophy attracted a growing number of workers. From 150,000 members in 1886, the AFL grew to 500,000 members by 1900 and more than one million by 1904.

3. **VISUAL EVIDENCE** Ask: What do the road signs say? How is the train engine labeled? Why did the cartoonist choose a wagon for some unions and a train for others?

3. *Efforts to form labor organizations were slowed by public distrust of unions. In this 1886 cartoon, the Knights of Labor and trade unions are pictured careening toward lawless disorder. In the background, the less militant Brotherhood of Locomotive Engineers is shown, by contrast, as orderly and lawful.*

1. **ECONOMICS** *The New York Times* agreed, commenting, "The object of trade is to get as much as you may and give as little as you can."

2. **READING** Gompers claimed that an employer regarded a worker "the same as a machine, thrown out as soon as all the work possible has been squeezed out of him."

Tension Between Labor and Management

Most company managers were hostile to unions. Owners felt they had the right to bargain with each worker individually. "If I wanted boiler iron," explained one railroad official, "I would go out on the market and buy it where I could get it cheapest, and if I employ men, I would do the same." Unions, he argued, interfered with his rights.

For their part, union officials scoffed at claims that employers had workers' best interests at heart. A few industrialists tried to provide their workers with such benefits as libraries and recreational facilities, but even those employers did not recognize the right of unions to exist. Suspicion and distrust persisted on both sides.

Consequently, violent strikes were not uncommon. The most serious strike erupted at Carnegie's Homestead steel plant in 1892. Angered by an unexpected wage cut, the Amalgamated Association of Iron and Steel Workers refused to accept the company's offer.

With a strike threatening, Henry Clay Frick, the plant manager, closed the plant. He put a wire fence around it and hired 300 Pinkerton guards. When the guards rafted down the Monongahela River to land at the plant, furious union workers attacked them. Gunfire erupted. Soon seven Pinkerton men and nine workers lay dead.

In response to the violence, the Pennsylvania National Guard surrounded the plant and arrested the strikers. Gradually, workers began to return to the steel mills, but no Amalgamated men got their jobs back, and wages fell by about 50 percent.

Since the steel workers' union at Homestead had been the AFL's largest union, the entire AFL suffered from this stunning defeat. The AFL continued to organize other industries, but the Homestead strike made it clear that unions faced a difficult battle for recognition.

Reaction to Unions

Employers were not the only Americans unsympathetic to unions. Courts often issued **injunctions,** orders prohibiting a given action, to stop strikes. Some courts held strikers personally responsible for employers' economic losses during a strike.

The press usually sided with employers during labor-management disputes. Newspaper publishers, who depended on local businesses for advertising revenue and who were employers themselves, often editorialized against what they saw as the unjustified demands of labor.

Furthermore, much of the public opposed unions. Even though most American unions took moderate positions, people often considered them radical organizations. Socialist activity in Europe probably influenced this view. In general, socialists believed that wealth derived from labor should be evenly distributed among the workers and that society as a whole, not profit-seeking individuals, should make economic decisions. In 1877, the Socialist Labor party was formed in the United States, but it remained small and had little influence.

The idea of collective bargaining also seemed foreign to many Americans. The tradition of individualism was strong, and people believed that individual effort was the way to advancement.

See p. T81.

SECTION 5 REVIEW

1. **Identify:** (a) Knights of Labor, (b) Terence V. Powderly, (c) American Federation of Labor, (d) Samuel Gompers.

2. **Define:** (a) anarchist, (b) craft union, (c) collective bargaining, (d) injunction.

3. (a) What were the goals of the Knights of Labor? (b) Who could join?

4. How did the Haymarket riot of 1886 affect the Knights of Labor?

5. (a) What were the goals of the American Federation of Labor? (b) Who could join?

6. How did much of the public react to unions in the late 1880s?

7. **Critical Thinking** How did industrialization affect the relationship between employees and employers?

3. **CITIZENSHIP** Strikebreakers were an effective weapon. "I can hire one half of the working class to kill the other half," railroad tycoon Jay Gould once sneered.

4. **ACTIVITY** Have students present a dialogue between a factory owner and a worker on such topics as working conditions, profits, and collective bargaining.

Summary

1. **After the Civil War, advances in communication and transportation helped stimulate the growth of industry.** The telegraph and later the telephone helped to speed business communication. Meanwhile, railroads increased efficiency by consolidating, and railroad owners looked for new ways to finance expansion.

2. **The growth of the American economy between 1865 and 1914 was due in part to industry's ability to innovate.** Enterprising industrialists seized on new inventions and used them to revolutionize old industries and create new ones. Americans adopted a pro-business philosophy.

3. **Business leaders explored new ways of doing business.** They built large corporations and tapped new sources of capital to pay for expansion. Leaders like Andrew Carnegie and John D. Rockefeller proved to be geniuses at devising new and more efficient forms of business organization.

4. **Industry also spread to the South, which formerly had an agricultural economy.** The "New South" based its industries on its natural resources, including cotton, timber, coal, and iron ore. But the industrial growth of the South still lagged behind that of the North and the West.

5. **Factory workers formed organizations to improve working conditions and work for common goals.** The Knights of Labor declined after the Haymarket riot of 1886. The American Federation of Labor, which organized only skilled workers and stressed limited goals, grew in the late 1800s. Still, many Americans continued to side with management against labor.

See p. T81.

Vocabulary

Match each term at left with its definition or description at right.

1. assets
2. rebate
3. pooling
4. dividend
5. monopoly
6. injunction

a. discount on normal charges
b. total control of an industry
c. order prohibiting an action
d. share of profits
e. property and cash
f. sharing of business

See p. T81.

Chapter Checkup

1. What technological developments in communication helped stimulate industrial growth?

2. (a) What problems resulted from the rapid growth of railroads between 1860 and 1900? (b) How did railroad owners try to solve these problems?

3. Explain how each of the following contributed to a new philosophy for business: (a) Carnegie's Gospel of Wealth; (b) social Darwinism; (c) laissez-faire economics; (d) Horatio Alger's stories.

4. (a) Why did corporations have less difficulty raising capital than proprietorships and partnerships? (b) How did corporations raise capital?

5. (a) Describe free enterprise. (b) Why did some people believe that giant corporations were abusing the free enterprise system?

6. Why did the growing industry of the South continue to lag behind that of the North?

7. (a) What conditions convinced many American workers to join unions in the late 1800s? (b) What attempts were made

to create a national labor organization? (c) Were they successful? Explain.

8. (a) What was the reaction of management to labor organizations? Why? (b) What was the reaction of the courts? (c) What was the reaction of much of the public? Why?

See p. T82.

Critical Thinking

1. **Supporting an Opinion**   Would you characterize the business leaders of the late 1800s as "robber barons" or as "industrial statesmen"? Give examples to support your answer.

2. **Evaluating**   Which invention discussed in this chapter do you think had the greatest impact on American daily life? Why?

See p. T82.

Connecting Past and Present

1. Consolidation is still an American business practice. Consult newspaper or magazine articles for examples of recent mergers or takeovers. How are such consolidations beneficial? In what ways are they harmful?

2. The Bessemer process revolutionized industry. How might recent innovations such as transistors and superconductors have equally far-reaching effects?

See p. T82.

Developing Basic Skills

1. **Comparing**   Make a chart with two columns and four rows. Label one column Knights of Labor and the other American Federation of Labor. Label the rows Date Founded, Goals, Types of Members, and Approved Tactics.
    Complete the chart. (a) How did the membership of the organizations differ? (b) What goals did both organizations have in common? (c) What goals were different? (d) Do you think any of the elements you identified may have made the AFL more likely to be successful? Explain.

2. **Comparing**   Review the description of vertical and horizontal integration on page 431. (a) What segments of an industry does a company control if it is vertically integrated? (b) What segments of an industry does a company control if it is horizontally integrated? (c) How might each give the company an edge over competition?

WRITING ABOUT HISTORY

Using Specialized Reference Books

Specialized reference books provide detailed information about a particular subject area. Some valuable specialized reference books in United States history are listed below.

Dictionary of American History—basic information about topics in American history

Encyclopedia of American History—description of events in American history in chronological order

United States Government Manual—information on government agencies

Statutes at Large—information about laws passed each year

Statistical Abstract of the United States—current economic and social statistics

Historical Statistics of the United States—economic and social statistics from colonial times to the present

Practice: In one of the books mentioned above, find additional information related to a subject discussed in Chapter 20. Identify the source and write a brief paragraph explaining what you have learned.

Politics and Reform

21

(1867–1900)

CHAPTER OUTLINE

1 **Political Corruption in a Gilded Age**

2 **Attempts at Reform**

3 **Politics in the New South**

4 **The Populist Crusade**

5 **The Decline of Populism**

CHAPTER OBJECTIVES After completing this chapter, students should be able to
1. describe political corruption in the late 1800s.
2. list attempts to end corruption.
3. describe politics in the South in the late 1800s.
4. explain the rise and fall of Populism.

CHAPTER PREVIEW Have students study the political cartoons on pp. 446 and 452. Ask them to summarize what each cartoon is attacking. Ask: Are there laws today aimed at stopping political corruption? What are they? Explain to the class that this chapter looks at corruption and at movements to end it in the late 1800s.

It was July 2, 1881, and President James Garfield had just been wounded by an assassin. All through that long, hot summer, the nation waited nervously as the President hovered between life and death. Would Vice President Chester Alan Arthur be moving into the White House? To many Americans, the man in line to take over the government seemed a poor choice for the job.

Arthur owed his position as Vice President to a political deal. Backers of Garfield for President in 1880 needed the support of Roscoe Conkling, the powerful and corrupt boss of the New York Republican machine. In return for that support, they agreed to accept Conkling's lieutenant, Chester Arthur, as Vice President. After all, Garfield was a young enough man; what reason was there to think he might not complete his term?

But now the unthinkable had happened. When Garfield died on September 19, Arthur became President.

"Elegant Arthur," known for his fashionable wardrobe, not his political ideals, would surprise everyone. As President, he proved to be his *own* boss. The new President prosecuted dishonest politicians. He also signed the landmark Civil Service Act, designed to ensure that government jobs went to those best qualified to fill them—not to those who had friends in high places. Arthur's actions so angered old time Republicans that, contrary to tradition, they denied the President his own party's nomination for reelection.

Throughout the second half of the 1800s, the overwhelming corruption at all levels of government became a serious issue. The reforms launched by President Arthur were just the first of many efforts to end abuse of the public trust. Later, politicians would attack big business and the banking interests. The Populist movement, drawing on farmers' discontent with the two major political parties, would become a major force for reform.

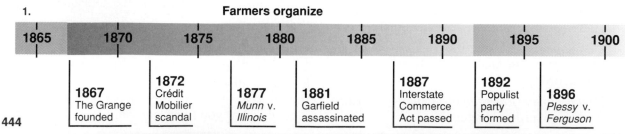

1.

Farmers organize

1865	1870	1875	1880	1885	1890	1895	1900

1867 The Grange founded

1872 Crédit Mobilier scandal

1877 *Munn* v. *Illinois*

1881 Garfield assassinated

1887 Interstate Commerce Act passed

1892 Populist party formed

1896 *Plessy* v. *Ferguson*

444

1. TIME LINE QUESTION Ask: How long after the Crédit Mobilier scandal was the Interstate Commerce Act passed?

1. Widespread corruption in the late 1880s did not dampen political loyalties. This lithograph, The Lost Bet, *by Chicago artist Joseph Klir, shows a Republican paying off an election bet. He pulls a carriage in which the Democratic winner of the bet rides in triumph.*

1. **VISUAL EVIDENCE** Joseph Klir was a Czechoslovakian immigrant. His landlord in Chicago was the winning candidate in this painting. The figures in the crowd were modeled after Klir's Czechoslovakian neighbors.

1 Political Corruption in a Gilded Age

READ TO UNDERSTAND

■ How some industrialists were able to wield political influence in the late 1800s.

■ How Congress came to assert its authority.

■ What scandals plagued the administration of President Grant.

In the years following the Civil War, rich industrialists could buy more than mansions and yachts with their money. They could buy political influence. Once, when told that some of his actions were against the law, railroad owner Cornelius Vanderbilt snorted: "Law! What do I care about the law? Haven't I got the power?"

Some industrialists, however, were concerned with more than a quest for money and power. After amassing an enormous fortune, Andrew Carnegie used his wealth for the benefit of society.

Bribery and Politics

In 1877, Collis P. Huntington, builder of the Central Pacific Railroad and a director of the Southern Pacific line, had a problem. A rival railroad tycoon had placed a bill before Congress aimed at breaking Huntington's control of rail routes to southern California. To Huntington, the solution was simple: Bribe the members of Congress and kill the bill. "It costs money to fix things," he explained. 2.

As industrialization transformed the country after the Civil War, dreams of power and riches corrupted some government officials. Representatives of wealthy special interests bribed members of Congress to pass favorable legislation. Cabinet members took advantage of their positions to make fortunes for themselves. Dishonesty infected state and local governments and even small businesses. **445**

2. **BACKGROUND** Huntington said, "If [another] man has the power to do great evil, and won't do right unless he is bribed to do it, it is a man's duty to go up and bribe the judge."

The author Mark Twain believed that such corruption was the underside of public life, the brass under a thin layer of gold. He la-1. beled the era the Gilded Age.

Wheeling and Dealing in Congress

Congress itself helped confirm the popular notion that politicians were interested only in enjoying the spoils of victory. The Senate, which wielded more power than the House, became known as a "rich man's club." Its members served six-year rather than two-year terms, and many had been able to stay in office for decades. Some had gained great personal wealth through their power and influence. As one observer noted, the country had a government "of the people, by the people, for the benefit of the Senate."

3. *Cartoonist Joseph Keppler criticizes President Grant by showing him as an acrobat using a cloth labeled "corruption" to hold up the evils of his administration. The scandals of the era provided rich material for satire. Keppler, an Austrian immigrant, founded* Puck, *the first successful humorous weekly in the United States.*

446

The House of Representatives had less influence, partly because it seemed too disorderly to function. Representatives often sat with their feet on their desks, smoking cigars or spitting tobacco juice. Some read newspapers or wrote letters instead of attending to business. Nevertheless, the House had some effective legislators and prominent national 2. figures.

Congress thought highly of itself despite its reputation. As you have read in Chapter 18, Congress used the impeachment of President Andrew Johnson to assert its authority over the executive branch. After Reconstruction, the presidency remained weak and Congress became stronger. Congressional leaders jealously protected their right to propose and make laws. The President, they believed, should only enforce laws passed by the legislative branch.

The Presidency in the Gilded Age

Overshadowed by Congress, the Presidents during the Gilded Age tended to be good politicians, but uninspiring leaders. Although some Presidents supported important reforms, they were generally willing to accept the greater power of the legislative branch.

Even if a President had wanted to lead vigorously, he would have found it difficult to do so. The executive staff was small. Without sufficient help, a President could not take the initiative on legislative issues. Moreover, no President between 1865 and 1897 had the advantage of having his own party in control of both houses of Congress throughout his full term of office.

Finally, Presidents were thwarted by the widespread political corruption of the period. Although most of them were personally honest, they were often surrounded by people who were not.

Scandals During the Grant Years

The worst examples of corruption at the national level took place during the administration of Ulysses S. Grant (1869–1877). An honest man and able general, Grant let loyalty to his friends cloud his judgment. He appointed many people who betrayed his trust.

1. In this cartoon, The Power of the Press, *Thomas Nast congratulates himself. Corrupt politicians are being crushed under a printing press on which cartoonist Nast sits.*

The first major scandal came to light in 1872. The New York *Sun* revealed how officials of the Union Pacific Railroad had created a fake construction company, the Crédit Mobilier, to line their pockets. The directors of the Union Pacific Railroad awarded favorable contracts to the Crédit Mobilier to lay track. On the basis of these contracts, Crédit Mobilier was able to sell stock and raise money.

Much of the stock was distributed to members of Congress "where it would do the most good." In return, the stockholding legislators voted funds for Union Pacific construction. Union Pacific then paid the Crédit Mobilier according to the contracts. Although the firm never laid a foot of track, Union Pacific officials and members of Congress received enormous dividends on their stock.

Further investigations revealed that at least five members of Grant's cabinet were dishonest. The most serious offender was Secretary of War William Belknap, who was involved in many of the shady dealings used by white traders to cheat Indians who lived on reservations. (See page 410.)

When Grant's secretary of the treasury resigned over yet another scandal, his re-

1. **BIOGRAPHY** In addition to attacking corruption, Nast also created the images of Uncle Sam, the Democratic donkey, the Republican elephant, and Santa Claus.

placement uncovered the Whiskey Ring. Hundreds of distillers had bribed treasury officials in order to avoid paying taxes. Even the President's personal secretary was involved. Although Grant ordered investigators to "let no guilty man escape," the President protected his secretary from punishment.

The scandals of the Grant administration damaged the office of the presidency and disillusioned the public. Yet the scandals also strengthened the movement to reform political life.

See p. T83.

SECTION 1 REVIEW

1. **Identify.** (a) Gilded Age, (b) Crédit Mobilier, (c) Whiskey Ring.

2. How did some wealthy industrialists use their money to influence the political process?

3. (a) How did Congress view its role in the period following the Civil War? (b) How did Congress view the President's role?

4. How did the scandals during the Grant administration affect the presidency?

5. **Critical Thinking** Which branch of government do you think is stronger today, the executive branch or the legislative branch? Explain.

2. **ACTIVITY** Have students choose one of the scandals described in this section and draw a political cartoon criticizing it.

2 Attempts at Reform

READ TO UNDERSTAND

■ How the Presidents who followed Grant contributed to reform.

■ How reform laws affected railroads and trusts.

■ What proposals radical reformers made.

■ *Vocabulary:* patronage system, holding company.

Angered by the corruption that was undermining the nation's institutions, Americans began to demand sweeping reforms. Once

447

3. **VOCABULARY** Have students look up these terms in the glossary before they begin reading.

1. **BACKGROUND** Nast enraged Boss Tweed of New York. Tweed said that most voters couldn't read, but they could look at pictures. He offered Nast $100,000 to "study art" in Europe, but Nast refused. When Tweed fled to Spain to avoid arrest, police there recognized him from one of Nast's cartoons.

2. *This 1880 cartoon shows James Garfield mowing down corruption on his way to the White House. Once he became President, however, Garfield was besieged by office-seekers. He lamented "in the agony of my soul against the greed for office and its consumption of my time."*

2. **VISUAL EVIDENCE** The caption of this cartoon is "Farmer Garfield Cutting a Swath to the White House." Garfield was the son of poor Ohio farmers.

begun, reform efforts were not limited to cleaning up politics, but were also aimed at curbing abuses by the powerful railroads and trusts.

The Mugwumps

One strong movement for reform came from a group of Republicans called Mugwumps, an Indian term meaning big chief. The Mugwumps opposed the spoils system begun under President Jackson. (See page 254.) They argued that this **patronage system,** the handing out of government jobs as rewards to loyal party workers, should be replaced by a civil service in which workers would be hired on the basis of merit.

The Mugwumps included two editors of well-known journals: E. L. Godkin of *The Nation* and George W. Curtis of *Harper's Weekly.* They exposed corrupt political machines and wrote editorials urging reform. *Harper's* cartoonist, Thomas Nast, caricatured greedy trusts and shady political bosses so

effectively that he broadened the movement to clean up government.

The Mugwumps never succeeded in firing the imagination of the average American, who did not share the reformers' distaste for the spoils system. Ignored by most politicians, the Mugwumps achieved only limited success.

Curtailing the Spoils System

The Mugwumps had small hopes that the three Republican Presidents who followed Ulysses S. Grant would advance the cause of reform. Yet Presidents Hayes (1877–1881), Garfield (1881), and Arthur (1881–1885) each took steps to reform the patronage system.

As you have read, President Rutherford Hayes won the 1876 presidential election through a political deal in which he was given the necessary electoral votes for a promise to end Reconstruction. (See page 391.) Upon taking office, Hayes appointed a noted reformer, Carl Schurz, to the cabinet as secretary of the interior. "Hayes has passed the Republican party to its worst enemies," grumbled one old timer.

President Hayes also launched an investigation into the New York customs house, in charge of collecting duties on imports. Investigators found that more than 200 officials in the customs house received salaries without doing any work. High officials pocketed some $1.5 million in duties each year. Despite the protests of influential Republicans, the President dismissed two senior customs house employees.

Hayes's successor, James Garfield, no sooner assumed office in 1881 than he found himself in the middle of a spirited struggle over patronage between two rival factions of the Republican party. One group was the "Halfbreeds," so called because of their half-hearted commitment to Reconstruction. The other was the "Stalwarts," who had supported a tough policy of Reconstruction. Each group lobbied Garfield to reward its followers with government jobs.

The efforts of both groups ended abruptly on July 2, 1881, when a disappointed office seeker, Charles Guiteau, shot President Garfield. His death in September from his

3. **PRESIDENTS** Although Hayes became President through party politics, he angered many Republicans by refusing to make full use of the spoils system.

4. **BACKGROUND** Remind students that they read a special feature about Schurz on p. 293.

1. wounds dramatized the need to reform the patronage system.

The Civil Service Act

Vice President Chester Arthur, who succeeded Garfield, was one of the customs house officials dismissed by President Hayes. Yet as President, Arthur put public service ahead of party politics.

Reacting to public outcry, in 1883 Congress passed the Civil Service Act, and President Arthur promptly signed it into law. The act classified approximately 15,000 federal jobs as civil service positions, to be awarded only to applicants who passed a competitive examination given by a Civil Service Commission. Furthermore, the act prohibited firing of civil service employees for political reasons.

Although the new legislation did not wipe out the spoils system overnight, it was an important step. The Civil Service Act allowed Presidents to expand the list of civil service jobs. Over the years, they did exactly that—often as a way of preventing their appointees from being dismissed by a new President. By 1897, more than half of the approximately 175,000 federal employees were in the civil service. 2.

Cleveland and Reform

Arthur's support for reform angered old-line Republicans, who refused to renominate him in 1884. In his place, they chose James G. Blaine, a Maine senator who headed the Halfbreed faction of the party.

This time, it was the Democrats who nominated a reformer, New York governor Grover Cleveland. Cleveland had won national attention by defying New York City's political bosses and running an honest administration. The voters chose Cleveland, and, for the first time in 25 years, a Democratic President moved into the White House. 3.

2. **PAST AND PRESENT** Have students find out what percentage of federal jobs is controlled by the Civil Service Commission today.

3. **PRESIDENTS** Grover Cleveland (1837–1908), born in New Jersey, battled corruption in Buffalo, New York, before becoming governor of the state.

---

4. *Honest management was a hallmark of Grover Cleveland's political career from the time he was mayor of Buffalo, New York. This 1895 cartoon shows him as the champion of civil service reform. President Cleveland's policy of selecting office-holders for competence rather than party loyalty disappointed many Democrats who hoped for jobs in the administration.*

4. **VISUAL EVIDENCE** Ask: What do the fence and the pasture represent? What do the two small inset cartoons in the upper left and upper right show?

VOICES OF FREEDOM

Civil Service Reform

The civil service system has been in place for over 100 years. Everyone knows someone who has taken a civil service examination to get a government job. But basing government employment on merit was not always seen as a good idea. In the 1870s, reform of the spoils system was a hotly debated issue. In the first reading below, a Republican senator predicts the consequences of a civil service system. In the second, written ten years after passage of the Civil Service Act, reformer Carl Schurz assesses the law's results.

Senator Oliver Morton:
In Favor of the Spoils System (1871)

In England the tenure of office in the civil service is for life. . . . Ten thousand men in this city [Washington] holding office for life would form a privileged class that would . . . [be] contrary to the fundamental principles of this government. . . .

Are the English clerks better qualified than those in our departments are? From the evidence I have, they are not. But they have one quality that our clerks have not got: that is, they have "the insolence of office" that results from a life tenure. . . .

I am not arguing against competitive examinations. I am in favor of them; but . . . men may pass an examination . . . and yet be utterly unqualified for the position.

Carl Schurz: The Results of Reform (1893)

The Fourth of March last a new administration went into power. Untold thousands of men poured into the national capital clamoring for office. . . . The office-hunting throng swept into the White House and into the departments like a cloud of locusts. . . . The Post Office Department was . . . snowed under with written applications . . . which in huge heaps covered the floors of the rooms. . . . Senators and members of the House of Representatives ran wildly about like whipped errand boys to press the claims of greedy constituents or mercenary henchmen.

But there is one part of the public service which now remains untouched by the . . . spoils carnival. . . . This is the "classified service," covered by Civil Service Law. . . . On [its doors] the words are written, "Nobody enters here who has not proved his fitness for the duties to be performed." The office-hunting mob reads this and recoils. [The public servant] depends upon his merit for his security and advancement, and this consciousness inspires his work.
See p. T83.

1. Contrast Senator Morton's view of a civil service worker with that of Carl Schurz.

2. **Critical Thinking** With which writer's view of an examination system for public servants do you agree? Why?

President Cleveland's administration was marked by angry confrontations with members of his own party. A man of principle, he insisted on appointing competent officeholders over party favorites who wanted their share of the spoils. Cleveland lost the 1888 election to Republican Benjamin Harrison, the grandson of President William Henry Harrison. When Harrison proved to be an undistinguished President, the voters gave Cleveland a second term in 1892.

Regulating the Railroads

Although Cleveland stressed civil service improvements, reform of the nation's railroads also became a pressing issue. As you have read in Chapter 20, cutthroat competition among railroads had resulted in practices such as rebates and pooling. Small shippers complained that the railroads unfairly gave their larger rivals lower rates. Often, too, railroads charged higher rates for haul-

450

1. **BACKGROUND** One railroad lawyer said that the ICC "satisfies the public clamor for regulation at the same time that regulation is almost wholly nominal."

2. **BACKGROUND** In 1906, the Hepburn Act greatly increased the powers and scope of the ICC, as students will read on p. 503.

ing freight short distances than they did for long hauls.

As early as 1837, a few state governments had acted to regulate railroads, but it was not until the 1870s that state regulatory commissions became widespread. The railroads argued that states had no power under the Constitution to regulate the railroad business. In 1877, in the case of *Munn* v. *Illinois,* the Supreme Court ruled that the states could indeed regulate railroads. But in 1886, the Court reversed itself in the case of *Wabash, St. Louis, & Pacific Railway Company* v. *Illinois.* Only Congress, the justices said, could regulate interstate commerce.

Interstate Commerce Act   Congress responded to the demands of reformers by passing the Interstate Commerce Act in 1887. The act banned rebating and pooling. It required the railroads to establish "reasonable and just" rates and to refrain from charging short-haul customers higher rates than long-haul customers. In addition, the act set up a five-member Interstate Commerce Commission (ICC) to investigate complaints and take action by filing suit in the courts.

The Interstate Commerce Act proved difficult to enforce. Supported by skilled lawyers and judges who believed the Constitution limited the government's regulatory powers, the railroads were able to blunt the force of the act. Between 1887 and 1906, the ICC lost almost every case brought before the Supreme Court. Yet the Interstate Commerce Act set an important precedent. In the years ahead, many federal commissions would be established to regulate other industries; and as the Supreme Court became more sympathetic to the regulation of business, the power of the ICC increased.

Attacking the Trusts

"The day of combination" had come to stay, according to John D. Rockefeller, yet many Americans viewed trusts with suspicion. They thought the trusts' size and power gave them an unfair advantage, which hindered the operation of the free enterprise system. Large trusts could drive smaller companies out of business by slashing prices. Once the competitors were out of the way, the trusts became monopolies, free to charge whatever prices they chose.

By ruthless use of monopoly power, trusts violated the public's sense of fair play. Cartoonists portrayed trusts as octopuses greedily grasping for more. In 1888, both Republicans and Democrats responded to public anger by endorsing trust regulation.

Sherman Antitrust Act   In 1890, Congress passed the Sherman Antitrust Act, the first federal effort to control trusts. The law prohibited monopolies, stating, "Every contract, combination in the form of trust or otherwise, or conspiracy in restraint of trade or commerce [that crosses state borders] . . . is hereby declared illegal." It thus became a crime for a business to conspire to destroy all competition.

The Sherman Antitrust Act looked good on paper, but there was no commission like the ICC to respond to antitrust complaints. To sidestep the law, corporations devised a substitute for the trust known as the **holding company.** Instead of merging separate companies into a trust, a holding company gained control of member companies by buying their stock. The "held" companies remained separate and business went on as usual, but the holding company controlled them just as effectively as a trust could.

The Supreme Court dealt a blow to the Sherman Act in 1895 in the case of *United States* v. *E. C. Knight Company.* The company had sold its sugar-refining properties to the American Sugar Refining Company. The government charged that the transaction made American Sugar one of the strongest monopolies in the country. Yet the Court ruled that the sale did not violate the Sherman Antitrust Act. The Court cited two reasons for its decision. First, the act barred monopolies in "trade or commerce." Knight's business was manufacturing. Second, the act applied to transactions that crossed state borders, while Knight refined all its sugar at plants within one state.

With industry assured that the Supreme Court would interpret the antitrust legislation narrowly, the number of holding companies and monopolies continued to grow throughout the 1890s.

3. **BACKGROUND** The Chicago *Tribune* warned, "Liberty and monopoly cannot live together."

4. **BACKGROUND** Although the Sherman Antitrust Act proved ineffective against most trusts, it was successfully used against labor unions on several occasions.

Trusts were complicated legal arrangements that concentrated control of an industry in the hands of
1. *a few people. As this 1889 cartoon shows, some people thought trusts were undermining traditional American liberties.*

1. **VISUAL EVIDENCE** Ask: What do the signs on Liberty's arm and chest mean? What does the wrecked boat mean?

The Radical Reformers

Reform of the civil service, railroads, and trusts was achieved by politicians who worked within the established economic and political system. Even the most militant Mugwumps accepted the basic idea of laissez-faire. But other Americans demanded more far-reaching change.

One radical reformer was Henry George, a self-taught economist whose book *Progress and Poverty* sold more than 2 million copies.
2. George believed that labor should be the basis of all wealth. Under the existing system, land might rise in value simply because a railroad ran near it; without performing any labor,

the owner of the land could thus make large profits. George proposed that Congress enact a single tax as a means of ending such "unearned" profits. This tax would be on income from the use of the bare land, but not on any improvements made to the land. All other taxes would be abolished.

Similarly, Edward Bellamy attracted considerable attention in 1888 with his novel *Looking Backward*. The novel pictured a utopia, or perfect society, in the year 2000. The government would run all industry with great wisdom, thus eliminating the "evils" of competition, and people would live in harmony. Bellamy's followers urged that his ideas be enacted into law.

Henry Demarest Lloyd aroused public opinion against the trusts when he published *Wealth Against Commonwealth* in 1894. Lloyd focused on Rockefeller's Standard Oil Company, marshaling facts and providing vivid examples of the trust's ruthless business practices.

These critics of American society were widely read, but their proposed solutions were too radical for most Americans. Still, they 3. drew public attention to problems that sorely needed solution.

See p. T83.

SECTION 2 REVIEW

1. **Identify:** (a) Chester Arthur, (b) Mugwumps, (c) Grover Cleveland, (d) Interstate Commerce Act, (e) Sherman Antitrust Act, (f) *United States* v. *E. C. Knight Company*.

2. **Define:** (a) patronage system, (b) holding company.

3. What steps did Presidents Hayes and Arthur take to end the abuses of the spoils system?

4. List three practices by the railroads that led to demands for regulation.

5. What were some of the more radical proposals made for reform?

6. **Critical Thinking** How did the growth of industry lead to the expansion of the federal government?

452

3. **DISCUSSION** Have students consider why Americans read critics of business but did not accept the remedies they proposed.

1. **VOCABULARY** Have students look up these terms in the glossary before they begin reading.

2. **ECONOMICS** Remind students that they read about Henry Grady's program for an industrialized "New South" on p. 433.

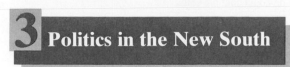

3 Politics in the New South

READceds TO UNDERSTAND

- What is meant by "the solid South."

- How Jim Crow laws deprived blacks of their rights.

- How the proposals for black progress of Booker T. Washington and W.E.B. Du Bois differed.

1. ■ *Vocabulary:* disenfranchise, poll tax, grandfather clause.

With the end of Reconstruction in 1877, the gains of blacks began to erode. White Democrats strengthened their grip on southern state governments so that the Republican party in the South all but disappeared.

Conservatives in Control

The Democrats, also known as Conservatives, who dominated southern politics after Reconstruction were not the same group of wealthy planters who had been in control before the Civil War. Many Conservatives were industrialists who shared the vision of a "New South," with an economy similar to that of

2. the industrial North.

Like business leaders in the rest of the country, southern industrialists opposed interference with their business activities by either state or national government. But southerners had a special reason for supporting laissez-faire. They had just gone through Radical Reconstruction, which seemed to them the height of government interference. With the end of Reconstruction, the Conservatives framed new institutions that severely limited the power of state governments to regulate economic affairs.

The Conservatives enjoyed widespread but not universal support. Graft and bribery flourished in the South as they did in the North. Whenever scandal erupted, Republicans and independents tried to attract voters to opposing candidates. But the Conservatives usually won.

Republicans, who were associated with the Union and Reconstruction, would be po-

litically crippled in the South for many years to come. The domination of the region's political affairs by a single party gave rise to the expression "the solid South," meaning solidly Democratic.

The Rise of Jim Crow

When Republican President Hayes toured the South in 1877, he told black citizens that their "rights and interests would be safer" if southern whites were "let alone by the general government." Hayes was, in effect, advocating a laissez-faire policy toward race relations. The federal government would maintain that policy for the next 75 years.

Southern Conservatives adopted what they felt was a moderate policy toward black citizens. The white politicians did not regard former slaves as equals, but they did accept that blacks should have some rights. Also, they courted black political support.

Throughout the 1880s and into the 1890s, blacks in the South continued to vote and hold minor political offices. Some were elected to state legislatures and the House of Representatives.

Trend Toward Segregation During the 1890s, however, southern state governments moved to deprive black Americans of their political rights and to segregate them by law from whites. In part, the reasons for this were economic. Falling farm prices and tightened credit during the depression of 1893 embittered white southern farmers. Many turned 3. their resentment toward blacks, demanding that they be segregated and be denied the right to vote.

Politics also contributed to the shift in policy. As you will read in the following section, rural southern reformers challenged Conservatives for power. To gain support from the white voters, the Conservatives abandoned their moderate racial policy and made direct appeals to racial hatred.

Voting Restrictions Although the Fifteenth Amendment to the Constitution guaranteed black American males the right to vote, between 1890 and 1907, southern states one by one adopted laws that effectively **disenfranchised,** or denied the vote to, black citizens. Rigid residency requirements prevented sharecroppers, who moved often, from

453

voting. Literacy tests and **poll taxes,** fees that
1. had to be paid in order to vote, further restricted the black vote.

Such voting restrictions worked against poor whites as well as blacks. Consequently, many southern states adopted so-called **grandfather clauses,** which permitted a man to vote if his father or grandfather had been eligible to vote in 1867. Because blacks had not been allowed to vote at that time, they could not qualify. (The Supreme Court declared grandfather clauses unconstitutional in 1915.)

Jim Crow Laws Southern legislatures also passed laws establishing strict social segregation. Blacks were forbidden to mingle with whites in railroad cars, buses, trolleys, passenger terminals, and other public facilities. Laws required blacks to drink from separate water fountains and sit in separate sections in theaters.

These segregation codes were called Jim Crow* laws. They received important sup-

---

*Jim Crow was a black stage character created by a white song-and-dance man in 1830. The character conveyed an unfavorable impression of black people.

port in 1896 when the Supreme Court decided the case of *Plessy* v. *Ferguson*. The Court ruled that segregation was legal as long as blacks were given "separate but equal" facilities. In other words, a state could require 2. that blacks and whites sit in separate railroad cars if accommodations in the cars were equal. Despite the Court's ruling, however, facilities for blacks, though separate, were rarely equal.

Sparked by racial hatred, lynch law and mob rule competed with justice. During the 1890s, almost 200 people were lynched each year in the United States. Four out of five lynchings took place in the South, and most victims in all areas of the country were black. Mark Twain, for one, was so shocked by the violence that he wrote an essay titled, "The United States of Lyncherdom."

The Response of Blacks

Faced with segregation and violence, black Americans searched for a solution to their plight. Some looked to the West as a land of opportunity. In the years following 1877, approximately 200,000 blacks moved west, many homesteading in Kansas or Oklahoma.

Thousands of blacks moved west in the late 1800s to escape racial segregation and
3. *violence. Those who sought the "freedom land" in Kansas were called Exodusters, after the Biblical Exodus in which Moses led his people out of slavery. Moses Speese and his family, shown here, homesteaded a farm in Kansas in 1885.*

454

3. **CRITICAL THINKING** Ask: How might life in Kansas differ from life in the South for the Speese family?

George Washington Carver, shown here in his laboratory at Tuskegee Institute,
was a creative agricultural scientist. He found more than 300 uses for the peanut,
including peanut butter. His discoveries helped make such crops as peanuts,
sweet potatoes, and soybeans more profitable, which in turn made the economy
of the South more diverse.

1. TECHNOLOGY Other peanut derivatives developed by Carver included milk, flour, inks,
plastics, soaps, cosmetics, and medicinal oils.

Most of the blacks who remained in the South continued to be sharecroppers and tenant farmers. Others worked at skilled trades such as carpentry, masonry, plastering, and painting, but even fewer opportunities existed in these trades than before the war. A few blacks founded their own businesses. Most notable was the North Carolina Mutual Life Insurance Company, organized in 1898. It soon became the largest black-owned business in the world.

Black Americans supported each other in these difficult times. Black schools and churches, established during Reconstruction, continued to grow. Fraternal lodges, mutual aid societies, and groups such as the National Negro Business League, an association of black business people founded in 1900, all responded to the needs of black citizens.

Booker T. Washington and Practical Education

Booker T. Washington emerged as a prominent black leader during these years. Born a slave, Washington eagerly pursued an edu-

cation after the war. He enrolled at Hampton Normal and Industrial Institute of Virginia, a school established by the Freedmen's Bureau to help blacks learn trades such as teaching and mechanics.

Washington decided to spread the Hampton ideal of practical education. In 1881, he founded the Tuskegee Institute in Alabama based on the philosophy that "knowledge must be harnessed to the things of real life." Tuskegee attracted hundreds of young blacks seeking vocational training. The distinguished black scientist George Washington Carver began teaching at Tuskegee in 1896. Carver discovered hundreds of uses for southern agricultural products, such as peanuts and sweet potatoes.

Throughout his career, Booker T. Washington insisted that conditions in the South made political equality for blacks an impossible goal. He suggested that blacks focus on achieving economic success. "Through the dairy farm, the truck garden, the trades, and commercial life . . . the negro is to find his way to the enjoyment of all his rights," he advised. Even without the vote, Washington

2. READING Interested students can read Booker T. Washington's autobiography, *Up From Slavery.*

3. ECONOMICS Before 1896, the peanut was not considered a major crop. By the time Carver died in 1943, it was the second largest cash crop in the South.

455

Handmade quilts preserve many American cultural traditions. Before the Civil War, slave women had drawn on the rich African textile-making tradition to add new techniques to the European art of quilting. In the late 1800s, Harriet Powers used these techniques to create stunning quilts like this one, which illustrates scenes from the Bible.

1. VISUAL EVIDENCE The quilt, which Powers worked on from 1895 to 1898, measures almost 6 feet by 9 feet.

---

2. BACKGROUND When Booker T. Washington was invited to dine at the White House in 1901, the invitation was criticized by many as an insult to white southerners.

noted, blacks had that "little green ballot," money, which could be deposited at the bank, where "no one will throw it out or refuse to count it."

Washington's message found its fullest expression in a speech he gave before an Atlanta business convention in 1895. He assured white business and political leaders that blacks were loyal to the southern way of life. Because of that loyalty, Washington maintained, blacks should have a chance to earn a decent living in the South. That speech, in which Washington abandoned social and political equality in return for prosperity, is
2. referred to as the Atlanta Compromise.

W.E.B. Du Bois Answers

In contrast to Booker T. Washington, William E. B. Du Bois (doo BOIZ) recommended vigorous protest against Jim Crow laws. Du Bois, who grew up in Massachusetts, was the first black to be graduated from Harvard with a
456 Ph.D. degree. Du Bois began teaching eco-

nomics and history at Atlanta University in 1896, about the time that Washington's views were receiving wide publicity.

The young Du Bois argued that blacks should fight for the right to vote and the right to enjoy equality of opportunity. In *The Souls of Black Folk,* published in 1903, Du Bois attacked Washington for abandoning the goal of equal rights. "Negroes must insist 3. continually," Du Bois wrote, "that voting is necessary to proper manhood, that color discrimination is barbarism, and that black boys need education as well as white boys." 4.

Inspired by Washington, Du Bois, and others, southern blacks slowly made economic progress. By 1900, one in five owned a home, and the combined worth of black farms was almost $500 million. While fewer than 5 percent of blacks could read in 1865, approximately 56 percent were literate in 1900. By 1915, blacks in the South owned 30,000 businesses, including grocery stores, dress shops, banks, and insurance companies.

Yet the hopes of black Americans in both the South and North were stifled by preju-

3. BACKGROUND Du Bois respected Washington's achievements, but once said, "So far as Mr. Washington apologizes for injustice, we must firmly oppose him."

4. READING Interested students can read sections of Du Bois's *Black Reconstruction.*

1. **VOCABULARY** Have students look up these terms in the glossary before they begin reading.

2. **READING** Interested students can read *The Populist Moment: A Short History of the Agrarian Revolt in America* by Lawrence Goodwyn.

dice. The road to full political and social equality stretched far into the future.

See p. T84.

SECTION 3 REVIEW

1. **Identify:** (a) "solid South," (b) Jim Crow laws, (c) *Plessy* v. *Ferguson,* (d) Booker T. Washington, (e) W.E.B. Du Bois.

2. **Define:** (a) disenfranchise, (b) poll tax, (c) grandfather clause.

3. List three ways in which southern blacks were discouraged from voting.

4. What kind of education was offered at Tuskegee Institute?

5. What did W.E.B. Du Bois urge black Americans to do?

6. **Critical Thinking** How would Booker T. Washington's ideas be received today? Why?

4 The Populist Crusade

READ TO UNDERSTAND

■ How economic problems in the 1870s and 1880s led farmers to organize.

■ What reforms were proposed in the Ocala Platform.

■ How the Populist party originated.

1. ■ *Vocabulary:* deflation, graduated personal income tax.

When times were good, few people were interested in change. But drought, debt, and depressions burdened farmers in the 1870s and 1880s. After years of hardship, farmers heeded a reformer's call to "raise less corn and more hell." Sweeping like wildfire across the prairies and the cotton fields, the protest movement sparked a new political party, the Populist party, which briefly challenged the 2. nation's traditional two-party system.

Roots of Discontent

Farmers faced an ironic problem in the late 1800s. As increased mechanization helped them produce more, they earned less. In 1880, 15 percent of the farmland in the United States yielded 30 percent of the world's grain. But American farmers competed on the world market with farmers in Australia, South America, and Canada. Plentiful supplies of food drove prices down. Mary Lease, a lawyer and fiery Kansas reformer, expressed the farmers' frustration:

> We were told two years ago to go to work and raise a big crop. . . . We plowed and planted; the rains fell, the sun shone, nature smiled, and we raised the big crop they told us to; and what came of it? Eight-cent corn, ten-cent oats, two-cent beef, and no price at all for butter and eggs—that's what came of it.

3.

4. **BACKGROUND** Her sharp tongue earned Mary Lease the nickname the "Kansas python."

Kansas orator and author Mary Lease was among 4. *the most articulate spokespersons for the Populist cause. Born in Pennsylvania, she moved to Kansas and became a lawyer. Populists represented a broad segment of American society, including farmers, small-town business people, and others who felt squeezed by the power of large monopolies.*

457

3. **ECONOMICS** In 1881, a bushel of wheat sold for $1.19. By 1894, the price had plunged to 49 cents. Corn prices fell from 63 cents to 18 cents a bushel in the same period.

As the amount of grain on the world market grew, prices dropped—resulting in
1. hardships for farmers. All but the very young members of farm families worked to
make ends meet. Several generations of women in this Alabama family are
spinning and weaving.

1. **VISUAL EVIDENCE** Ask: What kind of cloth do you think these women are weaving? Why?
Remind students that finished products fetch a higher price than raw materials.

Farmers saw the banks as the major cause of their problems. Farmers usually borrowed money to buy seed and machinery; they paid back their loans once crops were harvested and sold. But credit was hard to get during the 1880s and 1890s, and month after month the number of mortgage foreclosures increased.

Those farmers able to borrow money faced problems of another kind. These were
2. times of **deflation,** when the price of goods and services was dropping. For example, the dollar bought more in 1876 than it did in 1886. Farmers who borrowed money one year and paid it back several years later found that the money they paid back was worth more, and took longer to earn, than the money they had borrowed.

Farmers also pointed the finger of blame at railroads who transported their grain. The farmers claimed, quite rightly in many cases, that the rates the railroads charged in the West, where they had a monopoly, were two or three times higher than rates in the East.

Nature seemed to conspire against the
458 farmer, too. During the late 1880s, hard winters and summer droughts destroyed cattle and crops in the West. In the South, floods in the lower Mississippi Valley ruined much land.

Organizing for Action

As early as the 1860s, farmers had banded together to deal with their problems. In 1867, Oliver Kelley founded the Patrons of Husbandry, popularly called the Grange. Within seven years, more than 14,000 local Grange associations were formed. In midwestern states, their influence helped to pass laws to regulate railroad freight rates.

The Grange struggled to boost farm profits. Most farmers sold their harvested grain to distributors, who for a fee stored the grain in giant elevators and arranged to ship it to market. Grangers formed cooperatives that operated their own grain elevators and marketed the grain themselves. They also established stores to buy farm machinery and sell it to members at low prices.

The Grange was strongest in the Midwest and in Kentucky and Missouri, but even

2. **ECONOMICS** Have students give examples of what happens to prices in a deflationary time
compared to an inflationary time. Ask: Why would bankers fear inflation? Why would deflation
increase bank profits?

in these areas the organization waned when economic conditions improved in the late 1870s. In its brief heyday, the Grange had laid the pattern for future grass-roots movements. When conditions worsened again in the mid-1880s, new protest organizations gathered strength, especially in the South and the West.

1.   The Northwestern Farmers' Alliance, established in 1880, represented farmers in the Midwest. Among the southern groups, the Southern Farmers' Alliance achieved prominence. Begun in Texas in 1875, it spread throughout the South after 1886, under the direction of an energetic Methodist preacher named Charles W. Macune. At the same time, a separate Colored Farmers' National Alliance represented the interests of more than one million black farmers. The alliances adopted many of the Grangers' techniques. They organized cooperatives to purchase equipment and to market crops. They also published newspapers and ran lecture bureaus to spread their ideas.

2.

The Ocala Platform

As hard times spread, farmers came to believe that they had to take political action if they were to prosper. In 1889, some members of the Northwestern Alliance joined with the Southern Alliance to form the National Farmers' Alliance. The following year, leaders from alliances all over the country met at Ocala, Florida. They created a program for political reform, called the Ocala Platform.

     That platform demanded above all that the government make credit easier for farmers to obtain. Each year, farmers had to sell their crops immediately after harvest in order to pay back loans for seed and machinery. If prices were low at the time, farmers could not make enough money to pay back their loans. The Ocala Platform proposed that the government lend farmers up to 80 percent of the local market value of their crops. Farmers could then pay off their other debts and store their crops in warehouses until the market price rose.

     The Ocala Platform also advocated government action to discourage deflation. The government, it declared, should increase the amount of money in circulation. It could do this in part by minting silver coins. The increase in the money supply would inflate the currency; that is, money would be cheaper, an advantage to debtors.

     The Ocala Platform went on to argue that the government was aiding wealthy manufacturers at the expense of farmers and landowners. High tariffs protected domestic manufactured products from competition by cheaper European goods. Farmers had to pay higher prices for the protected products. Yet they were forced to sell their agricultural products in the international market without any similar government protection.

     Furthermore, most government taxes were based on the amount of land a person owned. The Ocala Platform recommended that wealth, not land, be taxed. It proposed a **graduated personal income tax,** that is, a tax in proportion to a person's income: Persons with higher incomes would pay a higher rate. Finally, the Ocala Platform called for strict regulation of the railroads. If regulation failed, the Alliance recommended that the government take over the railroads and run them fairly.

3.

Birth of the Populist Party

During the 1890 elections, the National Farmers' Alliance worked to elect representatives to Congress. In the South, where the Democratic party dominated, farmers demanded that Democratic candidates publicly support agrarian reform measures in return for the farmers' votes. In the West, many farmers formed independent parties.

     Candidates sympathetic to agrarian reform enjoyed great success in the election. In the South, the farmers' movement helped elect four governors, forty-four representatives, and three senators. In the West, Kansas and South Dakota each elected a reform senator, and Nebraska and Kansas elected several reform representatives.

     The sweetness of victory turned sour when the elected officials failed to carry out promised reform. Only Tom Watson of Georgia continued to support agrarian reform. In

459

2. **BACKGROUND** Both the Grange and the Farmers' Alliance faced bitter resistance from owners of grain elevators and from grain distributors.

3. **PAST AND PRESENT** Have students discuss which of the demands of the Ocala Platform have since been adopted by the federal government.

1. response, the farmers' alliances joined together to form a third political party. The Populist party, as it was called, met in Omaha, Nebraska, in 1892 to nominate a presidential ticket. This was no ordinary convention. From all over came farmers, ranchers, miners, small-town newspaper editors—people tired of the old parties and looking for change.

Many of the convention delegates appeared in broad-brimmed hats and dusty boots. They had nicknames like "Sockless Socrates" Simpson of Kansas, "Calamity" Weller of Iowa, and "Cyclone" Davis of Texas. But their demands for action were clear and direct.

The Populists chose two former Civil War generals as candidates, James B. Weaver of Iowa for President and James G. Field of Virginia for Vice President. The Populists ran on the Ocala Platform.

2. ginia for Vice President. The Populists ran on the Ocala Platform.

Although Democrat Grover Cleveland won the election of 1892 and returned for a second term as President after being out of office four years, the Populists did surprisingly well for a new party. Their ticket received one million popular and 22 electoral votes (from Kansas, Colorado, Idaho, Nevada, and North Dakota). As 1893 began, there were high hopes for further reforms.

2. DISCUSSION Ask: How did the choice of these two generals show that the Populists were trying to forge unity and overcome sectional feelings? See p. T84.

SECTION 4 REVIEW

1. **Identify:** (a) Grange, (b) National Farmers' Alliance, (c) Ocala Platform, (d) Populist party.

2. **Define:** (a) deflation, (b) graduated personal income tax.

3. (a) List three problems faced by American farmers in the late 1800s. (b) List three proposals outlined in the Ocala Platform.

4. (a) What were the results of the election of 1892? (b) How was the election significant for the Populist party?

5. **Critical Thinking** How was the Populist crusade similar to the labor movement of the late 1800s?

460

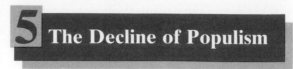

5 The Decline of Populism

READ TO UNDERSTAND

■ Why people wanted the unlimited coinage of silver.

■ How the silver issue led to a split in the Democratic party.

■ Why the Populist party declined.

■ *Vocabulary:* gold standard.

3.

Cheered by their strong showing in the 1892 election, Populists predicted that "the people" would soon triumph over "the plutocrats." Support for reform surged when the economy plunged into depression in 1893. Victory seemed nearer than ever—but victory was a mirage. Within a few brief years, the Populist movement would collapse.

The Depression of 1893

Shortly after his inauguration in 1893, President Grover Cleveland found himself facing the worst depression the nation had yet experienced. The financial collapse began when the Philadelphia and Reading Railroad went bankrupt. As panicked investors sold stock, prices fell on the New York Stock Exchange. Worried bank officers demanded that loans be repaid, but companies were in no position to make good on their debts. One by one, other major railroads declared bankruptcy, including the Erie, the Union Pacific, and the Santa Fe.

4.

The situation at the end of 1893 was grim. About 500 banks had failed and 1,500 businesses had gone bankrupt. Nearly 3 million workers were thrown out of work. Employers drastically cut wages.

President Cleveland strongly believed that the depression occurred because silver was circulating as part of the currency. Most economists today believe that government silver policies did little to either harm or benefit the economy, but Cleveland's belief and the actions he took provoked a political storm.

1. ECONOMICS The demand for silver coinage intensified when the discovery of new ore deposits in the 1870s drove down the price of silver.

GREAT DEBATE

Gold Versus Silver

For many years, Americans had engaged in heated debate about the nation's currency. Should money be based on gold alone? Or should both gold and silver be part of the currency? The way the issue was resolved could help determine which Americans made fortunes and which went hungry.

Supporters of silver believed that silver coinage would put money in their pockets and help pay off their debts. If the government bought silver to turn into coins or to back paper currency, the silver mines would prosper and the money supply would swell. If the money supply grew, prices would rise and farmers would get more for their crops, or so the reasoning went. Thus, farmers, miners, and rising business people who had started on borrowed money, especially in the

1. West, tended to favor "free silver."

Other Americans, however, strongly opposed silver. They wanted the government to maintain a **gold standard,** or currency based solely on gold. This would hold down the money supply and keep prices from rising. Supporters of the gold standard included bankers and established business people, especially in the East. Many workers also feared inflation and favored the gold standard.

Until 1873, the United States had minted gold and silver coins and printed paper money backed by gold and silver. In the Coinage Act of 1873, Congress declared that henceforth gold alone would be used. Farmers and other debtors voiced outrage. Trapped in a vise of falling prices and rising debt, they denounced "the Crime of 1873" and demanded that Congress restore the use of silver.

In 1878, Congress responded to such demands by passing the Bland-Allison Act over President Hayes's veto. This act required the government to buy a set amount of silver each year to be minted into coins. Then, in 1890, Congress passed the Sherman Silver Purchase Act. The act increased the amount of silver that had to be purchased yearly and allowed paper money backed by silver.

Subsequently, the depression in 1893 prodded President Cleveland to seek a return to the gold standard. He claimed that

This 1890 cartoon criticizes the Sherman Silver Purchase Act by showing Columbia, the symbol of the nation, drowning in silver coins. Senators who voted for the act have opened the floodgates in the background. Even the bill's sponsor did not think much of it.

2.

2. VISUAL EVIDENCE Ask: Who is the figure on the right? What is he trying to do?

basing the currency on gold and silver had weakened the economy. In his opinion, it had sapped the confidence of the business community, discouraged new investment, and created unemployment. But although Congress repealed the Sherman Act in 1893, the depression continued. ∎

Coxey's Army

With no relief in sight by 1894, more and more people blamed the President's policies. Among the most vocal critics was an Ohio stone-quarry owner, Jacob Coxey. Coxey himself was wealthy, but, like the Populists, he believed something had to be done for the millions of unemployed. He proposed a government road-construction program to provide work relief. If the treasury issued $500 million in new money, Coxey argued, it would create inflation, stimulate the economy, and pay for the road construction.

3.

Cleveland rejected all such schemes, as did Congress. Coxey angrily retorted that if Washington would not listen, he and his supporters would "send a petition to Washington with boots on." More than 500 followers marched from Massillon, Ohio, Coxey's home town, to Washington, D.C. Along the way, sympathetic crowds turned out to cheer the marchers, who became known as Coxey's Army.

461

3. BIOGRAPHY Jacob Coxey (1854–1951) was elected mayor of Massillon, Ohio, in 1931. As in 1894, he proposed to solve the hardships of the Great Depression with public works and inflated currency.

1. **CRITICAL THINKING** Have students discuss Bryan's imagery. Ask: Why might the speech have made a strong impression? How might it have offended some people?

2. **DISCUSSION** Have students consider how the two-party system tends to make it difficult to build support for third parties.

Coxey's Army was not welcome in Washington. The violence of labor strikes like the one at Carnegie's Homestead plant (see page 441) had led some government leaders to fear a revolution. Although Coxey's intentions were peaceful, police arrested him along with other leaders and dispersed his followers.

The Democrats Divide

Coxey's march demonstrated the depth of public discontent. President Cleveland also found growing opposition within his own party. Many southern and western Democrats despised Cleveland's commitment to gold. The President's unpopularity was reflected in the comment of Democratic Governor "Pitchfork" Ben Tillman of South Carolina: "I haven't got words to say what I think of that old bag of beef."

When the Democratic convention met in 1896, southern and western Democrats angrily outvoted Cleveland's eastern supporters. The party platform adopted many of the Populists' goals, including unlimited coinage of silver, a lower tariff, and an income tax.

In the debate on silver, a dramatic orator from Nebraska, William Jennings Bryan, held the delegates spellbound. "We have petitioned, and our petitions have been scorned; we have entreated, and our entreaties have been disregarded; we have begged, and they have mocked when our calamity came. We beg no longer; we entreat no more; we petition no more. We defy them!"

Referring to Cleveland's support of the gold standard, Bryan thundered, "You shall not press down upon the brow of labor this crown of thorns, you shall not crucify mankind upon a cross of gold!" The delegates roared their approval.

The Democrats nominated Bryan as their presidential candidate over the strong objections of Cleveland's supporters. Though only 36 years old, the Nebraskan was already well known throughout the South and West as the leading spokesman for the pro-silver faction.

The Populist party now faced a dilemma. Many members had hoped to succeed as a third party, but the Democrats had stolen much of their thunder by nominating Bryan.

Populist leaders wondered whether they too should support him. At their own convention, many Populists wanted to nominate a different candidate, but Tom Watson persuaded the delegates to place Bryan at the top of their ticket as the man most likely to beat the Republicans. Thus, Bryan was the candidate of two parties.

The Election of 1896

With the Democrats divided, the Republicans sensed victory. They selected Senator William McKinley from Ohio as their candidate. McKinley's nomination was the product of careful groundwork by Marcus "Mark" Hanna, a coal, iron, and shipping tycoon from Cleveland, Ohio.

The campaign of 1896 presented the voters with a dramatic contrast in style and policy. "Billy" Bryan moved at a hectic pace, traveling 18,000 miles (28,800 kilometers) to make more than 600 speeches. Always, his themes reflected the Populist creed: Regulate the railroads, curb the monopolies, and establish a currency backed by silver. The Bryan campaign gained the endorsement of reformers Henry George and Edward Bellamy, as well as labor leaders Eugene V. Debs of the Railway Union and Samuel Gompers of the AFL.

McKinley, for his part, remained in his home town of Canton, Ohio, throughout the campaign. Occasionally, he read speeches from his front porch to admirers who came to town to hear him. Such speeches contained quiet assurances that the nation's economic system was sound and that the gold standard was best for the country.

Meanwhile, Mark Hanna worked hard behind the scenes to round up campaign contributions from the trusts, railroad owners, large banks, and industrialists. Hanna raised well over $3 million, ten times as much as Bryan's campaign had. With so much money at his disposal, Hanna sent Republican speakers across the country to stump for their candidate. He distributed some 250 million pieces of literature.

McKinley triumphed by 600,000 popular votes, winning the northern labor vote and 60 percent of the electoral college. Without

3. **BIOGRAPHY** Marcus Hanna (1837–1904) was chairman of the Republican National Committee and served as senator from Ohio.

4. **PRESIDENTS** McKinley was the last former Civil War officer to become President.

1. This cartoon from the presidential election of 1896 shows William Jennings Bryan on the Democratic donkey leading a Populist army toward the White House. Included are Mary Lease, Jacob Coxey, Tom Watson, and "Pitchfork" Ben Tillman.

1. VISUAL EVIDENCE Ask: Do you think this cartoonist supported Bryan and the Populists? Why or why not?

2. BACKGROUND Many factory workers, like their employers, were afraid that Bryan's silver policy would damage the nation's industries.

support from the industrial sections of the country, Bryan's southern and western coalition had been unable to carry a presidential election.

The Populists' Fate

Bryan's defeat marked the end of the Populist movement. In part, the movement declined because of a failure of morale. The agricultural reformers had done their best, carrying every state west of the Mississippi and in the south. Yet they had fallen short. Furthermore, the Democrats had lured many Populists back into the Democratic party.

Improved economic conditions also hurt the Populist movement. In the first three years of McKinley's term, prosperity slowly returned to the nation. A wheat crop failure abroad in 1897 stimulated demand for American farm exports. Gold discoveries in Alaska helped expand the treasury's gold reserves. Ironically, the increase in the gold supply inflated the currency—which was exactly what the silver campaigners had been demanding. With conditions improving, the Populist drive lost its momentum.

Prosperity made McKinley's business principles appear sound. On the President's recommendation, Congress passed the Gold Standard Act of 1900 to put the nation back on the gold standard. The quiet acceptance of gold as the single basis of currency signaled the end of the long-running controversy. Few people objected when Congress set even higher tariff rates for industry in the Dingley Tariff Bill of 1897. In the next decade, other voices of reform would be raised, but the Populists' dramatic moment on the national scene had passed.

See p. T85.

SECTION 5 REVIEW

1. **Identify:** (a) Coinage Act, (b) Bland-Allison Act, (c) Sherman Silver Purchase Act, (d) Coxey's Army, (e) William Jennings Bryan, (f) William McKinley.

2. **Define:** gold standard.

3. According to President Cleveland, what caused the depression of 1893?

4. How did the Democratic party split at the presidential nominating convention in 1896?

5. What happened to the Populist movement after Bryan's defeat in 1896?

6. **Critical Thinking** How was the election of 1896 a victory for the Hamiltonian view of society over the Jeffersonian view?

3. READING Students can find primary source material about the Populists in *A Populist Reader*, edited by George Tindall. Secondary sources include *The Age of Reform* by Richard Hofstadter; *The Populist Response to Industrial America* by Norman Pollack; and *Tom Watson: Agrarian Rebel* by C. Vann Woodward.

CHAPTER 21 REVIEW

Summary

1. **The years after the Civil War were a time of political corruption.** The lure of great wealth tarnished the reputations of both Congress and the presidency, particularly during President Grant's administration.

2. **Reformers sought to end the abuses of power and wealth.** Congress passed the Civil Service Act to weaken the spoils system. The Interstate Commerce Act and the Sherman Antitrust Act were aimed at abuses in industry. But the railroads and giant trusts found ways to evade them.

3. **In the South, the Democrats consolidated their control over state governments.** During the 1890s, blacks lost much of what they had gained during Reconstruction. Booker T. Washington and W.E.B. Du Bois emerged as leaders of the blacks' struggle for a better life.

4. **American farmers facing economic hardship in the late 1800s began to organize to improve their lives.** Uniting at first in independent grass-roots movements, they eventually formed a new political party—the Populist party in 1892.

5. **The depression of 1893 created unrest and heightened the controversy over the coinage of silver.** Both the Democrats and the Populists nominated William Jennings Bryan for President in 1896, but Republican William McKinley won. As the major parties adopted many Populist ideas, and as prosperity returned, the Populist party declined.

See p. T85.

Vocabulary

On a separate sheet of paper, write the word or words that best complete each of the following sentences.

1. The practice of giving out government jobs as favors was the _____.

2. A (An) _____ buys stock in other corporations in order to control them.

3. People who are denied the vote are _____.

4. A (An) _____ is a fee paid for the right to vote.

5. _____ results in lower prices for goods and services.

See p. T85.

Chapter Checkup

1. How did the industrialists' great wealth contribute to political corruption ?

2. (a) What was the reputation of the Senate and the House of Representatives during the Gilded Age? (b) Why was Congress able to dominate the presidency? Give examples.

3. (a) How did state governments try to regulate railroads in the 1870s? (b) How did the Supreme Court rule on the states' power to regulate railroads in 1877? In 1886? (c) What were the provisions of the Interstate Commerce Act?

4. (a) How did southern state governments disenfranchise black voters? (b) What were Jim Crow laws? (c) How did the Supreme Court decision in *Plessy* v. *Ferguson* strengthen Jim Crow laws?

5. (a) How did Booker T. Washington urge southern blacks to respond to segregation? Why? (b) What response did W.E.B. Du Bois recommend? Why?

6. (a) Why did farmers find it increasingly difficult to make a living in the late 1800s? (b) What organizations did they form to deal with their problems? (c) What methods did these organizations use to help farmers?

7. (a) Why did farmers and miners favor the coinage of silver? (b) How did Congress react to pressure from the two groups? (c) Why did President Cleveland favor a gold standard?

8. (a) How did the Democratic party platform in 1896 reflect the goals of the Populists? (b) What developments led to the decline of the Populists after 1896?

See p. T86.

Critical Thinking

1. Analyzing (a) Why did Mark Twain label the decades after the Civil War the Gilded Age? (b) In what ways do you think it was a Gilded Age? Give examples.

2. Evaluating Why do you think the views of Booker T. Washington were more popular among white southerners than the views of W.E.B. Du Bois?

See p. T86.

Connecting Past and Present

1. Consult a current newspaper or magazine for information about a present-day political scandal. (a) Why do you think corruption is still a problem? (b) How is corruption dealt with today?

2. The Populist party was a third-party movement that waned when its ideas were taken over by the major parties. (a) What third parties exist today? (b) Have any of their goals been addressed by the major parties or major political figures? Explain.

See p. T86.

Developing Basic Skills

1. Analyzing Political Cartoons Political cartoons are valuable pieces of historical evidence. Study the cartoon on page 452: (a) Which economic development is the cartoon illustrating? (b) What impact does the cartoonist think this development is having on the people of the United States? (c) Do you think the cartoonist favors or opposes trusts? Why?

2. Comparing Make a chart with three columns. Label the first column Reform Actions. Label the second column Purpose and the third column Degree of Success. List the reform actions you learned about in this chapter in the first column. In the second column, describe the problem the action was to solve. In the third column, note how successful each of the actions was. (a) What problems were the reformers trying to solve? (b) How successful were they? (c) Why do you think this was the case?

WRITING ABOUT HISTORY

Evaluating a Source of Information

The quality of your research will depend in large part on your sources. To help evaluate a book, check the author's educational background and area of interest. Then look at the date of publication on the copyright page and the the name of the publisher. Recent books will probably be more up-to-date, while major publishers are usually careful about the quality of their publications.

Your library is a good source of information about periodicals. *Magazines for Libraries* reviews magazines for quality and possible bias. If you are consulting a newspaper, you will want to use a newspaper of record such as *The New York Times* or the Saint Louis *Post-Dispatch*. A newspaper of record reports major events in detail and carries the full text of important speeches and press conferences.

Practice: Using the preceding guidelines, review a magazine or book from your library. Tell why you think this book or magazine would or would not be a good source of historical information for a research paper.

Toward an Urban Age

22

(1865–1914)

CHAPTER OUTLINE

1 Beginning of an Urban Age

2 Immigrants and Cities

3 An Urban Way of Life

4 A Changing Society: Problems and Prospects

CHAPTER OBJECTIVES After completing this chapter, students should be able to
1. describe the rapid growth of American cities in the late 1800s.
2. explain how immigrants helped cities grow.
3. list cultural developments and problems of cities.
4. interpret thematic maps.

CHAPTER PREVIEW Have students brainstorm a list of differences between city and rural life, including such things as types of employment, transportation, housing, and entertainment. Ask: How would the absence of radio, television, and movies add to differences between urban and rural areas?

President Grover Cleveland first waved a magic wand, then pushed a button. Instantly, thousands upon thousands of electric lights dazzled the crowd. Mighty machines, dynamos, and motors lumbered into motion, and sparkling electric-powered fountains shot their spray high into the air. It was May 1, 1893, and the Columbian Exposition in Chicago was now officially open.

The fair was billed as a celebration of the 400th anniversary of Columbus's discovery of America. (It was such a huge project that it opened seven months late.) Primarily, however, the fair was a celebration of American industry and technology. Visitors to the fair marveled at the many displays of scientific ingenuity.

Since many fair-goers had never seen electricity at work before, this was the most awesome of the new wonders. Electricity powered cars, locomotives, fountains, elevators, and clocks. There was even an electric stove on which you could actually cook. And there were electric lights, thousands of them! Even today, photos of the "White City" look like the work of a Hollywood special-effects artist.

Other marvels included steam engines, hydraulic lifts, printing presses, refrigerators, machines for bookmaking and woodworking, and the world's fastest locomotive, New York Central's No. 999. For a fee, one could view the entire layout from the great Ferris wheel. The wheel, built by George Ferris himself, rose a dizzying 250 feet into the air. Suspended from it were 36 cars, each the size of a bus and each able to carry 36 people on the ride of their lives.

The Columbian Exposition was the proud symbol of the nation's strides in manufacturing, transportation, and communication. These forces, along with immigration, were relentlessly pushing America into an urban age. The developing cities would provide jobs, entertainment, and culture for millions—but they would also create serious social and political problems.

1.

"New" immigration increases

1865	1875	1885	1895	1905	1915

| **1869** Tweed Ring in New York City | **1871** Chicago becomes boom town | **1882** Chinese Exclusion Act passed | **1889** Jane Addams founds Hull House | **1893** Columbian Exposition opens | **1900** New York City grows to 3.5 million people | **1910** 8 million women hold jobs |

1. TIME LINE QUESTION Ask: Which events took place in the decade of the 1880s?

1. *New inventions transformed American cities. Thomas Edison brightened the cities with electric lights, which brought crowds onto the streets at night.*

2. *Streetcars and elevated trains, like the ones in this painting by Louis Sonntag, expanded the distances that people could travel to work, shop, or play.*

---

1. **TECHNOLOGY** Refer students to pp. 426 and 427 for a discussion of the contributions of Edison and George Westinghouse. Ask: Do you think the elevated train could have developed without Westinghouse's air brake?

 **Beginning of an Urban Age**

READ TO UNDERSTAND

■ Why cities grew rapidly in the late 1800s.

■ How Chicago symbolized urban America.

■ What problems urbanization brought.

"Those who labor in the earth are the chosen people of God," said Thomas Jefferson. Most Americans of his time agreed. Living mainly on farms or in villages, they tended to shun the cities as a breeding ground for sin. After the Civil War, however, many Ameri-cans sought the better life that cities promised. More and more of them decided to risk the temptations and move to cities in search of jobs. But the pace of urbanization caused serious problems.

The Rapid Growth of Cities

Industrial expansion fueled the explosive growth of cities in the late 1800s. Manufacturers built most of their new plants in cities in order to be near workers and transportation. The new jobs, in turn, drew even more people to the cities.

Population statistics reveal how rapidly cities grew in just 20 years. In 1880, fewer than 25 percent of Americans lived in cities. **467**

2. **VISUAL EVIDENCE** The date of this painting is 1895. Ask: How many forms of transportation are shown in the painting? Which ones would not have been available 20 years before? Which are still used today?

1. **BACKGROUND** A young man in a story by Hamlin Garland summed up the feelings of many farmers at the time: "I'm sick of farm life . . . It's nothing but fret, fret, and work the whole time, never going any place, never seeing anybody."

Then, between 1880 and 1900, the urban population doubled. New York City grew from fewer than 2 million people in 1880 to nearly 3.5 million in 1900. The population of Chicago more than tripled, from 440,000 to 1.7 million. The tilt toward the cities was sharpest in the Northeast, as people left farms for factory jobs. In the last 20 years of the 1800s, 60 percent of the rural townships of the Northeast lost population. 1.

By 1900, nearly 40 percent of the 70 million people in the United States lived in cities. Philadelphia had a population of more than one million. St. Louis, Boston, and Balti- 2.

2. **PAST AND PRESENT** Have students find out the populations of these cities today. Ask: Where do New York City, Chicago, and Philadelphia now rank on a list of the most populous cities in the U.S.?

SKILL LESSON

Urban Growth: Interpreting Thematic Maps

See p. T87.

Thematic maps are a valuable source of historical information. They show the distribution of such things as population, rainfall, or crop production. The key is particularly important on a thematic map because it explains the meaning of symbols used. To practice using thematic maps, study the maps below and on page 469. Then follow these steps.

1 **Decide what is shown on the maps.** (a) What is the topic of the maps? (b) What do the circles represent? (c) What do the areas shaded orange represent?

2 **Read the information on the maps.** (a) How many cities appear on the 1860 map? (b) On the 1900 map? (c) Which cities had 3.

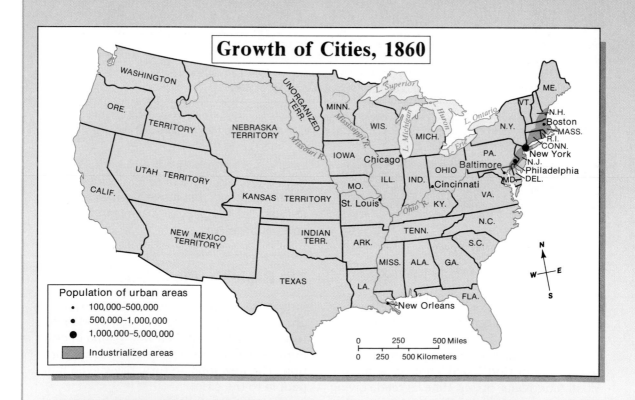

Growth of Cities, 1860

Population of urban areas
- · 100,000–500,000
- • 500,000–1,000,000
- ● 1,000,000–5,000,000
- ▢ Industrialized areas

468

3. **MAP READING** Ask: What was the westernmost city with a population of over 100,000 in 1860? In 1900?

1. **VOCABULARY** Children born in the U.S. of immigrant parents are called *first generation Americans;* their children are *second generation,* and so on. Ask how many students in your class are first or second generation Americans.

more each topped 500,000 people. Smaller cities like San Francisco, Milwaukee, Cleveland, and Detroit were also mushrooming. Although the majority of Americans still lived in rural areas, the trend was away from the country and toward cities. That trend would continue well into the 1900s.

An influx of immigrants further swelled city populations. By 1890, 68 percent of Chicago's population were foreign-born and another 10 percent were American-born children of immigrants. Indeed, Chicago, perhaps more than any other city, symbolized the growth of an urban America.

1.

2. **MAP READING** Ask: In which areas was there little urban growth between 1860 and 1900? What reasons can you suggest for this?

a population between one million and five million in 1860? (d) In 1900? (c) Which cities that appear on both maps grew in population between 1860 and 1900? (f) Which areas of the country were industrialized in 1860? (g) To which areas had industry spread by 1900? (h) Which cities are located on important waterways?

3 Draw conclusions. Use the text and maps to answer the following questions: (a) What relationship is there between industry and urban growth? (b) What relationship can you see between the location of cities and important waterways? (c) In which areas of the country did cities develop between 1860 and 1900?

2.

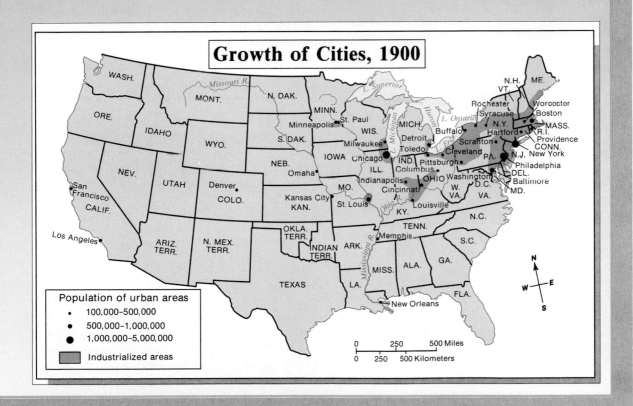

Growth of Cities, 1900

Population of urban areas
- · 100,000–500,000
- • 500,000–1,000,000
- ● 1,000,000–5,000,000
- ▨ Industrialized areas

0   250   500 Miles
0   250   500 Kilometers

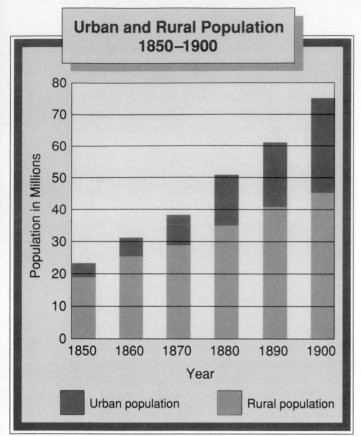

Urban and Rural Population 1850–1900

Population in Millions (y-axis: 0, 10, 20, 30, 40, 50, 60, 70, 80)

Year (x-axis: 1850, 1860, 1870, 1880, 1890, 1900)

■ Urban population   ■ Rural population

Source: *Historical Statistics of the United States*   See p. T87.

GRAPH STUDY   *The total population of the United States grew rapidly*

1. *in the late 1800s. As the graph indicates, the population of cities and towns grew faster in the 1880s and 1890s than did the population of rural areas. What ten-year period saw the biggest growth in urban population?*

1. **GRAPH READING** Ask: Approximately what percentage of the population was urban in 1860? In 1880? In 1900?

GEOGRAPHY AND HISTORY

Chicago: Symbol of an Urban Age

Early in 1893, a crew of 7,000 workers led by architect Daniel Burnham labored around the clock through the rain, sleet, ice, and snow of a Chicago spring. At times, their work-horses floundered belly-deep in mud. The hectic pace paid off, however. On May 1, 1893, the Columbian Exposition, marking the 400th anniversary of the landing of Christopher Columbus in the New World, was ready for the public. (See page 466.)

Congress had awarded Chicago the honor of playing host to the Columbian Exposition, billed as a celebration of American progress. The choice was apt, for Chicago—in poet

470

3. **ACTIVITY** Have interested students research the outbreaks of typhoid, cholera, and yellow fever that plagued American cities through the 1800s.

2. **BACKGROUND** The Chicago Fire of 1871 destroyed over three square miles. The need to rebuild quickly and replace old wooden buildings and sidewalks sped the city's transformation.

Carl Sandburg's words, "a tall bold slugger" of a city—typified both the vitality and the problems of the emerging urban scene. **2.**

Located on the southern shore of Lake Michigan, Chicago has a choice geographic location. It became a hub for rail and ship transportation. Trains brought travelers and goods from all over the nation, while ships moved raw materials in and finished prod-ucts out of the port on Lake Michigan. At-tracted by Chicago's advantages, many in-dustries located there. The new industries lured new manufacturers and people seeking jobs.

Pioneering business people in Chicago made fortunes in meatpacking, merchandis-ing, and steel. More than 200 self-made mil-lionaires lived in grand style in mansions lin-ing the lake front.

As manufacturing and industry pushed the city outward, it annexed nearby commu-nities that once had been politically inde-pendent. When the city's transportation sys-tem reached these outlying areas, some wealthy and middle-class residents moved out of the central city, leaving the downtown section to the poor and to commerce and industry.

Problems of a Growing City

Chicago's rapid growth created problems as well as fortunes. The stately mansions on the lake front stood in stark contrast to the crowded tenements of the Chicago slums. There, families lived in squalor, often with-out the most basic necessities, such as run-ning water. Diseases like typhoid regularly **3.** raged through the slums.

Tens of thousands of immigrants clus-tered in separate ethnic neighborhoods. Some sections became all Polish, some all Bohe-mian, Greek, Russian, or Chinese. African Americans also moved to Chicago from the South and formed their own neighborhoods. **4.**

Rich and poor alike endured some of the problems created by the city's rapid growth. As late as 1890, only one third of Chicago's streets were paved with cobblestones. When rain fell or snow melted, the streets became

4. **CRITICAL THINKING** Ask: Why do you think people from a particular country tended to settle together in one neighborhood?

1. READING Have a student read Carl Sandburg's poem "Chicago" aloud to the class. Lead a discussion on what kind of picture it paints of the city.

quagmires of mud. The droppings of thousands of horses pulling wagons, trolleys, and carriages also fouled the city streets. Grease, sewage, and dead animals floated down the Chicago River. So many chemicals had to be dumped into the river to purify it that wealthy residents refused to drink from the city water supply.

Rapid urban growth also offered rich pickings for corrupt politicians. Chicago, like most cities of the day, operated on graft and payoffs. (See page 482.) A bribe bought a city contract. Chicagoans nicknamed the members of their city council the "gray wolves." In a popular vaudeville skit, a hostess looked at several city officials sleeping at her feet after an evening's partying. She asked her husband, "Will I wake them?" "Leave them be," he replied. "While they sleep, the city's safe."

1. In 1893, even while the Columbian Exposition boasted displays of American genius and progress, many Americans bemoaned the
2. problems of Chicago and other cities. ■

3. MAP READING Have students compare this map with the map on p. 469. Ask: What other major cities grew up on the Great Lakes by 1900?

MAP STUDY By 1871, Chicago was a boom town of 300,000 people. By
3. 1900, its population had surged to 1.7 million. According to the map, why do you think Chicago became the major shipping point for the entire Midwest during this period? See p. T87.

Chicago, 1871

WI.

Area of city

—— Railroad lines

Elgin

Brickton (Park Ridge)

Evanston

Lake Michigan

Aurora

Cicero

Chicago

South Chicago

ILL.

Hammond

IND.

N
W—E
S

0 ——— 25 Miles
0 ——— 25 Kilometers

4. VOCABULARY Have students look up this word in the glossary before they begin reading.

See p. T87.

SECTION 1 REVIEW

1. Name two reasons manufacturers built plants in cities.

2. (a) Describe the change in United States population patterns that occurred between 1880 and 1900. (b) What were the causes of that change?

3. What characteristics did Chicago share with other expanding cities?

4. What two means of transportation made Chicago a transportation hub?

5. **Critical Thinking** How were the problems of cities in the late 1800s similar to the problems of cities today?

2. PAST AND PRESENT Ask: Which of these urban problems still exist today? Which have been solved?

2 Immigrants and Cities

READ TO UNDERSTAND

■ Why and how immigrants came to America.

■ Who the "new" immigrants were and where they settled.

■ What contributions immigrants made to their new country.

■ *Vocabulary:* pogrom.   4.

In 1884, the Statue of Liberty—a gift from France—was almost ready. But it still needed a pedestal. If "churlish millionaires" would not pay for a pedestal, Hungarian immigrant Joseph Pulitzer decided, then the people would. Pulitzer launched a campaign in his New York newspaper. Nickels and dimes poured in from 120,000 people—men, women, children. The pedestal was built. Fittingly, from this pedestal paid for by the common people, the majestic statue, standing at the entrance to New York Harbor, welcomed millions of immigrants in the years to come. 5. Most of these newcomers settled in the cities.

471

5. ACTIVITY Have students research the history of the Statue of Liberty and present their findings to the class.

2. **ECONOMICS** European farmers also faced competition from cheap American grain harvested in huge quantities on the Great Plains.

Between 1865 and 1900, about 13.5 million immigrants arrived in the United States. Most, like
1. *those in this photograph, came through the immigration station at Ellis Island in New York. They carried their few possessions in sacks, boxes, or on their backs. They also brought their desire for freedom, security, and a better way of life.*

1. **VISUAL EVIDENCE** Ask students to describe the emotions of the immigrants shown in this photograph.

The Pull of America

In the decades after the Civil War, a record number of immigrants reached the United States. From 1865 until the turn of the century, 13.5 million people came. Not until World War I interrupted the flow would the numbers dwindle.

Wars, famine, religious persecution, and overpopulation all prompted people to leave Europe and seek a better life in the United States. Some left their homeland in search of political or religious freedom. Some left because, in spite of their skills or education, they were unable to find work. Many left because their family's land had been so divided and subdivided among generations of children and grandchildren that their own plot
2. was now too small to farm profitably.
3. From the United States came word of a better life. Friends and relatives who had already made the trip wrote glowing letters home. One Polish immigrant wrote, "We eat here every day what we get only for Easter in our country." But getting to the new land was not easy.

Passage to the United States

Passage to the United States often cost a life's savings. Hotel operators, steamship companies, and ticket agents sometimes cheated immigrants shamelessly. Most newcomers bought the cheapest steamship ticket for accommodations in steerage. That gave them space in the noisiest part of the ship, near the engines and the rudder. Packed in like cattle, steerage passengers had little to eat and endured filthy conditions. Outbreaks of disease were common.

The crowded steerage frequently contained a diverse group of people. Many were poor farmers. Some were schoolmasters and skilled artisans looking for wider opportunities, or musicians and artists eager to see the world. No matter what their background, all had risked traveling into the unknown.

At journey's end, there was yet another ordeal—the immigration inspection. After 1890, the port of entry for most immigrants was Ellis Island in New York Harbor. There the humiliating process began. Waiting in long lines, the immigrants were tagged according to the language they spoke—one color for Greek, another for Italian, another for Armenian, Czech, and so on. Patiently, men, women, and children moved toward the dreaded moment before the immigration inspector.

With hundreds of immigrants to process daily, the overworked inspectors had just two minutes to ask 32 questions and complete a medical inspection. A newcomer who was found to have a contagious disease faced detainment and possibly shipment back home. Some immigrants had to accept a change in their name—from Bratkowski to Brown, for example—because the inspector did not want to struggle with the unfamiliar spelling. 4.

The "New" Immigration

Unfamiliar names like Bratkowski, Lagomarsino, and Koundakjian were but one sign of a dramatic shift in immigration. Before the 1880s, 8ᴐ percent of the immigrants to the United States came from Great Britain, Can-

472

3. **CITIZENSHIP** A Greek immigrant recalled, "Everybody was saying [the U.S.] was a land to make money, to have freedom, to do whatever you please."

4. **BACKGROUND** The first name of one Italian immigrant was changed from "Bartolomeo" to "Bill." His neighbor Mr. Miccio became "Mr. Mitchell."

1. **GEOGRAPHY** The kingdom of Bohemia in eastern Europe became part of the new nation of Czechoslovakia in 1914. (location)

ada, Germany, or Scandinavia. Many were Protestants, and a number spoke English. From 1881 to 1890, however, a flood of new immigrants arrived—an average of 500,000 each year. These new immigrants came increasingly from southern and eastern Europe, from Italy, Poland, Russia, Hungary, and
1. Bohemia.

People in this "new" immigration differed from Americans and from the "old" immigrants from northern and western Europe. The newcomers were often Catholic or Jewish. Their religion, language, and customs made them seem strange to many Americans.

The largest number came from Italy. Millions left the impoverished southern part of

2. **CRITICAL THINKING** Ask: Why do you think Lazarus called the statue "Mother of Exiles"?

THE AMERICAN EXPERIENCE

Emma Lazarus and "The New Colossus"

The poet Emma Lazarus, daughter of a prominent New York Jewish family, had worked tirelessly to help the thousands of immigrants who streamed into New York City from Europe. In 1883, to help raise money for a pedestal for the Statue of Liberty, Emma Lazarus agreed to write a poem. To her, the Statue of Liberty would be a symbol of hope for the newcomers to the nation.

Emma Lazarus called her poem "The New Colossus," comparing the Statue of Liberty to the Colossus of Rhodes, which had been considered one of the seven wonders of the ancient world. Today, visitors to the Statue of Liberty can see Emma Lazarus's poem inscribed on the pedestal.

2.

Not like the brazen giant of Greek fame,
With conquering limbs astride from land
   to land;
Here at our sea-washed, sunset gates
   shall stand
A mighty woman with a torch, whose flame
Is the imprisoned lightning, and her name
Mother of Exiles. From her beacon-hand
Glows world-wide welcome; her mild eyes
   command
The air-bridged harbor that twin cities
   frame.
"Keep, ancient lands, your storied pomp!"
   cries she

3.

With silent lips. "Give me your tired, your
   poor,
Your huddled masses yearning to breathe
   free,
The wretched refuse of your teeming
   shore.

Send these, the homeless, tempest-tost
   to me.
I lift my lamp beside the golden door!"

See p. T87.

1. Why did Emma Lazarus write her poem?

2. Critical Thinking What difference did Emma Lazarus see between the ancient Colossus of Rhodes and the new Statue of Liberty?

3. **VISUAL EVIDENCE** Have students compare this description of immigrants with the picture on p. 472.

the country because of drought, economic disaster, and cholera. Three out of four were men whose families stayed behind. Some planned to earn money in America and then go home.

In the next largest group were Jews from eastern Europe, mainly Russia. More than 3 million arrived between 1880 and 1920. Many had fled Europe to escape religious persecution. Jews in Russia and Poland had long been victims of **pogroms,** violent attacks against Jewish neighborhoods. Said one Russian Jew:

> Sympathy for Russia? How ironical it sounds. Am I not despised? Am I not urged to leave? . . . Do I not rise daily with . . . fear lest the hungry mob attack me . . . It is impossible that a Jew should regret leaving Russia.

Jewish immigrants, unlike many Italian immigrants, did not plan to return home. Whole families came to America together.

More than one million Slavs from Russia, the Ukraine, Poland, Croatia, Serbia, Bulgaria,

and Bohemia made up the third largest group of immigrants. Other immigrants arrived from Greece, Portugal, Armenia, and Turkey, and from China and Japan.

Patterns of Settlement

Most of the new immigrants settled in American cities, especially the industrial centers and ports. By 1900, two thirds of the foreign-born people in the United States lived in cities. One third of the residents of Boston and one fourth of the residents of Philadelphia were immigrants. In New York City, four out of five residents were either foreign-born or the children of immigrants.

Italians often became subway workers in New York, stockyard workers in Chicago, or miners in Illinois, Michigan, and Minnesota. Those who could afford to buy land often planted orchards or vineyards.

More than two thirds of the Jewish immigrants arrived as skilled workers. They entered New York's clothing industries by the thousands. By 1917, 70 percent of workers in the garment trades were Jewish. Other Jewish immigrants became bookbinders, teachers, and store owners.

Poles and other Slavs often moved to midwestern cities or to coal mining towns in Pennsylvania or the Midwest. Many Germans and Scandinavians bought farms in Iowa, Nebraska, and the Dakotas. Chinese and Japanese immigrants settled on the West Coast, usually in California. The surge of new immigrants in the late 1800s brought an outburst of nativism, or hatred of foreigners, recalling the similar outburst of the 1840s. (See Chapter 14.)

Reaction Against Immigrants

Some native-born citizens feared and resented the new immigrants, who competed for jobs. Desperate for work, they accepted lower wages and harsher working conditions than American-born workers. Thus, when economic conditions worsened, antiforeign feelings became even stronger. Groups such as the American Protective Association urged Congress to bar immigrants from certain countries. Founded in 1887, the American Protective Association attracted one million

GRAPH STUDY *Before 1880, nearly all immigrants to the United States came from the British Isles and northern*
1. *Europe. According to these graphs, how did the pattern of immigration shift after 1880?*
See p. T87.

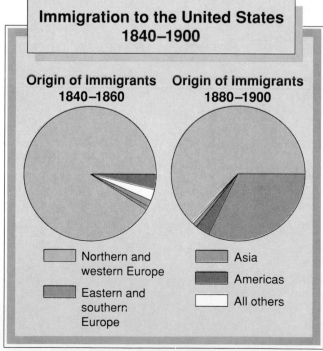

Immigration to the United States 1840–1900

Origin of Immigrants 1840–1860   **Origin of Immigrants 1880–1900**

- Northern and western Europe
- Eastern and southern Europe
- Asia
- Americas
- All others

Source: *Historical Statistics of the United States*

2. **VOCABULARY** The term *melting pot* is used to describe the U.S. as a place where immigrants from all over the world are blended into one society. It was the title of a 1908 play by Israel Zangwill.

members; their greatest resentment was against Roman Catholics.

Immigrants faced attacks by some American newspapers. One editorial, for example, charged that the United States was threatened by "an invasion of venomous reptiles . . . long-haired, wild-eyed, bad-smelling, atheistic, reckless foreign wretches, who never did a day's work in their lives."

The newcomers' languages, religions, and customs disturbed many Americans who traced their own heritage to northern and western Europe. The new immigrants faced discrimination. Jewish immigrants, for example, were excluded from the nation's better universities and had difficulty getting office jobs in New York City. In California, bands of ruffians terrorized Chinese immigrants. During the summer of 1877, gangs burned 25 Chinese laundries in San Francisco. Congress yielded to anti-Chinese feelings in 1882 and passed an exclusion act barring immigration from China.

Contributions to American Society

Although much scorned, the new immigrants made valuable contributions to the American economy. They helped build and staff the booming new industries. They laid track, built roads, stitched clothing, made shoes, and packed meat.

The new immigrants also enriched American culture. Each group brought with it traditions—foods, songs, theater, and literature—that added diversity and vitality to American life. Within the limits of one city, one might find a Polish newspaper, an Italian choral society, a Portuguese sewing club, a Greek theater group, and a Russian literary society.

Many new immigrants enriched urban life with their musical talent. When the growing cities started symphony orchestras and opera companies, most of the musicians and almost all the conductors were foreign-born. Italian, German, and Jewish immigrants filled the theaters to hear the music they remembered from Europe. Indeed, through music and other media, immigrants helped shape the look and feel of the cities and made a lasting mark on the evolving urban culture.

Israel Berlin and his parents came to the United States in 1893, fleeing the persecution of Jews in Russia. As a boy, Berlin began singing in Chinese and Jewish restaurants on the Lower East Side of New York City. He became famous as Irving Berlin when he wrote his first hit song, "Alexander's Ragtime Band," in 1911. Berlin went on to compose such popular songs as "White Christmas" and "God Bless America."

3.

See p. T88.

SECTION 2 REVIEW

1. **Define:** pogrom.

2. List three reasons Europeans came to the United States after the Civil War.

3. (a) Where did the largest groups of new immigrants come from? (b) Where did they tend to settle?

4. What factors contributed to antiforeign feelings among some Americans?

5. How did the immigrants contribute to American society and industry?

6. **Critical Thinking** How have immigrants enriched your community?

475

2. **BACKGROUND** Danish poet Adam Dan spoke for his fellow immigrants: "We came not empty-handed here/ But brought a rich cultural inheritance."

3. **PAST AND PRESENT** In 1988, Irving Berlin celebrated his one hundredth birthday.

1. **DISCUSSION** Ask: Can transportation help determine the way a city or an area develops today? How?

3 An Urban Way of Life

READ TO UNDERSTAND

■ How improvements in transportation affected life in the cities.

■ How retail stores and the newspaper industry changed.

■ How new leisure activities enriched people's lives.

"We cannot all live in cities," newspaper editor Horace Greeley commented, "yet nearly all seem determined to do so." Young people, he said, were looking for "hot and cold water, baker's bread, the theatre, and the streetcars."

As Greeley noted, the city's lure was not just jobs. It included comforts like piped-in hot water and entertainment like vaudeville. In a city, there was always something new to marvel at: a bridge, a skyscraper, a new trolley. And there were leisure activites to suit all tastes: classical music for the sophisticated, museums and theaters for the cultured,

2. **VISUAL EVIDENCE** Ask: What does this picture reveal about the customers and salespeople in early stores?

One of the pleasures of city life was shopping in department stores. At these large stores, different kinds of merchandise were sold in separate sections, or departments. Although early stores,

2. *like this one, were bare in appearance, competition gradually forced them to add more attractive furnishings and display cases.*

sporting matches for the fun-loving. With such attractions, cities grew bigger and bigger.

Urban Transportation

The urban centers of the East Coast had developed as "walking cities." Everything of importance was within walking distance. Only the rich rode in carriages. Everyone else walked. The omnibus, the horse-drawn streetcar, and the electric trolley changed that way of life. With the new modes of transportation, cities began to expand.

The electric trolley, with its fixed overhead wire, could go twice as fast and carry three times as many passengers as the horse-drawn streetcar. By 1895, 800 trolley lines were operating in the United States. Shops, housing, and businesses followed the transit lines out from the center of the city. 1.

With the electric trolley, urban working people gained greater mobility. People could now easily go for a picnic, to a library, or to the new department stores.

Department Stores

The new, all-purpose department store offered the shopper a chance to browse and buy a wide variety of goods. Instead of keeping the best merchandise out of sight, to be brought out only for wealthy customers, these stores invited everyone to look, touch, and buy.

R. H. Macy in New York, John Wanamaker in Philadelphia, Jordan Marsh in Boston, and Marshall Field in Chicago pioneered such stores. Others copied them. The aim was to sell in greater volume and at slightly lower prices than smaller shops. Department stores 3. also offered credit, free delivery, and something entirely new—a marked, set price. No longer could the customer haggle over the price with a salesperson.

F. W. Woolworth took the single-price idea a step further. He stocked his "five and ten" stores with inexpensive wares, mostly priced at a dime or under. The low prices tempted customers to buy items they did not need. Indeed, Woolworth's clerks were so busy taking cash they barely had time to stock shelves, never mind try to sell customers a particular item.

3. **ECONOMICS** Ask: Why were department stores able to sell goods at a lower price than small stores could?

The Streetcar and the American Dream

Around 1830, American city-dwellers began riding to work on public transportation. Horse-drawn carriages, dubbed "streetcars," picked up anyone who could pay a small fare. Before streetcars, most urban workers had to live within walking distance of their jobs, which often meant living in crowded city tenements.

In time, over 300 American cities had streetcars drawn by horses. But they were slow, and horses could not pull the cars up steep hills. In 1873, San Francisco began using heavy steel cables, powered by steam engines, to pull streetcars uphill. A year later, New York City first used electric streetcars, invented by Stephen Dudley Field.

Field solved the problem of transmitting electricity to a moving streetcar by stringing overhead wires along the streets. A long bar attached to the cars ended in a wheeled device, called a trolley, that slid along the wires. The chief difficulty—one that was never solved—was that the trolley sometimes slipped off the wire. The driver then had to get out and re-attach it while passengers waited. This gave rise to the expression, "He's off his trolley," to describe someone who acted crazy.

In 1888, Frank Julian Sprague built the first extensive trolley system in the United States in Richmond, Virginia. In only 90 days, he laid track and installed overhead wires along a 12-mile route.

1.

At the turn of the century, trolley-car companies built parks on the outskirts of cities to encourage customers to ride to the end of the line on weekends. Developers soon built relatively inexpensive houses on nearby land. These "streetcar suburbs" allowed many Americans to fulfill their dream of owning their own home. See p. T88.

1. What drawbacks did horse-drawn streetcars have?

2. **Critical Thinking** How have other developments in transportation affected where Americans live and work?

---

1. **TECHNOLOGY** In that time, Sprague also equipped 40 cars, built 80 motors, and set up a power plant.

Mass-Circulation Newspapers

"Read all about it," the newsboys shouted. Millions of Americans eagerly bought inexpensive newspapers in the late 1800s. Income from advertisers like the new department stores had enabled publishers to sell their papers for just pennies. And as newspaper circulation increased, advertising increased even more. Business people realized a single ad could reach more than one million readers, and they were willing to pay well for the exposure.

The mass circulation newspapers attracted readers with news of crime, sports, and gossip. No paper topped Joseph Pulitzer's

2. **ECONOMICS** The *World*'s circulation leaped from 15,000 a day in 1883 to 60,000 in 1884 and 1 million by 1898.

New York *World* in flamboyance. Pulitzer bought the *World* in 1883, and promptly cut the price to two cents. He called it a "people's paper." A master at devising ways to attract readers, Pulitzer once sent a reporter, Nellie Bly, on a race around the world. To keep interest high, he invited readers to guess the exact day, hour, and minute of her return.

2.

3.

Changing the Face of Cities

As more people and businesses moved to the cities, the price of land rose sharply. Innovative architects built upward, gaining more usable space from small parcels of land. One of the first to do so was Louis Sullivan, an

477

3. **BACKGROUND** On another occasion, Bly pretended to be insane to find out about care in a mental hospital. Her articles led to improved care for the mentally ill.

architectural genius who began using steel as the skeleton for the tall buildings known as skyscrapers. In 1889, Sullivan designed the first all-steel-skeleton building, the Auditorium Building in Chicago. A year later, the 26-story World Building was completed in New York. The "race to the skies" was on in earnest.

Retailers, too, sought a new kind of building in which to display their wares. The Cast Iron Palace in New York featured a huge first floor, ideal for browsing. Patrons rode to upper floors on the newly invented elevator. Through plate-glass windows, shoppers indulged in a new pastime, window-shopping.

Daniel Burnham was among the first advocates of city planning. At his urging, Chicago developed a long-range plan and set aside park land on the lake front. Other cities also hurried to build parks before all downtown land was paved over. In New York City, Frederick Law Olmsted designed Central Park in Manhattan and Prospect Park in Brooklyn. His parks gave people a sense of being in the country. Cities began to set aside land for botanical gardens, and several started zoos.

Music, Theater, and Art

With so many people, the cities could support leisure activities unavailable in most rural areas. Between 1862 and 1900, New York, Chicago, Pittsburgh, Cincinnati, and Philadelphia established symphony orchestras. In 1883, the Metropolitan Opera House opened in New York.

It was the heyday of vaudeville, with stand-up comedians, singers, dancers, and jugglers. Cheap theater tickets drew eager crowds. Plays ranged from fine Shakespearean works to popular but forgettable melodramas.

In towns small and large, an increasingly literate public wanted libraries. Over a period of years, Andrew Carnegie donated $60 million to start libraries across the country. By 1900, there were about 9,000 public libraries in the United States. Besides libraries, several cities started museums of fine arts. The new museums displayed paintings and sculpture from all over the world.

Many of the best American artists, like James McNeill Whistler, preferred to live in Europe. At home, however, major talents were at work. In Maine, Winslow Homer painted coastal scenes, capturing the flickering of sunlight on water. In Pennsylvania, Thomas Eakins painted realistic, often harsh, portraits and landscapes. His works were vivid renderings of the new industrial age.

Eakins and some of the artists who followed him were called the American Realists because they portrayed the not always pleasant realities of the life around them. This group and the American impressionist painters found few buyers in nineteenth-century America. In the early 1900s, however, their work began to draw international attention.

Sports

The big-city newspapers, with their crisply written sports articles, brought spectator sports such as baseball, football, and basketball into the mainstream of American life.

Popular myth credits Abner Doubleday with the invention of baseball at Cooperstown, New York, in 1839. During the Civil War, Union soldiers from New York taught men from other parts of the country how to play. For a time, the pitcher threw the ball underhand, the catcher caught it on the first bounce, and none of the players wore gloves.

The first professional baseball team was the Cincinnati Red Stockings. In 1876, eight teams organized the National League of Professional Baseball Clubs. A rival American League started some years later, and in 1903, the first World Series was held.

Basketball was introduced in 1891 in Springfield, Massachusetts, by Dr. James Naismith as a winter sport for young boys in his Young Men's Christian Association (YMCA). Basketball became a popular sport and soon spread to other nations.

Games of football using various rules from British soccer and rugby had been played in North America since colonial days. College students began playing the game before the Civil War, and its popularity increased once the war ended. By the 1890s, football games at Harvard, Yale, and Princeton were drawing huge crowds. In 1895, seven colleges in the Midwest began to organize what is now the Big Ten conference.

1. CRITICAL THINKING Ask: Why did so many forms of amusement develop in the cities?

1. With so many forms of entertainment available, cities were exciting places. But the glitter could not hide the problems that accompanied rapid urban growth.

See p. T88.

SECTION 3 REVIEW

1. **Identify:** (a) F. W. Woolworth, (b) Joseph Pulitzer, (c) Louis Sullivan, (d) Winslow Homer, (e) American Realists.

2. What was the importance of the electric trolley?

3. List two ways department stores differed from the shops of earlier eras.

4. How did newspapers like the New York *World* try to attract readers?

5. What new leisure activities emerged in the late 1800s?

6. **Critical Thinking** What attracts people to cities today?

4 A Changing Society: Problems and Prospects

READ TO UNDERSTAND

■ How reformers attacked urban social problems and political corruption.

■ What new opportunities were opening up for women.

■ Why progressive educators pioneered new ways of teaching children.

Despite all their splendors, cities suffered from crushing problems. People had crowded in too fast, packing into tenements, stuffing the streetcars to overflowing, choking the sewers with waste, and generally overwhelming the cities' services. Meanwhile, schools struggled to meet the needs of students from diverse backgrounds, slums bred disease and crime, and corrupt politicians stuffed their pockets with the people's money. Reformers yearned to clean up the mess. But where could they begin?

Boxing matches as well as football, baseball, and basketball games drew large crowds in the late 1800s. The nation's boxing hero was John L. Sullivan, who was heavyweight champion in the 1880s. Sullivan was the last champion to take part 2. in fights that lasted until one man could no longer continue. His longest fight lasted 75 rounds. Thomas Eakins, who painted this boxing scene, 3. was a leader of the group of painters known as American Realists.

3. **VISUAL EVIDENCE** Like many other painters, Eakins was interested in realistic studies of the human body. A number of his pictures depict athletes such as boxers, rowers, and pole vaulters.

Exposing Urban Problems

Grab the public's attention—that was the first task the reformers set for themselves. Tirelessly, they probed behind the scenes of urban problems, digging out the hidden truths.

The statistics could be grim indeed. One year, in one section of Chicago, 60 percent of all babies died before their first birthday. One New York social worker counted 1,231 people living in 120 rooms. Another could

479

2. **BACKGROUND** Boxers did not wear gloves until 1872. John L. Sullivan was the last of the bare-knuckle champions.

1. *Families in New York tenements lived in dark and dirty single rooms without toilets or running water. The only relief from the summer heat was the fire escape, where families slept on hot nights. The children in this Jacob Riis photograph would need determination to survive in the poor neighborhoods of the city. Photographs such as this one inspired public demand for improved housing and other reforms.*

1. **VISUAL EVIDENCE** Ask: How would these children's early years differ from the childhood of wealthy or middle-class children, or children in a rural community?

not find a single bathtub in three city blocks of tenements.

Jacob Riis, a Danish-born police reporter for the New York *Sun,* dug out the human stories behind the barroom murders, the suicides, and the fatal fires that were daily occurrences in parts of New York City. He detailed the wretched lives of slum dwellers—the ever-present stench, the filth, the blocked fire escapes that made any fire a deadly menace. Riis's 1890 book, *How the Other Half*
2. *Lives,* jolted many middle-class readers. Reformers like Riis helped create a public demand for decent living conditions for all.

Jane Addams and the Settlement House Movement

In several cities, hardheaded idealists were already at work. They moved into slums and established settlement houses, community centers that offered a wide range of services

to the poor. The best-known settlement house was Hull House in Chicago, founded in 1889 by Jane Addams and other young women.

On a trip to England, Addams had visited Toynbee Hall, a community center in the London slums. Impressed with the British achievements, Addams spearheaded the purchase of a decaying mansion in one of Chicago's worst neighborhoods. There she established Hull House.

Hull House provided a nursery and kindergarten for the children of working mothers. Adults could take courses in nutrition, health, and English. In time, a gymnasium and a theater group were added.

The women who operated Hull House documented the urgent problems of the neighborhood. Then, armed with facts, the reformers worked to get new laws passed. Alice Hamilton, a physician, treated the neighborhood's sick. She crusaded for laws to help control the spread of disease. Florence Kelley researched the harmful impact of industrial

480

2. **READING** In *How the Other Half Lives,* Riis beckoned to his readers: "Come over here. Step carefully over the baby—it is a baby, spite of its rags and dirt."

jobs on young children. She led a national campaign for child-labor laws.

By 1895, there were at least 50 settlement houses in American cities. The first settlement house operated by the Catholic church opened in 1898 in an Italian neighborhood of New York. Two years later, Brownson House opened in a Mexican section of Los Angeles.

Settlement houses became testing grounds for ideas about how to improve urban living. College professors and researchers came to visit and discuss ideas with social workers, teachers, and nurses. Bound together by cause and commitment, these professionals became the first effective group of urban reformers in the United States.

Despite their many successes, the reformers concluded that private efforts were not enough. "Private beneficence," said Jane Addams, "is totally inadequate to deal with the vast numbers of the city's disinherited." Government action, the reformers believed, was necessary to correct harmful conditions.

Women: New Opportunities and the Struggle for Rights

Influenced by the settlement house movement, many college-educated women chose professions, such as teaching or social work, that enabled them to serve the poor. Opportunities in other professions remained limited. For example, Iowa in 1869 was the first state to allow women to practice law, but not until 1920 could women practice law in all states. Despite restrictions and discouragement, there were 1,000 women lawyers and 7,000 women physicians by 1900.

Other opportunities opened for women after the Civil War. The invention of the typewriter, telegraph, and telephone created large numbers of clerical jobs, and women increasingly replaced men as office workers. The rise of department stores also created more jobs. By 1900, about 500,000 women worked in clerical and sales jobs. The number of women who held jobs outside the home rose dramatically, from 4 million in 1890 to 8 million in 1910.

Along with more job opportunities came greater legal equality for women. Increasingly in the late 1800s, state legislatures passed

laws giving married women control over their own property. By 1900, four western states—Wyoming, Colorado, Utah, and Idaho—had given women the right to vote in state elections. During the early 1900s, women like Alice Paul and Carrie Chapman Catt would continue the struggle for women's suffrage, as you will read in Chapter 23.

The Growth of Public Education

For many Americans before 1870, education meant a one-room school and a *McGuffey's Reader*. The average adult in 1870 had attended school for four years, and about one in five could not read or write. At the time, there were only 160 public high schools in the entire nation.

Born into a wealthy Illinois family, Jane Addams, below, turned her enormous energies and talents to improving conditions in the Chicago slums. Hull House, which she helped found, became a model for other settlement houses. It offered education, medical care, English classes, sports, and other activities for residents of the neighborhood in which it was located. By 1895, there were at least 50 settlement houses in American cities.

From 1870 to 1900, dozens of new colleges and universities opened. The graduates helped staff thousands of new elementary and high school classrooms. The public came to accept the idea of free tax-supported schools for all young people, and by 1900 there were 6,000 public high schools in the United States.

In the cities, however, traditional methods of teaching, such as drills and memorizing, did not work for many children. A child who spoke no English could make little sense of what was happening in the classroom. A frequent visitor to Hull House, Professor John Dewey of the University of Chicago, thought he had a solution.

Dewey urged schools to move away from rote learning. He and his wife, Harriet, tested their ideas at an experimental school at the university. Students could work in a kitchen, a carpentry shop, or a sewing room, as well as in classrooms.

Dewey's ideas were part of a broad movement to tailor education to fit the needs of students. The movement, often called progressive education, was part of a larger reform movement called progressivism. (You will read about progressivism in Chapter 23.)

Progressive teachers had three main goals. First, they wanted to widen school programs to include teaching about health, jobs, family, and community life. Second, they hoped to apply new discoveries in science and psychology to classroom teaching. Third, they aimed to use teaching techniques that would suit the kinds of children in the classroom. These new approaches, reformers hoped, would help improve the education of children living in an increasingly urban and industrial society.

Other Humanitarian Efforts

As you have read in Chapter 20, many Americans in the 1800s argued that government had no right to interfere in their lives. This belief in laissez-faire extended to social as well as economic life. Religious leaders had usually shared this view. But in the late 1800s, the social problems of the growing cities convinced some Christians that churches had to become actively committed to social reform.

Activist Protestant clergy developed what was called the Social Gospel. They argued that before churches could save souls, they had to improve the daily lives of the wretchedly poor.

Catholics also became more active in social reform. In 1889, Frances Xavier Cabrini arrived in the United States with a small group of Italian nuns to work among Italian immigrants. Before her death in 1917, Mother Cabrini founded 70 hospitals throughout the Americas.

During the late 1800s, a number of new organizations began to deal with social problems in a systematic way. One was the Salvation Army, established in London in 1878 by a Methodist minister, William Booth. Its purpose was to help house and feed the poor. One year later, an American branch was established. Living among slum dwellers, members of the Salvation Army set up soup kitchens for the poor and homeless.

The Red Cross, another new group, was founded in Europe in 1859 to aid soldiers wounded in war. Clara Barton, a former Civil War nurse, helped found the National Society of the Red Cross in the United States in 1881. It provided social services in the growing urban areas.

Governing the Cities

In the late 1800s, government in the growing cities continued as it had for over a century. Most cities required authority from state legislatures before they could pass major laws. Worse yet, corruption was widespread. Andrew White, president of Cornell University, wrote, "With few exceptions, the city governments are the worst in Christendom—the most expensive, the most inefficient, and the most corrupt."

City governments were often run by "machines" or "clubs" controlled by political bosses. The machine offered city jobs and contracts to those who had the right connections. A well-placed bribe could win a company a contract to pave streets, build schools, or operate trolley lines. "Boodle," payoffs to the bosses in return for contracts or official favors, was a way of life in many cities.

Yet the bosses and their machines did more than take bribes and offer favors. They

482

1. BACKGROUND Tweed died in a Manhattan jail in 1876. His family's request that flags in New York City be flown at half-staff in his honor was turned down.

often provided important services for poor city residents. An unemployed slum dweller could turn to the boss or one of his "ward heelers" for help in finding a job or for a loan to pay a medical bill. The machine sometimes offered English lessons or legal advice to immigrants and helped them apply for citizenship. It might hand out food baskets on holidays. In return for such assistance, the machine won the votes of most poor and immigrant city dwellers.

Perhaps the most notorious political boss of the era was William Marcy Tweed of New York City. "Boss" Tweed held no political office, but he controlled the Democratic political machine, popularly known as Tammany Hall. In three years, from 1868 to 1871, the "Tweed Ring" robbed the city of over $20 million, perhaps as much as $200 million. Such pilfering provided more than enough money to support the Tweed machine.

The Good-Government Movement

In city after city, reformers like Jane Addams teamed up with honest business people to reform city governments. The reformers often began by tackling specific abuses such as undependable garbage collection, unsafe building codes, and poor sanitation. Although they had some success, they soon saw that real change would require destruction of the "invisible government" of the political machines. They would have to beat the bosses.

Hard-fought election campaigns gave the reformers some stunning victories, and ambitious new mayors began to "clean house" in city after city. In Detroit, Mayor Hazen Pingree, elected in 1889, forced the transit authority to cut streetcar fares. Under his leadership, the city built more public parks and schools. When an economic depression struck, Pingree started a relief program for the unemployed. Mayors Tom Johnson of Cleveland and Samuel M. "Golden Rule" Jones of Toledo also earned reputations as enlightened leaders.

Urban reform was not without flaws, however. Many reformers believed that only well-educated professionals should run government. As some critics pointed out, however, such reform gave control to the upper and middle classes. Certain that most prob-

Cartoons by Thomas Nast, like this one of "Boss" Tweed, helped expose the corruption of the Tweed Ring in New York City. At one point, Nast was offered half a million dollars to stop his attacks on Tweed, but he persisted until Tweed was in jail.

3. VISUAL EVIDENCE Ask: What is the meaning of Tweed's costume in this cartoon?

lems could be solved by applying business methods to them, these new officials sometimes overlooked the poor, those whom the bosses had routinely "taken care of."

Although far from perfect, urban reform helped renew faith in government. Even more important, it paved the way for a national progressive movement.

See p. T89.

SECTION 4 REVIEW

1. **Identify:** (a) Jacob Riis, (b) Jane Addams, (c) John Dewey, (d) Social Gospel, (e) Frances Xavier Cabrini, (f) William Marcy Tweed.

2. What services did Hull House offer?

3. (a) What job opportunities opened for women in the late 1800s? (b) In which states had women won the right to vote in state elections by 1900?

4. Name the three main goals of progressive education.

5. (a) What did political machines offer the urban poor? (b) What reforms did urban reformers introduce?

6. **Critical Thinking** What services do people today expect to receive from city governments?

2. MAIN IDEA Ask: What is the "Golden Rule"? Why do you think the term was applied to Samuel M. Jones?

CHAPTER 22 REVIEW

Summary

1. **By 1914, the United States was becoming a nation of cities.** Although most Americans continued to live in small towns or rural areas, cities grew dramatically between 1865 and 1914. Cities like Chicago became the centers of industrial development. While growth brought prosperity to many, it also brought problems.

2. **Millions of immigrants poured into the United States in the late 1800s in search of a better life.** Mainly from southern and eastern Europe, these "new" immigrants were different from most previous immigrants in religion, language, and customs.

The newcomers made valuable contributions to American life.

3. **An urban way of life was developing.** City dwellers shopped in department stores, worked in skyscrapers, and rode in electric trolleys. They also enjoyed a wide variety of entertainment—from baseball to vaudeville.

4. **The rapidly growing cities suffered from major problems.** Reformers like Jacob Riis and Jane Addams worked to improve the lives of the poor. Other reformers fought for women's rights, progressive education, and good government.

See p. T89.

Vocabulary

Choose the answer that best completes each of the following sentences.

1. A term referring to city life is (a) suburban, (b) urban, (c) rural.

2. In an ethnic neighborhood, (a) people share the same language, customs, and culture, (b) there is a wide diversity of cultures, (c) young city dwellers are replacing older, poorer inhabitants.

3. Violent attacks against Jewish neighborhoods are (a) mugwumps, (b) potlatches, (c) pogroms.

4. Nativism is (a) hatred of foreigners, (b) an exaggerated loyalty to one's ancestors, (c) a study of a people's national heritage.

5. In city government, a "machine" was (a) the organization that controlled city jobs and contracts, (b) an unemployed slum dweller on welfare, (c) an organization of city reformers.

6. "Boodle" referred to (a) the steerage section of a ship, (b) payoffs in return for contracts or official favors, (c) neighborhoods in which immigrants settled.

See p. T89.

Chapter Checkup

1. What developments in the last half of the 1800s helped spark the growth of cities?

2. (a) What attracted industry to Chicago? (b) What problems did Chicago face as a rapidly growing city?

3. What attracted immigrants to the United States in the late 1800s?

4. (a) How did the "new" immigrants of the 1880s and 1890s differ from earlier immigrants to the United States? (b) How did these differences contribute to antiforeign feeling among some Americans?

5. Explain how each of the following affected life in the cities: (a) electric trolleys; (b) department stores; (c) rising land prices.

6. (a) What types of problems arose in the new urban areas? (b) How did settlement houses attempt to solve these problems?

7. How did the growth of industry and cities help create new job opportunities for women?

8. What role did political machines play in the government of many cities?

See p. T89.

Critical Thinking

1. **Recognizing Cause and Effect** How did the rapid growth of cities provide opportunities for both good and bad results?

2. **Identifying Relationships** (a) How did humanitarian groups like the Salvation Army and the Red Cross try to improve the lives of city residents? (b) How do the activities of such groups reflect the American tradition of voluntary action to improve society?

See p. T89.

Connecting Past and Present

1. Describe a condition in present-day American cities that you think needs reform. Tell why you feel as you do.

2. Religious leaders of many faiths still seek solutions to social problems. Give three examples of social action by religious groups today.

See p. T89.

Developing Basic Skills

1. **Reading Maps** Compare the map, Growth of Cities, 1900, on page 469 with the Population Distribution map on page 847. (a) Has the overall pattern of population distribution remained similar in the past 90 years? (b) Which are the areas of new development?

2. **Researching** Visit the library to learn about the history of a city near where you live. (a) Did the city grow rapidly during the late 1800s? Why or why not? (b) Did many "new" immigrants settle in the city? (c) If so, where did they come from?

WRITING ABOUT HISTORY

Bibliography Cards

To prepare a working bibliography, make out a separate bibliography card for each source you use. The information to include will depend on the type of publication.

If the source is a book, include the author (last name first), the title of the book (underlined), the place of publication, the name of the publisher, and the date of publication. Write the call number of the book in the upper right corner of the card.

If the source is an article, include the author, the title of the article (in quotation marks), and the name of the publication (underlined). For a magazine, add the date of publication and the page numbers. For a newspaper, add the date, edition, section, and page numbers. For a journal, add the volume, the year of publication (in parentheses), and the page numbers. For an encyclopedia, add the edition and the year of publication. If the article is unsigned, begin the card with the title of the article.

> 973
> B
>
> Burner, David et. al. America:
> A Portrait in History. 2nd ed.
> Englewood Cliffs, N. J.
> Prentice - Hall, Inc., 1978.

Practice: Prepare bibliography cards for the following items:

1. Your textbook. Use the call number 973.

2. An article entitled Jane Addams, published in the 1988 edition of The World Book Encyclopedia by World Book in Chicago.

3. An article entitled The Boom Towns, published in the June 15, 1987, issue of Time magazine on pages 14–17.

Mobility in America

The story of the movement of people is a common thread woven through the annals of history. The migration of the American people has been part of this pattern. Americans are mobile. They move not only from place to place (physical mobility), but also from one level of society to another (social and economic mobility).

Land of Opportunity   According to the social historian Max Lerner, there have been three kinds of physical mobility in American history. These are migrations across the oceans, migrations across the country to new frontiers, and the "internal crisscrossings" of people from farms to cities and cities to suburbs.

All three kinds of physical mobility have been closely linked to social and economic mobility. People have moved, in large part, to better their own lives or those of their children. As one turn-of-the-century Italian immigrant freely admitted, "If I could have worked my way up in my chosen profession in Italy, I would have stayed in Italy. But repeated efforts showed me that I could not. America was the land of opportunity, and so I came. . . ." Millions of others who migrated "across the oceans" did so for the same reason.

America was viewed as a land of opportunity as early as the 1600s. Indentured servants came to Massachusetts in the same ships as did Puritan settlers. Up and down the Atlantic coast, indentured servants were working to pay off their debt and then move on in search of land.

Many people who came to America left societies that still bore the imprint of feudalism. These societies accepted the idea that a person's social status and occupation were inherited. In America, differences existed between the rich and the

poor, but they were thought to be accidental, not the result of essential differences in people.

No better symbol of this belief could be found than Thomas Jefferson's order to replace the rectangular table in the White House with a round one. He did not want to decide which of his official guests should sit at the head of the table and which at the foot.

No better testing ground for this belief existed than the American frontier. There

1. **VISUAL EVIDENCE**   The cornucopia, shown here, is a common symbol of natural abundance. The word comes from a Greek phrase meaning "horn of plenty."

States competed with each other to attract ambitious immigrant workers. In this poster, California advertises its warm climate "without cyclones or blizzards." However, immigrants tended to move to areas with climates similar to their homelands. Scandinavians, for example, flooded into the northern grain-growing states of Minnesota and the Dakotas.

1.

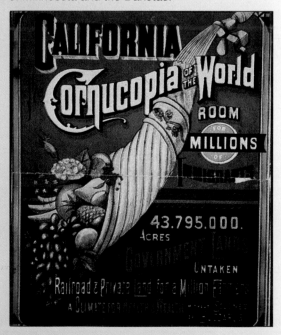

a person's rank was based on talent and ability, not on birth. The upper ranks of society were open to anyone willing and able to work.

Westward Migration   In the early 1800s, Americans moved steadily westward from the Atlantic coast. One English visitor said Americans seemed to suffer from "a disease of locomotion." Others thought this motion was temporary. The superintendent of the 1850 census claimed, "When the fertile plains of the West shall have been filled up, and men of scanty means cannot by a change of location acquire a home-stead, the inhabitants of each State will become comparatively stationary."

But other forces were at work to keep people moving. In the mid-1800s, a swelling stream of northern European immigrants traveled the canals, roads, and railroads that connected the older cities of the East with the West. By the time the census of 1890 showed that the frontier was closed, the country was in the midst of an industrial revolution. As economic and political problems disrupted southern and eastern Europe, booming industries welcomed immigrants to fill their need for workers.

The American Dream   Would these millions of immigrants achieve the American dream of opportunity and a better life? The expanding economy made it a possibility. As one New York banker said, "A man here may be a common day laborer, but if he has the right material in him, there is no reason why he should not occupy the best place in the nation."

To a native-born American, the idea that success could be earned was ordinary. But such was not always the case for the immigrant. Mario Puzo, author of *The Godfather,* writes of his own experience: "My mother wanted me to be a railroad clerk. . . . When I let everybody know that I was going to be a great writer . . . she quite simply assumed that I had gone off my nut. . . . Her peasant life in Italy made her believe that only the son of the nobility could possibly be a writer."

As millions of southern and eastern European immigrants were setting their

Industrialization spurred physical and social mobility. Many people took advantage of the new means of travel—the railroad. Railroad stations like this one hummed with arriving and departing passengers.

1.

1. **VISUAL EVIDENCE**   Ask: What social class do these train passengers probably belong to?

sights on the American dream, a great internal migration was beginning to take place. Thousands of black men and women were leaving small farms in the South to search for a better life in the urban North. During the industrial expansion caused by World War I, many black migrants envisioned a future bright with promise. One wrote, "I should have been here 20 years ago. . . . It's a great deal of pleasure in knowing that you have got some privilege. My children are going to the same school with the whites and I don't have to [bow] to anyone. I have registered—Will vote the next election."

But when the war was over, black workers who had been welcomed when they were needed began to see that welcome fade. Discrimination narrowed their opportunities. Then the depression hit. It was not until World War II that many African Americans saw a renewal of opportunity for economic and social mobility.

487

Mobility has helped form the American character. Unlike many Europeans, Americans who have achieved positions of power and influence have remained proud of their humble origins. The idea of "pulling up stakes" has become part of our national experience. And as a nation, we have made "change" and "progress" have almost the same meaning.

Today we are in the midst of new migrations. No longer do the majority of immigrants come across the Atlantic. Recent arrivals are far more likely to have crossed the Pacific Ocean or the Caribbean Sea. The South now competes with the West for migrants from the older urban areas. Yet these urban areas are themselves receiving new migrants—people who have returned to the cities to pursue new job opportunities. Americans continue to move to find a "better life."

See p. T90.

1. What are the three kinds of geographic mobility identified by Max Lerner?

2. **Critical Thinking** How do you think the size and natural wealth of the United States have helped shape the American character?

Notable Americans

Sarah Breedlove Walker

Like many Americans, Sarah Breedlove Walker was determined to achieve a better life. Through hard work and ingenuity, she overcame her humble beginnings and realized the American dream of wealth and fame.

Sarah Breedlove was born in Louisiana in 1868 to former slaves. An orphan at age 7 and a mother and widow by age 20, she learned very early to cope with poverty and responsibility.

Sarah Breedlove left Louisiana in 1888 and settled in St. Louis, Missouri. For many years, she worked as a maid, cook, and laundress—often for as little as $1.50 a day—to support herself and her child.

In her early thirties, however, Breedlove became concerned about financial security for her old age. According to one account, she thought of a money-making idea while balancing a basket of laundry on her head. Why not develop hair care products for blacks? For several years, she considered the idea and in her spare time developed formulas for salves and soaps.

At age 37, Sarah Breedlove uprooted herself again. She chose Denver, Colorado, as the place to start a hair-care business. Married to C. J. Walker, a newspaperman, she marketed her hair preparations under the name of Madame C. J. Walker.

Door-to-door sales in the Denver area proved successful. Soon Walker added

Sarah Walker (1867–1919) is seen here at the wheel of her automobile. Walker's rise from a laundress to a millionaire was a powerful testimony to her own determination and to American opportunity. The "Walker system" of beauty care was promoted by 5,000 saleswomen throughout the United States, the Caribbean, and South America.

1.

1. **VISUAL EVIDENCE** Ask: What other signs of Sarah Walker's prosperity are visible in this photograph?

cosmetics and toiletries to her line of products. Soaring profits enabled her to expand her business nationwide. Within a short period of time, she had established Walker schools of beauty culture across the country. From an initial investment of $1.25,

Walker was on her way to becoming the first black millionaire.

Walker's success did not end there. She took profits from her business and invested in real estate. Her holdings included valuable property in the West and the South and a fashionable mansion near New York City.

A more comfortable life was not the only satisfaction Walker derived from her newly gained wealth. In an interview two years before her death, she said that she wanted her money to benefit others. Besides making generous donations to support education and civil rights for blacks, she willed two-thirds of the profits of her company to charities.

Sarah Walker died in 1919 at age 51. The story of her rise from poverty was an inspiration to other struggling Americans. Her success proved that upward mobility in the United States was a reality.

See p. T90.

1. What were some of Sarah Walker's goals?

2. **Critical Thinking** How was geographic mobility related to Walker's economic success?

Voices of Freedom

An American Journey

In the late 1800s, some newly arrived immigrants followed a pattern of migration already familiar to native-born Americans: They set out from eastern cities to the sparsely inhabited West. Among them were Polish immigrants Isadore and Anna Solomon. In 1876, the Solomons left the East to open a general store in a primitive town in New Mexico. Their store was an immediate success, and the Solomons soon started a bank, a newspaper, and a hotel. The following is an account by Anna Solomon of the family's first months in New Mexico.

We sold everything we possessed except our three children and started on our journey for New Mexico. We had a very hard trip. . . .

When we reached La Junta, the end of the railroad in those days, [we] had to travel by stage, packed in like sardines day and night for six days. . . . When we got [to Las Cruces], I was tired out to death. . . . I lived [there] with the children for four months while my husband looked around for a location for our business. He finally found a place, and this is where we have been living now for thirty years.

When we were going to leave Las Cruces, we bought a two-seated wagon called a buck board, and a pair of horses. Into this we put a tent, some bedding, our cooking utensils, our provisions, our clothes, our children, ourselves. . . . It took us several days and nights to get there. How often I was frightened thinking I saw Indians. . . .

Now we had to start the housekeeping, but we had no furniture, no cooking stove, and nothing else that belongs to the comfort of the human race. [So] we cooked outside on the ground. We had a stove and other very necessary things coming from Las Cruces, being sent by an ox team with two loads of goods for the store that we were going to put up. But the wagons broke down on the road, and we had to send someone to repair them. They got here after three months. Until then we had no bed to sleep in, no stove to cook in, no table to eat off, no flour to bake bread. . . .

[Meanwhile] I took sick with chills and fever and my baby, Rose, also took sick. We had some very dark and sad times, but that did not hinder us from doing a good deal of business. We also started building—at first a bedroom, then a store. When that store was finished, I felt like the Queen of England.

Adapted from Kenneth Libo and Irving Howe, *We Lived There Too* (New York: St. Martin's/Marek 1984).
See p. T90.

1. What hardships did Anna Solomon encounter in New Mexico?

2. **Critical Thinking** How did the lives of the Solomons typify the quest for the American dream?

Unit Seven

ENTERING A MODERN AGE

Scientist George Washington Carver promoted the interests of black Americans.

1904 After work began, cutting the canal across Panama took ten grueling years.

	1900	1904	1908
POLITICS AND GOVERNMENT	**1900** La Follette is governor of Wisconsin	**1904** Roosevelt Corollary justifies intervention in Latin America	
SOCIETY AND CULTURE		**1903** Ida Tarbell exposes Standard Oil	**1909** NAACP founded
ECONOMICS AND TECHNOLOGY		**1903** Department of Commerce and Labor created	**1906** Pure Food and Drug Act bars use of harmful additives
WORLD EVENTS	**1900** Boxer Rebellion breaks out in China	**1904** War breaks out between Japan and Russia	
	McKinley	Roosevelt	

490

Conditions in crowded cities were one target of reformers in the early 1900s.

The campaign to prohibit the sale of alcohol eventually led to passage of the Eighteenth Amendment in 1917.

1912 Some Woodrow Wilson supporters tried to identify him with George Washington, as this song sheet shows.

1918 American soldiers helped stop a German counteroffensive at the Second Battle of the Marne.

1912	1916	1920

1913 Federal Reserve system created to regulate credit supply

1917 United States enters war on side of the Allies

1916 Interstate shipping of items produced by children is forbidden

1920 Women win right to vote

1911 Triangle Factory fire leads to factory safety regulations

1918 War Industries Board organizes industry in support of the war

1911 Mexican Revolution begins

1914 War begins in Europe

1919 Treaty of Versailles ends the war

Taft   Wilson   Harding

1917 Posters like this encouraged Americans to conserve food so soldiers would have enough.

1919 President Wilson and other Allied leaders hammered out the Treaty of Versailles to end the war.

The Progressive Era 23

(1900–1917)

CHAPTER OUTLINE

1 **Voices for Change**

2 **Reforms in Government**

3 **Theodore Roosevelt and the Square Deal**

4 **The Ordeal of William Howard Taft**

5 **Woodrow Wilson and the New Freedom**

May 4, 1912, was a sunny day in New York City. The weather was perfect for the parade that marched up Fifth Avenue. And for a change, so was the mood of the public.

First came the "cavalry"—50 smartly dressed women on horses, some riding side-saddle, some sitting astride their mounts, their three-cornered hats worn on an angle. Then followed a seemingly endless stream of women—women playing drums, women in carriages, women waving banners. The banners bore slogans like "How Long Must Women Wait for Liberty?" and "Votes for Women."

For hours the women marched by—seamstresses and society matrons, factory workers and housewives, and many more. As dusk crept over the city, the women lit flares and Japanese lanterns and kept marching. But there were not only women. In their midst marched representatives of the Men's League for Woman Suffrage—college students, Boy Scouts, even a grandfather carrying a baby.

It took spirit to march that day. Hecklers jeered at the men: "Who fixed breakfast this morning?" "Don't forget to do the dishes!" Spectators in suits and ties snickered at the women: "Where are your trousers?" But for the first time at a suffragist parade, the cheers of the spectators drowned out the hecklers, as 15,000 marchers stepped along the avenue. The next morning's New York *Tribune* called it "the greatest demonstration of women in all American history."

The women who fought for the right to vote—and the men who backed them—believed in change. They saw faults in American society, but they fervently believed in human progress. Faults could be eliminated. Society could be improved.

The suffragist drive was but one of many reforms that believers in progress championed in the early 1900s. Those believers in progress were called "progressives," and because of them historians refer to the first two decades of the 1900s as "The Progressive Era." During this period, the progressives were to achieve major reforms in the economy and the politics of the nation.

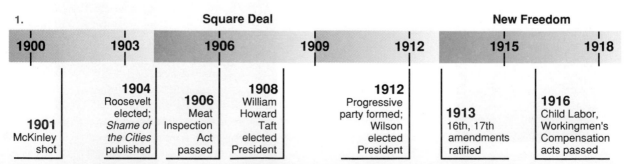

1.

		Square Deal				New Freedom	
1900	**1903**	**1906**	**1909**	**1912**		**1915**	**1918**

1901 McKinley shot

1904 Roosevelt elected; *Shame of the Cities* published

1906 Meat Inspection Act passed

1908 William Howard Taft elected President

1912 Progressive party formed; Wilson elected President

1913 16th, 17th amendments ratified

1916 Child Labor, Workingmen's Compensation acts passed

1. **TIME LINE QUESTION** Ask: What legislation on the time line was passed during Roosevelt's administration?

During the Progressive era, artists also broke with tradition. A group of painters, dubbed the "Ashcan School" by hostile critics, turned their talents to capturing the realities of urban life. In this painting, Six O'Clock, *John Sloan portrays New York City at evening rush hour.*

1.

1. **VISUAL EVIDENCE** John Sloan (1871–1951) worked as an illustrator at the Philadelphia *Inquirer* and later taught at the Art Students League in New York City.

1 Voices for Change

READ TO UNDERSTAND

- What goals inspired the progressives and the muckrakers.

- How black Americans fared during the progressive era.

- How workers and women gained new rights and benefits.

2. ■ *Vocabulary:* muckraker, women's suffrage.

The United States emerged from the 1800s a proud, strong nation. Yet it had achieved this position at a price. Political corruption, ruthless business practices, widespread poverty, racial and sexual inequality—all faced the United States as it moved into the new cen-

tury. The rising generation of progressive reformers resolved to right these wrongs.

Who Were the Progressives?

Kansas newspaper editor William Allen White joked that progressivism was simply Populism that had "shaved its whiskers, washed its shirt, put on a derby, and moved into the middle class." As White implied, progressivism was a middle-class movement. Progressive reformers were typically city dwellers and college-educated professionals. They sympathized with the downtrodden but were not among them.

3.

Some progressives began their careers in the settlement houses. There social workers met with reform-minded reporters, professors, teachers, doctors, nurses, and business people. Together, they formed the core of the progressive movement.

493

2. **VOCABULARY** Have students look up these terms in the glossary before they begin reading.

3. **LOCAL HISTORY** Have students research your area in the 1890s to discover if reformers were active there.

But the progressives were not all alike—far from it. They included Republicans and Democrats and socialists and people of many other political persuasions. Some focused on corruption in government and the need to make government more responsive to the needs of the people. Others worked to pass laws against unsafe working conditions, spoiled food, and slum housing. Still others battled for laws to regulate powerful monopolies. But all progressives shared the belief that the United States needed to be reformed. And all had confidence that it could be.

The Muckrakers

The first step in reforming society was exposing the conditions that needed reform. Many people read about the need for widespread reform in popular magazines. The pages of *McClure's,* a magazine that quickly took the lead, included exposés of lynching written by Roy Stannard Baker and articles by Lincoln Steffens on political corruption.

Steffens's articles were published as the book *The Shame of the Cities* (1904).

President Theodore Roosevelt found these journalists too negative. In a speech in Washington, he likened journalists such as Steffens and Baker to a man in a story who raked muck, or manure. That man, Roosevelt explained, was so intent on raking that he would not look up if he were offered a crown. From that story, these reporters gained the label **muckrakers.**

Despite the criticism aimed at them, the reform journalists caught the public's attention with their vivid writing. In his book *The Jungle* (1906), Upton Sinclair told how rats and dirt got ground up in meat, often from sick animals, which was then dyed to disguise its color. (See page 503.) John Spargo's book *The Bitter Cry of the Children* (1906) documented the grim poverty that caused thousands of children to go to school hungry. Ida Tarbell's *History of the Standard Oil Company* (1903) cataloged the ruthless tactics John D. Rockefeller used to build his oil monopoly.

Samuel S. McClure recognized that exposés increased magazine circulation. McClure's magazine, benefiting from his eye for journalistic talent, published some of the finest writers of the day. Recognizing the public's interest in trusts, McClure assigned Ida Tarbell, at left, to write a history of Standard Oil. The Christmas 1903 issue of the magazine, whose cover is shown here, carried the second installment of her series.

1. **ACTIVITY** Have students look through local papers for articles they consider to be "muckraking" and rewrite an article in a dramatic, crusading style.

Although the muckrakers did not offer their readers many solutions, they awakened a generation of Americans. Once made aware,
1. many people joined the crusade for reform.

Progressives and Black Americans

Overlooked by most progressives in their search for social justice was the plight of black Americans. Like many white Americans of the period, progressives tended to believe that white people were somehow superior to people with darker skin. In fact, many southern progressives worked to strengthen Jim Crow laws. (See page 452.) Many progressives in the North ignored, or even practiced, segregation and discrimination.

But some progressives felt outraged by the suffering inflicted on blacks. In 1908, an
2. anti-black riot in Springfield, Illinois, motivated the progressives to issue a declaration proposing an organization to protect the rights of blacks. Among the white signers of the declaration were the journalists Lincoln Steffens and Ray Stannard Baker; Jane Addams of Hull House; and John Dewey, the founder of progressive education. Among the black signers were W.E.B. Du Bois, Ida Wells-Barnett, and Mary Church Terrell, black rights advocates.

In 1909, this group of white and black reformers founded the National Association for the Advancement of Colored People (NAACP). Du Bois edited the association's official journal, *The Crisis,* but most of the officers during the early years of the organization were white. The NAACP was committed to a militant attack on all forms of racial oppression. The organization defended black citizens who had been arrested on questionable evidence. It investigated race riots and lynchings and fought for a federal antilynching law. By 1914, the NAACP had offices in 50 cities and a national membership of 6,000.

Advances for Workers

Social legislation and reform lagged behind the rapid industrialization and urbanization of the late 1800s and early 1900s. At the turn of the century, laborers in the steel industry worked 12 hours a day, 7 days a week. Textile workers, many of them women and children, worked from 60 to 84 hours a week.

2. **BACKGROUND** The riot occurred while Springfield was making plans to honor the centennial of Lincoln's birth.

"The problem of the twentieth century," wrote W.E.B. Du Bois in 1903, "is the problem of the color line." A historian and author, Du Bois was one of the founders of the National Association for the Advancement of Colored People, in 1909. He is shown here in his office at the NAACP journal, The Crisis, which he edited until 1934. 3.

3. **DISCUSSION** Have students explain the remark quoted in the caption. Ask: Has Du Bois's prediction come true?

Unemployment insurance was unheard of, and workers injured on the job received no disability pay. Few employers offered retirement pensions. Child labor and unsafe machinery were common in many plants.

Since many people viewed labor activists as "wild radicals" spouting foreign ideas, labor unions had difficulty winning concessions for workers. The progressives similarly did little to help the struggling unions. Rather, the progressives tried to reform business practices from the top down, fighting for legislation to protect working people.

They had some success, particularly during the early years of Woodrow Wilson's presidency (1913–1921). Between 1912 and 1917, 12 states passed minimum wage laws for women. Progressives also successfully pushed for state-sponsored insurance plans to cover industrial accidents. Thirty states had some system of industrial accident insurance by 1917. Many states passed laws that barred children from working at night. In 1911, a fire at the Triangle Shirtwaist Fac- 4. tory in New York City killed 146 women workers. After that, a number of state legislatures **495** passed factory safety regulations.

4. **BACKGROUND** The factory exits had been locked to keep the workers at their jobs. Many women leapt to their deaths.

1. **BIOGRAPHY** Kelley became chief factory inspector in Illinois. Due to her efforts, Illinois passed a law regulating conditions and prohibiting child labor.

2. **BACKGROUND** Remind students of the abolitionist and other reform activities of the early Quakers.

Women in the Progressive Era

By 1910, women held nearly one fourth of all jobs in the United States. Although the majority of women working outside the home were employed as maids and cooks, some women had ventured into office jobs, factory work, and professions such as teaching and nursing.

The so-called New Woman who worked outside her home was most visible and vocal in the settlement houses. Many of these women became highly skilled organizers and advocates of reforms.

1. Among the most successful was Florence Kelley, formerly of Hull House. As head of the National Consumers League, Kelley was known as "the impatient crusader" for her zeal in fighting against child labor and unsafe working conditions. Her league mobilized consumer pressure against industrial abuses. It asked shoppers to buy only products that carried the league's white label of approval.

Although women could not vote in most states, they were involved in a wide range of political and economic issues. The General Federation of Women's Clubs, which had almost a million members in 1910, concerned itself with factory conditions, political corruption, and law enforcement. While some clubs only talked about these problems, others pressed for state and local reform.

Women's Suffrage

Women's growing economic independence and experience in the progressive movement prompted them to demand the right to vote. Women reformers had concluded that without the vote they lacked the power needed to bring about political change.

By 1912, the impact of women in the work force and the general spirit of reform focused attention on the suffrage movement. Two groups led the field. The larger was the National American Woman Suffrage Association (NAWSA), headed by Carrie Chapman Catt. In state after state, the association pressured legislatures to extend suffrage.

A young Quaker, Alice Paul, left NAWSA 2. to help start a more militant group called the National Woman's party. On the day of Woodrow Wilson's inauguration in 1913, Paul organized a spectacular parade through

3. **MAP READING** Ask: What was the earliest state to grant full suffrage to women?

MAP STUDY

See p. T92.

By 1919, women in most states could vote in state and local elections. As the map shows, women had full suffrage in 15 states, mostly in the West. Only 11 states had no women's suffrage. What was the westernmost state in which women could not vote?

3.

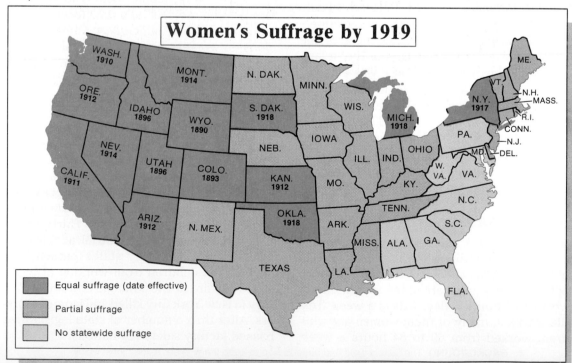

Women's Suffrage by 1919

WASH. 1910
ORE. 1912
MONT. 1914
N. DAK.
MINN.
IDAHO 1896
S. DAK. 1918
WIS.
ME.
VT.
N.H.
MASS.
N.Y. 1917
WYO. 1890
IOWA
MICH. 1918
NEV. 1914
NEB.
R.I.
CONN.
N.J.
PA.
OHIO
CALIF. 1911
UTAH 1896
COLO. 1893
ILL. IND.
MD. DEL.
W. VA. VA.
KAN. 1912
MO.
KY.
ARIZ. 1912
N. MEX.
OKLA. 1918
ARK.
TENN.
N.C.
S.C.
GA.
MISS. ALA.
TEXAS
LA.
FLA.

Equal suffrage (date effective)

Partial suffrage

No statewide suffrage

1. **BACKGROUND** Catt's first position was as a high school principal in Iowa. Within two years, she was promoted to superintendent of schools, an unusual position for a woman at that time.

NOTABLE AMERICANS

Carrie Chapman Catt: Fighter for Women's Rights

See p. T92.

Carrie Chapman Catt was a fiery woman from the northern plains. It took grit and determination to lead the fight for women's suffrage, and Catt had plenty of both. "To see her is like looking at sheer marble, flame-lit," wrote an awed reporter after one of her speeches.

The only woman in Iowa State College's class of 1880, Catt found her calling as a lecturer and fighter for women's rights. As head of the National American Woman Suffrage Association (NAWSA), Catt devised the strategy that succeeded in adding the Nineteenth Amendment to the Constitution.

One element of that strategy was a firm patriotism. Despite her own hatred of war, Catt helped persuade NAWSA to give strong support to the American effort in World War I. By impressing men with their patriotism, NAWSA leaders advanced the suffrage cause. Second, Catt's plan called for lobbying efforts on the state as well as the national level. Winning the vote in separate states sped the fight for a national amendment.

Catt spoke her mind plainly. "The United States has no right to talk about making the world safe for democracy as long as it believes in drawing the sex line," she declared. "Ours is not a true democracy."

After tireless efforts by Catt and other women, Congress voted the amendment in 1919. Catt set off on a "Wake Up America" tour. She spoke in thirteen states in eight weeks, urging women to work for ratification. Victory came at last in August 1920. "We are no longer petitioners," she rejoiced. "We are not wards of the nation but free and equal citizens."

1. What was Carrie Chapman Catt's strategy for winning full suffrage?

2. **Critical Thinking** Why do you think women won the right to vote during the progressive era?

2. **CITIZENSHIP** In 1920, Catt spent two months campaigning in Tennessee, the final state needed to ratify the Nineteenth Amendment.

Washington, D.C., to demonstrate support for **women's suffrage,** or right to vote. When Wilson refused to support a constitutional amendment granting women the right to vote, Alice Paul and her supporters began picketing the White House. The picketing went on daily for 18 months. Paul and other protesters were jailed and, when they went on a hunger strike, were force-fed. News coverage of the events dramatized the suffrage crusade.

One by one, states in the West and Midwest gave women the vote. By 1919, 15 states permitted full women's suffrage, and many other states allowed women to vote in local or state elections. Only 11 states, mostly in the East and South, did not allow women to vote at all. (See the map on page 496.) After a

3. **LOCAL HISTORY** Ask: In 1919, did your state have equal suffrage, partial women's suffrage, or no statewide women's suffrage?

1. **MAIN IDEA** Ask: Why was winning the right to vote so important to women such as Carrie Chapman Catt and Alice Paul?

2. **VOCABULARY** Have students look up these terms in the glossary before they begin reading.

major effort by the suffrage movement, Congress passed the Nineteenth Amendment in 1919. The states completed ratification of the amendment in August 1920.

1.   Catt observed a few years later: "It is doubtful if any man . . . ever realized what the suffrage struggle came to mean to women, . . . how much hope, how much despair went into it. It leaves the mark on one, such a struggle."

See p. T92.

SECTION 1 REVIEW

1. **Identify:** (a) Lincoln Steffens, (b) Ida Tarbell, (c) NAACP, (d) W.E.B. Du Bois.

2. **Define:** (a) muckraker, (b) women's suffrage.

3. List three concerns of the progressives.

4. What did the early NAACP accomplish?

5. List four types of legislation passed to protect working people.

6. What tactics did Alice Paul use to bring attention to the women's suffrage movement?

7. **Critical Thinking** What were the differences and similarities between muckrakers and progressives?

2 Reforms in Government

READ TO UNDERSTAND

■ How local and state governments became more democratic.

■ What changes were made in the way cities were governed.

■ How reformers changed the way United States senators were elected.

2. ■ *Vocabulary:* primary election, initiative, referendum, recall election, city manager.

In *The Shame of the Cities,* Lincoln Steffens charged that fraudulent voting lists used to stuff ballot boxes in Philadelphia contained the names of "dead dogs, children, and nonexistent persons." Progressives resolved to attack political corruption in two ways. They hoped to make government more responsive to the will of the people. They also wanted to employ experts to make government more efficient. Greater democracy and efficiency in government emerged as two pillars of progressive reform.

Agenda for Government Reform

"We are an inventive people," Steffens wrote, "and we all think that we shall devise some day a legal machine that will turn out good government automatically." The progressives certainly tried. Among the several ways they proposed for making governments automatically responsive to the people were primary elections, the initiative, the referendum, and the recall election.

Primary Elections Until the early 1900s, political party leaders largely controlled the choice of candidates for state and local government office. To make the process more democratic, progressives urged that voters pick party candidates in **primary elections,** or preliminary elections to be held before general elections. Voters in the primary election would choose among several candidates for the party nomination. Wisconsin adopted primaries in 1903. By 1916, all but three states used them.

Initiative, Referendum, and Recall Once voters had elected members of a city council or a state legislature, the people had little influence on the government until the next election. Traditionally, only members of the legislative body could introduce a bill. No formal means existed for citizens to submit their ideas directly to the lawmakers. To give voters a greater voice in lawmaking, the progressives proposed a device called the **initiative.** It allowed citizens to initiate, or propose, a bill by collecting a required number of signatures from registered voters.

Progressives also thought voters should 3. have a way to vote directly on some legislation. In a vote called a **referendum,** they could approve or reject a proposed law. By 1902, South Dakota, Utah, and Oregon had adopted the initiative and referendum.

3. **PAST AND PRESENT** If your state uses the referendum system, have students research recent referenda that have appeared on the ballot. Ask: What types of issues were voted on? Did voters approve the referenda?

"Make pictures from life" was the rallying cry of the "Ashcan School" of New York painters. Despite political corruption, the vigor of city life attracted artists. John
1. Sloan's enthusiasm for everyday events can be seen in this painting of women drying their hair on a rooftop.

1. **VISUAL EVIDENCE** Ask students what similarities they can see between this painting by Sloan and the one on p. 493.

Another progressive proposal, the **recall election,** let voters remove elected officials before they completed their terms. When a required number of voters signed a petition for a recall, a special election took place to decide whether or not to put someone out of office. By 1914, 11 states had provided for recall elections.

City Manager Plan As you have read, the progressives favored efficiency as well
2. as democracy. One means of improving efficiency was the **city manager,** a professional hired by an elected board of trustees to run a city government. Progressives believed that a professional manager with no political ambition would do the job better than elected officials who had no training in running a city.

Direct Election of Senators Until 1913, voters did not choose United States senators

directly. As specified in the Constitution, state legislatures elected the senators who represented the states in Congress. Progressives complained that political machines (see page 480) controlled some state legislatures, placing the election of senators in the hands of machine bosses.

As a cure for such abuses, progressives championed the direct election of senators. By 1910, two thirds of the states were giving voters a say about senatorial candidates in primary elections, and progressive newspaper editor William Allen White rejoiced: "It is safe to say that the decree of divorce between business and politics will be absolute within a few years."

In May 1912, Congress passed the Seventeenth Amendment, requiring direct election of senators in all states. The amendment was ratified the following year, but it was still too

499

2. **CITIZENSHIP** Ask students to find out if any cities in your area have city managers and, if so, when they adopted that form of administration.

1. *A small, wiry man with a bushy mane of hair, Robert M. "Battlin' Bob" La Follette was a passionate spokesman for progressive causes. As governor of Wisconsin and United States senator, La Follette never backed away from the fight for government that protected the common person from powerful economic forces.*

1. **VISUAL EVIDENCE** A friend described La Follette as a "barrel of wildcats" who would have made a good pirate.

early to speak of any "divorce" between business and politics.

La Follette and the Wisconsin Idea

While many cities and states experimented with progressive ideas for reform, Wisconsin took the lead. When voters there chose Robert La Follette as governor in 1900, progressives had elected someone who would test their full program on a statewide scale.

Nicknamed "Battlin' Bob," La Follette was a tough-minded progressive who used the tools of machine politicians to fight against the bosses themselves. "Every speech he made was an exercise in calisthenics," wrote Lincoln Steffens. La Follette, the orator, would punctuate his sentences by waving his "fight-

500

2. **CITIZENSHIP** La Follette ran for President in 1924 on the Progressive party ticket. His 4,822,856 vote total was among the largest for a third party candidate ever.

ing fists," defying the bosses, and appealing to the patriotism and self-interest of the people. His far-reaching reforms of state government came to be known as the Wisconsin Idea.

Under La Follette's leadership, the Wisconsin legislature established the direct primary in state elections. But La Follette realized that good government needed more than a voting public. Complicated problems, he believed, should be solved by experts. Borrowing heavily from the University of Wisconsin faculty, La Follette recruited a "brain trust" to help him solve state problems.

La Follette's experts focused on legislation and served on government commissions relating to railroads and public utilities. La Follette's railroad rate commission lowered rates and, as a result, increased the volume of freight traveling across the state. Their efforts benefited shippers and railroads alike and made railroading more efficient.

The Wisconsin Idea was so successful that it became a national model, a "laboratory for democracy." Several important progressive ideas became law in Wisconsin, including (in 1911) an income tax. The legislature also passed laws strengthening the civil service and protecting natural resources. In 1906, "Battlin' Bob" La Follette was elected to the United States Senate, where he continued to fight for progressive reforms.

See p. T92.

SECTION 2 REVIEW

1. **Identify:** (a) Robert La Follette, (b) the Wisconsin Idea.

2. **Define:** (a) primary election, (b) initiative, (c) referendum, (d) recall election, (e) city manager.

3. What were two main pillars of progressive reform?

4. How did the Seventeenth Amendment change the way senators were chosen?

5. **Critical Thinking** How did the progressives' ideas of democracy and government compare with those in the time of Andrew Jackson?

3. **BIOGRAPHY** Another progressive leader was "Holy Hiram" Johnson (1866–1912). As governor of California, he successfully wrested control of the state government from the powerful railroad interests.

3 Theodore Roosevelt and the Square Deal

READ TO UNDERSTAND

■ Why President Theodore Roosevelt fought big trusts.

■ What new laws protected consumers.

■ How Roosevelt promoted conservation of natural resources.

Late in the summer of 1901, Vice President Theodore Roosevelt took a camping trip into the Adirondack Mountains in upstate New York. On September 6, an assassin shot President McKinley at an exhibition in Buffalo, New York. After eight days of apparent improvement, McKinley took a turn for the worse. Informed of what was happening, Roosevelt climbed into a horse-drawn buckboard and rattled through the night over mountain roads to a railroad crossing, where a special train waited to rush him to Buffalo. By the time he arrived, McKinley was dead.

1. At the age of 42, Roosevelt became the youngest of all Presidents. He would use his new position to make progressivism a national force with a program that he called the Square Deal.

Roosevelt's Background

Although Theodore Roosevelt became President by accident, he was well qualified for the job. Energetic and intelligent, he also had broad experience in government on the city, state, and national levels.

This vigorous man began life as the sickly child of a wealthy New York couple. His father, whom he admired greatly, urged young Teddy to overcome his physical weakness through exercise—to build his body to match his active mind.

Shortly after graduation from Harvard University, Roosevelt began his political career as a member of the New York State legislature. Then tragedy struck. His young wife died in childbirth only hours after the death of his mother. Roosevelt was distraught. At the end of his elected term, Roosevelt quit

politics—he thought permanently. He bought two ranches in North Dakota, where he often worked on horseback for 12 hours a day.

Eventually, though, Roosevelt returned to public service. After a stint as commissioner of the New York City police force, he served as assistant secretary of the navy. As the Spanish-American War loomed in 1898, Roosevelt recruited cowboys, polo players, mounted policemen, and college athletes into a cavalry troop that was nicknamed the Rough Riders.

Emerging from the war as a hero, Colonel Roosevelt won election as governor of New York. With typical gusto, he set out to reform the state—much to the dismay of the state's other Republican leaders. In fact, it was partly to get him out of New York that those leaders engineered Roosevelt's nomination for the vice presidency. They considered the position a powerless one. However, not all the leaders were sure they had seen the last of Theodore Roosevelt. Mark Hanna, 2. who dominated the Republican Party, fumed, "Don't you realize there is but one heartbeat between the White House and this madman?"

GREAT DEBATE

Prosecuting the Trusts

When Theodore Roosevelt succeeded to the presidency, many Republican leaders feared that he was a radical determined to remake society. In fact, the President believed firmly in the established order and the free enterprise system. He welcomed the growth of industry, but he wanted government to have the authority to regulate the practices of giant corporations. He was called a "trust buster," but Roosevelt opposed only what he called "bad" trusts, those that used ruthless competitive tactics.

The President's first opportunity to regulate business came when he confronted the Northern Securities Company. That company had been created in 1901 by the merger of three railroads: the Great Northern; the Northern Pacific; and the Chicago, Burlington, and Quincy. It monopolized a significant portion of the national railroad system.

In 1902, Roosevelt ordered the attorney general to bring suit against Northern Secu-

501

3. ACTIVITY Have students draw cartoons about Roosevelt's handling of the coal strike, from either the owners' or the workers' point of view.

1. *In this political cartoon, Theodore Roosevelt is criticized for stopping his attorney general, Philander C. Knox, from enforcing antitrust laws. While some reformers wanted to ban all trusts, Roosevelt disagreed. He ordered the Department of Justice to bring suits against only those trusts he considered harmful.*

---

1. **VISUAL EVIDENCE** Have students give this cartoon an appropriate title or caption.

rities, charging it with violating the Sherman
2. Antitrust Act. (See page 451.) The act had been ineffective since the 1895 Supreme Court decision in *United States* v. *E. C. Knight Company.* The Northern Securities case was the President's invitation to the Court to revive the act.

In *Northern Securities Company* v. *United States* (1904), the Supreme Court ruled that Northern Securities had indeed violated the act. The Court ordered that the company be broken up. Roosevelt's victory prompted him to move next against the meat, oil, and tobacco trusts.

Despite these prosecutions, large corporations became more common during the Roosevelt years. Although Roosevelt prosecuted more trusts than previous Presidents, the two Presidents who followed him were to prosecute even more. ■

502

The Supervision of Business

Roosevelt was not an enemy of big business. He accepted large businesses as an important part of the modern economy and felt that many combinations made good economic sense. The President did move against big companies when he thought they acted irresponsibly, however, as in a 1902 strike by anthracite coal miners in Pennsylvania.

The miners' union had asked for an eight-hour day and a pay increase, but the coal operators refused to negotiate. Summer passed as coal supplies around the country dwindled. Schools and hospitals began to run out of fuel. Even after the union agreed to let an arbitrator settle the issues, the operators refused to negotiate.

The arrogant attitude of the owners outraged both the President and the public. Finally, Roosevelt threatened to send troops in to run the mines if the companies refused to bargain with the union. The coal operators were shocked. Other Presidents had used troops in labor disputes—but in support of employers, not workers. The owners backed down, and progressives hailed Roosevelt as a champion of working people.

In expanding government regulation of business, Roosevelt had stiff opposition from his own Republican party. The party "old-guard" traditionally represented business interests. Those politicians believed that government interference would weaken the free enterprise system. Thus, Roosevelt moved cautiously during his first years in the White House.

President in His Own Right

Roosevelt did not launch an overall program for reform until he had won the presidency in his own right and had proven that the voters supported his ideas. In 1904, the Republican convention nominated Roosevelt for President and Charles W. Fairbanks of Indiana for Vice President.

Since the Republicans were running as reformers, the Democrats tried to attract conservative voters by nominating Judge Alton B. Parker of New York. Parker ran a listless campaign. Roosevelt won by more

2. **ECONOMICS** Stock prices dipped at news of the lawsuit. "Wall Street is paralyzed at the thought that a President of the U.S. would sink so low as to try to enforce the law," one newspaper wrote.

popular votes than any previous President. He received 336 electoral votes to Parker's 140 and led in the popular vote by a stunning 2.5 million ballots.

1. The election of 1904 made Roosevelt the unchallenged leader of his party. More important, he and his programs received a clear vote of approval from the people. With typical energy, Roosevelt rushed to put his plans into effect.

A Series of Reforms

"These rats were nuisances," Upton Sinclair wrote in *The Jungle,* "and the packers put out poisoned bread for them; they would die, and then rats, bread, and meat would go into the hoppers together. . . . The meat would be shoveled into carts, and the man who did the shoveling did not trouble to lift a rat out even when he saw one." Sinclair's book, published in 1906, generated enormous public support for laws requiring strict federal inspection of meatpacking plants.

Although the muckrakers irritated Roosevelt, he read *The Jungle* with interest. He remembered that during the Spanish-American War hundreds of Americans soldiers had died from eating tainted meat. Roosevelt ordered a federal investigation of the meatpacking industry and threatened to publicize the findings if the industry did not accept regulation. The resulting Meat Inspection Act of 1906 set health and sanitary standards for all phases of the interstate meatpacking industry. In securing passage of this law, Roosevelt once again asserted government authority to regulate an industry that ignored the public interest.

Roosevelt also expanded government power to protect consumers from abuses in the food and drug industries. Investigators found canned foods that were contaminated with dangerous chemical additives. They showed how drug companies often exaggerated the curative powers of their products. Prodded by Roosevelt, Congress passed the Pure Food and Drug Act in 1906. The act banned harmful additives from foods and forbade the use of misleading statements in drug advertisements.

Farmers and owners of small businesses had long demanded stricter regulation of the railroads. Roosevelt and progressives in Congress proposed a bill that would let the Interstate Commerce Commission block unreasonable freight rates. Despite strong opposition from the railroads, Congress passed the Hepburn Act in 1906.

The Hepburn Act gave the Interstate Commerce Commission the power to set maximum freight rates. It also gave the commission authority to regulate other transportation facilities such as ferries and oil pipelines. Although Roosevelt was criticized for not going further to reform the railroads, he stated, "I believe in the men who take the next step; not those who theorize about the two-hundredth step."

The Democrats cried "blackmail" because Roosevelt received campaign contributions from big business in the 1904 presidential campaign. It was a futile attempt to stop a very popular President from getting reelected.

1. **ECONOMICS** Many of these abuses stemmed from the growing demand among city dwellers for processed foods.

AMERICAN ENTERPRISE

Protecting America's Food

In the early 1900s, when a person bought milk, he or she could never be quite sure what else was in the bottle. It was common knowledge in large cities that milk was diluted. Dealers commonly boosted two quarts of milk to a gallon of milk by adding water. And to improve the color, they often added molasses, chalk, or plaster. If, in fact, the milk was all milk, there was the chance that it came from a diseased cow living on garbage bought from a city government by the farmer.

1.   Other dairy products were equally suspect. The contents of some butter and cheese were best left to the imagination. A popular jingle of the day described conditions.

> Things are seldom what they seem;
> Skim milk masquerades as cream;
> Lard and soap we eat for cheese;
> Butter is but axle grease.

Demands for reform came from state and local governments, from the Department of Agriculture, from women's clubs, and from doc-

tors. As the food and drug industries gained a questionable reputation, honest business owners demanded that the crooks among them be weeded out. Conditions were so bad in the meatpacking industry that the demand in Europe for American meat dropped off.

Congress, prodded by progressive reformers and encouraged by legitimate business interests, swung into action. The lawmakers came to realize that in an age of mass production and mass marketing, individual consumers could do little to protect themselves. The fruits of the reform movement included the Meat Inspection Act and the Pure Food and Drug Act of 1906. Many other consumer-protection acts followed.

See p. T93.

1. What circumstances led to the demand for pure-food laws?

2. **Critical Thinking** Do you think pure-food laws are still needed today? Why or why not?

2. **BIOGRAPHY** Muir lived on his father's farm in Wisconsin until an accident nearly blinded him. After that, he wandered America, gratefully admiring its beauty.

Conserving the Wilderness

As an outdoorsman and former cattle rancher, President Roosevelt loved the American wilderness. Once, he camped out in a grove of giant sequoias with conservationist John Muir. "I stuffed him pretty well regarding the timber thieves, and the destructive work of the lumbermen, and other spoilers of the forest," said Muir. Roosevelt took Muir's words to heart, later lashing out at those who would "skin the land."

Although Roosevelt loved the forest, he did not share Muir's belief that all the wilderness should simply be left alone. The President's program called for balancing development with conservation. In 1906, he supported the Forest Homestead Act, which allowed the secretary of the interior to open up certain forest lands for agricultural use. Then, in 1907, he slowed the destruction of American for-

4. **BACKGROUND** At this time the first national monument—Grand Canyon National Monument—came into being.

ests by barring the cutting of trees on 150 million acres (60 million hectares) of government timberland. Roosevelt also promoted conservation by creating five national wilderness areas.

An Agenda for Further Reform

In 1907, a sharp financial panic and depression endangered Roosevelt's program for reform. Conservatives blamed the panic on Roosevelt's antibusiness speeches and actions. They said his trust busting had destroyed confidence in American business.

Fighting back, Roosevelt denounced "malefactors [evildoers] of great wealth" and promised to continue his campaign against "speculation, corruption, and fraud." Executives of large companies, he said, had opposed "every measure for honesty in busi-

504

3. **CITIZENSHIP** Roosevelt said: "To waste our national resources, to exhaust the land instead of using it so as to increase its usefulness, will result in undermining the very prosperity which we ought to hand down to our children amplified and developed."

ness that has been passed during the last six years."

In quick order, Roosevelt proposed a series of new reform measures. He called for inheritance and income taxes, more regulation of interstate commerce, and federal investigation of labor disputes. He proposed an eight-hour workday and workers' compensation. He also suggested federal regulation of the stock markets. Roosevelt's proposals alarmed business people and underscored a growing split between progressives and conservatives in the Republican party.

Passing the Reins to Taft

But Roosevelt's term was running out. Following a tradition that began with George Washington, Roosevelt chose not to run for a third term. He did, however, choose a successor—Secretary of War William Howard Taft. Taft had been a lawyer, judge, and governor-general of the Philippines.

The 1908 Republican convention nominated Taft on the first ballot, with James S. Sherman of New York for Vice President. The party platform had some progressive planks, but it was more conservative than either Roosevelt or Taft would have liked.

The Democrats tried to regain the presidency by appealing to progressive sentiments. Once again, they nominated William Jennings Bryan, who ran a strongly antitrust and prolabor campaign. However, Bryan did not rekindle the fiery support he had received in his earlier races. In the end, Taft won, partly because people identified him with Roosevelt. He carried 52 percent of the popular vote and won in the electoral college by a vote of 321 to 162.

With the White House securely in Republican hands of his own choosing, Roosevelt embarked on a hunting safari in Africa that kept him out of the country for more than a year. He left behind a record of leadership and dynamism that set high standards for 1. future Presidents. The presidency not only had regained the prestige it had lost after the Civil War, but it was becoming the most powerful branch of the government. Moreover, Roosevelt had given momentum to the

progressive movement, which was to dominate the next decade of national politics.

See p. T93.

SECTION 3 REVIEW

1. **Identify:** (a) Northern Securities Company, (b) Meat Inspection Act, (c) Pure Food and Drug Act, (d) Hepburn Act, (e) William Howard Taft.

2. (a) What was Roosevelt's attitude toward big business? (b) Why did Roosevelt want to dissolve certain trusts?

3. What steps did the Roosevelt administration take to protect the consumer?

4. What was Roosevelt's contribution to the conservation movement?

5. How did the panic of 1907 affect Roosevelt's program for reform?

6. **Critical Thinking** (a) What do you think Roosevelt meant by the following statement: "I believe in the men who take the next step; not those who theorize about the two-hundredth step"? (b) How did his actions support this view?

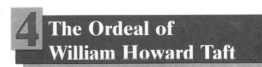

4 The Ordeal of William Howard Taft

READn TO UNDERSTAND

■ How President Taft continued the progressive tradition.

■ Why Theodore Roosevelt challenged President Taft for the nomination of the Republican party in 1912.

■ How the views of Woodrow Wilson, Theodore Roosevelt, and Eugene Debs differed on the issue of trusts.

The new occupant of the White House possessed none of Theodore Roosevelt's boisterous bravado. William Howard Taft was a 2. large and cautious man, a conservative at **505**

2. **PRESIDENTS** "Will" Taft, whose father was secretary of war and later attorney general under President Grant, graduated second in his class at Yale. After leaving the White House, Taft became the only President to also serve as the Chief Justice of the Supreme Court.

heart. Able and successful as a lawyer, Taft had wanted to be a Supreme Court justice, but his ambitious wife Helen had pushed him toward the presidency. While the White House had been an exciting challenge for Roosevelt, it became an ordeal for Taft.

Taft and the Tariff

Before he had been in office six months, Taft was in trouble. He and the progressives in Congress fell out over a tariff bill.

As long as tariffs protected American products from foreign competition, manufacturers could charge high prices. Progressives considered this practice unfair to consumers. Taft had pledged to reduce the tariff. Upon taking office in 1909, he called a special session of Congress to do so.

During that session, Republican Representative Sereno Payne of New York sponsored a tariff-reduction bill, which the House passed. But the Payne bill ran into trouble in the Senate. There, Senator Nelson Aldrich of Rhode Island added so many amendments to the bill that it actually raised the tariff on 500 frequently used items.

Instead of fighting to reverse the increases, Taft drifted into agreement with the Aldrich amendments. Thus, the Payne-Aldrich Tariff Act of 1909 cut tariffs on a few items, but its main effect was to raise tariffs and further insulate domestic manufacturers from foreign competition. When Taft called the tariff "the best bill that the Republican Party ever passed," progressives were dismayed. Taft was clearly an ineffective champion for their cause.

The Fight Against House Speaker Cannon

The growing tension between conservatives and progressives fueled another conflict. Throughout the first decade of the twentieth century and for many years before, the House of Representatives had been dominated by its speaker, Joseph G. Cannon of Illinois. Representative Cannon was noted for his salty language and rock-hard conservatism. As

Throughout his presidency, William Howard Taft worked under the shadow of Theodore Roosevelt. Comparisons between the two were made frequently. In this 1910 cartoon, Taft knits himself into a hopeless tangle of unsolved problems. Roosevelt turns a disapproving eye on the man he picked to succeed him.

1. **PAST AND PRESENT** Have students find out who the speaker of the House is today. Ask: How long has he held the job? What powers does he have?

3. **ACTIVITY** Have groups of students draw political cartoons presenting different points of view about the Ballinger-Pinchot controversy.

speaker of the House, Cannon chose members of all House committees. These appointments were extremely important to representatives. If, for example, a representative from a farm state wanted to sit on a committee that drafted farm legislation, only Cannon could put him there.

Furthermore, under the rules of the House, the speaker had the right to appoint a majority of the members of the Rules Committee, of which he was chairman. That committee determined when bills would be debated by the entire House. Cannon had often used his power to block reform legislation.

Taft disliked Cannon personally and opposed his stubborn, "standpat" conservatism. In 1909, when House progressives proposed to strip Cannon of some of his power, Taft pledged to support them.

But the President soon went back on his word. Conservative Republicans were six times as numerous as progressive Republicans, or "insurgents," in the House. The conservatives promised to cooperate with Taft on other issues if he would support Cannon. After calculating the political odds, the President agreed. Even without Taft, Republican insurgents and Democratic progressives were able to gather enough votes to limit the speaker's power.

The Conservation Controversy

Taft also disappointed many progressives on the conservation of natural resources. Although he set aside more national park and forest land than Roosevelt had, he emerged as a villain to conservationists.

The trouble began in 1910, when Taft's secretary of the interior, Richard A. Ballinger, issued an order allowing the government to sell certain wilderness areas in Wyoming and Montana. Ballinger's action enraged Gifford Pinchot, the chief of the United States Forest Service. Pinchot charged that Ballinger was trying to enrich corporations that wanted to exploit the resources of the area. Angry at the attack on his administration, Taft fired Pinchot.

The Ballinger-Pinchot controversy turned into a political disaster for Taft. The public came to doubt the President's commitment to conservation. Popular outrage against Ballinger forced Taft to ask for his resignation. Theodore Roosevelt resented Taft's treatment of his friend Pinchot and was impatient with Taft's seeming indifference to conservation. The controversy widened a growing gap between Taft and Roosevelt supporters within the Republican party.

Continuing Progressive Reform

President Taft's battles with reformers obscured the very real achievements of his administration. Although Roosevelt was known as the trust buster, Taft went after more trusts. Taft was an unlikely opponent of trusts. As a judge, he had a pro-business reputation, and as President he filled his cabinet with prosperous corporation lawyers. Yet Taft did not favor the trusts. His attorney general filed 90 antitrust lawsuits, compared to 44 during the Roosevelt administration. Cases against Standard Oil and the American Tobacco Company led to the reorganization of those giant firms.

President Taft fought for a graduated income tax. During the debate over the Payne-Aldrich tariff, Taft and the progressives had proposed an income tax to replace revenues that might be lost by lower tariff rates. But they had another ax to grind. In their eyes, a graduated income tax was much fairer than other taxes. It would place the greatest tax burden on those who had the highest incomes.

In 1895, the Supreme Court had ruled that an income tax was unconstitutional. To get around the Court's ruling, President Taft pushed for a constitutional amendment specifically permitting a federal income tax. Congress passed the proposal in 1909, and the states completed ratification of this Sixteenth Amendment in 1913. Legislation to establish a federal income tax came later that year under President Woodrow Wilson. (See page 511.)

President Taft took other progressive actions as well. He gave his support to the Mann-Elkins Act of 1910, which allowed the Interstate Commerce Commission to regulate railroad rates on commission members' initiative even without complaints from shippers. The act also gave the ICC power to regulate telegraph companies.

2. **BACKGROUND** Taft withdrew about 59 million acres of coal lands from public sale. By signing the Appalachian Forest Reserve Act, he protected large areas of the southern Appalachians and the White Mountains in N.H.

507

Under Taft, the Department of Commerce and Labor was split into two separate departments, and a Children's Bureau was set up in the Labor Department. Taft approved new safety regulations for mines and railroads. During Taft's term, Congress established an eight-hour workday for government employees and increased the number of government jobs filled by the Civil Service. But
1. unlike Roosevelt, Taft had no flair for publicity. He lacked the vital instinct for turning these actions into political gains. Republican progressives still saw Theodore Roosevelt as their leader.

The Return of Theodore Roosevelt

Progressive Republicans asked Roosevelt for support in the congressional elections of 1910. They felt that Taft and the conservatives were trying to crush progressivism in the Republican party. Convinced that Taft was "utterly

The point of this 1912 cartoon seems to be that the
2. *Progressive, or "Bull Moose," party was mainly a forum for Theodore Roosevelt. Yet the creation of the party did more than give Roosevelt a way to run for reelection. It also brought together reformers from both major political parties.*

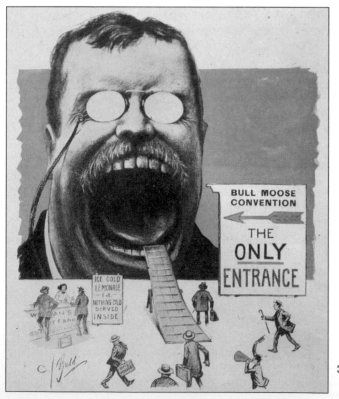

BULL MOOSE CONVENTION

THE **ONLY** ENTRANCE

ICE COLD LEMONADE

NOTHING COLD SERVED INSIDE

hopeless as a leader," Roosevelt decided to jump into the fray.

In a speech at Osawatomie, Kansas, on August 31, 1910, Roosevelt called for a "New Nationalism." This full package of progressive reforms urged strict regulation of business, social welfare laws, and a curb on the power of courts to nullify regulatory legislation. Fired with enthusiasm, Roosevelt at- 3.
tacked "local selfishness" and championed a strong national government that would "destroy privilege."

Conservative Republicans shuddered at what sounded to them like a deeply radical program, and they denounced Roosevelt for his "crime" at Osawatomie. With the Republicans badly split, the Democrats in 1910 won control of the House of Representatives for the first time in nearly 20 years. They also won many important governorships, including that of New Jersey, where Woodrow Wilson trounced the Republican opposition.

The Progressive Rebellion

As the 1912 election approached, Robert La Follette of Wisconsin challenged Taft for the Republican presidential nomination. La Follette drew strong support from Republican progressives. When La Follette collapsed while delivering a speech, Roosevelt decided to make a try for the Republican nomination. His move further splintered the Republican party. In the end, it helped put a Democrat in the White House for only the third time since the Civil War.

Taft refused to step aside for his former friend and sponsor, and the fight for the 1912 presidential nomination was on. Often, the fight turned rowdy, as Republican delegates to state conventions shouted, punched, and hurled chairs at one another.

President Taft controlled the Republican party apparatus that ran the national nominating convention held in June 1912. With skillful maneuvers, Taft filled the convention with loyal delegates. Roosevelt claimed fraud by "the representatives of reaction," and his supporters marched out of the hall. The remaining delegates nominated Taft.

Roosevelt and his supporters promptly launched the new Progressive party and

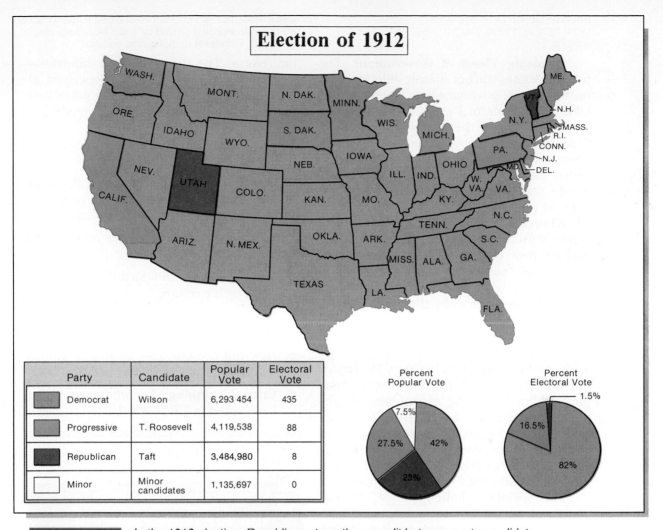

Election of 1912

Party	Candidate	Popular Vote	Electoral Vote
Democrat	Wilson	6,293 454	435
Progressive	T. Roosevelt	4,119,538	88
Republican	Taft	3,484,980	8
Minor	Minor candidates	1,135,697	0

Percent Popular Vote

7.5%
27.5%
42%
23%

Percent Electoral Vote

1.5%
16.5%
82%

MAP STUDY

See p. T94.

In the 1912 election, Republican strength was split between party candidate William Howard Taft and ex-President Theodore Roosevelt, who ran as a Progressive. As the table and graph show, Democrat Woodrow Wilson won a stunning victory in the electoral college. The popular vote was much closer. Who would have won the popular vote if Roosevelt's supporters had voted Republican?

1. **MAP READING** Ask: Which states cast electoral votes for Taft in 1912? Which states went to Roosevelt?

nominated Roosevelt. Roosevelt said he felt "as strong as a bull moose," so that animal became the party symbol. Now the Republican elephant and Democratic donkey had to contend with a fighting-mad bull moose.

The Bull Moose party platform called for the initiative and referendum (see page 498), women's suffrage, and direct presidential primaries. On the question of trusts, the platform called for government regulation of the activities of large corporations. The party also urged passage of a minimum wage, unemployment insurance, and workers' compensation insurance. The platform clearly reflected the New Nationalism Roosevelt had outlined in 1910.

New Freedom v. New Nationalism

With the Republicans split, the Democrats expected victory in 1912. They nominated Woodrow Wilson, a progressive who had been president of Princeton University and was currently governor of New Jersey. The Virginia-born Wilson was an attractive candidate, intelligent, honest, and sincerely dedicated to reform.

It soon became apparent that Taft had little chance for reelection. The contest boiled down to a two-way race between Wilson and Roosevelt. Wilson proposed a program that he called the "New Freedom." Roosevelt championed his own New Nationalism.

2.

509

2. **MAIN IDEA** Have students research the Square Deal and New Freedom and report to the class on their similarities and differences.

1. **BACKGROUND** Debs also ran for President in 1900, 1904, 1908, and 1920. The 1912 election was his best showing.

Opposing Views of Government The two candidates laid out sharply differing ideas on the role of government in American life. Like generations of Democrats before him, Wilson proclaimed the virtues of laissez-faire, the idea that "that government is best which governs least." Roosevelt, on the other hand, called for a more activist federal government—one that would take the lead in the fight for progress.

A burning issue was how to tame the giant trusts. Wilson's laissez-faire approach was to restore free competition by breaking up monopolies "so that the next generation of youngsters . . . will be free to go about making their own lives what they will." Wilson said Congress should pass laws that clearly prohibited monopolistic restraints on trade.

Roosevelt, however, believed that large-scale business was here to stay. He argued that the government should preserve competition by regulating monopolies in the public interest, not by breaking them up. Wilson feared that increasing regulation would make the government too powerful. Roosevelt feared that breaking up monopolies would undermine economic progress.

The Socialist Challenge Taft, Wilson, and Roosevelt were not the only candidates in 1912. Eugene V. Debs, founder of the American Railroad Union, ran as the presidential candidate of the Socialist party. Like other Socialists, Debs favored government ownership of all large-scale business. In this way, Debs differed from Roosevelt, who believed that government should supervise monopolies, and from Wilson, who believed they should be broken up.

1. In the election, Debs polled almost 900,000 votes, or 6 percent of the total popular vote. Debs's popularity was linked, in part, to the reform spirit of the period.

A Democratic Victory Taft and Roosevelt split the Republican vote in the 1912 presidential election, and Woodrow Wilson won handily. He received only 42 percent of the popular vote but won a majority in the electoral college. (See the graphs on page 509.) Democrats also won control of the House and the Senate and 21 governorships.

2. If the election was a defeat for Roosevelt's Progressive party, it was not a defeat

510

3. **VOCABULARY** Have students look up this term in the glossary before they begin reading.

2. **BACKGROUND** A 1912 cartoon depicted a mathematical equation: an elephant divided by a Bull Moose equaling a donkey. Ask students to explain this equation.

for reform. The three reform candidates—Wilson, Roosevelt, and Debs—received almost 11 million of the 15 million votes cast. Reform still topped the national agenda.

See p. T94.

SECTION 4 REVIEW

1. **Identify:** (a) Payne-Aldrich tariff, (b) Gifford Pinchot, (c) Progressive party, (d) New Freedom, (e) Eugene V. Debs.

2. Why did most progressives oppose high tariffs?

3. List three ways in which Taft continued progressive reform.

4. Why did Theodore Roosevelt leave the Republican party in 1912?

5. How did the attitudes of Wilson, Roosevelt, and Debs toward trusts differ?

6. **Critical Thinking** For whom would you have voted in 1912? Why?

5 Woodrow Wilson and the New Freedom

READ TO UNDERSTAND

■ What progressive reforms the Wilson administration carried out.

■ How the Federal Reserve System transformed the banking system of the United States.

■ How monopolies were regulated during the Wilson administration.

■ *Vocabulary:* interlocking directorate.   3.

Many people looked skeptically on the scholarly professor who had been elected President by less than half the voters. "Will this man be able to cope with the practical demands of national politics?" they asked. Any such doubts soon vanished. In his own way, 4. Woodrow Wilson was every bit as forceful as Theodore Roosevelt. An excellent leader, he knew how to inspire people. He believed the President should represent the highest na-

4. **PRESIDENTS** Wilson held a press conference 11 days after his inauguration. He was the first President to do so, setting a precedent that others have followed.

tional ideals, and he strengthened the presidency greatly during his eight years in office.

Tackling the Tariff

The issue of tariff reform soon tested Woodrow Wilson's ability to assert his leadership. As you have read, progressives had been outraged by the Payne-Aldrich tariff passed under President Taft. They expected Wilson to lower rates. Wilson opposed high tariffs because he believed that American industry would become more efficient if it had to face greater foreign competition. Competition would force American firms to improve their products and lower prices.

Immediately after taking office in 1913, Wilson called Congress into special session to reduce tariff duties. To dramatize the moment, the President appeared in Congress to deliver his message personally. No President since John Adams had done so, and the action riveted public attention on the tariff issue.

Under strong pressure from Wilson, the House passed a bill removing the tariff from many items and lowering duties on others. But the Senate proved less cooperative.

1. Denouncing the "insidious" lobbying of industrialists, Wilson took the tariff issue to the public. As the hot Washington summer wore on, he kept up the pressure on wavering senators. Finally, the President prevailed, and on October 3, 1913, he signed into law the Underwood-Simmons Tariff Act. The act substantially lowered the duty on imports for the first time since the Civil War, and many people believed it would lower the cost of living for the average citizen.

To replace revenues lost by cutting tariffs, the Underwood-Simmons Tariff Act included a provision that would have a lasting effect on American life. You have read that the Sixteenth, or Income Tax, Amendment had been ratified earlier in 1913. (See page 507.) The new tariff law also created a graduated income tax. The tax applied only to incomes of $4,000 or more, a princely sum in 1913, so it affected only a small minority of individuals. But it established the principle that people who had higher incomes should pay proportionately higher taxes—a principle still followed today.

The Federal Reserve Act

After the passage of the Underwood-Simmons Tariff Act, Wilson moved to reform the banking system. The financial panic of 1907 had alarmed business people and convinced many Americans that Wall Street banks were too powerful.

President Wilson believed that the government—not private banks—should regulate the supply of credit. He declared that **2.** "control must be public, not private, [and] must be vested in government itself, so that the banks may be the instruments, not the masters, of business and individual enterprise and initiative." After a long struggle that pitted the government, Wall Street banks, smaller banks, and progressives against one another, Congress achieved a compromise and passed Wilson's bill.

That bill, the Federal Reserve Act of 1913, thoroughly revised the banking system that had been in effect since the Civil War. For the first time, the federal government would

3. VISUAL EVIDENCE This portrait is by the British painter Sir William Orpen.

"Our duty is to cleanse, to reconsider, to restore every process of our common life," said Woodrow **3.** *Wilson in his inaugural address. Wilson backed up his words with vigorous action in the early years of his administration.*

1. **PAST AND PRESENT** Have students read recent newspaper and magazine articles about the Federal Reserve Board and summarize their findings for the class.

2. **VISUAL EVIDENCE** Ask students to consider how their lives would be different if they had been working at a job such as this since they finished eighth grade.

have a quick and effective way to raise or lower the money supply in times of economic stress.

The new system divided the nation into 12 districts and established a federal reserve bank for each district. Individual banks deposited a percentage of their monetary reserves in the federal reserve banks in their district. The Federal Reserve Board, headquartered in Washington, D.C., controlled the system by setting interest rates on loans made by the federal reserve banks to member banks. By lowering interest rates, the Federal Reserve Board made loans easier to obtain. That expanded the money supply. By raising interest rates, the Federal Reserve Board made loans more difficult to obtain and the money supply contracted.

At first, neither conservatives nor progressives were happy with the new system. Conservatives called it "socialistic." Progressives said Wilson had caved in to "the money
1. trust." But, as time passed, the federal reserve system gave the United States a centralized banking system.

Attacking the Trusts

As a candidate, Wilson seemed to favor breaking up trusts rather than regulating them. As President, however, he embarked on a more moderate course, moving toward Roosevelt's New Nationalism. This was partly because he lacked the congressional support to break up all trusts. It was also because Congress found it easier to legislate general rules and let a regulatory body determine on a case-by-case basis how they applied to particular situations. Wilson supported two major pieces of legislation that sought to control monopolies.

Clayton Antitrust Act In keeping with his goal of preserving competition, Wilson set out to strengthen the Sherman Antitrust Act of 1890. (See page 451.) Responding to the President's appeal, but having watered down many of his proposals, Congress passed the Clayton Antitrust Act of 1914. The new law prohibited pricing policies that might destroy competition. It outlawed the purchase of controlling stock by one company in a competing firm. It also forbade large corporations to have **interlocking directorates.** That is, it outlawed the practice of having the same individuals serve on the boards of directors of different firms in the same industry. That practice had been used to create monopolies.

The Clayton Act, unlike the Sherman Act, specified that labor unions were not "illegal combinations in restraint of trade." Furthermore, it recognized the right of workers to strike and picket. Samuel Gompers, leader of

The elimination of child labor was a key progressive goal. These young waterboys worked at the Homestead, Pennsylvania, steelworks. School ended at the eighth
2. grade or earlier for many young people. Although Congress passed the Child Labor Act, the Supreme Court later declared the law unconstitutional. A successful law banning child labor in industry was not passed until 1938.

the AFL, hailed the act as labor's "Magna Carta," but union leaders would find that they had gained little. Conservative judges would continue to interpret the laws in the interests of employers.

Federal Trade Commission Wilson embraced regulation even more explicitly by supporting the Federal Trade Commission Act of 1914. This law created a regulatory body called the Federal Trade Commission (FTC). The FTC aimed to preserve competition by preventing one firm from destroying another through unfair business practices. The commission could investigate complaints of unfair practices such as misleading advertising. If the commission found a complaint was justified, it would issue a "cease and desist" order barring the firm from continuing the misleading advertising.

Wilson did not see the FTC as a police officer waving a club over the heads of business people. Instead, said one of the drafters of the act, the President saw the FTC as "a counselor and friend to the business world." Under Wilson, that is what it became.

Wilson's Mixed Record on Social Issues

At the beginning of his administration, Wilson focused on economic fairness. He was reluctant to foster social legislation and had repeatedly opposed legislation that benefited only certain groups. But pressure from the progressive wing of the Democratic party and Democratic losses in the elections of 1914 made him more willing to support social-reform bills. These included the Seamen's Act of 1915, establishing minimum standards for the treatment of merchant sailors, and the Adamson Act of 1916, establishing an eight-hour workday for railroad workers.

Congress passed the Workingmen's Compensation Act in 1916. It provided financial aid to federal civil service employees who became disabled. The Child Labor Act of 1916 banned from interstate commerce any goods produced by child labor. The President also signed the Farm Loan Act in 1916, which made it easier for farmers to get loans.

Wilson resisted pressure to increase restrictions on immigration, even though many progressives favored the idea. Labor unions, in particular, wanted to reduce the number of immigrants who competed for jobs. Twice, the President vetoed bills to cut immigration. But, in 1917, Congress overrode his veto and enacted a bill requiring immigrants to pass a literacy test.

As you have read, only a minority of progressives were concerned with the problems of black Americans. During his campaign for President, Woodrow Wilson had promised them "absolute fair dealing." When he took office, however, his actions disappointed black leaders. For example, he approved the policy of official segregation in the federal government. According to this policy, black employees were forced to use separate rest rooms, and in some offices screens were placed between blacks and whites.

In 1913, a group of black leaders went to the White House to talk to Wilson about civil service segregation. After listening to their protest, the President told them that "segregation is not humiliating but a benefit, and ought to be so regarded by you gentlemen."

The opportunity for domestic reforms soon waned. By 1917, war loomed. President Wilson and the nation were forced to turn away from reform and pay closer attention to foreign affairs.

See p. T94.

SECTION 5 REVIEW

1. **Identify:** (a) Underwood-Simmons Tariff Act, (b) Federal Reserve Act, (c) Clayton Antitrust Act, (d) Federal Trade Commission.

2. **Define:** interlocking directorate.

3. (a) How did the Federal Reserve Act transform the banking system? (b) What action could the Federal Reserve Board take to increase the money supply?

4. Name two practices outlawed by the Clayton Antitrust Act.

5. What social-reform legislation was passed during Wilson's administration?

6. **Critical Thinking** How did Wilson's reforms reflect the growing industrialization of the United States?

513

Summary

1. **Progressivism was a reform movement that began about 1900.** Journalists roused public support against social and political injustice. Laws were passed to protect workers, and the Nineteenth Amendment gave women the right to vote. Black and white Americans founded the NAACP.

2. **Progressives promoted reforms to make local and state government more democratic and more efficient.** Among the measures adopted were primary elections, the initiative, and the referendum. The Seventeenth Amendment provided for direct election of United States senators.

3. **President Theodore Roosevelt brought progressivism to national government.** He filed lawsuits against major trusts and favored laws extending federal regulation of industry. Roosevelt also energized the movement to conserve America's natural resources. In 1908, Roosevelt handpicked William Howard Taft as his successor.

4. **President Taft promoted progressive reforms but alienated the progressives in Congress.** The Republican party split, and Theodore Roosevelt founded the Progressive party and ran against Taft and the Democrat Woodrow Wilson in the 1912 presidential election. Wilson won easily.

5. **During Wilson's presidency, Congress continued to pass progressive legislation.** It lowered the tariff, established federal control of the banking system, and strengthened antitrust laws.

See p. T94.

Vocabulary

Choose the answer that best completes each of the following sentences.

1. A writer who exposes corruption and bad business practices is called (a) a suffragist, (b) a muckraker, (c) an initiator.

2. Progressives believed party candidates should be chosen by means of (a) primary elections, (b) recall elections, (c) popular assemblies.

3. A means for people to propose bills to the legislature is the (a) referendum, (b) Wisconsin Idea, (c) initiative.

4. A direct vote by the people on a proposed bill is (a) a referendum, (b) an initiative, (c) an opinion poll.

5. An election to decide if an official should be removed from office before the expiration of his or her term is (a) a primary election, (b) an open election, (c) a recall election.

See p. T94.

Chapter Checkup

1. (a) What belief did most progressives share? (b) Did all progressives pursue the same reform goals? Explain.

2. (a) Who were the muckrakers? (b) How did they contribute to the growing reform efforts of the early 1900s?

3. (a) What was the attitude of most progressives toward the plight of black Americans? (b) What action did concerned progressives take to protect the rights of blacks?

4. (a) Why did Americans feel there was a need for federal guarantees of the purity of food and drugs? (b) How did Congress respond to that concern?

5. In what ways did Taft continue progressive reform? Give specific examples.

6. Describe the system established by the Federal Reserve Act.

See p. T95.

Critical Thinking

1. **Making a Judgment** (a) How did President Theodore Roosevelt increase the role of the federal government in the economy? (b) Do you think his actions were good for the country? Why or why not?

2. **Analyzing** What developments between 1850 and 1920 do you think helped women eventually gain suffrage?

3. **Comparing** Compare Roosevelt's New Nationalism and Wilson's New Freedom. Which of the two do you think offered a better way to deal with the giant trusts?

See p. T95.

Connecting Past and Present

1. (a) What laws regulate the hours and conditions under which teenagers can work today? (b) Do you think such laws are necessary?

2. (a) What are the major issues for reform in society and government today? (b) Describe a plan being considered to deal with one of the issues.

See p. T95.

Developing Basic Skills

1. **Doing Research** Visit your local library to find out whether the initiative, referendum, or recall election is allowed in your state. If any of them are, write a report about their use. Include information about the number of times each has been used and the issues involved.

2. **Comparing** Make a chart with three columns. In column 1, list the actions of President Roosevelt that reflected progressive goals. In column 2, list the actions of President Taft that reflected progressive goals. In column 3, list the actions of President Wilson that reflected progressive goals. Which President do you think best represents the progressive era?

WRITING ABOUT HISTORY

Preparing the Final Bibliography

The final bibliography is an alphabetical list of the sources you used to prepare your research paper. Since you wrote the author's last name first on each bibliography card, you can organize your bibliography by putting the cards in alphabetical order. Unsigned articles are alphabetized according to the first word of the title of the article. When there is more than one source by the same author, arrange them alphabetically by title. The author's name is written out only in the first entry; in all succeeding entries, three short dashes replace the author's name. Study the sample entries for style and punctuation.

Angle, Paul McClelland. <u>Crossroads: 1913</u>. Chicago, Rand McNally, 1963.

Johnson, D. E. and J. R. Johnson. "Three Hats in the Ring." <u>American History Illustrated</u>, November 19, 1984, pp. 12-17.

DiBacco, Thomas V. "Taxing Time." <u>Christian Science Monitor</u>. March 18, 1986, p. 14.

Practice: Arrange, capitalize, and punctuate the following bibliography entries.

1. An article entitled Carrie Chapman Catt, by Edna Lamprey Stantial, published in Collier's Encyclopedia, 1989 edition.

2. A book by Paolo Enrico Coletta entitled The Presidency of William Howard Taft, published in 1973 by the University Press of Kansas in Lawrence.

As the coach jolted along a dirt road, young Theodore Roosevelt glanced around. He was, in his own words, "a sickly boy, with no natural bodily prowess." He shared the coach with two other boys about 12 years old, "but very much more competent and also much more mischievous." The boys teased Theodore and soon a fight broke out. Theodore lost.

The experience changed Roosevelt's life. "I made up my mind," he wrote, "that I would not again be put in such a helpless position." The sickly boy built himself into a hardy, powerful adult. Although he was "a painfully slow and awkward pupil," he

1. **VOCABULARY** Point out that *culture* in the magazine title means "development."

The costumes have changed, but the activities
1. *remain the same. Physical fitness was in vogue in the early 1900s as people tried to improve themselves.*

William Muldoon
Horace Fletcher
Charlotte Perkins Gilman
Daniel Carson Goodman
Bernarr Macfadden

became an expert boxer and wrestler. He also took up hiking, fishing, and hunting.

Roosevelt never forgot his struggles. Throughout his life, he encouraged Americans to challenge themselves with rigorous exercise. Not only was "the strenuous life" good for the body—it was good for the spirit as well, Roosevelt believed.

Roosevelt's life reflected a long American tradition of striving for personal perfection. In the 1600s, the Puritans in Massachusetts exhorted people to eliminate sin from their lives. A career was not work for its own sake, but a calling to do God's work. In that spirit, Jonathan Edwards, whose preaching helped inspire the Great Awakening in 1738, wrote in his diary, "Resolved, never to lose one moment of time, but to improve it in the most profitable way I possibly can."

Striving for Perfection By the mid-1700s, Benjamin Franklin had transformed that religious ideal into a more worldly "Project for Arriving at Moral Perfection." In it, Franklin described 13 virtues that he wished to develop. They included frugality, industry, justice, moderation, cleanliness, and tranquility. Each week, Franklin concentrated on one virtue. At night, he noted in a book any offenses he was guilty of that day. At the end of 13 weeks, he started over.

Although few Americans have been as systematic as Franklin in seeking self-improvement, the values he upheld have had a wide influence on society. William Holmes McGuffey, a nineteenth-century educator and minister, published illustrated readers to teach reading and develop honesty, thrift, charity, and courage in schoolchildren. McGuffey's *Eclectic Reader* sold over 122 million copies from 1836 to 1920.

A Need for Books In the 1820s and 1830s, the public school system was teaching Americans to read. Yet many educated adults could not afford books. To fill this gap, several experiments in adult education were tried. One was the lyceum movement, founded by Josiah Holbrook. The lyceums began as local study groups and later presented lectures and debates. Holbrook hoped to provide "numerous cheap and practical tracts," which would be circulated to "branch lyceums, schools, academies, taverns, steamboats, and private families."

Meanwhile, another force was creating a need for some form of community education for adults. The nation was industrializing, and the growing cities were beset with problems of crime, alcoholism, and delinquency. Reformers saw education as a means of raising the level of morality and civic responsibility. In the 1830s, the combination of these forces led to the first tax-supported institution for the informal education of adults—the public library.

Chautauqua Movement In the late 1800s, a new movement developed that offered continuing education to adults. The Chautauqua movement was named after the lake in western New York State where its organizers first held meetings. It began as a program for training Sunday school teachers, but expanded in scope over the years.

By the 1880s, hundreds of men and women spent their summers in tents and cabins by the shore of Lake Chautauqua, improving their minds. They studied Hebrew, Latin, Greek, chemistry, music theory, and Shakespeare, among other courses. They listened to lectures on such timely topics as "The Importance of Science to the Religious Thinker," "Nature's Mechanics," and "Teaching in the West." Chautauquans improved their physical health with swimming, tennis, and other sports.

Soon, summer institutes modeled on Chautauqua were being held all over. The creators of Chautauqua also began a program of home reading so that those unable to go to camp could participate at home. One home reader began the program when he was 71 years old. At age 86, he wrote to

The accommodations at camp meetings were not luxurious, but people bent on self-improvement returned each year to refresh their minds .

1.

1. **VISUAL EVIDENCE** Have students compare this picture to the one on p. 314.

the founders to say, "I have enjoyed more of life in the last fifteen years than in all the years before." Over the years, the Chautauquas gave millions of Americans a vision of a better, more fulfilling life.

Not all movements for self-improvement have been as positive as the public library system or the Chautauquas. At times, some Americans have tried ridiculous schemes for instant results. In the 1920s, followers of French philosopher Émile Coué believed they would reach perfection simply by chanting, "Day by day in every way I am getting better and better." Others have tried cure-all diets, special baths, and various forms of mysticism. But many Americans believe there is no easy route to self-improvement. They would agree with Benjamin Franklin, who wrote, "There are no gains without pains."

See p. T95.

1. What were two underlying causes for the development of the public library system?

2. How would you account for the popularity of the Chautauqua movement?

3. **Critical Thinking** Do you agree with Benjamin Franklin's view that "there are no gains without pains"? Explain.

517

Ernest Thompson Seton

Ernest Thompson Seton, explorer, artist, and writer, was one of the best-known naturalists of his time. A gifted artist, he wrote and illustrated a series of popular wildlife books that drew attention to the nation's vanishing wilderness.

Perhaps most important of all, he founded an outdoor organization called the Woodcraft Indians, which later became the Boy Scouts of America. Through the Woodcraft Indians, Seton pioneered a way for young Americans to improve themselves through outdoor activities.

Ernest Thompson Seton was born in London in 1860. At age 6, he moved to Lindsay, Ontario, where his family started a farm. Before he was 10, Ernest had learned pioneer skills like herding cattle, felling trees, and casting rifle bullets from molten lead. He and his 13 brothers and sisters provided all the farm hands the family needed.

As a boy, Seton loved to listen to an old hunter who lived nearby tell about stalking bear and killing wolves. Slowly, however, he learned a different feeling for the animals of the deep Canadian woods. Once, Seton and his brothers pushed over a dead tree that a red squirrel had climbed. The tree crashed to the ground, killing the squirrel. "Now we experienced a surge of remorse," wrote Seton. "Why kill a helpless, harmless, beautiful wild thing for mere sport?" After that, Seton was interested in observing animals, not killing them. His dream "was to be with and study the wild creatures of the world about me."

Several obstacles threatened to keep Seton from reaching his dream. When he was 10, the farm at Lindsay failed, and his family moved to Toronto. Seton did not want to leave the birds and animals he loved. "But the spirit power, the will power, was driving," he discovered, "and each year showed that . . . even in the city the wild things came."

Seton's father presented another obstacle. His father wanted him to give up

Ernest Thompson Seton (1860–1946) helped found the Boy Scouts of America and wrote the first Boy Scout manual.

1.

1. **READING** Seton also wrote many nature books. The most popular was *Wild Animals I Have Known.*

nature study and become a painter. By sketching and painting birds, animals, and landscapes, Seton had become an accomplished artist. Yet Seton knew in his heart that he wanted to be a naturalist: "I thought I had a mission—to be the prophet of outdoor life." His father disagreed, telling him, "No, there is no opening, no future, for such a calling."

Seton obeyed his father, working hard and winning a scholarship to art school in London. But the lure of the wilderness drew him back to North America. He traveled widely, sketching birds and animals and writing nature stories. Through hard work, he made a career that combined his skill as an artist with his love of nature.

With money from his first book, Seton set up a nature sanctuary outside New York City. Here he intended to live and experiment with wildlife conservation. But local teenagers broke down the outer fence of the sanctuary and killed Seton's animals.

Friends urged Seton to call the police. Instead, he invited the youths to spend a weekend camping out in the sanctuary. At first, the youths greeted his offer with a stony silence. Much to Seton's surprise, however, 42 boys showed up on Friday.

From this incident, Seton saw that outdoor experience could help city youths, and he organized the Woodcraft Indians. Soon chapters opened all across the country, with young boys learning outdoor skills and crafts. For each skill they perfected, the "Indians" earned a feather. Seton's group became part of the Boy Scouts, which had begun in England in 1908. The feathers earned by Seton's Indians became the merit badges of the Boy Scouts.

Seton's road to success had not been easy. As one of 14 children, he had gotten little financial help from his parents. He worked hard to prove himself, and then used his success and love of the outdoors to benefit others. The key, he believed, was determination. "All things are possible to him that wills," he told a friend, "for will is the greatest power under the sun."

See p. T95.

1. What obstacles did Seton overcome to achieve his goals?

2. **Critical Thinking** How did Seton use nature study to help young people improve themselves?

The Woodcraft Indians

In the following passage, Ernest Thompson Seton describes his first outing with the boys who had vandalized his sanctuary. The group became the first Woodcraft Indians.

Now we set out on what was destined to be an epoch-making outing for the village boys, for myself, and for thousands of boys elsewhere. . . .

The boys wanted to wear feathers. I said: "Certainly, but remember, after the manner of the Indians. The good old Indian did not wear just any feather. . . . Each feather was conferred by the Council as the decoration for an exploit. I will give you a hundred exploits, each of which will entitle the doer to a feather. . . ."

I allowed a feather for all . . . who could walk four miles in an hour, or run 100 yards in eleven seconds. The only cheap one was for swimming. All who could swim one hundred yards, no matter how slowly, got the swimming feather.

In the second department, called Campercraft, I allowed honors to all who could light a campfire with rubbing sticks, could measure the width of a river without crossing it, etc.

The third department was nature study, and honors were allowed to all who could name correctly twenty-five trees, fifty flowers, fifty birds, etc. . . .

[The outing's] success far exceeded my highest expectations. Rough and wild boys may defy the teacher, and scoff at the opinions of their elders; but they cannot scoff at the public opinion of their playmates. . . .

In the final outcome, there was not one of these a bad boy. . . . Twenty-five years after this first camp we had a reunion. . . . Not one [of the group] went wrong. All have made good. What would have happened had I tried the compulsory—the military method, instead of the developmental, the Woodcraft Way?

Adapted from *Trail of an Artist/Naturalist: Autobiography of Ernest Thompson Seton,* ed. Keir B. Sterling (New York: Arno, 1978).

See p. T95.

1. How did Seton adapt the ways of the Indians to his organization?

2. **Critical Thinking** Why do you think Seton's methods worked to instill pride in the boys?

Becoming a World Power

24

(1865–1914)

CHAPTER OBJECTIVES After completing this chapter, students should be able to
1. explain reasons for U.S. expansion overseas.
2. list causes and results of the Spanish-American War.
3. analyze problems the empire created for the U.S.
4. describe Theodore Roosevelt's "big stick" policy.
5. explain U.S. involvement in Panama and Asia.
6. recognize propaganda.

CHAPTER PREVIEW Have students read the paragraphs and study the time line below. Ask: What areas outside the continental U.S. are part of the U.S. today? How did they become so? Which are states? Which are territories? Write down student responses and have the class add to and correct their list as they read the chapter.

"Did you ever see such a fleet and such a day?" exclaimed a grinning Teddy Roosevelt to the cheering crowd at Hampton Roads, Virginia. "By George, isn't it magnificent?" It was December 16, 1907, and the optimistic President was proudly watching 16 battleships of the Great White Fleet steam out to sea.

In the early 1900s, a nation's naval strength was the standard by which its prestige was rated. Consequently, Roosevelt was sending this armada of gleaming white ships around the world as a sign of the coming of age of the United States.

The gesture, however, was not entirely symbolic. Roosevelt was worried about the growing strength of Japan, which had just thrashed the Russians in the Russo-Japanese war of 1904–1905. Japanese-American relations were tense, and wild rumors were flying that the Japanese meant to seize the Panama Canal or Hawaii or the Philippines—or all three! So Roosevelt had good reason to test the readiness of his fleet.

The voyage was an immense success. South American capitals competed for the honor of holding the grandest reception, and the Australians threw an eight-day party. The only tense moment came when the fleet entered Yokohama harbor in Japan. Some American officials feared the Japanese were plotting to sink the battleships. But the welcome was gracious. The friendly feelings peaked when a temporary arch built to honor the fleet caught fire and an American marine climbed it to pluck the Japanese flag from the flames. The crowd went wild and paraded the Yankee hero around on their shoulders.

In the decades after the Civil War, Americans were preoccupied with healing the wounds of the ruinous conflict. But when the United States acquired overseas territory as a result of the Spanish-American War, the nation found it had become an empire—with all the ensuing responsibilities. The Great White Fleet was a symbol that the United States was taking its place in the arena of world affairs.

1.

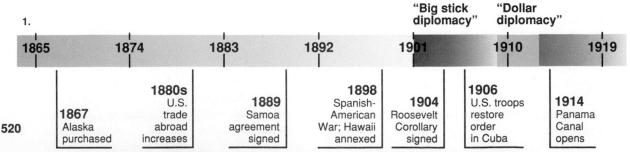

1865	1874	1883	1892	1901	1910	1919

"Big stick diplomacy" "Dollar diplomacy"

1867 Alaska purchased

1880s U.S. trade abroad increases

1889 Samoa agreement signed

1898 Spanish-American War; Hawaii annexed

1904 Roosevelt Corollary signed

1906 U.S. troops restore order in Cuba

1914 Panama Canal opens

520

1. TIME LINE QUESTION Ask: How long after the Spanish-American War did U.S. troops restore order in Cuba?

1. *The Great White Fleet, seen here steaming into the harbor in San Francisco, proclaimed the new role of the United States in the world. Reminiscing about the fleet in his autobiography, Theodore Roosevelt called it "the most important service that I rendered to peace."*

1. **VISUAL EVIDENCE** Boatloads of sightseers, such as those shown here, greeted the fleet in every port.

2. **VOCABULARY** Have students look up this word in the glossary before they begin reading.

1 The Dream of Expansion

READ TO UNDERSTAND

■ How the United States acquired new territory after the Civil War.

■ What ideas led Americans to seek further expansion.

■ Why American leaders revived the Monroe Doctrine in the late 1800s.

2. ■ *Vocabulary:* imperialism.

In 1880, the cost-conscious ruler of Turkey decided to close his diplomatic missions in such "minor" countries as Sweden, Belgium, and the United States. This was but one indication of how little other nations regarded the United States at that time. But this attitude was soon to change, as the United States joined Great Britain, France, and other countries in building its own overseas empire.

Europe's Imperial Drive

For hundreds of years, European nations had been setting up colonies in distant places. Then, in the late 1800s, there was a new spurt of activity as Great Britain, France, Russia, and latecomers like Germany and Italy eagerly sought new lands to rule and exploit. Thus began the era of modern **imperialism,** when powerful nations created empires by dominating other lands.

In most cases, it was the Industrial Revolution that spurred the rise of imperialism. The wealth and productivity created by the growth of industry had stimulated the quest for both new markets and sources of raw materials. The colonies and possessions of imperial nations thus served a double purpose. They provided markets for manufactured goods that could not be consumed at home and supplied raw materials from which to make those goods.

The technology that made colonies desirable also made them more accessible than ever before. Steamships had increased the

521

3. **BACKGROUND** Italy did not become a unified nation until 1870. Germany was not unified until 1871.

1. **READING** Have students read Kipling's poem "The White Man's Burden." Discuss the ideas and attitudes expressed in the poem.

speed of ocean travel, and the transoceanic cable had accelerated communication between nations. And if distant peoples should resist the empire builders, new weapons like improved rifles and the Maxim gun, an early type of machine gun, could persuade them to change their minds.

Also important in the development of the new imperialism was the growing belief among Europeans that they had a moral duty to bring civilization to the "backward" peoples 1. of the world. In the words of the British writer Rudyard Kipling, this was the "white man's burden."

By the late 1800s, the colonizing nations of Europe, joined by Japan, had claimed huge chunks of the world, principally in Asia, Africa, and the Pacific. In the scramble for empire, sharp rivalries developed among the empire builders. Sometimes, they managed to settle their differences through diplomatic means. Occasionally, they resorted to armed skirmishes and even wars. These imperial

2. **VISUAL EVIDENCE** Ask: Why do you think these women risked hardships to reach the Klondike?

Before the discovery of gold in the Yukon, the purchase of Alaska from Russia in 1867 had been ridiculed as "Seward's Folly." By 1898, however, when this photograph was taken, prospectors were
2. *racing to Alaska. The two women prospectors in this photograph faced a hazardous journey over treacherous mountain passes to reach the Klondike.*

rivalries would contribute to the outbreak of World War I in 1914.

Early Signs of American Expansionism

While European nations were expanding their power throughout the world, the United States was looking inward. For a time after the Civil War, Americans poured their energies into building industry, settling the West, reviving the war-torn South, and meeting the challenges of the Gilded Age. Most Americans had little interest in events beyond their own shores. The New York *Sun* even sug- 3. gested that the Department of State, which was in charge of foreign relations, had "outgrown its usefulness" and should be abolished.

One public figure who did not share this isolationist sentiment was William H. Seward. Seward, who served as secretary of state under Presidents Lincoln and Johnson, believed that the United States should expand into a vast empire. To do this would require reducing the influence of other nations in North America.

Seward's first opportunity came in 1866, a year after the end of the Civil War. During the war, Emperor Napoleon III of France had set up a puppet government in Mexico headed by Archduke Maximilian of Austria and backed by French troops. While the United States was fighting the Civil War, it was in no position to act against this clear challenge to the Monroe Doctrine. But with the war over, Seward sent the French a strong note demanding that they withdraw their troops. Fearful that the United States might enforce its demand with military power, the French gave in. They agreed to evacuate their army and left Maximilian to the mercy of Mexican rebels, who executed him.

In 1867, Seward found another opportunity to extend American interests. When Russia expressed its desire to sell Alaska to the United States, Seward persuaded Congress to appropriate the asking price of $7.2 million—about 2 cents an acre (.4 hectare). Initially mocked as "Seward's Folly," the purchase was to prove its value many times over. Thirty years later, an Alaskan gold rush yielded millions of dollars worth of gold.

3. **BACKGROUND** By 1885, the Department of State had only 60 employees.

1. **GEOGRAPHY** The census of 1890 declared that for the first time "there can hardly be said to be a frontier line" in the American West. (regions)

With these two actions, Seward eliminated French and Russian influence in North America and at the same time acquired a huge territory for the United States. During this same period, Seward also tried to buy the Danish Virgin Islands in the Caribbean. The Senate, however, refused to ratify a treaty he had worked out with Denmark.

During the administration of President Grant, proposals for extending American territorial claims found little public support. A Philadelphia newspaper expressed the popular mood when it stated, "The true interests of the American people will be better served . . . by a thorough and complete development of the immense resources of our existing territory than by any rash attempts to increase it."

During the 1880s, dreams of empire began to surface. Faced with an excess of food and manufactured goods, Americans began to export more to other countries. Exports increased from $450 million in 1870 to more than $1 billion by the early 1890s. Slowly, the United States began to penetrate world markets previously dominated by European nations. But such competition increased the likelihood that Americans would become involved in foreign conflicts.

A Rationale for Expansion

New interest in overseas markets and territories required a new point of view about foreign affairs. Among those who argued for United States expansion were historian Frederick Jackson Turner, naval officer Alfred Thayer Mahan, and Congregationalist minister Josiah Strong.

The Disappearing Frontier Frederick Jackson Turner was a young professor of history at the University of Wisconsin during the 1890s. He maintained that the availability of free land along the frontier throughout most of America's history had enabled poor or restless Americans to move West and pros-

1. per. As settlers moved west, the frontier disappeared. Turner feared that the loss of opportunity might lead to domestic upheavals. Indeed, labor unrest and political turmoil between 1870 and 1900 seemed to suggest that Turner was right.

Public sentiment in favor of expanding United States influence abroad was strong. Many Americans believed it was a continuation of manifest destiny. In this 1897 cartoon, critical of expansionism, Uncle Sam waits for Hawaii, Canada, Cuba, and Central America to fall into his basket.

2.

2. **VISUAL EVIDENCE** Ask: Which apples have already fallen into the basket?

For many Americans, the "closing of the frontier" sparked an urge to seek opportunities abroad. Leaders like Senator Henry Cabot Lodge of Massachusetts, John Hay of Ohio, and young Theodore Roosevelt of New York argued that the United States should expand overseas to preserve its vitality and avoid social conflict at home. World markets would provide an outlet for the excess production of American farms and factories. And wider trade would lessen the threat of economic depressions that had struck in every decade since the Civil War.

Protecting World Markets Captain Mahan shared the expansionists' view. In 1890, he published an influential book called *The Influence of Sea Power Upon History.* Mahan maintained that the future prosperity of the United States depended on access to world markets. Those markets could be acquired 3. through trade, not colonies. All great trading nations had to have a strong navy to protect trade routes, since the loss of trade to enemy powers could weaken the nation.

Mahan thus urged the government to add modern steam-powered battleships to its **523** fleet. He also proposed that the United States

3. **CRITICAL THINKING** Ask: How might competition for foreign markets lead to war?

annex Hawaii and build a canal across Central America. Hawaii would provide an important naval base in the Pacific, and the canal would allow American ships to pass quickly between the Atlantic and Pacific oceans.

Civilizing the World   Josiah Strong, in his 1885 book *Our Country, Its Possible Future and Its Present Crisis,* envisioned an American Christian empire that would spread across the Pacific into Asia. He argued that the "white race," represented by the United States, had been divinely chosen to "civilize" the rest of the world. Strong had his own interpretation of Charles Darwin's theory of the "survival of the fittest." (See page 428.) In Strong's opinion, the white race was the "fittest" and thus the American empire would survive and prosper.

While Mahan and Turner were primarily interested in the expansion of trade, Strong stressed territorial expansion. Their ideas influenced both the public and politicians as the United States took its first steps toward gaining greater influence in the Pacific.

When Lydia Kamekeha came to the Hawaiian throne, American residents on the island believed she would support their interests. But as Queen Liliuokalani, she proved a strong nationalist who tried to reduce the power of foreign merchants on the island. She ruled from 1891 to 1893 as the last Hawaiian monarch. Afterward, she received a small pension from the United States government.

A Foothold in the Pacific

Americans had traded with Asian nations since the 1700s, and this activity increased greatly during the 1800s. The United States signed a commercial treaty with China in 1844, opened trade with Japan in 1854, and arranged a trade treaty with Korea in 1882.

Share of Samoa   By the 1880s, the United States was showing interest in the Pacific island of Samoa (sah MOH ah), where the fine harbor of Pago Pago (PAHNG oh PAHNG oh) could serve as a naval base and commercial port. Germany and Great Britain, however, also realized the value of the harbor, and the three powers competed for dominance. For several months in 1889, a clash seemed imminent as German and American sailors eyed each other nervously from gunboats anchored at Pago Pago. Then, just as tensions were at their highest, a powerful storm sank the ships of both countries and the threat of war began to ease.

In 1899, the three nations finally settled the issue. Samoa was divided between the United States and Germany, and Britain was given territories elsewhere in the Pacific. The events in Samoa, nevertheless, had demonstrated that the United States would assert its power in the Pacific Ocean.

The Annexation of Hawaii   Although agreeing to cooperate with Germany in Samoa, the United States wanted sole control of Hawaii. Europeans and Americans had first learned of the Hawaiian Islands in 1778, after British sea captain James Cook landed there seeking fresh water and trade.

During the 1800s, Hawaii attracted traders from China, France, Spain, and the United States. Americans, especially, valued the islands as a stopover for their growing trade with China. Descendents of American missionaries who settled in Hawaii became prosperous sugar growers who dominated the islands' economy and government.

In 1891, Queen Liliuokalani (lih LEE uh OH kuh LAH nee), a strong nationalist, came to the throne. She tried to restore the power of the Hawaiian monarchy and reduce the privileges of foreign merchants. But in January 1893, American residents, with the help of United States marines, overthrew her. They then set up a new government and sent a delegation to Washington, D.C., to negotiate a treaty.

1. President Benjamin Harrison supported an annexation treaty with the new Hawaiian government. However, Grover Cleveland, who succeeded Harrison in 1893, voiced outrage at the high-handed actions of the American sugar growers and the role of the marines in the revolt. Consequently, he withdrew the treaty from the Senate. Debate over the annexation of Hawaii continued until 1898, during President McKinley's administration. At that time, Congress passed a joint resolution annexing Hawaii to the United States.

Applying the Monroe Doctrine

The United States had always maintained a special interest in Latin America and the Caribbean. This interest had been formalized in 1823, when President James Monroe issued the Monroe Doctrine. (See page 234.) The Monroe Doctrine stated that the United States would oppose all European intervention in the affairs of independent nations in the Americas. But for many years after 1823, it was the British navy that enforced the Monroe Doctrine. Most Americans forgot about it.

After the Civil War, however, Americans became more concerned with Latin America.
2. As United States industry and interests expanded, American merchants and manufacturers looked with interest at Latin America's raw materials. Military leaders considered many parts of the region to be strategically important. Also, American leaders talked of building a canal across Central America that would shorten the voyage between the Atlantic and Pacific oceans by thousands of miles.

In the 1870s, a French company set out to build such a canal across Panama. President Rutherford B. Hayes angrily revived the Monroe Doctrine, declaring that Panama was "virtually a part of the coast line of the United States." He said, "The policy of this country is a canal under American control." Although the French ignored Hayes, other difficulties forced them to abandon the canal project in 1889.

Meanwhile, south of Panama, a border dispute in 1895 between Venezuela and the colony of British Guiana (ghee AH nah) brought the United States and Britain close to war. The boundary between Venezuela and British Guiana had long been contested. The discovery of gold in the disputed area increased the stakes of the claim and the tension between the two nations. At Venezuela's request, the United States demanded that Britain submit the dispute to arbitration. Britain replied with a firm "no," shrugging off Secretary of State Richard Olney's claim that "today the United States is practically sovereign on this continent."

President Cleveland saw Britain's reply as a challenge to the Monroe Doctrine. He threatened war if the British seized new territory. The British, preoccupied with German threats to their interests in Africa, wanted to avoid conflict with the United States. In 1897, Great Britain agreed to have an independent commission settle the boundary dispute, and the crisis ended. The events in Panama and Venezuela showed that Americans were coming to see the Monroe Doctrine as a vital force in United States policy toward Latin America.

See p. T96.

SECTION 1 REVIEW

1. **Identify:** (a) William H. Seward, (b) Frederick Jackson Turner, (c) Alfred Thayer Mahan, (d) Josiah Strong, (e) Queen Liliuokalani.

2. **Define:** imperialism.

3. (a) How did Secretary of State Seward end French influence in North America? (b) How did he end Russian influence?

4. What arguments did each of the following make for expansion? (a) Frederick Turner; (b) Captain Mahan; (c) Josiah Strong.

5. (a) How did the United States gain a foothold in Samoa? (b) Why was the United States interested in acquiring Hawaii?

6. How did Britain challenge the Monroe Doctrine?

7. **Critical Thinking** How were industrialization and the growth of empires related?

525

2 Spanish-American War

READ TO UNDERSTAND

■ How the press helped to provoke the Spanish-American War.

■ What major battles took place during the Spanish-American War.

■ How the United States acquired an empire of its own.

1. ■ *Vocabulary:* jingoism, reconcentration, yellow journalism.

2. For many years, Americans had cast covetous glances at Cuba, a rich tropical island only 90 miles (144 kilometers) off the coast of Florida. Secretary of State John Quincy Adams, in a memorable reference in 1823, had compared Cuba to an apple that a tempest might tear "from its native tree" (that is, the Spanish empire) and drop into American hands.

By the 1890s, Spain's American empire had been pruned back to two islands—Cuba and Puerto Rico. Bitter unrest in Cuba led the United States toward war with Spain.

3. **VISUAL EVIDENCE** Ask: Why would a cartoon like this have a strong effect on the American public?

3. *Cartoonists actively pushed the United States toward war with Spain. In this pro-war cartoon, a romantic figure of Cuban liberty is being fried by Spanish misrule.*

Moving Toward War

Although activity in foreign affairs during the late 1800s had brought the United States close to war several times, the nation had managed to avoid armed conflict. The successful outcome of the disputes in Samoa, Venezuela, and Hawaii, along with growing naval strength, had made American citizens and their leaders confident of the nation's power.

This confidence, however, threatened to develop into **jingoism,** an exaggerated and belligerent national pride. Jingoists often advocated an aggressive, more warlike foreign policy. In 1891, they demanded war with Chile after two American sailors were killed and seventeen were injured in a riot in Valparaiso, Chile. President Harrison ordered the navy to prepare for war. Faced with American threats, the Chilean government offered compensation and the crisis ended.

The trouble in Cuba, however, was different—and far more dangerous. Americans had invested money in Cuba since before the Civil War, mainly in the rich sugar plantations. They wanted to protect those investments. Some Americans wanted to annex Cuba outright, even though it still belonged to Spain.

In 1895, Cuba's hatred of Spanish rule and its frustration with falling sugar prices led to a bloody revolt. Some rebels set fire to sugar fields and blew up trains. Choosing repression instead of reform, Spain sent a new and ruthless governor, General Valeriano Weyler (WAY ee lair). The American press soon dubbed him "Butcher Weyler" because of his brutal treatment of prisoners and his cruel policies. Under one policy, known as **reconcentration,** Weyler's troops herded Cuban villagers into concentration camps, where many died from hunger and neglect.

Inhuman conditions in these camps outraged many Americans. A group of Cubans in New York fanned anti-Spanish feeling by spreading stories of Spanish atrocities. Two New York City newspapers, Joseph Pulitzer's *World* and William Randolph Hearst's *Journal,* further fed the anti-Spanish hysteria. Describing Weyler as a "mad dog" or "human hyena" while playing down brutal deeds of the rebels, they intentionally tried to whip up the emotions of their readers.

Lola Rodríguez de Tió: Poet and Patriot

Undaunted by Spanish terror, Lola Rodríguez de Tió used the skills of a poet and orator to help her native Puerto Rico and her adopted Cuba to throw off Spanish rule. Rather than bullets, she fired words at her oppressors, and today she is remembered as a true patriot.

Born in Puerto Rico in 1843, Lola Rodríguez refused to play the role of a traditional woman. She had urgent thoughts of her own and insisted on expressing them. Thus, she became the first Puerto Rican woman to deliver a public speech on the island and the first woman to join the men of her native town in literary and political discussions.

After marrying Bonocio Tió Segarra, a journalist and poet, Lola Rodríguez de Tió joined the struggle to win Puerto Rican independence from Spain. In 1887, when a cruel Spanish governor unleashed a reign of terror in Puerto Rico, the poet appealed for help to the government in Spain. Soon after, she and her family fled to Cuba.

In Cuba, the Tió home became a meeting place for Cubans eager to put an end to despotic Spanish rule. Rodríguez de Tió penned verses that called for freedom—verses that Cuba's rulers considered subversive. A poem called "A Cuba" ("To Cuba") especially angered the Spanish. Fearing arrest, Rodríguez de Tió

and her family fled once again, this time to New York.

In the United States, Rodríguez de Tió continued to recite her patriotic poems and to work for the independence of Cuba. After the Spanish-American War, she returned to Havana, to receive a hero's welcome.

1.

> Es libre aquél que lo quiere,
> Hombre llámese, o mujer,
> Que aspirar puede al derecho
> Quien reconoce el deber.
>
> Niega todo lo que quieras,
> Si negar es tu desgracia,
> Mas, no me niegues tres cosas
> El alma, Dios y la patria.
>
> Freedom comes if you want it,
> Be you called a man or woman,
> If you can aspire to justice
> If you recognize duty.
>
> Deny all that you like,
> If denying is your misfortune,
> But do not deny me three things:
> Spirit, God and nation.

See p. T97.

1. What political goal did Rodríguez de Tió express in her poems?

2. **Critical Thinking** Why might Cuba's Spanish rulers have feared those poems?

1. **CRITICAL THINKING** Ask: What ideals expressed in this poem would be shared by many people in the U.S.?

Pulitzer and Hearst were indulging in a style of reporting called **yellow journalism.** Paying scant attention to the facts, the yellow press tried to sell newspapers by featuring screaming headlines and sensational stories, with Spain as the villain. Hearst was so confident of his ability to sway public opinion that he reputedly told one photographer who was heading for Cuba, "You supply the pictures. I'll supply the war." Swayed by the yellow press, many Americans called for a war to liberate Cuba from Spanish rule.

On the Brink of War

When riots erupted in Havana, the Cuban capital, in 1898, President William McKinley ordered the battleship *Maine* into Havana's

harbor to protect United States citizens and property. On February 15, 1898, a huge explosion destroyed the battleship, killing 260 American sailors. An investigation failed to reveal why the *Maine* blew up, although 78 years later an official study would say that all evidence pointed to an accident. But people in the United States, inflamed by hysterical news stories, angrily blamed Spain. (See page 530.)

For several weeks after the sinking of the *Maine,* the United States hovered on the brink of declaring war. President McKinley, however, held back. In March 1898, he proposed a cease-fire between Spanish troops and Cuban rebels. He offered to mediate talks between Spain and Cuba, but he clearly indicated that the outcome should be Cuban

2.

527

2. **BACKGROUND** Theodore Roosevelt was irate at McKinley's hesitation. "McKinley has no more backbone than a chocolate eclair," Roosevelt fumed.

independence. Spain rejected McKinley's proposal.

War fever ran high. Expansionists, such as Captain Mahan and Assistant Secretary of the Navy Theodore Roosevelt, foresaw a victory over Spain as the beginning of an empire for the United States. Many social reformers, labor leaders, and religious leaders favored a war as a moral crusade to improve conditions in Cuba. And millions of ordinary citizens, outraged by the sinking of the *Maine* and by Weyler's atrocities, also demanded war against Spain.

Most business leaders, except the few with large holdings in Cuba, opposed war. Industrialists believed that war would disrupt the United States economy, but they were not powerful enough to hold back the tide of war.

President McKinley presented Spain with a series of demands, including the withdrawal of Spain from Cuba. Spain would agree to meet only some of these demands, however, and McKinley decided to ask Congress for a declaration of war against Spain. Congress complied on April 20, 1898.

War in the Pacific

Surprisingly, the first fighting of the war did not take place in Cuba. It took place on the other side of the world, in the Philippine Islands, which were controlled by Spain. The United States had begun preparations for a Pacific war soon after the sinking of the *Maine*. On February 25, Theodore Roosevelt, as assistant secretary of the navy, had sent a message to Commodore George Dewey, commander of the United States fleet based in Hong Kong. If war came, Roosevelt said, Dewey's mission would be to destroy the Spanish fleet at Manila Bay in the Philippines.

1.

2. **MAP READING** Ask: Between what two islands did American troops sail to reach Puerto Rico from Cuba?

MAP STUDY The sea battle between the United States and Spain ended quickly in the Pacific, when ships under Admiral George Dewey sank the Spanish fleet stationed in the Philippines. In the Caribbean, the United States Navy sank a Spanish squadron in a one-sided battle near Santiago. American ground troops defeated the Spanish in Cuba and Puerto Rico. Why was the naval attack more complicated in the Caribbean than in the Pacific? See p. T97.

2.

Spanish-American War

CHINA

FORMOSA (Japan)

Hong Kong (Br.)

DEWEY

PACIFIC OCEAN

SOUTH CHINA SEA

PHILIPPINE ISLANDS

Manila

Manila Bay

BRITISH NORTH BORNEO

The Philippines

FLORIDA

Tampa

GULF OF MEXICO

Key West

Battleship *Maine* sunk

Havana

CUBA

San Juan Hill

Santiago

CARIBBEAN SEA

JAMAICA (Br.)

ATLANTIC OCEAN

BAHAMA ISLANDS (Br.)

HAITI

DOMINICAN REPUBLIC

San Juan

PUERTO RICO

The Caribbean

| 0 | 150 | 300 Miles |
| 0 | 150 | 300 Kilometers |

- - - → United States Navy
——→ United States Army
——→ Spanish fleet
✴ United States victories

| 0 | 150 | 300 Miles |
| 0 | 150 | 300 Kilometers |

The 10th Cavalry was one of the regiments sent to fight the Spanish in Cuba in 1090. General John J. Pershing, who may be one of the white officers in this painting, had served earlier as an officer with the black regiment on the western frontier. When war broke out with Spain, Pershing wangled a transfer back to the 10th Cavalry. Pershing's nickname, "Black Jack," came from his years with the regiment.

When Congress declared war, Dewey and the fleet steamed toward Manila Bay. At dawn on May 1, Dewey's guns opened fire and succeeded in sinking or capturing the entire Spanish fleet, with only one American casualty. The Spanish still held Manila, however, so Dewey asked McKinley to send more troops. Meanwhile, Dewey also joined forces with Emilio Aguinaldo (AH gwee NAHL doh), the leader of Filipino rebels fighting for independence from Spain. McKinley sent 11,000 troops plus naval support. On August 13, 1898, rebel and United States forces took Manila.

Even anti-expansionists in the United States thrilled at Dewey's victory. The expansionists especially admired the stunning naval performance in Manila Bay. Those who dreamed of empire believed that they were seeing the dawn of a new age of American expansion.

War in the Caribbean

While American forces were crushing the Spanish in the Philippines, preparations were under way for an invasion of Cuba. Eager to fight in what Secretary of State John Hay called a "splendid little war," 200,000 men volunteered to join the army.

During the spring of 1898, 17,000 troops gathered at a military base in Tampa, Florida. The army, however, was not equipped to launch an invasion. While cavalry troops waited in vain for horses, soldiers bound for tropical Cuba were issued heavy woolen uniforms. Riots broke out between frustrated white soldiers and black soldiers.

529

SKILL LESSON

1. ACTIVITY Have students bring in examples of propaganda from current newspapers, magazines, pamphlets, speeches, or other sources.

Sinking the *Maine:* Recognizing Propaganda

Propaganda is a deliberate attempt to manipulate the truth about people or events to further one's own cause or to damage an opposing cause. Propaganda often includes many accurate facts, but propagandists may distort the facts to fit the impression they want to convey.

1.

Many types of historical evidence may contain propaganda. Thus, it is important to recognize propaganda. Propaganda, for example, may have influenced the outbreak of the Spanish-American War. Two pieces of evidence about the sinking of the *Maine* are reproduced below. One is the dispatch sent by the captain of the *Maine* to the secretary of the navy immediately after the incident. The second is the headline of a newspaper.

See p. T97.

1 Identify the facts. A fact is something that is true or that can be proven. An opinion is a judgment that reflects a person's feelings, beliefs, or attitudes. (a) List the facts in Captain Sigsbee's message. (b) What opinions can you identify in his message? (c) List the facts in the *World* report. (d) Is any of the information in the report based on opinions? Give examples.

2 Identify distortions of fact. (a) What does Captain Sigsbee say about the cause of the explosion? (b) What does the *World* imply about Sigsbee's opinion of the cause?

3 Analyze the emotional appeal. (a) Does Captain Sigsbee seem interested in arousing public opinion against the Spanish? (b) What effect might the picture of the explosion in the *World* report have on the public? Why? (c) What impact might the use of the word enemy in the third headline have on the reader? (d) Find three other words that are likely to have an emotional appeal. What emotion is each likely to arouse?

4 Reach conclusions. Use your text and the two documents to answer the following questions: (a) What overall message is conveyed by the author of the *World* report? (b) Why might the author want to present a distorted account of the incident? (c) What effect do you think reports such as the one in the *World* had on the outbreak of the war?

Message From Captain Sigsbee to the Secretary of the Navy, February 15, 1898

Maine blown up in Havana Harbor at nine-forty tonight and destroyed. Many wounded and doubtless more killed or drowned. Wounded and others on board Spanish man-of-war and Ward Line steamer. Send lighthouse tenders from Key West for crew and the few pieces of equipment above water. No one has clothing other than that upon him. Public opinion should be suspended until further report. All Spanish officers, including representatives of General Blanco, now with me to express sympathy.

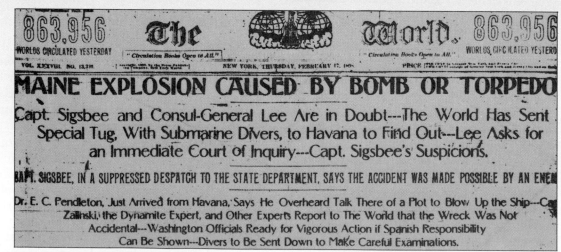

863,956 WORLDS CIRCULATED YESTERDAY — The World — 863,956 WORLDS CIRCULATED YESTERDAY

"Circulation Books Open to All." "Circulation Books Open to All."

VOL. XXXVIII. NO. 13,319. NEW YORK, THURSDAY, FEBRUARY 17, 1898. PRICE [illegible]

MAINE EXPLOSION CAUSED BY BOMB OR TORPEDO

Capt. Sigsbee and Consul-General Lee Are in Doubt---The World Has Sent a Special Tug, With Submarine Divers, to Havana to Find Out---Lee Asks for an Immediate Court of Inquiry---Capt. Sigsbee's Suspicions.

CAPT. SIGSBEE, IN A SUPPRESSED DESPATCH TO THE STATE DEPARTMENT, SAYS THE ACCIDENT WAS MADE POSSIBLE BY AN ENEMY

Dr. E. C. Pendleton, Just Arrived from Havana, Says He Overheard Talk There of a Plot to Blow Up the Ship---Capt. Zalinski, the Dynamite Expert, and Other Experts Report to The World that the Wreck Was Not Accidental---Washington Officials Ready for Vigorous Action if Spanish Responsibility Can Be Shown---Divers to Be Sent Down to Make Careful Examinations.

Despite this confusion, the invasion force sailed on June 14. (See the map on page 528.) Among the troops was the spirited Theodore Roosevelt. He had resigned his desk job in the Navy Department so that he could be second in command of a volunteer unit called the Rough Riders, a mixed crew of cowboys, college students, and adventurers. Roosevelt came to symbolize national enthusiasm for the fight against Spain.

By the end of June, United States troops had established a beachhead near Santiago on the eastern tip of Cuba. Again, inefficiency hindered the war effort. Some soldiers died of food poisoning after eating badly preserved meat.

Finally, on July 1, troops engaged the Spanish defenders of Santiago. In a bloody fight, United States forces attacked the ridges surrounding the city. Roosevelt's Rough Riders and black soldiers of the 9th and 10th Cavalry regiments charged up San Juan Hill. Under withering fire, they suffered heavy casualties—more than 200 men killed and more than 1,100 wounded. The Spanish army, however, was demoralized and short of ammunition, and the Americans took the hill. Then, on July 3, an American fleet sank a Spanish squadron that was trying to escape from Santiago harbor. This blow ended Spanish resistance in Cuba.

The United States then turned to the Spanish-ruled island of Puerto Rico. American troops landing in Puerto Rico during late July met little opposition and quickly conquered the island. On August 12, 1898, the Spanish signed a truce. The war had lasted three months.

Results of the War

In a peace treaty signed on December 10, 1898, the United States acquired Puerto Rico, the Philippines, and the Pacific island of Guam. Cuba became an independent nation. The United States Senate ratified the treaty in 1899. Although most Americans were pleased by their newly won status as a great power, they were soon to learn that power brought with it great, and sometimes troublesome, responsibilities.

See p. T97.

SECTION 2 REVIEW

1. **Identify:** (a) Valeriano Weyler, (b) William Randolph Hearst, (c) the *Maine,* (d) George Dewey, (e) Theodore Roosevelt.

2. **Define:** (a) jingoism, (b) reconcentration, (c) yellow journalism.

3. What methods did the press use to stir up hatred against Spain?

4. What effect did Dewey's victory in Manila Bay have on Americans?

5. (a) List the territories that the United States acquired as a result of the Spanish-American War. (b) What status did Cuba achieve as a result of the war?

6. **Critical Thinking** Who benefited from the sinking of the *Maine?*

2. **VOCABULARY** Have students look up these terms in the glossary before they begin reading.

3 Responsibilities of Empire

READ TO UNDERSTAND

■ How the United States treatment of Cuba and the Philippines differed.

■ Why the United States adopted the Open Door policy.

■ How President Roosevelt modified the Monroe Doctrine.

■ *Vocabulary:* protectorate, sphere of influence. 2.

The United States emerged from the Spanish-American War with far-flung overseas holdings. The nation now had colonies in the Pacific and Latin America, and its navy patrolled the waters of the Atlantic and Pacific. The easy victory over Spain made Americans confident that the United States could continue to expand. While some Americans were thrilled by the challenge of empire, others were troubled by the responsibilities.

531

The Cuban Problem

The conclusion of the war with Spain did not end United States involvement in Cuba. The resolution by which Congress had declared war on Spain in 1898 had included a provision called the Teller Amendment. In this provision, the United States promised not to annex Cuba and to withdraw from the island as soon as order was restored. The war, however, left Cuba in chaos: Government was at a standstill, sanitation almost nonexistent, and disease rampant. Seeing this, President McKinley installed a military government to administer the island. Under the leadership of General Leonard Wood, the Americans worked to wipe out yellow fever and improve Cuban education and agriculture.

In 1900, when Cubans began to draft a constitution, the United States insisted that they include a provision known as the Platt Amendment. Under the Platt Amendment, Cuba promised not to make treaties or incur debts that might result in foreign intervention. It also agreed to let the United States establish two naval stations on the island. Finally, Cuba recognized the right of the United States to send troops to Cuba in order to preserve law and order.

In effect, the Platt Amendment made Cuba a **protectorate** of the United States. A protectorate is a country that is technically independent but whose government and economy are controlled by a stronger power. The United States pulled its army out of Cuba in 1904, but intervened again in 1906 (see page 536) and 1917.

In theory, at least, Cuba was an independent nation. The Philippines, however, fell under complete United States control and gave the nation a new role as an imperial power.

GREAT DEBATE

Acquiring the Philippines

At the end of the Spanish-American War, President McKinley was not sure how the United States should treat the Philippines. He paced the floor of the White House night after night before deciding that the United States must rule the Philippines. The President argued

532

3. **BACKGROUND** Some historians claim that more than 100,000 Filipinos died before the Philippine Insurrection, as it was known, finally ended.

that the Filipinos "were unfit for self-government" and that Americans had a duty to "uplift and civilize and Christianize them." He said this despite the fact that for hundreds of years a majority of the Philippine population had belonged to the Roman Catholic Church and thus were already Christian.

Most Americans probably shared McKinley's view that governing the Philippines was the responsibility of the United States. But some people insisted that colonialism—the practice of owning colonies—was wrong. They maintained that taking over the Philippines violated Americans' belief in liberty. Some were also concerned that an overseas empire would drag the country into war with other powers. Finally, critics argued that the Constitution made no provision for governing colonies.

Complicating the American debate over annexation was a Filipino rebellion. In 1896, Filipino nationalists had risen in revolt against Spanish rule. The revolutionaries, led by Emilio Aguinaldo, had hoped that an American victory in the Spanish-American War would bring independence to the Philippines. But while the Senate debated the peace treaty ending the Spanish-American War, President McKinley ordered American troops to occupy the Philippines. Aguinaldo then took up arms against the United States.

The Senate ratified the peace treaty and made the Philippines an American colony. But for two years, Aguinaldo's troops fought for independence. Finally, the United States captured Aguinaldo and crushed the revolt in 1901. The war against Aguinaldo's nationalists had lasted longer, killed more people, and cost more money than the original war against Spain in 1898. The long and bitter struggle showed that acquiring an empire was easier than running one. ■

The Open Door Policy

United States interest in Asia, especially China, grew after the annexation of the Philippines and Guam. Americans saw those islands as stepping stones to China. Missionaries wanted to convert the Chinese to Christianity, and merchants wanted a share of the profitable China trade.

1. **ACTIVITY** Have students research the Boxer Rebellion. Ask them to agree or disagree with this statement: The Boxer Rebellion was a patriotic movement like the American Revolution.

Those hopes were threatened in the late 1800s as the European powers and Japan sought to divide China into **spheres of influence,** or areas in which one power or another would be dominant. Taking advantage of Chinese military weakness, Russia seized Port Arthur in the north, Japan claimed the island of Formosa, Britain held Hong Kong, Portugal held Macao, and Germany claimed the port of Kiachow in central China. Those spheres of influence restricted United States participation in the China trade. (See the map on page 540.)

After the Spanish-American War, the United States decided to try to open China to all nations on an equal basis. In 1899, Secretary of State John Hay sent letters, known as the Open Door notes, to the nations already involved in China.

Hay asked those powers to respect three principles: no power would prevent others from trading in its sphere of influence; tariffs in China would be collected only by the Chinese, and, within its sphere, no power would ask for harbor or railroad duties that discriminated against the other powers. Although most of the nations were unenthusiastic about the Open Door letters, Hay announced that the Open Door policy was in effect since no power had rejected it outright.

The Boxer Rebellion

No sooner had the great powers ended their diplomatic maneuvering over the Open Door policy than they were faced with the Boxer Rebellion. In the spring of 1900, a secret Chinese society known as the Boxers rose up to expel the "foreign devils." They killed more than 200 Europeans and attacked buildings in Peking owned by foreign governments. The uprising lasted for nearly two months, until

2. **VISUAL EVIDENCE** Have students identify the other nations whose armies are shown in this painting.

The Boxers, whose Chinese name means "society of harmonious fists," wanted to expel all foreigners. American diplomats and Christian missionaries were among those trapped in Peking. As seen in this painting, United States troops were part of the international force that defeated the Boxers. China was forced to pay $333 million in reparations for the action.

troops from several European countries and the United States broke the siege.

Hay feared the triumphant powers would now carve the rest of China into separate spheres. He sent another series of Open Door notes to the European powers and Japan. This second series of notes not only upheld the principles of the first notes but also stressed that the United States believed in maintaining an independent China.

Only Great Britain, France, and Germany accepted the second Open Door notes. However, Japan and Russia, fearing that any attempt to divide China might lead to an open war, quietly observed Hay's policy. As a result, China remained open to American trade.

Policing the Western Hemisphere

Unlike McKinley, President Theodore Roosevelt had a truly global strategy. He believed his country had a "superior" civilization that

obligated it to take the lead in world affairs. Indeed, Roosevelt believed that "superior" nations like the United States had the "most regrettable but necessary international police duty which must be performed for the sake of the welfare of mankind."

This belief was embodied in Roosevelt's foreign policy, which came to be called the "big stick" policy. "I have always been fond 1. of the West African proverb, 'Speak softly and carry a big stick, you will go far,'" he declared.

The Venezuelan Affair In 1902, an incident involving a naval blockade of Venezuela gave Roosevelt an opportunity to assume the role of policeman in Latin America, which he willingly undertook. The situation in Venezuela was typical of that in a number of Latin American countries at the turn of the century. After overthrowing Spanish rule, the Venezuelans had failed to establish a stable system of government. They looked to Euro-

2. *This cartoon portrayed Roosevelt as a boy wading in the Caribbean, carrying his "big stick" and towing the American fleet behind him. Although the United States was able to impose its will on its smaller neighbors, it created a legacy of bitterness that remains to this day.*

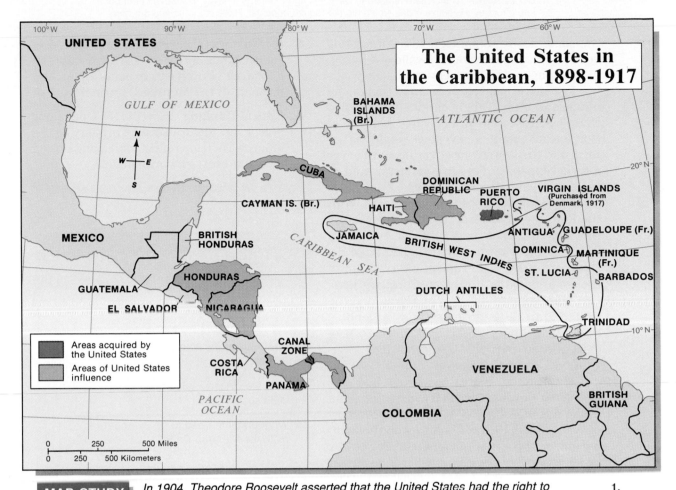

MAP STUDY In 1904, Theodore Roosevelt asserted that the United States had the right to exercise "international police power" over the neighboring Caribbean area. What areas in the Caribbean did the United States control by 1917?

See p. T98.

1.

1. **MAP READING** Have students figure the distance from the U.S. mainland to Cuba, Puerto Rico, the Canal Zone, Nicaragua, and the Dominican Republic.

pean nations for help. Bankers in Great Britain, Germany, and Italy had lent them money.

2. When Venezuela failed to repay the loans, the three nations blockaded its ports and destroyed several Venezuelan vessels.

At the Venezuelans' request, Roosevelt stepped in to persuade the European powers to accept arbitration to settle the dispute. He proposed that the issue be taken to the newly created Permanent Court of Arbitration at The Hague in the Netherlands. Despite initial German resistance, the court at The Hague eventually decided the case.

The Venezuelan incident had great significance. Although the United States had not specifically invoked the Monroe Doctrine, the doctrine gained new strength, since Great Britain, Germany, and Italy had followed the wishes of the United States. Believing that further European intervention in the West-

ern Hemisphere could endanger the area's stability, as well as United States interests, Roosevelt began to formulate a new policy for the Americas.

The Roosevelt Corollary In December 1904, President Roosevelt took advantage of a crisis in the Dominican Republic to announce his new Latin American policy. This policy was known as the Roosevelt Corollary to the Monroe Doctrine. With it, the United States asserted the right to exercise "international police power" in Latin America.

Like Venezuela, the Dominican Republic had fallen into debt to European financiers. At first, Roosevelt hesitated to get involved. 3. Nevertheless, he was certain that the European powers would intervene if the United States did not. In deciding to act, the President claimed he had no plans to make the Dominican Republic a colony. "I have about **535**

2. **ECONOMICS** Have students read recent periodicals to find out how debt problems affect relations between Latin American nations and the U.S. today.

3. **BACKGROUND** Roosevelt warned Secretary of War Elihu Root, "If we intend to say 'Hands off' to the powers of Europe, sooner or later we must keep order ourselves."

the same desire to annex it as a gorged boa constrictor might have to swallow a porcupine wrong-end-to," he remarked.

1. Instead, Roosevelt persuaded Dominican officials to submit their national finances to United States control. Forty-five percent of Dominican customs revenues would be returned to the Dominican government to cover internal expenses. Fifty-five percent would go toward paying off foreign debts.

Applying the Roosevelt Corollary With the Roosevelt Corollary, the use of power by the United States had taken a new turn. Whereas the Monroe Doctrine had been designed to prevent European intervention in the Americas, the Roosevelt Corollary justified intervention in the Americas by the United States. Countries such as Argentina, Brazil, and Chile, all strong enough to take care of their own affairs, did not face intervention. But weaker nations did.

2. The United States again applied the Roosevelt Corollary in 1906 when a rebellion broke out in Cuba. Roosevelt sent Secretary of War William Howard Taft to stop the fighting and set up a new government. Backed by 5,000 troops, American civilians governed Cuba for 28 months. Yet, Roosevelt said, "The United States wishes nothing of the Cubans save that they shall be able to preserve order among themselves and therefore to preserve their independence." When order returned, the Americans withdrew—at least for the time being.

See p. T98.

SECTION 3 REVIEW

1. **Identify:** (a) Teller Amendment, (b) Platt Amendment, (c) Emilio Aguinaldo, (d) Open Door notes, (e) Boxer Rebellion, (f) Roosevelt Corollary.

2. **Define:** (a) protectorate, (b) sphere of influence.

3. (a) How did Cuba become a protectorate of the United States? (b) How did the Philippines become an American colony?

4. (a) Which nations had spheres of influence in China? (b) What was the purpose of the Open Door notes sent by Secretary of State Hay?

5. (a) What was the significance of the Venezuelan affair in 1902? (b) How did the Roosevelt Corollary expand upon the meaning of the Monroe Doctrine?

6. **Critical Thinking** How did the Open Door policy and the Roosevelt Corollary to the Monroe Doctrine reflect increasing United States interest in world affairs?

4 The Panama Canal

READATO UNDERSTAND

■ Why Americans wanted a canal across Panama.

■ How the United States acquired the right to build such a canal.

■ What problems had to be overcome to complete the Panama Canal.

Ever since 1513, when Balboa sighted the Pacific Ocean from a mountain peak in Panama, Europeans and Americans had recognized the importance of that narrow isthmus of land separating the Atlantic and Pacific oceans. American merchants and admirals alike yearned for a canal across Panama. By avoiding the trip around South America, ships could shorten the journey from New York to San Francisco by more than 7,500 miles (about 12,000 kilometers). A canal would reduce the cost of shipping and enable the United States to avoid the heavy expense of keeping separate navies in the Atlantic and Pacific oceans.

Early Plans for a Canal

In the Clayton-Bulwer Treaty of 1850, the United States and Great Britain had agreed to joint control of any future canal in Panama or Nicaragua. Later, the French made a separate agreement with Colombia, which controlled Panama. In 1882, a French company led by engineer Ferdinand de Lesseps began digging a canal in Panama. The proj-

536

2. **BACKGROUND** The Roosevelt Corollary was later used to justify intervention in Nicaragua and Honduras.

3. **BACKGROUND** Philip II of Spain sent surveyors to study the feasibility of building a canal as early as 1567.

ect was a failure. The French company lacked money and adequate tools, and malaria killed 20,000 of the canal workers. After eight years of trying, de Lesseps was finally forced to abandon the project.

In 1898, the Spanish-American War rekindled American interest in building a canal across the isthmus. The battleship *Oregon* had to steam from San Francisco around South America to join the fighting in Cuba. Congress thus saw the strategic importance of an interocean canal. The Clayton-Bulwer Treaty, however, limited American ability to undertake a canal project on its own.

"I Took the Canal Zone"

In 1901, the Roosevelt administration negotiated the Hay-Pauncefote Treaty with Great Britain. The treaty gave the United States a free hand to build, operate, and fortify a canal across Panama or Nicaragua. The United States could now proceed with plans for a canal. After studying different routes, a commission of experts recommended the Panama route. Meanwhile, Congress authorized the President to negotiate with Colombia to purchase land for the canal.

Colombia rejected the President's offer of $10 million plus an annual rent of $250,000 as too low. Taking the issue to the press, Roosevelt called the Colombians "inefficient bandits" and the "blackmailers of Bogotá." His comments encouraged Panamanian nationalists, who, according to Roosevelt's count, had revolted against Colombia 53 times in 57 years.

From their rooms in the Waldorf-Astoria Hotel in New York City, a group of Panamanian conspirators plotted another revolt, this time with United States knowledge. The leader of the plot, a French citizen named Philippe Bunau-Varilla (byoo NOH vah REEL yah), met with Secretary of State John Hay and President Roosevelt. Although Roosevelt made no specific promises, Bunau-Varilla left the meeting with the impression that the United States would not help Colombia suppress the Panamanian rebels and might even support the rebellion.

Not by coincidence, a United States warship, the USS *Nashville*, steamed into the Panamanian port of Colón on November 2, 1903. Encouraged by this display of American support, the Panamanians immediately revolted. The Colombian army, sent to stop the revolt, was blocked by United States naval forces. On November 3, Panama declared its independence from Colombia, and three days later the United States officially recognized the new nation.

Less than two weeks afterward, the Panamanian government granted the United States a larger canal zone than the Colombians had proposed, yet with the same terms. Years later, Roosevelt bragged, "I took the Canal Zone and let Congress debate." 1.

GEOGRAPHY AND HISTORY
Digging the Big Ditch

With the Canal Zone under United States control, Americans set about completing the task undertaken by de Lesseps some 20 years earlier. British author James Bryce called the building of the Panama Canal "the greatest liberty Man has ever taken with Nature."

When the operation began in 1904, the greatest obstacle was disease. Colonel Wil-

The greatest obstacle to building a canal in Central America was yellow fever. Carried by mosquitoes in the region, the disease had helped to thwart an earlier French attempt to build a canal in the area. U.S. Army medical officer William Gorgas led a program that eliminated yellow fever in two years. 2. 3.

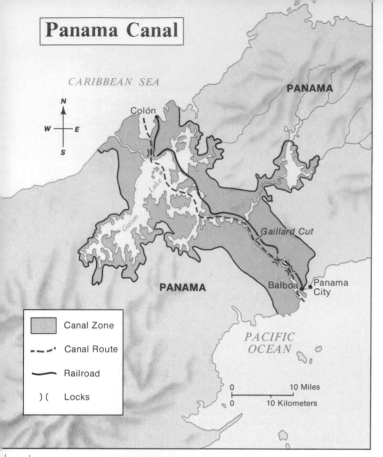

Panama Canal

CARIBBEAN SEA

PANAMA

Colón

Gatun Lake

Gaillard Cut

PANAMA

Balboa · Panama City

PACIFIC OCEAN

N
W E
S

Legend:
- Canal Zone
- Canal Route
- Railroad
-)(Locks

0   10 Miles
0   10 Kilometers

1. **MAP READING** Point out to students that the Atlantic side of the canal is farther west than the Pacific side.

to form Gatun Lake, and constructed three pairs of locks to lift and lower ships.

On August 15, 1914, the passenger-cargo ship SS *Ancon* completed the first trip through the canal. The words on the official seal of the Canal Zone had at last come true: "The Land Divided, the World United." At a cost of thousands of lives and $400 million, the United States had provided its ships with easy access between the Atlantic and Pacific. The nation now had greater ability to extend its power and influence to other parts of the world. ■

See p. T98.

2.

MAP STUDY *Carving a canal through the dense jungle of Panama took*
1. *seven years and the work of 43,400 laborers. A series of locks raised and lowered water levels for ships moving through the canal. Why was the canal important for both merchants and the navy?*

See p. T98.

liam C. Gorgas, a physician who had wiped out yellow fever in Cuba after the Spanish-American War, mounted a campaign to destroy the mosquitoes that spread yellow fever and malaria in the canal zone. Gorgas and his workers drained swamps, cut brush, and destroyed grassy marshes where mosquitoes bred. They also worked to eliminate the rats that carried bubonic plague. By 1906, their work was almost complete.

Now, construction began on a canal that could raise or lower ships more than 100 feet (30 meters) as they crossed between the Atlantic and Pacific oceans. Over a period of seven years, a work force of 43,400, under the supervision of army engineer Colonel George W. Goethals, removed 211 million cubic yards (161 million cubic meters) of earth before finishing the "big ditch." Crews dug the Gaillard Cut, dammed the Chagres River

SECTION 4 REVIEW

1. **Identify:** (a) Clayton-Bulwer Treaty, (b) Hay-Pauncefote Treaty, (c) William C. Gorgas.

2. List the major advantages of a canal across Panama.

3. (a) How did the government of Colombia react to the United States offer to buy land for a canal? (b) How did the United States acquire the land?

4. **Critical Thinking** How did geography influence President Theodore Roosevelt's foreign policy?

5 The United States in Asia

READ TO UNDERSTAND

■ How President Roosevelt mediated a peace settlement between Russia and Japan.

■ Why tensions increased between the United States and Japan.

■ How the foreign policy of President Taft differed from that of President Roosevelt.

William Howard Taft, President Roosevelt's secretary of war and his successor as President, once said of Roosevelt that he "believes

2. **READING** Students interested in an exciting account of the building of the Panama Canal can read *The Path Between the Seas* by David McCullough.

1. CRITICAL THINKING Ask: Do you think it is a good idea for a nation's foreign policy to benefit its business interests?

2. CRITICAL THINKING Ask students to suggest reasons why the interests of the people of Manchuria and Korea were not considered in making the Treaty of Portsmouth.

in war and wishes to be a Napoleon and to die on the battlefield." Whether or not the assessment was accurate, the fact is that in foreign affairs, Roosevelt spent much effort trying to end a war between Japan and Russia and to improve relations between Japan and the United States. Roosevelt's interest in Asia, however, was not purely idealistic. He knew that American businesses looked there for markets and outlets for investment and that they would expect the United States government to support them.

United States Interests in China

President Roosevelt did not believe the United States had any vital interests in China, but he knew that Americans had been previously involved there and might become so again. For example, John D. Rockefeller's Standard Oil Company had made huge investments in China, and the American China Development Company had engaged in railroad construction there. Roosevelt thus championed the Open Door policy, begun under President

1. McKinley. (See page 532.) He believed that no nation seeking investment opportunities in China should be shut out.

During Roosevelt's administration, there was a great deal of rivalry between Russia and Japan over influence in China. Roosevelt disliked the Russians and hoped that the Japanese-Russian competition would keep China free of Russian domination. He also hoped that, with each side checking the power of the other, American businesses would be free to pursue their interests without direct involvement by the United States government. However, the rivalry between Japan and Russia soon flared into war.

The Russo-Japanese War

Japan, a densely populated nation with few natural resources, needed raw materials to fuel its growing industry. The best source for these materials seemed to be China's northernmost province of Manchuria, which was quite near Japan. Russia, however, wanted to exclude Japan from China and seal off Manchuria for itself. Great Britain, long the most powerful European nation trading in Asia, had its own interests in China and favored the Japanese. In 1902, Britain signed a secret treaty with Japan, agreeing to cooperate in restricting Russian expansion into Manchuria.

For more than a year, tensions between Russia and Japan ran high. Then, in February 1904, Japan launched a surprise torpedo attack on the Russian fleet anchored at Port Arthur in Manchuria. To the delight of many Americans, the Japanese followed their initial success with more victories. President Roosevelt especially enjoyed the fact that the "utterly insincere and treacherous" Russians were being humiliated.

By the spring of 1905, the warring nations were exhausted and eager to make peace. President Roosevelt invited Russia and Japan to send representatives to a peace conference at Portsmouth, New Hampshire. There, largely through Roosevelt's diplomatic efforts, the two nations worked out an agreement that ended the war.

The Treaty of Portsmouth, signed in September 1905, recognized the Japanese victory, the first for an Asian country over a European power. Japan was awarded Port Arthur, the southern half of Sakhalin Island, control of the Manchurian railroads, and, in effect, control of Korea. In turn, Japan gave 2. up its demand that Russia pay for war damages. Manchuria remained part of China.

To satisfy United States interests, Japan and Russia pledged that China would be kept open to trade with all nations. Thus, through the Treaty of Portsmouth, the United States maintained the Open Door in China. Never before had an American President played a central role in an international crisis not directly involving the United States. For his 3. efforts, Roosevelt won the 1906 Nobel Peace Prize.

Japanese-American Relations

While Roosevelt's efforts at Portsmouth impressed Europeans and Americans alike, they won the friendship of neither the Russians nor the Japanese. The Russians blamed Roo- **539** sevelt for their losses under the Treaty of Portsmouth. The Japanese wanted Manchurian resources, and they feared that less of those raw materials would flow into Japanese factories as more nations took advantage of the Open Door policy.

The United States still saw Japan as an important counterbalance to Russian influence. As a result, President Roosevelt decided to negotiate his own set of agreements with Japan. Shortly before the Portsmouth conference, he sent Secretary of War William Howard Taft to Japan. Taft offered Japan full recognition of Japanese control over Korea. In return, the Japanese pledged to allow the Philippine islands to remain under United States control.

Meanwhile, events within the United States were challenging Japanese-American relations. When Japanese immigration to the United States increased as a result of the Russo-Japanese War, a wave of anti-Japanese agitation swept the West Coast. Many Americans resented the Asian newcomers because they competed for jobs and seemed so different in their customs and beliefs. In 1906, the San Francisco Board of Education placed the city's 93 Asian pupils in a separate school. Japan protested, and Roosevelt intervened to soften what the Japanese regarded as a racial insult.

The President denounced the school board's action as a "wicked absurdity." He persuaded the school board to accept a compromise under which the board would return the Asian children to regular schools, and he would take steps to restrict further Japanese immigration.

2. **MAP READING** Have students locate Japan, its possessions, and its spheres of influence. Ask: Which country had the largest sphere of influence? Why do you think this was so?

MAP STUDY

See p. T99.

Many foreign powers claimed territory in Asia. Several countries also controlled trade in their "spheres of influence" in China. Which nation claimed Indochina? Who had a sphere of influence that included the city of Shanghai?

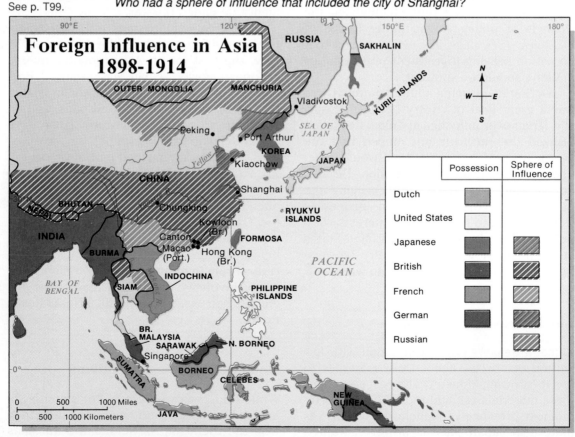

Foreign Influence in Asia 1898-1914

	Possession	Sphere of Influence
Dutch		
United States		
Japanese		
British		
French		
German		
Russian		

The Great White Fleet

During the San Francisco schools crisis, jingoists on both sides of the Pacific called for war. Although the President had no intention of using military force, he wanted to make sure that no one interpreted his actions as a sign of weakness. Consequently, in 1907, Roosevelt undertook a dramatic demonstration of military strength.

1.   The President sent the entire United States battle fleet on a cruise around the world. (See page 520.) Congress objected to the expense of the voyage, and some people questioned its value. But Roosevelt was determined.

When the Great White Fleet, as it was known, entered Japanese waters, leaders there were duly impressed. With its 16 battleships, the United States had the third largest navy in the world. Only the British and Germans had larger fleets. As one sure indication that Japanese-American relations were improving, Japanese schoolchildren welcomed the naval visitors by singing "The Star-Spangled Banner"—in English.

By the time the fleet returned to the United States in 1909, Secretary of State Elihu Root and Japanese Ambassador Kogoro Takahira (tah kah HEE rah) had exchanged notes settling most of the differences between the two countries. Both nations agreed to preserve stability in the Pacific, mutually respect territorial claims, maintain the Open Door in China, and use peaceful methods to protect Chinese independence.

Dollar Diplomacy

President Roosevelt's successor took a different tack when dealing with foreign policy. In 1909, when William Howard Taft succeeded Roosevelt as President, he decided to modify Roosevelt's "big stick" policy by "substituting dollars for bullets." He reasoned that American economic activity abroad would bring stability to troubled regions and power and profit to the United States without the use of force. With this policy of "dollar diplomacy," President Taft encouraged commercial ventures that would advance United States foreign policy. For example, Taft supported investments in China to "give the voice of the United States more authority in that country."

But dollar diplomacy had a more dramatic effect in Latin America than in Asia. Now that it had the Panama Canal to protect, the United States wanted to remove any European pretext for military intervention in the Americas. Thus, Taft encouraged New York bankers to replace European financiers as the major lenders to countries like Nicaragua and Haiti.

Although Taft's dollar diplomacy was intended to make military intervention less likely, it did not eliminate intervention altogether. In 1911, after Nicaragua defaulted on its foreign debts, the Taft administration arranged for bankers to take over the operation of Nicaragua's customs service. Nicaraguans who opposed this arrangement rose in revolt, and in 1912 Taft sent marines to protect American interests. One unintended 2. outcome of dollar diplomacy in Latin America was a growing distrust of the United States among Latin Americans.

See p. T99.

SECTION 5 REVIEW

1. **Identify:** (a) Treaty of Portsmouth, (b) dollar diplomacy.

2. (a) What role did President Roosevelt play in ending the war between Russia and Japan? (b) How did Russia and Japan react to the settlement terms?

3. How did increased Japanese immigration to the United States lead to friction between Japan and the United States?

4. Why did President Roosevelt send the Great White Fleet around the world?

5. What were the short-term and long-term effects of Taft's policy of dollar diplomacy in Latin America?

6. **Critical Thinking** Do you think Roosevelt's foreign policy was based on idealism or on realism? Explain.

CHAPTER 24 REVIEW

Summary

1. **Interest in foreign affairs revived in the 1890s.** In the Pacific, the United States acquired Samoa and Hawaii. Closer to home, the nation showed new interest in Latin America, reviving the Monroe Doctrine.

2. **Cuba was a trouble spot that led the United States into war with Spain.** The Spanish-American War of 1898 transformed the United States into a world power. The United States defeated Spain, acquiring Puerto Rico, Guam, and the Philippines.

3. **The United States now had the responsibilities of empire.** The Philippines became an American colony and Cuba, a protectorate. President McKinley responded to American business interests by supporting an Open Door policy in China. McKin-

ley's successor, Theodore Roosevelt, proclaimed the Roosevelt Corollary to the Monroe Doctrine.

4. **In 1903, Roosevelt acquired the land necessary to construct the Panama Canal.** The canal was completed in 1914. It gave easy access between the Atlantic and Pacific and greatly increased United States power.

5. **Roosevelt maintained the Open Door policy by helping negotiate an end to the Russo-Japanese War.** Discrimination against Japanese immigrants in California disrupted Japanese-American relations, but peace was maintained. Roosevelt's successor as President, William Howard Taft, played down military strength and promoted a policy of "dollar diplomacy."

See p. T99.

Vocabulary

On a separate sheet of paper, write the word or words that best complete each of the following sentences.

1. Seizing control of other lands to create an empire is called _____.

2. _____ is exaggerated and belligerent national pride.

3. _____ was a system of control of Cuba's civilian population.

4. _____ is sensational, sometimes untruthful, newspaper reporting.

5. A country whose government and economy are controlled by a stronger nation is called a (an) _____.

6. Taft's policy of using financial investments rather than military force to influence a foreign country is called _____.

See p. T99.

Chapter Checkup

1. (a) What was the attitude of most Americans toward foreign affairs after the Civil War? (b) What changed that attitude?

2. (a) Describe the events that led to the annexation of Hawaii. (b) Why did President Cleveland oppose the annexation?

3. Explain how each of the following contributed to the outbreak of the Spanish-American War: (a) jingoism; (b) yellow journalism; (c) sinking of the *Maine*.

4. (a) Why were Americans interested in China in the late 1800s? (b) What action did Secretary of State Hay take to improve the United States position in China?

5. (a) What was the Roosevelt Corollary? (b) How did Roosevelt apply his corollary in Cuba? (c) How did President Taft apply it in Nicaragua?

542

6. What steps did Roosevelt take to gain control of a canal zone for the United States?

7. (a) What role did the United States play in ending the Russo-Japanese war? (b) What did the United States gain as a result of the peace treaty?

8. Was dollar diplomacy more successful in Asia or in Latin America? Why?

See p. T100.

Critical Thinking

1. **Evaluating** William G. Sumner was one American who opposed the annexation of the Philippines. He argued that the notion of a civilizing mission would lead the United States down the path of intervention and war. Do you think developments in the Philippines between 1899 and 1901 confirm or refute Sumner's argument? Cite specific evidence to support your answer.

2. **Analyzing** It has been said that, although the Monroe Doctrine protected Latin America from European powers, it did not protect the region from the United States. Based on this chapter, do you agree or disagree with the appraisal? Why?

See p. T100.

Connecting Past and Present

1. Compare American goals in China in the late 1800s with American goals there today. What similarities and differences can you find?

2. In 1979, the United States agreed to end American control over the Panama Canal by 1999. Do you think the United States is any less dependent on the canal now than in the past? Why or why not?

See p. T100.

Developing Basic Skills

1. **Placing Events in Time** Review this chapter and construct a time line of United States actions in world affairs from 1866 to 1914. (a) In which decades did the United States acquire new territories? (b) In which decades did the United States intervene militarily in other nations?

2. **Map Reading** Study the map of foreign influence in Asia on page 540. (a) Which nations claimed spheres of influence in China? (b) Which nations claimed territory in Asia?

WRITING ABOUT HISTORY

Writing a Preliminary Thesis Statement

In preparing a paper, it is useful to write down the main idea, or thesis, of what you plan to say in your paper. The main idea, stated in a declarative sentence, is called a thesis statement. Writing the thesis statement helps you to limit your topic and guide your research. Of course, you may have to revise your preliminary thesis because you cannot find the information to support it or because you find evidence that your thesis is incorrect.

A possible thesis statement for a paper on the United States in world affairs is the following: The Roosevelt Corollary marked a major change in United States foreign policy toward Latin America.

Practice: Write a thesis statement for each topic below.

1. The Changes in United States Foreign Policy Beginning in the Late 1800s

2. Theodore Roosevelt's Role in Obtaining the Canal Zone

3. American Influence on Asian Affairs in the Early 1900s

The World at War

25

(1912–1919)

CHAPTER OUTLINE

1 Woodrow Wilson and Moral Diplomacy

2 War in Europe

3 The Home Front

4 The United States in the War

5 Search for a "Just Peace"

CHAPTER OBJECTIVES After completing this chapter, students should be able to
1. describe Woodrow Wilson's "moral diplomacy."
2. explain why the U.S. moved from neutrality to involvement in World War I.
3. describe life on the home front during the war.
4. explain the role of the U.S. in both the war and the peace negotiations.
5. analyze fiction as historical evidence.

The boys had formed a little group called the "Lightfoot Club," which met in the hayloft belonging to Tommy Wilson's father. One day, they decided it would be fun to hold a debate, just like college men. The subject was to be "Is the pen mightier than the sword?"

Tommy prepared very hard, thinking up all the reasons why the written word was indeed more powerful than any army. But when the time came, he drew the other side—that the sword was mightier. "I can't take that side," he protested. "I don't believe it." The other boys tried to convince him that it was just a game, but Tommy would not go along. "I can't argue for something I don't believe in," he said. "It would be dishonest."

Thomas Wilson would eventually drop his first name in favor of his middle name. A half-century later, he was known throughout the world as Woodrow Wilson, President of the United States.

Before Wilson became President, he expressed the belief that war was a poor way to carry out international policy. When he ran for a second term of office, one of his campaign slogans was "He kept us out of war." But Wilson also held that "when men take up arms to set other men free, there is something sacred and holy in the warfare."

In 1917, Wilson went before Congress, asking for a declaration of war and speaking with the same conviction he had once demonstrated in his father's hayloft. "We will fight," he said, "for the ultimate peace of the world and the liberation of its peoples . . . The world must be made safe for democracy."

CHAPTER PREVIEW Have students read the paragraphs above and study the time line below. Ask them to speculate on what events or developments could have pushed the U.S. into a war that began in Europe. Ask: How do you think World War I differed from earlier wars? How would a world war today differ from World War I?

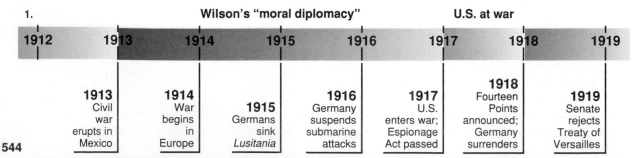

1.

Wilson's "moral diplomacy"   U.S. at war

| 1912 | 1913 | 1914 | 1915 | 1916 | 1917 | 1918 | 1919 |

1913 Civil war erupts in Mexico

1914 War begins in Europe

1915 Germans sink *Lusitania*

1916 Germany suspends submarine attacks

1917 U.S. enters war; Espionage Act passed

1918 Fourteen Points announced; Germany surrenders

1919 Senate rejects Treaty of Versailles

544

1. TIME LINE QUESTION Ask: How many years did World War I last? For how many years did the U.S. take part in the war?

Although President Wilson wanted to keep the United States out of World War I, events made that impossible. Once involved, American troops fought hard on the battlefields of France. Captain Harvey Dunn, one of a team of artists sent to the front by the War Department, painted this American soldier fighting on as his comrade lies dead at his feet.

1.

---

1. **VISUAL EVIDENCE** Refer students to Dunn's painting of a prairie family on p. 417. Have students speculate on what it might feel like for a boy from a rural area to find himself on a battlefield in France.

1 Woodrow Wilson and Moral Diplomacy

READONLY TO UNDERSTAND

■ How President Wilson's idealism influenced his foreign policy.

■ Where moral diplomacy failed.

■ Why the United States became entangled in Mexico's civil war.

Woodrow Wilson, who was elected President in 1912, had little interest in world diplomacy. "It would be the irony of fate if my administration had to deal chiefly with foreign affairs," he remarked to a friend upon taking office. But fate was fickle. World crises forced President Wilson to pay close attention to foreign affairs.

Wilson and his secretary of state, William Jennings Bryan, shared a burning ideal-

ism and moral fervor. They disliked the assertive policies of Roosevelt and Taft. Instead, they proposed something they called "moral diplomacy"—a policy that would make the United States in effect the conscience of the world. "The force of America is the force of 2. moral principle," Wilson said, and he set out with missionary zeal to condemn colonialism, spread democracy, and promote peace.

Moral Diplomacy in Action

In 1913, Secretary of State Bryan set in motion a plan for achieving world peace through a series of "cooling-off" treaties. Thirty nations agreed to submit their disputes to a permanent international committee. While the committee conducted an inquiry, the nations agreed to refrain from acts of war for a one-year period.

Bryan and humanitarian groups hailed the treaties as a stride toward peace. But Theo-   **545**

---

2. **CRITICAL THINKING** Have students consider whether U.S. foreign policy today supports or contradicts the view that "the force of America is the force of moral principle."

dore Roosevelt and other advocates of military strength saw the treaties as unenforceable and therefore meaningless.

1.   In Asia, Wilson pursued moral diplomacy by ending United States support for a six-nation Chinese railway project encouraged by President Taft. He viewed this project as an uncalled for interference in Chinese affairs. At the same time, he recognized the new republic of China, the first leader of a major nation to do so.

Moral Diplomacy Falters

Relations with Japan posed a number of problems for the concept of moral diplomacy. In California, legislators seeking favor with local agriculture and labor groups had enacted a law that prohibited noncitizens from owning land. Japanese immigrants, who were most directly affected by the law, protested angrily.

2. **VISUAL EVIDENCE** Ask: What title might be given to this painting by a U.S. marine? By a citizen of the Dominican Republic?

"The United States will never again seek one additional foot of territory by conquest," proclaimed Woodrow Wilson in a 1913 speech. Despite that
2. *promise, the sight of American marines raising the flag in a Caribbean country was common during Wilson's administration.*

President Wilson played down the issue and ignored the racist overtones of the California law. He thus failed to enforce a treaty obligation to treat Japanese immigrants fairly. Only public outrage in Japan motivated the President to act. He sent the secretary of state to California, but Bryan could not persuade state officials to change their policy.

Japanese-American relations worsened in 1915. With Europe involved in war, Japan felt free to present 21 demands to China. Had China agreed to the demands, it would have become little more than a Japanese protectorate. However, the United States objected that the 21 demands violated the Open Door policy, and Japan eased its pressure on China, at least for the moment.

Reversals in Latin America

Although President Taft had been unable to make dollar diplomacy work in Asia, where European nations had carved out their own interests, he had applied the policy freely in Latin America. There, the United States faced much less competition from Europe.

Denouncing Taft's dollar diplomacy, Woodrow Wilson declared that he had no similar wish to support any "special group or interests." The stated goals of Wilson's Latin American policy were to promote democracy and ensure the security of the Panama Canal. At times, the goals clashed.

One early instance involved a treaty the Taft administration had drafted giving the United States a permanent option to build a second canal across Nicaragua. For this and other privileges, the United States was to pay Nicaragua the small sum of $3 million. Although this seemed to go against their principles, Wilson and Bryan realized that the treaty could prevent another nation from gaining control of a competing canal route. 3.

Despite his opposition to imperialism, Wilson ordered military intervention in Latin America more often than any prior President. Wilson's answer to upheavals in the Caribbean nations of Haiti in 1915 and the Dominican Republic in 1916 was to send in the marines. Haiti was pressured to permit the United States to make it a protectorate. As Wilson and Bryan saw it, the United States

3. **BACKGROUND** Bryan had a provision added to Taft's original treaty authorizing U.S. intervention in Nicaraguan internal affairs.

was restoring order and protecting property, much of which was owned by United States citizens. As many Latin Americans viewed it, the United States was violating the Caribbean nations' independence.

1.   Wilson's plan to aid the Latin American nations and prepare them for democracy failed. Instead, he created an "American lake" in the Caribbean and inspired hatred rather than friendship.

Civil War in Mexico

While the United States kept a close eye on all of Latin America, it had a special interest in Mexico. The two nations shared a common border and close cultural ties, dating back to Spanish settlement of Mexico and the Southwest some 400 years before. Yet political unrest in Mexico finally led Wilson to substitute military power for moral diplomacy.

In 1911, Mexicans overthrew a dictator. Two years later, General Victoriano Huerta (WEHR tah) seized power from the new revolutionary government. Huerta favored the wealthy landowners in Mexico and was proba-

2. bly supported by foreign oil interests. Venustiano Carranza (kahr RAHN zah) led the resistance to the Huerta regime. A bloody civil war raged in Mexico, and for a time Wilson adopted an attitude of "watchful waiting." He hoped that Mexico would set up a democratic government that would help the masses of people in Mexico and be friendly to the United States.

The civil war dragged on, however, and Huerta proclaimed himself military dictator of Mexico. First, Wilson banned arms shipments to Mexico. Then he offered to mediate the dispute between Huerta and Carranza. Somewhat indiscreetly, he even offered to support the Carranza faction if it would guarantee the orderly establishment of constitutional government. Carranza refused.

The situation reached a breaking point. In April 1914, Mexican soldiers in Tampico, Mexico, arrested members of the crew of the USS *Dolphin.* Although the sailors were promptly released with an apology, Wilson took strong action. Without waiting for con-

gressional approval, the President ordered the navy to capture the port of Vera Cruz before a German ship could land a cargo of arms for Huerta's forces. The Mexicans resisted, and in the battle that followed, 126 "Huertistas" and 19 Americans died. 3.

The minor importance of the *Dolphin* arrests contrasted with the severity of Wilson's reaction. This brought outcries of protest from Huerta, his rival Carranza, and newspaper editors throughout the world. Wilson and Bryan averted war by allowing Argentina, Brazil, and Chile to mediate the crisis at a conference held in Niagara Falls, Canada.

In July 1914, Huerta accepted defeat and abandoned Mexico City. Carranza took power on the eve of the outbreak of World War I in Europe.

United States Involvement

The dispute might have ended had not Francisco "Pancho" Villa (VEE yah), a Mexican revolutionary, led a revolt against Carranza. In October 1915, the United States recognized the Carranza government. Villa retaliated with a series of anti-American raids. In January 1916, his men removed 17 United States citizens from a train in Mexico and shot them. In March, Villa and his band crossed the Rio Grande to attack and burn the town of Columbus, New Mexico, killing 19 Americans.

A reluctant Carranza agreed to let United States troops pursue Villa. American Brigadier General John Pershing led an expedition to capture Villa dead or alive. Far exceeding the spirit of the agreement, 6,000 troops pursued Villa deep into Mexico.

In April 1916, when Carranza demanded that the United States end its "invasion," Wilson refused. The rebel Villa suddenly swung north and attacked Glen Springs, Texas. Outraged Americans called for war.

But neither Carranza nor Wilson wanted to fight. Carranza had pressing domestic problems, and war in Europe occupied Wilson's attention. In July 1916, a joint commission set to work to resolve matters. Early the following year, Wilson pulled American troops out of Mexico.

547

2. **PRESIDENTS** Wilson would not recognize Huerta as the rightful leader of Mexico—the first time any President had refused to recognize a government in power.

3. **DISCUSSION** Ask: Do you think these events justified U.S. intervention in Mexico? Why or why not?

Wilson said of events in Mexico, "We will never condone iniquity [wickedness] just because it is most convenient to do so." But the occupation of
1. *Vera Cruz caused a public outcry against the United States in Mexico.*

1. **VISUAL EVIDENCE** This snapshot shows two American sailors guarding a sick Mexican woman at Vera Cruz.

As the soldiers headed home, Americans realized that their nation had undergone remarkable changes since 1898. Now, the United States kept troops and ships in both Asia and Latin America. American business interests spanned the globe. The United States had become too much a part of the world community to ignore the war that had been raging in Europe since 1914.

See p. T101.

SECTION 1 REVIEW

1. **Identify:** (a) moral diplomacy, (b) Victoriano Huerta, (c) Venustiano Carranza, (d) Francisco "Pancho" Villa, (e) John Pershing.

2. What was the purpose of the "cooling-off" treaties negotiated by Secretary of State Bryan?

3. In which two Latin American countries did Bryan and Wilson resort to the use of troops during 1915 and 1916?

4. Why did Wilson oppose Huerta's government in Mexico?

5. **Critical Thinking** Why do you think Mexicans referred to the United States as the "Colossus of the North"?

548

2. **BACKGROUND** The 19-year-old assassin, Gavrilo Princip, also shot and killed the archduke's wife, Sophie.

2 War in Europe

READ TO UNDERSTAND

■ Why war erupted in Europe in 1914.

■ What circumstances made it difficult for the United States to maintain neutrality.

■ What events drew the United States into the war.

Most Americans were probably unimpressed by newspaper headlines on June 29, 1914. The day before, a Bosnian nationalist had 2. assassinated an archduke in Bosnia, a province of Austria-Hungary on the Balkan peninsula in southeastern Europe. Not many Americans knew or cared much about Archduke Francis Ferdinand, although he was next in line for Austria-Hungary's throne. But for the leaders of Europe, it was a different matter. The young assassin belonged to the Black Hand, a terrorist group seeking to unite Bosnia with the independent nation of Serbia (now part of Yugoslavia). There was reason to believe that Serbia had plotted the murder. How would Austria-Hungary respond?

World War I Begins

The assassination of Archduke Francis Ferdi- 3. nand has been described as the spark that ignited a powder keg. Strong nationalist feelings in the Balkans and imperialist rivalries (see page 521) were already threatening the peace in Europe. By 1914, the major powers of Europe were involved in competing alliances. On one side was the Triple Alliance of Austria-Hungary, Germany, and Italy. On the other side was the Triple Entente (ahn TAHNT) of France, Great Britain, and Russia. This system of alliances played an important part in turning the archduke's assassination into a major war.

After the assassination, Austria-Hungary got assurances of German support and then made demands on Serbia. Austria-Hungary claimed Serbia was behind the attack. Not satisfied with the Serbian reply and spurred on by Germany, Austria-Hungary declared war

3. **BACKGROUND** In the spring of 1914, an American diplomat in Europe wrote to President Wilson, "Everybody's nerves are tense. It only requires a spark to set the whole thing off."

on Serbia. Russia, competing with Austria-Hungary for power in southeastern Europe, backed the Serbs. Russia's ally France supported this move. Then on August 1, 1914, Germany declared war on Russia and two days later on France.

The Central Powers, as Austria-Hungary and Germany were called, anticipated a swift victory. They planned to march rapidly west to defeat France, before the slow-moving Russians could mobilize for action. The shortest route to France was through neutral Belgium. Germany asked permission to move troops through Belgium and offered King Albert payment for any damages. The king refused, saying, "Belgium is a nation, not a road." Nevertheless, on August 3, German forces invaded Belgium. The next day, Brit-

1.

2. MAP READING Ask: Which Allied powers bordered Germany? What battle site was due west of Brussels? In which direction did the Allied offensive push?

MAP STUDY *Most European nations participated in the war as either Allied Powers or Central Powers. For more than four years and at incredible loss of human life, fighting shifted back and forth on the western front. After large numbers of United States troops reached France in 1918, an Allied counteroffensive finally defeated the Central Powers. Which countries remained neutral in the war? Approximately how close did the German forces get to Paris?* See p. T101.

2.

ain, committed to defend Belgium, declared war on Germany.

Within weeks, Turkey and Bulgaria joined the Central Powers and Japan sided with the Allies, as Britain, France, and Russia were called. Waiting to see which side would offer most for its assistance, Italy entered the war in 1915 on the side of the Allies.

A brave defense by 200,000 Belgian soldiers failed to stop the Germans, but it did delay them while the Allies mobilized. The year 1914 ended with the German advance halted in France. On both the eastern and the western battlefronts, opposing armies dug an extensive network of trenches from which they could fire on enemy lines. On both sides, thousands of soldiers died to advance just a few yards. Despite the slaughter early in the war, most European leaders remained hopeful. Surely victory would come soon!

American Neutrality

President Woodrow Wilson and most of his advisers favored the Allies. Wilson considered Germany a "lawless" nation as well as a threat to United States interests in Latin America. But Wilson thought the Allies could win without United States involvement, so he adopted a policy of formal neutrality. The President urged Americans to be "impartial in thought as well as in action."

But few Americans could remain uninvolved, much less neutral. This was a nation of immigrants with strong emotional ties to distant homelands. A majority shared language and ancestry with the British. Traditional friendship with France also drew the United States to the Allies.

Many Americans, however, favored the Central Powers. Eight million German Americans saw the war as a defense of German soil against French and Russian aggression. Four million Irish Americans, bearing an ancient hatred of the British, generally sided with the Central Powers. Similarly, American Jews harbored strong anti-Russian sentiments and tended to sympathize with the Germans.

Supporters of both sides used propaganda to try to influence public opinion. Most of the major American newspapers backed the Allies, so supporters of the Central Powers focused on German, Irish, and other immigrant newspapers. They tried to convince Americans that the Allies had caused the war and that Germany was fighting to save Western Europe from a "Slavic peril."

Allied propaganda probably had the greater impact. After the invasion of neutral Belgium, the British spread stories of German atrocities against Belgian civilians. The Germans were more easily portrayed as aggressors, since most of the fighting was on Allied soil. German experiments with such new weapons as submarines and poison gas struck Americans as brutal and immoral. Many Americans also believed the Allies were fighting to defend civilization. They saw the Germans as militaristic, believing in obedience rather than freedom.

Economic Impact

American economic ties to the Allies made strict neutrality unlikely, as those nations looked to the United States for supplies. A deluge of orders from the Allies soon created an economic boom. Almost overnight, a great munitions industry sprang up. Within three years, the United States sent $1 billion worth of arms and explosives to the Allies. Allied orders caused American steel, copper, oil, grain, and food production to increase. Trade with the Allies grew from $500 million in 1914 to $3.5 billion in 1917.

At the same time, a British naval blockade disrupted trade with the Central Powers. To make the blockade effective, the British navy mined the North Sea. The British also acted to block United States trade with neutral Holland and Denmark and forced American ships into port for inspection. President Wilson's protests had little effect.

The British, however, did try to soften the impact of the blockade on the United States economy. For example, they prevented a slump in the cotton market by purchasing the cotton that would normally have been sold to Germany. In light of such activities, the Germans considered the United States a silent partner of the Allies. Wilson insisted, however, that the United States was not violating neutrality.

550

1. **BACKGROUND** Before the ship sailed from the U.S., the German embassy warned in a newspaper ad: "Travellers are reminded that vessels flying the flag of Great Britain are liable to destruction."

The Submarine Controversy

Although American reaction to the British blockade was mild, the German use of a new weapon, the submarine, or U-boat, provoked outrage. In 1914 and 1915, while the British blockade bottled up the German navy in the North Sea, German submarines began attacking Allied ships.

The use of submarines raised new issues. International law required a ship to warn that it was about to sink an enemy vessel, so that the crew might escape. But submarines were slow and could not warn of an attack without surfacing and exposing themselves to ramming or other attack.

Early in 1915, asserting that Allied ships sometimes disguised themselves as neutrals, the Germans warned that any ships entering a war zone around Great Britain risked being attacked without warning. President Wilson, however, refused to interrupt trade by declaring the zone off limits to American shipping. When Americans began losing their lives in submarine attacks, the American public became incensed.

On March 28, 1915, a German torpedo sank the British liner *Falaba* in the Irish Sea, and one American drowned. Then, six weeks later, on May 7, a German submarine torpedoed the *Lusitania,* a sleek British passenger ship. Among the 1,200 passengers who died were 128 Americans. President Wilson demanded that the Germans end submarine attacks on unarmed ships, although the *Lusitania* was probably carrying munitions. Upset by Wilson's hard line, Secretary of State Bryan resigned.

Claiming a right of "just self-defense," the Germans continued their attacks. After the French passenger ship *Sussex* was torpedoed in March 1916, Wilson issued another protest. Not wanting to push the United States into the war on the side of the Allies, the Germans then agreed to suspend unannounced submarine attacks.

Peace and the Election of 1916

Submarine warfare and the relationship of the United States to the European powers became major political issues at home. Former President Theodore Roosevelt sharply criticized President Wilson and urged the United States to build up its armed forces in preparation for war.

2. **ACTIVITY** Have students find and read a contemporary newspaper account of the *Lusitania*'s sinking. Ask them to describe what the report shows about the public mood at the time.

3. *A British admiral in 1902 had called the U-boat "underhanded, unfair, and un-English." Submarines depended on surprise attacks and had no extra room on board, so the accepted rules of saving passengers and crew of an enemy ship could not be followed. When trench fighting on land produced a stalemate, Germany turned to submarine warfare to break the British blockade. After a submarine sank the* Lusitania, *anti-German feelings ran high in the United States. Germans were called "savages drunk with blood."*

3. **VOCABULARY** The name U-boat was short for *unterseeboot,* German for "underwater boat." German submarines were all marked with a large "U" followed by a number.

1.   Disturbed by the thought of a large standing army during peacetime, Wilson resisted Roosevelt's calls for a major program of preparedness. Yet he could not ignore the possibility that the United States might be drawn into the war. Thus, in 1916, the President doubled the size of the regular army and urged the construction of a "navy second to none."

    Yet, as the presidential election of 1916 approached, the nation still seemed to favor peace. The Republicans nominated Charles Evans Hughes for President. Democrats labeled Hughes a "war candidate" despite his moderate position on the war. They portrayed Wilson as a man who would keep the nation out of war. "Wilson and Peace with Honor, or Hughes with Roosevelt and War?" they asked the voters.

    The race was close. Hughes went to bed election night convinced he had won, while glum Democrats awaited the final count. By morning, however, late returns from the South and West had given the victory to Wilson. He took 49.4 percent of the popular vote, against 46.2 percent for Hughes. The American desire for peace brought Wilson victory, but peace would not last long, for the tragedy in Europe was deepening.

The End of Neutrality

Wilson had long hoped to negotiate an end to the war in Europe. Twice he sent his trusted friend and adviser Colonel Edward House to mediate between the opposing sides, and twice House failed. In late 1916, Wilson tried once more to bring Europe to the peace table.

2.   In December, the President worked on a diplomatic note pledging the United States to help arrange a peace. Before he had finished his draft, the Germans announced they were ready to negotiate an end to the war. Confident of victory, they demanded territory from Belgium, France, and Luxembourg, in addition to concessions along the Baltic Sea and in Africa. Such demands were unacceptable to the Allies.

    In January 1917, Germany unleashed its submarines to sink all ships, enemy or neutral, in the war zone. German officers antici-

pated victory before the United States could enter the war. In response, Wilson broke off relations with Germany, but hesitated to do more.

    An event in early March ended Wilson's reluctance. Britain intercepted a message known as the Zimmermann Telegram from German Foreign Minister Arthur Zimmermann to a German envoy in Mexico. Newspapers trumpeted the news: Germany was trying to lure Mexico and Japan (one of the Allies) over to its side. The message suggested that Mexico might regain land it had lost to the United States in 1848, including Texas. Such a direct threat shook Wilson's resolve to maintain American neutrality.

    Later that month, events in Russia removed Wilson's last doubts about entering the war. A revolution overthrew the autocratic czar and set up a constitutional government. Spared the embarrassment of allying with an absolute monarch, the President could more easily claim that the Allied cause was just. He asked Congress for a declaration of war on Germany, which it voted on April 6. The United States was officially at war.   3.

See p. T101.

SECTION 2 REVIEW

1. **Identify:** (a) Central Powers, (b) Allies, (c) *Lusitania,* (d) Charles Evans Hughes, (e) Zimmermann Telegram.

2. What circumstances led to the outbreak of war in Europe in 1914?

3. (a) How did the Central Powers and Allies try to influence American public opinion? (b) Which effort was more successful? Explain.

4. (a) How did Wilson react to German submarine attacks on unarmed ships? (b) What was the German response?

5. What three events eventually led to United States entry in the war?

6. **Critical Thinking** How could you have predicted Theodore Roosevelt's reaction to the war in Europe?

3 The Home Front

READ TO UNDERSTAND

■ What methods the United States used to raise an army.

■ How the war benefited business people, workers, women, and minorities.

■ How the war stirred up hatred and threatened the rights of dissenters.

Americans rushed into the war with reckless abandon. At a church in New England, a speaker cried that the German kaiser, or king, should be captured and then boiled in oil. People stood on chairs to cheer his words.

The people of Britain and France, weak from endless months of turnips and cabbage and demoralized by the slaughter of their soldiers, had long since lost such enthusiasm.

1. Once the United States declared war, President Wilson and his advisers were shocked to learn just how desperate the Allies were. Down to their last reserves, the Europeans begged for massive supplies of men
2. and materials. To save the Allies, Americans

poured their resources and patriotic fervor into winning the war.

Raising an Army

Even before the United States entered the war, Congress had debated raising an army. Should soldiers be recruited or drafted? President Wilson favored the draft as more democratic, but his selective-service bill caused a long debate in Congress. Not until May 7, 1917, was Wilson able to sign the bill, which set a minimum draft age of 21.

Some officials feared the draft would lead to riots, as it had during the Civil War, but patriotic appeals sparked massive support. By June 5, 1917, almost 10 million men between the ages of 21 and 31 had registered. Through voluntary enlistments and the draft, the American military had almost 5 million soldiers under arms by November 1918.

Blacks responded as enthusiastically as whites. Yet they had to serve in all-black units and faced the same discrimination in the armed forces as they knew at home. Of 371,000 blacks in uniform, only a few thousand ever saw combat. The rest were restricted to menial duties.

2. ACTIVITY Ask students to find recordings of such World War I songs as "Over There" or "Keep the Home Fires Burning." After listening to the songs, discuss how they might have affected the American public.

3. *Clubs for servicemen, called canteens, were set up in many cities as recreation centers for soldiers who would soon be leaving to fight in Europe. Women volunteers worked at canteens such as this one in Newark, New Jersey.*

3. VISUAL EVIDENCE Ask: Why do you think canteens were set up for soldiers?

1. **CITIZENSHIP** The 371st and 372nd black regiments were commended by the French general Goybet. He recalled, "The heroic rush of the colored American regiments . . . the most formidable defense, the nests of machine guns, the best organized positions, the artillery barrages most crushing, could not stop them."

1.   For the black soldiers overseas, Europe offered a marked contrast to life at home. The French, for example, had no history of racial conflict. They treated black soldiers much like their white comrades. When a black regiment demonstrated great courage, the grateful French government awarded two of its members, Henry Johnson and Needham Roberts, the Croix de Guerre (CWAH duh GAIR), a high military honor.

Wartime Industry

Although an army had been mobilized, the declaration of war caught the nation short of supplies. On hand were just 600,000 rifles, about 2,000 machine guns, and fewer than 1,000 artillery pieces. Chaos threatened as the military competed with the Allies and private industry to buy scarce materials.

By the summer of 1917, President Wilson knew that bold action was needed. He established the War Industries Board (WIB) to spur production and coordinate war industries. After months of frustration and failure, the WIB accomplished its goals under the direction of Bernard Baruch, a former Wall Street tycoon. (See the feature below.) The WIB strictly controlled scarce materials, set prices, and standardized production.

Similar efforts brought order to the shipping and railroad industries. Edward Hurley left the Federal Trade Commission to build a merchant marine. President Wilson asked Secretary of the Treasury William Gibbs McAdoo,

2. **BIOGRAPHY** After graduating from college, Bernard Baruch (1870–1965) went to work as an office boy in a linen company. He later amassed a fortune through stock speculations.

AMERICAN ENTERPRISE

Mobilizing Industry for War

2.   During 1918, as the trickle of American soldiers to the French battlefront became a flood, a tall, courtly man named Bernard Baruch set out to bring the American government and business into a partnership. Baruch, a Wall Street genius, was appointed by President Wilson to take over as head of the War Industries Board (WIB). He succeeded where others had failed.

For months, the WIB had been trying, without success, to impose order on the chaos of American industry. War industries did not get the copper and steel they needed; government agencies bid against one another for scarce supplies; Allied governments pleaded for more munitions.

Like many progressives of the time, Baruch believed there must be a way to tame the seeming chaos of the free enterprise system. As head of the WIB, he used his wartime powers to create order by forcing cooperation between the business community and the government in the interest of the war effort.

Was the navy short of steel for its ships? The WIB would procure enough steel for two warships by persuading the garment industry to stop putting stays in women's corsets. Did the French lack steel for artillery shells? The WIB would call two Pennsylvania steel mills and have the steel on its way within six days.

Not since the Civil War had the federal government taken such a direct role in running the nation's economy. Yet protests were muted, since most people fervently believed in the priority of the war effort. The business community went along, if not willingly at least grudgingly. Corporate profits had soared from 1914 to 1917 and continued rising even under the wartime controls. As one steel executive said, "We are all making more money out of this war than the average human being ought to."

Sensitive to charges that big business was "infiltrating" the government, President Wilson dissolved the WIB at the end of the war. The WIB's legendary leader, Bernard Baruch, lived into the 1960s, becoming an adviser to several Presidents.

See p. T102.

1. What was the purpose of the War Industries Board?

2. **Critical Thinking** How can war create a need for adjustments to the free enterprise system?

his son-in-law, to organize all the rail lines into one national network.

The government supported the massive mobilization by increasing taxes and selling bonds. McAdoo organized five Liberty Loan drives. Amid parades and patriotic appeals, volunteers knocked on doors to sell Liberty Bonds—in effect borrowing money for the government. Meanwhile, at school, children chipped in 25 cents at a time to buy "thrift stamps." A filled thrift card bought a war savings stamp worth $5, and a filled war savings card bought a $50 Liberty Bond.

At home, parents showed their patriotism by hanging out a red-and-white service flag with a blue star for each family member at war. Sometimes, a flag bore a gold star, for a son who had died at the front.

Workers During the War

Help from American workers was central to the mobilization of industry. In April 1918, President Wilson created the National War Labor Board to unify labor policies and settle disputes between management and labor. The board sometimes sided with management, but more often with workers. Mandatory mediation produced an unusual period of labor peace.

Wilson threw the full force of the government behind workers' rights, helping labor win major gains during the war. Union membership rose sharply. The American Federation of Labor grew from just over 2 million members in 1916 to nearly 3.3 million in 1920.

The federal government also helped to improve working conditions. In some cases it insisted on an eight-hour workday. It set standards for the employment of women and children, and it demanded that employers pay fair wages. Despite the rapid inflation of the war years, real income rose 14 percent in 1917 and 20 percent more in 1918.

The need for war workers opened up new jobs for women. Many women worked in steel mills and munitions factories. For the first time, government agencies opened their doors to women lawyers and doctors.

Most of the new opportunities lasted only as long as the war. By 1920, the percentage of women holding jobs was lower than in 1910. One union spokesman expressed the

WAR GARDENS OVER THE TOP

The Seeds of Victory Insure the Fruits of Peace

Copyright, 1919, National War Garden Commission.

Posters like the one above were created to bolster Americans' support of the war effort.

attitude of many when he declared that "the same patriotism that induced women to enter industry during the war should induce them to vacate their positions after the war."

The war also gave new opportunities to blacks, who had been moving north in growing numbers since 1900. In the five years after 1914, jobs in war industries attracted about 500,000 more blacks to northern cities. Yet the opportunities were short-lived. Once the war ended, many blacks were thrown out of work or had to accept lower-paying jobs.

Producing Food

When the United States entered the war, the people of France, Britain, and Italy were suffering widespread hunger. Thus, increasing American food production became a top priority. President Wilson appointed Herbert Hoover, an engineer and self-made millionaire, as head of the Food Administration. Hoover was known worldwide as the man who had organized a massive food-relief program to Belgium after the German invasion. The Lever Act of August 1917 gave Hoover full authority over food production, distribution, and farm supplies.

The top food priorities were wheat, pork, and sugar. Poor harvests kept wheat supplies low, but Americans cut back to save food. They voluntarily accepted "Wheatless Mon-

1. **CITIZENSHIP** During the war, nearly the entire leadership of the Industrial Workers of the World (the Wobblies) and the Socialist party were arrested. Altogether, some 1,600 people were jailed.

days," "Meatless Tuesdays," and "Porkless Thursdays." To supplement the food supply, children grew vegetables on school playgrounds and parents planted "victory gardens" in back yards. The results were amazing. Without rationing or great sacrifice, Americans almost tripled the amount of food sent to the Allies.

Influencing Public Opinion

President Wilson wanted Americans to know that they were fighting a just war. He explained: "The world must be made safe for democracy. . . . We have no selfish ends to serve. We desire no conquest, no domination." To enlist public support for the war, Wilson set up the Committee on Public Information (CPI) and named journalist George Creel to head it.

Creel showed resourcefulness and zeal in stirring up patriotism. He enlisted more

2. **ECONOMICS** In its first five bond drives, the government raised $21.5 billion.

2. *The bloody hand of the "Hun," a name that compared modern Germans to the barbarian Huns, appeared on posters urging Americans to buy Liberty Bonds. The Committee on Public Information enlisted some of the finest artists and advertising people to support the war effort.*

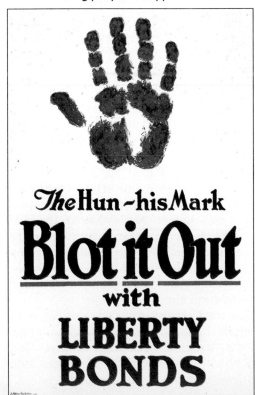

than 150,000 citizen lecturers in a big propaganda drive. They pointed out that the war was being fought for freedom and democracy. They also warned that disloyalty and sabotage threatened the war effort.

The CPI spurred the sale of Liberty Bonds, cut job absenteeism, and raised morale, but it also stirred suspicion and fear. German Americans, especially, became the victims of hate campaigns. Schools stopped teaching the German language. People renamed sauerkraut "liberty cabbage" and called German measles "liberty measles." Pacifists and socialists who criticized the war suffered verbal and physical abuse. Socialist leader Eugene V. Debs went to jail for speaking out against the war. A New York socialite was sentenced to ten years in jail for preaching "discontent with the government." Dissent had become the same as treason. 1.

Wartime legislation also stifled dissent. For example, the Espionage Act of 1917 imposed fines of up to $10,000 and jail sentences of up to 20 years for aiding the enemy or obstructing recruitment. The law gave sweeping authority to the postmaster general to confiscate material considered disloyal. The Sedition Act of 1918 punished any expression of disloyalty to the American government, flag, or military uniforms.

See p. T102.

SECTION 3 REVIEW

1. **Identify:** (a) War Industries Board, (b) Bernard Baruch, (c) William McAdoo, (d) National War Labor Board, (e) Herbert Hoover.

2. How did the United States raise an army?

3. List two ways the government improved conditions for American workers during the war.

4. How did the American public help increase food supplies during the war?

5. What was the purpose of the Committee on Public Information?

6. **Critical Thinking** Why are civil liberties endangered when dissent is treated as treason?

4 The United States in the War

READY TO UNDERSTAND

■ How the United States contributed to an Allied victory.

■ Why Germany surrendered in November 1918.

■ What kind of peace Wilson sought in proposing his Fourteen Points.

1. ■ *Vocabulary:* convoy, reparations, territorial integrity, self-determination.

Soon after declaring war, Congress called on administration officials to outline their war plans. At a Senate hearing in April 1917, a War Department official ticked off a $3 billion shopping list of needed supplies. "And we may have to have an army in France," he remarked. "Good grief!" declared Senator Thomas S. Martin of Virginia. "You're not going to send soldiers over there, are you?"

As it turned out, the United States sent more than 2 million soldiers to France during the next 19 months. Mobilization proceeded slowly at first. As late as March 1918, fewer than 300,000 American fighting men were in Europe. But then the troops poured in.

War at Sea

The British navy dominated the surface of the oceans, but German submarines continued to disrupt Allied shipping. Unescorted

2. **READING** Have interested students read Erich Maria Remarque's classic novel *All Quiet on the Western Front*, which describes war in the trenches from the point of view of a German infantryman.

SKILL LESSON

An American Experience in the World War: Analyzing Fiction as Historical Evidence

2.

Novels, short stories, and other works of fiction can be used as historical evidence. Below is an excerpt from *Three Soldiers*, a 1919 novel by John Dos Passos. Dos Passos was disillusioned by the brutal realities of modern warfare. Analyze the text as historical evidence. See p. T102.

1 **Identify the nature of the source.** (a) What type of document is it? (b) Who wrote it? (c) When was the document written?

2 **Interpret the source's content.** (a) Who is Chrisfield? (b) Where is he? (c) How would you describe his state of mind?

3 **Analyze the account as an historical source.** (a) What was the author's attitude about the war? (b) Does his attitude seem to have influenced his description of the event? Explain.

4 **Study the source to learn about an historical event.** (a) What can you learn about the war by reading this excerpt? (b) In what ways is the excerpt limited as historical evidence?

John Dos Passos

Chrisfield . . . could hardly hear the tramp of feet on the road, so loud was the pandemonium of the guns ahead and behind. Every now and then a rocket would burst in front of them and its red and green lights would mingle for a moment with the stars. But it was only overhead he could see the stars. Everywhere else white and red glows rose and fell as if the horizon were on fire.

As they started down the slope, the trees suddenly broke away and they saw the valley between them full of the glare of guns and the white light of star shells. It was like looking into a stove full of glowing embers. The hillside that sloped away from them was full of crashing detonations and yellow tongues of flame. In a battery near the road, that seemed to crush their skulls each time a gun fired, they could see the dark forms of the artillerymen silhouetted against the red glare. Stunned and blinded, they kept marching down the road. It seemed to Chrisfield that they were going to step any minute into the flaring muzzle of a gun.

1. **BACKGROUND** Russia reached a separate peace with Germany in the Treaty of Brest-Litovsk, signed in March 1918. Russia ceded much territory to Germany under the treaty.

merchant vessels were too easy a target. U-boats were destroying ships faster than they could be replaced. American troops and supplies would be useless if they could not cross the Atlantic.

Soon after the United States entered the war, Admiral William S. Sims convinced the British to use **convoys** to reduce the danger of attack. In convoys, destroyers and other warships escorted vessels across the ocean, providing protection against U-boats. The method was effective. Convoys transported American soldiers to Europe without the loss of a single life. They also delivered supplies to Europe more quickly than had been anticipated, further strengthening the war effort.

American industry strained to produce warships, especially destroyers and submarine chasers. The effort was so successful that by the end of the war, the United States Navy had grown to include more than 500,000 sailors and 2,000 ships.

The American Expeditionary Force

President Wilson chose General John J. Pershing to lead American troops, known as the American Expeditionary Force (AEF). General Pershing angered the Allies by insisting that American soldiers be trained before heading for Europe. This meant few troops would arrive before 1918. Pershing also insisted that the American force keep its identity and not be used merely to fill gaps in the French and British armies. Allied leaders, desperately needing troops, resented his attitude.

The first years of the war had consisted mainly of trench warfare. Both sides dug defensive trenches, often within 100 yards of each other, fired devastating artillery barrages, and mounted occasional infantry charges. The loss of life was immense, with little territorial gain by either side.

In November 1917, the second revolution in a year forced Russia to drop out of the war. Germany could now focus on the west-

2. **ACTIVITY** Have students imagine that they are American soldiers or nurses in France. Have them write letters home describing their experiences. Students might want to do additional research.

2. *Both American women and men served in France. The Red Cross sent women to provide medical and nursing services to American fighting men. These medical workers had to treat a new kind of casualty—soldiers sickened by poison gas. Poison gas added a new dimension of terror to warfare. Although gas masks were uncomfortable and stuffy, they became a standard piece of equipment for American soldiers.*

After Russia abandoned the war in the east, German armies massed their strength on the western front. At first, Allied forces reeled backward. Then they began a
1. massive counteroffensive. United States forces were assigned the section between Meuse and the Argonne Forest, shown here. One tenth of them were killed or wounded in the savage fighting,

1. **VISUAL EVIDENCE** An American soldier who fought in the trenches recalled, "The men slept in mud, washed in mud, ate mud, and dreamed mud."

2. **VOCABULARY** At Belleau Wood, the fierce attacks of U.S. Marines caused German soldiers to call them *teufelhunden. Devil dogs* remains their nickname.

ern front. In the spring of 1918, the Germans attacked the Allied lines, breaking the defensive pattern of the war. Allied leaders appointed Field Marshal Ferdinand Foch of France to command all Allied forces in Europe. Pershing agreed to cooperate.

2. In May 1918, the Germans launched a major offensive that advanced to within 50 miles (80 kilometers) of Paris. A combined force of French and American troops stopped the Germans and drove them back in the battles of Chateau Thierry and Belleau Wood. By autumn, the arrival of more American troops allowed Pershing to control his own fighting force, the American First Army. He quickly mounted offensives against German lines in the south. American successes there contributed to British and French victories elsewhere, and the Allies pressed on to vic-
3. tory. On November 11, 1918, German delegates met with Marshal Foch and signed an armistice.

American troops and supplies had helped turn the tide of battle. The "Yanks" not only gave the Allies a numerical advantage but raised the spirits of the exhausted British and French troops. While more than 100,000 American soldiers had died, the Allied toll was far higher. Britain lost nearly 1 million people, France 1.5 million, and Russia 1.7 million.

Diplomacy and War

As early as 1914, President Wilson had suggested the outlines of a "liberal" peace. He called for disarmament to halt the arms race among nations and for public diplomacy to end the system of secret treaties that had helped start the war. Wilson also urged rejection of territorial gains by the victors and of payment of **reparations,** or penalties for damages, by the losers. Such leniency, he felt, might lead to a more permanent peace.

In 1916, Wilson declared that the United States wanted a peace treaty that guaranteed the **territorial integrity** of nations, that is, one that preserved their boundaries. The peace should also guarantee the right of the nations involved to **self-determination,** or to form their own government without outside interference; freedom of the seas; and pro-

559

3. **PAST AND PRESENT** Wilson proclaimed this the first Armistice Day. In 1954, Congress changed the name to Veterans Day to honor all American soldiers.

Woodrow Wilson: A Proposal for Peace

1.

In early 1917, President Wilson was still hopeful that peace could be negotiated between the Allies and the Central Powers. He outlined proposals for that peace in a speech to the Senate on January 22, 1917. The final part of Wilson's speech is printed below.

I am proposing, as it were, that the nations should with one accord adopt the doctrine of President Monroe as the doctrine of the world: that no nation should seek to extend its polity over any other nation or people, but that every people should be left free to determine its own polity, its own way of development—unhindered, unthreatened, unafraid, the little along with the great and powerful.

I am proposing that all nations henceforth avoid entangling alliances which would draw them into competitions of power, catch them in a net of intrigue and selfish rivalry, and disturb their own affairs with influences intruded from without.

I am proposing government by the consent of the governed; that freedom of the seas which in international conference after conference representatives of the United States have urged with the eloquence of those who are the convinced disciples of liberty; and that moderation of armaments which makes of armies and navies a power for order merely, not an instrument of aggression or of selfish violence.

These are American principles, American policies. We could stand for no others. And they are also the principles of forward-looking men and women everywhere, of every modern nation, of every enlightened community. They are the principles of mankind and must prevail.

See p. T102.

1. What principles did President Wilson outline in his speech?

2. **Critical Thinking** What steps have nations taken recently to try to implement some of these principles?

1. **CRITICAL THINKING** Ask: Why did Wilson wish to extend the application of the Monroe Doctrine? How did his extension of the Doctrine differ from Roosevelt's?

tection from aggression. These were grand ideas, but until the United States entered the war, Wilson had little influence. The American role in ending the war strengthened the President's hand.

Early in 1918, with his country actively involved in the war, Wilson proposed a plan for peace called the Fourteen Points. The first five points called for open treaties, freedom of the seas, free trade, arms reductions, and impartial adjustment of colonial claims. Points six through thirteen dealt with national self-determination and the realignment of borders that had been changed during or prior to the war. The fourteenth point was essential to Wilson's personal vision of world peace. It called for the establishment of an international organization to settle disputes between nations and prevent future wars.

As the war neared an end, the President tried to guarantee a peace built around his Fourteen Points. Under pressure from Wilson, German Kaiser Wilhelm II gave up his throne on November 9. The Germans then set up a

560

democratic government in an attempt to win more lenient treatment from the victorious Allies. Now Wilson had to persuade Allied leaders, and Americans as well, to accept his version of peace.

2.

See p. T102.

1. **Identify:** Fourteen Points.

2. **Define:** (a) convoy, (b) reparations, (c) territorial integrity, (d) self-determination.

3. What helped turned the tide of the war in 1918?

4. How did Germany try to win leniency from the Allies?

5. What was Wilson's "liberal" peace plan?

6. **Critical Thinking** President Wilson felt that a lenient peace treaty might lead to a more permanent peace. Do you agree or disagree? Explain.

5 Search for a "Just Peace"

READ TO UNDERSTAND

■ Why Wilson faced resistance to his peace plan in the United States.

■ What were the major terms of the Treaty of Versailles.

■ Why the Senate rejected the Treaty of Versailles.

1. When the guns fell silent, the world rejoiced. But no one knew what kind of peace would follow. That would depend on negotiations between the victors and the vanquished. Allied leaders, intent on punishing Germany and preventing it from ever becoming a major power again, openly scoffed at many of Wilson's high-minded proposals. French Premier Georges Clemenceau is said to have remarked, "God gave us His Ten Commandments, and we broke them. Wilson gave us his Fourteen Points; we shall see."

Resistance at Home

Wilson's ideas met resistance not only from Allied leaders but also from many Americans. One source of domestic opposition lay in two-party jockeying for political advantage. The Republicans did not want the Democrats to use the peace to win votes. Many Americans also questioned whether the United States should join a world organization, as called for in the fourteenth point. Staying out of European affairs had been a longstanding American tradition. Now that the German threat was over, many Americans wanted to return to that tradition.

The President's own actions stirred further trouble. When Wilson tried to build support for his plan by making the 1918 congressional elections a referendum on his policies, the effort backfired. Republicans gained con-

2. *On the battlefield, the silence was complete. "All we did was stand and stare and stare," wrote an American private. But in the Allied capitals, joyful demonstrations of victory broke out. The American impressionist painter Childe Hassam was in Paris during the war, and he painted* Allied Flags, *seen here. The American flag flies above the flags of 11 other nations in this festive picture. The artist painted himself into the crowd—the man with the portfolio.*

trol of both houses of Congress. Republican leaders proclaimed the election results a rejection of Wilson's foreign policy.

The President lost support in an already hostile Congress when he failed to name any influential Republicans to the negotiating team that would go to Paris. As a result, Republicans in Congress would look on any treaty as a Democratic one, open to partisan attack.

1. Wilson also provoked criticism when he decided to lead the delegation to Paris himself. No President had ever traveled abroad on a diplomatic mission. Many Americans felt that the President should stay home and help the nation deal with the problems of readjusting to peace.

2. **MAP READING** Have students compare this map with the one on p. 549 and list the changes that were made.

MAP STUDY

The map of Europe after the peace conference looked very
2. *different from the map five years earlier. (See page 549.) Many new nations were created as the old empires of Austria-Hungary and Russia collapsed. What new nation was created entirely out of territory lost by Austria-Hungary?* See p. T103.

Europe After the War

Territories lost by:
Austria-Hungary
Bulgaria
Germany
Russia

0   200 Miles
0   200 Kilometers

Another difficulty arose when other countries demanded that the negotiations be secret. Secrecy angered American reporters, who wanted to cover the peace talks. It also seemed to violate the first of Wilson's Fourteen Points, which called for open agreements. Despite such concerns, President Wilson left for Europe in December 1918 with high hopes.

The Versailles Peace Conference

President Wilson visited several countries before the peace conference, which began in January 1919 at Versailles (vehr SI), near Paris. Wildly enthusiastic crowds greeted him in London, Paris, and Rome. Wilson considered his reception a sign of great popular support for his ideas. Actually, few Europeans fully understood the President's plan for peace. Rather, they saw him as a great leader whose nation had helped end the terrible war engulfing their countries. Their reception, however, only strengthened Wilson's determination to make the peace treaty fit his plan.

At Versailles, Wilson encountered equally **3.** determined men. Premier Georges Clemenceau (KLEHM uhn soh) of France, Prime Minister David Lloyd George of Britain, and Prime Minister Vittorio Orlando of Italy had two major concerns. They all sought to protect the interests of their own countries and punish Germany for the damages the Allies had suffered in the war. The Treaty of Versailles, which they forced Germany to sign on June 28, 1919, reflected those goals.

Austria-Hungary had collapsed, and the treaty recognized several new nations created out of the old empire. (See the map at the left.) France regained Alsace-Lorraine from Germany, acquired mining rights in the Saar Valley, and gained the right to occupy the Rhineland for 15 years. Lloyd George, Clemenceau, and Orlando persuaded Wilson to agree to demands that Germany pay huge reparations to France and Britain and that the treaty include a clause blaming Germany for the war.

Although much of the treaty seemed a violation of Wilson's original goals, he agreed to it because it included the covenant, or constitution, of the League of Nations. Wilson

3. **ACTIVITY** Have interested students prepare biographical sketches of these European leaders and present them to the class.

believed that the League could help prevent future wars through negotiation.

The President was aware that many Republican senators opposed the League of Nations. In fact, during the negotiations, 39 Republican senators—enough to block ratification of a treaty—had signed a petition
1. calling the treaty unacceptable. The senators, led by Henry Cabot Lodge of Massachusetts, especially objected to Article 10 of the League's covenant. Article 10 guaranteed the territorial integrity of member states and called for possible economic and military sanctions against violators. These senators did not want an international body making decisions for the United States.

Wilson negotiated changes in the covenant in order to make it more acceptable. In its final form, the covenant allowed withdrawal from the League, made participation in sanctions optional, and recognized the importance of the Monroe Doctrine in the Western Hemisphere. With the revised treaty in hand, the President returned to the United States to seek Senate ratification.

Defeat of the Treaty

Woodrow Wilson delivered the 264-page Treaty of Versailles to the Senate in person. Democrats applauded. The Republican majority sat silent.

Most Americans probably favored the treaty and the League, although German and Irish Americans, along with many liberals, thought the treaty was too harsh on Germany. In the Senate, opinion broke along party lines. All but 4 of the 47 Democrats stood loyally with Wilson. While some of the 49 Republicans leaned toward strict isolation, most supported a series of amendments proposed by Henry Cabot Lodge.

Senator Lodge wanted to "Republicanize" the treaty so that the Democrats could not use it to partisan advantage. More important, he saw the League of Nations as a threat to American sovereignty. He said his goal was to avoid United States involvement in the internal affairs of other nations and to protect Congress's authority to declare war.

Wilson refused to accept any but the mildest changes in the treaty. Failing to gain Sen-

ate support, he went to the people. Early in September 1919, he began a cross-country trip to explain the treaty. In Omaha, Nebraska, he warned, "I can predict with absolute certainty that within another generation there will be another world war if the nations of the world do not concert . . . to prevent it." The crowds were friendly and enthusiastic, but that did not change Senate votes.

The trip destroyed the President's fragile health. On September 25, Wilson collapsed. 2. A week later, he suffered a stroke that paralyzed his left side. For months, he remained almost helpless in bed.

In November 1919, the Senate defeated the treaty, which included Lodge's amendments. Wilson had called on Democrats to vote against the treaty as long as it contained those amendments. In March 1920, another amended version of the treaty came before the Senate, and again it lost. Wilson so opposed Lodge's changes that he was willing to lose the entire treaty rather than accept them. By rejecting the Treaty of Versailles, the Sen- 3. ate dashed Woodrow Wilson's dream of a new world order. The League of Nations began its peacekeeping mission without the United States.

See p. T103.

SECTION 5 REVIEW

1. **Identify:** (a) Treaty of Versailles, (b) League of Nations, (c) Henry Cabot Lodge, (d) Article 10.

2. Why did President Wilson face domestic opposition to his peace plan?

3. (a) How did the Treaty of Versailles violate Wilson's principles? (b) What changes did Wilson negotiate in the covenant of the League of Nations to make it more acceptable to the Senate?

4. Why did the Senate reject the Treaty of Versailles?

5. **Critical Thinking** How could the fact that 1920 was an election year have affected the chances for the ratification of the treaty?

Summary

1. **Woodrow Wilson and his secretary of state, William Jennings Bryan, brought moral zeal to American foreign policy.** They wanted to bring world peace and democratic governments to all people. Yet they also advanced United States interests, especially in Latin America, although their actions made enemies as well as friends.

2. **When war broke out in Europe, President Wilson urged Americans to remain neutral.** But neutrality was hard to achieve. After many provocations, Congress declared war on Germany in April 1917.

3. **The United States now turned its full attention to the war effort.** Millions of men were drafted, and industry reached new heights. The War Industries Board coordinated war production. The National War Labor Board helped unify labor policy. Extreme patriotic feeling sometimes resulted in attacks on German Americans, pacifists, and socialists.

4. **The American Expeditionary Force bolstered Allied military efforts.** Arriving in Europe in 1918, the AEF helped turn the tide of war. Hopeful that President Wilson's Fourteen Points would form the basis for a lenient peace, Germany signed an armistice on November 11, 1918.

5. **Allied leaders demanded a peace treaty that would punish Germany.** The Treaty of Versailles forced Germany to give up territory and to pay reparations. President Wilson agreed to the treaty because it provided for the League of Nations, but the Senate refused to ratify it.

See p. T103.

Vocabulary

Match each term at left with its definition or description at right.

1. neutral

2. convoy

3. reparations

4. territorial integrity

5. self-determination

a. right to form a government without interference

b. protected boundaries

c. a protective escort

d. payment of costs of war

e. nonaligned

See p. T103.

Chapter Checkup

1. What actions did Wilson take in each of the following countries? (a) Nicaragua; (b) Haiti; (c) Dominican Republic.

2. (a) How did Wilson try to influence the outcome of the Mexican civil war? (b) Why did the United States send troops into Mexico in 1916?

3. (a) What policy did the United States proclaim at the outbreak of war in Europe? (b) Why was it difficult to maintain that policy?

4. (a) How did the German use of the submarine violate international law? (b) Why did the Germans agree to stop unannounced attacks in 1916?

5. (a) How did the American government mobilize industry to support the war effort? (b) What actions did the government take to win the support of workers?

6. How did the arrival of United States troops help the Allies win the war?

7. (a) Briefly describe President Wilson's Fourteen Points. (b) Which provisions of the Treaty of Versailles seemed to contradict the Fourteen Points? (c) Why was

Wilson willing to accept the treaty despite such contradictions?

8. (a) How did Wilson alienate many Americans even before the peace conference began? (b) Why did most Republican senators oppose the treaty? (c) Why did Senator Lodge propose amendments?

See p. T104.

Critical Thinking

1. Comparing Compare Wilson's "moral diplomacy" to Roosevelt's "big stick" and Taft's "dollar diplomacy." (a) How did the theories behind the policies differ? (b) Did the policies differ in action? Explain.

2. Supporting an Opinion (a) What do you think the union official meant by his comment that "the same patriotism that induced women to enter industry during the war should induce them to vacate their positions after the war"? (b) Do you agree with him? Why or why not?

See p. T104.

Connecting Past and Present

1. United States relations with Nicaragua and Mexico have made news in recent years, just as in Wilson's time. (a) Why have American leaders taken such a keen interest in those nations' affairs? (b) How do past disputes with those nations influence present-day relations?

2. Although the United States refused to join the League of Nations, it has been a leading member of the United Nations, formed at the end of World War II in 1945. Why might the United States be more inclined today than in 1919 to participate in such a world body?

See p. T104.

Developing Basic Skills

1. Map Reading Compare the two maps on pages 549 and 562. (a) Which new countries were created after the war? (b) Which nation no longer existed after the war? (c) Which nations lost territory? (d) Which nations gained territory?

2. Using a Primary Source Read the excerpts from President Wilson's foreign policy speech on page 560. (a) Why is this document a primary source? (b) What can you learn about Wilson's goals for peace by reading it? (c) How does this primary source differ from a diary account?

WRITING ABOUT HISTORY

Preparing a Preliminary Outline

A preliminary outline helps you to focus on areas of research. The first steps in preparing a preliminary outline are to write down the title and thesis statement of your paper. Then formulate questions about the topic. Using the questions as a guideline, draw up a simple outline. Study the following example.

Title: The United States Home Front Mobilizes for War

Thesis statement: Once the United States entered World War I, the nation marshaled its human and material resources to help the Allied effort.

1. The government builds up the armed forces.

2. The government organizes industry.

3. Industry responds.

4. The government encourages public participation.

5. The public responds.

Practice: Choose a topic from Chapter 25 and prepare a preliminary outline.

THE YEARS BETWEEN THE WARS

Ben Shahn's tribute to immigrants shows Albert Einstein, with the violin case, among the unknown masses.

Because of the work of jazz singers, such as Ruby Green, the 1920s are often called the Jazz Age.

	1918	1921	1924	1927
POLITICS AND GOVERNMENT		**1919** Fear of radicals leads to the Red Scare	**1924** Fall indicted in Teapot Dome scandal	
SOCIETY AND CULTURE		**1920** First commercial radio station broadcasts	**1924** Congress cuts immigration from southern and eastern Europe	
ECONOMICS AND TECHNOLOGY		**1919** Strikes in steel and coal industries	**1926** Hurricane ends the Florida land boom	
WORLD EVENTS	**1918** Armistice ends fighting in the war	**1922** Mussolini comes to power in Italy	**1926** Germany joins the League of Nations	

Wilson | Harding | Coolidge

Farmers did not share in the prosperity of the Roaring Twenties.

The automobile, shown in this 1920s advertisement, helped transform American society.

UNIT OUTLINE

1932 As the depression deepened, pressure grew for more government action.

WPA murals often emphasized the theme of self-improvement and hard work.

1927	1930	1933	1936	1939

1931 Bonus Army leaves for Washington   **1933** New Deal begins

1927 *Jazz Singer* is first talking movie

1930 Grant Wood's *American Gothic* depicts a farm couple

1935 Social Security Act provides pensions for the elderly

1929 Stock market crash leads to the Great Depression

1933 TVA created

1935 WPA puts people to work on public works projects

1930 Depression spreads in Europe

Hoover — Roosevelt

By the late 1920s, millions of Americans were speculating on Wall Street.

1932 The drought that lasted until 1936 turned farmland into dust.

Life in the 1920s

26

(1919–1929)

CHAPTER OUTLINE

1 The Rocky Road to Peacetime

2 The Politics of Normalcy

3 A Decade of Material Progress

4 The Jazz Age

5 Changing Times

At ten o'clock in the evening of May 21, 1927, a tiny silver airplane made a few circles in the sky high above the Eiffel Tower in Paris. The weary pilot, who had not slept in nearly three days, spied the lights of Le Bourget airfield, headed his craft toward them, and touched down about 20 minutes later.

When he looked out of the plane's door, he saw, to his astonishment, a mob of 100,000 people racing toward him. As he attempted to leave the plane, the cheering crowd seized him, hoisted him in the air, and paraded him around for a full half-hour.

This was just the beginning of the nearly hysterical enthusiasm that would engulf this tall, slim, shy 26-year-old Minnesotan named Charles Lindbergh. He had just completed the first solo nonstop airplane flight from New York to Paris, a trip that took 33½ hours. He had no map, no parachute, and no radio, and his plane, *The Spirit of St. Louis,* had only one engine.

America idolized "Lucky Lindy" as it has idolized few persons. One newspaper called his achievement "the greatest feat of a solitary man in the records of the human race." A speaker at a dinner honoring the flier proclaimed it "the most marvelous day that this old earth has ever known."

In the excitement of the 1920s, many Americans were disturbed by newspaper stories about crime, corruption, greed, rising divorce rates, and the general loss of traditional values. Lindbergh represented what most people liked to think was best about America—courage, intelligence, honesty, and the ability to make science work for the benefit of humanity. In a way, Lindbergh combined the past and the future. He stood for "old-fashioned" virtues, yet pointed to a future full of technological wonders. The world was changing, and Lindbergh, at least briefly, enabled people to face the future with optimism.

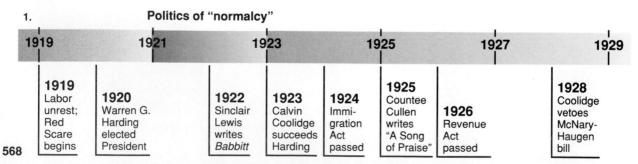

1.

Politics of "normalcy"

1919	1921	1923	1925	1927	1929

1919 Labor unrest; Red Scare begins

1920 Warren G. Harding elected President

1922 Sinclair Lewis writes *Babbitt*

1923 Calvin Coolidge succeeds Harding

1924 Immigration Act passed

1925 Countee Cullen writes "A Song of Praise"

1926 Revenue Act passed

1928 Coolidge vetoes McNary-Haugen bill

568

1. TIME LINE QUESTION Ask: Which President was responsible for the politics of "normalcy"?

Lindbergh's flight was a high point of the "Roaring Twenties." Americans seemed to revel in the new freedoms brought by prosperity, technology, and mobility.

1. *Howard Thain captured the spirit of the decade in this painting,* Times Square.

---

1. **VISUAL EVIDENCE** Ask: What words would you use to describe the mood of this painting? Does it present a positive or negative picture of the city?

1 The Rocky Road to Peacetime

READt TO UNDERSTAND

■ What problems the United States faced after World War I.

■ How the country reacted to fears of revolution.

■ Why black Americans became disillusioned.

2. ■ *Vocabulary:* general strike, quota system.

After the war, almost every city and town in the United States welcomed back its soldiers and sailors with parades and celebrations. It would not be very long, however, before Americans began to realize that peace also brought problems. Thousands of veterans flooded the job market. Factories had to switch from producing war supplies to producing consumer goods. The rise in the cost of living outpaced earnings.

Returning to Normal

When World War I ended in 1918, President Wilson asked for a rapid end to government operation of industries such as railroads. Congress quickly agreed. No plans had been made, however, for easing soldiers and sailors back into civilian life or for avoiding the economic problems that might result from the end of government regulation of industry.

569

2. **VOCABULARY** Have students look up these terms in the glossary before they begin reading.

The armed forces discharged 4 million men after the war. Other government departments cut hundreds of thousands of wartime employees. All of these people needed jobs. Yet the pool of available jobs shrank even further, as many factories closed in order to retool for peacetime production. By 1921, unemployment engulfed almost 5 million people.

Meanwhile, the American economy faced another unsettling condition. At the end of the war, many consumers went on a spending spree, buying goods that had been unavailable during the war. Shortages of these goods soon increased inflation. For example, the price of a pound of sugar increased from 10 cents in 1918 to 20 cents in 1920. As prices soared, the cost of living doubled from what it had been in 1913.

1. To make matters worse, between 1920 and 1922, the country slid into a recession. Farmers were hit hard by falling prices. For example, the price of wheat sank from a wartime high of $2.26 a bushel to less than $1 a bushel in 1922.

Postwar Labor Unrest

The close of the war brought an end to peaceful relations between factory owners and workers. During the war, management and labor had worked together in a spirit of patriotism to solve problems without strikes or lockouts. Rising prices after the war, however, fueled workers' demands for higher wages. With a large pool of replacement workers available, employers could refuse to comply. Many unions responded by going on strike. Workers in the clothing, textile, telegraph, and telephone industries won higher pay, but unions in other industries were less successful.

Business and labor leaders tried to portray each other as enemies of American values. Many employers charged that unions were run by radicals who aimed to undermine the American economy. Some union activists argued that factory owners became wealthy at the expense of workers.

The first serious confrontation took place in the steel industry. In September 1919, a newly formed steelworkers' union demanded higher wages, a six-day work week, and an end to the twelve-hour work day. Management refused to negotiate, and the union called a strike. Within a week, 365,000 steel-2. workers across the country had walked out. When violence erupted, local police and state militia helped steel companies break the picket lines. Companies hired strikebreakers to replace the union workers. After 20 deaths and the loss of $100 million in wages, the union called off the strike on January 9, 1920. It had won nothing.

A 1919 strike in the coal industry was more successful. After federal officials se-3. cured a court order against the strike, United Mine Workers leader John L. Lewis urged the miners to return to work. "We are Americans. We cannot fight our government," he said. But, as Lewis expected, the workers stayed out. Finally, the coal companies agreed to settle the dispute, and the workers won a 27 percent wage increase.

Two strikes in particular convinced many Americans that foreign radicals might be causing the labor unrest: a general strike in Seattle, Washington, and a police strike in Boston, Massachusetts.

In 1919, the Central Labor Council of Seattle called a **general strike,** a strike by the members of all unions, in support of striking shipyard workers. Many Americans considered the general strike a radical tactic imported from Europe. When Seattle Mayor Ole Hanson used troops to crush the strike, he became a national hero—except among union workers.

The strike by Boston police was of even greater concern to most citizens. Police officers walked off the job in September 1919 after the police commissioner fired 19 officers who had tried to organize a union. With police protection suspended, looting broke out in the city. Actual damage was small, but waves of fear swept across the nation. Massachusetts Governor Calvin Coolidge condemned the strike as a threat to public safety and called out the National Guard.

These strikes and hundreds of others hardened the public attitude toward unions. After several major defeats, membership in the American Federation of Labor sank from

2. **TECHNOLOGY** Lead a discussion on the impact on the economy of a strike in an industry such as steel.

3. **BIOGRAPHY** John L. Lewis (1880–1969) later founded the Congress of Industrial Organizations (CIO), which organized unskilled workers in the 1930s.

1. **PAST AND PRESENT** Have students compare and contrast these arrests with those that took place at the time of the Alien and Sedition acts.

2. **CITIZENSHIP** Many of the people arrested were not allowed to contact a lawyer. Those who visited the prisoners often were arrested also.

more than 5 million in 1920 to about 3.6 million in 1923.

The Red Scare

As you have read in Chapter 25, a revolution overthrew Russia's government in 1917. It was led by a radical group of communists called the Bolsheviks, or Reds. The Bolsheviks advocated worldwide revolution and called on the workers of the world to unite and overthrow capitalism.

Many Americans feared the spread of communist revolutionary ideas in the United States. The strikes of the postwar years and a series of terrorist incidents increased their anxiety. Postal workers found packages containing bombs addressed to prominent citizens. In 1919, the home of Attorney General A. Mitchell Palmer was bombed. The following year, a bomb exploded in New York City's financial district, killing 38 people and injuring hundreds more.

For many people, these acts of terrorism, combined with labor unrest, heightened the fear of a communist revolution. During this "Red Scare," few Americans could see the difference between criminal terrorists and peaceful protestors or strikers. As a result, during 1919 and early 1920, socialists and other radicals were frequently harassed by citizens and government authorities. Such attacks often targeted immigrants, especially those from eastern Europe.

In response to public demands for action, Attorney General Palmer organized a series of raids to arrest suspected communists. In January 1920, authorities seized more than 6,000 people in 33 cities. Almost none had committed any crime. Of those arrested, about 550 were deported. Yet the Palmer raids did not uncover a single plot to overthrow the government.

At first, people responded enthusiastically to Palmer's actions. Eventually, however, a growing number of Americans, including a former Supreme Court justice, began to condemn the government's violations of constitutional rights. Furthermore, people soon realized that revolution was not imminent. By late 1920, the Red Scare had faded.

Sacco and Vanzetti

One of the underlying causes of the Red Scare was hostility to immigrants. Many Americans believed that the "new immigrants," most of whom came from southern and eastern Europe, would not fit into American society.

The extent of this attitude toward immigrants was revealed in a murder case in Massachusetts. In April 1920, armed bandits robbed a shoe factory in South Braintree, Massachusetts, killing a paymaster and a guard. Two Italian immigrants, Nicola Sacco and Bartolomeo Vanzetti, were accused of the crime. Both were anarchists, people opposed to organized government. In 1921, they were tried, found guilty, and sentenced to be executed.

Many people believed that the verdict was based on inconclusive evidence and that the judge was prejudiced against the two men. They believed that Sacco and Vanzetti had been convicted because they were immigrants and held unpopular political views.

A series of strikes and terrorist acts caused many Americans to fear the spread of communism. In this 1919 cartoon, a Bolshevik is shown creeping out from under the American flag. It appealed to the deepest fears of the Red Scare—that communist revolutionaries could change the American way of life.

1. **PAST AND PRESENT** Have students find out what kind of restrictions on immigration exist today.

2. **BACKGROUND** Refer students to p. 540 for a reminder of earlier actions that limited Japanese immigration to the U.S.

The case attracted international attention. Many prominent persons demanded that Sacco and Vanzetti be given a new trial. An equally vocal group believed the men were guilty and dismissed the critics as radicals and agitators. After many futile appeals, the two were executed in 1927. Fifty years later Governor Michael Dukakis of Massachusetts, citing trial irregularities, cleared their names.

Restrictions on Immigration

Following World War I, a record flood of immigrants came to the United States, raising concern among many Americans. Business people feared that immigrants would spread radical ideas. Workers worried that immigrants would compete for jobs and drive wages down. As a result, the government was pressured to restrict the numbers of immigrants entering the country.

Congress responded to public demands for immigration restriction by passing the Emergency Quota Act of 1921. This law introduced a **quota system** that set limits on the number of people who could immigrate. Under the system, the number of immigrants from each nation was limited to 3 percent of the number of people of that nationality living in the United States in 1910. The act also limited the total number of immigrants to 357,000 each year. 1.

After the Emergency Quota Act failed to reduce the flow of southern and eastern European immigrants substantially, Congress passed the Immigration Act of 1924. The new law lowered the quota from 3 percent to 2 percent and changed the base year from 1910 to 1890, a year when few southern and eastern Europeans were living in the United States. This provision greatly reduced the number of new immigrants from those regions. The act dealt even more harshly with the Japanese, barring them altogether as "aliens ineligible to citizenship." 2.

Another law in 1929 further reduced the annual quota of immigrants to 150,000. None of the quota laws applied to immigrants from Canada and Latin America. But immigration from Asia and Africa was sharply curtailed.

GRAPH STUDY *New immigration laws changed the pattern of immigration to the United States. The graph, below, left, shows the percentage of immigrants from various areas before the new laws went into 3. effect. The new laws set no limit on newcomers from the Western Hemisphere. How is this fact reflected in the graph below, right?* See p. T106.

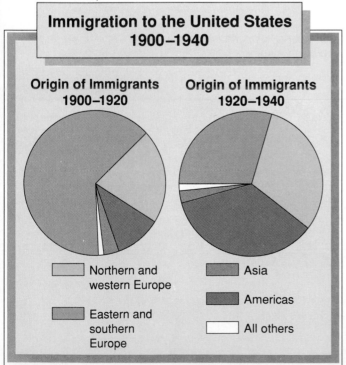

Immigration to the United States 1900–1940

Origin of Immigrants 1900–1920

Origin of Immigrants 1920–1940

- Northern and western Europe
- Eastern and southern Europe
- Asia
- Americas
- All others

Source: *Historical Statistics of the United States*

Black Americans Are Disillusioned

New job opportunities in war industries had raised the aspirations of many black Americans. Between 1917 and 1925, about 600,000 blacks migrated to northern industrial cities.

During both the war and the postwar years, however, blacks faced discrimination in jobs and housing. As unemployment rose, they suffered greatly. Many white workers resented blacks competing for jobs. And blacks were not welcome in all-white neighborhoods in northern cities.

In 1919, racial tensions sparked riots in more than 20 cities. The worst riot began when whites attacked a black youngster swimming in a "white" area of Lake Michigan in Chicago. Before the riot ended, more than 500 people were injured and 38 were killed.

3. **GRAPH READING** Ask: From 1920 to 1940, about what percentage of immigrants came from eastern and southern Europe? From northern and western Europe?

After World War II, many blacks moved from the South to settle in such northern cities as Detroit, New York, Chicago, and St. Louis. Although blacks met prejudice in the North, too, they also found new opportunities, as pictured in this painting by
1. Jacob Lawrence called *The Library*. Lawrence's paintings of black life vibrate with intense color and interweave complex groups of geometric figures.

1. **VISUAL EVIDENCE** Interested students can look at other paintings from Lawrence's series entitled *The Migration of the Negro*.

See p. T106.

The revival of the Ku Klux Klan reflected the intolerance of the period. The new Klan formed in Georgia in 1915 and spread quickly from the South to parts of the Midwest and West. While the original Klan, founded after the Civil War, had terrorized freed slaves and whites who sympathized with them, the new Klan had a broader goal: to preserve the United States for white, native-born Protestants. Consequently, the Klan attacked not only blacks, but also immigrants, Catholics, and Jews.

2. By 1923, the Ku Klux Klan claimed 4 million members and had become a political force in Texas, Oregon, Georgia, Oklahoma, Alabama, and Indiana. Klan-supported candidates won governorships in Oklahoma and Oregon. The political power of the Klan declined after 1924, however, once the corruption and illegal activities of many of its leaders were exposed.

SECTION 1 REVIEW

1. **Identify:** (a) Calvin Coolidge, (b) Bolsheviks, (c) A. Mitchell Palmer, (d) Sacco and Vanzetti.

2. **Define:** (a) general strike, (b) quota system.

3. (a) Why was there labor unrest after World War I? (b) How did it contribute to the Red Scare?

4. Which nationalities were most affected by the new legislation restricting immigration?

5. Why were blacks disillusioned after the war?

6. **Critical Thinking** How can economic problems lead to social unrest?

573

2. **READING** Interested students might read relevant chapters in *Hooded Americanism: The History of the Ku Klux Klan* by David M. Chalmers.

2 The Politics of Normalcy

READ TO UNDERSTAND

■ What strengths and weaknesses marked the Harding administration.

■ How business fared under President Coolidge.

■ Why some Americans failed to share in the overall prosperity of the 1920s.

1. ■ *Vocabulary:* normalcy, parity, migrant worker.

Warren G. Harding, the Republican nominee for President in 1920, caught the mood of the country when he said that what Americans needed was a return to **"normalcy,"** his word for normality. For Harding and the Republicans, normalcy meant an end to wartime experiments and postwar unrest. It meant that business should not be burdened with government regulation, but, if necessary, government should be ready to aid business. Harding and his successor, Calvin Coolidge, presided over government during this "era of normalcy" in the United States.

The Election of 1920

The Republicans anticipated an easy victory in the presidential election of 1920. With the Democrats badly split over the Versailles Treaty, the Republicans knew they need only

2. find an attractive candidate to win. In a backroom compromise, party leaders chose Senator Warren G. Harding of Ohio. "This Harding's no world beater," they admitted, "but . . . he's the best of the bunch." Convention delegates agreed, adding Governor Calvin Coolidge of Massachusetts to the ticket as the vice presidential nominee.

The Democratic presidential nominating convention cast 44 ballots before choosing Governor James Cox of Ohio. For Vice President, they picked Franklin D. Roosevelt, Wilson's assistant secretary of the navy.

2. **PRESIDENTS** Harding was a printer's apprentice before attending college. He later bought and made himself editor of an Ohio newspaper, the *Marion Star.*

In the first national election in which women had full suffrage, Harding polled a record 16 million votes, compared to Cox's 9 million. Harding urged the country to seek "not heroism but healing, not nostrums but normalcy." No one had heard the word "normalcy" before the 1920 campaign, but everyone knew what Harding meant.

The Harding Administration

Harding's election began 12 years of Republican leadership. Throughout the 1920s, Republicans controlled both the presidency and Congress.

The affable Harding fit the image of President. Distinguished, gray-haired, and handsome, he cut an impressive figure. From a start as a small-town Ohio politician and newspaper editor, he had risen to the United States Senate. But as President, Harding often felt 3. inadequate, and he nearly worked himself to death trying to meet the demands of the office. Unfortunately, he was probably correct when he said, "I knew this job would be too much for me." Harding had created many of his own problems by appointing some of his poker-playing friends to major government positions.

The man who dominated Harding's administration, however, was not one of Harding's poker pals. He was the able Secretary of the Treasury Andrew Mellon, a wealthy banker and industrialist. Mellon shared the 4. pro-business stance of the Harding administration. Thus, he favored a high tariff that would protect American business from foreign competition. Accepting Mellon's view, Congress passed the Fordney-McCumber Act in 1922, raising tariffs to a new high.

Mellon also believed that taxes on large incomes should be cut. If taxes were lowered, he argued, the wealthy would have more money to invest. More investment would create more jobs, which would mean more income for middle- and lower-income people. A majority of Congress agreed with Mellon's reasoning. Congress passed the Revenue Act of 1921 and other new tax laws that slashed taxes on higher incomes.

3. **PRESIDENTS** Harding once said, "I listen to one side and they seem right. I talk to the other side and they seem just as right."

4. **BIOGRAPHY** Mellon donated his vast art collection to the public and helped endow Carnegie-Mellon University in Pittsburgh.

In his drive to promote efficiency and economy in government, Mellon instituted a much-needed budgeting process for government departments. Working with the new budget director, Charles Dawes, Mellon reduced the national debt and balanced the budget. Government expenses fell from $6.4 billion in 1920 to $2.9 billion in 1927.

The determination of the Harding administration to cut costs led to conflict with the American Legion and other veterans' groups. Many veterans wanted to be compensated for the money they could have earned as civilians instead of having served at low pay in the armed forces. In 1922, Congress passed a "bonus bill" to give veterans a bonus for every day they served. But Harding vetoed the bill as too costly. In 1924, however, Congress passed a bill over Harding's veto giving the average veteran about $1,000 worth of paid-up life insurance.

Corruption in Government

Although President Harding himself was honest, his administration was riddled with swindlers and corrupt officials. Attorney General Harry Daugherty and his friend Jesse Smith made fortunes selling government favors, immunities from prosecution, and pardons. Charles Forbes, head of the Veterans Bureau, sold shipments of bandages, drugs, and bedding and pocketed the money.

But the biggest scandal of Harding's tenure was the Teapot Dome affair. In 1921, Secretary of the Interior Albert B. Fall leased the navy's oil reserves at Teapot Dome, Wyoming, and Elk Hills, California, to two oil men, Harry F. Sinclair and Edward L. Doheny. In exchange for the oil reserves, Sinclair and Doheny "lent" Secretary Fall about $100,000 and made him "gifts" of over $300,000. Fall was sentenced to one year in jail for accepting the bribes, thus becoming the first cabinet officer in history to be sent to prison.

President Harding never learned the full extent of the corruption in his administration. He died of a heart attack on August 2, 1923. The task of restoring the nation's faith in government fell to his Vice President, Calvin Coolidge.

Calvin Coolidge

Calvin Coolidge took the oath of office, administered by his father, a justice of the peace, in the living room of the Vermont farmhouse that five generations of Coolidges had called home. Because the new President rarely smiled and spoke little, he struck people as cold. A college student once told Coolidge that she had bet her roommate that she could get him to say more than three words. "You lose," was Coolidge's reply.

Despite his reserved nature, Coolidge succeeded in restoring confidence in government. And no man was more committed to

President Harding posed with Madame Marie Curie (to his right) and a group of women visitors. Madame Curie, the great French scientist, won the Nobel Prize in 1911 for her work on radium. She toured the United States in 1921, accompanied by her daughters. The President presented her with a gram of radium, purchased with funds contributed by American women.

Who Says a Watched Pot Never Boils?

During the election of 1924, the Democrats tried to tie in Republican candidate Calvin Coolidge with the corruption that had stained the Harding
1. *administration. The political cartoon above refers to the Teapot Dome scandal, which involved the leasing of valuable government-owned oil fields by Harding cronies.*

1. **VISUAL EVIDENCE** Have students explain the meaning of the cartoon's caption.

the business community. "The man who builds a factory builds a temple," he commented. As the economy improved during the 1920s, Coolidge became more convinced that business principles should guide the United States. Thrilled by the nation's prosperity, Coolidge proudly proclaimed that "the business of America is business."

The Election of 1924

As the 1924 presidential election neared, a united Republican party nominated Coolidge. The Democrats, however, battled for 17 days in a July heat wave before agreeing on a can-

didate and a platform. Millions of Americans listened on a new contraption called the radio to the convention struggle between the rural followers of William Jennings Bryan and the urban supporters of Tammany Hall politicians from New York.

The most hotly contested issue at the Democratic convention was a proposed plank in the party platform condemning the Ku Klux Klan. The plank lost by just one vote out of more than 1,000 cast. After 103 ballots, the 2. exhausted Democrats nominated John W. Davis, a conservative corporate lawyer closely associated with Wall Street banking interests. Both parties thus chose candidates with a strong business orientation.

Dismayed by the conservatism of the candidates of the two major parties, farmers, social reformers, socialists, and progressives formed a new Progressive party and rallied behind the candidacy of Robert La Follette of Wisconsin. La Follette supported government ownership of railroads, abolition of child labor, and the right of unions to organize and engage in collective bargaining.

Americans voted overwhelmingly to "keep cool with Coolidge," giving him victory in 35 states. Davis won 12 states; La Follette won only his home state of Wisconsin.

Business Under Coolidge

Coolidge did not disappoint his supporters in the business community. In 1926, he signed a revenue act that drastically slashed taxes on high incomes. He appointed friends of business to run the Interstate Commerce Commission, the Federal Reserve Board, and the Federal Trade Commission, agencies that had been created to regulate business practices. (See pages 451, 511, and 513.) The President's appointments provoked progressive Senator George Norris of Nebraska to remark:

The effect of these appointments is to set 3. the country back more than twenty-five years. It is an indirect but positive repeal of congressional enactments, which no administration, however powerful, would dare to bring about by any direct means. It is the nullification of federal law by a process of boring from within.

576

3. **MAIN IDEA** Have students restate the quotation in their own words. Ask: In what sense was Coolidge's policy bringing about "the nullification of federal law"?

Nevertheless, Coolidge's pro-business program won widespread praise as the nation enjoyed a period of dazzling prosperity. Between 1921 and 1929, the output of industry nearly doubled. Profits and wages grew, and unemployment shrank. While not everyone became rich, more people could afford to buy more products than ever before.

The Farm Problem

Among those who did not share in the general prosperity of the 1920s were the nation's farmers. During the war, American farmers had increased production by planting more acres, and prices soared because of the great demand from Europe. When the war ended, European agriculture resumed production. In addition, increased harvests in nations such as Canada and Australia contributed to worldwide overproduction. As a result, crop prices fell sharply, while the prices farmers paid for seeds, fertilizer, farm machinery, and interest on their bank loans did not.

Caught in a painful squeeze, farmers looked to the federal government for help. Legislators from agricultural districts voted together as a "farm bloc" to pass bills that would help farmers. One such proposal was the McNary-Haugen bill.

The aim of the McNary-Haugen bill was to keep farmers' purchasing power constant, even if market prices dropped. The goal was **parity,** or equality, between farmers' standard of living in good years and their standard of living in bad years. The McNary-Haugen bill provided for the government to buy up surpluses of certain crops, such as wheat and corn, in bad years, and to sell them abroad. Thus, when the market price was low, farmers would receive a higher price, called a parity price, from the government.

President Coolidge vetoed the McNary-Haugen bill in 1927 and again in 1928, observing that "farmers have never made money." The overall prosperity of the 1920s hid the severity of the farm problem as well as other flaws in the economy.

2. VOCABULARY The word *bloc* originally indicated a temporary alliance. It has come to mean a group of legislators that cooperate on an issue without regard to party affiliations.

AMERICAN ENTERPRISE

A View of Business in the 1920s

When President Calvin Coolidge proclaimed that "the business of America is business," he was expressing the opinion of many people. Seldom in American history has the business community been so admired as during the 1920s. The extent of that admiration can be seen in the following excerpts from an article written by Edward E. Purinton in 1921.

Among the nations of the earth today American stands for one idea: *Business.* . . . Through business, properly conceived, managed, and conducted, the human race is finally to be redeemed. . . .

What is the finest game? Business. The soundest science? Business. . . . The fullest education? Business. The fairest opportunity? Business. . . . You may not agree. That is because you judge business by the crude, mean, stupid, false imitation of business that happens to be located near you.

The finest game is business. The rewards are for everybody, and all can win. There are no favorites. And in this game there is no "luck." The speed and size of your winnings are for you alone to decide.

The fullest education is business. A proper blend of study, work, and life is essential to advancement. . . . In the school of business, moreover, you teach yourself and learn most from your own mistakes. What you learn here you live out, the only real test.

See p. T106.

1. What is the author's attitude toward business?

2. Critical Thinking How does your attitude toward business compare to the author's?

3. CRITICAL THINKING Ask: Why does Purinton say that "the fullest education is business"? Do you agree or disagree? Explain.

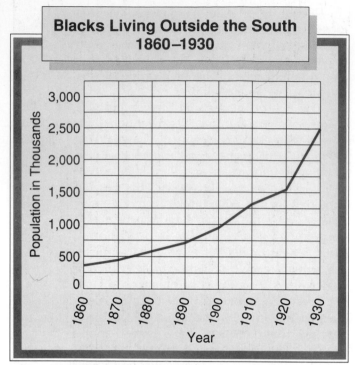

Blacks Living Outside the South 1860–1930

Population in Thousands (y-axis): 0, 500, 1,000, 1,500, 2,000, 2,500, 3,000

Year (x-axis): 1860, 1870, 1880, 1890, 1900, 1910, 1920, 1930

Source: United States Bureau of the Census   See p. T106.

GRAPH STUDY   *The exodus of black Americans from the South,*
1. *which began after the Civil War, picked up momentum around 1900. Most blacks moved to the North and the West for better jobs. Some, however, hoped to escape segregation. During what ten-year period did the number of blacks living outside the South increase the most?*
1. **GRAPH READING**   Ask: How many blacks lived outside the South in 1860? In 1900? In 1930?

Others Bypassed by Prosperity

The struggle of the farmers was matched by that of blacks and other minorities. Black sharecroppers* in the South were particularly hard hit. The boll weevil was destroying millions of acres of the South's main crop, cotton. At the same time, new synthetic fabrics such as rayon were competing with cotton and holding its price down.

Few blacks who fled to northern cities during the so-called Great Migration of the 1920s fared any better than those who remained in the South. Most labor unions excluded black workers, and blacks generally got only the lowest-paying jobs.

_____

*As you have read in Chapter 18, sharecroppers farmed someone else's land. They shared the crops they raised with the landowner.

The prosperity of the 1920s also bypassed Indians and Mexican immigrants. The authors of the Dawes Act of 1887 had hoped to see Indians assimilated into the general population. (See page 410.) But that did not happen. Instead, Indians lost over 60 percent of the land they had owned before 1887. Furthermore, the Dawes Act weakened Indian culture and traditions. A 1926 report on conditions among Indians declared that a majority were "extremely poor" and suffered from poor health and inadequate education.

In 1900, about 100,000 people of Mexican birth were living in the Southwest. During the period of the Mexican Revolution, from 1910 to 1917, many more Mexicans fled to the United States. By 1930, more than one million Mexicans had crossed the border.

Mexicans were drawn to the United States by jobs in the vegetable fields, orchards, and factories of the Southwest. Mexican workers lived under difficult conditions. Many were 2. **migrant workers,** who traveled from farm to farm, employed only as long as necessary to harvest a crop. Usually receiving very low wages, these migrant workers could find only squalid housing. Others were factory workers, crowded into the most dilapidated, poverty-stricken districts of cities. For most, prosperity remained only a dream.

See p. T106.

SECTION 2 REVIEW

1. **Identify:**   (a) Warren G. Harding, (b) Andrew Mellon, (c) Fordney-McCumber Act, (d) McNary-Haugen bill.

2. **Define:**   (a) normalcy, (b) parity, (c) migrant worker.

3. What were the key features of Andrew Mellon's economic program?

4. Describe three scandals that tarnished the Harding administration.

5. How did Calvin Coolidge's administration support business?

6. How did some groups miss out on the prosperity of the 1920s?

7. **Critical Thinking**   What conditions affecting farm income are largely beyond the control of farmers?

578

2. **PAST AND PRESENT**   Have students use the *Readers' Guide* to learn about migrant workers today. Ask: How has life changed for these workers since the 1920s?

1. **VOCABULARY** Have students look up these terms in the glossary before they begin reading.

3 A Decade of Material Progress

READD TO UNDERSTAND

- ■ Why industry became more efficient in the 1920s.

- ■ What Henry Ford contributed to industry.

- ■ How the automobile changed American life.

1. ■ *Vocabulary:* scientific management, assembly line.

For thousands of American families in the 1920s, the replacement of an old-fashioned icebox with a modern electric refrigerator was an important step on the road to a better life. Factories poured out a steady stream of consumer products, and for a time increasing numbers of people could afford them. The 1920s also saw industrial innovations and improved technology increase productivity and the nation's material wealth.

A Surge of Electrical Power

After 1900, the output of electricity soared as a result of new production methods that made more efficient use of coal. Between 1902 and 1929, the production of electric power increased by 19 times. Increased electric output not only boosted industrial production, it also made home life more pleasant. While only 20 percent of American homes had electricity before World War I, by the late 1920s, 70 percent were electrified.

Abundant electricity allowed Americans to enjoy a wide range of consumer goods. Refrigerators, washing machines, vacuum cleaners, and other new appliances helped to transform American homes during the 1920s. Annual sales of major household appliances more than doubled during the decade.

2. **DISCUSSION** Have students imagine how their lives would change if they had to go a week without electricity.

More Efficient Industry

Although the number of industrial workers remained the same, the production of goods in the United States increased 25 percent between 1921 and 1928. The growing use of electrically powered equipment was partially

3. **ACTIVITY** Ask students to try applying scientific management techniques to an everyday activity, such as dressing or brushing their teeth.

responsible. Electric power enabled a worker to do more in less time. Between 1920 and 1929, output per working hour went up 35 percent, twice the increase of the previous decade.

Scientific management, the systematic study and improvement of worker efficiency, also made industry more productive. The leading advocate of scientific management was Frederick W. Taylor. Taylor conducted careful time-and-motion studies. For example, he might count the number of steps a worker took to perform a job or note how often a worker picked up a particular tool. Taylor would then redesign the work space or the work pattern to eliminate useless steps. Factories that followed Taylor's suggestions were able to boost output by as much as 300 percent with no increase in the work force. Although Taylor died in 1915, other "efficiency experts" continued to apply his scientific management methods in the 1920s.

4. **VISUAL EVIDENCE** Ask: How is the human worker pictured? What is his relationship to the machinery?

Improved technology and management methods increased business productivity in the 1920s. Advertisements hailed the up-to-date machinery used in the manufacturing process. Machinery itself was glorified by artists, as can be seen in this painting by Paul Kelpe.

1. **DISCUSSION** Ford reduced working hours and raised wages of his employees. Ask: Why do you think Ford was able to make these concessions to workers?

Henry Ford

Henry Ford was an industrialist who applied electric power and scientific management to the production of an item the public wanted to buy. In doing so, he revolutionized the automobile industry.

In 1914, Ford introduced an electrically powered assembly line at his Highland Park, Michigan, plant. On the **assembly line,** workers stood at their work stations while unfinished cars moved past them on a conveyor belt. Each worker performed one simple task on each car as it passed by. Ford's efficiency experts determined what each individual task should be and how long it should take. A Model T Ford, which had taken 14 hours to complete in 1913, was now being built in 93 minutes.

Ford believed that more people would buy a car if the price was low. With his efficient assembly lines, Ford could produce cars inexpensively. In 1914, a new Model T sold for $490. By 1924, Ford had reduced the price to $260, and a car rolled out of a Ford plant every ten seconds. Although the Model T

2. **VISUAL EVIDENCE** The man in the straw hat is a government inspector checking the safety of the pump.

Early motorists carried a can of gasoline to refuel their cars. Soon, "filling stations" like this one sprang up along American roads to service the growing numbers of automobiles. In 1920, when this picture was taken, there were about 1,500 filling stations. By 1929, there were more than 120,000.

3. **ECONOMICS** Ford's main competitor was General Motors, founded by William C. Durant. G.M. won customers by offering a choice of colors.

came in only one color—black—people flocked to Ford showrooms.

As other automobile manufacturers instituted Ford's techniques, the industry prospered. The annual production of American cars soared from 4,000 in 1900 to 4.8 million in 1929.

The Impact of the Automobile

About 9 million automobiles were registered in the United States in 1920. By 1930, registrations had more than tripled. These millions of new cars created new demands. In 1920, highways were often nothing more than rutted dirt roads, and driving was often hazardous. In 1921, Congress passed the Federal Highway Act to encourage road building. State governments imposed taxes on gasoline to raise money for highway construction. As a result of these efforts, surfaced road mileage in the United States almost doubled between 1921 and 1929. The Bronx River Parkway, which opened in New York in 1927, was the first of many limited-access highways in parklike settings.

With good roads, car owners no longer found it necessary to live close to their jobs in the city. The new mobility caused a surge in the growth of suburbs. For example, during the 1920s, the population of Cleveland's suburb of Shaker Heights increased tenfold, and the population of Scarsdale, a New York City suburb, nearly tripled.

An offshoot of the booming suburbs was a demand for homes, schools, churches, libraries, and stores. New construction provided work for many thousands of carpenters, bricklayers, masons, and other skilled workers.

Automobile production also generated jobs in industries that supplied materials used to build cars, including the rubber, steel, and glass industries. New roadside food stands and tourist cabins met the needs of motorists. By 1930, one out of nine workers had a job related to the automobile industry. Each new industry, in turn, generated more jobs, providing workers with money to spend on goods such as sewing machines, refrigerators, and, of course, cars.

4. **BACKGROUND** Other brand names of cars came from pioneers of the auto industry—Ransom Olds, James Packard, Louis Chevrolet, and David Buick.

5. **TECHNOLOGY** Cars weighed more than carriages and buggies and often bogged down in mud. This prompted many communities to pave roads.

See p. T107.

SECTION 3 REVIEW

1. **Identify:** (a) Frederick W. Taylor, (b) Henry Ford.

2. **Define:** (a) scientific management, (b) assembly line.

3. How did Frederick Taylor's studies have an impact on productivity?

4. How did Henry Ford revolutionize the automobile industry?

5. Describe two ways in which the automobile changed American life.

6. **Critical Thinking** Name one industry other than the automobile industry that has had a major impact on society. Explain your choice.

1. **VOCABULARY** Have students look up this word in the glossary before they begin reading.

4 The Jazz Age

READ TO UNDERSTAND

■ Why the 1920s were called the Jazz Age.

■ How the black community reflected the spirit of the Jazz Age.

■ What effect the 1920s had on art and literature.

1. ■ *Vocabulary:* expatriate.

The novelist F. Scott Fitzgerald called the period between the war and 1929 the Jazz Age. "My candle burns at both ends," wrote Edna St. Vincent Millay, offering an image that captured the restless spirit of the 1920s. This was the decade in which the world discovered American jazz and when American playwrights, novelists, and poets created enduring works of art that also reflected the spirit of the times.

Jazz—the American Sound

Of all the music that poured from the radio, none was more uniquely American, more original, or more controversial than jazz.

3. **ACTIVITY** Play the class several recordings of early jazz or blues. Ask students to compare it with today's popular music.

2. **BIOGRAPHY** Bessie Smith (1898?–1937) was known as "Empress of the Blues" to her devoted fans. Her first recording, "Down Hearted Blues," sold over 2 million copies.

Born in New Orleans, jazz blended West African rhythms, black work songs and spirituals, and European harmonies. Jazz also had roots in the ragtime rhythms of composers like Scott Joplin as well as in another United States creation, the blues. Musicians improvised on a theme to make jazz what it was: flexible, alive, and ever-changing.

The first great jazz musicians were black. They included composer "Jelly Roll" Morton, singer Bessie Smith, and trumpet player, singer, and improviser Louis Armstrong. Jazz soon transcended color, however, and musicians of all backgrounds adopted it.

2.

3.

Jazz spread from New Orleans to Chicago, Kansas City, and the black section of New York City known as Harlem. One of the many black musicians who performed there was Duke Ellington. His jazz band played at the well-known Cotton Club.

The Harlem Renaissance

Jazz found a warm reception in Harlem. Harlem was the black cultural capital of the United States and home to many black musicians, writers, artists, and performers. During the 1920s, their work produced a flowering of creativity that became known as the Harlem Renaissance.

While jazz celebrated liberation, much of the poetry of the Harlem Renaissance protested the prejudice of white America. Poet Langston Hughes, probably the best-known figure of the Harlem Renaissance, proudly reminded his readers of black Americans' African heritage. Countee Cullen, a Harvard graduate and New York City schoolteacher, also wrote poems that swelled with black pride, as did Claude McKay. McKay's powerful verse cast a penetrating light on the problem of discrimination in the United States.

4.

Other figures of the Harlem Renaissance wrote scholarly books and articles about black Americans. Carter G. Woodson, a pioneer in the field of black history and the founder of Black History Week (later Black History Month), established the *Journal of Negro History* in 1916. W.E.B. Du Bois (see pages 456 and 495) wrote about the history of black people. As one of the leaders of the National Association for the Advancement of **581**

4. **READING** Students might like to read works by writers of the Harlem Renaissance. Suggest "If We Must Die" by Claude McKay or a poem by Langston Hughes.

Colored People, he believed that blacks should work within the system in fighting for equal rights.

Marcus Garvey offered another route to black fulfillment. Garvey, who came to New York from Jamaica in 1916, advocated black pride and held that blacks must rely on themselves for their salvation. This would not come in the United States, he claimed. Therefore, he urged American blacks to go "back to Africa" to set up a nation there.

Garvey's weekly paper, *Negro World,* spread the message of pride and tried to popularize the idea of returning to Africa. Although Garvey never did establish an American black community in Africa, a new self-awareness affected African Americans.

1. **VISUAL EVIDENCE** Ask: Why do you think paintings such as this one outraged so many Americans?

1. *Pablo Picasso was the most influential artist of the 1900s. One of the founders of cubism, he experimented with many different styles in his long career. The harlequin, or clown, seen in this cubist work, is one of many that Picasso painted. In some, Picasso painted his own face on the clown.*

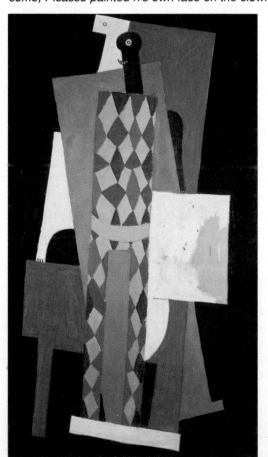

582

Modern Art

On February 17, 1913, a huge art show opened 2. at the 69th Regiment Armory in New York City. The Armory Show had "The New Spirit" for its motto. The exhibition was the first major display of modern art in the United States. It immediately became the subject of a public outcry.

While traditional European and American 3. artists tried in some ways to represent reality in their work, modern artists let their imaginations roam more widely. Much of modern art is abstract. For example, Pablo Picasso, a Spanish artist, painted his figures in geometric shapes: cubes, spheres, and cones.

The new styles of work shocked and angered many art lovers. An abstract painting by Marcel Duchamp titled *Nude Descending a Staircase* became the object of countless jokes. One skeptic parodied Duchamp's work by painting *The Rude Descending a Staircase,* a rather jumbled picture of the New York subway at rush hour.

Although modern art remained controversial, by the 1920s, many American artists and critics began to accept the new forms. In 1929, the Museum of Modern Art opened in New York City and its exhibits began to bridge the gap between traditional and modern art. It displayed not only paintings and sculpture but also the work of architects, designers, photographers, and filmmakers. It thus helped the public understand that these fields were also "art."

While the museum tried to define art trends, individual painters pursued their own visions, sometimes far outside the "modern" framework. Edward Hopper's landscapes captured both the isolation of rural farmhouses and the lonely anonymity of big cities. Grant Wood painted scenes of rural America, including his memorable portrait of a somber farm couple, *American Gothic* (1930). Georgia O'Keeffe celebrated urban landscapes of skyscrapers before turning to southwestern themes. These artists and many others helped capture the spirit of the age.

The Lost Generation

While the nation was enjoying the prosperity of the 1920s, some of its most prominent writers were expressing disillusionment. Horri-

3. **CRITICAL THINKING** Ask: Do you think the development of photography in the 1800s affected the growth of nonrealistic painting? Explain.

1. Grant Wood studied painting in Paris but returned to his native Iowa, where he found the inspiration for much of his work. This detail of the picture Dinner for Threshers depicts farm workers enjoying a hearty dinner after a long day in the fields. Wood was one of a group of artists known as the American Scene realists.

1. **VISUAL EVIDENCE** This painting is autobiographical. Wood was depicting the kind of threshing dinners he had attended as a young boy in Iowa.

3. **VOCABULARY** The word *babbitt* became a popular term for any self-satisfied, small-minded businessman.

fied by the devastation of World War I, these writers had come to distrust the ideas and values of the past. At the same time, they rejected the emphasis on pleasure that had emerged after the war. In their works, these writers painted a picture of an uncertain, meaningless world.

Many American writers of the period became **expatriates,** leaving the United States and settling in Europe, sometimes permanently. One of the most influential expatriates was Gertrude Stein, who coined the phrase "Lost Generation" to describe those who shared her sense of detachment. Stein's Paris home became a refuge for many other American writers, including Sherwood Anderson, Ernest Hemingway, and F. Scott Fitzgerald.

During the 1920s, both Hemingway and Fitzgerald earned international acclaim with 2. their works about contemporary life. In his novel *The Sun Also Rises* (1926), Hemingway depicts a group of British and American expatriates seeking to escape from their unbearable sense of uncertainly and inner despair. Fitgerald's novel *The Great Gatsby* (1926) tells of a self-made tycoon's tragic quest to live the American dream.

Many other members of the Lost Generation also earned lasting reputations. Sinclair Lewis became the first American writer to 3. earn the Nobel Prize in literature. His novels, including *Main Street* (1920) and *Babbitt* (1922), satirized the smugness and material-

ism of the period. The brilliant American poet T. S. Eliot wrote *The Waste Land* (1922), a complex and lengthy poem that expressed his view of contemporary society as fragmented and empty. Eugene O'Neill wrote eighteen plays during the 1920s and earned four Pulitzer Prizes by writing dramas in which he exposed the uncontrollable inner selves of his characters.

See p. T107.

SECTION 4 REVIEW

1. **Identify:** (a) Harlem Renaissance, (b) Langston Hughes, (c) Marcus Garvey, (d) Gertrude Stein, (e) Ernest Hemingway, (f) F. Scott Fitzgerald, (g) Sinclair Lewis, (h) T. S. Eliot.

2. **Define:** expatriate.

3. (a) What were the origins of jazz? (b) Why did the music give its name to an era?

4. How did blacks contribute to the culture of the 1920s?

5. (a) How did art reflect the trends of the 1920s? (b) How did the Lost Generation react to the prosperity of the 1920s?

6. **Critical Thinking** How do art, music, and literature today reflect the values and ideals of contemporary society?

583

2. **READING** Interested students can read a short story by Hemingway, such as "A Day's Wait," "Old Man at the Bridge," or "A Clean, Well-Lighted Place."

1. **VOCABULARY** Have students look up this word in the glossary before they begin reading.

2. **DISCUSSION** Lead a discussion on the ways in which the radio brought the nation closer together and helped foster a national culture.

5 Changing Times

READ TO UNDERSTAND

■ What new forms popular entertainment took.

■ How people reacted to changes in society.

■ How the lives of women changed in the 1920s.

1. ■ *Vocabulary:* flapper.

During the 1920s, millions of Americans gathered around the radio in the evening to listen to their favorite programs. On Friday or Saturday night, they hopped in their cars to drive to the local movie theater to see the latest film. These experiences helped to shape a new popular culture in America, one that celebrated new heroes and enjoyed new fads. Yet not everyone approved. Newly emerging values challenged the religious and moral beliefs of many Americans, who struggled to defend the traditional vision of America.

Radio

Although experimental radio stations had begun to broadcast around 1915, the radio audience before 1920 was composed mainly of hobbyists who built their own radios. In November 1920, station KDKA in Pittsburgh made the first commercial broadcast, a transmission of the presidential election returns. In 1921, those who had radios could hear a blow-by-blow account of the heavyweight fight between Jack Dempsey and the French war hero Georges Carpentier and a play-by-play account of the World Series. By 1924, millions of Americans were able to tune in to the Democratic convention.

2. The popularity of radio spread across the United States with stunning speed. Two years after the first commercial broadcast, annual sales of radios totaled $60 million. By 1929, $843 million was being spent annually on radios and about 40 percent of American homes had one. The government began assigning wavelengths to stations in 1927. A new style of life developed as families gathered together to listen to the radio after dinner. Favorite programs included comedy series, popular and classical music, news reports, and sports broadcasts.

The Movies

The motion picture also became a popular pastime during the 1920s. In Hollywood, the newly established movie capital of the world, movie studios turned out hundreds of films that transported viewers to a world of glamour, romance, and adventure. The age of the movie star began as Clara Bow, John Barrymore, Mary Pickford, Gloria Swanson, Greta Garbo, Charles Chaplin, Lillian Gish, and many others became celebrities. Audiences thrilled to the fearless exploits of Douglas Fairbanks in *The Three Musketeers* (1921) and adored the romantic Rudolph Valentino in *The Sheik* (1921). In the "westerns," actors such as Tom Mix and William S. Hart played tight-lipped, heroic cowboys.

3. Until 1927, movies were silent—they had no sound track. Audiences read title cards that appeared on the screen to follow the plot, while an organist or pianist played background music. Then, on October 6, 1927, with 4. *The Jazz Singer,* the talking movie appeared. The great success of *The Jazz Singer,* starring Al Jolson, signaled the end of the silent era. Audiences delighted in the new "talkies." Movie attendance rose from 60 million paid admissions per week in 1927 to 110 million per week in 1929.

Heroes and Fads

Radio was even more accessible to the public than movies and brought nearly immediate reports of news into millions of homes. This era of improved communication helped create instant heroes and fads.

In 1926, after Gertrude Ederle became the first woman to swim the English Channel, her home town of New York City gave her a ticker tape* parade. A year later, an even larger parade welcomed aviator Charles A. Lindbergh.

---

*Offices in the Wall Street area were equipped with ticker tape machines, devices that record telegraphed stock quotations on strips of paper or tape. During a ticker tape parade, office workers would throw shreds of ticker tape out of windows.

3. **TECHNOLOGY** Ask if any students have seen a silent movie. Have them describe their impressions to the class.

4. **BACKGROUND** The first words Jolson spoke in *The Jazz Singer* were prophetic: "You ain't heard nothin' yet!"

In May 1927, news of Lindbergh's solo nonstop flight across the Atlantic captivated Americans. Upon his return, New Yorkers gave him a tumultuous welcome. Newspapers estimated that street cleaners swept up 1,800 tons (about 1,600 metric tons) of paper after Lindbergh's ticker tape parade. Lindbergh became the hero of the decade, widely admired for his skill and modesty.

1. Sports greats such as auto racer Barney Oldfield, tennis player Helen Wills, and boxer Jack Dempsey also captured the imaginations of many Americans. Fans filled major league baseball stadiums to see Babe Ruth, Ty Cobb, and other stars. College football, with stars like Red Grange, also drew thousands of spectators. Sports events of all kinds—horse and auto racing, tennis, and golf, among others—enjoyed rising attendance.

When Lindbergh returned to the United States, the 3. acclaim was even greater than it had been in Europe. This ticker tape parade in New York City was one of several parades in his honor.

3. **READING** Interested students can read Lindbergh's autobiography, *The Spirit of St. Louis*.

Prohibition

While radio and movies were celebrating the culture of the time, others in America were debating the nation's cultural values. A long-running debate of the 1920s involved the prohibition of alcohol. Ever since the mid-1800s, reformers had preached against the evils of liquor and had demanded that its manufacture be outlawed. This "temperance movement" gained momentum during World War I, on the grounds that banning liquor would save much-needed grain.

In 1917, Congress approved the Eighteenth Amendment, which prohibited the manufacture, sale, and transportation of alcoholic beverages. The so-called Prohibition Amendment was ratified by the states in January 1919, and Congress passed the Volstead Act to enforce it.

Although the nation became officially "dry," violation of the law was widespread throughout the 1920s. Many people had no intention of giving up beer, wine, and liquor.

2. "Bootleggers" smuggled large amounts of "booze" into the United States to satisfy the demand. Much of the trade in liquor was carried on by gangsters, who waged gang wars over distribution rights in their "territories." Drinkers could buy booze in illegal nightclubs, known as "speakeasies" because customers had to whisper a password to get in. Efforts

to enforce the law were largely futile, and by 1930 most Americans agreed that prohibition had failed. A strong sentiment developed for repealing the Eighteenth Amendment.

In Defense of Traditional Values

The debate over prohibition reflected a concern of many Americans. Millions of Americans, especially those living in small towns and rural areas, believed that the rapid social and economic changes of the years that were called the Roaring Twenties were destroying a way of life. To counteract what they considered an immoral force, these people worked to strengthen and defend their own values.

Church membership grew throughout the 4. 1920s, and books on religion multiplied. Revival meetings attracted large audiences. All over the nation, people went to church socials, rodeos, and country fairs—pastimes far removed from city life. To many Americans, Henry Ford represented the strength of traditional values. He had risen from modest origins. Even as a rich man, he championed the values of honesty and thrift. At his museum at Dearborn Village, Ford tried to preserve rural life. Yet because Ford fiercely resisted labor unions and financed an anti- **585**

2. **VOCABULARY** The term *bootlegger* was first used in the 1850s to refer to someone who smuggled illegal whiskey in a tall boot.

4. **ACTIVITY** The Scopes trial of 1925 showed the conflict between traditional values and new ideas. Interested students might research and report on the Scopes trial.

THE AMERICAN EXPERIENCE

Izzy and Moe: Prohibition Agents

Music wafted from a New York speakeasy. The doorman peered through the peephole. Outside, a fat man clutched a pail of dill pickles. Although the doorman did not recognize the fellow, he opened the door. Who could suspect a person selling pickles? The pickle salesman, however, was a federal prohibition agent. It was his duty to enforce the Eighteenth Amendment to the Constitution, which prohibited making, selling, or transporting alcoholic beverages.

Isadore "Izzy" Einstein stood five feet, five inches tall and weighed 225 pounds. His partner, Moe Smith, was a bit taller and heavier. They frequently made newspaper headlines as the zaniest and most effective prohibition agents in the country.

Izzy Einstein was a master of disguise. He could move easily through New York's diverse neighborhoods, for he spoke five languages fluently and was comfortable in four others. On the waterfront, he would dress as a fisherman, lugging along a string of fish.

Between them, Izzy and Moe made more than 4,000 arrests. In their five-year career, they seized $15-million worth of alcohol and much equipment for making alcohol. Few agents could approach their record of success.

1. By the mid-1920s, bootlegging, the illegal manufacture and sale of alcohol, was a billion-dollar-a-year business in the United States.

About half a million people took part in bootleg operations. Fleets of boats brought alcohol across the Great Lakes from Canada. Rum-runners from Cuba landed easily on the long coastline of Florida. Cars with "booze" hidden in false bottoms crossed the Mexican border. Thousands of backyard stills turned out home-brewed concoctions. Fifteen hundred federal prohibition agents were charged with shutting down these diverse operations. They had an entire country to patrol.

Izzy and Moe went from city to city. On the road, Izzy timed how long it took a stranger (himself) to find and buy an illegal drink. His report: New Orleans, 35 seconds; Pittsburgh, 11 minutes; Atlanta, 17 minutes; Washington, D.C., one hour. His experience showed that, while millions of Americans might support prohibition, millions more—including many elected officials and police officers—opposed it and openly flouted the law. When Izzy wrote a book about his exploits, he dedicated it "to the 4,392 persons I arrested, hoping they bear me no grudge for having done my duty."

See p. T108.

1. What accounted for Izzy and Moe's successful apprehension of many bootleggers?

2. **Critical Thinking** Why do you think prohibition was called a "noble experiment," but was repealed?

1. PAST AND PRESENT Have interested students research current activities and policies of the League of Women Voters and report their findings to the class.

Semitic newspaper, many Americans rejected his example.

Changes for Women

As American society modernized in the 1920s, the lives of women underwent changes that were more social than economic or political. In 1920, women had won the right to vote under the Nineteenth Amendment. (See page 892.) Many reformers believed that this victory would usher in an age of complete equality, but they were wrong. Women did not concentrate their newly gained political power on women's rights causes or candidates. The League of Women Voters, for example, supported a wide range of reform measures, not just "women's" issues.

Few women achieved economic independence in the 1920s. Although more women were working outside the home, they received far from equal treatment in the job market, and usually held jobs with low pay and little prestige. Most married women, whether they worked outside the home or not, continued to bear the responsibility of running the home. Homemakers did, however, find some of their tasks simplified by new electrical appliances and by a trend to smaller houses and apartments.

One aspect of the changed status of women in the 1920s was symbolized by the **flapper.** The flapper was a new woman, restless, always on the move, eager to try something different. She shocked her elders—and many of her contemporaries—with her clothes, her slang, her dancing, and her refusal to follow traditional rules.

Clothes were the outward expression of the flapper's defiance of tradition. Unlike her mother, she refused to wear petticoats or squeeze into a corset. She shocked her elders by shortening her skirts right up to her knees and rolling her stockings (silk, not cotton) down to meet them. She "bobbed" her hair short for comfort and simplicity. And while the well-bred woman of an earlier age rarely "painted" her face, the flapper wore bright red lipstick. She even smoked cigarettes and drank liquor in public. Yet the flapper was more than a giddy symbol of the Jazz Age. She also represented the new social freedom of women.

After winning the right to vote in 1920, young women took up the free style of dress and conduct that made the "flapper" the symbol of the age. Flappers were celebrated in story, song, and movies. Many women maintained their traditional values, but even they might imagine themselves in the place of the flapper on this magazine cover of the 1920s.

See p. T108.

SECTION 5 REVIEW

1. **Identify:** (a) *The Jazz Singer,* (b) Gertrude Ederle, (c) Charles A. Lindbergh, (d) Eighteenth Amendment, (e) League of Women Voters.

2. **Define:** flapper.

3. How did the radio affect American life?

4. How did Americans respond to the changing values of the period?

5. What kinds of change did women experience during the 1920s?

6. **Critical Thinking** How can material progress benefit a society? How can it harm a society?

587

2. VISUAL EVIDENCE This cover was illustrated by John Held, Jr. His popular drawings of flappers in the 1920s influenced more young women to take up the "shocking" new styles and manners.

Summary

1. **The years immediately after World War I were a troublesome time in American life.** Veterans had difficulty finding jobs, and labor unrest spread. A rash of strikes and concern that the Russian communists would start a world revolution led to a Red Scare. Anti-immigrant, anti-radical, and anti-black sentiment influenced the times.

2. **Under President Coolidge, the nation enjoyed a period of "normalcy."** Despite the corruption of the Harding administration, business prospered. Prosperity generally missed farmers, blacks, Indians, and Mexican immigrants, however.

3. **The 1920s were years of impressive material progress.** The use of electric power increased, and industry became more efficient. Factories produced large quantities of consumer goods, especially electrical appliances for household use. The automobile industry grew rapidly, thanks largely to Henry Ford's assembly line.

4. **The restless 1920s were known as the Jazz Age.** The period saw the flourishing of black culture with the Harlem Renaissance. It also saw the flowering of art and literature. Some of the best American writers criticized the materialism they saw in modern society.

5. **The 1920s saw changes in the culture and values of many Americans.** Radio and motion pictures became popular forms of entertainment and contributed to changing values. Yet while many Americans accepted the new values, others maintained their traditional beliefs. Women achieved social gains, but were still not equal economically.

See p. T108.

Vocabulary

Match each term at left with its definition or description at right.

1. general strike
2. quota system
3. migrant worker
4. assembly line
5. expatriate

a. person who goes to live in another country

b. plan to curb immigration

c. walkout by members of all unions at once

d. continuous factory process with specialized tasks for workers

e. worker who travels from farm to farm

See p. T108.

Chapter Checkup

1. (a) What economic problems did the United States face when World War I ended? (b) How did those problems cause social tensions?

2. (a) What developments contributed to anti-foreign feeling after the war? (b) How did the immigration acts of 1921, 1924, and 1929 affect the number and origin of immigrants who came to the United States?

3. (a) Identify the pro-business actions of the Harding administration. (b) Of the Coolidge administration. (c) How did progressives such as George Norris react to the government's pro-business policies?

4. (a) Why were the 1920s a difficult time for farmers? (b) How did President Coolidge regard the farmers' problems?

5. (a) How did the use of electricity change American home life between 1900 and 1930? (b) How did it affect industry?

6. What were the major themes of the Harlem Renaissance?

7. (a) Who were the Lost Generation? (b) What were the main ideas they expressed?

8. Explain how each of the following contributed to changes in American life during the 1920s: (a) radio; (b) motion pictures; (c) prohibition.

See p. T108.

Critical Thinking

1. **Analyzing** (a) List the actions taken during the Harding and Coolidge administrations that could be considered pro-business. (b) Describe how you believe each action would help business.

2. **Supporting a Point of View** (a) How did the writers of the Lost Generation describe the America of the 1920s? (b) Do you agree or disagree with their assessment? Write a paragraph, citing specific examples, to support your point of view.

3. **Identifying Supporting Details** (a) How might you explain the growth in the popularity of radio during the 1920s? (b) What evidence of that growth can you cite?

See p. T109.

Connecting Past and Present

1. Federal laws give unions greater protection today than in the 1920s. (a) Describe the importance of unions in our economic and social life. (b) Why have recent years been hard on unions?

2. Consider the role that television plays in contemporary society. (a) In what ways do you think radio played a similar role in the 1920s? (b) How has the role of radio changed since the 1920s?

See p. T109.

Developing Basic Skills

1. **Graph Reading** Compare the graphs on immigration on pages 474 and 572. (a) From which region did the largest percentage of immigrants come between 1900 and 1920? (b) How did the origin of immigrants to the United States change since the 1840s?

2. **Using Primary Sources** Studying works of art or literature can help you understand the time in which the painter or poet lived. Choose an artist or writer who was active during the 1920s and study one of his or her works. Write a report in which you explain what you learned about the 1920s from the work.

WRITING ABOUT HISTORY

Taking Notes

If you have followed the suggestions in the previous lessons, you are now ready to begin serious note-taking. Compare your bibliography cards with your preliminary outline and select the sources you think will be most relevant. Use a separate note card for each source and for different subjects from the same source. Write the subject in the right-hand corner so you will be able to organize the cards according to your outline. In the upper left-hand corner, write the title, author, and publishing information you will need for footnotes. Record the pages from which you have obtained each fact, idea, or quotation. Write notes on the front of the card only.

Practice: Write a sample note card on the subject "American culture." Use your textbook as the source.

Sports in America

On July 21, 1921, some 91,000 spectators poured into Boyle's Thirty Acres in Jersey City, New Jersey, to see Jack Dempsey knock out "Gorgeous" Georges Carpentier in the fourth round. That was boxing's first million dollar gate—the first time Americans had spent $1 million to watch a single sporting event. Again that year, crowds broke records to see the New York Yankees' Babe Ruth hit 59 home runs and the New York Giants beat the New York Yankees in the World Series. Each Saturday afternoon in the fall, thousands of fans flocked into huge new college football stadiums to cheer on their heroes. The United States had entered the Golden Age of Sports.

Americans had not always had such a passion for games. In the colonial era,

1. **VISUAL EVIDENCE** Have students compare this magazine cover to the one on p. 587.

---

1. *Women's new role in society—and their less confining clothing—drew them into outdoor sports. America's best woman golfer in the 1920s was Glenna Collett. She won six U.S. National Amateur women's championships, more than any other golfer, male or female, has ever won.*

Distance Lends Enchantment

Puritan ministers preached against "gaming," or playing games for stakes. "The path of amusement can become the broadway to destruction," warned the *New York Magazine* in the 1700s. James Fenimore Cooper, the nineteenth-century novelist, still felt it necessary to caution that time devoted to games and relaxation was time "misspent."

Disapproval of idleness and games reflected the realities of life in pre-industrial America. Faced with obtaining the necessities of life by their own hand, Americans had little time for recreation. Work was the key to survival. "Contests" and "bees" such as corn huskings and log rollings were fun and provided sport, but work, not recreation, was their main purpose.

With the onset of the Industrial Revolution in the mid-1800s, a higher standard of living and more leisure time transformed Americans' dim view of recreation. Foreign travelers reported that ordinary Americans were much taken with "amusements, spectacles, and distractions." Moralists now worried that with less physically demanding labor, people would lose their "muscular vigor." "Who, in this community, really takes physical exercise?" one concerned writer asked in 1858. He urged his readers to take up the strenuous activities of their childhood.

Development of Sports The rapid growth of factories and cities after the Civil War further spurred the development of sports. By the late 1800s, football, baseball, ice hockey, track and field, golf, and tennis had taken root. To keep active in winter, Americans even invented an indoor sport—basketball. Newly formed associations set up rules for amateur and professional sports. *Strike, ball,* and *foul* took on new meanings. Newspapers fueled public interest with vivid reports of the latest games.

"The craze for sports, contents, and 'events' is a feature of the modern world," one writer of the 1880s observed.

The sports craze kept pace with the rapid spread of industry. By the 1920s, the average American family spent only half of its income for the necessities of life, and the average work week was down to 48 hours. The stage was set for a new era—the Golden Age of Sports. Record numbers of people participated in sports. Even greater numbers of Americans became spectators at sports events.

Sports and American Values Sports were looked on as a training ground for life. In 1911, Albert Spaulding, a former baseball player and an organizer of the National League, claimed that the person who achieves as an athlete "has within him the elements of pronounced success in other walks of life." He proclaimed baseball the "national game" because "it is the exponent of American courage, confidence, combativeness; American dash, discipline, determination; American energy, eagerness, enthusiasm; American pluck, persistency, performance; American spirit, sagacity, success; American vim, vigor, virility."

For some, sports were expressions of traditional values. Roderick Nash, a historian, claims that during the 1920s, sports provided "living testimony of the power of courage, strength, and honor of the self-reliant individual." "The athletic hero," he explains, "was the twentieth-century equivalent of the pathfinder or pioneer."

Equally important, sports provided a common ground for *all* individuals to achieve. In 1947, Jackie Robinson became the first black athlete to play in the major leagues. This breakthrough marked the beginning of racial integration in many other sports as well. A significant gain for women came in the Educational Amendment Act of 1972. It signaled that schools would have to devote more money to women's sports than they had in the past.

Sports Today Americans still have a passion for sports. And they still embrace sports as an antidote to the problems of

Although prejudice was still an obstacle for black athletes, Jesse Owens (at left) thrilled the world at the 1936 Olympic Games held in Berlin. His three gold medals struck a blow against the "master race" theories of Adolf Hitler. Hitler left the stadium rather than be present for the ceremony giving Owens his medals.

1. **BACKGROUND** Some black athletes had considered boycotting the 1936 Olympics to protest Hitler's racist policies as well as discrimination in the U.S.

society. In the 1980s, Americans have made great strides in achieving physical health through sports. Popular magazines feature articles on the "fitness craze," and shopping malls all over the country have stores devoted solely to sporting goods. But some old and new questions still remain. How can schools best integrate sports and study? Have sports become too commercial? Should we expect professional athletes to serve as role models? These and other questions deserve attention because the influence of sports and sports figures on American life cannot be ignored.

See p. T109.

1. Why were sports considered important in industrial America?

2. **Critical Thinking** How can emphasis on sports benefit or harm a society?

591

The 1927 Yankees

Many outstanding athletes and teams stood in the sports spotlight during the 1920s. None, however, won greater fame and success than the New York Yankees of 1927. That season, the "Bronx Bombers" and their "Murderers' Row" of power hitters captured the hearts and minds of Americans with their spectacular feats on the baseball field.

The stars of the team were baseball legends George Herman "Babe" Ruth—the "Bambino"—and Lou Gehrig—the "Iron Horse." Ruth's batting average of .356, 164 runs batted in, and 60 home runs stunned Yankee opponents and thrilled Yankee fans. Gehrig's statistics were equally impressive: a batting average of .373, 175 runs batted in, and 47 home runs.

Other power hitters, including Bob Meusel, Earl Combs, and "Push-em-up" Tony Lazzeri, contributed to the Yankees' reputation as the "Window Breakers." At the season's end, Yankee players led the American League in home runs, triples, doubles, hits, slugging average, total bases, and runs batted in.

To the delight of their fans, the Yankees frequently unleashed all of their power in a single inning—usually the eighth. In an on-slaught that was dubbed "five o'clock lightning," the Yankees often came from behind to soundly defeat their bewildered opponents.

Yankee power hitting translated into a Yankee winning season. Maintaining first place from their second game to their last, the Yankees boasted a sensational record in October: 110 victories, a winning percentage of .714, and a finish 19 games ahead of the second place Philadelphia Athletics. As the American League champions, the Yankees faced the Pittsburgh Pirates in the 1927 World Series.

Some baseball historians claim the series was over before it began. During batting practice before the first game, the Yankees demoralized the Pittsburgh nine by belting one long drive after another into the outfield seats. Paced by the awesome hitting of Ruth and Gehrig, the Yankees won the series in four straight games.

The World Series was a dramatic end to one of the greatest seasons achieved by any team in American sports history.

1. VISUAL EVIDENCE Babe Ruth is standing in the back row, third from the left.

---

1. *The 1927 New York Yankees have been called the greatest baseball team of all time. In that year, Babe Ruth set his legendary record of 60 home runs. When reporters pointed out that his salary was higher than the President's, Ruth quipped, "Yeah, but I had a better year than he did."*

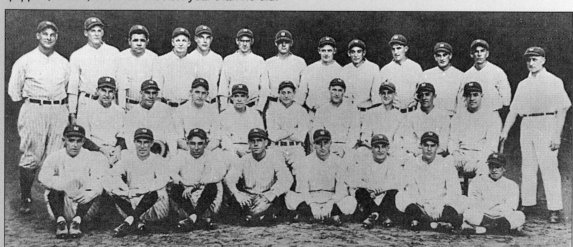

Many other Yankee teams went on to win championships, but none has outshone the "Bronx Bombers" of 1927. That team and its heroes still serve as a wonderful example of the magic, the fantasy, the spectacle of American sports.

See p. T109.

1. How did the 1927 New York Yankees capture the imagination of the public?

2. **Critical Thinking** What American values did the 1927 New York Yankees reflect?

Voices of Freedom

Red Grange—Sports Hero

During the 1920s, newspapers heightened the public's passion for sports by portraying athletes as heroes. In this colorful account of a college football game, sports reporter Harry Cross hails the extraordinary Red Grange, halfback for the University of Illinois.

Philadelphia, Oct. 31, 1925—The golden yellow headgear of Red Grange of Illinois flashed over Franklin Field this afternoon while 65,000 spectators, gathered from all over the East, saw him almost single-handedly defeat Pennsylvania's great eleven by a score of 24 to 2. The speed, cleverness, and uncanny intuition of any other football player have never made such an impression on the Eastern gridiron as Grange's meteoric flights over a slippery, muddy field today.

The East has heard of the great achievements of this football player and has taken them with a grain of salt. They did not believe that he could be as great as the Middle West said he was. But he is. That is the strange part about it. Red Grange is human. He is not a myth. He dashes and dodges over the gridiron with a speed of foot and an alertness of mind which set him high up on a pedestal among this generation of football players.

Three times this afternoon Grange raced majestically through the Pennsylvania eleven to touchdowns. Not only that, but he carried the ball thirty-six times in today's battle and gained 363 yards in his mad dashes. Twice did Grange gallop 60 yards. Once he left the Quakers trailing 40 yards behind him and another time he raced 24 yards through a compact defense before he was dragged into the mud from behind.

One of the assets of this irrepressible Grange is mental. He thinks quicker than the players who try to stop him. He is a flash at picking openings and his real skill begins when the tacklers of the opposition begin to twine their arms about him. This afternoon Pennsylvania tacklers dropped off Grange like the leaves fall from a tree in autumn. . . .

His left arm is a rod of steel. When he shoots it out straight at the onrushing opposition, they bowl over like so many tenpins. And how the boy can keep his feet! . . . In every scrimmage which marked Pennsylvania's downfall, Red Grange was the last player to go down. The other players . . . piled about him, but there he stood, the last contestant on his feet, and he did not topple over until the last inch had been gained.

Pennsylvania suffered terrible shock in the humiliation of the Red and Blue this afternoon. This eleven was triumphantly pointed toward an Eastern and even a national championship. It was proud of its strength and boastful of its achievements. It . . . was so certain that the wet and muddy field today would be Grange's undoing that it was prepared for nothing but the sweetness of victory. It tasted nothing but bitterness.

Adapted from "Grange Shows the East," by Harry Cross, *The New York Times,* October 31, 1925.
See p. T109.

1. According to Harry Cross, what special qualities does halfback Red Grange have as a football player?

2. **Critical Thinking** Does television capture the excitement of sports events as well today as did Harry Cross in this 1925 newspaper article?

593

From Prosperity to Despair (1928–1932)

27

CHAPTER OUTLINE

1 The Bubble Bursts

2 The Grim Years Begin

3 Failure of Traditional Remedies

CHAPTER OBJECTIVES After completing this chapter, students should be able to
1. identify weaknesses in the economy in the 1920s.
2. describe causes and symptoms of the depression.
3. describe Hoover's response to the depression.
4. synthesize pieces of evidence.

CHAPTER PREVIEW Ask students to study the graphs on pp. 602–603. Ask: What information does each convey? What was the apparent state of the economy during most of the 1920s? When did this change? How can you tell? How do the graphs illustrate the chapter title?

When Walter W. Walters, a cannery worker in Portland, Oregon, lost his job in 1932, he joined the ranks of millions of unemployed Americans. It was the worst year of the Great Depression, and the unemployment rate was a staggering 24 percent. But Walters regained hope when he heard about a bill before Congress. Back in 1924, Congress had voted a bonus for every World War I veteran, payable in 1945. Now, a new bill had been introduced calling for immediate payment. It would give Walters and other veterans a new start.

Walters reasoned that the odds in favor of the bill's passage would be greatly improved if a group of veterans, like himself, demonstrated in the nation's capital. So he and about 300 other unemployed veterans, traveling by freight train, began a cross-country trek to Washington, D.C.

Little did Walters know what he was starting. As word of his journey spread, thousands of jobless veterans from all over the country joined in. One reporter described the march as "a supreme escape gesture—a flight from hunger, from the cries of starving children, . . .

from the harsh rebuffs of prospective employers." By June, about 20,000 Bonus Marchers, some with their families, had arrived in the city.

The Bonus Army was orderly and patient as it camped out in the capital. A list of camp rules read: "1. Stay until the bonus is granted. 2. No radical talk. 3. No panhandling. 4. No booze." But on June 17, 1932, the bad news came. The Senate had killed the bonus bill. Disappointed, many marchers returned to their homes. But thousands stayed, and after some veterans scuffled with the police, President Herbert Hoover called in the army to disperse them.

On July 28, United States cavalry, infantry, and a mounted machine gun squadron marched down Pennsylvania Avenue. Armed with tear gas and bayonets, the army scattered the veterans and set fire to their camp. The image of the Bonus Army, their hopes smoldering in the ashes, was in sharp contrast to American life only a few years before. The gaiety and optimism of the 1920s seemed gone forever.

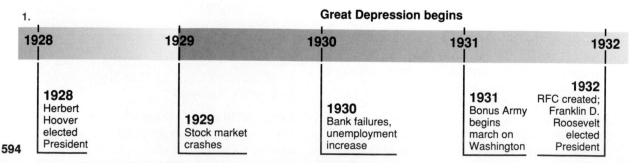

Great Depression begins

1.

| 1928 | 1929 | 1930 | 1931 | 1932 |

1928 Herbert Hoover elected President

1929 Stock market crashes

1930 Bank failures, unemployment increase

1931 Bonus Army begins march on Washington

1932 RFC created; Franklin D. Roosevelt elected President

594

1. TIME LINE QUESTION Ask: Who was President when the stock market crashed?

1. Like the Bonus Marchers, people throughout the country needed jobs during the Great Depression. Painter Isaac Soyer captured the soul-crushing despair of being out of work and out of hope in this painting, Employment Agency.

1. **VISUAL EVIDENCE** Have students write and act out a dialogue among the four people shown in the painting.

2. **VOCABULARY** Have students look up these terms in the glossary before they begin reading.

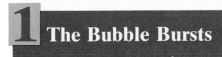 **The Bubble Bursts**

READ TO UNDERSTAND

■ What caused a slowdown in the economy by the end of the 1920s.

■ How the candidates for President in 1928 differed.

■ Why the stock market crashed in 1929.

2. ■ *Vocabulary:* on margin, margin call.

The glitter of the Roaring Twenties blinded the nation to its growing economic problems. Workers in many industries found it increasingly difficult to live well on what they earned. Unsold goods began to pile up on store shelves. Many farmers risked losing their land because prices for their products were so low. People were borrowing heavily to finance get-rich-quick schemes. Although signs of impending trouble were evident by 1927, few took them seriously.

Signs of a Slowdown

Although industrial workers saw their wages 3. rise during the 1920s, these increases could not keep up with the rising cost of goods. Workers found it more and more difficult to buy the very products they made. As spending decreased, the demand for some goods fell. Before long, factories laid off workers, decreasing demand for goods even further. In 1929, a study in Muncie, Indiana, revealed that in 40 percent of working families, a   **595**

3. **ECONOMICS** To most people, these events looked like a typical economic downturn. Interested students might research and graph the business cycle from 1915 to 1930.

AMERICAN ENTERPRISE

The Stock Market

In London, they met in coffee houses. In New York, they could be found conducting business under a buttonwood tree on Wall Street. These were the stockbrokers—agents who matched stocks for sale with those who wanted to invest in corporations.

As the Industrial Revolution spread and the corporation became a common form of business organization, these casual markets became more structured. London's first stock exchange was organized by brokers in 1773. Nearly 20 years later, the brokers on Wall Street organized the New York Stock Exchange.

The New York Stock Exchange is often called the nation's marketplace because it is the largest center in the world for buying and selling stock in American and foreign businesses. The New York Stock Exchange and the American Stock Exchange, which is also located in New York, account for 90 percent of the stocks bought and sold in the United States.

The prices of stocks are not set like the prices in a retail store. Although stock prices respond to a variety of factors, their rise and fall is largely determined by supply and demand. When many people want to buy stocks, prices rise, and it is said that there is a "bull market." When many people want to sell and there are fewer buyers, prices fall, and it is said that there is a a "bear market."

The terms "bull market" and "bear market" are derived from the way the two animals attack. A bull attacks by tossing its horns up in the air; a bear sweeps its paws downward. A bullish investor believes that prices will go up and buys in anticipation of a market advance. A bearish investor expects stock prices to fall and sells with the hope of buying back later at a lower price.

See p. T110.

1. What is the difference between a bull market and a bear market?

2. **Critical Thinking** What economic conditions probably affect people's willingness to buy stocks?

1.

---

1. **ECONOMICS** Have students study the stock pages of a local newspaper for a week. Ask: Does the current market seem to be a bull market or a bear market?

---

worker had been laid off at least one month that year.

Some industries, such as textiles and soft-coal mining, never shared in the prosperity of the 1920s. For workers in those industries, a booming economy was something they only read about in the newspapers. The words on a Pennsylvania mining town tombstone reflect their plight:

2.
> For forty years beneath the sod
> With pick and spade I did my task
> The coal king's slave, but now, thank God,
> I'm free at last.

Even in healthier industries, there were signs of trouble. By 1929, the pace of the construction industry had slowed. Production in the automobile industry, one of the fastest-growing industries of the decade, began to decline. Conditions in agriculture were even more disturbing.

American farm families faced grim economic conditions throughout much of the decade. Farm expenses rose much faster than the prices for farm products. The efficiency of farmers contributed further to their financial problems, since overproduction kept prices low. (See page 577.)

As the 1928 presidential election neared, most people saw the farm situation as the nation's major economic problem. They failed to notice the other warning signals.

The Election of 1928

Had he run for reelection, Calvin Coolidge might have won easily. He surprised nearly everyone, however, by announcing in his typically concise fashion, "I do not choose to run for President in 1928."

Republicans had little difficulty choosing Herbert Hoover to replace Coolidge. Hoover,

596

---

2. **ACTIVITY** Have groups of students compose similar epitaphs for farmers, blacks, textile workers, and others who did not share in the good times of the 1920s.

Coolidge's popular and experienced secretary of commerce, had the confidence of party leaders. As a successful consulting engineer, he had worked on projects throughout the world. After World War I, he directed a massive famine relief program in Europe that fed millions of people. As secretary of commerce for eight years, he actively promoted the development of American business. To many Americans, Hoover represented several ideals: He was a self-made man, an efficiency expert, and a humanitarian.

1. The Democrats picked a candidate who contrasted sharply with Hoover in background, style, and beliefs. They chose Al Smith, the outspoken four-time governor of New York. He was the first candidate of a major party born and bred in a big city.

The son of Irish immigrant parents, Smith grew up in New York City. His initial rise in politics had been through the New York City Tammany Hall political machine. A Roman Catholic, he attracted the support of many of the "new immigrants" from southern Europe who had settled in cities. In contrast, Hoover, born in West Branch, Iowa, seemed to represent traditional small-town Protestant America. He also typified prosperous, middle-class society.

2. The positions of the two candidates were also quite different. Hoover believed in what he called "rugged individualism." He realized that farmers were suffering, but he felt that their problems could be solved through their own efforts and through cooperation. Government, he claimed, should not meddle in farmers' problems or in those of business.

In contrast, Smith believed government should play a more active role. He stood for public ownership of some electric power companies. Furthermore, the Democratic platform urged strong government action to help farmers. As the first Roman Catholic to run for the presidency, Smith became the focus of a savage anti-Catholic campaign. In addition, his pledge to end prohibition drew fierce attacks from "dry" forces.

3. On election day, Hoover swept 40 of the 48 states, including Smith's own New York. The Republican victory reflected the belief that the nation was healthy and, in general, prosperous. During the campaign, Hoover had capitalized on this belief when he declared, "We in America today are nearer to the final triumph over poverty than ever before in the history of any land."

Get-Rich-Quick Fever

In the 1920s, newspaper stories about people who made quick fortunes convinced many Americans that they too could strike it rich. The quickest way to wealth, most thought, was to speculate in land or stocks.* The object was to buy a piece of land or a stock at a low price, wait for the price to rise, and then sell the stock or property for a handsome profit.

All across the country, people speculated in land. The building of suburbs drove land

*As you learned in Chapter 20, stocks are shares of ownership in a corporation.

3. PAST AND PRESENT America's first Catholic President was John F. Kennedy, elected in 1960.

Among the many get-rich-quick schemes of the 1920s was investment in Florida land. This 1925 drawing for the cover of Life *magazine mocks a couple who bought Florida land sight unseen, only to learn that their "land" was in a swamp.*

4.

2. PRESIDENTS Hoover was the son of a Quaker blacksmith. He grew up in Oregon and attended Stanford University, where he graduated as a mining engineer.

4. BACKGROUND To spur land sales, realtors hired the famed orator William Jennings Bryan to lecture on the benefits of the Florida climate.

The long-lasting bull market of the 1920s deluded many into thinking it would last forever. But in 1929, the bears took over, as indicated by this cartoon, and dragged many investors to disaster.

1. **VISUAL EVIDENCE** Ask: Why does the cartoonist show the buildings swaying in the background?

prices skyward, but nowhere did land values soar as much as in Florida. The warm Florida climate attracted speculators, who saw the area as an ideal spot for vacation resorts. People bought any land available, including swamps. They did not plan to build on the land, but rather to resell it later for profit. And indeed, those who bought early made huge profits. But the Florida land boom, already weakening, came to an abrupt halt in 1926, after two devastating hurricanes roared through the state.

If land speculation seemed too risky, there was always the stock market. Only a small number of Americans, about 4 million, actually bought stocks during the 1920s. And the great majority were inexperienced investors who rarely paid attention to the financial health of the companies in which they were buying stock. Fascinated by the widespread stories of stock market success, they assumed that prices would simply keep rising no matter how the companies did.

To attract investors, many brokers sold shares of stock **on margin.** That is, the investor paid only part of the selling price in cash and borrowed the rest from the stockbroker. The broker in turn borrowed money from banks and corporations in order to cover loans made to investors. If the investor could not repay the loan, the broker took the stock. Investors had to pay interest on the loan, but if the price of the stock went up, the buyer could repay the loan and interest and still make a profit.

The Crash

During most of the 1920s, the system seemed to work, and stock prices rose steadily. But in March 1928, stocks began to soar. Speculation by individuals increased, and the stock market boomed through the summer of 1929. By September, stock prices were 400 percent higher than they had been five years earlier. Some cautious investors began to worry that prices were overinflated and started to sell. The majority, however, shared the view of a prominent economist who proclaimed that "stock prices have reached what looks like a permanently high plateau." Nevertheless, with fewer buyers, prices began to edge downward.

In early October, stock prices slid badly as orders to sell outnumbered orders to buy. Then on Thursday, October 24, a flood of sell orders sent prices tumbling. On Monday, after reviewing their accounts over the weekend, brokers put out **margin calls** to cover investor loans. That is, the brokers asked investors who had bought on margin to put up more money to cover their loans on stocks that were now worth less. Some investors, unable to put up the extra money, lost their stocks. These margin calls produced more selling, as investors tried desperately to raise money. Meanwhile, banks and other creditors called in their loans to brokers.

On Tuesday, October 29—Black Tuesday, as it is now called—there was a devastating panic in the market. Orders to sell at any price swamped the stock market, but there were almost no buyers. The price of stocks plummeted, and the market crashed. Stocks

2. **BACKGROUND** In 1921 alone, seven new counties were formed in Florida.

4. **ECONOMICS** An example of the rise in stock prices is provided by RCA stock. From 1928 to 1929, the price of a share rose from $85 to $505.

1. in many companies became virtually worthless. Fortunes vanished in hours on the worst day in stock market history.

Business leaders and bankers met hurriedly to find ways to avert a panic. In an attempt to restore public confidence in the economy, John D. Rockefeller announced, "My son and I have for some days been purchasing some common stocks." When he heard this, comedian Eddie Cantor replied, "Sure, who else has any money left?"

See p. T110.

SECTION 1 REVIEW

1. **Identify:** (a) Herbert Hoover, (b) Al Smith.

2. **Define:** (a) on margin, (b) margin call.

3. Why did most Americans fail to notice the economic trouble signs during the 1920s?

4. How did Hoover and Smith differ on the question of government help for farmers?

5. What two types of investments attracted many speculators during the 1920s?

6. **Critical Thinking** How did the public, business, and government contribute to the conditions that led to the crash?

2. **VOCABULARY** Have students look up these terms in the glossary before they begin reading.

2 The Grim Years Begin

READ TO UNDERSTAND

■ What caused the Great Depression.

■ How the depression affected businesses.

■ What impact unemployment had on American society.

2. ■ *Vocabulary:* durable goods, business inventory.

The stock market crash was the first bombshell to shatter the American public's hopes for a secure economic future. Other disasters, such as bank failures and job layoffs, followed soon after. As the nation slipped into an economic depression, few escaped the effects of the collapse. Millions of unemployed workers joined food lines to wait for handouts of bread. Selling apples on street corners became a symbol of the economic despair of the era. For most Americans, it was the worst of times.

The Causes of the Depression

Many factors contributed to the onset of the Great Depression. One was a sharp imbalance between supply and demand. For a free enterprise system to operate effectively, the supply of products should equal the demand for those products. But demand had begun to fall during the late 1920s.

During the 1920s, the increasing use of mass production in American industry resulted in the production of more goods than ever before. Yet demand for these goods was weak. As you have read earlier in this chapter, workers could not afford to buy more goods because wages were not keeping pace with increased prices. Weaknesses in agriculture also meant that farm families could afford to buy few products.

Furthermore, many of the items produced were **durable goods,** or products designed to last several years before being replaced, such as automobiles, stoves, and tractors. By 1929, many people either owned the durable goods they wanted or could not afford to buy more, even on credit. Thus, the demand for such goods decreased.

As demand fell, **business inventories,** or the quantity of unsold goods on hand, crept upward. In response, factories cut back pro- 3. duction and laid off some workers. Since laid-off workers were unable to buy durable goods, job layoffs cut consumer demand still further.

The weakness of the banking system also contributed to the economic collapse. Many banks had made risky loans, such as those to speculators. In the wake of the stock market crash, some banks failed when borrowers could not pay back their loans. Each bank closing shook the confidence of depositors in other banks, and people began withdrawing their money. Such withdrawals further decreased the nation's money supply and led to additional bank failures. Nearly 5,000 banks 4. failed between 1929 and 1932.

599

The ripple effects of economic collapse wiped out many fortunes. In the 1932 cartoon at right, a once-rich man sells apples on the street to earn money. But the humor was based on tragic reality. One-time millionaire, Fred Bell, at left, was photographed selling apples on a San Francisco corner in 1931. He was not alone. Apple growers faced with a surplus of unsold apples offered them on credit to anyone willing to sell them. In New York City, 6,000 people accepted the offer.

1.

2.

1. **VISUAL EVIDENCE** The cartoon is titled "Democracy." Ask students to explain the meaning of the title.

2. **VISUAL EVIDENCE** Ask: Why do you think this image became an enduring symbol of the Great Depression?

3.   The onset of depression in the United States had international repercussions. Faced with their own economic troubles, European investors also withdrew money from banks in the United States. The failure of a key Vienna bank in 1931 signaled a worldwide economic breakdown. The collapse of the German economy came next. The Great Depression had begun.

Economic Collapse

The spread of depression in the United States was swift and relentless. A chain reaction was set in motion. Industrial areas suffered first, as payrolls dropped by one third. In 1930,

26,355 businesses failed. Two million fewer cars rolled off the assembly lines than in 1929. Trying to save money, employers cut the work week to three days, then two, then one. Finally, they laid workers off.

Unemployed workers could buy little more than food. Most people did not have enough savings to tide them over difficult times. Old clothes were patched and mended. Families fell behind on credit payments and lost their radios, cars, and homes. People who fell behind on rent were evicted. Construction of new housing came to a halt, throwing still more people out of work.

Hundreds of thousands of people saw what savings they had wiped out in bank fail-

3. **MAIN IDEA** Have students draw a chart summarizing the causes of the Great Depression in the U.S.

1. **LOCAL HISTORY** Have interested students interview relatives or neighbors who lived through the depression and compile an oral history of the period.

ures. For those who were already poor, life became even more desperate. Poet Langston Hughes noted that the depression took everyone down a peg or two, but that blacks had fewer pegs to fall. For Hughes and other writers of the Harlem Renaissance, the depression signaled the end of an exciting era.

Impact of the Collapse

1. The United States had experienced depressions before, but the Great Depression was unique. During earlier depressions, many people lived on farms and could grow their own food. But in 1930, the farm population was smaller. Instead, millions depended on industrial jobs for their livelihood. When factories closed, they had no jobs and no food or land on which to grow it.

The Great Depression did more than reduce people's standard of living. It also sapped their sense of personal worth. Traditional American values of hard work and individual responsibility were severely tested. In 1930, there were 4 million Americans out of work. By 1932, the figure had risen to

2. **CRITICAL THINKING** Ask: Judging from the graph of stock prices, was the author of "This Prosperity" justified in writing as he did in 1927? What did he fail to take into account?

SKILL LESSON

The Economy of the Roaring Twenties: Synthesizing Pieces of Evidence

To make the best use of historical evidence, you must be able to synthesize, that is, put pieces of evidence together to form a whole.

To practice the skill of synthesizing, use the graph of the index of common stock prices on page 602; the graph of workers' average yearly wages on page 603; the picture on page 597; and the quotation, at right, published in 1927. Follow the steps below:

See p. T110.

1. **Analyze each piece of evidence.** (a) According to the graph on page 602, what was the index of common stock prices in 1925? (b) How had it changed by 1929? (c) According to the graph on page 603, how did the average yearly income of farm workers change between 1922 and 1929? (d) Which group of workers had the largest increase in yearly wages between 1922 and 1929? (e) What economic development is portrayed in the picture on page 597? (f) What did the writer of the quotation predict about business cycles?

2. **Compare the pieces of evidence.** (a) If you looked only at the graph of stock prices between 1925 and 1929, what would you conclude about the economy of the 1920s?

(b) Would the data about the wages of farm workers confirm that conclusion or conflict with it? (c) Does the picture give you the same impression of the economy of the 1920s as the quotation does? Explain.

3. **Synthesize the evidence in order to draw conclusions.** (a) Were the 1920s generally a period of economic prosperity? Explain. (b) What economic problems can you identify? (c) Write a paragraph describing the economy of the 1920s.

From "This Prosperity"

Business has attained a degree of stability in this country that is quite beyond any previous precedent. It is wholly probable that the old abrupt business cycles, with their rapid ascents from depression, to recovery, and on up to prosperity in about two years, and their still more rapid descents through general decline back down to depression in about another year are things of the past. The country is now too wealthy, and our credit supplies are too ably administered through the Federal Reserve System, to permit a return to those . . . recurring conditions.

Index of Common Stock Prices, 1920–1932

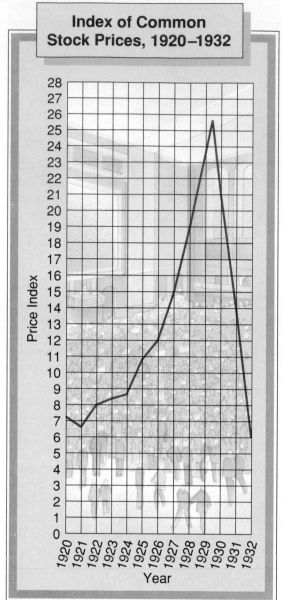

Source: *Historical Statistics of the United States*

GRAPH STUDY *There are many ways to measure changes in the national economy. The graphs on this and the following page show pieces of the economic pattern between 1920 and 1932. The graph at left traces the climb in the price index of common stocks in the 1920s, the sharp break in 1929, and the plummet after the crash. The index of common stocks is a weighted average of the prices of selected stocks. The numbers along the vertical axis of the graph measure price movements. Between which years did stock prices rise most sharply? Between which years did they fall most sharply?*

602

Gross National Product 1920–1932

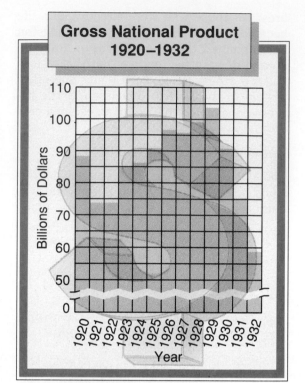

Source: *Historical Statistics of the United States* See p. T110.

GRAPH STUDY *The gross national product, or GNP, is the total dollar value of all goods and services produced by a country in one year. It is considered a good measure of overall economic health. What rose more steadily from 1922 to 1929, stock prices or the GNP?* 1.

1. **GRAPH READING** Ask: About how high did the price index go at its peak? How far had it fallen by 1932? Why do you suppose both graphs showed a dip in 1921 to 1922?

12 million, almost one quarter of the work force.

Such statistics, however, tell little of the daily misery of broken people. They tell little of whole families scavenging for food at city dumps and in restaurant garbage cans, or of men leaving their families to roam the land in search of work. Nor do they tell of the 2. homeless living in condemned buildings, abandoned railroad boxcars, or shacks built of tin, cardboard, or orange crates. Finally, they do not tell of the lines—lines of people waiting to apply for a job, lines of people waiting for free soup, lines of people waiting for donated clothing. For the first time, these images of despair were carried to every corner of the nation by newspapers, magazines, and radio.

2. **ECONOMICS** In 1932, 20% of New York City's students were malnourished. A child who was told to go home and eat replied, "I can't. This is my sister's day to eat."

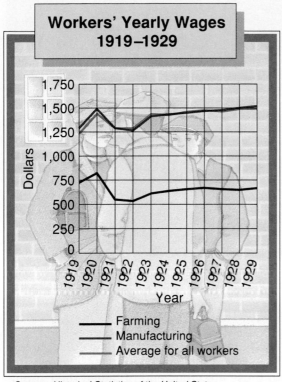

Workers' Yearly Wages 1919–1929

Dollars

1,750
1,500
1,250
1,000
750
500
250
0

1919 1920 1921 1922 1923 1924 1925 1926 1927 1928 1929

Year

— Farming
— Manufacturing
— Average for all workers

Source: *Historical Statistics of the United States*

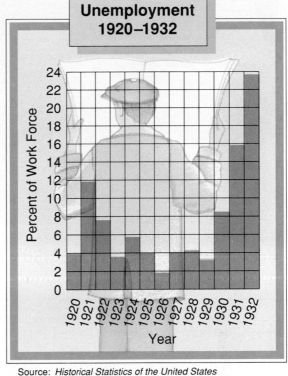

Unemployment 1920–1932

Percent of Work Force

24
22
20
18
16
14
12
10
8
6
4
2
0

1920 1921 1922 1923 1924 1925 1926 1927 1928 1929 1930 1931 1932

Year

Source: *Historical Statistics of the United States*

GRAPH STUDY

See p. T110.

Most workers earned more as the 1920s progressed. But farmers did not share in this prosperity because of falling world prices for farm products. Another way of measuring a nation's economic health is to look at the percentage of people who cannot find work. Note the rise and fall in unemployment in the 1920s, then the steep jump in unemployment after 1929. In what year did both unemployment and wages drop?

See p. T110.

SECTION 2 REVIEW

1. **Define:** (a) durable goods, (b) business inventory.

2. Why were supply and demand imbalanced in the late 1920s?

3. How did the stock market crash affect banks?

4. Why was the economic collapse like a chain reaction?

5. Why was the Great Depression more devastating than previous depressions?

6. **Critical Thinking** Based on the graphs above and on page 602, what is the relationship between the gross national product and unemployment?

1.

2.

1. **GRAPH READING** Ask: In which year was the gap between manufacturing wages and farming wages the smallest? The widest?

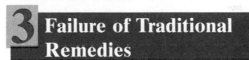

3 Failure of Traditional Remedies

READ TO UNDERSTAND

■ What action President Hoover took to end the depression.

■ How the Bonus Army affected the public's opinion of Hoover.

■ Why Roosevelt was elected President by such a large margin in 1932.

In the first years of the depression, President Hoover stood steadfastly by his belief that government should not intervene directly in the economy. "Economic wounds must be healed by . . . producers and consumers them- **603**

2. **GRAPH READING** Explain that unemployment figures reflect the number of people who are looking for work but cannot find it. When people become too discouraged even to look, they drop out of the statistics.

Across the United States, thousands of men, women, and children stood in lines. They stood in lines at factories and employment offices, hoping to get a job. Some lined up and waited for hours just to get a free meal, as in this photograph taken on Christmas Day in 1931.

1. **VISUAL EVIDENCE** In cities, bread lines extended for blocks. One New Yorker observed, "You'd see these men, silent, shuffling along in line. Shabby clothes, but you could see they had been pretty good clothes."

selves," he said. But the severity and persistence of the Great Depression forced him to modify his views. He eventually authorized programs that assisted businesses in the belief that prosperity would "trickle down" to the workers and consumers. Unfortunately, his efforts were too little, too late.

An Initial "Hands-Off" Policy

The President's advisers believed that both depression and recovery were an inevitable part of the economic cycle. Thus, they urged Hoover to allow the depression to proceed without government intervention. Andrew Mellon, now Hoover's secretary of the treasury, believed that the depression was a good thing. "People will work harder, live a more moral life, . . . and enterprising people will pick up the wrecks from less competent people."

Despite such advice, President Hoover did attempt to turn the economy around. To restore the public's confidence in the economy, he told Americans that conditions were improving. In May 1930, he stated, "We have now passed the worst, and with continued unity of effort we shall rapidly recover." A month later, the President announced that the "depression is over."

In another effort to bolster confidence, Hoover invited business leaders to the White House for a series of economic conferences. He pleaded the cause of business expansion to those attending and obtained their promise not to reduce wages and prices. Such well-intentioned agreements, however, failed to survive worsening conditions. By September 1931, most of the nation's major industries had been forced to cut wages in order to maintain profits.

President Hoover also advocated public works, suggesting that federal funds be used for projects such as dams and highways. Such projects, he argued, would increase employment and put money back into the economy. He opposed, however, federal borrowing to pay for these projects. Hoover insisted that federal public-works projects be funded only to the extent that there was cash to pay for them. By the end of Hoover's presidency, the federal government was spending $500 million more a year on public works than it had in 1928.

Hoover urged state and local governments to spend more money on public works as well. With revenues reduced sharply by the depression, however, few governments had the needed money.

Hoover's "hands-off" policy soon began to erode public support. By 1930, voter discontent returned the control of the House of Representatives to the Democrats for the first time since 1916.

604

2. **CRITICAL THINKING** Ask: How do you think unemployed people felt about Mellon's comments? Explain.

1. PAST AND PRESENT N.Y.C.'s subways still house the homeless. Have students prepare a report comparing today's homeless with those of the 1930s.

3. VISUAL EVIDENCE Have students imagine that they are one of the people in this picture. Ask them to write a letter about going to or working at the soup kitchen.

The Reconstruction Finance Corporation

As pressure for more government action mounted, Hoover proposed the creation of a government agency to stop bank failures and business closings. In 1932, Congress created the Reconstruction Finance Corporation (RFC), giving it power to make loans to banks, railroads, and insurance companies. Congress also went beyond Hoover's intentions and gave the RFC the right to lend money to local communities for public-works programs.

The RFC was not as effective as Hoover or Congress had hoped. RFC officials were reluctant to loan the money that Congress had given the agency. Banks that did receive loans often used the funds to strengthen their own finances rather than extend credit to the community. The RFC virtually ignored the congressional goal of financing public works.

The RFC reflected Treasury Secretary Mellon's "trickle-down" theory. According to Mellon, the benefits from help given to business and industry would trickle down to ordinary people. Whether or not the theory was valid was difficult to determine, as conditions rapidly worsened.

By the winter of 1931–1932, despair was everywhere. In New York City, hundreds of homeless people rode the subways all night long because that was warmer than sleeping on a park bench. There were 800,000 jobless in the city. In Detroit, some 223,000 people had no jobs. In Chicago, 40 percent of all workers were jobless.

Most people who had jobs did not work a full day. Social workers strove tirelessly to find money to feed the unemployed and to force the government to act. "Have you ever seen the uncontrolled trembling of parents who have gone half starved for weeks so the children may have food?" demanded Lillian Wald of the Henry Street Settlement House in New York.

A Question of Relief

Although President Hoover opposed direct government relief, he strongly urged private, voluntary agencies to provide it. Organizations such as settlement houses, the Salvation Army, the YMCA, community chests, church groups, and others worked to feed and shelter the jobless millions. But the sheer numbers of unemployed overwhelmed the effort.

Public relief in the first years of the depression was provided strictly on a local basis. Neither the states nor the federal government took part. In rural areas and in some cities and towns, no public relief was available at all. In other places, only a small number of people could be cared for. Local relief programs had not been designed and funded to handle the needs of millions.

Furthermore, just when communities needed more money for relief, income from taxes was shrinking. As a result, some cities were forced to reduce the amount of relief provided to each family. In the desperate winter of 1931–1932, for example, New York City was able to give each family on relief just $2.39 a week. Many areas did not even have that much to offer.

Most early relief efforts were private, church-sponsored, or run by local communities. "Soup kitchens" like this one in Chicago offered a bowl of soup to anyone who asked—as long as the soup held out. Poverty brought everyone down to the same level. Some of the people waiting for soup in this picture appear prosperous, but their fine clothes are only relics of a happier past.

2. READING Students interested in learning more about the period can read *The People Talk: American Voices from the Great Depression* by Benjamin Appel, or *Hard Times: An Oral History of the Great Depression* by Studs Terkel.

1. BACKGROUND One baby later died from the effects of the tear gas. A seven-year-old boy was bayoneted in the leg when he turned back for his pet rabbit.

2. BACKGROUND The government finally paid the bonus to veterans in 1936.

By 1932, about 100 cities had run out of funds. Only about one in four unemployed Americans was receiving any kind of relief. Twelve million Americans were jobless, and the number was growing monthly. Those who did have jobs sometimes worked for five or six cents an hour.

At a national conference of social workers, Jacob Billikopf, executive director of the Federation of Jewish Charities, warned that private efforts, however valiant, were failing. Government, he said, "will be compelled, by the cruel events ahead of us, to step into the situation and bring relief on a large scale."

The Bonus Army

It was as the depression deepened that the group of veterans from Oregon set out on their widely publicized journey to Washington, D.C., to demand immediate payment of World War I bonuses. (See page 594.) Once the Bonus Army reached the city, most camped in makeshift tents or shacks on the Anacostia Flats, a swampy area near the Potomac River. The Washington chief of police, Pelham Glassford, rode there daily helping people to find food, lodging, and medicine. A former brigadier general, Glassford had led some of the veterans in the war and still considered them "his boys." His concern helped keep the peace when the Senate overwhelmingly rejected the bill and thousands of veterans decided to stay in Washington "until 1945."

But President Hoover refused to meet with the veterans' leaders. After some disorder broke out, he ordered the army to tear down the makeshift camp. Under the command of General Douglas MacArthur, cavalry troops used tear gas to clear out the veterans and their families. Newspaper and magazine photos and movie newsreels of the event shocked the public. The government had used its power against its own people, not to help them. Such actions destroyed what little remained of Hoover's prestige.

The Election of 1932

President Hoover took more government action to relieve economic problems than any President before him. Yet because of the widespread misery in 1932, he became the object of anger and scorn. People living in shantytowns called their poor communities

3. BACKGROUND While they were encamped, the Bonus Marchers kept strict military discipline, including bugle calls and chow lines.

As seen in this photo, the Bonus Marchers camped in the nation's capital, living in cars, tents, and shacks. After the army drove them out of Washington, they scattered throughout the country. President Hoover declared, "A challenge to the authority of the United States government has been met, swiftly and firmly."

Presidential Election Results, 1928 and 1932

Year	Party	Candidate	Popular Vote	Percent of Popular Vote	Electoral Vote
1928	Republican	Herbert Hoover	21,391,993	59	444
	Democratic	Alfred Smith	15,016,116	41	87
1932	Republican	Herbert Hoover	15,758,901	40	59
	Democratic	Franklin Roosevelt	22,809,638	58	472
	Minor	Minor candidates	881,951	2	0

CHART STUDY *The decline of Herbert Hoover's popularity can be seen in this table comparing the 1928 and 1932 presidential elections. In 1928, with the nation enjoying unparalleled prosperity, Hoover swamped Alfred Smith. Four years later, Hoover was buried in a landslide for Franklin Roosevelt. Did minor candidates affect the outcome of the election?* See p. T111.

1.

1. **GRAPH READING** Have students convert the information in this table into four circle graphs—two showing the popular and electoral vote breakdown in 1928 and two showing the same in 1932.

Hoovervilles. Empty pockets turned inside out were called Hoover flags. Day-old newspapers were known as Hoover blankets.

The President became gloomier as time went on. One observer noted, "If you put a rose in Hoover's hand, it would wilt." The Republican party knew that Hoover could not win the 1932 election, but the loyal delegates nominated him for a second term.

As Democrats smelled victory, several well-known leaders sought the nomination. The party's choice was Franklin Delano Roosevelt, the governor of New York. A distant cousin of Theodore Roosevelt, the candidate bore a name recognized by most Americans.

As governor of New York, Roosevelt had acted quickly when the depression hit. His state was the first to set up a relief plan for the unemployed. Roosevelt also started a program to create jobs on land conservation projects and proposed a plan for unemployment insurance.

Once nominated, Roosevelt broke tradition by flying to the convention to deliver his 2. acceptance speech in person. "I pledge myself," he told the delegates, "to a new deal for the American people."

During the election campaign, Hoover was dreary and pessimistic while Roosevelt radiated charm and confidence. Although Roosevelt did not outline a specific program, he insisted that something must be done. "The country needs bold, persistent experimentation," he said. "It is common sense to take a method and try it. If it fails, admit it frankly and try another. But above all, try something."

A majority of Americans agreed with Roosevelt, electing him by a landslide of 57 percent of the popular vote. Hoover carried only six states, in the Northeast.

Roosevelt's support came from city dwellers, immigrants, workers, and farmers. He also won the "solid South," where Democrats had been in control since the end of Reconstruction. These groups began to form a coalition of voters that would make the Democrats a majority party for the first time since the Civil War.

See p. T111.

SECTION 3 REVIEW

1. **Identify:** (a) Reconstruction Finance Corporation, (b) Bonus Army, (c) Franklin Delano Roosevelt.

2. What did President Hoover think he should do at the onset of the depression?

3. How did Congress go beyond Hoover's intentions when it created the RFC?

4. How did Hoover's reaction to the Bonus Army affect people's opinion of him?

5. What was Roosevelt's position during the campaign?

6. **Critical Thinking** How did American reaction to hardship reflect faith in democratic institutions?

2. **PRESIDENTS** One reason for this action was Roosevelt's desire to show that, although paralyzed by polio, he was still healthy and vigorous enough to tackle the difficult job ahead.

CHAPTER 27 REVIEW

Summary

1. **In the late 1920s, few people noticed the signs of a weakening economy.** Confident in the future when they elected Herbert Hoover President in 1928, many Americans were willing to speculate in land or stocks. When stock prices fell in late 1929, the flood of orders to sell led to a stock market crash.

2. **The economy of the United States slipped into a deep depression.** Businesses and banks closed, and people lost their jobs, their cars, and even their homes. For many Americans, it was a time of deep despair.

3. **President Hoover opposed government interference in the economy.** He did, however, propose the Reconstruction Finance Corporation to halt business and bank failures. He also urged local agencies to provide relief, but the problem overwhelmed their resources. In 1932, the voters signaled their desire for change by electing Franklin D. Roosevelt as President.

See p. T111.

Vocabulary

Choose the answer that best completes each of the following sentences.

1. Speculation is the act of buying land or stock for the purpose of (a) long-term investment, (b) making a quick profit, (c) gaining a tax advantage.

2. Buying stock with money borrowed from a broker is buying (a) on the cuff, (b) on margin, (c) on review.

3. A request by a broker for an investor to put up more money to cover a loan for the purchase of stocks that are worth less than when they were bought is a (a) margin call, (b) credit call, (c) stock option.

4. Products designed to last several years before being replaced are (a) perennial goods, (b) consumable goods, (c) durable goods.

5. Unsold goods on hand are (a) stocks, (b) stock lists, (c) business inventories.
See p. T111.

Chapter Checkup

1. What were the signs of economic problems underlying the prosperity of the 1920s?

2. Describe the personal and political differences between Herbert Hoover and Al Smith, the presidential candidates in 1928.

3. (a) How did speculators try to "get rich quick" during the 1920s? (b) What ended the Florida land boom? (c) How were investors able to buy stocks without paying the full price in cash?

4. Describe how each of the following contributed to the onset of the Great Depression: (a) imbalance of supply and demand; (b) production of more durable goods; (c) rising business inventories; (d) bank closings.

5. (a) How did the depression affect Americans? (b) What were the international repercussions of the onset of depression in the United States?

6. (a) What did President Hoover's advisers urge him to do about the depression? Why? (b) How did Hoover try to restore public confidence? (c) What types of public works programs did Hoover support?

7. (a) What powers did Congress grant the Reconstruction Finance Corporation? (b) How did it use those powers?

8. (a) How did Hoover propose to provide relief? (b) Was this strategy successful? Explain.

See p. T112.

Critical Thinking

1. **Analyzing** (a) How was the Reconstruction Finance Corporation an example of the "trickle-down" theory? (b) Why did Hoover support that theory?

2. **Evaluating** Why do you think almost 60 percent of American voters cast their ballots for Franklin Roosevelt in 1932?

See p. T112.

Connecting Past and Present

1. What problems do American farmers face today that are similar to the problems faced by farmers in the late 1920s?

2. Compare the stock market crash of 1929 and the stock market crash of 1987.

3. How is the role of government in the economy today different from what it was during the Hoover administration?

See p. T112.

Developing Basic Skills

1. **Using Primary Sources** In the library, look at copies of a newspaper from October 1929. What evidence can you find that the stock market was collapsing?

2. **Using Statistics** Study the table on page 607. (a) How many electoral votes did Roosevelt receive in 1932? (b) How many popular votes did the Democratic candidate receive in 1932? (c) How many more popular votes did Hoover receive in 1928 than in 1932? (d) How might you explain this change?

WRITING ABOUT HISTORY

Deciding When to Document

There are certain circumstances in which you must document, or identify, the sources of the information you include in a research paper. Generally, these include the following: (a) any direct quotation, even if it is only a phrase; (b) the summary of an author's ideas; (c) statistical facts; (d) a fact that is not common knowledge or a fact that is disputable. By citing sources, you give the proper credit to a person for the work he or she has done. You also provide valuable information for readers if they want to do further research themselves.

There are times when documentation is not necessary. You do not have to identify the source of any fact that is generally known, even if you did not know the fact yourself. Basic biographical information about a public figure, such as his or her birthplace, education, public offices, and accomplishments, is usually considered general knowledge. A rule of thumb is that a fact that appears un-documented in several sources need not be documented.

It is not necessary to document proverbs and quotations that are familiar. For example, you need not document the adage, "A stitch in time saves nine," or the quotation, "The business of America is business."

Practice: Copy the items from the following list that would require documentation in a research paper.

1. The date of the 1929 stock market crash.
2. The gross national product for 1930.
3. The economist John Kenneth Galbraith's theory of the cause of the depression.
4. A passage from Herbert Hoover's inaugural address.
5. The amount of money invested in real estate in Florida in 1932.
6. A person's account of how the depression affected her life.
7. The fact that thousands of people were homeless during the depression.

A New Deal

28

(1933–1935)

CHAPTER OUTLINE

1 The Roots of the New Deal

2 The First Hundred Days

3 Critics of the New Deal

4 The Second New Deal

CHAPTER OBJECTIVES After completing this chapter, students should be able to
1. identify the ideas behind the New Deal.
2. summarize the programs of the first hundred days.
3. explain why some people opposed the New Deal.
4. describe the programs of the second hundred days.

Millions of Americans gathered expectantly around their radios that Saturday afternoon, March 4, 1933. From the tinny radio speakers came the unmistakable voice of President Franklin D. Roosevelt—strong, vigorous, and self-assured. In his inaugural speech, the President gave his listeners exactly what they needed—confidence in themselves and confidence in the ability of their government to fight the depression.

The situation could not have been bleaker. The banking system was near collapse, and one quarter of the population had virtually no income. As desperation mounted, so did outbursts of panic. In January 1933, several hundred jobless people surrounded a New York City restaurant and demanded free food. In February, 5,000 unemployed people besieged the Seattle County–City Building, demanding help for themselves and their families.

No wonder, then, that Americans found hope in Roosevelt's powerful words: "This great nation will endure as it has endured, will revive and will prosper. So, first of all, let me assert my firm belief that the only thing we have to fear is fear itself . . ."

And Roosevelt promised that government would act. "In their need they [the people] have registered a mandate that they want direct, vigorous action. They have asked for discipline and direction under leadership. They have made me the present instrument of their wishes. In the spirit of the gift I take it."

Roosevelt kept his word. Having promised "a new deal for the American people," he initiated bold new federal programs for relief, recovery, and reform. Yet, while many Americans applauded the New Deal, others protested either that the government had done too little or had interfered too much.

CHAPTER PREVIEW Have students review Chapter 27, then describe the country's situation in 1932. Ask them how most Americans probably felt when FDR said, "The country needs bold, persistent experimentation. It is common sense to take a method and try it. If it fails, admit it and try another. But above all, try something." Ask: Why is an economic depression more difficult to respond to than a natural disaster?

1.

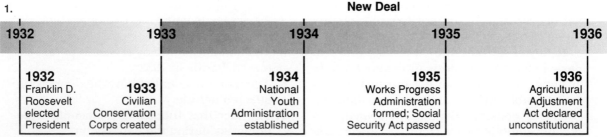

New Deal

1932	1933	1934	1935	1936
1932 Franklin D. Roosevelt elected President	**1933** Civilian Conservation Corps created	**1934** National Youth Administration established	**1935** Works Progress Administration formed; Social Security Act passed	**1936** Agricultural Adjustment Act declared unconstitutional

1. TIME LINE QUESTION Ask: What programs were passed during the New Deal?

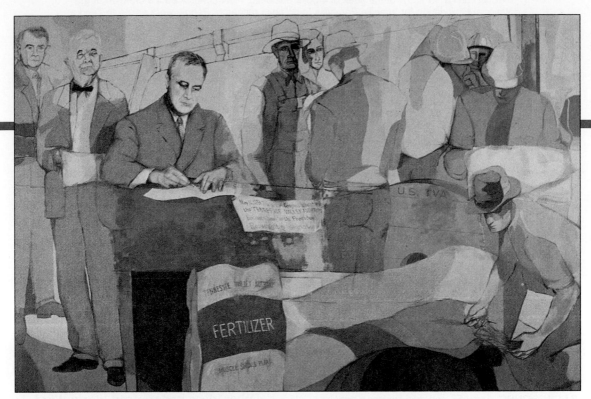

President Roosevelt's first hundred days in office produced a flood of legislation. The sight of the President signing bill after bill encouraged the country. This
1. section of a mural at Wilson Dam in Tennessee commemorates one of Roosevelts's most enduring achievements, the Tennessee Valley Authority.

1. **VISUAL EVIDENCE** Ask: What three groups of people are shown in this mural? Why are they included?

1 The Roots of the New Deal

crisis. The responsibility to lead fell to President Franklin D. Roosevelt.

Franklin D. Roosevelt

READ TO UNDERSTAND

- How Roosevelt's background influenced his political philosophy.

- What ideas provided the basis for Roosevelt's New Deal.

- How Roosevelt's outlook differed from that of Herbert Hoover.

Social workers, sociologists, economists, political scientists, and lawyers streamed into
2. Washington in 1933. They came with new ideas, plans for action, and, above all, enthusiasm. Even the public joined in, flooding President Roosevelt with letters outlining ideas for ending the depression. The goal of all was to pull the nation out of economic

Like his distant cousin Theodore, Franklin Roosevelt came from a wealthy background. As a boy, Roosevelt grew up in the genteel atmosphere of Hyde Park, New York, amid the rolling country estates lining the Hudson River. His strong-willed mother taught him that the wealthy and privileged had an obligation to help the less fortunate.

As a young man, Roosevelt had studied history and government at Harvard College and law at Columbia University. In 1905, he married Anna Eleanor Roosevelt, niece of then President Theodore Roosevelt.

The young Roosevelt rejected a Wall Street law practice for what he hoped would be a more exciting career in politics. In quick succession, he became a New York State

611

2. **BACKGROUND** Popular songs accented the positive, such as "Life Is Just a Bowl of Cherries" and "The Best Things in Life Are Free." FDR's theme was "Happy Days Are Here Again."

1. **PRESIDENTS** In 1937, at the peak of a polio epidemic, FDR announced the creation of the National Foundation for Infantile Paralysis to do polio research. People were asked to send a dime to the White House; this became the March of Dimes.

senator, then assistant secretary of the navy during the war, and, in 1920, the Democratic candidate for Vice President. After the Democrats lost the 1920 election, Roosevelt returned to private life.

The following summer, while vacationing at Campobello Island in Canada with his family, Roosevelt was stricken with polio. His legs paralyzed as a result of the disease, Roosevelt thought at age 39 that his political career was over. But his wife and his devoted political adviser Louis Howe thought otherwise. With their encouragement, Roosevelt endured seven years of grueling exercise and therapy. Once strong enough to walk with the help of heavy metal braces, he resumed his political career.

In 1928, Franklin Roosevelt ran successfully for governor of New York State. The stock market crash and the onset of the Great Depression occurred during his first year in office. As governor, Roosevelt saw the de-

2. **BACKGROUND** The AFL opposed Perkins's appointment because she had never been a union official. But her firm stand on workers' rights won the AFL's respect.

---

2. *Frances Perkins, the first woman cabinet officer, served as Roosevelt's secretary of labor. She had begun her career as a social worker in Jane Addams's Hull House in Chicago. As chairwoman of the New York State Industrial Board, she won reduction of the work week for women in New York from 54 to 48 hours. Here, she wears a hard hat while inspecting the construction of San Francisco's Golden Gate Bridge in 1935.*

pression in terms of the human suffering it caused. He believed that the government was responsible for ending the depression and helping its victims.

Roosevelt had absorbed the lesson that his wealth obliged him to help others. His illness had given him a sense of compassion for victims of misfortune. His background and his belief that government should help people in need shaped his political philosophy. That philosophy provided the foundation for the New Deal.

Ideas for Action

Many of the ideas underlying the New Deal were not new. Some reflected the aims that progressives had worked for early in the century: conserving natural resources, breaking up monopolies, regulating business, and improving working conditions.

Other ideas had roots in World War I. To fight the war against Germany, government planning agencies had coordinated the production of food and manufactured goods. (See page 554.) Many of Roosevelt's advisers urged the creation of similar federal agencies to fight the war against economic depression.

But Roosevelt did not look only to the past. He was willing to experiment and sought out people with untried ideas. Among these were a group of advisers called Roosevelt's brain trust, so named because several of them were university professors. Led by Raymond Moley and Rexford Tugwell, these experts in economics, social planning, and law helped Roosevelt chart the course of the early New Deal. They believed that centralized planning was the key to avoiding overproduction and wasteful competition.

Roosevelt sought for his cabinet the best people, not the best Democrats. Harold Ickes, the new secretary of the interior, had been a progressive Republican and a leader of reform politics in Chicago. Henry A. Wallace, another progressive Republican, fought for new farm programs as secretary of agriculture. Roosevelt called on Frances Perkins, a social work administrator, to take the post of secretary of labor. She was the first woman ever to hold a cabinet position.

3. **ACTIVITY** Have students research the careers of these and other members of Roosevelt's cabinet and present their findings to the class. They should suggest why Roosevelt chose each one for their position.

Although Roosevelt began the New Deal with few concrete plans, he had a wealth of ideas from which to choose. Furthermore, the goals of the New Deal were clear: to provide immediate relief for the unemployed, to bring about the recovery of the economy, and to enact reforms to correct the conditions that had contributed to the economic crisis.

A New Beginning

1. On inauguration day, March 4, 1933, Herbert Hoover and Franklin Roosevelt rode together in an open car down Pennsylvania Avenue toward the Capitol. Relations between the two men had been tense since the election. Hoover had asked Roosevelt for a pledge to carry out certain policies that the Republican President thought essential. Roosevelt, who rejected his predecessor's economic policies, had refused. As they rode along, they barely acknowledged each other.

   When they spoke to the country at large that day, they expressed opposite points of view. Upon leaving office, Hoover had lamented privately, "We are at the end of our rope. There is nothing more we can do."

2. Roosevelt, on the other hand, voiced confidence and optimism. Promising a dramatic change in economic policy, the President concluded, "The nation asks for action and action now. We must act and act quickly."

See p. T113.

SECTION 1 REVIEW

1. **Identify:** (a) brain trust, (b) Harold Ickes, (c) Henry Wallace, (d) Frances Perkins.

2. How might Roosevelt's background have affected his attitude toward fighting the Great Depression?

3. List sources of ideas for the New Deal.

4. Compare Roosevelt's outlook on the depression with that of Herbert Hoover.

5. **Critical Thinking** Why do you think Franklin Roosevelt attracted progressive Republicans to his administration?

---

2 The First Hundred Days

READ TO UNDERSTAND

■ How President Roosevelt dealt with the banking crisis.

■ How New Deal programs provided relief for workers and farmers.

■ What New Deal programs were aimed at industrial recovery.

Immediately upon taking the oath of office, President Roosevelt plunged into action. He called Congress into special session, drafted legislation, and kept in constant touch with the American people. During the first three months of his administration, Roosevelt persuaded Congress to pass 15 major pieces of legislation, each designed to fight the Great Depression. This period of frenzied action came to be called "the hundred days."

Relieving the Banking Crisis

In the four months between Roosevelt's election and his inauguration, the nation's banking system reached the brink of collapse. People swarmed to banks to withdraw their money. They stashed it in mattresses, under floorboards—anywhere but in the banks. As the money flowed out, more banks failed. In a last-ditch effort to save the banks in Detroit, the governor of Michigan ordered them all to close. Officials in Chicago and New York planned similar closings.

On his second day in office, Roosevelt declared a national "bank holiday." In an unprecedented action, he closed every bank in the country until further notice. The "holiday," Roosevelt hoped, would stem the tide of bank failures by preventing people from withdrawing their money.

At the same time, the eager President ordered his secretary of the treasury to draft legislation to save the banking system. Five days later, he called a special session of Congress. With shouts of approval, Congress

613

1. **ACTIVITY** Find a recording of FDR's fireside chats and play excerpts for the class. Have students discuss how the chats reassured Americans during the depression.

passed the Emergency Banking Relief Act almost unanimously.

According to the new law, only those banks with enough funds to meet depositors' withdrawal requests could reopen. Sound banks could borrow federal funds to reopen. Those banks judged unsound were to remain closed.

1. A few nights later, Roosevelt went on nationwide radio with the first of many "fireside chats," informal talks he made to the American people. In clear and convincing terms, he explained the Emergency Banking Relief Act. He urged his listeners to return their money to the reopened banks. "I can assure you," he said, "it is safer to keep your money in a reopened bank than under the mattress."

During those first days, Roosevelt sent Congress a government economy bill that reduced the salaries of all federal employees and cut veterans' pensions. Two days later, Congress passed the bill despite the vehement opposition of veterans. The President

2. **VISUAL EVIDENCE** About 200,000 blacks served in the CCC. Since applicants were selected by state and local relief agencies, some areas excluded blacks.

2. *One of the most successful New Deal programs was the Civilian Conservation Corps, which provided jobs and training for men between the ages of 18 and 25. Members of the CCC planted 17 million acres of forests, built dams, and created parks. The CCC also offered medical care for its members. This corpsman is learning the use of a surveyor's transit.*

4. **BACKGROUND** Young men in the CCC worked hard. A typical day began at 6 A.M. In addition to housing, clothing, food, and training, the men received $30 a month.

3. **PRESIDENTS** Rogers went on, "If he burned down the Capitol, we would cheer and say, 'Well, we at least got a fire started anyhow.'"

also submitted a proposal to legalize the sale of beer and light wines. Again Congress agreed, this time over the opposition of the prohibitionists.*

The speed with which the new administration converted proposals into action heartened many Americans. Will Rogers, the 3. popular humorist, summed up Roosevelt's first week in office: "The whole country is with him, just so he does something."

Relieving the Employment Crisis

In 1933, over 13 million Americans were out of work. These people desperately needed money for the bare essentials: food, clothing, and shelter. During the first months of the new administration, Congress passed major legislation to help Americans meet these needs.

Civilian Conservation Corps The Civilian Conservation Reforestation Relief Act had the dual purpose of conserving natural resources and giving jobs to young people. The act set up the Civilian Conservation Corps (CCC). The CCC enlisted unemployed single 4. men between the ages of 18 and 25 to plant trees, dig reservoirs, build bridges, and develop parks all over the nation. The federal government paid for the men's housing, clothes, and food, so part of their salary could be sent home to help their families. By the end of the 1930s, more than 2.5 million young men had served in the CCC.

Federal Emergency Relief Act Next, Congress passed the Federal Emergency Relief Act (FERA). It gave money to local and state welfare agencies to distribute to the unemployed.

Roosevelt appointed Harry Hopkins to head the FERA. Hopkins, who had administered a relief program in New York, moved to Washington, D.C., set up a desk in a federal office building, and distributed $5 million in his first two hours on the job. Hopkins, 5. however, felt that the program was inadequate. In his view, the unemployed needed

---

*Later in 1933, the Twenty-first Amendment to the Constitution, repealing the earlier Prohibition Amendment, was ratified.

5. **BACKGROUND** Hopkins urged swift passage of relief bills, declaring "Hunger is not debatable."

1. The Civilian Conservation Corps was for men only, and other New Deal job programs also favored men. Both married women and single women, like the protestors shown here, felt the government was overlooking their needs. Many married women were the sole support of their families, and single women argued that they had a right to a job.

1. **CRITICAL THINKING** Ask: Why do you think many of the New Deal programs gave preference to men?

jobs, not handouts, to rebuild their lives and self-respect.

Civil Works Administration President Roosevelt agreed with Hopkins. As a result, he authorized Hopkins to establish the Civil Works Administration (CWA). The CWA offered jobs rather than relief. Within a few months, it employed over 4 million people.

Hopkins displayed a genius for creating jobs. Working for the CWA, construction crews built roads, athletic fields, and airports. Opera singers toured rural areas giving concerts, and archaeologists excavated prehistoric mounds. Despite such achievements, the CWA came under fire. Critics accused the agency of spending funds on unnecessary "make-work." Concerned that the country might grow overly dependent on the CWA, the President ended the program early in 1934.

Planning for Agricultural Recovery

American farmers were well acquainted with economic depression. As you have read in Chapters 26 and 27, farm profits had fallen steadily throughout the 1920s. Much of the problem resulted from chronic surpluses of crops such as wheat, corn, and cotton. As farm prices fell, farmers planted more crops to try to cover their expenses. The increased planting caused even greater surpluses, driving farmers further into debt.

Agricultural Adjustment Act The vicious cycle of overproduction, falling prices, and shrinking farm income demanded drastic action. Roosevelt's advisers thought that the prices of major crops would rise only if production were reduced. They proposed setting limits on crop production, promising that the government would pay the farmers for what they did not plant. The money for these payments would come from taxes on the processors of farm products, such as millers, canners, and meatpackers.

By April 1933, a draft of these proposals was ready for Congress. It was none too soon. Growing numbers of farmers faced bank foreclosures of the mortgages on their farms, and unrest was rippling through the countryside. Moreover, spring had come and farmers were beginning to plant their crops. As one Agri-

2.

615

2. **DISCUSSION** Ask: Why was the money to help farmers raised by taxing mills and packing houses? Do you think this policy was fair or unfair? Why?

culture Department official put it, "We were racing against the sun."

Even so, it was May before Congress passed the Agricultural Adjustment Act, forming the Agricultural Adjustment Administration (AAA). By that time, over 40 million acres (16 million hectares) of cotton had been planted. Another surplus was expected.

Destruction of Crops Roosevelt and Congress decided to pay the farmers to destroy some of their crops by plowing them under the soil. Agriculture agents traveled across the South in the late spring and summer of 1933, persuading farmers to sign up for the campaign. One of the biggest difficulties was persuading the mules. Trained to walk be-

VOICES OF FREEDOM

The Fireside Chats

When Franklin D. Roosevelt became President in March 1933, the American people needed constant reassurance that the nation could recover. To Franklin Roosevelt, radio broadcasts seemed ready-made for this purpose. He could sit in his study and give "fireside chats" that explained government programs to Americans everywhere.

Roosevelt's fireside chats gave the American people new hope. The broadcasts made them feel that he had the people's interests at heart and was working to improve their lives. Secretary of Labor Frances Perkins described the chats:

When he talked on the radio, he saw them [the people] gathered in the little parlor, listening with their neighbors. He was conscious of their faces and hands, their clothes and homes. His voice and his facial expression as he spoke were those of an intimate friend. After he became President, I often was at the White House when he broadcast, and I realized how unconscious he was of the twenty or thirty of us in that room and how clearly his mind was focused on the people listening at the other end. As he talked, his head would nod and his hands would move in simple, natural, comfortable gestures. His face would smile and light up as though he were actually sitting on the front porch or in the parlor with them. People felt this, and it bound them to him in affection.

I have sat in those little parlors and on those porches myself during some of the speeches, and I have seen men and women gathered around the radio, even those who didn't like him or were opposed to him politically, listening with a pleasant, happy feeling of friendship. The exchange between them and him through the medium of the radio was very real. I have seen tears come to their eyes as he told them of some tragic episode. . . . I have also seen them laugh. . . . [T]he laughter of those gathered around radios of the country was a natural, sincere, and affectionate reaching out to this man.
See p. T113.

1. What mannerisms and gestures did Perkins notice when Roosevelt gave his fireside chats? What reactions from the people did she notice?

2. **Critical Thinking** How can a President's ability to communicate with the public affect his or her ability to deal with the other branches of the government?

Thanks to modern machinery and fertile land, American farms were among the most productive in the world. But their very success created the problem of farm surpluses. The more the farmers produced, the less their crops would bring in the marketplace. This painting, Threshing on the High Plains, is by Thomas Hart Benton, one of the American Realist painters who captured the spirit of the nation in their scenes of rural life.

1.

1. VISUAL EVIDENCE Benton was born in Missouri and died in Kansas. Another of his paintings of farm life is found on p. 8.

---

2. PAST AND PRESENT Have students research price supports for farm products today and report their findings to the class.

tween rows of cotton, they now had to be taught to trample the plants.

2. Since there was also a surplus of pork, the AAA bought and disposed of 5 million pigs. Who could escape the bitter irony that food was destroyed while thousands of Americans went hungry? Secretary of Agriculture Henry Wallace, himself a farmer, regretfully pointed out that "to destroy a standing crop goes against the soundest instincts of human nature." Yet the plan seemed to work—for the farmers at least. In later years, farmers limited production as planned, and bad weather helped reduce production further. As a result, prices and farm income rose.

Planning for Industrial Recovery

Like agriculture, industry was trapped in a downward economic spiral. One fourth of the labor force was out of work. Those with jobs were being paid less as employers cut wages to lower costs. Competition for sales was fierce as demand for goods decreased. This decreased demand led to lower production, which caused more unemployment. There seemed no end to the dismal cycle.

Once again, the administration sprang into action. Several members of the brain trust urged that government and industry cooperate in planning industrial production. They suggested using the War Industries Board, which had set priorities and production quotas during World War I, as a model.

National Industrial Recovery Act In June 1933, Congress passed the National Industrial Recovery Act. In its main provision, the act set up trade associations in each industry to draft codes for the industry. The purpose of the codes was to stabilize production, to end the price cutting that forced businesses to cut wages and lay off workers, and to establish decent standards of wages, hours, and working conditions.

To further this last aim, Section 7A of the 3. act forbade employers to interfere with workers' attempts to organize unions. It also guaranteed unions the right to bargain with employers about wages, hours, and working conditions. Union leaders called 7A a "Magna Carta" for labor.

National Recovery Administration To enforce the codes, the National Recovery Industrial Act created the National Recovery **617**

3. CRITICAL THINKING Labor leader John L. Lewis compared Section 7A to the Emancipation Proclamation. Ask students to explain why he made that comparison.

1. Administration (NRA). Under the colorful leadership of former army general Hugh Johnson, the agency began its work during the summer of 1933 with all the fanfare of a national crusade.

The NRA emblem, a Blue Eagle over the slogan "We Do Our Part," became a rallying point for Americans. Eager to show that they followed NRA codes, business people stamped the symbol on their products and posted it in store windows, on factory doors, and on delivery trucks. Huge parades lent drama to the crusade and inspired Americans to buy only products stamped with the symbol. In New York City, a quarter of a million people, ranging from factory workers to stockbrokers to actors, marched down Fifth Avenue behind the NRA Blue Eagle.

However, the NRA needed more than fanfare to succeed. Before long, problems surfaced. NRA regulations resulted in codes for the production of hair tonic, shoulder pads, dog leashes, and even musical comedies. More important, many businesses simply ignored the codes. Industrialist Henry Ford refused to cooperate with the NRA from the start. Labor leaders complained that the NRA kept wages too low. Although the NRA helped to stop the price-cutting–wage-cutting cycle in large industries, enforcing its codes became increasingly difficult.

Public Works Administration The National Industrial Recovery Act also set up the Public Works Administration (PWA), headed by Secretary of the Interior Harold Ickes. Like the CWA, the new agency tried to stimulate employment by spending large sums of money on public works projects. Ickes stressed honesty and quality, so the PWA started slowly. Eventually, PWA workers built a municipal auditorium in Kansas City; the Triborough Bridge in New York City; a water-

2. **MAP READING** Ask: Which cities are located along the Tennessee River? In which states were major dams built? What other river was part of the TVA?

MAP STUDY *The vast Tennessee Valley Authority project affected seven states, harnessing the power of the Tennessee River and others nearby. In addition to electricity, TVA dams created lakes that spurred recreational development in the region. The map shows the major TVA dams and the total area provided with electric power. In which state was a dam built outside the area served by the TVA?*

2.

See p. T113.

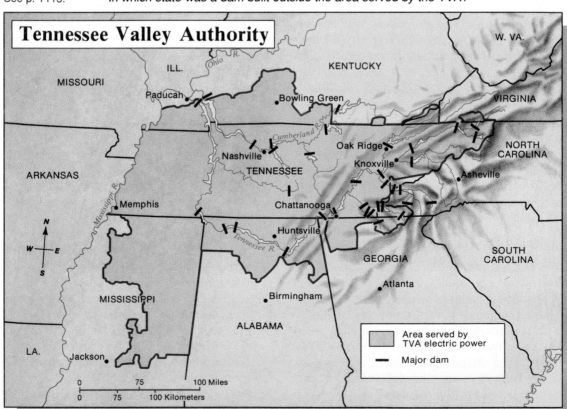

Tennessee Valley Authority

W. VA.
MISSOURI
ILL.
Ohio R.
KENTUCKY
Paducah
Bowling Green
VIRGINIA
Cumberland R.
Oak Ridge
NORTH CAROLINA
Nashville
Knoxville
TENNESSEE
ARKANSAS
Asheville
Mississippi R.
Memphis
Chattanooga
Huntsville
Tennessee R.
SOUTH CAROLINA
GEORGIA
Atlanta
MISSISSIPPI
Birmingham
ALABAMA
LA.
Jackson

Area served by TVA electric power
— Major dam

N W E S

0   75   100 Miles
0   75   100 Kilometers

Norris Dam, shown here, was the first of the great TVA projects to be completed,
1. in 1936. It was named after Senator George Norris of Nebraska, who first urged creation of the TVA and other public-power projects. Though a Republican, Norris strongly supported Roosevelt's programs, and he faced heavy criticism from his party for doing so.

---

1. **BIOGRAPHY** George Norris (1861–1944) was a Senator from 1912 to 1943. A progressive, he often went against his party. Norris once said that he "would rather be right than regular."

2. supply system in Denver; a deep-water port for Brownsville, Texas; new schools in Los Angeles; and two aircraft carriers for the navy.

GREAT DEBATE

Remaking a Region: TVA

In a time of bold experimentation, perhaps no program was more daring than the Tennessee Valley Authority (TVA). The TVA transformed the entire Tennessee River Valley from a backwater of poor farms into a rich and productive region. Never before had a nation embarked upon a conservation and social planning effort on such a grand scale.

3. The area, extending over parts of seven states, had fallen victim to careless use of resources. Loggers had cut down most trees in the area, loosening the soil and causing massive erosion. This poor land use, along with the frequent flooding of the Tennessee River, made farming difficult. Personal income in the region was half the national average, and living conditions were abysmal.

Impact of the TVA The TVA changed the face of the area. Engineers built a series of dams along the Tennessee River and its tributaries. Then the TVA constructed hydroelectric power plants to supply electricity to homes and farms in the valley and to attract industry and new jobs. The dams helped control flooding and created recreation areas. (See the map on page 618.)

The TVA channeled some of the newly created power into the manufacture of fertilizer, selling it to farmers at cost. With fertilizers, farmers improved the land and were able to increase harvests. The TVA also planted millions of trees in the valley to stop erosion. Finally, the authority introduced many educational, recreational, and health services into the region to improve economic and social conditions.

Criticism of the TVA The TVA stirred angry controversy. Power companies in the area objected to government production and sale of power. They charged that such government competition was unfair. Other crit-

619

2. **TECHNOLOGY** The aircraft carriers were the *Yorktown* and *Enterprise*. The PWA also built Boulder Dam and a new sewer system in Chicago.

3. **GEOGRAPHY** Have students use the map on p. 618 to name the seven states. (regions)

See p. T113.

ics objected to "social planning" by the TVA.
1. They maintained that the federal government
had no right to interfere in the region and
that problems there were matters of state
and local concern. Some residents resisted a
change in their way of life and the introduction of "this newfangled pipe water" running
into their homes. Despite such criticism, the
mammoth project transformed the region and
continues to operate today. ■

Other Hundred Days Measures

The legislation passed during the first
hundred days of Roosevelt's administration
was not part of a unified plan for recovery.
Rather, each law was an attempt to solve a
particular problem or to change a particular
condition plaguing the nation.

The Truth-in-Securities Act was aimed at
the wild stock market speculation that helped
bring on the crash. This law required full
public disclosure of all appropriate financial
information about corporation stocks. Mis-
representation became a criminal offense.

The Glass-Steagall Banking Act reformed
the banking system. It created the Federal
Deposit Insurance Corporation (FDIC), which
to this day insures savings accounts. The law
provided that if an FDIC-insured bank failed,
the government would reimburse the depositors. Reassured customers began depositing
rather than withdrawing savings.

The Farm Credit Administration (FCA)
was established to provide farmers with low-
interest loans to help pay their debts. During
the mid-1930s, the FCA helped as many as
300 farmers a day save their farms from fore-
closure and bankruptcy.

The Home Owners' Loan Corporation
(HOLC) performed a similar service for home
owners. Owners could get low-interest, long-
term loans that reduced their monthly house
payments. The HOLC helped almost 1,000
families a day keep their homes during the
mid-1930s.

The hundred days ended in the early
hours of June 16 as Congress adjourned. The
weary legislators expressed the hope that
their efforts would bring the depression to a
swift conclusion. But the economic crisis was
not so easily solved.

620

SECTION 2 REVIEW

1. **Identify:** (a) fireside chat, (b) Harry
Hopkins, (c) Blue Eagle.

2. How did President Franklin Roosevelt try
to relieve the banking crisis?

3. (a) What was the purpose of the Federal
Emergency Relief Act? (b) How did the
purpose of the Civil Works Administration differ from that of the FERA?

4. (a) What was the main provision of the
National Industrial Recovery Act? (b) What
was the main purpose of the Public Works
Administration?

5. List three actions of the Tennessee Valley
Authority.

6. **Critical Thinking** How did Roosevelt's
economic policies differ from those of
Herbert Hoover?

3 Critics of the New Deal

READ TO UNDERSTAND

■ What proposals were made by New Deal
critics Senator Long, Father Coughlin, and
Dr. Townsend.

■ Why Roosevelt was concerned about the
issues his critics raised.

■ How the Supreme Court viewed New Deal
measures.

A noted political writer, Walter Lippmann, 2.
praised the first hundred days of the New
Deal: "At the end of February, we were a
[collection] of disorderly panic-stricken mobs
and factions. In the hundred days from March
to June, we became again an organized nation confident of our power to provide for
our own security and to control our own
destiny."

Not all Americans, however, were enthusiastic about the New Deal. Some critics believed that the government was interfering

1. **READING** For a look at Long and other colorful figures of the 1930s, interested students can read *Just Around The Corner*, by Robert Bendiner.

too much in people's lives. Others believed that the administration should take more drastic steps to aid the American people. Many of these people had originally supported Roosevelt. Now they attacked the New Deal in growing numbers.

Demands for Stronger Action

The depression was stubborn, and in two years even the most dramatic New Deal programs had failed to turn the economy around. Throughout the nation, some people began to look to those who offered simple answers to complex problems.

1.   From Louisiana came Senator Huey Long, preaching the gospel of Share the Wealth. Originally a supporter of Roosevelt, the Kingfish, as he was called, felt that the New Deal had done nothing to redistribute the nation's wealth more evenly. Long suggested that the government confiscate "the swollen fortunes" of the rich and tax 100 percent of all income over $1 million a year. The senator wanted the money redistributed to provide every family with a house, a car, education for the children, a pension for the elderly, and an income of $2,000 to $3,000 a year. Long's idea had little practical basis, but it attracted millions of supporters, especially among the poor.

2.   Father Charles Coughlin, another vocal critic of Roosevelt and the New Deal, broadcast his views over the airwaves from Detroit. Each week, the "radio priest" told at least 10 million listeners that the depression was the fault of an international conspiracy of bankers. Before the 1932 election, Coughlin had backed Roosevelt, telling his listeners that they could choose "Roosevelt or ruin." But Coughlin lost his enthusiasm for the New Deal, believing that stronger actions should be taken against "banking and money interests."

    Dr. Francis E. Townsend, a retired California physician, wanted the government to help older citizens. He proposed that the government pay every person over age 60 a monthly pension of $200. In return, the recipient would agree to retire, freeing a job for someone else. The pensioner would also agree to spend the entire $200 within the month, thereby further stimulating the econ-

Cartoonists and critics often made fun of the many "alphabet agencies" created by the New Deal. In his election campaign, Roosevelt had promised to try new remedies to end the depression. If those remedies failed, he said, he would abandon them and try others. Can you supply the full names of the programs indicated with letters in this cartoon?

3. **VISUAL EVIDENCE** Ask: What does the cartoon suggest about the relationship between FDR and the Congress?

omy. No matter how impractical Townsend's plan was, it attracted members to Townsend Clubs all over the country.

    Roosevelt and his advisers knew that they could not ignore these critics. "In normal times, the radio and other appeals by them would not be effective," said Roosevelt. "However, these are not normal times; the people are jumpy and very ready to run after strange gods." Furthermore, the rise of dictators in Italy and Germany (see page 652) had shown to what extremes desperate nations might go. Consequently, the planners of the New Deal began to reconsider their positions regarding taxation, banking, and aid to the elderly.

The Conservative Reaction

While Long, Coughlin, and Townsend wanted the government to do more, many critics wanted it to do less. These conservatives saw   **621**

2. **BIOGRAPHY** One 1930s poll showed that Coughlin (1891–1979) was second only to FDR in national popularity. When he began broadcasting pro-Nazi views, his radio program was canceled, and his superiors in the Roman Catholic Church reassigned him to a small parish in New York.

the new laws as a threat to individual liberty.

1. Many business people argued that excessive taxes and regulations were crippling them. Raymond Moley, who had been a member of Roosevelt's brain trust, charged that the free-enterprise system was at risk.

In 1934, conservatives founded the American Liberty League. Its members included wealthy Americans like Pierre Du Pont, as well as bitter Roosevelt rivals. Al Smith, Roosevelt's one-time ally, belonged to the League. According to League members, the government had a duty to encourage private enterprise and use of property. Attacks by the wealthy had little popular appeal, however, and provided Roosevelt additional arguments to rally support for the New Deal.

Attack by the Supreme Court

Administration officials viewed the depression as a national emergency, similar to war, which justified an expansion of government power. They believed the government needed that power to revitalize the nation's economic and social well-being.

From the outset, however, many of Roosevelt's advisers worried that the Supreme Court might find this expansion of federal power unconstitutional. Their concerns proved justified. On May 27, 1935, the Supreme Court handed down a decision involving a New York chicken processor who had been convicted of violating an NRA code. In *Schechter* v. *United States,* the Court decided that the National Industrial Recovery Act was unconstitutional because the federal government had no power to regulate intrastate commerce, commerce within the boundaries of one state.

In 1936, the Court struck down the Agricultural Adjustment Act. The Court ruled that Congress could not tax food processors to pay farmers for cutbacks in production. It was unconstitutional to take "money from one group for the benefit of another."

2. In the same session, the Court declared three other New Deal laws unconstitutional. In each case, the Court ruled that the federal government had gone beyond the limits of constitutional authority. Roosevelt complained that the Court's decisions reflected

a "horse and buggy," or old-fashioned, interpretation of what the Constitution allowed, but the decisions stood.

See p. T114.

1. **Identify:** (a) Huey Long, (b) Charles Coughlin, (c) Francis E. Townsend, (d) American Liberty League, (e) *Schechter* v. *United States.*

2. Describe the program suggested by each of the following: (a) Senator Long; (b) Father Coughlin; (c) Dr. Townsend.

3. Why did Roosevelt and his advisers feel that they could not ignore the criticisms of Long, Coughlin, and Townsend?

4. List two New Deal laws the Supreme Court declared unconstitutional.

5. **Critical Thinking** Why do you think the Great Depression led to the development of some extreme proposals?

3. **VOCABULARY** Have students look up this term in the glossary before they begin reading.

The Second New Deal

READ TO UNDERSTAND

■ How the Works Progress Administration and Wagner Act benefited workers.

■ How public utilities were regulated.

■ What benefits were provided under the Social Security Act.

■ *Vocabulary:* utility company.   3.

Attacks on the New Deal inspired President Roosevelt to new action. In January 1935, he reminded Congress, "We have not weeded out the over-privileged, and we have not effectively lifted up the under-privileged." In this spirit, the determined President and Congress launched a "second hundred days" of legislative action, a "second New Deal." From July into September 1935, Congress once again addressed the triple problems of relief, recovery, and reform.

622

1. **LOCAL HISTORY** Have interested students find out what projects the WPA undertook in your area. They might begin their research by calling a local historical society.

Putting People to Work

The human suffering caused by unemployment still plagued the nation as the New Deal entered its third year. Twenty million people relied on public assistance and welfare to survive. Roosevelt decided that only a massive public works program could provide the jobs needed to bring relief. After some pressure from the administration, Congress passed the Emergency Relief Appropriations Act, which created the Works Progress Administration (WPA).

Roosevelt named Harry Hopkins, former head of the Civil Works Administration, to head the new agency. Hopkins distributed huge sums of money to provide jobs and get money into circulation. As with the CWA, Hopkins was accused of creating "make-work" projects that would not benefit the country in the long run. "People don't eat in the long run," Hopkins replied with exasperation. "They eat today."

1. The WPA immediately put people to work on a wide variety of construction projects. WPA workers built or improved 2,500 hospitals, 5,000 schools, 13,000 parks and playgrounds, and 1,000 airports. But such projects employed only construction workers. Hopkins set about providing jobs for other workers as well.

2. Soon the WPA established several projects for people in the arts. The Federal Theatre Project hired actors and directors to put on plays, vaudeville shows, and circuses across the country. Often traveling to remote rural areas, the entertainers performed for people who had never seen a theater production before. The Federal Writers' Project employed authors to write historical and geographical guides for every state in the nation. The Federal Art Project hired artists to paint murals in public buildings. Despite providing work for millions of people, the WPA fell far short of providing work for all the able-bodied unemployed.

Nearly 3 million families were still on relief, and youngsters in such households often had to quit school to look for a job. In so doing, young people lost the opportunity for an education and more often than not wound up on the unemployment rolls.

2. **BACKGROUND** Millions of Americans heard free concerts or took free music or art classes.

An extension of the WPA, the National Youth Administration (NYA) attacked that problem. The NYA offered young people a way to earn money while in school by providing part-time jobs in and around the schools. The agency helped 600,000 students work their way through college and another 1.5 million to stay in high school.

Reforming Labor Relations

When the Supreme Court declared the National Industrial Recovery Act unconstitutional, the protections that Section 7A of the act gave to organized labor were struck down with it. Senator Robert F. Wagner of New York took up the workers' cause in Congress. In 1935, he introduced a new bill to guarantee workers' rights to organize and bargain collectively. The bill also banned as unfair cer-

3. **ACTIVITY** Have students find and present copies of other murals painted by WPA artists.

Roosevelt wanted to provide people with jobs, not handouts. "What I am seeking," he said, "is . . . to substitute work for relief." To further this goal, the WPA created over 1.4 million individual projects. They included murals and paintings like the one shown here, titled Paper Workers. *The artist depicts the workers almost as parts of the machine on which they work. The idea that modern industry is dehumanizing was a popular theme of the 1930s.*

Mary McLeod Bethune

It was an encounter of great importance. Two highly energetic and determined Americans were meeting for the first time. Mary McLeod Bethune was reporting to President Franklin Delano Roosevelt on what the National Youth Administration meant to minority groups.

Mrs. Bethune spoke emphatically. "We are bringing life and spirit to these many thousands who for so long have been in darkness! Now I speak, Mr. President, not as Mrs. Bethune but as the voice of 14 million Americans who seek to achieve full citizenship. . . . We want to continue to open doors for these millions." President Roosevelt, moved by Mrs. Bethune's plea, pledged his support.

Mary McLeod Bethune had traveled a long road to become adviser to the President. Born in 1875, she was the youngest of 17 children. Her parents were poor sharecroppers who had been slaves. She grew up with a deep religious faith and a profound love of learning. In 1904, with only $1.50 in her pocket and six students, Bethune started a college for blacks. The school became the successful Bethune-Cookman College.

1.

President Roosevelt made Mary McLeod Bethune a member of his Black Cabinet—a group of black Americans who advised him on programs and policies. In 1936, when the Division of Negro Affairs of the NYA was estab-

lished, she was named its director. Bethune was the first black American to head a government agency.

Mary McLeod Bethune worked tirelessly in government service and education. Greeting her one day, President Roosevelt said, "I am always glad to see you, Mrs. Bethune, because you never ask for anything for yourself."

See p. T114.

1. What were two of Mrs. Bethune's accomplishments?

2. **Critical Thinking** Why was Mrs. Bethune's first meeting with President Roosevelt so important for black Americans during the depression?

1. **ACTIVITY** Have students research the careers of other members of the Black Cabinet, such as Robert C. Weaver and Ralph Bunche. Have them present their findings to the class.

tain practices employers used to discourage employees from organizing. Such practices included firing workers who joined unions or infiltrating unions with company spies.

Many business people opposed the bill vehemently, insisting that it defined unfair action by management but said nothing about unfair action by labor. Nevertheless, Congress passed the National Labor Relations Act in

2. July 1935. The Wagner Act, as it was known, established the National Labor Relations Board (NLRB) to administer the law. The NLRB had the authority to determine when there was sufficient worker demand to warrant union representation in an industry. In such matters, the business community often

accused the NLRB of routinely favoring labor over management.

Regulating the Utilities

By the 1930s, huge holding companies had taken control of **utility companies,** which distributed gas and electricity in various sections of the country. These utilities closed out competition in many areas. Thus, they could set rates at levels of their own choosing, and customers had no choice but to pay. The Roosevelt administration watched this development with growing concern.

To break these monopolies and lower customer rates, Roosevelt urged Congress to

2. **PAST AND PRESENT** Have interested students use the *Readers' Guide* to find articles about recent actions of the NLRB and report their findings to the class.

pass the Public Utilities Holding Company Act. Under this act, the government could prohibit holding companies from owning more than one utility company in any one part of the country. The government could dissolve any holding company that could not prove that it was servicing a local area efficiently.

The powerful utilities mounted a million-dollar campaign to defeat the legislation. But

1. Congress passed it nonetheless. The Public Utilities Holding Company Act ended most of the large utility empires and put the rest under the direct supervision of government agencies.

GREAT DEBATE

Providing Social Security

Should a community be responsible for its helpless? For Secretary of Labor Frances Perkins, the answer was yes. One of her top priorities was providing security against poverty in old age and against wage loss during unemployment. In fact, Perkins was so concerned that she refused to take her cabinet post until Roosevelt accepted her ideas for a program of old age and unemployment insurance. Once in office, she mobilized support for the program and, with the help of Senator Wagner, guided the legislation through Congress.

In September 1935, Congress passed the last piece of legislation of the second hundred days: the Social Security Act. The act created a national system of pensions for the elderly, supported by payments from employers, employees, and the federal government. It also established state-run insurance programs to provide unemployment compensation for people who lost their jobs. Finally, the act granted states money to provide support for the handicapped and dependent children.

Criticism of the Social Security Act was varied. Some people thought the bill did not go far enough in providing for the unemployed or the elderly. They argued that too many workers were not eligible to take part. Other people feared the idea of a public rather

3. than a private insurance program. One business leader claimed it would ruin the nation "by destroying initiative, discouraging thrift,

The Social Security Act created a separate fund in the federal treasury for old age and disability benefits. Critics said that Social Security was the first step toward socialism. To some, the idea of issuing a number to identify each citizen was an attack on American individualism.

2. **VISUAL EVIDENCE** Ask: Do you agree with the cartoonist that widespread use of Social Security numbers has depersonalized America?

and stifling individual responsibility." Despite the criticism, the Social Security Act continues as law today. ■

See p. T114.

SECTION 4 REVIEW

1. **Identify:** Robert F. Wagner.

2. **Define:** utility company.

3. (a) What problem led to creation of the Works Progress Administration? (b) How did the WPA try to solve the problem? (c) What did the National Youth Administration accomplish?

4. What rights did the Wagner Act guarantee to workers?

5. (a) What groups of people did the Social Security Act of 1935 affect? (b) Describe its major provisions.

6. **Critical Thinking** How are the services provided by utilities different from those provided by other companies?

625

Summary

1. **President Franklin Roosevelt instituted the New Deal to end the Great Depression.** Although he did not have a specific plan, he had a wealth of ideas, experiences, and advisers on which to rely.

2. **During the first hundred days, the Roosevelt administration drafted a flood of legislation to provide relief and recovery.** These laws aimed to end bank failures, distribute money for food and clothing, and ease unemployment. The AAA and NRA were created to further the recovery of agriculture and industry.

3. **The New Deal encountered considerable opposition.** Some critics thought the programs did not do enough to help the American people. Others argued that the actions of the government threatened the free-enterprise system. In 1935, the Supreme Court ruled several New Deal laws unconstitutional.

4. **The second hundred days saw renewed efforts to legislate relief, recovery, and reform.** The WPA put people to work. Organized labor won important rights in the Wagner Act, and utility companies were regulated by the Public Utilities Holding Company Act. The elderly and unemployed gained protection from financial ruin through the Social Security Act.

See p. T115.

Vocabulary

On a separate sheet of paper, write the word or words that best complete each of the following sentences.

1. The _____ was a nickname for a group of Roosevelt's advisers.

2. The closing of banks for an indefinite period was referred to as the _____.

3. The _____ were Roosevelt's radio broadcasts that explained government policies.

4. _____ commerce is commerce within the boundaries of one state.

5. A (An) _____ is a company that distributes gas and electricity.

See p. T115.

Chapter Checkup

1. How did Franklin Roosevelt's past experiences help shape his policies?

2. Explain how each of the following contributed to the ideas of the New Deal: (a) progressivism; (b) lessons from the world war; (c) the brain trust.

3. (a) Why did Congress pass the Emergency Banking Relief Act? (b) What were its major provisions?

4. (a) What two pieces of legislation did Congress pass during the first hundred days to provide immediate relief to the unemployed? (b) Describe the provisions of each act. (c) What was the purpose of the Civil Works Administration?

5. (a) Describe the Agricultural Adjustment Act. (b) What extraordinary actions did the government take to implement it?

6. (a) How did the National Industrial Recovery Act try to stop the downward economic spiral in industry? (b) What problems arose in implementing the act?

7. (a) What was the purpose of the Tennessee Valley Authority? (b) Why did the TVA stir up controversy?

8. Explain why each of the following criticized the New Deal: (a) Huey Long; (b) Charles Coughlin; (c) Francis E. Townsend; (d) Raymond Moley.

9. (a) Why did the Supreme Court rule the National Industrial Recovery Act (NIRA) unconstitutional? (b) The Agricultural Adjustment Act (AAA)?

10. What legislation made up the second hundred days?

See p. T115.

Critical Thinking

1. Comparing (a) What advances did organized labor make during the New Deal? (b) How did those advances compare with the situation of labor during the early 1920s? (See Chapter 26.) (c) How might you explain the difference?

2. Supporting an Opinion (a) Why did some critics fear that the New Deal programs would undermine the free-enterprise system? (b) Do you think their concern was justified? Explain.

See p. T115.

Connecting Past and Present

1. The TVA was created to help Americans living in a poverty-stricken region of the United States. (a) Which regions of the country have high levels of poverty today? (b) Would a TVA-type program help end poverty in these regions? Why or why not?

2. Which New Deal measures would provide protection from hardship should another depression occur today?

See p. T115.

Developing Basic Skills

1. Classifying Make a chart with three columns. In the first column, list the New Deal laws described in this chapter. In the second column, describe the problem or problems each law tried to solve. In the third column, list the groups of people each law affected.

After completing your chart, answer the following questions: (a) Which problem generated the largest number of laws? (b) What groups of people were most affected by the laws? Explain.

2. Researching Find out whether the Works Progress Administration sponsored any projects near where you live. (You might consult the local chamber of commerce or local historical society.) How do you think the WPA contributed to your community?

WRITING ABOUT HISTORY

Avoiding Plagiarism

Plagiarism is copying information word for word or paraphrasing information without giving credit to the original source. Proper documentation can mean the difference between plagiarism and a well-written paper.

Practice: Compare each of the following paragraphs with the last paragraph in the Chapter Opener on page 610. Which paragraph is an example of plagiarism? Why?

1. As he promised, Roosevelt led the nation with courage and action. He worked toward "a new deal for the American people" by implementing bold federal programs aimed at relief, recovery, and reform. Many Americans supported his programs. Others, however, felt that the government had done too much or too little.

2. Roosevelt's formula for economic recovery seemed simple enough: Courage plus action equals a new deal for the American people. Soon after taking office, Roosevelt tested the formula with bold government programs for relief, recovery, and reform. As time passed, however, the New Deal experiments drew fire.

The New Deal Continues (1936–1939)

29

CHAPTER OUTLINE

 1 New Deal Gains and Losses

 2 Further Reform

 3 Life During the New Deal Years

CHAPTER OBJECTIVES After completing this chapter, students should be able to
1. explain why a new recession began in 1937.
2. discuss New Deal reforms of FDR's second term.
3. describe the impact of the New Deal on American society.
4. analyze oral evidence.

CHAPTER PREVIEW Have students study the paintings on pp. 629 and 635. Explain that drought and dust ravaged the heartland of America during the mid-1930s. Ask them what they know about the Dust Bowl and discuss the information and mood the paintings convey.

As the curtain rose, the spotlight centered on "Thomas Edison," proudly holding up his new creation—the light bulb. A group of business people crowded around him, eager to market the product. In a later scene, a woman nagged an old bearded farmer to "raise holy blazes" to get electricity on his farm.

The scenes were part of *Power,* a play produced by the Federal Theatre Project, which provided jobs for people in the arts. The New Deal FTP program made it possible for writers to write, musicians to perform, artists to paint, and theater people to practice their crafts.

Within two years of its founding in 1935, the FTP could successfully boast 13,000 theater people back to work, shows open all across the country, and a total audience of 25 million people. Tour groups traveled the byways of depression America, bringing Shakespeare to Florida and the ballet to Iowa.

Many FTP productions carried a New Deal message. *Power,* for example, focused on the need for cheap electricity. And in *Pinocchio,* a children's favorite, the puppet Pinocchio encouraged generosity by offering money to the poor.

Audiences approved, but congressional conservatives argued that some of the plays produced by FTP were outright propaganda. They bristled at spending tax money to support what they considered extremist ideas. In 1939, Congress cut off funds for the Federal Theatre Project. Staging a dramatic protest, the producers of *Pinocchio* laid the puppet in a pine coffin. On it, they inscribed the following words: "Born December 23, 1938; Killed by Act of Congress, June 30, 1939."

At one time, the New Deal could do no wrong in the eyes of Congress. In 1933, one senator had commented, "Whatever law the President thinks he may need to end the depression, Congress will jump through a hoop to put through." By 1936, the legislators would jump no more.

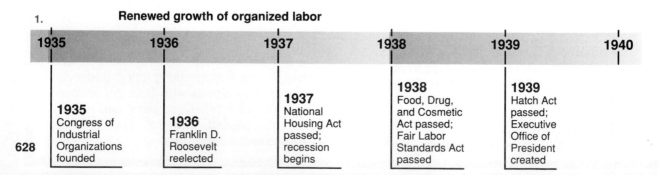

1.

Renewed growth of organized labor

1935	1936	1937	1938	1939	1940
1935 Congress of Industrial Organizations founded	**1936** Franklin D. Roosevelt reelected	**1937** National Housing Act passed; recession begins	**1938** Food, Drug, and Cosmetic Act passed; Fair Labor Standards Act passed	**1939** Hatch Act passed; Executive Office of President created	

628

1. TIME LINE QUESTION Ask: In what year was there a new economic downturn?

New Deal programs stimulated production in all the arts. In The Annual Move, a
1936 painting by Texas artist Otis Dozier, a family is packing up its belongings to
1. seek a better life elsewhere. Parts of the Midwest suffered from a long drought during
the early 1930s. Many farm families headed for California, in hope of a new start.

1. **VISUAL EVIDENCE** Have students list details in the painting that illustrate this family's
economic state.

1 New Deal Gains and Losses

READ TO UNDERSTAND

■ How Roosevelt built a new coalition that
transformed the Democratic party.

■ Why Roosevelt tried to "pack" the Supreme
Court.

■ Why the nation experienced a new economic
crisis in 1937 and 1938.

2. ■ *Vocabulary:* deficit spending.

How did the people react to the New Deal? In
1934, they had voted their approval. That
year, the Democrats gained 20 new seats in
the Senate and 18 in the House. But the big
test would be the presidential election of 1936.

Roosevelt's critics began their assault.
The powerful Chicago *Daily Tribune* led the
anti–New Deal charge, repeatedly urging vot-

ers to "turn the rascals out." As election
day, 1936, approached, the *Tribune* ran a daily
reminder in italic type: "*Only 201 [200,
199 . . .] days remain in which to save your
country. What are you doing to save it?*"

The Election of 1936

The Republicans named Governor Alfred M.
Landon of Kansas as their presidential candidate. Given Roosevelt's overwhelming popularity, Landon seemed to be their most
electable prospect. A moderate Republican,
he had accepted many New Deal efforts to
use government power to fight the Great Depression. Also, Landon had an impressive
political record. In 1934, when Democrats
swept many state and congressional elections,
he had been the only Republican governor to
win reelection.

Besides moderate Republicans, Landon's
campaign attracted business people and others who attacked Roosevelt's programs as a
threat to the free-enterprise system. The op-

629

2. **VOCABULARY** Have students look up this term in the glossary before they begin reading.

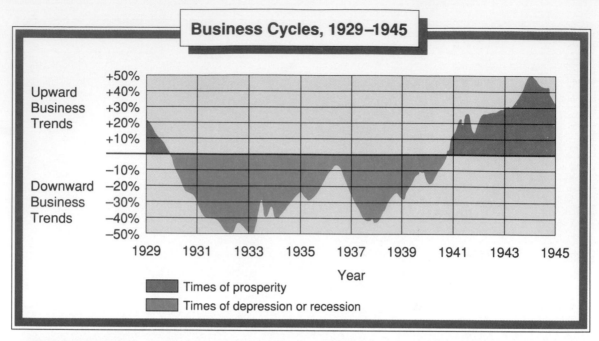

Business Cycles, 1929–1945

Upward Business Trends: +50% +40% +30% +20% +10%

Downward Business Trends: −10% −20% −30% −40% −50%

Year: 1929 1931 1933 1935 1937 1939 1941 1943 1945

■ Times of prosperity
■ Times of depression or recession

GRAPH STUDY This graph traces fluctuations in the business cycle beginning with the stock market crash of 1929 and ending with the close of World War II in 1945. Economic recovery from the Great Depression seemed near in 1936, but the deep slump of 1937–1938 signaled a new recession. As the graph shows, the depression did not finally end until the United States geared up for war production in 1941. How would you describe the state of American business during 1936? See p. T116. **1.**

1. GRAPH READING Ask: In what year did the business cycle reach its lowest point?

position of some critics was so fierce that it bordered on hatred. The family of millionaire J. P. Morgan, Jr., for example, cautioned visitors not to say the President's name around Morgan; it might cause his blood pressure to rise sky high.

2. Roosevelt met the opposition head on. In a campaign speech at Madison Square Garden in New York City, he lashed out against his critics in business. "Never before in all our history have these forces been so united against one candidate as they stand today," he told the cheering crowd. "They are unanimous in their hate for me—and I welcome their hatred."

At first, Landon did not call for an end to New Deal programs. Instead, he argued that Republicans could manage the programs more effectively, waste less money, and achieve better results. But when this strategy brought little support, Landon stepped up his attack. By November, he was denouncing the Social Security Act as "unjust, unworkable, stupidly drafted, and wastefully financed."

On election day, the people gave the President and the New Deal a huge vote of

confidence. Roosevelt carried every state except Maine and Vermont. Equally impressive was the popular vote: Roosevelt, 61 percent; Landon, 37 percent; and the Union party, formed by followers of Father Coughlin, Dr. Townsend, and Huey Long, only 2 percent.

The Roosevelt Coalition

Much of the New Deal's success at the polls stemmed from the Democratic coalition Roosevelt had carefully built since 1932. Each group in the coalition had its own reasons for backing the Democratic party.

Before 1936, the Democrats had been the smaller of the two major parties. They drew membership from two very different sources. One source was the "solid South," where distaste for the Republican party had run high since the Civil War and Reconstruction. The other source was the political machines of many large eastern and midwestern cities. Those party organizations could deliver votes for Democratic candidates with the regularity of well-oiled machinery. Most of the votes came from immigrant groups that had recently settled in the cities.

630

2. BACKGROUND Landon's campaign symbol was the sunflower. FDR joked that the sunflower was yellow, had a black heart, and died in November.

1. **CITIZENSHIP** Before FDR, many blacks had felt, as Frederick Douglass said, that "the Republican party is the ship, all else the sea."

To that base, Roosevelt added organized labor. The Wagner Act (see page 624) had guaranteed workers the right to organize and to bargain collectively with employers. As a result, the Democrats could now count on organized labor not only for votes but also for hefty campaign donations.

1. Roosevelt also attracted blacks to the Democratic party. Abraham Lincoln had issued the Emancipation Proclamation, and for years blacks had remained loyal to the Republicans, "the party of Lincoln." However, under the New Deal, the government began taking an active interest in the conditions of black life. Eleanor Roosevelt, especially, tried to see that New Deal programs did not discriminate by race. Blacks also received appointments to important government positions. (See page 624.)

Finally, Roosevelt drew intellectuals to the Democratic party. Although few in number, they had significant influence. Including teachers, university professors, and writers, they helped mold public opinion by publicizing and popularizing Democratic party ideas and candidates.

2. The new coalition, first evident in 1936, helped to change the face of American politics. It not only strengthened the Democratic party, but also made it the majority party for decades to come.

An Attack on the Supreme Court

Roosevelt opened his second term as President with a startling proposal. In February 1937, he asked Congress to redesign the federal judiciary. Pointing to long delays in the hearing of cases, he argued that there were too few federal judges.

3. **Roosevelt's Plan** The heart of the problem, Roosevelt claimed, was the Supreme Court. In his opinion, the Court needed not only more justices but also younger ones. To that end, he recommended that the President have the power to appoint one additional justice for every justice age 70 or over who refused to retire. The maximum number of Supreme Court justices would increase from nine to fifteen.

Roosevelt was not really concerned about the efficiency of the federal judiciary. As you have read, the Supreme Court had already

3. **BACKGROUND** Roosevelt scornfully referred to the Supreme Court as "the nine old men."

2. **PAST AND PRESENT** Have students use the *Readers' Guide* to find what groups supported each major party in the last presidential election.

struck down several key pieces of New Deal legislation. (See page 622.) The President feared that the Social Security Act and the Wagner Act might also fail a Court test.

Admittedly, the Court posed a major roadblock to the administration's plans. Four justices usually supported New Deal measures. But the "Four Horsemen," as the conservative judges were called, neutralized these supporters. The fate of most cases, therefore, rested with the Court's ninth member, Justice Owen Roberts, who often voted with the conservatives. The appointment of additional justices, Roosevelt believed, would break through this roadblock and create a sympathetic majority.

The Battle Begins Roosevelt's political instincts had failed him, however. Critics in both major parties accused him of trying to "pack" the Court with supporters of his programs. Opponents of the New Deal who had worried all along that Roosevelt was out to destroy constitutional government saw their suspicions confirmed. Even those who supported Roosevelt on other issues began to desert him on this one. Upon hearing of Roosevelt's Court plan, one supporter of the New Deal in Congress turned to reporters

4. **VISUAL EVIDENCE** Have students write a paragraph explaining the cartoon.

Roosevelt's plan to increase the number of justices on the Supreme Court was widely seen as an attack on the Court itself. This cartoon shows Roosevelt asking Secretary of the Interior Harold Ickes for money from the Public Works Administration (PWA) to carry out his plan.

4.

and said, "Boys, here's where I cash in my chips."

1. Few people believed the President's claim that he sought only to improve the Court's efficiency. Chief Justice Charles Evans Hughes pointed out that there was no significant delay in cases coming before the Court. He insisted that an increase in the number of justices might itself delay decisions.

The Outcome After a six-month battle, Roosevelt finally accepted defeat and withdrew his proposal for Court reform. But the fight had been a costly one. The President had lost congressional and public support and created divisions in the Democratic party.

In the end, however, two unforeseen developments gave Roosevelt the sympathetic majority he wanted. First, the Court suddenly began upholding New Deal legislation. Justice Roberts voted with the President's supporters to uphold key provisions of the Social Security Act, the Wagner Act, and a state minimum-wage law.

Second, the retirement of a conservative justice gave Roosevelt the opportunity to make an appointment. In fact, by the end of 3. his presidency, Roosevelt had appointed eight associate justices and one chief justice. Looking back on the Court fight of 1937, Roosevelt claimed that although he had lost the battle, he had won the war.

The Economy Takes Another Plunge

No sooner had the Supreme Court battle subsided then another crisis loomed. This time, the nation faced a painful economic setback.

Cuts in Spending During 1935 and 1936, the economy had slowly improved. By early 1937, several Roosevelt advisers believed it was time to phase out New Deal programs aimed at stimulating economic recovery. For example, the advisers called for cuts in public works and employment programs. As Secretary of the Treasury Henry Morgenthau, Jr., later said, "this was the moment . . . to strip off the bandages, throw away the crutches, and see if American private enterprise could stand on its own two feet."

The President agreed: The time was right to cut government spending. Congress drastically slashed existing WPA programs and allocated no funds for new programs.

Meanwhile, however, two other developments reduced the total amount of private spending. First, the Federal Reserve Board had raised interest rates. Because of the increased cost of bank loans for new factories

2. **MAP READING** Ask: How much higher was unemployment in 1933 than in 1938?

GRAPH STUDY *This graph of the percentage of people out of work between 1932 and 1945 shows a rise in*

2. *employment between 1933 and 1937. It seemed for a time that the end of the Great Depression was in sight. But with another recession in 1937 and 1938, joblessness rose again. How did the country's entry into World War II in 1941 affect unemployment?* See p. T116.

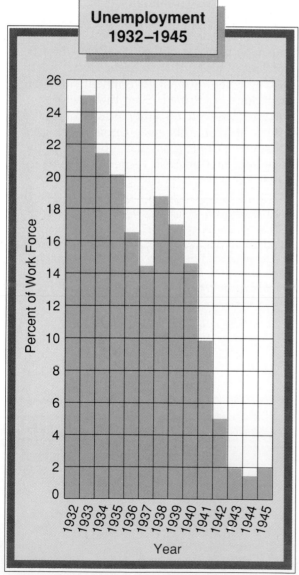

Unemployment 1932–1945

Source: *Historical Statistics of the United States*

The recession of 1937–1938 caused more misery for a nation that was just
beginning economic recovery. Joseph Vavak's painting Women of Flint *conveys*
1. *the bleak mood that again enveloped the country. The city of Flint, Michigan, was*
dependent on automobile factories, where unemployment was particularly high.

---

1. **VISUAL EVIDENCE** Ask: What is lying on the ground at the center of the picture? Why does
the artist include this object?

and equipment, companies began to cut back.
Second, new Social Security taxes on employers and employees left businesses and
consumers with less money to spend.

Recession Hits The double blow of cuts
in both government and private spending sent
the economy reeling. A **severe recession**
developed in the fall of 1937. By the spring of
1938, just seven months later, 4 million more
workers were out of work. Large inventories
piled up in warehouses as wage cuts and
unemployment slashed consumer spending.
Across the nation, the economic collapse was
actually sharper than in the first months of
the Great Depression. Nearly all of the gains
in employment and production were wiped
out.

Despite the severe conditions, Roosevelt
at first hesitated to act. He hoped that private business could reverse the downward
trend of the economy without renewed government spending for jobs and relief. By
March 1938, however, the President decided
that the government had to resort to deficit
spending in order to stimulate the economy.

Deficit spending is the practice of spending 2.
more money than is taken in from taxes.

For many Americans, the recession of
1937–1938 was a rude awakening. They realized that the New Deal policies had failed to
bring about full recovery.

See p. T116.

SECTION 1 REVIEW

1. **Identify:** Alfred M. Landon.

2. **Define:** deficit spending.

3. What was Alfred Landon's original attitude toward the New Deal?

4. Describe the new Democratic coalition of
1936.

5. What happened to the economy in the
fall and winter of 1937–1938?

6. **Critical Thinking** Why do you think even
Roosevelt's supporters opposed his plans
for the Supreme Court?

633

2. **ECONOMICS** Ask: How does the federal government fund deficit spending? What are the
dangers of this practice?

2 Further Reform

READ TO UNDERSTAND

■ How the New Deal helped labor unions.

■ Why agricultural reforms were an important part of the New Deal.

■ What other reforms took place during Roosevelt's second term.

1. ■ *Vocabulary:* industrial union, sitdown strike.

Roosevelt began his new term in 1937 with a passionate plea for reform. "I see tens of millions . . . denied . . . the necessities of life . . . ," he proclaimed in his second inaugural ad-
2. dress. "I see one third of a nation ill-housed, ill-clad, ill-nourished." Roosevelt soon proposed a sweeping new series of reform measures to benefit those hardest hit by the Great Depression—workers, farmers, and the poor.

The Growth of Organized Labor

Labor leaders took the Wagner Act of 1935
3. as a signal to organize. The American Federation of Labor began a massive drive to recruit one million more workers and thereby increase union bargaining power.

Conflict in the AFL One faction of AFL union leaders criticized the recruiting drive for moving too slowly. They also faulted the AFL for concentrating on skilled workers such as pipe fitters, machinists, and printers. In their view, the AFL should form unions in large industries—such as steel, textile, and automobile manufacturing—that employed great numbers of unskilled laborers.

Leading that faction was John L. Lewis, president of the United Mine Workers (UMW). At the 1935 AFL convention, he argued for **industrial unions**—unions that represent every worker in an industry, not just workers in skilled crafts. Many AFL leaders opposed this idea. In the heated debate that followed, Lewis punched William "Big Bill" Hutcheson of the Carpenters' Union and knocked him down. Although Lewis won the fight, he did not win AFL support for his plan.

Rival Unions Still determined, Lewis and several other AFL union leaders formed a rival group of unions, later called the Congress of Industrial Organizations (CIO). The CIO proceeded to organize workers in whole industries as Lewis had demanded. Inevitably, many employers resisted CIO efforts to organize, despite the Wagner Act.

In response to such resistance, workers in the Goodyear tire factory in Akron, Ohio, developed a new strategy, the **sitdown strike.** One night at exactly 2:00 A.M., the workers stopped the production line. They sat down next to the idle machines and refused to leave the factory until their employers recognized the union. Fearing destruction of factory property, the employers decided against using force to remove the workers.

Soon sitdown strikes spread to other industries—even gravedigging. A common tactic of plant managers was to turn off the heat to try to force sitdown strikers out of a factory. Undaunted, the workers often sang, danced, and roller-skated to keep warm.

Breakthroughs The first large industry to be successfully organized was the auto industry. In 1937, a six-week sitdown strike closed several General Motors plants in Flint, Michigan. The company called in the police and the National Guard, but the union held out. Eventually, General Motors recognized the United Automobile Workers as the employees' union, the first in the industry.

The steel industry proved more resistant. Union organizers recalled the bloody battles of the early 1920s, when the steel industry had defeated several strikes. In 1937, the huge United States Steel Corporation unexpectedly agreed to recognize the Steel Workers Organizing Committee of the CIO. Other steel companies refused to follow that example, however. In what became known as the Memorial Day Massacre, police shot and killed ten strikers at the Republic Steel Plant in Chicago. The National Labor Relations Board then stepped in and forced the steel industry to negotiate with the union.

Total union membership grew from fewer than 3 million in 1933 to nearly 9 million in 1939. Organized labor had clearly attained more economic and political power under the New Deal than ever before.

634

1. BACKGROUND Puerto Rico also faced hardships during the depression. The average worker there earned only 12 cents a day. Puerto Rican leaders persuaded Congress to help the island recover.

The Fair Labor Standards Act

1. Many workers still did not belong to unions. For these millions, working conditions remained harsh. Shoe factory workers in New England earned an average of only $853 a year. Cotton factory workers in the South averaged less than 40 cents an hour. Most worked twelve hours a day, six days a week throughout the year.

In 1937, Roosevelt proposed a bill to improve wages and conditions for all workers in the country. He urged a federal wages-and-hours law that would "put a floor below which wages shall not fall, and a ceiling beyond which the hours of industrial labor shall not rise."

The bill aroused strong opposition. Business owners felt that government once again was threatening private enterprise. Farmers objected that they could not pay workers as much as industries could. Only by excluding a wide range of workers, such as agricultural laborers and domestic servants, did supporters of the bill save it.

Finally, in June 1938, Congress passed the Fair Labor Standards Act. The act set minimum wages and maximum hours of work in industries whose products crossed state lines. It also banned child labor under age 16 in industries engaged in interstate commerce. Most important, the act was a precedent for federal laws to improve working conditions.

GEOGRAPHY AND HISTORY

The Dust Bowl

Suffering severe hardships since the end of World War I, many farmers found it nearly impossible to survive the Great Depression. Then, in the midst of the depression, from 2. 1932 to 1936, drought struck large sections of the Midwest, from Texas to the Dakotas. (See page 413.) The blistering sun scorched and withered wide expanses of grass and crops. The skies darkened as vast clouds of dust arose from the sun-dried land, giving the area a new name, the Dust Bowl.

At times, the dust clouds became so thick that train engineers were unable to read signal lights. Winds dropped trails of grit and dirt everywhere. As far east as Cleveland and Memphis, people wore masks as protection from the "black blizzards." Red snow fell on New England, and sailors in the Atlantic found traces of Nebraska soil.

2. PAST AND PRESENT The Great Plains could be threatened again. The world's largest underground lake, stretching from Texas to South Dakota, may be drying up.

3. *Images of death and starvation haunt Alexandre Hogue's* Drought Stricken Area. *In the mid-1930s, parts of the once-fertile Midwest became known as the Dust Bowl. After years with little or no rain, the topsoil turned into dust and was carried off by the wind.*

3. VISUAL EVIDENCE Ask: Why does the artist show these two animals but no people?

The FSA Photographs: Faces of Rural America

1. Crops froze in the California pea fields in the spring of 1936. Photographer Dorothea Lange recalled the scene:

> I saw and approached the hungry and desperate mother as if drawn by a magnet. . . . She asked me no questions. . . . I did not ask her name. . . . She said that they had been living on frozen vegetables from the surrounding fields, and birds that the children had killed. She had just sold the tires from the car to buy food.

Lange's photograph of that mother and her children (right) is one of the best known in an extraordinary collection. Lange and ten other photographers, including Walker Evans and Ben Shahn, worked for the Historical Section of the Farm Security Administration (FSA). Their assignment was to create a pictorial record of life in rural America during the Great Depression.

FSA photographers shot pictures during New England winters. They recorded cotton pickers in Mississippi, elderly couples in the Midwest, and a thousand other scenes. It was the stark images of sharecroppers in wretched shacks, of dusty migrant families, and of the haunted eyes of parents unable to feed their children that lingered longest. In an era before television, these photographs, available free to newspapers and magazines, brought home the urgency of rural suffering.

Dorothea Lange

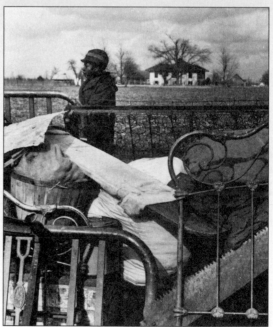
Arthur Rothstein

See p. T117.

1. Why did the FSA hire Lange and other photographers?

2. Critical Thinking How do you think the FSA photo collection was politically helpful to supporters of the New Deal?

1. **ACTIVITY** In 1939, Lange published a collection of her photographs titled *An American Exodus: A Record of Human Erosion.* Interested students can study this book and make a presentation.

2. Midwestern farmers watched helplessly as the soil blew away and banks and land companies took over what was left of their farms. Many thousands of families sadly loaded their possessions into old cars or trucks and headed west.

636

Over a million "Okies" from Oklahoma or "Arkies" from Arkansas traveled westward along Highway 66. They sought work in the orchards, orange groves, and lettuce fields of Washington, Oregon, and California. For many, the end of the journey brought not 3.

2. **BACKGROUND** One migrant explained why he packed his things and headed west. "Do you reckon I'd be out on the highway if I had it good at home?"

3. **READING** Students might enjoy reading John Steinbeck's classic novel about the Okies, *The Grapes of Wrath.*

1. **TECHNOLOGY** In 1930, only 10% of the farms in the U.S. had electricity. By 1941, 40% did.

2. **TECHNOLOGY** Ask: How would the "shelter belt" and the Soil Conservation and Domestic Allotment Act help prevent another Dust Bowl?

work, but eviction by sheriffs and self-appointed vigilantes. Westerners had their own unemployment problems. They wanted no outside competition. ■

Tenant Farming and Sharecropping

The poorest of the poor during the depression included the tenant farmers and sharecroppers of the southern cotton belt. Unable to buy land of their own, these farmers rented a few acres and struggled to scratch out a meager living. Each spring, they borrowed money from a bank or the landowner to plant a crop, usually cotton. At harvest time, they paid off the loan. Any money that was left over, they kept to get them through the winter. As the economy worsened, there was almost nothing left. Each year, these farmers sank deeper into debt.

The early New Deal actually intensified the plight of tenant farmers and sharecroppers. By reducing the number of acres in production in order to cut surpluses, the Agricultural Adjustment Act forced these people off the land they worked. Unlike landowners, who received money for not producing, tenants and sharecroppers got nothing in return.

Agricultural Reforms

The Roosevelt administration eventually faced up to the problems of rural poverty and sought new ways to overcome it. The Resettlement Administration (RA), formed in 1935, resettled poor farmers on good land and provided sufficient equipment and advice for them to make a fresh start. But funds were short, and the program received little support. The RA resettled only 4,441 families, far short of its goal of 500,000.

In 1937, the Farm Security Administration (FSA) replaced the RA. The FSA helped tenants and sharecroppers to buy farms and equipment. By 1940, it had provided short-term loans to more than 800,000 families and long-term farm-purchase loans to another 13,600.

One other New Deal plan helped ease the 1. drudgery for many farmers. The Rural Electrification Administration (REA) lent money for building power lines, thus extending electricity to isolated rural areas.

Allied with the problems of the farmers was the need for soil conservation. At President Roosevelt's urging, the Forest Service planted a "shelter belt" of trees across the open plains. These trees blocked wind, held moisture and soil, and provided a refuge for animals.

In 1936, President Roosevelt signed the Soil Conservation and Domestic Allotment Act. The act encouraged farmers to stop grow- 2. ing soil-depleting crops like corn, tobacco, and cotton on part of their land. They were to substitute soil-enriching land cover like grass and soybeans to revive the fertility of the soil. Participating farmers received payments from the government to compensate them for lost crops.

A New Agricultural Adjustment Act

When the Supreme Court struck down the Agricultural Adjustment Act in 1936, the government lost a way of limiting farm surpluses. As the four-year drought ended, surpluses reappeared, threatening the gains farm prices had made earlier. Secretary of Agriculture Henry Wallace ironically complained that if there were a good harvest, "we would be sunk." To ward off surpluses, Congress passed the second AAA in 1938.

Under the new act, the government could once again pay farmers to limit their crops. But payments would not come from a processing tax, which was the Supreme Court's objection to the first AAA. Instead, Congress would appropriate the money. Crop production could be limited either through crop allotments—set amounts that each farmer was allowed to grow—or by taking land out of production for soil conservation. The second AAA also insured wheat farmers against drought losses.

Finally, the act put into practice Wallace's plan for an "ever-normal granary." Under this plan, farmers were not allowed to sell crop surpluses on the open market. Instead, the government would buy the crops and store them for use in times of poor harvests. In 3. this way, farm products would be available in steady supply.

Other New Deal Reforms

Lack of affordable housing was a problem shared by rural and urban communities. To relieve the shortage, Congress passed the National Housing Act of 1937. The act extended loans to local public agencies to encourage the construction of housing for low-income families. It also created the United States Housing Authority, which in a few years helped fund more than 150,000 new housing units.

To protect consumers, Congress passed the Food, Drug, and Cosmetic Act in 1938. This was a much stronger law than the 1906
1. Pure Food and Drug Act. For the first time, manufacturers of certain foods, drugs, and cosmetics had to list the ingredients on the package. The new law also required rigid testing of new drugs before they could be sold.

The Hatch Act, passed in 1939, targeted abuses of power by federal officials. The act grew out of scandals linked to the WPA. Some officials had granted people relief payments in return for promises to vote for Democratic candidates. One series of newspaper stories charged that a Kentucky senator's reelection had been "bought with WPA votes." The Hatch Act barred the use of official favors to influence elections. It also forbade federal employees, except those in policy-making positions, to take an active part in political campaigns.

One reform, little noticed at the time, was to have far-reaching consequences. In 1939, in response to the growing demands on the presidency, Roosevelt issued Executive Order 8248, which created the Executive Office of the President. The new office included administrative assistants, press secretaries, budget officers, legal advisers, and other assistants. As later Presidents added more positions, the Executive Office played an increasingly important role in helping the President meet the demands of his office.

See p. T117.

SECTION 2 REVIEW

1. **Identify:** (a) John L. Lewis, (b) Congress of Industrial Organizations, (c) Farm Security Administration, (d) second Agricultural Adjustment Act.

2. **Define:** (a) industrial union, (b) sitdown strike.

3. What type of workers did John L. Lewis want to organize?

4. What were the two major provisions of the Fair Labor Standards Act?

5. (a) Describe the Dust Bowl. (b) How did it affect the lives of midwestern farmers?

6. **Critical Thinking** (a) What arguments can you make for the Hatch Act? (b) Against the act?

3 Life During the New Deal Years

READ TO UNDERSTAND

■ How Americans escaped the depression through entertainment.

■ What minority groups gained and lost during the 1930s.

■ What impact the New Deal had on American life and thought.

No one who lived through the Great Depression ever forgot the hardships and the fear. A job—gone. Savings—vanished. Loved ones—hungry. For a child, the pain came from seeing a parent helpless and overwhelmed. "I remember how, after dinner, my father would just lie on the couch in utter despair, night after night for hours," recalled one adult many years later.

What had happened to the American dream? Americans had worked hard, saved their money, and then lost everything. Could people still believe in themselves? Could they still believe in traditional values of hard work, thrift, and security? If not, where was hope?

The Search for Entertainment

Depression-bound Americans sought escape from daily worries. Radio and talking pictures 2. were two popular sources of entertainment. People who could not afford to buy a radio

638

1. sometimes built their own. Movie theaters charged only 25 cents for admission—and gave away free dishes one night a week.

The 1930s were the golden years of the American film industry, and Hollywood, California, was its headquarters. Before the New Deal, many movies questioned traditional values. Gangsters were heroes. In films such as *Little Caesar, Public Enemy,* and *Scarface,* gangsters combined ambition, hard work, and loyalty in order to get ahead in a chaotic world. Those who were normally expected to uphold law and order—police, lawyers, politicians—often were shown as dishonest and corrupt. Social disorder was even the subject of movie comedies such as the Marx Brothers' *Duck Soup* and Mae West's *She Done Him Wrong.*

During the New Deal, Hollywood took a new direction. Comedies with stars like Cary Grant, Katharine Hepburn, and Irene Dunne showed how, even when the world seemed confused, the social order still worked. Dramas made heroes of federal agents who relentlessly stalked criminals. Lavish musicals, film versions of the classics of literature, and huge epics such as Margaret Mitchell's Civil War story *Gone With the Wind* gave audiences a chance to escape, for a few hours at least, from the troubles of the real world.

The Great Depression had badly shaken Americans' faith in their society. Hollywood set out to restore that faith and rebuild confidence in the value of hard work, perseverance, and moderation. For example, Walt Disney's Mickey Mouse embodied the ideals of initiative and enterprise. In *Three Little Pigs,* Disney used an old story that captured the purposeful spirit of the New Deal. When the pigs in the cartoon sang "Who's Afraid of the Big, Bad Wolf?" some in the audience saw the wolf as a symbol of the depression.

2. Director Frank Capra introduced Americans to populist heroes in *Mr. Smith Goes to Washington,* starring James Stewart, and *Mr. Deeds Goes to Town* and *Meet John Doe,* both starring Gary Cooper. Capra's heroes battled corrupt power. They met humiliation and frustration, but, with the help of "ordinary" people, they accomplished their missions.

Like the movies, radio thrived in hard times. As the depression forced vaudeville theaters to close, talent flooded the airwaves.

Americans wanted to dream of a better, happier time, and popular entertainment provided such dreams. For the price of admission, usually 25 cents, people could escape their troubles with a night at a movie like A Star Is Born.

3.

3. **PAST AND PRESENT** *A Star Is Born* was remade twice: in 1954 with Judy Garland and in 1976 with Barbra Streisand.

Such stars as George Burns, Gracie Allen, Jack Benny, Mary Livingston, Ed Wynn, and Fred Allen offered listeners comic relief. With so many people out of work and at home, daytime serials drew large audiences. These radio shows were called soap operas because soap makers often sponsored them.

Art Reflects the Times

American artists and writers powerfully portrayed the cruelty of the depression years. One of the best-known novels of the 1930s was John Steinbeck's *The Grapes of Wrath.* In it, the author traced the heartbreaking migration of Okies and Arkies westward to California.

Dorothea Lange captured pitiful Dust Bowl scenes in photographs later published in *An American Exodus.* In *You Have Seen Their Faces,* photographer Margaret Bourke-White vividly portrayed rural poverty in the South, as did photographer Walker Evans and writer James Agee in *Let Us Now Praise Famous Men.* Richard Wright's novels *Uncle*

639

Many WPA artists created works that celebrated ordinary people. Some art reflected the misery, anger, and despair that many people felt. This painting,
1. *Subway, by Lily Furedi, shows a subway car filled with commuters. They represent the quiet dignity of those who carried on with their lives in the face of hardship and poverty.*

1. **VISUAL EVIDENCE** Ask: What different segments of society are shown in this painting?

Tom's Children and *Native Son* opened many Americans' eyes to what it meant to grow up black during the Great Depression.

WPA-supported projects in literature, painting, and sculpture gave work to many writers and artists. Often, the work reflected the search for common themes that could
2. bind the country together. The past was given a new emphasis, as writers compiled state histories and wrote biographies of notable Americans such as Benjamin Franklin and Abraham Lincoln. In tribute to the American worker, painters decorated public buildings with giant murals showing farmers at work in the countryside and construction workers
3. at their labors in the cities. In praise of American Presidents, Gutzon Borglum sculpted massive heads of Washington, Jefferson, Lin-

640

3. **BACKGROUND** Borglum died the year work was completed. It took six and a half years.

coln, and Theodore Roosevelt on Mount Rushmore in the Black Hills of South Dakota.

Black Americans and the New Deal

Even before the depression, black Americans faced an intolerable situation. They still suffered racial discrimination in both the North and South. Many could live only in segregated areas, and most received less pay for their work than whites.

The depression only deepened the wounds. Victims of a "last hired, first fired" policy, black workers were usually the first to be laid off in any cutback. Many black tenant farmers and sharecroppers in the South were forced off the land they worked as a

2. **LOCAL HISTORY** The WPA produced a series of guidebooks called the American Guide. They provided a history and geography of every state and many smaller regions of the country. Some of the guides have been reissued recently. Students might enjoy reading about your state.

1. **DISCUSSION** Ask: Do you agree with Roosevelt's reasons for not backing the bill? Why or why not? How do you think black leaders reacted?

2. **BACKGROUND** Collier wrote, "So intimately is all of Indian life tied up with the land . . . that to think of Indians is to think of land."

result of surplus reduction policies. Most terrifying, however, was an increase in black lynchings. Frustrated by their own economic plight, white mobs killed more than 60 blacks between 1930 and 1934.

1. Roosevelt denounced lynchings as "collective murder." He refused, however, to back a bill in Congress to make lynching a federal crime. Southerners controlled key committees in both houses, and the President needed their support for his economic programs. "I did not choose the tools with which I must work," he explained to black leaders. "If I come out for an anti-lynching bill now, they will block every bill I ask Congress to pass, to keep America from collapsing. I just can't take that risk."

Blacks did make some gains during the New Deal, however. As you have read, Eleanor Roosevelt, as well as Harry Hopkins and Harold Ickes, tried to prevent discrimination against blacks in relief and job programs. Thousands of young black men learned a trade through the Civilian Conservation Corps. And more blacks than ever before held important government positions. Although the New Deal did not include civil rights or anti-discrimination laws, it did offer black Americans new hope for political and social improvement.

Attempts to Improve Life for American Indians

Intent on a new deal for American Indians, President Roosevelt appointed John Collier to head the Bureau of Indian Affairs. Outspoken and determined, Collier fought to include Indians in New Deal relief and job programs.

2. One of Collier's main goals was to help the Indians use their land more effectively. An important first step was to stop the sale by individual Indians of land allotted to them by the government. Collier's campaign also included the Indian Emergency Conservation Work Group, a special branch of the CCC. This group employed Indians in programs of soil erosion control, irrigation, and land development.

Preservation of the Indians' tribal way of life was also a priority for Collier. The Indian Reorganization Act, passed in 1934, aimed to restore tribal ownership of land, expand tribal land holdings, and encourage tribal self-government. Funds were also set up to provide scholarships and to help Indians set up their own businesses.

Expulsion of Mexican Americans

As you have read, hundreds of thousands of Mexicans had been migrating to the Southwest since the early 1900s. (See page 578.) Most labored as migrant workers or found jobs in mines or local industries. As the Dust Bowl took hold and as factories and mines closed during the depression, many Americans who once welcomed the cheap labor now feared Mexican workers as competitors for jobs.

3. Popular unrest in the Southwest convinced government officials to adopt a deportation policy. Thousands of families were uprooted and sent back to Mexico. Many deported children had been born in the United States and therefore were American citizens. Still, the government refused to honor their rights.

Small Gains for Women

During the 1920s, women had entered the work force in greater numbers and acquired jobs with higher status and incomes. But when the depression struck, opportunities for women faded. Employees often fired women and hired men to replace them. Many companies refused to hire a woman if her husband had a job. After all, it was reasoned, men were the "breadwinners" in the average family, so they should have what jobs were available.

Impetus for a new deal for women came largely from Mary Dewson. Roosevelt had appointed Dewson to coordinate women's activities in his 1932 presidential campaign and later in his administration. Seizing the initiative, she worked for equal treatment of women in New Deal programs. She also persuaded Roosevelt to appoint women to important posts. The most notable appointment was Frances Perkins as secretary of labor. Other appointments included the first women to serve as minister to a foreign nation, as

641

1. **ACTIVITY** Have interested students do research on Eleanor Roosevelt's role in FDR's presidency and present oral reports to the class.

director of the United States mint, and as judge in a circuit court of appeals.

1.   Eleanor Roosevelt, however, was the New Deal's most visible champion of rights for women. After her husband's election, she held her own press conferences—for women reporters only. Since her activities and statements often became front-page news, women reporters got first crack at some major stories. The First Lady also captured the spotlight through her own syndicated newspaper column, "My Day," and her own radio program. Her many other interests included the League of Women Voters and the Women's Trade Union League.

    Mary Dewson, Frances Perkins, and Eleanor Roosevelt contributed to New Deal popularity. Their efforts and achievements convinced many women that they might gain more political, social, and economic equality by supporting the New Deal.

Impact of the New Deal

After 1938, the New Deal lost most of its momentum. Americans began to turn their attention to events in Europe and Asia that

2. **VISUAL EVIDENCE** Ask: How do you think these miners felt about Eleanor Roosevelt's visit?

Eleanor Roosevelt became the eyes and ears of her husband, whose disability kept him in the White House. He sometimes began meetings by saying, "You know my Missus gets around a lot and she says . . . ." An advocate for the jobless,

2. *the disadvantaged, and minorities, Eleanor Roosevelt is seen here inspecting a coal mine.*

3. **DISCUSSION** Ask: Do most people today still accept the ideas behind the New Deal? What evidence supports your opinion?

were propelling the world toward war. Also, although 6 million Americans were still unemployed, the worst of the depression seemed to be over.

Despite its short history, the New Deal had profound and lasting effects. Americans had learned that a democratic republic could survive a severe crisis without a dictatorship. Through the New Deal, their government had taken a moderate course. It had preserved the free-enterprise system by reforming it.

New Deal programs greatly increased the size and scope of the federal government. The government now had a much larger role in the economy. True, the government had taken steps before to regulate business and control monopoly. But New Deal banking, securities, and public utility legislation were bold expansions of the concept. Also, for the first time, the government acted as an employer of last resort and a sponsor of work projects.

People's views about the responsibility of government changed during the New Deal. Before the 1930s, most people viewed government help for the needy as charity; it was a humiliation to those who accepted it. But the New Deal fostered the idea that people were entitled to public assistance when they became victims of economic conditions over which they had no control.

Before 1933, most Americans considered the federal government remote from their lives. By 1939, it was hard to find anyone in the nation who did not have a friend or relative who owed a job, house, farm, education, or some other benefit to a New Deal program. Defenders of the New Deal pointed to that fact with pride. Never before, they argued, had people had security against old age or unemployment.

Critics charged, however, that the growth of the federal government threatened American values and traditions. The ideals of individual initiative and free enterprise, they argued, were being undermined.

Debate about whether the changes brought about by the New Deal were good for the nation has continued. Yet few people deny that the New Deal had a major impact on government, the economy, and society.

4. **MAIN IDEA** Have students summarize the ways in which the New Deal affected American life and government.

SKILL LESSON

A View of the New Deal: Analyzing Oral Evidence

A tape-recorded oral account of an event can be a valuable historical document. It can help you understand how historical events affect people and can give you insight into what it was like to live during a specific time. The extract at right is part of an interview with David Kennedy in the late 1960s. Kennedy served on the Federal Reserve Board during the New Deal. At the time of the interview, he was head of a major company. Follow the steps below to analyze the document.

See p. T117

1 **Identify the source of the document.** (a) Who was interviewed? (b) When did the interview take place?

2 **Describe the evidence.** (a) What was the person's original attitude toward Roosevelt? (b) How did his attitude change? Why?

3 **Decide how reliable the evidence is.** (a) What was the person's role in the events being described? How might his role affect his interpretation? (b) How long after the event did the interview take place? How might that affect the person's account? (c) How might the person's position at the time of the interview affect his account?

4 **Study the evidence to learn more about an historical event.** (a) How does the person think Roosevelt helped the nation early in the New Deal? (b) What can you learn about the New Deal from this document?

David Kennedy

Roosevelt gave us quite a bit of hope early. He probably saved us from complete collapse in that sense. But he did not answer the things. Many of his programs were turned on and off, started and stopped . . . shifting gears. Because we had never been in anything like this.

Planning had not been done. So they'd go out and sweep the mountains and clean up the debris, and then the wind comes along and blows it back again. It gave some work. But the people that got the money in some ways were benefited and in other ways were hurt. They didn't like to see the waste. . . . They had mixed reactions.

I was enthusiastic when Roosevelt came in. I thought: We're in serious trouble. Something has to be done, and here's a man that's going to do it. I voted for him his first term and his second. After that, I voted against him. It wasn't just on the two-term basis, although that was important. The packing of the Supreme Court and the fact that we were not making the progress I thought our country was capable of making . . . I became terribly disenchanted.

He was a dramatic leader. He had charm, personality, poise, and so on. He could inspire people. But to me, he lacked the stick-to-it-iveness to carry a program through.

Source: Studs Terkel, *Hard Times* (New York: Avon, 1970).

See p. T118.

SECTION 3 REVIEW

1. **Identify:** (a) Frank Capra (b) John Steinbeck, (c) Margaret Bourke-White, (d) Richard Wright, (e) Mary Dewson.

2. What role did movies play during the depression?

3. What was the main activity of the Indian Emergency Conservation Work Group?

4. What impact did the depression have on Mexican workers in the United States?

5. What government posts did women hold in Roosevelt's administration?

6. **Critical Thinking** How did artists and writers contribute to an understanding of the effects of the depression?

Summary

1. **Despite a landslide victory, President Roosevelt met growing resistance from Congress during his second term.** Even some of his strongest supporters questioned his attempt to "pack" the Supreme Court. A severe recession in 1937 and 1938 revealed that the problems underlying the depression had not been solved.

2. **Roosevelt's second administration worked for reform measures that would benefit workers and farmers.** The CIO helped unskilled workers organize in unprecedented numbers, while the Fair Labor Standards Act improved conditions for all workers. Congress passed several new laws to help farmers hard hit by a severe drought in the 1930s.

3. **The depression and the New Deal affected American culture and thought.** Popular entertainment and fine art reflected the values and themes that bound the country together. In some ways, the spirit of reform improved conditions for black Americans, American Indians, and women. The New Deal also encouraged the rapid growth in the size and influence of the federal government.

See p. T118.

Vocabulary

On a separate sheet of paper, write the word or words that best complete each of the following sentences.

1. _____ is the practice of spending more money than is taken in.

2. _____ represent all workers in a particular industry.

3. During a _____, workers refuse to leave the work place until their demands are met.

4. The _____ is a term that refers to the area in the Midwest beset by drought during the Great Depression.

5. Dispossessed farm families from Oklahoma who set out westward to find work were called _____.

See p. T118.

Chapter Checkup

1. (a) What groups made up Roosevelt's coalition in the 1936 election? (b) How had the Democrats won the support of organized labor and black Americans?

2. (a) What did Roosevelt hope to accomplish by redesigning the Supreme Court? (b) Was he successful? Explain?

3. (a) What developments led to a severe recession in 1937–1938? (b) Why did Roosevelt hesitate to increase government spending?

4. (a) What types of workers did the Congress of Industrial Organizations represent? (b) What new tactic did workers use to achieve their goals in the 1930s? (c) Was that tactic successful? Explain.

5. What actions did the second Roosevelt administration take to try to alleviate the problems of farmers?

6. (a) Why was the Great Depression a particularly difficult time for many black Americans? (b) In what ways did the situation for blacks improve during the New Deal?

7. (a) How did John Collier try to improve conditions for American Indians? (b) What

did the Indian Reorganization Act of 1934 offer?

8. (a) How did the onset of the depression affect women working outside the home? (b) How did Mary Dewson try to improve women's position?

See p. T118.

Critical Thinking

1. **Evaluating** (a) What lasting impact did the New Deal have on the federal government? (b) In what other ways do you think the New Deal permanently affected American life? (c) Do you think the New Deal was good for the nation in the 1930s? (d) Do you think its long-term effects have been positive or negative? Explain.

2. **Supporting a Point of View** Many observers believed that President Roosevelt's plan to add justices to the Supreme Court would have upset the system of checks and balances. Do you agree or disagree with that view? Why?

3. **Analyzing** (a) How did movies and radio help Americans cope with the effects of the great Depression? (b) What values did many movies try to reinforce?

See p. T118.

Connecting Past and Present

1. Workers were a key part of the Democratic coalition of 1936. Why do you think the Republicans have won many workers away from the Democrats in recent years?

2. Compare the themes of movies in the 1930s with themes today.

3. List five ways the federal government directly affects your life today.

See p. T118.

Developing Basic Skills

1. **Using Visual Evidence** The painting on page 640 was done as a WPA project. (a) What is shown in the painting? (b) What message do you think the artist was trying to convey to people living during the Great Depression? (c) What can you learn about the period from the painting?

2. **Collecting Evidence** In this chapter you have read an oral history. (See page 643.) Talk with someone you know who lived during the 1930s and ask what life was like during the Great Depression. Write a report about what you learned.

WRITING ABOUT HISTORY

Organizing Note Cards

To organize the information you have gathered for your research paper, look at the subject you have written in the corner of each note card. Match the cards with the divisions in your preliminary outline. Choose those cards that support your thesis statement and are related to the outline topics. Decide on the order of supporting information you will use under each topic. (See page 113.) Arrange the cards in that order.

Practice: Suppose that one of the subheadings in an outline you have prepared for a paper on the New Deal is "New Deal Reforms." Which of the following note card topics correlate with that subhead? Explain your choices.

1. Supreme Court
2. sitdown strike
3. Fair Labor Standards Act
4. "black blizzards"
5. Agricultural Adjustment Act
6. National Housing Act
7. Food, Drug, and Cosmetic Act
8. Hatch Act

Unit Nine WAR AND THE SEARCH FOR PEACE

1940 The British defense against German attack created sympathy for Britain among Americans.

"above and beyond the call of duty"

DORIE MILLER

1941 Dorie Miller received the Navy Cross for his valor at Pearl Harbor.

	1940	1945	1950
POLITICS AND GOVERNMENT	**1941** Japanese attack U.S. ships at Pearl Harbor	**1944** D-Day invasion of France	
SOCIETY AND CULTURE	**1942** Japanese Americans on Pacific Coast are relocated inland	**1947** Jackie Robinson first black major league baseball player	
ECONOMICS AND TECHNOLOGY	**1942** War Production Board created to manage the economy	**1945** Atomic bombs dropped on Japanese cities	
WORLD EVENTS	**1943** Allies invade Italy	**1945** Germany surrenders	
		Roosevelt	Truman

Women Ordnance Workers took jobs in arms factories to support the war effort.

"THE GIRL HE LEFT BEHIND" IS STILL BEHIND HIM **She's a WOW**

This watch, found in Hiroshima, marks the moment the atomic bomb hit.

Kansas City Spirit by Norman Rockwell reflects the renewed postwar energy.

Campaign buttons are a popular gimmick in presidential elections.

1950	1955	1960
1950 McCarthy makes charges about communists		**1960** U-2 incident
Early 1950s Rock 'n' roll emerges	**1955** Montgomery bus boycott	**1960** "Sit-in" protests begin
1950 Sale of televisions soars	**1957** *Sputnik I* launched	
1950 North Korea invades South Korea	**1956** Hungarians revolt against Soviet control	
Truman	Eisenhower	Kennedy

1950 United States troops fought in Korea as part of a United Nations force.

As suburbs grew in the 1950s, more and more people took trains to work in the cities.

647

Prelude to Another World Conflict (1920–1941)

CHAPTER OUTLINE

1 **American Diplomacy From Harding to Hoover**

2 **International Challenges During the 1930s**

3 **The Threat of War**

4 **Between Peace and War**

CHAPTER OBJECTIVES After completing this chapter, students should be able to
1. outline American foreign policy in the 1920s and 1930s.
2. list the events that led to World War II.
3. describe U.S. aid to the Allies and American entry into the war.

CHAPTER PREVIEW Have students read the paragraphs and study the time line below. Have students review Article 1, Section 8, of the Constitution. Then ask: Who has the power to declare war? Why might the President be concerned about the feelings of the American people toward the British?

It was a fine afternoon for a picnic, and the setting was perfect—a green hill above the Hudson River in New York State. Friends and neighbors enjoyed hot dogs, baked beans, doughnuts, and gingerbread, all washed down with soda and coffee. But although the food was ordinary picnic fare, the picnickers were not ordinary folk. Quite the contrary, President and Mrs. Franklin D. Roosevelt were entertaining the king and queen of England.

Originally, King George VI and Queen Elizabeth had planned a trip only to Canada. With world tensions mounting in 1939, the royal family sought to strengthen the bonds of the British Empire. When President Roosevelt learned of the trip, he invited the royal couple to the United States. He hoped to discuss the growing possibility of war in Europe. More important, he hoped that the king and queen would charm the American people and arouse pro-British sentiment.

After the picnic, the Roosevelts accompanied their guests to the railroad station near Hyde Park, the Roosevelts' country estate. As the train pulled out, the royal couple waved to the crowd. Then, as Eleanor Roosevelt later described it, "Somebody began singing 'Auld Lang Syne,' and then everybody was singing and it seemed to me that there was something of our friendship and our sadness and something of the uncertainty of our futures in that song that could not have been said as well in any other words. I think the king and queen . . . were deeply moved. I know I was."

Friendship, sadness, uncertainty—there was good reason for such strong feelings among the picnickers that day. Unprovoked aggression by Japan, Germany, and Italy threatened world peace. Once again, Great Britain and the United States found themselves faced with the possibility of a long and bloody world war. Indeed, a bare three months after the picnic, Britain took up arms. Two years later, following a desperate effort to steer clear of war, the United States joined Britain in the battle against the Axis powers.

1.

Aggression in Europe and Asia

1921	1925	1929	1933	1937	1941

1921
Washington Naval Conference

1924
Dawes Plan adopted

1928
Kellogg-Briand Pact signed

1931
Japan invades China

1933
Hitler seizes power in Germany

1936
Germany invades Rhineland; Spanish Civil War begins

1939
Germany invades Poland; World War II begins

1941
Japan attacks Pearl Harbor; U.S. enters World War II

1. TIME LINE QUESTION Ask: What event took place the same year the U.S. entered the war?

1. In his painting War and Peace, *Peter Hurd depicts bombers taking off from a farmer's field in Great Britain. For two years, Americans debated the role they should take in the war that was engulfing Europe. The desire to help the British was offset by the strong isolationist sentiment that gripped the United States in the 1930s.*

1. **CRITICAL THINKING** Ask: Why do you think the British air force was using farmers' fields as runways?

2. **VOCABULARY** Have students look up these terms in the glossary before they begin reading.

1 American Diplomacy From Harding to Hoover

READ TO UNDERSTAND

■ What role the United States played in world economic and political affairs in the 1920s.

■ How United States policy changed toward Latin America.

■ How the United States reacted to Japanese aggression in China.

2. ■ *Vocabulary:* isolationist, internationalist.

During the 1920s, most Americans, and the Presidents they elected, were cautious of foreign involvements. Presidents Harding, Coolidge, and Hoover all tried to avoid a major American role in world affairs. Even so, the United States adopted some policies requiring limited cooperation with other nations.

GREAT DEBATE

Isolation Versus Intervention

Most government officials and citizens in the 1920s were **isolationists.** The United States, they believed, should avoid alliances and entangling agreements with other nations. Isolationist feelings, in fact, had kept the United States from signing the Treaty of Versailles, which provided for membership in the League of Nations. As President Harding proudly declared in 1923, the United States "does not propose to enter [the League] now by the side door, or the back door, or the cellar door."

A minority of the American public, on the other hand, felt that the United States should not divorce itself from world affairs. These **internationalists** believed that as a great power, the United States must take an active role. Events in Japan seemed to reinforce the internationalist view.

After World War I, Japan, interested in creating a Pacific empire, had begun build-

3.

649

3. **BACKGROUND** A 1937 poll showed that 70 percent of Americans thought the United States had erred in entering World War I.

ing a powerful navy. Great Britain and the United States opposed this action. Soon all three nations were embarked on a naval arms race.

Washington Naval Conference In 1921, President Harding asked representatives of nine Asian and European nations to meet in Washington to discuss ways to ease tensions in the Pacific. After much debate, the delegates to the Washington Naval Conference negotiated three treaties.

The Five-Power Treaty banned the construction of large warships for ten years and limited the tonnage each nation could have. For every five tons of ships the United States or Britain owned, Japan could have three tons, and France and Italy could have one and three-fourths tons. In the Four-Power Treaty, the United States, Britain, France, and Japan agreed to respect each other's territorial rights in the Pacific and to refer future disputes to a conference. The Nine-Power Treaty was a formal acceptance of the Open Door policy in China.

The Washington Naval Conference seemed to be an important step toward peace. It eased the arms race and tensions in the Pacific. Soon, however, the Conference agreements unraveled. Nations sidestepped them by building smaller warships and submarines.

1. Moreover, Japan continued its quest for a Pacific empire.

Kellogg-Briand Pact To counteract increasing international tensions in the late 1920s, United States Secretary of State Frank B. Kellogg and French Foreign Minister Aristide Briand proposed a treaty to guarantee peace. In 1928, 14 nations signed the Kellogg-Briand Pact, outlawing war except in cases of self-defense. Although 63 nations eventually ratified the pact, there was no system to enforce it. As one senator complained, the

2. pact was worth no more than a postage stamp.

Trade Barriers During the 1920s, the United States also took part in many League of Nations conferences on international trade, communications, and transportation. Nevertheless, United States tariff policy reflected strong isolationist sentiments. The Fordney-McCumber Act of 1922, for example, established high tariff rates. The Hawley-Smoot Act,

650

passed in 1930, raised rates even more. These highly protective tariffs disrupted world trade and worsened economic conditions for all nations.

The United States in the World Economy

Economic problems in Europe forced the United States to take a more direct role in the world economy. Devastated by wild inflation in 1923, Germany had failed to make reparation payments to France.* In reaction, French troops occupied the Ruhr region of Germany, threatening the delicate balance of power. To help Germany pay its reparations, the United States proposed the Dawes Plan in 1924.

According to the plan, named after banker Charles G. Dawes, the United States would lend money to Germany. Germany would use this loan to pay reparations to France and the other Allies. The Allies, in turn, would then have the money to pay their wartime debts to the United States. The Dawes Plan rescued Germany from economic ruin and enabled the Allies to repay the United States. At the same time, however, it involved the United States more directly in the European economy.

Still another economic development conflicted with United States isolationism. During the 1920s, the nation experienced tremendous growth in its international trade and investments. Between 1913 and 1925, the volume of United States exports almost doubled. American companies built factories in Europe and established oil interests in the Middle East. No amount of isolationist sentiment, it seemed, could stem the tide of American economic expansion. ■

Policy Toward Latin America

United States policy toward Latin America was not isolationist. In fact, unstable conditions in Latin American nations prompted the United States to send in troops to restore order.

*As you read in Chapter 25, reparations were penalty payments that Germany was to make to the Allies for war damages.

2. **BACKGROUND** Other critics called it an "international kiss."

3. **MAIN IDEA** Have students give the main features of American foreign policy in the 1920s.

During the early 1920s, American soldiers were stationed in Panama, the Dominican Republic, Haiti, and Honduras. American marines, having withdrawn from Nicaragua in 1. 1925 after a stay of nearly 13 years, returned there in 1926 when civil war broke out. Their mission was to fight anti-government forces and ensure a free election.

By the late 1920s, however, this pattern of military intervention was ending. Under fire from progressives in his own party, President Coolidge placed less emphasis on armed intervention in Latin America.

Developments in Mexico tested Coolidge's ability to deal with a Latin American neighbor without resorting to force. In 1927, the Mexican congress passed a law limiting the period of United States ownership of Mexican oil resources to 50 years. President Coolidge appointed Dwight W. Morrow, a promi-2. nent banker, to negotiate with the Mexican government. Instructed to "keep us out of war," Morrow worked out an agreement allowing United States corporations to keep oil properties acquired before 1917. Morrow's success encouraged the United States to continue a more peaceful approach to Latin American affairs.

Under Herbert Hoover, the United States departed even further from a policy based on force in Latin America. In 1928, President Coolidge's undersecretary of state, J. Reuben Clark, had drawn up a memorandum stating that the United States had no right to intervene militarily in Latin American nations. The Clark Memorandum was officially released in 1930 by the Hoover administration. President Hoover soon showed that he meant to honor the principle of nonintervention. He refrained from sending troops to El Salvador in 1932 when that country failed to pay some debts. He also agreed to withdraw United States troops from Nicaragua.

War in Asia

Isolationism faced a crucial test in 1931. In the fall of that year, Japanese troops began to occupy the northern Chinese province of Manchuria. When China petitioned the League of Nations for help, the League asked the United States to participate in an economic

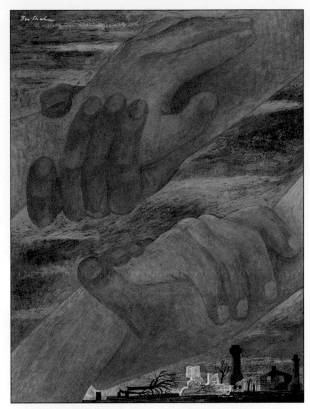

In the late 1920s, the United States shifted its policy in Latin America from military intervention to greater cooperation and aid. This shift improved relations between the United States and its Latin neighbors. This poster, created by artist Ben Shahn, reflects the new feelings of brotherhood.

3.

3. **VISUAL EVIDENCE** What symbols does Shahn use to convey a spirit of brotherhood? Are they effective?

boycott against Japan. The Hoover administration refused, and in the end, the League took no action. Now easy prey, Manchuria fell in January 1932, and Japan set up a "puppet" government, that is, one controlled by Japan.

Although Japanese aggression outraged Americans, President Hoover did not want to become involved in an Asian war. Unable to make even mild threats, Secretary of State Henry L. Stimson instead issued a statement that the United States would refuse to recognize Japanese territorial gains in China. The so-called Stimson Doctrine, however, included no proposals for concrete action against Japan.

Most Americans feared involvement in Asia and supported President Hoover's cautious policy. Internationalists, however, were **651**

The Japanese justified their invasion of the
1. Chinese province of Manchuria in 1931 as "pacific [peaceful] and natural expansion." But, as this cartoon shows, the aggression violated an assortment of international agreements. Most Americans, preoccupied by the Great Depression, paid little attention to events in Manchuria. "The American people," said an editorial in the Philadelphia Record, "don't give a hoot in a rain barrel who controls North China."

1. **BACKGROUND** Remind students that Japan's attempt to win control of Manchuria had contributed to the Russo-Japanese War in 1905 (p. 539).

opposed to his policy. They warned that American inaction would encourage hostile acts by aggressive powers. Events soon proved their warning correct.

See p. T120.

SECTION 1 REVIEW

1. **Identify:** (a) Kellogg-Briand Pact, (b) Dawes Plan, (c) Clark Memorandum, (d) Stimson Doctrine.

2. **Define:** (a) isolationist, (b) internationalist.

3. What was the purpose of the Washington Naval Conference?

4. How did United States policy toward Latin America change during the 1920s?

5. **Critical Thinking** Why do you think many historians consider that the Stimson Doctrine was ineffective?

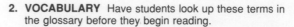

International Challenges During the 1930s

READl TO UNDERSTAND

■ How dictators came to power in Germany and Italy.

■ How Congress tried to keep the United States neutral.

■ How President Roosevelt tried to secure the friendship of Latin American countries.

■ *Vocabulary:* totalitarian state, devalue.

2.

The Great Depression dominated the lives of nearly all Americans during the 1930s. Problems such as jobs, food, clothing, and shelter seemed more important than international events. But aggressive actions by Germany, Italy, and Japan eventually forced the United States to become more involved in world affairs.

Rise of Totalitarian Dictatorships

By the mid-1930s, dictators had established totalitarian governments in Italy and Germany. In a **totalitarian state,** the government is supreme and individuals have few rights. All political opposition is forbidden.

In 1922, Benito Mussolini established himself as dictator of Italy. He and his followers, known as fascists, suspended elections, 3. put the Italian economy under strict government supervision, and began to modernize the armed forces. Fascist leaders loudly supported an active campaign of territorial expansion. They promised that Italy would become a great power in the Mediterranean region and in Africa.

Even more ominous was the rise of Adolf Hitler and his National Socialist, or Nazi, party in Germany. The Nazis had grown increasingly popular during the 1920s and early 1930s because of Hitler's fierce attacks on the Treaty of Versailles. Hitler expressed the feelings of many Germans who believed their nation had been unfairly punished by the treaty. He also proclaimed that the Germans were a "master race" and blamed the German defeat in World

3. **VOCABULARY** The word *fascist* comes from the Latin word *fasces,* meaning a bundle of sticks. Since a single stick can be broken but a bundle of sticks cannot, the Italian word *fascio* was used for a political association.

War I on the Jews within Germany. Once in power, Hitler and the Nazis established totalitarian control and secretly began to build up the German military in preparation for aggressive expansion.

After 1930, Japan, too, came under leadership intent on expansion and empire. A military clique gradually assumed more and more control, and Emperor Hirohito became little more than a figurehead. Aggression in Manchuria (see page 651) was only the beginning of an effort to secure markets and raw materials essential to a new and powerful Japan.

Economic Issues

The worldwide depression during the 1930s increased support of totalitarian dictatorships. With industry at a standstill, many nations had erected high tariff barriers to protect their failing businesses from foreign competition. High tariffs, in turn, contributed to a collapse of trade, which made the depression worse. American exports, for example, had dropped 50 percent between 1929 and 1933.

Boosting International Trade President Roosevelt and Secretary of State Cordell Hull believed that a revival of trade could ease the depression. If the United States exported more goods, they reasoned, then production would rise and unemployment would fall.

One strategy was to **devalue** the currency, that is, to reduce the value of the dollar in relation to other currencies. With devaluation, American products would be less expensive on the world market. Roosevelt began to devalue the dollar in 1933, but the tactic had little impact on trade.

In another attempt to improve foreign trade, Roosevelt pressed for lower tariffs on imports. Congress responded by passing the Trade Agreements Act in 1934. This act gave the President power to lower existing tariffs as much as 50 percent. Roosevelt had hoped that by lowering tariffs, he would encourage other nations to do the same, thus increasing American exports. But the worldwide depression suppressed demand for American products, and exports increased only modestly.

By 1933, Adolf Hitler controlled the government in Germany. His Nazi party solidified its support with huge party rallies like the one shown here. As thousands of onlookers cheered, seemingly endless rows of uniformed party members marched into the stadium with military precision. They carried vivid red flags adorned with the swastika, the Nazi party symbol.

3.

Desire for foreign trade also influenced the United States to grant diplomatic recognition to the Soviet Union in 1933. The United States had refused to recognize the Bolshevik government after the revolution in 1917. (See page 571.) Even with recognition, however, vigorous trade with the Soviet Union did not materialize.

Payment of War Debts The worldwide depression also affected the repayment of war debts. During the war, the Allies had borrowed almost $10 billion from the United States. According to the Dawes Plan of 1924, the Allies would pay their debts to the United States by collecting reparations from Germany. The reparations, as you will recall, were partly financed by United States loans. When the depression struck, the United States stopped aid to Germany, and Germany slowed its payments to the Allies. Consequently, the Allies were unable to pay their debts to the United States.

In 1931, President Hoover attempted to relieve the Allies' burden by suspending all debt payment for a year. But when payments **653**

2. **CRITICAL THINKING** Japan was a latecomer to the scramble for territories. Ask: How might this fact help explain the "aggressiveness" of its foreign policy?

3. **BACKGROUND** The swastika is an ancient symbol used by Byzantines, Greeks, Celts, Buddhists, and North American and South American Indians.

came due again, many debtor nations were still unable to fulfill their obligations. The United States eventually collected only about one quarter of the money owed by the Allies. (Only Finland met its full obligation.) Americans resented the Allies for not paying their full share of the cost of the war effort. This resentment helped strengthen isolationist sentiment during the 1930s.

The Isolationist Impulse

Findings of a congressional inquiry further fueled isolationist sentiment during the 1930s. From 1934 to 1936, Senator Gerald Nye of North Dakota chaired a committee investigating United States entry into World War I. According to the committee, international bankers who had financed the Allied war effort had drawn the United States into war. Eager for repayment, these bankers had lob-

bied for United States entry in the hope of speeding up an Allied victory.

The Nye committee further charged that munitions industries, anticipating increased profits, had also pressed for American entry into the war. With each new accusation, isolationist feelings increased.

Confident of public support, congressional isolationists introduced legislation to promote their cause. The Neutrality Act of 1935 authorized the President to bar arms sales to warring nations. The first test came almost immediately, when Italy invaded Ethiopia in October. Invoking the Neutrality Act, Roosevelt refused to sell arms to either nation. Since Italy was stronger militarily, the act worked against Ethiopia.

In 1936, Congress extended neutrality legislation by forbidding all loans to belligerents. Later in the year, civil war broke out in Spain between supporters of the republican government and fascists led by Francisco

VOICES OF FREEDOM

Conflict Over Neutrality

The conflict over neutrality was played out in the Senate during the 1930s. The following excerpts are from speeches delivered in the Senate on the issue of neutrality legislation. Senator Thomas T. Connally, the head of the Senate Foreign Relations Committee, rejected neutrality. Senator Arthur H. Vandenberg was an isolationist leader.

Senator Connally

Is it an expression of neutrality to say to two warring nations, one of which has ambitions for territorial conquest, the other unprepared, the other weak, the other trying to pursue its own destiny—is it neutral to say to those nations, "We shall give arms to neither of you," thereby insuring the triumph of the prepared nation, the covetous nation, the ambitious nation, the nation which seeks by force of arms to impose its will on a weaker and defenseless nation?

Senator Vandenberg

In the midst of foreign war and the alarms of other wars, we are asked to depart basically from the neutrality which the American Congress has twice told the world, since 1935, would be our rule of conduct in such an event. . . .

Consciously or otherwise, but mostly consciously, we are asked to depart from it in behalf of one belligerent whom our personal sympathies largely favor, and against another belligerent whom our personal feelings largely condemn. In my opinion, this is the road that may lead us to war, and I will not voluntarily take it. . . .

See p. T120.

1. What is the view of Senator Connally? Of Senator Vandenberg?

2. **Critical Thinking** With which senator's view do you agree? Why?

1. **TECHNOLOGY** The Germans used the Spanish Civil War to test new weapons and equipment.

Franco. Franco received military support from

1. Germany and Italy, while the Soviet Union aided the republicans. Despite widespread

2. American sympathy for the republicans, President Roosevelt called for neutrality. A joint resolution of Congress in January 1937 banned United States aid to either side.

Congress asserted its neutrality policy again later in 1937. A new Neutrality Act banned the shipment of nonmilitary goods to warring nations, as well as travel by Americans on the ships of belligerents. Without doubt, isolationism dominated United States foreign policy during the 1930s. However, increasing aggression by Germany, Italy, and Japan would soon challenge that policy.

The Good Neighbor Policy

Faced with aggressive dictatorships in Europe and Asia, President Roosevelt tried to secure the friendship of the Latin American nations. In his inauguration speech in March 1933, Roosevelt proclaimed that the United States would follow "the policy of the good neighbor."

In late 1933, Secretary of State Cordell Hull attended the Seventh Pan-American Conference in Montevideo, Uruguay. There Hull supported the principle that "no state has the right to intervene in the internal or external affairs of another." In 1934, Roosevelt implemented the "good neighbor" policy by withdrawing United States marines from Haiti and nullifying the Platt Amendment, which had restricted Cuban independence.

The "good neighbor" policy benefited the United States. In 1936, President Roosevelt attended an inter-American conference on peace in Buenos Aires, Argentina, and received an enthusiastic welcome. In his address to the conference, he stressed the unity of the United States and Latin America. He told his listeners that nations outside the Western Hemisphere seeking "to commit acts of aggression against us will find a hemisphere wholly prepared to consult together for our mutual safety and our mutual good." Latin American friendship proved important to the United States when world war broke out.

"We shun political commitments which might entangle us in foreign wars," said President Roosevelt a month after the outbreak of the Spanish Civil War. With the threat of general war in Europe growing, most Americans hoped the United States would not become involved. As this 1938 cartoon shows, many Americans recalled the battle casualties of World War I and the failure of European nations to repay their war debts.

... 3.

See p. T120.

SECTION 2 REVIEW

1. **Identify:** (a) Benito Mussolini, (b) Adolf Hitler, (c) Nye committee, (d) "good neighbor" policy.

2. **Define:** (a) totalitarian state, (b) devalue.

3. (a) What issues helped Hitler gain popularity in Germany? (b) On whom did he blame Germany's defeat in World War I?

4. What events tested the neutrality policy of the United States?

5. **Critical Thinking** Would the government of the United States be likely to isolate the nation from European affairs today? Explain.

655

2. **BACKGROUND** Thousands of Americans went to Spain as private citizens to fight on the side of the republicans. Among them was Ernest Hemingway.

3. **VISUAL EVIDENCE** The cartoon implies that American experiences as a result of World War I would color U.S. reaction to a threat of war.

3 The Threat of War

READ TO UNDERSTAND

■ How Japan and Germany expanded their borders.

■ Why European nations gave in to Hitler's demands.

■ How war broke out in Asia and Europe.

1. ■ *Vocabulary:* appeasement, blitzkrieg.

Agreements to promote peace and cooperation failed to prevent aggressive acts by Italy, Japan, and Germany during the 1930s. But as threatening as these aggressions were, Europe's democracies took little action. The memory of World War I was still strong, and most Europeans feared a second bloody war in their lifetime. With aggression proceeding unchecked, the world drew closer to another major conflict.

Japanese Militarism in Asia

United States foreign policy in Asia changed little after Franklin Roosevelt became President. In 1934, Congress passed the Tydings-McDuffie Act, which promised the Philippines complete independence within a decade.* The United States appeared ready to withdraw from a military or political role in Asian affairs.

Meanwhile, Japanese aggression continued. In 1937, Japan launched a full-scale war
2. against China, seizing Peking, Shanghai, and other cities. Because of American sympathy for China, President Roosevelt did not invoke the neutrality acts, which would have barred the sale of arms and nonmilitary goods to both sides. Although the President hoped his action would help China, in fact, it benefited the Japanese more. They were able to acquire more arms and war materials because they had more merchant ships to transport them.

---

*As you read in Chapter 24, the United States had taken control of the Philippines after the Spanish-American War.

656

Alarmed by events, President Roosevelt cautiously began to challenge isolationist policy. In a major speech in Chicago in 1937, he warned Americans that nations must take positive action "to preserve world peace" if they did not wish to become embroiled in war. Comparing war to a highly contagious disease, Roosevelt urged a "quarantine" of armed conflict wherever it might occur.

Despite Roosevelt's efforts to alter isolationist sentiment, events soon demonstrated that he had not succeeded. On December 12, 1937, Japanese bombers sank the American gunboat *Panay,* on patrol on the Yangtze River in China. Two crew members were killed in the *Panay* incident. The United States took no action. Instead, the government accepted a Japanese apology and payment of $2 million for damages.

Fearing a similar incident might lead to war, many Americans voiced approval of a proposed constitutional amendment. The 3. Ludlow Amendment would have required a national vote before the United States could enter a war, except in the case of invasion. Although the amendment failed to clear Congress, the vote was very close, reflecting the strong national desire to avoid war at any cost.

Germany on the March

Once, when an adviser cautioned Adolf Hitler against angering other European powers, Hitler assured him that the rest of Europe would "never act! They'll just protest. And they will always be too late." Events throughout the 1930s proved Hitler correct. Germany's accelerated military buildup, and its aggressive actions went virtually unchallenged.

In 1936, German soldiers marched into the Rhineland, German territory located between the Rhine River and the French and Belgian borders. In so doing, Germany violated the Treaty of Versailles. Fearful of war, however, France offered no resistance, and the German army remained.

This passive agreement to Hitler's demands became known as **appeasement.** To avoid war, both France and Britain continued to allow German aggression in Europe.

1. **BACKGROUND** Hitler had written of his plans for empire in *Mein Kampf* (My Struggle) in 1923, but few people had taken the book seriously.

Sooner or later, the European leaders believed, Hitler would satisfy his desire for conquest.

In 1938, Germany annexed Austria to the Third Reich.* Again, Hitler met no resistance, either from the Austrians or the rest of Europe. Later that same year, Hitler demanded that Germany be given possession of the Sudetenland, a region in western Czechoslovakia. He argued that the Sudetenland should be part of Germany because 3 million Germans lived there. This time, Hitler met resistance. Czechoslovakia was prepared to fight, and a crisis arose.

Appeasement in Munich Hitler met with French and British leaders at a conference in Munich, Germany, in 1938, in an effort to resolve the crisis. The French and British agreed to German demands in Czechoslovakia in return for Hitler's promise to end German expansion. In addition, Italy and Germany joined Britain and France in a pledge that none of the four would ever make war on the others. Czechoslovakia protested the loss of the Sudetenland, but without support from

*The Third Reich was the name of the German state under the Nazis.

2. **MAP READING** Have students locate the area controlled by Italy in September 1939. Ask: What areas had Germany taken over by September 1939?

MAP STUDY

In 1935, Italy under Mussolini invaded Ethiopia. Then, between 1936 and 1939, Hitler sent the German army to win control of several areas bordering Germany. From the evidence on this map, do you think Hitler's invasion of Poland could have been predicted? Explain.

2.

See p. T121.

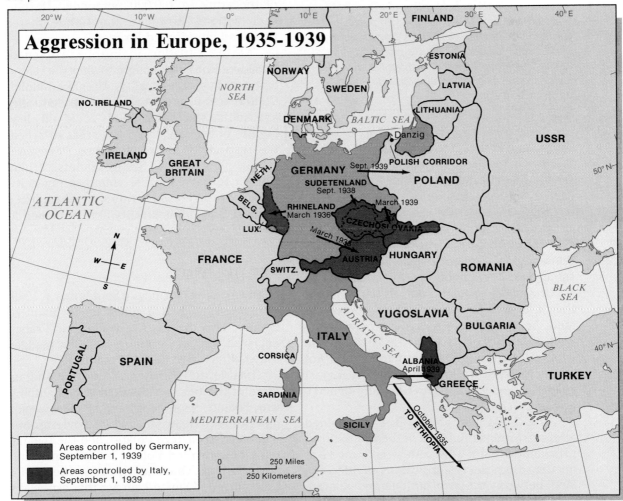

Aggression in Europe, 1935–1939

Areas controlled by Germany, September 1, 1939

Areas controlled by Italy, September 1, 1939

0   250 Miles
0   250 Kilometers

Reaction to German occupation of the Sudetenland ran the full range of emotions. German inhabitants greeted the Nazis warmly, and Czechs felt despair. In this picture, it is hard to know whether the woman at right is crying for
1. joy or sorrow as she and others salute the arriving Germans.

1. **BACKGROUND** One Sudeten woman, tossing a bouquet of roses to a passing Nazi automobile, accidentally hit Hitler in the face.

Britain and France it was powerless to resist. Returning to Great Britain, Prime Minister Neville Chamberlain proclaimed that he had gained "peace with honor" and "peace for our time."

Despite Hitler's assurances that he had no interest in more territory, he annexed the remainder of Czechoslovakia in 1939. In the same year, Italy conquered Albania.

A German-Soviet Pact Hitler realized that if he was to continue seizing European land, he would have to avoid war with the Soviet Union. For its part, the Soviet Union wanted assurance that Germany would not target its territory for expansion. In August 1939, the Soviet Union and Germany signed a nonaggression pact.

The Molotov-Ribbentrop Pact, named
2. after the foreign ministers of the two nations, proclaimed that neither side would wage war on the other. Secret provisions divided Poland between the two nations and guaranteed that Germany would not interfere if the

658

Soviet Union invaded Finland. The pact helped set the stage for war.

Early Preparations

Although Chamberlain forecast peace, European nations had begun preparing for war. At the time, the United States had almost no military force. Following the end of war in 1918, Congress had ordered drastic reductions in the nation's armed forces. Hitler had such disdain for the United States military that he mocked, "The inferiority and decadence of this allegedly new world power is evident in its military inefficiency."

The United States did expand the army and navy somewhat in the mid- and late 1930s. President Roosevelt authorized the construction of additional cruisers and aircraft carriers. And in 1935, Congress increased the size of the army to 165,000 personnel. Despite such actions, however, the United States remained unprepared for war.

As the situation in Europe worsened, President Roosevelt sought to alter the United States policy of neutrality. After the Munich Conference, he tried to revise the neutrality acts so that the United States could aid allies in case of war. He urged Congress to repeal the restrictions on selling arms. "I've fired my last shot," he told Senate leaders. "I think I ought to have another round in my belt." But Congress refused to honor the President's request, and the neutrality acts remained in effect.

The War Begins

At dawn on the morning of September 1, 1939, Germany launched a full-scale invasion of Poland. Two days later, Britain and France declared war on Germany, fulfilling pledges they had made to defend Poland.

Unable to withstand the tremendous force of the German **blitzkrieg,** or lightning war, Poland surrendered in just a few weeks, on October 6, 1939. Meanwhile, Soviet troops had invaded eastern Poland, and the two nations now divided Poland into German and Soviet zones. One month later, the Soviet Union invaded Finland, an act that especially outraged Americans, since Finland had been

2. **CRITICAL THINKING** Have students look at the map on p. 657. Explain that the Molotov-Ribbentrop Pact freed Hitler from the danger of a two-front war. Ask: Why did Hitler want to avoid a war on two fronts?

the only nation to continue repayment of its World War I debts.

Two days after the outbreak of war in Poland, President Roosevelt issued a proclamation of neutrality. He commented, however, that Americans need not "remain neutral in thought." Even while declaring neutrality, Roosevelt made further efforts to repeal restrictions on arms sales. Isolationists in Congress fought his proposals.

Finally, the President and Congress reached a compromise. The United States could sell arms to the Allies on a "cash-and-carry" basis, that is, as long as the Allies paid cash and transported the materials on their own ships. At the same time, Roosevelt assured Americans that there was not "the remotest possibility of sending the boys of American mothers to fight on the battlefields of Europe."

German Victories

After the occupation of Poland, there was a long lull in the fighting. American newspapers began to write about the "phony war." The lull was shattered by the rumble of tanks in April 1940, when Germany attacked and overran Norway and Denmark.

The Fall of France   One month later, German forces invaded Belgium and the Netherlands before driving deep into France. Italy entered the war by attacking France from the south. "The hand that held the dagger," said Roosevelt angrily, "has struck it into the back of his neighbor."

French and British forces buckled before the crushing Nazi blitzkrieg. Retreating to the coast of France, the British army was miraculously saved from destruction at the beaches of Dunkirk. Hundreds of small boats rushed

2. **VISUAL EVIDENCE** According to this painting, from where was the German attack on these troops coming?

In one of the most spectacular rescue operations ever, more than 300,000 British soldiers were evacuated from the beach where they were trapped at Dunkirk, France. Hundreds of small boats of every shape and size, manned by every variety of British seaman, rushed across the English Channel to save the exhausted troops. In this painting by Richard Eurich, the defiant British battle the enemy while awaiting what has become known as the "Miracle of Dunkirk."

across the English Channel to evacuate the exhausted troops. France surrendered to Germany on June 22, 1940.

A New Resolve Britain now stood alone. Neville Chamberlain resigned, and Winston
1. Churchill, a longtime critic of appeasement, succeeded him as prime minister. As Britain braced itself for attack, Churchill told his people he could offer them only the prospect of "blood, toil, sweat and tears." He inspired the British and Americans by pledging "to wage war, by sea, land and air, with all our might and with all the strength God can give us."

In the United States, a major shift in public opinion allowed preparations for war to begin in earnest. Congress authorized huge sums of money to modernize the army and navy. Within five months, over $17 billion was appropriated for defense.

In 1940, Prime Minister Churchill pleaded with Roosevelt for ships to reinforce the Royal Navy. At first, Roosevelt hesitated. But as German submarine attacks on British shipping continued, the President agreed to a deal. In exchange for a 99-year lease on naval and air bases in Newfoundland and the Caribbean, the United States transferred 50 old but usable destroyers to the British fleet. Roosevelt called the destroyer agreement "the most important action in the reinforcement of our
2. national defense that has been taken since the Louisiana Purchase."

See p. T121.

SECTION 3 REVIEW

1. **Identify:** (a) *Panay* incident, (b) Munich Conference, (c) Neville Chamberlain, (d) Winston Churchill.

2. **Define:** (a) appeasement, (b) blitzkrieg.

3. How did the United States respond to the Japanese attack on China in 1937?

4. What event prompted Britain and France to declare war on Germany?

5. **Critical Thinking** What factors might account for the difference between President Roosevelt's reaction to war in Europe in the 1930s and President Wilson's reactions to World War I?

---

4 **Between Peace and War**

READ TO UNDERSTAND

■ How the United States lent or leased supplies to Britain.

■ What ideas Churchill and Roosevelt outlined in the Atlantic Charter.

■ How events in Asia drew the United States into the war.

Night after night, from September 1940 to May 1941, German planes dropped bombs on London and other British cities. The Royal Air Force took to the skies and, at a terrible cost of life and aircraft, managed to fight off the German bombers. In the United States, people gathered nightly in front of their radios to hear Edward R. Murrow and other war correspondents reporting directly from London. As they listened to these reports from war-ravaged Britain, Americans wondered how much longer the United States could stay out of the war.

A Third Term for Roosevelt

Meanwhile, two candidates battled for the presidency of the United States. Wendell Willkie, the Republican candidate, was a corporate executive from Indiana. As president of a public utilities holding company, he had led the fight against the Tennessee Valley Authority during the early years of the New Deal.

In an unprecedented move, Franklin Roosevelt announced that he would seek a third term as President. He cited the crisis in 3. Europe and his established relations with European leaders as reasons for breaking the two-term tradition established by George Washington. By the summer of 1940, international events had overshadowed the third-term issue, and the Democrats renominated Roosevelt.

Willkie was an internationalist who supported many of Roosevelt's foreign policy actions, including increased aid to Britain. He also approved of the Selective Service Act instituting the first peacetime draft, which was scheduled to take effect in the fall of 1940. As the presidential campaign continued, Willkie found it more and more difficult to find an issue on which to challenge Roosevelt.

Late in the campaign, Willkie began accusing Roosevelt of maneuvering the country into war. The President responded with his old promise: "I have said this before, but I shall say it again and again: Your boys are not going to be sent into any foreign wars."

1. Roosevelt easily won the election with 54 percent of the popular vote.

End of Isolationism

In May 1940, when the German blitzkrieg struck France, President Roosevelt had proclaimed that the European conflict created an "unlimited national emergency" for the United States. He urged an all-out effort to strengthen national defense. Roosevelt's proclamation pleased internationalist groups, which had long advocated preparation for war.

Lend-Lease At this time, as you recall, Britain was buying supplies from the United States under the cash-and-carry arrangement. By the end of 1940, however, the British were running out of money. Despite sympathy for Britain, many Americans, including members of Congress, were hesitant about lending money. They remembered the Allies' failure to repay war debts after World War I.

Faced with this dilemma, President Roosevelt proposed a solution: The United States would lend Britain whatever supplies it needed to wage war against Germany. He compared this to helping neighbors whose house was on fire. If the neighbors needed your garden hose to put out the fire, Roosevelt pointed out, you would not waste time arguing about the cost of the hose or how it would be paid for. You would simply give your neighbors the hose and tell them to return it after the fire was out.

Congress approved Roosevelt's plan and passed the Lend-Lease Act in early 1941. The act gave the President the authority to sell, exchange, lend, or lease war materials to any
2. country whose security he deemed vital to the defense of the United States. Roosevelt

told Americans that the nation must now become the "arsenal of democracy."

In June 1941, Germany launched a surprise attack on the Soviet Union. German troops pushed deep into Soviet territory, overrunning the Ukraine and approaching Moscow and Leningrad. The United States immediately extended the Lend-Lease Act to include the Soviet Union. Roosevelt and Churchill agreed that even though Stalin's government was oppressive, it was essential to help the Soviet Union ward off the German invasion.

The Battle of the Atlantic Getting the Lend-Lease materials across the Atlantic to Britain proved difficult. "Wolf packs" of German submarines sank many supply ships throughout the spring of 1941. Some advis-

By 1940, England stood alone against the German war machine. Prime Minister Winston Churchill vowed, "We shall fight on the beaches . . . and in the streets. . . . We shall never surrender." Between September 1940 and May 1941, German planes bombed London nightly. Although damage was extensive, as seen in the blasted stores and bus in 3. *this picture, Londoners' spirits remained high.*

ers urged Roosevelt to order navy destroyers to escort the ships on the dangerous Atlantic crossing. But the President hesitated to take such a drastic step.

Repeated German attacks on British supply vessels finally forced Roosevelt's hand. In July 1941, the President announced that United States warships would accompany British freighters as far as Iceland. From there, the British navy would escort the merchant ships to British ports. At first, the Germans did nothing to challenge America's actions. During September and October, however, German submarines attacked the American destroyers *Reuben James* and *Kearny*. An undeclared naval war erupted on the Atlantic.

Isolationist Arguments Weaken A vocal group of isolationists continued to argue vigorously against foreign involvements. The America First Committee led the opposition to the Lend-Lease Act and all other aid to the Allies. As events in Europe worsened, however, the isolationists' position became increasingly unpopular.

Most Americans had mixed feelings about the war. They wanted to see Germany defeated, but without direct United States participation. To satisfy public opinion, policy makers continued to seek a middle road between isolationism and war.

Alliance With Britain Although still officially neutral, the United States continued to move toward an alliance with Britain. Military leaders of the two countries met secretly in Washington, D.C., to plan a joint strategy should the United States enter the war.

In August 1941, Roosevelt and Churchill met aboard a warship off the coast of Newfoundland. Although Roosevelt still refused to commit fighting forces, the leaders did agree on a statement of "certain common principles" on which to base "a better future for the world."

In this statement, the Atlantic Charter, the United States and Britain agreed to seek no territorial gain and to support "the right of all peoples to choose the form of government under which they will live." They urged all nations to cooperate economically to raise the general standard of living in the world. They also proposed the disarmament of all aggressor nations after the defeat of Nazism,

and "the establishment of a wide and permanent system of general security." But even while Roosevelt and Churchill discussed the war in Europe, the danger of a wider war in Asia grew.

Embargo Against Japan

As you have read, relations between Japan and the United States had been strained since 1937. (See page 656.) Tensions increased in the spring of 1940, when France and the Netherlands fell to Germany. French and Dutch colonies in Asia were now ripe for the picking.

In September 1940, Secretary of State Cordell Hull informed Japan that the United States would not tolerate a Japanese military presence in European colonies in Asia. Before the month ended, however, Japan had reached an agreement with the government of occupied France giving Japan control of military bases in French Indochina (now the nations of Vietnam, Cambodia, and Laos).

The United States responded by placing an embargo on the export of scrap metal, oil, and aviation fuel to Japan. Since Japan depended on the United States for 90 percent of its scrap metal and 60 percent of its oil, the embargo would seriously cripple Japan. On the following day, Japan announced that it had formed a military alliance with Germany and Italy.

War in the Pacific loomed in the summer and fall of 1941. In July, Japan occupied French Indochina. In response, the United States froze all Japanese accounts in American banks. This prevented Japan from buying any goods from the United States.

In November 1941, Secretary of State Hull met with Japanese diplomats in Washington, D.C. The Japanese asked the United States to end aid to China and restore full economic relations with Japan. Hull countered that the United States would end the embargo if Japan withdrew from China and Indochina. The talks continued without agreement.

Pearl Harbor

Even while the Japanese diplomats were meeting with Hull, their country was preparing to attack the United States. At 7:55 A.M. on

662

"Surprise attack successful," was the message sent to the military high command from the Japanese fleet. On Sunday morning, December 7, 1941, a Japanese air raid destroyed the United States Pacific fleet at Pearl Harbor. Nineteen ships
1. *were sunk or put out of commission, and more than 180 planes were destroyed. Luckily, the aircraft carriers stationed at Pearl Harbor were not in port at the time. The sneak attack united Americans in their desire to go to war.*

---

1. **CITIZENSHIP** The attack on Pearl Harbor was so devastating that full details of the damage suffered by the Pacific fleet were not disclosed for a year.

Sunday, December 7, 1941, a wave of Japanese bombers struck the United States fleet at Pearl Harbor, the American naval base in Hawaii. The United States Navy was taken by surprise. American military leaders had been warned of a possible Japanese attack, but they expected it in southeast Asia, not Pearl Harbor. Thus, no special precautions had been taken, and most of the fleet was caught at anchor. Of the large ships based at Pearl Harbor, only the aircraft carriers were not docked at the time of the attack.

Pearl Harbor was a catastrophe for the United States. Nineteen ships, including six battleships, sank or suffered severe damage. Japanese planes destroyed more than 180 aircraft still on the ground. More than 2,300
2. American soldiers and sailors died, and nearly 2,000 more were wounded.

The next day, a visibly grim and shaken President addressed a special joint session of Congress. The hall was silent as Roosevelt described the "sudden and deliberate attack" on United States forces on "a day which will live in infamy." Roosevelt asked Congress to declare a state of war between the United States and Japan.

Within hours, Congress approved a declaration of war, with only one negative vote. Three days later, Japan's European allies, Germany and Italy, declared war on the United States. Congress immediately passed a declaration of war against the two European powers. For the second time in less than 25 years, the United States was at war.

See p. T121.

SECTION 4 REVIEW

1. **Identify:** (a) Wendell Willkie, (b) Lend-Lease Act, (c) Atlantic Charter.

2. How were the positions of Roosevelt and Willkie similar?

3. What development led Roosevelt to propose the policy of Lend-Lease?

4. How did the war in Europe give Japan opportunities to expand in Asia?

5. **Critical Thinking** Was the entry of the United States into World War II inevitable? Explain.

663

2. **LOCAL HISTORY** Have students interview relatives or neighbors who remember the day Pearl Harbor was attacked. They should find out where the person was when news of the attack broke and how they reacted.

CHAPTER 30 REVIEW

Summary

1. **During the 1920s, most Americans shared isolationist feelings.** Still, the United States adopted a policy of limited cooperation in world affairs. United States policy in Latin America slowly changed from one of military intervention to peaceful diplomacy.

2. **During the 1930s, totalitarian dictatorships arose in Germany and Italy.** The United States tried to remain uninvolved in Europe's problems by passing neutrality acts. To secure friendly relations with the nations of Latin America, President Roosevelt adopted a "good neighbor policy."

3. **Japanese and German aggression met little resistance during the 1930s.** Fearing involvement in another world war, Britain and France adopted a policy of appeasement toward Hitler. The German invasion of Poland in 1939 finally prompted France and Britain to declare war. In 1940, France fell, and Britain stood alone against the Nazis.

4. **After the fall of France, the United States struggled to find a middle road between isolationism and war.** To halt Germany, it lent or leased war supplies to Britain and later the Soviet Union. To halt Japan, it imposed an embargo on oil and scrap iron. A Japanese attack on Pearl Harbor in December 1941 finally drew the United States into the war.

See p. T121.

Vocabulary

Match the term at left with its definition or description at right.

1. isolationist
2. internationalist
3. totalitarian state
4. devalue
5. appeasement

a. giving in to demands to avoid conflict
b. country where the government is supreme
c. favors minimum foreign involvement
d. to reduce the value of the dollar
e. favors an active role in world affairs

See p. T121.

Chapter Checkup

1. How did the United States support world cooperation during the 1920s?

2. Describe the United States role in the world economy in the 1920s.

3. (a) How did United States policy toward Latin America change under Presidents Coolidge and Hoover? (b) What was Franklin Roosevelt's policy toward Latin America?

4. (a) How did the Nye committee investigation strengthen isolationist sentiment during the mid-1930s? (b) Describe three pieces of isolationist legislation passed during the period.

5. (a) What actions by Japan alarmed the United States in the 1930s? (b) How did the United States respond to each of these actions?

6. (a) Describe the policy of appeasement pursued by Britain and France. (b) How did war begin in 1939?

7. (a) What was the Lend-Lease Act? (b) How did it allow the United States to help Britain and the Soviet Union?

8. (a) What economic actions did the United States take to stop Japanese aggression in the early 1940s? (b) What finally led the United States to declare war on Japan?

See p. T122.

Critical Thinking

1. **Evaluating** How do you think the mood of the Roaring Twenties (see Chapter 26) may have contributed to the feeling of isolationism during that decade?

2. **Supporting an Opinion** No President had ever served more than two terms, yet Franklin Roosevelt was elected for a third term in 1940. Why do you think that happened? Cite specific evidence to support your answer.

3. **Classifying** Construct a chart with two columns and two rows. Label column 1 Isolationist and column 2 Internationalist. Label row 1 1920s and row 2 1930s. Classify the events of each decade as isolationist or internationalist and write them in the appropriate box. Based on your chart, in which decade does the United States appear to have been more isolationist? Explain.

See p. T122.

Connecting Past and Present

1. The failure of isolationism to keep the United States out of war was not forgotten after World War II. How is the role of the United States in international affairs today different from its role during the 1920s and 1930s?

2. The policy of appeasement toward Germany in the 1930s has drawn much criticism. How do nations today respond to aggressive or otherwise unacceptable policies of other nations?

See p. T122.

Developing Basic Skills

1. **Comparing** Review the events that led to United States entry into World War I in 1917. (See Chapter 25.) How did the circumstances surrounding United States entry into World War II differ from those leading to involvement in World War I? Were there any similarities? Explain.

2. **Analyzing Political Cartoons** Study the cartoon on page 655. (a) The cartoon is titled "A Good Time for Reflection." What do you think Uncle Sam is reflecting on? (b) Based on the cartoon, how do you think the cartoonist viewed the threat of war in Europe? (c) Would you consider this cartoon isolationist, internationalist, or neither? Explain.

WRITING ABOUT HISTORY

Preparing a Topic Outline

Once you have organized your notecards and classified them according to topics, you should prepare a topic outline. A topic outline helps you to focus on the main idea and the supporting details. Look at the portion of a topic outline below. The main topics are identified with Roman numerals. Subtopics are labeled with capital letters. Supporting details are labeled with Arabic numerals.

  I. Introduction
 II. Isolation Versus Intervention

   A. Washington Naval Conference
      1. Five-Power Treaty
      2. Four-Power Treaty
      3. Nine-Power Treaty
   B. Kellogg-Briand Pact
   C. Trade barriers
      1. Fordney-McCumber Act of 1922
      2. Hawley-Smoot Act of 1930
III. The United States in the World Economy

Practice: Complete the topic outline based on Section 1 of Chapter 30.

The Second World War (1941–1945)

31

CHAPTER OUTLINE

1 A World War

2 On the Home Front

3 The Allies on the Offensive

4 Wartime Diplomacy and Politics

5 Victory

CHAPTER OBJECTIVES After completing this chapter, students should be able to
1. describe how the Allies progressed during 1942.
2. discuss life on the home front.
3. explain Allied victories in Europe and the Pacific in 1943 and 1944.
4. describe how the war ended and summarize Allied plans for the postwar world.

CHAPTER PREVIEW Have students read the paragraphs and study the time line below. Then ask them to look at the chart on p. 668 and the maps on pp. 676 and 679. Help them use the maps to trace the main fighting of the war. Ask: How do the maps and chart show that World War II was global?

The wail of sirens pierced the night. It was an air raid drill. People scurried inside and drew the curtains. Americans could not be sure that they would not share the same fate as people in Britain. As World War II raged in Europe and Asia, the nation prepared for the worst.

"Put those lights out!" prodded volunteer air raid wardens. After all, in a real air raid, the "blackout" could prevent enemy pilots from spotting their targets. One newspaper characterized the periodic blackouts that became part of the home-front routine as symbols of "the awesome night that war has brought to the world." And a warden described how the blackouts did "something to you. . . . There is no physical fear. But the war is no longer far off in London or Chungking."

While citizens at home dutifully drew their curtains and turned out their lights, others were scanning the skies on the lookout for enemy planes. Men, women, and even children volunteered for this lonely task. One 14-year-old described her job: "We were . . . taught the shapes and silhouettes of the planes, and we were supposed to tell how many miles away they were. It was terribly confusing in the beginning," she later recalled.

What was anticipated, of course, never happened. Only one enemy pilot ever bombed the United States, and his mission was to set a forest fire in Oregon. Yet the volunteers' knowledge that they were doing what they could to help gave them a satisfying sense of shared achievement. As one former volunteer remembered, ". . . there was a solidarity, a unity, in the United States, a feeling that we're all in this together, and through our technological know-how and our determination and our downright good Americanism, we were going to win."

The victory did not come easily. The nation experienced defeat and disappointment, at first. But in the end, the Americans and their allies were able to stem the tide of German and Japanese advances to win the war.

1.

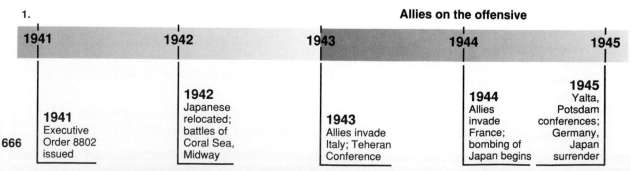

Allies on the offensive

| 1941 | 1942 | 1943 | 1944 | 1945 |

1941 Executive Order 8802 issued

1942 Japanese relocated; battles of Coral Sea, Midway

1943 Allies invade Italy; Teheran Conference

1944 Allies invade France; bombing of Japan begins

1945 Yalta, Potsdam conferences; Germany, Japan surrender

1. **TIME LINE QUESTION** Ask: How long after the bombing of Japan began did that nation surrender?

As the people at home prepared for the worst, American soldiers and sailors engaged in the grim struggle against Germany and Japan. This painting shows
1. the fighting in the North Atlantic, where American ships faced attacks by surface ships and "wolf packs" of German submarines.

1. **BACKGROUND** Surviving a U-boat attack required endurance. Three merchant sailors lasted for 83 days on raw fish, birds, and rainwater before being rescued from their raft.

1 A World War

READ TO UNDERSTAND

■ Why the Allies had to fight two separate wars.

■ What military strategy the Allies adopted.

■ What major battles stemmed the Axis advance by early 1943.

Those who lived through World War II recall it as "the Big One"—the largest, most destructive, and most deadly war in human history. Before it ended, over 50 nations took part.

The Allies Against the Axis Powers

In terms of numbers, the war would seem to have been lopsided. Aligned on one side were the Axis powers: Germany, Italy, Japan, and only six other nations. On the other side were 26 Allied powers, led by the United States, Great Britain, and the Soviet Union. By the end of the war, the Allies encompassed 49 nations.

The Allies' advantage in numbers was offset, in part, by the need to maintain long supply lines and fight two separate wars. One war took place in the Pacific, where the United States, Great Britain, Australia, and New Zealand clashed with Japan. Fighting there stretched for 5,000 miles (8,000 kilometers) north to south from Alaska to Java, and for 7,000 miles (about 11,000 kilometers) east to 2. west from Hawaii to India.

The second war took place on three major fronts, or battle zones, in Europe and Africa. On the eastern front, the Soviet Union faced Germany, Bulgaria, Finland, Hungary, and Romania. On the southern front, United States, British, and Australian troops grappled with the Germans and Italians in North Africa and Italy. On the western front, the Allies staged the greatest air-sea-land military

667

2. **GEOGRAPHY** Have students locate these places on a world map or globe. (location)

Allies and Axis Powers

Allies

Argentina (1945)	Ethiopia (1942)	New Zealand (1939)
Australia (1939)	France (1939)	Nicaragua (1941)
Belgium (1940)	Great Britain (1939)	Norway (1940)
Bolivia (1943)	Greece (1940)	Panama (1941)
Brazil (1942)	Guatemala (1941)	Paraguay (1945)
Canada (1939)	Haiti (1941)	Peru (1945)
Chile (1945)	Honduras (1941)	Poland (1939)
China (1941)	India (1939)	San Marino (1944)
Colombia (1943)	Iran (1941)	Saudi Arabia (1945)
Costa Rica (1941)	Iraq (1943)	South Africa (1939)
Cuba (1941)	Lebanon (1945)	Syria (1941)
Czechoslovakia (1941)	Liberia (1944)	Turkey (1945)
Denmark (1940)	Luxembourg (1940)	U.S.S.R. (1941)
Dominican Republic (1941)	Mexico (1942)	United States (1941)
Ecuador (1945)	Mongolian People's	Uruguay (1945)
Egypt (1945)	Republic (1945)	Venezuela (1945)
El Salvador (1941)	Netherlands (1940)	Yugoslavia (1941)

Axis Powers

Albania (1940)	Italy (1940)
Bulgaria (1941)	Japan (1941)
Finland (1941)	Romania (1940)
Germany (1939)	Thailand (1942)
Hungary (1940)	

Neutral Nations

Eire (Ireland)
Portugal
Spain
Sweden
Switzerland

CHART STUDY *Few nations remained neutral in World War II, as this chart shows. The dates in parentheses are the years in which each country entered the war. How many nations were involved in the war on each side by the end of 1941?* 1.

See p. T123.

1. ACTIVITY Interested students might like to research why the neutral nations remained neutral. They can report their findings to the class.

2. operation in history—an invasion of Europe across the English Channel.

Dark Days of 1942

By early 1942, the Allies faced a grave situation in the Pacific. The Japanese had conquered many islands in the western Pacific as well as a large area of eastern and southern Asia. Chinese resistance had worn down, India faced threats from east and west, and Australia braced itself for a Japanese invasion.

The Allied outlook in Europe and Africa was equally grim. Germany and its allies held most of the European mainland. In the spring of 1942, Hitler's armies renewed their onslaught against the Soviet Union. Driving deep into Soviet territory, they threatened oil fields

in the south and advanced on the city of Stalingrad. Meanwhile, in Africa, the Germans had nearly pushed the British out of Egypt. The Axis was close to controlling North Africa, the Suez Canal, and the oil fields of the Middle East.

While Axis victories increased tension during 1942, the Allies groped for an effective military strategy. American Admiral Ernest King and General Douglas MacArthur proposed that the United States focus on the defeat of Japan. But Roosevelt had already accepted the British view that the Allies' 3. prime target should be Germany and Italy.

In 1942, American Generals George C. Marshall and Dwight D. Eisenhower urged that the Allies invade France across the English Channel by the spring of 1943. The Soviets were enthusiastic, hoping that such an inva-

668

2. GEOGRAPHY Have students locate each of the three major fronts on the map on p. 676. (location)

3. CRITICAL THINKING Ask: Why do you think the British favored defeating Germany and Italy first?

sion would force Hitler to divert some of his troops from the eastern to the western front. British Prime Minister Churchill argued that the Allies were not prepared to strike at Germany from the west and persuaded Roosevelt to support an alternative strategy, Operation Torch.

The War in North Africa

Operation Torch called for an invasion of North Africa, to be followed by advances into the Mediterranean area. In November 1942, combined British and United States forces under General Eisenhower landed on the coast of French North Africa in Morocco and Algeria. The Allied troops easily defeated soldiers of Vichy (VEE shee), France,* who were stationed in North Africa.

Moving eastward, the Allies reached Tunisia. There they met stiff resistance from the German Afrika Korps, led by Field Marshal Erwin Rommel. After initial setbacks, the Allied troops drove the Germans toward the Mediterranean Sea. In May 1943, the greatly outnumbered Axis forces surrendered.

1.

---

*After France fell to Germany in 1940, some French officials decided to cooperate with the Germans. They formed a government at Vichy, in southern France.

Victory in North Africa gave the Allies their first major breakthrough. As Prime Minister Churchill had foreseen, it opened the Mediterranean Sea to Allied shipping and made an invasion of southern Europe possible. The Allied offensive was under way.

A Holding Action in the Pacific

The Japanese had followed the attack on Pearl Harbor with a string of victories. Guam, Wake Island, and Hong Kong fell within three weeks. Singapore followed two months later. In May 1942, after a heroic defense of Bataan and Corregidor, American and Filipino forces surrendered the Philippine Islands. Before evacuation, however, General Douglas MacArthur promised the Filipino people, "I shall return." Meanwhile, Japanese forces advanced from Indochina into Burma, threatening India to the west and Australia and New Zealand to the south.

The adoption of a "beat Hitler first" strategy did not mean abandoning the Pacific theater. Fortunately, the United States aircraft carriers in the Pacific had survived the attack on Pearl Harbor. Relying on the carriers, a naval task force engaged a Japanese fleet in the Coral Sea near Java in early May 1942. After a three-day battle, the Japanese fleet turned back.

2. **GEOGRAPHY** Have students locate the Coral Sea on the map on page 679. (location)

The battle of the Coral Sea was a milestone in naval military history. It was the
2. *first major battle in which surface ships did not fire a shot. All the fighting was done by aircraft from the carrier ships, or "flattops."*

1. **READING** Interested students might like to read *Pacific War Diary, 1942–1945,* by James J. Fahey, an American sailor in the Pacific.

2. **BACKGROUND** In the battle for Stalingrad, which ended in January 1943, more than 200,000 Germans died and 80,000 were taken prisoner.

One month later, the United States Navy won a major victory at Midway Island in the central Pacific. Between them, the Americans and the Japanese lost more than 400 planes in that battle. Later that summer, United States Marines began a long, bitter struggle for control of Guadalcanal in the Solomon Islands. The island was secured by February 1943.

By early 1943, the Allies sensed eventual victory for the first time. The United States forces had stopped the Japanese advance. Allied troops had driven the Axis powers out of North Africa. And in the Soviet Union, Soviet soldiers and civilians, along with extreme winter conditions, had halted the German advance into their country.

See p. T123.

SECTION 1 REVIEW

1. **Identify:** (a) Allies, (b) Axis, (c) Douglas MacArthur, (d) Dwight D. Eisenhower.

2. In what two areas of the world was most of World War II fought?

3. What was the strategy of Operation Torch?

4. (a) List two reasons why the Allied victory in North Africa was significant. (b) What other victories helped the Allies?

5. **Critical Thinking** Why do you think the early days of the war went badly for the Allies?

2 On the Home Front

READ TO UNDERSTAND

■ How the United States prepared for World War II.

■ What impact the war had on the economy and daily life in the United States.

■ How the war affected women and minority groups.

"Remember Pearl Harbor" became a rallying cry for the American people. Although the United States was not subject to prolonged enemy attack, Americans rolled up their sleeves and joined in the war effort. The "V for Victory" became a familiar symbol. Businesses displayed it on buildings and merchants hung it in store windows. Radio stations even broadcast it in Morse code as their sign-on and sign-off signal.

Building the Armed Forces

After declaring war, Congress swiftly built up United States fighting forces. Six million men and women volunteered for service. Almost 10 million men were drafted. Women enlisted in the WAACS (army), WAVES (navy), SPARS (coast guard), and the women's branch of the marines.

Fighting a world war posed training problems. Soldiers might have to fight in jungles on Pacific islands, in African deserts, or in the European countryside. To meet this challenge, the armed forces had to create an organization and supply network that truly spanned the globe.

Organizing for Wartime Production

The war had to be won in the factories as well as as on the battlefields. President Roosevelt announced staggering production goals for 1942: 60,000 airplanes, 45,000 tanks, 20,000 antiaircraft guns, and 8 million tons (7.3 million metric tons) of merchant shipping.

As in World War I, the federal government played a major role in developing a wartime economy. To supervise conversion from a peacetime to a wartime economy, Roosevelt created the War Production Board (WPB). By retooling and redesigning their assembly lines, factories produced mosquito netting instead of shirts, bomb fuses instead of model trains, and cartridge cases instead of kitchen sinks. In fact, after 1942, all automobile makers changed to full-time production of tanks, trucks, armored personnel carriers, and aircraft.

This massive effort required a complex network of federal agencies. When the WPB failed to meet production demands, Roosevelt replaced it with the Office of War Mobilization (OWM). The OWM smoothed out the bottlenecks that had hindered the earlier efforts. Guided by these agencies, United States industry and workers met the most rigorous

3. **VOCABULARY** The term GI Joe, used for American troops, first appeared in a comic strip in 1942. GI, for "general issue," was stamped on everything issued to soldiers.

production demands and in some cases even surpassed them.

With increased production of war materials, consumer goods became scarcer and more expensive. To control inflation, Roosevelt established the Office of Price Administration (OPA). The OPA set price ceilings on most items, including rents, since housing was scarce throughout the war. The agency also supervised a rationing system for such items as gasoline, tires, coffee, canned food, and meat.

To address the problems of labor, Roosevelt empowered other agencies. The War Manpower Commission (WMC) determined which industries needed workers most. The National War Labor Board (NWLB) helped settle disputes. By enforcing the Wagner Act (see page 624), the board encouraged the growth of union membership. It also allowed wage increases to offset rising prices and at the same time tried to limit inflation. In fact, the wages of most Americans climbed steadily from 1941 to 1945.

To pay for the war, the government raised 1. taxes, especially on high incomes. In addition, it borrowed huge amounts of money by selling war bonds. Spectacular drives used movie stars and comic book heroes such as Batman and Dick Tracy to sell bonds and bolster patriotic spirit.

The Return of Prosperity

The United States economy grew tremendously during the war. Between 1939 and 1945, the gross national product rose from $91.1 billion to $213.6 billion. During 1942 alone, war production rose over 300 percent, surpassing that of Germany, Italy, and Japan combined.

Much of the economic growth was due to increased output of aircraft and ships. In 1939, a total of 47,000 workers produced 5,900 planes; five years later, 2.1 million workers were producing almost 100,000 planes annually. Between 1941 and 1943, the shipbuilding industry increased its production of tonnage by 1,900 percent.

Not only was such production crucial to the Allied war effort, it also ended the depression, as demand for manufactured goods skyrocketed. When industries geared up,

unemployment decreased dramatically. Growing demand for agricultural products brought farmers a level of prosperity they had not enjoyed since World War I. Between 1940 and 1945, crop prices doubled. Production increased even though farm population and acreage declined.

Resisting Government Controls

Various labor groups protested against controls set by the NWLB. In January 1943, coal miners in Alabama struck. John L. Lewis, president of the United Mine Workers, asked the miners to return to the coal fields while he negotiated with the board. But negotiations continually broke down, and the miners called further strikes.

In May, the President seized the mines. He threatened to draft the striking miners and replace them with soldiers. The miners, however, refused to give in. By November, negotiations had broken down again, and 530,000 men were on strike. The government finally agreed to some of the union's demands. The 11-month struggle had won the miners a pay raise of $1.50 per day.

2. **VISUAL EVIDENCE** Ask: How does this poster get its message across?

The government cautioned Americans that enemy spies could pick up valuable information even from informal gossip. "Loose lips sink ships," was a wartime slogan. This poster warns citizens against talk about shipping schedules.   2.

Other challenges came from business. Montgomery Ward, a large mail-order firm, refused to recognize its workers' union. When the workers went on strike, the National War Labor Board ordered Sewell Avery, the company president, to negotiate with the union. Avery ignored the order. President Roosevelt then invoked the wartime Smith-Connally Act, which gave him power to seize any strike-bound plant necessary to the war effort. Newspapers across the country ran a front-page picture of two soldiers carrying Avery out of his office after he refused to leave. For the rest of the war, the government ran the company.

Changes in Daily Life

The war demanded many sacrifices of Americans on the home front. Family separation, frequent relocation, and worry about men and women stationed overseas were concerns

1. VISUAL EVIDENCE One aircraft company popularized a mythical woman worker called "Rosie the Riveter."

1. As factories worked around the clock to produce items needed for war, women assumed jobs formerly open only to men. In this painting, a woman works on a bomber in California.

2. BACKGROUND Women were told, "If you can drive a car, you can run a machine."

shared by many Americans. Such experiences gave people a common sense of purpose.

Commitment to the war effort took different forms. Backyards became "victory gardens" to stretch the food supply. Scrap-rubber and scrap-iron collection drives brought in scarce materials. Americans dutifully saved ration coupons and stood in long lines to buy scarce items.

Business also lent its support to the war effort. Newspaper, magazine, and radio advertisements prodded Americans to make do with less. Industries mounted campaigns explaining that certain purchases would best be put off until after the war. One tire manufacturer asked consumers to conserve rubber by driving less, using the slogan, "Hitler smiles when you waste miles."

The role of women changed dramatically during the war, although in many cases only temporarily. Hundreds of thousands of women joined the military service. They piloted bombers across the Atlantic Ocean, repaired airplanes and land vehicles, drove trucks, operated radios, and did clerical and technical work of all kinds.

As the demand for workers rose, women joined the civilian work force in record numbers. By the end of the war, one out of every **2.** three workers in industry and business was a woman. Traditional barriers against hiring women in such industries as steel and shipbuilding fell away. Through song and story, women received praise for keeping American production lines moving.

Changes in clothing, appearance, and hair styles reflected women's new work roles. More important, however, was a change in how women saw themselves. Besides pride in a job well done, women gained confidence **3.** that they could have both a family and a job or career.

African Americans During the War

The war years produced some gains for African Americans. Some 2 million blacks held jobs in aircraft factories, steel mills, and shipyards. In both the North and the South, blacks enjoyed more social acceptance and economic well-being. Lynchings stopped almost completely. In a joint effort to fight racial mis-

3. LOCAL HISTORY Have students interview relatives or neighbors who remember life at home during World War II and compile their findings into an oral history.

1. **CITIZENSHIP** Some German prisoners had more privileges than black Americans. At one camp, POWs sat in front for shows, while black guards sat in back.

understanding, black and white leaders formed the Southern Regional Council.

President Roosevelt himself took a stand on behalf of African Americans. In 1941, A. Philip Randolph, head of the Brotherhood of Sleeping Car Porters, threatened to lead a march on Washington, D.C., to protest prejudice against black workers. Roosevelt responded by issuing Executive Order 8802. The order banned discrimination in all government agencies, in job training programs, and in all companies doing business with the federal government. It also established the Fair Employment Practices Committee to ensure equal treatment for blacks and other minorities in war industries.

Yet discrimination persisted—even in the armed forces. During much of the war, official policy was to have all-black units of soldiers or sailors commanded by white officers. In the navy, most blacks could only be porters. Black soldiers on leave from training camps in the South faced the indignity of 1. segregated eating places, movie houses, and recreational facilities.

In the North, an influx of southern blacks aggravated racial tensions. Whites resented black competition for both jobs and housing. In one instance, streetcar workers in Philadelphia struck to protest the upgrading of black workers to motormen. The President sent in troops to maintain operation of vital war industries in the city.

Sometimes resentment flared into violence. In Detroit, efforts to move blacks into a federal housing project aroused anger among whites. In the summer of 1943, a riot broke out. Before police and federal troops restored order, 25 blacks and 9 whites were killed.

Other Victims of Discrimination

Mexican Americans continued to face discrimination, especially in the cities of the Southwest. Like other minority groups throughout the country, Mexican Americans often were crowded into run-down urban areas, suffered high unemployment rates, and found longtime residents hostile.

Young Mexican Americans in Los Angeles became the object of frequent violent at-

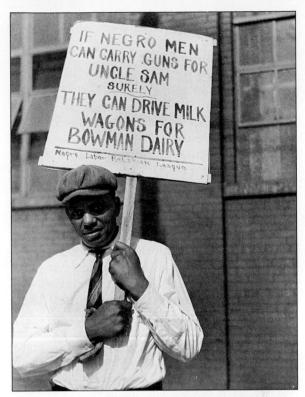

The need for workers in war industries opened jobs to groups that had often been excluded. By 1944, 2 million African Americans were working in war industries. But prejudice persisted, as can be seen from this picketer protesting a dairy's exclusion of black drivers. The sign underscores 2. *the message that black soldiers were defending the country while black drivers were being denied a job.*

2. **VISUAL EVIDENCE** Ask: Do you think the picketer had a strong argument for being given a job?

tacks. During the early 1940s, young Mexican American men adopted a flamboyant style of dress, sporting "zoot" suits and wearing their long hair slicked back into "duck tails."

In July 1943, groups of sailors and soldiers home on leave roamed the streets, beating up the "zooters," tearing their clothes and cutting their hair. Newspaper and radio reports blamed the violence on the zooters. 3. However, a citizens' committee appointed by California Governor Earl Warren revealed the truth about the incident and the need for improved housing for Mexican Americans.

Italian Americans and German Americans also felt the sting of discrimination from fellow citizens during the war. Some changed their names to conceal their family's country of origin. However, their experiences with discrimination were not nearly so painful as those experienced by Japanese Americans.

673

3. **BACKGROUND** In her newspaper column, Eleanor Roosevelt wrote that the riots resulted from "longstanding discrimination against the Mexicans in the Southwest."

Japanese Americans Lose Their Liberties

The bombing of Pearl Harbor by Japan created a wave of anger against Americans of Japanese ancestry. Although Japanese Americans were loyal citizens, many other Americans held them responsible for the Japanese attack. And since most of them lived on the Pacific coast in small, identifiable communities, they became easy targets for systematic discrimination.

Once at war, the United States feared a Japanese invasion of the Pacific coast, the area of the country closest to Japan. Warning of possible sabotage, in February 1942, defense officials labeled Japanese Americans living on the Pacific coast "a menace to be dealt with." Yielding to pressure, President Roosevelt granted the War Department full authority to forcibly relocate thousands of innocent Japanese Americans.

With little or no warning, 110,000 Japanese Americans were uprooted and moved to internment camps in the middle of the country. They had to sell their homes, businesses, and most of their personal possessions for whatever prices they could get on short notice. Home for the evacuees, two thirds of whom were American-born citizens, was a wooden barracks, with one room per family.

Despite this unfair and humiliating treatment, Japanese Americans remained loyal to their country. More than 1,200 internees petitioned the President to give them a chance to serve. They were allowed to form the 100th Infantry Battalion, which became one of the most highly decorated fighting units in United States military history.

The nation's Japanese Americans were detained in the isolated camps for most of the war. In 1944, the Supreme Court upheld the forced relocation as a justifiable wartime measure. Not until 1945, when Allied victory seemed certain, were these people allowed to return to their communities to rebuild their shattered lives. 1.

As the years passed and the emotions of war faded, Americans began to recognize the injustice that had been done. Finally, in 1988, Congress voted overwhelmingly to formally apologize to Japanese Americans who were driven from their homes in World War II and to give $20,000 to each surviving internee. Although it was acknowledged that nothing

"Herd 'em up, pack 'em off, and give 'em the inside room in the Badlands," recommended one newspaper columnist as the appropriate treatment for
2. *Japanese Americans. In 1942, more than 100,000 Japanese Americans living on the West Coast were loaded onto trucks, like those at left, and transported to isolated camps roped off by barbed wire. Even so, thousands of young Japanese Americans volunteered for the United States armed forces. The mother at right, interned with her younger son in a "temporary" camp, proudly displays a picture of her son in the United States Army.*

was adequate to right the enormous wrong of the past, the action by Congress helped Americans to close this unfortunate chapter in their history.

See p. T123.

SECTION 2 REVIEW

1. **Identify:** (a) War Production Board, (b) Office of War Mobilization, (c) Office of Price Administration, (d) War Manpower Commission, (e) National War Labor Board, (f) A. Philip Randolph, (g) Executive Order 8802.

2. Give two examples of how industry converted to wartime production.

3. How did conditions for workers improve as a result of the war?

4. (a) What type of work opened up to women as a result of the war? (b) What benefits did black workers gain?

5. How were Japanese Americans treated during the war?

6. **Critical Thinking** Why are people more likely to tolerate increased government intervention during a war?

3 The Allies on the Offensive

READ TO UNDERSTAND

■ What offensive the Allies took on the southern front.

■ What help Stalin requested from the other Allied nations.

■ How the Allies launched an invasion of France across the English Channel.

1. ■ *Vocabulary:* leapfrogging.

By 1943, the tide of war had turned. Bolstered by American supplies and soldiers, the Allies had finally stopped Axis advances in Europe and the Pacific. The Allies now took to the air, land, and seas in bold offensives on all

fronts. Meanwhile, Germany itself faced an onslaught of Allied air assaults.

Air War Over Germany

Using British bases, the Allies had begun air attacks on German cities as early as the summer of 1942. Their aim was to disrupt the German war machine however and wherever possible. During 1943 and 1944, the attacks increased in intensity. Night after night, day after day, Allied squadrons rained bombs on German transportation lines, industrial plants, and military installations.

By 1945, the Allied air effort had severely disrupted German transportation and destroyed many vital war industries. Nevertheless, German war production continued to increase until the Allies gained control of the skies over Europe, almost at the end of the war. The air war over Germany was costly. The Allies lost more than 158,000 pilots and crew members and more than 40,000 planes.

The Invasion of Italy

As the air war over Germany intensified, the Allies planned an invasion of Italy from the bases they had captured in North Africa. (See Section 1.) Italy, they thought, was the weak point in the Axis empire. Churchill wanted to knock Mussolini out of the war, to open what he dubbed the "soft underbelly" of Europe.

In July 1943, paratroopers of the 82nd Airborne Division parachuted into Sicily in the first large-scale Allied airborne assault of the war. Despite bad weather and poor coordination between army assault forces and naval bombardments, the invasion of the island was successful. Encouraged by the success of the invasion, the Italians overthrew Mussolini, who had already fallen from favor.

From Sicily, Allied forces pushed on to the Italian mainland, assaulting Salerno in September 1943. Just days before, the new Italian government had surrendered to the Allies. Hitler, however, ordered German troops to resist the Allied advance.

Bitter fighting marked almost every mile of the advance up the Italian peninsula. The Germans dug in and halted the Allied drive at Monte Cassino, in central Italy. In January

675

1944, however, the Allies made an amphibious landing, that is, a landing by sea, on the beaches at Anzio, near Rome. After six months of fighting, Rome was liberated. The Allies then continued north, but German forces in Italy did not surrender until the war had nearly ended more than a year later.

The Eastern Front

For almost three years, the Soviet Union battled the advancing German army within its borders. Soviet Premier Joseph Stalin had asked the Allies for three things: massive supplies, territorial concessions in eastern Europe, and a second front in western Europe. He had been disappointed on all three.

Contrary to Allied suspicions that Stalin might make a separate peace with the Axis powers, Soviet resistance was fierce and effective. During the winter of 1941–1942, Soviet troops halted the German advance outside Moscow. One year later, the advancing Soviet army lifted the 900-day German siege of Leningrad that claimed the lives of nearly 1.5 million Soviet citizens.

Meanwhile, the Allies found ways to deliver critical supplies to the Soviet Union. German submarines, on occasion, had cut off Allied shipping to the northern Soviet port of Murmansk. As a result, the United States

2. **MAP READING** Ask: When did the Allies first invade Italy? France? Germany? When did Allied troops reach Austria? Which Allied nation retook Poland and Romania?

MAP STUDY

See p. T124.

By the time the United States entered the war at the end of 1941, Axis powers controlled virtually all of western Europe and North Africa. Arrows indicate the important Allied campaigns between 1942 and 1945. Which major Allied advances began in 1943?

World War II in Europe and North Africa, 1942-1945

and Great Britain shifted some of their supply operations to a longer but safer route north through the Persian Gulf and across Iran.

The turning point in the east came in 1943 at the city of Stalingrad. There, after months of fierce house-to-house fighting, the Soviets forced the Germans to surrender. The Red Army, as the Soviet army is called, now went on the offensive, mounting a massive drive against Germany from the east.

The Soviet offensive helped the British and Americans launch an invasion of Europe from Britain. Now that the Allies had fulfilled Stalin's requests for supplies and a second front, only his territorial demands threatened to drive the Allies apart.

GEOGRAPHY AND HISTORY

D-Day in France

In early 1944, the Supreme Allied Command made final plans for the long-awaited invasion across the English Channel from England into France. General Eisenhower was appointed supreme allied commander of the European theater of operations. The invasion, code-named Operation Overlord, was scheduled for the late spring of 1944.

The success of Overlord depended on three conditions. First, the Allies had to build up an enormous reserve of troops and of supplies: ammunition, trucks, food, construction equipment, medical supplies, tanks, artillery, and countless other items. Artificial harbors, made of concrete, had to be towed across the channel and used for the landing and for unloading supplies. Second, secrecy had to be maintained. Although the Germans expected an attack, they did not know when or where it might come. Third, the weather had to be clear. An unexpected storm or fog would make paratroop landings behind German lines and landings on the beaches from boats all but impossible.

At 6:30 A.M. on June 6, 1944, now known

1. as D-Day, the largest amphibious invasion in history began. Nearly 6,000 Allied ships ferried 150,000 men and their supplies across the English Channel from the southern coast of England to beachheads in northern France.

2. Even though the Germans had expected the

On June 6, 1944, Allied forces stormed the beaches of Normandy. Despite heavy advance bombing of German positions, losses in the first landing wave were staggering. But the troops that got through established a beachhead for reinforcements, like those shown here, wading ashore. A highly successful operation, the Normandy invasion marked the beginning of the end for Nazi Germany.

3. **BACKGROUND** Many Allied soldiers drowned leaving the landing craft; others died on the beaches of Normandy.

invasion at Calais, where the channel is narrower, they rapidly mobilized heavy resistance on the beaches of Normandy. At one beachhead, American casualties in the first assault groups on the beach were 60 percent.

Six weeks passed before the Allies fully secured landing areas. By that time, other Allied troops had moved into northern France and captured the port of Cherbourg, which became a major receiving point of supplies for the rest of the war. On August 25, the rapidly advancing Allied armies liberated Paris after four years of German occupation.

General Eisenhower did not believe the Allies had sufficient supplies to launch a single drive into the heart of Germany. Instead, he decided to move along a broad front. In August, he ordered an invasion across the Mediterranean into southern France. As the winter of 1944–1945 approached, Eisenhower's armies had recaptured most of western Europe. Now they planned the final assault on Germany.

677

2. **BACKGROUND** German leaders debated the likely invasion. Rommel said, "An attempt must be made to beat off the enemy landing on the coast and to fight the battle in a . . . fortified coastal strip." Hitler concurred.

1. **ACTIVITY** Have students choose one battle in the Pacific and write a short report on it. They should include a map.

Taking the Offensive in the Pacific

While the Allies battled to regain Europe, an equally important war raged in the Pacific. At first, General MacArthur and Admiral Chester Nimitz, commanders of the Allied forces there, disagreed on the best "road to Tokyo." MacArthur preferred a southern Pacific route, pushing northward from Australia through New Guinea and the Philippines and on to Japan. Nimitz favored an advance toward Japan by way of the islands of the central Pacific.

The military commanders finally decided to follow both strategies. They succeeded by **leapfrogging.** Rather than take Japanese-held islands one by one as they came to them, the Allies decided to invade a few strategic islands and bypass others. The theory was that the Japanese would not be able to supply their forces on islands that the Allies had leapfrogged. Isolated, these islands would have to surrender.

2. **BACKGROUND** Remind students that MacArthur vowed "I shall return" when he was forced to evacuate the Philippines in 1942 (p. 669).

In 1943 and 1944, the United States Marine Corps, with naval support, assaulted the islands of Tarawa (tuh RAH wuh), Kwajalein (KWAHJ uh luhn), and Guam in the central Pacific. Meanwhile, MacArthur's troops captured New Guinea in the south. Fierce Japanese resistance resulted in heavy Allied casualties. At Tarawa, for example, casualties in some marine units reached 50 percent. But the technique of amphibious landings—requiring close coordination among air bombings, naval support, and troop movements—steadily improved.

In October 1944, General MacArthur's forces began an invasion of the Philippine Islands. MacArthur himself landed on the island of Leyte (LAY tee), where he proclaimed, "People of the Philippines, I have returned." In the battle of Leyte Gulf, which followed, the United States Navy sank an entire Japanese fleet. By late 1944, United States bombers had begun steady aerial attacks on the islands of Japan itself. ■

3. **GEOGRAPHY** Have students locate the Philippines and Leyte Gulf on the map on page 679. (location)

In the Pacific, the war was fought island by island, inch by inch, often against Japanese snipers who were prepared to die rather than surrender. Besides the Japanese, American troops faced other enemies in the island jungles: savage heat, insects, malaria, and fungus infections. This painting, Ghost Trail, by combat artist Kerr Eby, shows the marines trudging through the dense tropical jungle of Bougainville in the Solomon Islands.

4. **VISUAL EVIDENCE** Have students imagine they were on the Solomon Islands in 1943. Have them write a letter home about the action shown in this picture.

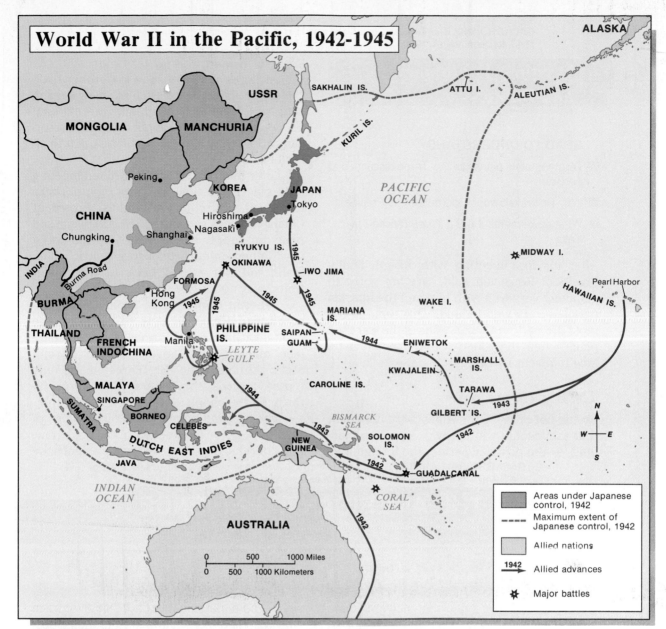

World War II in the Pacific, 1942-1945

ALASKA

MONGOLIA

MANCHURIA

USSR

SAKHALIN IS.

ATTU I.

ALEUTIAN IS.

KURIL IS.

Peking

KOREA

JAPAN

Tokyo

PACIFIC OCEAN

CHINA

Hiroshima

Nagasaki

Chungking

Shanghai

MIDWAY I.

RYUKYU IS.

1945

OKINAWA

INDIA

Burma Road

FORMOSA

IWO JIMA

Pearl Harbor

HAWAIIAN IS.

Hong Kong

1945

1945

1945

WAKE I.

BURMA

1945

MARIANA IS.

THAILAND

PHILIPPINE IS.

SAIPAN

GUAM

1944

ENIWETOK

FRENCH INDOCHINA

Manila

LEYTE GULF

MARSHALL IS.

KWAJALEIN

MALAYA

CAROLINE IS.

TARAWA

SINGAPORE

1944

GILBERT IS.

1943

SUMATRA

BORNEO

CELEBES

BISMARCK SEA

1943

SOLOMON IS.

1942

N

DUTCH EAST INDIES

NEW GUINEA

1943

JAVA

1942

W E

GUADALCANAL

S

INDIAN OCEAN

1942

CORAL SEA

AUSTRALIA

0   500   1000 Miles

0   500   1000 Kilometers

1942

	Areas under Japanese control, 1942
- - -	Maximum extent of Japanese control, 1942
	Allied nations
1942 →	Allied advances
✵	Major battles

See p. T124.

MAP STUDY

By 1942, Japan controlled much of China, the nations of eastern and southern Asia, and a string of Pacific islands. But at the battle of Midway, the United States Navy stopped the Japanese fleet. For the next two years, Allied forces attacked Japanese-held islands in a "leapfrog" pattern. At times, casualties numbered as many as half the troops involved. How far had Allied troops advanced by 1942?

1.

See p. T124.

1. MAP READING Ask: What islands are southeast of Midway? In what year did Allied troops reach Guam? Iwo Jima? Okinawa?

SECTION 3 REVIEW

1. **Identify:** (a) Joseph Stalin, (b) D-Day (c) Operation Overlord, (d) Cherbourg, (e) Chester Nimitz.

2. **Define:** leapfrogging.

3. What event led to the overthrow of Mussolini in Italy?

4. What three things did Stalin request from his allies?

5. List the three conditions necessary for the success of Operation Overlord.

6. **Critical Thinking** Study the map above and the map on page 676. Why would the Soviet Union want to delay declaring war on Japan as long as possible?

1. **BACKGROUND** The Teheran Conference was held in the capital of Iran from November 28, 1943, to December 1, 1943.

4 Wartime Diplomacy and Politics

- What tentative plans the Big Three discussed at Teheran.
- Why Roosevelt won a fourth term as President.
- What agreements the Big Three reached at Yalta.

After his first meeting with Joseph Stalin, President Roosevelt said, "We are going to get along very well with him and the Russian people—very well indeed." But some of the most dramatic confrontations of the war took place when the Allied leaders met face-to-face to discuss strategy.

The Big Three Confer

By the fall of 1943, the Allies were confident that they would win the war. Intent on planning for the postwar period, the foreign ministers of Britain, the Soviet Union, and the United States met in Moscow in October 1943. They discussed the creation of a new organization of nations to maintain international peace and security. Membership in the organization, they agreed, would be open to all nations.

Later that fall, yet another Allied meeting took place, this time in Cairo, Egypt. There Roosevelt, Churchill, and Chinese President Chiang Kai-shek (jyahng ky SHEHK) discussed plans for supply lines through Burma and a new Chinese military offensive against Japan. Stalin did not attend because the Soviet Union was not at war with Japan.

Teheran Conference From Cairo, Roosevelt and Churchill flew to Teheran, the capital of Iran, for Roosevelt's first face-to-face meeting with Soviet Premier Joseph Stalin. Although the "Big Three" made only tentative plans, the Teheran Conference influenced the shape of the postwar world. 1.

The meeting opened with discussions of the strategy for final defeat of the Axis powers. Churchill and Roosevelt made a final com-

2. **BACKGROUND** In 1864, Kit Carson and the U.S. Army destroyed the homes and farms of the Navajo. The Navajo remain the largest Indian group in the United States.

THE AMERICAN EXPERIENCE

The Code That Was Never Broken

About 350 Navajos in the United States Marine Corps made a major contribution to the Allied victory in World War II. They did not drop bombs or lead an invasion. They simply talked to each other.

Secret codes have long been an important weapon in battle. By using codes, military leaders can safely transmit information on troop deployment and instructions to commanders in the field. But thousands of lives may be lost if an enemy breaks the code.

During World War II, the United States military developed a code system that was virtually foolproof. The Marine Corps trained a group of Navajos to work as "code talkers" in the Pacific. Instead of using an artificial code, these code talkers simply used their own language. Because the Navajo language is very difficult to learn and is still unwritten, few people other than the Navajo themselves are able to speak it.

The Navajo code talkers were a familiar sight in command posts or huddled over radio sets in combat zones, transmitting messages. They assigned the names of birds, fish, and animals to military terms and then transmitted the code words in Navajo. A member of the team on the receiving end would then translate the Navajo words into English.

Thanks to the code talkers, calls to headquarters for airplanes or artillery could be sent in complete secrecy. The Japanese were never able to break the Navajo "code." This unique contribution by the Navajos was invaluable to the advancing Allied forces and helped them to achieve eventual victory over Japan. 2.

See p. T125.

1. Why was the Navajo code unique?

2. **Critical Thinking** Why do you think the marines were quite certain that the Japanese could not break the Navajo code?

mitment to the cross-channel invasion of France. Stalin, in turn, promised a spring offensive to coincide with the cross-channel landing. He further promised to enter the Pacific war once Germany surrendered. Other topics of discussion included the proposed international organization and the postwar fate of Germany.

At the end of the conference, the three leaders declared, "We leave here, friends in fact, in spirit, and in purpose." The Teheran meeting represented the high point of Allied goodwill. A troubled road lay ahead.

Other Meetings Diplomatic discussions after the Teheran Conference continued to focus on postwar settlements. Economic ministers meeting in Bretton Woods, New Hampshire, in 1944 drew up plans for the International Monetary Fund and the International Bank for Reconstruction and Development. These organizations would aid postwar recovery and finance long-range improvements in war-ravaged countries. At Dumbarton Oaks, in Washington, D.C., delegates from the United States, Britain, China, and the Soviet Union made further plans for an international peacekeeping organization, to be known as the United Nations.

The Election of 1944

At the height of the war, Americans began to ask if their President would seek a fourth term in office. "All that is within me cries to go back to my home on the Hudson," Roosevelt told reporters in the summer of 1944. Nevertheless, citing the need for continuity in leadership during the war, Roosevelt decided to run again.

The President had almost no opposition within his party. However, the Democrats had some difficulty selecting a candidate for Vice President. After rejecting the current Vice President, Henry Wallace, as too liberal, the nominating convention settled on Senator Harry S. Truman of Missouri.

The Republican party selected Thomas E. Dewey, the governor of New York, to oppose Roosevelt. Dewey chose to avoid international issues in the campaign. Instead, he focused on the failure of Democratic economic policies. Only the war, he charged, had ended the depression. A peacetime economy would require better management, Dewey warned American voters.

Although the strain of his years in office had aged Roosevelt noticeably, the President made special efforts to show he was still in good health. At one point, he spent an entire day in New York City campaigning from an open car during a rainstorm.

Roosevelt's popularity remained high, and a majority of voters did not want to change leaders during the war. As a result, Roosevelt won election to an unprecedented fourth term as President with 54 percent of the popular vote and 432 of 531 votes in the electoral college.

The Meeting in Yalta

In February 1945, Roosevelt, Churchill, and Stalin met at the winter resort of Yalta in the Soviet Union. They continued to discuss strategy in Asia, postwar settlements in Europe, and plans for the United Nations. Above all, Roosevelt wanted a firm commitment from Stalin to enter the war against Japan. The island campaigns in the Pacific had made clear that many hundreds of thousands of Americans would be killed or wounded in an assault on Japan.

At Yalta, Stalin again agreed to declare war on Japan three months after the surrender of Germany. In exchange for this promise, Roosevelt and Churchill accepted Stalin's demands for postwar control of the Kurile Islands and southern Sakhalin Island, Japanese territories off the Pacific coast of the Soviet Union. They also agreed that the Soviet Union would retain control of Outer Mongolia in northern China. It would also keep shipping rights in the harbor of Port Arthur and control over railroads in Manchuria.

The Big Three reached other agreements at Yalta. Countries occupied by Germany during the war would have free elections as soon as possible. Germany would have four zones of occupation, governed by American, British, French, and Soviet forces. And a conference of the United Nations would meet in San Francisco in April 1945. There they would draw up a charter for a permanent peacekeeping organization.

By April 1945, as it prepared for the final attack on Germany, the Red Army already

681

In 1945, the war-weary Allied leaders—from left
1. to right, Churchill, Roosevelt, and Stalin—met at
Yalta to plan their final strategy. At Yalta, Stalin
repeated his pledge to bring the Soviet Union
into the war against Japan. The Big Three also
discussed the founding of the United Nations
and the postwar treatment of Germany.

1. **VISUAL EVIDENCE** Ask: What effect would photos like
this one have on people in these leaders' countries?

occupied much of eastern Europe. Roosevelt
and Churchill could only hope that Stalin
would honor the Yalta commitment to free
elections in the occupied nations. Churchill
would later comment, "Our hopeful assump-
tions were soon to be falsified. Still, they were
the only ones possible at the time."

See p. T125.

SECTION 4 REVIEW

1. **Identify:** (a) Chiang Kai-shek, (b) Big
   Three, (c) United Nations, (d) Harry S.
   Truman, (e) Thomas E. Dewey.

2. What promises did Stalin make at Teheran?

3. What issue did Dewey stress in the election of 1944?

4. What did the Big Three decide at Yalta
   about the fate of Germany after the war?

5. **Critical Thinking** Why do you think
   Roosevelt was in a stronger position to
   influence the Allies than Wilson had been?

682

---

2. **VOCABULARY** Have students look up this term in the
glossary before they begin reading.

5 Victory

READLY TO UNDERSTAND

- What events led to the end of war in Europe.

- Why the Japanese surrendered.

- What was the legacy of World War II.

- *Vocabulary:* kamikaze.   2.

In the last days of the Third Reich, Hitler
sent 14-year-olds into battle. In the Pacific,
Japanese pilots carried out suicide attacks
against American ships. These desperate acts
showed that the final days of the war would
be costly. Experts thought that an invasion
of Japan would take one million men. But the
United States was working to develop a secret weapon—the atomic bomb.

Ending the War in Europe

In December 1944, German troops launched
one last counteroffensive in the Ardennes
Forest. Their successful attack made a large
bulge in the Allied offensive line. American
soldiers at the small town of Bastogne found
themselves surrounded. But when the German command asked Brigadier General Anthony C. McAuliffe to surrender, he replied,
"Nuts." The Allies stopped the German advance, but the Battle of the Bulge slowed the 3.
Allied invasion of Germany by six weeks.

The German war machine was falling
apart. In the east, the Soviets pushed across
Poland, Czechoslovakia, and Hungary into
Germany. Allied bombers pounded Berlin,
Hamburg, and other German cities. One particularly severe fire bombing leveled the entire center of the city of Dresden. In March, a
small American force captured a key bridge
across the Rhine River. Soon Allied armies
crossed the Rhine and began the conquest
of Germany.

A Final Strategy At that point, General
Eisenhower faced a difficult decision. He
could concentrate his forces and make a swift
advance across Germany to meet the Red
Army near Berlin. Or he could spread his
armies out to pursue German troops in the

---

3. **BACKGROUND** The Battle of the Bulge was the biggest battle fought on the western front. More
than one million soldiers were involved. Hitler devised the attack against the advice of his generals.

1. **VOCABULARY** The systematic killing of a whole national or ethnic group was termed *genocide* by a historian after the war. The word combined the Greek root *geno,* meaning race, and *cide,* meaning kill.

southern provinces. Churchill urged Eisenhower to push on to Berlin. The British prime minister did not trust Stalin's promise for free elections in postwar Europe. He wanted the United States and Britain to occupy as much of Germany and eastern Europe as possible before the war ended.

Eisenhower, however, believed that the military goal of defeating Germany as completely as possible should outweigh postwar political considerations. The general encouraged his field commanders to move slowly and to do a thorough job of conquering the Germans. Shortly before the war ended, American and Russian troops met at the Elbe River, nearly 100 miles (160 kilometers) west of Berlin.

The Third Reich was now in almost total ruin. Hitler had committed suicide in Berlin on April 30. One week later, on May 7, General Eisenhower accepted Germany's unconditional surrender, effective the next day, thereafter known as V-E Day.

The Holocaust

The joy that greeted the end of the war in Europe was soon dampened by news stories coming out of Germany. Throughout the war, vague reports of Nazi "death camps" had reached the Allies. But it was not until Allied troops liberated the camps after the war that their full horror was revealed.

Hitler hated all Jews and had made them a scapegoat for Germany's problems. He created the concentration camps to carry out the "final solution of the Jewish question," the seemingly innocent term he invented for the extermination of all the Jews in Europe. The worst of the camps were located at Auschwitz, Maidanek, and Treblinka in Poland; others were located in Germany, in places like Buchenwald and Dachau. Jews from all over Europe—men, women, and children—were rounded up at gunpoint and shipped in locked boxcars to these camps. There, they were stripped, forced into spe-

2. **VISUAL EVIDENCE** Have students imagine they were with the soldiers liberating the concentration camp at left. Have them describe what they saw.

No rumors of the horrors of Nazi concentration camps could prepare Americans for the scenes they found when they liberated the camps. The stench of death hung in the air. At Auschwitz alone, shown at right, more than one million died. At Buchenwald, at left, Allied forces found slave laborers nearly starved to death. The man at the far right of the second tier of bunks is Elie Wiesel, whose postwar writings and testament about the Holocaust later brought him the Nobel Peace Prize.

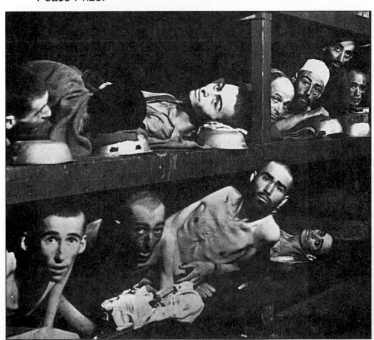

cial chambers, and gassed; their bodies were burned in specially constructed ovens. In all, some 6 million Jews—one third of Europe's total Jewish population—were killed in Nazi concentration camps. This systematic murder of Europe's Jews by the Nazis has come to be called the Holocaust, from the Greek word for "burned." Another 6 million people whom the Nazis considered "inferior"—Slavs, Gypsies, the physically and mentally disabled—as well as political enemies also perished in the Nazi camps.

President Truman Takes Office

On April 12, less than one month before the German surrender, President Roosevelt died at his vacation home in Warm Springs, Georgia. Americans mourned his loss with the greatest public outpouring of grief since the death of Abraham Lincoln.

On the afternoon of April 12, Eleanor Roosevelt told Vice President Harry S. Truman that her husband had died. Shocked, Truman asked if there was anything he could do for her. "Is there anything we can do for *you?*" she replied. "For you are the one in need of help now."

Certainly, Truman had not been prepared for the responsibilities he now assumed. He had no information about the atomic bomb that American scientists were developing. He knew little of the Yalta agreements. He had never entered the secret map room of the White House. "I felt," Truman admitted, "like the moon, the stars, and all the planets had fallen on me." Nevertheless, Truman, a veteran of Missouri and national politics, moved quickly to take up the unfinished business of Roosevelt's administration.

One of Truman's first acts was to announce that the United States would take part in the United Nations conference in San Francisco later that month, as planned. With Truman's approval, the conference drafted and adopted the Charter of the United Nations. Congress consented to United States membership in the world organization in July 1945.

Meanwhile, planning of the final offensive against the Japanese continued. Hard-won battles on the islands of Iwo Jima (EE woh JEE muh) and Okinawa (oh kuh NAH wuh) brought United States forces within striking distance of Japan. Those battles had shown, however, that Japanese fighter pilots would resort to **kamikaze** tactics, sacrificing their lives by deliberately crashing their planes, loaded with explosives, into Allied ships. There was every reason to think the Japanese would put up an even more bitter and bloody struggle if the United States were to invade Japan.

A New Weapon

On July 14, 1945, a blinding light illuminated the early morning sky over the New Mexico desert. Windows cracked over 75 miles (about 120 kilometers) away. In Potsdam, Germany, at a final meeting of the Big Three, President Truman received word that American scientists had set off an atomic bomb.

The atomic device was the result of a massive research effort known as the Manhattan Project. Since 1942, the United States had spent over $2 billion to design and build three atomic bombs. The project employed more than 120,000 people, including many of the most respected nuclear physicists from the United States, Britain, and Canada as well as European scientists who had fled Nazi tyranny.

For Truman, news of the successful nuclear test came as a great relief. Now that the United States had the atomic bomb, Soviet help was no longer crucial to defeating Japan. American leaders, therefore, would not be so hard-pressed to compromise with Stalin in discussions over Poland, Germany, and other difficult postwar problems.

When Truman told Stalin about an unspecified new American weapon, Stalin encouraged him to use it. In the declaration that emerged from the Potsdam Conference, the Allies warned the Japanese that they faced complete destruction if they did not agree to unconditional surrender. Unaware of what the warning really meant, the Japanese ignored it.

On August 6, 1945, the *Enola Gay,* a specially fitted B-29 bomber, dropped an atomic bomb on Hiroshima, Japan, leveling the city. Three days later, a second atomic bomb was dropped on Nagasaki. More than 150,000

684

"Saw city, destroyed same," was the message from the pilot of the Enola Gay.
The atomic bomb he dropped, the first ever used in warfare, leveled Hiroshima.
1. *The intense heat and the windblast that followed swept away virtually everything
inside the city. American combat artist Standish Backus, Jr., made this pencil
sketch of Hiroshima after the bombing.*

1. **VISUAL EVIDENCE** Have students compare this picture with the picture of the Hiroshima watch on p. 646.
Ask: Why do you think the scientists who developed the bomb almost hoped it would not work?

Japanese died in the two explosions. Thousands more were injured by the radiation from the bomb. Overwhelmed by these disasters and by the Soviet entry into the war **2.** on August 8, the Japanese surrendered on August 14.

The Legacy of World War II

World War II brought unequaled destruction to the nations of the world. More than 55 million civilians and soldiers died in the conflict, nearly 30 million in the Soviet Union alone. The American toll was about 290,000 dead and 670,000 wounded.

The war also changed the map of the world. Former colonial powers, such as France, the Netherlands, Germany, Italy, Japan, and Great Britain, found their empires in ruin. Nations formerly under imperial rule in Asia and Africa were seeking independence and would soon enter the world community as free states. The Soviet Union had become the dominant power in Europe and a powerful force on the international scene. The United States had shown that it had the most powerful military force in the world.

World War II revealed the enormous potential of science and technology to either advance civilization or destroy it. The mushroom clouds over Hiroshima and Nagasaki would linger in memory as the dreaded symbols of a new age. But if put to peaceful use,

experts argued, science could improve the human condition.

Americans entered the postwar era hopeful that their arsenal of weapons and their good will could serve the cause of peace. These hopes were soon tested. Questions about boundaries and free elections that had divided the Allies during the war threatened the peace they had struggled to achieve. A new era of confrontation was dawning.

See p. T125.

SECTION 5 REVIEW

1. **Identify:** (a) the Holocaust, (b) Manhattan Project.

2. **Define:** kamikaze.

3. (a) What did General Eisenhower think was the most important Allied goal in 1945? (b) What strategy did Churchill think the Allies should follow? Why? (c) What strategy did the Allies adopt?

4. What was the "final solution of the Jewish question"?

5. (a) What secret weapon did the United States develop? (b) How was it used?

6. **Critical Thinking** In Japanese culture, surrender was considered a disgrace. How do you think this attitude affected Japanese conduct of the war?

2. **DISCUSSION** Ask students if they think the United States was justified in dropping atomic bombs on civilian targets.

Summary

1. **By the time the United States entered World War II, the future appeared bleak for the Allies.** The German army was invading the Soviet Union, and the Japanese had extended their control in Asia and the Pacific. The Allied leaders concentrated their forces in Europe, but naval victories in the Pacific stopped the Japanese advance.

2. **The American effort on the home front was crucial to Allied victory.** Industrial production increased dramatically, and the Great Depression came to an end. Minorities made some gains but still faced discrimination. Japanese Americans were relocated to internment camps.

3. **By 1943, the Allies had begun to take the offensive.** American and British troops invaded Italy, and Soviet forces moved into eastern Europe. On D-Day, June 6, 1944, the Allies began the invasion of France. Meanwhile, bitter battles raged for control of the Pacific.

4. **Leaders of the United States, Britain, and the Soviet Union met for discussions.** At Teheran, they made plans for an international organization and discussed the postwar fate of Germany. Later, at Yalta, the Big Three discussed strategy in Asia and agreed on free elections for countries occupied by Germany during the war.

5. **Germany surrendered in May 1945, but the war in the Pacific raged on.** In August, the United States dropped atomic bombs on Hiroshima and Nagasaki, forcing the Japanese to surrender.

See p. T125.

Vocabulary

On a separate sheet of paper, write the word or words that best complete each of the following sentences.

1. Japanese Americans were detained in _____ during World War II.

2. A landing by sea is a (an) _____ landing.

3. The strategy of seizing certain Japanese-held islands while bypassing others was called _____.

4. The _____ was the systematic murder of Europe's Jews by the Nazis.

5. _____ attacks were suicide attacks by Japanese airplane pilots.

See p. T125.

Chapter Checkup

1. (a) Why was 1942 a dark year for the Allies? (b) How did Operation Torch improve the Allied situation in Europe? (c) Why did the Allied position in the Pacific improve by early 1943?

2. Explain how each of the following helped mobilize American industry for war: (a) War Production Board; (b) Office of War Mobilization; (c) Office of Price Administration; (d) War Manpower Commission; (e) National War Labor Board.

3. Explain how the war affected each of the following groups: (a) organized labor; (b) women; (c) African Americans; (d) Mexican Americans; (e) Italian and German Americans; (f) Japanese Americans.

4. (a) Why did the Allies decide to invade Italy? (b) Were they successful? Explain.

5. (a) Describe Operation Overlord. (b) Was it successful? Explain.

6. (a) What strategies did MacArthur and Nimitz propose to defeat Japan? (b) What strategy did they adopt?

7. (a) Where did diplomatic conferences between Allied leaders take place during the war? (b) What topics did they discuss at these conferences?

8. (a) Why did American leaders believe the final assault on Japan would be very costly? (b) How did possession of the atomic bomb alter the attitude of American leaders toward Stalin?

See p. T126.

Critical Thinking

1. **Supporting an Opinion**   The war that lasted from 1914 to 1918 is usually called World War I, while the war that lasted from 1939 to 1945 is called World War II. Would you agree that World War II was actually more "worldwide" than World War I? Use facts from the text to support your opinion.

2. **Comparing**   (a) How were Japanese Americans treated during World War II? (b) How does their treatment compare to the way German Americans were treated during World War I? (c) How might you explain the difference?

See p. T126.

Connecting Past and Present

1. World War II offered women, blacks, and other minorities greater participation in American life. How does the treatment of these groups today differ from that before World War II? What role did the war play in these changes? Give specific examples to support your answer.

2. During World War II, the United States unleashed the power of the atom. How has the existence of nuclear weapons altered the relationships among nations?

See p. T126.

Developing Basic Skills

1. **Comparing**   Review how the government mobilized industry during World War I. (See Chapter 25, Section 3, "The Home Front.") (a) In what ways was the mobilization effort during World War II similar to the effort in World War I? (b) In what ways was it different? (c) How might you explain the similarities and the differences?

2. **Analyzing Fiction as Historical Evidence** Review the steps for analyzing fiction in the Skill Lesson on page 557. Then write a brief report about a story that you have read or a movie or TV program that you have seen about World War II. Include (a) the type of source you used; (b) when the source was written or produced; (c) what you know about the author or producer of the source; (d) what you learned from the source about World War II; (e) how the source is limited as historical evidence.

WRITING ABOUT HISTORY

Writing and Revising a First Draft

When revising your first draft, ask yourself the following: Does the introduction lead into the thesis logically? Does each paragraph develop one idea related to the thesis? Are the paragraphs organized in a logical order? Is all the information relevant? Are direct quotes smoothly incorporated into the text? Does the conclusion reinforce the thesis? Is your language appropriate?

Practice: Rewrite the paragraph below to improve the organization and style.

In October 1944, General MacArthur who had said "I shall return," returned to the Philippines. In two humongous battles, Japan's sea power was done in. This was at the battle of the Philippine Sea and the battle for Leyte Gulf. Japan's air force was now reduced to kamikazes who could not turn the tide. MacArthur liberated Manila in February 1945.

687

Volunteerism

On December 7, 1941, Japanese airplanes bombed the United States fleet at Pearl Harbor. The next day, President Roosevelt asked Congress to declare war on Japan and began to ready the nation for the battles ahead.

The government had the power to draft soldiers, levy taxes, and order factories to produce war materials. But winning the war depended on Americans giving wholehearted support to the struggle, and this the government could not order.

On December 9, President Roosevelt spoke to the American people over the

1. **VISUAL EVIDENCE** The "V for Victory" sign was popularized by Winston Churchill.

Americans on the home front did their part in the war effort. These blind children with farm tools on
1. *their shoulders form a "V for Victory" around their garden. Their school had formerly grown flowers on the spot. But, like other Americans, they now planted tomatoes, beans, beets, and leafy green vegetables to help alleviate wartime food shortages.*

radio. "We are now in this war," he said. "We are all in it—all the way. Every single man, woman, and child is a partner in the most tremendous undertaking in American history." He asked Americans to help voluntarily in any way they could.

The Volunteer Spirit Americans responded generously to the President's plea. The nation faced a critical shortage of rubber, vital for many military uses. Roosevelt asked Americans to turn in "old tires, old rubber shoes, bathing caps. . . ." Within a few weeks, Americans had dug some 450,000 tons of scrap rubber from their attics, garages, and basements. The scrap rubber was boiled down and made into tires for jeeps and airplanes.

Even children did their part for the war effort. War industries were constantly short of iron, steel, aluminum, and copper. So all around the country, children organized groups like "Uncle Sam's Scrappers" and the "Tin Can Colonels." They scoured their neighborhoods for old cans, car parts, and other scrap metal. By 1945, scrap scavengers were supplying much of the steel and half the tin needed for the war effort. Americans also helped finance the war by buying war bonds—some $49 billion worth from 1941 to 1945.

The volunteer spirit Americans showed during World War II had its roots deep in American history. As far back as 1717, Boston had a volunteer fire department. During the Revolution, thousands of Americans volunteered to serve in state militias. And so many Tennesseans responded to the call to arms in the Mexican War that Tennessee has been known as the "Volunteer State" ever since.

By the 1800s, the new nation had thousands of voluntary groups. When Alexis de Tocqueville visited the United States in the 1830s, he noted, "Americans of all ages, all conditions, and all dispositions constantly form associations. . . . The Americans make associations to give entertainments, to found seminaries, to build inns, to construct churches, to diffuse books . . . ; in this manner they found hospitals, prisons, and schools."

Women's Role Women took a leading role in the voluntary associations of the mid-1800s. By then, mass-produced goods had eased housekeeping duties of middle-class women. Many women seized the chance to do challenging and rewarding work outside the home. They became the leadership as well as the rank-and-file of literary societies and of temperance, antislavery, and women's suffrage groups.

During the Civil War, women of all social and economic classes on both sides pitched in to help. They organized aid societies to collect money, make blankets and bullets, and care for wounded soldiers. At first, Union and Confederate armies refused to allow women nurses to work near the battle line. But as the war dragged on, both armies were forced to change this policy. Women worked in field hospitals just out of cannon range, and some even helped take wounded men from the field after battles.

Clara Barton set the model for selfless volunteerism during the Civil War. She risked her life helping the wounded on both sides of the fray. From her experience, Barton saw the need for a relief organization that would have access to both sides during wartime. In 1881, she founded the American Red Cross to meet this need. As president of the Red Cross, Barton fought for an international agreement designating the Red Cross as a neutral agency. Today, Red Cross volunteers are often the only people allowed to visit prisoners in totalitarian countries.

In today's fast-paced world, many functions once carried out by volunteers are now performed by professionals. Nurses, firefighters, and police are usually

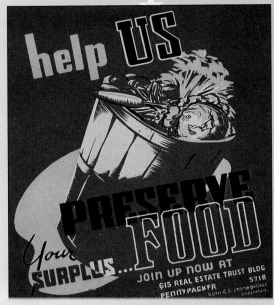

War puts unusual strains on a society. During World War II, volunteers helped provide food for the home front while the United States sent tons of food to Europe.

1.

1. **VISUAL EVIDENCE** Have students compare this poster to the World War I poster on p. 555.

salaried employees. Major charities have staffs of paid professionals.

Yet the volunteer spirit is very much alive in the United States today. Business organizations such as the Rotary and Kiwanis, and fraternal organizations like the Knights of Columbus and Elks, are supported by volunteer work and contributions. So are the Little League and 4-H. There are citizen action groups like Common Cause or the American Enterprise Institute, as well as professional societies from the Police Benevolent Association to the American Historical Association. In the 1990s, Americans will continue to nurture democracy, not only through participation in government, but also through the variety of their voluntary associations.

See p. T126.

1. How did Americans display a spirit of volunteerism during World War II?

2. What special contributions have American women made as volunteers?

3. **Critical Thinking** How can volunteer work benefit the volunteer as well as society?

Lillian Gilbreth

There is a saying, "If you want something done, ask a busy person." No better example could be found to support this idea than Lillian Moller Gilbreth. Lillian Gilbreth was the mother of 12 children, holder of several Ph.D.s, and a world-famous efficiency expert who ran her own business. Yet like many other Americans, she found an astounding amount of time for volunteer work.

Lillian Moller grew up in Oakland, California. She studied psychology at the University of California, where she was the first woman to speak at a commencement. Not long after, on a visit to Boston, Lillian met Frank Gilbreth. They were married in 1904.

At the time, Frank Gilbreth was a pioneer in the field of scientific management. He was constantly seeking more efficient ways to use time and labor. The Gilbreths made their home a laboratory for experiments in efficiency. A "Family Council" of parents and children managed day-to-day business, since the Gilbreths believed democracy increased cooperation. The council assigned all the household chores. Other jobs, like painting or repairing, went to the child who bid the lowest price. Two of the Gilbreth children later told the story of their unusual upbringing in the book *Cheaper by the Dozen.*

In 1924, Lillian's efficiency was put to the ultimate test. That year her husband died, leaving her with 11 surviving youngsters to raise alone. Lillian Gilbreth had to convince clients that she could carry on without her husband. Soon, she confirmed her own reputation as an expert in scientific management.

In the 1930s, Gilbreth became concerned with problems faced by the handicapped. She found that houses, furniture, and appliances were not built with the needs of the handicapped in mind. Gilbreth designed a model kitchen for the handicapped and wrote *Normal Lives for the Disabled,* which suggested ways for dis-

Although Lillian Gilbreth (1878–1972) was the mother of 12 children, she still found time for many volunteer activities and a career as an efficiency expert. She designed a model kitchen for the handicapped and suggested ways to make housework easier for them. In her community, she did volunteer work in churches and libraries and was an education adviser to the Girl Scouts. Her educational expertise also helped her serve as an adviser to the Office of War Information.

1.

1. **DISCUSSION** Have students suggest the kinds of activities Gilbreth might get involved in today.

abled people to do housework. She also donated her talents to help several groups that did physical rehabilitation.

Despite her heavy work schedule, Gilbreth made time to do other volunteer work as well. She helped churches and libraries in her community and was an educational adviser to the Girl Scouts of America. In the first years of the Great Depression, she served on the Emergency Committee for Unemployment Relief formed by President Roosevelt. During World War II, she was a consultant on education to the Office of War

Information. Following the war, she served as a member of the Civil Defense Advisory Commission. In 1966, she was the first woman to receive the Hoover medal for distinguished public service by an engineer.

Lillian Gilbreth remained an active writer and lecturer well into her eighties. Today, many of her ideas about rehabilitating the handicapped are still studied. Most of all she is remembered as a woman whose full, active life combined business, scholarship, family, and public service.

See p. T126.

1. What did Lillian Gilbreth do to help the physically handicapped?

2. **Critical Thinking**   In what ways is Lillian Gilbreth an example of the spirit of volunteerism?

Voices of Freedom

Entertaining the Troops

World War II brought the voluntary spirit in the United States to a peak. The United Service Organizations (USO) put together touring companies of actors, comedians, bandleaders, singers, and dancers to entertain the armed forces overseas. The following account of one of these traveling shows is from The New York Times *of April 2, 1944.*

The stage is a rough board affair, supported by freshly hewn logs. On it a girl, dressed in a simple cotton dress like those you see on the boardwalk . . . on a summer afternoon, is singing. Behind her two other entertainers are sitting on camp stools and to the right an accordionist pumps his arms. . . .

The scene is in New Guinea. It is hot—115 degrees in back of the stage, 130 plus under the arc lights that are powered by a mobile Army generator standing nearby. . . . The accordion's tones swell to a crescendo for the closing phrases. The singer's last note is cut short by a roar that breaks across the jungle stillness. A thousand pairs of hands are clapping. Men are shouting and whistling.

The singer and the performers with her in New Guinea make up an overseas company of the Camp Shows branch of the United Service Organizations. At the present time, eighty such companies are out of the country, giving shows in bomb-damaged opera houses in Italy, in rickety Nissen huts in North Africa, in storage barns in Alaska and the Aleutians, in jungles, deserts, mountain hideouts—in fact, wherever American boys are stationed.

Camp Shows over the past two and a half years has built a far-flung global circuit. . . . Camp Shows' job—with the help of the Hollywood Victory Committee—is primarily one of finding talent and molding it into variety-type shows. The talent falls into two classifications. First there are the paid USO Camp Show performers, hired from theaters, vaudeville companies, night clubs, and shows. . . . In the second class are Broadway, Hollywood, and radio volunteers who offer their services for a minimum of six weeks. . . .

Letters flood . . . into USO-Camp Shows from soldiers and sailors in the fighting zones and from their parents at home attesting the gratitude of the servicemen for the "live shows." There is not an actor who has returned who has not had mail and telephone calls from parents in all parts of the United States to tell how much their sons liked their performances.

Adapted from John Desmond, *New York Times Magazine,* April 2, 1944.

See p. T126.

1. Why would members of the armed forces be so responsive to the live shows?

2. **Critical Thinking**   What motivated Americans to such a high degree of volunteerism during World War II?

The Postwar International Scene (1945–1960)

CHAPTER OUTLINE

1 The Postwar World

2 A Cold War Begins

3 The Korean War

4 New Directions in Foreign Policy

5 The Challenge of Nationalism

CHAPTER OBJECTIVES After completing this chapter, students should be able to
1. describe postwar tensions and define the cold war.
2. explain causes and results of the Korean War.
3. describe Eisenhower's foreign policy.
4. explain how nationalism affected international relations in the 1950s.

CHAPTER PREVIEW Have students read the paragraphs and look at the time line below. Explain that a major feature of international relations after World War II was rivalry between the U.S. and the U.S.S.R. Ask: Why do you suppose the wartime alliance between the two countries fell apart? To what extent do these countries compete today?

He was not known as an exciting public speaker, but on this occasion he inspired the audience with his eloquence. "In the last six terrible years," he said, "unnumbered men have died to give humanity another chance. We too have a job of work to do if we are not to fail those men. Let us do it with courage, modesty, and dispatch [speed]. Let us do it now." The audience cheered.

It was April 25, 1945, and the speaker was Anthony Eden, the British secretary of state for foreign affairs. He was addressing the first session of a new organization—the United Nations. The audience was composed of delegates from nations around the world. They were gathered in the San Francisco Opera House, newly redecorated for the occasion. World War II was in its final stages, and the delegates had come together to form an organization that would prevent such devastation from occurring ever again.

A new pattern of world power was already emerging that would test their resolve. Only mutual hatred of the Nazi regime had supported the alliance between the United States and the Soviet Union. When the Soviet delegation showed up in San Francisco with a small army of security guards, it was clear that deep distrust divided the communist bloc and the western democracies. The Soviet ambassador immediately got things off to a rocky start when he challenged the right of the American representative to host the conference.

An international organization to guarantee peace had been tried before—the League of Nations after World War I—and it had failed. But in a mood of "cautious optimism," as one writer put it, the nations of the world were ready to try again. While the tensions between the former allies were a cause of serious concern, the United Nations offered at least some hope that the postwar world would be different.

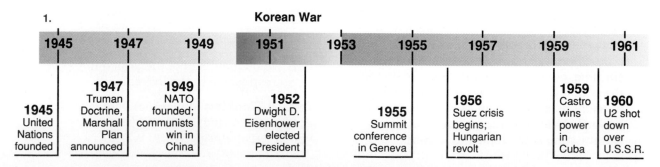

1.

Korean War

| 1945 | 1947 | 1949 | 1951 | 1953 | 1955 | 1957 | 1959 | 1961 |

1945 United Nations founded

1947 Truman Doctrine, Marshall Plan announced

1949 NATO founded; communists win in China

1952 Dwight D. Eisenhower elected President

1955 Summit conference in Geneva

1956 Suez crisis begins; Hungarian revolt

1959 Castro wins power in Cuba

1960 U2 shot down over U.S.S.R.

1. TIME LINE QUESTION Ask: Who was elected President during the Korean War?

The people of the world looked forward to a better life after the war's end. This
1. *feeling of hope is captured in Ben Shahn's* Reconstruction, *painted in 1945. The children of war emerge from the ruins to play and explore again. Throughout his career, Shahn used social and political themes in his art. "I hate injustice," he said, "and I hope to go on hating it all my life."*

---

1. **VISUAL EVIDENCE** Ben Shahn (1898–1969), born in Lithuania, came to the U.S. at the age of eight. During World War II, he designed many posters for the Office of War Information.

1 The Postwar World

READ TO UNDERSTAND

■ How communism made inroads in eastern and southern Europe.

■ What actions the United Nations took to prevent conflicts.

■ How the end of World War II affected Japan, Korea, and China.

"A new era is upon us. . . . The utter destructiveness of war now blots out this alternative. We have had our last chance." Those were the words General Douglas MacArthur broadcast to the world from the battleship *Missouri* after the signing of the Japanese surrender. Against tremendous odds, a new international organization, the United Nations, would try to keep the peace in this new era.

Roots of Conflict in Europe

From the moment the Bolsheviks seized power in 1917, most Americans viewed the Soviet Union with a mixture of mistrust and fear. Although World War II had brought the 2. Soviet Union and the United States together as allies, their relations were often troubled.

Wartime Suspicions During the war, Soviet Premier Joseph Stalin had doubted the Allies' willingness to help the Soviet Union. In his view, the British and Americans had delayed the cross-channel invasion of Europe in order to prolong the Soviet struggle against Germany. Stalin also resented Allied rejection of his argument that the Soviet Union needed a buffer zone of friendly states in eastern Europe as protection from future German attack.

On the other hand, many Americans, including some Department of State officials, distrusted the Soviet Union. They believed that the Soviets were plotting worldwide

693

2. **BACKGROUND** After World War I, Woodrow Wilson sent soldiers to fight with other Allies against the Bolsheviks. The effort failed and created ill will.

1. revolution and territorial expansion. Soviet actions after the war seemed to confirm such suspicions.

Tensions in Eastern Europe In 1944 and 1945, the Red Army had driven German troops out of Soviet territory and continued to pursue them west. (See page 677.) As a result, the Soviet Union occupied much of eastern Europe at the end of the war.

During the wartime conferences of Allied leaders, Stalin had agreed to certain concessions, such as allowing free elections in Poland after the war. But instead, the Soviets installed a communist-dominated government in Warsaw. A similar fate befell the other eastern European nations, including Czechoslovakia, Hungary, and Romania: The Red Army kept order while Soviet-backed communists set up governments.

A Divided Germany Meanwhile, conflict arose over the future of Germany. As you have read, during the war, the Big Three had agreed to divide Germany into four zones

MAP STUDY *At the end of World War II, the Allied powers divided Germany*

2. *into four zones of occupation. Although the German capital, Berlin, was in the Soviet-occupied zone, all four Allies shared control of the city.*

See p. T127. *Which countries controlled Germany's seaports?*

of occupation. (See the map at left.) The capital city of Berlin, located deep in the Soviet zone, was also divided into four sectors. However, the agreement did not guarantee free access to Berlin through the Soviet zone. Nor did the Allies reach an understanding as to the future reunification of Germany. Soviet actions in Berlin and eastern Europe would soon widen the split between the United States and the Soviet Union.

The United Nations

While the war was still in progress, the Allies had made plans for an international peacekeeping organization. (See page 681.) In April 1945, diplomats from 50 nations met in San Francisco and adopted a charter for this new organization, the United Nations (UN). According to the charter, the United Nations would try to prevent wars from occurring and stop those that did break out. Member states pledged to seek peaceful solutions to international disputes, as well as to work together to eliminate hunger, disease, and illiteracy. Many people hoped that the United Nations would succeed where the [3.] League of Nations had failed.

The UN charter provided for six major bodies within the organization. (See the diagram on page 695.) All member nations belong to the General Assembly, which discusses world problems and recommends action.

The Security Council is the UN body most directly responsible for maintaining world peace. Originally, only 11 nations sat on the Security Council, but that number has increased to 15. Five major powers—the United States, Great Britain, France, the Soviet Union, and China—have permanent seats. The remaining members are elected for two-year terms by the General Assembly.

The Security Council investigates conflicts between nations and recommends solutions. It also has the authority to organize peacekeeping forces made up of troops from member nations. However, the council has no power to enforce its decisions. Further-[4.] more, any permanent member of the Security Council can veto council resolutions. The Soviet Union used this veto power frequently during the early postwar years.

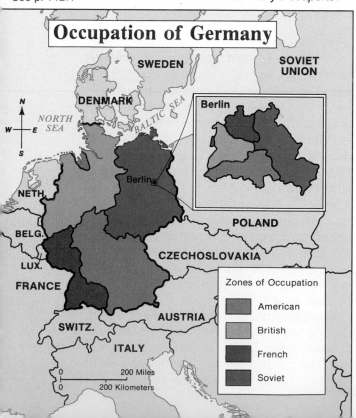

Occupation of Germany

SWEDEN

SOVIET UNION

DENMARK

Berlin

NORTH SEA

BALTIC SEA

Berlin

NETH.

POLAND

BELG.

CZECHOSLOVAKIA

LUX.

FRANCE

Zones of Occupation

AUSTRIA

American

SWITZ.

British

ITALY

French

0   200 Miles

0   200 Kilometers

Soviet

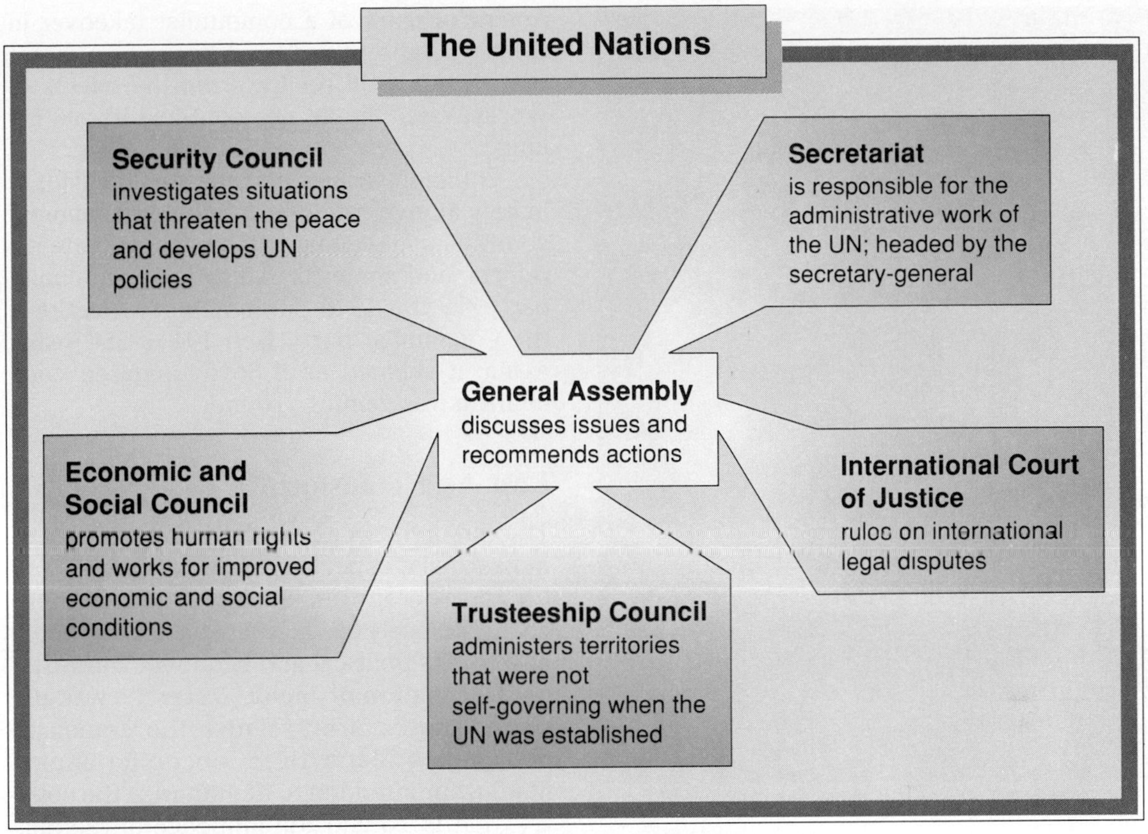

The United Nations

Security Council
investigates situations that threaten the peace and develops UN policies

Secretariat
is responsible for the administrative work of the UN; headed by the secretary-general

General Assembly
discusses issues and recommends actions

Economic and Social Council
promotes human rights and works for improved economic and social conditions

International Court of Justice
rules on international legal disputes

Trusteeship Council
administers territories that were not self-governing when the UN was established

CHART STUDY *Representatives of 50 nations met in San Francisco in 1945 to adopt the Charter of the United Nations. The diagram shows the six major bodies of the United Nations. Which body would probably deal with the treatment of political prisoners by a member nation?* See p. T127.

1.

1. **CHART READING** Ask: Which body promotes human rights? Which discusses world problems? Which is headed by the secretary-general?

2. **BACKGROUND** In 1947, there were about 1,091,000 Muslim Arabs, 614,000 Jews, and 146,000 Christians living in Palestine.

UN Actions in the Middle East

The first case to come before the Security Council involved a dispute between the United States and the Soviet Union over Iran. During World War II, Soviet, British, and American troops had occupied Iran to guard its vital oil fields and protect the main supply route to the Soviet Union. When the war ended, the United States and Britain removed their troops from Iran. The Soviets, however, refused to leave. Instead, they encouraged revolution in northern Iran, and used their troops to prevent the Iranian government from restoring order.

Supported by the United States, Iran brought a complaint before the UN Security Council. Finally, in April 1946, after forcing an oil concession from the Iranians, the Soviets withdrew and the crisis ended.

The United Nations also tried to settle a crisis in Palestine, a Middle Eastern territory administered by Great Britain. After World War II, British rule in Palestine became increasingly unpopular. The British presence angered both the Arabs who made up a majority of the population and resident Jews, many of whom had fled from Europe during the 1930s to escape Nazi persecution.

In 1947, a UN commission recommended that Palestine be divided into an Arab and a Jewish state. When the British withdrew in 1948, the Jewish residents of Palestine proclaimed the nation of Israel. President Truman immediately recognized the new nation. Neighboring Arab states, however, vowed to reclaim what they considered their land, and attacked Israel. The United Nations arranged an armistice in 1949, which restored an uneasy peace to the area.

2.

3.

695

3. **BIOGRAPHY** Ralph Bunche (1904–1971), a member of FDR's "Black Cabinet," helped organize the UN. In 1949, he was awarded the Nobel Peace Prize for helping to negotiate an end to the first Arab-Israeli conflict.

Printed by permission of the Estate of Norman Rockwell, Copyright © 1961 Estate of Norman Rockwell

An early description of the UN was "a town meeting of the world." Norman Rockwell illustrated the ideals behind the UN with his painting The Golden Rule. *Rockwell spent five months working on it, using as models people from his hometown area in Vermont. He won praise for his depiction of people of different races and nationalities working together to build a better world.*

1. **VISUAL EVIDENCE** Ask students how many different nationalities, races, and religions they can identify in this painting.

Turmoil in Southern Europe

World War II plunged much of southern Europe into political and economic turmoil. After the Allies drove the Nazis out of Greece in late 1944, a bitter civil war erupted between supporters and opponents of the Greek monarchy. A truce in January 1945 ended the fighting temporarily, but civil war broke out again in 1946. Meanwhile, the Greek economy was in ruins, and starvation was widespread.

Major opponents of the monarchy, primarily communists, received aid from Yugoslavia, a communist nation bordering Greece. The monarchy received aid from Britain.

American fears of a communist takeover in Greece heightened when it became apparent that Britain, still reeling from the effects of World War II, could not continue its aid for long.

Communists also became a political force in Italy after World War II. Difficult economic conditions made many Italians desperate for reform, and some turned to the Communist party. In the 1946 parliamentary elections, the Communist party won 104 of 556 seats. Again, it seemed as if Soviet-inspired communism was gaining ground.

East Asia Transformed

The end of the war brought dramatic changes in East Asia, especially in Japan, Korea, and China. The United States watched these changes closely to see what effects they would have on its political and economic interests.

Occupation of Japan After the war, the United States Army, under the command of Douglas MacArthur, occupied Japan. MacArthur intended to demilitarize the country, that is, to end the influence of the military on Japanese society and government. To accomplish this, he drafted a constitution for Japan that called for representative government and that removed the power of the emperor. Traditional educational practices, family-controlled land trusts, state-supported religion, and Japan's large standing army all were abolished.

2.

Japan's defeat and demilitarization left a power vacuum in East Asia. To fill that vacuum, the United States and the Soviet Union competed for influence in the region. Korea, which had been under Japanese control since 1910, became a major area of conflict.

Division of Korea During World War II, the United States and the Soviet Union agreed to divide Korea along the 38th parallel. The Soviet Union was to disarm Japanese troops in the northern zone, and the United States was to do the same in the southern sector. The two powers also agreed to national elections for a unified Korea at a later date.

After the war, however, the Soviet Union set up a communist government in its zone and refused to cooperate in national elections. Meanwhile, an American-educated Korean,

696

2. **CITIZENSHIP** The new constitution left the emperor as symbolic head of the government. It also gave Japanese women the right to vote.

1. **VOCABULARY** Have students look up this word in the glossary before they begin reading.

2. **PRESIDENTS** Harry Truman was present for Churchill's speech in Fulton. He nodded in agreement at the points Churchill was making.

Syngman Rhee (SIHNG muhn REE), was elected president in the south. By 1948, Korea had, in effect, become two nations: North Korea, backed by the Soviet Union, and South Korea, backed by the United States.

Civil War in China Conditions in China also alarmed United States officials. Civil war had raged in that nation since the early 1930s, with communist forces led by Mao Zedong (MOW zuh DUNG) opposing the nationalist government of Chiang Kai-shek. Once World War II was over, the civil war in China intensified.

The communists had an army of 500,000 troops, less than one fourth the strength of the nationalists. In addition, the nationalist army was more modern, largely trained and equipped by the United States. The nationalist government of Chiang Kai-shek, however, was corrupt. Eventually, the corruption crippled the nationalists' fighting ability and drove many Chinese to the communist side.

In December 1945, President Harry Truman sent General George C. Marshall to China to negotiate the formation of a unified nation under a government acceptable to both sides. Shortly after Marshall's arrival, a cease-fire was declared, and negotiations began. But neither side was willing to compromise, and a year later, the civil war resumed.

See p. T127.

SECTION 1 REVIEW

1. **Identify:** (a) United Nations, (b) General Assembly, (c) Security Council, (d) Syngman Rhee, (e) Mao Zedong.

2. Identify three sources of tension between the Soviet Union and the United States after World War II.

3. What role did the United Nations play in the creation of Israel?

4. What were the two opposing forces in the Chinese civil war?

5. **Critical Thinking** To what was General MacArthur referring when he said, "A new era is upon us. . . . The utter destructiveness of war now blots out this alternative"?

2 A Cold War Begins

READ TO UNDERSTAND

◼ How the Marshall Plan aimed to prevent the spread of communism.

◼ Why the United States joined NATO.

◼ What events led President Truman to develop a stronger military policy.

◼ *Vocabulary:* containment.

1.

In 1946, in a speech at Fulton, Missouri, Winston Churchill declared that an "iron curtain" had fallen across Europe, separating the democratic nations of western Europe from the communist nations of eastern Europe. Increasingly, the United States assumed the role of leader of those democratic nations and attempted to "contain" the spread of communism. Despite increasing tensions, the opposing superpowers—the United States and the Soviet Union—avoided direct warfare with each other. Instead, they engaged in a "cold war."

2.

The Truman Doctrine

United States policy toward the Soviet Union after World War II drew heavily on the ideas of George Kennan, who had served in the United States embassy in Moscow. Kennan attributed aggressive Soviet actions largely to Stalin's fear that "hostile capitalist" nations would encircle the Soviet Union. In Stalin's view, Kennan explained, the Soviet Union needed to take all possible steps to prevent such encirclement. Kennan argued that the United States should "contain" aggressive Soviet actions by applying counterforce at strategic political and geographic locations.

3.

Events in Greece and Turkey soon gave the Truman administration an opportunity to apply this policy of **containment.** In February 1947, the British informed the United States that they could no longer afford to assist the Greek monarchy in its civil war. (See page 696.) President Truman feared that

697

British withdrawal would mean victory for the communists. Meanwhile, Turkey was also desperate for foreign aid. Political unrest rocked the nation, and the Soviet Union was demanding part of Turkish territory.

Truman decided to ask Congress to appropriate $400 million in aid to Greece and Turkey. Before a joint session of Congress, the President declared that "it must be the policy of the United States to support free peoples who are resisting attempted subjugation by armed minorities or by outside pressures." This statement became known as the Truman Doctrine.

In his speech, Truman formally recognized the existence of a "cold war" between democratic and communist nations. Economic and military aid, he said, would be the major weapons of the United States in this cold war. The Truman Doctrine proved effective in both Greece and Turkey. Bolstered by American aid, the Greek monarchy defeated the communist uprising, and order was restored in Turkey.

The Marshall Plan

In 1947, Secretary of State George C. Marshall returned from a trip to Europe deeply upset by the dire need of the nations and people he had seen there. "The patient is sinking while the doctors deliberate," he warned in a somber radio address to the nation.

Focusing now on western Europe, the Truman administration moved quickly. The Europeans desperately needed financial aid to rebuild their devastated economies. Marshall urged European leaders to draw up a plan for recovery. He purposely did not exclude the Soviet Union or the nations of eastern Europe, known as the Soviet bloc.

VOICES OF FREEDOM

The Truman Doctrine

A major turning point in United States foreign policy took place in early 1947. Warned that Greece and Turkey were likely to give in to Soviet pressure if they did not receive help, on March 12, President Harry S. Truman addressed a joint session of Congress to ask for financial and military aid for these nations. This policy of supporting nations threatened by communism became known as the Truman Doctrine. A portion of Truman's speech is printed below.

I believe that it must be the policy of the United States to support free peoples who are resisting attempted subjugation by armed minorities or by outside pressures. I believe that we must assist free peoples to work out their own destinies in their own way. I believe that our help should be primarily through economic and financial aid, which is essential to economic stability and orderly political processes.

Should we fail to aid Greece and Turkey in this fateful hour, the effect will be far-reaching to the West as well as to the East. We must take immediate and resolute action. . . .

The seeds of totalitarian regimes are nurtured by misery and want. They spread and grow in the evil soil of poverty and strife. They reach their full growth when the hope of a people for a better life has died. We must keep that hope alive. The free peoples of the world look to us for support in maintaining their freedoms. If we falter in our leadership, we may endanger the peace of the world—and we shall surely endanger the welfare of our own nation.

Great responsibilities have been placed upon us by the swift movement of events. I am confident that the Congress will face these responsibilities squarely.

See p. T128.

1. According to Truman, what conditions help totalitarian regimes to grow powerful?

2. **Critical Thinking** How was the Truman Doctrine a significant departure from prewar isolationism?

1. **ECONOMICS** Even before the Marshall Plan, the U.S. had funneled about $11 billion in aid to Europe through the UN.

In June 1947, a Soviet delegation arrived in Paris to meet with delegations from Great Britain and France. Three days later, however, the Soviets left, refusing to accept the French and British recovery plan for Europe as a whole. Within a week, the Soviet Union had devised its own economic plan for eastern Europe.

Meanwhile, representatives from 16 other nations met in Paris and worked out a recovery plan. It called for $16 billion in American aid over a period of four years. The Truman administration now launched a lobbying effort to get the plan through Congress.

President Truman pointed out that such aid would benefit the United States as well as Europe. Economic recovery would help western European nations both to resist domestic communist threats and to strengthen their military capacity. Furthermore, Truman argued, the demand for American exports would increase, thereby improving the United States economy.

The key to the European Recovery Plan, or Marshall Plan, as it was known, was the economic recovery of Germany, the industrial heartland of Europe. "Without a revival of German production," Marshall told Congress, "there can be no revival of Europe's economy." Though fearful of a strong Germany, other European nations agreed, since they would also benefit from the aid.

The Marshall Plan became the crowning achievement of the United States containment policy. In four years, over $12 billion went to rebuild the war-torn economies of western Europe. As prosperity returned to Europe, the likelihood of communist victories subsided. The decision to help rebuild western Germany, however, was to lead to future conflict with the Soviet Union.

2. **CRITICAL THINKING** Have students compare the treatment of Germany after World War I and after World War II.

The Berlin Blockade

As you have read, Germany had been divided into four zones of Allied occupation after the war. (See page 694.) Britain, France, and the United States worked closely to administer the western sectors of the country, while the Soviet Union took charge of the eastern sector. After years of fruitless discussions with the Soviets about the reunification of Germany, on June 7, 1948, the United States,

"Operation Vittles" was the code name for the daring Berlin airlift operation. When the Soviet Union closed off all road, rail, and river traffic to West Berlin in 1948, the United States launched an airlift to supply the encircled city. An American cargo plane delivering food and other vital supplies is closely watched by West Berliners standing in the midst of the bombed-out city.

Britain, and France announced their intention to merge the western zones into an independent German nation.

The Soviet Union, fearful of a strong, unified Germany under western influence, reacted quickly. On June 24, 1948, the Soviets blocked all road, rail, and river traffic to West Berlin, which, as you recall, was in the middle of the Soviet-controlled zone. Supplies were cut off to more than 2 million residents. The Soviets hoped that the blockade would drive the other Allies out of Berlin and lay the basis for the unification of Germany under Soviet influence.

President Truman met the Soviet challenge. He ordered a massive airlift to take supplies to the distressed West Berliners. Each day for 321 days, the Berlin airlift delivered thousands of tons of food, coal, and clothing to the city. In May 1949, convinced

699

3. **VISUAL EVIDENCE** Ask: How do you think these Berliners felt when British and American planes, which had bombed them only three years before, began flying in supplies?

of American determination to preserve West Berlin independence, the Soviet Union ended the blockade. The western powers went on with their plan to combine their occupation zones into a single, independent country. This nation, the German Federal Republic, is commonly known today as West Germany. At the same time, the Soviet zone became the German Democratic Republic, or East Germany.

Growing Commitment

In the turmoil of the postwar world, the United States broke with its isolationist past and entered a peacetime military alliance with the nations of Western Europe.

NATO In March 1948, Britain, France, Belgium, the Netherlands, and Luxembourg signed the Brussels Treaty, pledging assistance should any of them be attacked. In April

1. **VISUAL EVIDENCE** Ask: Do you think this poster is an example of propaganda? Why or why not?

European concern about Soviet aggression was a major reason for the founding of NATO.

1. _This French poster shows the Soviet military threatening Europe. The figures in the background are Soviet citizens being sent into exile in Siberia. Stalin is the small figure in the center._

1949, the Brussels Treaty nations, joined by Denmark, Norway, Portugal, Italy, Iceland, Canada, and the United States, signed a mutual defense treaty creating the North Atlantic Treaty Organization (NATO).* The treaty stated that an attack on any one of the NATO nations would be considered an attack on all of them. For the United States, NATO was an essential element in its struggle to prevent the spread of communism. In 1955, the Soviet Union formed an opposing alliance, the Warsaw Pact, with Albania, Bulgaria, Czechoslovakia, East Germany, Hungary, Poland, and Romania. (See the map on page 701.)

United States membership in NATO not only represented the nation's commitment by treaty to the defense of Europe, it also represented America's commitment to a role of leadership in the postwar world. Possession of nuclear weapons made the United States the most important member of the alliance, and the commander of NATO military forces was always an American general.

Point Four Truman won reelection in 1948. Encouraged by public support for his first-term foreign policy, he now proposed yet another commitment—this time to areas outside Europe. His Point Four program, so called because it was the fourth point of his 1949 inaugural address, would provide economic aid to newly independent nations anywhere in the world. After 18 months of debate, Congress agreed to earmark $27 million for this purpose. The aid program thereafter was modest, but it had some effect. For example, American assistance helped the Iranians wipe out malaria.

Challenges to Postwar Confidence

Even as democratic nations joined together to form NATO, two events in late 1949 demonstrated the growing power of the communist world. Both signaled an increase in cold war tensions.

People's Republic of China The first event occurred in China. Each month of 1949 brought news of another victory for Mao

---

*Turkey and Greece joined NATO in 1952, West Germany in 1955, and Spain in 1982; France withdrew from NATO in 1966.

3. **BACKGROUND** According to a Chicago reporter, Americans sensed that "relentless forces are prowling the earth and that somehow they are bound to mean trouble for us."

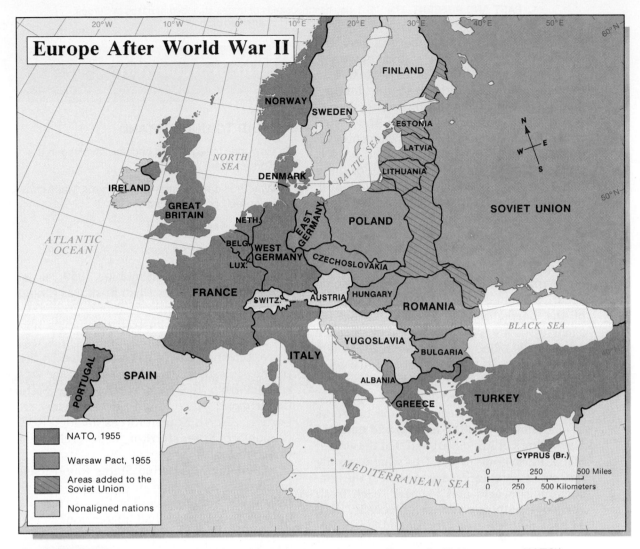

Europe After World War II

FINLAND
NORWAY
SWEDEN
ESTONIA
LATVIA
LITHUANIA
DENMARK
IRELAND
GREAT BRITAIN
NETH.
EAST GERMANY
POLAND
SOVIET UNION
BELG.
WEST GERMANY
LUX.
CZECHOSLOVAKIA
FRANCE
SWITZ.
AUSTRIA
HUNGARY
ROMANIA
YUGOSLAVIA
ITALY
BULGARIA
PORTUGAL
SPAIN
ALBANIA
GREECE
TURKEY
CYPRUS (Br.)

NORTH SEA
ATLANTIC OCEAN
BALTIC SEA
BLACK SEA
MEDITERRANEAN SEA

NATO, 1955
Warsaw Pact, 1955
Areas added to the Soviet Union
Nonaligned nations

0   250   500 Miles
0   250   500 Kilometers

MAP STUDY

See p. T128.

The United States joined with nations of western Europe in 1949 to create NATO. NATO countries agreed that an attack on one was an attack on all. Countries under Soviet influence later formed the Warsaw Pact. As the map shows, few countries in Europe remained outside the two alliances. Compare this map with the map of Europe after World War I on page 562. What countries were independent in 1918 but not in the 1950s? What happened to them?

1.

1. **MAP READING** Ask: Which NATO nations border Warsaw Pact nations?

Zedong's communist forces over the nationalist armies of Chiang Kai-shek. By the end of the year, the communists had taken control of mainland China and established the People's Republic of China. The nationalists had retreated to the island of Formosa, now known as Taiwan.

Truman refused to recognize the communist government on the mainland. Instead, the United States recognized the nationalists on Taiwan as the legitimate government of 2. China. In 1950, the United States began providing military protection for Taiwan.

Mao's victory over the nationalists provoked a storm of criticism against Truman's foreign policy. Critics charged that Truman had "lost China" by concentrating military and economic aid in Europe. More aid to the Chinese nationalists, some Americans insisted, would have saved Chiang's regime.

Soviet Nuclear Test Another event in 1949 dampened American hopes for a quick end to the cold war. In September, President Truman announced that the Soviet Union had successfully tested an atomic device. United States monopoly on atomic power was over.

2. **PAST AND PRESENT** The U.S. finally recognized the communist government in 1972. That year, the People's Republic of China took over Taiwan's permanent seat on the UN Security Council.

As Senator Arthur Vandenberg of Michigan grimly put it, "This is now a different world."

In response to the Soviet nuclear test, President Truman authorized the development of the even more powerful hydrogen bomb. Over the next two years, the United States also began rebuilding its conventional, or nonatomic, forces, such as land armies, tanks and guns, and air power. All of these
1. had been greatly reduced after World War II. Many of the rebuilt forces became part of the NATO command in Europe.

NSC 68   The end of American atomic supremacy also forced Truman to reassess the nation's foreign policy. To examine possible new strategies, he turned to the National Security Council (NSC). The NSC, consisting of the heads of defense and intelligence agencies, along with the Central Intelligence Agency (CIA), had been set up in 1947 when Congress passed the National Security Act.

In 1950, the NSC presented President Truman with a classified document called NSC 68. This document described the future as "an indefinite period of tension and danger." The authors of NSC 68 argued that the United States must commit itself to whatever military steps were necessary to protect the noncommunist world and to meet "each fresh challenge promptly and unequivocally." NSC 68 provided the basis for United States foreign policy throughout much of the 1950s and 1960s.

See p. T128.

SECTION 2 REVIEW

1. **Identify:**   (a) Truman Doctrine, (b) Marshall Plan, (c) NATO, (d) NSC 68.

2. **Define:**   containment.

3. What was the main purpose of the Marshall Plan?

4. (a) Why was NATO formed? (b) Why did the United States join NATO?

5. What two events in 1949 increased cold war tensions?

6. **Critical Thinking**   Why do you think the United States did not return to the isolationism that followed World War I?

702

3 The Korean War

READE TO UNDERSTAND

READ TO UNDERSTAND

■ How the United States became involved in the Korean War.

■ Why President Truman and General MacArthur disagreed on war objectives.

■ How the war was ended.

■ *Vocabulary:* limited war.   2.

On a Saturday evening in June 1950, Assistant Secretary of State Dean Rusk was dining at the home of friends in Washington, D.C. Most other top administration officials had left the city to escape the summer's first heat wave. Unexpectedly, Rusk was called to the phone. He listened intently as a message was relayed from the code room of the State Department: "According to Korean army reports . . . North Korean forces invaded ROK (Republic of Korea) territory at several points this morning. . . ."

Suddenly, the United States found itself involved in a new kind of situation—neither fully at war nor at peace. The UN also faced a difficult test: Could it halt aggression?

The War Begins

After World War II, Korea was divided along the 38th parallel into a northern zone allied with the Soviet Union and a southern zone supported by the United States. (See page 696.) Negotiations on the unification of Korea had been unsuccessful, and by 1950, the potential for trouble was high.

The arrest of several northern delegates by the South Korean government on June 11 provided tinder for an already explosive situation. On June 25, the armies of communist North Korea swept across the 38th parallel and invaded South Korea.

Defense of South Korea   At an emergency meeting held later that same day, the UN Security Council passed a resolution condemning the invasion and demanding the immediate withdrawal of North Korean forces. Two days later, the council adopted a second resolution, this time calling for UN

1. **BACKGROUND** The UN Security Council voted 7 to 1 to "repel the armed attack." The lone no vote was cast by Yugoslavia.

action to aid South Korea. Had the Soviet representative been present, he probably would have vetoed both votes. But the Soviets were boycotting the council because the UN had not granted membership to the People's Republic of China.

On the same day that the United Nations voted to aid South Korea, President Truman ordered American planes and ships to back up the South Korean army. Three days later, on June 30, he ordered American ground forces into South Korea. One week later, in accord with a UN vote, he appointed General Douglas MacArthur to command a joint UN fighting force. About four fifths of this force would be American troops.

The goal of the UN action, as described by Truman, was to drive the North Koreans out of South Korea and reestablish the border at the 38th parallel. But the UN troops, primarily Americans rushed in from Japanese bases, were poorly prepared to fight, and the South Koreans lacked vital equipment.

Meeting little resistance, Soviet-supplied North Korean troops pushed southward. By August 1950, they had captured virtually all of South Korea. In September, however, General MacArthur launched a surprise attack at Inchon, far behind North Korean lines. Within two weeks, UN forces had recaptured most of South Korea.

Invasion of North Korea According to its stated objectives, the UN mission was complete. But the momentum of MacArthur's assault now began to take over. In October, with the approval of both Truman and the UN General Assembly, UN forces crossed the 38th parallel into North Korea. The United Nations revised its objectives, calling for "the establishment of a unified, independent, and democratic Korea."

The invasion of North Korea brought disastrous consequences. Communist China had warned that it would not "sit back with folded hands" if United States troops marched into North Korea. But American leaders had paid little attention to such warnings, believing that China would never intervene. The American leaders were wrong. In late November, hundreds of thousands of Chinese soldiers poured across the Yalu River into North Korea and forced UN troops to retreat with heavy losses across the 38th parallel.

3. **READING** Interested students can read more about MacArthur in *American Caesar* by William Manchester.

2. **BACKGROUND** An American soldier wrote of the retreat, "All day and night we ran like antelopes. We didn't know our officers. They didn't know us."

A Clash Between Truman and MacArthur

The Korean conflict was now, in General MacArthur's words, "an entirely new war." How that war should be fought became the focus of a disagreement between General MacArthur and President Truman.

Differences in War Objectives In Truman's view, a major land war in Asia to defeat North Korea and China might provoke

4. **MAP READING** Ask: How close to the Chinese border did UN troops advance? When?

MAP STUDY *When North Korea drove deep into South Korea, a United Nations force came to the assistance of the south. UN troops under General Douglas MacArthur landed at Inchon and went on to recapture most of South Korea. How many times did the city of Seoul change hands between the first North Korean advance and the armistice?* See p. T128.

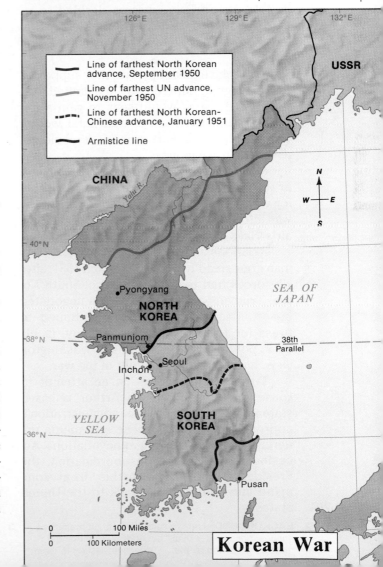

Line of farthest North Korean advance, September 1950
Line of farthest UN advance, November 1950
Line of farthest North Korean-Chinese advance, January 1951
Armistice line

USSR
CHINA
Yalu R.
40°N
SEA OF JAPAN
Pyongyang
NORTH KOREA
38°N
Panmunjom
38th Parallel
Seoul
Inchon
YELLOW SEA
36°N
SOUTH KOREA
Pusan
0   100 Miles
0   100 Kilometers

Korean War

President Eisenhower, shown here sharing a combat meal with a soldier, kept his
campaign pledge to go to Korea. Ike's three-day visit boosted the morale of
American troops, who fought over rough terrain in bitterly cold weather.

1. **VISUAL EVIDENCE** At this time, Eisenhower had been elected but had not yet taken office.

the Soviets to retaliate in Europe or elsewhere in Asia. He and his advisers decided to revive the original objective of the war: restoring the boundary between North and South Korea.

To achieve that objective, they supported the strategy of **limited war.** In a limited war, the United States would seek to gain a few specific objectives rather than total victory over North Korea. Furthermore, it would not use nuclear weapons.

MacArthur did not accept that concept. In war, he declared, "there is no substitute for victory." MacArthur wanted to extend the war into China and urged the use of massive air strikes against targets in that country.

Relations between MacArthur and Truman grew steadily worse. By March 1951, after UN forces had recovered most of South Korea, Truman was ready to seek a negotiated peace. MacArthur, however, continued to press for total defeat of the enemy. In his eyes, political considerations in Washington were hampering his conduct of the war.

Truman Under Fire In an attempt to rouse public opinion, MacArthur released statements criticizing the administration's approach to the war. These statements undercut Truman's attempt at negotiations. Accusing the general of insubordination, the President removed MacArthur from command and ordered him back to the United States.

MacArthur returned home to a hero's welcome and received a standing ovation when he addressed a joint session of Congress. A congressional committee began investigating Truman's dismissal of MacArthur. For a time, support of the general was strong, but Truman successfully defended his decision. By upholding his role as commander in chief, the President had reaffirmed the principle of civilian control of the military.

Cease-Fire

Negotiations for a cease-fire in Korea began in July 1951, but they dragged on for two years. During the presidential election campaign of 1952, Republican candidate General Dwight D. Eisenhower pledged that, if elected, he would personally go to Korea and get the stalled peace negotiations moving again.

Eisenhower won the election and visited Korea within a few weeks of his victory. By then, both sides were eager for a cease-fire. The only remaining problem was the return of prisoners of war. The two sides finally agreed to turn this issue over to an international commission.

A cease-fire agreement ending the hostilities in Korea was signed on July 27, 1953. The agreement reestablished fixed borders between North and South Korea. Although relations between the two nations remained tense, war did not break out again.

704

2. **BACKGROUND** Truman said, "Debate on matters of national policy is . . . vital," but added, "Commanders must be governed by the . . . directives issued to them."

3. **DISCUSSION** Ask: Why was MacArthur seen as a hero by many Americans? Was Truman wrong to recall him? What was at stake?

See p. T128.

SECTION 3 REVIEW

1. **Identify:** (a) 38th parallel, (b) General Douglas MacArthur.

2. **Define:** limited war.

3. What action did the UN take when North Korea invaded South Korea?

4. Describe the opposing positions of Truman and MacArthur regarding the conduct of the Korean War.

5. **Critical Thinking** Do you think that the military should be under civilian control? Why or why not?

4 New Directions in Foreign Policy

READ TO UNDERSTAND

■ How the foreign policy of the Eisenhower and Truman administrations differed.

■ Why Soviet-American relations improved during the 1950s.

■ What caused a setback in Soviet-American relations.

1. ■ *Vocabulary:* massive retaliation, arms race.

President Eisenhower's secretary of state, John Foster Dulles, warned that "the threat of Soviet Communism . . . is not only the gravest threat that ever faced the United States but the gravest threat that has ever faced what we call Western civilization." A strong anti-communist, Dulles envisioned a broader, more idealistic, and more aggressive foreign policy than Truman's.

President Eisenhower, however, was more restrained than Dulles. Having firsthand experience of the horrors of war, he was eager to end tensions that might lead to war. The Soviet premier, Joseph Stalin, had died in 1953. The new Soviet leadership offered an opportunity for the United States and the Soviet Union to move toward more peaceful relations.

2. **DISCUSSION** Ask students how they think George Kennan and Douglas MacArthur would have felt about Dulles's policies.

1. **VOCABULARY** Have students look up these terms in the glossary before they begin reading.

A Different Approach

Secretary of State John Foster Dulles believed that communism was an immoral system of government. He rejected the Truman administration's policy of containment, which tolerated Soviet power where it already existed. To Dulles, United States foreign policy should aim to destroy communism.

Dulles developed two basic strategies to carry out his foreign policy principles. First, the United States should encourage the "liberation of the captive peoples" in eastern Europe through political pressure and propaganda. Thus, radio broadcasts by Voice of America and Radio Free Europe urged people in eastern European nations to overthrow their communist governments.

Second, the United States should adopt a new strategy of **massive retaliation** to stop communist aggression. Instead of using conventional forces to support local efforts to

2.

3. **VISUAL EVIDENCE** Ask: Would this poster have a greater impact in Europe or in the U.S.? Why?

After the Soviet Union broke the United States monopoly on atomic bombs, the two countries competed in a world-threatening arms race. Growing stockpiles of weapons led to a disarmament movement during the 1950s. Artist Tadeus Trepkowski created this 1952 poster showing a falling bomb that contains a bombed-out building. The German word for "never" warns against the danger of the arms race.

3.

705

resist communist aggression, as in Korea, the United States should retaliate directly against the Soviet Union or China, with nuclear weapons if necessary. Thus, during the 1950s, the United States competed against the Soviet Union in an **arms race** to accumulate sophisticated nuclear arsenals.

By the late 1950s, however, Dulles's aggressive policy had produced few gains. Changes in the Soviet Union led President Eisenhower to seek to reduce tensions in the cold war.

A "Thaw" in the Cold War

After Stalin's death in 1953, Soviet policy underwent several changes. First, Soviet leaders began to concentrate on improving living conditions within the Soviet Union. They hoped to impress young nations in Asia, Africa, and Latin America with the superiority of communism as an economic system. In addition, the Soviet leadership now stated that war between the Soviet Union and the West* was unnecessary. Peaceful competition, they boasted, would establish the superiority of the Soviet system.

These new directions in Soviet policy offered an opportunity for a "thaw" in the cold war. Resisting advice not to negotiate with the Soviets, President Eisenhower cautiously moved to relax tensions between the two powers.

The Geneva Summit The first indication of a thaw was a summit conference in Geneva, Switzerland, in 1955. At this conference, President Eisenhower met with the leaders of the Soviet Union, Britain, and France to discuss disarmament and the reunification of East and West Germany. The western powers wanted Germany to be reunited. The Soviets, however, still feared a powerful reunited Germany, especially one allied with the West, and put up stiff resistance.

Talks on disarmament were more successful. Both sides had come to realize the terrible danger of continuing the nuclear arms race. Although they reached no specific agreement at Geneva, disarmament discussions continued after the meeting was adjourned. In 1958, the Soviet Union, the United States, and Britain agreed to suspend the testing of nuclear weapons while they worked to bring about a permanent halt to the arms race.

A Soviet Visit The high point of the thaw in American-Soviet relations came in the summer of 1959. Nikita Khrushchev (nuh KEET uh kroosh CHAWF), the new premier of the Soviet Union, made a two-week visit to the United States. The Soviet leader toured factories, attended a midwestern barbecue, discussed raising corn with an Iowa farmer, and visited Hollywood.

Khrushchev concluded his tour with a lengthy series of talks with President Eisenhower at Camp David, the presidential retreat outside Washington. The two leaders agreed to hold a new summit meeting the following year in Paris. Hopes for a further relaxation of tensions ran high as the "spirit of Camp David" warmed Soviets and Americans alike.

A Setback to Peaceful Relations

The spirit of Camp David was soon destroyed by the U-2 incident. A U-2 is a high-altitude plane specially equipped to take detailed photographs of ground activities. In 1956, American U-2s had begun making flights over the Soviet Union to photograph such things as the movements of Soviet troop convoys and the locations of Soviet missiles.

In May 1960, ten days before the planned Paris summit conference, Khrushchev announced that a U-2 plane had been shot down over the Soviet Union. The captured pilot had admitted that his job was to photograph Soviet military facilities. Several days later, President Eisenhower stated that he had authorized the U-2 flights in the interest of national security.

In an effort to save the summit conference, Eisenhower announced to the Soviets that he had suspended U-2 flights. Khrushchev, however, was not satisfied. On his arrival in Paris, he demanded an apology. Eisenhower refused, and the summit collapsed.

---

*The United States, nations of western Europe, and other nations opposed to Soviet expansion were known as the "West" or the "western powers." The Soviet Union and its allies became known as the "East" or the "eastern powers."

See p. T129.

SECTION 4 REVIEW

1. **Identify:** (a) John Foster Dulles, (b) Nikita Khrushchev.

2. **Define:** (a) massive retaliation, (b) arms race.

3. (a) What was the basis of the foreign policy of John Foster Dulles? (b) What two strategies did Dulles use to promote his foreign policy?

4. What was the high point of the thaw in the cold war in the late 1950s?

5. What effect did the U-2 incident have on the thaw?

6. **Critical Thinking** How does the present United States policy toward the Soviet Union compare with the policy after World War II?

5 The Challenge of Nationalism

READ TO UNDERSTAND

■ How the Soviet Union and the United States responded to nationalist movements during the 1950s.

■ Why the United States became involved in Southeast Asia.

■ What events in the Middle East and Latin America challenged United States policy.

1. ■ *Vocabulary:* domino theory.

Throughout the postwar world, the nationalist impulse grew stronger. People in farflung corners of the world struggled to free their lands from foreign influence and determine their own destiny. The focus of the cold war thus shifted away from western Europe to Asia, the Middle East, and Latin America.

The Hungarian Uprising

Aware that the Soviet Union had begun to relax political and economic controls within its own borders, eastern Europeans began to

2. **VOCABULARY** Have students define nationalism and discuss how it can lead to independence movements.

1. **VOCABULARY** Have students look up this term in the glossary before they begin reading.

demand more freedom for themselves. In 1956, strong nationalist feelings erupted in two eastern European nations. The first uprising occurred in Poland, where workers protested Soviet rule and won greater control of their own government.

Encouraged by the Polish example, Hungarian nationalists also staged an uprising. They called for replacement of pro-Soviet officials in the Hungarian government, withdrawal of Soviet troops, and legalization of noncommunist political parties. Students and workers organized huge demonstrations in support of these demands.

Soviet tanks and troops moved swiftly to crush the uprising. Although the western powers welcomed those Hungarians who escaped, they sent no direct aid to the rebels in Hungary. For some Americans, the inability of the United States to help the Hungarians was proof that Secretary Dulles's strategy of "liberation" of eastern Europe was not a practical one.

3. **CRITICAL THINKING** Ask: Why do you think Hungarian crowds would storm a Soviet bookstore?

This Hungarian man protests communism by burning a picture of Lenin, leader of the 1917 Russian revolution. The picture came from a Soviet bookstore in Budapest that was stormed by angry crowds.

1. **GEOGRAPHY** At that time, these colonies were known as Indochina. Have students locate the region on the map on pp. 842–843. (location)

2. **DISCUSSION** Ask: Why did Eisenhower reject Dulles's plan? Do you think he was right? How might the rest of the world have reacted to a nuclear attack on Vietnam?

War in Southeast Asia

After the defeat of Japan, the French, in 1945, tried to reestablish control over their former 1. colonies of Vietnam, Cambodia, and Laos in Southeast Asia. Opposing the French were Vietnamese forces led by Ho Chi Minh (HOH CHEE MIHN), a communist. These Vietnamese rebels were continuing a struggle for independence they had been waging since the 1930s.

In the late 1940s, the French threatened to leave NATO if the United States did not support them in Southeast Asia. For almost five years, the United States contributed money and supplies to the French war effort. But even so, France was unable to defeat Ho's guerrilla forces.

Ho's armies continued to grow in strength and popular support. In the spring of 1954, they trapped a large French force at Dien Bien Phu (DYEHN BYEHN FOO). The French asked the United States to send in troops. President Eisenhower, fearing another war like the Korean conflict, refused. He also re-
2. jected Dulles's advice to use nuclear weapons against the Vietnamese. The French were forced to surrender Dien Bien Phu.

Soon after, the nations involved met in Geneva to negotiate terms. The agreements they reached, called the Geneva Accords, temporarily divided Vietnam into two sectors and provided that elections would be held later to reunify the country.

Ho Chi Minh's communist government retained control of North Vietnam. In South Vietnam, the government of Ngo Dinh Diem (noh din ZEE em), supported by the United States, took control. Diem resisted holding elections to unify the two Vietnams, and the country remained divided.

With the defeat of France, the United States became the leading western power in Southeast Asia. Many people justified the American presence by citing the **domino theory.** According to this theory, if one nation became communist, neighboring nations would topple to the communists like a set of falling dominoes. United States policy was to prevent the first domino from falling.

As part of this policy, the United States sponsored the creation of the Southeast Asia Treaty Organization (SEATO).* Under the terms of this alliance, the United States pledged to aid member nations threatened by aggression. Furthermore, in 1955, under the SEATO pact, the United States began sending military advisers to South Vietnam to help train that country's armed forces. The United States also pledged to come to the aid of Taiwan if it were attacked by mainland China.

The Middle East

In 1954, Gamal Abdel Nasser became president of Egypt as the result of a revolution. He soon made an arms agreement with the Soviets and recognized communist China. In response, the United States withdrew its offer to help the Egyptians build a dam across the Nile River. In 1956, Nasser seized control of the Suez Canal from the British and excluded Israeli ships.

Israel, already at odds with its Arab neighbor, attacked Egyptian forces. With the outbreak of war, the British and the French began bombing Egyptian targets, claiming they were protecting the strategically located canal. They expected the United States to join them and were surprised when Dulles and Eisenhower refused. Fearing a larger conflict, the United States pressed Britain and France to stop the fighting. It also sponsored a UN resolution condemning the attack. Faced with combined UN and United States pressure, the French and British backed down.

Although the Soviet Union had not been directly involved in the Suez Crisis, it had offered military and economic aid to Egypt. In turn, President Eisenhower announced that the United States would offer financial aid to Middle Eastern countries that requested help against communist aggression. This policy became known as the Eisenhower Doctrine. In 3. 1958, the United States used this doctrine to justify landing American marines in Lebanon as a show of force to end civil war there.

Revolution in Latin America

In the 1950s, dictators held power in many Latin American countries. The United States maintained friendly relations with those dic-

*The original members of SEATO included the United States, Great Britain, France, Australia, New Zealand, Thailand, Pakistan, and the Philippines.

tators in the hope that these leaders would prevent revolution in the region. According to many Latin Americans, the United States had, in fact, helped to install the dictatorships to protect investments of its corporations.

Vice President Richard Nixon's visit to Peru and Venezuela in 1958 revealed the depth of anti-American feeling. Angry mobs threw stones and eggs at the Vice President and attacked his limousine. Shocked at this outburst, the administration began efforts to improve relations with its Latin American neighbors. But hostile nationalist movements were on the rise in the region.

Rise of Castro in Cuba In 1959, Fidel Castro led a successful revolution in Cuba against the dictator Fulgencio Batista (bah TEES tah). President Eisenhower recognized the new government a week after Castro took power. During the following months, however, Castro's policies resulted in increasingly tense relations with the United States.

The Cuban economy was heavily dependent on the United States. For example, Americans owned 80 percent of the Cuban utilities industry, 40 percent of its sugar plantations, and 90 percent of its mineral resources. Castro believed that to strengthen the Cuban economy, he would have to lessen the control of American businesses.

A Rift With Cuba In June 1960, the Cuban government seized several American-owned oil refineries. President Eisenhower retaliated by reducing the quota on United States sugar imports from Cuba. When Cuba seized more American businesses, relations worsened, and President Eisenhower placed an embargo on trade with Cuba.

During this period, Cuba formed close ties with the Soviet Union. In July 1960, Premier Khrushchev announced that the Soviet Union would protect Cuba from any military attack by the United States. The Soviets also began supplying Cuba with economic and military aid. By the end of 1960, Cuba was clearly moving into the Soviet camp. As a result, President Eisenhower broke off diplomatic relations with Cuba on January 3, 1961, 17 days before his term of office ended.

Between 1945 and 1960, the United States had strengthened its relationship with the industrialized nations of Europe and Asia. In

After Castro overthrew the dictator Fulgencio Batista, the United States immediately offered diplomatic recognition to his regime. The relationship soured as Castro turned to the Soviet Union for aid. This poster celebrating Castro's sixth year in power shows the Cuban leader wearing his trademark army fatigues.

3. **VISUAL EVIDENCE** Ask: Why do you think Castro has chosen always to wear army fatigues in public?

the competition with the Soviet Union for the allegiance of other nations, however, the results were less certain. Furthermore, the arms race between the two powers continued to threaten the entire world.

See p. T129.

SECTION 5 REVIEW

1. **Identify:** (a) Ho Chi Minh, (b) Dien Bien Phu, (c) SEATO, (d) Gamal Abdel Nasser, (e) Eisenhower Doctrine, (f) Fidel Castro.

2. **Define:** domino theory.

3. How did the Soviet Union respond to the Hungarian uprising?

4. What led to United States involvement in Vietnam?

5. How did the United States respond to the Suez crisis?

6. **Critical Thinking** How might Dulles's foreign policy have encouraged the Hungarian uprising?

Summary

1. **World tensions did not end with Allied victory in World War II.** Pro-communist governments took hold in eastern Europe, and communism threatened the stability of southern Europe. The United Nations dealt with crises in the Middle East. Events in Asia set the stage for future conflicts.

2. **After World War II, the United States adopted a policy of containment.** Application of the Truman Doctrine and the Marshall Plan helped to rebuild western European economies and stem communist aggression. Membership in NATO reflected growing commitment to European defense. A communist victory in China and Soviet nuclear capability presented new challenges.

3. **In June 1950, communist North Korea invaded South Korea.** United Nations and United States troops defended South Korea. The advance of UN troops into North Korea brought China into the war. A cease-fire agreement in 1953 established North and South Korea as separate nations.

4. **John Foster Dulles urged a foreign policy based on "liberation of captive peoples" and massive retaliation.** New Soviet leadership, however, offered a "thaw" in relations. President Eisenhower moved to relax tensions, but the U-2 incident caused a setback.

5. **Nationalism became an important force during the 1950s.** A Hungarian uprising challenged Soviet control. A communist-led revolution in Vietnam forced out the French and launched the United States on the road to involvement in Southeast Asia. New leaders in Egypt and Cuba asserted their independence and looked to the Soviet Union for support.

See p. T129.

Vocabulary

On a separate sheet of paper, write the word or words that best complete each of the following sentences.

1. _____ is a foreign policy aimed at holding Soviet influence within existing limits.

2. A (An) _____ is fought to achieve selected objectives rather than total victory.

3. The strategy of _____ called for direct retaliation against the Soviet Union or China, with nuclear weapons if necessary.

4. The _____ is the Soviet-American competition to develop a nuclear arsenal.

5. According to the _____, if one Asian nation became communist, neighboring nations would follow.

See p. T129.

Chapter Checkup

1. (a) What wartime suspicions contributed to postwar tensions between the United States and the Soviet Union? (b) What postwar Soviet actions fueled American mistrust?

2. (a) What were the goals of the United Nations? (b) What was the main responsibility of the Security Council? (c) What could the council do to fulfill that responsibility? (d) How was its power limited? (e) What actions did the UN take in the Middle East in the late 1940s?

3. (a) What was the Marshall Plan? (b) In what way was it a part of the policy of containment? (c) Was it successful? Explain.

4. (a) How did the United States react to the North Korean invasion of South Korea? (b) Why did the goal of the UN and the United States change in October 1950? (c) What was the consequence of the invasion of North Korea?

5. (a) What led to a "thaw" in the cold war during the late 1950s? (b) What resulted from the 1955 summit conference between Khrushchev and Eisenhower? (c) What ended the thaw?

6. (a) What was the first reaction of the United States to the revolution led by Fidel Castro in Cuba? (b) Why did the American attitude toward Castro change?

See p. T130.

Critical Thinking

1. Defending an Opinion   Would you agree with Senator Vandenberg that after the Soviets exploded their first atomic weapon, it was "now a different world"? (See page 702.) Why or why not?

2. Evaluating   Do you think the policy of containment was generally successful between 1947 and 1960? Why or why not?

See p. T130.

Connecting Past and Present

1. Summit meetings between Soviet and American leaders have continued to explore ways to end tensions. Describe a recent summit meeting and tell what it accomplished.

2. The United Nations was formed to promote world peace and understanding. What steps has the United Nations taken in recent years to accomplish those goals?

See p. T130.

Developing Basic Skills

1. Map Reading   On the map on page 701, locate: the members of (a) NATO; (b) the Warsaw Pact. (c) What countries remained nonaligned? (d) Why do you think so few countries remained nonaligned?

2. Using Visual Evidence   Study the photograph on page 699. (a) What is shown in the photograph? (b) How would you describe the mood of the people pictured? (c) What issue led to the dispute over the city of Berlin? (d) How was it resolved?

WRITING ABOUT HISTORY

Proofreading Your Paper

After you have revised your first draft, you should proofread it for spelling, capitalization, and punctuation errors. The standard proofreading symbols are listed at the right.

Practice: Rewrite this paragraph, using the proofreading symbols at the right to make necessary changes:

The United states replaced Frnace as the leading Western power in Southea st Asia. many justified America presence there by what became known as the domino theory According to this theory if one nation accepted communist, neidhboring nations would topplelike a set of falling dominoes.

Symbol	Meaning of symbol
b̲	Capitalize a letter.
∕	Lower-case a letter.
op̬e̬n	Insert a letter or punctuation mark.
℘	Delete a word, letter, or punctuation mark.
w⌢as	Close up a space.
and⧽in	Add a space.
⌒of	Transpose letters.
¶This	Begin a new paragraph.
⊙	Add a period.
⌃	Add a comma.
Truman's	Add an apostrophe.
stet never	Keep what is crossed out.

A Search For Stability (1945–1960)

33

CHAPTER OUTLINE

1 From War to Peace
2 The Cold War at Home
3 Stability Under Eisenhower
4 A Deceptive Calm

CHAPTER OBJECTIVES After completing this chapter, students should be able to
1. describe achievements of the Truman administration.
2. discuss the rise and fall of Joseph McCarthy.
3. describe American life in the 1950s.
4. explain early steps to end segregation.

The rookie could do it all. Smart, fast, and strong, he could hit to either field, bunt, play defense, and steal a base before the opposing pitcher knew what was happening. And yet, no ballplayer had ever been treated with such contempt. Opposing players scorned him and tried to push him off the base paths. When his team was on the road, fans jeered him and hotels and restaurants turned him away. Some of his own teammates would not speak to the newcomer.

The baseball outcast was Jackie Robinson. He was born in Georgia, had attended UCLA, and served in the army in World War II. His only offense was that he was black—the first black ballplayer in the major leagues. The year was 1947, and Branch Rickey, general manager of the Brooklyn Dodgers, had decided to make the first move toward ending segregation in baseball. But the first black player would need more than talent—he would need the character and restraint to endure the

inevitable snubs and insults without returning the hostility. Robinson succeeded on all counts.

In his first season, Robinson batted .297, led the National League in stolen bases, and was voted Rookie of the Year. By 1949, his batting average had soared to .342 and it remained over .300 for the next five years. Even more important, he won the respect of fans everywhere. By the end of his rookie year, national polls rated him the second most popular person in America, close behind singer Bing Crosby.

Jackie Robinson became a symbol of change for blacks in America. Having fought in the war and worked in wartime industries, blacks were no longer willing to be second-class citizens. The acceptance of Jackie Robinson and other black players who followed smashed the color barrier in sports. Meanwhile, the President, the Congress, and the Supreme Court were whittling away at segregation in other ways.

CHAPTER PREVIEW Ask students what television shows and movies from (or about) the 1950s they have seen. Have them brainstorm words or phrases that describe that era. Ask: How did the 1950s differ from today? Have the class review their list after reading this chapter.

1.

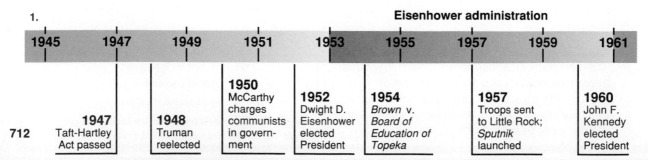

Eisenhower administration

| 1945 | 1947 | 1949 | 1951 | 1953 | 1955 | 1957 | 1959 | 1961 |

1947 Taft-Hartley Act passed

1948 Truman reelected

1950 McCarthy charges communists in government

1952 Dwight D. Eisenhower elected President

1954 *Brown* v. *Board of Education of Topeka*

1957 Troops sent to Little Rock; *Sputnik* launched

1960 John F. Kennedy elected President

1. TIME LINE QUESTION Ask: Who became President after Dwight D. Eisenhower?

for full employment after the war
REGISTER · VOTE
C I O POLITICAL ACTION COMMITTEE

Americans hoped for peace and prosperity after the sacrifices of World War II.
1. *This poster by Ben Shahn urges people to use the vote as a weapon to guarantee a booming economy in the postwar years.*

1. **VISUAL EVIDENCE** Remind students that other posters by Ben Shahn appear on pp. 651 and 693.

1 From War to Peace

READ TO UNDERSTAND

■ What economic problems the United States faced after the war.

■ How the government fought unemployment and high prices.

■ What the results of Truman's Fair Deal program were.

2. ■ *Vocabulary:* closed shop.

On August 14, 1945, automobile horns blared, church bells pealed, and crowds of people poured into the streets to celebrate—the war was over! But clouds still loomed on the horizon. Would the new President follow the path of Franklin Roosevelt and extend New Deal benefits? Or would he end the reforms, as many Roosevelt critics urged? Above all, Americans feared that the end of wartime spending might mean a return to the high unemployment of the depression years.

Economic Issues

After the war, the nation had to adapt the economy to the demands of peacetime. Two problems made the task more difficult: inflation and labor unrest.

During the war, a low unemployment rate, high wages, and shortages of consumer products had enabled Americans to save a total of $44 billion. Once the war was over, they were eager to spend those savings. But economic conditions frustrated their efforts. As wartime ceilings on prices and rents were lifted, inflation soared. In an example of the law of supply and demand at work, prices rose sharply as too much money chased too few goods. By 1948, prices were 48 percent higher than in 1945.

713

2. **VOCABULARY** Have students look up this term in the glossary before they begin reading.

1. **ECONOMICS** Have students compare and contrast the economic situation after World War II with that after World War I (pp. 569–570).

3. **CITIZENSHIP** Republicans also sponsored the Twenty-second Amendment to the Constitution, ratified in 1951, which limited a President to two full terms in office.

1. Workers had accepted limits on their way of life while the country was at war, but were no longer willing to do so when the war was over. As inflation cut into their buying power, workers demanded large wage increases. When employers resisted, the workers went on strike. The first strike occurred just one month after the war ended. In January 1946, strikes in the steel, automobile, meatpacking, and electrical appliance industries almost paralyzed the nation.

A walkout by railroad workers in May 1946 especially angered Truman. "What decent American would pull a strike at a time like this?" the President asked. After Truman's efforts to resolve the dispute failed, he stunned the nation by asking Congress for emergency power "to draft into the armed forces of the United States all workers who are on strike against their government."

The results were predictable. Under that kind of pressure, the union quickly agreed to end the strike. Both liberals and conservatives condemned the President's request as an abuse of the draft system, and labor leaders never quite forgave Truman.

For the most part, however, Truman worked hard to smooth the conversion to peacetime. To ease the reentry of American servicemen into civilian life, Congress had passed the Servicemen's Readjustment Act in 1944. Sometimes called the GI* Bill, it granted veterans a variety of benefits, including a year of unemployment insurance for veterans unable to find work, financial aid for veterans to attend college, and government loans for veterans to build homes and start businesses.

In the spirit of the New Deal, Truman also asked Congress to make "maximum employment, production, and purchasing power" a government responsibility and a national goal. Because of conservative opposition to increased government spending, however, the Employment Act passed in 1946 did little to

2. spur employment, although it did make "full employment" a national goal. Unemployment

rose to about 6 percent during the late 1940s, but did not return to the levels of the Great Depression. The act also set up a Council of Economic Advisers to guide the President on economic matters.

The Eightieth Congress

By the 1946 congressional elections, many voters blamed the President for inflation, shortages, and strikes. One critic joked, "To err is Truman." Using the campaign slogan, "Had enough?" the Republicans won a majority in both houses of Congress.

Most members of the new Eightieth Congress believed that much of Roosevelt's New Deal legislation had undermined private enterprise and initiative. As a result, Congress refused to pass new bills to provide federal funds for public housing or education and rejected a federally financed medical insurance plan. 3.

The most far-reaching action of the Eightieth Congress was the passage of the Taft-Hartley Act in 1947 over Truman's veto. The act reflected the anti-union feeling generated by the postwar strikes. It enabled the attorney general to apply for a court order to delay for 80 days any strike endangering the public's health or safety. Other provisions banned union contributions to political campaigns and the **closed shop,** in which all workers in a particular business or factory are required to be union members.

The Election of 1948

The Republicans' stunning gains in the 1946 congressional elections led them to expect victory in the presidential election of 1948. Once again, they nominated Governor Thomas E. Dewey of New York. Although Truman's sagging popularity seemed to indicate that he could be defeated easily, he won the Democratic nomination.

Truman's candidacy was badly hampered by a three-way split of the Democratic party. Southern Democrats, angry at Truman's support for civil rights legislation, broke with the Democratic party and established the States' Rights party. They nominated Gover-

---

*GI refers to a member of the United States armed forces. The term originated in soldiers' jokes that they, like their equipment, were "government

714   issue."

Printed by permission of the Estate of Norman Rockwell,
Copyright © 1948 Estate of Norman Rockwell

The 1948 election was a spirited race as President Truman carried out his promise to "give 'em hell." In the painting at left, by Norman Rockwell, a young
1. *couple argue over their choice for President. At right, a triumphant Harry Truman displays the Chicago* Tribune's *blooper. On the basis of polls and early returns, it too hastily declared Thomas Dewey the winner.*

1. **VISUAL EVIDENCE** The painting at the left appeared on a magazine cover only five days before the photo at the right was taken. The same newspaper is shown in both.

nor Strom Thurmond of South Carolina for President. Other Democrats, unhappy with Truman's containment policy, formed a new Progressive party and turned to Henry Wallace, Vice President during Franklin Roosevelt's third term. Truman supporters feared that Thurmond and Wallace would draw Democratic voters away from the President.

Undaunted, Truman crisscrossed the country by train on a "whistle-stop" campaign. Speaking to crowds from the rear car of the train, he made nearly 300 speeches in eight weeks. Truman attacked what he called the "do-nothing" Eightieth Congress and lashed out at the Republicans for opposing his social legislation.

On election day, few people doubted that Dewey would be the next President. As the night wore on, Dewey supporters celebrated the anticipated victory. The morning headline of the Chicago *Daily Tribune* proclaimed, "Dewey Defeats Truman." But the vote count
2. told a different story. Truman was the victor,

having achieved the political upset of the century.

The Fair Deal

After the election, the President declared that "Every segment of our population and every individual has the right to expect from his government a fair deal." Truman's Fair Deal included a broad package of reforms. He worked for passage of the National Housing Act of 1949, a measure that helped finance low-income housing. In the same year, Congress extended two New Deal measures. It amended the Fair Labor Standards Act (see page 635), raising the minimum hourly wage from 40 to 75 cents. The Social Security Act of 1950 increased the number of people covered under the old-age insurance provisions of the Social Security Act of 1935.

Despite these successes, Truman failed to accomplish some major objectives. Congress refused to repeal the Taft-Hartley Act **715**

2. **PRESIDENTS** Truman had won 49.5 percent of the popular vote to Dewey's 45 percent. In the electoral college, he had 303 votes to Dewey's 189.

1. **MAIN IDEA** Have students explain the main goals of the Fair Deal.

3. **BACKGROUND** Only two blacks served on the 15-member committee—Sadie T. Alexander and Dr. Channing Tobias.

and again rejected bills to provide federally financed health insurance. Bills to ban the

1. poll tax* and discrimination in employment were also defeated.

Extending Civil Rights

Racial segregation persisted after World War II. In the North, it took the form of de facto segregation, that is, segregation that existed in fact if not in law. In the South, Jim Crow laws separated the races. Blacks could not sit at the counters in most coffee shops. They attended segregated schools and were restricted to separate sections on buses and in other public facilities.

Yet some change was apparent. In 1947, Jackie Robinson became the first black to play on a major league baseball team. Blacks had previously been allowed to play only in all-black leagues. During and after the war, there were also public demonstrations against

---

*As you have read in Chapter 21, poll taxes were fees a person had to pay in order to vote. They had been used to prevent poor blacks from voting.

2. **BACKGROUND** Robinson also became the first black player elected to the Baseball Hall of Fame.

Jackie Robinson broke the "color line" when he became the first black major league baseball
2. *player, in 1947. For ten years, he played infield for the Brooklyn Dodgers, delighting fans with his daring style of play. Robinson's breakthrough opened the door for blacks in baseball and other sports.*

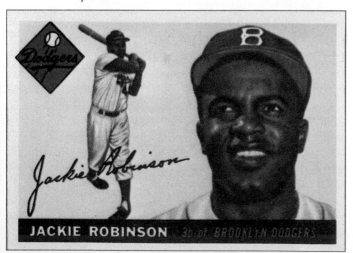

JACKIE ROBINSON 3b of BROOKLYN DODGERS

segregation in dining and recreational facilities.

Although Truman was unable to persuade Congress to pass civil rights legislation, he did use his influence as chief executive to fight discrimination against black Americans. The President publicly condemned lynchings, declaring that Americans could not tolerate "acts of intimidation and violence in our . . . communities." He also created the President's Committee on Civil Rights. Its 1947 report, 3. entitled *To Secure These Rights,* called for "the elimination of segregation from American 4. life."

In 1948, Truman issued an executive order proclaiming that it was "the policy of the President that there shall be equality of treatment and opportunity for all persons in the armed services." Although desegregation of the military proceeded slowly, by 1951 most units in the Korean War were integrated.

Truman also reaffirmed Franklin Roosevelt's executive order banning discrimination in firms doing business with the federal government. In 1952, the President created the Committee on Contracts Compliance to investigate cases of discrimination against minorities. The committee's lack of enforcement powers, however, limited its ability to curb discrimination. Nonetheless, President Truman's visible support of greater civil rights contributed to a movement that would grow stronger in the 1950s and 1960s.

See p. T131.

SECTION 1 REVIEW

1. **Identify:** (a) Taft-Hartley Act, (b) Thomas E. Dewey, (c) States' Rights party, (d) Progressive party.

2. **Define:** closed shop.

3. How did American workers react to postwar inflation?

4. What did the GI Bill of Rights provide?

5. List three measures of the Fair Deal.

6. **Critical Thinking** What means does a President have to overcome an uncooperative Congress?

4. **CITIZENSHIP** After receiving the report, Truman sent a message to Congress that said: "Unfortunately there still are examples—flagrant examples—of discrimination which are utterly contrary to our ideals."

1. **VOCABULARY** Have students look up these words in the glossary before they begin reading.

2. **ACTIVITY** Have students write and act out a dialogue between a member of HUAC and a person opposed to the "blacklist" system.

2 The Cold War at Home

READ TO UNDERSTAND

■ Why President Truman created the Loyalty Review Board.

■ Why Americans feared that communist agents were working within the United States.

■ How Senator Joseph McCarthy increased fears of communist subversion.

1. ■ *Vocabulary:* blacklist, McCarthyism.

On February 9, 1950, in a speech delivered at Wheeling, West Virginia, Senator Joseph R. McCarthy of Wisconsin waved a piece of paper before the crowd. He said it was a list of 205 state department officials who were members of the Communist party. McCarthy's charges were never proven, but for a time they made him one of the most powerful people in the United States. Like the "Red Scare" after World War I, such accusations played on Americans' fear of communist agents.

A Question of Loyalty

The tensions of the cold war fed the American public's fear of communism within the United States. Although the Communist party in the United States had little influence, many people worried that it might harbor Soviet spies.

Recognizing the public's concern, President Truman created the Loyalty Review Board in 1947 to guarantee the "unswerving loyalty" of all federal employees. Truman, himself, did not believe that there were disloyal employees. When the board revealed that some people of "doubtful loyalty" were on the federal payroll, Truman's critics charged that he was unmindful of the dangers of communism.

Un-American Activities Committee Other investigations increased public concern about the potential influence of communists in the United States. The House of Represen-

tatives had created the Committee on Un-American Activities (HUAC) in 1938 to investigate possible subversive activity by fascists or communists.

In 1947, under the control of conservative Republicans, HUAC launched a series of widely publicized and inflammatory investigations to reveal communist activity in the nation. The committee turned first to the movie industry. Although the committee produced little evidence, its hearings tarnished the reputations of a number of writers, producers, and performers. The committee also pressed film-makers to adopt a **blacklist,** a list of suspected communists, who 2. would be refused employment.

In 1948, HUAC began an investigation of disloyalty in government. Whittaker Chambers, a former communist agent, testified that a State Department official, Alger Hiss, had been a Communist party member during the 1930s. Furthermore, he testifed, Hiss had given him secret State Department documents. Chambers produced microfilms of the documents. Hiss, who denied the charges, was never tried for espionage. He was, however, convicted of perjury, or lying under oath, because he had denied knowing Chambers.

Spy Ring Revealed The disclosure in February 1950 that a respected British scientist, Dr. Klaus Fuchs, had betrayed atomic secrets to the Soviets heightened American fears of communist spies. Fuchs had been a member of the research team that developed the atomic bomb at Los Alamos, New Mexico. After his arrest, Fuchs testified that he had given the Soviets full details of the manufacture of the atomic bomb. He also agreed to reveal the workings of the Los Alamos spy ring.

Investigation of Fuchs's information led to the arrest of Ethel and Julius Rosenberg, an obscure New York couple, in the summer of 1950. The Rosenbergs were both members of the Communist party. The government claimed that the Rosenbergs had masterminded a conspiracy. Although the couple vehemently denied any guilt, a jury found them guilty of espionage. The judge sentenced 3. them to death, and they were executed on June 19, 1953.

717

McCarthyism

The widely publicized cases of Hiss and the Rosenbergs increased public anxiety about
1. communism and contributed to the rise to prominence of Republican Senator Joseph R. McCarthy from Wisconsin.

McCarthy's 1950 speech at Wheeling, West Virginia, received widespread coverage. In a later speech, he altered his charge, citing "205 bad security risks" in the State Department, rather than 205 Communist party members. Only 57 employees, he now said, were communists. In still other speeches, he used different numbers. Although he was unable to back his charges with proof, his fame grew. In the climate of the times, McCarthy attracted a large following of Americans. He persuaded millions that he was protecting national security.

During the next four years, McCarthy's claims grew more sensational. He charged that the Democratic party had been guilty of "twenty years of treason." He called for Truman's impeachment and maintained that General George C. Marshall had been "an instrument of the Soviet conspiracy." After the election of President Eisenhower, he hinted that the new President was not sufficiently anticommunist.

Soon people came to use the term **"McCarthyism"** to refer to the senator's technique of making sweeping accusations without producing conclusive evidence. For several years, McCarthy terrorized public life. The senator's influence was so great that few people risked publicly opposing him. The publicity he created and the accusations he made, though unproved, ruined the reputations of many public figures.

McCarthy's Fall

McCarthy's recklessness, which had been his source of strength, eventually caused his downfall. When his assistant, David Schine, was drafted into the army in 1954, McCarthy allowed his top aide, Roy Cohn, to press the army to make Schine an officer. The army rebuffed Cohn's efforts. In response, Senator McCarthy charged that the army base at Fort Monmouth, New Jersey, was infested with communists.

In April 1954, the Senate held televised hearings to air the differences between the senator and the army. On some days, as many

2. CRITICAL THINKING Ask: Why do you suppose McCarthy was able to carry on his attacks for so long before he was finally censured?

Senator Joseph McCarthy charged that communists had infiltrated many areas of American life. Here, the senator testifies at the Army-McCarthy hearings that brought about his downfall. At left is the army counsel, Joseph Welch. The
2. *televised hearings weakened McCarthy's popularity, and in December 1954, the Senate censured him for "conduct unbecoming a member."*

as 20 million people watched the Army-McCarthy hearings. The television cameras exposed McCarthy's abrasive manner. They also allowed the public to watch the army's lawyer, Joseph Welch, subject McCarthy's arguments to intense examination. To many Americans, McCarthy was revealed as a bully, not a hero.

In December 1954, the Senate passed a resolution condemning McCarthy for "conduct unbecoming a member." This censure resolution eroded McCarthy's popular appeal and his national political power.

See p. T131.

SECTION 2 REVIEW

1. **Identify:** Committee on Un-American Activities.

2. **Define:** (a) blacklist, (b) McCarthyism.

3. List two developments that created public concern about communism in the United States in the 1950's.

4. (a) How did Joseph McCarthy rise to national prominence? (b) What led to McCarthy's decline?

5. **Critical Thinking** How was McCarthy's reaction to communists similar to the Red Scare? How was it different?

3 Stability Under Eisenhower

READ TO UNDERSTAND

■ How President Eisenhower shifted the role of government in the American economy.

■ Why many Americans moved to the suburbs in the 1950s.

■ What role women played in American life and popular culture.

In 1952, a popular figure made his entrance on the American political scene. Former World War II General Dwight D. Eisenhower,

courted by both major parties, accepted the Republican nomination for President. Eisenhower's broad smile and friendly, secure manner were reassuring. His campaign slogan, "We Like Ike," summed up the feelings of the millions of Americans who went to the polls to elect the first Republican President in 20 years.

Victory for the Republicans

President Truman, his popularity greatly diminished, declined to enter the presidential contest in 1952. The Democratic party nominated Governor Adlai E. Stevenson of Illinois for President and Senator John J. Sparkman of Alabama for Vice President. The Republican party chose Dwight D. Eisenhower for President and Senator Richard M. Nixon of California as his running mate.

The race was uneven from the start. Adlai Stevenson was virtually unknown outside Illinois, and opponents labeled him an overly intellectual "egghead." Eisenhower, on the other hand, was a national hero. He had commanded the United States forces in Europe during World War II and the American occupation forces in Germany after the war. The Republicans fought a hard campaign. They accused Democrats of being "soft on communism" at home and blamed them for the stalemate in the war in Korea. Eisenhower promised to break the deadlock by going to Korea personally. (See page 704.)

Eisenhower won by a landslide, receiving nearly 34 million votes to 27 million for Stevenson. In 1956, Eisenhower would beat Stevenson again by an even larger margin.

As President, Eisenhower took a moderate political course. He condemned two of Senator McCarthy's assistants, although he refused to denounce McCarthy himself until the senator's power declined. While Eisenhower resisted demands to dismantle New Deal programs, he also refused to work for new social legislation.

Government and the Economy

President Eisenhower and the Republican-controlled Congress tried to reduce the government's role in the economy. Congress **719**

1. BACKGROUND As he left office, Eisenhower said, "America is today the strongest, the most influential, and most productive nation in the world."

limited federal aid for public housing and ended the wage and price controls that had been established by the Truman administration. Furthermore, Congress transferred offshore oil fields, previously under federal control, to state control. The secretary of agriculture reduced federal aid to farmers.

1.   The Eisenhower years were prosperous ones for most Americans. Unemployment remained at about 5 percent, and industrial wages increased slightly. Inflation lowered purchasing power but was not as serious as it had been in the years immediately following World War II. The gross national product, the total of goods and services produced by a nation during a given year, climbed until 1957, when the economy was hit by a serious recession, or economic downturn.

2. VISUAL EVIDENCE Another Norman Rockwell cover for the *Saturday Evening Post* appears on p. 715.

---

2.   *This cover for a 1957 issue of the* Saturday Evening Post *captures the dilemma of the period. Norman Rockwell's cover painting* After the Prom *portrays a teenage couple, beaming and innocent. Above them, the headline asks, "How Will Americans Behave If H-Bombs Fall?"*

The Saturday Evening

POST

May 25, 1957 · 15¢

I Call on Groucho
By PETE MARTIN

How Will America Behave
IF H-BOMBS FALL?

Printed by permission of the Estate of Norman Rockwell, Copyright © 1957 Estate of Norman Rockwell

3. GEOGRAPHY In the 1950s, 14 of the nation's 15 largest cities lost population. New York lost 2 percent, while its suburbs gained 58 percent. (movements)

Eisenhower's handling of the 1957–1958 recession reflected his belief that government should not control the economy. When unemployment reached 6.8 percent in 1958, Democrats called for New Deal-style public works projects to stimulate the economy. But Eisenhower refused, declaring that it was wrong to believe "that when the economy starts to slow up, only a vast outpouring of . . . tax dollars will pump us out of trouble."

Eisenhower maintained that increased federal spending would create a false prosperity and increase inflation. "Huge programs," he argued, "would have only enfeebled the economy." The economy slowly recovered, and by 1959 unemployment had returned to 5 percent.

Life in the 1950s

The 1950s were a period of great social change. One of the most pronounced shifts was the vast migration of people to the suburbs. New communities of mainly young married couples sprouted up almost overnight where cornfields had been.

    Several factors encouraged that growth. A postwar "baby boom" created a need for new housing, while the prosperity of the period enabled many people to buy their own homes. The GI Bill provided federal aid for home-loan mortgages for veterans. And a massive postwar road-building program linked suburban homes to city jobs.

    Managing a home in the suburbs and raising a family became the goal of many women during the 1950s. The suburbs, in turn, became increasingly self-contained, marking the beginning of the decline of the inner cities. While suburban residents of the 1920s had depended on the city for entertainment and shopping, the postwar suburbanite could find a wide variety of goods in nearby supermarkets.

    Television was especially important in reinforcing the view that women's role was in the home. The popularity of television had risen dramatically since the beginning of national network broadcasting in 1946. During the 1950s, almost 7 million television sets were sold each year. Most television com-

4. LOCAL HISTORY Have students research population changes in your area since 1945 and plot their findings on a graph.

The 1950s brought a change in American homes and American home life. After two decades of depression and war, the United States went on a building binge. Techniques of mass production helped produce suburbs like Levittown,
1. Pennsylvania, shown above. In their new suburban homes, people gathered around television sets. National network broadcasting began in 1946, and by the 1950s television had become the center of families' entertainment, as well as their window on the world.

1. **BACKGROUND** This Levittown and another in New York State were among the first totally preplanned suburban communities in the U.S. Levittown, N.Y., had 17,477 low-priced houses, all with the same floor plan.

mercials showed women doing work around the house. Popular programs such as *Father*
2. *Knows Best* seldom portrayed women who worked outside the home.

Religion was especially important in the United States during the 1950s. Church membership grew twice as fast as the population. The Reverend Norman Vincent Peale's best seller, *The Power of Positive Thinking,* stressed the need for religion in a successful life. Religion on television was also influential. Bishop Fulton J. Sheen was the host of a popular program, and the Reverend Billy Graham led a television crusade that brought his ministry national attention.

Among many Americans, increased religious feeling grew out of a search for stability and peace. Religious faith thus became closely linked with patriotism. As President Eisenhower stated, "Our government makes no sense unless it is founded in a deeply felt religious faith." In 1954, Congress added the words "under God" to the Pledge of Allegiance to the Flag.

See p. T132.

SECTION 3 REVIEW

1. **Identify:** Adlai E. Stevenson.

2. What was Eisenhower's view of the government's role in the economy?

3. List two factors that encouraged the growth of suburbs after World War II.

4. What was the goal of many American women during the 1950s?

5. **Critical Thinking** Why do you think both the Democrats and the Republicans wanted General Eisenhower as their presidential candidate?

721

2. **BIOGRAPHY** Lucille Ball (1911–1989) starred in the most popular comedy program of the 1950s, *I Love Lucy.* She played a housewife whose husband refused to let her work outside the home. But in real life, Ball became the first woman to own and run a Hollywood studio.

1. **VOCABULARY** Have students look up this term in the glossary before they begin reading.

2. **BIOGRAPHY** In 1967, Marshall became the first black Supreme Court justice.

4 A Deceptive Calm

READ TO UNDERSTAND

- What gains African Americans made during the 1950s.

- Why the launch of *Sputnik I* caused changes in American education.

- What new music and art forms developed in the 1950s.

1. ■ *Vocabulary:* civil disobedience.

Beneath the surface calm of the Eisenhower years, there flowed deep currents of change and discontent. African Americans pressed to overturn a system that kept them separate and unequal. Other Americans rebelled against the conformity they saw in middle-class suburbs. And while "baby boomers" rocked to the strains of Buddy Holly and Elvis Presley, their shocked parents suddenly discovered that the nation had lost its technological superiority and that its education system was in crisis.

GREAT DEBATE

Separate but Equal

In the 1896 case *Plessy* v. *Ferguson,* the Supreme Court had ruled that separate facilities for blacks and whites were constitutional, so long as the facilities for blacks were "equal" to those for whites. (See page 454.) For over 50 years, that decision had served as the legal basis for segregation. But African Americans chafed under the "Jim Crow" system that made them second-class citizens.

2. In the 1930s and 1940s, young Thurgood Marshall, an attorney for the National Association for the Advancement of Colored People (NAACP), traveled the South, providing legal help for blacks. He sued for equal pay on behalf of black teachers, and he defended a man accused of murder in a town where the Ku Klux Klan remained strong. Often, his office was the back seat of his beat-up '29 Ford.

For years, Marshall and the NAACP had opposed the "separate but equal" doctrine. By the late 1940s, the Supreme Court indicated some sympathy with the NAACP position. In cases involving the "white" law schools of the Universities of Texas and Oklahoma, the Court ruled against arrangements that were separate but clearly unequal. As a result, some blacks were admitted to several all-white southern colleges. But elementary and secondary schools remained segregated.

Then in the early 1950s, the NAACP filed suit against the Board of Education of Topeka, Kansas, on behalf of Linda Brown. The board had denied Brown admission to an all-white public elementary school near her home. The case reached the Supreme Court in 1954. As Brown's lawyer, Marshall charged that public school segregation violated the "equal protection" clause of the Fourteenth Amendment to the Constitution. Separate could never be equal, he argued, because the very act of segregating black children lowered their morale and motivation.

In its decision in *Brown* v. *Board of Education of Topeka,* the Supreme Court accepted Marshall's argument. "The doctrine of 'separate but equal' has no place in public education," it declared. In another decision a year later, the Court ordered school integration 3. to proceed "with all deliberate speed."

The Fight Against Segregation Continues

Encouraged by the Supreme Court decision, some southern blacks turned to public protest. The most effective challenge began in Montgomery, Alabama, in December 1955. Rosa Parks, a black woman tired after a long day's work, was arrested for refusing to give up her bus seat to a white man. Her arrest prompted local black citizens to organize a boycott of the bus line.

The boycott took a new turn with the arrival of the Reverend Martin Luther King, Jr., a young minister from Atlanta, Georgia. Like Marshall, King represented a new generation of college-educated black leaders who were unwilling to accept second-class citizenship. But King also drew on his Christian upbringing and his study of the Gospels. To battle segregation, he advocated the use of **civil disobedience,** that is, nonviolent opposition to unjust laws. He spoke boldly to his opponents, in the lilting rhythms of a south-

3. **BACKGROUND** Desegregation proceeded slowly. Ten years after *Brown,* only one percent of black students in the South attended school with white children.

1. **BACKGROUND** King said, "If we are arrested every day, if we are exploited every day, if we are trampled over every day, don't ever let anyone pull you so low as to hate them. We must use the weapon of love."

ern preacher. "In winning our freedom," he said, "we will so appeal to your heart and conscience that we will win you in the process."

The bus company finally agreed to integrate the buses and hire black drivers after the Supreme Court ruled that bus segregation violated the Constitution. Early on the morning of December 21, 1956, the Reverend King signaled the end of the boycott by boarding one of Montgomery's newly integrated buses.

Many white southern leaders were determined to resist integration. They viewed the Supreme Court's decision in *Brown* v. *the Board of Education* as a threat to state and local authority. President Eisenhower himself was reluctant to use federal power to force integration. But in 1957, a crisis in Little Rock, Arkansas, forced him to act.

In Little Rock, Governor Orval Faubus had called in the National Guard to prevent black students from attending Central High School. Since Faubus had defied a federal court order, Eisenhower felt he had to uphold the law. He also recognized that "our enemies are gloating over this incident and using it everywhere to misrepresent the whole nation." Eisenhower ordered federal troops to Little Rock to protect the black students from hostile crowds. Under the protection of the troops, a handful of black students entered Central High. A year later, however, Governor Faubus closed the school, and it did not reopen as an integrated school until 1959.

Meanwhile, protest against segregation increased as Eisenhower's term drew to a close. On February 1, 1960, a group of black college students refused to leave their seats when they were denied service at a lunch counter in Greensboro, North Carolina. After several months of "sit-ins," the lunch counter was integrated. Over time, the spread of sit-ins wore down resistance to integrated eating facilities. But protest would not end before both the South and the North experienced a virtual revolution in race relations. ■

One day in 1955, in Montgomery, Alabama, Rosa Parks refused to give up her bus seat to a white person. She was promptly arrested. A year later, a Supreme Court decision outlawed segregation on public transportation. Rosa Parks, above, enjoys the view from a front seat on a Montgomery bus.

3. **BACKGROUND** Parks later said, "I don't know why I wouldn't move. There was no plot or plan at all. I was just tired from shopping. My feet hurt."

boom" children created overcrowded classrooms and double session school days. Furthermore, American teachers were notoriously underpaid. In October 1957, educational reformers received a boost from an unexpected and unwelcome source. Americans were stunned to learn that the Soviet Union had launched the first satellite into orbit around the earth.

Superior technology had kept the United States ahead of the Soviet Union in the cold war. But the Soviet's successful launch of *Sputnik I* shattered Americans' confidence. Even worse, the first attempts by the United States to launch a satellite ended in failure. Not until January 1958 did the United States put *Explorer I* into orbit.

Why had the Soviets been able to leap ahead in space? Many people pointed an accusing finger at the American educational system. *Life,* a popular weekly magazine, ran

A Crisis in Education

During the 1950s, Americans had grown increasingly dissatisfied with the nation's educational system. The new wave of "baby

2. **READING** Interested students can read Althea Gibson's *I Always Wanted to Be Somebody.* Gibson was the first black woman to win a tennis championship at Wimbledon.

VOICES OF FREEDOM

The Struggle at Little Rock

Nine African American students, six young women and three young men, attempted to integrate Central High in Little Rock, Arkansas, in September 1957. Daisy Bates, the Arkansas State President of the NAACP, fought to keep the students in Central High. She guided and counseled the students until they all graduated.

The following passage is an account told to Daisy Bates by one student, Elizabeth Eckford, of what is was like to be a black student in Little Rock.

The crowd moved in closer and then began to follow me, calling me names. I still wasn't afraid. Just a little bit nervous. Then my knees started to shake all of a sudden and I wondered whether I could make it to the center entrance a block away. It was the longest block I ever walked in my whole life. . . .

I stood looking at the school—it looked so big! Just then the guards let some white students go through. The crowd was quiet. I guess they were waiting to see what was going to happen. When I was able to steady my knees, I walked up to the guard who had let the white students in. He didn't move. When I tried to squeeze past him, he raised his bayonet and then the other guards closed in and they raised their bayonets.

They glared at me with a mean look and I was very frightened and didn't know what to do. I turned around and the crowd came to-

ward me. They moved closer and closer. Somebody started yelling, "Lynch her! Lynch her!" I tried to see a friendly face somewhere in the mob—someone who maybe would help. I looked into the face of an old woman and it seemed a kind face, but when I looked at her again, she spat on me.

Adapted from Daisy Bates, *The Long Shadow of Little Rock* (New York: David McKay, 1962).

See p. T132.

1. How did some people in Little Rock react to school integration?

2. **Critical Thinking** What do you think motivated Elizabeth Eckford and other students like her to face a hostile crowd in order to attend an integrated school?

1. **ACTIVITY** Have students draw editorial cartoons about the integration of Central High in Little Rock.

a series of articles called "The Crisis in Education." The articles reported that American educational standards were "shockingly low." Many parents agreed that the schools had failed to challenge young people.

In response, many schools began to emphasize science and mathematics courses, believing these subjects held the key to victory in the "space race." Congress also passed the National Defense Education Act in 1958. The act provided federal aid to schools and colleges, especially for projects designed to improve instruction in science and math.

New Popular Culture

The undercurrents of change in society in the 1950s were reflected in music and art. During the 1930s and 1940s, popular music had been dominated by the smooth melodies of such "crooners" as Bing Crosby and Frank Sinatra and by the "big band" sounds

724

2. **PAST AND PRESENT** Ask: What subjects are emphasized in American education today? Why?

1. **BACKGROUND** Some people wanted to ban rock 'n' roll. But one rock group, Danny and the Juniors, responded by singing, "I don't care what people say/Rock 'n' roll is here to stay!"

of Glenn Miller and Duke Ellington. In the early 1950s, radio disk jockeys began playing a new type of music—rock 'n' roll. Rock 'n' roll blended elements from country-and-western music with the rhythm-and-blues songs of black artists. American teenagers loved the strong beat, simple harmonies, and loud volume.

Rock's driving beat stood in sharp contrast to the quiet tone of much of the Eisenhower era. Many adults were shocked by the slicked-back hairdos and hip-swinging performance styles of rock stars like Elvis Presley, Chuck Berry, and Buddy Holly. Some worried that rock music would contribute to teenage crime and immorality. Despite such objections, American youth quickly adopted rock. Rock stars became idols, and rock 'n' roll filled the air waves.

The visual arts also were transformed. American artists led an international movement away from realistic painting to a form known as abstract expressionism. Visitors to art galleries were often puzzled by what appeared to be little more than randomly splashed paint on canvases. But the abstract expressionists were serious artists. Some, such as Jackson Pollock, used swirling colors to absorb the viewer in emotion. Others offered interesting repetitions of colors and lines.

A Sense of Disillusionment

With prosperity, Americans could buy bigger cars, fancy lawnmowers, and elaborate kitchen appliances. But while most Americans seemed content with the society during the 1950s, others wondered whether bigger cars and greener front lawns concealed an emptiness. One group, labeled "beatniks," refused to conform to traditional ways of dressing, speaking, and acting. Wearing sweatshirts and jeans, they "hung out" in coffee houses, listening to "cool" jazz and poetry. Instead of striving for material success, they searched for spiritual inspiration. The leader of the "beat" movement was Jack Kerouac, who celebrated its code of freedom and poverty in a series of anti-establishment novels,

2. **BIOGRAPHY** Jackson Pollock (1912–1956) developed a technique of painting without a brush. Instead, he poured or dripped paint onto a canvas. Although most art critics admired Pollock's work, *Time* magazine called him "Jack the Dripper."

The new sound of the 1950s was rock 'n' roll. Like jazz, rock was an American musical form that appealed to people around the world. The British pop artist Peter Black used the decade's music idols as the subject of his painting
3. *Got a Girl. Pictured from left to right are Fabian, Frankie Avalon, Rick Nelson, Bobby Rydell, and Elvis Presley twice.*

3. **VISUAL EVIDENCE** Other early rock 'n' roll singers included Little Richard, Jerry Lee Lewis, Fats Domino, and the Everly Brothers.

1. READING Students might enjoy reading works by "beat generation" writers such as Kerouac or poet Allen Ginsberg.

1. the best-known of which is *On the Road* (1957).

Some social scientists warned that the growth of large businesses involved disturbing trends. William H. Whyte argued in his book *The Organization Man* (1956) that the

2. VISUAL EVIDENCE Have students suggest why paintings such as this one confused museum goers.

By the 1950s, a group of painters called abstract expressionists had become a major force in the art world. Because many of them worked or exhibited their art in New York City, they were also known as the New York School. One of the movement's most influential figures was Hans Hofmann, whose untitled painting from 1955 is shown here. Energetic brush strokes of vibrant color

2. *characterize his work. "At the time of making a picture," Hofmann has written, "I want not to know what I'm doing; a picture should be made with feeling, not with knowing."*

3. READING Interested students can read and report on Kennedy's Pulitzer Prize-winning book *Profiles in Courage.*

bureaucracies of big business stifled creativity and individuality. To rise on the corporate ladder, Whyte claimed, employees were encouraged to conform rather than to think for themselves.

Other critics voiced different concerns. David Riesman, a Harvard sociologist, suggested in his book *The Lonely Crowd* (1950) that Americans of the 1950s cared too much about other people's opinion of them. Instead of relying on their own judgment, they bowed to pressures from friends and neighbors.

In 1959, a scandal on a popular television quiz show convinced some critics that their concerns about American society were well founded. Charles Van Doren, a Columbia University instructor, revealed that the show's producers had given him the correct answers in advance. The producers had even coached him on how to make his answers entertaining.

Some Americans saw signs of national decline in the scandal. Novelist John Steinbeck claimed, "On all levels, American society is rigged. . . . I am troubled by the cynical immorality of my country. It cannot survive on this basis." An article in *Look* magazine lamented the emergence of the "freedom to chisel." Such feelings of disillusionment became a campaign issue in the presidential election of 1960.

The Election of 1960

In 1960, the Republicans nominated Vice President Richard M. Nixon as their presidential candidate and Henry Cabot Lodge, Jr., of Massachusetts as his running mate. The Democratic party nominated John F. Kennedy, a young senator from Massachusetts, for President, and Senator Lyndon B. Johnson of Texas as Vice President. 3.

Kennedy focused his campaign on the theme that the country had been drifting under Eisenhower. The senator promised to "get America moving again." In nationally televised debates between Kennedy and Nixon, Kennedy seemed confident and vigorous while Nixon appeared nervous and unsure of 4. himself.

4. BACKGROUND There were four televised debates. Nixon claimed that his refusal to wear makeup caused him to look unattractive and unhealthy to television viewers.

Televised debates between Richard Nixon (right) and John F. Kennedy (left) in 1960 reflected the growing importance of television. For the first time, millions of
1. voters could watch and compare the candidates as they discussed the issues. Kennedy's TV performance helped him win the election. But people who listened only on radio told pollsters that they believed Nixon had won the debate.

1. **BACKGROUND** Between 65 and 70 million Americans watched the first televised debate.

During the campaign, Kennedy argued that the Republicans had allowed the Soviet Union to achieve nuclear superiority over the United States. He promised to close the "missile gap" if elected President. Nixon campaigned on Eisenhower's record, stressing the peace and prosperity of the Eisenhower administration. Although neither candidate made an issue of the fact that Kennedy was Catholic, his religion probably gained him votes in eastern cities and hurt his candidacy in rural areas and in the West.

The election was extremely close. Kennedy received 34,227,096 popular votes to Nixon's 34,108,546, although in the electoral college Kennedy won by 303 to 219. At age 43, John F. Kennedy became the youngest
2. person and first Catholic elected President of the United States.

See p. T132.

SECTION 4 REVIEW

1. **Identify:** (a) Rosa Parks, (b) Martin Luther King, Jr., (c) *Sputnik I,* (d) beatniks, (e) Richard M. Nixon, (f) John F. Kennedy.

2. **Define:** civil disobedience.

3. What did the Supreme Court rule in *Brown* v. *Board of Education of Topeka?*

4. What protest tactics did black Americans use against segregation during the 1950s?

5. How did Congress react to the launch of *Sputnik I?*

6. **Critical Thinking** How did writers and artists of the 1950s reflect concerns similar to those expressed in the 1920s?

727

2. **PRESIDENTS** Theodore Roosevelt was younger when he assumed the office after McKinley's assassination, but Kennedy was the youngest elected President.

CHAPTER 33 REVIEW

Summary

1. **The transition to peacetime was troubled by unemployment, inflation, and strikes.** In 1947, Congress passed the Taft-Hartley Act, limiting the power of unions. Despite public discontent with the economy, Truman was elected in 1948. He instituted a Fair Deal program and worked against racial discrimination.

2. **The cold war contributed to anxieties about the threat of communism at home.** In an atmosphere of suspicion, Senator Joseph McCarthy charged that communists were active in government. His manner and his failure to produce hard evidence led to a decline in his popularity.

3. **Dwight Eisenhower, who was elected in 1952, pursued a moderate course.** He tried to reduce government's role in the economy but did not dismantle New Deal programs. Although a fairly stable period, the Eisenhower years saw significant social changes. Millions of Americans moved to the suburbs, and women resumed roles as homemakers.

4. **A 1954 Supreme Court ruling outlawing segregation in public schools encouraged blacks to protest their second-class status.** Dr. Martin Luther King, Jr., who advocated civil disobedience, rose to prominence by leading a bus boycott in Montgomery, Alabama. The Soviet launching of *Sputnik I* led to demands for educational change. In 1960, John F. Kennedy was elected President.

See p. T133.

Vocabulary

On a separate sheet of paper, write the word or words that best complete each of the following sentences.

1. The Servicemen's Readjustment Act was sometimes called the _____.

2. In a (an) _____, all workers are required to be union members.

3. A (An) _____ is a list of workers who would be refused employment.

4. The term _____ refers to the making of sweeping accusations, without evidence.

5. _____ is nonviolent protest against an unjust law or condition.

See p. T133.

Chapter Checkup

1. (a) What economic problems confronted the nation after World War II? (b) What were the basic causes of those problems? (c) What actions did the government take to try to solve them?

2. (a) Why did the Republicans win a majority in both houses of Congress in 1946? (b) What impact did the Eightieth Congress have on President Truman's legislative program? (c) What parts of Truman's Fair Deal did Congress pass after the 1948 election? (d) What parts of the Fair Deal failed to pass?

3. (a) How did segregation differ in the North and the South? (b) Describe how President Truman advanced the civil rights of black Americans.

4. Identify two events that caused the American public to become increasingly concerned about the potential danger of communist activity at home.

5. (a) What charges did Senator Joseph McCarthy make? (b) What effect did he have? (c) Why did he eventually cease to be a political force?

728

6. (a) Describe general economic conditions during President Eisenhower's administration. (b) How did Eisenhower react to the recession of 1957–1958? Why?

7. (a) Why did suburbs grow dramatically during the 1950s? (b) How were they different from the suburbs of the 1920s?

8. (a) How did the Supreme Court decision in *Brown* v. *Board of Education of Topeka* differ from the 1896 Court decision on racial segregation? (b) What arguments did the NAACP lawyer make against "separate but equal" facilities?

9. (a) Why was the launching of *Sputnik I* by the Soviet Union a shock to most Americans? (b) What did many people blame for that development?

10. Why were some people disillusioned by American society during the 1950s?

See p. T133.

Critical Thinking

1. **Recognizing Relationships** Review what you have learned about the attitude of the United States toward the Soviet Union after World War II. (See Chapter 32.) What relationship do you see between foreign policy and the domestic politics you studied in this chapter?

2. **Comparing** How did Eisenhower's attitude toward government involvement in the economy differ from Truman's?

See p. T133.

Connecting Past and Present

1. In the 1950s, new forms of music and visual arts began to become part of the popular culture. What new music and art forms have emerged in the past 10 to 15 years?

2. During the 1950s, the country was challenged by important economic issues. Compare the economic issues facing the country today with those of the 1950s.

See p. T133.

Developing Basic Skills

1. **Using Visual Evidence** A popular song in 1962 described suburban homes as little boxes that all looked the same. Study the photograph on page 721. (a) Using that picture as evidence, do you think the words of the song are accurate? (b) In what way is the evidence limited? (c) Find out if there are any suburbs that developed in the 1950s near where you live. Does the song accurately describe those suburbs?

2. **Collecting Evidence** Interview a friend or relative who lived during the 1950s. Ask the person what he or she remembers about the following topics: McCarthyism, television programs, the launching of *Sputnik,* the beginning of rock 'n' roll. Compare the person's recollections with what you have read in the text. (a) How are they similar? (b) How are they different?

WRITING ABOUT HISTORY

Informal Documentation

As you recall, there are times when you must cite a source used for a research paper. (See page 609.) The two common types of citations are informal citations and footnotes. Informal citations are placed immediately after the facts or quote you have taken from a source. To write informal citations, include in parentheses the author's name, the title of the source, and the page number where the information can be found. For example: (Thomas Bailey, *Diplomatic History of the United States,* 316–317). Of course, each of the sources you identify must also appear in your bibliography.

Practice: Using your textbook as your source, write an informal citation.

Unit Ten TOWARD THE NEXT CENTURY

1963 Martin Luther King, Jr., led a huge demonstration in Washington, D.C., to demand an end to discrimination.

1972 Richard Nixon's visit to China opened the door for improved relations.

	1960	1965	1970	1975
POLITICS AND GOVERNMENT		**1963** John Kennedy assassinated		**1973** Watergate scandal comes to light
SOCIETY AND CULTURE		**1965** Voting Rights Act allows federal officials to register voters	**1971** Twenty-sixth Amendment ratified	
ECONOMICS AND TECHNOLOGY	**1962** John Glenn orbits the earth			**1973** Alaskan Pipeline is approved
WORLD EVENTS	**1961** Bay of Pigs invasion	**1967** Six-Day War breaks out		

Eisenhower	Kennedy	Johnson	Nixon	Ford

1964 The Beatles were one of the British rock groups that revolutionized American music.

The Vietnam Veterans Memorial is enscribed with the names of all Americans missing or killed in Vietnam.

730

1986 The centennial of the Statue of Liberty showed the renewed patriotism of the late 1980s.

Interest in physical fitness extends to the highest levels of government.

1975	1980	1985	PRESENT

1978 Camp David agreement signed

1984 Reagan reelected President

1988 George Bush elected President

1976 Nation celebrates bicentennial

1981 Sandra Day O'Connor appointed to Supreme Court

1980 Inflation rate is 13.5 percent

1989 Massive oil spill in Alaskan waters

1975 Helsinki Accords spell out human rights standards

1987 U.S. and U.S.S.R. agree to INF Treaty

Carter	Reagan	Bush

1988 The Republican National Convention, held in New Orleans, nominated George Bush for the presidency.

Lasers are important to many scientific advances, from medicine to music.

731

A Turbulent Decade

34

(1960–1969)

CHAPTER OBJECTIVES After completing this chapter, students should be able to

1. describe American foreign relations under John Kennedy.
2. explain the goals and accomplishments of the New Frontier and Great Society.
3. discuss the rights movements of minorities and women.
4. describe U.S. involvement in Vietnam and the domestic reaction to it.

CHAPTER PREVIEW Read to students these words from John Kennedy's inaugural address: "Let the word go forth from this time and place . . . that the torch has been passed to a new generation of Americans . . ." Then have them read the paragraphs below and study the pictures and captions in this chapter. Ask: Were most Americans in a hopeful mood in 1960? What events altered this mood?

For days, the President had tried to preserve an atmosphere of calm. But as he prepared to go before the television cameras on that October 22, 1962, John F. Kennedy knew that what he was about to say would push the world dangerously close to an all-out nuclear war.

"This government, as promised, has maintained the closest surveillance of the Soviet military build-up on the island of Cuba," he said. "Within the past week, unmistakable evidence has established the fact that a series of offensive missile sites is now in preparation on that imprisoned island. The purpose of these bases can be none other than to provide a nuclear strike capability against the United States. . . ."

The President declared that the presence of missiles in Cuba could not be tolerated. "I have directed the Armed Forces to prepare for any eventualities," he warned. "It shall be the policy of this nation to regard any nuclear missile launched from Cuba against any nation in the Western Hemisphere as an attack by the Soviet Union on the United States, requiring a full retaliatory response upon the Soviet Union. . . . We will not prematurely or unnecessarily risk the costs of worldwide nuclear war in which even the fruits of victory would be ashes in our mouth, but neither will we shrink from that risk at any time it must be faced."

Kennedy's words shook the country. What would the Soviets do? Would they back down and remove the missiles or would they risk nuclear war? Five days later, Nikita Khrushchev, the Soviet leader, announced that the missiles would be removed. The world breathed a collective sigh of relief as the threat of war was averted.

The Cuban missile crisis clearly demonstrated the dangerous world tensions of the 1960s. Before the close of this stormy era, one President would be assassinated and another's political career would be destroyed by intense opposition to his foreign policy.

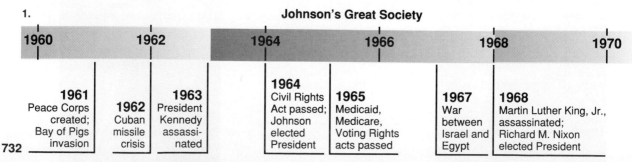

1.

Johnson's Great Society

1960	1962	1964	1966	1968	1970

1961
Peace Corps created; Bay of Pigs invasion

1962
Cuban missile crisis

1963
President Kennedy assassinated

1964
Civil Rights Act passed; Johnson elected President

1965
Medicaid, Medicare, Voting Rights acts passed

1967
War between Israel and Egypt

1968
Martin Luther King, Jr., assassinated; Richard M. Nixon elected President

732

1. TIME LINE QUESTION Ask: What acts were passed in the first three years of Johnson's Great Society?

Competition with the Soviet Union extended into space. After a slow start, the United States launched its own space exploration program. Here, *Apollo 8* lifts off

1. from Kennedy Space Center in Florida, carrying astronauts Frank Borman, James Lovell, and William Anders.

1. **VISUAL EVIDENCE** The *Saturn V* space vehicle in this photograph was 363 feet high.

1 Increased World Tension

READ TO UNDERSTAND

■ Why the Bay of Pigs invasion failed.

■ How President Kennedy responded to crises in Cuba and Berlin.

■ How the Cuban missile crisis contributed to the adoption of a nuclear test-ban treaty.

2. ■ *Vocabulary:* strategic forces.

"Ask not what your country can do for you— ask what you can do for your country," declared John F. Kennedy on the blustery, cold day of his inauguration. The new President thrilled Americans with the promise that the nation would "pay any price, bear any burden, meet any hardship, support any friend, oppose any foe to assure the survival and success of liberty." During Kennedy's presidency, international crises tested this resolve and threatened to change the cold war into a hot one.

The Kennedy Team

John Fitzgerald Kennedy brought to the White House a combination of youth, intelligence, and ideals, tempered by an eye for practical politics. Kennedy was the youngest person ever elected President, however, and he recognized that his youth might work against him. As a result, he chose his cabinet and advisers carefully. He appointed respected 3. experts from the military and from the academic world, including a few Republicans.

733

2. **VOCABULARY** Have students look up this term in the glossary before they begin reading.

3. **READING** Interested students might read parts of *The Best and the Brightest* by David Halberstam, which chronicles the Kennedy years.

The youngest person ever elected President,
1. John Kennedy radiated a special charm and appeal. He used a rocker in his White House office to ease recurring back pain resulting from football and war injuries. After the White House released photographs like this one, sales of rocking chairs soared.

1. **BACKGROUND** In his inaugural address, Kennedy stressed that he was the first President born in this century.

The man who most symbolized the energy of the new administration was Secretary of Defense Robert McNamara. McNamara had been part of a young group of managers known as the "whiz kids," who helped rebuild the Ford Motor Company during the 1950s. McNamara was president of Ford when Kennedy asked him to become a member of the Cabinet.

A Shift in Foreign Relations

President Eisenhower had followed a moderate defense policy. Upon leaving office, he warned against the "unwarranted influence" of the "military-industrial complex," as he labeled the military establishment and the industries that support it.

During the 1960 campaign, however, John Kennedy spoke of a "missile gap." He claimed that the Soviet Union had a better supply of military weapons, especially long-range missiles. Consequently, once in office, he stepped up military spending.

2. **ACTIVITY** If possible, you might arrange for a former Peace Corps volunteer to speak to the class about his or her experiences in the program.

The rivalry with the Soviet Union was closer to home than ever before. In 1959, a revolution in Cuba had established a pro-Soviet government on that island. Premier Khrushchev pledged support for such "wars of liberation." As a counterbalance, President Kennedy wanted United States armed forces prepared to combat Soviet-supported revolutions. To this end, the Kennedy administration developed **strategic forces,** specially trained units that could be moved quickly anywhere in the world they were needed. They were an attempt to move away from Dulles's massive retaliation policy.

But Kennedy's response to the Soviet challenge went beyond military measures. He proposed a new type of foreign aid through the Peace Corps. Peace Corps volunteers would teach or give technical advice in the developing countries of Africa, Asia, and South America. President Kennedy hoped that 2. such aid would convince these nations that democracy offered the best way to achieve peace, stability, and economic growth.

In an attempt to improve relations with Latin America, the administration organized the Alliance for Progress in 1961. The United States pledged over $20 billion in aid over a ten-year period. Latin American nations were to invest some $80 billion of their own funds for economic development.

In return for aid, members of the Alliance agreed to make their economic and social systems more democratic, and thereby reduce the chances of violent revolution. President Kennedy warned that "those who make peaceful revolution impossible will make violent revolution inevitable." Although 3. few governments wanted to carry out reforms, the Alliance for Progress did improve the image of the United States in Latin America.

Trouble in the Bay of Pigs

Whatever goodwill the United States gained through the Alliance for Progress, however, was soon lost in an attempt to overthrow Castro.

When President Kennedy came into office, he was told that the Central Intelligence Agency (CIA) had already begun to train anti-Castro Cuban exiles to overthrow the Cuban government. The plan was to land a secret

3. **CRITICAL THINKING** Have students restate Kennedy's statement in their own words. Ask: Do any recent events illustrate the point Kennedy was making?

1. invasion force trained in Guatemala at the Bay of Pigs in Cuba. Anti-Castro forces in the mountains were to join the assault group and march on Havana, the capital.

Convinced that Castro lacked the support of the Cuban people, Kennedy overcame his doubts and let the invasion begin on April 17, 1961. It was a disaster. The "secret" training activities in Guatemala had been reported in *The New York Times,* and Cuban intelligence officials had apparently briefed the military about the invasion. Consequently, the Cubans were well prepared. In addition, Kennedy, who wanted to be able to deny direct involvement, had canceled promised American air support. And no anti-Castro uprising supported the invaders. Within four days, the mission had collapsed and some 1,200 invaders were captured.

Kennedy was upset and embarrassed by the episode. But he took full responsibility. "All my life, I've known better than to depend on the experts," he remarked privately. "How could I have been so stupid, to let them go ahead?" The failure of the Bay of Pigs demonstrated the difficulties of using covert military tactics to gain broad political goals.

Growing Tension in Europe

In June 1961, Kennedy traveled to Vienna, Austria, to meet with Premier Nikita Khrushchev. He encountered a demanding Soviet leader. Too many East Germans were crossing over into West Berlin, Khrushchev complained. And NATO forces posed a threat to East Germany and should leave West Berlin before the end of the year. If his demands were not met, Khrushchev threatened, the Soviet Union would sign a separate peace treaty with East Germany. Western access to Berlin would then have to be cleared with East Germany, and the Soviet Union implied it would protect East Germany from attack.

Khrushchev may have challenged Kennedy because he considered the President weak in light of the Bay of Pigs. Kennedy, however, did not back down. Returning home, 2. he called up reserve military units and asked Congress for money to enlarge the armed forces. He also launched a program to build fallout shelters throughout the United States in case of a nuclear attack.

Then suddenly, on August 13, the East Germans built a wall between East and West Berlin. The wall effectively cut off the flow of East Germans to the West, and tensions eased somewhat. It also proved to be a valuable propaganda weapon for the western powers. The Berlin Wall was a sharp reminder that the communist governments of eastern Europe had to use force to prevent their people from running away.

In 1963, President Kennedy visited West Berlin. He was greeted by enormous crowds who heard him declare, *"Ich bin ein Berliner"*

In 1961, the East German authorities built a high, bleak wall between East and West Berlin. Their aim was to put an end to the steadily increasing flow of East Germans to the West. In a demonstration of support for the people of the divided
3. *city, in 1963, President Kennedy stood before a cheering crowd at the Berlin Wall and declared in German, "Ich bin ein Berliner" ("I am a Berliner").*

("I am a Berliner"). With that statement, he assured the residents of West Berlin that the United States would maintain its support of the city.

The Cuban Missile Crisis

In the midst of the heightened tensions over Berlin, President Kennedy learned that Premier Khrushchev had placed offensive weapons in Cuba. Aerial photographs revealed the construction of missile launch pads there.

The President immediately called together a group of advisers to consider a response. For six days, while his staff weighed alternatives, the President carried on as if nothing had happened. Finally, his advisers presented Kennedy with two options: blockade Cuba or launch an air strike against the missile sites.

On October 22, 1962, the President told a shocked nation of the presence of the launch pads. (See page 732.) He informed the public that he had ordered a naval blockade to prevent further entry of offensive weap-
1. ons into Cuba. He had also placed the armed forces on full alert.

As Soviet ships steamed steadily toward Cuba, tensions mounted. If the ships ran the blockade, would the Americans attack? And would the Soviets then strike back? Suddenly, the ships stopped. "We're eyeball to eyeball," reported Secretary of State Dean Rusk, "and I think the other fellow just blinked." Convinced of American determination, Premier Khrushchev ordered the ships to turn back and the missile bases to be taken apart. In
2. return, the United States promised that it would not invade Cuba.

The crisis was over, but the prospect of a nuclear war had been sobering indeed. To help avoid similar confrontations in the future, the Americans and Soviets set up a direct telephone link, known as the "hot line," between Washington and Moscow.

The crisis also raised interest in limiting tests of nuclear weapons. In July 1963, the Soviet Union and the United States concluded a treaty banning nuclear tests in the atmosphere. As President Kennedy proclaimed:

If we cannot end now all our differences, at least we can help make the world safe for

diversity. For . . . we all inhabit this small planet. We all breathe the same air. We all cherish our children's future. And we are all mortal.

Although the treaty still allowed underground tests, it helped ease international tensions that had plagued the previous two decades.

See p. T134.

SECTION 1 REVIEW

1. **Identify:** (a) Robert McNamara, (b) Peace Corps, (c) Alliance for Progress.

2. **Define:** strategic forces.

3. (a) Why did Kennedy agree to go forward with the Bay of Pigs invasion? (b) What was the result?

4. What two actions did President Kennedy's advisers suggest as possible responses to the building of missile bases in Cuba?

5. **Critical Thinking** What do you think were the benefits of having the Peace Corps made up of volunteers?

2 The New Frontier

READ TO UNDERSTAND

■ What goal President Kennedy set for the exploration of space.

■ How President Kennedy tried to control inflation.

■ What advances were made in civil rights during the Kennedy administration.

Undaunted by international tensions, President Kennedy called on the nation to raise its sights. Recalling the past triumphs of Americans in forging a nation and conquering the wilderness, Kennedy challenged Americans to find a "new frontier." As President, he led the way, tackling the problems of the exploration of space, economic development, and civil rights.

1. **VOCABULARY** American space pilots are called *astronauts,* from the Greek words for star and sailor. Soviet space pilots are called *cosmonauts.*

The Frontier of Space

The Soviet Union launched numerous satellites in the late 1950s, pulling ahead in the race to explore space. In April 1961, the Soviets captured the headlines, when Yuri Gagarin (YOO ree guh GAHR uhn) became the first person to orbit the earth. One month later, United States Navy Commander Alan Shepard, Jr., rode a tiny Mercury capsule in a suborbital flight of 300 miles (about 500 kilometers). Shortly afterward, President Kennedy pledged the United States to "landing a man on the moon and returning him safely to earth" by 1970.

On February 20, 1962, Lieutenant Colonel John Glenn was launched into orbit from Cape Canaveral, Florida. In contrast to Soviet secrecy about its space program, the National Aeronautics and Space Administration (NASA) permitted live press and television coverage of its manned flights. Millions of Americans heard the slow countdown, watched the rocket's takeoff, and followed Glenn's conversations with ground control. Glenn orbited the earth three times and returned home safely in what he called a "fireball of a ride."

Other manned and unmanned launches followed. Telstar, a commercial communications satellite, orbited the earth, relaying live television broadcasts over long distances. The Mariner series of space probes came within 21,000 miles (34,000 kilometers) of the planet Venus and radioed back information. With each success, interest in space grew.

Economic Policies

Having come into office while the economy was sluggish and unemployment was increasing, President Kennedy tried a variety of measures to "get the country moving again." An alliance of Republicans and conservative Democrats in Congress resisted the President's attempts to increase government spending for education, but Congress did agree to raise the minimum wage. It also began a debate on a tax cut that Kennedy proposed. Many economists claimed that lower taxes would stimulate the economy by leav-

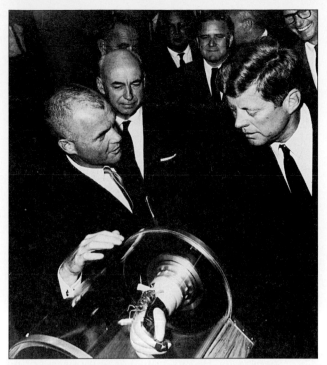

On a tour of the NASA installation in Houston, Texas, astronaut John Glenn showed President Kennedy how a space glove operated. The President strongly supported the United States space program.

2. **PAST AND PRESENT** Glenn was elected to the U.S. Senate from Ohio in 1974. He won reelection in 1980 and 1986.

ing the taxpayer more money to spend on consumer products.

Government spending on space and defense helped spur the economy but also contributed to inflation. To control inflation, Kennedy set "wage-price guideposts" that he hoped business and labor would follow. He was particularly concerned about wages and prices in the steel industry. Because steel was used in many other industries, an increase in steel costs would affect the entire economy.

In April 1962, the administration persuaded steelworkers to accept a contract with a modest wage increase. The union agreed, with the understanding that the steel companies would not raise steel prices. But U.S. Steel and other major producers surprised the President by announcing a steep price increase. Kennedy condemned the steel companies' actions. The Defense Department then announced it would purchase steel only from those companies that had not raised prices.

Many smaller companies kept their prices down. This forced other producers to return to the old price levels. Kennedy had won a

3. **ECONOMICS** Have students investigate the 1981 tax cuts urged by the Reagan administration and report on how they affected the economy and the federal deficit.

major battle against inflation, but his attack on the steel companies damaged administration relations with big business.

President Kennedy also urged Congress to pass several programs designed to reduce poverty. These programs were aimed especially at urban slums and poor rural areas such as Appalachia, an area stretching south from Pennsylvania through West Virginia, Kentucky, Tennessee, and Alabama. Local residents were to help plan economic programs suited to local needs.

Civil Rights

Although Kennedy had long supported civil rights legislation, as President he moved cautiously because he needed the backing of southern Democrats in Congress for other programs. He did, however, support a voting rights bill and a proposal for a Twenty-fourth Amendment to the Constitution, prohibiting poll taxes. This amendment was passed in August 1962 and ratified in 1964. (See page 895.) Kennedy also appointed blacks to key positions, including Robert Weaver as head of the Housing and Home Finance Agency and Thurgood Marshall as a federal judge.

In February 1960, rather than serve these black customers, this store in North Carolina closed its lunch counter. The sit-in was a popular civil rights
2. *tactic because it was easy to use anywhere. Civil rights protestors held sit-ins at segregated rest rooms, bus station waiting rooms, movie theaters, and hotel lobbies.*

Tactics of Nonviolence Many civil rights leaders were unhappy with the slow pace of reform. Unwilling to wait for the government, they adopted the tactic of nonviolent opposition advocated by the Reverend Martin Luther King, Jr. His organization, the Southern Christian Leadership Conference, was joined by others, including the Congress of Racial Equality (CORE) and the Student Nonviolent Coordinating Committee (SNCC). The National Association for the Advancement of Colored People continued to work through the courts, where it filed suits against acts of discrimination.

As you have read in Chapter 33, a movement against segregated public facilities in the South began in 1960, when a group of young blacks refused to leave an "all-white" lunch counter. Other civil rights workers—both black and white—took up the struggle. "Freedom riders" refused to be segregated on buses and trains. Groups marched to protest the denial of voting rights. Protestors led campaigns to desegregate schools. In the North, advocates of civil rights organized rent strikes to protest poor housing conditions and boycotted stores that refused to hire blacks.

These nonviolent tactics often produced a violent response. Angry mobs attacked buses of freedom riders. Police sometimes scattered protestors with water hoses, police dogs, or electric cattle prods. Civil rights workers were imprisoned and fined. Sometimes, they deliberately sought arrest to attract national attention to their cause.

Government Action Attorney General Robert Kennedy, the President's brother, dealt firmly with violations of civil rights. In 1961, he sent federal troops to Alabama to protect blacks trying to integrate buses and trains. He personally supervised the case of James Meredith, a black Air Force veteran who tried to enroll at the all-white University of Mississippi. Riots broke out when Meredith registered for classes in 1962. The attorney general ordered 5,000 federal troops to the campus to restore order. Several hundred 1. soldiers remained there until Meredith graduated.

In Alabama, Governor George Wallace got national attention by personally barring the door as federal marshals tried to escort black

I Have a Dream

The throng of over 200,000 people gathered in front of the Lincoln Memorial on August 28, 1963, was the largest civil rights demonstration of the decade. As Martin Luther King, Jr., rose to speak, the crowd hushed. The great civil rights leader stirred African Americans and white Americans alike with what many think was his greatest speech. A portion of it is printed below.

I say to you today, my friends, that in spite of the difficulties and frustrations of the moment I still have a dream. It is a dream deeply rooted in the American dream.

I have a dream that one day this nation will rise up and live out the true meaning of its creed: "We hold these truths to be self-evident; that all men are created equal."

. . . I have a dream that my four little children will one day live in a nation where they will not be judged by the color of their skin but by the content of their character. . . .

When we let freedom ring, when we let it ring from every village and every hamlet, from every state and every city, we will be able to speed up that day when all of God's children, black men and white men, Jews and Gentiles, Protestants and Catholics, will be able to join hands and sing in the words of the old Negro

spiritual, "Free at last! Free at last! Thank God Almighty, we are free at last!"

See p. T135.

1. What quotation from the Declaration of Independence did Dr. King use to remind his audience that some Americans still did not enjoy their basic rights?

2. **Critical Thinking** Judging from this speech, how do you think Dr. King would have responded to those radical black leaders who proposed that blacks separate from white society?

1.

---

1. **DISCUSSION** Play a recording of King's speech to the class and discuss how his delivery adds to the impact.

student Autherine Lucy into the formerly all-white University of Alabama. Like Meredith, Lucy continued her education with the protection of federal troops.

Proposing Legislation In June 1963, President Kennedy presented Congress with a proposal for a comprehensive civil rights program. The proposed legislation would ban discrimination in employment, in public accommodations, in voting, and in state programs receiving federal aid. In a television message, the President asked:

> Are we to say to the world—and much more importantly, to each other—that this is the land of the free except for the Negroes; that we have no second-class citizens, except Negroes; that we have no class or caste system, no ghettos, no master race, except with respect to Negroes?

March on Washington On August 28, 1963, more than 200,000 blacks and whites gathered in Washington, D.C., to demand racial equality. Waving banners and singing hymns, they listened as civil rights leaders called for justice. The high point of the day was a ringing speech of hope by Martin Luther King, Jr. "I have a dream," he proclaimed, and then painted a picture of a nation where all people were equal and he and his children would be "free at last!"

2.

Tragedy in Dallas

On November 22, 1963, President Kennedy arrived in Dallas, Texas, on a political tour. As the presidential motorcade proceeded to the center of the city, the crowd was friendly and enthusiastic. The President and his wife,

739

2. **READING** Interested students can read part of one of King's books, such as *Stride Toward Freedom* and *Why We Can't Wait*.

On the plane carrying the body of John Kennedy to Washington, Lyndon Johnson
1. took the oath of office as President. With his hand on Kennedy's Bible, Johnson
was sworn in by Judge Sarah T. Hughes, with Lady Bird Johnson to his right and
Jacqueline Kennedy to his left. Afterward, the new President thanked Mrs.
Kennedy for being present. "You're so brave to do this," he said.

1. **VISUAL EVIDENCE** Only one cameraperson—White House photographer Cecil Stoughton—
recorded Johnson's swearing-in. This painting is based on that photograph.

Jacqueline, waved and smiled warmly in response.

Suddenly, rifle shots rang out. The President lurched, then slumped in his seat. Amid the ensuing confusion, the presidential limousine sped to Parkland Memorial Hospital, but it was too late—John F. Kennedy was dead. That afternoon, aboard an Air Force jet bound for Washington, Vice President Lyndon Johnson was sworn in as the thirty-sixth President of the United States.

2. In Dallas, Lee Harvey Oswald was arrested and charged with the assassination. Two days later, millions watching a live television broadcast gasped in disbelief as they saw Oswald, under police escort, shot to death by Jack Ruby, a local nightclub operator.

The nation and the world viewed the events of that November weekend with horror and grief. Americans wept as television cameras followed the flag-draped casket carrying the President's body to Arlington National Cemetery. Although President Kennedy had not been in office long enough to test the full measure of his leadership, his vigor and idealism had kindled a spirit of hope in many Americans.

See p. T135.

SECTION 2 REVIEW

1. **Identify:** (a) Alan Shepard, (b) John Glenn, (c) Telstar, (d) James Meredith, (e) George Wallace.

2. What goal did Kennedy set for the exploration of space?

3. (a) How did Kennedy try to control inflation? (b) What industry was he especially concerned about? Why?

4. Describe the tactics used by civil rights supporters in the early 1960s.

5. **Critical Thinking** Why would the term the "new frontier" have special symbolism for Americans?

740

2. **BACKGROUND** The Warren Commission, headed by Chief Justice Earl Warren, investigated
the assassination and concluded that Oswald had acted alone and not as part of a conspiracy.

1. **PRESIDENTS** In 1958, LBJ wrote, "Government can waste the people's resources by inertia quite as much as by vigor." As they read further, ask students to consider how Johnson's policies illustrate this belief.

3 Building the Great Society

READ TO UNDERSTAND

■ What Kennedy programs were enacted during the Johnson administration.

■ What programs President Johnson enacted to help the poor and elderly.

■ How President Johnson expanded black voting rights.

Lyndon Johnson, the new President, owed his success to a shrewd political mind and his celebrated powers of persuasion. Senator George Smathers of Florida recalled the "Johnson treatment" as being like "a great overpowering thunderstorm that consumed you as it closed in around you." President Johnson used his persuasive abilities to carry through the program that John F. Kennedy had begun earlier and to win support for his own program, which he called the "Great Society."

The Great Society, stated Johnson, "asks not only how much, but how good; not only how to create wealth, but how to use it; not only how fast we are going, but where we are headed."

The Great Society Begins

When Johnson arrived in Washington on November 22, 1963, he said simply, "I'll do my best. That's all I can do." It was a rare moment of modesty for this powerful man.

Few leaders in Washington had more experience for the job of President than Lyndon Johnson. First sent to the House of Representatives by Texas in 1937, Johnson was elected to the Senate in 1948 and by 1953 was Senate Democratic minority leader. When Johnson became Senate majority leader in 1958, he was perhaps the most influential politician on Capitol Hill.

As President, Johnson immediately urged Congress to pass the major bills that had been proposed by the Kennedy administra-tion. He won over opponents to Kennedy's tax cut proposal by promising a more effi-cient federal budget. And he successfully urged Congress to pass Kennedy's civil rights program as the Civil Rights Act of 1964.

President Johnson called on the nation to join him in a "War on Poverty." In 1964, some 30 million Americans—16 percent of the population—lived below the "poverty line," the minimum income level people need to subsist. The keystone of Johnson's program to help the poor was the Economic Opportunity Act of 1964. The act provided job training programs, loans to encourage rural farm cooperatives and urban businesses, and aid to migrant laborers. It also created VISTA (Volunteers in Service to America), a domestic Peace Corps.

3. **VISUAL EVIDENCE** This section of Kentucky was one of the poorest in the U.S. in the 1960s.

"This administration," announced President Johnson in 1964, "here and now, declares unconditional war on poverty in America." In rural areas such as Appalachia, people had not felt the effects of prosperity. Still, this elderly woman shows her self-reliance and pride as she tends her vegetable garden.

2. **BACKGROUND** Five days after the assassination, Johnson told Congress that the best way to honor Kennedy's memory was to pass the tax bill and Civil Rights Act.

1. **TECHNOLOGY** One Johnson commercial did not even mention Goldwater. It showed a child pulling petals from a flower. Her counting turned into a missile countdown and a mushroom cloud suddenly filled the TV screen.

A Democratic Landslide

Johnson's active first year in office assured his nomination as the Democratic presidential candidate in 1964. As his running mate, he chose Hubert H. Humphrey, a well-known liberal senator from Minnesota.

The Republicans nominated Senator Barry Goldwater of Arizona for President and New York Congressman William Miller for Vice President. Goldwater, a strong believer in states' rights, represented the Republican party's conservative wing. In accepting the nomination, he squarely faced the charge by party moderates that his views were too extreme. "Extremism in the defense of liberty is no vice," he said. "Moderation in pursuit of justice is no virtue."

During the campaign, Johnson and Humphrey portrayed themselves as moderate, less dangerous alternatives to the conservative Goldwater. Democratic political advertisements stressed that Goldwater had questioned the Social Security system and that he seemed too willing to use nuclear weapons in a crisis. The tactic worked. Johnson won 61 percent of the popular vote, the biggest victory since that of Franklin Roosevelt in 1936. The Democrats also won a large majority in both houses, giving Johnson the votes he needed to enact his Great Society programs.

A Flood of Legislation

During the campaign, Lyndon Johnson summed up what he believed most Americans wanted. "They want education for their children and an improving life for their families. They want to protect liberty and pursue peace. They expect justice for themselves and are willing to grant it to others." To enable Americans to fulfill these goals, Johnson proposed a broad program of social legislation, much of which was passed in 1965.

One of the most far-reaching pieces of legislation was the Medicare Act. It provided hospital coverage for citizens over age 65 and allowed them to join a program that helped pay other medical expenses. An associated Medicaid program provided funds to assist poor people of all ages who were not covered by Medicare. The passage of the Medicare Act guaranteed a minimum level of health care for Americans for the first time.

President Johnson also pressed for stronger civil rights laws. He redoubled his efforts after a civil rights worker was killed

2. **BACKGROUND** Johnson supporters chanted his campaign slogan, "All the Way with LBJ." Goldwater's slogan was "In your heart, you know he's right."

Each of the presidential candidates, Lyndon Johnson and Barry Goldwater, had supporters in this crowd in South Carolina. Although Johnson could have won reelection without leaving the White House, he barnstormed through the country speaking and shaking hands.

1. **DISCUSSION** Ask: Have students compare Johnson's Great Society to the New Deal.

2. **VOCABULARY** Have students look up these terms in the glossary before they begin reading.

during a voter registration campaign in Selma, Alabama. The Voting Rights Act of 1965 authorized federal officials to register voters in states where official racial discrimination continued. The enforcement of this law resulted in the registration of more than one million new black voters by the 1968 election.

But the reforms did not end there. The Immigration Act of 1965 removed quotas based on race or national origin that had existed since the 1920s. (See page 572.) The Housing Act provided federal funds for constructing low- and middle-income housing. The Department of Housing and Urban Development (HUD) was created. It was headed by Robert Weaver, the first black to serve in a presidential cabinet. Congress also expanded Social Security benefits, provided aid to higher education, began efforts to curb water pollution, and created the National Foundation for the Arts and Humanities.

After Congress adjourned in October 1965, the President proudly presented a display case of 50 pens to members of the White House press. The inscription read, "With these fifty pens President Lyndon B. Johnson signed into law the foundations of the Great Society, which was passed by the historical

1. and fabulous first session of the Eighty-ninth Congress."

See p. T135.

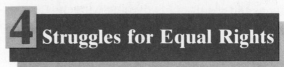

4 Struggles for Equal Rights

READ TO UNDERSTAND

■ Why the black civil rights movement became more militant.

■ What problems Hispanic Americans, American Indians, and women faced.

■ What progress the nation's minority groups made in gaining equal rights.

■ *Vocabulary:* de facto segregation, bracero.

2.

The movement for full rights for all Americans exploded during the 1960s. A raised fist became the symbol of the "black power" movement. Hispanic Americans and American Indians began to protest their second-class status. And women—who were actually a majority of Americans—announced their intention to gain equal rights.

A More Militant Black Movement

After 1963, a growing number of African American leaders came to believe that non-violent tactics did not work fast enough. These radical leaders were especially concerned with the problems of northern blacks. **De facto segregation**, that is, segregation created by housing patterns, not by law, kept most northern blacks in run-down ghettos, 3. where they lived in decayed buildings with inadequate plumbing and heating. Although the average income of blacks had risen since 1950, their incomes remained lower than those of whites and their unemployment rate was higher.

Radicals demanded immediate and drastic action to wipe out such conditions. One group, the Black Muslims, believed that African Americans should separate completely from white society. These views were spread in the early 1960s by a Black Muslim minister named Malcolm X. By 1964, however, Malcolm X had rejected separatism in favor of "a society in which there could exist honest white-black brotherhood." Malcolm X was shot and killed in February 1965, presuma- **743**

SECTION 3 REVIEW

1. **Identify:** (a) VISTA, (b) Hubert H. Humphrey, (c) Barry Goldwater.

2. Name two Kennedy programs that President Johnson persuaded Congress to pass.

3. (a) Why did Johnson feel the need for a "War on Poverty"? (b) List two provisions of the Economic Opportunity Act of 1964.

4. What did the Medicare Act provide?

5. What civil rights legislation was passed by the Johnson administration?

6. **Critical Thinking** Why do you think the "Great Society" has been called the "second Reconstruction"?

3. **VOCABULARY** The word *ghetto* originally referred to a segregated Jewish sector in a European city. In the U.S., it has come to mean any inner-city slum.

bly as the result of his dispute with the Black Muslims. His ideas, expressed in the *Autobiography of Malcolm X,* have remained influential.

Militant black leaders such as Stokely Carmichael and Floyd McKissick rejected cooperation with whites and instead issued a demand for "black power." Blacks, they argued, should take control of the economic and political aspects of their lives even if it required violent revolution. The Black Panthers urged their black "brothers" to arm themselves and to fight for their rights when necessary.

While accepting the idea of black power, moderate black leaders stressed that it should take the form of self-reliance and pride, not violence. Opinion polls revealed that most African Americans preferred the goal of integration and favored the more moderate interpretation of black power. However, the more violent language of the radical groups attracted widespread attention.

Violence Erupts By the middle of the decade, frustration and despair in black ghettos erupted into violence. In the summer of 1964, rioting tore through Harlem and Rochester, New York. In August 1965, even greater violence exploded in the Los Angeles ghetto known as Watts. Rioting, burning, and looting raged for five days. By the time 14,000 troops of the National Guard restored order, 34 people were dead, 4,000 had been arrested, and property damage was $35 million. In 1966 and 1967, riots broke out in other major cities, including Newark, Cincinnati, Atlanta, and Detroit.

The riots caused great destruction and despair in the black communities where they occurred. They also increased "white backlash," or negative feelings toward blacks' demands for equality.

Kerner Commission President Johnson appointed the Kerner Commission, headed by Illinois Governor Otto Kerner, to study the causes of the riots. The commission's report, issued in 1968, noted that African Americans had made significant progress. Freedom riders had largely succeeded in desegregating public places, and millions of blacks were voting. And the Civil Rights Act of 1968 had declared that no person could be denied housing on account of race.

But, warned the report, more remained to be done. "Our nation is moving toward two societies," the commission declared, "one black, one white—separate but unequal." According to the report, only a "commitment to national action—compassionate, massive, and sustained," could bring equality for all.

Assassination of Dr. King As if to underscore the fact that the nation's divisions were far from healed, on April 4, 1968, a sniper's bullet, fired by a white segregationist, struck down Dr. Martin Luther King, Jr. King had gone to Memphis, Tennessee, to support a strike called by sanitation workers there. Speaking to his followers on the night before his death, King seemed prophetic when he declared, "I've seen the Promised Land. I may not get there with you. But I want you to know tonight that we as a people will get to the Promised Land."

The body of Dr. King, who had won the Nobel Peace Prize "for the furtherance of brotherhood among men," was laid to rest at Morehouse College in Atlanta, Georgia. Inscribed on his gravestone are the words, "Free at last, free at last, thank God Almighty I'm free at last."

Hispanic Americans

Inspired by the black civil rights movement, Hispanic American, or Latino, groups began to work more actively to overcome inequalities. Such efforts were often more regional than national, however, because various Hispanic groups were scattered throughout the nation.

During the 1600s, small groups of Spanish farmers had settled in what is now the southwestern United States. Many of their descendants, known as Hispanos, continued to live in the rural uplands and mountains of New Mexico and Colorado. The majority of them raised sheep or tended small farms, as their ancestors had done.

A much larger Hispanic minority were descendants of Mexicans who had been living in the Southwest when the United States annexed it in the Mexican War. Over the years, Mexicans continued to migrate to this area, especially after 1910. (See page 578.) By 1960, approximately 3.5 million Mexican Americans lived in the Southwest.

744

In December 1967, Martin Luther King's Southern Christian Leadership Conference decided to mount a Poor People's Campaign the following summer. After Dr. King's assassination in April 1968, the Conference leadership decided the campaign would go on. In May, black demonstrators—young, old, families—marched through the streets of Atlanta, Georgia, on what became known as the Poor People's March.

1.

1. **ACTIVITY** Have students find and bring in recordings of songs sung by civil rights marchers, such as "We Shall Overcome" and "Keep Your Eyes on the Prize."

In the eastern United States, most Hispanics trace their roots to Puerto Rico. The United States had annexed the island in 1898 and granted American citizenship to its residents in 1917. In 1952, Puerto Rico became a self-governing commonwealth of the United States. It had its own constitution and elected its own governor and legislature. At the same time, Puerto Ricans continued to have all the rights of United States citizens and were thus free to settle on the mainland United States.

Before World War II, only about 70,000 Puerto Ricans had moved to the mainland, most of them to New York City. After the war, the population of Puerto Rico expanded rapidly, and the numbers who left the island increased. By 1960, some 600,000 Puerto Ricans had come to the mainland. Many continued to settle in New York, but some moved to other cities, including Chicago, San Francisco, and Bridgeport, Connecticut.

A third major Hispanic group was of Cuban origin. When Fidel Castro set up a communist state in the early 1960s, thousands of Cubans sought to leave their country. Between 1961 and 1970, more than 200,000 Cubans immigrated to the United States.

Most Cubans settled in southern Florida, where they resumed careers in medicine, law, and teaching. Miami, the city with the greatest number of Cuban immigrants, acquired a new appearance. Shop windows displayed signs in Spanish. Cuban restaurants opened, and Spanish-language radio stations began broadcasting. As their numbers grew, Cuban Americans became an increasingly significant force in southern Florida.

2.

Forms of Discrimination

Hispanic Americans faced many forms of discrimination. They lived in a land in which the dominant culture was English. Few schools had programs to teach English to students whose first language was Spanish. Consequently, Hispanic students found themselves at a disadvantage. The lack of a good education in turn made it more difficult to obtain good jobs. Even well-educated Hispanic Americans encountered discrimination among employers.

A government program begun in the 1950s created special problems for Mexican-American migrant workers. Under that program, Mexicans could obtain temporary permits to work in the United States. **Braceros,** as the Mexican laborers were known, worked for very low wages under harsh conditions. They received none of the benefits, such as medical insurance, offered to other workers, and they competed with migrant workers for jobs. The program was halted in 1965.

745

2. **GEOGRAPHY** Ask: How did geography influence the settlement patterns of Hispanics in the United States? (movement)

Fighting for Equality Hispanics fought discrimination with a variety of tactics. In 1962, Cesar Chavez (SAY zahr CHAH vays) began a movement to unionize California grape pickers. The majority of grape pickers were Mexican Americans. Chavez believed that a strong union would help migrant workers gain higher wages and better working conditions. He adopted a nonviolent strategy, similar to that of Martin Luther King, Jr. He organized sit-ins and demonstrations. During the late 1960s, Chavez spearheaded a nationwide boycott of grapes that forced an

1. increasing number of growers to accept the union by 1970.

In southwestern Texas, José Angel Gutiérrez (hoh SAY AHN hehl goo TYEHR rehs) sought power for Mexican Americans through political action, generally concentrating on local elections. "Mexicanos need to be in control of their destiny," declared Gutiérrez. "We have been complacent for too long." His political party, La Raza Unida (The United People), called for bilingual education in public school systems, improved public services, and an end to job discrimination.

By the end of the 1960s, Hispanic groups had made definite gains. Cesar Chavez's ef-

forts to unionize migrant grape pickers spread to other fruit and vegetable industries. A growing number of Americans of Spanish heritage gained access to better jobs. In addition, some school districts had become more sensitive to the needs of Hispanic Americans. Yet a conflict over assimilation or maintaining ethnic identity splintered Hispanic politics. Large numbers of Hispanics continued to face economic hardship and discrimination.

American Indians

Toward the end of the 1960s, American Indians also adopted the techniques of protest. Like other minorities, they faced discrimination in many forms. But Indians were also embittered by the government's long history of contradictory and changing policies.

As you read in Chapter 19, the Dawes Act of 1887 sought to break up the reservation system by dividing reservation lands among individual Indians. In 1934, the government reversed that policy. The Indian Reorganization Act encouraged Indians to govern themselves in traditional groups.

In the 1960s, the struggle for equal rights for all Americans exploded in full force. The movement took many forms and had many faces, two of which are shown below. At left is Cesar Chavez, who organized Mexican American grape pickers for higher wages and better working conditions. At right is Navajo Annie
2. *Wauneka; President Johnson is presenting her with the Presidential Medal of Freedom for her tireless efforts to improve the conditions of her people.*

1. **READING** Students interested in the situation of American Indians in the 1960s can read *Custer Died for Your Sins* by Vine Deloria, Jr., a Sioux.

The National Congress of American Indians was founded in 1940 in reaction to years of discrimination. The National Congress regularly petitioned Congress for greater recognition of Indian rights. During the 1950s, government policy shifted again. This time, the federal government sought to turn over Indian programs to the states. Such inconsistency brought sharp protests from the National Congress and other Indian groups.

In the 1960s, the federal government once again endorsed a return to a tribal system. But by the late 1960s, an estimated 50 percent of all Indians lived off the reservations, mainly in urban areas. City life weakened traditional tribal ties and customs. Urban youth, especially, began to make more radical demands for Indian rights.

1. One group, led by Dennis Banks and Clyde Bellecourt, organized the militant American Indian Movement (AIM) in 1968. In March 1973, AIM members seized the trading post at Wounded Knee, South Dakota, site of a massacre of Indians by army troops in 1890. (See page 408.) AIM demanded reforms in the tribal government and strict adherence to old Indian treaties. Federal law officers quickly surrounded the area. Occasional gunfire left two Indians dead and a federal agent paralyzed. After 71 days, failing to get support from other Indians, the AIM militants surrendered.

Like the movements led by Hispanics and blacks, Indian protests signaled a new attitude among minority groups. Indians demonstrated increasing pride in their heritage, confidence in their ability to contribute to the diversity of American society, and willingness to act to achieve their goals.

The Women's Rights Movement

Women in the 1960s had full political rights, and many worked outside the home. Yet some contended that women continued to be victims of discrimination. Betty Friedan, an early leader of the women's rights movement, made the point strongly in her book *The Feminine Mystique,* published in 1963.

2. According to Friedan, after World War II, society had forced women to retreat from the job market back into the home. The busi-

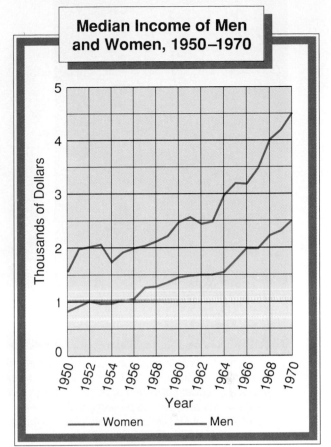

Median Income of Men and Women, 1950–1970

Source: *Historical Statistics of the United States*   See p. T136.

GRAPH STUDY *Incomes of women lagged far behind those of men.* 3.
The graph shows the median incomes of men and women from 1950 to 1970. Although women's incomes rose, men's incomes rose faster. ("Median" income is a kind of "middle" income: Half of all incomes are above the median, and half are below the median.) In what year did women's median income reach what men's had been in 1950?

3. **GRAPH READING** Ask: In what year were men's and women's median income closest? What year were they farthest apart?

ness world continued to be dominated by men, she said. Women's jobs were limited primarily to a few professions, such as nursing, teaching, and secretarial work. When women did perform the same jobs as men, women's salaries were usually lower.

In 1966, Friedan founded the National Organization for Women (NOW) to press for legislation that would give women greater freedom and equality. The organization sought equal pay for equal work and new opportunities for women at all levels of employment. It also campaigned for the provision of day-care facilities for the children of mothers who worked outside the home.

747

2. **BIOGRAPHY** Betty Goldstein Friedan (1921–) was born in Peoria, Illinois. She led a nationwide Women's Strike for Equality in 1970, the fiftieth anniversary of women's winning the right to vote.

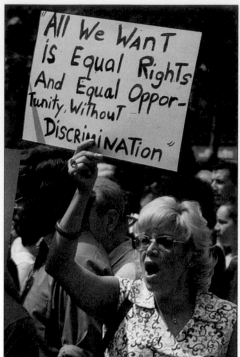

Controversy swirled around the Equal Rights Amendment from the time it was proposed by Congress in 1972. Those in favor argued that it protected women by guaranteeing equal rights and opportunities. Opponents claimed that it could
1. destroy traditional roles and protections for women. When the amendment was sent to the states for ratification, both sides demonstrated to persuade state legislatures to vote their way.

1. **VISUAL EVIDENCE** Have students act out a conversation between the women shown at the right and at the left.

See p. T136.

Through the women's rights movement, women began to assume more diverse roles during the 1960s. The Equal Pay Act of 1963 guaranteed equal pay for equal work, and the Civil Rights Act of 1964 banned job discrimination on the basis of sex as well as on race or ethnic origin. Although those acts were not always vigorously enforced, they provided a legal basis for greater equality. In the late 1960s and early 1970s, women entered the work force in record numbers. Many companies made special efforts to promote women to management positions.

A proposed constitutional amendment forbidding discrimination by sex was passed by Congress in 1972. However, this Equal Rights Amendment (ERA) met with strong opposition from many Americans of both sexes, who believed that it would undermine traditional values. Opponents also argued that the amendment was unnecessary, since
2. women already had equal rights. Although the ERA was not ratified, women continued
748 their campaign for greater equality.

SECTION 4 REVIEW

1. **Identify:** (a) Kerner Commission, (b) Cesar Chavez, (c) Dennis Banks, (d) American Indian Movement, (e) Betty Friedan.

2. **Define:** (a) de facto segregation, (b) bracero.

3. (a) Why did African Americans abandon the nonviolent tactics of Martin Luther King, Jr.? (b) What tactics did militant blacks advocate? (c) What were two important results of the rioting by urban blacks?

4. (a) In which areas did each of the following make gains in the 1960s: Hispanics; American Indians; women? (b) What problems remained for each?

5. **Critical Thinking** Why do you think the black civil rights movement had an effect on other minorities?

2. **DISCUSSION** Have students compare the situation of women in the 1960s with that of blacks, Hispanics, and American Indians in terms of problems, methods used to correct them, and progress made.

1. **VOCABULARY** Have students look up this word in the glossary before they begin reading.

2. **PAST AND PRESENT** Have interested students research current U.S. policy toward South Africa and report their findings to the class.

5 Growing Involvement in World Affairs

READ TO UNDERSTAND

■ Why the United States intervened in some Third World nations.

■ How the United States became increasingly involved in Vietnam.

■ How the Vietnam War divided public opinion in the United States.

1. ■ *Vocabulary:* apartheid.

"If I left that war and let the communists take over South Vietnam, then I would be seen as a coward and my nation would be seen as an appeaser," Lyndon Johnson told a writer after he had left the presidency. "Containing" communist expansion was the keystone of United States foreign policy during the 1960s. In Southeast Asia, this policy involved the United States in an expanding war in Vietnam that left Americans sharply divided over whether the fate of Vietnam was truly vital to American security.

A Time of Tensions

By the 1960s, the United States and the Soviet Union were competing in a new arena. Each sought friends among the developing nations of Asia, Africa, and Latin America, many of which had gained independence since World War II. These nations made up the Third World: They belonged neither to the "first world" (the United States and its allies) nor the "second world" (the Soviet bloc). Superpower competition in the Third World contributed to a number of conflicts during the 1960s.

Africa In 1960, the Belgian Congo became the independent Congo. (It is now Zaire.) When opposing groups fought over control of the new government, President Kennedy decided to aid the pro-American side. Many Africans resented American involvement, especially since white mercenaries from South Africa took part.

For many years, the governments of South Africa and Rhodesia (now Zimbabwe) practiced **apartheid** (uh PAHRT hayt), a policy of racial separation by law. Although the majority of the population was black, the governments were controlled by the white descendants of European colonists.

For the United States, to oppose the white regimes was to risk the loss of valuable economic resources and strategic naval bases in South Africa. But to endorse the government would violate principles of justice, as well as alienate newly independent African nations. For a while, the United States compromised by publicly condemning apartheid while trading with South Africa and Rhodesia for important resources.

2.

Latin America Another area of conflict was Latin America. Here the United States claimed a special role under the Monroe Doctrine. President Johnson wanted to make sure that Cuban-style communism did not spread in the region. He was particularly worried about the Dominican Republic.

In 1962, voters in that Caribbean island nation had elected Juan Bosch as their first democratic leader. Ousted by the military after seven months, Bosch and his followers tried to regain power in April 1965. This ignited a civil war. Calling the situation "grave," President Johnson sent in 23,000 American marines and called for a cease-fire. With the aid of the United States, the Dominican military remained in control.

The United States had intervened, Johnson explained, to protect American civilians living in the Dominican Republic and to prevent communists from exploiting the situation and taking over. Critics, however, claimed that the communist threat was more imagined than real. Bosch, an advocate of democratic reform, was bitter. "This was a democratic revolution smashed by the leading democracy in the world," he lamented.

3.

The Middle East In the Middle East, the United States balanced Soviet aid to Egypt by sending military aid to Israel. In 1967, Israel drove Egyptian forces out of the Sinai Desert and across the Suez Canal during a six-day war. Israeli troops also forced Syrian forces from the Golan Heights and seized all

749

3. **MAIN IDEA** Ask: What point was Juan Bosch making? Do you agree or disagree with him?

1. **MAP READING** Ask: Why was the Gulf of Tonkin important to North Vietnam?

2. **DISCUSSION** Ask: Do you think the U.S. should have pressured Diem to allow the elections even though the Vietnamese people were likely to vote for a communist?

of Jerusalem and lands on the West Bank of the Jordan River.

During the crisis, American and Soviet leaders used the Moscow-Washington telephone hot line for the first time. They assured each other that they would not intervene in the conflict. However, continuing hostilities between Egypt and Israel signaled that the Middle East would remain a dangerous hotspot.

The Sino-Soviet Split As you have read, after Mao Zedong's victory in the Chinese civil war, the United States refused to recognize the People's Republic of China. (See page 700.) Mao's China received Soviet aid and supported the Soviet position in international affairs. Many Americans saw it as part of a unified communist bloc directed from Moscow.

In the late 1950s, the Soviets and Chinese had a series of quarrels. Relations between the two great communist powers began to cool. Despite this development, United States policy makers did not attempt to move closer to China. They were aware of the hostility of many Americans toward communist China. Americans' attitude toward China hardened in 1964, when China tested its first nuclear weapons. The Chinese defended their action. "China cannot remain idle and do nothing in the face of the ever-increasing threat posed by the United States," they argued.

Growing Involvement in Vietnam

As you have read in Chapter 32, when France withdrew from Vietnam in 1954, the armistice left the country divided into two sections: North Vietnam, led by communist Ho Chi Minh; and South Vietnam, led by Ngo Dinh Diem. Diem was backed by the Eisenhower administration, which began sending aid, including a small number of military advisers, to South Vietnam.

Elections to unify the country were to be held in 1956, but President Diem refused to allow them. Ho Chi Minh would easily win in the North. Even in the South, his reputation 2. as a nationalist made him popular.

At the end of 1960, encouraged by the North Vietnamese, Diem's opponents formed the National Liberation Front (NLF), or Viet Cong. Viet Cong influence spread throughout South Vietnam, particularly in the villages where most of the population lived. Using guerrilla warfare tactics, the Viet Cong killed village officials supporting Diem and tried to replace them with their own "shadow government." Their disciplined commitment and ruthless tactics brought them success in many areas. They also profited because Diem had been equally ruthless in suppressing his opponents. As a result, Diem was not a popu- 3. lar leader.

When John F. Kennedy entered the White House, Diem's government was in deep trouble. Kennedy, as a young politician, had

MAP STUDY The long war in Vietnam eventually affected most of
1. Southeast Asia. The Ho Chi Minh Trail, shown on this map, was a main supply line from North Vietnam to Viet Cong guerrillas. How did the Ho
See p. T136. Chi Minh Trail tend to widen the conflict?

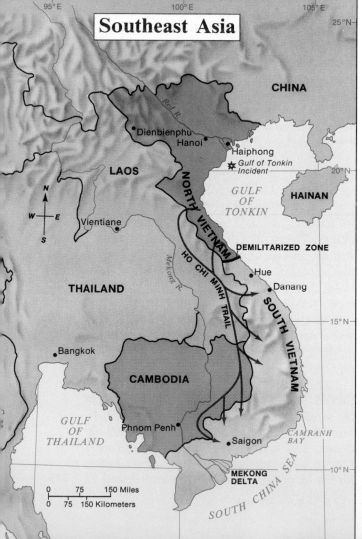

3. **BACKGROUND** Diem, a Catholic, also began widespread imprisonment of Buddhists, who opposed his government.

backed the Vietnamese drive for independence against the French. But as President, Kennedy believed that communism should be stopped in South Vietnam. He therefore increased the number of military advisers and the amount of military equipment the United States was sending to aid South Vietnam's army of 150,000 men. By the end of 1963, approximately 16,000 American troops were serving in Vietnam as advisers. The Viet Cong, estimated to number 15,000, were resourceful fighters, however, and continued to hold their own.

Meanwhile, Diem continued repressive measures against Buddhists and demonstrators, further weakening his support. In October 1963, a group of South Vietnamese military officers assassinated Diem. A month later, Kennedy was dead and the problem of Vietnam was left to his successor.

The Gulf of Tonkin Resolution

During the early stages of the war, most Viet Cong guerrillas were South Vietnamese. North Vietnam had sent supplies and only a few guerrilla fighters south. But gradually, both American and North Vietnamese involvement increased. In 1964, 7,000 North Vietnamese troops traveled south along the Ho Chi Minh Trail, a system of jungle and mountain roads linking the two parts of the country.

Then, on August 2, 1964, North Vietnamese torpedo boats attacked the United States destroyer *Maddox* in the Gulf of Tonkin, not far from the North Vietnamese coast. The *Maddox* had been patrolling the Gulf of Tonkin while South Vietnamese gunboats raided North Vietnamese islands in the gulf.

Two nights later, in the midst of a heavy thunderstorm, radar operators on another American destroyer, the *C. Turner Joy,* reported a second torpedo attack. The bad weather conditions, however, made it difficult to determine whether enemy ships had actually been near the scene. In any case, North Vietnam argued that it had the right to chase attackers from its territorial waters. President Johnson, on the other hand, contended that the attack had been unprovoked. In response, he ordered immediate air strikes against North Vietnam.

At the same time, the President asked Congress for the authority to take "all necessary steps" to "prevent further aggression" by the North Vietnamese. The Gulf of Tonkin resolution, granting this far-reaching power, passed the House by a vote of 415 to 0 and the Senate by a vote of 88 to 2. Johnson would 1. eventually use the resolution to send more than 500,000 American fighting men to Vietnam.

The War Escalates

For the rest of 1964, however, the United States took few actions in Vietnam. Johnson, in the midst of his election campaign against Goldwater, promised that he would not send "American boys to do the fighting" that should be done by the South Vietnamese. This promise later came back to haunt him.

In February 1965, the Viet Cong attacked an American air base at Pleiku in South Vietnam, killing eight Americans. The President reacted by ordering another air strike on North Vietnam. In March, Johnson stepped up the air attacks and started a continuous bombing campaign, known as Rolling Thunder. It was intended to stop the North from supplying the Viet Cong.

To conduct the bombing campaign, the United States needed additional air bases in Vietnam, which it quickly built. The Viet Cong responded by attacking these new installations. To protect the bases, President Johnson ordered 3,500 marines into Vietnam. That decision marked a fateful turning in the war. For the first time, American troops were in Vietnam not merely as military advisers, but to engage in combat.

As the Viet Cong attacks continued, American involvement rose sharply. In April, President Johnson ordered another 20,000 troops into Vietnam. By June, General William Westmoreland, the commander of United States forces in Vietnam, had asked for an additional 200,000 troops. They were soon engaged in major operations against the Viet Cong. American forces grew to 385,000 by 2. the end of 1966 and reached 536,000 by 1968.

The United States commitment to South Vietnam, which had been growing very slowly since the early 1950s, had suddenly become quite substantial. By sending troops, John-

751

In this 1965 photograph, American soldiers wade waist deep in water during a
1. mission to "search and destroy" Viet Cong forces. The American military tried to engage the Viet Cong in pitched battles where the Americans' superior firepower and air support could prevail. But the communists avoided such battles, and United States troops had to comb jungles, swamps, and high "elephant grass" to find their hidden enemy.

1. **ACTIVITY** Have students interview Vietnam veterans. They might ask how the veterans' experience differed from the view Americans were given by television.

son had committed the United States to supporting South Vietnam. Although American forces had the edge in military technology, the Viet Cong were determined in their opposition. They were also backed by increased aid from North Vietnam.

The Viet Cong were an elusive enemy. They carried out sudden ambushes, then faded back into the jungle or disappeared into a village. It was often difficult to tell hostile villagers from friendly ones. American troops were sent on "search and destroy" missions, to find the enemy, but there were no clear battle lines. Troops would take territory, "pacify" it, and move on—only to have the Viet Cong infiltrate it once again.

Under such conditions, combat duty became particularly nerve-wracking. Troops never knew when booby traps set by the Viet Cong might explode along roads and trails. "It was very frustrating," recalled one American soldier, "because how do you fight back against a booby trap? You're just walking along and all of a sudden your buddy doesn't have a leg. Or you don't have a leg." Such uncertainty led to attacks on Vietnamese villages like My Lai, where in 1968 American soldiers killed more than 200 civilians, including women and children.

As the war progressed, President Johnson periodically interrupted the bombing campaign to seek negotiations with North Vietnam. Neither side, however, could agree on conditions for peace. North Vietnam demanded a place for the National Liberation Front in any postwar government. The United States rejected such terms, and the fighting continued.

GREAT DEBATE

The Hawks and the Doves

As you have read, President Johnson received overwhelming support for the Gulf of Tonkin resolution in 1964. As more and more American troops were sent to Vietnam, however, opposition to the war began to grow. Many Americans felt betrayed. Despite optimistic claims by the government that the war was going well, each day increasing numbers of American soldiers were killed.

In 1966, the Senate Foreign Relations Committee held hearings on the conduct of the war. The hearings showed that even 2. government officials were sharply divided between those who supported the war ("hawks") and those who opposed American involvement ("doves").

752

2. **BACKGROUND** These televised hearings were chaired by Senator J. William Fulbright of Arkansas, a critic of Johnson's conduct of the war.

1. **TECHNOLOGY** Years after the war, a number of Vietnam veterans claimed that they had come down with cancer through exposure to Agent Orange, a chemical defoliant.

3. **PRESIDENTS** Johnson said, "I do not believe that I should devote an hour or a day of my time to any duties other than the awesome duties of this office. . . ."

The hawks maintained that the war had been forced on the United States by North Vietnamese aggression against the South. They claimed that the United States, in fighting communism in South Vietnam, was preventing a communist takeover of all of Southeast Asia. Doves argued that the United States had no compelling reason to justify the enormous sacrifice in lives and money. They charged that the United States was not fighting communist aggression but interfering in a civil war.

The doves also pointed to the staggering costs of the war—$20 billion in 1967 alone. Rising defense budgets put pressure on Johnson to cut back on his Great Society social programs. The United States could not afford both "guns and butter." In February 1967, Martin Luther King, Jr., declared, "The promises of the Great Society have been shot down on the battlefield of Vietnam."

King, like some other clergy and citizens, also saw the conduct of the war as a moral issue. American air attacks were devastating the Vietnamese countryside in both the North and South. More explosives were dropped on Vietnam than were used on Europe and Asia in World War II. Planes sprayed chemicals on South Vietnam's forests and farmland to destroy the enemy's hiding places and deny them food supplies.

The Tet Offensive

Johnson and military commanders like General Westmoreland assured Americans that they were winning the war. However, on January 30, 1968, as the celebration of Tet, the Vietnamese New Year, began, the Viet Cong launched attacks on major cities throughout South Vietnam. They even stormed the walls of the American embassy in the capital of Saigon. Although they were eventually pushed back by American and South Vietnamese forces, the Viet Cong had won an important political victory. The Tet offensive showed that, despite the presence of about half a million American troops, no part of Vietnam was safe from the Viet Cong.

The Tet offensive further divided public opinion within the United States. Thousands of college students protested American involvement in the war. Adopting many of the tactics of the civil rights movement, they staged marches and sit-ins. They conducted teach-ins to educate others on the issues of the war. They publicly burned their draft cards and counseled others to avoid the draft. Some marchers carried the Viet Cong flag.

By now, many advisers to President Johnson were convinced that this was a war the United States could not win. Johnson was also aware that public support for the war had eroded. He turned down a request by General Westmoreland for an additional 200,000 men. Finally, on March 31, Johnson announced that he was suspending the bombing of North Vietnam. In response, North Vietnam agreed to enter into peace negotiations in Paris. ∎

The Election of 1968

The Vietnam War played a major role in the presidential election of 1968. The doves within the Democratic party rallied around an antiwar candidate, Minnesota's Senator Eugene McCarthy. Supported by an army of student volunteers, McCarthy entered the New Hampshire primary in opposition to President Johnson. Although McCarthy lost, he gathered a surprisingly large number of votes.

Then, in March, in the same speech in which he announced the suspension of the bombing of North Vietnam, Johnson stunned the nation by saying that he would not run for reelection.

With Johnson out of the running, Robert Kennedy and Vice President Hubert Humphrey entered the race. Humphrey cautiously supported administration policies in Vietnam. Kennedy, who had at first supported American intervention in Vietnam, by 1968 was speaking out against the war. His energetic campaign produced an impressive string of victories over McCarthy and Humphrey. The greatest of these came in the important California primary of June 1968.

But on the evening of Kennedy's victory speech in Los Angeles, a young Palestinian named Sirhan Sirhan, angered by Kennedy's support of Israel, shot and killed him. The nation, still recovering from the assassination of Martin Luther King, Jr., only two months earlier (see Section 4), mourned yet another leader.

753

1. **PAST AND PRESENT** Recent popular songs that deal with social and political issues include John Cougar Mellencamp's "Rain on the Scarecrow" (about farm problems) and Tracy Chapman's "Fast Car" (about poverty and homelessness).

Robert Kennedy's death left Hubert Humphrey a clear path to the Democratic presidential nomination. The party gathered for its nominating convention in Chicago in August. Antiwar activists from around the country gathered in Chicago, too.

As Chicago police patrolled outside the convention hall, violence broke out. Demonstrators heckled the police with obscenities and threw bricks, bottles, and garbage. The police reacted with surprising force. Hundreds of demonstrators, as well as some policemen, were injured. In addition, 49 reporters were arrested, beaten, or sprayed with a caustic chemical designed for crowd control. Inside the hall, the convention delegates nomi-

ARTS IN AMERICA

The Music of Protest and Change

During the turbulent 1960s, political themes found their way into popular music. The song "Where Have All the Flowers Gone?" for example, protested war, while "What Have They Done to the Rain?" voiced concern about radioactive fallout. When Bob Dylan sang that "the times they are a changin'," he expressed the central mood of the 1960s.

Folk singers such as Joan Baez, Judy Collins, below, and Bob Dylan attracted a large following among students. Dylan became the leader of musical protest. Through his songs, he spoke out against bigotry and injustice. At a massive antiwar demonstration in Washington, D.C., on November 15, 1969, Dylan led the crowd of 250,000 people in singing "We Shall Overcome," the rousing civil rights anthem that the antiwar protestors borrowed.

Rock music also underwent a revolution in the early 1960s. In 1964, a British group called the Beatles took the United States by storm. Not satisfied with singing "silly love songs," the Beatles created experimental, musically complex pieces. Their immensely popular 1967 album, *Sergeant Pepper's Lonely Hearts Club Band,* paved the way for later rock artists who sang harder-edged songs about the problems of society.

From Detroit, in the meantime, came the "Motown" rhythms that attracted wide audiences to black stars. Black record producer Berry Gordy created a multimillion dollar business by discovering such performers as Smokey Robinson, Stevie Wonder, and the Supremes. Along with Aretha Franklin, these black artists consistently topped the pop music charts.

A three-day outdoor rock festival in August 1969 was a fitting climax to the 1960s. More than 300,000 young people swarmed into a field near Bethel, New York, for the Woodstock Music and Art Fair. Those who gathered at Woodstock celebrated not only their music, but also their protest against conventional society. Woodstock offered the nation a glimpse of the "counter culture" that was forging new values and lifestyles for a generation of American youth.

See p. T136.

1. List four things that popular songs protested during the 1960s.

2. **Critical Thinking** How can protest songs affect people's emotions in ways that speeches and articles cannot?

As the Vietnam War escalated, so did the size of the marches protesting American involvement. The peace movement included a wide range of groups, from radical to mainstream, who came together for huge demonstrations, like this one in Washington, D.C.

1.

---

1. **VISUAL EVIDENCE** Ask: How would seeing news photographs like this affect U.S. soldiers in Vietnam?

See p. T137.

nated Humphrey, who chose Senator Edmund Muskie of Maine as his running mate.

Reacting to the antiwar movement and to the urban riots that had been disrupting the nation, Alabama Governor George Wallace became a third-party candidate for President. He campaigned on the pledge to restore "law and order" to the nation.

2.

In Miami, the Republicans turned again to Richard Nixon as their candidate. His nomination was the result of a remarkable political comeback. Defeated as the Republican presidential candidate in 1960 and as a candidate for governor of California in 1962, Nixon had spent the following six years repairing his political career. In 1968, with his running mate, Spiro Agnew, governor of Maryland, Nixon narrowly won the election, with 43.4 percent of the popular vote against Humphrey's 42.7 percent. George Wallace polled 13.5 percent. The election results underscored the divisions in American society that prompted Nixon's campaign promise to "bring us together."

SECTION 5 REVIEW

1. **Identify:** (a) Third World, (b) Viet Cong, (c) William Westmoreland.

2. **Define:** apartheid.

3. Why did President Johnson intervene in the Dominican Republic?

4. List the actions taken in Vietnam by Presidents Eisenhower and Kennedy.

5. What was the main purpose of the Rolling Thunder bombing campaign instituted by President Johnson against North Vietnam?

6. What two actions did President Johnson take in March 1968 in response to growing opposition to the war in Vietnam?

7. **Critical Thinking** How did the Gulf of Tonkin resolution mark a turning point in the Vietnam conflict?

755

2. **BACKGROUND** Remind students that George Wallace had opposed the desegregation of the University of Alabama in 1962 (see pp. 738–739).

Summary

1. **The first two years of Kennedy's presidency were marked by foreign policy crises.** Kennedy faced problems with a failed invasion of Cuba and a crisis in Berlin. A confrontation over Soviet missile sites in Cuba brought the world to the brink of nuclear war. After the Cuban missile crisis, the superpowers negotiated a nuclear test ban treaty.

2. **On the home front, the 1960s began with high hopes.** The space program was launched vigorously. Kennedy pursued civil rights goals cautiously, but when civil rights demonstrators met with violence or illegal resistance, he enforced the law. In 1963, President Kennedy was assassinated in Dallas, Texas, and Vice President Lyndon Johnson become President.

3. **President Johnson persuaded Congress to pass many of Kennedy's programs.** After being elected in his own right in 1964, Johnson introduced legislation to create the Great Society. His administration's achievements included Medicare and Medicaid, a voting rights law, and the removal of immigration quotas based on race or national origin.

4. **The movement for civil rights exploded in the 1960s.** Many civil rights leaders adopted the nonviolent methods of Martin Luther King, Jr., but others demanded more radical action. Inspired in part by the black movement, Hispanic Americans, American Indians, and women began to organize to end discrimination.

5. **By the end of the decade, the United States was deeply involved in a war in Vietnam.** The Gulf of Tonkin incident led to increased American involvement in Vietnam. Opposition to the war grew as the nation's commitment increased. Richard Nixon was elected President in 1968 and inherited the tasks of ending the war and healing the divisions it had caused.

See p. T137.

Vocabulary

On a separate sheet of paper, write the word or words that best complete each of the following sentences.

1. _____ are specially trained military units that could be moved quickly to any part of the world.

2. The _____ is the minimum income level considered necessary to live a decent life.

3. Segregation created by housing patterns and not by law is known as _____.

4. A (An) _____ is a Mexican who holds a temporary permit to work in the United States.

5. The systematic separation of races by law is called _____.

See p. T137.

Chapter Checkup

1. (a) What developments increased tensions between the United States and the Soviet Union in 1961 and 1962? (b) What event led to a nuclear test ban treaty? Explain.

2. How did President Kennedy begin to move toward his New Frontier goals in each of the following areas: (a) space exploration; (b) the economy; (c) civil rights?

3. What was the purpose of each of the following: (a) Peace Corps; (b) Alliance for Progress?

4. (a) What did President Johnson mean by the "Great Society"? (b) Describe the major piece of legislation Congress passed as part of the Great Society.

5. (a) What tactics did African Americans use against segregation in the early 1960s? (b) Why did some black leaders demand more radical tactics?

6. (a) What groups in addition to blacks struggled for equality in the 1960s? (b) What kinds of discrimination did each group face?

7. (a) What factors contributed to American involvement in Vietnam? (b) What caused opposition to the war to increase?

8. (a) Who were the "hawks"? What arguments did they use to support their position? (b) Who were the "doves"? How did they support their position?

See p. T137.

Critical Thinking

1. **Analyzing** How did the Kerner Commission offer both warning and cautious hope?

2. **Comparing** (a) How did United States involvement in the Vietnam War differ from its involvement in the Korean War? (b) From its involvement in World War II? (c) How can you relate those differences to public attitudes toward each of the wars?

See p. T137.

Connecting Past and Present

1. As the Voting Rights Act increased black voter registration, more black candidates began to run for office. Name some prominent black elected officials serving today.

2. Since the 1960s, the role of women in society has changed greatly. How do women's roles today differ from their roles before World War II?

See p. T137.

Developing Basic Skills

1. **Placing Events in Time** Construct a time line of major developments from 1930 to 1968 in the struggle of black Americans for greater equality. (a) In which period was there the most progress? Why? (b) In which period was there the most government activity?

2. **Graph Reading** Study the graph on page 747. (a) What happened to the median income of men between 1950 and 1970? (b) What happened to the median income of women? (c) What happened to the relationship between men's and women's median incomes during the period? (d) What conclusion can you draw about men's and women's incomes from the graph?

WRITING ABOUT HISTORY

Footnotes for Books

Footnotes are an important means of documentation for a research paper. They show the reader that you have used sources and provide information about those sources. To write a footnote, place a small number just after and slightly above the quotation, fact, or idea that you are taking from your source. Then identify the source at the bottom of the page or on a separate numbered list at the end of the paper. Study the examples of footnotes that follow.

[1] James Alonzo Bishop, *The Days of Martin Luther King, Jr.* (New York: Putnam, 1971), p. 387.

[2] Bishop, *The Days of Martin Luther King, Jr.,* pp. 411–412.

[3] Edwin S. Gaustad, ed., *A Documentary History of Religion in America Since 1865* (Grand Rapids, Michigan: William B. Eerdmans Publishing Co. 1983), p. 512.

Practice: Write two sample footnotes, using your textbook as the source.

Challenges at Home and Abroad (1969–1980)

35

CHAPTER OUTLINE

1 A Balance of Power

2 The Politics of Stability

3 A Crisis in the Presidency

4 A New Start

5 The Carter White House

CHAPTER OBJECTIVES After completing this chapter, students should be able to
1. describe Richard Nixon's foreign and domestic policies.
2. discuss the Watergate affair and its aftermath.
3. list the main events of the Ford years.
4. discuss the challenges Jimmy Carter faced.

CHAPTER PREVIEW Have students review the events of the 1960s, covered in Chapter 34. Ask: After the turbulence of the 1960s, what do you think most Americans hoped for in the 1970s? From the chapter outline at left and the time line below, do you think the new decade unfolded as Americans hoped it would? Explain.

In 1901, H. G. Wells wrote the science fiction adventure *The First Men on the Moon*. On July 20, 1969, science fiction became science fact. That day, an estimated 600 million people around the world gathered in front of their television sets to share the experience. As the American spaceship *Columbia* orbited the moon, its smaller lunar landing craft, the *Eagle,* detached itself from the mother ship and approached the moon's surface. On board the *Eagle* were two astronauts, Neil Armstrong and Edwin "Buzz" Aldrin.

At 4:17 P.M., Eastern Daylight Time, the *Eagle* touched down on the moon's Sea of Tranquility. Millions on Earth listened in awe as Armstrong radioed back across a quarter-million miles of space to Mission Control in Houston: "Houston. Tranquility Base here. The *Eagle* has landed."

Armstrong and Aldrin remained in their lunar module for six and a half hours before Armstrong descended the ladder to the moon's surface. A television camera on the outside of the landing craft beamed his picture and message back to Earth: "That's one small step for a man, one giant leap for mankind."

After the astronauts had explored for about 50 minutes, they received a call from the White House. President Richard Nixon expressed the sentiments of millions when he said, "This certainly has to be the most historic telephone call ever made. I just can't tell you how proud we all are. . . . Because of what you have done, the heavens have become a part of man's world."

For Americans, the moon mission was an important reassertion of pride and accomplishment at a time of great national turmoil. The nation was still divided by the Vietnam War. Several of its leaders had been killed by assassins. When Neil Armstrong first stepped on the moon, the United States seemed ready once again to meet the challenges that faced it at home and abroad.

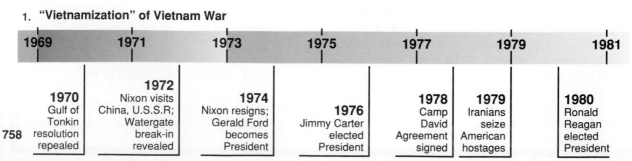

1. "Vietnamization" of Vietnam War

1969	1971	1973	1975	1977	1979	1981

1970 Gulf of Tonkin resolution repealed

1972 Nixon visits China, U.S.S.R.; Watergate break-in revealed

1974 Nixon resigns; Gerald Ford becomes President

1976 Jimmy Carter elected President

1978 Camp David Agreement signed

1979 Iranians seize American hostages

1980 Ronald Reagan elected President

758

1. **TIME LINE QUESTION** Ask: Who was President when the Camp David Agreement was signed?

During the 1970s, more space exploration took place than ever before. Five other moon landings followed the first one. Here, Astronaut David R. Scott salutes the
1. United States flag planted on the moon during the Apollo 15 *mission in 1971. To the right is part of the lunar module, and in the background is the Hadley Delta mountain.*

---

1. **VISUAL EVIDENCE** In outer space, there is no atmosphere to scatter light. Astronauts use special cameras that are extremely light-sensitive.

1 A Balance of Power

READA TO UNDERSTAND

READ TO UNDERSTAND

■ How President Nixon's foreign policy redefined the American role in the world community.

■ How United States involvement in Vietnam ended.

■ Why President Nixon visited China and the Soviet Union.

2. ■ *Vocabulary:* détente.

Richard Nixon's election as President in 1968 was the final step in an amazing political comeback. Six years before, after losing a race for governor of California, he had announced

his retirement from politics. In a bitter press conference, he had blamed his loss—and his earlier defeat in the 1960 presidential 3. election—on the press. But he remained active in politics and in 1968 emerged from retirement to achieve his dream of becoming President.

The New President

"You need a President for foreign policy; no secretary of state is important." Thus President Nixon foretold the direct role he would take in determining the nation's foreign policy. Nixon's interest in foreign affairs overshadowed his concern for domestic affairs. He claimed, in fact, that the nation "could run itself domestically without a President."

As Vice President under Eisenhower, Nixon had traveled to many foreign coun-

759

2. **VOCABULARY** Have students look up this word in the glossary before they begin reading.

3. **PRESIDENTS** "You won't have Richard Nixon to kick around anymore," Nixon angrily told reporters.

tries and had taken an active role in foreign affairs. He came to the presidency with a new
1. approach to foreign policy that surprised both his friends and foes.

Nixon chose a Washington outsider as his chief White House foreign policy adviser. Henry Kissinger had fled from Germany to the United States in 1938 to escape the Nazis and had then served in the United States Army during World War II. A Harvard professor, Kissinger impressed Nixon with his views on Vietnam. During Nixon's presidency, Kissinger would carry out secret diplomatic missions and have a major say in policy. He shared Nixon's view that the United States had to redefine its role in the world community.

Nixon and Kissinger believed that the world could no longer be viewed as divided into opposing communist and noncommunist blocs. Rather, they thought, there were now many centers of power, including Europe, Japan, the People's Republic of China, the Soviet Union, the Middle East, and the United States. Accordingly, United States foreign policy should pursue different goals with each of these power centers.

Both Nixon and Kissinger believed that the United States had overextended itself militarily. As a result, the administration moved to reduce American obligations abroad. In a policy that became known as the Nixon Doctrine, the President stated:

> The United States will participate in the defense and development of allies and friends, but cannot—and will not—conceive all the plans, design all the programs, execute all the decisions and undertake all the defense of the free nations of the world. We will help where it will make a real difference and is considered in our interest.

The War in Vietnam

When Nixon took office in January 1969, more than 540,000 American troops were in Vietnam. To plug what he saw as a serious drain on American resources, Nixon announced a
2. policy of "Vietnamization." Under Vietnamization, South Vietnam would take increased
760 responsibility for fighting the war. In June

1969, Nixon announced the withdrawal of 25,000 American troops from Vietnam.

The President, however, could not abandon South Vietnam completely. Like Lyndon Johnson, he did not want to "lose" to communism. Without informing either Congress or the American public, Nixon ordered a resumption of the bombing of North Vietnam to try to force a political settlement of the war. He also formed plans to stop the flow of
3. enemy supplies along the Ho Chi Minh Trail through Laos and Cambodia.

Invasion of Cambodia Throughout the war, the Viet Cong had used Laos and Cambodia as "sanctuaries," places of refuge where they could go to escape American and South Vietnamese troops. President Johnson had forbidden American troops to enter those countries. He feared that such a move would bring China into the war. In April 1970, Nixon announced that American and South Vietnamese troops were invading enemy sanctuaries in Cambodia.

The Cambodian invasion raised a storm of protest across the United States. Even average citizens who had once regarded opponents of the war as disloyal began to have doubts. The mood of crisis deepened on May 4. On that day, four students were killed and nine others injured when National Guard troops opened fire at an antiwar demonstration at Kent State University in Ohio. At Jackson State College in Mississippi, a similar incident a week later left two students dead and twelve injured.

The day after the Kent State killings, the President announced that troops would be withdrawn from Cambodia within two months. But the antiwar movement was gathering momentum. On May 9, nearly 100,000 protestors assembled in Washington, D.C., to demonstrate opposition to the war. In December 1970, Congress repealed the Gulf of Tonkin resolution, which had provided the legal basis for conducting the war. But Nixon ignored the action. He believed that his role as commander in chief gave him authority to keep troops in Vietnam.

Cease-fire In contrast to the rising pitch of protest was the gradual withdrawal of American troops. By September 1972, only 60,000 remained in Vietnam. Meanwhile,

2. BACKGROUND Nixon also announced a "protective-reactive" policy: Instead of seeking out the enemy, American troops would fight only when attacked.

3. BACKGROUND Remind students that President Johnson had suspended the bombing on March 31, 1968, and that North Vietnam had agreed to negotiate as a result (p. 753).

Henry Kissinger was conducting secret negotiations with the North Vietnamese. In October 1972, just before the presidential election, Kissinger announced that a tentative agreement had been reached: "Peace is at hand."

But optimism was premature. When negotiations broke down in December, Nixon ordered new bombings of the North. These raids were some of the most destructive of the war. The following month, the two sides returned to the conference table and signed a cease-fire. Over the next few months, the remaining American combat forces left the country.

Communist Victory Although the cease-fire brought about the complete withdrawal of American forces, it did not bring peace to the region. The cease-fire broke down, and fighting resumed between North and South Vietnam. In April 1975, the North launched an invasion that crushed the South Vietnamese army. American television viewers watched in horror as desperate South Vietnamese fought with American embassy personnel for space on the last helicopters that flew out of Saigon before the Viet Cong took over the city.

On May 1, North Vietnamese tanks crashed through the gates of the Presidential Palace in Saigon. Saigon was renamed Ho Chi Minh City. North and South Vietnam were reunited under communist rule.

The Vietnam Balance Sheet

The Vietnam War was the longest war in the nation's history. More than 58,000 American soldiers lost their lives and more than 300,000 were wounded. The economic costs of the war were enormous—about $150 billion. For many years to come, the specter of Vietnam would haunt the nation. Americans would wonder why and how the nation had become involved in a war so far away.

3. *As the North Vietnamese massed to attack Saigon, the last Americans prepared to leave the city. After communist rocket fire closed the airport, the largest helicopter rescue mission in history swung into action. Shuttling between the roof of the American embassy and aircraft carriers off the coast, a fleet of 70 helicopters carried more than 1,000 Americans and almost 6,000 Vietnamese to safety.*

1. READING Students who want to learn more about the experiences of Americans in Vietnam can read *Everything We Had: An Oral History of the Vietnam War by 33 American Soldiers Who Fought It,* edited by Al Santoli.

The Vietnam War also led to a limit on presidential power. Troubled by the fact that two Presidents had sent troops into battle without a formal declaration of war, Congress passed the War Powers Act in November 1973. The act declared that a President could not send United States military forces into action for longer than 60 days unless authorized to do so by Congress. Congress hoped that such a measure would prevent similar interventions in the future.

Nixon's Visits to China and the Soviet Union

In perhaps the most unexpected move of his presidency, Nixon acted to restore relations between the United States and China, the most populous communist country in the world. Nixon had been a strong anticommunist throughout his political career. As Nixon saw it, the split that had developed between China and the Soviet Union in the

THE AMERICAN EXPERIENCE

Vietnam Veterans War Memorial

They come as pilgrims to mourn the loss of a son, a sweetheart, a buddy. Some kneel and cry; others salute; still others rub their hands over the polished black surface. The place where they come is officially known as the Vietnam Veterans Memorial. Most visitors refer to it simply as "the Wall."

In the late 1970s, a competition was held to decide the design of a Vietnam War memorial to be erected in Washington, D.C. Judges chose the design of architecture student Maya Ying Lin over 1,420 other entries. She designed a memorial made of two black granite walls, each 250 feet (75 meters) long, that slope down into the ground and meet to form a *V.* The names of more than 58,000 Americans who lost their lives in the Vietnam War are etched on the wall. Lin said of her design, "It does not glorify the war or make an antiwar statement. It is a place for private reckoning."

Since its completion in 1982, millions of visitors have come to the Wall. They have left all manner of mementos behind, among them flags, military medals, lyrics of a favorite song, letters, toys, candles. The National Parks Service has gathered and stored these mementos as historical artifacts. One visitor left a message that read, "Dear Michael: Your name is here but you are not. I made a rubbing of it, thinking that if I rubbed hard enough I would rub your name off the wall and you would come back to me."

When Vietnam veterans returned home, they did not get the enthusiastic welcome that veterans of previous wars had received. Too many at home were not ready to appreciate what the veterans had done. The Wall has helped to heal the national wounds caused by the war. Jack Wheeler, who played a key role in getting the memorial built, said, "It exposes, and thereby ends, the denial that has characterized the country's reaction to the war. It is probably the single most important step in the process of healing and redemption."

See p. T138.

1. What purpose did the designer of the Vietnam Veterans Memorial have in mind?

2. Critical Thinking How do you think the memorial has helped to heal the wounds of the war?

2. DISCUSSION Ask if any students in the class have visited the Vietnam War memorial, or if they have any relatives whose names are inscribed on the wall.

Following the communist victory in China's civil war, there was no direct contact between the People's Republic of China and the United States for more than 20 years. When relations between the two countries thawed during the
1. early 1970s, teen-agers on an American table tennis team became the first American visitors to China. Part of the group is shown here with interpreters on the Great Wall of China.

1. **BACKGROUND** The visit of the American table tennis team was popularly referred to as "Ping-Pong diplomacy."

late 1950s (see page 750) provided an opportunity for the United States to make diplomatic gains. In July 1971, Henry Kissinger made a secret trip to China to arrange a visit by President Nixon the following February. After 22 years of silence between the two nations, China and the United States began a dialogue.

During Nixon's visit, he toured the Great Wall of China, attended banquets, and met with Chinese leader Mao Zedong. The two leaders agreed on scientific and cultural exchanges and expressed an interest in increasing trade. A year later, China and the United States took steps toward formal recognition.

Any change in the United States relationship with China was bound to affect its relationship with China's rival, the Soviet Union. Consequently, Nixon made a gesture to improve relations with the Soviet Union. In May 1972, he visited that nation, the first President to do so since World War II. His trip marked the beginning of an era of **détente** (day TAHNT), a relaxation of tension between the two superpowers.

While in Moscow, the President and Soviet leaders signed an arms control agreement, the Strategic Arms Limitation Treaty (SALT). This treaty restricted the types and numbers of nuclear warheads and missiles that each country could deploy. President Nixon's visit also opened new avenues of international cooperation and trade, including scientific cooperation and the sale of American wheat to the Soviet Union. Most Americans, eager to reduce international tensions and the threat of nuclear war, approved of détente.

See p. T138.

SECTION 1 REVIEW

1. **Identify:** (a) Henry Kissinger, (b) SALT.

2. **Define:** détente.

3. (a) What was Nixon's approach to foreign policy? (b) Describe the Nixon Doctrine.

4. How did United States military involvement in Vietnam end?

5. What agreement did Nixon reach with China during his 1972 visit?

6. **Critical Thinking** Why would Nixon's reputation as an anticommunist have helped him win acceptance of his foreign policy?

763

2. **ECONOMICS** Farmers were especially pleased because wheat sales to the Soviet Union increased the price of their grain. However, many consumers in the U.S. complained about a rise in domestic food prices.

2 The Politics of Stability

READ TO UNDERSTAND

■ What decisions the Supreme Court made regarding the rights of people accused of crimes.

■ What new approaches Nixon took toward social programs and civil rights.

■ How rising oil prices affected the lives of Americans.

1. ■ *Vocabulary:* impound, stagflation.

In winning the 1968 election, Nixon had the support of many Americans who felt that the protest and reform movements of the 1960s had gone too far. They did not join in demonstrations in the streets against the war, racism, or injustice. Rather, this "silent majority" was more concerned with issues and problems that affected them more directly, such as crime and inflation.

GREAT DEBATE

The Supreme Court and Crime

Throughout his election campaign, Nixon had stressed law and order issues that concerned many Americans. As President, he supported anticrime measures that increased the power of law enforcement officials. But Nixon's most lasting influence on criminal justice probably resulted from his four appointments to the Supreme Court.

The Warren Court Nixon was a strong critic of Chief Justice Earl Warren, whom he considered too liberal. During the 1960s, under Warren, the Supreme Court had handed down several rulings that increased the rights of people accused of crimes. In *Gideon* v. *Wainwright* (1963), for example, the Court held that states had to provide free legal repre-
2. sentation for defendants who could not afford to hire lawyers.

Other Warren Court decisions restricted methods used by police to gather evidence against suspected criminals. In *Mapp* v. *Ohio*

(1961), the Supreme Court ruled that items illegally seized by police could not be used as evidence against the accused. In *Miranda* v. *Arizona* (1966), the Court held that, before questioning accused persons, police must inform them of their rights to remain silent and to be represented by a lawyer.

Many Americans agreed with Nixon's view that the Warren Court rulings restricted the power of the police too much. These critics argued that the Court had tipped the balance of justice in favor of accused persons at the expense of victims and society.

In 1969, poor health forced Chief Justice Warren to resign from the Court. President Nixon appointed Warren Burger, a respected judge from Minnesota, to replace him. Burger shared Nixon's concern that the Court had been too liberal in protecting criminal suspects. Nixon later filled three more vacancies on the Court, selecting Harry Blackmun of Minnesota, Lewis F. Powell of Virginia, and William H. Rehnquist of Arizona.

The Burger Court Chief Justice Burger steered the Supreme Court along a more conservative path. Although the Court did not reverse earlier criminal procedure decisions, it did limit their scope. For example, the Court held that even if police violated the *Miranda* rule in obtaining a pretrial confession, that confession could still be used to discredit trial testimony of the defendant.

The Burger Court also narrowed the scope of the *Mapp* decision. It ruled that questions based on illegally seized evidence 3. could be asked at a grand jury hearing, even if they could not be asked in a jury trial.

But the final word on balancing the rights of the accused against the rights of society had not yet been heard. The issue remains a subject of concern. ■

Nixon's Domestic Policies

President Nixon found himself at odds with Congress over President Johnson's Great Society. (See page 741.) Concerned about inflation, Nixon vetoed several major bills that provided funds to continue Johnson's social programs. Congress, whose support for the

2. **READING** Students interested in the law might like to read and report on *Gideon's Trumpet* by Anthony Lewis, an account of the Gideon case.

3. **MAIN IDEA** Have students contrast the Burger Court's rulings on the rights of the accused with those of the Warren Court.

Great Society remained strong, overrode the Nixon vetoes. In response, the President **impounded,** or refused to spend, funds that
1. Congress had appropriated. Despite such actions, federal spending for social programs continued to rise during the Nixon years.

Nixon did not support the rights of minorities as vigorously as his predecessor had. His administration opposed the extension of the Voting Rights Act of 1965 and denounced court-ordered busing to achieve racial integration of the nation's schools. The White
2. House also relaxed federal guidelines governing school desegregation.

Nixon's civil rights programs did, however, seek to increase employment for black workers and to assist black-owned businesses. During the Nixon administration, the number of small, black-owned businesses increased. Still, most blacks considered Nixon's record disappointing.

Economic Problems

The Vietnam War gave rise to a number of economic problems that continued to trouble the nation into the 1970s. Military spending during the war had stimulated inflation; by 1970, the annual rate of inflation had reached 5 percent. At the same time, growth of the economy had stalled, or become stagnant; recession now joined inflation. Finally, thousands of Vietnam veterans had returned home looking for jobs. But jobs were not available, and unemployment rose to 6 percent. Economists called this combination of economic conditions—inflation, recession, and high unemployment—**stagflation.**

As a conservative, President Nixon disliked government interference in the economy. So he surprised Americans when he ordered a temporary freeze on wages, prices, and rents in August 1971 to control inflation. The freeze soon changed to price controls monitored by a Cost of Living Council. Although these measures were effective temporarily, prices soared when Nixon lifted the controls in early 1973. Inflation increased further that year as a result of an oil embargo in the Middle East.

Arab Oil Embargo In 1960, the major oil-exporting nations formed the Organization of Petroleum Exporting Countries (OPEC). OPEC demanded a voice in setting oil prices and production quotas. They had little success until 1973.

In October 1973, Egyptian and Syrian troops launched a surprise attack on Israel on the Jewish holiday of Yom Kippur. The fighting continued for several weeks. Henry Kissinger, now secretary of state, flew back

3. **GRAPH READING** Ask: What was the purchasing power of the dollar in 1960? In 1970? In 1980?

GRAPH STUDY *As a result of inflation, the* 3. *purchasing power of the dollar declined steadily between 1960 and 1980. This graph shows how much a 1967 dollar could have bought in each of the years shown. During what year did the dollar drop to half its 1960 value?* See p. T139.

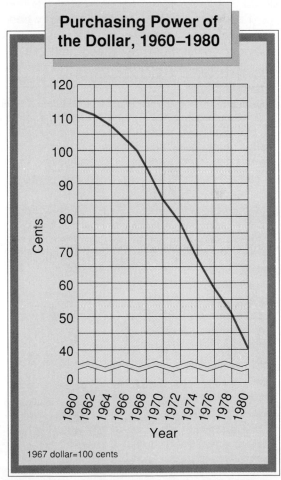

Purchasing Power of the Dollar, 1960–1980

1967 dollar=100 cents

Source: U.S. Department of Labor, Bureau of Labor Statistics

765

1. **ECONOMICS** The oil embargo was also imposed on Europe and Japan, which suffered even more than the United States because they imported more of their oil.

2. **BACKGROUND** Remind students that Kennedy's ambitious space program was in part a response to the Soviet success with *Sputnik I.*

and forth between the Arab and Israeli capitals. As a result of his "shuttle diplomacy," he was finally able to arrange a cease-fire.

Although Kissinger helped end the fighting, the Arab nations resented the United States policy of support for Israel. During the October War, the United States had supplied Israel with military and economic aid. In retaliation, the Arab oil-producing nations embargoed, or stopped, oil shipments to the United States. Because the United States 1. imported about 25 percent of the oil it used, the embargo seriously disrupted American life.

Oil Shortage at Home Americans soon found themselves waiting in long lines to buy gasoline—if they could get any at all. The price of fuel oil quadrupled, and costs soared for thousands of other petroleum-based products, such as plastics, medicines, and fertilizers.

President Nixon encouraged energy conservation to ease the crisis. He asked the states to lower highway speed limits to 55 miles per hour to improve gas mileage. In an effort to increase domestic oil production, he authorized construction of an oil pipeline in Alaska.

Although the Arab nations lifted the oil embargo in March 1974, OPEC, which included several non-Arab nations, became a powerful force. OPEC continued to raise the price of oil throughout the 1970s. The lesson was clear: Americans needed to become more careful about the ways they used energy.

A Lunar Triumph

"Men have landed and walked on the moon." So began a news report of one of the brightest moments of the Nixon administration. In 1961, President Kennedy had vowed to have a man on the moon by 1970. That pledge 2. became a reality a year ahead of schedule.

In July 1969, Commander Neil Armstrong led the three-man mission that orbited the moon and descended to its surface in a lunar

3. **LOCAL HISTORY** Have students interview local residents or read local newspapers to learn how your area was affected by the oil embargo.

The oil embargo was a rude jolt to the American people. It demonstrated the nation's dependence on foreign sources of energy. Gas stations with signs saying, "Sorry, we're dry," were common sights for motorists. To conserve fuel oil, 3. *homes, businesses, and schools lowered their thermostats. The children in this Kansas classroom wear heavy coats, gloves, and hats to keep warm.*

2. **TECHNOLOGY** Interested students might like to research and report on other ways that space technology has benefited consumers.

The Election of 1972

The year 1972 was the high point of Nixon's presidency. The economy appeared stable, and most people approved of the President's policy of détente. Nixon and Vice President Agnew easily won renomination at the Republican convention that year.

The Democratic party, on the other hand, was badly split. Senator George McGovern of South Dakota won the presidential nomination, but many Democrats felt he was too liberal. McGovern's problems mounted when he felt obliged to drop his running mate, Senator Thomas Eagleton of Missouri, from the ticket because Eagleton had once suffered an emotional illness. McGovern replaced him with Sargent Shriver, former director of the Peace Corps and a brother-in-law of John Kennedy.

Meanwhile, President Nixon based a well-organized and well-financed campaign on his record in foreign policy. American involvement in Vietnam was winding down, and many Americans saw him as a decisive and competent leader. Nixon won the election by a landslide, carrying every state but Massachusetts and winning almost 61 percent of the popular vote. Nixon thus began his second term with a strong mandate. Few could have predicted that within two years his political career would be in shambles.

See p. T139.

The space program was a source of pride to Americans. Space exploration in the 1970s provided more information on Earth's neighbors than had been gathered in all previous human history. This lithograph, Splashdown, by Robert T. McCall, shows the Apollo spacecraft returning from a successful mission. The billowing shapes of
1. the red, white, and blue parachutes capture the patriotic mood of the moment.

---

1. **VISUAL EVIDENCE** Ask: Does this picture still stir patriotic feelings? Why or why not?

module. (See page 758.) Five other lunar landings followed, with the last occurring in December 1972.

The space program brought benefits beyond the thrill of exploration. Space satellites improved communications, navigation, and weather forecasting on Earth. The use of small computers aboard space capsules stimulated the microelectronics industry. Other space research led to the production
2. of more efficient insulating materials, devices that generated solar energy, and freeze-dried foods.

SECTION 2 REVIEW

1. **Identify:** (a) Earl Warren, (b) Warren Burger, (c) OPEC, (d) Neil Armstrong, (e) George McGovern.

2. **Define:** (a) impound, (b) stagflation.

3. What did the Supreme Court rule in the case of *Miranda* v. *Arizona*?

4. What actions did the Nixon administration take regarding social programs and civil rights?

5. What role did the United States play during the Arab-Israeli war of October 1973?

6. **Critical Thinking** What advantages does a President in office have in an election campaign?

3. **CITIZENSHIP** In 1971, the Twenty-sixth Amendment to the Constitution had lowered the voting age to 18. Many of these young first-time voters supported McGovern, an antiwar candidate, in 1972.

3 A Crisis in the Presidency

READ TO UNDERSTAND

■ How a break-in of Democratic party headquarters led to a Senate investigation that shocked the nation.

■ What actions led to calls for President Nixon's impeachment.

■ How the Watergate affair demonstrated the strength of the system of checks and balances.

During the 1972 presidential campaign, a mysterious break-in took place at the Democratic party headquarters in Washington, D.C. Almost unnoticed at the time, this incident would force Richard Nixon to become the first President to resign from office.

A Puzzling Burglary

At 2:30 A.M. on June 17, 1972, in the nation's capital, police arrested five men who had broken into the Democratic National Committee headquarters, located in the Watergate apartment complex. One of the Watergate burglars, James McCord, had worked as a security consultant for the Committee to Re-elect the President (CRP). An address book carried by the burglars contained the name of another White House employee.

When asked about the incident, White House Press Secretary Ronald Ziegler called the incident a "third-rate burglary attempt." The President dismissed the break-in as a "bizarre incident" and insisted that no one in the White House was involved.

Yet, during the months that followed, other disturbing facts came to light, many of them uncovered by *Washington Post* reporters Bob Woodward and Carl Bernstein. Reports pointed to the existence of a $350,000 "slush fund" controlled by CRP and used to finance undercover projects to discredit Democratic party rivals. Other information suggested that Nixon's former attorney general, John Mitchell, knew of the fund and might even have approved the illegal activities.

On the day sentences were imposed on the convicted Watergate burglars, the judge revealed the contents of a letter from James McCord. McCord charged that certain high officials had pressed the burglars to plead guilty so their trial would be concluded quickly.

The Cover-up Unravels

The suspicion that the White House had something to hide increased. Investigations linked high-level officials to the cover-up, including John Mitchell and President Nixon's two closest aides, H. R. Haldeman and John Ehrlichman.

In May 1973, a special committee set up by the Senate met to hear testimony about Watergate. Senator Sam Ervin of North Carolina, who headed the Senate committee, was determined to discover what the President knew about the Watergate burglary and cover-up. For three months, the televised committee hearings gave the public a close look at the Watergate investigation.

The most astonishing testimony came from John Dean, the former White House counsel. In a quiet voice, Dean related a detailed sequence of events and accused President Nixon of suppressing information about the Watergate break-in. Dean charged that the President had approved plans to pay the Watergate burglars "hush money" to remain silent.

The White House denied Dean's charges. The case against the President seemed to rest on Dean's word alone. Then, in July, a White House aide surprised committee members when he revealed that all of the President's conversations had been routinely tape-recorded.

The Investigation Continues

Meanwhile, Nixon had moved to dispel charges that he was obstructing the Watergate investigation. The President had in-

2. **PAST AND PRESENT** Also sentenced was G. Gordon Liddy, a lawyer for CRP. In the 1980s, Liddy became an actor, appearing on such television shows as *Miami Vice.*

3. **BACKGROUND** Committee member Howard Baker, a Tennessee Republican, doggedly asked each witness, "What did the President know and when did he know it?"

1. **ACTIVITY** Have students write a newspaper article about the Saturday Night Massacre that includes a headline.

structed his attorney general, Elliot Richardson, to appoint an independent special prosecutor to handle the case. Richardson chose Archibald Cox, a respected Harvard University law professor.

Cox moved quickly to gain access to White House records, including the tapes. Nixon refused to release the tapes. He claimed that "executive privilege" allowed him to withhold certain tapes for reasons of national security. Thereupon, on July 23, Cox requested a subpoena, a legally binding order, directing the President to turn over selected tapes to the special prosecutor's office.

In growing desperation, Nixon ordered Richardson to fire Cox. Richardson refused and promptly resigned, as did his immediate subordinate. Solicitor General Robert Bork carried out the order, firing Cox on Saturday, October 20.

1. Reporters dubbed the resignations and firing the Saturday Night Massacre. Letters of protest poured into Congress, where 16 separate bills were introduced calling for impeachment of the President. The House Judiciary Committee, under Chairman Peter Rodino of New Jersey, began impeachment deliberations.*

Agnew's Undoing

While Nixon's situation in the Watergate affair became more difficult, another inquiry was in progress. Officials charged that Vice President Agnew, both while governor of Maryland and while Vice President, had accepted bribes from construction companies doing business with the state of Maryland.

2. Faced with a strong case against him and the prospect of going to prison, Agnew resigned as Vice President on October 10, 1973. According to the Twenty-fifth Amendment, the President must select a new Vice President when that position becomes vacant. Accordingly, President Nixon chose Repre-

---

*The House of Representatives can impeach, or accuse, a President of high crimes and misdemeanors. The Senate then tries the case, and if it votes to convict, the President is removed from office.

"The finest thing to come out of the mind of man," is the way Senator Sam Ervin, chairman of the Watergate hearings, described the United States Constitution. Ervin's "country-lawyer" style could not conceal his keen mind as he sharply questioned witnesses involved in the Watergate scandals. The televised Watergate hearings educated the American public on the process of the American constitutional system in a time of crisis.

3.

3. **DISCUSSION** Ervin stated that he considered Watergate the greatest tragedy in U.S. history.

sentative Gerald Ford of Michigan to fill the vacant office and Congress confirmed the appointment on October 12.

The Crisis Deepens

With the pressures against him mounting, President Nixon appointed a new special prosecutor, Leon Jaworski of Texas. The President also agreed to release the subpoenaed tapes. But embarrassed White House lawyers were forced to tell the court that some of the tapes were missing. Even worse, an apparently crucial 18½-minute segment of one tape had been erased. Experts testified that the erasures were probably deliberate.

In March 1974, the grand jury investigating Watergate matters indicted Mitchell, Hal-

2. **BACKGROUND** To avoid a trial, Agnew pleaded "no contest" to income tax evasion. In exchange, prosecutors dropped the other charges. Agnew was fined $10,000 and sentenced to three years on probation.

deman, Ehrlichman, and several other Nixon aides for perjury and obstruction of justice. The grand jury named the President as an
1. unindicted co-conspirator. In April, Special Prosecutor Jaworski and the House Judiciary Committee requested additional tapes. The President refused to supply them. In July, the Supreme Court ruled that Nixon must turn the tapes over to Jaworski.

Later that month, the Judiciary Committee passed three articles of impeachment against the President. The articles claimed that the President had obstructed justice, misused his presidential powers, and refused

---

2. *Here, President Nixon gives a final wave before beginning his trip back to California on his last day in office. While Nixon flew westward on Air Force One, Gerald Ford was sworn in as the 38th President of the United States.*

to comply with the committee's request for evidence.

Nixon finally relented and released transcripts of the tapes in question. The evidence of the President's involvement in the Watergate cover-up was clear—and shocking. The transcripts revealed that only days after the burglary, the President had ordered the FBI to stop its investigation of the break-in. Impeachment by the House seemed certain.

To forestall the inevitable, President Nixon appeared on national television on August 8, 1974, and announced his decision to resign. He became the first President in the history of the republic to take such an action. Gerald Ford then succeeded Nixon as President, the first person to assume this office without having been elected as either President or Vice President.

The Imperial Presidency

Even before Watergate, some critics had charged that recent Presidents were creating an "imperial presidency" by assuming too much power. During the Nixon years, the White House staff grew to 500 persons, more than double the size of any previous presidential staff. Members of the White House staff do not have to be confirmed by the Senate, as cabinet members do. Thus, influential staff members, such as H. R. Haldeman and John Ehrlichman, were not responsible to anyone but the President.

Furthermore, critics were concerned that recent Presidents had exceeded presidential authority, as defined by the Constitution. Nixon, for example, had defied Congress by impounding funds Congress had appropriated. He had also raised questions of constitutionality when he claimed the right to refuse to allow members of the executive branch to testify before congressional committees.

The events of Watergate focused attention on the powers of the President and brought demands for reform. Congress responded with several new laws. The Congressional Budget and Impoundment Act of 1974 revised congressional budget-making practices and forbade a President to impound funds appropriated by Congress. The Fed-

2. CRITICAL THINKING Have students consider the irony of the circumstances in which Nixon, the "law-and-order candidate" in 1968, was forced from office.

1. **LOCAL HISTORY** Have students interview relatives and neighbors about their recollections of the Watergate scandal. Students might ask: Have your opinions about Watergate and President Nixon changed since 1974?

eral Campaign Reform Act of 1974 provided tax funds for candidates for federal office and placed limits on private campaign contributions. Congress also strengthened the 1966 Freedom of Information Act, giving the public greater access to information on government activities.

Watergate in Retrospect

1. The Watergate crisis was a traumatic experience for the nation. Yet, it also demonstrated the strength of the system of checks and balances. Congress and the Supreme Court had successfully checked the power of the President when he appeared to be abusing that power. The balance of powers outlined in the Constitution had been maintained.

While Watergate revealed the dangers of an "imperial presidency," it also demonstrated that no President is above the law. As Gerald Ford commented upon taking office, "Our great republic is a government of laws and not of men." That no President can

2. ignore the law seems to be one enduring lesson of the Watergate experience.

To some observers, Nixon's resignation in August 1974 marked the real end of the turbulent decade of the 1960s. Strong feelings about the Vietnam War and Watergate had sharply divided the nation. It was now up to Gerald Ford to try to heal the nation's wounds.

See p. T139.

SECTION 3 REVIEW

1. **Identify:** (a) John Mitchell, (b) Sam Ervin, (c) John Dean, (d) Archibald Cox, (c) Gerald Ford, (f) Leon Jaworski.

2. What was the Saturday Night Massacre?

3. Why were the tapes important in the Watergate case?

4. What charges did the House Judiciary Committee make against Nixon?

5. **Critical Thinking** Why do you think many Americans in recent years favored a strong President?

4 A New Start

READ TO UNDERSTAND

■ What controversies affected the Ford presidency.

■ How President Ford attempted to deal with economic problems.

■ How Ford continued Nixon's foreign policies.

"Our long national nightmare is over," President Gerald Ford proclaimed after taking the oath of office. Indeed, after the turmoil the nation experienced as a result of Vietnam and Watergate, the public desperately wanted a return to stability.

The Unexpected President

Gerald Ford had served his congressional district in Michigan for 25 years, earning a reputation for hard work and dependability. His colleagues in the House liked him and
3. had warmly supported his selection as Vice President when Spiro Agnew resigned.

After the disillusionment caused by the Watergate affair, Ford seemed an ideal person to hold the presidency. He was outgoing and scrupulously honest, and people responded to his simple lifestyle. Ford's pledge of "openness and candor" drew wide praise. So, too, did his promise to hold regular news conferences and to make himself available to the nation.

As President, Ford moved quickly to assure stability and to restore confidence in government. He selected Nelson Rockefeller, a former governor of New York, as his Vice President. He retained Henry Kissinger as secretary of state and promised to follow the foreign policy established by Nixon.

New Controversies

Ford's popularity soon suffered a severe setback. Only a month after taking office, President Ford issued a pardon that freed Richard Nixon from prosecution for any crimes

2. **ACTIVITY** Have students draw a political cartoon about one event or lesson of the Watergate affair.

3. **PRESIDENTS** "The nicest thing about Jerry Ford," said Senator Robert Griffin, "is that he just doesn't have enemies."

President Ford promised to "bind up the nation's wounds." His down-to-earth style was welcome. Two weeks after becoming President, Ford visited Chicago to
1. *address the Veterans of Foreign Wars. Leaving his car in the motorcade, Ford plunged into the crowd to shake hands and sign autographs.*

1. **PRESIDENTS** In September 1975, two different women attempted to assassinate President Ford. The President was shaken but unhurt.

2. **ACTIVITY** Have students write a letter to President Ford either supporting or opposing his pardon of Nixon.

he might have committed while in office. Ford stated that he wanted to spare the country the agony of putting a former President on trial.

The pardon set off a storm of controversy and suspicion. The White House was flooded with phone calls and telegrams critical of
2. Ford's action. Many people questioned the justice of allowing Nixon to escape punishment while many of his subordinates had gone to jail. There were even charges of a secret deal between Nixon and Ford. President Ford defended the pardon decision vigorously. Nevertheless, he would never entirely regain the good will and support he had had when he first took office.

Disclosures of FBI and CIA misconduct also startled the nation. In December 1974, the press revealed that the CIA had spied on and kept files on American citizens, in direct violation of the agency's charter. And in February 1975, it was discovered that J. Edgar

Hoover, the longtime head of the FBI, had kept secret files on prominent Americans. President Ford appointed a high-level commission to investigate the charges against the CIA. At the same time, Congress set up special committees to investigate both agencies and moved to restrict their undercover activities.

Ford sparked another controversy when he offered amnesty, or pardon, to those who had illegally avoided military service during the Vietnam War. The President said he wanted to heal the social divisions caused by the war. Critics charged that Ford's plan 3. was too lenient on people who had refused to fight for their country. In any case, few people took advantage of the amnesty offer. Some refused because they opposed Ford's requirement that they perform some kind of alternative national service. To them, accepting the offer would be an admission that their resistance to military service had been wrong.

3. **CRITICAL THINKING** Have students discuss Ford's pardon of Nixon and his offer of amnesty to draft evaders. Ask: What do the two actions reveal about Ford?

1. **ECONOMICS** Make sure students understand why Ford thought cutting taxes would help end the recession and why cutting government spending would slow inflation.

2. **BACKGROUND** A high point of détente occurred in July 1975. A Soviet and an American spacecraft docked in space, and the two crews performed joint experiments.

A Troubled Economy

Ford's political problems were matched by serious economic difficulties. Steep increases in the price of oil had caused a sharp jump in the inflation rate. To counter rising prices, Ford began a voluntary program of controlling prices and wages called WIN (Whip Inflation Now).

Instead of improving, the economy got worse, and the nation soon entered the worst recession since the 1930s. Many factories closed, and consumer demand for goods dropped sharply. The rate of unemployment rose steadily, reaching about 9 percent by late 1975.

To stimulate the economy, Ford persuaded Congress to approve a tax cut. While the cut contributed to a modest economic recovery, it also sparked a new round of inflation. The economy seemed stalled in a pattern of alternating periods of recession and growing inflation. President Ford tried to control inflation by cutting government spending. He vetoed a number of spending bills passed by Congress. But inflation continued to plague the nation.

Continuity in Foreign Policy

In foreign affairs, President Ford maintained the policies of the Nixon administration. With Henry Kissinger as his secretary of state, Ford extended détente. He visited the Soviet Union in November 1974 and met with Soviet President Leonid Brezhnev to discuss a new treaty to limit nuclear arms.

The following year, the President traveled to Helsinki, Finland, where he signed an agreement with the Soviet Union, Canada, and 32 other nations in western and eastern Europe. The agreement, known as the Helsinki Accords, recognized the national boundaries set up after World War II. It also spelled out human rights standards that the signing nations pledged to observe.

Despite these signs of cooperation, by 1976, relations with the Soviet Union had begun to cool. Critics of détente charged that the Soviet Union had cheated on nuclear arms

3. **BIOGRAPHY** Golda Meir (1898–1978) was born in Kiev, Russia. Her family moved to Milwaukee, Wisconsin, when she was eight. In 1921, she settled in Palestine, where she worked for the creation of a Jewish state. In 1969, she became Israel's first woman prime minister.

Henry Kissinger was an important force in American foreign policy for many years. As secretary of state in both the Nixon and Ford administrations, Kissinger was a strong advocate of "personal diplomacy" and traveled the world conferring with foreign leaders. Here, he is shown meeting with Israeli Prime Minister Golda Meir.

1. **LOCAL HISTORY** Have students find out if Vietnamese refugees settled in your area and how they adjusted to life here. You might have a refugee talk to the class.

agreements and had steadily increased its arsenal of weapons. They contended that the Soviet Union had encouraged Egypt to attack Israel in 1973 and that it was arming other countries in the Third World. Many still viewed the Soviet Union as an adversary rather than a partner in détente.

Foreign Policy in Southeast Asia

Although the United States was no longer actively involved in the Vietnam War during the Ford administration, the aftershocks were still being felt. In 1975, the nation witnessed the defeat of South Vietnam by the North, as well as the evacuation of American embassy personnel from Saigon. Immediately after the communist takeover (see page 761), more than 100,000 South Vietnam-
1. ese fled their country, many coming to the United States.

2. **VISUAL EVIDENCE** "Operation Sail" involved 225 sailing ships and 300 nations.

President Ford told Americans to "break out the flag, strike up the band, light up the sky," for the bicentennial, and the nation gladly complied. In New York City, old-fashioned sailing ships from many nations sailed through the harbor. "Operation
2. *Sail" ended with a spectacular fireworks display at the Statue of Liberty.*

At approximately the same time, the pro-American government of neighboring Cambodia also collapsed and was replaced by a communist regime led by Pol Pot. The suffering inflicted on the Cambodian people by the Pol Pot regime was enormous. More than one million Cambodians are believed to have starved or been executed.

In May 1975, Cambodia's new regime seized the American merchant ship *Mayaguez* after the ship had entered Cambodian waters. President Ford called the seizure an "act of piracy." He sent a naval force and about 2,000 marines to free the crew of 39. Although 15 Americans died and 50 were wounded in the operation, most Americans supported the President.

The 1976 Election

While the Ford administration had little time to forge its own policies, the President's honesty and goodwill helped the nation recover from the Watergate affair. Most Americans welcomed the positive mood as they celebrated the nation's bicentennial on July 4, 1976.

Nonetheless, President Ford faced a strong challenge for the 1976 Republican presidential nomination. Ronald W. Reagan, former governor of California, had the support of the conservative wing of the Republican party. Ford won a narrow victory at the party convention, but echoes of the Watergate scandal weakened his chances for election.

Former Georgia Governor Jimmy Carter carried the Democratic banner. Little known outside Georgia two years earlier, Carter's effective campaigning won him the nomination. He promised the American people, "I will never lie to you," a reminder of the scandals of the Nixon presidency.

Neither candidate offered well-defined programs on the major issues of the campaign—inflation, unemployment, and energy shortages. However, Jimmy Carter's strong civil rights record as governor brought him overwhelming support from black voters. Carter won a slim popular majority, with
3. 40.8 million popular votes to 39.1 million for Ford. In the electoral college, Carter won 297 votes to 241 for Ford.

3. **PRESIDENTS** Jimmy Carter is the only graduate of the U.S. Naval Academy to be elected President.

When Jimmy Carter told his mother in 1974 that he was going to run for President, she replied, "President of what?" Carter is shown at left campaigning on a "Democratic Whistlestop" tour in Pennsylvania. At the Republican nominating convention, before facing Carter in the election, President Ford faced a stiff challenge from Ronald Reagan. Some of Reagan's conservative supporters are shown at right.

1.

1. **VISUAL EVIDENCE** In a "whistlestop" tour, a candidate travels in a train, speaking to crowds at each stop from the back of the train. Have students suggest reasons why a candidate might use this method today.

See p. T140.

SECTION 4 REVIEW

1. **Identify:** (a) Nelson Rockefeller, (b) WIN, (c) Helsinki Accords.

2. What revelations about the CIA and FBI startled the nation?

3. (a) How did President Ford try to stimulate the economy? (b) What effect did this measure have?

4. On what grounds did some Americans criticize the policy of détente during the mid-1970s?

5. **Critical Thinking** Do you think that President Ford's pardon of Nixon benefited or harmed the nation? Explain.

5 The Carter White House

READ TO UNDERSTAND

■ What difficult economic problems President Carter faced.

■ How Carter made human rights the centerpiece of his foreign policy.

■ How the Iran hostage crisis contributed to Carter's defeat.

"Why not the best?" asked Jimmy Carter during the 1976 presidential campaign. With few ties to official Washington, he promised to bring new faces and ideas to national government. As an "outsider," however, Carter

2.

775

2. **PRESIDENTS** Jimmy Carter declared: "I have been accused of being an outsider. I plead guilty. Unfortunately, the vast majority of Americans . . . are also outsiders."

1. **DISCUSSION** Ask: What might be the advantages and disadvantages of appointing advisers who were new to Washington?

2. **VISUAL EVIDENCE** Ask: How do you think Carter's informal style helped him become President in the post-Watergate atmosphere of the mid-1970s?

had to convince the traditional leadership in Washington to enact his programs. The task was a difficult one in light of both inflation and recession at home and mounting world tensions.

New Leadership in Washington

When James Earl Carter announced he would seek the Democratic nomination for President, few people thought he could win. Carter had served as governor of Georgia but had little experience in national or international politics. In addition, no candidate from the deep South had won the presidency since before the Civil War. Finally, Carter lacked support from Democratic party leaders. He proved, however, to have wide appeal among rank-and-file Democrats.

Carter promised honest government to a nation still struggling to forget Watergate. Many Americans welcomed his low-key, folksy manner and deep religious convictions. They thought that such a President would surely bring the federal government back in touch with the people. Carter planned to appoint people to his administration who were new 1. to national government.

At his inauguration, Carter showed that he intended to transplant much of his simple, down-home style to Washington. He substituted a business suit for the formal attire Presidents usually wore for the inauguration ceremony. And in administering the presidential oath of office, the Chief Justice of the Supreme Court used Carter's nickname, "Jimmy," rather than his given name, James Earl. Afterward, rather than ride in the presidential limousine, Carter walked from the Capitol to the White House.

A Stalemate With Congress

As President, Carter faced several particularly difficult issues. These including a spiraling inflation and a severe energy crisis. At

"He helps me with everything," Rosalynn Carter told reporters about her husband.

2. The Carters brought their relaxed, down-home style to Washington. Shown here on the White House veranda, they look as if they might be back in their home town of Plains, Georgia.

the same time, he also faced an assertive Congress, eager to limit presidential authority after Vietnam and Watergate.

Carter's personal style of operation sometimes added to his problems. Never having served in Congress, he did not have close ties with the Democratic leadership in the House and Senate. Many of his advisers were also new to Washington. Furthermore, Carter's critics charged that the President became bogged down in details and failed to emphasize broad goals for his administration.

In his first year in office, Carter showered Congress with almost a dozen major bills covering tax reform, social security, energy, and other pressing matters. Faced with strong opposition, however, no bill passed without major alterations. For example, the President initiated a bill to lower income taxes for the poor. It also closed certain tax "loopholes" that allowed many people to avoid paying taxes, no matter how much they earned. While the bill that Congress passed did lower some taxes, it also raised the Social Security tax. The result was an increased tax bill for most Americans.

In April 1977, Carter sent a National Energy Plan to Congress. As you have read, an energy crisis loomed large even before Carter assumed the presidency. After the Arab oil embargo of 1973, enormous oil shortages rocked the nation and oil prices soared. (See page 765.) Energy policy was thus a priority for the Carter administration.

Carter's energy plan called for a new cabinet office, the Department of Energy, and funds for research on alternative energy sources. The bill also proposed high taxes on crude oil to encourage conservation. The revenues would be used to pay for mass public transportation. The energy bill passed the House with only minor changes. But by the time it passed the Senate, few of the President's ideas were left. Critics pointed to this as evidence that Carter had not displayed effective leadership.

In 1979, a crisis occurred in Iran. (See page 780.) Since this Middle Eastern country is a leading oil producer, the events there stimulated further action on energy. Congress authorized $100 million for solar energy research. And President Carter called for phas-

ing out controls on the price of domestic crude oil to allow domestic oil prices to rise to world levels.

In 1980, the United States paid $62 billion for imported oil, twice the 1976 figure. However, Carter's energy program had begun to have its effects. Higher prices had stimulated a boom in exploration and domestic drilling. They had also brought a decline in oil consumption, as individuals and industries tried to conserve the more expensive fuel.

A New Emphasis in Foreign Policy

"Our commitment to human rights must be absolute," Jimmy Carter told the nation in his inaugural address. "Because we are free we can never be indifferent to the face of freedom elsewhere." Human rights* became the centerpiece of the Carter foreign policy.

President Carter required the State Department to use compliance with human rights guidelines as a criterion for giving aid to needy nations. His administration suspended military aid to several nations guilty of severe violations of rights. Yet some of the most loyal allies of the United States had long records of political abuse. For example, the shah of Iran, a harsh military dictator, was an important ally of the United States in the Persian Gulf region. While Carter might quietly urge the shah to improve his nation's human rights record, he did not want to embarrass an important ally. As a result, nations less important to United States foreign policy interests were held to stricter standards.

Africa The application of Carter's human rights policy led to a more active American role in Africa. In South Africa, the Carter administration condemned apartheid—as you have read, the policy of strict separation of the races enforced by law. In neighboring

---

*"Human rights" refers to the opportunities of people to make political choices, to express their beliefs without the threat of persecution or violence, and to own personal property. Traditionally, governments in democratic countries such as Great Britain, Sweden, Japan, and the United States respect human rights more than do military dictatorships or governments in Soviet bloc nations.

1. **MAP READING** Ask: Which countries border Israel? Which of these countries claims territory occupied by Israel?

Rhodesia, the Carter administration took part in negotiations between representatives of the country's ruling white minority and its black majority. As a result of the negotiations, the white government agreed to withdraw. Rhodesia was renamed Zimbabwe, and majority rule was established.

MAP STUDY

1. *Israel gained territory in each of three wars fought in the Middle East. In the 1978 Camp David Agreement, the leaders of Egypt and Israel took initial steps toward resolving the long Middle East dispute. Israel agreed to withdraw from the Sinai Peninsula, the Gaza Strip, and part of Jordan over a five-year period. The withdrawal from the Sinai was completed in 1982. From the map, why do you think control of the Sinai might be important to Egypt?* See p. T140.

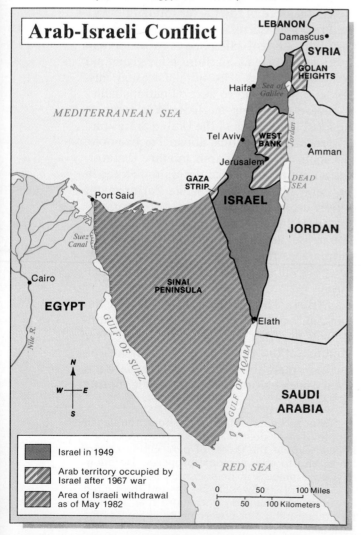

Arab-Israeli Conflict

LEBANON
Damascus●
SYRIA
GOLAN HEIGHTS
Haifa
Sea of Galilee
MEDITERRANEAN SEA
Tel Aviv
WEST BANK
Jordan R.
Jerusalem
Amman
DEAD SEA
GAZA STRIP
Port Said
ISRAEL
JORDAN
Suez Canal
Cairo
SINAI PENINSULA
EGYPT
Nile R.
GULF OF SUEZ
Elath
N
W—E
S
GULF OF AQABA
SAUDI ARABIA
RED SEA

0   50   100 Miles
0   50   100 Kilometers

■ Israel in 1949
▨ Arab territory occupied by Israel after 1967 war
▨ Area of Israeli withdrawal as of May 1982

2. **ACTIVITY** Have students draw a political cartoon that indicates a position on the Panama Canal treaties.

Panama President Carter achieved an important success for his human rights policy in Central America. Negotiations between Panama and the United States over the status of the Panama Canal had dragged on for years. In 1978, Carter agreed to a series of treaties granting Panama control over the canal zone by the year 2000.

Carter believed that the treaties would improve the United States image in Latin America. He also thought that the danger of sabotage to the canal would be reduced if the Panamanians gained control. After bitter debate, in which opponents charged that Carter was giving away American property, 2. the Senate voted its approval of the treaties in March 1978.

China Although President Nixon had encouraged a thaw in United States relations with the People's Republic of China, negotiations to normalize relations had faltered. In 1979, Carter concluded a series of agreements that included formal diplomatic recognition and increased opportunities for trade.

Even though most Americans supported Carter, diplomatic recognition of China caused considerable controversy. The communist government of Beijing had insisted that the United States withdraw its recognition of the nationalist government in Taiwan as the official government of China. Conservative Republicans accused Carter of abandoning a longtime ally of the United States.

The Camp David Summit

President Carter's greatest success in foreign affairs resulted from his efforts to settle the longstanding dispute between Israel and Egypt. Progress in reducing the tensions between Egypt and Israel came in 1977. In that year, President Sadat visited Israel, the first 3. Arab head of state to do so. Shortly thereafter, Israeli Prime Minister Menachem Begin returned the visit. In a cordial meeting, the two leaders agreed to work toward a peaceful settlement of their nations' differences.

When negotiations stalled in 1978, President Carter invited Begin and Sadat to the United States to discuss their differences. For 12 days, the three leaders met at the President's Camp David retreat in Maryland. In

3. **BACKGROUND** Sadat wanted to ease tensions with Israel in order to concentrate on improving life for Egyptians at home.

The crowning achievement of the Carter presidency was the Camp David summit in 1978. President Carter brought together President Anwar el-Sadat of Egypt (left) and Prime Minister Menachem Begin of Israel (right) for private talks on the
1. Middle East. Here, the three joyful statesmen shake hands outside the White House after signing the "Framework for Peace in the Middle East."

---

1. **READING** Interested students might like to read Jimmy Carter's account of the Camp David summit in his book *Keeping Faith*.

September 1978, the tired but elated heads of state signed the "Framework for Peace in the Middle East." The document laid the groundwork for a peace treaty between Egypt and Israel. In March 1979, in Washington, D.C., Sadat and Begin signed a formal peace treaty, ending 30 years of war between Egypt and Israel. An emotional President Carter signed as a witness.

Changing Relations With the Soviet Union

President Carter took office eager to conclude a new arms agreement with the Soviet Union. American and Soviet negotiators had been meeting regularly since the Ford administration to seek a formula for extending the nuclear missile limitations agreed to in the 1972 SALT treaty. (See page 763.) In June 1979, President Carter flew to Vienna, Austria, to meet Soviet President Leonid Brezhnev. After a round of talks, the two men signed SALT II.

However, Carter found it easier to reach agreement with Brezhnev than with treaty opponents in the United States Senate. Critics of SALT II argued that the treaty would give the Soviets a dangerous advantage in warheads and missiles. Supporters of the treaty thought it a necessary step toward reducing the danger of nuclear war. The controversy ended when the Soviet Union invaded Afghanistan in December 1979. The 2. Soviet action destroyed any chance of Congress ratifying SALT II.

Reacting to the invasion, President Carter angrily declared, "The Soviet Union must pay a concrete price for its aggression." He ordered a series of economic and political measures against the Soviet Union, including

2. **GEOGRAPHY** Have students locate Afghanistan on a map. Ask: Why might control of Afghanistan be important to the Soviet Union? (location)

779

a ban on the sale of high-technology equipment and a severe reduction in grain sales to the Soviet Union. Carter also ordered United States athletes to boycott the 1980 summer Olympics in Moscow.

After the Soviet invasion of Afghanistan, President Carter warned that the United States would fight if the Soviets made any 1. military moves toward the Persian Gulf, the oil lifeline of the west. He also announced that he would increase the American military budget and that the United States would install new nuclear weapons in western Europe. Détente was clearly over.

Crisis in Iran

A crisis in Iran caused an even greater emotional response in the United States. In January 1979, right-wing Islamic fundamentalists, people who believed in strict adherence to the laws and traditions of Islam, overthrew the shah of Iran. Their religious leader, the 2. Ayatollah Khomeini (i uh TOH luh hoh MEH nee), assumed the leadership of Iran when the shah fled the country. The Ayatollah had a fanatic hatred for the West, particularly the United States, which he called "the Great Satan."

In November 1979, the Carter administration allowed the exiled shah to enter the United States for medical treatment. In response, militant Iranians stormed the American embassy in the Iranian capital of Teheran. They took more than 50 Americans hostage. American diplomatic efforts and economic measures were unable to free the hostages. A daring rescue mission failed because of mechanical difficulties.

The hostage crisis dominated newspaper headlines. Each evening, television news brought anti-American demonstrators, shaking their fists and shouting "Death to the United States," into American living rooms. Rarely in its history had the United States been so humiliated or seemed so powerless in an international situation.

The situation grew increasingly tense as the United States built up its military presence in the Indian Ocean and the Persian Gulf. When war broke out between Iran and Iraq

in September 1980, Iran blamed it on United States influence. Meanwhile, the hostage negotiations remained deadlocked. There seemed little President Carter could do without creating a grave threat to the hostages' lives. Yet, until the last hours of his presidency, Carter devoted his energies to freeing the hostages.

A Weakening Economy

The revolution in Iran did more than weaken the strategic position of the United States in the Persian Gulf region. It also weakened the nation's economy. Iran's oil exports dropped to practically nothing. The resulting shortage helped drive up the price of oil from about $13 per barrel in 1978 to over $31 in 1980.

The rise in oil prices contributed to a sharp increase in the inflation rate. By 1980, the prices of goods were rising by 13.5 per- 3. cent per year. At the same time, rising interest rates made it more difficult for consumers to borrow money for major purchases such as cars and homes, or for businesses to borrow for investments in new plants and equipment. Unemployment also increased, jumping from 5.8 percent in 1979 to 7.1 percent in 1980. Black Americans were particularly hard hit as their unemployment rate reached over 13 percent. As a result, Americans faced the 1980 election worried about the health of the economy.

The 1980 Election

The combination of economic distress and the long, drawn-out hostage crisis undermined President Carter's popularity. Nonetheless, when the Democratic convention met, Carter easily won renomination. The Republican party rallied behind Ronald Reagan of California and his running mate, George Bush of Texas. Only the defection of John Anderson of Illinois, who ran for President as an independent, marred GOP unity.

Jimmy Carter did little active campaigning. Ronald Reagan made the economy and the hostage crisis major issues of his campaign. He asked voters whether they were

1. The oil shortages of the 1970s brought about a new emphasis on finding alternative sources of energy. Researchers sought to develop nuclear, solar, and wind energy. In this solar home in New Mexico, several energy systems are at work. The water in drums along one side of the house stores the sun's heat, solar panels are on the roof, and power is generated by a windmill.

1. **LOCAL HISTORY** Have students find out whether your local area experimented with alternative energy sources in the 1970s. Ask: What are the main sources of energy in your area today?

better off in 1980 than in 1977, when Jimmy Carter took office. Double-digit inflation and high interest rates led many Americans to answer "no" to Reagan's question. Reagan also stressed his determination to reduce the role of the federal government in the lives of Americans and to strengthen national defense. The Democrats argued that Reagan's promise to lower the cost of government
2. while greatly increasing defense spending did not make sense.

On election day, Ronald Reagan won 51 percent of the popular vote compared to 41 percent for Carter and 7 percent for Anderson. In the electoral college, Reagan won 489 electoral votes and Carter 49.

Furthermore, for the first time in 26 years, the Republicans gained a majority in the Senate, winning 53 seats. Although the Republicans also made gains in the House of Representatives, claiming 191 seats, they remained a minority in that body. Many tradi-

tional Democratic voters in labor unions, large cities, and the South had shifted to the Republicans. 3.

See p. T140.

SECTION 5 REVIEW

1. **Identify:** (a) Anwar el-Sadat, (b) Menachem Begin, (c) Ayatollah Khomeini.

2. How did Congress thwart Carter's legislation on domestic issues?

3. How did President Carter try to make concern for human rights an important part of United States foreign policy?

4. What effect did the Iran hostage crisis have on the United States economy?

5. **Critical Thinking** How might dependence on foreign oil affect United States foreign policy?

781

2. **PRESIDENTS** Before he became Reagan's running mate, George Bush had called this plan "voodoo economics." He later came to support Reagan's economic program.

3. **DISCUSSION** Have students suggest reasons why many groups that traditionally voted Democratic supported Ronald Reagan in 1980.

Summary

1. **Under President Nixon, the United States began to disengage from the war in Vietnam.** Nixon worked to improve relations with China and the Soviet Union, initiating a period of détente.

2. **Nixon stressed law and order at home.** His conservative appointees to the Supreme Court limited the scope of earlier decisions in the area of criminal rights. Economic problems such as inflation still plagued the nation and were aggravated by the rapid rise of oil prices after 1973.

3. **The Watergate crisis led to the resignation of Richard Nixon.** Although the nation was shaken by the events of Watergate, the crisis demonstrated that the system of checks and balances worked.

4. **Gerald Ford, Nixon's successor, hoped to restore stability and confidence in government.** But Ford's administration was plagued by economic problems, including the worst recession since the 1930s. The new President was also hurt by criticism of his pardon of Richard Nixon. In the 1976 presidential election, Ford lost to Democrat Jimmy Carter.

5. **Jimmy Carter tried to take a fresh approach to the problems facing the nation.** His personal style was simple and relaxed, while his foreign policy was based on human rights concerns. He successfully negotiated a peace treaty between Israel and Egypt. But rising inflation and the Iran hostage crisis contributed to Carter's defeat by Ronald Reagan in 1980.

See p. T140.

Vocabulary

On a separate sheet of paper, write the word or words that best complete each of the following sentences.

1. _____ was the United States policy aimed at increasing the responsibility of South Vietnam for fighting the Vietnam War.

2. _____ was the relaxation of tension between the United States and the Soviet Union that took place during President Nixon's second administration.

3. In 1973, Nixon _____, or refused to spend, funds appropriated by Congress.

4. _____ is an economic condition characterized by simultaneous inflation, recession, and high unemployment.

5. Traveling back and forth between nations to negotiate a treaty is sometimes called _____.

6. A _____ is a legally binding order.

See p. T140.

Chapter Checkup

1. How did President Nixon reduce tensions with China and the Soviet Union in 1972?

2. (a) Why did Arab nations impose a boycott on oil shipments to the United States in 1973? (b) What impact did the boycott have on American life? Why?

3. (a) Why did the House Judiciary Committee begin hearings on the impeachment of President Nixon? (b) What did the committee decide? (c) What was Nixon's reaction?

4. (a) What economic problems faced the nation during the Nixon-Ford years? (b) What policies were implemented to deal with those problems? (c) To what extent were those policies successful?

5. Describe the controversies surrounding the following aspects of Jimmy Carter's foreign policy: (a) human rights; (b) Panama Canal treaties; (c) recognition of the People's Republic of China; (d) ratification of SALT II.

See p. T141.

Critical Thinking

1. **Analyzing** Why do you think President Nixon probably faced less opposition in his efforts to improve relations with China and the Soviet Union than he would have had he not been known as a strong anti-communist?

2. **Evaluating** The Constitution established a system of checks and balances. (See pages 166–167.) How well did that system work during the Watergate crisis? What specific actions reflected the operation of a system of checks and balances?

See p. T141.

Comparing Past and Present

1. Richard Nixon's presidency could be seen as the culmination of a trend toward an "imperial presidency." (a) How does the power of the President today compare to the power of the presidency in the 1960s and 1970s? (b) Does the current President seem able to carry out his programs? Why or why not?

2. The revolution that brought the Ayatollah Khomeini to power in Iran and the Iran hostage crisis were serious threats to American interests in the Middle East. What effect do the nation of Iran and its policies have on the United States today?

See p. T141.

Developing Basic Skills

1. **Writing a Report** Investigate one or more of the products you use that was developed through space technology. (You could begin with the products described on page 767, but there are many others.) Write a report in which you describe how the product was used in the space program and how it has been adapted for everyday use.

2. **Graph Reading** Study the graph of the purchasing power of the dollar on page 765. (a) What happened to the purchasing power of the dollar between 1960 and 1980? (b) In terms of 1967 dollars, how much could a dollar buy in 1980? (c) How do you think the average American was affected by this development? Explain.

WRITING ABOUT HISTORY

Footnotes for Signed and Unsigned Articles

Footnotes for different types of sources require different kinds of information. Notice the variations in the following footnotes.

Signed and unsigned magazine articles:

[1] D. M. Alpern, "Nixon in Prime Time," *Newsweek,* April 16, 1984, p. 34.
[2] "What's Wrong with the Way We Pick Our Presidents," *U.S. News and World Report,* July 23, 1984, p. 29.

Signed and unsigned newspaper articles:

[1] Philip Geyelin, "Sh! Says Richard Nixon," *Washington Post,* May 25, 1986, p. C7.
[2] "10 Years Later," *Washington Post,* August 9, 1984, p. A22.

Signed and unsigned encyclopedia articles:

[1] *Academic American Encyclopedia,* 1985 ed., "Gerald R. Ford," by Stanley W. Cloud.
[2] *The New Columbia Encyclopedia,* 1975 ed., "Gerald R. Ford."

Practice: Rewrite the following footnotes correctly.

1. *The New York Times,* December 23, 1986 "OPEC Pact Sends Oil Prices Up," p. D1, by Lee A Daniels.

2. Richard Corliss, Platoon, January 26, 1987, *Newsweek,* pp. 54-55.

3. Henry Kissinger, *The New Columbia Encyclopedia,* 1975 ed.

New Directions

36

(1981–Present)

CHAPTER OBJECTIVES After completing this chapter, students should be able to
1. describe Ronald Reagan's domestic and foreign policies.
2. describe the challenges facing George Bush.
3. discuss social and economic issues facing the nation.
4. explain how various groups worked for equality.

CHAPTER PREVIEW Have students look at the pictures and captions and skim the section titles and subtitles in this chapter. Then ask them to make a list of the main issues Americans faced in the 1980s. Have them report on which issues are in the news today.

CHAPTER OUTLINE

1. **The Reagan Revolution**
2. **Foreign Affairs During the Reagan Years**
3. **Bush Takes Over**
4. **Examining Social Issues**
5. **Striving for Equality**

Incoming Presidents have often used inaugurations to make symbolic gestures. Abraham Lincoln's second inaugural parade was the first to include black marchers—a clear symbol that slavery was over. Theodore Roosevelt took the oath in 1905 bareheaded. He was an outdoorsman and wanted everyone to know it. Dwight D. Eisenhower's first inaugural in 1953 featured 22,000 marchers from the military service, a strong sign that the United States had become a world military power.

In a break with tradition, in 1981, Ronald Reagan gave his inaugural address on the West Front of the Capitol rather than the East Front. It was a symbolic gesture. Reagan came from the West, and the West provided the popular base from which he launched his bid for the presidency.

The symbolism of George Bush's inauguration in 1989 included his choice of music. Country music, blues, and a Mexican mariachi band showed that he considered himself a Texan who shared the culture and tastes of many other Americans.

The inauguration of George Bush as President on January 20, 1989, marked the two hundredth anniversary of the government of the United States under the Constitution. Beginning with the swearing in of George Washington as the nation's first President in 1789, the inauguration ceremony itself has become a treasured institution.

Inaugurations represent the strength and the unique nature of the American system of government. For 200 years, the banner of leadership has passed in orderly fashion from President to President, regardless of any difference of political views that may exist between the officeholder and his successor. In 1933, conservative Herbert Hoover handed over the reins of government to liberal Franklin D. Roosevelt. In 1969, liberal Lyndon Johnson gave way to conservative Richard Nixon.

Inauguration ceremonies mark both an end and a beginning. The outgoing President, his achievements now part of history, remains in the background as the spotlight focuses on his successor.

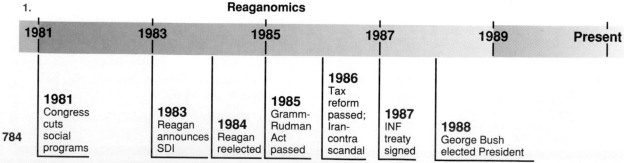

1.

Reaganomics

1981 — 1983 — 1985 — 1987 — 1989 — Present

1981 Congress cuts social programs

1983 Reagan announces SDI

1984 Reagan reelected

1985 Gramm-Rudman Act passed

1986 Tax reform passed; Iran-contra scandal

1987 INF treaty signed

1988 George Bush elected President

784

1. **TIME LINE QUESTION** Ask: How long after Reagan announced SDI was the INF treaty signed?

George Bush and his wife, Barbara, are shown at left at his inauguration as the
1. forty-first President of the United States. At right are Vice President Quayle and
his wife, Marilyn. In his inaugural address, Bush declared that "A new breeze is
blowing. . . . A nation refreshed by freedom stands ready to push on. . . ."

1. **VISUAL EVIDENCE**
This picture was
taken on the steps of
the Lincoln Memorial.

2. **VOCABULARY** Have students look up these words in
the glossary before they begin reading.

3. **ACTIVITY** Have students draw political cartoons that
agree or disagree with Reagan's comment.

1 The Reagan Revolution

READD TO UNDERSTAND

■ What economic issues faced the Reagan
administration.

■ How President Reagan applied his belief in a
free market to the nation's economic problems.

■ How President Reagan's appointments made
the Supreme Court more conservative.

2. ■ *Vocabulary:* deficit, deregulation.

Ronald Reagan's election in 1980 marked a
new direction in American politics. Since the
1930s, the federal government had expanded
its control of social and economic programs.
In contrast, in his first inaugural speech,
Reagan stressed his basic political belief:

"Government is not the solution to our problems. Government is the problem." During 3.
the next eight years, Reagan attempted to
limit federal spending and federal regulation
in a "conservative revolution."

The President's Style

Ronald Reagan seemed an unusual choice as
a Republican President. When elected in 1980,
he was 69 years old, the oldest person elected
to the presidency. Until the 1960s, he was
better known nationally as a movie and television actor than as a politician. After start- 4.
ing his political life during the depression
years as a liberal Democrat, he switched to
the Republican party in 1962 and was elected
governor of California four years later. By
1976, Reagan had emerged as the leader of
the conservative wing of the Republican
party.

4. **CRITICAL THINKING** Ask: How might Reagan's background in film and television have
helped him become President?

2. **ECONOMICS** Reagan favored supply-side economics, in which inflation and unemployment are seen as problems solvable by adjusting the supply of goods, rather than the demand for goods, as in Keynesian economics.

Ronald and Nancy Reagan brought the glamour of
1. *Hollywood to Washington, welcoming celebrities to the White House. The Reagans are shown here with singer Ray Charles at the 1981 inauguration.*

1. **BIOGRAPHY** Before marrying Reagan, Nancy Davis had also acted in Hollywood.

The first day of the Reagan administration was one of drama and suspense. Intense negotiations in the final hours of the Carter administration had produced an agreement to free the 52 American hostages held in the United States Embassy in Iran. Minutes after Ronald Reagan took the oath of office, word came of their release. With the return of the hostages, who had been held captive for 444 days, the Reagan administration began on a high note.

From the beginning, Reagan stamped the presidency with his own style. Leaving the details of government to his aides while he devoted his energies to selling his program, he sometimes appeared uninformed about his administration's activities.

Reagan had a relaxed and good-humored manner. Only two months into his admini-

786

stration, he was shot by a would-be assassin. As Reagan was rushed to the hospital, bleeding heavily, he smiled at the doctors and cracked, "I hope you are all good Republicans." His humor, along with a stubborn courage, were qualities that endeared him to many Americans.

The Reagan Economic Program

The state of the economy had been a major issue in the 1980 campaign. Calling it "the worst economic mess since the Great Depression," Reagan listed five economic problems: too much government spending, high taxes and interest rates, inflation, and unemployment. With the intention of trying "something different," Reagan introduced what became known as Reaganomics. It was a program designed to stimulate the economy and cut 2. back on the growing budget **deficit,** as the government spent more than it took in.

Features of Reaganomics Reagan's economic plan called for a reduction in personal and business taxes, coupled with reduced government spending. Reducing taxes, Reagan believed, would enable people to save more and to spend more. As a result, business could expand and employ more people. More people would pay taxes. Even with lower tax rates, the government would collect more money. If everything went as planned, the budget would become balanced.

Reagan hoped to pair increased revenue with decreased government spending. He opposed cuts in defense spending because he had promised to increase American military strength. Widespread public resistance prevented cuts in social security, so the President targeted social programs. Reagan clearly signaled he would limit programs begun by Roosevelt's New Deal and maintained or expanded by each President since.

Reagan also hoped to "get government off the back of the people" by reducing government restrictions on business and industry. This process, known as **deregulation,** freed industries such as banking, trucking, and the airlines from government regulation. In addition, the President signed an execu- 3. tive order abolishing price controls on most domestic crude oil.

3. **MAIN IDEA** Have students explain the main features of Reaganomics.

2. **CITIZENSHIP** This initial slippage in the economy helped the Democrats gain 26 new seats in the House in the 1982 congressional elections.

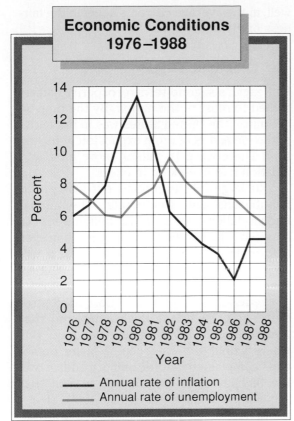

Economic Conditions 1976–1988

Percent / Year

— Annual rate of inflation
— Annual rate of unemployment

Source U.S. Bureau of Labor Statistics

GRAPH STUDY   *A high rate of inflation was a problem during*
1. *much of the 1970s. The rate of inflation dropped in the early 1980s, as this graph shows, but unemployment rose as a result of a deep recession. In what years did both the inflation rate and unemployment rate fall?*   See p. T141.

1. **GRAPH READING** Ask: What was the highest rate of inflation? When did it occur?

Congress passed much of Reagan's economic program during his first term. In 1981, it approved plans to cut federal income taxes and to slash $35 billion from social programs, including food stamps, Medicaid, Medicare, and the school lunch program.

Issues Raised Reagan's program, however, was not without its critics. Some said it showed disregard for the weakest members of society. "Across the board" tax cuts of 25 percent, they argued, helped the rich far more than the poor. Cuts in government programs hurt the needy even more.

Deregulation also sparked criticism. Government regulations were designed to limit unfair or reckless business practices. Some people worried that government supervision

was necessary to protect Americans from toxic spills and unsafe products.

At first, the economy slipped, causing a recession and a 10 percent unemployment rate. But then the high rate of inflation began to drop. With so many people out of work, consumers spent less, and businesses lowered prices. Inflation also decreased because the supply of oil increased, driving down prices for gasoline and petroleum products.

By 1983, the economy had begun to improve. Employment increased and the average family income rose for the first time in four years. Support for Reagan's policies increased.

The Election of 1984

Ronald Reagan entered the 1984 election race confidently. Among the Democrats, however, eight candidates sought their party's nomination, including Jesse Jackson, the first black man to vie for the presidential nomination of

Jesse Jackson was the country's most important African American leader in the 1980s. "Our time has come," he roared to enthusiastic crowds when he competed for the presidential nomination in 1984. Jackson won some Democratic state primaries—the first black ever to do so. His showing in the 1988 campaign was even stronger.

3. **VISUAL EVIDENCE** This photograph shows Jackson announcing his candidacy in November 1983, as enthusiastic crowds chanted "Run, Jesse, run!"

1. **CITIZENSHIP** Mondale also considered three mayors: Dianne Feinstein of San Francisco, Henry Cisneros of San Antonio, and Thomas Bradley of Los Angeles.

3. **CRITICAL THINKING** Ask: Does the need to run for reelection every two years make it hard for members of Congress to support cuts in social programs?

a major political party. Walter Mondale, Vice President under Jimmy Carter, finally emerged as the party's choice. For his running mate, Mondale chose Geraldine Ferraro, the first woman to be the vice presidential candidate of a major political party.

Ronald Reagan won 59 percent of the popular vote. With this impressive mandate as support, he began his second term by tackling two thorny tasks: tax reform and federal deficit reduction.

Tax Reform

Tax reform is difficult to achieve. No matter how taxes are changed, someone will be unhappy. Determined to beat the odds, Reagan gave tax reform and tax simplification high priority in his second term.

Over the years, lawmakers had added many deductions and loopholes to the tax laws. Often, only certain groups of people benefited. To keep their advantages, some of these groups lobbied strongly against serious reform. Tax simplification, they argued, would remove deductions that encouraged positive goals, such as charitable contributions.

Despite the opposition to the proposed changes, politicians realized that most Americans believed the tax system was unfair and needed reform. Key Democrats, including Senator Bill Bradley of New Jersey, had long advocated reform. After months of work, Congress passed a major tax reform plan in 1986. The new tax code sharply limited many loopholes and lowered and simplified the tax rates. But many people in the middle class saw their taxes rise significantly. They charged that the poorest and richest in society had received the greatest benefits under the new plan.

Most experts agreed that the long-range effects of the new tax code could not be predicted. Some critics felt that the new system would bring in less revenue than before and result in greater deficits. Lawmakers, on the other hand, hoped the elimination of many loopholes and deductions would produce more revenue. They foresaw an increase, as well, in the average citizen's belief in the fairness of the tax system.

The Economic Legacy

By Reagan's second term, prosperity had returned to most of the nation. By the time he left office, the United States was in the midst of the longest economic expansion of its history. There were 16 million more jobs, and inflation had been kept in check.

But large deficits continued to worry both Republicans and Democrats. The annual budget deficit averaged $1.8 billion per year between 1982 and 1988—far higher than ever before. The federal debt reached $2.6 trillion, largely because of increased military spending. (See page 790.)

Federal Deficit In an effort to control the deficit, President Reagan insisted that Congress cut government spending. But where would the cuts come? Many Democrats complained that the military budget was too high. Reagan Republicans argued that social programs should be cut.

In response, Congress passed the Balanced Budget and Emergency Control Act of 1985, or Gramm-Rudman Act. This law provided for automatic spending cuts if the President and Congress disagreed over how to get the job done. Year by year, the Gramm-Rudman law would increase the required cuts, until the budget was balanced. The solution was popular because the threat of automatic cuts was designed to force Congress and the President to make difficult choices.

But, in 1986, the Supreme Court struck down the provision of the Gramm-Rudman Act that automatically triggered across-the-board budget cuts. It held that Congress could not give up its constitutional role as budget-maker. Nevertheless, the idea behind Gramm-Rudman has continued to attract support.

Trade Deficit A serious trade deficit also plagued the nation's economy. Each year, the value of the nation's imports greatly exceeded the value of its exports, causing an enormous trade imbalance.

There were two major reasons for the trade deficit. Americans bought more from abroad than they sold to foreign nations. And

2. **BIOGRAPHY** Bill Bradley, a member of the Basketball Hall of Fame, played for Princeton University and the New York Knicks. He was elected to Congress in 1978 and 1984. Another sports figure, football quarterback Jack Kemp, served in the U.S. Congress and on President Bush's cabinet.

1. **BACKGROUND** Although a conservative, O'Connor had supported the Equal Rights Amendment. As a result, some conservative groups opposed her nomination.

in relation to other world currencies, the dollar was strong. The high value of the dollar made it more expensive for foreigners to buy American products and less expensive for Americans to buy foreign products.

The government took action. It devalued the dollar, hoping to make American goods more competitive in foreign markets. It also negotiated a free trade agreement eliminating tariffs with Canada in the hopes of creating a larger market for American goods. Despite these efforts, the trade deficit remained high, and Americans continued to import more than they exported.

The 1987 Crash On October 19, 1987, the stock market plunged 508 points, losing 25 percent of its value in one day. Although experts did not agree on what caused the crash, many thought that it was a warning that the economy was unsound. They claimed that the nation could not continue to support huge budget and trade deficits. Despite the severity of the crash, the country did not fall into a recession. On the contrary, the economy seemed to recover quickly.

The Supreme Court

President Reagan's conservative agenda extended beyond his economic policies. He favored allowing school prayer and opposed legalized abortion. Since cases involving these and other far-reaching issues come before the Supreme Court, many people wondered whom Reagan would appoint. The President considered the Court too liberal and hoped to shift the balance on the side of the conservatives.

Early in Reagan's first administration, a vacancy on the Court gave the President his first opportunity. In July 1981, Reagan announced the nomination of Sandra Day O'Connor as an associate justice of the Supreme Court. Confirmed by the Senate by a vote of 99 to 0, she became the first woman on the Court. She has generally aligned herself with the other conservative justices.

Reagan's next Supreme Court appointment came in 1986, when Chief Justice Warren Burger retired. The President named Associate Justice William Rehnquist to be

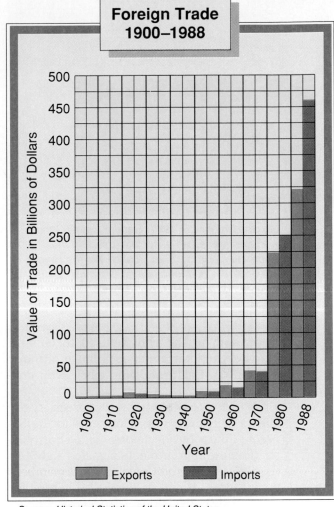

Foreign Trade 1900–1988

Source: *Historical Statistics of the United States;* U.S. Department of Commerce

GRAPH STUDY *On this chart, you can trace imports and exports from 1900 to 1988. In recent years, the United States trade deficit has increased sharply. In what year shown on the graph were imports first more than exports?* See p. T142.

2. **GRAPH READING** Ask: How big was the trade deficit in 1980? In 1988?

Chief Justice and nominated Antonin Scalia to replace Rehnquist as associate justice. Both justices were known for their strong conservative views.

In 1987, Reagan's nomination of Judge Robert Bork erupted in controversy. Many Democrats, and a few Republicans, thought Bork was too conservative. Some minorities feared that his presence on the Court would threaten to weaken, or even reverse, the social and political gains of recent years. A Senate committee questioned Bork on his

789

3. **BACKGROUND** Remind students that Bork, as solicitor general, had fired the special prosecutor investigating the Watergate burglary and cover-up in 1973 (see p. 769).

1. On September 25, 1981, Sandra Day O'Connor was sworn in as an associate justice of the Supreme Court by Chief Justice Warren Burger. She took the oath of office on two family Bibles held by her husband, John J. O'Connor.

1. **BIOGRAPHY** O'Connor (1930–) had been an assistant attorney general for Arizona and a state senator.

views and, in the end, refused to confirm him. Reagan later nominated Judge Anthony Kennedy of California, who easily won confirmation.

It is not possible to predict precisely the effects of Reagan's appointments to the Supreme Court, but decisions made shortly after the new appointments signaled a shift to the right. While the Court still had members regarded as liberal, it would be harder for them to sway decisions.

See p. T142.

SECTION 1 REVIEW

1. **Identify:** (a) Reaganomics, (b) Sandra Day O'Connor.

2. **Define:** (a) deficit, (b) deregulation.

3. (a) What did Reagan see as the cause of the nation's economic problems? (b) What parts of his economic program did Congress enact in 1981?

4. What was the purpose of the Gramm-Rudman Act?

5. **Critical Thinking** What changes might be expected in Supreme Court decisions based on President Reagan's appointments?

2. **VOCABULARY** Have students look up these words in the glossary before they begin reading.

2 Foreign Affairs During the Reagan Years

READ TO UNDERSTAND

■ How President Reagan dealt with Soviet challenges and initiatives.

■ What Reagan's foreign policy objectives were toward Latin America.

■ How Reagan handled challenges in the Middle East and Africa.

■ *Vocabulary:* glasnost, divestiture.

2.

In foreign policy, President Reagan began his presidency as a vocal critic of the policy of détente and ended on a relationship of mutual regard with the premier of the Soviet Union. The President tended to view conflicts throughout the world as part of a global struggle between the United States and the "evil empire," as he once called the Soviet Union. Yet he was willing to initiate and respond to proposals to reduce tensions between the two superpowers.

President Reagan believed that to gain peace, the United States had to be strong. Calling on Americans to "stand tall," he helped revive the national pride that had been lagging since the Vietnam War.

A Tough Stand

In the beginning, Reagan took a firm stand against Soviet actions. Charging that the Soviet Union assumed the right "to commit any crime, to lie, to cheat to attain its ends," he spoke out against Soviet repression at home and abroad. He particularly condemned the continued Soviet presence in Afghanistan and repression of the Solidarity labor movement in Poland.

3.

Reagan's strong words were matched with action. Claiming that the Soviets were ahead in the arms race, Reagan began to pour billions of dollars into defense. To counter any threat, Reagan proposed, and Congress passed, the largest peacetime military buildup in the nation's history. Over the next eight years, the outflow reached $2 trillion.

3. **BACKGROUND** Several other incidents strained U.S.-Soviet relations. In 1983, a Soviet fighter plane shot down an unarmed South Korean airliner flying over Soviet territory; 269 passengers, some of them American, were killed. In 1984, the Soviet Union boycotted the Olympic Games held in Los Angeles, claiming that the U.S. would not give adequate protection to Soviet athletes.

1. **BACKGROUND** After leading the Soviet Union for 18 years, Leonid Brezhnev died in 1982. His two successors each died after about a year in office.

In 1983, Reagan proposed developing a weapons system in outer space to shield the nation from incoming enemy missiles. Despite a projected cost of billions of dollars and disagreement among scientists about whether it could ever work, Congress voted funds to begin work on the Strategic Defense Initiative (SDI). The somewhat futuristic sound of the plan earned it the nickname "Star Wars."

The size of the arms buildup worried many people. Would the race to put missile platforms in outer space heighten world tension? Between 1982 and 1985, the Soviet Union went through a succession of three leaders before Mikhail Gorbachev (GOR buh chawf) became premier. Any major improvement in the relationship between the United States and the Soviet Union was unlikely in a period of such instability.

Reagan and Gorbachev

Gorbachev was part of a new generation of Soviet leaders. Younger and more open, he supported a policy of **glasnost,** or speaking out honestly about social and political ills. Gorbachev blasted corruption and inefficiency as he set out to reform the lagging Soviet economy. But an intense arms race with the United States would undermine his efforts. The Soviet economy could not support both more consumer goods and more weapons. If for no other reason, the time was ripe for reducing world tensions.

In a move aimed at stopping the development of the SDI, Premier Gorbachev called for a discontinuation of testing of all nuclear weapons and halted such testing by the Soviet Union in 1985. The Reagan administration, however, continued underground testing, believing it was necessary to ensure effective weapons. In 1987, the Soviets resumed underground testing.

President Reagan and the Soviet premier first met in Geneva, Switzerland, in 1985, to get acquainted and to explore grounds for agreement between the two countries. While no arms control agreements were reached, the leaders got to know each other.

Reagan and Gorbachev met again on several occasions to discuss arms control. Early

Mikhail Gorbachev brought a new kind of leadership to the Soviet Union. His easy charm and openness attracted admirers throughout the West. President Reagan and Premier Gorbachev developed a good working relationship and applauded each other after signing the INF treaty in Washington.

2. **BIOGRAPHY** Gorbachev (1931–) was the first Soviet leader born after the Russian Revolution of 1917.

disappointments gave way to progress. In 1987, the two leaders signed a treaty to limit intermediate-range nuclear forces (INF). The INF treaty banned all medium-range nuclear missiles from Europe.

"The use of force no longer can or must be an instrument of foreign policy." The words were those of Premier Gorbachev in a speech to the United Nations in 1988 as he offered a series of proposals to promote peace. The measures included a unilateral reduction of the Soviet military presence in eastern Europe. That is, the Soviet Union would cut back its troops and equipment even if NATO did not. Gorbachev also announced the withdrawal of all Soviet troops from Afghanistan.

Some people had doubts, but the Soviet Union under Gorbachev seemed to be following a less aggressive foreign policy. NATO officials promised to discuss possible arms reductions at a meeting scheduled in Vienna in 1989.

Dealing with Latin America

The Reagan administration developed a firmly anticommunist foreign policy in Latin America. While President Carter had concentrated

3. **READING** Interested students can read Lee Blessing's *A Walk in the Woods,* a fictional play about arms control negotiations between the U.S. and the Soviet Union.

1. BACKGROUND The day before the story broke, an American kidnapped in Lebanon had been freed after 17 months in captivity. Extremists still held six other Americans, as well as several French and British hostages.

on poverty and human rights, President Reagan tended to view problems in Latin America within the framework of the larger superpower struggle. As a result, his administration intervened actively in Latin American affairs, supporting governments that opposed communism, even if those governments were military dictatorships.

Nicaragua   In 1979, a revolution in Nicaragua overthrew the dictator Anastasio Somoza. The new leaders were from a leftist group called the Sandinistas, named after a Nicaraguan who had fought against American marines in the 1930s. At first, the Carter administration supported the Sandinista government. But relations between Nicaragua and the United States soured when the Sandinistas established close ties with Cuba.

Reagan feared that Castro and the Soviet Union would set up a base in Nicaragua. As a result, he authorized the CIA to support the contras, a group of rebels who were fighting the Sandinistas. The Reagan policy was controversial. Some Americans feared that a commitment to the contras would lead to the involvement of United States troops. Others felt that it was illegal to support the overthrow of a government with which the United States maintained diplomatic relations. Criticism mounted when it was discovered that the CIA had been involved in mining a Nicaraguan harbor. But that was a minor incident compared to the furor that arose in 1986.

Iran-Contra Scandal   In late 1986, a Lebanese newspaper reported that the United States government had secretly sold arms to Iran in order to help free American hostages being held there. The report seemed unbelievable since the United States had banned arms shipments to Iran. But a few days later, the government admitted that arms had been sold. Not only that, but the proceeds from the sale had been diverted to the contras in Nicaragua. This happened at a time when United States military aid to the contras had been prohibited by law.

As concern mounted, Congress set up a committee to look into the matter. The investigation revealed that most of the operation had been led by a Marine lieutenant colonel, Oliver North, who said he was following orders from higher officials in gov-

2. VISUAL EVIDENCE Ask: What impression of North is given in this photograph?

The Iran-contra hearings were the focus of national attention in the summer of 1987. The high point of the televised Senate investigation was the four days of riveting testimony by 43-year-old marine Oliver North. North's clean-cut good looks and emotional answers to congressional questions won him popularity with the television-viewing public.

ernment. According to a report issued later, the plot was known to only a few people in the government.

Critics compared the affair to the Watergate scandals during the Nixon administration. (See page 768.) But no evidence tied President Reagan directly to North's activities. By the end of the congressional hearings, the President was already regaining his popularity. In 1989, North stood trial for his part in the affair. The jury found him guilty on three criminal charges, including destroying documents, but acquitted him on nine others, including lying to Congress. North vowed to appeal until he was "fully vindicated."

El Salvador Nicaragua's neighbor El Salvador also experienced a leftist rebellion against a military dictatorship. The Reagan administration backed the Salvadoran government, claiming that the Nicaraguan Sandinistas were secretly aiding the rebels. In 1983, the people of El Salvador elected a civilian government led by moderate José Napoleón Duarte. Duarte opened talks with the rebels, but the differences between the two sides remained. In 1989, the people elected a more conservative government that pledged a harder line with the rebels. Fighting continues to plague the country.

Other Developments In October 1983, President Reagan sent United States military
1. forces to Grenada. The Reagan administration believed that Grenada's new radical government was building an airfield for Soviet and Cuban use. As a result of the invasion, a government more favorable to the United States was restored. In 1988, the United States government indicted General Manuel
2. Noriega, the dictator of Panama, for drug dealing. However, he remained in power.

Other changes in Latin America have been encouraging. During the 1980s in Argentina, Brazil, Uruguay, and Ecuador, military rulers stepped down and democratically elected governments took their place. An elected government also replaced a dictator in Honduras. It remains to be seen, however, whether these new governments will be able to deal with the economic and social problems that beset much of Latin America.

The Middle East

President Reagan's primary goals in the Middle East were to prevent Soviet gains there and promote stability in a region that was considered strategic to United States interests. The Middle East links Europe, Asia, and Africa and has large oil reserves. Relations with Israel, America's most important ally in the area, became closer for most of the Reagan years.

Israel faced opposition from Palestinians, who wanted to set up an independent state on Israeli-controlled land on the west bank of the Jordan River. Although talks had been held under the Carter administration concerning the establishment of Palestinian self-rule in the area, no further action had been taken. As a result, Palestinian unrest increased, leading to periodic outbursts of violence.

Trouble in Lebanon Since the mid-1970s, rivalry between Christians and Muslims in Lebanon threatened to tear the country apart. The situation was made worse by the arrival in Lebanon, over the years, of many Palestinian refugees. Some of the Palestinians belonged to the Palestine Liberation Organization (PLO), a guerrilla group that launched repeated attacks on Israel.

In the summer of 1982, Israel invaded Lebanon to destroy PLO military bases. Despite criticism from many countries, including the United States, Israeli troops swept northward to the Lebanese capital of Beirut. A cease-fire was finally arranged, and PLO leaders were allowed to leave the country under the protection of an international peacekeeping force.

The situation in Lebanon between rival groups grew worse. In an effort to support the Lebanese government, the United States stationed naval ships in the Mediterranean Sea off Lebanon's coast and had United States marines protect an area around Beirut's airport. In October 1983, a terrorist truck loaded with explosives crashed into the marine barracks, killing 241 Americans. The deaths of these men raised grave questions about American involvement in Lebanon. President Reagan withdrew United States forces in February 1984.

3.

2. **BACKGROUND** In 1989, elections were held in Panama. However, U.S. observers immediately accused Noriega of tampering with the election. Some even charged that soldiers had stolen some ballots at gunpoint.

3. **BACKGROUND** Since Lebanon won its independence in 1943, the president of Lebanon had always been a Maronite (an ancient Roman Catholic community).

793

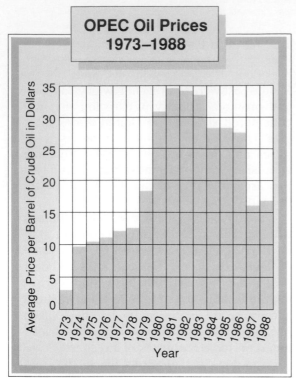

OPEC Oil Prices 1973–1988

Average Price per Barrel of Crude Oil in Dollars — Year

Source: U.S. Department of Energy

GRAPH STUDY *OPEC oil prices rose steadily between 1973*

1. *and 1981, as this graph shows. However, a world surplus of oil in the mid-1980s began to bring oil prices down. What year saw the sharpest rise in oil prices? How many years later did the sharpest fall take place?* See p. T142.

1. **GRAPH READING** Ask: What was the average price of oil in 1973? In 1980? In 1988?

The Iran-Iraq War American relations with Iran became increasingly troubled in the late 1980s. The United States was officially neutral in the war between Iran and Iraq, which had been going on since 1980. But it regarded Iran under the Ayatollah Khomeini as an unfriendly nation and charged that Iran had encouraged terrorist acts against the United States. Therefore, the United States banned arms shipments to Iran and urged others to do the same. Americans and American allies were thus shocked by the revelations of the Iran-contra affair.

As the Iran-Iraq war continued, it threatened to disrupt shipping in the Persian Gulf, which was in the war zone. Many nations, including the United States, depend on the oil shipments that flow through the gulf. When the United States sent its navy to escort tankers carrying vital oil supplies, it showed its willingness to protect the free flow of oil. The American action helped push Iran and Iraq 2. to end the war through negotiation.

Terrorism

Conflicts in the Middle East have contributed to a worldwide increase in terrorism, with Americans often the targets. The taking of American hostages in Lebanon was just one of several incidents. In 1985, Lebanese Muslim terrorists hijacked a TWA plane and took it to Beirut. There, the passengers were kept hostage for two weeks. Later in 1985, Palestinian terrorists hijacked a Mediterranean cruise ship and killed one American passenger. This time, the United States intercepted the hijackers and forced their escape plane to land.

The Reagan administration blamed Libyan dictator Muammar Qaddafi (kuh DAHF ee) for many of the terrorist activities. After a bomb killed an American serviceman in Berlin in April 1986, American planes bombed Libya's capital city, Tripoli. American strate- 3. gists hoped that this action would lead to Qaddafi's overthrow, but he retained his hold on the country.

A Policy Toward South Africa

South Africa's policy of apartheid forced the Reagan administration into a difficult situation. Under President Carter, relations with South Africa had been cool, and contacts between the two countries were limited. President Reagan also rejected apartheid, but argued that severe actions against South Africa, by destroying jobs, would hurt the black majority more than it would the white government. Moreover, Reagan believed that South Africa's strategic location and mineral resources made it important in the global struggle against the Soviet Union.

As a result, the Reagan administration adopted a policy known as "constructive engagement" in South Africa. American policymakers used quiet diplomacy and kept public criticism of the South African government to a minimum. Members of Congress, on the other hand, rejected the cautious approach.

794

1. **LOCAL HISTORY** Ask students to find out if their state has followed a policy of divestiture in response to events in South Africa.

2. **DISCUSSION** Ask: Do you think the government should restrict imports from Japan? What effect would such restrictions have on your life?

They called for economic sanctions, or limits on trade and investment, to pressure the South African government into changing its apartheid policy. In October 1986, Congress passed a sanctions bill over President Reagan's veto. The economic sanctions included a ban on new investments in South Africa and the prohibition of imports of South African products.

Many American universities and some state governments have followed a policy of **divestiture,** or selling off stock in companies
1. that have operations in South Africa. Many United States businesses have also withdrawn their sales outlets and factories from South Africa. The object of these actions is to put pressure on South Africa to change its apartheid policy.

Asia and the Pacific

In recent years, East Asia has become important to the United States, primarily because of its rapid economic development. The United States has sought closer economic ties with the People's Republic of China since full diplomatic relations were established in 1979. Under the leadership of Deng Xiaoping (DUHNG syow PIHNG), the Chinese government began to allow private enterprise and trade.

The United States, anticipating the prospect of gaining access to China's enormous market, has helped to provide economic expertise. The Reagan administration, looking to China as a check on the Soviet Union, agreed to sell advanced weapons to the Chinese. Despite differences, the two nations maintain a strong relationship based on their mutual needs.

Japan has enjoyed good relations with the United States. But the Japanese have resented pressure from Congress to restrain their exports to the United States. Some Americans have claimed that Japanese companies sell products for less than it costs to make them in order to establish markets abroad. Although Japan has encouraged its people to buy American goods, the country
2. has not lifted heavy restrictions against such American exports as farm products.

South Korea has taken a lesson from Japan's economic success. Since the 1970s, South Korea has enjoyed a booming economy. The South Koreans have begun to sell electronic goods and automobiles in the United States, where South Korean products compete favorably with Japanese-made goods. Economic prosperity, however, has not brought political harmony to South Korea. But, after years of authoritarian rule, South Korea has taken steps toward a more democratic government.

The Philippines The United States granted the Philippines its independence in 1946. For a considerable time, democracy flourished. In 1965, Ferdinand Marcos was elected president of the Philippines. He was a staunch anticommunist and friend of the United States. However, his government gradually became corrupt and repressive. In 1972, Marcos declared martial law and ruled as a dictator. The importance of American naval bases in the Philippines discouraged the United States from taking action against him.

In 1983, agents of the Philippine government gunned down Marcos's political rival Benigno Aquino. In 1986, Corazon Aquino, the

Corazon Aquino has sought help from the United States to rebuild the weakened Philippine economy. Aquino attended school in the United States and lived here in exile with her husband. 3.

3. **BIOGRAPHY** Corazon Aquino (1933–), born to a wealthy family in the Philippines, studied French at Mt. St. Vincent College in New York. She began studying law in Manila, but quit when she married. She first entered public life as a spokesperson for her husband when he was imprisoned in 1972.

slain man's widow, challenged Marcos in the presidential elections. A revolt threatened when Marcos tried to steal the election. The United States refused to support him, and Marcos fled the Philippines to seek asylum in Hawaii.

Although a new, popularly approved constitution went into effect, Corazon Aquino faces challenges from communist guerrillas and Marcos's supporters. Democracy remains a fragile commodity in the Philippines. See p. T142.

SECTION 2 REVIEW

1. **Identify:** (a) Mikhail Gorbachev, (b) INF treaty, (c) contras.

2. **Define:** (a) glasnost, (b) divestiture.

3. (a) What was President Reagan's policy toward the Soviet Union? (b) How did relations between the two nations change?

4. (a) What was the basis of Reagan's foreign policy in Latin America? (b) Why was Reagan's policy toward Nicaragua controversial?

5. What limitations has Congress placed on South African relations with the United States?

6. **Critical Thinking** Compare the foreign policy goals of President Carter and President Reagan. How did they differ?

3 Bush Takes Over

READ TO UNDERSTAND

■ What role television played in the 1988 election.

■ How Bush signaled a shift from the policies of the Reagan era.

■ What issues Bush faced upon taking office.

As 1988 approached, so did the end of Ronald Reagan's second term as President. By law, he could not run again. His Vice President,

George Bush, who had served beside him loyally, launched his drive for the presidency. Bush was an amiable and easygoing man. But because he had been so loyal to the President, he had no strong public identity of his own. History was also against him. No serving Vice President had been elected to the presidency since Martin Van Buren succeeded Andrew Jackson in 1837. Yet, Bush won the election and faced the challenge of continuing the Reagan revolution.

The Election of 1988

The Democrats had an abundance of candidates eager to run for President. Michael Dukakis, the governor of Massachusetts, and Jesse Jackson soon led the pack. Jackson, who in 1984 had sought the Democratic party's nomination for President, tried again in 1988. He won widespread support from blacks, whom he preferred to address as African Americans, and many liberal whites. In the end, though, the Democrats chose Michael Dukakis, a more middle-of-the-road candidate, at their convention in Atlanta. The vice presidential nominee was Senator Lloyd Bentsen of Texas.

The Republicans, meeting in New Orleans, chose George Bush. To the surprise of many, he chose as his running mate a relatively young, unknown conservative senator from Indiana, J. Danforth "Dan" Quayle.

In general, the campaign was one of style over substance. The candidates spoke only in general terms about the economy, the drug problem, reducing the deficits, curbing crime, and honesty in government. George Bush pointed to the Reagan economic recovery while Michael Dukakis declared that the supposedly healthy economy was like Swiss cheese—full of holes. He said the nation needed competent leaders.

More so than other recent campaigns, the 1988 contest for the White House was played out on the television screen. Both Republican and Democratic campaign directors organized their candidates' activities so that they could be presented in short "soundbites" on the evening television news programs. Inevitably, the use of these short film clips emphasized the candidates' appearance

1.

2.

Some of the traditional political hoopla survived in the 1900 campaign. Here,
1. Michael Dukakis marches in a parade in his honor in an Ohio neighborhood,
while George Bush campaigns with his wife in his home state of Texas.

1. **CITIZENSHIP** Dukakis, the son of immigrants, was the first American of Greek descent to run for President.

and manner rather than the substance of what they said.

In a campaign fought through paid television advertisements, both sides frequently emphasized the negative aspects of their opponent rather than the strengths of their candidate. Bush's "spots," for example, portrayed Dukakis as weak on crime, pollution, and foreign affairs. Dukakis's advertisements portrayed Bush as insensitive to social issues and to the plight of the poor. By the end of the campaign, many Americans were up-
2. set at the nasty tone of some of the political advertisements.

On election day, the public responded to the peace and prosperity of the Reagan era and chose Bush. He received 53 percent of the popular vote to Dukakis's 46 percent, and 426 electoral votes to Dukakis's 111. The Democrats, however, continued to hold a majority in both the House of Representatives and the Senate.

The New President

Raised in a wealthy family and educated at prestigious schools, George Herbert Walker Bush had all the traditional virtues: honesty, decency, loyalty, and courage. A veteran of World War II, successful in business, a former member of Congress, ambassador, and

3. **PRESIDENTS** Bush, in his victory speech, addressed those who had voted against him: "My hand is out to you, and I want to be your President, too."

head of the CIA, he seemed a capable successor to President Reagan. His staunch loyalty to Reagan caused some people to wonder how Bush could establish his own identity.

In his inaugural address, Bush signaled a departure from some of the ideas and attitudes of the Reagan era. Proclaiming a "new breeze," he promised a "kinder, gentler nation." "Use power to help people . . . ," he said. "We are not the sum of our possessions. . . . We cannot hope only to leave our children a bigger car, a bigger bank account. We must hope to give them a sense of what it means to be a loyal friend, a loving parent, a citizen who leaves his home, his neighborhood and town better than he found it."

Also significant was Bush's call for bipartisan government. Bush hoped to heal some of the rifts between the Democrats and Republicans. Bush hoped that the country's 3. problems could be solved with more cooperation between the parties and between the executive and legislative branches.

Issues to Be Faced

When Bush assumed office in January 1989, he had to decide how far to continue the Reagan revolution. Ronald Reagan had called for less government regulation. Should Bush follow that course? Reagan had begun his

2. **DISCUSSION** Ask: Do you think that television has had a positive or a negative effect on presidential campaigns? What steps would you take to prevent the misuse of television by political candidates?

1. **BIOGRAPHY** James Baker (1930–) was born in Houston, Texas. During the Reagan administration, he served as White House chief of staff and as secretary of the treasury. He managed George Bush's campaign for President in 1980 as well as in 1988.

term as a staunch foe of the Soviets. Yet, he had softened his attitude after meeting with Premier Gorbachev. In the early months of the presidency, the Bush administration expressed caution about the Soviet move to reduce its troop strength in eastern Europe. While agreeing that these and other moves were positive steps, Secretary of State James A. Baker was concerned that they might threaten the unity of the North Atlantic alliance. George Bush was not ready to declare that the cold war was over.

As a part of his Middle East policy, the President continued the Reagan effort to arrange for an international conference to settle the dispute between Israel and Palestinians. In 1988, the Palestine Liberation Organization had reluctantly acknowledged Israel's right to exist and pledged to avoid using terrorism. The Bush administration took advantage of the PLO's new stance to hold talks with the Palestinians in an effort to move the peace process along. At the same time, the President tried to persuade Israeli Prime Minister Itzhak Shamir to modify his long-standing refusal to meet with the PLO.

On the Asian front, President Bush took pains to cultivate relations with Japan, China,

2. **VISUAL EVIDENCE** The poster at left shows Mao Zedong, founder of the People's Republic of China.

President Bush was an "old friend" of China, having headed the United States diplomatic mission there in the mid-1970s. Returning as President in February 1989, Bush, as shown here, was warmly greeted by a crowd in Beijing. Later, Bush hosted a banquet for Chinese leaders. The menu was a Texas-style barbecue.

and South Korea. After attending the funeral of Japanese Emperor Hirohito in February 1989, Bush made a whirlwind tour of the region to meet with Asian leaders. At each stop, his message conveyed a wish to balance change with a desire for continuity. This was particularly evident in China, where he promised not to exploit the American improved relations with the Soviet Union to China's disadvantage.

In Central America, President Bush took a less confrontational approach than Reagan had. Although the Bush administration looked suspiciously on Nicaraguan President Daniel Ortega's promise to hold elections in his country, it did not press for military aid to the contra rebels. Instead, it worked out a bipartisan agreement with Congress to provide them with food, clothing, shelter, and medical supplies. President Bush also sent a bipartisan committee to Panama to observe the 1989 elections.

Domestic Policy On the home front, President Bush had to find a way to reduce the federal budget deficit. Bush could not raise taxes to close the gap, because he had firmly pledged not to do so. His call for increased volunteerism—"a thousand points of light"—was seen by most as a sign that the President would ask for reductions in federally funded programs.

At the same time, the issues of education and drugs seemed to call for increased spending. During the presidential campaign, Bush had vowed to become the "Education President" and to devote serious attention to improving education. He also had to confront the drug crisis that was causing a rise in crime in many neighborhoods. Building on Reagan's "Just Say No" anti-drug campaign, Bush appointed former Secretary of Education William Bennett as the nation's "drug czar." The President indicated, however, that the deficit problem would rule out an expensive crackdown.

A financial crisis that had been brewing came to a head in the early months of the Bush administration. The system of savings and loan banks, deregulated under Reagan, was in danger of collapse. The Federal Savings and Loan Insurance Corporation did not have enough money to pay off the millions of depositors who had invested their life sav-

3. **BACKGROUND** Three months later, Mikhail Gorbachev also visited China, the first Soviet leader to do so in over 20 years.

ings in the failed banks. The administration tightened bank regulations. But even so, the bank crisis seemed likely to cost Americans over $100 billion to solve.

See p. T142.

SECTION 3 REVIEW

1. **Identify:** (a) George Bush, (b) Jesse Jackson, (c) Michael Dukakis, (d) James A. Baker.

2. How did Bush and Dukakis use television to wage their presidential campaigns?

3. What solutions did President Bush offer for dealing with the federal deficit?

4. How did Bush propose to solve the nation's drug crisis?

5. **Critical Thinking** Why is it so difficult for a Vice President to be elected to succeed the President he served?

4 Examining Social Issues

READ TO UNDERSTAND

■ Why Americans have sought a return to traditional values.

■ What changes the American family has undergone.

■ How homelessness, education, and drugs have become political issues.

The election of Ronald Reagan in 1980 had signaled a victory for those who wanted a less active role for the federal government. But in many ways, the Reagan revolution was social as well as political. Many Americans of the 1980s called for a return to what they viewed as traditional American values.

Traditional American Values

During the stormy years of the 1960s, college students often marched for civil rights or protested the war in Vietnam. They rejected the traditional clothing and haircuts of their parents in favor of blue jeans, "love" beads, and long hair. Some critics complained that the students were too idealistic and impractical.

In the late 1970s, a shift occurred. Many young people turned their attention away from social and political issues. They chose a more conventional lifestyle and displayed a new interest in the older values. Students concentrated more on their future careers and getting ahead in the world. Now, many observers complained that "yuppies"—young 1. urban professional workers—had become overly concerned with money, possessions, and comfort.

Were people becoming too materialistic? Would worldly lifestyles erode the religious foundations of American culture? Groups such as the Moral Majority, organized by the Reverend Jerry Falwell of Lynchburg, Virginia, led campaigns to make Christianity more prominent in American life. Ministers, like the Reverend Pat Robertson, used television to 2. present their message.

Religious groups, of course, had long played a part in American life. Like religious groups of the 1950s and 1960s that worked for civil rights, these newer organizations used the political process to further causes they considered important. They campaigned for these issues and supported candidates who favored their views.

Mixing religious values with politics, however, has always been a sensitive business. The United States is a pluralistic society with people of many different religious beliefs. Members of some religious groups fear that their constitutional right of religious freedom will suffer if values become political issues. They, as well as other Americans with no religious beliefs, argue that values should remain a matter for family and religion, not government. It was for this reason that Thomas Jefferson and the others of the founding generation insisted that the government should not make any laws limiting religious freedom.

The Family

The supporters of the return to traditional values have placed special emphasis on the role families play in American life. They have

1. *A mother waving goodbye to her child at a day-care center is now a common American sight. Economic changes and increased opportunities for women have produced a sharp rise in the number of working mothers. Finding quality day care at an affordable price is a challenge for families where both parents are employed outside the home.*

campaigned to improve the stability of the family as an institution.

Strains on the Family As a result of the increased divorce rate, single-parent families, usually headed by women, make up over 10 percent of all American households. With only 2. one wage-earner, these households face severe economic strain.

Teen-age pregnancy places yet another strain on the family. The illegitimacy rate in the United States is one of the highest among industrialized nations. According to predictions, one out of every ten girls between the ages of 13 and 19 will probably become pregnant out of wedlock.

The increasing role of women in the work place has also affected the family. Today, more women are working outside the home than ever before. In some cases, fathers help in raising the children. For the most part, however, parents rely on professional child care.

Nonparental Child Care Nonparental child care has become a pressing national concern. To meet the need, day-care centers have mushroomed throughout the country. Businesses have established day-care centers within the work place to accommodate employees.

Many psychologists, however, question whether day-care centers or babysitters can answer children's needs as effectively as parents. As defenders of the traditional family point out, the family has always been the primary source of children's intellectual growth and system of values.

Some children must fend for themselves while their parents work. Known as "latchkey children" because they have the key to the home, these children often have no supervision, even at a very young age.

Many people have suggested that society may be harmed by some of these changes.

The Homeless and Welfare Families

In recent years, the problem of homelessness in our society has been growing. Homeless people can be seen in cities across the country. They haunt the streets, bus and train stations, parks, and abandoned buildings, eating whatever they can find and sleeping under rags and newspapers.

Although some of the homeless are mentally ill, many simply have not been able to find jobs or affordable housing. Calling homelessness a "national shame," the Bush administration has promised a vigorous approach 3. to the problem.

In a slightly better position are people on welfare. Over the years, the federal government has spent billions of dollars on welfare. Critics claim that the welfare system has created a permanent underclass dependent on assistance. According to them, many of this underclass are single women whose daughters will also probably go on welfare.

Some experts today call for reform in the welfare system. A bill passed in 1988 provided funds—beginning with $600 million in 1989 and increasing to $1.3 billion in 1995—to combat welfare dependency. Under this legislation, some welfare parents will receive job training, job search assistance, education, and work experience. Those who refuse these programs will lose welfare payments.

800

2. **BACKGROUND** Another result of the increased divorce rate is the "blended family": a single household containing children of more than one marriage.

3. **ACTIVITY** Have students use the *Readers' Guide* to research recent efforts to help the homeless. Ask them to present their findings to the class.

1. **DISCUSSION** Have students explain the meaning of this statement. Ask: Why was the report titled "A Nation at Risk"?

The Education System

In the early 1980s, many people voiced increasing concern about the nation's educational system. Some critics blamed the lowered standards of the 1960s, when schools allowed nontraditional subjects in the curriculum. The more recent "back-to-basics" movement reflects both the need to improve American education and a return to more traditional values.

"A Nation at Risk" In 1983, the Department of Education issued a report condemning the nation's educational system. Titled "A Nation at Risk," the report stated, "If an unfriendly power had attempted to impose on America the mediocre educational performance that exists today, we might well have viewed it as an act of war." 1.

In its report, the Department of Education included two recommendations: more time in school each year and more required

2. **VISUAL EVIDENCE** The man at the left is Edward James Olmos, who played Escalante in the movie *Stand and Deliver*. Olmos called Escalante "an American hero."

NOTABLE AMERICANS

2.

Jaime Escalante

A teacher was giving his new class a talk about *ganas,* a Spanish word for desire. "The only thing you got to do over here, you got to work with *ganas.* You don't have to have a high IQ. . . . Myself, I have a negative IQ. So the only thing I require of you is the *ganas.*"

This was Jaime Escalante, seen at the far right, the only high school math teacher ever to become the hero of a movie. *Stand and Deliver* told the true story of how Escalante turned a class full of unprepared, uninterested students into a team of calculus wizards.

Escalante joined the faculty of Garfield High School in 1974. At the time, nobody expected much from its students. The school, located in a low-income section of East Los Angeles, was plagued by drugs and gang violence. Half of all the students dropped out.

But Escalante was determined. He had been a teacher in his native Bolivia before coming to America. Speaking no English, he scrubbed floors while studying at night. Now that he was qualified to teach in his new country, he wanted to make a difference.

Escalante got his students' attention any way he could. His teaching props included meat cleavers and windup toys. He translated calculus operations into basketball terms and bounced around the classroom yelling instructions like "give and go." Inattentive students might suddenly find themselves hit with a little red pillow.

Most important, Escalante built his students' *ganas* and confidence. He challenged them to meet high standards. Under the clock, he hung a sign reminding them that *"Determination + Discipline + Hard Work = Way to Success."* Escalante knew that these students could achieve more than they or anyone else ever expected.

By 1987, Garfield's advanced calculus students ranked fourth in the United States. Best of all, gangs and drugs were on the way out at Garfield High School.

3.

See p. T143.

1. What did *ganas* mean to Escalante?

2. **Critical Thinking** How could success in an activity like calculus have an effect on drug use and gang fighting?

3. **BACKGROUND** One student said of Escalante, "He made us feel powerful, that we could do anything."

courses in basic subjects such as English, mathematics, science, and social studies.

State legislatures and boards of education have responded to the criticism. Among the changes they have made in public schools are a longer school year, more required courses, and competency exams as a requirement for graduation from high school.

Education and Democracy An effective education system is crucial to a democratic
1. society. Since democracy rests on the idea that a citizen can and should make important decisions, the ideal citizen is an informed one. Citizens who can understand issues are, in effect, essential to the survival and strength of a democracy.

The Drug Crisis

Drugs have long been a problem in America. Abuse of substances such as marijuana, heroin, and cocaine is not a new phenomenon.

2. **BACKGROUND** Despite problems in the educational system, more students are staying in school and graduating than ever before.

---

2. *Education is an important part of preparing for a productive life. The nation needs educated workers to be able to compete in tomorrow's world.*

But their increasing and widespread use has created a major crisis.

A National Threat Drug use has become increasingly costly to society. In 1986, the government estimated that drug use contributed to $33 billion in lost employee productivity. Moreover, between 1982 and 1986, the federal budget for drug enforcement nearly doubled, although money appropriated for treatment of drug abuse declined sharply.

Drug testing has added to costs. Fearful that drug use would hamper employee performance, about one third of the country's major corporations instituted drug testing for their employees. Federal and local governments also have required drug testing for employees whose jobs involve public safety.

By 1986, the drug crisis worsened with the appearance of a highly addictive form of cocaine known as crack. The use of this powerful drug had become widespread in such cities as Los Angeles, Houston, Miami, and New York. Youth addiction and drug-related 3. crime soared.

Government Action The federal government has taken some steps to meet the drug crisis. In 1988, Congress passed a stiff anti-drug bill to punish users as well as dealers of illegal drugs. Users caught with even a small amount of drugs face possible fines of up to $10,000. Drug dealers who murder while committing a drug-related crime face a possible death penalty.

Also in 1988, representatives from 47 nations met in Vienna, Austria, and signed a United Nations accord to freeze and seize bank accounts of suspected drug traffickers. The accord reflected the world's recognition that no country can successfully attack the drug problem alone; it will take an international effort.

AIDS Another serious concern in recent years has been the spread of the disease known as Acquired Immune Deficiency Syndrome, or AIDS. AIDS is caused by a virus that cripples the body's ability to fight off infection. Research shows that a person can contract AIDS through sexual contact with an infected partner or by sharing contaminated needles while taking drugs. But as yet, there is no cure for nor means of immunization against AIDS.

3. **LOCAL HISTORY** Tie this section in with current anti-drug programs in your community or school.

1. **VISUAL EVIDENCE** Point out that this photo shows various groups (teachers, students, organizations like Phoenix House) cooperating to combat drugs.

3. **VOCABULARY** Have students look up these terms in the glossary before they begin reading.

The use of crack, a cheap form of cocaine,
1. *endangers some areas as crack dealers carry on open warfare for control of the business. The rapid spread of the use of crack has spurred communities into action. Concerned citizens have joined to fight drug abuse in all its forms.*

2. **BACKGROUND** By October 1988, at least 75,000 Americans had contracted AIDS.

Concerned parents, community leaders, and health care professionals are at work trying to educate young people and other citizens who may be at risk. As research continues into the control and prevention of
2. AIDS, the disease is being treated as a serious public health problem.

See p. T143.

SECTION 4 REVIEW

1. Why has nonparental child care become a national concern?

2. What changes in education did "A Nation at Risk" recommend?

3. How has the drug crisis affected American society?

4. **Critical Thinking** Why is the dispute over values such a difficult one in a pluralistic society?

5 Striving for Equality

READN TO UNDERSTAND

■ What progress women and African Americans have made toward equality.

■ Why Hispanics are a significant minority in the United States.

■ How American Indians have worked to gain new rights.

■ *Vocabulary:* affirmative action, mainstream.   3.

One of the most important trends in United States history has been the struggle for equality among the nation's diverse groups. Discrimination has often stimulated groups to organize to combat disadvantages. In the 1970s, the emphasis of the struggle for equality shifted as the federal government played a less significant role in supporting groups that had traditionally been the targets of discrimination.

Gains for Women

The defeat of the Equal Rights Amendment in 1982 forced leaders of the women's movement to reconsider their tactics. Action shifted to the courts. Groups and individuals brought suits against businesses and government agencies that were accused of discriminating against women.

Still, the 1980s were a time of great achievement for American women. In record numbers, women entered careers that traditionally were dominated by men. The armed forces, police, and fire departments have seen an influx of women. In the 1980s, Sally Ride became the first American woman astronaut, and Kathryn Sullivan was the first 4. American woman to walk in space. Women have also made significant inroads in other careers, such as business management and engineering.

Yet on the average, women workers still earn only about 65 percent of what men do. One reason is that a majority of women con- **803**

4. **BACKGROUND** Only two other women, both Soviet, had been in space before Ride. Ride, who has a Ph.D. in astrophysics, insisted that being the first American woman in space was "no big deal."

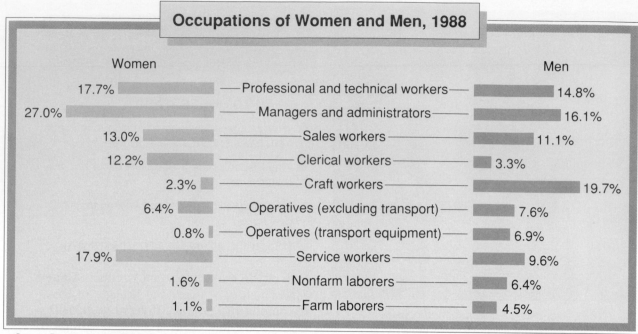

Occupations of Women and Men, 1988

Women		Men
17.7%	——Professional and technical workers——	14.8%
27.0%	——Managers and administrators——	16.1%
13.0%	——Sales workers——	11.1%
12.2%	——Clerical workers——	3.3%
2.3%	——Craft workers——	19.7%
6.4%	——Operatives (excluding transport)——	7.6%
0.8%	——Operatives (transport equipment)——	6.9%
17.9%	——Service workers——	9.6%
1.6%	——Nonfarm laborers——	6.4%
1.1%	——Farm laborers——	4.5%

Source: Bureau of Labor Statistics

GRAPH STUDY *Since the 1960s, women have entered the work force in unprecedented numbers, and many more women have taken professional or managerial jobs. This chart shows the percentage of men and women in various occupations. In which occupations do more than 15 percent of women work? In which do more than 15 percent of men work?* See p. T143.

1.

1. **GRAPH READING** Ask: Is homemaking included in the graph? Do you think it should be? Why or why not?

tinue to hold such traditional occupations as secretary, sales clerk, and registered nurse. These jobs tend to be low-paying, in spite of the fact that they require a skill level equal to that needed for higher-paying jobs traditionally held by men.

African Americans

2. Historically, unemployment has been higher among blacks, especially black youths. Since the mid-1970s, **affirmative action** programs have been set up to compensate for past discrimination and increase opportunities for minorities and women.

But government programs that have enabled blacks to make gains in the past have come under scrutiny in recent years. Critics sometimes describe affirmative action as "reverse discrimination." One interpretation of affirmative action was the decision of the Supreme Court in the case of *Regents of the University of California* v. *Bakke* in 1978. In this case, Allan Bakke, a white, sued to be admitted to the University of California medical school. He argued that he had been refused admission because the university set aside places for less-well-qualified blacks. The Supreme Court ordered that Bakke be admitted to the medical school. However, while the Court ruled that a rigid quota system based on race was unconstitutional, it did decide that race could be considered in formulating admissions policy.

In 1987, however, another Supreme Court ruling once more adjusted the ground rules for affirmative action. To provide relief for the proven discrimination against black Alabama state troopers, a federal court had ordered that for each white trooper promoted, one black trooper had to be promoted. In a 5–4 decision in the case of *United States* v. *Paradise,* the Supreme Court upheld the strict promotion quota.

During President Reagan's administration, some members of the Civil Rights Commission objected to the methods used to promote civil rights in the past. Reagan at first

2. **BACKGROUND** In 1983, when the unemployment rate for the total population of the U.S. was 9.6 percent, the unemployment rate among blacks was 19.5 percent.

1. **BACKGROUND** The new holiday was celebrated for the first time on January 20, 1986. King was actually born on January 15, but the holiday is celebrated on the Monday closest to King's birthday.

1. opposed extension of the Voting Rights Act, claiming that it was no longer needed. In 1982, Congress eliminated busing as a tool for integrating schools. On the other hand, Congress proclaimed the birthday of Martin Luther King, Jr., a national holiday in recognition of his contributions to the nation.

Many African Americans feel that some of the gains of the earlier civil rights movement have been lost. But there has been progress for some. Because more blacks were completing high school and attending college, more of them moved into the middle class and entered the professions than ever before. The percentage of blacks in professional and technical jobs almost tripled be-

tween 1960 and 1980, and the number of blacks in managerial positions doubled. Yet the median family income of African Americans remains between 50 and 60 percent of the median family income of whites.

Hispanic Americans

According to the 1980 population census, there are 15 million people of Hispanic heritage in the United States. Hispanics thus make up the second largest minority group, after black Americans. They form important percentages of the populations of such cities as Miami, New York, Los Angeles, and San Antonio. They have come from all parts of the

2. **GRAPH READING** Ask: What percentage of professional and technical jobs did blacks hold in 1960? In 1980? What percentage of clerical jobs did blacks hold in 1960? In 1980?

GRAPH STUDY *Since 1960, the percentage of African Americans in white-collar jobs has grown dramatically. On the graph, these jobs are labeled Professional and technical workers, Managers and administrators, Sales workers, and Clerical workers. Despite this growth, however, the incomes of blacks continue to trail the incomes of whites. In which occupations has the percentage of black workers dropped between 1960 and 1988?* See p. T143.

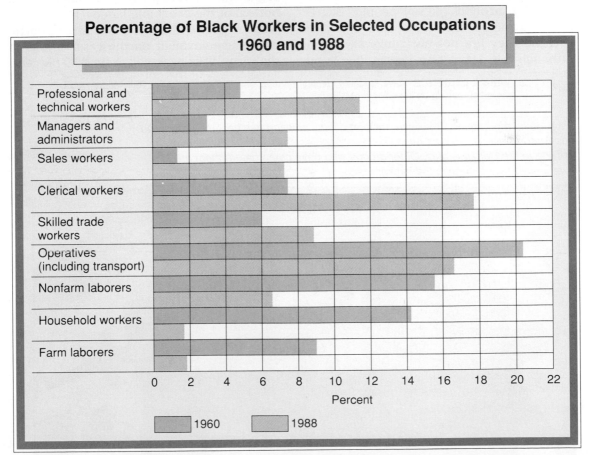

Percentage of Black Workers in Selected Occupations
1960 and 1988

Source: Bureau of Labor Statistics

1. ACTIVITY Ask interested students to prepare a report on the history of Puerto Rico. Suggest that they also discuss why Puerto Rico has remained a commonwealth instead of becoming a state.

Spanish-speaking world, but mainly from Cuba, Mexico, and Puerto Rico.

In the past 20 years, large numbers of Cubans have come to the United States. As you have read in Chapter 34, in 1980 more than 100,000 Cuban refugees arrived in the United States. They were fleeing the communist regime of Fidel Castro, and their exodus became known as the Freedom Flotilla. Many of the new arrivals settled in Florida, and today Miami is an important center of Cuban American life. (See page 745.)

Most Mexican Americans, who make up the largest Hispanic group, live in the Southwest. All the major cities in this area have large Mexican American communities. In recent years, Mexican Americans have played an increasingly important role in the political and social life of that area.

The largest Puerto Rican community is in New York City, although smaller Puerto Rican communities are found in Chicago and Newark, New Jersey. Puerto Ricans make up about 10 percent of the population of New York City, around 700,000 people. Puerto Ricans are unique among Hispanic Americans because they are not an immigrant group. Although it is not a state, Puerto Rico is po-

litically part of the United States, and all its people are United States citizens.

American Indians

By 1980, 1,400,000 Indians lived within the United States. About 54 percent of them now live in urban areas. Others have chosen to retain their Indian nation identity and customs on Indian reservations.

Under President Nixon, government policy was to promise Indians a degree of "self-determination." They were encouraged to develop tradional life on the reservations. The government pledged assistance in educational and economic development, housing, and vocational training. By 1973, Indians made up a majority of the members of the federal Bureau of Indian Affairs.

Recently, there has been a small increase of Indians in the professions. American Indians have become lawyers, doctors, and engineers. But many have remained at the bottom of the economic ladder. Mainly as a result of poor education and lack of opportunity, unemployment on the reservations in the early 1980s averaged around 50 percent.

2. VISUAL EVIDENCE Have students identify the flags shown in this painting. Ask: What point is the artist making by including these flags?

Through immigrants, the Mexican tradition of wall painting has become part of the Los Angeles scene. This mural in East Los Angeles shows new Latin immigrants arriving in the United States. Other groups who have come before them are symbolized by the flags in the background.

Some Indian groups have sued to recover land taken from them earlier. The Taos Pueblo in New Mexico recovered the Blue Lake, which was sacred to their tribe and which formed part of a national park. In Maine, Indians sued for the recovery of more than one third of the state. The courts awarded them $81 million with the provision that they be allowed to purchase 300,000 acres of land in Maine.

Because they are spread among more than 450 scattered groups, many speaking different languages, Indians have found it difficult to cooperate for national action. Ancient conflicts have also weakened their strength, as in the case of the Hopi and the Navajo, who have fought over rights to the same land in the Southwest.

Handicapped Americans

During the 1970s, the handicapped started to move into the mainstream of American life. Inspired by gains made by other minorities, they organized to demand equal advantages that had been denied them in the past. The Rehabilitation Act of 1973 forbade discrimination against the handicapped in jobs, education, and housing.

Federal and local governments have responded to lobbying by the handicapped by taking their special needs into account. Many public buildings and transportation systems now can meet the needs of handicapped Americans. For example, elevators often have Braille numbers to designate the floors. Ramps provide access to buildings for people in wheelchairs. Convenient parking spaces are designated for use by the handicapped.

In 1975, Congress passed the Education for All Handicapped Children Act. This required public schools to provide suitable education for children with physical or mental handicaps. Schools were to **mainstream** handicapped children, that is, allow them to attend classes with the nonhandicapped, rather than in special facilities. Critics of mainstreaming say that handicapped children might need special attention or facilities that are not available in a regular classroom. Supporters argue that the benefit of being in a normal school environment outweighs any drawbacks.

Handicapped people are pursuing the same pleasures of life as other Americans. In sports, the Special Olympics gives them an opportunity to compete on the international level. This man is playing in a tennis tournament in California.

2.

See p. T143.

SECTION 5 REVIEW

1. **Identify:** Sally Ride.

2. **Define:** (a) affirmative action, (b) mainstream.

3. In what areas have women recently made progress?

4. (a) What gains have African Americans made in the 1970s and 1980s? (b) What setbacks have they faced?

5. Why have Hispanic Americans become a significant minority in the United States?

6. What gains have the handicapped made in recent years?

7. **Critical Thinking** What characteristics of American society make it possible for minorities to become part of the mainstream of society?

CHAPTER 36 REVIEW

Summary

1. **President Reagan promised to improve the economy with his program of Reaganomics.** By the mid-1980s, a recovery was underway. He also focused on tax reform and reduction of the budget deficit.

2. **In foreign affairs, Reagan acted firmly.** Meetings with Soviet Premier Gorbachev, coupled with changes in Soviet policy, improved relations between the United States and the Soviet Union. Policies in Latin America and the Middle East were influenced by the superpower conflict.

3. **George Bush signaled a shift away from the Reagan era.** Promising a "kinder and gentler" nation, President Bush had to deal with new issues as well as with unresolved problems left behind by the previous administration.

4. **During the 1980s, many Americans sought a return to more traditional values.** Religious groups, in particular, have actively supported the revival of traditional beliefs and values. At the same time, America faces a wide range of social issues.

5. **Minorities have struggled to gain equal political, social, and economic rights.** Although each group has had varying success, the trend has generally been toward equality. The success of one group has spurred on others.

See p. T144.

Vocabulary

Choose the answer that best completes each of the following sentences.

1. Decreasing government involvement in business is known as (a) divestiture, (b) deficit, (c) deregulation.

2. Spending more than one takes in results in a (a) surplus, (b) deregulation, (c) deficit.

3. The Soviet policy of speaking out honestly about problems is called (a) apartheid, (b) New Federalism, (c) glasnost.

4. The refusal to keep stock in a company doing business in South Africa is called (a) apartheid; (b) deregulation; (c) divestiture.

5. Young urban professionals are also known as (a) yuppies, (b) conservatives, (b) incumbents.

6. Offering opportunities to minorities applying for jobs or school admission is known as (a) mainstreaming, (b) affirmative action, (c) glasnost.

See p. T144.

Chapter Checkup

1. (a) What did President Reagan consider the major economic problems of the nation when he first took office? (b) How did he deal with them?

2. (a) How did the Reagan administration try to eliminate the federal deficit? (b) The trade deficit?

3. What changes took place in United States relations with the Soviet Union during Reagan's presidency?

4. Describe President Reagan's foreign policy toward (a) Latin America, (b) the Middle East, (c) South Africa.

5. What signals did President Bush give that his administration would be a change from the Reagan era?

6. (a) What major issues did George Bush face upon taking office? (b) What were his early moves to deal with these issues?

7. What factors have contributed to a weakening of the American family?

8. Describe recent gains and problems of: (a) women; (b) blacks; (c) Hispanic Americans; (d) Indians; (e) the handicapped.

Critical Thinking

1. **Comparing** Compare Ronald Reagan's response to the recession of the early 1980s with Franklin D. Roosevelt's response to the Great Depression of the early 1930s. (See Chapters 28 and 29.) (a) How did the basic approach of the two Presidents differ? (b) What developments of the past 50 years might help explain why their approaches were different?

2. **Analyzing** How can policies of the federal government affect the direction in which society develops?

Connecting Past and Present

1. Make a list of the foreign policy problems faced by the United States during the 1970s and 1980s. Compare these problems with the issues facing the United States after World War II. (See pages 693–709.) What are the similarities and differences between the two periods?

2. The 1980s, according to many people, can be characterized as a time when people's commitment has been primarily to themselves rather than to society. Compare this period with the 1960s. What similarities or differences are there between people's attitudes during these two periods?

Developing Basic Skills

1. **Writing a Report** Using materials available in the library, investigate the change in relations between the United States and the Soviet Union during the Reagan years. Write a report in which you describe how Mikhail Gorbachev has succeeded in presenting a different image from previous Soviet leaders. Explain why the United States has declared a "wait-and-see" attitude toward Soviet initiatives.

2. **Studying a Graph** Study the graph on page 787. (a) In what year was the unemployment rate the highest? (b) In what year was the inflation rate highest? (c) What generalization about the economy between 1980 and 1982 can you make from the information on the graph?

WRITING ABOUT HISTORY

Creating a Graph

A graph can present a great deal of information clearly in a limited amount of space. You may find it useful to develop a graph to illustrate a research paper when you have statistical data that support your thesis. The most common types of graphs are circle graphs, line graphs, and bar graphs. Circle graphs show the relationship of a part to a whole. Bar graphs and line graphs are useful to show comparisons and changes over a period of time. Your choice of graph type will depend on the information you want to display and the impact you want to make.

Practice: Use the following table of federal debt from 1979 to 1988 to create a graph that shows trends in the federal debt. Figures are in millions of dollars (add 000,000).

Year	Millions of Dollars	Year	Millions of Dollars
1979	833,751	1984	1,576,748
1980	914,317	1985	1,841,748
1981	1,003,941	1986	2,120,082
1982	1,146,941	1987	2,345,578
1983	1,381,886	1988	2,600,753

Source: Office of Budget and Management

The United States: Today and Tomorrow

37

CHAPTER OUTLINE

1 **Governing a Growing Nation**

2 **A Changing Population**

3 **Advances in Science and Technology**

4 **The American Economy Today**

5 **The United States and the World**

It is early afternoon when you get to Burgerland. The tables are full of people, and there are lines at every order station. But there are no employees to be seen—no human ones, that is. When you step up to the counter, a metallic voice comes out of a speaker: "May I take your order?" You answer, "A Buddy Burger Deluxe, chef's salad, and milk." The speaker squawks, "That will be $4.05. Please deposit bills in the slot and coins in the cup." The money is whisked away and, in moments, a blinking light announces your change.

Out in the kitchen, the scene is somewhat the same. One robot plucks the hamburger from the grill and drops it onto the bun, another adds the fixings, a third dishes out salad, and a fourth uses its delicate mechanical fingers to arrange your order on a tray. The only sound other than a sizzling grill is the whirr of tireless little machines. Strange? No, you are used to robots by now. After all, they vacuum your rugs, walk your dog, drive your car, and play chess with you. This is the twenty-first century, isn't it?

Science fiction? Maybe—and maybe not. Researchers have already created a robot that can place hamburgers onto buns, and fastfood chains are investigating the possibility of a completely robot-run restaurant. Other scientists, looking farther into the future, foresee robots equipped with "artificial intelligence," which will give the impression that the robots can think.

An adventurous desire to test and explore the limits of technology has characterized the United States since its earliest days. The challenges ahead are great. If technological and engineering know-how is combined with a sensitivity to humanity's spiritual and cultural needs, the future will hold wonders indeed.

1.

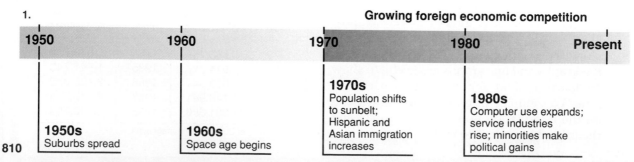

Growing foreign economic competition

| 1950 | 1960 | 1970 | 1980 | Present |

1950s Suburbs spread

1960s Space age begins

1970s Population shifts to sunbelt; Hispanic and Asian immigration increases

1980s Computer use expands; service industries rise; minorities make political gains

810

1. **TIME LINE QUESTION** Ask: Which development shown on the time line has had the largest impact on your life? How long ago did it occur?

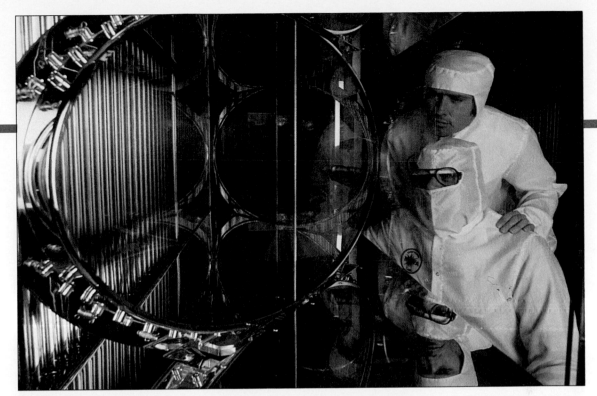

Lasers, devices that create concentrated beams of light, are an example of
1. *technology that is changing American life. Lasers are used in sophisticated weapons, light shows, CD players, and medicine. Shown here is NOVA, the world's largest laser, at Livermore Laboratory in California.*

1. **TECHNOLOGY** Arthur Schawlow, who developed one of the first lasers, predicted that "lasers will make practical what can barely be done today, and make possible what is not yet even dreamed of."

1 Governing a Growing Nation

READ TO UNDERSTAND

■ How the role of the federal government has changed.

■ Why the power of political parties has weakened.

■ What political gains have been made by women and minority groups.

2. ■ *Vocabulary:* special interest group.

In the first presidential election of this century, William McKinley staged a "front porch" campaign. He stayed at home, gave few speeches, and occasionally came out on his front porch to answer reporters' questions. The simple campaign style suited the scale of government in the early 1900s. Few Ameri-

cans had much contact with Washington in McKinley's time. The federal govenment delivered the mails, collected tariffs, maintained harbors and roads, ran the federal courts, managed the public domain, and organized the armed forces. Today, things are different. The federal government now touches all aspects of American life.

The Role of Government

The role of government today differs greatly from what it was even 50 years ago. Until the 1930s, few people believed the federal government should play a major part in providing social services. Today, federal spending
3. on social programs is roughly 500 times as great as it was in 1929.

The enlarged role of the federal government goes beyond providing social services to trying to improve the quality of life in general. Federal regulations affect such things as the content of hot dogs and the air quality

2. **VOCABULARY** Have students look up this term in the glossary before they begin reading.

3. **BACKGROUND** Remind students that government response to the Great Depression brought about much of the increase in the 1930s.

811

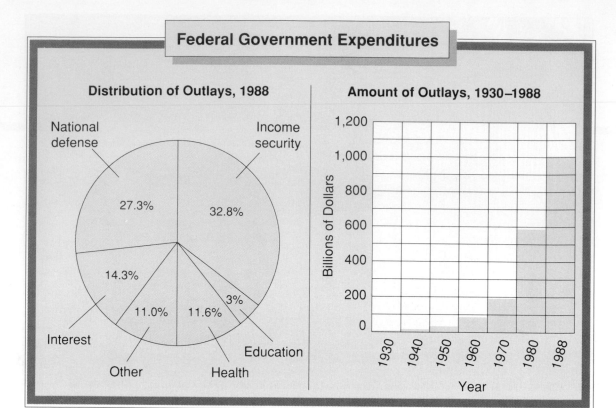

Federal Government Expenditures

Distribution of Outlays, 1988

National defense — 27.3%
Income security — 32.8%
Interest — 14.3%
Other — 11.0%
Health — 11.6%
Education — 3%

Amount of Outlays, 1930–1988

Billions of Dollars (vertical axis: 0, 200, 400, 600, 800, 1,000, 1,200)

Year (horizontal axis: 1930, 1940, 1950, 1960, 1970, 1980, 1988)

Source: *Historical Statistics of the United States;* Office of Management and Budget

GRAPH STUDY

See p. T145.

These graphs show two ways of looking at federal spending. The circle graph at left shows how federal funds were allocated in 1988. The bar graph at right traces the increase in federal expenditures from 1930 to 1988. About how many billions of dollars were spent on education in 1988?

1.

1. **GRAPH READING** Ask: In 1988, what percentage of government expenditures went for health? For national defense? Name one thing that might have been included in "Other."

in textile mills. Government officials examine the food Americans eat, the clothes they wear, the cars they drive, and the safety of their environment.

During the late 1970s, the federal agencies that administer these standards came under attack. Critics cited the many thousands of regulations that required vast amounts of time, money, and paperwork to administer. They argued that often the benefits did not justify the expense. The deregulation efforts of the Reagan administration (see page 786) were a response to these criticisms.

The Role of Political Parties

The Republican and Democratic parties have dominated American politics since the Civil War. They built coalitions of diverse groups that cooperated to win elections. People often voted for the party, rather than the indi-

vidual. Today, the ability of candidates to appeal directly to the voters through radio and television has weakened political parties. Independent voters often hold the balance of power in today's elections.

Special Interest Groups Political parties have also been weakened by the growth of **special interest groups**—organizations devoted to promoting a single political issue. Special interest groups lobby for or against such issues as gun control, abortion rights, and increases in social security. Through political action committees (PACs), they donate money to candidates who support their point of view. PAC money has become an important factor in winning elections.

2.

The growth of special interest groups has caused concern. Critics charge that these groups have an influence on candidates and government that is out of proportion to their size. Through organized letter-writing cam-

2. **BACKGROUND** In 1982, 3,479 PACs contributed $90 million to congressional campaigns. One critic charged, "Dependency on PACs has grown so much that PACS, not constituents, are now the focus of a congressman's attention."

paigns and demonstrations, they may earn more than their share of attention. On the other hand, special interest groups galvanize people into action and provide a way for Americans to participate in government.

Elections and the Media Accompanying the decline of political parties has been the growing importance of television. Television appearances allow candidates to reach far more people than they ever could by visiting towns and cities around the country. Thus, campaign managers develop strategies geared to television.

A thoughtful, well-reasoned comment is less likely to be reported on television than a quick slogan expressed in a "sound bite" that will fit into a television news broadcast. Television advertisements enable candidates to control the message they want the public to hear. Analysts use public-opinion polls to determine the issues the public feels most strongly about—and the candidates tailor their advertisements accordingly.

The need for television advertising has greatly increased the cost of political campaigns. Some political observers fear that the trend toward more expensive campaigns may keep qualified people out of politics because they do not have the money to run. Candidates may also shy away from issues that might offend groups that provide funds.

Recognizing the powerful influence of the media, many candidates now engage in televised debates with their opponents. A candidate's success or failure often depends on how well he or she comes across on the television screen.

Minorities in Government

As the minority population of the United States has increased, more minority members have won positions in government through election and appointment. African Americans used their dramatic gains in voting rights to enter politics in a major way. In Congress, black representatives formed the Black Caucus in 1970 to discuss ways of promoting issues of importance to minorities. The caucus helped mobilize support for the divestiture campaign against South Africa. And Jesse Jackson's campaigns for the Demo-

cratic nomination for the presidency in 1984 and 1988 attracted major support. Blacks are now commonly appointed to cabinet positions.

The most impressive gains for blacks have been at the state and local levels. Blacks have held the position of mayor in some of the country's most important cities—Los Angeles, Chicago, Philadelphia, Washington, D.C., and Detroit. They have also demonstrated their political power by electing sheriffs and mayors of small towns in the South.

Hispanic Americans made dramatic gains in the late 1970s and 1980s. By 1989, more than 3,000 Hispanic Americans held appointive or elective offices at all levels of government. The city of Miami elected a Cuban mayor, Xavier L. Suarez. Bob Martinez, whose grandparents came from Spain, became Florida's governor in 1986. Mexican Americans have been politically successful throughout the Southwest. New Mexico has had a senator and two governors who were Mexican Americans.

3. **BIOGRAPHY** Dole, a senator from Kansas since 1969, was Gerald Ford's running mate in 1976. His wife, Elizabeth, was secretary of transportation under Ronald Reagan.

Senator Robert Dole, campaigning during the 1988 New Hampshire primary, is surrounded by cameras and reporters. Media coverage is an important part of campaigns.

Women continue to make great gains in political representation. The candidacy of Geraldine Ferraro for Vice President in 1984 reflected the growing strength of women in politics.

Extending Voting Rights

From 13 states hugging the eastern coast, the United States has grown to 50 states that span a continent and extend into the Pacific. The American population has expanded from about 4 million to over 240 million people.

In most of the original 13 states, the right to vote was restricted to white male Protestant property owners. When the Constitution

GRAPH STUDY *As you can see on this graph, more people vote in presidential elections than in elections when only members of Congress are being chosen. How would you describe the general trend in voting based on the graph?* See p. T145.

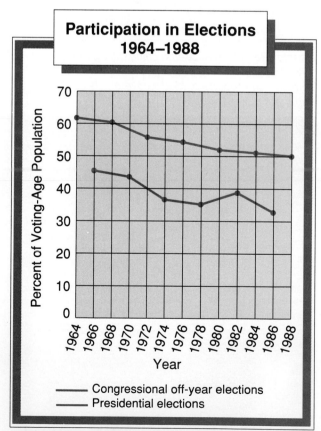

Participation in Elections 1964–1988

Percent of Voting-Age Population

—— Congressional off-year elections
—— Presidential elections

Source: U.S. Bureau of the Census; Committee for the Study of the American Electorate

was ratified in 1789, the barriers of religion and property began to fall. By the 1830s, most states had granted the vote to all white males.

The Fifteenth Amendment to the Constitution, ratified in 1870, stated that citizens could not be denied the right to vote on the basis of race. By the 1880s, however, southern states were preventing black citizens from voting. Voting rights legislation in the 1960s finally guaranteed the right to vote to all African Americans. The Twenty-fourth Amendment, ratified in 1964, outlawed the poll tax.

The long struggle for women's suffrage ended in 1920 when the states ratified the Nineteenth Amendment. The Twenty-sixth Amendment, ratified in 1971, guaranteed the right to vote to persons 18 years of age or older.

For the American political process, one of the most distressing developments since World War II has been the declining number of people who vote. As the percentage of the population who could vote grew, the percentage that did vote dropped. (See the graph at left.)

In recent years, several attempts have been made to get more people to vote by simplifying the registration process. In some areas, citizens can register by mail. In others, volunteers register people in malls and on street corners.

See p. T145.

SECTION 1 REVIEW

1. **Identify:** (a) PAC, (b) Black Caucus.

2. **Define:** special interest group.

3. How has the role of the federal government changed in recent times?

4. How has television affected the power of political parties?

5. Describe the political gains won by minorities and women in recent years.

6. **Critical Thinking** Why do you think special interest groups are so effective in getting their viewpoints across?

2 A Changing Population

READb TO UNDERSTAND

READ TO UNDERSTAND

■ How immigration patterns have changed.

■ What challenges are presented by the aging of the population.

■ Why urban areas have experienced a renewal.

1. ■ *Vocabulary:* bilingual education, zero population growth.

"Here is not merely a nation but a teeming Nation of nations," wrote the poet Walt Whitman. In that spirit, with a burst of fireworks, the United States celebrated the 100th birthday of the Statue of Liberty in 1986. New arrivals are still helping to mold the United States. At the same time, population shifts within the country and an aging popuation present new challenges.

A Land of Immigrants

The United States has always been a land of immigrants. Over time, the sources of immigration have changed. The most recent changes resulted from the Immigration and
2. Nationality Act of 1965. The act abolished the national origins quotas for immigrants that were first introduced in 1921 (see page 572). Since 1965, most new Americans have come from Asia, Latin America, and the Caribbean islands rather than from Europe.

Asians are the fastest growing group of immigrants to the United States. In the 1960s, 13 percent of the people who immigrated to the United States came from Asia. The figure jumped to over 50 percent at times in the 1980s. Nearly 7 million Asian Americans included refugees from Vietnam and Cambodia fleeing the turmoil in their homelands, as well as immigrants from China, Japan, Korea, the Philippines, and the Indian subcontinent.

Asian immigrants have achieved considerable success in their new land. The high value traditionally accorded to education in many Asian countries has been transplanted to the United States. Asian American students are represented in large numbers at the best colleges and universities in this country.

Many educated Asian immigrants have used their skills to win places in the professions and business management. Others have opened small businesses, such as dry cleaning stores, self-service laundries, and fruit, vegetable, and fish markets. Today, Americans of Korean origin have a greater proportion of self-employed people than any other American ethnic group.

3. **GRAPH READING** Ask: During what period did immigration to the U.S. from all sources decline?

GRAPH STUDY *Since the 1960s, immigrants have come increasingly from the nations of the Americas and Asia. From which region did the most immigrants come in the period from 1951 to 1970? From 1971 to 1987?* See p. T146.

3.

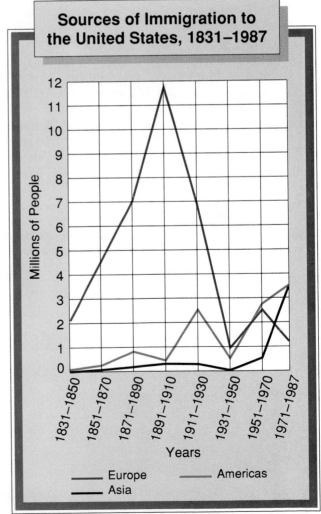

Sources of Immigration to the United States, 1831–1987

Millions of People / Years

Europe — Americas — Asia

Source: U.S. Department of Justice; Immigration and Naturalization Service

815

2. **CITIZENSHIP** The Nationality Act set an annual limit of 120,000 immigrants from the Western Hemisphere and 170,000 immigrants from all other nations, with no more than 20,000 from any one country. Relatives of U.S. citizens and people with special skills are given preference.

A large number of immigrants continues to come from Latin America and the Caribbean. About half of these new arrivals come from Mexico, but Central Americans, South Americans, and Haitians are also heavily represented. Many of these immigrants are fleeing from the poverty and political instability that limits opportunities in their homelands. Hispanics are expected to be the largest minority group in the United States by the end of the 1990s.

In 1986, Congress acted to control illegal immigration. It provided penalties for employers who hire people without proper documents. Congress provided for the illegal immigrants already here by granting amnesty to those who had lived in the United States before January 1, 1982. About 300,000 aliens have received legal status through the amnesty program.

Cultural Diversity

The flow of immigrants has infused new energy into American life and increased the nation's cultural diversity. Historians used to describe the United States as a "melting pot" in which the cultures brought by the immigrants would blend to form a single American culture. More recently, observers have used the "salad bowl" as an analogy for American society. Like the various elements in a salad, many different cultures exist side by side, united by the political ideals of a free society.

Immigrants adopt some ways of American life, while at the same time preserving parts of their home cultures. Whether it is a "melting pot" or a "salad bowl," the United States has gained from the rich cultural heritage of its many immigrant groups. These traditions can be seen in many aspects of American life—in the names of towns and cities, in the variety of food and clothing, and in the different forms of religious worship and festivals.

Some of these foreign traditions have become part of mainstream American culture. Today, tacos and enchiladas are as "American" as pizza and frankfurters—which were contributed by earlier Italian and German immigrants.

Yet cultural diversity presents problems as well. For many newcomers, adjusting to new ways of living and a new language is a challenge. Schools have tried to help immigrant children overcome the language barrier with **bilingual education**—allowing stu-

GRAPH STUDY *The variety of religions in the United States is evidence of the nation's cultural diversity. This graph shows the five main religious groups, some of which contain many smaller religious denominations. How would you describe the number of Protestants as compared to the four other groups combined?* See p. T146.

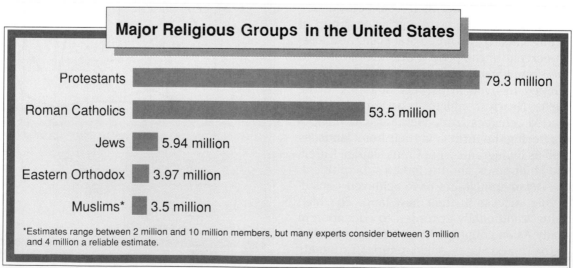

Major Religious Groups in the United States

Protestants — 79.3 million
Roman Catholics — 53.5 million
Jews — 5.94 million
Eastern Orthodox — 3.97 million
Muslims* — 3.5 million

*Estimates range between 2 million and 10 million members, but many experts consider between 3 million and 4 million a reliable estimate.

Source: *Yearbook of American and Canadian Churches, 1989;* University of Massachusetts

Immigrants have adapted to American customs while preserving their own traditions. The Vietnamese at left attend an adult education class to learn English.

1. The young women at right are taking part in a folk festival in New Jersey, dressed in the national costume of the Ukraine, a part of the Soviet Union.

1. **LOCAL HISTORY** Ask: What celebrations take place in your community that underscore the various heritages of its people?

2. **LOCAL HISTORY** If your school has a bilingual program, have students report on its effectiveness.

dents to take some courses in their native language while they are learning English.

Bilingual education programs have provoked much controversy. Critics say these programs discourage children from learning English. They are also very expensive and strain the resources of many school districts. Responding to these criticisms, some states with large foreign-born populations have passed laws making English the official language. Supporters of bilingual education counter that allowing children to use their native languages until they master English eases their transition into a new society.

An Aging Population

The nation's population is changing in other ways. One trend is slower population growth. Americans in general are marrying later and having fewer children. Some experts predict that by the year 2050 the United States

Helping the rapidly growing population of older citizens lead satisfying lives is an important challenge. These senior citizens are painting ceramics at a community center in Miami, Florida.

3.

3. **VISUAL EVIDENCE** Ask: What other kinds of activities do you think this community center might offer?

Distribution of United States Population by Age and Sex

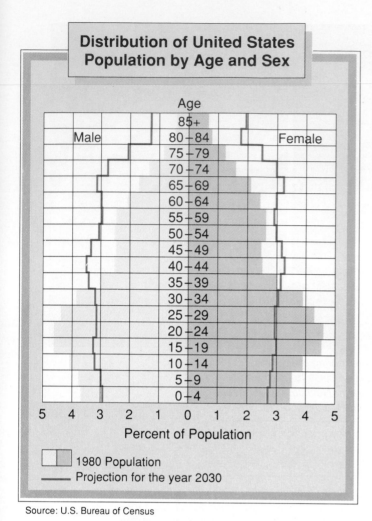

Age

Male — Female

85+
80–84
75–79
70–74
65–69
60–64
55–59
50–54
45–49
40–44
35–39
30–34
25–29
20–24
15–19
10–14
5–9
0–4

5 4 3 2 1 0 1 2 3 4 5

Percent of Population

☐ 1980 Population
— Projection for the year 2030

Source: U.S. Bureau of Census

Expenditures for Medicare and Medicaid, 1972–1987

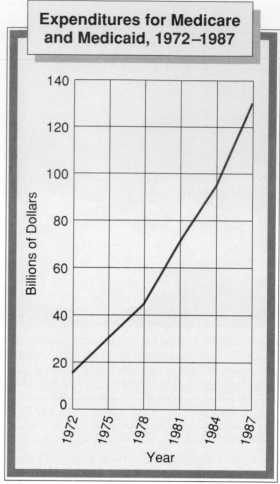

Billions of Dollars

140
120
100
80
60
40
20
0

1972 1975 1978 1981 1984 1987

Year

Source: Health Care Financing Administration

GRAPH STUDY *These graphs illustrate the aging of the population of the United States. The graph at left is called a population pyramid. It shows the percentage of men and women in various age groups. How will the shape of the pyramid change by the year 2030? What effect do you think that change will have on the expenses for Medicare and Medicaid, shown in the graph at right?*

See p. T146.

1.

1. **GRAPH READING** Ask: What percentage of females was 80 to 84 in 1980? Have students locate the projection for their own age group in 2030.

will reach **zero population growth.** In other words, the number of children born will equal the number of people who die.

The population is also becoming older. As fewer babies are born, the percentage of young people in the population drops. At the same time, with improvements in health care, older people live longer. (See the graphs above.) Today, one out of every eight Americans is 65 years of age or older. That figure is expected to rise as the "baby boomers," the people born between 1945 and 1960, reach old age in the early years of the twenty-first

2. **CRITICAL THINKING** Ask: How might the older population affect government services? What industries might expand because of the older population?

century. This will mean that a smaller proportion of the population will be part of the work force.

The over-65 segment of the population has demonstrated its political strength through such organizations as the Gray Panthers and the American Association of Retired Persons (AARP). To these groups, no political issue is more sensitive than social security, which provides older Americans with pensions and medical care. They have been successful in persuading Congress to maintain benefits.

2.

3.

3. **BIOGRAPHY** Representative Claude Pepper of Florida helped reorganize the Social Security system in the 1980s. Earlier, he had sponsored a bill raising mandatory retirement ages. In 1988, he won reelection to Congress at the age of 88. He died in 1989.

A Mobile Population

By the end of the 1800s, an increasing number of Americans were moving to the rapidly growing industrial cities of the Northeast and Midwest. That movement continued throughout the mid-1900s. The United States, which had begun as a rural nation, became an urban one.

Suburbs The post–World War II growth of suburbs continued into the 1980s. In the 1990s, more Americans will live in the suburbs than in cities and rural areas. Indeed, the growth of the suburbs has been so great that many suburban communities outside large cities have themselves become cities.

At first, suburban areas were composed of entirely white neighborhoods. However, many African Americans who prospered after the civil-rights gains of the 1960s began to buy homes in suburbia. Also, as many businesses moved from cities to the suburbs, minority employees followed. As a result, the suburban population is more diverse today than it has been in the past.

Changes in the Cities Large cities suffered from many problems. Especially in the Northeast and Midwest, urban populations experienced rising unemployment as businesses and factories moved elsewhere. Poverty, decay, and crime caused the flight of many middle-class residents. Yet office buildings in the downtown areas of large cities continue to be the workplaces for city dwellers and commuters.

When the price of gasoline rose in the late 1970s, city living became more attractive as commuting became more expensive. Indeed, many cities are undergoing massive face lifts as businesses and middle-class families return to the urban areas. "Urban homesteaders" are renovating factories, lofts, waterfront warehouses, and old houses. A new generation of younger Americans is repairing homes in once-blighted areas.

Sunbelt and Frostbelt Throughout the 1970s and 1980s, many people moved to the sunbelt, a nickname for the warm, sunny states of the Southeast and Southwest. During that decade, the population of the West and South grew almost twice as fast as did that of the country as a whole.

Most of the growth occurred in three states: Texas, California, and Florida. Six sunbelt cities—Los Angeles, Houston, Dallas, San Diego, Phoenix, and San Antonio—now rank among the nation's ten largest cities. As of 1990, one out of every nine Americans lived in the state of California. Because so many people have moved to the sunbelt, northeastern and midwestern states—the so-called frostbelt—have lost congressional seats to the sunbelt states.

VISUAL EVIDENCE Ask: What other tasks can you see that this couple will have to do?

Plenty of elbow grease is what is needed to renovate old houses, warehouses, and factories to make them livable. The energy of young couples like this one is changing the face of many city neighborhoods and giving the pride of home ownership to many who otherwise could not afford it.

Water in the Southwest

In the 1800s, people prospected for gold. In the 1900s, they drilled for oil. In the 2000s, the search may be for pure water.

People of the Southwest already face a chronic water shortage. The low average rainfall has created a need for an elaborate water transfer system. As early as 1922, the seven states that make up the drainage area of the Colorado River (Arizona, Nevada, California, Wyoming, Utah, Colorado, and New Mexico) signed a pact allotting the river's water. In 1944, a treaty with Mexico guaranteed that nation a share. Recent controversy over supply and use has resulted in bitter lawsuits.

Most of California's share of the Colorado River is diverted into the All-American Canal near Yuma and used to irrigate crops in the Imperial and Coachella valleys. A smaller share enters the Colorado River Aqueduct for delivery to Los Angeles and San Diego. Much of Arizona's share supports the expansion of Phoenix and Tucson and irrigates farms. Nevada's supply supports life in the Las Vegas oasis.

As more people move to the Southwest, water supply becomes a more pressing issue. People who favor expansion talk of tapping the Columbia River farther north and perhaps transporting water from Canada. Conservationists, alarmed over excessive irrigation, seek less water for farm use and more for cities and industry. Whatever the solution, the debate will challenge people's ability to compromise and to adjust to a limited resource.
See p. T146.

1. How has the water from the Colorado River been allotted?

2. Critical Thinking What are some of the choices people have to make when water is a limited resource?

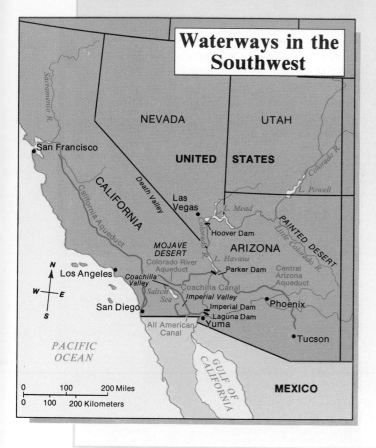

Waterways in the Southwest

Sacramento R.
San Francisco
NEVADA
UTAH
UNITED   STATES
CALIFORNIA
California Aqueduct
Death Valley
Las Vegas
Colorado R.
L. Powell
L. Mead
Hoover Dam
MOJAVE DESERT
PAINTED DESERT
ARIZONA
Little Colorado R.
L. Havasu
Colorado River Aqueduct
Parker Dam
Central Arizona Aqueduct
Los Angeles
Coachella Valley
Salton Sea
Coachilla Canal
Imperial Valley
Imperial Dam
Phoenix
San Diego
Laguna Dam
Yuma
All American Canal
Tucson
PACIFIC OCEAN
GULF OF CALIFORNIA
MEXICO

N / W / E / S

0   100   200 Miles
0   100   200 Kilometers

1.

1. LOCAL HISTORY Ask: What is the chief source of water for your area? Have there been any threats to your water supply in recent years? If so, what steps have been taken to solve the problem?
See p. T146.

SECTION 2 REVIEW

1. Identify: (a) sunbelt, (b) frostbelt.

2. Define: (a) bilingual education, (b) zero population growth.

3. What areas of the world provided the most immigrants to the United States in the 1980s?

4. How will the aging population affect the economy?

5. What factors promoted a revival of the nation's cities?

6. Critical Thinking Why do you think the question of language and bilingual education is such an emotional issue?

1. **VOCABULARY** Have students look up these terms in the glossary before they begin reading.

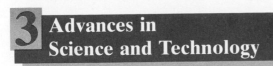

3 Advances in Science and Technology

READ TO UNDERSTAND

- How advances in medical science have prolonged life.

- Why computers are expected to change Americans' everyday lives.

- How lasers are being used.

1. *Vocabulary:* genetic engineering, modem, artificial intelligence, laser.

In the past, American families considered the day they got their first telephone, first car, or first television as important milestones. The generation of 1990s will more likely ask, "Remember when we got our first computer?" Computers suddenly began popping up on desks in homes, schools, and offices everywhere in the 1980s. Computers are among the technologies that have revolutionized communications, education, and medical care.

Toward a Healthier Life

People now in their forties can remember the time when polio was a crippling childhood disease. Now, vaccines to prevent polio have virtually eliminated this disease. Throughout the 1900s, improvements in nutrition, medical care, and public sanitation have extended life expectancy. Americans born in 1920 could expect to live about 54 years. Today, the expected life span is more than 20 years longer.

Researchers have found ways to affect the very nature of living things. A technology known as **genetic engineering** can alter the genetic code of cells to fight diseases or
2. produce new kinds of plants and organisms. Scientists have inserted human genes into bacteria to produce insulin, needed by the millions of people who suffer from diabetes. The day may not be far off when birth defects will be eliminated by altering the cells in human embryos. Such power, however, will create questions about the wisdom and

3. **ACTIVITY** Have students research recent U.S. winners of the Nobel Prize for medicine and report on their achievements or discoveries.

2. **TECHNOLOGY** In 1988, scientists developed a strain of genetically engineered mice for use in cancer research. These mice became the first animals to be patented.

morality of affecting life in so fundamental a way.

Advances in technology have also improved medical treatment. Surgeons use nylon thread thinner than a human hair to reattach severed arms and legs. Doctors can look inside the brain and other organs of the body using computer assisted X-ray scanning—CAT scan, for short. Paraplegics may be able to regain control of their muscles with the help of computers, although this is still in the experimental stage. Electronic devices have been developed to assist or replace the body's own organs. Pacemakers regulate the rhythm of irregular heartbeats, and dialysis machines cleanse the blood of patients whose kidneys have failed.

The progress of medical technology has created problems and ethical questions as

4. **GRAPH READING** Point out that the graph shows life expectancy for people born in a particular year.

GRAPH STUDY *Medical advances such as the development of vaccines and improved methods of treatment have increased the number of years most Americans live. In 1900, the average person lived to age 47. Based on the graph, what is the average life expectancy of people today?* See p. T146.

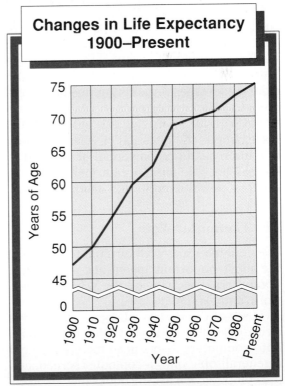

Changes in Life Expectancy 1900–Present

Years of Age (y-axis): 0, 45, 50, 55, 60, 65, 70, 75
Year (x-axis): 1900, 1910, 1920, 1930, 1940, 1950, 1960, 1970, 1980, Present

Source: *Statistical Abstract of the United States; Historical Statistics of the United States*

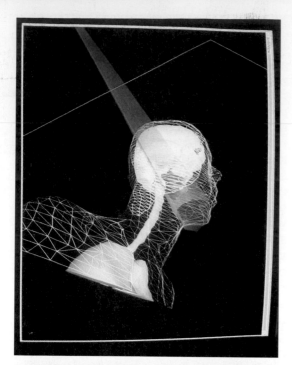

A new technique creates a computer-generated image that lets doctors look inside the body's organs. The computer makes a hologram, or three-dimensional image, that can be turned so that doctors can see it from all sides. In this picture, the reddish area inside the green cone of light indicates a diseased portion of the brain that needs radiation treatment.

1. **VISUAL EVIDENCE** Ask: Why would a hologram like this be more useful than an X-ray?

well. Advances in medical treatment have contributed to soaring medical costs. As medical techniques enable people to live longer, the need for nursing homes for the elderly increases. In addition, medical technology sometimes extends the days or years of life without improving the quality of life. For example, the question of when the body of a brain-dead person should be allowed to die has become an imporant moral issue as doctors' power over life and death increases.

The Computer Age

The computer may well turn out to be one of the most important inventions of all time. Computers are changing the way we study, work, and even play.

Uses of Computers Large libraries have already begun to transfer their card catalogs onto computers. Users need merely type out a general topic onto a computer screen, and the computer will list the books that are likely

822

to have information on the topic. Someday, the complete text of every book ever printed may be available to anyone with a home computer. In 1988, Stephen Jobs, one of the inventors of the Apple computer, presented a new computer that comes with the works of Shakespeare and a large dictionary already in its memory.

Computers have produced a revolution in offices and factories. In some modern factories, humans are needed only to service the computer-controlled robots that do all the assembly-line work. Computers order and ship parts automatically. They also perform office tasks such as record-keeping, payroll accounting, and billing.

A device called a **modem** can connect a computer through telephone lines to any similarly equipped computer. With a modem, people at home can link their computers into businesses, schools, and libraries. Many businesses now have employees who never come to the office—all their work is done at home on a computer and transmitted by modem.

Consumers will soon be able to shop by computer. Electronic mail already delivers letters via computers, and newspapers may someday follow. Some handicapped people are using computers to attend college. Video games using computer technology are changing the way many Americans use their leisure time.

Challenges of the Computer Age Some people are uneasy about the dawning age of computers. Scientists are working on the development of **artificial intelligence**—programs that will allow computers to make deductions, draw inferences, and learn through experience. The idea of a "thinking" computer frightens many Americans. Experts point out, however, that it is humans who design and write the programs for computers.

Without computer technology, the United States could not have sent satellites or people into space. Yet that same technology has made modern weapons far more accurate and destructive than ever before. Also, computer weapons systems operate so swiftly that human control of them has lessened. There is concern that a computer might react to a false radar image and launch a missile.

1. **ACTIVITY** Some shuttle flights have carried out experiments designed by students. Have interested students find out more about these experiments and then suggest their own for a future space flight.

Are computers a threat to privacy? More and more information about people's personal lives is stored in government and business computers. This information is supposed to be confidential. Yet "hackers," or expert hobbyists, have been able to tap into some of these computers. Hackers have even invaded computers containing secret scientific and military information.

Space Technology

On May 5, 1961, Alan Shepard rocketed into space on *Mercury 3,* and the United States entered the space age. (See page 737.) From the beginning, the space program has been a source of pride. It represented the triumph of American technology.

Today, communications satellites transmit television signals around the globe. A space telescope launched in 1983 lets scientists scan parts of the universe previously beyond the range of the human eye. Two unmanned spacecraft launched in 1977 continue to provide a glimpse of the far reaches of the solar system by sending back pictures of the outer planets. In November 1980, *Voyager 1* came close enough to Saturn to send back clear pictures of the planet's rings. *Voyager 2,* which is carrying artifacts representing life on Earth, is headed beyond the solar system to visit unknown parts of the universe.

In the 1980s, a reusable space shuttle was developed. Huge disposable rockets took the shuttle into orbit. Afterward, the small passenger-carrying craft returned to Earth's atmosphere, where it landed like an airplane. 1. By the mid-1980s, the space shuttle was making regular trips into space.

Then, on January 28, 1986, disaster struck. With millions of Americans watching on television, the space shuttle *Challenger* exploded seconds after leaving the launch pad. All seven persons on board were killed. One of the dead was Christa McAuliffe, a New Hampshire social studies teacher who had been 2. chosen to be a citizen observer on the flight. The space program was put on hold as a result of the tragedy. After changes in engineering and procedures, a new space shuttle resumed Americans' journey toward the stars in September 1988.

2. **BACKGROUND** Only a few months earlier, U.S. Senator Jake Garn of Utah had been the first civilian to fly on a shuttle mission.

Laser Technology

In the 1930s and 1940s, science fiction writers described such futuristic weapons as ray guns. These weapons would shoot beams of light rather than bullets. Today, the laser has brought that fictional vision closer to reality. The term **laser** was coined in 1957 when scientist Gordon Gould created a device for Light Amplification by Stimulated Emission of Radiation (LASER). Lasers create intense light on a narrow range of wavelengths.

Lasers used in medicine are so precise they can burn away diseased tissue without harming the healthy tissue around it. Military planners are also investigating the use of lasers. Experimental weapons using laser beams to destroy distant targets have already been developed.

Lasers are already part of everyday life. Most people are familiar with the black bar

3. **DISCUSSION** Ask: Why are scientists interested in discovering intelligent life elsewhere in the universe?

This radio telescope at Socorro, Mexico, is probing the universe for "news" from outer space. It is part of the SETI Program, or Search for Extraterrestrial Intelligence. Aimed toward distant galaxies, the radio telescope listens for sounds that may signal intelligent life.

code on packages in supermarkets. At the checkout counter, the package is passed across a laser beam connected to a computer, which automatically gives the price and records the sale.

The use of lasers promises to revolutionize entertainment and communications. Recordings on compact discs (CDs) are played with a laser beam, rather than a needle or stylus. Thus, CDs cannot scratch or wear out. They also produce a clearer sound. Electronic messages can be sent by amplified light over flexible glass fiber wires called fiber-optic cables. These cables are far cheaper to make and install than copper cables. Used in con-

2. **VISUAL EVIDENCE** Ask: Why is the task performed by this laser valuable?

Lasers are more precise than the sharpest knife. This specialized laser is used to clean and conserve old paintings. It can remove varnish,
2. *discolorations, and dirt without damaging the paint underneath.*

junction with computers, fiber optics will make it practical to transmit vast amounts of data stored on computer systems.

The Information Explosion

New technology has revolutionized the way information is gathered. News organizations and businesses are linked electronically to their offices around the world. News and information are spread almost instantaneously across the country and around the globe. 1. Space satellites gather information about distant countries. The rapid increase in the amount of data has created what has been called an information explosion.

Today, families can create elaborate information and entertainment systems at home. The videocassette recorder (VCR) has made it possible for people to record television programs and view them whenever they wish. They can also rent or buy videotapes that provide everything from televison programs and movies to exercise programs and rock concerts.

Television programming expanded dramatically when cable TV systems began operation in the mid-1970s. In some areas, large satellite dishes have sprouted in backyards to bring in hundreds of far-away TV channels from other cities. High-density television will 3. greatly improve picture quality.

See p. T146.

SECTION 3 REVIEW

1. **Define:** (a) genetic engineering, (b) modem, (c) artificial intelligence, (d) laser.

2. Describe three recent medical advances.

3. How have computers increased the amount of information available to the average person?

4. How have lasers changed communications and entertainment?

5. **Critical Thinking** Do you think the computer has changed the lives of Americans more than such technological advances as the telephone and the automobile? Explain.

4 The American Economy Today

READ TO UNDERSTAND

■ How the basis of the American economy has changed.

■ How agricultural productivity is both a benefit and a problem.

■ Why environmental concerns can conflict with economic needs.

1. ■ *Vocabulary:* productivity, givebacks.

When Soviet Premier Nikita Khrushchev visited this country in the 1960s, he was amazed to see huge parking lots full of cars outside the factories where ordinary people worked. The United States has indeed created a high standard of living. Yet the nation now faces important challenges to its economy.

A Record of Growth

The United States has had an impressive history of economic growth. The gross national product (GNP), the total value of goods and services produced, has grown steadily. As the number of products available to Americans has increased, so has their income. From 1930 to 1980, the average real income of Americans tripled. More than 80 percent of American families own at least one car. Nearly all Americans own a refrigerator and a television set. The percentage who own VCRs, computers, and microwave ovens increases daily.

The basis of American economic strength has been changing. In the early 1900s, manufacturing was the basis of the American econ-
2. omy. In the last 50 years, professions and service industries have increased in importance. During the 1960s, service jobs such as salespeople, computer technicians, and the professions overtook manufacturing as the major source of jobs.

Recently, American business has been working to maintain the clear-cut economic supremacy it enjoyed in the past. Although American manufacturing jobs have been lost

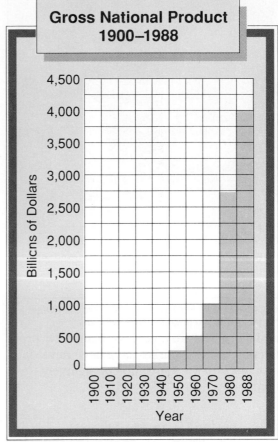

Gross National Product 1900–1988

Billions of Dollars (y-axis): 0, 500, 1,000, 1,500, 2,000, 2,500, 3,000, 3,500, 4,000, 4,500

Year (x-axis): 1900, 1910, 1920, 1930, 1940, 1950, 1960, 1970, 1980, 1988

Source: *Historical Statistics of the United States;* U.S. Department of Commerce   See p. T147.

GRAPH STUDY   *The United States emerged from World War II with the world's strongest economy. One measure of economic strength is the gross national product (GNP). The GNP is the total dollar value of goods and services produced in a year. How did the GNP of the United States change between 1960 and 1980?*

3. **GRAPH READING** Ask: What was the GNP in 1910? In 1960? How much greater was the GNP in 1988 than in 1970?

to overseas competition, millions of new jobs have been created in other areas of the economy. Many of the expanding industries, dubbed sunrise industries, have been in high technology. The world's most important computer manufacturer, International Business Machines (IBM), is an American company.

A major force in high-technology industries has been the independent business person, the entrepreneur. In contrast to the manager who is an employee of a large corporation, the entrepreneur is self-employed

2. **ECONOMICS** Companies that manufacture basic items such as automobiles and steel are referred to as *smokestack industries.*

1. *Service jobs are a high-growth sector of the American economy. Fast-food restaurants are leading employers of teen-agers and retired persons.*

2. **TECHNOLOGY** Ask students what factors probably contributed to the great increase in productivity.

and more likely to take risks. Many new products on today's market have been developed as a result of the innovation of relatively small companies.

Maintaining Competitiveness

One key to strengthening the American economy is to increase productivity. From 1890 to 1970, the **productivity,** that is, the output per hour of work, of American workers more

2. than quadrupled. This means that a worker in 1970 produced four times as much dollar value per hour as did a worker in 1890. Although American productivity is still increasing, the rate of increase has been slower than that in Japan, South Korea, Taiwan, and some European countries. As a result, American products cost more to produce and are less competitive on the world market.

Other factors have increased the com-
3. petitiveness of foreign goods. In some cases, foreign companies sell their products in the United States for less than it costs to produce them. This practice is known as "dumping." The United States government has tried to discourage dumping by monitoring the prices charged by foreign businesses. In some foreign countries, the government subsidizes key industries, allowing its companies to sell

826 at lower prices and still make a profit.

3. **ACTIVITY** Have students make a list of products in their homes that were manufactured in other countries.

Industry and government in the United States have taken action. Companies are investing in new, more efficient plants and equipment and some are giving workers a larger role in solving on-the-job problems. The United States government has made agreements with foreign governments to reduce the number of foreign products that can be sold in the United States. Japan has agreed to limit the number of Japanese cars it may export to the United States. Sterner measures have also been proposed. Some officials favor imposing higher tariffs on imported goods. The issue of what measures to take has sparked heated public debate.

Labor Unions

Labor unions have also had to adjust to changes in industry. Traditionally, the strength of the labor movement has been in

4. **GRAPH READING** Ask: When did union membership peak? During what period did it decline most rapidly?

GRAPH STUDY *Membership in labor unions has not grown as* 4. *fast as the labor force. In fact, the percentage of workers in unions has dropped in recent years, as this graph shows. By what percent did union membership drop between 1970 and 1988?*

See p. T147.

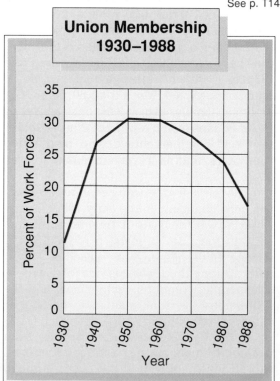

Union Membership 1930–1988

Source: *Statistical Abstract of the United States; Historical Statistics of the United States;* U.S. Bureau of Labor Statistics

basic industries such as steel and automobiles. But it is these industries that have been hurt by competition from abroad and that have had to cut down on their work force. As a result, membership in labor unions declined from 30 percent of the labor force in the 1950s to about 18 percent in 1989. This loss contributed to a decline in the political and economic influence of unions.

In recent years, unions have not been able to get the kind of favorable contract terms they won in the past. Instead, new contracts, particularly in heavy industry, have sometimes included **givebacks,** that is, the reduction or elimination of previously won benefits. But unions are meeting these new conditions. Many unions have placed greater emphasis on a new range of issues, such as working environment, flexible schedules, and maternity leaves.

Agriculture in the United States

Until the late 1800s, the United States was chiefly a farming nation. By the 1980s, fewer than one out of every 25 American workers was involved in agriculture. Yet farm production increased significantly because of the use of improved equipment, fertilizers, and plant and animal breeding techniques. Today, one farmer produces enough to feed 75 people, over four times as much as the farmer was able to produce as recently as the 1950s. But owners of small family farms have not had an easy time. Only large-scale farming, or agribusiness, which is often owned by large corporations, is consistently profitable.

The major reason for the farmers' dilemma has been that farmers are not able to adjust the supply of their product to the demand. Federal farm programs have tried to deal with this problem. The government has guaranteed a certain price level for particular crops. If a farmer's market price falls below that level, then the government buys the crops at the higher price. The government has also paid farmers not to plant on some of their land. These policies have not cut farm production enough, because advances in agricultural technology continue to bring ever greater yields per acre.

GREAT DEBATE

A Healthy Living and Working Environment

One of the challenges facing Americans in the nation's third century is to strike a balance between the economic needs of a community and the need for a healthy environment. How much risk is the country willing to run to produce needed chemicals and energy? How much is it willing to pay for a healthy environment?

Americans enjoy the freedom and convenience of owning and using their own automobiles. But these advantages are paid for with traffic jams and air pollution. Growing communities are finding that their original plans for waste disposal cannot keep pace with expansion and development. They are searching for economical and environmentally sound ways to dispose of garbage and industrial waste, including radioactive wastes from nuclear power plants.

New scientific discoveries often benefit society, but some have had unexpected side effects. Some industrial chemicals, for example, have been linked to cancer and other

No matter what problems face farmers, many love the land too much to give up easily. As one farmer, facing the drought of 1988, put it, "You hunker down, you survive."

827

The need to clean up contaminated soil from a chemical plant that has stopped operations is an example of the problem of toxic-waste disposal. The plant had manufactured Agent Orange, which contains the deadly poison dioxin. The contaminated soil is being stored in the large red containers.

1. **TECHNOLOGY** Agent Orange had been used extensively by the army to destroy vegetation in Vietnam (see p. 753).

serious disorders in humans. Fumes, wastes, and chemicals can contaminate the air people breathe, the water they drink, and the food they eat. Chemical wastes containing powerful poisons have seeped into the public water supply, posing a grave health risk. Emissions from oil- and coal-burning plants in the Ohio River Valley have fallen in the form of acid rain on New England and Canada, damaging the forests, lakes, and wildlife of these areas.

Two events in foreign countries emphasized the dangers of ignoring environmental standards. In December 1984, an accidental release of poison gas at a Union Carbide plant in Bhopal (boh PAHL), India, killed thousands of people and blinded or otherwise disabled thousands more. In April 1986, the world's worst nuclear plant accident occurred in the Soviet city of Chernobyl (chern NOH bul). An explosion shot a huge cloud of radioactive gas into the sky. It contaminated hundreds of square miles of land and killed 30 people. Traces of radioactivity were detected as far away as the United States.

In the 1970s, the federal government set standards to ensure safe water and air. These new regulations did not quiet the demand for stricter laws to protect the health of workers and local residents. But factory owners claimed that there were enough environmental laws. They contended that further regulations would add to their expenses, causing higher prices, without vastly improving the environment. Workers, who feared the loss of jobs, also opposed regulations they considered too strict. Yet, a major oil spill in the waters off Alaska in 1989 once more showed that the balance between the economy and the environment has still not been found. ∎

See p. T147.

SECTION 4 REVIEW

1. **Identify:** (a) sunrise industry, (b) dumping.

2. **Define:** (a) productivity, (b) givebacks.

3. (a) How has the basis of the American economy changed? (b) How has this change affected labor unions?

4. How has the federal government tried to ease the problems of the farmer?

5. **Critical Thinking** Why is it difficult to find a balance between a healthy living environment and a healthy economy?

2. **CITIZENSHIP** In 1970, Congress passed the Clean Air Act and Clean Water Act and set up the Environmental Protection Agency (EPA) to enforce the laws.

5 The United States and the World

READ TO UNDERSTAND

■ How the United States has become part of an interdependent world.

■ What problems are faced by Third World nations.

■ How the United States is helping poorer countries.

1. ■ *Vocabulary:* default.

Nicholas Jacobs lives on the edge of the Kalahari Desert in the African nation of Botswana. He started a one-room shoe factory with loans from the Botswana Development Bank. About half of the bank's funds had come from foreign aid from the United States. The aid gave Jacobs a chance for a more productive life. Through such programs as the one that helped Nicholas Jacobs, the United States can help raise living standards elsewhere.

A Changing World Scene

Following World War I, Americans sought a return to peace, and for many that meant isolation from world affairs. But after World War II, the United States could no longer choose isolationism. It was now the world's most powerful nation, both economically and militarily.

As Japan and the nations of western Europe recovered from World War II, they entered a period of rapid economic growth. By the 1970s, they were competing successfully with the United States in world markets. And the rest of the world had become more interdependent. Political and economic developments in one area of the world affected other areas. Nearly every country, for example, was affected by a sharp rise in the cost of oil in the 1970s and early 1980s.

Fashioning a Successful Foreign Policy

For many years after World War II, American foreign policy was primarily concerned with containing the power of the Soviet Union. In a world dominated by two superpowers, the United States was the leader of the free world. As you have read, the United States sent vast

2. **VISUAL EVIDENCE** The dock shown is in Oakland. Almost 6 million tons of foreign goods pass through Oakland each year.

2. *These Japanese cars being unloaded on a California dock are just one of the many products that pass through American ports each year. The growing interdependence of nations has increased international trade.*

1. **ACTIVITY** Have students do research about one country that is pursuing an independent course in Africa, Asia, or Latin America. Ask: Has the country received aid from the U.S.? From the Soviet Union? What is current U.S. policy toward the government of this nation?

amounts of aid to western Europe and Japan to help rebuild their economies. Alliances such as NATO were aimed at checking Soviet strength.

By the 1980s, however, most Americans realized that the world's economic and political balance was becoming increasingly complex. With the new leadership of Mikhail Gorbachev in the Soviet Union (see page 791), American policy makers began to explore the possibilities of a different relationship between the two superpowers.

Policy makers have found that classifying nations as pro-Soviet or pro-American is not as easy as it once was. Nor is it as meaningful. Major communist powers such as China are pursuing independent courses, as are many smaller nations in Africa, Asia, and 1. Latin America. The United States must take into account the interests of its traditional allies when it makes foreign policy decisions. For example, in arms talks with the Soviet Union, the United States has to consider the defense concerns of its European allies.

Finally, the United States government has to fashion a foreign policy that is domestically acceptable. This can be difficult. Con-flicts often arise between Congress and the President over foreign policy. Since the Vietnam War, Congress has demanded a greater voice in foreign affairs. President Carter was unable to persuade the Senate to ratify SALT II, and President Reagan faced strong congressional opposition to his policies on Central America.

Problems of the Third World

Events in the less developed countries, or Third World, affect the lives of Americans. These nations are important markets for American products and are sources of raw materials important to the United States economy. Some of them are of strategic importance to the defense of the United States. Therefore, the United States is concerned about an increasing gap between the Third World and the more developed countries. The poverty of many Third World countries is tied to illiteracy and poor health conditions, which hinder development.

In the 1970s, many Third World countries borrowed large amounts of money from banks in Europe and the United States to

SKILL LESSON

Trends in American History: Forecasting Alternative Futures

See p. T147.

In this chapter, you have reviewed several trends in American history. But what lies ahead for the United States? Will the rate of technological change expand, or will it slow down? Will the American people find a solution to the farm crisis? Will they learn how to balance the needs of the environment with the needs of the economy? Will the United States maintain its economic position? These are just a few of the questions you might ask about the future.

While no one can predict exactly what will happen, you can forecast, or suggest, possible developments. Such forecasts can influence your decisions and actions in the present. For example, if you forecast that energy costs will continue to rise, you may decide to buy an energy-efficient automobile or a solar-heated house. Use the steps below to practice the skill of forecasting.

1 Identify a trend. Review this chapter and select one of the trends discussed. Write a paragraph in which you describe the trend in your own words.

2 Project alternative future developments. (a) What might happen if the trend continues? (b) What type of future events might change the trend? (c) How might each event affect the trend?

3 Determine the likelihood of possible developments. To complete this step, use current news magazines, newspapers, and books. After researching the possible developments, decide which is most likely to occur and which is least likely to occur. Write a report explaining your conclusions about possible future developments.

1. **ACTIVITY** Have students research the debt problem in Mexico, Argentina, or Brazil. They should also report on the effect of the problem on the U.S.

strengthen their economies. However, a world recession lowered demand for the minerals, metals, and farm products these nations export. Thus they have found it difficult to pay their debts. If a nation **defaults,** or fails to pay its debts, the soundness of the lending banks could be threatened. Economists worry that the failure of an important bank could trigger a worldwide panic.

A Tradition of Generosity

It has been part of the American tradition to give freely to less fortunate nations. Through the Food for Peace program, the United States has used its surplus food to help feed the hungry throughout the world. A special financial agency that helps underdeveloped countries is the Agency for International Development (AID). This agency, part of the State Department, gives low-interest loans to projects that AID workers believe are particularly deserving of help.

In the mid-1980s, Americans became aware of the drought that was causing famine in sub-Saharan Africa. One of the hardest hit was the country of Ethiopia, ruled by a left-wing government. Despite the government's hostility, Americans generously gave money and food. Many citizens volunteered to help distribute the aid. Moreover, the Reagan administration authorized the largest amount of aid given by any single government.

The Peace Corps, established during the Kennedy administration (see page 734), continues to help Third World countries. By working with people in different lands, the Peace Corps promotes a better understanding among people. Former Peace Corps members have recalled their experiences abroad as enriching ones.

Many corporations and private organizations help to fund aid programs. They have made possible fisheries programs in Burundi and agricultural training in other African countries. Private groups donate grain and vegetable seeds for backyard gardens. Volunteers provide nutrition education in many countries. American generosity has had a positive impact on the lives of people all over the world.

The fireworks that exploded over Washington, D.C., to celebrate President Bush's inauguration symbolize the enthusiasm with which the United States faces new challenges.

3. **VISUAL EVIDENCE** Have students identify the buildings shown in this photograph.

A Challenge for You

In this book, you have read about the people and events that have shaped the history of the American republic. You have the opportunity, even the responsibility, to build on the traditions passed to you. The year 1992 marks the 500th anniversary of the landing of Columbus in the Western Hemisphere. The daring spirit that inspired Columbus and his sailors challenges you to explore new frontiers. The history of the next century will be your story.

See p. T147.

SECTION 5 REVIEW

1. **Define:** default.

2. How has United States foreign policy changed since World War II?

3. What problems face Third World nations?

4. How has the United States tried to help less developed countries?

5. **Critical Thinking** What do you consider the greatest challenge facing the United States in the twenty-first century? Why?

2. **BACKGROUND** Another program begun in the 1960s, Food for Peace, distributed surplus food to help feed the hungry throughout the world.

Summary

1. **The role of the federal government and of political parties has changed over the years.** The nation has become more democratic as voting rights have expanded to include minorities, women, and people 18 years of age or older.

2. **Today, most immigrants come from Asia and the Americas.** Their cultural diversity continues to enrich American life. A long-term trend is the aging of the American population, which will have significant consequences in the next century.

3. **Advances in science and technology have led to significant contributions in many fields, including medicine and communications.** Computers have revolutionized both the work place and leisure time for many Americans. Lasers have important new uses, particularly in communications.

4. **The American economy has been challenged by foreign trade and by the need to balance economic growth and a healthy environment.** Jobs in traditional industries have been lost while the service and technical sectors have increased in importance.

5. **Today, the United States faces an increasingly complex world.** Foreign policy decisions are complicated by concerns for Third World nations and the need to consider the interests of traditional allies. The United States continues its tradition of generosity to people, regardless of the political stand of their government.

See p. T148.

Vocabulary

On a separate sheet of paper, write the word or words that best complete each of the following sentences.

1. People with similar interests who band together to influence legislators are called a (an) _____.

2. _____ is the point at which the number of children born in a place equals the number of people who die.

3. _____ is a technology that allows scientists to alter the genetic code of cells.

4. With _____, computers will be able to make deductions, draw inferences, and learn through experience.

5. A (An) _____ is a device for amplifying and concentrating light into a narrow beam.

6. _____ are previously won benefits that unions have had to give up in order to get new contracts.

See p. T148.

Chapter Checkup

1. How does the federal government's role today differ from that of 50 years ago?

2. (a) How has television affected how election campaigns are conducted? (b) How have public-opinion polls affected election campaigns?

3. How has the pattern of immigration to the United States changed since 1965?

4. How has the pattern of population distribution changed in the United States in recent years?

5. Identify three recent medical advances and their effects.

6. How has technology contributed to the information explosion?

7. (a) What factors have enabled foreign companies to compete with American industry? (b) How has the United States combated foreign competition?

8. (a) Describe three environmental problems facing the nation. (b) What steps have been taken to deal with these problems?

9. (a) What are some of the issues that must be considered by those who shape American foreign policy?

10. How has the United States helped foreign nations to overcome economic problems?

See p. T148.

Critical Thinking

1. **Supporting an Opinion** What role did the various forms of media play in forming your opinions about the candidates in the most recent national and local elections? Which form was most important? Why?

2. **Analyzing** Few aspects of life today are unaffected by computers. How do you think computers will directly affect your life in the next ten years?

See p. T148.

Connecting Past and Present

1. The federal government had a very limited role in the 1800s. As you have read, there was even strong debate in the Congress over whether or not the federal government should build roads. (a) In what areas today is there controversy over the role of the federal government? (b) Do you think that government in the United States has grown too large? Why or why not?

2. As you have read, when this nation was young so was its population. Now the percentage of the population that is older is increasing. How will these changes in the population affect the future of the economy, politics, and society?

See p. T148.

Developing Basic Skills

1. **Ranking** List the challenges facing the United States during the 1980s and rank them from most to least important in your opinion. Then write an essay describing the possible consequences of not meeting the most important challenge.

2. **Reading Graphs** Study the circle graph on page 812. (a) What information is shown on the graph? (b) In what category does the government spend the most money? (c) What percentage of the budget does the government spend on defense? (d) If the national debt continues to rise, how will this graph change?

WRITING ABOUT HISTORY

Typing the Final Draft

The appearance of a report reflects the care with which it was prepared. The following are general guidelines to follow.

Handwritten Paper:
    Lined, white $8^1/_2$" x 11"
    Ruled left margin
Text: Written or printed neatly in ink
    One side only
    Indent all paragraphs
    Single space
    Light corrections allowed

Typewritten or Wordprocessed Paper:
    Unlined, white $8^1/_2$" x 11"
Text: One side only
    Double space
    Margin settings — 10 left, 75 right
    5-space indent for paragraphs
    Light corrections allowed
All pages should be numbered. Your last name should be written on each page.

Practice: Analyze a report that you have done. Note how it compares with the guidelines above.

What do the following words all have in common: *honcho, A-OK,* and *byte?* The answer is that they are all relatively new words added to the English language by Americans.

Honcho ("He's the head honcho on the day shift") originated from a Japanese term meaning squad leader. It was adopted by the Americans who occupied Japan after World War II. A-OK became popular in the 1960s, when astronauts assured launch commanders that their systems were "All okay." Byte, a product of the computer era, refers to a piece of data stored. These are only three examples from the "recent history" of American English.

Indeed, languages have histories every bit as rich as the histories of nations. Before the Normans invaded England in 1066, people in England spoke Anglo-Saxon, a Germanic tongue. After the conquest, they adopted many French words. Most short English words, like *can, get,* and *hit,* come from Anglo-Saxon. Longer words, like *civilization* and *communication,* come from French. Century after century, the language grew. Today, some 80 percent of all English words can be traced to other languages.

In America, English developed even quicker. For example, settlers adopted many Native American terms, including *raccoon, moose, squash, pecan, canoe, moccasin,* and *toboggan.* And the number of place names taken from Indian languages is staggering. More than half of the 50 states have Native American names, from Massachusetts and Connecticut to the Dakotas and Hawaii.

American English did not develop simply by borrowing words. In sprawling, decentralized America, many local variations in language sprang up. The process began almost immediately in the colonies. A youngster might get wet feet in a *kill* (Catskill) in New York, in a *brook* (Seabrook) in New England, in a *run* (Bull Run) in Virginia, and in a *creek* almost everywhere else.

By the 1800s, the United States was known as the seedbed of hundreds of new words. Purists objected to the new terms. As one English magazine put it, "If the pure well of English is to remain undefiled, no Yankee should be allowed henceforth to throw mud into it." But Thomas Jefferson had recognized long before that the "new circumstances" in America called "for new words, new phrases, and the transfer of old words to new objects." Jefferson himself coined a word, *belittle,* which is still used today, although snobbish English critics of his day belittled the contribution!

Local regions have contributed their own phrases. When miners in the far West found a site that "panned out," they rushed to "stake a claim." Lumberjacks in the

1. **LOCAL HISTORY** Ask: Do any towns in your area have American Indian names?

1. *Many words, such as* skunk, tomahawk, *and* tepee, *were adopted from American Indian languages by the early settlers.*

Pacific northwest used the term *backlog* for timber waiting to be shipped. Today *backlog* means unfinished work. In New England in the early 1900s, Moxie was a popular soft drink. Soon, if a person had "moxie," it meant that he or she had the courage or pluck to face difficult situations.

Contributions of Immigrants The mix of people in America also gave rise to new words. Immigrants brought with them many phrases that are now a part of our language. In fact, the word immigrate itself is American and was first used in 1789. Spanish-speaking people have contributed more words to American English than has any other group. Spanish gave us the words we use when we take a stroll in the *plaza,* run for cover from a *tornado,* or witness a *stampede* of *mustangs.* French contributed familiar words such as *depot, dimes, cents, chowder,* and *gopher.*

Each group of immigrants added their own terms. Dutch Americans ate *coleslaw, cookies,* and *waffles.* They thought that wild stories were *poppycock,* even if the story was told by their *boss.* German Americans asked for the *check* when they paid the bill at their local *delicatessen,* told *hoodlums* to *scram,* sent their children to *kindergarten,* and said *phooey!* Italian immigrants contributed words like *pizza, ravioli, macaroni, broccoli,* and *zucchini* to American cuisine as well as musical terms like *opera, virtuoso,* and *allegro.* Yiddish-speaking Jews from eastern Europe called a sentimental play or movie *schmaltz* and said that shoddy merchandise was *schlock.*

Contributions of Blacks Black Americans have given many words to the language as well. *Okra* and *gumbo* are found on many menus. And most people know what it means to *bad-mouth* someone. Perhaps most striking are the words used for the different kinds of music black Americans pioneered. *Spirituals* were first spoken of widely in the 1860s, *blues* in the 1870s, *ragtime* in the 1890s, *jazz* at the turn of the century, *boogie woogie* in the 1920s, *jitterbug* in the 1940s, *rhythm and blues* in the 1950s, *soul* in the 1960s, and *rap* in the 1980s.

As this menu board from a French cafe shows, English has absorbed words from other languages and other languages have adopted words from English. 1.

1. **VISUAL EVIDENCE** Point out that two other items on this menu originated in other cultures: *sandwich* (British) and *pizza* (Italian).

The growth of American English shows no signs of slowing. Critics will no doubt try to keep it in check, as they have for hundreds of years. (Even in the 1660s, the English essayist Jonathan Swift complained of the "Enthusiastic Jargon" creeping into the language.) Some new words will quickly die out, while others will remain.

But "speaking American" will always involve words from all backgrounds and walks of life. As the poet Walt Whitman noted, English is not "an abstract construction of dictionary makers," but a language that has "its basis broad and low, close to the ground." In that sense, it is a democratic language, a language of the people.

See p. T148.

1. What are some of the ways that new words are introduced into American English?

2. **Critical Thinking** How does American English exemplify American society?

S. I. Hayakawa

Language has been important to S. I. Hayakawa as a student, teacher, and author. It has also been important to him as a citizen concerned with the quality and effectiveness of public communication.

Hayakawa, the son of Japanese immigrants, was born in Canada in 1906. After earning his undergraduate and graduate degrees in English Literature in Canada, he studied for his doctorate at the University of Wisconsin.

During the 1930s, Hayakawa recognized the role of propaganda in the rise of European dictatorships. He analyzed how dictators twisted words to mold public opinion. For example, Hitler used the innocent-sounding word "resettlement" to mask the movement of Jews into death camps.

Hayakawa wanted Americans to be able to detect superstition, propaganda, and faulty reasoning in what they read and heard. He set out to make people aware of how words can be used and abused.

Scholars had studied the meaning and use of words, but Hayakawa brought the discussion from the lecture hall to the living room. In 1941, he published *Language in Action*—a book on language for the everyday reader. The book was an immediate success. Extensively revised in 1949 as *Language in Thought and Action,* it has remained in print for over 40 years.

Except for brief periods as a college president and United States senator, Hayakawa has devoted most of his adult life to teaching and writing about language. Even in his eighties, he has remained outspoken on the topic of public communication. In recent years, this interest has embroiled him in the controversy over bilingualism.

Hayakawa is the honorary chairman of U.S. English, a group that seeks a constitutional amendment establishing English as the country's official language. He has stated, "We can speak any language we want at the dinner table, but English is the

Former Senator S. I. Hayakawa has devoted many years to the study of semantics, or the development, meaning, and use of words.

1.

1. **READING** Have students read current newspapers and magazines to find examples of misleading or unclear language.

language of public discourses, of the marketplace, and of the voting booth." If you allow people to avoid learning English, Hayakawa argues, you deny them the full opportunities of American life.

Hayakawa's critics believe that a law making English the official language is unnecessary and is an insult to Americans whose home language is not English. They argue that non-English speakers are well aware that they must be able to speak English in order to better their economic situation. According to one Hispanic leader, "If you don't speak English, you're a dishwasher."

Hayakawa's ideas about bilingualism have stirred much controversy throughout the nation. But at the same time, they have contributed to a much needed evaluation of language in a pluralistic society. Americans pay him tribute for his ideas on communication and the use and abuse of language. In effect, Hayakawa has focused attention on the power of the spoken and written word.

See p. T148.

1. What did Hayakawa hope to accomplish with *Language and Thought in Action?*

2. **Critical Thinking** Do you support Senator Hayakawa's view that English should be the country's official language? Explain.

Public and Private Language

Richard Rodriguez, a writer and lecturer, grew up in California, the son of Mexican immigrant parents. At home, his family spoke in Spanish, but he recognized the need to learn English also. In the following excerpt from his autobiography, Rodriguez describes his first days in an English-speaking school.

I remember to start with that day in Sacramento—a California now nearly thirty years past—when I first entered a classroom, able to understand some fifty stray English words.

The nun said in a friendly but oddly impersonal voice, "Boys and girls, this is Richard Rodriguez." (I heard her sound out: Rich-heard Road-ree-guess.) It was the first time I had heard anyone name me in English. "Richard," the nun repeated more slowly, writing my name down in her black leather book. . . .

Memory teaches me what I know of these matters; the boy reminds the adult. I was a bilingual child, . . . the son of working-class parents, both Mexican immigrants. . . . In public, my father and mother spoke a hesitant, accented, not always grammatical English. And they would have to strain—their bodies tense—to catch the sense of what was rapidly said by *los gringos*. At home they spoke Spanish. . . . The words would come quickly, with ease. Conveyed through those sounds was the pleasing, soothing, consoling reminder of being at home.

I learned my first words of English overhearing my parents speak to strangers.

At five years of age, I knew just enough English for my mother to trust me on errands to stores one block away. No more.

I was a listening child, careful to hear the different sounds of Spanish and English. . . . First, there were English (gringo) sounds. So many words were still unknown that when the butcher or the lady at the drugstore said something to me, exotic polysyllabic sounds would bloom in the midst of their sentences. Often, the speech of people in public seemed to be very loud, booming with confidence. The man behind the counter would literally ask, "What can I do for you?" But by being so firm and so clear, the sound of his voice said that he was a gringo, he belonged in public society.

But then there was Spanish. *Español:* my father's language. *Español:* the language that seemed to me a private language. I'd heard strangers on the radio and in the Mexican Catholic church across town speaking in Spanish, but I couldn't really believe that Spanish was a public language, like English. . . . Spanish seemed to be the language of home. . . . It became the language of joyful return.

Adapted from Richard Rodriguez, *Hunger of Memory* (Boston: David R. Godine).
See p. T148.

1. Why does Rodriguez view Spanish as a private language?

2. **Critical Thinking** What does he consider to be the essential importance of English in a bilingual family?

Reference Section

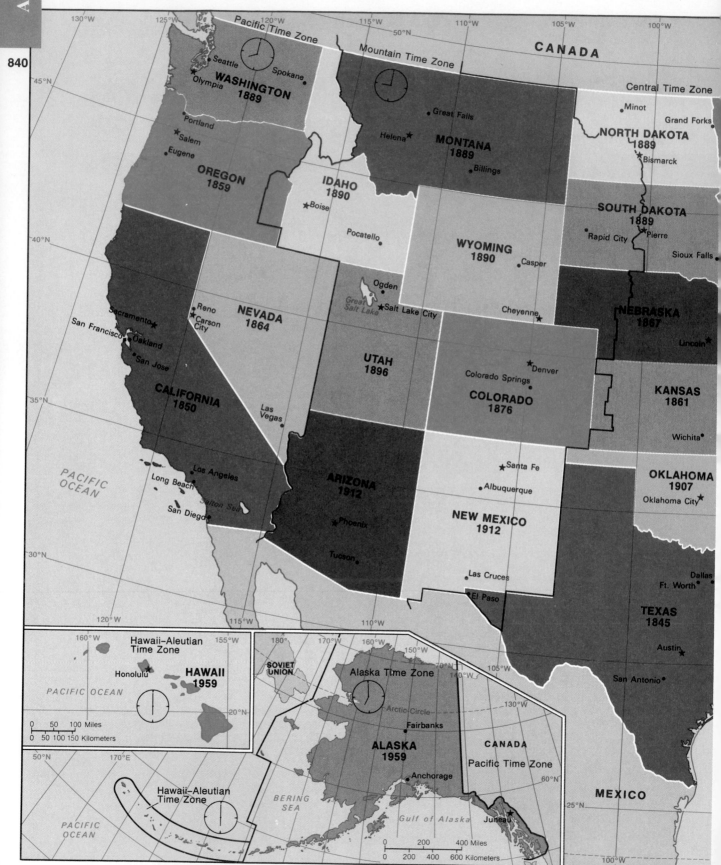

Pacific Time Zone

Mountain Time Zone

CANADA

Central Time Zone

Seattle
Spokane

WASHINGTON 1889
Olympia

Portland

Salem

Eugene

OREGON 1859

IDAHO 1890
Boise

Pocatello

Great Falls

MONTANA 1889
Helena

Billings

Minot

Grand Forks

NORTH DAKOTA 1889
Bismarck

SOUTH DAKOTA 1889
Rapid City
Pierre

Sioux Falls

WYOMING 1890
Casper

Cheyenne

NEBRASKA 1867
Lincoln

Reno
Carson City

NEVADA 1864

Sacramento

San Francisco
Oakland
San Jose

Ogden

Great Salt Lake
Salt Lake City

UTAH 1896

Denver

Colorado Springs

COLORADO 1876

KANSAS 1861

Wichita

CALIFORNIA 1850

Las Vegas

Los Angeles

Long Beach

San Diego

Salton Sea

ARIZONA 1912

Phoenix

Tucson

Santa Fe

Albuquerque

NEW MEXICO 1912

Las Cruces

El Paso

OKLAHOMA 1907
Oklahoma City

TEXAS 1845

Dallas
Ft. Worth

Austin

San Antonio

PACIFIC OCEAN

MEXICO

Hawaii–Aleutian Time Zone

HAWAII 1959
Honolulu

PACIFIC OCEAN

0 50 100 Miles
0 50 100 150 Kilometers

SOVIET UNION

Alaska Time Zone

Arctic Circle

Fairbanks

ALASKA 1959

CANADA

Pacific Time Zone

Anchorage

BERING SEA

Hawaii–Aleutian Time Zone

PACIFIC OCEAN

Gulf of Alaska

Juneau

0 200 400 Miles
0 200 400 600 Kilometers

The United States

★ Capital city

• Other city

1787 Year of admission to the Union

— Boundaries of time zones

| 0 | 100 | 200 | 300 Miles |

| 0 | 100 | 200 | 300 | 400 Kilometers |

MAINE 1820

VT. 1791   N.H. 1788

MASS. 1788

CONN. 1788   R.I. 1790

NEW YORK 1788

NEW JERSEY 1787

PENNSYLVANIA 1787

MD. 1788   DEL. 1787

WEST VIRGINIA 1863

VIRGINIA 1788

OHIO 1803

INDIANA 1816

ILLINOIS 1818

MICHIGAN 1837

WISCONSIN 1848

MINNESOTA 1858

IOWA 1846

MISSOURI 1821

KENTUCKY 1792

TENNESSEE 1796

NORTH CAROLINA 1789

SOUTH CAROLINA 1788

ARKANSAS 1836

MISSISSIPPI 1817

ALABAMA 1819

GEORGIA 1788

LOUISIANA 1812

FLORIDA 1845

Atlantic Time Zone

Eastern Time Zone

CANADA

ATLANTIC OCEAN

Gulf of Mexico

Tropic of Cancer

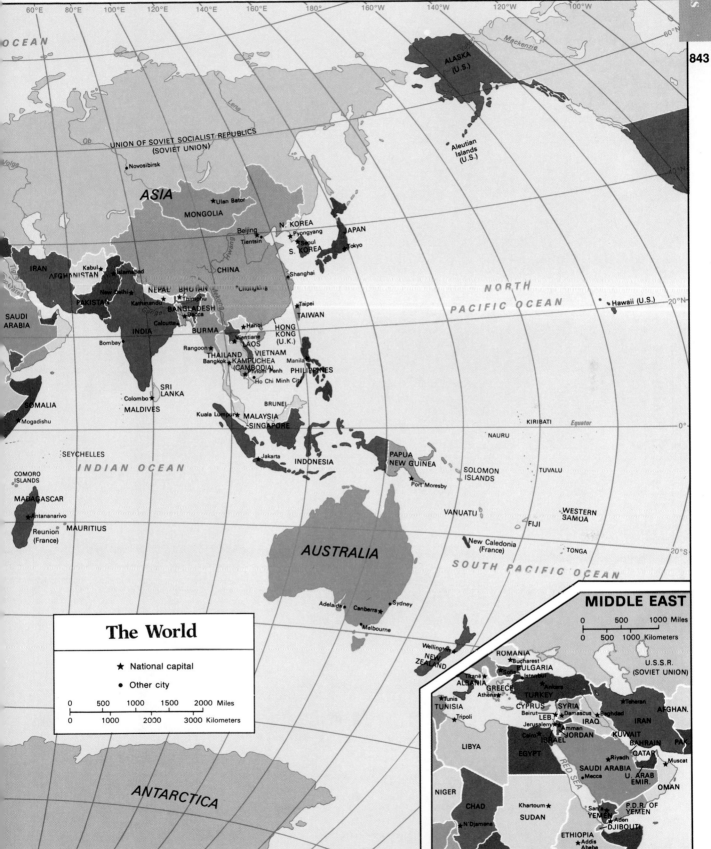

60°E 80°E 100°E 120°E 140°E 160°E 180° 160°W 140°W 120°W 100°W

OCEAN

60°N

Mackenzie

ALASKA (U.S.)

Ob

UNION OF SOVIET SOCIALIST REPUBLICS (SOVIET UNION)

Lena

40°N

Volga

•Novosibirsk

Aleutian Islands (U.S.)

ASIA

★Ulan Bator

MONGOLIA

Hwang

N. KOREA

JAPAN

Beijing★

★Pyongyang

•Tientsin

Seoul★

S. KOREA

•Tokyo

IRAN

Kabul• ★ •Islamabad

CHINA

Chungking•

AFGHANISTAN

•Shanghai

NORTH

PACIFIC OCEAN

New Delhi★

NEPAL BHUTAN

Kathmandu• ★Thimphu

•Taipei

20°N

Hawaii (U.S.)★

SAUDI ARABIA

PAKISTAN

Ganges

BANGLADESH

•Dacca

Calcutta•

•Hanoi★

HONG KONG (U.K.)

INDIA

BURMA

Mekong

TAIWAN

Bombay•

Rangoon★

Vientiane★

LAOS

VIETNAM

THAILAND

KAMPUCHEA (CAMBODIA)

Manila★

SRI LANKA

Bangkok★

Phnom Penh★

PHILIPPINES

SOMALIA

Colombo★

•Ho Chi Minh City

MALDIVES

BRUNEI

0°

Equator

•Mogadishu

Kuala Lumpur★

MALAYSIA

KIRIBATI

SINGAPORE

SEYCHELLES

NAURU

INDIAN OCEAN

COMORO ISLANDS

•Jakarta

INDONESIA

PAPUA NEW GUINEA

SOLOMON ISLANDS

TUVALU

MADAGASCAR

★Antananarivo

Port Moresby★

Reunion (France)

MAURITIUS

VANUATU

WESTERN SAMOA

FIJI

20°S

New Caledonia (France)

TONGA

SOUTH PACIFIC OCEAN

AUSTRALIA

Adelaide•

Canberra★

•Sydney

•Melbourne

Wellington★

NEW ZEALAND

The World

★ National capital

• Other city

0   500   1000   1500   2000 Miles

0   1000   2000   3000 Kilometers

ANTARCTICA

MIDDLE EAST

0   500   1000 Miles

0   500   1000 Kilometers

ROMANIA

★Bucharest

U.S.S.R. (SOVIET UNION)

BULGARIA

•Sofia

•Istanbul

Tiranë★

ALBANIA

GREECE

★Ankara

★Teheran

AFGHAN.

Athens★

CYPRUS

TURKEY

SYRIA

•Tunis

Beirut•

★Damascus

★Baghdad

IRAN

TUNISIA

LEB.

IRAQ

•Tripoli

Jerusalem★

★Amman

KUWAIT

PAK.

ISRAEL

JORDAN

BAHRAIN

Cairo•

QATAR

LIBYA

EGYPT

SAUDI ARABIA

•Riyadh

U. ARAB EMIR.

•Muscat

NIGER

Red Sea

•Mecca

OMAN

CHAD

Khartoum★

P.D.R. OF YEMEN

N'Djamena★

SUDAN

Sana•

YEMEN

•Aden

DJIBOUTI

ETHIOPIA

•Addis Ababa

Physical Features

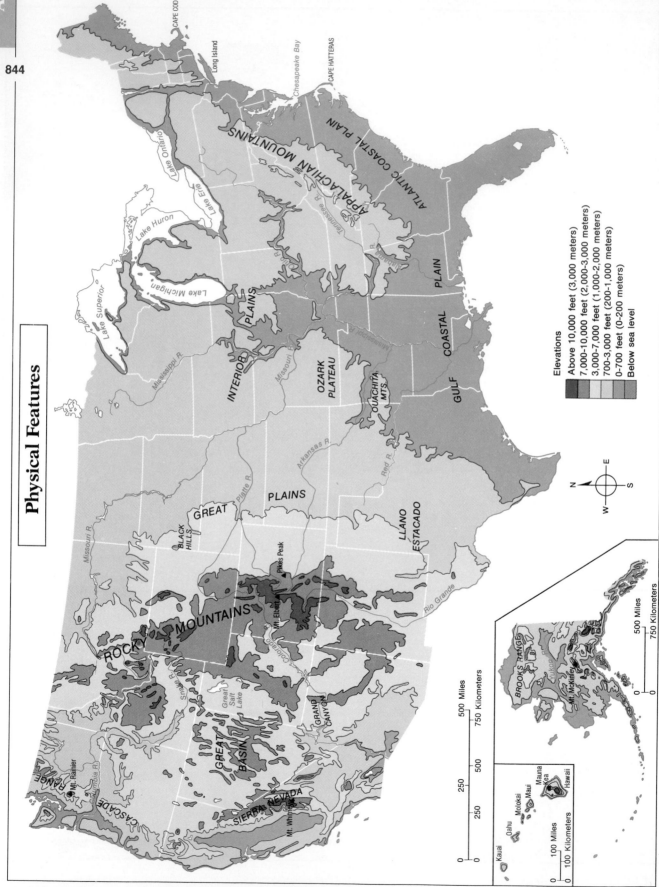

CAPE COD

Long Island

Chesapeake Bay

CAPE HATTERAS

Lake Ontario

Lake Erie

APPALACHIAN MOUNTAINS

ATLANTIC COASTAL PLAIN

Lake Huron

Lake Superior

Lake Michigan

Tennessee R.

Ohio R.

COASTAL

PLAIN

INTERIOR

PLAINS

Mississippi R.

Missouri R.

OZARK
PLATEAU

Mississippi R.

GULF

OUACHITA
MTS.

Arkansas R.

Red R.

Missouri R.

GREAT

PLAINS

Platte R.

BLACK
HILLS

Pikes Peak

LLANO
ESTACADO

ROCKY

MOUNTAINS

Mt. Elbert

Colorado R.

Rio Grande

Mt. Rainier

CASCADE RANGE

Columbia R.

Snake R.

GREAT
SALT
LAKE

GRAND
CANYON

GREAT
BASIN

SIERRA NEVADA

Mt. Whitney

Elevations

Above 10,000 feet (3,000 meters)
7,000–10,000 feet (2,000–3,000 meters)
3,000–7,000 feet (1,000–2,000 meters)
700–3,000 feet (200–1,000 meters)
0–700 feet (0–200 meters)
Below sea level

N
W E
S

0   250   500 Miles
0   250   500   750 Kilometers

BROOKS RANGE

Yukon R.

Mt. McKinley

0   500 Miles
0   750 Kilometers

Kauai
Oahu
Molokai
Maui
Mauna
Kea
Hawaii

0   100 Miles
0   100 Kilometers

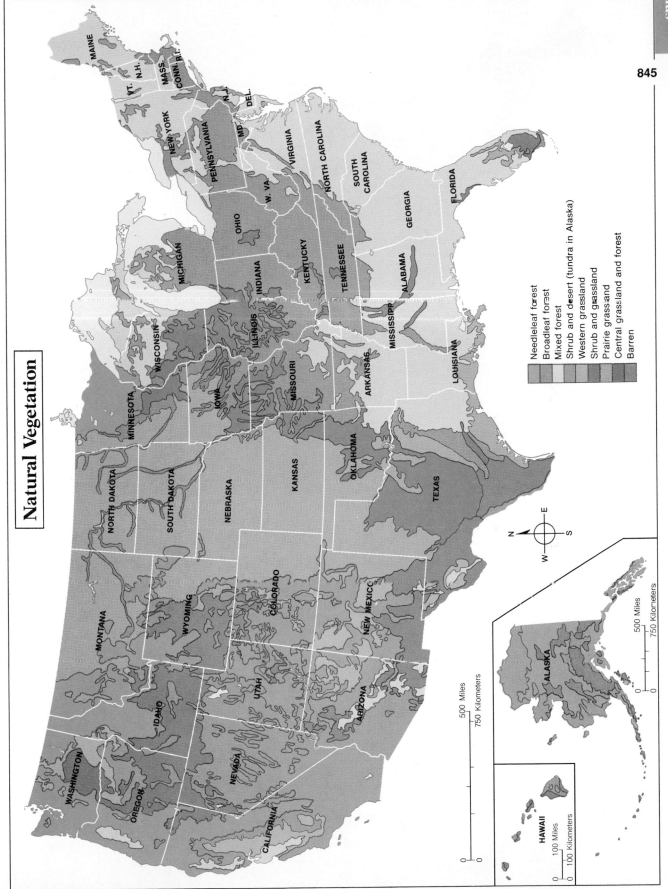

Natural Vegetation

MAINE
VT. N.H.
MASS.
CONN. R.I.
NEW YORK
N.J.
DEL.
PENNSYLVANIA
MD.
VIRGINIA
W. VA.
NORTH CAROLINA
SOUTH CAROLINA
FLORIDA
OHIO
GEORGIA
MICHIGAN
INDIANA
KENTUCKY
TENNESSEE
ALABAMA
ILLINOIS
MISSISSIPPI
WISCONSIN
MISSOURI
ARKANSAS
LOUISIANA
IOWA
MINNESOTA
OKLAHOMA
NORTH DAKOTA
SOUTH DAKOTA
NEBRASKA
KANSAS
TEXAS
COLORADO
NEW MEXICO
MONTANA
WYOMING
UTAH
ARIZONA
IDAHO
NEVADA
WASHINGTON
OREGON
CALIFORNIA

Needleleaf forest
Broadleaf forest
Mixed forest
Shrub and desert (tundra in Alaska)
Western grassland
Shrub and grassland
Prairie grassland
Central grassland and forest
Barren

N
E
S
W

500 Miles
750 Kilometers

ALASKA
500 Miles
750 Kilometers

HAWAII
100 Miles
100 Kilometers

Patterns of Settlement

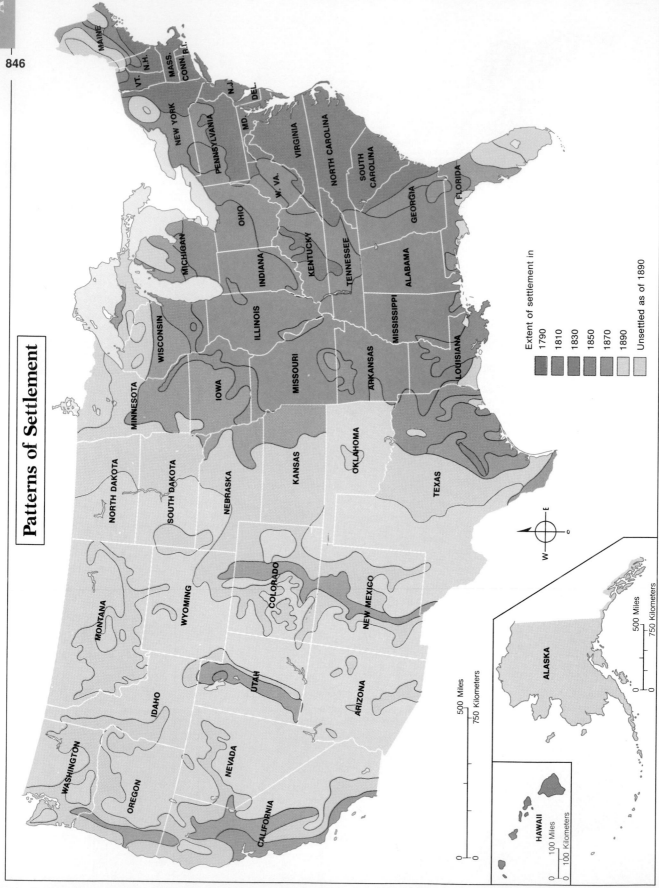

Extent of settlement in
1790
1810
1830
1850
1870
1890
Unsettled as of 1890

MAINE
VT. N.H. MASS. CONN. R.I.
NEW YORK
N.J.
PENNSYLVANIA
MD. DEL.
W. VA. VIRGINIA
OHIO
MICHIGAN
INDIANA
KENTUCKY
NORTH CAROLINA
SOUTH CAROLINA
TENNESSEE
GEORGIA
ALABAMA
FLORIDA
ILLINOIS
WISCONSIN
MISSISSIPPI
LOUISIANA
IOWA
MISSOURI
ARKANSAS
MINNESOTA
NORTH DAKOTA
SOUTH DAKOTA
NEBRASKA
KANSAS
OKLAHOMA
TEXAS
COLORADO
NEW MEXICO
WYOMING
MONTANA
UTAH
ARIZONA
IDAHO
NEVADA
WASHINGTON
OREGON
CALIFORNIA

ALASKA
500 Miles
750 Kilometers

HAWAII
100 Miles
100 Kilometers

500 Miles
750 Kilometers

N
E
W
S

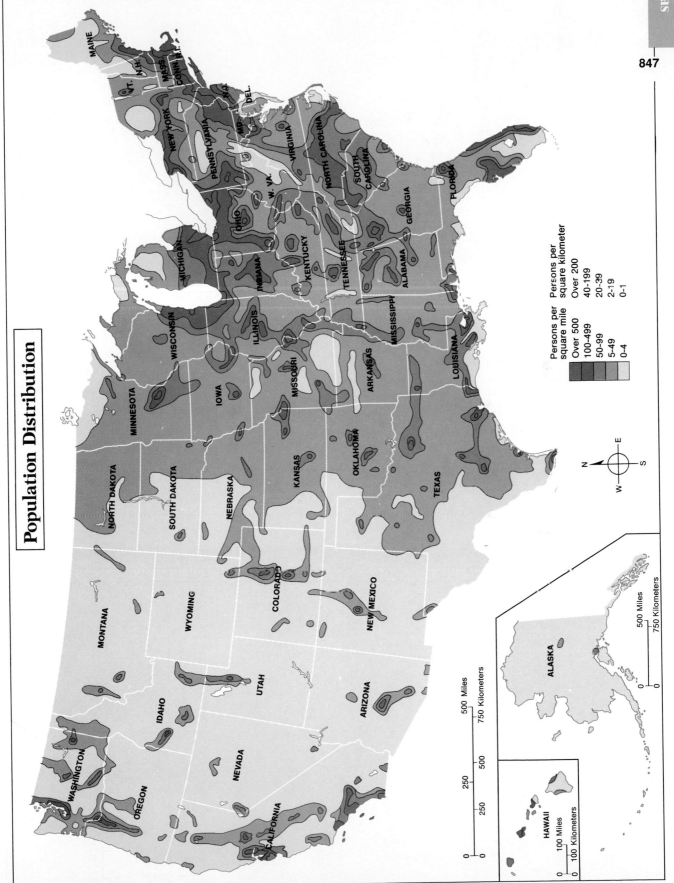

Population Distribution

Persons per square mile
- Over 500
- 100-499
- 50-99
- 5-49
- 0-4

Persons per square kilometer
- Over 200
- 40-199
- 20-39
- 2-19
- 0-1

Mineral Resources

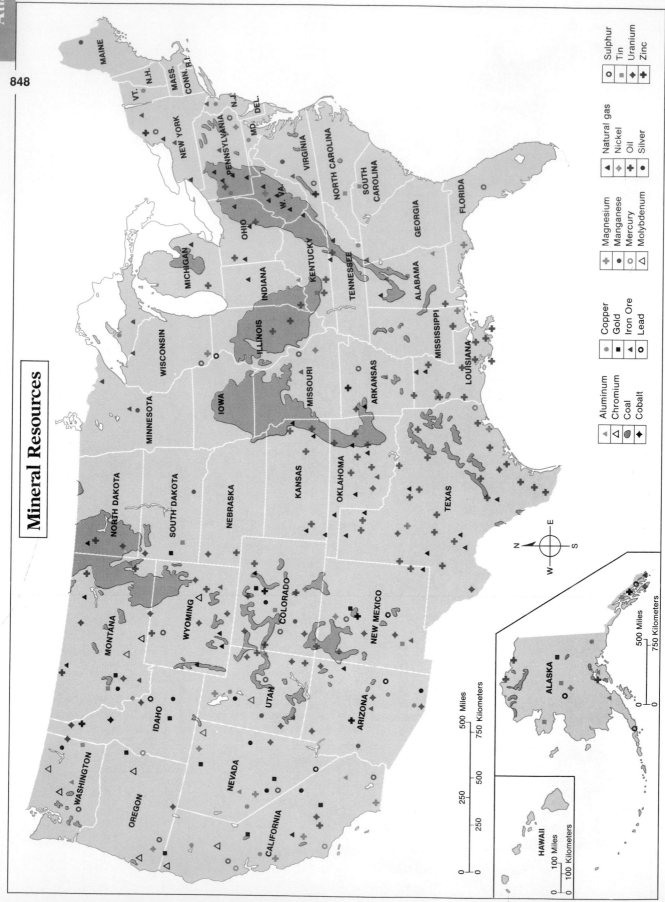

Legend

Aluminum	Chromium	Coal	Cobalt
Copper	Gold	Iron Ore	Lead
Magnesium	Manganese	Mercury	Molybdenum
Natural gas	Nickel	Oil	Silver
Sulphur	Tin	Uranium	Zinc

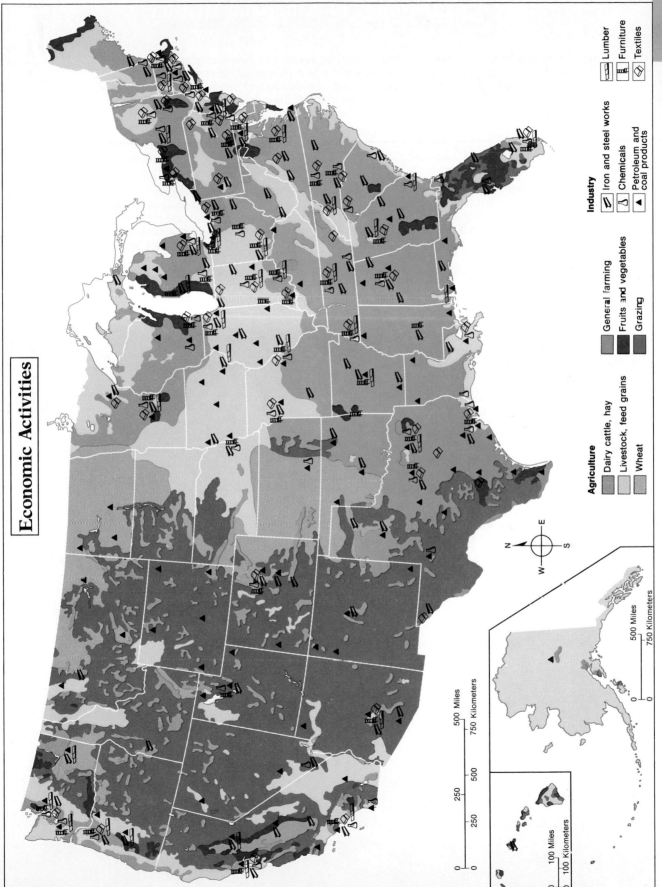

Economic Activities

Agriculture

- Dairy cattle, hay
- Livestock, feed grains
- Wheat
- General farming
- Fruits and vegetables
- Grazing

Industry

- Iron and steel works
- Chemicals
- Petroleum and coal products
- Lumber
- Furniture
- Textiles

N
W E
S

500 Miles
250   500
250   750 Kilometers
0

500 Miles
0
0   750 Kilometers

100 Miles
0
0   100 Kilometers

A Chronology of American History

This chronology includes some of the most important events and developments in American history. It can be used to trace developments in politics and government, exploration and innovation, society and economics, and culture and religion. The number following each entry refers to the chapter in which the event or development is discussed in the text.

	Politics and Government	Exploration and Innovation
Prehistory– 1499	Mayan Empire reaches its height 1 Crusades for Holy Land begin 1 Aztecs establish empire in Mexico 1 Strong monarchies develop in Europe 1 Incas establish empire in South America 1	Mayas predict eclipses of sun 1 Aztecs develop accurate calendar 1 Marco Polo travels to China 1 Columbus sails to America 2 Vasco da Gama reaches India 1
1500– 1599	Cortés defeats Aztecs 2 Pizarro captures Inca capital 2 Spanish enact Laws of the Indies 2 English colony established at Roanoke 2 English defeat Spanish Armada 2	Spanish explore North America 2 Magellan's expedition circles the globe 2 Cartier sails up St. Lawrence River 2 Drake sails around the world 2
1600– 1649	House of Burgesses set up in Virginia 2 Mayflower Compact signed 2 Massachusetts Bay colony founded 2 Maryland becomes first proprietary colony 3	English joint stock companies sponsor settlement in North America 2 Champlain founds Quebec 2 Spanish found Santa Fe 4 West Indian tobacco adapted to Virginia 2
1650– 1699	Town meetings held in New England 3 Restoration of Charles II in England 3 Royal colonies develop 3 France claims Louisiana 4 Glorious Revolution in England 3	Spanish explore Pacific coast 4 Joliet and Marquette explore Mississippi River 4 La Salle reaches Mississippi Delta 4
1700– 1749	Georgia founded 3 Molasses Act passed 4 English settlers move into Ohio Valley 4	Indigo developed as cash crop 3 Benjamin Franklin develops scientific approach to medicine 3
1750– 1799	French and Indian War 4 Intolerable Acts passed 5 Declaration of Independence signed 6 Revolutionary War 6 Articles of Confederation ratified 7 Constitution ratified 9	Watt patents steam engine 11 Fitch launches first steam-powered boat 11 Slater sets up textile mills in New England 11 Eli Whitney invents cotton gin 11

Society and Economics	Culture and Religion	
Agriculture develops in Americas 1 Rise of merchants and bankers in Europe 1 Trade between Europe and Asia expands 1 Northwest Coast Indians hold potlatches 1	Mayas develop system of writing 1 Aztecs build Tenochtitlán 1 Renaissance begins in Europe 1 Incas construct great cities 1	**Prehistory– 1499**

Native American population of Spanish
  America declines 2
Slave trade begins in Americas 2
French develop fishing and fur trading in
  North America 2
	Spanish try to convert Native Americans to
	  Christianity 2
	Universities open in Spanish America 2
	John White paints watercolors of life in
	  North America 2
		**1500–
		1599**

John Smith organizes life in Jamestown 2 Slavery introduced in Virginia 2 Bible-based society in Massachusetts 2	Persecution of Puritans in England 2 Harvard founded 3 Public school law passed in Massachusetts 3 Religious tolerance granted in Maryland 3	**1600– 1649**

New England becomes shipbuilding
  center 3
Navigation Acts passed 4
Royal African Company established 3
Bacon's Rebellion 3
	Quakers seek religious freedom in
	  Pennsylvania 3
	Spanish missions in Southwest 4
	Primer created in New England 3
	College of William and Mary founded 3
		**1650–
		1699**

Triangular trade flourishes 4 Immigration to Middle Colonies grows 3 Plantations expand in Southern Colonies 3 Growth of port cities 3	Yale College founded 3 First weekly newspaper in colonies founded 3 Great Awakening begins 3 John Peter Zenger arrested for libel 3	**1700– 1749**

Proclamation of 1763 5
Parliament passes Sugar, Quartering, Stamp,
  Currency, and Townshend acts 5
Colonies boycott British goods 5
Northern states abolish slavery 7
Northwest Ordinance takes effect 7
	Southern states disestablish Episcopal
	  Church 7
	Noah Webster promotes an American
	  language 7
	National capital designed and built 9
		**1750–
		1799**

851

Politics and Government	Exploration and Innovation
1800–1824	
Louisiana Purchase 10	Lewis and Clark expedition 10
War of 1812 10	Steamboats improved 11
Missouri Compromise passed 17	Steam-powered locomotives developed 14
Monroe Doctrine 12	
1825–1849	
Jacksonian democracy 12	Erie Canal opened 11
Indian Removal Act passed 12	Mechanical reaper, steel plow, and telegraph developed 14
Texas wins independence 13	First commercial railroads in use 14
Oregon divided along the 49th parallel 13	Gold discovered at Sutter's Mill 13
Mexican War 13	
1850–1874	
Compromise of 1850 16	Passenger elevator, sleeping car, and air brake invented 20
Kansas-Nebraska Act passed 16	Bessemer process developed 20
Civil War 17	Pony Express founded 19
Reconstruction 18	Ironclad ships used in Civil War 17
Alaska purchased from Russia 24	Transcontinental railroad completed 19
Warfare on the Great Plains 19	
1875–1899	
Battle of Little Big Horn 19	Refrigeration in meatpacking developed 20
Populist movement 21	Telephone, phonograph, incandescent light bulb invented 20
ICC created 21	First skyscraper built 22
Sherman Antitrust Act passed 21	
Spanish-American War 24	
1900–1924	
Progressive era 23	Panama Canal built 24
Roosevelt Corollary 24	Assembly line introduced 26
World War I 25	Scientific management introduced 26
Fourteen Points 25	Model T Ford becomes popular 26
Treaty of Versailles rejected 25	Electric appliances become widespread 26
Red Scare 26	
1925–1949	
Bonus Army 27	Lindbergh flies across Atlantic 26
New Deal 28, 29	Talking films introduced 26
World War II 30, 31	TVA dams constructed 28
Truman Doctrine and Marshall Plan 32	Atomic bomb developed 31
NATO created 32	National television broadcasts begin 33
1950–1974	
Korean War 32	*Explorer I* launched into orbit 33
McCarthyism 33	First laser developed 37
Cuban missile crisis 34	First communications satellite launched 34
Vietnam War 34, 35	American astronauts land on moon 35
Watergate crisis 35	
1975–Present	
Diplomatic recognition of China 35	Genetic engineering, computers, lasers, and pacemakers advance medicine 37
First woman on Supreme Court 36	Computers become common in homes and offices 37
Sanctions imposed on South Africa 36	*Voyager I* passes Saturn 37
INF Treaty limits some nuclear missiles 36	

Society and Economics

Culture and Religion

Glossary

This glossary defines many important historical terms and phrases. Most of the entries appear in boldface the first time they are used in the text. The page number following each definition refers to the page on which the term or phrase is first discussed in the text.

Pronunciation Key

When difficult terms or names first appear in the text, they are respelled to aid pronunciation. A syllable in LARGE CAPITAL LETTERS receives the most stress. Syllables with a secondary stress appear in SMALL CAPITAL LETTERS. The key below lists the letters used for respelling. It includes examples of words using each sound and shows how they would be respelled.

Symbol	Example	Respelling
a	hat	(hat)
ay	pay, late	(pay), (layt)
ah	star, hot	(stahr), (haht)
ai	air, dare	(air), (dair)
aw	law, all	(law), (awl)
eh	met	(meht)
ee	bee, eat	(bee), (eet)
er	learn, sir, fur	(learn), (ser), (fer)
ih	fit	(fiht)
ī	mile	(mīl)
ir	ear	(ir)
oh	no	(noh)
oi	soil, boy	(soil), (boi)
oo	root, rule	(root), (rool)
or	born, door	(born), (dor)
ow	plow, out	(plow), (owt)

Symbol	Example	Respelling
u	put, book	(put), (buk)
uh	fun	(fuhn)
yoo	few, use	(fyoo), (yooz)
ch	chill, reach	(chihl), (reech)
g	go, dig	(goh), (dihg)
j	jet, gently, bridge	(jeht), (JEHNT-lee), (brihj)
k	kite, cup	(kīt), (kuhp)
ks	mix	(mihks)
kw	quick	(kwihk)
ng	bring	(brihng)
s	say, cent	(say), (sehnt)
sh	she, crash	(shee), (krash)
th	three	(three)
th	then, breathe	(thehn), (breeth)
y	yet, onion	(yeht), (UHN-yuhn)
z	zip, always	(zihp), (AWL-wayz)
zh	treasure	(TREH-zher)

abolitionist reformer in the 1800s who worked for an immediate end to slavery (page 322)

abstinence giving up of all alcohol (page 315)

adobe sun-dried clay brick used by the Pueblo to construct buildings (page 14)

affirmative action a policy or program set up to compensate for past discrimination and increase opportunities for minorities and women (page 804)

amend to alter the Constitution (page 171)

anarchist a person who opposes all organized government (page 439)

apartheid a policy of complete racial separation by law as practiced in South Africa (page 749)

appeasement a policy of giving in to an aggressor to avoid war; specifically, the policy followed by European leaders in the 1930s of granting Hitler's demands for more territory (page 656)

arms race the competition between the United States and the Soviet Union since 1949 to accumulate sophisticated nuclear arsenals (page 706)

artificial intelligence programs that will allow computers to make deductions, draw inferences, and learn through experience (page 822)

assembly line a system in which work passes from one worker to another, each performing one task in the production of an item; introduced by Henry Ford (page 580)

assets the property, equipment, and cash of a business or individual (page 424)

assimilate to merge into another culture by adopting its standards and values (page 294)

assumption the taking over of state debts by the federal government after the Revolutionary War (page 181)

astrolabe an invention of the Renaissance era that enabled a sailor to fix a ship's position by finding the altitude of the stars (page 20)

bank note paper money backed by a bank's reserves of gold or silver (page 225)

Bessemer process a method of producing strong steel quickly and cheaply by heating iron in a furnace and then introducing cold air to burn out the impurities (page 425)

bicameral legislature a legislature that has two houses, upper and lower (page 146)

bilingual education a system that allows students to take some courses in their native language while they are learning English (page 816)

bill of attainder a law allowing a person charged with a serious crime to be fined or imprisoned without a trial; prohibited by the Constitution (page 172)

blacklist the practice of barring employment to anyone suspected of being a communist (page 717)

blitzkrieg in German, "lightning war"; a sudden, swift, large-scale invasion, used by Germany during World War II (page 658)

bond a certificate that earns interest and is redeemed for cash on a given date (page 424)

bounty a sum paid to a recruit for signing up for military service; used by the Union during the Civil War (page 355)

bounty jumping a practice of enlisting for military service more than once during the Civil War in order to receive payment for each enlistment (page 355)

bracero a Mexican worker who, under a government program started in the 1950s, obtained a temporary permit to work in the United States (page 745)

brain trust a group of scholars and technical experts who advised President Franklin Roosevelt during the New Deal (page 612)

business inventory the quantity of unsold goods on hand (page 599)

capital money invested in a business (page 220)

caravel a sixteenth century ship that could sail into the wind (page 21)

carpetbagger a northerner who settled in the South after the Civil War and supported Radical Reconstruction (page 386)

cash crop a crop grown to be sold at a profit rather than to be consumed by the farmer (page 65)

caucus a secret meeting in which a few members of Congress decided on their party's presidential candidate; replaced in the mid-1800s by a nominating convention (page 250)

checks and balances a system established under the Constitution by which each branch of government can check or control the power of the other branches (page 166)

circumnavigate to sail around the globe; first accomplished by Magellan's expedition in 1522 (page 27)

city manager a professional administrator hired by an elected board of trustees to manage a city government (page 499)

civil disobedience a form of nonviolent protest against an unjust law in which the protestor violates the law but is willing to accept the penalties (page 722)

climate the average weather of a place over a period of 20 or 30 years (page 9)

clipper ship a fast sailing vessel of the mid-1800s (page 289)

closed shop a system where all workers in a particular industry are required to be members of a union (page 714)

collective bargaining negotiation between organized workers and management to reach

855

an agreement on wages, hours, and working conditions (page 440)

compass an invention of the Renaissance era that enabled a sailor to tell direction (page 20)

compulsory education the requirement that every child attend school until a certain age (page 317)

concurrent powers powers granted by the Constitution to both the national and state governments (page 164)

confederation an alliance of independent states (page 148)

conquistador a professional Spanish soldier who explored and conquered lands in the New World (page 27)

consolidate to combine into a single unit, as to combine smaller companies into a larger one (page 423)

containment foreign policy first outlined in 1947 stating that the United States would contain, or hold, Soviet influence within its existing limits (page 697)

contraband merchandise smuggled across enemy lines; used to describe a fugitive slave behind Union lines during the Civil War whom the North refused to return to a southern master (page 363)

convoy a protective escort provided by navy warships for vessels crossing the ocean during wartime (page 558)

copperhead a northerner who opposed the Civil War or supported the Confederacy (page 365)

corduroy road a road made up of tree trunks laid side by side (page 229)

coureur de bois a French fur trader in New France (page 84)

crack a highly addictive form of cocaine (page 802)

craft union a union in which all members practice the same occupation (page 440)

dame school classes for girls and younger children that were held in colonial homes (page 72)

de facto segregation segregation that exists in fact, although not by law (page 743)

856 **default** to fail to pay a debt (page 831)

deficit a condition when government expenses exceed government income (page 786)

deficit spending a government practice of spending more money than is taken in from taxes (page 633)

deflation an economic condition in which the price of goods and services declines (page 458)

delegated powers powers given by the Constitution exclusively to the national government and forbidden to the states (page 164)

depression an economic condition marked by a drastic decline in production and sales and a severe increase in unemployment (page 258)

deregulation a reduction of government regulation on business and industry (page 786)

détente a relaxation of tensions between the United States and the Soviet Union, beginning in the early 1970s (page 763)

devalue to reduce the value of the dollar in relation to other currencies (page 653)

disenfranchise to take away the right to vote (page 453)

divestiture a refusal to hold stock in companies that have operations in South Africa (page 795)

dividend a share of a company's profits issued to stockholders on a periodic basis (page 432)

dollar diplomacy President Taft's policy of encouraging financial investment in foreign countries as a means of increasing U.S. influence (page 541)

domino theory the idea that if one nation became communist, neighboring nations would follow (page 708)

due process protection that guarantees individuals accused of crimes a fair, standardized, and open legal process (page 172)

durable goods products designed to last several years before being replaced (page 599)

economic sanctions limits on trade with a nation until it changes its policies (page 795)

electoral college an assembly elected by the states to formally elect the President and Vice President of the United States (page 168)

elevation the height of an area of land measured from sea level (page 6)

emancipation the freeing of slaves (page 322)

embargo a complete halt to trade with another nation (page 206)

encomienda the right granted to conquistadores to demand a tax from Native Americans living on a given piece of land (page 32)

enumerated commodity a colonial product that Parliament said could be shipped only to England (page 78)

established church an official church supported by taxes on citizens regardless of their personal beliefs (page 70)

expatriate a person who leaves his or her homeland to live in another country (page 583)

ex post facto law a law that makes an act a crime after it has been committed; prohibited by the Constitution (page 172)

factory system a system in which all workers in a manufacturing process are brought together under one roof (page 220)

fall line the area east of the Appalachian Mountains in which inland rivers begin dropping toward sea level (page 63)

federalism a system of government in which authority is divided between national and state governments (page 164)

feeder line a railroad route that carried freight to a river or a canal (page 287)

feudalism the political and social system of Europe during the Middle Ages, characterized by self-sufficient manors and obligations of service and loyalty among classes (page 18)

fireside chat an informal talk on nationwide radio by President Roosevelt (page 614)

flapper a woman of the 1920s who defied tradition with shocking or unconventional clothes, slang, dancing, and behavior (page 587)

freedman a former slave freed as a result of the Civil War (page 378)

free enterprise a system in which private individuals can make economic decisions, such as what products to make, how much to produce, and what prices to set (page 432)

free state a state in which slavery was prohibited before the Civil War (page 333)

funding a process by which a government raises or borrows money to pay off a debt (page 180)

gang system a system of field work in which slaves worked together in gangs under an overseer (page 301)

general strike a strike by the members of all unions in a particular location (page 570)

genetic engineering a technology that alters the genetic codes of cells to fight disease and produce new organisms (page 821)

geography the study of people, their environments, and their resources (page 3)

givebacks previously won benefits that workers have to give up in order to negotiate a new labor contract (page 827)

glasnost policy of speaking out openly about problems in the Soviet Union, instituted by Mikhail Gorbachev (page 791)

gold standard a system in which a nation's currency is based on the value of gold (page 461)

graduated personal income tax a system in which the tax rate is proportionate to a person's income (page 459)

grandfather clause voting regulation adopted by a number of southern states after Reconstruction; allowed a man to vote if his father or grandfather had been eligible to vote in 1867 (page 454)

Grange an organization of farmers founded in 1867 for social reasons; later campaigned for state regulation of railroads and other reforms (page 458)

gross national product the total value of all the goods and services produced by a country (page 825)

history an account of what has happened in the life or development of a people, a nation, or a civilization (page 3)

holding company a company that gains control of other companies by buying their stock (page 451)

Holocaust the systematic murder of more than 6 million Jews by the Nazis before and during World War II (page 684)

horizontal integration   form of business organization in which a company controls one area of production (page 431)

impeach   to accuse the President of wrongdoing; power given by the Constitution to the House of Representatives (page 167)

imperialism   the effort by a powerful nation to create an empire by dominating other nations (page 521)

impound   to refuse to spend funds appropriated by Congress (page 765)

impressment   the British practice of forcing sailors to serve in the British navy during the early 1800s (page 205)

inalienable rights   rights that governments cannot take away from citizens (page 147)

indentured servant   a person who agreed to work for an employer in colonial America for a specified period of time in return for the cost of passage (page 66)

indigo   a West Indian plant used to make blue dye; grown for profit in the southern Colonies (page 65)

industrial union   a union that represents every worker in a single industry (page 634)

inflation   a decline in the value of money as more money is printed, resulting in increased prices (page 125)

information explosion   the rapid increase in the amount of data available in the 1980s (page 824)

initiative   a procedure that allows citizens to propose a bill by collecting a specific number of signatures from registered voters (page 498)

injunction   a court order prohibiting a given action; used frequently to stop strikes (page 441)

interchangeable parts   identical component parts that can be easily used in place of one another in the manufacturing process (page 221)

interlocking directorate   a system under which the same people serve on the boards of directors of several firms within the same industry (page 512)

internationalist   person in the 1920s and 1930s who believed that the United States should take an active role in world affairs (page 649)

isolationist   person in the 1920s and 1930s who believed that the United States should minimize its involvement in foreign affairs (page 649)

jingoism   an exaggerated and belligerent national pride (page 526)

joint stock company   a form of business organization devised around 1600 by European nations to finance business ventures; pooled the funds of many investors by selling shares in the company (page 38)

judicial review   the power of the Supreme Court to review all acts passed by Congress and reject those it considers unconstitutional (page 198)

kamikaze   a tactic whereby Japanese fighter pilots during World War II deliberately crashed their planes into Allied ships (page 684)

kiva   an underground room at the center of a Pueblo town where the men conducted religious ceremonies (page 14)

laissez-faire   noninterference of government in the lives of individuals (page 199)

laissez-faire economics   school of thought that rejects government regulation of industry and the economy (page 428)

lame duck   an elected official serving only until his or her successor takes office (page 348)

laser   a beam of intense light used in medicine and military technology; stands for Light Amplification by Stimulated Emission of Radiation (page 823)

latitude   distance north or south of the equator (page 4)

leapfrogging   the technique used by the Allies in World War II of invading a few strategic Japanese-held islands and bypassing others (page 678)

limited liability   system by which an investor's personal responsibility for the debts of a corporation is limited to his or her initial investment (page 220)

limited war   a war in which specific objectives are sought, rather than total victory over the enemy (page 704)

literacy rate the proportion of a population that can read and write (page 72)

localism the tendency of states or areas to act independently and not as part of a unified nation (page 124)

long drive a cattle drive in which a large herd was moved across hundreds or thousands of miles to a railhead, from which the cattle would be shipped to market (page 412)

longitude distance east or west of the Prime Meridian (page 4)

loose construction an interpretation of the Constitution holding that the federal government has more powers than those actually listed (page 182)

mainstream to place handicapped students in classes with nonhandicapped students rather than in special facilities (page 807)

manifest destiny a commonly held belief in the first half of the nineteenth century that the United States had a mission to expand its borders to incorporate all land between the Atlantic and Pacific Oceans (page 274)

manor during the Middle Ages, a large estate owned by a lord where peasants produced all the necessities (page 18)

manumission the freeing of slaves (page 144)

margin call a request by a stockbroker that an investor who has bought on margin put up more money to cover loans on stocks that have decreased in value (page 598)

massive retaliation a military strategy proposed during the cold war of the 1950s in which the United States would retaliate directly against the Soviet Union or China, with nuclear weapons if necessary (page 705)

matrilineal describing a society where descent is traced through the mother's line (page 14)

McCarthyism the technique used by Senator Joseph McCarthy in the 1950s of making sweeping accusations of disloyalty without producing conclusive evidence (page 718)

mercantilism an economic system prevalent in Europe after the Middle Ages in which each nation attempted to sell more than it bought in order to increase its supply of gold (page 77)

migrant worker an agricultural worker who travels from farm to farm doing seasonal work (page 578)

minuteman a member of a colonial Massachusetts militia ready to fight the British on a moment's notice (page 111)

modem a device that connects one computer to another through telephone lines (page 822)

monopoly complete control of a product or service in a particular market by a single company (page 432)

moral diplomacy a term describing President Wilson's approach to foreign policy, which emphasized the use of negotiation and arbitration rather than force (page 545)

mortality rate death rate (page 265)

muckraker early twentieth-century American journalist who tried to reform society by exposing political corruption, health hazards, and other social problems (page 494)

Mugwumps reformers within the Republican party who crusaded to end political corruption during the late 1800s (page 448)

nativist a person who wanted to limit immigration and preserve the virtues and way of life of native-born Americans (page 294)

naturalized citizen a person who gives up citizenship in one country to become a citizen of another (page 205)

nomadic moving from place to place instead of living in permanent villages (page 14)

nonimportation agreement a promise made by colonial merchants and planters not to import certain goods taxed by the Townshend Acts (page 101)

normalcy President Warren G. Harding's term for the return to peace and normal business conditions after World War I (page 574)

nullify to declare a law invalid (page 193)

on margin refers to the practice of buying stock in which the buyer pays only part of the selling price and borrows the rest from a broker (page 598)

pacifism opposition to the use of force for any reason (page 122)

parity a system in which the government supports the price of certain farm products in order to maintain the purchasing power of farmers (page 577)

party platform a political party's declaration of its principles and programs (page 247)

patronage system the practice of giving out government jobs as favors to loyal party workers (page 448)

patroon a landowner in the Dutch colonies who received rent, taxes, and labor from tenant farmers (page 63)

pictogram a picture drawn on rock by the Anasazi that conveyed their ideas about life (page 14)

piedmont region a region of rolling hills; in the south, the piedmont lies between the Appalachian Mountains and the tidewater region (page 65)

planter an aristocratic plantation owner of the South who planted cash crops and employed a large number of slaves (page 65)

pogrom a violent attack against a Jewish neighborhood in eastern Europe (page 474)

poll tax a fee that had to be paid in order to vote; instituted in the South after the Civil War to prevent blacks from voting; rendered unconstitutional by the Twenty-fourth Amendment (page 454)

pooling an illegal agreement among railroad administrators to divide the total volume of freight among their lines (page 424)

popular sovereignty the principle that a government's power or authority comes from the people (page 163)

potlatch a feast held by an early Native American family of the northwest Pacific coast to demonstrate its prosperity (page 13)

presidio a Spanish settlement in the New World built for military activities (page 31)

primary election an election held before a general election to choose candidates for office (page 498)

primer a small textbook that taught Puritan children reading, spelling, and the tenets of the Puritan faith (page 70)

productivity the total output of a worker per hour of work (page 826)

prohibition the ban on the sale and manufacture of alcoholic beverages resulting from ratification of the Eighteenth Amendment in 1919 (page 585)

proprietor an individual who received colonial land in America from the king of England and who was expected to administer that land in accordance with the laws of England (page 54)

protective tariff a tax on imports designed to protect manufacturers from foreign competition (page 183)

protectorate a country that is technically independent, but whose government and economy are controlled by a stronger power (page 532)

public domain land that belongs to the nation rather than to individuals (page 405)

pueblo a Spanish settlement in the New World established for farming, trade, and town life (page 32)

quadrant an invention of the Renaissance era that enabled a sailor to take bearings from the sun or the stars in order to plot a ship's position on a map (page 20)

quota system a system that set limits on the number of immigrants and where they come from (page 572)

ranchero a Mexican ranch owner (page 265)

ratify to officially approve a proposal (page 149)

rebate in the 1800s, an illegal discount on railroad shipping charges (page 424)

recall election a special election that allows voters to remove an elected official before the completion of his or her term (page 499)

reconcentration a policy of General Weyler of Spain in 1896 whereby Cuban villagers were herded into detention camps (page 526)

referendum the process by which people can vote directly on a proposed law (page 498)

relief the rate of change in the elevation of the land (page 6)

reparations payments made by nations defeated in war as a penalty for damages (page 559)

reservation an area of land specifically set aside by the federal government for Native Americans (page 409)

reserved powers powers retained by the states because they are not expressly given to the federal government nor denied to the states by the Constitution (page 164)

revival a meeting held to renew people's religious faith (page 314)

royal colony an American colony in which the governor and council were appointed by the king (page 57)

sachem one of 50 specially chosen leaders who, along with the chiefs of each tribe, governed the Iroquois League during the 1500s (page 15)

scalawag a white southerner who supported Radical Reconstruction (page 386)

scientific management the systematic study and improvement of worker efficiency (page 579)

sea dogs English sailors who pirated Spanish ships carrying precious minerals from the New World back to Spain (page 35)

secede to withdraw from a large political body (page 200)

segregated separated on the basis of race (page 143)

self-determination the freedom of a country to determine its own future and form of government without outside interference (page 559)

self-sufficient having the resources to get along without outside help, as a farm family in the New England colonies (page 58)

separation of powers a system in which legislative, executive, and judicial powers are divided among separate branches of government (page 166)

serf a peasant of the Middle Ages who was bound to a lord's land (page 18)

sharecropper an agricultural worker who works part of another person's land, receives supplies and equipment from the landowner, and in return gives the landowner part of the harvest (page 385)

sitdown strike a strike in which workers sit down on the job and refuse to leave the work place until their demands are met (page 634)

slave code set of laws regulating the conduct of slaves before the Civil War (page 69)

slave state a state in which slavery was permitted before the Civil War (page 333)

special interest group an organization of people with common interests devoted to promoting a single political issue (page 812)

sphere of influence an area in China during the late 1800s where trade was controlled by a foreign power (page 533)

spoils system the practice of dismissing government job holders affiliated with a defeated party and replacing them with supporters of the victorious party (page 254)

squatter a person who settles on land without a legal right to do so (page 151)

stagflation an economic condition of both inflation and recession (page 765)

stock certificate a document stating that the holder owns a share of a corporation (page 424)

strategic forces specially trained armed forces units that can be moved quickly to any part of the world (page 734)

strict construction a literal interpretation of the Constitution, holding that the federal government has only those powers specifically listed in the Constitution (page 182)

strike an organized work stoppage by employees, conducted for the purpose of improving pay or working conditions (page 290)

subsistence farming a level of farming at which farmers produce just enough to feed their families (page 58)

sunbelt a term referring to southeastern and southwestern states known for their mild climates and expanding economies (page 819)

task system a system by which individual slaves were assigned specific jobs each day (page 301)

temperance movement a campaign against alcoholic beverages (page 315)

tenant an agricultural worker who rents land from another person and pays the rent either in cash or by giving the landowner a portion of the crop; tenants provide their own seed and supplies (page 385)

territorial integrity preservation of a nation's boundaries (page 559)

tidewater region a flat coastal plain where the land is so low that rivers crossing it flow backwards with incoming tides (page 65)

totalitarian state a country in which the government is supreme and individuals have few rights (page 652)

town meeting a meeting in which residents of a town in the New England colonies discussed matters of importance and elected representatives to the colonial assembly (page 60)

trade deficit a situation in which the value of a nation's imports exceeds the value of its exports (page 788)

triangular trade the pattern of trade during the colonial era in which merchant ships traveled a triangular route, stopping in New England, Africa, and the West Indies (page 80)

trunk line a heavily traveled railroad route that links major cities (page 287)

trust a form of business organization, widespread during the late 1800s, in which investors in independent corporations exchanged their stock certificates for trust certificates issued by a giant firm; they received dividends but lost their say in management (page 432)

unconstitutional refers to a legislative act or executive action that violates the Constitution (page 167)

underground railroad the network of people who helped slaves escape to the northern states or to Canada (page 324)

union an association of workers formed to improve wages and working conditions (page 290)

utility company a company that distributes gas and electricity (page 624)

utopian ideal; a term referring to communities of the 1800s that were founded to demonstrate how an ideal society should work (page 318)

vassal a lord who received land from a king, an emperor, or a higher lord during the Middle Ages in return for loyalty (page 18)

vertical integration a form of business organization in which a manufacturer controls all the steps required to turn raw materials into a finished product (page 431)

veto an action by which an executive rejects a bill submitted by a legislature (page 146)

vigilante a self-appointed enforcer of the law (page 404)

watered stock worthless shares of ownership in a company, backed by exaggerated assets (page 424)

white manhood suffrage voting by all white males (page 249)

women's suffrage the right of women to vote (page 497)

workingmen's party an organization of workers of the early 1800s that sought universal white manhood suffrage, free public education, and abolition of debtor imprisonment laws (page 291)

writ of assistance a document issued by British authorities during the colonial period that allowed officials to conduct unrestricted searches (page 101)

writ of habeas corpus a court order releasing a person arrested without specific charges (page 172)

yellow journalism a style of newspaper writing in the late 1890s that featured sensational headlines and stories (page 527)

yuppie a young urban professional of the 1980s, overly concerned with money and possessions (page 799)

zero population growth a point at which the number of births equals the numbers of deaths in a population (page 818)

The Fifty States

State	Capital	Date of Entry to Union (Order of Entry)	Area in Square Miles	Resident Population	Number of Representatives in House
Alabama	Montgomery	1819 (22)	51,705	4,102,000	7
Alaska	Juneau	1959 (49)	591,004	524,000	1
Arizona	Phoenix	1912 (48)	114,000	3,489,000	5
Arkansas	Little Rock	1836 (25)	53,187	2,395,000	4
California	Sacramento	1850 (31)	158,706	28,314,000	45
Colorado	Denver	1876 (38)	104,091	3,301,000	6
Connecticut	Hartford	1788 (5)	5,018	3,233,000	6
Delaware	Dover	1787 (1)	2,044	660,000	1
Florida	Tallahassee	1845 (27)	58,664	12,335,000	19
Georgia	Atlanta	1788 (4)	58,910	6,342,000	10
Hawaii	Honolulu	1959 (50)	6,471	1,098,000	2
Idaho	Boise	1890 (43)	83,564	1,003,000	2
Illinois	Springfield	1818 (21)	56,345	11,614,000	22
Indiana	Indianapolis	1816 (19)	36,185	5,556,000	10
Iowa	Des Moines	1846 (29)	56,275	2,834,000	6
Kansas	Topeka	1861 (34)	82,277	2,495,000	5
Kentucky	Frankfort	1792 (15)	40,409	3,727,000	7
Louisiana	Baton Rouge	1812 (18)	47,751	4,408,000	8
Maine	Augusta	1820 (23)	33,265	1,205,000	2
Maryland	Annapolis	1788 (7)	10,460	4,622,000	8
Massachusetts	Boston	1788 (6)	8,284	5,889,000	11
Michigan	Lansing	1837 (26)	58,527	9,240,000	18
Minnesota	St. Paul	1858 (32)	84,402	4,307,000	8
Mississippi	Jackson	1817 (20)	47,689	2,620,000	5
Missouri	Jefferson City	1821 (24)	69,697	5,141,000	9
Montana	Helena	1889 (41)	147,046	805,000	2
Nebraska	Lincoln	1867 (37)	77,355	1,602,000	3
Nevada	Carson City	1864 (36)	110,561	1,054,000	2
New Hampshire	Concord	1788 (9)	9,279	1,085,000	2
New Jersey	Trenton	1787 (3)	7,787	7,721,000	14
New Mexico	Santa Fe	1912 (47)	121,593	1,507,000	3
New York	Albany	1788 (11)	49,108	17,909,000	34
North Carolina	Raleigh	1789 (12)	52,669	6,489,000	11
North Dakota	Bismarck	1889 (39)	70,703	667,000	1
Ohio	Columbus	1803 (17)	41,330	10,855,000	21
Oklahoma	Oklahoma City	1907 (46)	69,956	3,242,000	6
Oregon	Salem	1859 (33)	97,073	2,767,000	5
Pennsylvania	Harrisburg	1787 (2)	45,308	12,001,000	23
Rhode Island	Providence	1790 (13)	1,212	993,000	2
South Carolina	Columbia	1788 (8)	31,113	3,470,000	6
South Dakota	Pierre	1889 (40)	77,116	713,000	1
Tennessee	Nashville	1796 (16)	42,144	4,895,000	9
Texas	Austin	1845 (28)	266,807	16,841,000	27
Utah	Salt Lake City	1896 (45)	84,899	1,690,000	3
Vermont	Montpelier	1791 (14)	8,614	557,000	1
Virginia	Richmond	1788 (10)	40,767	6,015,000	10
Washington	Olympia	1889 (42)	68,138	4,648,000	8
West Virginia	Charleston	1863 (35)	24,231	1,876,000	4
Wisconsin	Madison	1848 (30)	56,153	4,855,000	9
Wyoming	Cheyenne	1890 (44)	97,809	479,000	1
District of Columbia			69	617,000	1 (nonvoting)

Presidents and Vice Presidents of the United States

President	Term(s) Served	Political Party	Vice President	Term(s) Served
1. George Washington (b. 1732, d. 1799)	1789–1797	None	John Adams	1789–1797
2. John Adams (b. 1735, d. 1826)	1797–1801	Federalist	Thomas Jefferson	1797–1801
3. Thomas Jefferson (b. 1743, d. 1826)	1801–1809	Dem.-Rep.	Aaron Burr George Clinton	1801–1805 1805–1809
4. James Madison (b. 1751, d. 1836)	1809–1817	Dem.-Rep.	George Clinton Elbridge Gerry	1809–1812 1813–1814
5. James Monroe (b. 1758, d. 1831)	1817–1825	Dem.-Rep.	Daniel D. Tompkins	1817–1825
6. John Quincy Adams (b. 1767, d. 1848)	1825–1829	Dem.-Rep.	John C. Calhoun	1825–1829
7. Andrew Jackson (b. 1767, d. 1845)	1829–1837	Democrat	John C. Calhoun Martin Van Buren	1829–1832 1833–1837
8. Martin Van Buren (b. 1782, d. 1862)	1837–1841	Democrat	Richard M. Johnson	1837–1841
9. William H. Harrison (b. 1773, d. 1841)	1841	Whig	John Tyler	1841
10. John Tyler (b. 1790, d. 1862)	1841–1845	Whig	*	
11. James K. Polk (b. 1795, d. 1849)	1845–1849	Democrat	George M. Dallas	1845–1849
12. Zachary Taylor (b. 1784, d. 1850)	1849–1850	Whig	Millard Fillmore	1849–1850
13. Millard Fillmore (b. 1800, d. 1874)	1850–1853	Whig	*	
14. Franklin Pierce (b. 1804, d. 1869)	1853–1857	Democrat	William R. King	1853
15. James Buchanan (b. 1791, d. 1868)	1857–1861	Democrat	John C. Breckinridge	1857–1861
16. Abraham Lincoln (b. 1809, d. 1865)	1861–1865	Republican	Hannibal Hamlin Andrew Johnson	1861–1865 1865
17. Andrew Johnson (b. 1808, d. 1875)	1865–1869	Republican	*	
18. Ulysses S. Grant (b. 1822, d. 1885)	1869–1877	Republican	Schuyler Colfax Henry Wilson	1869–1873 1873–1875
19. Rutherford B. Hayes (b. 1822, d. 1893)	1877–1881	Republican	William A. Wheeler	1877–1881
20. James A. Garfield (b. 1831, d. 1881)	1881	Republican	Chester A. Arthur	1881
21. Chester A. Arthur (b. 1829, d. 1886)	1881–1885	Republican	*	
22. Grover Cleveland (b. 1837, d. 1908)	1885-1889	Democrat	Thomas A. Hendricks	1885
23. Benjamin Harrison (b. 1833, d. 1901)	1889–1893	Republican	Levi P. Morton	1889–1893
24. Grover Cleveland (b. 1837, d. 1908)	1893–1897	Democrat	Adlai E. Stevenson	1893–1897
25. William McKinley (b. 1843, d. 1901)	1897–1901	Republican	Garret A. Hobart Theodore Roosevelt	1897–1899 1901
26. Theodore Roosevelt (b. 1858, d. 1919)	1901–1909	Republican	Charles W. Fairbanks	1905–1909
27. William H. Taft (b. 1857, d. 1930)	1909–1913	Republican	James S. Sherman	1909–1912
28. Woodrow Wilson (b. 1856, d. 1924)	1913–1921	Democrat	Thomas R. Marshall	1913–1921
29. Warren G. Harding (b. 1865, d. 1923)	1921–1923	Republican	Calvin Coolidge	1921–1923
30. Calvin Coolidge (b. 1872, d. 1933)	1923–1929	Republican	Charles G. Dawes	1925–1929
31. Herbert C. Hoover (b. 1874, d. 1964)	1929–1933	Republican	Charles Curtis	1929–1933
32. Franklin D. Roosevelt (b. 1882, d. 1945)	1933–1945	Democrat	John N. Garner Henry A. Wallace Harry S. Truman	1933–1941 1941–1945 1945
33. Harry S. Truman (b. 1884, d. 1972)	1945–1953	Democrat	Alben W. Barkley	1949–1953
34. Dwight D. Eisenhower (b. 1890, d. 1969)	1953–1961	Republican	Richard M. Nixon	1953–1961
35. John F. Kennedy (b. 1917, d. 1963)	1961–1963	Democrat	Lyndon B. Johnson	1961–1963
36. Lyndon B. Johnson (b. 1908, d. 1973)	1963–1969	Democrat	Hubert H. Humphrey	1965–1969
37. Richard M. Nixon (b. 1913)	1969–1974	Republican	Spiro T. Agnew Gerald R. Ford	1969–1973 1973–1974
38. Gerald R. Ford† (b. 1913)	1974–1977	Republican	Nelson A. Rockefeller	1974–1977
39. Jimmy Carter (b. 1924)	1977–1981	Democrat	Walter F. Mondale	1977–1981
40. Ronald Reagan (b. 1911)	1981–1989	Republican	George Bush	1981–1989
41. George Bush (b. 1924)	1989–	Republican	J. Danforth Quayle	1989–

*Prior to ratification of the Twenty-fifth Amendment in 1967, there was no constitutional provision for replacing a Vice President if that office became vacant.

†Inaugurated August 9, 1974, to replace Nixon, who resigned the same day.

Presidents and Vice Presidents

When in the course of human events it becomes necessary for one people to dissolve the political bands which have connected them with another and to assume, among the powers of the earth, the separate and equal station to which the laws of nature and of nature's God entitle them, a decent respect to the opinions of mankind requires that they should declare the causes which impel them to the separation.

We hold these truths to be self-evident, that all men are created equal; that they are endowed by their Creator with certain unalienable rights; that among these are life, liberty, and the pursuit of happiness. That, to secure these rights, governments are instituted among men, deriving their just powers from the consent of the governed; that, whenever any form of government becomes destructive of these ends, it is the right of the people to alter or to abolish it, and to institute a new government, laying its foundation on such principles, and organizing its powers in such form, as to them shall seem most likely to effect their safety and happiness. Prudence, indeed, will dictate that governments long established should not be changed for light and transient causes; and, accordingly, all experience hath shown that mankind are more disposed to suffer, while evils are sufferable, than to right themselves by abolishing the forms to which they are accustomed. But when a long train of abuses and usurpations, pursuing invariably the same object, evinces a design to reduce them under absolute despotism, it is their right, it is their duty, to throw off such government and to provide new guards for their future security. Such has been the patient sufferance of these colonies, and such is now the necessity which constrains them to alter their former systems of government. The history of the present King of Great Britain is a history of repeated injuries and usurpations, all having, in direct object, the establishment of an absolute tyranny over these States. To prove this, let facts be submitted to a candid world:

He has refused his assent to laws the most wholesome and necessary for the public good.

He has forbidden his governors to pass laws of immediate and pressing importance, unless suspended in their operation till his assent should be obtained; and, when so suspended, he has utterly neglected to attend to them.

He has refused to pass other laws for the accommodation of the large districts of people, unless those people would relinquish the right of representation in the legislature: a right inestimable to them and formidable to tyrants only.

He has called together legislative bodies at places unusual, uncomfortable, and distant from the depository of their public records, for the sole purpose of fatiguing them into compliance with his measures.

He has dissolved representative houses, repeatedly for opposing, with manly firmness, his invasions on the rights of the people.

He has refused, for a long time after such dissolutions, to cause others to be elected: whereby the legislative powers, incapable of annihilation, have returned to the people at large for their exercise; the state remaining, in the meantime, exposed to all the danger of invasion from without and convulsions within.

He has endeavored to prevent the population of these States; for that purpose, obstructing the laws for naturalization of foreigners, refusing to pass others to encourage their migration hither, and raising the conditions of new appropriations of lands.

He has obstructed the administration of justice by refusing his assent to laws for establishing judiciary powers.

He has made judges dependent on his will alone for the tenure of their offices and the amount and payment of their salaries.

He has erected a multitude of new offices and sent hither swarms of officers to harass our people and eat out their substance.

He has kept among us, in time of peace, standing armies, without the consent of our legislatures.

He has affected to render the military independent of, and superior to, the civil power.

865

He has combined with others to subject us to a jurisdiction foreign to our Constitution and unacknowledged by our laws, giving his assent to their acts of pretended legislation—

For quartering large bodies of armed troops among us;

For protecting them by a mock trial from punishment for any murders which they should commit on the inhabitants of these States;

For cutting off our trade with all parts of the world;

For imposing taxes on us without our consent;

For depriving us, in many cases, of the benefit of trial by jury;

For transporting us beyond seas to be tried for pretended offences;

For abolishing the free system of English laws in a neighboring province, establishing therein an arbitrary government, and enlarging its boundaries, so as to render it at once an example and fit instrument for introducing the same absolute rule into these colonies;

For taking away our charters, abolishing our most valuable laws, and altering, fundamentally, the powers of our governments;

For suspending our own legislatures and declaring themselves invested with power to legislate for us in all cases whatsoever.

He has abdicated government here by declaring us out of his protection and waging war against us.

He has plundered our seas, ravaged our coasts, burnt our towns, and destroyed the lives of our people.

He is, at this time, transporting large armies of foreign mercenaries to complete the works of death, desolation, and tyranny already begun with circumstances of cruelty and perfidy scarcely paralleled in the most barbarous ages, and totally unworthy, the head of a civilized nation.

He has constrained our fellow citizens, taken captive on the high seas, to bear arms against their country, to become the executioners of their friends and brethren, or to fall themselves by their hands.

He has excited domestic insurrections amongst us and has endeavored to bring on the inhabitants of our frontiers, the merciless Indian savages, whose known rule of warfare is an undistinguished destruction of all ages, sexes, and conditions.

In every stage of these oppressions, we have petitioned for redress in the most humble terms; our repeated petitions have been answered only by repeated injury. A prince whose character is thus marked by every act which may define a tyrant is unfit to be the ruler of a free people.

Nor have we been wanting in attention to our British brethren. We have warned them, from time to time, of attempts made by their legislature to extend an unwarrantable jurisdiction over us. We have reminded them of the circumstances of our emigration and settlement here. We have appealed to their native justice and magnanimity, and we have conjured them, by the ties of our common kindred, to disavow these usurpations, which would inevitably interrupt our connections and correspondence. They, too, have been deaf to the voice of justice and consanguinity. We must, therefore, acquiesce in the necessity which denounces our separation, and hold them, as we hold the rest of mankind, enemies in war, in peace, friends.

We, therefore, the representatives of the United States of America, in general Congress assembled, appealing to the Supreme Judge of the world for the rectitude of our intentions, do, in the name and by the authority of the good people of these colonies, solemnly publish and declare, that these united colonies are, and of right ought to be, free and independent states: that they are absolved from all allegiance to the British Crown, and that all political connection between them and the state of Great Britain is, and ought to be, totally dissolved; and that, as free and independent states, they have full power to levy war, conclude peace, contract alliances, establish commerce, and to do all other acts and things which independent states may of right do. And, for the support of this declaration, with a firm reliance on the protection of Divine Providence, we mutually pledge to each other our lives, our fortunes, and our sacred honor.

The Constitution of the United States of America

The text of the Constitution is printed against a white background. Annotations are printed against a tan background. The titles of articles, sections, and clauses have been added for clarity. They are not part of the original document. The portions of the Constitution in brackets have been changed by amendments or no longer apply. Page numbers in the annotations refer to relevant material in your textbook. Difficult terms in the Constitution are italicized and defined in the annotations.

Preamble

We, the people of the United States, in order to form a more perfect Union, establish justice, insure domestic tranquillity, provide for the common defense, promote the general welfare, and secure the blessings of liberty to ourselves and our posterity, do ordain and establish this Constitution for the United States of America.

The Preamble introduces the purposes of the government established by the Constitution. It does not have the force of law. Therefore, parties to lawsuits cannot base claims on the provisions contained in the Preamble.

Article 1. The Legislative Branch

Legislative powers refers to the power to make law. The Senate and the House of Representatives make up the federal government's legislative branch.

Section 1. A Two-House Legislature

All legislative powers herein granted shall be vested in a Congress of the United States, which shall consist of a Senate and House of Representatives.

Through custom other branches of the federal government also possess lawmaking power. When judges interpret the Constitution, they are, in effect, making law (pages 218–219). Furthermore, such regulatory agencies as the Federal Trade Commission can make rules that have the effect of law. The powers of the federal regulatory agencies, however, are subject to the control of Congress.

Section 2. House of Representatives

1. Election of Members The House of Representatives shall be composed of members chosen every second year by the people of the several states, and the electors in each state shall have the qualifications requisite for electors of the most numerous branch of the state legislature.

Clause 1 *Electors* refers to voters. Members of the House run for election every two years. The original Constitution does not specify voting qualifications. It provides that people qualified to vote in elections for the largest house of the state legislature must be allowed to vote in elections for the House of Representatives. Four amendments to the Constitution—the Fifteenth, Nineteenth, Twenty-fourth, and Twenty-sixth—have restricted state power to limit the right to vote.

2. Qualifications No person shall be a Representative who shall not have attained to the age of twenty-five years, and been seven years a citizen of the United States, and who shall not, when elected, be an inhabitant of that state in which he shall be chosen.

Clause 2 A member of the House must live in the state he or she represents, but members need not be legal residents of the district they represent. Tradition, however, dictates that candidates run for election in the districts in which they legally reside.

3. Determining Representation Representatives [and direct taxes] shall be apportioned among the several states which may be

Clause 3 *Persons bound to service* refers to indentured servants, while *all other persons* refers to the slave population. The *enumeration* that will be made every ten years refers to a census.

A state's representation in the House is based on its population. According to the original clause, the state's entire free population is counted for the purpose of representation, but only three fifths of the slaves were to be counted. This arrangement resulted from a compromise at the Constitutional Convention (page 162). The so-called three-fifths clause became meaningless when the Thirteenth Amendment, which freed the slaves, was added to the Constitution. An act of Congress has fixed the number of members in the House at 435.

Clause 4 *Executive authority* refers to the governor of a state. A *writ of election* is an order to hold an election. When a member of the House leaves office prior to the end of his or her term, the governor must fill that vacancy by calling a special election.

Clause 5 The *speaker of the House* is a member who acts as its presiding officer. By modern practice, the speaker is chosen by the party that has a majority in the House. The speaker applies House rules and determines when members will be allowed to address the House. *Impeachment* is an accusation of misconduct that can be made against the President and Vice President, federal judges, and other high federal officials. Impeachment and removal from office are discussed in Section 3.

Clause 1 According to the original clause, the legislature of each state was to elect two senators. This clause was nullified by the Seventeenth Amendment, ratified in 1913.

Clause 2 Unlike the House, in which the terms of all members expire at the same time, the terms of only one third of the senators expire in any congressional election year. Thus every two years one third of the Senate stands for reelection. Normally only one of a state's senators would run in any election year. The election of the Senate by thirds ensures that the body will not be totally transformed in any one election.

This clause allows the governor, the *executive,* to fill vacancies that occur between elections by making temporary appointments if the state legislature is not in session. Under this clause, when the legislature reconvenes it has the power to fill any existing vacancies. The method for filling vacancies was changed by the Seventeenth Amendment.

868

included within this Union, according to their respective numbers [which shall be determined by adding to the whole number of free persons, including those bound to service for a term of years, and excluding Indians not taxed, three-fifths of all other persons]. The actual enumeration shall be made within three years after the first meeting of the Congress of the United States, and within every subsequent term of ten years, in such manner as they shall by law direct. The number of Representatives shall not exceed one for every 30,000, but each state shall have at least one Representative; [and until such enumeration shall be made, the state of New Hampshire shall be entitled to choose three; Massachusetts, eight; Rhode Island and Providence Plantations, one; Connecticut, five; New York, six; New Jersey, four; Pennsylvania, eight; Delaware, one; Maryland, six; Virginia, ten; North Carolina, five; South Carolina, five; and Georgia, three.]

4. Filling Vacancies When vacancies happen in the representation from any state, the executive authority thereof shall issue writs of election to fill such vacancies.

5. Selection of Officers; Power of Impeachment The House of Representatives shall choose their Speaker and other officers; and shall have the sole power of impeachment.

Section 3. The Senate

1. Selection of Members The Senate of the United States shall be composed of two Senators from each state [chosen by the legislature thereof], for six years, and each Senator shall have one vote.

2. Alternating Terms; Filling Vacancies Immediately after they shall be assembled in consequence of the first election, they shall be divided as equally as may be into three classes. [The seats of the Senators of the first class shall be vacated at the expiration of the second year, of the second class at the expiration of the fourth year, and of the third class at the expiration of the sixth year,] so that one-third may be chosen every second year; [and if vacancies happen by resignation, or otherwise, during the recess of the legislature of any state, the executive thereof may make temporary appointments until the next meeting of the legislature, which shall then fill such vacancies.]

3. Qualifications No person shall be a Senator who shall not have attained to the age of thirty years, and been nine years a citizen of the United States, and who shall not, when elected, be an inhabitant of that state for which he shall be chosen.

4. President of the Senate The Vice-President of the United States shall be president of the Senate, but shall have no vote, unless they be equally divided.

5. Election of Senate Officers The Senate shall choose their other officers, and also a president *pro tempore*, in the absence of the Vice-President, or when he shall exercise the office of the President of the United States.

6. Impeachment Trials The Senate shall have the sole power to try all impeachments. When sitting for that purpose, they shall be on oath or affirmation. When the President of the United States is tried, the Chief Justice shall preside; and no person shall be convicted without the concurrence of two-thirds of the members present.

7. Penalties Upon Conviction Judgment in cases of impeachment shall not extend further than to removal from office, and disqualification to hold and enjoy any office of honor, trust, or profit under the United States; but the party convicted shall nevertheless be liable and subject to indictment, trial, judgment, and punishment, according to law.

Section 4. Times of Elections and Meetings
1. Election of Congress The times, places, and manner of holding elections for Senators and Representatives shall be prescribed in

Clause 3 The qualifications for membership in the Senate are more restrictive than qualifications for membership in the House. The age qualifications must be met at the time the oath of office is taken.

Clause 4 The Vice President of the United States is the president of the Senate. As presiding officer, he or she applies the rules of the Senate. The president of the Senate may vote only to break a tie. The first Vice President, John Adams, cast 20 votes during his term in office. Besides filling a vacancy created by the President's death or resignation, these are the only powers the Constitution assigns to the Vice President.

Clause 5 *Pro tempore* means temporary. The president pro tempore must be a member of the Senate. He or she presides over the Senate in the absence of the Vice President. Under the Presidential Succession Act of 1947, the president pro tempore of the Senate follows the Vice President and the speaker of the House in the line of succession if the office of President becomes vacant.

Clause 6 The *Chief Justice* refers to the Chief Justice of the Supreme Court. By a majority vote the House may impeach the President and Vice President, federal judges, and cabinet officers for "treason, bribery, or other high crimes and misdemeanors." (See Article 2, Section 4.)
The Senate acts as a jury in impeachment cases. A two-thirds vote against the accused results in conviction. Although several federal judges have been convicted by the Senate, no President has ever been convicted. The House impeached President Andrew Johnson in 1868, but the Senate acquitted him of the charges (page 384). President Richard Nixon faced the possibility of impeachment and conviction, but his resignation ended the impeachment proceedings in progress (page 770).

Clause 7 *Judgment* in this clause means conviction by the Senate. Government officials convicted in impeachment proceedings are removed from office and barred from holding office in the future. The Senate does not have the power to impose any other penalty on convicted officials. However, they may be tried subsequently in criminal courts.

Clause 1 Under this clause the state legislatures are free to determine the time and manner of congressional elections unless Congress acts. Prior to 1842 Congress allowed the states to regulate congressional elections. In some states members of the House were chosen on a state-wide basis. In 1842 Congress required the states to create congressional districts. One representative was to be elected from each district. In 1872 Congress provided that congressional elections be held in every state on the same date in even-numbered years.

Clause 2 The Twentieth Amendment changed the date for the beginning of each congressional session to January 3 unless Congress resolves to meet on another day.

Clause 1 A *quorum* is the minimum number of members required to be present for the conduct of business. Each house of Congress has the right to decide the qualifications of its members. Until 1969 it was generally held that Congress could impose qualifications not specified in the Constitution. Thus some members have been barred from Congress because they were found to have engaged in misconduct.

For example, in 1967 the House of Representatives refused to seat Adam Clayton Powell of New York because of "gross misconduct." When Powell's suit challenging his exclusion reached the Supreme Court, the Court held that the Constitution does not permit Congress to exclude legally elected members who have met all the requirements specified in Article 1, Section 2.

Clause 2 This clause gives both houses of Congress wide power to conduct their business. The Senate, for example, has established rules for debate that allow *filibustering*, the practice of giving lengthy speeches for the purpose of obstructing pending legislation. In 1917 the Senate passed a *cloture* rule, a rule allowing the Senate to vote to stop a filibuster. The right to filibuster does not exist in the House.

Clause 3 The *Congressional Record*, published daily, prints all speeches made on the floor of the House and the Senate. It also records the votes cast.

Clause 4 Neither the House nor the Senate can adjourn for more than three days without the approval of the other body. This clause requires the two houses of Congress to meet in the same place. For example, the House cannot adjourn its session in Washington, D.C., and reconvene in another place.

Article 2, Section 3 gives the President the power to adjourn both houses of Congress if they cannot agree on a time to adjourn. To date the President has never exercised this power.

each state by the legislature thereof; but the Congress may at any time by law make or alter such regulations, except as to the places of choosing Senators.

2. Annual Sessions The Congress shall assemble at least once in every year, [and such meeting shall be on the first Monday in December, unless they shall by law appoint a different day.]

Section 5. Rules for the Conduct of Business

1. Organization Each house shall be the judge of the elections, returns, and qualifications of its own members, and a majority of each shall constitute a quorum to do business; but a smaller number may adjourn from day to day, and may be authorized to compel the attendance of absent members, in such manner, and under such penalties, as each house may provide.

2. Procedures Each house may determine the rules of its proceedings, punish its members for disorderly behavior, and with the concurrence of two-thirds, expel a member.

3. A Written Record Each house shall keep a journal of its proceedings, and from time to time publish the same, excepting such parts as may in their judgment require secrecy; and the yeas and nays of the members of either house on any question shall, at the desire of one-fifth of those present, be entered on the journal.

4. Rules for Adjournment Neither house, during the session of Congress, shall, without the consent of the other, adjourn for more than three days, nor to any other place than that in which the two houses shall be sitting.

Section 6. Privileges and Restrictions

1. Salaries and Immunities The Senators and Representatives shall receive a compensation for their services, to be ascertained by law and paid out of the Treasury of the United States. They shall in all cases, except treason, felony, and breach of the peace, be privileged from arrest during their attendance at the session of their respective houses, and in going to and returning from the same; and for any speech or debate in either house, they shall not be questioned in any other place.

Clause 1 The salary for members of Congress is set by an act of Congress. Members with special responsibilities, such as the speaker of the House, receive larger salaries.

This clause provides that when Congress is in session its members shall enjoy an immunity from arrest in civil cases. Thus the clause protects members of Congress from imprisonment for debt. The clause does not provide immunity from arrest in state or federal criminal cases.

A member of Congress is protected from libel and slander suits for things he or she says in Congress while it is in session. This provision also protects members of Congress from lawsuits concerning their written words. Immunity under the speech and debate provision does not extend to words spoken outside Congress.

2. Restrictions on Other Employment No Senator or Representative shall, during the time for which he was elected, be appointed to any civil office under the authority of the United States, which shall have been created, or the emoluments whereof shall have been increased, during such time; and no person holding any office under the United States shall be a member of either house during his continuance in office.

Clause 2 *Emolument* means salary. The first part of this clause bars a member of Congress from holding a federal office that was created or the salary of which was increased during his or her term in Congress. The second part of the clause prevents officeholders in the executive and judicial branches from serving in Congress. This provision strengthens the separation of powers.

Section 7. Law-Making Process

1. Tax Bills All bills for raising revenue shall originate in the House of Representatives; but the Senate may propose or concur with amendments as on other bills.

Clause 1 *Revenue* is income raised by a unit of government through taxation. Under this clause, federal revenue bills must originate in the House. This was a democratic measure because when the Constitution was written, the House was the only branch of government elected directly by the people. The Senate can amend revenue legislation. By custom, bills authorizing the expenditure of federal money also originate in the House.

2. How a Bill Becomes a Law Every bill which shall have passed the House of Representatives and the Senate shall, before it become a law, be presented to the President of the United States; if he approve, he shall sign it, but if not, he shall return it, with his objections, to that house in which it shall have originated, who shall enter the objections at large on their journal, and proceed to reconsider it. If after such reconsideration two-thirds of that house shall agree to pass the bill, it shall be sent, together with the objections, to the other house, by which it shall likewise be reconsidered, and, if approved by two-thirds of that house, it shall become a law. But in all such cases the votes of both houses shall be determined by yeas and nays, and the names of the persons voting for and against the bill shall be entered on the journal of each house

Clause 2 A *bill* is a proposal for a law. Bills passed by a majority of the House and Senate are presented to the President. If the President signs the bill it becomes law. A bill can also become law without the President's signature. The President can refuse to act on a bill. If Congress is in session at the time, the bill becomes law ten days after the President receives it.

The President can *veto*, or reject, a bill in two ways. He or she can veto it by sending it back to the house where it originated or by refusing to take any action on it. If the President withholds action and Congress adjourns within ten days of the President's receipt of the bill, the bill is dead. This method of killing a bill without taking action is known as the *pocket veto.*

A bill vetoed by the President can still become law if it is passed again by a two-thirds vote in each house of Congress. This clause is an important part of the system of checks and balances established by the Constitution (pages 166–167).

Clause 3 This clause was inserted to prevent Congress from bypassing the President by calling pieces of legislation resolutions rather than bills. *Joint resolutions* go through the same process as bills and have the force of law. Such resolutions are passed when there is no need for prolonged examination of a measure before Congress. For example, proposals to renew an existing piece of legislation sometimes take the form of a joint resolution.

Concurrent resolutions are the expression of the will of Congress. They are not submitted to the President and do not have the force of law. Changes in rules of legislative procedure typically take the form of concurrent resolutions. Congressional resolutions proposing constitutional amendments are not presented to the President.

Clause 1 *Duties* are tariffs, and *excises* are taxes on the production or sale of particular goods. *Imposts* refers to taxes generally. This clause gives Congress the power to tax and to spend tax revenues.

The clause does not give Congress unlimited taxation power. For example, Congress may not tax exports (see Section 9, Clause 5) or the activities of state governments. Until the ratification of the Sixteenth Amendment in 1913, Congress could not impose an income tax unless the tax was apportioned among the states according to population. Taxes under this clause must be imposed uniformly.

Clause 2 Congress may authorize the sale of bonds to the public to raise money for the operation of the government. The government thus borrows money from the bond holders. People and banks invest in bonds on the assumption that the government will meet its obligations to creditors. The Constitution sets no limit on the total indebtedness of the federal government.

Clause 3 This clause gives the federal government exclusive power to regulate foreign and interstate trade. For example, only the federal government may impose tariffs on foreign goods or regulate the freight rates of railroads crossing state lines. The so-called commerce clause provided the constitutional basis for the Interstate Commerce Act (page 451), the Sherman Antitrust Act (page 451), as well as other federal regulatory legislation.

Clause 4 *Naturalization* is the process by which a citizen of one country becomes a citizen of another country. This clause requires that the naturalization process be the same throughout the United States. A business or in-

respectively. If any bill shall not be returned by the President within ten days (Sundays excepted) after it shall have been presented to him, the same bill shall be a law, in like manner as if he had signed it, unless the Congress by their adjournment prevent its return, in which case it shall not be a law.

3. Resolutions Passed by Congress Every order, resolution, or vote to which the concurrence of the Senate and House of Representatives may be necessary (except on a question of adjournment) shall be presented to the President of the United States; and before the same shall take effect, shall be approved by him, or being disapproved by him, shall be repassed by two-thirds of the Senate and House of Representatives, according to the rules and limitations prescribed in the case of a bill.

Section 8. Powers Delegated to Congress
The Congress shall have power

1. To lay and collect taxes, duties, imposts, and excises, to pay the debts and provide for the common defense and general welfare of the United States; but all duties, imposts, and excises shall be uniform throughout the United States;

2. To borrow money on the credit of the United States;

3. To regulate commerce with foreign nations, and among the several states, and with the Indian tribes;

4. To establish a uniform rule of naturalization, and uniform laws on the subject of bankruptcies throughout the United States;

5. To coin money, regulate the value thereof, and of foreign coin, and fix the standard of weights and measures;

6. To provide for the punishment of counterfeiting the securities and current coin of the United States;

7. To establish post offices and post roads;

8. To promote the progress of science and useful arts by securing for limited times to authors and inventors the exclusive right to their respective writings and discoveries;

9. To constitute tribunals inferior to the Supreme Court;

10. To define and punish piracies and felonies committed on the high seas and offenses against the law of nations;

11. To declare war, [grant letters of marque and reprisal,] and make rules concerning captures on land and water;

dividual is *bankrupt* when it is unable to pay its debts. The clause empowers Congress to pass laws to supervise the collection of debts from bankrupt businesses or individuals.

Clause 5 Under this clause Congress is authorized to coin metallic currency. The clause also provides the legal basis for the printing of paper currency by the government. The government determines the metallic content of coins and the amount of gold and silver that backs printed currency. It also has the power to adjust the value of the dollar in relation to foreign currencies.

Clause 6 *Counterfeiting* is the act of making an unauthorized copy of United States currency for the purpose of using it as legal tender. Law enforcement agents from the Treasury Department investigate this crime.

Clause 7 By virtue of this clause Congress has the power to establish a government monopoly over delivery of mail.

Clause 8 Under this clause Congress may pass *copyright* laws that enable a person to register his or her work in the United States Copyright Office. Once copyrighted, a work may not be used or copied without the author's permission. A copyright registered prior to January 1978 lasts for 28 years and may be renewed for an additional 28 years. A copyright registered after January 1978 lasts for the author's lifetime plus 50 years.

The clause also allows Congress to enact legislation to protect the work of inventors. The government issues *patents* to people who invent new goods or manufacturing processes. An invention registered with the Patent Office may not be manufactured and sold without the permission of the patent holder. Patents for inventions last for 17 years.

Clause 9 Article 3, Section 1, establishes the Supreme Court. This clause gives Congress the power to create *inferior,* or lower, federal courts.

Clause 10 *Piracy* is robbery of ships on the high seas. Under this clause United States courts have jurisdiction over piracy cases even though the crime may have been committed outside national territorial limits.

Clause 11 *Letters of marque and reprisal* are documents issued by the government authorizing an armed merchant vessel to attack ships of an enemy nation.

Congress has the exclusive power to declare war. Declarations of war are granted upon request of the President. This procedure was followed in the War of 1812, the Spanish-American War, and the two world wars. But the United States has engaged in armed conflict without a congressional declaration of war, as in Korea and Vietnam. The legal basis of a war fought without congressional declaration is the President's authority as commander-in-chief (Article 2, Section 2, Clause 1) to order American forces into action. During the late 1960s and early 1970s the Supreme Court refused to review claims that challenged the constitutionality of the Vietnam War. The War Powers Act of 1973 placed restrictions on the

President's power to engage American forces without an official declaration of war (page 762).

Clauses 12, 13, 14 These clauses subordinate the military to the control of Congress. Congress determines the level of funding of the army and navy, and it has the power to fix the size of the armed forces. Although these clauses do not mention a military draft, the power "to raise and support armies" suggests the authority to establish a draft. Clause 14 empowers Congress to write a code governing military discipline.

Clauses 15, 16 *Militia* refers to the various state militias. The militia exists to protect the United States from insurrection and foreign invasion. Although the militia, now called the National Guard, is organized along state lines and is under the command of the governor of each state, it can be placed under the command of the President. President Eisenhower placed the Arkansas National Guard under federal control during the Little Rock school integration crisis (page 723).

Clause 17 This clause provides that the site of the nation's capital be outside the jurisdiction of any state. It calls upon the federal government to exercise full control over the district in which the capital is located. In 1790, after much discussion, Congress made Washington, D.C., the nation's capital (page 181). Congress has the power to legislate for Washington, D.C., but in 1973 it gave the district's residents the right to elect local officials.

Clause 18 The first 17 clauses in this section list the powers that the Constitution specifically delegates to Congress (page 164). The framers of the Constitution realized that Congress could not deal with the changing needs of the nation if it was limited to only those powers explicitly listed. They therefore added this clause. Under this clause Congress may pass legislation that is "necessary and proper" for implementing its delegated powers. It is sometimes called the elastic clause because it allows Congress to stretch the meaning of its delegated powers.

Clause 1 This clause, which deals with the importation of slaves, was the result of a compromise between supporters and defenders of the slave trade (pages 162–163). To satisfy slave owners, the Constitution barred Congress from immediately prohibiting the importation of slaves. But the Constitution did provide that Congress could prohibit the slave trade after 1808. The $10 import tax was never imposed. This clause is now obsolete.

12. To raise and support armies, but no appropriation of money to that use shall be for a longer term than two years;

13. To provide and maintain a navy;

14. To make rules for the government and regulation of the land and naval forces;

15. To provide for calling forth the militia to execute the laws of the Union, suppress insurrections, and repel invasions;

16. To provide for organizing, arming, and disciplining the militia, and for governing such part of them as may be employed in the service of the United States, reserving to the states, respectively, the appointment of the officers, and the authority of training the militia according to the discipline prescribed by Congress;

17. To exercise exclusive legislation in all cases whatsoever, over such district (not exceeding ten miles square) as may, by cession of particular states, and the acceptance of Congress, become the seat of government of the United States, and to exercise like authority over all places purchased by the consent of the legislature of the state in which the same shall be, for the erection of forts, magazines, arsenals, dock-yards, and other needful buildings;—and

18. To make all laws which shall be necessary and proper for carrying into execution the foregoing powers, and all other powers vested by this Constitution in the government of the United States, or in any department or officer thereof.

Section 9. Powers Denied to the Federal Government

1. The Slave Trade [The migration or importation of such persons as any of the states now existing shall think proper to admit shall not be prohibited by the Congress prior to the year 1808; but a tax or duty may be imposed on such importation, not exceeding $10 for each person.]

2. Writ of Habeas Corpus The privilege of the writ of *habeas corpus* shall not be suspended, unless when in cases of rebellion or invasion the public safety may require it.

Clause 2 A *writ* is a court order directing an action. A *writ of habeas corpus* is a court order directing government officials to bring a prisoner to court and explain why he or she is being held. The writ of habeas corpus is an important safeguard against unlawful imprisonment. A judge can order the release of a prisoner if he or she finds that there are insufficient grounds for the prisoner's detention.

The clause allows for the suspension of the writ of habeas corpus in times of rebellion or invasion. But it does not state which branch of government has the power to suspend the writ. In 1861, in the case of *ex parte Merryman*, Chief Justice of the Supreme Court Roger B. Taney ruled that Congress, not the President, has the power to suspend the writ of habeas corpus. Congress subsequently passed legislation authorizing the President to suspend the writ. President Abraham Lincoln suspended the writ of habeas corpus during the Civil War.

3. Bills of Attainder and Ex Post Facto Laws No bill of attainder or *ex post facto* law shall be passed.

Clause 3 A *bill of attainder* is a legislative act declaring that a person is guilty of a particular crime. *Ex post facto* laws impose penalties on acts that were committed when the conduct was not forbidden by law.

Bills of attainder punish the accused without giving him or her the benefit of a trial by jury. For example, during World War II Congress prohibited the payment of salaries to three government officials accused of being unpatriotic. In 1946 the Supreme Court nullified the act, holding that the legislation constituted a bill of attainder. Legislation requiring communists to register with the government, however, has been held not to constitute a bill of attainder.

There have been many court decisions explaining what constitutes an ex post facto law. For example, in 1972 a United States district court held that a law barring the payment of government pensions to persons previously found guilty of *perjury,* or lying under oath, in national security matters constituted an ex post facto law and thus could not be enforced. In this case the people claiming the pensions had not been federal employees at the time the pension law was passed.

4. Apportionment of Direct Taxes [No capitation or other direct tax shall be laid, unless in proportion to the census or enumeration herein before directed to be taken.]

Clause 4 A *capitation tax* is a tax levied directly on each person. Direct taxes, according to this clause, can be imposed only if they are divided among the states according to population. The Sixteenth Amendment gives Congress the right establish an income tax without regard to the population of the states.

5. Taxes on Exports No tax or duty shall be laid on articles exported from any state.

Clause 5 Congress is explicitly barred from taxing exports. The clause was inserted at the insistence of southern states, since their economies depended on exporting agricultural products (page 163).

6. Special Preference for Trade No preference shall be given any regulation of commerce or revenue to the ports of one state over those of another; nor shall vessels bound to, or from, one state, be obliged to enter, clear, or pay duties in another.

Clause 6 To *enter* means to report to the customs house. A vessel is *cleared* when it obtains the proper documents at the customs house. The clause bars Congress from passing legislation that would promote the commerce of one state to the disadvantage of others. It also prohibits states from imposing tariffs on interstate commerce.

Clause 7 The federal government may not spend any money unless Congress has authorized its expenditure. Thus the President is prohibited from drawing money from the treasury for programs that have not been approved by Congress. This power provides Congress with an important check on the President.

Whether the President must spend money authorized by Congress is unclear. For example, President Lyndon Johnson refused to release federal aid for highway funds to the states, and President Richard Nixon refused to spend food stamp money appropriated by Congress. The refusal of the President to spend money authorized by Congress is called *impoundment.*

Clause 8 Meeting at a time when feeling against monarchy ran high, the framers inserted a clause prohibiting the government from awarding titles of nobility. American citizens are not allowed to accept titles of nobility from foreign governments without the consent of Congress. Consistent with the provisions of this clause, Congress has passed legislation permitting government officials to receive small gifts from foreign officials. But gifts that exceed "minimal value" must be accepted in behalf of the United States and become the property of the nation.

Clause 1 See Article 1, Section 8, Clause 11, for letters of marque and reprisal. Some of the powers denied to the states are similarly denied to the federal government. The prohibition against bills of attainder, ex post facto laws, and the creation of titles of nobility fall into this category.

Other prohibitions apply only to the states. For example, the states are barred from making treaties and coining money. The framers of the Constitution feared the prospect of a nation divided by conflicting diplomatic obligations and separate currencies. The obligations of contracts provision bars a state from nullifying valid contracts, that is, from declaring them void.

The prohibitions listed in this clause are unconditional. Congress cannot pass a law granting these powers to the states.

Clauses 2, 3 Powers listed in Clauses 2 and 3 are denied to the states, but Congress can lift the prohibitions by passing appropriate legislation.

Clause 2 bars the states from taxing imports and exports unless permitted by Congress. The clause allows the states to charge inspection fees on goods entering the states if approved by Congress. Fees collected by the states must be turned over to the United States Treasury.

Tonnage refers to the carrying capacity of a ship. A duty on tonnage would be based on a ship's cargo capacity. States may not impose tonnage taxes unless authorized by Congress.

Clause 3 forbids the states to maintain an army and navy without the consent of Congress. The states are similarly barred from entering into agreements with foreign nations or engaging in war unless the threat of invasion is imminent.

7. Spending No money shall be drawn from the Treasury, but in consequence of appropriations made by law; and a regular statement and account of the receipts and expenditures of all public money shall be published from time to time.

8. Creation of Titles of Nobility No title of nobility shall be granted by the United States; and no person holding any office of profit or trust under them, shall, without the consent of the Congress, accept of any present, emolument, office, or title, of any kind whatever, from any king, prince, or foreign state.

Section 10. Powers Denied to the States

1. Unconditional Prohibitions No state shall enter into any treaty, alliance, or confederation; grant letters of marque and reprisal; coin money; emit bills of credit; make anything but gold and silver coin a tender in payment of debts; pass any bill of attainder, *ex post facto* law, or law impairing the obligation of contracts, or grant any title of nobility.

2. Powers Conditionally Denied No state shall, without the consent of the Congress, lay any imposts or duties on imports or exports, except what may be absolutely necessary for executing its inspection laws; and the net produce of all duties and imposts, laid by any state on imports or exports, shall be for the use of the Treasury of the United States; and all such laws shall be subject to the revision and control of the Congress.

3. Other Denied Powers No state shall, without the consent of Congress, lay any duty of tonnage, keep troops, or ships of war in time of peace, enter into any agreement or compact with another state, or with a foreign power, or engage in war, unless actually invaded, or in such imminent danger as will not admit of delay.

Article 2. The Executive Branch

Section 1. President and Vice-President

1. Chief Executive The executive power shall be vested in a President of the United States of America. He shall hold his office during the term of four years, and together with the Vice-President, chosen for the same term, be elected as follows:

2. Selection of Electors Each state shall appoint, in such manner as the legislature thereof may direct, a number of electors, equal to the whole number of Senators and Representatives to which the state may be entitled in the Congress; but no Senator or Representative, or person holding an office or trust or profit under the United States, shall be appointed an elector.

3. Electoral College Procedures [The electors shall meet in their respective states, and vote by ballot for two persons, of whom one at least shall not be an inhabitant of the same state with themselves. And they shall make a list of all the persons voted for, and of the number of votes for each; which list they shall sign and certify, and transmit sealed to the seat of the government of the United States, directed to the president of the Senate. The president of the Senate shall, in the presence of the Senate and House of Representatives, open all the certificates, and the votes shall then be counted. The person having the greatest number of votes shall be the President, if such number be a majority of the whole number of electors appointed; and if there be more than one who have such majority, and have an equal number of votes, then the House of Representatives shall immediately choose by ballot one of them for President; and if no person have a majority, then from the five highest on the list the said House shall in like manner choose the President. But in choosing the President the votes shall be taken by states, the representation from each state having one vote. A quorum for this purpose shall consist of a member or members from two-thirds of the states, and a majority of all the states shall be necessary to a choice. In every case, after the choice of the President, the person having the greatest number of votes of the electors shall be the Vice-President. But if there should remain two

Clause 1 As chief executive the President is responsible for enforcing laws passed by Congress. Whether the President has additional power as chief executive has been a matter of dispute. President Theodore Roosevelt believed that the President could do "anything that the needs of the nation demanded unless such action was forbidden by the Constitution and the law." Others have argued that the authority of the chief executive should be limited to enforcing the law. See Article 2, Section 2, for a further discussion of the powers of the President.

Clauses 2, 3 Some of the framers of the Constitution feared allowing the people to elect the President directly (pages 167–168). Consequently, the Constitutional Convention established the electoral college. According to Clause 2 each state's electoral vote is to equal its combined number of senators and representatives. The states may decide the procedure for selecting electors. Members of Congress and federal officeholders are barred from serving as electors. This much of the original electoral college system is still in effect.

Clause 3 called upon each elector to vote for two candidates without designating one for President and one for Vice President. The candidate who received the most electoral votes (provided it was a majority) would become President. In cases in which no candidate won a majority of the electoral vote, the House would choose the President, and the Senate would choose the Vice President.

The election of 1800 revealed a defect in the original electoral college system (page 193). Thomas Jefferson was the presidential candidate of the Republican party, and Aaron Burr was the vice presidential candidate. But since the vote ended in a tie, either could have become President. The House finally elected Jefferson. The Twelfth Amendment altered electoral college procedures.

or more who have equal votes, the Senate shall choose from them by ballot the Vice-President.]

4. Time of Elections The Congress may determine the time of choosing the electors, and the day on which they shall give their votes; which day shall be the same throughout the United States.

Clause 4 According to legislation passed in 1792 electors are chosen on the Tuesday following the first Monday of November every four years. Congress has required that the electors of each state meet to cast their ballots on the first Monday after the second Wednesday in December, following the election in November. The votes of the electoral college are counted in the House of Representatives on January 6.

Today voters in each state cast ballots for slates of electors pledged to presidential candidates. The candidate receiving most of a state's popular vote wins that state's electoral vote. Neither the Constitution nor federal law requires electors to vote for the candidate to whom they are pledged. However, according to custom, electors nearly always do so. Thus the general election in November settles the issue of who will be the next President, and the balloting in December attracts little interest.

Clause 5 The first seven Presidents of the United States could not claim to be natural-born citizens of the United States, because they were born subjects of the British crown. But they qualified for the presidency because they were citizens "of the United States at the time of the adoption of this Constitution."

Although the issue has never been resolved by the courts, scholarly opinion suggests that the children of American citizens born abroad meet the citizenship requirements of this clause. Note that natural-born and native-born are not identical terms. A child of American parents who is born abroad is a natural- but not a native-born citizen of the United States.

5. Qualifications for President No person except a natural-born citizen [or a citizen of the United States, at the time of the adoption of this Constitution], shall be eligible to the office of the President; neither shall any person be eligible to that office who shall not have attained to the age of thirty-five years, and been fourteen years a resident within the United States.

Clause 6 This clause states that the powers of the President shall pass to the Vice President if the President leaves office or is unable to discharge the duties of the office. The language of this clause caused confusion the first time a President died in office. When President William Henry Harrison died, it was uncertain whether Vice President John Tyler should remain Vice President and simply act as President or actually be sworn in as President. Tyler persuaded a federal judge to swear him in, and the precedent was created that the Vice President assumes the office of President when that office becomes vacant. The Twenty-fifth Amendment superseded this clause.

6. Presidential Succession In case of the removal of the President from office, or of his death, resignation, or inability to discharge the powers and duties of the said office, the same shall devolve on the Vice-President, and the Congress may by law provide for the case of removal, death, resignation, or inability, both of the President and Vice-President, declaring what officer shall then act as President, and such officer shall act accordingly, until the disability be removed, or a President shall be elected.

Clause 7 In 1983 the President received a salary of $200,000. The Constitution prohibits the salary from being increased or decreased during a President's term. This clause bars the President from accepting any other federal or state position during his or her term in office.

7. Salary The President shall, at stated times, receive for his services, a compensation, which shall neither be increased nor diminished during the period for which he shall have been elected, and he shall not receive within that period any other emolument from the United States, or any of them.

Clause 8 By custom the presidential oath is administered by the Chief Justice of the Supreme Court. But this has not always been the case. After President John Kennedy's assassination, Vice President Lyndon Johnson was sworn in by a federal district judge.

8. The Oath of Office Before he enter on the execution of his office, he shall take the following oath or affirmation:—"I do solemnly swear (or affirm) that I will faithfully execute the office of President of the United States, and will to the best of my ability, preserve, protect, and defend the Constitution of the United States."

Section 2. Powers of the President

1. Commander in Chief of the Armed Forces The President shall be Commander in Chief of the Army and Navy of the United States, and of the militia of the several states, when called into the actual service of the United States; he may require the option, in writing, of the principal officer in each of the executive departments, upon any subject relating to the duties of their respective offices, and he shall have power to grant reprieves and pardons for offenses against the United States, except in cases of impeachment.

2. Making Treaties and Nominations He shall have power, by and with the advice and consent of the Senate, to make treaties, provided two-thirds of the Senators present concur; and he shall nominate, and by and with the advice and consent of the Senate, shall appoint ambassadors, other public ministers and consuls, judges of the Supreme Court, and all other officers of the United States, whose appointments are not herein otherwise provided for, and which shall be established by law; but the Congress may by law vest the appointment of such inferior officers, as they think proper, in the President alone, in the courts of law, or in the heads of departments.

3. Temporary Appointments The President shall have power to fill up all vacancies that may happen during the recess of the Senate, by granting commissions which shall expire at the end of their next session.

Clause 1 This clause, combined with the provisions outlining congressional control over the military (see Article 1, Section 8, Clauses 11–15), established the principle of civilian control of the armed forces. Although the President may not serve in the armed forces while in office, he or she occupies the highest position in the military chain of command. President Harry Truman exercised the principle of civilian control of the military during the Korean War. He relieved General Douglas MacArthur of his command after MacArthur criticized Truman's handling of the war (page 704).

Since President Lincoln's administration, the definition of the commander-in-chief's powers has expanded beyond narrowly military actions. For example, Lincoln based his issuance of the Emancipation Proclamation on this power (page 363). During World War II President Franklin Roosevelt supervised labor relations, claiming that his power as commander-in-chief enabled him to impose sanctions on employers and employees who threatened industrial peace.

A *reprieve* suspends punishment prescribed by law. A *pardon* issued before trial bars prosecution. If a pardon is issued after conviction, it wipes out the judgment of the court. The President may not issue pardons in impeachment cases. President Gerald Ford's pardon of Richard Nixon barred the government from prosecuting the former President for possible criminal offenses (page 771). Because Nixon had already resigned from office, impeachment was no longer an issue.

Clause 2 As a part of the system of checks and balances, this clause requires that treaties negotiated by the President be approved by two thirds of the Senate. The Senate defeat of the Versailles Treaty in 1919 illustrates the President's dependence on the consent of the Senate (page 563).

Executive agreements made with foreign heads of state are not subject to Senate approval. For example, President Franklin Roosevelt bypassed the Senate in the 1940 bases-for-destroyers deal with Britain. Roosevelt declared that his power as commander-in-chief enabled him to execute that agreement. The Supreme Court has sanctioned executive agreements as a valid exercise of presidential power.

This clause also requires that the President's appointments to high public office be confirmed by the Senate. Most presidential appointments are routinely confirmed, but the Senate refused to confirm two of President Nixon's nominations to the Supreme Court.

Clause 3 If the Senate is recessed, the President may fill high government posts with temporary appointments.

This section has helped make the President a legislative leader. The President has the power to recommend the enactment of legislation. Section 3 requires the President to give a state of the union address to Congress. This address is given in January, and since 1913 it has been delivered in person by the President.

The provision empowering the President to receive ambassadors and other public ministers, together with the powers to command the armed forces and negotiate treaties, gives him or her a predominant role in shaping foreign policy.

This section also requires that the President "take care that the laws be faithfully executed." President Dwight Eisenhower's dispatch of troops to Little Rock, Arkansas, during the 1957 school integration crisis was an application of this principle (page 723). Administration of programs created by Congress is a primary example of the President's execution of the law.

Civil officers include federal judges and members of the cabinet. The role of Congress in the impeachment and removal process is discussed in Article 1, Section 2, Clauses 6 and 7.

The term *high crimes and misdemeanors* is ambiguous. When applied to the impeachment of judges, the phrase has included violations of particular laws as well as general noncriminal misconduct. Because only one President—Andrew Johnson—has been impeached, the courts have not had occasion to decide whether "high crimes and misdemeanors" must include violations of law when applied to impeachment of a President. During the Watergate affair President Nixon's lawyers insisted that impeachable offenses must be violations of law. But some members of the House argued that noncriminal misconduct could provide the basis for impeachment.

Judicial refers to the courts. The Constitution created the Supreme Court, but it does not specify the size of the Court, nor does it establish additional federal courts. The framers left these tasks to Congress. This section does provide, however, that all federal judges shall serve for life, dependent upon good behavior.

According to the Judiciary Act of 1789 the membership of the Supreme Court was fixed at six (nine justices now sit on the Court), and a system of lower courts was established (page 180). Congress created 13 district courts and three courts of appeals. Today there are 94 district courts and 13 courts of appeals.

District courts conduct trials of criminal and civil cases. Courts of appeals hear claims that a district court committed errors in the conduct of a trial or pretrial proceedings. While the Congress may abolish the district courts or courts of appeals, it may not abolish the Supreme Court.

Clause 1 *Jurisdiction* refers to the right of a court to hear a case. The distinction between courts of law and courts of equity is now largely obsolete. Federal courts can decide only cases brought by parties to a lawsuit. Federal courts cannot make rules of law when no lawsuit exists.

Section 3. Duties

He shall from time to time give to the Congress information of the state of the Union, and recommend to their consideration such measures as he shall judge necessary and expedient; he may, on extraordinary occasions, convene both houses, or either of them, and in case of disagreement between them, with respect to the time of adjournment, he may adjourn them to such time as he shall think proper; he shall receive ambassadors and other public ministers; he shall take care that the laws be faithfully executed, and shall commission all the officers of the United States.

Section 4. Impeachment and Removal From Office

The President, Vice-President, and all civil officers of the United States, shall be removed from office on impeachment for, and conviction of, treason, bribery, or other high crimes and misdemeanors.

Article 3. The Judicial Branch

Section 1. Federal Courts

The judicial power of the United States shall be vested in one Supreme Court, and in such inferior courts as the Congress may from time to time ordain and establish. The judges, both of the Supreme and inferior courts, shall hold their offices during good behavior, and shall, at stated times, receive for their services a compensation, which shall not be diminished during their continuance in office.

Section 2. Jurisdiction of Federal Courts

1. Scope of Judicial Power The judicial power shall extend to all cases, in law and equity, arising under this Constitution, the laws of the United States, and treaties made or which shall be made, under their authority; to all cases affecting ambassadors, other public ministers and consuls; to all cases of admiralty and maritime jurisdiction; to controversies to which the United States shall be a party; to controversies between two or more states; [between a state and citizens of another state;] between citizens of the same state claiming lands under grants of different states, and between a state or the citizens thereof, and foreign states, citizens, or subjects.

2. The Supreme Court In all cases affecting ambassadors, other public ministers and consuls, and those in which a state shall be a party, the Supreme Court shall have original jurisdiction. In all the other cases before mentioned, the Supreme Court shall have appellate jurisdiction, both as to law and fact, with such exceptions, and under such regulations as the Congress shall make.

3. Trial by Jury The trial of all crimes, except in cases of impeachment, shall be by jury; and such trial shall be held in the state where the said crimes shall have been committed; but when not committed within any state, the trial shall be at such place or places as the Congress may by law have directed.

Section 3. Treason
1. Definition Treason against the United States shall consist only in levying war against them, or in adhering to their enemies, giving them aid and comfort. No person shall be convicted of treason unless on the testimony of two witnesses to the same overt act, or on confession in open court.

2. Punishment The Congress shall have power to declare the punishment of treason, but no attainder of treason shall work corruption of blood or forfeiture except during the life of the person attainted.

Federal courts are empowered to hear cases *under this Constitution.* This means that the federal judiciary can determine the constitutionality of acts of Congress and state legislatures as well as of actions of the President and other government officials.

The right of a court to rule on the constitutionality of laws and and official acts is known as *judicial review.* Already exercised by the state courts, the doctrine was reaffirmed in *Marbury* v. *Madison* (page 198), when the Supreme Court held that "a legislative act, contrary to the Constitution, is not law." Federal courts also have jurisdiction in cases involving ambassadors and cases in which the United States is a party. The provision allowing federal jurisdiction in cases "between a State and citizens of another State" has been modified by the Eleventh Amendment.

Clause 2 *Original jurisdiction* refers to the power of a court to hear a case when it originates. Typically courts of original jurisdiction find the facts of a case and determine the issue of guilt or liability. Courts of *appellate jurisdiction* do not decide the question of guilt or liability. They review claims that a lower court judge made legal errors in conducting the trial or pretrial proceedings.

Under this clause the Supreme Court exercises original jurisdiction over a narrow range of cases: disputes in which a state is involved and cases involving ambassadors or public ministers. In recent times the Supreme Court has exercised its original jurisdiction infrequently. Instead it functions almost exclusively as an appellate court.

Clause 3 This clause does not guarantee trial by jury in *civil cases,* legal disputes that do not involve allegations of criminal wrongdoing. Nor does it require the states to provide jury trials. The clause applies to federal criminal prosecutions. See the Sixth Amendment for a more extended discussion fo the right to trial by jury.

Clause 1 An *overt act* refers to a concrete action, not merely a state of mind.

Clause 2 This clause allows Congress to punish traitors, but it forbids punishment of the traitor's children for the crime of the parent. *Attainder* refers to the loss of rights that accompanies conviction for a serious crime. Under English law, attainder of treason was transmitted to the children of traitors. In England, corruption of blood meant that the children of criminals could not inherit or retain property owned by the parents. Such a punishment is prohibited by this clause, and it has been abolished in England.

The purpose of this section is to guarantee that the official records and acts of one state are recognized by the other states. For example, the section requires a state to recognize valid marriage certificates issued by another state.

Clause 1 Despite this clause, the Constitution, as interpreted by the courts, does not forbid state residence requirements for lower tuition rates, and for hunting, fishing, and professional licenses.

Clause 2 *Extradition* is the process of returning an alleged criminal or fugitive found in one state to the state in which he or she is sought. The Supreme Court has ruled that federal courts are powerless to order a governor to extradite a fugitive from justice. The court interpreted this clause to mean that governors may deliver an escaped criminal to the authorities of another state but are not required to do so.

Clause 3 *Person held to service or labor* refers to slaves and indentured servants. This clause required states to return runaway slaves to their owners. See pages 338–339 for a discussion of the fugitive slave controversy. The Thirteenth Amendment nullified this clause.

Clause 1 This clause gives Congress the power to admit new states. However, Congress does not have unrestricted authority to set conditions for admission. For example, when Oklahoma applied for admission to the Union, Congress made the location of the state capital a condition for admission. In *Coyle* v. *Smith* (1911), the Supreme Court held that Congress may not set admission requirements in areas exclusively under state control.

Clause 2 Congress can make rules for the administration of land owned by the United States. This includes territories not organized into states and federal land located within a state. See pages 151–152 for a description of how Congress administered the Northwest Territory. The Supreme Court has prohibited states from taxing federal property.

Article 4. Relations Among the States

Section 1. Official Records and Acts
Full faith and credit shall be given in each state to the public acts, records, and judicial proceedings of every other state. And the Congress may by general laws prescribe the manner in which such acts, records, and proceedings shall be proved, and the effect thereof.

Section 2. Privileges and Rights of Citizens
1. Privileges The citizens of each state shall be entitled to all privileges and immunities of citizens in the several states.

2. Extradition A person charged in any state with treason, felony, or other crime, who shall flee from justice, and be found in another state, shall on demand of the executive authority of the state from which he fled, be delivered up, to be removed to the state having jurisdiction of the crime.

3. Return of Fugitive Slaves [No person held to service or labor in one state, under the laws thereof, escaping into another, shall in consequence of any law or regulation therein, be discharged from such service or labor, but shall be delivered up on claim of the party to whom such service or labor may be due.]

Section 3. Admission of States and Governing Territories
1. New States New states may be admitted by the Congress into this Union; but no new state shall be formed or erected within the jurisdiction of any other state; nor any state be formed by the junction of two or more states, or parts of states, without the consent of the legislatures of the states concerned as well as of the Congress.

2. Federal Lands The Congress shall have power to dispose of and make all needful rules and regulations respecting the territory or other property belonging to the United States; and nothing in this Constitution shall be so construed as to prejudice any claims of the United States, or of any particular state.

Section 4. Guarantees to the States

The United States shall guarantee to every state in this Union a republican form of government, and shall protect each of them against invasion; and on application of the legislature, or of the executive (when the legislature cannot be convened) against domestic violence.

A *republic* is a form of government in which the voters have supreme authority and power is exercised by elected representatives. According to this section the United States government must protect the existence of a republican form of government in every state. The federal government must also protect the states from foreign invasion and supply armed forces to suppress disorder when asked to do so by a state. The President may also, on his or her own initiative, send troops to a state to enforce the laws and preserve order. See Article 2, Section 2, Clause 1.

Article 5. Amendment of the Constitution

The Congress, whenever two-thirds of both houses shall deem it necessary, shall propose amendments to this Constitution, or, on the application of the legislatures of two-thirds of the several states, shall call a convention for proposing amendments, which, in either case, shall be valid to all intents and purposes, as part of this Constitution, when ratified by the legislatures of three-fourths of the several states, or by conventions in three-fourths thereof, as the one or the other mode of ratification may be proposed by the Congress; provided that [no amendments which may be made prior to the year 1808 shall in any manner affect the first and fourth clauses in the Ninth Section of the First Article; and that] no state, without its consent, shall be deprived of its equal suffrage in the Senate.

This article provides that amendments to the Constitution can be proposed by a two-thirds vote of both houses of Congress or by a national convention called by Congress at the request of two thirds of the state legislatures. No amendment has ever been proposed by the latter method. Proposed constitutional amendments can be ratified either by the legislatures of three fourths of the states or by three fourths of special state conventions. The latter method has been used only once. Congress determines by which method a proposed amendment will be ratified.

The Constitution does not specify the period of time in which a proposed amendment must be ratified. However, Congress may establish a time limit for ratification. Since the passage of the Twentieth Amendment, Congress has provided that proposed amendments will be void unless ratified within seven years. Such a limitation has been upheld by the Supreme Court.

In October 1978 Congress extended the ratification deadline for the proposed Equal Rights Amendment. The constitutionality of that resolution is the subject of debate. The question of whether a state may rescind, or withdraw, its ratification of an amendment is also disputed. Several state legislatures rescinded their approval of the proposed Equal Rights Amendment, but the legality of the action has not yet been determined by the Supreme Court.

Article 6. Other Provisions

Section 1. Prior Public Debts

All debts contracted and engagements entered into, before the adoption of this Constitution, shall be as valid against the United States under this Constitution, as under the Confederation.

According to this clause the United States government agreed to pay debts incurred prior to the adoption of the Constitution.

Section 2. Supreme Law of the Land

This Constitution, and the laws of the United States which shall be made in pursuance thereof, and all treaties made, or which shall be made, under the authority of the United States, shall be the supreme law of the land; and the judges in every state shall be bound thereby, anything in the constitution or

This section makes the Constitution, acts of Congress, and treaties ratified by the Senate the "supreme law of the land." The Supreme Court has held that a state may not regulate the operation of any federal activity. For example, a state may not examine the qualifications of federal mail truck drivers, nor may it impose dietary standards in federal institutions.

The section requires state judges to strike down state laws that conflict with the Constitution or an act of Congress. State courts are bound by the decisions of the United States Supreme Court, although the extent to which they must follow the rulings of lower federal courts is less clear.

State and federal officeholders must take an oath to support the Constitution. Person whose conscience does not permit the swearing of oaths may affirm their support of the Constitution.

During the colonial period England and all the colonies except Rhode Island imposed a religious test for the holding of public office. Typically, the religious test required an officeholder to profess belief in the faith of one of the Protestant denominations. Intent on barring this practice in the United States, the framers of the Constitution provided that religious affiliation may not be a qualification for office holding.

During 1787 and 1788 the states held conventions to ratify the Constitution. By October 1788 the required nine states had ratified the Constitution. The Constitution went into effect on the first Wednesday of March 1789.

laws of any state to the contrary notwithstanding.

Section 3. Oaths to Support the Constitution

The Senators and Representatives before mentioned, and the members of the several state legislatures, and all executive and judicial officers, both of the United States and of the several states, shall be bound by oath or affirmation, to support this Constitution; but no religious test shall ever be required as a qualification to any office or public trust under the United States.

Article 7. Ratification

The ratification of the convention of nine states shall be sufficient for the establishment of the Constitution between the states so ratifying the same.

Done in Convention, by the unanimous consent of the states present, the seventeenth day of September, in the year of our Lord one thousand seven hundred and eighty-seven, and of the independence of the United States of America the twelfth. *In Witness* whereof, we have hereunto subscribed our names.

Attest:

William Jackson,
Secretary

George Washington,
President and Deputy from Virginia

New Hampshire
John Langdon
Nicholas Gilman

Massachusetts
Nathaniel Gorham
Rufus King

Connecticut
William Samuel Johnson
Roger Sherman

New York
Alexander Hamilton

New Jersey
William Livingston
David Brearley
William Paterson
Jonathan Dayton

Pennsylvania
Benjamin Franklin
Thomas Mifflin
Robert Morris
George Clymer
Thomas Fitzsimons
Jared Ingersoll
James Wilson
Gouverneur Morris

Delaware
George Read
Gunning Bedford, Jr.
John Dickinson
Richard Bassett
Jacob Broom

Maryland
James McHenry
Dan of St. Thomas Jennifer
Daniel Carroll

Virginia
John Blair
James Madison, Jr.

North Carolina
William Blount
Richard Dobbs Spaight
Hugh Williamson

South Carolina
John Rutledge
Charles Cotesworth Pinckney
Charles Pinckney
Pierce Butler

Georgia
William Few
Abraham Baldwin

The Constitution

Amendments to the Constitution

The first ten amendments, which were added to the Constitution in 1791, are called the Bill of Rights. Originally the Bill of Rights applied only to actions of the federal government. However, the Supreme Court has used the due process clause of the Fourteenth Amendment to extend many of the rights to protect individuals against action by the states.

Amendment 1. Freedoms of Religion, Speech, Press, Assembly, and Petition

Congress shall make no law respecting an establishment of religion, or prohibiting the free exercise thereof; or abridging the freedom of speech, or of the press; or the right of the people peaceably to assemble, and to petition the government for a redress of grievances.

The First Amendment prohibits the government from *abridging*, or limiting, freedom of expression. Freedom of the press protects all forms of the press from government control or censorship. Freedom of assembly is the right to peaceably gather to express a point of view. *Petition* refers to the expression of complaints directly to government officials. *Redress* means to set right, or correct. Americans have the right to present grievances to the government and ask that the source of the grievances be eliminated.

An *established religion* is one that is officially recognized by a government and has privileges denied other denominations. During the colonial period, established churches were common (page 70). The authors of the First Amendment wanted to separate government and religion. Defining the government's proper relationship to religion, however, has presented problems for the courts. The Supreme Court has upheld state aid for the transportation of students to parochial schools, but it has invalidated devotional Bible reading in public schools. The First Amendment also bars government restriction on the *free exercise of religion*. This means, in part, that the state cannot penalize an individual for the exercise of his or her religious beliefs.

Determining the range of conduct protected by the free speech clause has been an important task of the courts. In *Schenk* v. *United States* (1919) the Court upheld Schenk's conviction for distributing antidraft pamphlets during World War I. It ruled that Schenk's actions presented a "clear and present danger" to the United States. In the absence of "clear and present danger" the courts have generally not upheld restrictions on freedom of speech.

Amendment 2. Right to Bear Arms

A well-regulated militia, being necessary to the security of a free state, the right of the people to keep and bear arms shall not be infringed.

This amendment guarantees the right of a state militia to keep weapons. Courts have generally ruled that government can regulate the ownership of weapons by private citizens.

Amendment 3. Lodging Troops in Private Homes

No soldier shall, in time of peace, be quartered in any house, without the consent of the owner; nor in time of war, but in a manner to be prescribed by law.

During the colonial period the British lodged soldiers in private homes without the consent of the owners (page 105). This amendment restricts the government's right to use private residences as military barracks.

This amendment protects Americans from unreasonable searches and seizures. A reasonable search is defined as one authorized by a judge who issues a search warrant. A warrant is issued only if there is *probable cause*. This means that it is likely the search will produce evidence that a particular crime has been committed. A warrant must specify the exact place to be searched and the things to be seized.

Courts have ruled that in some cases searches are permissible without a warrant. For example, courts have held that police may search a person who is under arrest. The Supreme Court has also upheld the right of police to stop and search a person if the officer reasonably concludes that the suspect may be armed. Furthermore, a warrant is not need if a person freely consents to a search.

The Supreme Court has ruled that items discovered in the course of an unlawful search may not be used as evidence against the accused during trial for a criminal offense. This ban is called the *exclusionary rule*.

A *capital* crime is one for which the penalty may be death. An *infamous* crime is one punishable by imprisonment or loss of political privileges. According to the Fifth Amendment prosecutions of both types of crimes in federal court must be based on the accusation of a grand jury. The *grand jury*, a panel of between 12 and 23 citizens, may issue an *indictment*, or accusation, at the request of the public prosecutor. *Presentments*, now rarely used, are grand jury accusations not sought by the public prosecutor.

Double jeopardy is forbidden by the Fifth Amendment. This means that an accused person may not be tried twice for the same crime. The double jeopardy rule does not bar prosecution when the original conviction was set aside by an appellate court.

This amendment also prohibits the government from forcing accused persons to testify against themselves. Thus an accused person may not be required to testify in his or her own defense during trial. Nor can the prosecutor suggest to the jury that failure to testify is a sign of guilt.

Due process refers to fair procedure. In the context of criminal procedure, due process includes the right of the accused to be heard, to be represented by a lawyer, and to confront prosecution witnesses. In noncriminal matters, due process requires authorities to provide a forum in which the affected individual can be heard. The last provision of the amendment bars the government from seizing private property without compensating the owner.

The Sixth Amendment does not require a trial by jury in cases in which the maximum punishment is six months in prison or less, or in cases in military courts. Although juries traditionally have 12 members, convictions by six-person juries have been upheld by the courts. The amendment does not require unanimous verdicts.

Amendment 4. Search and Seizure

The right of the people to be secure in their persons, houses, papers, and effects, against unreasonable searches and seizures, shall not be violated; and no warrants shall issue but upon probable cause, supported by oath or affirmation, and particularly describing the place to be searched, and the persons or things to be seized.

Amendment 5. Rights of the Accused

No person shall be held to answer for a capital, or otherwise infamous, crime, unless on a presentment or indictment of a grand jury, except in cases arising in the land or naval forces, or in the militia, when in actual service in time of war or public danger; nor shall any person be subject for the same offense to be twice put in jeopardy of life and limb; nor shall be compelled, in any criminal case, to be a witness against himself; nor be deprived of life, liberty, or property, without due process of law; nor shall private property be taken for public use, without just compensation.

Amendment 6. Right to Speedy Trial by Jury

In all criminal prosecutions, the accused shall enjoy the right to a speedy and public trial, by an impartial jury of the state and district wherein the crime shall have been committed, which district shall have been previously ascertained by law, and to be informed of the nature and cause of the accusation; to be confronted with the witnesses against him; to have compulsory process for obtaining witnesses in his favor, and to have the assistance of counsel for his defense.

Defendants have the right to a speedy trial, although this does not mean that courts are bound to try defendants within a specified period of time. However, delays that are purposeful and that prejudice the defendant's right to a fair trial may result in a dismissal of the charge. The requirement that trials be public does not prohibit trial judges from excluding television camera crews and newspaper photographers from the courtroom. The requirement that a jury be *impartial* means the jury members must lay aside their opinions and render a verdict based solely on the evidence presented in court. The *compulsory process* provision refers to a defendant's right to force witnesses to testify by issuing *subpoenas*, legal orders requiring a person to appear in court.

Since 1942 the federal government has been obligated to provide free legal counsel to defendants in criminal trials if the defendents cannot afford to hire a lawyer. In 1963 the Supreme Court imposed the same requirement on the states (page 764).

Amendment 7. Jury Trial in Civil Cases

In suits at common law, where the value in controversy shall exceed $20, the right of trial by jury shall be preserved, and no fact tried by a jury shall be otherwise re-examined in any court of the United States than according to the rules of the common law.

Common law refers to rules of law established by judges in past cases. This amendment establishes the right to a jury trial in civil cases in which the amount of money disputed meets a specified dollar limit.

The second part of the amendment limits the power of federal appellate courts to reexamine facts tried by juries in civil cases. This means that an appellate court may not overturn a verdict solely because it disagrees with the jury's interpretation of the evidence. An appellate court may set aside a verdict only on the grounds that the trial court committed errors in law that deprived the defendant of his or her right to a fair trial.

Amendment 8. Bail and Punishment

Excessive bail shall not be required, nor excessive fines imposed, nor cruel and unusual punishments inflicted.

Bail is money a defendant gives to the court as a pledge that he or she will appear for trial. The amendment prohibits unreasonable denial of bail. The decision to deny bail depends on such factors as the defendant's family and community ties, the seriousness of the charge, and the weight of the evidence.

Courts have held that bail is excessive if it is set at a figure higher than necessary to secure the appearance of the accused at trial. A defendant's inability to pay bail is not in itself proof that excessive bail has been imposed.

Cruel and unusual punishments are barred by the amendment. These include various forms of physical and mental abuse.

Amendment 9. Powers Reserved to the People

The enumeration in the Constitution, of certain rights, shall not be construed to deny or disparage others retained by the people.

This amendment asserts that people have rights not listed in the Constitution. It assumes that there are rights so basic that they exist even though not specifically mentioned. This amendment was added to satisfy critics of the original Constitution who feared that a Bill of Rights would be used to limit rights to only those listed (page 172).

This amendment limits federal power by providing that the states shall exercise those powers that are neither denied to them nor specifically delegated to the federal government. The powers reserved to the states are not listed in the Constitution.

See the note for Article 3, Section 2, Clause 1.

Before the adoption of this amendment the candidates for President and Vice President were not specified. The candidate who received the most electoral votes became President, and the runner-up became Vice President. See the note for Article 2, Section 1, Clause 3. The Twelfth Amendment sought to prevent a repetition of the deadlocked election of 1800. It provides that there be separate ballots for President and Vice President.

According to this amendment, the House of Representatives elects the President if no candidate receives a majority in the electoral college (pages 245–246).

Amendment 10. Powers Reserved to the States

The powers not delegated to the United States by the Constitution, nor prohibited by it to the states, are reserved to the states respectively, or to the people.

Amendment 11. Suits Against States

Passed by Congress on March 4, 1794. Ratified on January 23, 1795.

The judicial power of the United States shall not be construed to extend to any suit in law or equity, commenced or prosecuted against one of the United States, by citizens of another state, or by citizens or subjects of any foreign state.

Amendment 12. Election of President and Vice-President

Passed by Congress on December 9, 1803. Ratified on June 15, 1804.

The electors shall meet in their respective states, and vote by ballot for President and Vice-President, one of whom, at least, shall not be an inhabitant of the same state with themselves; they shall name in their ballots the person voted for as President, and in distinct ballots the person voted for as Vice-President, and they shall make distinct lists of all persons voted for as President, and of all persons voted for as Vice-President, and of the number of votes for each, which lists they shall sign and certify, and transmit, sealed, to the seat of government of the United States, directed to the President of the Senate; the President of the Senate shall, in the presence of the Senate and House of Representatives, open all the certificates and the votes shall then be counted; the person having the greatest number of votes for President shall be the President, if such number be a majority of the whole number of electors appointed; and if no person have such majority, then from the persons having the highest numbers not exceeding three on the list of those voted for as President, the House of Representatives shall choose immediately, by ballot, the President. But in choosing the President, the votes shall be taken by states, the representation from each state having one vote; a quorum for this purpose shall consist of a member or members from two-thirds of the states, and a majority of all the states shall be necessary to a choice. And if the House of Representatives shall not choose a President whenever the right of choice shall devolve upon them, [before the fourth day of March next following,] then the Vice-President shall act as President, as in the case of the death or other constitutional disability of the President. The person having the greatest number of votes as Vice-President, shall be the Vice-President, if such number be a majority of the whole number of electors appointed, and if no person have a majority, then, from the two highest numbers on the list, the Senate shall choose the Vice-President; a quorum for the purpose shall consist of two-thirds of the whole number of Senators, and a majority of the whole number shall be necessary to a choice. But no person constitutionally ineligible to the office of President shall be eligible to that of Vice-President of the United States.

Amendment 13. Abolition of Slavery

Passed by Congress on January 31, 1865. Ratified on December 6, 1865.

Section 1. Neither slavery nor involuntary servitude, except as a punishment for crime whereof the party shall have been duly convicted, shall exist within the United States, or any place subject to their jurisdiction.

Section 2. Congress shall have power to enforce this article by appropriate legislation.

Amendment 14. Rights of Citizens

Passed by Congress on June 13, 1866. Ratified on July 9, 1868.

Section 1. Citizenship All persons born or naturalized in the United States and subject to the jurisdiction thereof, are citizens of the United States and of the state wherein they reside. No state shall make or enforce any law which shall abridge the privileges or immunities of citizens of the United States; nor shall any state deprive any person of life, liberty, or property, without due process of law; nor deny to any person within its jurisdiction the equal protection of the laws.

The Emancipation Proclamation, issued by President Lincoln in 1863, freed only those slaves residing in states controlled by the Confederacy (page 363). This amendment completed the emancipation process.

In addition to abolishing slavery, the amendment prohibits *involuntary servitude,* or labor done against one's will. This does not apply to persons convicted of a crime. Courts have held that forced labor in payment of a debt violates the ban on involuntary servitude.

This section defines citizenship for the first time in the Constitution, and it extends citizenship to blacks. It also prohibits states from denying the rights and privileges of citizenship to any citizen. The guarantee of due process contained in the Fifth Amendment applies to the federal government, while this section forbids states to deny due process of law.

During the late nineteenth and early twentieth centuries, the due process clause was used to strike down state laws that regulated business practices and labor conditions. The courts held that state regulatory legislation deprived corporations of the right to manage their property as they saw fit. Since the 1930s, however, courts have generally held that the due process clause does not necessarily invalidate regulatory legislation. Courts have ruled that legislation protecting the health and safety of citizens is not prohibited by the due process clause.

Section 1 also guarantees all citizens "equal protection under the law." The authors of the amendment included this clause to prevent states from discriminating against black citizens. In 1896, however, in *Plessy* v. *Ferguson*, the Supreme Court ruled that separate facilities for blacks and whites did not violate this clause as long as the facilities were equal (page 454). This view was upheld until the 1954 ruling in *Brown* v. *Board of Education* that separate facilities were inherently unequal (page 722).

This section provides that states would have their representation in the House of Representatives reduced if they infringed on the right of citizens to vote. This specific provision has never been enforced. However, federal voting legislation passed during the 1960s largely ended voting discrimination.

This section prohibited persons who had been federal or state government officials before the Civil War and who had participated in the Confederate cause from serving again as government officials. In 1872 Congress restored the political rights of former Confederate officials.

The validity of debts owed to the United States was recognized by this section, but it barred the repayment of debts owed by the Confederacy. Thus the Confederacy's creditors were punished for aiding the rebellion. The states of the former Confederacy were also barred from compensating slave owners for the loss of slaves.

Section 2. Apportionment of Representatives Representatives shall be apportioned among the several states according to their respective numbers, counting the whole number of persons in each state, excluding Indians not taxed. But when the right to vote at any election for the choice of electors for President and Vice-President of the United States, Representatives in Congress, the executive and judicial officers of a state, or the members of the legislature thereof, is denied to any of the male inhabitants of such state, being twenty-one years of age and citizens of the United States, or in any way abridged, except for participation in rebellion, or other crime, the basis of representation therein shall be reduced in the proportion which the number of such male citizens shall bear to the whole number of male citizens twenty-one years of age in such state.

Section 3. Former Confederate Officials No person shall be a Senator or Representative in Congress, or elector of President and Vice-President, or hold any office, civil or military, under the United States, or under any state, who, having previously taken an oath, as a member of Congress, or as an officer of the United States, or as a member of any state legislature, or as an executive or judicial officer of any state, to support the Constitution of the United States, shall have engaged in insurrection or rebellion against the same, or given aid or comfort to the enemies thereof. But Congress may, by vote of two-thirds of each house, remove such disability.

Section 4. Government Debt The validity of the public debt of the United States, authorized by law, including debts incurred for payment of pensions and bounties for services in suppressing insurrection or rebellion, shall not be questioned. But neither the United States nor any state shall assume or pay any debt or obligation incurred in aid of insurrection or rebellion against the United States or any claim for the loss or emancipation of any slave; but all such debts, obligations, and claims shall be held illegal and void.

Section 5. Enforcing the Amendment The Congress shall have power to enforce, by appropriate legislation, the provisions of this article.

Congress passed a Civil Rights Act in 1875 that barred segregation in hotels, public transportation, theaters, and other public places. But in 1883 the Supreme Court struck down the act, holding that the Fourteenth Amendment applied only to discriminatory actions by the states, not by individuals. The Court has held that the amendment does apply to businesses if they rent their premises from the state.

Amendment 15. Right of Suffrage

Passed by Congress on February 26, 1869. Ratified on February 2, 1870.

Section 1. Extending the Right to Vote The right of citizens of the United States to vote shall not be denied or abridged by the United States or any state on account of race, color, or previous condition of servitude.

This section bars voting discrimination on the grounds of race or "previous condition of servitude." It thus extended suffrage to former slaves and to blacks who had been free before the Civil War. Despite the Fifteenth Amendment, during the late nineteenth century the southern states began to deny the right to vote to blacks through the use of grandfather clauses, literacy tests, and poll taxes (page 454).

Section 2. Enforcement The Congress shall have power to enforce this article by appropriate legislation.

The Twenty-fourth Amendment prohibited the use of poll taxes in national elections. The Voting Rights Act of 1965 suspended literacy tests and authorized federal supervision of voter registration in places where a pattern of discrimination had been found (page 743).

Amendment 16. The Income Tax

Passed by Congress on July 12, 1909. Ratified on February 3, 1913.

The Congress shall have power to lay and collect taxes on incomes, from whatever source derived, without apportionment among the several states, and without regard to any census or enumeration.

In 1894 the Supreme Court invalidated an income tax law by ruling that the Constitution prohibited a "direct tax" unless it was collected in proportion to each state's population. Congress had not provided for this method of collection in 1894 tax legislation. This amendment provides that income taxes can be collected without regard to a state's population (page 507). It thereby nullifies Article 1, Section 9, Clause 4.

Amendment 17. Election of Senators

Passed by Congress on May 13, 1912. Ratified on April 8, 1913.

Section 1. Method of election The Senate of the United States shall be composed of two Senators from each state, elected by the people thereof, for six years; and each Senator shall have one vote. The electors in each state shall have the qualifications requisite for electors of the most numerous branch of the state legislatures.

This amendment replaces Article 1, Section 3, Clause 1. According to the amendment senators are directly elected by the people of each state. The amendment reflected the efforts of progressives to make the election process more democratic (page 499).

Section 2. Vacancies When vacancies happen in the representation of any state in the Senate, the executive authority of such state shall issue writs of election to fill such vacancies: *Provided* that the legislature of any state may empower the executive thereof to

When a Senate seat becomes vacant, the governor of the state must order an election to fill the vacancy. The state legislature may empower the governor to make a temporary appointment until an election is held.

The terms of senators who had already been elected by state legislatures were not affected by the Seventeenth Amendment.

This amendment banned the manufacture, sale, and transportation of alcoholic beverages (page 585). It was repealed by the Twenty-first Amendment.

Both the states and the federal government had the power to pass legislation to enforce the amendment.

The Eighteenth Amendment was the first to include a specific time limit for ratification by the required number of states.

According to this amendment neither the federal nor the state governments can deny the right to vote on account of sex. Prior to the enactment of the amendment many individual states had extended suffrage to women (pages 497–498).

This section changes the date of the beginning of presidential terms from March 4 to January 20. This shortened the waiting period between the November election and

make temporary appointments until the people fill the vacancies by election as the legislature may direct.

[**Section 3. Those Elected Under Previous Procedure** This amendment shall not be so construed as to affect the election or term of any Senator chosen before it becomes valid as part of the Constitution.]

Amendment 18. Prohibition of Alcoholic Beverages

Passed by Congress on December 18, 1917. Ratified on January 16, 1919.

[**Section 1. Ban on Alcohol** After one year from the ratification of this article the manufacture, sale, or transportation of intoxicating liquors within, the importation thereof into, or the exportation thereof from, the United States and all territory subject to the jurisdiction thereof for beverage purposes is hereby prohibited.

Section 2. Enforcement The Congress and the several states shall have concurrent power to enforce this article by appropriate legislation.

Section 3. Method of Ratification This article shall be inoperative unless it shall have been ratified as an amendment to the Constitution by the legislatures of the several states, as provided in the Constitution, within seven years from the date of the submission hereof to the states by the Congress.]

Amendment 19. Women's Suffrage

Passed by Congress on June 4, 1919. Ratified on August 18, 1920.

Section 1. The Right to Vote The right of citizens of the United States to vote shall not be denied or abridged by the United States or by any state on account of sex.

Section 2. Enforcement Congress shall have power to enforce this article by appropriate legislation.

Amendment 20. Presidential Terms; Sessions of Congress

Passed by Congress on March 2, 1932. Ratified on January 23, 1933.

Section 1. Beginning of Term The terms of the President and Vice-President shall end at noon on the 20th day of January, and the terms of Senators and Representatives at noon on the 3rd day of January, of the years in which such terms would have ended if this article had not been ratified; and the terms of their successors shall then begin.

Section 2. Congressional Sessions The Congress shall assemble at least once in every year, and such meeting shall begin at noon on the 3d day of January, unless they shall by law appoint a different day.

Section 3. Presidential Succession If at the time fixed for the beginning of the term of the President, the President-elect shall have died, the Vice-President-elect shall become President. If a President shall not have been chosen before the time fixed for the beginning of his term, or if the President-elect shall have failed to qualify, then the Vice-President-elect shall act as President until a President shall have qualified; and the Congress may by law provide for the case wherein neither a President-elect nor a Vice-President-elect shall have qualified, declaring who shall then act as President, or the manner in which one who is to act shall be selected, and such person shall act accordingly until a President or Vice-President shall have qualified.

Section 4. Elections Decided by Congress The Congress may by law provide for the case of the death of any of the persons from whom the House of Representatives may choose a President whenever the right of choice shall have devolved upon them, and for the case of the death of any of the persons from whom the Senate may choose a Vice-President whenever the right of choice shall have devolved upon them.

[Section 5. Date of Implementation Sections 1 and 2 shall take effect on the 15th day of October following the ratification of this article.

Section 6. Ratification Period This article shall be inoperative unless it shall have been ratified as an amendment to the Constitution by the legislatures of three-fourths of the several states within seven years from the date of its submission.]

the inauguration of the President. It also changed the date for the beginning of congressional terms from March 4 to January 3.

According to this section annual sessions of Congress are to begin on January 3 rather than in December. Prior to the amendment members of Congress who were defeated in November served in a new session of Congress from December until March. Such members were known as *lame ducks.* Thus the amendment is often called the lame duck amendment. By establishing the same date for the beginning of a member's term and the beginning of a new session, the overlap was eliminated.

If the President-elect dies, the Vice President-elect will become President.

Congress is empowered to pass legislation to deal with a situation in which a presidential candidate dies while an election is being decided by the House. Similar authorization is given to Congress in cases in which the Senate elects the Vice President.

Congress directed that special state conventions be called to ratify the amendment. Prohibition ended on December 5, 1933. This is the only time an amendment was ratified by state conventions rather than by state legislatures.

Each state remained free to ban the sale or manufacture of alcoholic beverages within its borders. This section makes the importation of liquor into a so-called dry state a federal offense.

Before Franklin D. Roosevelt no President served for more than two terms (pages 660 and 681). Roosevelt's four-term presidency convinced many Americans that the two-term tradition should be reinforced by a constitutional amendment.

Amendment 21. Repeal of Prohibition

Passed by Congress on February 20, 1933. Ratified on December 5, 1933.

Section 1. Repeal of National Prohibition
The eighteenth article of amendment to the Constitution of the United States is hereby repealed.

Section 2. State Laws
The transportation or importation into any state, territory, or possession of the United States for delivery or use therein of intoxicating liquors, in violation of the laws thereof, is hereby prohibited.

[Section 3. Ratification Period
This article shall be inoperative unless it shall have been ratified as an amendment to the Constitution by conventions in the several states, as provided in the Constitution, within seven years from the date of the submission hereof to the states by the Congress.]

Amendment 22. Limit on Number of President's Terms

Passed by Congress on March 12, 1947. Ratified on March 1, 1951.

Section 1. Two-Term Limit
No person shall be elected to the office of the President more than twice, and no person who has held the office of President, or acted as President, for more than two years of a term to which some other person was elected President shall be elected to the office of the President more than once. [But this Article shall not apply to any person holding the office of President when this Article was proposed by the Congress, and shall not prevent any person who may be holding the office of President, or acting as President, during the term within which this Article becomes operative from holding the office of President or acting as President during the remainder of such term.]

[Section 2. Ratification Period
This Article shall be inoperative unless it shall have been ratified as an amendment to the Constitution by the legislatures of three-fourths of the several states within seven years from the date of its submission to the states by the Congress.]

Amendment 23. Presidential Electors for District of Columbia

Passed by Congress on June 16, 1960. Ratified on April 3, 1961.

Section 1. Determining the Number of Electors The District constituting the seat of Government of the United States shall appoint in such manner as the Congress may direct:

A number of electors of President and Vice-President equal to the whole number of Senators and Representatives in Congress to which the District would be entitled if it were a State, but in no event more than the least populous State; they shall be in addition to those appointed by the States, but they shall be considered, for the purposes of the election of President and Vice-President, to be electors appointed by a State; and they shall meet in the District and perform such duties as provided by the twelfth article of amendment.

Section 2. Enforcement The Congress shall have power to enforce this article by appropriate legislation.

This amendment gives residents of Washington, D.C., the right to vote in presidential elections. Washington, D.C., has three electoral votes.

Amendment 24. Abolition of Poll Tax in National Elections

Passed by Congress on August 27, 1962. Ratified on January 23, 1964.

Section 1. Poll Tax Banned The right of citizens of the United States to vote in any primary or other election for President or Vice-President, for electors for President or Vice-President, or for Senator or Representative in Congress, shall not be denied or abridged by the United States or any state by reason of failure to pay any poll tax or other tax.

Section 2. Enforcement The Congress shall have the power to enforce this article by appropriate legislation.

No state can impose the payment of a poll tax as a requirement for voting in national elections. Some states had used poll taxes to deprive blacks of the right to vote. The amendment bars poll taxes only in presidential and congressional elections. A Supreme Court decision in 1966 nullified poll taxes in state elections on the grounds that such taxes constitute a denial of equal protection of the laws under the Fourteenth Amendment.

This section clarifies Article 2, Section 1, which ambiguously provides that in case of the President's death his or her powers "shall devolve on the Vice-President." Amendment 25 states simply that "the Vice-President shall become President" in the event of the President's death or resignation from office.

When Vice President Lyndon Johnson became President after the death of President John Kennedy, the vice presidency remained vacant for the balance of Johnson's first term in office. The problem of a vacant vice presidency was remedied by the Twenty-fifth Amendment, which provides that the President shall fill vacancies in the vice presidency. Acting under this amendment President Richard Nixon appointed Gerald Ford Vice President after Spiro Agnew resigned (page 769). The amendment was used a second time, after Nixon resigned as President. Gerald Ford, who succeeded Nixon, appointed Nelson Rockefeller Vice President.

During the twentieth century there have been times when poor health prevented a President from exercising the powers of office. Presidents Woodrow Wilson and Dwight Eisenhower both fell gravely ill while in office. The Constitution, as it stood, did not prescribe who should exercise presidential powers if a President became disabled. This section states that the Vice President will serve as Acting President if the President declares in writing that he or she is unable to execute the powers of office.

This section provides that the Vice President and the cabinet may declare that the President is unable to execute the powers of the office, whereupon the Vice President becomes Acting President. In turn, the President may declare that no disability exists and resume office. However, the Vice President and cabinet may challenge the President's assertion of no disability. At that point the Congress would determine whether the President was in fact disabled.

Amendment 25. Presidential Succession and Disability

Passed by Congress on July 6, 1965. Ratified on February 11, 1967.

Section 1. President's Death or Resignation In case of the removal of the President from office or his death or resignation, the Vice-President shall become President.

Section 2. Vacancies in Vice-Presidency Whenever there is a vacancy in the office of the Vice-President, the President shall nominate a Vice-President who shall take the office upon confirmation by a majority vote of both houses of Congress.

Section 3. Disability of the President Whenever the President transmits to the President pro tempore of the Senate and the Speaker of the House of Representatives his written declaration that he is unable to discharge the powers and duties of his office, and until he transmits to them a written declaration to the contrary, such powers and duties shall be discharged by the Vice-President as Acting President.

Section 4. Whenever the Vice-President and a majority of either the principal officers of the executive departments or of such other body as Congress may by law provide, transmit to the President pro tempore of the Senate and the Speaker of the House of Representatives their written declaration that the President is unable to discharge the powers and duties of his office, the Vice-President shall immediately assume the powers and duties of the office as Acting President.

Thereafter, when the President transmits to the President pro tempore of the Senate and the Speaker of the House of Representatives his written declaration that no inability exists, he shall resume the powers and duties of his office unless the Vice-President and a majority of either the principal officers of the executive department or of such other body as Congress may by law provide, transmit within four days to the President pro tempore of the Senate and the Speaker of the House of Representatives their written declaration that the President is unable to discharge the powers and duties of his office. Thereupon Con-

The Constitution

gress shall decide the issue, assembling within 48 hours for that purpose if not in session. If the Congress, within 21 days after receipt of the latter written declaration, or, if Congress is not in session, within 21 days after Congress is required to assemble, determines by two-thirds vote of both houses that the President is unable to discharge the powers and duties of his office, the Vice-President shall continue to discharge the same as Acting President; otherwise, the President shall assume the powers and duties of his office.

Amendment 26. Suffrage for Persons 18 Years or Older

Passed by Congress on March 23, 1971. Ratified on July 1, 1971.

Section 1. Lowering of Voting Age The right of citizens of the United States, who are 18 years of age or older, to vote shall not be denied or abridged by the United States or any state on account of age.

Section 2. Enforcement The Congress shall have the power to enforce this article by appropriate legislation.

Proposed Amendment. Representation for the Capital District

Passed by Congress on August 27, 1978.

Section 1. District Treated as a State For purposes of representation in the Congress, election of the President and Vice-President, and Article V of this Constitution, the District constituting the seat of government of the United States shall be treated as though it were a State.

Section 2. Enforcement The exercise of the rights and powers conferred under this article shall be by the people of the District constituting the seat of government, and as shall be provided by the Congress.

Section 3. Effect on the Twenty-third Amendment The twenty-third article of amendment to the Constitution of the United States is hereby repealed.

Prior to ratification of the amendment most states disqualified persons under age 21 from voting. Legislation passed by Congress in 1970 lowered the minimum voting age to 18 for state and federal elections, but the Supreme Court ruled the same year that Congress could not set minimum age qualifications for state elections. As a result, this amendment was proposed and ratified.

The Constitution

Italicized page numbers refer to illustrations. The *m, c,* or *p* preceding the number refers to a map *(m),* chart *(c),* or picture *(p)* on that page. An *n* following a page number refers to a footnote. *Painting* indicates a work by the listed artist.

Index

---

403 SI; 405 The Thomas Gilcrease Institute of American History and Art, Tulsa, Okla.; 406 The Thomas Gilcrease Institute of American History and Art, Tulsa, Okla.; 409 National Gallery of Canada; 411 The Anschutz Collection; 413 The Granger Collection; 414 Wichita Art Museum; 417 Pugsly Union, South Dakota State University; 421 The Granger Collection; 422 The Granger Collection; 423 The Granger Collection; 425 Bethlehem Steel Corporation; 427 National Portrait Gallery; 429 Culver Pictures; 431 National Portrait Gallery, SI, Gift of Mrs. Margaret Carnegie Miller; 432 The Granger Collection; 434 Atlanta Historical Society; 436 Metropolitan Life Insurance Company; 439 The Granger Collection; 440 NYPL; 445 Chicago Historical Society; 446 LC; 447 The Granger Collection; 448 The Granger Collection; 449 The Granger Collection; 452 NYPL; 454 Nebraska State Historical Society; 455 LC; 456 MFA, M. and M. Karolik Collection; 457 Kansas State Historical Society; 458 U.S. Department of Agriculture; 461 The Granger Collection; 463 The Granger Collection; 467 MCNY; 472 Culver Pictures; 473 MCNY; 475 The Granger Collection; 476 The Granger Collection; 477 Culver Pictures; 479 Philadelphia Museum of Art; 480 Culver Pictures; 481 LC; 483 Culver Pictures; 486 NYHS, Bella Landauer Collection; 487 Bettmann Archive; 488 Rosetta Records.

UNIT SEVEN Page 490 tl, tr The Granger Collection; bl Los Angeles County Museum of Art: br Scala/Art Resource; 491 tl NYHS; tr The Granger Collection; bl LC; br Imperial War Museum; 493 The Phillips Collection; 494 l LC, r Culver Pictures; 495 NAACP; 497 Culver Pictures; 499 Addison Gallery of American Art, Phillips Academy, Andover, Massachusetts; 500 LC; 502 The Granger Collection; 503 J. Doyle DeWitt Collection, University of Hartford; 506 Theodore Roosevelt Collection, Harvard Library; 508 LC; 511 National Portrait Gallery, SI; 512 LC; 516 International Sports and Games Research Collection, Notre Dame; 517 Bettmann Archive; 518 The Boy Scouts of America; 521 U.S. Naval Academy Museum; 522 LC; 523 The Granger Collection; 524 LC; 526 The Granger Collection; 529 LC; 530 The Granger Collection; 533 LC; 534 The Granger Collection; 537 The Granger Collection; 545 SI; 546 SI; 548 Culver Pictures; 551 SI; 553 NA; 555 Culver Pictures; 556 The Granger Collection; 558 l, r Culver Pictures; 559 NA; 561 Kennedy Galleries.

UNIT EIGHT Page 566 tl Scala/Art Resource; tr The Granger Collection; bl SEF/Art Resource; br LC; 567 tl LC; tr San Francisco Art Museum; bl LC; br Giraudon/Art Resource; 569 NYHS; 571 The Granger Collection; 573 National Museum of American Art, Smithsonian; 575 Culver Pictures; 576 LC; 579 National Museum of American Art, Smithsonian Institution; 580 Culver Pictures; 582 Art Resource; 583 The Fine Arts Museum of San Francisco, Gift of Mr. and Mrs. John D. Rockefeller 3rd; 585 Culver Pictures; 586 Bettmann Archive; 587 LC; 590 The Granger Collection; 591 Bettmann Archive; 592 National Baseball Hall of Fame; 595 Whitney Museum of American Art; 597 LC; 598 The Granger Collection; 600 l Wide World, r The Granger Collection; 604 UPI/Bettmann Newsphotos; 605 LC; 606 UPI/Bettmann Newsphotos; 611 TVA; 612 UPI/Bettmann Newsphotos; 614 National Archive; 615 UPI/Bettmann Newsphotos; 616 UPI/Bettmann Newsphotos; 617 The Anschutz Collection; 619 TVA; 621 LC; 623 National Museum of American Art, Smithsonian; 624 Bettmann Archive; 625 LC; 629 Dallas Museum of Art, Gift of Eleanor and Tom May; 631 LC; 633 National Museum of American Art, Smithsonian; 635 Dallas Museum of Art, Dallas Art Association Purchase; 636 LC, Farm Security Administration (both); 639 Photofest; 640 National Museum of American Art, Smithsonian Institution; 642 UPI/Bettmann Newsphotos.

UNIT NINE Page 646 tl The Granger Collection; tr LC; bl Courtesy of the Franklin Delano Roosevelt Library; br John Launois 1982/Black Star; 647 tl Hallmark Cards, Inc.; tm, tr The Granger Collection; bl UPI/Bettmann Newsphotos; br Saturday Evening Post cover, 1946, The Curtis Publishing Co.; 649 U.S. Army Center of Military History; 651 NA; 652 The Granger Collection; 653 Keystone/The Image Works; 655 LC; 658 UPI/Bettmann Newsphotos; 659 National Gallery of Canada, Massey Collection; 661 William Vandivert, Life Magazine © Time Inc.; 663 The National Maritime Museum, London; 667 U.S. Merchant Marine Academy; 669 Navy Combat Art Collection; 671 LC; 672 U.S. Army Center of Military History; 673 LC; 674 l LC, r War Reloca-tion Authority, NA; 677 UPI/Bettmann Newsphotos; 678 Navy Combat Art Collection; 682 U.S. Army; 683 l The Bettmann Archive, r Art Resource; 685 Navy Combat Art Collection; 688 UPI/Bettmann Newsphotos; 689 LC; 690 The Bettmann Archive; 693 Collection of Whitney Museum of American Art; 696 Courtesy of the Norman Rockwell Museum at the Old Corner House, Stockbridge, Mass.; 699 Walter Sanders, Life Magazine © 1948 Time Inc.; 700 LC; 704 D. B. Owen/Black Star; 705 The Granger Collection; 707 UPI/Bettmann Newsphotos; 709 The Granger Collection; 713 Collection, The Museum of Modern Art, New York. Gift of the CIO Political Action Committee; 715 l Harry S. Truman Library and Museum, r UPI/Bettmann Newsphotos; 716 The Granger Collection; 718 UPI/Bettmann Newsphotos; 720 Courtesy of the Norman Rockwell Museum at the Old Corner House, Stockbridge, Mass.; 721 t © Van Bucher/Photo Researchers; b A. Y. Owen, Life Magazine © 1954 Time Inc.; 723 UPI/Bettmann Newsphotos; 724 © Burt Glinn/Magnum Photos; 725 The Bridgeman Art Library/Art Resource; 726 Art Resource; 727 UPI/Bettmann Newsphotos.

UNIT TEN Page 730 tl AP/Wide World Photos; tr © Wally Mc-Namee/Woodfin Camp & Associates; bl UPI/Bettmann Newsphotos; br © Peter Marlow/Magnum Photos; 731 tl © J. P. Laffont/Sygma; tr © Dennis Brack 1987/Black Star; bl © Paul S. Conklin 1988; br © Chuck O'Rear/Woodfin Camp & Associates; 733 NASA, 734 © Fred Ward/Black Star; 735 LC; 737 NASA; 738 © Bruce Roberts/Photo Researchers; 739 UPI/Bettmann Newsphotos; 740 LC; 741 © Michal Heron 1971; 742 © Max Schler 1964/Black Star; 745 © Jim Amos/Photo Researchers; 746 l © Bob Fitch/Black Star, r UPI/Bettmann Newsphotos; 748 l © Werner Wolff/Black Star, r © Jan Lukas/Photo Researchers; 752 LC; 754 © Jason Laure/Woodfin Camp & Associates; 755 © Rick Winsor/Woodfin Camp & Associates; 759 NASA; 761 © Nik Wheeler 1975/Black Star; 762 © Peter Marlow/Magnum Photos; 763 Frank Fishbeck, Life Magazine © Time Inc.; 766 l © Dennis Brack 1973/Black Star, r UPI/Bettmann Newsphotos; 767 NASA, gift of the artist; 769 © Fred Ward 1973/Black Star; 770 © Dennis Brack 1974/Black Star; 772 © J. P. Laffont 1974/Sygma; 773 © David Rubinger 1973/Black Star; 774 © Dan Budnik/Woodfin Camp & Associates; 775 l © Dennis Brack 1976/Black Star; r © Dennis Brack 1976/Black Star; 776 © Dennis Brack 1977/Black Star; 779 © Sygma; 781 © Tom McHugh/Photo Researchers; 785 © Rick Friedman 1989/Black Star; 786 © Dennis Brack 1981/Black Star; 787 © Jean Louis Atlan 1983/Sygma; 790 © Breese 1981/Gamma; 791 © Larry Downing 1987/Woodfin Camp & Associates; 792 Terry Ashe/Time Magazine; 795 © John Ficara/Woodfin Camp & Associates; 797 l © Rick Friedman 1988/Black Star, r © Villafuerte/Texastock; 798 AP/Wide World Photos; 800 © Jacques Chenet 1985/Woodfin Camp & Associates; 801 AP/Wide World Photos; 802 © Jan Halaska 1980/Photo Researchers; 803 © A. Tannenbaum/Sygma; 806 © Lester Sloan 1979/Woodfin Camp & Associates; 807 © Spencer Grant/Photo Researchers; 811 © Roger Ressmeyer 1989/Starlight; 813 © Paul Conklin; 817 tl © Blair Seitz 1985/Photo Researchers, tr © Guy Gillette 1984/Photo Researchers, b © Michal Heron 1986/Woodfin Camp & Associates; 819 © John Marmaras/Woodfin Camp & Associates; 822 © David M. Grossman 1989; 823 © T. J. Florian 1986/Rainbow; 824 © Chuck O'Rear/Woodfin Camp & Associates; 826 © Michal Heron 1987; 827 © Jim Richardson 1988; 828 © Ted Spiegel 1987/Black Star; 829 © George Hall/Woodfin Camp & Associates; 831 © Dennis Brack 1989/Black Star; 834 Newberry Library; 835 Mark Antman/The Image Works; 836 World Wide.

REFERENCE SECTION Page 838 tl MFA, tr SEF/Art Resource, ml Mystic Seaport Museum, Mystic, Conn., mr NYHS, bl © Peter Marlow/Magnum Photos, br The Granger Collection, 839 tl Los Angeles County Museum of Art, tr The Granger Collection, b Architect of the Capitol; 850 l Independence National Historical Park, r Peale Museum; 851 Colonial Williamsburg Foundation (both); 852 l Chicago Historical Society, Solomon D. Butcher Collection, r Thomas Gilcrease Institute of American History and Art, Tulsa, Okla.; 853 l Bethlehem Steel Corporation, r Joslyn Art Museum.

BACK COVER
from top to bottom Royal Ontario Museum, Toronto; MMA; City Library, DeSmet, S. Dak.; San Francisco Art Museum; © J. P. Laffont/Sygma.

917